HISTORY OF NORTHWEST MISSOURI

CHARLES D. ZOOK. As a merchant and banker Mr. Zook has been identified with Oregon most of his life. He has been successful in business to the degree that he is now rated as one of the wealthiest men in Holt County. In many ways he has shown his public spirit in community affairs, and as a banker and lender of money has often assisted individuals in their struggles to gain a home. It is only expressing one phase of his general local reputation to say that Charley Zook, as he is familiarly called by his friends, has never yet foreclosed a mortgage. While Mr. Zook does business on thorough business principles, he has at the same time endeared himself to many personal friends by his aid to them when they needed assistance. His father and uncle were pioneers in business affairs in Northwest Missouri, and few names have more important associations with large business and financial management in this section of the state than Zook.

Levi Zook, father of Charles D., came from Marion County, Ohio, to Northwest Missouri in 1842, only five years after the Platte Purchase. He possessed a fair education, but most of it was acquired as a result of his individual study. Levi Zook was the son of G. F. and · Annie (Forney) Zook. In 1850 Levi Zook engaged in the general merchandise business with his brother William, who a number of years later died in St. Joseph, Missouri. At the end of five years Levi Zook retired from the firm, owing to poor health, and later went into business with Hiram Patterson for six years under the name of Zook & Patterson. From 1857 until 1861 their establishment was located at Forest City, Missouri, then moving to Mills County, Iowa, where they closed out in 1862. In 1864 he reopened business in Oregon, with Jonas Lehmar, and business was continued until 1869. In 1867 Levi Zook opened a private bank, the first financial institution in Holt County. This bank had its quarters in the front end of the store, and was conducted as Zook & Scott, bankers. Levi Zook again retired on account of poor health, and on re-entering banking business was associated with Robert Montgomery, under the name Zook & Montgomery. The firm dissolved in 1875. In 1881 Levi Zook superintended the construction of the courthouse at Oregon. He was a man of great business ability, possessed a judgment and character which made him a leader in every community, and left an honored name. During the war he was a strong Union man, assisted in raising volunteers, though his own health did not permit active service. He was affiliated with Forest City Lodge No. 214, A. F. & A. M., and was an active member of the Presbyterian Church. Levi Zook was married November 3, 1859, to Minnie Van Lunen, who was born in Prussia, and was brought in childhood to Pennsylvania. She died November 2, 1864, and her husband passed away in April, 1895.

Charles D. Zook was born at Oregon July 24, 1860, was educated in his native town, attended the University of Missouri during 1879-80, and then started a mercantile store in Atchison County for himself. Later he was a member of the banking firm of Zook & Thomas at Mound City, sold his interests there and engaged in the wholesale boot and shoe business at Kansas City from 1885 to 1890, and since that time has been chiefly identified with his banking business at Oregon. This is one of the oldest banking institutions of Northwest Missouri, and under his individual management has in many ways proved its service and its standing in the county. The bank is now conducted under the name of Zook & Roecker, with Mr. Zook as president. Its cashier for many years was the late Albert Roecker, one of the prominent men of Holt County. Beside his position as a banker, Mr. Zook is one of the principal stockholders in the wholesale dry goods business at Omaha conducted under the name Byrne & Hanmer Dry Goods Company.

Mr. Zook was married February 19, 1884, to Emma Curry, daughter of James and Mary M. Curry. They have one daughter, Mary, the wife of Dr. S. B. Hibbard of Kansas City. In politics Mr. Zook is a democrat, but his activities have never been in seeking office for himself, but always for the benefit of the party organization and for local betterment. He was on the democratic state committee one term, and has found many opportunities to exercise his business prominence for the good of his home locality. In 1911 Mr. Zook was appointed superintendent of the rebuilding of the Holt County Courthouse, a work that was accomplished in a thoroughly creditable manner, to the satisfaction of the County Court and the public in general. His broad interest in public affairs has found a special subject in the public schools, and for a number of years he served as member of the school board.

R. E. SEATON. A man of unquestioned ability and integrity, R. E. Seaton occupies a position of prominence among the leading manufacturers of Clinton County, being manager of the Noremac Chemical Company, at Cameron, one of the largest manufacturing plants of the kind in Northwestern Missouri. This enterprising company has established a substantial business in the manufacture of household remedies, extracts, spices, and all kinds of stock remedies and food. During the ten years the company has been located at Cameron, the products of its plant have been successfully used in relieving the suffering and helping the sick, throughout Missouri and adjoining states, while through the timely use of its stock remedies and food thousands of blooded cattle, horses and hogs have been saved from death, and their owners from great financial losses. One hundred different articles are made in the plant, the greater number of which are of medicinal value in the treatment of diseases to which human flesh is heir, or those which afflict cattle, horses, hogs, poultry and sheep. The plant, which is 45 by 85 feet, and well equipped for manufacturing purposes, is located at the corner of Third and Walnut streets. The company, which is wide-awake and progressive, employs traveling salesmen who, with team and wagons, cover all of the territory of Northwestern Missouri and Nebraska.

R. E. Seaton was born in Perrin, Clinton County, Missouri, in 1884, a son of Thomas B. Seaton, a native of the same county. He is of early pioneer ancestry, his grandfather, John R. Seaton, and his great grandfather, Solomon Seaton, having migrated from their native state, Tennessee, to Missouri at a very early day, becoming pioneers of Clinton County. Thomas B. Seaton, a life-long resident of Clinton County, married Alice Potter, also a native of Clinton County. For many years R. E. Seaton was traveling salesman for the company of which he is now manager, having Nebraska as his special territory, with the thriving city of Ord as his headquarters.

Mr. Seaton married, at the age of twenty-three years, in De Kalb County, Missouri, Miss Bertha Smith, a daughter of Rev. F. A. Smith, and into their pleasant home three children have been born, namely: Thomas O., Ruth P., and Helen. Mr. and Mrs. Seaton are both members of the Methodist Episcopal Church and contribute liberally towards its support.

J. E. PARK. Conspicuous among the leading stockmen of Northwest Missouri is J. E. Park, of Cameron, proprietor of the Park Stock Farm, and an extensive dealer in imported and home-bred Percherons. As a man and a citizen he is held in high repute, and by his excellent character and straightforward business dealings he has won the esteem and confidence of the general public, and built up an extremely large and lucrative patronage, everything he says regarding his stock being as he represents, and his prices being ever right. He was born on a farm in Clinton County, Missouri, in 1859. His father, William Park, was a native of Clay County, but after his marriage settled in Clinton County, where he devoted his energies to the improvement of a farm. During the Civil war he served as a soldier in the Confederate army. He married Jane Hall, and of their children two are now living in California; one son, William, resides at Mulhall, Oklahoma; and J. E. is the subject of this brief sketch.

Brought up on the home farm, J. E. Park obtained a good common school education, and an excellent training in the habits of truth, honesty and justice. Finding the life of a farmer congenial to his tastes, he decided to devote his time and attentions to the independent occupation to which he was reared, and in which he had gained some experience. Turning his attention more especially to stock breeding and growing, Mr. Park, in 1889, bought twenty acres of land adjoining the City of Cameron, and has here established one of the finest stock barns in Clinton County. His first purchase was a native bred registered Percheron, four years old, and weighing 2,100 pounds. Meeting with much success in his venture, Mr. Park gradually enlarged his operations, and now has in his stables some of the finest Percheron stallions and jacks to be found in the country, and also a valuable bunch of high-class jacks and jennets, 14½ to 16 hands high, with plenty of bone and quality. His Percheron stallion, "Merton," weighing 2,200 pounds, is one of the best to be found in the State of Missouri, and would be eligible for stock shows in any state of the Union. Another important member of Mr. Park's stables is a beautiful dapple grey stallion, "Waterloo," that is worthy of a place among the prize winners of any state. The quality of his horses, Kentucky jacks and jennets, and their low prices, sell them very readily, the buyers being sure of a safe guarantee when trading with Mr. Park. He has dealt with people from all of the Central and Western states, doing thousands of dollars worth of business, and invariably winning friends with each deal.

Mr. Park married, November 6, 1884, Miss Frances Harlan, a daughter of Price Harlan. Politically Mr. Park is identified with the democratic party; fraternally he belongs to the Independent Order of Odd Fellows, and Mrs. Park to the Daughters of Rebekah; religiously both Mr. and Mrs. Park are members of the Christian Church.

JOHN C. VAN TRUMP. One and one-half miles south of the attractive little town of Millville, Ray County, in Grape Grove Township, is situated the well improved homestead farm of Mr. Van Trump, who is one of the representative agriculturists and stock growers of the county, who is imbued with progressiveness and marked civic liberality and whose circle of friends is coincident with that of his acquaintances.

Mr. Van Trump finds a due mede of satisfaction in reverting to the historic Old Dominion commonwealth as the place of his nativity and he is a scion of one of the old families of Virginia, the lineage on the paternal side being remotely traced back to staunch Holland-Dutch stock. Mr. Van Trump was born in Rockingham County, Virginia, on the 7th of March, 1852, and is a son of Reuben and Diana (Carnes) Van Trump, both likewise natives of Rockingham County, where the former was born November 24, 1826, and the latter on the 27th of May, 1828. Of the six children three died in infancy and of those who attained to years of maturity John C., of this review, is the eldest; Americus V. and Medisia Belle are likewise residents of Ray County, Missouri, and the latter is the widow of Marshall Hyder. In 1854, when the subject of this sketch was about two years of age, his parents removed from Virginia to Wayne County, Indiana, and shortly afterward they established their residence in Rochester Township, Fulton County, that state, where the father continued to be actively identified with agricultural pursuits until 1875. He then came to Ray County, Missouri, and established his home on a farm near Russellville, but in 1884 he sold his property and removed to the northwestern part of the county, near Lawson, where he continued as a substantial and honored representative of the agricultural industry until his death, on the 1st of October, 1888, his loved and devoted wife having been summoned to the life eternal on the 23d of November, 1883. He was a lifelong democrat in his political adherency and he was actively affiliated with the Odd Fellows' fraternity, the precepts of which he exemplified in his worthy and successful life.

John C. Van Trump was reared and educated in the State of Indiana, where he duly availed himself of the advantages of the public schools of Fulton County and where he gained practical experience in connection with the activities of the home farm. He remained at the parental home until the time of his marriage, in 1888, he having been about twenty years of age at the time of the family removal from Indiana to Ray County, Missouri. After his marriage Mr. Van Trump engaged in farming near Lawson, and in 1891 he purchased his present fine farm, which comprises 150 acres and upon which he has made many excellent improvements, the entire appearance of the place giving distinctive evidence of thrift and prosperity. He is giving special attention to the raising of horses and jacks, as well as Duroc Jersey swine, and he is recognized as one of the broad-minded and progressive agriculturists and stock-raisers of the county. He redeemed his farm from a run-down condition, as it had been greatly neglected prior to the time when he purchased the property, and he now has the satisfaction of knowing that he has one of the valuable farms of the county and that much of its improvement and embellishment has been due to his own well ordered industry and up-to-date policies.

In politics Mr. Van Trump is a staunch adherent of the democratic party and in the autumn of 1906 he was given definite assurance of public esteem in his home county, in that he was elected presiding judge of the County Court, a position of which he continued the incumbent for four years, having assumed his official prerogatives in January, 1907. Within his term of office was completed the first permanent bridge work in Ray County, the construction being of concrete, and another important and gratifying work completed in his regime was the building of the substantial and attractive county home for poor at Richmond. Mr. Van Trump is affiliated with the Independent Order of Odd Fellows and is an elder of the Christian Church at Millville, his wife and children likewise being zealous members of this church.

On the 23d of December, 1888, Mr. Van Trump wedded Miss Mary Cummins, who was born on a farm near Knoxville, Ray County, Missouri, on the 12th of July, 1862, and who is a daughter of Artemas Ward Cummins and Lucy (Watson) Cummins, the father having been born in Ohio on the 15th of November, 1841, and the mother having been born in Tennessee, July 25, 1834. Mrs. Van Trump is the second eldest of the six surviving children, there having been eight children in the family. Eliza A. is the wife of Laban Daus, of Yale, Oklahoma; Thomas A. is a resident of Coffeyville, Kansas; Sarah E. is the wife of James Cavender, of Holt, Clay County, Missouri; Laura remains at the parental home; and Florence is the wife of Lee Clark, of Lathrop, Clinton County, this state. Mr. Cummins was a child of two years at the time of his parents removal from Ohio to Missouri, in 1843, and the family home was established on a farm near Knoxville, Ray County, where he was reared to manhood and where he wedded Miss Lucy Watson. In 1861, when but eighteen years of age, he enlisted for service as a soldier in the Union army, and he continued in active service until the close of the great Civil war. He took part in numerous engagements and in one of the same he received a severe wound in the thigh. In 1880 he removed to Lathrop, Clinton County, where he has since lived retired and where he and his devoted wife are enjoying the fruits of former years of earnest endeavor. Mr. and Mrs. Van Trump have shown signal appreciation of the value of education, in that they have given to each of their four children the best possible advantages, the three elder children all being graduates of Western College at Odessa, Lafayette County, Missouri, and the younger of the two daughters having completed a course in the school for the blind that is maintained in the City of St. Louis. Ruby E., who was born November 27, 1889, is now a successful and popular teacher in the public schools of her native state; Sidney K. likewise is proving an able representative of the pedagogic profession; Charles W., who was born November 22, 1894, remains at the parental home, as does also Laura C. B., who was born March 14, 1897.

CHARLES E. RUSH. The connection of Charles E. Rush with library work began with his college days in 1902, and he has since that time been continuously identified with library work, either in a public or private capacity. He has gone into the work with an enthusiasm that has made him one of the most successful and sought after librarians in the state, and he has been at the head of the St. Joseph Public Library since 1910.

Mr. Rush was born at Fairmount, Indiana, on March 23, 1885, and is a son of Reverend Nixon and Louisa (Winslow) Rush. Both parents were Quakers, of North Carolina ancestry. The paternal grandsire of Mr. Rush was a slave holder in North Carolina, but he became early convinced of the error of owning human property, so that in 1830 he freed his slaves and moved north to Indiana, where the family has since been established. The father of Mr. Rush is a Quaker minister, who added farming to his ministerial activities and became one of the most useful men in his community.

Charles E. Rush was educated in the common schools of the Town of Fairmount and at the Fairmount Friends Academy. He had his A. B. degree from Earlham College in 1905, after which he entered the Library Summer School at Madison, Wisconsin, of which he is a graduate, and received the degree of B. L. S. from the New York State Library School at Albany in 1908. He planned a career as librarian when he was a boy, and so arranged his studies from his college days. He was a student-assistant in the library at Earlham College in Richmond, Indiana, from 1903 to 1905, and served a year as an assistant at the Wisconsin University Library at Madison in 1905 and 1906. He was an assistant in the Free Public Library in Newark, New Jersey, in 1907, and in 1907 and 1908 was engaged as a special cataloguer in the Pruyn Private Library in Albany, New York. In 1908 he became librarian of the Public Library at Jackson, Michigan, and two years later he came to St. Joseph to assume the duties of librarian of the public library here, where he has continued his work successfully and with all satisfaction to the public and to the board of library directors.

Mr. Rush is a member of the American Library Association and of the Missouri Library Association, serving as vice president of the latter organization in 1912 and as president in 1913. As one who is deeply interested in civic and social work, Mr. Rush is concerned in making the library a thing of practical value in the community, not alone for the young readers and students, but for the laboring man, the busy merchant and business man of every order. He has prepared a number of pamphlets and magazine articles bearing upon the splendid possibilities that are to be found from a more intimate knowledge of the "people's university," among them might be mentioned "Library Publicity," "The Man in the Yards," and "Two Books a Year for My Child." His "Reading List for the Boy Scouts of America" was the first library pamphlet published on the subject and it has been well received wherever it has been shown.

Mr. Rush is an active member of the St. Joseph Commerce Club and in 1912 was chairman of the luncheon and entertainment committee. In 1913 he was a member of the art and publicity committees of the club, and has been active in the work of the organization in varied ways.

In 1910 Mr. Rush was married to Miss R. Lionne Adsit, a daughter of Rev. Spenser M. Adsit, of Albany, New York, who is a Presbyterian minister. Mrs. Rush is a graduate of Vassar College, at Poughkeepsie, New York, class of 1906, receiving the degree of A. B., and is also a graduate of the New York State Library School at Albany, class of 1908, with the degree of B. L. S. She spent two years as chief of the information department in the Public Library at Washington, D. C., prior to her marriage.

In 1911 Mrs. Rush was president of the Federation of Women's Clubs of St. Joseph, Missouri, and since that time has been a member of the executive committee of the Federation. She is active in the church work of the First Presbyterian Church of St. Joseph, of which she is a member, and is president of the Kings Daughters Society, an auxiliary organization of the church. She is one of the prominent women of the city and takes a leading place in the representative social club and civic activities of the city.

BENJAMIN H. CARTER. Noteworthy among the little group of Cameron people that are rendering the Government active and able service is Benjamin H. Carter, rural mail carrier on Route 3. He was born, October 8, 1857, on the parental homestead in Platte County, Missouri, of Scotch-Irish descent. Benjamin H. Carter, Sr., his father, was born and reared in Kentucky. He came to Missouri in 1844, spent one year in Clay County, and in 1857, in pioneer days, located in Platte County. Choosing the occupation of a farmer, he was engaged in agricultural pursuits until his death, at the age of seventy-three years. A man of integrity, upright and fair in all his dealings, he won the confidence of the community in which he resided for so many years, and though during the Civil war his sympathies were with the Union men his own life was such that he was never molested, and he was enabled on one or two occasions to save the lives of others. He was a republican in politics. He married Melinda A. Vermillion, and of their eight children two daughters are living in Platte County, one son resides in El Paso, Texas, and another son, L. O. Carter, is a prominent lawyer of Kansas City, where he has served a judge of bankruptcy.

Benjamin H. Carter, the special subject of this sketch, grew to manhood on his father's farm in Platte County, acquiring his early education in the public schools. He became familiar with farm work while young, and still owns a good farm. In 1902 he was appointed rural mail carrier on Route 6 from Cameron, and continued on that route for six years. He was then transferred to Route 3, which covers 25⅜ miles to the southwest from Cameron, and in the discharge of his duties he travels annually a distance of approximately eight thousand miles. He has carried the mail on foot, on horseback, in cart or carriage, but now owns and uses an automobile whenever the roads, which are usually good, permit. He has a pleasant home at 221 West Cornhill Street, in a desirable part of the town, and there he and his family enjoy the comforts of life.

Mr. Carter married, in 1880, Miss Permelia S. Frazer, a daughter of George Frazer, of Platte County, and into their household two children have been born, Ruth J. and James B. Ruth J. Carter was educated in the Wesleyan College at Cameron and became a successful and popular teacher. She was appointed rural mail carrier and served on Rural Route 4 for nine months and is now her father's deputy or substitute. James B. Clark is a clerk in the Cameron Postoffice, also a graduate of Missouri Wesleyan College Business Department and of Lincoln-Jefferson University of Law, Hammond, Ind. He married Miss Grace English, and they have one son, Raymond English Carter.

Religiously Mr. Carter is an active member of the Methodist Episcopal Church, in which he has served as class leader and steward and as superintendent of the Sunday school. Fraternally he belongs to the Order of Masons.

JOHN COSTIN. With all of honor and consistency may be entered in this publication a tribute to the venerable pioneer citizen whose name introduces this paragraph and who has maintained his home in Worth County for a period of virtually sixty years. He has passed the eightieth milestone on the journey of life, has ordered his course on a high plane of integrity and honor, has achieved worthy success through his own efforts, and has at all times stood exponent of the most loyal and worthy citizenship. He has served in various offices of public trust within the long years of his residence in Worth County, and also has the distinction of being one of the gallant citizens of Missouri who went forth in defense of the Union in the Civil war. A man of deep piety, of strong and noble nature and of utmost tolerance and kindliness, Mr. Costin has made his life count for good in all its relations and is well worthy of the unqualified confidence and affection that are accorded him by all who know him, so that he may recall in gracious retrospect the incidents of an earnest and useful life now that its shadows begin to steal gently from the golden west.

John Costin was born in Jefferson County, Kentucky, on the 18th of September, 1830, and is a scion of sterling pioneer families of that fine old commonwealth, within whose borders were born his parents, Lewis and Catherine (Smock) Costin, both of whom passed the closing period of their lives in the State of Indiana. In the year 1843, when the subject of this review was a lad of about thirteen years, the family removed from Kentucky to Owen County, Indiana, where the father purchased a tract of wild land and instituted the reclamation of a farm. John Costin, owing to the vicissitudes and conditions of time and place, received most meager educational advantages in his boyhood and youth, but fully has he profited through self-discipline and association with the practical affairs of life, with the result that he is a man of broad mental ken and mature judgment. As a mere boy Mr. Costin gained close fellowship with toil, in connection with the work of the home farm, and he became also a wage-earner when he was but eight years old, modest recompense being given him for the work of cutting cornstalks for neighbors near the old home in Kentucky.

At the age of twenty years Mr. Costin made his first independent investment, by purchasing a tract of land in Decatur County, Iowa. On this place he remained only one year, at the expiration of which, in 1855, he came to Worth County, Missouri, which has represented his home during the long intervening years. Here he purchased 160 acres of swamp land, and he applied himself to the arduous work of providing a proper system of drainage and to bringing the land under effective cultivation. On his originally uninviting farm he eventually produced very fine crops of wheat, corn and other cereals, and with increasing prosperity he added to his landed estate from time to time, until he is now the owner of a fine demesne of 1,000 acres, in sections 13, 65 and 32, Worth Township.

In 1860, while still giving careful supervision to his farm, Mr. Costin established a general store at West Point, the nucleus of the village now known as Oxford. He sold this store and business eleven months later, and thereafter he continued successfully in the mercantile trade, by establishing, in turn, stores at Grant City, Worth and Smithton. He eventually disposed of each of these establishments, the one at Worth having been sold to his son, Nicholas F., who still continues the enterprise and who is known as one of the successful business men of Worth County, individual record concerning him being given on other pages of this work.

In response to President Lincoln's first call for volunteers to aid in maintaining the integrity of the Union, Mr. Costin enlisted as a member of a regiment largely recruited in Worth and adjoining counties, and after serving about thirteen months, principally in Missouri and Arkansas, he received his honorable discharge. In politics Mr. Costin has ever been arrayed as a staunch supporter of the cause of the democratic party, and he has been called upon to serve in various positions of local public trust. In 1864 he served as treasurer of Worth County and in 1868 he was elected county sheriff and collector, to which dual office he was elected in 1870, so that he served, and with marked ability, for four consecutive years, later having been the incumbent of the office of county coroner. He also served for a number of years as a member of the school board of his district, and his influence and aid have at all times been given in the furtherance of measures tending to conserve the educational, moral and general civic welfare of the community, in later years his zeal having been specially notable in connection with the promotion of the good roads movement in this section of the state. Mr. Costin and his gracious wife are most zealous and devout members of the Christian Church, in which he is now an elder of the church at Worth, his service having previously been given for a number of years in the position of deacon.

At Greenup, Cumberland County, Illinois, in the year 1852, was solemnized the marriage of Mr. Costin to Miss Louisa Asher, daughter of Lewis and Alice (Brown) Asher, who were residents of Illinois at the time of their death, Mrs. Costin having been born in Warren County, Indiana, on the 24th of August, 1835. Mr. and Mrs. Costin became the parents of five children, concerning whom brief record is given in conclusion of this review: John D., who was born March 4, 1877, and who wedded Miss Leora Barnes, of Worth County, is one of the prosperous farmers of this county; Nicholas F. is engaged in business at Worth and is the subject of an individual sketch on other pages of this volume; Martha Jane, who died in December, 1896, was the wife of James Martin, who is a representative farmer of Worth County, and she is survived by three children, Zula May, Gettis and Maggie Vera. The second daughter, Florence, born in 1864, is the wife of Reuben Swain, and they live in Nodaway County and have had three children, Arthur,

John S. Amick

Minnie and Blanche, but Arthur died in 1913. Zula May, youngest of
the children of Mr. and Mrs. Costin, was born March 27, 1873, and is the
wife of Ira Wells, engaged in farming near Ravenswood, Nodaway
County, and they have one son, Darl Ford.

NICHOLAS F. COSTIN. Bearing a name that has been most honorably
and prominently linked with the history of Worth County for more than
half a century, Mr. Costin is in every sense upholding the high prestige
of his patronymic and is numbered among the progressive merchants
and loyal and enterprising citizens of his native county, where he is
engaged in the general merchandise business in the Village of Worth,
as successor of his honored father, John Costin, concerning whom consistent and more specific mention is made on other pages of this publication, so that further review of the family history is not demanded in
the present connection.

Nicholas Ford Costin was born on the old homestead farm, in Middle-
fork Township, Worth County, Missouri, on the 25th of December, 1878,
so that he became a right welcome Christmas guest in the family home,
as the youngest of the four children. The public schools afforded to Mr.
Costin his early educational advantages, and this discipline was supplemented by a course in the Gem City Business College, in which he was
graduated in 1896. In pursuance of higher academic training he
entered Stenbury College, in 1892, prior to taking his course in the
business college, and he there pursued the normal or teacher's curriculum
until 1894, when he returned to his home and became actively associated
with the work and management of the farm. In the same year also he
became his father's coadjutor in establishing the general store at Worth,
and he continued as his father's partner in the business until 1910, since
which time he has been the sole proprietor. He has brought to bear most
progressive policies and has made his store effective in service, with a
stock carefully selected to meet the demands of the trade and with
punctilious care to fair and honorable treatment of all patrons. On the
11th of October, 1913, Mr. Costin removed from his original building to
new and more eligible quarters in an adjoining building, the second
floor of which is nicely fitted up as a village opera house or theater.

Mr. Costin has strong vantage-place in the confidence and esteem of
the people of his native county, and it may legitimately be said that here
his circle of friends is limited only by that of his acquaintances. At the
county seat he is affiliated with Grant City Lodge No. 66, Ancient Free
and Accepted Masons, besides which he holds membership in the adjunct
organization, the Order of the Eastern Star, and is a member of Worth
Lodge No. 614, Independent Order of Odd Fellows. In politics he is
unswerving in his support and advocacy of the cause of the democratic
party and he has served as clerk of various elections held in the county.

On February 22, 1903, Mr. Costin was married to Miss Adella Mc-
Cray, who was born in Nodaway County and who is a daughter of
James A. and Amanda E. (Mullen) McCray, whose fine homestead farm
is situated near Gilman City, Daviess County, where they have resided
for many years, Mr. McCray being a prominent democrat of that county
and having served as its sheriff. Mrs. Costin completed special course
in literature and music at Grand River College, and is a woman whose
gracious personality makes her a favorite in the social life of her home
community. Here both she and her husband are affiliated with Hall of
Sunshine Chapter No. 222, Order of the Eastern Star, and she is eligible
likewise for membership in the Society of the Daughters of the American Revolution. Mr. and Mrs. Costin have no children.

JOHN S. SMITH. There is no financial institution in Northwest
Missouri which more thoroughly deserves and enjoys to a greater degree

the confidence of the community which it serves than the Holt County Bank, at Mound City, which has had a long and prosperous career of more than thirty years. The bank was organized in February, 1880, by Hugh Montgomery, Albert Roecker and Robert Montgomery. Its first president was Robert Montgomery, and its first cashier was Hugh Montgomery. This bank began as a small private institution, started more for the convenience of a limited patronage than as a general public utility, and its growth has been in proportion to the development of the community and the constantly growing patronage voluntarily accorded it. Its first location was in the rear of the William Hoblitzell store, now the Wehrli store, subsequently it was moved to the corner where the Riffe & Company's store is now located, and after that building burned was moved to its present location.

It is an axiom that the strength of any banking institution depends upon the personnel of the men behind it and in its organization. To an important degree the success of the Holt County Bank has been due to Mr. John S. Smith, who is now serving as its president, and was its cashier from 1887 to 1900, when promoted to his present office.

John S. Smith has made a typical American success. He started life as a section hand and has risen to leadership in his community, both as a banker and citizen. His father was killed during the Civil war, and his widowed mother had six small children dependent upon her. In such conditions it was necessary for the son John early to take up work that would help support the household, and all the education he received was acquired by self study during the meager opportunities of hard labor.

John S. Smith was born in Holt County, April 11, 1855, a son of Moses and Sarah Louise (Currier) Smith. Diligence, ambition and integrity have been the characteristic features of Mr. Smith's career. He worked only a few years as a common laborer, then found employment in a hardware store in Mound City, from that got into the lumber business, and had a small independent establishment of his own. The people of this community from the first had recognized his thorough integrity in all his dealings, and as he was prosperous himself and a man of rare judgment, many found it convenient to intrust him with the task of looking after their financial surplus. In this way Mr. Smith was led to engage in banking in a small way, and his institution was one of the constituent elements in the formation of the Holt County Bank. From the position of cashier in that institution he was promoted to the presidency, and is the owner of most of the stock in the bank. His nephew, B. P. Smith, was for several years cashier, and is now vice president, while the present cashier is B. H. Watson.

Besides his interest as a banker, Mr. Smith is the owner of a thousand acres of land in the vicinity of Mound City, and is easily one of the most substantial citizens of that section. He also has extensive business interests in Kansas, Colorado and other states. He has attained thirty-two degrees in Scottish Rite Masonry and is affiliated with the Independent Order of Odd Fellows and the Woodmen of the World. His chief public service has been as a member of the school board, and for more than thirty years he has served as its president. Since he began as a business man at Mound City no enterprise affecting the welfare of the community has been advanced without his loyal support and frequent cooperation. He is a well-known citizen in Northwest Missouri, and particularly in banking circles of this section of the state.

Mr. Smith was married July 19, 1874, to Miss Mary N. Denmark, who was born at Black River Falls, Wisconsin. To their marriage have been born nine children, and the four still living are: Bertha B., at home; Charles C., who married Margaret Corsant and lives in Mound

City, engaged in the oil producing business, operating chiefly in the Oklahoma fields; Helen H. is the wife of C. T. Hall, assistant cashier of the Holt County Bank; and Colene, a student in Rockford College at Rockford, Illinois.

MILLARD FILLMORE STIPES. This Jamesport editor and publisher has lived actively and usefully in Northwest Missouri forty-five years, at first as a teacher and surveyor, and close on to thirty years in journalism. A newspaper man is also in an important sense a public man, and Mr. Stipes has in addition given much time to the formal duties of office in his city and state.

Millard Fillmore Stipes is a lineal descendant, twelfth in line, from Sir Edward, Lord North, the first baron of that name, created by Henry VIII of England. Capt. George North, an officer in the Pennsylvania line during the American Revolution, who fought so valiantly against his kinsman, the British premier, was the great-grandfather of the Missouri editor.

Mr. Stipes was born at the old Cruzen home in Saline County, Missouri, November 12, 1851. Growing up on his father's farm, he attended district school near by except for a year or so during the Civil war, and during 1867-68 was a student in the Miami Male and Female Institute, a private school conducted by John C. Hamner, A. M., of Virginia. In the spring of 1869 his parents removed to a new home in Carroll County, and he began work on a farm and as a surveyor, a calling he had learned under the instruction of Professor Hamner. For two years he was deputy county surveyor, and in January, 1870, began teaching, his regular occupation for the next fifteen winters and for about half of the intervening summers. Mr. Stipes was a student in the Kirksville Normal during the spring and summer of 1873 and again in 1874. His teaching was chiefly in the country districts of Carroll and Saline counties, but for three years, 1880 to 1883, he was at the head of the graded schools in Norborne, and at Jamesport the following year and at Jameson the next, all in Missouri.

On January 1, 1885, Mr. Stipes took charge of the Jameson Reporter, which he edited and published until September 1, 1886, when he purchased the Jamesport Gazette, of which he has been editor and publisher continuously to the present writing. Few members of the profession in Northwest Missouri have held an editor's chair with one paper for a longer time.

While not a professional politician, Mr. Stipes has for a number of years been interested in politics and the problems of government. In 1892 he represented his county in the democratic state convention at Sedalia and again at Kansas City in 1894, and has often been called to preside over democratic county and local conventions. By appointment from Governor Folk, he served four years, February 1, 1907, to February 1, 1911, as a member of the board of control of the State Industrial Home for Girls at Chillicothe, and during that time was treasurer of the institution. In his home city Mr. Stipes served for twenty-one years on the school board, all the time as president or secretary.

December 28, 1881, he married Emma Lee Kieffer, at the home of her parents near Miami. Her death occurred April 22, 1891, and one child survives, Mrs. Opal Arnold. He married Amy Louise Ried, June 6, 1893, at the home of her parents in Kirkwood, Missouri. Three children were born to them, two of whom, Ruth and Florence, survive.

SOPER J. TAUL. One of the comparatively young men in Clay County citizenship, Mr. Taul has achieved the success which consists in accumulation of a substantial share of the world's goods and in an honorable position among his fellows. Largely through his own efforts he has prospered as a farmer, and for the past four years has justified the confidence of the community through his work in the office of county collector.

Soper J. Taul was born in Platte Township of Clay County, November 22, 1877. His parents were Ben I. and Patsy Ann (Spencer) Taul. His father was born in Clark County, Kentucky, in 1821, and the mother in Nicholas County of the same state on August 26, 1832, and is still living, while the father died July 26, 1886. They were married in their native state—came out to Missouri before the war, the father coming through by land-working cows—and they settled in Clay County, but owing to the troubles incident to war times returned to Kentucky. When peace was restored they found permanent homes in Missouri, and the father took up farming east of Smithville. He started with 390 acres, and had an estate of 270 at the time of his death. For this time he was reckoned among the successful farmers. He was a democrat, and with his family worshipped in the Methodist faith. Of the eleven children, nine are still living, as follows: Elizabeth, wife of S. H. Lewis of Paradise, Missouri; James, of Clay County; Mollie, wife of Noah Neff, of Liberty; W. K., of Kearny; Margaret, deceased; J. T., who is farming on the home place; R. C., living at Paradise; Maxie, wife of Hayden Settle, of Kearny; Benjamin, of St. Joseph; C. D., deceased; and Soper J.

The youngest of the family, Soper J. Taul was only nine years old when his father died, and as the necessities of the homestead demanded all hands, he stopped his schooling at an early age, having attended several winter terms in the country. He worked at home until his marriage, and when that event was celebrated at the age of twenty-one he started out to provide for his own family. On December 21, 1898, he married Minerva Davis, who was born in the same neighborhood November 12, 1877, a daughter of Cephas and Falitta Jane (Britt) Davis. Her mother is still living at the age of sixty-five.

As a part of his earlier experience Mr. Taul had worked for three years, between the ages of fifteen and seventeen, at wages of 50 cents a day, so he had a thorough apprenticeship in the school of labor. After his marriage he continued on the home place a short time, then rented land for three years, after which he bought a place adjoining the old homestead. For about ten years he carried on his enterprise as a progressive farmer citizen, and still owns and operates a farm of 160 acres north of Liberty.

Mr. Taul has taken considerable part in democratic politics, and was the choice of his party and many friends for the office of county collector in the fall of 1910, and after four years of capable work was renominated and elected without opposition in 1914. Mr. Taul belongs to the Knights of Pythias and Independent Order of Odd Fellows, and he and his wife are Methodists. They are the parents of two children: May Neff and Dorothy Eleanor.

G. W. STONER. Noteworthy among the oldest and best known real estate men of Northwest Missouri is G. W. Stoner, of Cameron, who has been a resident of that city since 1868, and during the time that has since elapsed has been conspicuously identified with the highest interests of town and county, ever using his influence to promote the public welfare.. Mr. Stoner was born, January 13, 1835, in South Bend, Indiana, and when he was about twelve years old the family removed to Montgomery County, that state, locating not far from Crawfordsville.

Jacob Stoner, his father, was a native of Virginia, was of German descent, and inherited in a large measure the habits of thrift and industry characteristic of his forefathers. Migrating with his family to

Indiana in pioneer days, he bought land in Montgomery County, and in addition to carrying on general farming, he for many years had a well producing sugar orchard on his place. He married, in Botetourt County, Virginia, Polly Beath, who was of English ancestry, and to them five children were born, two sons and three daughters, and of these three children are living, as follows: David, a resident of Kansas; Mariah Brawton, of Lathrop, Missouri; and G. W., the subject of this review. Both parents died on the home farm in Indiana, the father dying at the age of seventy-seven years, he having survived his wife for a number of years. He was a republican in politics, and both he and his wife were members of the Christian Church.

G. W. Stoner acquired his education in the district schools of his native county, and developed into manhood on the parental homestead, where he was trained to the habits of industry and thrift that became the foundation of his present success in business and have gained for him the respect of the community in which he lives. As a young man he was ambitious to take advantage of the opportunities offered in a new and undeveloped country, and in 1857 located in Daviess County, Missouri, where he followed farming for a few years. Settling in Cameron in 1868, he established himself in the real estate business, which he has since followed with deserved success, his dealings being extensive and profitable. Mr. Stoner has an intimate acquaintance with land values throughout the central west, his dealings in realty extending to all parts of Missouri, Kansas, Oklahoma and Texas.

He married, in 1862, more than fifty years ago, Susan Rogers, of Daviess County, Missouri, who has, indeed, proved herself a true helpmate and a most congenial companion. Three children blessed their union, namely: Jacob, Ida and B. F., but the last named, the youngest of the three, died in 1868. Jacob Stoner, the first born, died in April, 1912, his death being mourned as a public loss. He was one of the best known traveling salesmen of the state, and was also active in local affairs, having served his constituents most faithfully and ably in various offices, more especially as mayor of Cameron. For many years he was drum major in the Cameron Military Band, which was one of the finest musical organizations in this section of the country, and was often in demand throughout Missouri, playing in all its large cities. He was a member of the Independent Order of Odd Fellows and of the Knights of Pythias. He married Alice Smith, a native of Missouri.

Mr. G. W. Stoner is public spirited and a highly useful member of the community, active in advancing the things which make for the welfare and progress of town and county, being especially interested in the cause of education and religion. Both Mr. and Mrs. Stoner united with the Christian Church when young.

GENERAL BENJAMIN M. PRENTISS. For many years one of the most distinguished citizens of Missouri as well as of the nation was the late Gen. Benjamin M. Prentiss, who for twenty years lived at Bethany, where his death occurred on February 8, 1901. General Prentiss was a soldier of two wars, rose to the rank of major general, U. S. Volunteers, during the Civil war and was the hero of the great battle of Shiloh. In his political career he was an associate of Lincoln and other distinguished leaders of Illinois, and in the later years of his life was one of the most admired orators and leaders in the republican party of Missouri.

Benjamin M. Prentiss was born at Belleville, Virginia, November 23, 1819. He was a direct descendant from Valentine Prentiss who came to America from England in 1620. Another direct ancestor was the noted Elder Brewster, of the Mayflower colony. Valentine Prentiss (1) with his wife, Alice, came to Roxbury, Massachusetts, in 1631, and died about 1633. His son John Prentiss (2) born in England, came over with his parents in 1631, married Hester ———; died in 1691. His son Jonathan Prentiss (3), born July 15, 1657, married Elizabeth Latimer; died July 28, 1727. His son John Prentiss (4), born 1705, married Sarah Christophers; died January, 1746-47. His son John Prentiss (5), born November 23, 1740, married Esther Richards; died November 22, 17—. His son Henry Leonidas Prentiss (6), born July 4, 1788, married Rebecca Mayberry; died December 24, 1849.

Henry Leonidas Prentiss, father of General Prentiss, was born in New London, Connecticut, in 1788, and died at Quincy, Illinois, in 1849. He was a public-spirited man and a politician. At one time he was a member of the Legislature from Wood County, Virginia. He married Rebecca Mayberry, and General Prentiss was one of two sons, the other being Henry Clay, who died in Knox County, Missouri. The daughters were Mrs. Amelia Adair, Mrs. Lucy Bowles, Mrs. Mary Goodno.

General Prentiss spent his early childhood in Virginia, and from there his parents moved to Quincy, Illinois. His education came from the country schools of Virginia, and afterwards from a private military school. Migrating west in 1836, he located in Marion County, Missouri, and engaged in the manufacture of cordage. In the spring of 1841 he went to Quincy and established himself in the same business with his father. During the Mormon excitement at Nauvoo, Illinois, he was in the service of the state, and at the opening of the Mexican war he was appointed adjutant of the First Illinois Infantry. With this regiment he served through the entire war, first as first lieutenant and afterwards as captain of Company I, which he commanded under General Taylor at the battle of Buena Vista.

It was during his residence at Palmyra, Missouri, that the mettle of General Prentiss' character was tested. A small man in physical stature, but with extraordinary courage and force of intellect and will, he never hesitated in the presence of anyone to uphold his ideas of morals and politics. He possessed decided convictions on the subject of slavery and other economic questions which finally were settled by the arbitrament of war, and expressed himself characteristically and freely in whatever community he lived. Palmyra at that time was a hotbed of secession sentiment, and young Prentiss was constantly persecuted because of his anti-slavery views. In a contest of wits and logic he was an easy victor, but not all his battles were of that character. He frequently engaged in personal combat, though not as an aggressor, and it became almost a common practice for the southerners in that town to set upon the valiant young abolitionist the strongest bully who could be induced to attack him. So far as can be ascertained, there was never a case in which Prentiss did not prove himself master of the situation, and when he left Palmyra he had at least the thorough respect if not the friendship of every resident. After his return to Quincy and also after the war, General Prentiss was engaged in business as a commission merchant and also as a manufacturer of cordage. With the outbreak of hostilities between the North and South he was one of the first to respond with the offer of his services. At the first call for troops he sent a telegram to the governor of Illinois, tendering two companies, and has the distinction of having been the first officer commissioned by the state. Beginning as a captain, he was promoted to major, from that to colonel, and then to the rank of brigadier-general before reaching the actual scene of hostilities. General Prentiss was placed in command at Cairo at the beginning of the war and established a blockade of the Mississippi River. While there he was waited upon by a delegation of Kentuckians, who protested against the landing of troops on Kentucky soil. This delegation reminded him that Kentucky was a sovereign state, the peer of Illinois, but to this General Prentiss replied that when the President called for troops to defend the Union, Illinois promptly furnished her quota, while Kentucky had failed to respond, and consequently her wishes were not entitled to the same consideration.

After leaving Cairo General Prentiss was ordered by General Fremont to Jefferson City, Missouri, to take command of all North and Central Missouri. He fought at Mount Zion and a number of other minor engagements in the state. Subsequently being ordered to the field by General Halleck, he proceeded to Pittsburg Landing, Tennessee, where he arrived April 1st, and organized and took command of the Sixth Division, Army of the Tennessee. It was there that his reputation as a military leader was secured beyond all peradventure. The historians of that great battle have all united in giving General Prentiss' command credit for maintaining the integrity of the Union position during the first day, and thus insuring what amounted to a virtual victory for the Union arms. It will be recalled that the other federal generals in council doubted that the Confederates were massed in force at Shiloh, and at his own request General Prentiss was permitted to send a small force forward to ascertain whether the enemy was not there in force. Five companies from General Prentiss' division were selected for that task, and these troops while reconnoitering received the first onslaughts of the enemy, arrested their charge and thus gave the Union army time to form the line of battle. The Confederates attacked in such force and with such energy that General Sherman's corps and all the other commands were compelled to give ground, and General Prentiss himself had to retire to a better position. At his command his troops finally took position in the old Sunken Road, and there their resistance was so deadly that the Confederates called the place the "Hornet's Nest," and there the most sanguinary struggle of the day was centered. It was while General Prentiss was holding this line that General Grant came up, and requested him to hold the road until sundown at all hazards. General Prentiss gave his promise, and he afterwards stated that again and again he looked for the setting sun, and was almost convinced from the slowness with which that luminary moved toward the western horizon, that it had surely caught upon a snag. No reinforcements were sent to his hard-pressed troops, and at 5.30 in the evening General Prentiss and his 2,200 soldiers were captured. For the following seven months he endured the rigors of Confederate prisons. It was during this time that newspapers published the report that the Confederates had surprised and taken General Prentiss out of bed early in the morning on the first day. This report went all over the Union, and for a number of years remained without formal contradiction. General Prentiss declined to defend himself officially from the falsehood until 1880, when at the urging of his friends and in justice to the troops captured with him, he issued a

"On the morning of April 6, 1862, the Union forces encamped at Pittsburg Landing consisted of five divisions, commanded respectively by: First, McClernand, 7,028 men; second, W. H. L. Wallace, 7,564 men; fourth, Hurlbut, 7,302 men; fifth, Sherman, 8,830 men; sixth, B. M. Prentiss, 5,463 men; total, 36,187 men.

"About 20 per cent of this number did not engage in the action on account of sickness, detailed for other duty and temporary absence, leaving 28,950 on active duty; with sixty-one regiments of infantry, three regiments of cavalry, and twenty-one batteries of artillery, exclusive of the Third Division, commanded by Gen. Lew Wallace, at Crump's Landing, seven miles below, numbering 7,564 men, not engaged in the first day's battle.

"Gen. U. S. Grant was in command of all Union forces in the vicinity of Savannah and Pittsburg Landing.

"Gen. Albert Sydney Johnston was in command of all Confederate forces in Tennessee.

"General Hickenlooper."

SIXTH DIVISION

"On the 26th day of March, 1862, General Grant, by Special Order No. 36, assigned General Prentiss to the command of unattached troops then arriving at Pittsburg Landing, with directions to organize these regiments, as they arrived upon the field, into brigades, and the brigades into a division, to be designated the Sixth Division.

"Under this order one brigade of four regiments, commanded by Colonel Peabody, had been organized and was encamped on west side of Eastern Corinth Road, 400 yards south of the Barnes Field. Another brigade, commanded by Colonel Miller, Eighteenth Missouri, was partially organized. Three regiments had reported and were in camp on the east side of the Eastern Corinth Road. Other regiments on their way up the Tennessee River had been ordered to report to General Prentiss, but had not arrived.

"The Sixteenth Iowa arrived on the field on the 5th and sent its morning report to General Prentiss in time to have it included in his report of present for duty that day; it was not fully equipped and did not disembark from the boat until the morning of the 6th. The Fifteenth Iowa and Twenty-third Missouri arrived at the landing Sunday morning, April 6, 1862. The Twenty-third Missouri reported to General Prentiss at his third position about 9:30 A. M., and was placed in line at once as part of his command. The Fifteenth and Sixteenth Iowa were, by General Grant's order, sent to the right to reinforce McClernand. They reported to him at his fifth position in Jones' Field, and were hotly engaged from about 1 P. M. to 2:30 P. M. Hickenlooper's Fifth Ohio Battery and Munch's First Minnesota Battery and two battalions of Eleventh Illinois Cavalry had been assigned to the division and were encamped in the rear of the infantry. One company from each regiment was on picket one mile in front of the camps. On Saturday, April 5th, a reconnoitering party under Colonel Moore, Twenty-first Missouri, was sent to the front. Colonel Moore reported Confederate cavalry and some evidences of an infantry force in front, but he failed to develop a regular line of the enemy. Prentiss doubled his pickets, and at 3 A. M. Sunday sent out another party of three companies of the Twenty-fifth Missouri, under Major Powell, to reconnoiter well to the front. This party encountered the Confederate picket under Major Hardcastle in Fraley's Field at 4.55 A. M. These pickets at once engaged, and continued their fire until about 6:30 A. M., when the advance of the main line of Hardee's Corps drove Powell back.

"General Prentiss, hearing the firing, formed his division at 6 A. M. and sent Peabody's brigade in advance of his camp to relieve the retiring pickets and posted Miller's brigade 300 yards in front of his camp, with batteries in the field at right and left of the Eastern Corinth Road. In this position the division was attacked at 8 A. M. by the brigades of Gladden, Shaver, Chalmers, and Wood and driven back to its camp, where the contest was renewed. At 9 A. M. Prentiss was compelled to abandon his camp and fall back to his third position, which he occupied at 9:05 A. M. in an old road between the divisions of Hurlbut and W. H. L. Wallace. Hickenlooper lost two guns in first position and Munch had two disabled. Each brought four guns into line at the Hornet's Nest. Prentiss was here joined by the Twenty-third Missouri, which gave him about one thousand men at his third position. With this force he held his line against the attacks of Shaver, Stephens and Gibson, as described in account of Tuttle's brigade, until 4 P. M., when Hurlbut fell back and Prentiss was obliged to swing his division back at right angles to Tuttle in order to protect the left flank. When Tuttle's left regiments marched to the rear Prentiss fell back behind them towards the Corinth Road and was surrounded and captured at 5:30 P. M., near the forks of the Eastern Corinth Road. Hickenlooper and Munch withdrew just before they were surrounded, Hickenlooper reporting to Sherman and becoming engaged in the 4:30 action on the Hamburg Road. Munch's battery reported to Colonel Webster was in position at mouth of Dill Branch, where it assisted in repelling the last attack Sunday night.

"Maj. D. W. Reed,
"Historian and Secretary, Shiloh National
Military Park Commission."

THE HORNET'S NEST

"Slowly we retired from one defensible position to another, at each receiving the fire of well-served opposing battery, until we reached a roadway which ran at right angles to the one upon which we had been moving, well known as the "Sunken Road," having been cut some distance through a low hill. Thus nature supplied a breastwork, a defensive line upon which to rally, with a prominent knoll upon which to place the battery, with front covered by almost impenetrable growth of underbrush. The Confederates made repeated charges and desperate assaults but the Union force could not be routed from their place of vantage. The dead and wounded fell like hail. A great number of the troops that fought like tigers in the "Sunken Road" were raw, had never been in battle before. The day wore on, the Union line slowly melting away, ammunition nearly exhausted. The enemy's lines were plainly seen crossing to the peach orchard in our rear, toward the only road over which escape was possible. Then General Prentiss informed me that he feared it was too late to withdraw his infantry, but I must pull out, and, if possible, reach the reserve forces in the rear. I bade the general good-bye, and under whip and spur, the remnant of our battery dashed down the road, barely escaping capture. Prentiss remained with his devoted followers, and with them accepted captivity rather than abandon the position he had been ordered to hold to the last.   General Hickenlooper."

"Shiloh was the severest battle fought at the West during the war, and but few in the East equaled it, for hard, determined fighting. I saw an open field, in our possession on the second day, over which the Confederates had made repeated charges the day before, so covered with dead that it would have been possible to walk across the clearing, in any direction stepping on dead bodies, without a foot touching the ground. On our side, National and Confederate troops were mingled together in about equal proportions, but on the remainder of the field nearly all were Confederates. On one part, which had evidently not been plowed for years, bushes had grown up, some to the height of eight or ten feet. There was not one of these left standing unpierced by bullets. The smaller ones were all cut down.

"Gen. U. S. Grant."

"The chivalry of the South was to be met by the sturdy manhood of the North. Perhaps neither Gettysburg nor any other battlefield of the war furnished a greater scene of courage and carnage than that afforded in and about that 'Peach Orchard.' It was simply an exhibition of valor, and it was splendid. * * * Prentiss took his third position a few minutes after 9 o'clock, and here he was joined by the Twenty-third Missouri Infantry, which added about six hundred to his fragment of a division. In Prentiss' morning fights and retreat his command had dwindled to less than a thousand men, but these men gave a good account of themselves before the night fell. * * * There was much good fighting in different parts of the field, though not of such magnitude as in and about the 'Peach Orchard'' and in front of the 'Hornet's Nest.' * * * The heroic stand of Prentiss and Wallace in the old road near Duncan field had served the Union cause well. Prentiss was a prisoner in the hands of the enemy, and W. H. L. Wallace lay mortally wounded on the field held by the Confederates, but the stubborn fight, waged from half-past nine in the morning until half-past five in the afternoon, taking the whole strength of the Confederates to subdue the spirited resistance, had saved the day to the Federal Army.   Maj. Geo. Mason,

"Secretary Illinois Shiloh Battlefield Commission."

"The first collision was in the quarter of Gladden's brigade, on our right, with a battalion of five companies of the Twenty-first Missouri of Prentiss' division dispatched well to the front by General Prentiss, of his own motion, as early as 3 A. M. But for this incident, due solely to the intelligent soldierly forethought of an officer not trained for the business of war, the whole Federal front would have been struck wholly unawares, for nowhere else had such prudence been shown.

"General Beauregard."

"I think it is now generally conceded that but for the foresight of General Prentiss in sending Colonel Moore to the front, the Rebels would have reached Sherman's and Prentiss' camp before 6 o'clock. It is also conceded that the heroic fight made by Prentiss at 6 o'clock, in advance of his camp, was the most important event of the battle. He checked the enemy for more than an hour, and their heavy infantry and artillery firing made it so plain to the rest of the army that a battle was unexpectedly upon them, that they moved to its sound without orders.   Colonel Andreas."

"With Hurlbut gone, and Wallace gone, Prentiss was left isolated, struck in front, in rear, and upon either flank, cut off in every attempt to escape, about half-past 5 o'clock what was left of Prentiss' division surrendered. It was this division which had received the first blow in the morning, and made the last organized resistance in the afternoon. The whole Confederate line advanced, resulting at first in the confusion of the enemy, and then in the death of W. H. L. Wallace and the surrender of Prentiss. These generals have received scant justice for their stubborn defense. They had agreed to hold their position at all odds, and did so until Wallace received his fatal wound, and Prentiss was surrounded and captured, with nearly three thousand men. This delay was the salvation of Grant's army.

"Col. Wm. P. Johnston."

"Prentiss' vigilance gave the first warning of the actual danger, and, in fact, commenced the contest. This spirited beginning gave the first alarm to the divisions of Sherman and Prentiss. The latter promptly formed his division and moved a quarter of a mile in advance of his camp, where he was attacked before Sherman was under arms. With the rawest troops in the army, his vigilance gave the earliest warning of danger, and offered absolute resistance to its approach; though broken in the advance, he rallied in line with Hurlbut and Wallace and firmly held his ground until completely surrounded.

"General Buell."

"The final victory of that battle was one of the most important which has ever occurred on this continent.. It dissipated forever that nonsense of 'one southern man whipping a dozen Yankees.' It gave us the prestige which we had only to follow up, as we did at Corinth, Iuka, Vicksburg, Chattanooga, Atlanta, Columbia, and Raleigh—yea, to the end of the war—to insure absolute success.

"General Sherman."

After being exchanged, General Prentiss was commissioned a major general of volunteers for his gallantry at the battle of Shiloh. He served on the court-martial in the case of Gen. Fitz John Porter, and he was the last member of that court to pass away. At the close of this trial he was ordered to report to General Grant at Milliken's Bend, by whom he was assigned the command of the eastern district of Arkansas, with headquarters at Helena. Here on the 4th of July, 1863, he commanded the Union forces in the battle of Helena, gaining a decided victory over the enemy, whose forces were equal to four times his number.

The political career of General Prentiss began a number of years before the war. He was a republican from the organization of the party, and in 1860 was nominated by the Quincy district for Congress. During that year he spoke from the same platform with Oglesby, Ingersoll, Palmer, Yates and Lincoln, and was a companion of Lincoln when the latter spoke in his district. On the first occasion in which General Prentiss spoke with Mr. Lincoln, the future president made a characteristic speech, and said about all there was to be said. When he sat down "Captain Prentiss" was introduced as a candidate for Congress, and being sadly embarrassed by the presence of Mr. Lincoln, leaped from his chair and landed flat-footed on the table in the center of the stage. He did this to attract the attention of the audience and perhaps also it removed some of his embarrassment. When he started into his speech he began in his usual fiery and entertaining way and kept the audience laughing for a few minutes and then sat down. Lincoln with his ready sympathy had divined his predicament and understood the reason for his action, and at the conclusion of his speech leaned over and said, "Young man, when you come in contact with great men, rub up against them and you will find there is not much difference after all." In that campaign General Prentiss was defeated, since that congressional district was not yet ready to accept the doctrines of a new party, but throughout the remaining years of his Illinois residence was in great demand as a speaker in the campaigns.

During his residence at Quincy, General Prentiss was appointed United States pension agent by General Grant, and filled the office eight years. In 1878 he moved to Missouri, spent a short time in Sullivan County, and then engaged in the practice of law at Kirksville. After moving to Bethany in 1881 he continued the practice of law, and in 1888, after the election of President Harrison was appointed postmaster, and received the same honor from President McKinley. In 1880 General Prentiss served as a delegate-at-large to the republican national convention which nominated General Garfield, and was a delegate to the national convention of 1884 which placed Blaine and Logan in the field as the national republican candidates and seconded the nomination of John A. Logan for president. He frequently attended the Missouri conventions of his party, and was one of the most influential and popular leaders in the state. He took part in every campaign until his death. Those who recall General Prentiss as a political orator will agree with the opinion that no speaker of his time could stir up more enthusiasm among his followers, and at the same time do more to convince the lukewarm and disaffected.

After the election of General Harrison, General Prentiss went to Washington, met the president, and was asked what he wanted. General Prentiss, considering his distinguished services was exceedingly modest, and his request was for the postmastership at Bethany, but, he said, he did not wish that office until the then incumbent's term had expired. The president assured him that the office should be his, but expressed himself as desirous to accommodate General Prentiss with something more suitable. However, the latter declined any further favors. While in Washington he went to the office of General Noble, then secretary of the interior, and told the secretary that he was to be the postmaster of Bethany after a few months, and in the meantime inquired if there was not some service that he could render during the interval. General Noble in response made him special agent of the general land office and sent him to Denver, Colorado. While there General Prentiss became so occupied with his duties that he almost forgot the Bethany postoffice, until notified of the resignation of its former incumbent, returned just in time to receive his commission. In religion General Prentiss was a member of the Methodist Church.

The first wife of General Prentiss was Margaret Sowdosky. Their children were: Harrison Tyler; Guy Champlain, who marched with Sherman to the sea and died in Quincy; Jacob Henry, who spent his last years in Bethany, where his family survive him; Ella, who married Doctor Blackburn and still lives in Bethany; Benjamin M., Jr., of Colorado; Clay, of Bethany. The oldest of these children, Harrison Tyler, known better as "Tip," was a drummer boy at Shiloh under General Sherman. The story is related that during the battle he met his father's aide and inquired "where is the old man?" "He's out there where you hear all that fighting," was the reply. "Well," said the drummer boy, "if he's out there one member of the family in the fight is enough, I'm going to the river." For many years after the war, Tip Prentiss was a river pilot on the Mississippi, and died in Bethany.

General Prentiss' second wife was Mary Worthington Whitney, a daughter of Joseph Ingram Whitney, who came from Maine. Mrs. Prentiss was born in Pennsylvania, December 16, 1836, and died in Bethany July 28, 1894. Her children were: Joseph W., of Bethany; Arthur Oglesby, who died in California; Edgar Worthington; and Mrs. Mary Cover, of Harrison County.

Edgar Worthington Prentiss, who has spent most of his life in Bethany, was born in Quincy, Illinois, November 21, 1870. He has lived in Bethany since December 16, 1881. For a number of years he was the companion of his father during numerous political campaigns. While his father was postmaster at Bethany he served as assistant through both the Harrison and McKinley administrations, and then succeeded his father in the office and was himself postmaster for two terms. Since leaving the Bethany postoffice Mr. Prentiss has engaged in business.

On July 14, 1909, Mr. Prentiss was married at Bethany to Miss Lillian C. Neville, a daughter of James M. Neville. A short time previously Mrs. Prentiss had retired from her office as county superintendent of schools, and about the same time Mr. Prentiss left the postoffice, their marriage marking the conclusion of their official career. Mrs. Prentiss was born in Harrison County, was for a number of years engaged in educational work, served in committees in the State Teachers' Association, and has been actively identified with musical and literary circles at Bethany. She is a graduate of the Bethany High School and the Warrensbrug State Normal School. Mrs. Prentiss is now regent of the Daughters of the American Revolution in the Elizabeth Harrison Chapter at Bethany. Mr. Prentiss and wife are active members of the Methodist Church; he is a trustee and she is president of the Ladies' Aid Society.

REV. GEORGE SHERMAN MURPHY, D. D. A man of broad culture, earnest convictions, and strong character, Rev. George Sherman Murphy, pastor of the First English Lutheran Church at St. Joseph, is well known throughout this section of the county as an active and effective worker in all religious and charitable undertakings. He was born, March 4, 1865, near Lewistown, Mifflin County, Pennsylvania, a son of Joseph Murphy, and grandson of Andrew Murphy, both natives of Juniata County, Pennsylvania. His great-grandfather, Patrick Murphy, was born and reared in Ireland, and on coming to this country located in Juniata County, Pennsylvania, where he spent his remaining days. Andrew Murphy was a farmer by occupation, and spent his entire life in his native county. He was a man of great piety, and a faithful member of the Scotch Covenanter Church.

Growing to manhood in Juniata County, Joseph Murphy embarked in mercantile pursuits when young, settling in Reedsville, Mifflin County, where he was actively and prosperously engaged in business until his death, while yet in manhood's prime, having been but thirty-one years old when called to the realms above. The maiden name of his wife was Mary Wherry. She was born in Mifflin County, Pennsylvania, a daughter of George and Sarah (Hoyt) Wherry, coming from German and English ancestry. She is now living with her son George, a bright and active woman, seventy-four years young.

The only son of his parents, George Sherman Murphy attended the rural schools until fourteen years of age, and then began clerking in a store at Yeagertown, Pennsylvania, from that time being self-supporting. He subsequently entered the employ of the William Mann Company, proprietors of the largest axe factory in the world, located in Mifflin County, and there, as a metal polisher, earned money with which to advance his education. Entering Susequehanna University, at Selinsgrove, Pennsylvania, at the age of twenty-three years, Mr. Murphy continued his studies there two years, and then became a member of the sophomore class of Wittenberg College, in Springfield, Ohio, and in 1893 was graduated from that institution with second honors. He was immediately engaged as tutor in Greek at that college, and ere long was advanced from tutor to professor of Greek, and occupied that chair until 1903.

At the age of nineteen years Mr. Murphy had united with the Lutheran Church, and was licensed to preach at a meeting of the Wittenberg Synod, at Plymouth, Ohio, September 29, 1895, and ordained at a meeting of the East Ohio Synod, in Canal Dover, on October 21, 1900. His first charge was at Lucas, Ohio, where he had a successful pastorate. In 1906 he was called to St. Paul's Church, at Peabody, Kansas, where he was stationed six years. An enthusiastic worker while there, Mr. Murphy inspired his congregation to such an extent that a church was built at a cost of $20,000, and was dedicated free of debt.

In 1912 Mr. Murphy came to St. Joseph as pastor of the First English Lutheran Church. He at once set about raising funds for a new church, and that was completed and dedicated on January 18, 1914, a new parsonage also being finished at that time. The church building is a beautiful structure of stone, built in modern style, and containing various rooms for Sunday school and social meetings aside from the main auditorium. There is also a large kitchen and dining room, handsomely finished and furnished, that add much to the equipment of the building. The entire cost of this handsome structure was $62,000, every dollar of which has been paid.

On December 29, 1896, Mr. Murphy was united in marriage with Miss Rebecca Webber, who was born at Penn Grove, New Jersey, a daughter of William and Mary (Harris) Webber, and a lineal descendant on the maternal side of Roger Williams. Mr. and Mrs. Murphy have one child, George W. Murphy, born August 12, 1899.

Fraternally, Mr. Murphy is a member of Clarke Lodge No. 101, Ancient Free and Accepted Masons, of Springfield, Ohio; of Mitchell Chapter No. 14, Royal Arch Masons, of St. Joseph; of Newton Commandery No. 9, Knights Templar, of Newton, Kansas; of Wichita Council No. 12, Royal and Select Masters, of Wichita, Kansas; of Isis Temple, Ancient Arabic Order of Nobles of the Mystic Shrine, of Salina, Kansas; and of all the bodies of the Ancient and Accepted Scottish Rite, thirty-second degree, St. Joseph, Missouri. . He is also a member of the Phi Kappa Psi Fraternity. For six years Mr. Murphy was president of the Peabody, Kansas, Chautauqua. In June, 1914, the honorary degree of doctor of divinity was conferred on him by Midland College, Atchison, Kansas.

ROBERT HUGH MILLER. It is doubtful if, throughout the newspaper world of Northwest Missouri, there has been a better known or more greatly beloved figure than the late Robert Hugh Miller, of Liberty, who for forty years successfully guided the destiny of the Liberty Tribune. A pioneer citizen of Clay County, he started life as a poor boy, and worked his own way steadily upward through the force of sheer merit. Kindly natured and generous in his disposition and at all times thoughtful for others, he was a man in a thousand, whose friends were numbered by the hundreds and who was universally respected, admired and esteemed. Quiet and unassuming at all times, he was yet a man of infinite resource and absolutely fearless in his denunciation of whatever he believed to be an evil or an injustice. Talented and most capable, strong in good qualities and firm in his character, faithful to every duty which devolved upon him, a loyal and true friend, he was a credit at once to his forebears, his community and his craft, and when he passed away, February 14, 1911, he left a void in the hearts of those who knew him which time has not yet filled nor will for many years.

Robert Hugh Miller was born November 17, 1826, in the City of Richmond, Virginia, a son of John E. and Mary (Rogers) Miller, the father a native of Scotland, and the mother a native of the Old Dominion, her parents being patriots of the Revolution. The father was a kinsman of High Miller, the eminent Scottish geologist and writer, author of "Old Red Sandstone." John E. Miller died in 1829, and soon thereafter the mother removed with her children to Glasgow, Barren County, Kentucky, from whence, three years later, she made her way to Paris, Monroe County, Missouri, where, in order to keep her little family together, she secured a position as a school teacher, her son being among her pupils. She remarried in Missouri and died in 1870, and was buried in a secluded cemetery, but in later years the son had her remains carefully disinterred and laid to rest in the public cemetery at Bowling Green, Missouri, where a handsome monument marks her grave.

In 1840, when fourteen years of age, Mr. Miller was apprenticed to the printer's trade in the office of the Patriot, a newspaper published at Columbia, Missouri, and when that sheet was discontinued Mr. Miller joined the force of the Statesman, where, under the editorship of the late Col. William F. Switzler, he gained experience which was invaluable to him in later years, and was thrown in contact with such men as Warren Woodson, James S. Rollins, Dr. William Jewell, James L. Stephens, old Doctor Duncan, the Todds, the Basses, the Clarksons, the Hickmans and the great lawyer, old Jack Gordon. Having completed his apprenticeship, January 1, 1846, he set about securing a location wherein to establish a newspaper, and with the late John B. Williams chose Liberty, Missouri, as a field of operation and founded the Liberty Tribune. The first issue bore the date of April 4, 1846, and the partnership continued for less than a year, Mr. Miller buying Mr. Williams' interest, and from that time until Mr. Miller sold the Tribune plant to the late John Dougherty, in September, 1885, he continued as its sole owner, the last issue while he was in charge bearing the date of the last Friday in September. Hence, he was sole editor and proprietor of the Tribune for nearly thirty-eight years, continuously.

In an article written by a lifelong friend, D. C. Allen, which was published in the Tribune at the time of Mr. Miller's death, Mr. Allen says, in part: "As can be understood, the Tribune remained stanchly whig until in 1852, when the whig party went down in defeat under Scott and Graham, leaving 'trailing clouds of glory' all over its past. With the characteristic devotion of old whigs to the names of Clay, Webster, Crittenden and their compeers, it declined to support the democracy in 1856 and 1860, but in those years gave its countenance respectively to Fillmore and Donelson, and Bell and Everett. After 1860 it gave its adherence to the democratic party, and remained one of the truest democratic newspapers in Missouri. During the whole time of Mr. Miller's connection with the Tribune it gave its earnest advocacy to every measure calculated to advance the interests of his community and state. It stood for William Jewell College, first, last and all of the time. In 1860 it urged the people of the county to vote $200,000 in bonds for the construction of the Kansas City, Galveston and Lake Superior railroad, designed to connect Kansas City with the Hannibal railroad at Cameron. The tone of the Tribune was ever moderate and it was always on the side of law, of order, of faith, of the Constitution. In its columns, extending from April 4, 1846, until in September, 1885, is stored very much the larger portion of the facts which go to making up the history of the people of our county, socially, educationally and politically. There is no contrivance which can measure the influence of those facts as they were gathered and disseminated.

"The education of Mr. Miller did not extend beyond the primary studies. This he supplemented by the education of the printing office, which had its advantages not elsewhere attainable. Above all, it stored his mind and memory with an infinite mass of facts. In addition he read a good deal outside of the printing office. All this made of him a man of extensive and valuable information. In estimating the character of Mr. Miller, one must not forget a combination in him of very high qualities. These were the highest integrity, a strong sense of justice, fine courage, an unusual call to duty, deep tenderness of feeling, great reverence for the past, earnest devotion to principle, a lofty conception of the obligations of friendship—all under the control of strong, massive common sense.

"His reverence for the past constantly urged him to seek out and accumulate objects of antiquity, curios connected with his own family, old papers and documents illustrating the history of the county and state, and family relics. He obtained every little object which had any association with his mother. He loved to gather articles connected with the Revolutionary war. His tenderness to persons, especially the poor, and to dumb animals, could, if necessary, be shown by many facts. He could not endure ill treatment of dumb animals. His horse, his cows, his dog, any pet about the place, must receive proper attention. There seemed to be a sympathy and personal attachment between him and his old riding horse. He was a very hospitable man, loved the best food, and provided a great abundance of food in his household. He loved to sit down to his dinner table surrounded by his friends and kinfolks, with viands in lavish abundance.

"It seems hardly necessary to add that he was a most valuable citizen. He was one of the most faithful of friends. No one can charge him with ingratitude. His word or promise was as good as gold. No one will pretend there was in our community a truer or more faithful man. He gave to charitable purposes as a prudent man should—that is, with discrimination and judgment—but he always gave where there was any merit. He was replete with kindness in his family and among his friends. He went in and out before the people of Clay County for sixty-five years. He was an appreciable part of the community. Since Mr. Miller retired from editorial work, he had allowed himself more ease and leisure than formerly. He was one of the most industrious, energetic men we have had in this county—during his earlier years constantly at work—and was gifted with rare business acumen. By 1885 he had achieved a handsome competence. By prudence, good management and safe investment, before his death he had added to this. Mr. Miller was a man of great order and method. He had a place for everything and insisted that everything should be in its place. In his office work he demanded that everything be exact. He allowed no negligence. His pride was in the mechanical neatness and beauty of the Tribune. He was one of the rare few who made a fortune in the printing office.

"At his death, he belonged to no denomination of Christians, but he was never known to utter a word against Christianity. Why or how he attained and retained this attitude towards the church is inscrutable—at least he left no explanation."

Mr. Miller was married first June 28, 1848, to Miss Enfield (Enna) F. Peters, daughter of John R. Peters, of Clay County, and five children were born to this union: Millard Fillmore, who died in youth; Belle, deceased, who was the wife of J. J. Stogdall, of Liberty; Julia, who is the wife of Edwin Withers, of Liberty; Hugh, a resident of Kansas City; and Irving, a resident of Junction City, Kansas. Mr. Miller's first wife died December 3, 1867, and May 3, 1871, he was married to Miss Louise Wilson, daughter of Hon. John Wilson, of Platte County. Five children were born to this union: Roy, who died in early manhood; Bessie, who married first a Mr. Day, and then L. Noel, and now resides at Glasco, Kansas; Ida, who is the wife of Prof. A. V. Dye, of Bisbee, Arizona; Clark, now a resident of Richmond, Missouri; and Mary, the wife of Harry Smith, of Richmond, Missouri.

Mrs. Louise (Wilson) Miller was born in Platte County, Missouri, August 7, 1844, a daughter of John and Elizabeth (Trigg-Clark) Wilson. Hon. John Wilson was born in Christian County, Kentucky, February 13, 1804, and about the year 1828 moved to Booneville, Missouri, where he married, and, entering the practice of law, became prosecuting attorney for all of Southwest Missouri. In 1841 Mr. Wilson came to Platte County, settling on the old Norton farm adjoining Platte City, where his name was enrolled as a practicing attorney of Platte County, July 13th of that year. In 1856, 1862 and 1864 he was elected to the Legislature of the state, and opposed secession, but in 1865 voted against emancipation. In the latter year he was appointed county attorney, an office in which he served several years. In his early days he was an ardent whig and gloried in the fact that he was the first man to propose General Taylor for president. Mr. Wilson was a member of the circle of lawyers who framed the constitution of Missouri, and was associated with such leading men as Doniphan, Atchison, Burnett, Rees and Wood, and other history makers of the state. Far and wide he was known as "Hon. John Wilson from Platte," "The Old Line Whig" and "The Loud Voiced Orator." At different times his name was mentioned in connection with the offices of supreme judge, governor and United States senator.

Mr. Wilson became the father of twelve children, of whom five are living at this time: James B., a resident of Kansas; Hon. Robert P. C., of Platte City; Charles B., of Oklahoma; John, of Kansas City; and Louise, who is now Mrs. Miller.

Elizabeth Trigg Clark, the mother of Mrs. Miller, was the daughter of Robert P. and Malinda (Trigg) Clark, the latter being a daughter of Col. Stephen and Elizabeth (Clark) Trigg, of Virginia and Kentucky. Colonel Trigg was a member of that distinguished Virginia family which furnished four congressmen to the nation. He was a member of two patriotic conventions that met at Williamsburg, Virginia, in 1774 and 1776, and among his compeers are found Jefferson, Harrison, Randolph, Lee, Marshall, McDowell, Henry and Peyton. In 1779 Colonel Trigg was sent to Kentucky by the governor of Virginia and after he had fulfilled his commission he decided to make the "Dark and Bloody Ground" his home. At the head of a band of brave and hardy men he pursued the Indians and established a barricade near Harrodsburg, known as Trigg's Station. Subsequently he was elected to the Legislature, was a trustee of the original towns of Louisville and Covington, and fell covered with blood and glory at the battle of Blue Licks, Kentucky, August 17, 1782. He married Elizabeth Clark, and had a family of nine children, of whom Elizabeth Clark, Mrs. Miller's mother, was the fifth in order of birth.

son, who married Judith Adams. The latter's children were: Robert, William and John. Of these, Robert married Susannah Henderson, and had a family of thirteen children, one of whom, Christopher, was a member of Congress from Virginia during Jefferson's administration. Another son, James, was a member of Congress from Kentucky in 1812-16, and governor of his state in 1838. Another of the sons of Robert Clark, Bennett Clark, came to Missouri, settled in Howard County, and was the father of Robert P. Clark, the grandfather of Mrs. Miller.

Gen. John P. Clark, Sr., was for many years a member of Congress, a Confederate state senator and a brigadier-general in the Confederate army. He was the grandfather of John B. Clark, Jr., who was also a brigadier-general of the Confederacy and a member of Congress from 1872 to 1882; and of Robert C. Clark, now head of one of the public institutions of Missouri. Robert P. Clark, the grandfather of Mrs. Miller, was prominent in the affairs of Missouri as a territory, and was a member of the convention which framed the constitution under which Missouri was admitted to the Union as a state.

Mrs. Miller, who still survives her distinguished husband and resides at Liberty, was educated at Platte City, and at the Ladies' College, Liberty. She is a member of the Daughters of the American Revolution, and is well known in social circles of the city.

NOAH H. KING. Years of familiarity with financial affairs gave to Noah H. King an experience that fitted him most admirably for his present position as manager of the Tootle Estate, the business of which runs into many millions of dollars, and in which work he has been engaged since January, 1910. Mention of this magnificent estate is made elsewhere in this work in connection with the sketch of the late Milton Tootle, Sr., who created the estate, so that further details concerning the scope and magnitude of Mr. King's activities will not be necessary at this point in regard to his connection with the Tootle affairs.

Mr. King is not a Missourian by birth. He claims the State of Illinois for his natal state, and he was born there in 1873, the son of William A. and Elizabeth (Wilkins) King. The King family is directly allied with the family of which Austin A. King was a member. It will be remembered by Missourians that he was governor of the State of Missouri from 1848 to 1852 and furthermore that he was the first judge of Buchanan County, to which office he was elected in 1837. The family had its origin in Tennessee, the grandfather of Noah H. King having come to Buchanan County, Missouri, prior to Civil war days, and he was killed while serving as a soldier in the Union army.

William A. King was born in Tennessee, and was engaged in farming activities in Missouri practically all his maturer life, with the exception of two years spent in Illinois about the time of his marriage, during which time Noah H. of this review was born.

Noah H. King was educated in the country schools of his home community, and reared on his father's farm, there remaining until 1890, when he came to St. Joseph and started in business life as an office boy with the Buell Manufacturing Company, manufacturers of woolen goods in St. Joseph. The boy remained with them for three years, and in 1893 went with the State National Bank of St. Joseph. He continued with that fiscal institution until it was liquidated, in 1896, when he became discount teller with the Tootle-Lemon National Bank, remaining with them until January 1, 1910, when he became the active manager of the Tootle estate, which position he still is filling with all of satisfaction to those most concerned.

It will be seen that Mr. King's actual banking experience from the time he began up to the time when he became associated with his present business did not extend over more than seven years, but much of close familiarity with the business was crowded into that period. While discount teller for the Tootle-Lemon National Bank he also served a term as manager of the St. Joseph Clearing House Association.

Mr. King has also been connected with other business enterprises, among them being his association with the Davis Milling Company of St. Joseph, of which he has been secretary since 1910.

Mr. King is fraternally identified by his relations with the Benevolent and Protective Order of Elks, Lodge No. 40, of St. Joseph, and he is socially prominent as a member of the St. Joseph Country Club and the Highland Golf and Country Club.

In 1898 Mr. King was married to Miss Mary Cannon, a daughter of Thomas Cannon of St. Joseph, who came to St. Joseph in about 1870 and here engaged extensively in the starch and glucose business. He is now living retired in this city. Mr. and Mrs. King have a son, Horace J. King. The family home is at No. 2638 Folsom Street.

JAMES H. MEYER. Through a period of more than six decades the name of Meyer has been prominently connected with the history of Holt County. It is an honored name and one that is familiar to the people of this part of Northwest Missouri by reason of the honorable and useful lives of those who have borne it. James H. Meyer, of Hickery, is a worthy representative of the family whose history forms a connecting link between the past and the present. He saw Holt County in the days when its land was but little improved, its pioneer homes widely scattered and its evidences of development few. In the work of progress and development that has since wrought marvelous changes he has borne his part and today ranks among those valued and substantial citizens of the community who laid the foundation of the present prosperity of the county.

James H. Meyer was born in Holt County, Missouri, December 31, 1853, and is a son of Andrew and Mary (Secrist) Meyer. The father, a native of Germany, emigrated to the United States about 1835, and for several years, while seeking a capital with which to establish himself as a farmer, accepted such honorable employment as came his way, working in the City of Saint Joseph when there were but two white men in that place. In 1849, attracted by the discovery of gold, he made his way across the plains to California with an ox-team, the journey consuming four months, and after sixteen months of hard and successful effort returned to Missouri with $6,000 in gold. This he invested, in 1850, in a farm of 440 acres, located about four miles south of Mound City. About ten acres of this land had been cleared, but there were few improvements, and the family home was a small log cabin with a clapboard roof, in the construction of which not a nail had been used. During the Civil war Mr. Meyer invested heavily in land, prospered wonderfully through his wise and judicious business dealings, and accumulated some two thousand three hundred acres of land, on which he made various valuable improvements. When his wife died he gave up active pursuits, and from that time until his own death lived among his children. He was a man of exemplary habits, a faithful member of the Presbyterian Church, and was highly esteemed by his fellow citizens who elected him county judge of Holt County. The thirteen children, all born in this county, were as follows: Anna E., who married W. A. Long; James H., who married Fannie L. Pointer; Mary M., who married Charles Corsaut and died at the age of twenty-one years; Alfred A., who married Edna Phillip; an infant, deceased; Willard P., who married Hettie Case; Armilda C., who married Charles Corsaut; George W., who married Mamie Fry; Robert F., who married Lena Rosebury; Charles, who married Anna Patterson; Emma J., who married W. Rayburn; Marvin E., who married Cora Henning; and Don C., who married Alma Duncan.

James H. Meyer divided his boyhood between working on his father's farm during the summer months and attending the country district schools in the short winter terms, and thus grew to sturdy manhood and adopted the vocation of agriculturist. At the time of his marriage he entered upon a career of his own, settling on his farm in the vicinity of Mound City, in a small three-room frame house, which was destroyed by fire and replaced by the present modern residence. From time to time, following his father's example, Mr. Meyer added to his property, until at one time he was the owner of 400 acres, but of this has since sold 120 acres to his son Logan, and eighty acres to his son William A. An energetic and skilled agriculturist, Mr. Meyer made a success of his undertakings, and at this time is living in semi-retirement on his farm. He has made a specialty of raising stock, horses, hogs and cattle, and has the reputation of being one of the best judges of stock in the country. He has ever been a friend of modern ideas, and has contributed to the development of the community by the erection of buildings, including the residence on the farm of his son William F. While not a politician, he has supported democratic candidates and policies, and has served for a period of twelve years as a member of the school board. With his family, he attends the Presbyterian Church.

Mr. Meyer married Fannie L. Pointer, October 21, 1875, and to this union there have been born six children, as follows: William A., who married Cora Trimmer, and they have three children, Harvin A., Earl and Dorothy, all born in Holt County; Ralph M., who married Mabel Terry and has four children, Galen, born in Nodaway County, and Ralph M., Jr., Lucy and Clinton, born in Holt County; Logan A., who married Hattie Wakeley and has four children, Ellen, Mary, Hazel and William H., all born in Holt County; James H., Jr., who married Floy Seepen, has three children, Frances Marguerite and Thomas L., born in Wayne County, and David Winter, born in Florida; Edgar R., who married Miriam Hayhurst, has three children, Errol and Barbara, born in Texas, and Ned H., born in Holt County; and Dr. Frances P., who married Virgil Carter, and has one child, Marguerite J., born in St. Joseph, Buchanan County, Missouri.

ALVAH PATEE CLAYTON. St. Joseph as a city of trade and industry has been fortunate in the possession of a fine body of citizenship, including men of ability and integrity to direct the large enterprises which have given this city distinction among the larger centers of Missouri. During the last quarter of the century, one of these building builders and upholders of local prosperity has been Alvah Patee Clayton, president of the Sheridan-Clayton Paper Company, a former mayor of St. Joseph, bearing a name which has long had a distinctive place in the city's history, and one of the foremost Masons of Northwest Missouri. Mr. Clayton has had a long and varied career, which has made him both a witness and a participant of many eras of achievements and social and business advancement.

The Sheridan-Clayton Paper Company, located at 302-308 South Third Street, and of which Mr. Clayton has been president since 1902, is the largest wholesale and jobbing house of its kind in St. Joseph, and has a history going back thirty years or more. The company makes a specialty of wrapping paper, stationery, school supplies, holiday goods, toys, woodenware, and drug sundries. The territory over which its goods are distributed through a large force of traveling representatives comprises the states of Missouri, Kansas, Oklahoma, Texas, Nebraska, Iowa, Colorado, Utah, Wyoming and Idaho.

Alvah Patee Clayton is a native of the State of Ohio, born at Ashley, December 27, 1860, a son of James Wellington and Almira Elizabeth (Patee) Clayton. After his father's death in Ohio, in 1864, the mother, who was a daughter of Alvah Patee, and a niece of John Patee, both of whom helped make business and civic history in St. Joseph, herself came to this city, bringing her son Alvah in 1865, and she lived here until her death, December 24, 1912. Thus Mr. Clayton has been a resident of St. Joseph practically all his life. The public schools gave him his early education, and later he was a student in the Christian Brothers College at St. Joseph. His practical business career began with the old wholesale stationery firm of Williams Brothers, and though his identification with paper trade has not been continuous, it was that early experience which really gave him the start towards his permanent career. In 1881 Mr. Clayton engaged in the general merchandise trade at Eleventh and Penn streets, in St. Joseph, as a member of the firm of Skiles, Hull & Clayton. This partnership continued until 1884, in which year Mr. Clayton went on the road as traveling representative for the Beaumont-Sheridan Paper Company of St. Joseph. He sold paper for this firm over a territory with satisfactory success until 1886. Then he was out of the paper business for one year, and was traveling salesman, representing R. T. Davis Milling Company of St. Joseph. Returning to his old firm, which in the meantime had reorganized and taken the title of Ashton-Sheridan Paper Company, Mr. Clayton in 1888 himself bought a one-third interest in the business, and it was then reorganized and incorporated as the Sheridan-Clayton Paper Company, with John J. Sheridan as president and A. P. Clayton as vice president. Upon Mr. Sheridan's retiring from the business, in 1902, Mr. Clayton became president, but the old title of the firm is still kept.

Few business men have so popular a place in community and general social esteem as Mr. Clayton. Outside of the paper company, his business interests include the relation of vice president of the Park Bank of St. Joseph, director of the Bartlett Trust Company of St. Joseph, and director of the Mueller-Keller Candy Company of St. Joseph. Having long been prominently identified with business affairs, being considered one of the leading business men, and a man whose efficiency was beyond a question of doubt, Mr. Clayton was prevailed upon to accept the nomination for the office of mayor, and was elected two terms, his period of service running from 1908 to 1912. He also served two terms as president of the St. Joseph Commercial Club, was president of the Lotus Club for two terms, and president of the Jefferson Club two terms. His interests in many lines are indicated by the various honorary memberships which have bestowed upon him, and these include honorary membership in the following orders: International Typographical Union; International Bricklayers,, Plasterers, and Masons' Unions; International Plumbers' and Steamfitters' Union; Missouri State Retail Merchants' Association; Master Bakers' Association of America; Master Bakers' Association of Kansas.

His Masonic record is also noteworthy. He has taken thirty-two degrees in the Scottish Rite, and in the work of the Mystic Shrine is one of the most accomplished men in the entire country, and known among Mystic Shriners from coast to coast. In 1906, Mr. Clayton was elected to the exalted office of Imperial Potentate of North America, of the A. A. O. Nobles of the Mystic Shrine, serving during the year 1907. His local membership is with Moila Temple, of the Mystic Shrine, and he was potentate for eight years, from 1899 to 1906. He has an honorary life membership in forty shrines in North America, and is an honorary member of Pacific Lodge of New York City, A. F. & A. M., a lodge composed of actors and theatrical managers. Perhaps his greatest distinction in Masonic work was his activity in organizing, in January, 1907, the first shrine in a Latin country, the Republic of Mexico. In January, 1908, he instituted and delivered the charter to Aneva Temple, A. A. O. N. M. S., at the City of Mexico, and conferred the order upon President Diaz and other prominent Mexicans. Mr. Clayton has been affiliated with the Masonic Order since he was twenty-one years of age, and is a life member of Charity Lodge No. 331, A. F. & A. M., receiving his life membership card for thirty years of active service. His other relations are with St. Joseph's Chapter, R. A. M.; Hugh DePayen Commandery No. 51, K. T., and all the Scottish Rite bodies, including St. Joseph Consistory No. 4, A. A. S. R.

In 1887 Mr. Clayton married Miss Mattie Gunn, a daughter of Dr. Robert Gunn, a well known physician of St. Joseph, and also a very prominent Mason. They are the parents of three sons: Robert Griffin Clayton, Edward Smith Clayton, and Alvah Patee Clayton, Jr. Their home is at 208 North Nineteenth Street.

Mr. Clayton's career has been a busy one, and filled with accomplishments in various lines. His ability to do many things perhaps comes from his splendid physical and mental efficiency, and his stature of six feet two inches, with weight of more than two hundred and fifty, is suggestive of his general bigness, not only physically, but in every characteristic. He is one of the men of action, and of large and distinctive influence in the city.

OLAF T. ANDERSON. In the career of Olaf T. Anderson there are to be found lessons for the youth of any land. The son of wealthy and refined parents, he came to the United States as a youth of nineteen years to carve out his own career, and here, after a long period of struggle, he has eventually reached the goal of his ambition. For a number of years after his arrival, it seemed that fate had destined Mr. Anderson to ignominious defeat and failure. Time and again he fought his way to a substantial start in life, only to see his earnings swept away by disasters over which he had no control, but his native pride and his fine self-reliance would not allow him to admit himself beaten, and he kept persistently, doggedly and energetically working, until through the sheer force of his exertions he overcame obstacles, thrust aside discouragements, and emerged triumphant, with a clear title to a position among American self-made men. Now, in the evening of life, with his struggles behind him, he may contentedly look back over the years of his arduous labors, secure in the knowledge that the success which is his has been honestly and legitimately gained, and that his position in the esteem and respect of those among whom he has labored rests upon no questionable action.

Olaf T. Anderson was born at Helsingburg, Sweden, March 9, 1847, a son of Anderson Bengtson and wife, natives of that country, where both died. There were five sons in the family: Peter, who died at the home of his brother, Olaf T.; Bengt, who died at Des Moines, Iowa; Nels, who is a resident of Alta, Iowa; John, who lives at Butte, Montana, and Olaf T., of this review. Mr. Anderson was educated in the public schools of his native land and was given more than ordinary advantages in this direction. It would have been possible for him to have remained at home, where his father would have placed him in business, but the young man was of an independent nature, and on reaching his nineteenth year decided to come to the United States in the search for fortune and position. Making his way to England, he there took a vessel which brought him to New York, and from that city he went to Kansas City, Missouri, and secured employment in the construction gang which was engaged in building a bridge for the Hannibal & St. Joseph Railway. Here the misfortunes of the young foreigner began, for unscrupulous persons stole all of his clothes and he was left destitute, although he was partly reimbursed by a kind-hearted section boss, who gave him five dollars. After a number of hardships he eventually made his way to the vicinity of Holt, in Clay County, where he purchased forty acres of land. There he labored faithfully for four years, but not being familiar with American methods, or soil and climatic conditions, his strenuous work failed to bring the desired results, and he lost all his holdings and was compelled to send to Europe for a loan. When this arrived, he felt that his fortunes might change in another locality, and he subsequently went to Nodaway County, Missouri, where in the vicinity of Guilford (to the east) he purchased a quarter section of land, on which he located in 1873. This was absolutely raw property, and by the time he had placed improvements thereon, he found himself deeply in debt, and again in 1875 was compelled to go to work again as a laborer. Mr. Anderson's next venture was in the Willamette Valley of Oregon, where he ditched and drained land through the winter for six months, and during this time it rained for fifty-three days, although Mr. Anderson lost only one day's labor in this time.

Returning to Nodaway County, Missouri, in 1876, with some small capital, Mr. Anderson within three years had cleared himself from debt and had purchased 160 acres of land, well stocked, making in all 320 acres. It was at that time that his fortunes took a turn for the better, and from that time to the present his advance has been steady and consecutive. In 1880 he sold this tract of land to a Mr. Jacob Pugh, and came to Gentry County, here buying sixty acres of land near Alanthus Grove, which he subsequently sold and went west to his cattle ranch, located seventy-five miles northwest of Garden City, Kansas. There he remained with some success until 1884, when he returned to Alanthus Grove and purchased seven farms, the greater part on time, as his capital was but $3,000. This property comprised 900 acres, but later he disposed of a part of the property, retaining 404 acres in sections 25, 30, 31 and 36, township 64, range 32, the only improvement on this land being fencing. Here he settled down to farming and stock-raising, and during the years that followed put in improvements valued at $15,000, all of which were paid for by the yield of the land. In 1914 he sold this property to his daughter, Mrs. Augusta Pierce, for the sum of $50,000 cash, and March 1, 1915, took up his residence in his beautiful home which he had erected at Albany.

While the greater part of Mr. Anderson's activities have been devoted to agricultural pursuits, he has also been interested in a number of other ventures, and is at present a stockholder in the Farmers and Mechanics Bank at Stanberry and the First National Bank of Albany. In 1880 he was one of the organizers of the Mutual Insurance Company of Gentry County, and is now a director of this concern, which handles about $2,000,000 worth of insurance. A republican in politics, in 1905 he was nominated for the office of county judge, but owing to the great democratic majority in the county met with defeat. Fraternally he is connected with Alanthus Grove Blue Lodge, No. 262, A. F. & A. M. He has been active in religious work, and is treasurer of the Baptist Church at Alanthus Grove. In every walk of life Mr. Anderson has displayed a strict adherence to high principles, and no man of his community is held in higher general confidence and esteem.

Mr. Anderson was married in 1873, in Clay County, Missouri, to Miss Johanna Pearson, of Sweden, whose parents, farming people, died in that country. To this union there have been born the following children: Augusta, the widow of John Pierce, who died September 15, 1908, purchased her father's farm, which she rents for a yearly sum of $2,400, and is the mother of two children, Ruth and Bonnie; Alma, the wife of W. R. Cook, has the following children: Beatrice, Lilian, Chester, Stella, Mabel, Ray, Bertha, Emma, Gladys, Delbert and John, of whom Beatrice married Albert Wilson of Gentry County, and has one son and a daughter; Emma, who became the wife of. Tom Jennings, of Gentry County, and died June 19, 1906, at the age of thirty-three years, leaving one child, Bertha; Oscar, a farmer of Twin Falls, Idaho, married Kate Hall, and has three children, Olaf, Valeta and Nanny; Mary, who married Harry Carter, a farmer of Gentry County, and has two children, Ross and Eileen; and John, a farmer of Nodaway County, married Ethel Wilson and has two children, Geneva and Victor.

WILLIAM ROLEKE. Among the mayors of the various cities in Northwest Missouri, perhaps none has a better record of administration than William Roleke, now chief executive of the City of Bethany. William Roleke has been identified with Bethany since 1886, is a successful business man, and at the same time one of the keenest observers, practical workers and leaders in local affairs. While never neglecting his business nor failing to provide for the needs of his own household, Mr. Roleke since taking out his naturalization papers as an American citizen has had a fair idea of politics, and has been both a thinker and an actor in his home town.

William Roleke was born in the Province of Hanover, Germany, in the City of Papenburg. He belonged to a family of the official class. His father, Karl Roleke, who was born in the same locality, entered the army at the age of sixteen, and after the required military service was appointed to a position in the civil service, and finally became a revenue officer. He was retired on a pension some twenty years before his death, which occurred in July, 1914, at the age of eighty-five. His wife, whose first name was Augusta, died in 1870. Only three children reached mature years; John, a business man in Hamburg, Germany; George, in business at Papenburg; and William.

William Roleke attended school during the required time until fourteen years of age, and then began learning the tailor's trade in Papenburg. He subsequently lived in the free City of Hamburg, and escaped the regular requirement of military service by "drawing himself out," as he explains it. William Roleke was born January 15, 1864, and in 1886, at the age of twenty-two, left his native land, traveled about Northern Germany and in Belgium, "having a good time," as he expresses it, and at Antwerp, Belgium, took passage on the Belgenland of the Red Star Line, and landed in New York. He progressed leisurely through the states, stopping a time in New York, Chicago and St. Louis, and having some means was able to select his future home with care and a proper regard for future opportunities. It was after arriving in Bethany that Mr. Roleke mastered the English language, which he did readily enough, and eagerly embraced every opportunity to prepare himself for the responsibilities of American citizenship. He soon declared his intentions of naturalization, and cast his first vote as an American citizen for Grover Cleveland. He has since been affiliated with the democratic party in national politics. On coming to Bethany, Mr. Roleke entered the employ of his cousin, Herman Roleke, and subsequently they were in the tailor business as partners, under the firm name of H. and W. Roleke, for fifteen years. William Roleke since 1903 has been sole proprietor of the business and has built up an establishment that is the leading one of its kind in Harrison County. Mr. Roleke is also one of the directors and was one of the organizers of the First National Bank of Bethany.

During his active business career and residence at Bethany, Mr. Roleke came to be known among his fellow citizens as an advocate of progressive improvement. His judgment in such matters was entitled to consideration since he studied the needs of the town and was prepared for discussion, and when the occasion arose was also a practical worker in any movement in which he took part. It was these qualifications that first brought him election in 1908 to the office of mayor, and he has been reelected four times, having succeeded Mayor Cruzan in the office. His administration in the past six years has been responsible for all the modern improvements in Bethany. These include the laying of pavement around the public square and in some of the side streets and alleys, and also the concreting of Central Street. Another important municipal improvement was the construction of a new electric light plant and the installation of a new filter system at the waterworks, besides a general clean up of the town. Mr. Roleke was one of the first to advocate these public improvements, and Bethany citizens have kept him in office because they recognized his able leadership and ability to carry out constructive measures. His first election came by a small majority of thirty votes, but the confidence of the people in his work has been shown by his election the second time by a majority of two to one, while in the next election his vote was three to one, and the last time it was by almost a unanimous choice that he entered the office.

Mr. Roleke has represented his local lodge of Knights of Pythias in the Grand Lodge seven times, is affiliated with both the subordinate lodge and encampment of the Independent Order of Odd Fellows, and is also a member of the Order of Yeomen. At Bethany on September 2, 1888, Mr. Roleke married Miss Anna Schulze. She was born in Berlin, Germany, a daughter of Gustav Schulze, a capitalist. Mrs. Roleke came to the United States to visit her cousin, Herman Roleke, and at Bethany made the acquaintance of William Roleke and they were married here. Their children are: Dr. Helen, who is a graduate of the Kirksville College of Osteopathy, and for two years practiced at Joplin, Missouri, until her marriage to J. T. Parks, and they now live in Kansas. Carl, who is in the plumbing business at Bethany; and Catherine, a student in the Bethany High School.

SAMUEL BOB STOCKWELL. One of the progressive, enterprising and intelligent stockmen and farmers of Harrison County, whose property is located in the vicinity of Bethany, is Samuel Bob Stockwell, who is one of the first generation removed from the founder of the family in this part of Northwest Missouri. His father, Shelton M. Stockwell, brought his family hither after the close of the Civil war, in 1867 to be exact, from Ray County, Missouri, where he had spent a few years and where he had lived during the war, in which he served as a member of the Missouri State Militia. He had gone to Ray County to take up farming from Rush County, Indiana, having received a limited education in the district schools of the Hoosier state, and in Rush County was married to Amanda Ellis, daughter of Judge Ellis, a farmer and Christian preacher who came to Missouri and settled in Harrison County about the time of Mr. Stockwell's migration. Judge Ellis died here as did his wife, their home being located about six miles south of the Town of Bethany.

On coming to Harrison County, Shelton M. Stockwell settled three miles west of Bethany, purchasing the Jo Riggs farm, on which he carried on farming and stock-raising in a thorough and successful manner, doing the substantial improvement necessary to make a productive farm and erecting buildings for the comfort of his family and the shelter of his stock, grain and implements. He was one of the early feeders here and for his own use bred the Poland-China hog, while the Short Horn cattle stocked his pastures and were of his own breeding. He was a man close to the people, his neighbors, without political ambitions, although strong as a republican. He favored public education and always gave it his moral and financial support, although he had had but few advantages in his own youth, and in this respect his wife was much like him, although her opportunities had, perhaps, been a little greater. She still survives and resides at Bethany, her eighty-eighth birthday having occurred November 17, 1914. She is identified with the Christian Church, and Mr. Stockwell's membership therein dated from early life. He was unfriendly to secret organizations, and in his intercourse with men never essayed to speak in public. Mr. Stockwell passed away, universally respected and esteemed, on his farm in Harrison County, July 13, 1895, when his community lost a strong, stirring and helpful citizen. The children of Shelton M. and Amanda Stockwell were as follows: Alonzo, a resident of Bethany; Belle, who is the wife of J. W. Kerlin, of Albany, Missouri; Viola, who married Charles McCoy, of White Oak Township, Harrison County; Alice, who is the wife of W. M. Claytor, also of White Oak Township; Elizabeth, who is the widow of the late R. A. Cowan, and resides at Bethany; Jennie, who is the wife of J. B. Rhodus, of that place; and Samuel B.

The father of Shelton M. Stockwell was a native of Bourbon County, Kentucky, who had all the Kentuckian's love for fine horseflesh and was a dealer in and breeder of that animal, also engaging in general farming pursuits. Some time after his marriage to Miss Goff, a German woman whose family was prominently known in Bourbon County, he moved to Rush County, Indiana, and there continued to be engaged as a farmer during the remainder of his life. He was also a local preacher of the Christian Church, and both he and his wife are buried in Indiana. Their children were as follows: Eliza, who became the wife of a Mr. Cowan and spent her life in Indiana; Parson, who died in Missouri; Elisha, who died in Ray County, Missouri; Shelton M., the father of Samuel B., and born in Bourbon County, Kentucky; Margaret, who married Hugh Cowan and died in Indiana; and Robert, who passed away in Harrison County, Missouri.

Samuel Bob Stockwell was born on the farm on which he now lives, December 28, 1870. His life as a boy and youth was brought into close connection with stock and he began buying cattle when he was but thirteen years of age, in the meantime securing his education in the community schools, and in which, to use Mr. Stockwell's own words, "he went as far as he could." He was about eighteen years of age when he became manager of the home farm, and eight years later was put in full control of it. He fed his first load of cattle in 1896, and has been identified with feeding every year since, his operations gradually increasing in scope and importance until he is now accounted one of the leading stockmen of the county. Mr. Stockwell's ranch comprises land in sections 12 and 13, in township 63, range 29, aggregating 240 acres; in Bethany Township he owns land in sections 7 and 18, same township and range, aggregating 160 acres, all joining and making a handsome ranch devoted to horses, mules and cattle; and he also operates a leased ranch near Hatfield, Missouri, an important part of his industry.

In politics Mr. Stockwell is a republican, but he is entirely without political ambitions, and has never even attended local or other conventions. He cast his first presidential vote for Benjamin Harrison, in 1892. Possessing a pleasing personality and being an intelligent and interesting conversationalist, Mr. Stockwell has formed many acquaintances in Harrison County and has retained them as friends. He is a member of the Odd Fellows and Knights of Pythias, having taken some interest in fraternal matters, and with Mrs. Stockwell attends the Christian Church, with which both are affiliated.

Mr. Stockwell was married April 17, 1910, at Saint Joseph, Missouri, by Rev. M. M. Goode, to Miss Sadie J. Sutton, a daughter of John H. and Ellen (Hubbard) Sutton, of Rush County, Indiana. Mr. Sutton was reared in Davies County, Missouri, and has lived in Harrison County since 1888, has been a prominent contractor for many years, and has four sons following the same line of work. The children of Mr. and Mrs. Sutton are: Leonard H., Henry G., Fred K., Ralph H., Mrs. Stockwell, Nell K., who is county superintendent of schools of Harrison County, John H., Jr., and Herbert D.

GEORGE W. BARLOW. In the many years of his active practice at Bethany, George W. Barlow has distinguished himself for solid ability as a lawyer, and at the same time has devoted much of his time and energy to the public welfare. Mr. Barlow began practice in Harrison County in September, 1879, and for many years has been known as one of the leaders of the local bar, and at the same time the community has often looked to his interest and support for many enterprises and movements that would advance the city and surrounding country. Among Missourian republicans, Mr. Barlow has been a strong and influential leader and has a large acquaintance with leading members of the party both in the state and throughout the nation.

George W. Barlow came to Harrison County in 1869 and to the State of Missouri in 1865, at which time his parents settled in Chillicothe, Livingston County. They were from Jackson, Ohio, where George W. Barlow was born October 14, 1855. He was well educated in the public schools, but worked for his higher education, and after taking the normal course at the University of Missouri engaged in teaching school for forty months in Harrison County. It was through his profession as a teacher that he first impressed himself upon this section, and came to know hundreds of people young and old. His work as a teacher was done in the country schools, and from the means acquired through that profession he took up the study of law and in 1878 was graduated from the law department of the State University. Having finished his education and training for his profession, Mr. Barlow returned to Bethany, and in September, 1879, formed a partnership with Thomas D. Neal, as Neal & Barlow. After the death of Mr. Neal he formed a partnership with Judge George W. Wanamaker in 1882, and they were long regarded as the leading firm in Harrison County. Their associations continued until the elevation of Judge Wanamaker to the district bench in 1905. Since then Mr. Barlow has been in practice with his brother, Gilbert Barlow, and the firm was Barlow & Barlow from January 1, 1905, to January 1, 1914, at which time L. R. Kautz was admitted to the firm, which is now Barlow, Barlow & Kautz.

Mr. Barlow entered politics as a republican, casting his first presidential ballot for Rutherford B. Hayes, and for nearly forty years has never missed a presidential election. He has been in many local conventions, was assistant sergeant-at-arms of the national convention at St. Louis in 1896, which nominated McKinley, was a delegate from his congressional district in 1908 and cast a vote for President Taft, and in 1912 was a spectator in the national convention at Chicago, and witnessed the turbulent scenes which marked the walkout of the progressive element of the party. Mr. Barlow was chairman of the committee on credentials in the famed Excelsior Springs District Republican Convention of 1912, one of the first held in the state, and one whose acts were reported as important political news all over the country, and resulted in severe criticism. Mr. Barlow wrote a history of that convention from intimate knowledge of its inside workings, and published the article in the press dispatches just before the meeting of the republican leaders held in Indianapolis that year, and his article had an important bearing on the consultations in that meeting.

As to his own public service, Mr. Barlow in the fall of 1888 was elected prosecuting attorney of Harrison County, and was reelected in 1890, having succeeded Judge W. H. Skinner in that office. His administration was one of aggressive and efficient service, during which time he convicted more men for crimes than had been the record of any of his predecessors. Mr. Barlow traced up through Pinkerton detectives one man charged with rape who had crossed the Gulf of Mexico, and after getting him back to the Missouri courts prosecuted him and sent him to the penitentiary for ten years. During his term, Mr. Barlow continued his partnership with Judge Wanamaker, who was his assistant in the office, and at the close of his second term resumed his large private practice. For many years Mr. Barlow has been local attorney for the Burlington Railway, and his firm now handles the litigation for that company. He was one of the organizers of the Grand River Coal & Coke Company of Harrison County, the largest corporation in the county, and is a director and attorney for the company. Mr. Barlow was also one of the chief stockholders and builders of the Heilbron Sanatorium at Bethany, and is still chief stockholder and treasurer of the company. He and his brother built in Bethany the Barlow Block, the best business building in the county. He is the owner of other property in the city, and has one of the best residences located in the midst of spacious grounds on Elm Street, and it is easily one of the most attractive homes in the county. The residence contains ten rooms, is modern throughout, and is finished in oak and walnut, with floors of heavy oak.

Mr. Barlow was married October 9, 1879, in Bethany to Miss Elizabeth Hockridge, daughter of Nelson A. and Maretta (Hart) Hockridge. The Hockridge family formerly lived in the vicinity of Utica, New

and Emma, who died as Mrs. F. H. Nally. Mr. and Mrs. Barlow have a daughter, Mabel, wife of L. R. Kautz, a young lawyer of Bethany, and they have a son, George Barlow Kautz. Mr. Barlow also has as a member of his family Maretta Barlow, the daughter of Mrs. Emma Nally, sister of Mrs. Barlow. She has been reared in the Barlow home since childhood, and is being educated and trained as carefully as if she were an own child. Mr. Barlow is a Knight Templar Mason and also affiliated with the Knights of Pythias, and some years ago served as judge advocate of the Missouri Division of the Sons of the Revolution.

George W. Barlow comes from an old Virginia family. His grandparents were George and Sarah (Ubanks) Barlow, both natives of Virginia and born about 1786 and 1789, respectively. They were married in 1811. George Barlow enlisted as a private during the War of 1812, but was soon detached from the field service and sent out as a recruiting officer. He died in Jackson County, Ohio, in 1854, and his wife passed away in 1866. They were members of the Baptist Church.

James Barlow, father of the Bethany lawyer, was born in Caroline County, Virginia, in 1832, and spent his active career as a farmer. In 1836 his parents moved to Ohio, and he was married in Jackson County of that state to Miss Lucinda Nally, daughter of William and Patsy Nally, who were likewise from Virginia. James Barlow, in 1863, enlisted in Company I of the One Hundred and Seventy-second Ohio Volunteer Infantry, served as sergeant of his company, and was in several engagements before he was discharged in the fall of 1864. During the Morgan raid through Ohio he was captured, but was soon released. James Barlow was a republican, and one of the active influential men of Northwest Missouri after his removal to this state in 1865. He became a prominent Methodist Church leader in Harrison County, and built there a church largely by his own funds. His death occurred in April, 1907, and he is survived by his wife. Their children are: Emma, wife of Frank P. Burris of Harrison County; William C., assistant cashier of the Bethany Savings Bank; Henry A., a farmer in Harrison County; Lola, wife of John Ballard, of Bethany; Howard, of Daviess County, Missouri; Dr. Edward, a prominent physician at Pattonsburg, Missouri, where he died in 1902; Harvey K., a Harrison County farmer; and Gilbert, who practices law in partnership with his brother, George W.

CHARLES F. DAUGHERTY. For twenty-five years Mr. Daugherty has been one of the active educators in Missouri, has been in all branches of public school work, from a country school to the organized city system, and since 1913 has been superintendent of the Bethany public schools. Mr. Daugherty early in life chose school work as his profession, and his experience and talent have constituted him an able executive, a successful worker among the young, and he has likewise taken a prominent part in the organized activities of teachers and has performed his part in raising the standard of education in this state.

Mr. Daugherty began his work as a country teacher in the Carlock School near Dadeville in Dade County, Southwestern Missouri. His early training had been largely of the country, with a country school education, and he has a keen appreciation of educational conditions as they were in the rural districts twenty or thirty years ago. Early in his career he was a student for some time in the Ash Grove Christian College, alternating his work as a student with teaching in the country, and later was a student in Drury College at Springfield, in the Springfield Normal, and also in the University of Missouri. He finished the course in the normal schools, and is at the present time eligible to a degree at the State University.

Professor Daugherty began his greatest school work as principal at Everton, and afterwards was at Republic, Fairplay and Willard, then became superintendent of the Monett schools, followed by a similar position at Deepwater, and for four years was supervising principal in the Joplin schools. Thus his early experiences were all in the Southwest Missouri counties. From Joplin Professor Daugherty went out of the state for a brief time, and was superintendent at Fredonia, Kansas. Returning to Missouri, he became superintendent at Albany, spent three years there, and then accepted his present position at Bethany in 1913.

Aside from his regular work in the various schools mentioned, Mr. Daugherty has on various occasions been an instructor in county teachers' institutes. He was at one time secretary of the Southwestern Teachers' Association, and in the Missouri Teachers' Association was a member of the committee on time and place in 1910 and 1913, and is now one of the directors of the School Peace League, which originated with the State Teachers' Association, and continues to work as an independent league for the preservation of peace among nations and people. Professor Daugherty has frequently appeared on the programs of state meetings with papers on educational topics, and is a man who has progressive ideas on school work, and his formal papers and informal discussions have always been worth listening to. Among his many papers and addresses there is no occasion to speak with particularity but an address on the subject of "Youth" delivered at the commencement exercises at Fairplay was considered by his friends and associates as probably one of his best efforts. Mr. Daugherty is a member of the executive board of the Athletic Association of Northwest Missouri. He drew up the courses of study for the schools of Deepwater, and at Fredonia, and is credited with having placed Fredonia, Deepwater and Albany on the eligible list of schools for affiliation with the higher state educational institutions. During his career as superintendent Professor Daugherty has graduated about one hundred and thirty pupils, and he states that twenty-six per cent of them have followed him into school work. During the past four years forty-five per cent of the graduates have entered colleges and universities for higher education. Out of a class of twenty-nine in 1914 at the Bethany High School, fifteen are now attending higher institutions of learning. Fourteen were graduated from the teacher's training course, and of this number one is now in the State University while twelve are teaching in Harrison County. Mr. Daugherty is unmarried. He is affiliated with the Independent Order of Odd Fellows and the Rebekahs, the Knights of Pythias, and the Lodge, Chapter and Commandery of Masons. His church is the Christian.

Charles F. Daugherty was born in Tazewell County, Virginia, December 28, 1866. He has lived in Missouri since 1868 when his parents came to this state, spent a short time at Albany and then went into Southwest Missouri and located in Dade County. Professor Daugherty grew up in Dade and Greene counties. Mr. Daugherty's remote American ancestor is said to have brought a cargo of silk to New York, and after selling it settled in North Carolina. He was a native of Ireland. The grandfather of Professor Daugherty was John L. Daugherty, who spent his life in Virginia, and was a local official and proprietor of a hotel at Tazewell, where he died. His children were: Isaac, James, David, John, George and Mary. George G. Daugherty, father of Charles F., was a native of Tazewell County, early in the war entered the Confederate service, was captured and in a northern prison until exchanged, then returned to his command and continued until the close of the war. He was a tailor by trade, and after coming to Dade County followed farming until his death in 1881 at the age of fifty-six. George G. Daugherty married Mary Jane Gillespie, daughter of William Gillespie, a Virginia farmer. This family of Gillespies furnished also the maternal ancestors for James Gillespie Blaine, the great statesman and presidential candidate of the republican party in 1884. George Daugherty and wife were members of the Methodist Church, South. His wife died in 1895. Her children were: John L., who died in Hiattville, Kansas, in 1908; James W., of Fort Collins, Colorado; Mrs. M. C. Potter, of Bolivar, Missouri; Charles F. Daugherty; and Miss Maggie A., of Kansas City.

ASHMAN H. VANDIVERT, M. D. One of the old and honored families of Harrison County, belonging to the pioneer age in this section, members of which have been identified with commercial, agricultural activities and various learned professions in this state and elsewhere for generations, is that of Vandivert. Dr. Ashman H. Vandivert, who is the son of a pioneer physician in Harrison County, has practiced medicine at Bethany for more than thirty-five years, and by his native ability and devotion to his calling has won high distinction in his profession.

The Vandivert family was established in America by Holland-Dutch ancestors, who came from Holland with Peter Stuyvesant and settled at New Amsterdam, now New York. During the Revolutionary war there were four New York soldiers named "Vandervoort." The grandfather of Doctor Vandivert was Barnett Vandivert, who died in Jackson County, Ohio, at the age of ninety-six. He married a Miss Henry, and among their children were: Joseph, John, James, Barnett, Dr. Robert, Mrs. Moore, Mrs. Akin, and Samuel. Joseph was a graduate of the Mussey Medical College at Cincinnati, went South and entered the Confederate army when the Civil war came on, had a home in Mississippi, and after losing his family subsequent to the war went West and died at Empire, Colorado. The son Samuel came West and died in Harrison County, Missouri. Barnett moved to Illinois and died in the southern part of that state. John and James both died in Ohio, and the daughters spent their years in the same state.

The late Dr. Robert H. Vandivert, father of Dr. Ashman H., came to Harrison County, Missouri, in 1856, locating in the country south of Bethany and spending most of his active career in that vicinity. He was born November 14, 1819, and it is believed that Pennsylvania was his native state. The family afterwards located in Muskingum County, Ohio, and he graduated in medicine from the Starling Medical College at Columbus about 1850, practiced in Muskingum County until his removal to the West, and made the journey to Missouri by railroad as far as St. Louis, and then by boat up the Missouri River to St. Joseph. He was accompanied by his wife and three sons.

After coming to Harrison County, Dr. Robert H. Vandivert invested his surplus money in land, and after the war bought some large tracts in Daviess County. While busy with his profession, he did something toward the improvement of the land and was known as a farmer and stock raiser. The practice of his profession he carried on after the war until 1875. He was a member of the state militia until he passed the military age, and as a republican was present at the first meeting by that party in Harrison County in 1860 and was elected chairman. Just one week later, it is a matter of interest to note, the democrats organized for the campaign of 1860, and his brother presided over that meeting. The senior Doctor Vandivert, in 1868, was elected to fill an unexpired term in the State Senate, and in 1870 was elected for the full term. His service for six years covered the period of the building of the Lincoln Institute, the colored school at Jefferson City, one of the early institutions of the kind for the race. While Doctor Vandivert was not gifted as a speaker, he was an organizer and worker, and a man of varied interests and did a large and important service to his community and state. Fully impressed with the value of public education, he advocated schools as long as he lived, and educated his own children liberally. His oldest son, J. Worth, was graduated from the College of the Christian Church at Canton, and died as a lawyer at the age of twenty-six. Another son, Arthur Hubert, finished the course in pharmacy at the University of Michigan, but died as a farmer in Harrison County in April, 1913. Samuel W., another of his children, graduated from the law department of the University of Michigan, became district judge in Kansas, subsequently went East and while living in New Jersey became prominent as a lawyer in New York City, but is now engaged in the newspaper business at Russellville, Arkansas. Dr. Robert Vandivert was married in Belmont County, Ohio, to Agnes Hannah Berry, daughter of Samuel Berry. She died in June, 1858, leaving children as follows, some of whom have already been mentioned: Joseph Worthington; Dr. Ashman H.; Arthur H.; Samuel W.; Harriet Agnes, wife of Prof. Ben L. Remmick of the State Agricultural College of Kansas. While Doctor Vandivert was identified with the Christian or Disciples Church, his wife was an adherent of the Quaker faith.

Dr. Ashman H. Vandivert was born in Muskingum County, Ohio, April 6, 1853, and was about three years of age when the family came to Northwest Missouri. His education was supplied by the public schools of Bethany, and in 1874, at the age of twenty-one, he took up the study of medicine in the office of Doctor Walker at Bethany. In 1877, Doctor Vandivert was graduated M. D. from the University of Michigan, then returned to Harrison County and has since been actively identified with his large practice in town and country, with the exception of four years. In April, 1909, Doctor Vandivert was appointed by the board of control as a physician at Hospital No. 2 in St. Joseph and gave four years to that work. Doctor Vandivert is identified with the Harrison County Medical Society, and at one time served as vice president of the Missouri State Medical Association, and is a member of the American Medical Association.

Doctor Vandivert is a republican and has been actively identified with the party. In 1888 was an alternate delegate to the National Republican Convention, and during his long professional career has endeavored wherever possible to serve his community with the disinterested public spirit which has always been his characteristic. He was for fifteen years a member of the school board of Bethany, finally resigning that office. Doctor Vandivert is a large, broad-shouldered man, and with his splendid physical make-up combines earnest sincerity in all his work, and has a highly successful and influential position in Harrison County. He is the owner of the Vandivert Drug Store at Bethany, is a stockholder in the Bethany Republican Printing Company, and owns farm lands in the vicinity.

Doctor Vandivert was married, in June, 1878, to Rosa Templeman, daughter of William A. Templeman. At her death, in February, 1880, she left a daughter, Bessie Agnes, who is now a teacher in the public schools of Seattle, Washington. Doctor Vandivert was again married on September 29, 1886, to Emma Buckles. She was the oldest of nine

Margaret W. Halstead

children, all of whom are living, and was born near Grafton, Illinois, a daughter of William and Harriet (Ripson) Buckles, who were early settlers of Illinois, and her mother is still living. Doctor Vandivert and wife have the following children: Robert Henry, who died July 1, 1912, while serving as foreman with the Arnold Construction Company at Evansville, Indiana, and was unmarried; Dr. William Worthington, who graduated from the University Medical College of Kansas City in 1913, is in practice at Bethany, and married Lillian Guise of Dale, Indiana; Ashman Hubert, the youngest, died in infancy.

DR. JOSEPH S. HALSTEAD. At the time of this publication there are probably no men in the medical profession and very few citizens in Northwest Missouri who have so long a retrospect over the past as the venerable Dr. Joseph S. Halstead of Breckenridge.

Doctor Halstead has farmed and practiced medicine in Caldwell County since 1860, though for a number of years his activity has been merely nominal, and he is now suffering from the infirmities of age and his time has been largely spent in retirement and in association with the past. Doctor Halstead was born at Louisville, Kentucky, March 4, 1818. Incidental to the date of his birth it may be noted that Doctor Halstead is opposed to the proposed change for the date of inauguration of presidents. He says the nation has been observing his birthday every four years for ninety-six years, and he wants the same consideration he has always had. At the time of his birth James Madison was still President of the United States. The greatest statesmen, soldiers and leaders in the field of the arts and literature during the nineteenth century in America were at that time hardly at the beginning of their careers. As a boy, youth and young physician in Kentucky, Doctor Halstead knew such great personalities as Henry Clay and Gen. Andrew Jackson, and met General Lafayette on his last visit to America. The span of this one man's life practically covers every phase in the development of the United States from the beginning of the era of westward expansion. Missouri was not admitted as a state until after he was born, and he was in the full pride of manhood when the Mexican war was fought and gave to the United States its great possessions in the Southwest.

The father of Dr. Joseph S. Halstead was Alexander Halstead, who was born in Geneseo County, New York, and was a tailor by trade. He married Margaret Singer, a native of Philadelphia. They came to the West among the pioneers in the western movement and settled in Lexington, Kentucky, and in 1832 moved to Jennings County, Indiana. The father died at the age of ninety-four and his wife aged forty-five. The mother was a member of the Methodist Church, and the father was a whig and later a republican. There were eleven sons and two daughters. One of them, James C., served as a soldier in the Union army.

Doctor Halstead grew up in Kentucky, acquired a good education for his time, and finished the course in the Transylvania College in the medical department in 1840. He began practice in Kentucky, and was married in 1852 to Margaret Wickliffe. For sixty-two years she has been his devoted companion and wife, and is now eighty-five. Her great-grandfather was the noted Gen. Ben Logan of Kentucky. Doctor Halstead and wife became the parents of eight children, five sons and three daughters: Nat W., who is an attorney at Beardstown, Kentucky; Anna Lucy Rozell, of Salt Lake City, Utah; Margaret B., of Chillicothe, Missouri; Joseph D., of Phoenix, Arizona, in the lumber business; Charles W., of Breckenridge, Missouri; Jasper N., a lumberman in Iowa; Logan, of Hamilton, Missouri; Mary Clifford, of Breckenridge. The children were all well educated, and fitted for their respective spheres of usefulness in the world. Doctor Halstead has thirty-four grandchildren and twelve great-grandchildren. Of the large family covering four generations, there have been only three deaths in sixty-two years, and one of them accidental.

Doctor Halstead came to Caldwell County, Missouri, in 1860, took up the practice of medicine, and gave his services to the community throughout the Civil war and for a great many years afterwards. He is one of the old-style gentlemen, and has outlived practically all his contemporaries, and now in his ninety-sixth year his mind and memory dwell chiefly in the scenes of a long distant past. He is fond of talking of old times, and particularly of events that occurred more than three-quarters of a century ago.

One of the most interesting special articles that appeared in a recent issue of the Kansas City Star had Dr. Halstead as its subject under the title "Henry Clay's Family Physician Is Still Living in Missouri." Without repeating some of the matter of this article already covered, the following will add to the many interesting facts that should be preserved in a sketch of this venerable Breckenridge citizen:

"Dr. Halstead was living in Kentucky during the height of Henry Clay's greatness, except during part of 1841 and 1842, when he came up the river in a steamer and stopped at Richmond, Missouri. There he practiced medicine, but answered the call of his former practice and returned to Kentucky, where he remained until 1860. Then he returned and bought a section of land near Breckenridge, part of which he still owns.

"To the Clay home Dr. Halstead was called many times and he has a very vivid remembrance of the occasion when the 'great pacificator' made his famous statement, 'I would rather be right than be president.' A party of New England capitalists and manufacturers had called upon him to get him to modify his views in some particulars. 'It will defeat you if you don't,' they said. Then he dismissed them with the statement which has become history.

"The cane of which the people of Breckenridge are so proud and which Dr. Halstead carries only on special occasions has engraved on the staghorn handle 'W. H. Jenifer, 1819.' Jenifer was representing Missouri in the fight for admission to the Union. Clay made a great speech which virtually brought the state in, and Jenifer gave the cane to Clay after the address, and told him its history. He had cut an olive branch from a spot near the birthplace of Cicero and had had a cane made of it. Clay prized it very highly and after his death Tom Clay, the son, gave it to Dr. Halstead.

"Dr. Halstead was in Kentucky during the great cholera outbreak and his exposure and lack of sleep and food while waiting on the victims caused him to drop from a weight of 140 pounds to 92 pounds. This weight he never regained, and he figures curiously enough that that experience was beneficial rather than detrimental.

"When he came to Missouri in 1860 for the second time, landing at Lexington with his wife and carrying his money in gold in saddlebags, he rode to Plattsburg and bought from the Government 640 acres of land near Breckenridge. This choice area was obtained for two dollars and a half per acre. Dr. Halstead says of his farm that its first owner was the King of Spain, the second Napoleon Bonaparte, with the United States third, and he was the fourth and first individual owner. When he came to Caldwell County it was with the intention of giving up medical practice and engaging as a farmer. However, the Civil war upset his plans. It left him the only physician in the county, and he proved himself a real neighbor, even though his farm often was raided in his absence.''

J. LEE CROSS. One of the foremost attorneys of Clinton County, J. Lee Cross, of Cameron, belongs to a family distinguished for its many able members of the legal profession, his father and four brothers all being lawyers of note in Missouri. A native of Caldwell County, he was born, in 1868, in Mirabile, then a frontier village, being the eldest of the five sons of John A. Cross, founder of the well-known legal firm of Cross & Sons, of Lathrop, Clinton County, and of whom a brief biographical sketch appears on another page of this volume.

Having completed his college course, J. Lee Cross, who inherited in no small measure many of the natural gifts of his distinguished father, began the study of law under the direction of his father, receiving advantages and training of exceptional value, he and his brothers seemingly imbibing legal knowledge in the atmosphere of law surrounding the Cross home. One of the first trials that made any very vivid impression upon the minds of the sons of John A. Cross was that of the Crusaders, which was won by their father, and made the name of Cross familiar and famous from the East to the West. In 1894 Mr. J. Lee Cross was admitted to the bar, and since taking up his residence in Cameron he has established a large and constantly growing practice, and is numbered among the esteemed and valued citizens of this section of Clinton County.

Mr. Cross married Miss Maud Green, who was born, in Fayette, Missouri, a daughter of the late W. J. Green. Fraternally Mr. Cross is a member of the Knights of Pythias.

CARLTON S. WINSLOW. The constantly increasing tendency of men learned in the law—the natural result of a profession which equips its followers for success in various lines of endeavor—to engage in occupations outside their immediate sphere of activity, has resulted in numerous advantages, among these being the raising of commercial standards, an avoidance of legal complications, and a general simplifying of conditions through a knowledge of fundamental principles. In this connection, an illustration is given in the career of Carlton S. Winslow, of Bethany, a thoroughly learned member of the Harrison County bar, who, as president of the Crescent Jersey Farm Company, is known as one of the leading stockmen of Northwest Missouri.

Mr. Winslow was born February 9, 1860, in Rutland County, Vermont, and is a son of William L. and Julia (Cheedle) Winslow. The family is traced back to the Mayflower and to Massachusetts, and Mr. Winslow's grandfather was Nathaniel Winslow, who was perhaps the founder of the Vermont branch. The grandfather, who was a farmer and passed his life in the Green Mountain State, married as his first wife Miss Clarissa Pettigrew, and their eight sons and two daughters were: Henry, who died in Vermont; Russell, who died at Toledo, Ohio; Ephraim, who spent his life near Monroe, Michigan; Samuel, who spent the greater part of his life in Michigan but died in Vermont; Harris, who lived near Monroe, Michigan, and died there; Stephen, who died in Vermont; Lewis I., who also passed away in that state; William L.; Clarissa, who died at Deerfield, Michigan, as Mrs. Thomas Logan; and Mary, one of the older children of the family, who married Mr. Pierce, and died near Petersburg, Michigan.

William L. Winslow was born in Addison County, Vermont, where he was brought up as a farmer and secured his education in the public schools. He lived a quiet and uneventful life as an agriculturist and was successful as a financier, winning prosperity from his business ventures. His connection with the Civil war was confined to his duties as selectman of his town in Vermont, in which capacity, whenever a draft was made for troops, he saw that the bounty was paid and the men raised. In politics he was a republican, he belonged to no fraternity, and his religious faith was that of the Methodist Church, of which he was a member. Mr. Winslow married Julia Cheedle, a daughter of an artisan and blacksmith who died in Vermont and whose wife was Minerva Snow. The Cheedle children were four in number: John; Elizabeth, who married Almon Cunningham; Timothy B.; and Mrs. Winslow. The last named passed away in 1907, at Bethany, and was laid to rest beside her husband in the Miriam Cemetery. Their children were: Jane E., of Hale Center, Texas, widow of John S. Pryor; Carlton S., of this review; and Hattie A., the wife of U. G. Long, of Harrison County.

Carlton S. Winslow was a lad of eight years when he accompanied his parents to Sherman Township, Harrison County, and remained under the parental roof until reaching the age of seventeen years, at which time he was sent to take a commercial course in Grand River College, Edinburg, Missouri. Succeeding this, he took up the study of law with Alvord & Faucett, of Bethany, with whom he completed his studies, and was admitted to the bar at Gallatin, February 3, 1880, before Judge Samuel A. Richardson. He was the first aspirant to be examined under the law requiring the presence of the entire bar in open court, and in his case there were about forty lawyers on hand, the greater part of a night being spent in completing the proceedings with this lone applicant.

After securing his admission Mr. Winslow started seeking a place for locating, and after a brief stop at Concordia, Kansas, was induced to open an office at Atwood, Kansas, expecting the location of a land office there, but, being disappointed in this, came to Missouri and located at Bethany. He was associated first with Judge W. H. Skinner, as Skinner & Winslow, and later on with E. H. Frisby, as Frisby & Winslow. His primary cases were not of spectacular interest, and the very first one was tried at Atwood, Kansas, where he built the first house on the present townsite. He was defending cattle men and the conditions out there at that time demanded that cattle men carry pistols for personal protection, and on this occasion the court room was full of them.

In 1886, Mr. Winslow left Bethany because of pulmonary trouble and sought the climate of Central Kansas, locating at Marion. While in Kansas he was the western attorney for Lord Scully, the English land baron. He was a factor in republican politics also, and aided in the overthrow of the populist, Judge Doster, from the district bench, after having urged his election as a republican four years before. Mr. Winslow continued his practice and carried on banking, recuperated his health so as to pass two examinations for life insurance, and left after six years and went to Chicago, Illinois. There he was associated with Frank M. Cox and Spencer Ward, as Cox, Winslow & Ward, and each of these men made a professional standing as a lawyer and a citizen. They were in civil practice and Mr. Winslow's work was confined to corporation and chancery business. While in Chicago he was a member of the Hamilton Club, the leading republican organization of Chicago and one of the most prominent in the United States, and was a member of the republican committee of Lake View. Mr. Winslow left Chicago upon the death of his father, in 1899, and returned to Bethany, where he resumed the practice of law. He was for five years city attorney, and was the candidate of the Law and Order League before the primaries in 1914 for the office of prosecuting attorney of Harrison County. He is a past chancellor of the Knights of Pythias and was a member of the Illinois Grand Lodge for four years, and while in Chicago was the deputy for the district in which Evanston is located.

Aside from his legal practice, Mr. Winslow has been extensively engaged in breeding Jersey cattle and handling his dairy farm, located two miles northwest of Bethany. His dairy barn in 32 by 54 feet, of brick, with concrete floors, mangers and gutters, and extends into a frame barn, 26 by 64 feet, with shed room and iron stanchions, accommodating forty-three head of cattle. He built the second silo in the county. "Golden Jubilee's Lad," No. 94,792, a grandson of "Golden Grand," No. 53,568, that splendid son of "Golden Lad," P. S. 1,242 H. C., the most prepotent bull ever imported to this country, heads the herd on Crescent Jersey Farm. He has also a great-grandson of "Diploma," No. 16,219, sire of fifty-five in list, including "Merry Maiden," sweepstakes cow at the Chicago World's Fair, and of "Stoke Pogis of Prospect," No. 29,121, sire of sixty-nine in list. Mr. Winslow has recently added "Undulata Gamboge Chief," No. 120,886, from the herd of R. A. Long of Kansas City, Missouri. "Undulata Gamboge Chief," a son of "Fountain Chieftan," grand champion of Chicago National Dairy Show, 1911, which sold for $5,100, and a grandson of "Noble of Oakland," which sold for $15,000, and a great-grandson of "Gamboge Knight," which brought $6,700.

Mr. Winslow was married July 7, 1880, to Miss Anna M. Bolar, a daughter of William and Eveline (Boyce) Bolar, farming people of Harrison County. Mrs. Winslow is the second in a family of thirteen children. One son has been born to Mr. and Mrs. Winslow, Waldo W., born April 16, 1881, educated in the grammar, high school and the academy of the Northwestern University, Chicago, and now a Harrison County farmer. He married Gertrude Wormouth, a county school teacher and resident of Kansas City, Missouri, where she graduated from the Manual Training High School. Two children have come to this union: Alexander, born in January, 1904; and Edith Ilene, born in February, 1912.

WILLIAM McCULLOCH DUNN. The distinguishing quality of William M. Dunn during his residence of nearly fifty years in Bethany was his activity as a merchant. For nearly forty years Mr. Dunn was one of the men who sold goods and developed the commercial interests of Bethany. To his thorough experience and natural ability as a merchant, Mr. Dunn brought that integrity of character which always goes with the successful merchant, and his record throughout has been without a stain. He is now retired from merchandising, but is still a director in the Harrison County Bank at Bethany.

William McCulloch Dunn was born in Washington County, Virginia, January 9, 1839. His early environment was that of a farm boy, his father being a small planter, and he grew up with the other children in the rural districts of old Virginia. His education came from one of the old Field schools of Virginia, and the building which he knew as a schoolhouse was constructed of logs with perhaps better than ordinary furnishings and equipments. By attendance at school he gleaned a knowledge of geography, grammar, history and physics and thus acquired sufficient knowledge to qualify him as a teacher. Not long after reaching manhood, the terrible struggle between the states began, and early in the year 1861 he enlisted for service, and was for four years a member of the Southern army battling for the Confederacy. He was commissioned captain, quartermaster and paymaster, and assigned to the Thirty-sixth Virginia Regiment of Infantry. That regiment was a part of the army of Northern Virginia, but his first service was in Western Virginia and in the Mississippi Valley. In 1861 he participated in his first battle at Gauley, under the command of General Floyd, and was also present at Cloyd's Farm and several other minor engagements. He was with the troops that in the early part of 1862 were concentrated along the Cumberland and Tennessee rivers, and was under the command of Floyd at Fort Donelson. Just before the surrender of that post he and his command escaped by boat up the Tennessee River and he traveled on the same boat on which Generals Pillow and Floyd were partners. Later he saw service under the noted Gen. Jubal A. Early, up and down the Shenandoah Valley, and was at the battle of Winchester, Cedar Creek, and was captured at Waynesboro, but managed to make his escape a few minutes later, leaving behind all his money and his surplus clothes down to his tooth brush. He walked across the country to Lynchburg, and there joined Breckenridge's command. Towards the end of the war his regiment was at Christiansburg on its way to Petersburg and Richmond to join Lee's army, and the command was disbanded, its commander being then General Echols. Though in service for four years, Mr. Dunn escaped wounds, and was acting quartermaster of a brigade when the war closed.

Mr. Dunn resumed civil pursuits in Virginia as a teacher, but a single term of that experience sufficed and he then turned to a more congenial field in commercial pursuits. It was in 1866, not long after the war, that Mr. Dunn came west and located in Bethany. He traveled by railroad as far as Chillicothe, and there took a stage across country to Bethany. Here he found a town twenty years old, with several hundred inhabitants, and the center of a good trading community. His career began as clerk for H. M. Cuddy, and after a year he became partner of Mr. Cuddy. A year later he bought an interest in the firm of Munson & McGeorge, and for several years the firm of McGeorge & Dunn had a large share of the local trade. Mr. McGeorge then sold out to Robert H. Dunn, a brother of William M., and the firm became William M. Dunn & Brother. Somewhat later a nephew, W. F. Cuddy, came into the firm, and it was then reorganized as Dunn Bros. & Co. After more than thirty years of active merchandising Mr. Dunn retired from the firm in 1902, and has since been engaged with his private interests.

While a democrat, Mr. Dunn has never been identified with politics, except as a voter. Fraternally he is affiliated with the Independent Order of Odd Fellows. In 1870, at Bethany, Mr. Dunn married Miss Desdemona Munson, a daughter of Thomas Munson, who came to Missouri from Kentucky. When Mrs. Dunn died, in 1874, she left a son, William Victor, who for a time was associated with his father in business, then went to Kansas City, was a successful real estate dealer there and died March 12, 1907. William Victor Dunn married Louisa Morrison, and she is now living in Kansas City with her son, Stewart William Victor Dunn, aged fifteen.

Mr. Dunn comes of an old Virginia family of Scotch-Irish stock, and besides his own record as a soldier of the Confederacy the descendants are entitled to membership in the patriotic societies that commemorate service in the early Colonial and Revolutionary wars. His grandfather was William Dunn, who came from Ireland and founded the family in Virginia. He reached America in time to take part in the Revolutionary war as a soldier. His children were: William; John; Doctor Samuel; Mary, who married Caleb Logan; Katie, who married Shaw Logan; Lydia, who married Jonas Smith. William Dunn of these children came to Missouri, but all the others spent all their lives in Virginia.

John Dunn, father of the Bethany business man, was born in Washington County, Virginia, and died there in 1845. He married Mary McCulloch, a daughter of Robert McCulloch and a granddaughter of Thomas McCulloch, the McCullochs having come originally from Scotland. Grandfather Thomas McCulloch was a Colonial soldier during the Revolution and was killed in the battle of Kings Mountain. Robert McCulloch married Sarah Clark. Mrs. John Dunn died in Virginia in 1891, when nearly eighty-six years of age. She was a member of the Methodist Church. Her children were: Mary, who married David Cuddy, and spent her life in Virginia; Theophilus, who was a soldier in the Thirty-seventh Virginia Infantry during the war, was wounded in the battle of Kernstown under Stonewall Jackson, was for many years a Virginia merchant, came to Missouri in 1904 and now lives at Gilman; William M., who was next among the children; Robert H., of Bethany; and John F., who was also a Confederate soldier and is a farmer in Washington County, Virginia.

HERMAN ROLEKE, who has lived at Bethany since 1880, and who has been a merchant tailor all these years, is, as his name would indicate, of German birth, his native province being that of Hanover and his town the city of that name. He was born April 2, 1862, and was reared in the home of a tailor, his father being Joseph Roleke, a tailor and a native of the same locality, where he spent his life as had his ancestors back to 1640. The family seems to have included a long line of mechanics, and all soldiered when needed by the fatherland, an uncle of Mr. Roleke being a distinguished German army officer during the Franco-Prussian war. Joseph Roleke married Amelia Schulze, and to them there were born seven children, of whom Herman, of this review, is the only one of the family to come to the United States.

Herman Roleke secured his education in the public schools and the commercial college of Hanover, and learned his trade under the capable preceptorship of his father. He learned something of the opportunities in America from having a cousin who came over before the Civil war and was lost as an engineer in the Federal navy during that struggle, and while the young man, of course, did not gain his knowledge of America from that uncle, the impetus which started him westward and across the Atlantic was that given by the presence of the uncle here. Mr. Roleke sailed from the City of Bremen, Germany, on the German Lloyd steamer Rhein, bound for New York, and landed after a trip devoid of special incident some fourteen days later. Subsequently, while en route west he stopped at Chicago and Quincy, Illinois, and chanced to make some acquaintances before Bethany was reached, these influencing him to stop at this point. At that time this town was the end of the railroad and he was forced to stop here, so that he had an excellent chance of noting the opportunities and advantages, and finally decided to make this place his permanent home. For two years Mr. Roleke was employed at his trade for the old tailor here at that time, one McCurry, and then established a place of business of his own.

During the next thirty-two years, Mr. Roleke's history as a business man of Bethany is expressed briefly by a career of industry. He displayed his interest in public affairs, was one of the promoters of the

Young Men's Improvement Club, and was elected himself to the town council more than twenty years ago. The stimulating cry at that time was for macadam roads, electric lights and waterworks, and this was achieved by bonding the town, the first issue of bonds for any purpose by the corporation. After serving a term Mr. Roleke refused to again become a candidate for the position of alderman, and his career was ended as a public official, although he has never ceased his "boosting." Mr. Roleke laid out the "Park Addition" to Bethany, being associated with McCollum Brothers in that movement. This comprised an addition in the east part of the town, the best one here. Mr. Roleke subsequently built Roleke Park, called by Bob Taylor, Hobson and other chautauqua men "Beautiful Roleke Park," and in it the chautauqua meetings of Bethany have been held for nine years. Mr. Roleke has built there one of the most beautiful landscape gardens to be found in Missouri, this comprising ten acres laid off by Mr. Roleke himself from a barren tract of land, and its improvements have given Bethany a park which rivals anything in the state in attractiveness. The Allen Park, in the east part of Bethany, is also a product of Mr. Roleke's genius for park building. It is a small plaza at the junction of three streets, and is equipped with a fountain. The place was once a mere wallow and an eyesore to the town. When Mr. Roleke took up the question of making a park of it and urged it, as only he can, it assumed other shape than an "undesirable spot" rapidly.

The laying out of the grounds of the County Home near Bethany also fell to Mr. Roleke's lot. He was chosen for this labor by the County Court, and it, too, presents wonders in the direction of landscape beautification. He financiered and promoted the erection of the Pythian Castle, at Bethany, in 1900, built upon the mediæval style of architecture and at a cost of about twenty thousand dollars. Quoting from the address of the grand chancellor of the Knights of Pythias of Missouri, with reference to this matter, we find the following: "I have not sufficient command of language to describe this building, nor space had I the words, but this I will say—it is and always will be a fitting monument to one of the best men and truest friends I ever knew, Herman Roleke."

Mr. Roleke joined the Knights of Pythias in 1883, passed all the chairs here, and has been a member of the Grand Lodge since 1895. He has been grand master of the exchequer for eleven years, or treasurer of the Missouri Order. After ten years of service as such the honors of past grand chancellor of the state were bestowed upon him in honor of his labors. That occasion was marked by the presentation to Mr. Roleke of a solid gold emblem by the Grand Lodge with appropriate inscription as to his faithful service.

In politics Mr. Roleke started out as a voter as a protective democrat, following Randall of Pennsylvania, but when the democratic party parted from Randall's lead he abandoned it and cast his lot with the republicans. He followed the fortunes of this party until 1896 when he voted for William J. Bryan. In 1912, having resumed republicanism, he resented the methods used at the republican convention at Chicago and followed the cause of Colonel Roosevelt.

Mr. Roleke was married at Bethany, Missouri, in March, 1882, to Miss Rachel Mainwaring, a daughter of Josiah Mainwaring, who came from Liverpool, England, in 1839 and married Elizabeth Henry. Mrs. Roleke was the youngest of six children living. To Mr. and Mrs. Roleke there have been born the following children still living: Helena, the wife of Earl Poland, of Bethany; Gertrude, the wife of Harvey J. Burris, of Denver, Colorado; Joseph, a resident of Sioux Falls, South Dakota; Hazel, the wife of Alvin Bartlett, of Bethany; and Agnes, the youngest, who is single and resides with her parents.

ALFRED CARROLL REYNOLDS, M. D.   During the past twenty-seven years the name of Dr. Alfred Carroll Reynolds has been increasingly identified with the best tenets of medical and surgical science in Harrison County. By many of the longest established and most conservative families his skill, resource and obliging temperament have come to be regarded as indispensable, and there exist many who are indebted to him for their restoration to health, happiness and usefulness. Doctor Reynolds came to Harrison County, Missouri, in 1887 from Woodland, Iowa, where he had spent two years in the practice of his profession, going there from Davis City, that state. At the latter place he had practiced two years, and had gone there from the homestead farm in Marion County, Iowa, where he was born June 25, 1854, a son of Mortimer S. and Nancy (Nossaman) Reynolds.

Silas Reynolds, the grandfather of Doctor Reynolds, was born in Virginia and there passed his entire life. His widow, who was formerly Minerva See, came to the West with her children, settled in Iowa, and there passed the remaining years of her life in Marion County. The children were: Mortimer S.; Carroll; Morris; John; Leaher, who became the wife of Jack Hegwood; Lutitia, who married John DeMoss; and Jane, who became the wife of "Tap" Hegwood. Mortimer S. Reynolds was born in the Old Dominion State, in 1828, and during the early '40s migrated to the West, settling in Iowa, where he entered land in Marion County which he improved, and there made his home for many years. Later in life he came to Missouri and took up his residence near Martinsville, which was the scene of his abode for twenty years. He was a stalwart democrat, was a member of the Baptist Church, and a Master Mason. Mr. Reynolds married Mary Nossaman, a daughter of Adam Nossaman, who came to Iowa from Kentucky, but was formerly a resident of Indiana. Mrs. Reynolds' parents died near Indianapolis, Indiana, while her own death occurred at Martinsville, Missouri, in March, 1907. Her children were as follows: Dr. Alfred Carroll, of this notice; Dr. Vernon, who is a practicing physician of Oklahoma; Samantha, a resident of Harrison County, Missouri, and wife of Charles Chandler; Dr. Mortimer S., Jr., a resident of Yates Center, Kansas; Dr. Allen, who is a resident of Caledonia, Iowa; Levi, who resides in Montana; Ida, who became the wife of Mr. McConkey and died in Iowa, without issue; and Charles, who died single.

Alfred Carroll Reynolds grew up as a country boy amid rural surroundings and secured his literary education at Pella, Iowa. He began his career as a farmer and took up the study of medicine with his brother, Dr. Vernon Reynolds, at Durham, Iowa, and took lectures at the Keokuk Medical School and the College of Physicians and Surgeons, Keokuk. After his graduation, in 1882, he established himself in practice at Davis City, as before related. Doctor Reynolds belongs to the Harrison County Medical Society and the Missouri State Medical Society, and has always practiced in and among the rural precincts. His first location in Harrison County was at Martinsville, where he remained until February, 1914, and at that time came to Bethany.

Doctor Reynolds was married in Marion County, Iowa, in February, 1874, to Miss Hannah J. Teter, a daughter of Samuel E. Teter, of Iowa, who died in Marion County, this state, in 1881, leaving these children: Dr. Elda M., a practicing physician of Union Star, Missouri, married

Nora Funk; and three children who·died in childhood. Doctor Reynolds married his second wife at Davis City, Iowa, in 1884, she being Miss Flora Norman, a daughter of Samuel and Kate (Robinson) Norman. The children in the Norman family were: Clara, the wife of Lemuel Grindle; and Mrs. Reynolds. Doctor and Mrs. Reynolds have the following children: Wilda, Wanda, Vaughn, Vern, A. C., D. O. and Berman.

Doctor Reynolds is identified with the Christian Church. He erected his home in the east part of Bethany, a residence of eleven rooms, on his 7½ acre tract, and it is one of the splendid homes of this town. It would seem that Doctor Reynolds has taken a rather silent part in his community affairs, but his profession and his business have absorbed his attention almost to the exclusion of other matters. For twenty years he has owned a farm, which he has operated, and also had a drug store at Martinsville and helped to promote the bank there as a stockholder, and is still such. He supports the candidates of the democratic party.

GEORGE WESLEY BARRY, who for thirty-four years has been a factor in the commercial life of Bethany, came to this town and engaged in the harness business before he was twenty-one years old and has been on duty every day since. He came from Gentry County, Missouri, where, near Darlington, he grew up and was educated, and was a schoolmate of Woodson Peery, his seat-mate and now Northwest Missouri's eminent legal light, and George Holden, now prominent in business affairs of Albany, was another schoolmate. Mr. Barry began learning the harness maker's trade the day he was fifteen years of age, with George Pierce, of Albany, and remained in that shop until he completed his trade and engaged in business on his own account at Bethany.

Mr. Barry's first store was located over Dunn Brothers'. dry goods establishment, at Bethany, there being at that time five harness shops here, while since then there have been as high as seven shops at one time. He remained upstairs over the Dunns for several years and then, desiring larger quarters, moved to the old Elmo Hotel property, which he purchased. A few months later he bought a lot on Main Street and moved his store to·it, and there, in 1890, he erected his new brick store, a one-story structure, which has been his establishment to the present time. Mr. Barry started into business at Bethany with a capital of about one hundred and fifty dollars, in addition to which he secured an advance of $100 worth of merchandise from his Albany employer. He brought a partner, Andrew Lord, from Albany, who was to share in the profits of the business with him, and they began business here May 17, 1878, but Mr. Lord became dissatisfied with the meagre earnings of their first two weeks, wanted full pay for more time than he had worked, and finally brought suit for a balance of $15, which Mr. Barry paid, thus setting Lord free. Some time later Mr. Barry took his brother in as partner and they were together twenty years, and still later he took in another brother, J. B. Barry, who died in the firm, since which time George W. Barry has been alone.

George Wesley Barry was born in Lee County, Iowa, May 21, 1859, a son of William C. Barry. His grandfather, a native of Ireland, bearing the name of O'Barry, died in Maryland, the father of these children: William C.; a son who disappeared many years ago and whom it is believed went to California; Wesley, of Denver, Colorado; and James, a son by a second marriage, who lives near Chillicothe, Missouri. William C. Barry was born in Maryland, and as a child left his native state and went to Lee County, Iowa, where he grew up and was married to Nancy

Wells, who died at Bethany, Missouri, in 1881. After his marriage Mr. Barry moved to Pettis County, Missouri, and lived on a farm near Sedalia until the Civil war broke out, when he left his farm and returned to Iowa, there residing until about the time of the close of hostilities. He then went to Mount Vernon, Ohio, but soon returned to the West, and after a short stay in Iowa came to Gentry County, Missouri. Having acquired a good education in his youth, he secured employment as a teacher in the public schools, but finally established himself in the butcher business at Albany. Prior to the Civil war Mr. Barry was a democrat, but at the time that struggle broke out he transferred his support to the republican party. His religious faith was that of the Presbyterian Church, while his wife, who was a daughter of Aaron Wells, was a Methodist. Their children were as follows: William L., of Leon, Iowa; George Wesley, of this notice; Belle, who married Mr. Hair, of California; Anna, who married Mr. Horner, of Indiana; Emma, who married Arden Butler and died at Darlington, Missouri; Miss Hattie, whose home is in Chicago; Lou, who married Charles E. Fitch, of Wheaton, Illinois; Myrtie, who died single; Charles, of Trenton, Missouri; and J. Blaine, who died at Bethany.

George Wesley Barry was married at Bethany, Missouri, March 20, 1890, to Miss Ann Hubbard, a daughter of E. Little Hubbard, a native of Vermont, who came to Missouri as a pioneer and here engaged in farming and stock raising. There were five children in the Hubbard family: Wallace; Henrietta; Mrs. Barry; Emma, who married W. S. Walker; and Ed, a resident of Bethany. To Mr. and Mrs. Barry there have been born four children: Gordon, who died at the age of seventeen years; and Ross, Nell and Everett, all at home.

In addition to his prosperous and steadily growing business at Bethany, Mr. Barry is the owner of suburban property in this vicinity, and is the proprietor of the only harness shop at Stanberry. He is a republican in politics, but is not an office seeker, and belongs neither to a secret organization or a church. He is a tall, muscular man, who has demonstrated his effectiveness in business, and who, at the same time, has established a reputation as a good and public-spirited citizen.

WILLIAM FRANK CUDDY. Since the year 1875, when he wrapped up his first package of goods at Bethany, William Frank Cuddy has been connected with the mercantile interests of Bethany, and during this time has firmly established himself in the confidence of the people, both as a reliable and honorable merchant and as a thorough-going and progressive citizen. He was born in Washington County, Virginia, March 13, 1854, where he grew up on a farm of modest size, and without the environment of slavery, being under the parental roof until of age, and his coming West was the first start he made in life independent of others.

The Cuddy family originated in Ireland, from whence the progenitor, the grandfather of William Frank Cuddy, emigrated to the United States. Among his children there were no daughters, but his sons included Henry, Lilburn and David, the last named being the father of William F. David Cuddy was born in Washington County, Virginia, August 30, 1829, and died there December 15, 1911. He was a man of somewhat limited education, passed his life in the pursuits of the soil, and had no political career. He was originally opposed to secession, but when his state left the Union he lent it his moral support, and had two brothers who were soldiers in the Confederate army. Mr. Cuddy was a democrat in his political views, and he was an unwavering member of the Methodist Episcopal Church, South, and almost felt that members of other denominations would have difficulty in reaching their final reward. He was an exceedingly active man in the church and served prominently as an official and a church supporter. Mr. Cuddy married Mary J. Dunn, a sister of William M. and Robert Dunn, of Bethany. As estimated by her son she was the best woman that ever lived, and passed away at the age of seventy-two years, having been the mother of the following children: William Frank; Robert H., a resident of Washington County, Virginia; John H., who is associated with his brother in the store at Bethany; and four daughters who died in childhood.

William Frank Cuddy came to Bethany, Missouri, with only a common school education and with no business experience of any nature. He secured employment with the firm of McGeorge & Dunn, merchants, at a salary of $20 per month, and for eighteen months thus continued to be engaged, paying his board and supporting himself with these meagre wages. He was then offered and accepted $30 a month with the firm of Hubbard & Price, at that time located at Bethany, and continued to spend eighteen months with this firm also. Mr. Cuddy's uncle, William Dunn, then offered him a working interest in a store here whose stock he had purchased at a bankrupt sale, and Mr. Cuddy accepted his offer and assisted him in the disposition of the goods, his part of the profits from the arrangement being $1,200. On the closing out of this venture, Mr. Dunn gave him a working interest in the store or business of McGeorge & Dunn, and that arrangement continued for perhaps five years and Mr. Cuddy invested his savings in the stock, which gave him a fourth interest in the business. When the firm was changed to Dunn Brothers & Company, Mr. Cuddy was a silent partner of it and he has clung to the store tenaciously for the whole period of nearly forty years without losing a day of unnecessary time. The firm of Cuddy & Dunn came into existence some twelve years ago, and Mr. Cuddy remains as the head of it. He has rarely identified himself with other business enterprises, and has never connected himself with the official life of the town, although he is a director of the Harrison County Bank at Bethany.

When Mr. Cuddy has participated in politics it has been merely as a democrat and as a voter. He cast his first vote for Tilden and Hendricks in 1876, and has never missed voting at a presidential election since, and has supported the regular nominee of the party, save when William J. Bryan was supporting the "Free Silver" issue, when he voted for Major McKinley for president. He supported Mr. Bryan, however, the last time he was a candidate and gladly gave his vote to Mr. Wilson in 1912, and is more than pleased with the condition of affairs under his administration. In church matters Mr. Cuddy has never identified himself with any particular religious denomination, but is an attendant of the Presbyterian Church, in which Mrs. Cuddy holds her membership. He belongs to no fraternal society save the Knights of Pythias.

Mr. Cuddy was married at Osceola, Iowa, March 8, 1888, to Miss Jean Morrison, a daughter of James and Marian (Stewart) Morrison. The Morrisons and the Stewarts came from Glasgow, Scotland, and Mrs. Cuddy was born at Osceola, Iowa, in 1867. Her brothers and sisters were: James, who died in Iowa; Mrs. Louisa Lapsley and Mrs. Jessie Cuddy, both residents of Kansas City, Missouri; and Polly, who died as Mrs. Robert Cuddy. Mr. and Mrs. W. F. Cuddy have one daughter, Mildred, who is ten years of age.

O. O. Meredith, M. D.

OSCAR O. MEREDITH, M. D. The medical profession in Breckenridge has no stronger member than Doctor Meredith, who during the past ten years in his practice in that city and vicinity has built up a splendid reputation as a skillful physician and surgeon and enjoys a constantly growing prestige and influence throughout his home community. Doctor Meredith located at Breckenridge in 1905. He is a graduate of the class of 1903 from Eclectic Medical College of St. Louis, and spent his first two years after graduation at Cowgill, Missouri.

Though Doctor Meredith has spent nearly all his life in this part of Northwest Missouri, he is a Hoosier by birth, born at Bloomfield, Greene County, Indiana, January 9, 1880. His father, Samuel G. Meredith, was a physician. In 1882 he brought his family to Northwest Missouri and he died in Cowgill at the age of sixty-two. Samuel G. Meredith married Rachel Pethtel, who was born in Ohio. Their family comprised five children: Edgar F., who is a resident of Kirkwood, Missouri; Oscar O.; Forest Lee, of Webster, Iowa; Herma Jennie Griffing, of Gault, Missouri, and Effie Craig Butts, who died December 25, 1914. The parents were active members of the Christian Church, in which the father served as an elder, and was also affiliated with the Masonic order and the Independent Order of Odd Fellows.

Dr. O. O. Meredith received his education in the public schools, spent a year in the University of Missouri at Columbia, and previous to taking up the practice of medicine was for one year connected with the department of instruction in histology at the Eclectic Medical University of Kansas City, Missouri. Doctor Meredith took the full course in the medical college, and since graduating has devoted himself untiringly to the interests of his medical clients.

In 1905 Doctor Meredith married Maud Foreman, a daughter of John P. Foreman. Doctor Meredith is affiliated with the Independent Order of Odd Fellows, and is also a member of the Caldwell County Medical Society, the Missouri State Medical Association and the Eclectic State and National Medical Society, as was his father. He is and has been local registrar for preservation of vital statistics in registration district No. 94, Caldwell County, since 1910. He is a man of athletic build, has great vitality and energy as well as skill for the prosecution of his duties as a physician, and is one of the studious and hard-working members of the profession.

TAYLOR EDWARD STONE. A resident of Harrison County since 1871, Taylor E. Stone came to this section of Missouri as a poor man, and his achievements of the past forty years are measured in the accumulation of a handsome farming estate, a beautiful city home at Bethany, where he has lived since 1900, and by valuable service to both the church and civic affairs of his home community.

Taylor Edward Stone was born in Licking County, Missouri, July 3, 1847. His father was Edward Stone, who came from Maryland and died in Ohio in 1862 at the age of one hundred and four years. He served as a soldier during the War of 1812 and afterwards in the Blackhawk war. As a result of his military experience he received three wounds. The Federal Government granted him a land warrant for his services during the War of 1812, but it was never commuted into land, and no trace of the document is now to be found. Edward Stone was three times married, and there were children by all the wives. His last wife was Mary Ellen Morris, who died in 1859 and is buried beside her husband at Hanover, in Licking County, Ohio. Her children were: Mary, who married John Harper; Lila, who married Burr Beard; Thomas, of Knox County, Ohio; Frank N., of Cleveland, Ohio; Taylor

E.; Jesse, of Licking County, Ohio. By his former marriages Edward Stone had children named as follows: John, George, Theodore and Ivan, who spent their lives in Ohio; Jennie, who married Andrew Thompson; and Henrietta, who was the wife of George English.

Taylor E. Stone was left an orphan during his boyhood, and reached maturity with only a country school education; he learned no trade, and industry has been the key with which he has unlocked the door to prosperity. Before reaching his majority he went away from home to enlist in the Union army, and in 1864 became a private in Company G of the One Hundred and Ninety-seventh Ohio Infantry, under Captain Owens and Colonel Austin. His regiment was used chiefly for guard duty, at Baltimore and Washington and in the State of Delaware, being stationed at cities in the guarding of bridges, and at the close of the war Mr. Stone was at Dover, Delaware. On returning home from the army, he began work as a farm laborer at daily wages, and continued in that way until 1871, when he started west. A railroad took him as far as Osceola, Iowa, and as there was no railroads in Harrison County, Missouri, at that time, he came overland to join some friends in that locality. Here he easily found work on farms, though the wages were low, a dollar a day being a big price for labor at that time. Land in Harrison County at that time sold for $2.50 to $25 an acre, depending upon improvements. Mr. Stone located in Clay Township, began as a renter, and finally bought land in township 66 of range 26. It was unimproved, and Mr. Stone erected his first house with lumber hauled from Princeton. That was the nucleus around which he has since accumulated the possessions which mark him as one of Harrison County's thrifty and substantial citizens. In that vicinity he still owns his quarter section of land, and lived there and engaged in general farming and stock raising until his removal to Bethany in 1900. During the time his home was in the country, Mr. Stone assisted in the organization of a Presbyterian church in that community. In Bethany Mr. Stone has a splendid home, with large grounds.

During the past fourteen years he has been very active as a citizen of Bethany, and is now in his fourth term as an alderman. During the eight years of his service all the important public improvements have been instituted at Bethany, including paving, installation of waterworks and the removal of the plant from its old location, the laying of concrete sidewalks all over the town and many other improvements. When the Roleke administration came into power the municipality was issuing scrip to discharge its obligations, but the city is now practically out of debt, and in the meantime a large amount has been expended in local betterment. Mr. Stone takes much interest in Grand Army matters, is an active member of the T. D. Neal Post, has attended the national encampment of the order, and· in his home post has done much committee work in preparing for soldiers' reunions. He is affiliated with all branches of the Independent Order of Odd Fellows, is a past grand of the lodge, is a member of the Knights of Pythias, and is assistant scout master of the boy scouts. His political action has identified him with the republican party. Mr. Stone is one of the leading laymen in the Presbyterian Church, and one of the elders in the Bethany Church. He has been a member of the Presbytery and has attended the synods, and was a delegate to the convention at Decatur, Illinois, where the union of the old school and the Cumberland churches was consummated.

In April, 1871, Mr. Stone married Miss Jennie Cullins, daughter of an Ohio settler. Mrs. Stone died in Bethany without children.

On December 29, 1907, he married Mrs. Hattie Hohr. Mrs. Stone is a daughter of William A. and Emeline Templeman, and represents two of the distinguished families of Northwest Missouri.

William A. Templeman, who was born in Fauquier County, Virginia, February 14, 1835, was brought to Harrison County, Missouri, as a child. His father, Thornton Hume Templeman, came to Missouri during the decade of the '40s and located at Bethany in 1853. Thornton H. Templeman was a native of Virginia, and a son of Fielding Templeman, who was of Scotch ancestry. Thornton Templeman married Harriet Holmes in Stafford County, Virginia. On locating at Bethany he engaged in the dry goods business, and was postmaster of the town before and during the war. First a whig, he later entered the republican party, and his religious affiliation was with the Christian Church. His death occurred in 1874, and his devoted companion in the home and in church work followed him a few years later. Their children were: William A.; Sarah A., who married William Collier and died in Bethany; Frances, who married Joseph Collier, and is now Mrs. William Gale of Bethany; Mildred, married Jefferson Nordyke and died in Bethany.

William A. Templeman acquired his education in the Bethany schools, and had his early experience in business in the store of his father. He afterwards acquired the store and was a merchant here for a number of years. He finally moved out to Colorado, and followed merchandising and mining at Leadville, and on his return to Bethany was a real estate man until his retirement. William A. Templeman conducted one of the early newspapers of Bethany, having been editor of the Bethany Union during the Civil war. He was a war democrat, and was enrolled with the state militia, and on one occasion accompanied his company to Chillicothe to defend that town against threatened trouble. He served in the office of county collector and throughout his active career was one of the leading men of Bethany. He was an elder in the Disciples Church and superintendent of its Sunday school.

William A. Templeman was married August 9, 1855, to Miss Emeline Allen. Their children were: Mrs. Rosa A. Vandivert, now deceased; Mrs. Judge Wanamaker, of Bethany; John Allen, of Austin, Texas; Harriet, wife of Taylor E. Stone; Nancy, who died in childhood; Mrs. Emma Oxford; William Thornton, of Bethany; and Marian, wife of Virgil Yates of Bethany.

Mrs. William A. Templeman was a daughter of the Rev. John S. Allen, and mention of his name recalls one of the most noted pioneer families of Northwest Missouri. He had come into this section when a number of the present counties were under the jurisdiction of Daviess County. Rev. John S. Allen was born in Overton County, Tennessee, June 26, 1814, a son of William and Mary (Copeland) Allen, Overton County farmers. John S. was one of a family of thirteen children, and judged by the standards of the time possessed a liberal education. In 1832 he left Tennessee, settled in Illinois, and in Woodford County of that state married Nancy Childress, who was born in Kentucky, November 4, 1813. From Illinois Reverend Allen was one of the leaders in a party of pioneers who came to Harrison County at the beginning of civilization in this section. The other members of that caravan were: John W. Brown, Thomas Tucker, Thomas Brown, W. R. Allen, C. L. Jennings, Ephraim Stewart and A. A. Allen, the last named being unmarried. These families all settled near Bethany, and gave their character as industrious, moral and religious people to the community. In this new country Reverend Allen soon constituted himself a leader not only in his church but also as a citizen and business man. He was a strong Union sympathizer and attended the secession convention of Missouri as a delegate, where he used his influence to keep Missouri from joining the Confederacy. He was a democrat in politics. The work of this devout man was felt everywhere, both in Harrison and adjoining counties in the early days. His voice was raised for God throughout all these counties, and those converted under the spell of his preaching numbered legion. In business affairs he was a merchant, and was one of the organizers and for twenty years president of the First Bank of Bethany. John S. Allen's family comprised the following children: Mrs. William A. Templeman, who was born in Woodford County, Illinois, March 22, 1837, and grew up in the pioneer community of Bethany; James R., who died in Bethany; Mrs. Dr. King of Bethany; Mrs. Elizabeth Roberts of Bethany; and Willard Cass, who died in Bethany.

THOMAS JEFFERSON FLINT. An honored resident of Bethany, where he lives retired, Thomas J. Flint has spent the greater part of seventy years in Northwest Missouri, mainly in Daviess and Harrison counties. He knew this country when it was a wilderness, and few men still living have so broad a scope of experience and recollection in the things that made for development and history in this fair portion of Missouri. He has been a teacher, a soldier, a county official, a farmer and a merchant, and in the manifold relations of a long life has steered a course directed by the positive and high-minded qualities of his character.

Thomas Jefferson Flint was born in Franklin County, Indiana, August 4, 1835. His grandfather, John Flint, was an Englishman, and with four brothers came to America about 1788, his settlement being in Maryland, while the others located in other colonies. He was a sailor, and was lost at sea while his family were living in Maryland. By his marriage to Temperance Humphrey he had the following children: John, who was lost at sea with his father; Dorcas, who was born in 1795, married Samuel Davis and died near Mexarville, Indiana; Thomas, born in 1798, came to Missouri and settled on a farm in Harrison County in 1838, was one of the first officials in Bethany when it was founded and later county clerk of Harrison County, and died on his farm here, but was buried in the McCleary Cemetery in Daviess County, where his brother George also rests; George, whose career is the subject of the following paragraph; Maria, born in 1804, married about 1822 Oliver Thurston and died near Mexarville, Indiana, in 1868; Joseph H., born in 1807, was a Baptist preacher and physician, and spent many years at Ottumwa, Iowa, where he died.

Rev. George Flint, whose name deserves remembrance among the pioneers of Northwest Missouri, was born in Maryland, July 19, 1801. After the death of his father his mother brought her family to Hamilton County, Ohio, where she died about 1820. The circumstances of his youth in a new country and with a meagerness of family resources left him little opportunity for gaining an education, and his regular schooling was confined to three months. His studious nature and ambition for a life of usefulness enabled him to overcome this handicap, and in time he became a man of intellectual attainments far above the average. By the light of a fire kindled by hickory bark, he studied arithmetic, grammar, geography and some history, consuming the contents of the limited store of books which he could buy or borrow, and eventually even entered the field of the classics, and was able to read both Greek and

Latin. Both in early and later life he taught many terms of school, chiefly in the country districts. His talent as a conversationalist and public speaker led him into the ministry. As an illustration of his familiarity with the Bible, it is recalled that he once repeated from memory the whole of Paul's letter to the Hebrews, thirteen chapters. He was never identified with any secret order. In politics, before the war, he was a democrat, and in 1860 voted for Stephen A. Douglas for president, as did his sons, but his next ballot went to Mr. Lincoln, and his sons followed his example.

Rev. George Flint brought his family out to Missouri in the early '40s, and entered land in Daviess County. About 1844 he opened a store on his land in Washington Township and continued as a merchant until 1849. Soon afterward, selling his farm, he moved to Saline County, and while there lived in the Town of Miami and was an active preacher. He organized the Christian Church at Arrow Rock and preached in Brunswick. While in Daviess County he organized a church in the Ford Schoolhouse, and the society afterwards erected a house of worship at Coffey. Soon after the close of the Civil war the Rev. Mr. Flint moved to Coffey, then an inland village, and remained there until his death, September 21, 1871.

The maiden name of the wife of this early Missouri divine was Nancy Foster, of Hamilton County, Ohio. Her father, who was born in 1776, moved from Kentucky to Ohio, subsequently to Indiana and finally to a farm in Missouri, where he died in 1850. He married Rachel Thomas, who died in 1854. The Foster children were: Elizabeth, who became the wife of Ancel Terry and died near Coffey, Missouri; Rachel, who married Thomas Flint and died in Harrison County, Missouri; John, who spent most of his life near Bethany as a farmer; Nancy Flint; Nelson, who started from Daviess County to California in 1849, but died en route while near Cheyenne, Wyoming; and Thomas, who crossed the plains to California in 1850 and spent the rest of his life in and about Sacramento.

The Rev. George and Nancy Flint's children were: William F., born April 4, 1828, in Hamilton County, Ohio, spent his life largely as a teacher and farmer, and also during the war served in the Missouri State Militia and afterward for a year was captain of Company F of the Forty-third Missouri Infantry; he married Mary Ann Ford, and left eight children. Rachel Temperance, born September 7, 1830, married John R. Maize, and died near Bethany in 1892, leaving seven children. Louisa Ann, born November 23, 1832, married Alanson Alley, and died near Bethany, July 12, 1874. The next in order of birth is Thomas J., of whom more is given in following paragraphs. Maria R., born January 13, 1838, married Isaac N. Thomas and died in Bethany, October 25, 1869. John Logan, born July 10, 1840, was a volunteer soldier of Company D of the Twenty-seventh Missouri Infantry, from which he was discharged for disability, in 1888 went to California, and now lives at Fowler. Andrew S., born September 21, 1842, in the flush of young manhood entered Company D of the Twenty-seventh Missouri Infantry, and died during the siege of Vicksburg. Asby C., born December 27, 1844, married Harlan T. Gerrish of Patoka, Illinois. Larkin S., born March 1, 1847, during the last year of the war served as fifer in Company F of the Forty-third Missouri Infantry, and is now a farmer near Bethany.

The preceding account shows that Thomas Jefferson Flint comes of a family with excellent characteristics. His own career has been in keeping with his inheritance. He was about old enough when the family moved to Missouri so that the journey left some impression on his boyish memory, and he grew to manhood in Daviess County, and attended the country schools. Later he was in the Bethany schools when Judge Howell was a teacher. At the age of eighteen he himself was recruited for service in the schoolroom, at wages of $15 a month. His first term was taught in the Glover School, now the Maize School. It was a log house, with mud-and-stick chimney and a big open fireplace into which the big boys rolled the logs on cold winter days. School was called at 8 in the morning. Everything went by a code of rules, tacked up on the wall where all could see, and one of the Monday morning duties was the reading aloud of these rules for the guidance of the scholars. Boys and girls were not permitted to play together, a situation that prevailed when Mr. Flint and his wife were schoolmates together in Daviess County. The rules also forbade whispering, skating, snowballing and wrestling, scuffling and fighting.

Mr. Flint abandoned the schoolroom and went from Daviess County into the army. In September, 1861, he enlisted in the Missouri State Militia in Captain Broomfield's company of six months' militia. The company marched out a few times during the following winter, but never came in sight of the enemy. In September, 1862, he enlisted in the regular service, in Company D of the Twenty-seventh Missouri Infantry, under Capt. William A. Talby and Col. Thomas Curley. He and his comrades were rendezvoused and drilled at Benton Barracks in St. Louis, and in January, 1863, proceeded to Rolla. There Mr. Flint was discharged after having contracted pneumonia, resulting in bronchitis. He came home to resume work in the schoolroom, and in the spring became a pupil again in the Bethany schools. In July, 1864, he reenlisted, entering Company F of the Forty-third Missouri, and was discharged June 30, 1865. His regiment was in no engagements during this time and was kept on duty in its home state.

After the war Mr. Flint resumed teaching, and his last school was in the summer of 1868 in the Marlar district. About this time he became active in local politics, and after one term as treasurer of Daviess County was elected sheriff, serving four years. It was while he was in the office of county treasurer that the James boys killed Capt. John W. Sheets, mistaking him for Major Cox, whom they sought to kill to avenge his act in slaying the notorious Bill Anderson. At that time Mr. Flint was a Gallatin merchant, and had the county safe in his store there. He witnessed the flight of the bandits after they had completed their act of venegeance and had taken some of the funds of the local bank. After leaving the sheriff's office he resumed merchandising at Gallatin and was associated with John J. Broadbeck until 1882, when he left Missouri and located at Great Bend, Kansas. Besides keeping a store, he also did farming and proved up on a claim in Ness County. His home was in Great Bend for twenty years, and in the meantime he made two trips to California, visiting his brother. His return to Missouri was in 1904, and since then his home has been in Bethany, and he has been retired from active business.

On September 4, 1859, Mr. Flint married Miss Lydia A. Adams, a daughter of William and Elizabeth (Beall) Adams, her father being a farmer from Henry County, Indiana. Mrs. Flint was the third of four children. At Great Bend, Kansas, Mr. Flint married for his second wife, on March 28, 1883, Mrs. Lucretia E. Crail, a daughter of Ruel and Mamie (Thomas) Nimocks, the former an Ohio man. Mrs. Nimocks was a cousin of Mr. Flint's mother. The Nimocks children were: Mrs. Flint, born December 8, 1842; George, who was a Union soldier from

Iowa, and died at Great Bend in 1902; Albert, of Barton County, Kansas; Link, of Vesalia, California; Frank, of Ottumwa, Iowa; Clara, who lives in Eldon, Iowa; Mrs. Vina Foster, of Eldon; and Mrs. Lucy Cramer, of Eldon. Mrs. Flint died August 27, 1903. On November 9, 1904, he married for his present wife, at Bethany, Mrs. Sallie A. Zimmerlee, a daughter of Milton and Emily (Jones) Higgins. Her father came from Clarksburg, Indiana, to Daviess County, Missouri, where Mrs. Flint was reared. By her first husband, Edward Zimmerlee, she had the following children: Emily, wife of Charles Barnes, of Bethany; Mattie, wife of William Hill, of St. Louis; Maud, who married D. W. Coe, of New York City; and Katherine, wife of George H. Pannell, of Los Angeles.

Mr. Flint has always acted with the republican party, and while in Kansas was active in the party. He was a delegate to the congressional convention at St. Joseph when Mr. Parker was nominated by the republicans of this district. He belongs to the Christian Church, in which he has served as elder.

JOHN LOUIS COLE. Half a century of honorable business activity and citizenship comprises a record such as any man should be proud to possess. It was nearly fifty years ago when John L. Cole of Bethany, then a young man, with hardly a dollar to his name, and with only manual labor as his dependence, came to Harrison County and began a career which has since brought him a generous success so far as his own material means are concerned, and has also identified his name with much that is profitable and worthy in the community. His career has in it much of encouragement for those who begin life under a handicap, and in the face of difficulties that discourage those lacking in self-reliance and industry.

John Louis Cole was born in Cincinnati, Ohio, January 6, 1843, a son of Jacob and Mary C. (Smoker) Kohl. His father was a Pennsylvania German, and spelled his name in the true German manner. The mother was a native of Germany. Both the parents died of the cholera scourge at Cincinnati in 1849, and they left the following children: Sophia, who married Charles Lowe and spent her life in Indianapolis; Caroline, who married Henry Anderson and also lived in Indianapolis; Mary C., who became the wife of Dr. Samuel E. Strong and died at Ironton, Missouri; John L.; and Dr. William C., who at the time of his death was a physician at the Hospital for the Insane at Jacksonville, Illinois, and left two children.

After the death of his parents John L. Cole, then six years of age, was taken into the home of comparative strangers, and until eighteen years of age lived with Noah Boyce in Morgan County, Illinois. He was still under age when the Civil war broke out. In 1861 he enlisted, and was assigned to Company I in the Fourteenth Illinois Infantry. He joined his command at Rolla, Missouri, whither it had gone to the front. His first captain was Captain Mitchem and later Capt. Ernest Ward. The first colonel of the regiment was John M. Palmer, a distinguished Illinoisan, and later Colonel Cam and finally Col. Cyrus Ball commanded the regiment. The regiment went into Southern Missouri to reinforce General Lyon's army at Wilson Creek, but did not reach the battleground to participate in that crucial engagement, and the troops were then ordered South to Fort Henry and Fort Donelson. Mr. Cole began to see active service during the siege of Fort Donelson, and after the fall of that post proceeded to Shiloh. Subsequently the command made an effort to reach Vicksburg by way of Holly Springs, but the

Confederates cut off their line of communication, and they had to retreat, and finally reached the vicinity of Vicksburg by way of the Mississippi River. In front of Vicksburg the Union forces were employed in digging a canal to change the course of the river, and later Mr. Cole's command was engaged in the siege of the city, being posted southeast of the river stronghold. Mr. Cole says the happiest day of his life was when Pemberton surrendered the Vicksburg garrison. After some further employment in the campaigns of Mississippi, the Fourteenth Regiment joined Grant's army at Chattanooga, and was present but not in action during the battles of Missionary Ridge and Lookout Mountain. In the general advance toward Atlanta, the Fourteenth was assigned to McPherson's corps, and fought in the battle of Resaca, and in many of the other engagements during the almost continuous fighting between Chattanooga and Atlanta, including the battles of Buzzard's Roost, Dalton, Ringgold Gap, Peachtree Creek, where General McPherson was killed, and then in front of Atlanta on July 22d and again on July 28, and finally at Jonesboro. Jonesboro was the last engagement in which Mr. Cole participated. He had enlisted on September 7, 1861, and his three year term expired just before the fall of Atlanta, but he remained twenty days over time because of inability to get through the lines to the North. Mr. Cole was discharged at Big Shanty. Although he had many close calls he came out unwounded. At Vicksburg he was on one occasion stationed behind a clump of sprouts as a sharpshooter using his gun against a picket in the rebel fort, and was fired on in return and the ball passed through the edge of his cap just above his ear. At Shiloh Mr. Cole's cartridge box was pierced by a pullet.

After leaving the army the veteran soldier, though still under age, returned to Illinois. Having no trade, he took Horace Greeley's advice to "go West and grow up with the country," and thus arrived in Harrison County, Missouri, in 1865. His circumstances were such that he could be classed only as a "laboring man," he had no money, and unable to find employment, in a short time his feet were almost on the ground. Through the kindness of Mr. Casebolt, who is still living in this vicinity, he received a pair of boots, and thus protected his bare feet until the winter was over. That winter was spent in the home of William H. Bowler, a son-in-law of the man with whom Mr. Cole had spent his youth in Illinois.

With the opening of the spring of 1866, Mr. Cole rented a farm, and with one horse which he owned and one that he borrowed put in a crop, and as his efforts were seconded by a propitious season, he seemed fairly started toward prosperity. Hogs were worth at that time 8 cents a pound, and he believed it wise to buy hogs and feed his corn to them. Corn was so cheap as almost to be a drug on the market, but after he had fed all his own crop and had bought 500 bushels more, the price of hogs had declined so that he was compelled to kill them and peddle the pork around his home vicinity at 4 cents a pound. Thus his first year proved almost disastrous, and he was left deeply in debt. He still possessed the sympathy and confidence of his neighbors, and the following year rented a farm from Mr. Baber, raised another crop of corn, on the half shares, and again, on the advice of Mr. Baber, bought and fed hogs, and this year conditions were in his favor, and he more than made up for the losses of the previous season. With this varying success Mr. Cole continued as a renter for three years, and then bought eighty acres of land in Sherman Township. Forty acres were under fence and a poor house that deserved the name of shanty was the principal improvement. Mr. Cole engaged to pay $20 an acre for the property, and by several seasons of unflagging work struggled out from under the load of debt, and after that his progress toward success was marked by only the ordinary incidents and ups and downs of the Missouri farmer. The farm which he bought more than forty years ago was his permanent home, and he kept increasing his acreage until his accumulations were measured by 600 acres, and he continued as active manager and supervisor of this large estate until 1902. That year Mr. Cole moved to the City of Bethany, and bought the old Doctor Vandivert home, which had later been the home of General Prentiss. Aside from his large farming interests Mr. Cole was for a time interested in the Cole hardware store at Bethany, and was one of the organizers and is now president of the Harrison County Bank of Bethany.

Although in politics he has been a vigorous advocate of the economic policies maintained by the republican party, Mr. Cole has been chiefly characterized through his strict temperance views, and has refused to vote for any man who uses alcoholic drinks as a beverage. He has served as one of the trustees of the Methodist Episcopal Church, and since 1865 has been identified with the Independent Order of Odd Fellows, in which organization he has served as noble grand.

On May 31, 1871, Mr. Cole was married in Harrison County to Miss Ellen Meek. Her parents were Rev. George W. and Mary (Chockley) Meek, her father a United Brethren minister who came to Missouri from Indiana. Mrs. Cole was the third in a family of seven children. The children of Mr. and Mrs. Cole are: William C., a hardware merchant of Bethany; Charles L., who is now active manager of the home farm; George E., a merchant at Carnegie, Oklahoma; Maud and Roy, twins, the former the wife of Dod Planck, a Sherman Township farmer, and Roy, a farmer in Harrison County.

HENRY LEWIS GEORGE has been identified with the business life of St. Joseph for a period of forty-five years, and during this time it has been his privilege to realize many of his worthy ambitions and through the exercise of good judgment and business sagacity to wrest from his opportunities financial and general success. In his evolution from grocer's clerk at a meager salary to the head of one of St. Joseph's leading commission enterprises he has supplied an inspiring example of the compelling power of strong determination and perseverance and the high worth of homely, sterling virtues. Mr. George was born in the City of Philadelphia, Pennsylvania, in November, 1849, and his family history, as traced in a genealogy now in Mr. George's possession, runs back several centuries in Austria. His great-great-great-grandfather, John George George, who spelled the name Jorger, was born in Austria about the year 1686, came to America with his brother Peter and here founded the family in Pennsylvania, where they were granted all the privileges allowed natural born British subjects. He became a land owner and spent the remainder of his life in Pennsylvania, where he passed away at a ripe old age, in the faith of the Lutheran Church. Peter George and his son, Joseph, served in the Revolutionary war, in Capt. Thomas Fitzsimmons' company, in the Third Battalion, commanded by Col. John Cadwalader, and participated in the battles of Trenton, Princeton, Brandywine and Monmouth and wintered at Valley Forge. The Third Battalion was delegated by General Washington for special service. Peter George subsequently took an active part in public affairs in Philadelphia, where he was married to Sybella Rennin or Renninger. Joseph George, who conducted the Fox Chase Inn at Philadelphia prior to the

Revolution, married Anna Barbara Somers, a daughter of Henry and Veronica Somers.

The family name in Pennsylvania has been variously spelled, as Jorg, Jorge, Jarger, Jurigher, Jerger, Yerger, Yeriger, Yorger, Gerger, Georger and George. Peter George, the great-great-grandfather of Henry L. George, was born about 1720, in Philadelphia. Among his sons was Joseph George, who was born in that city about 1752, and the latter's son, also named Joseph George, was born there October 24, 1785. He served as a soldier during the War of 1812 from August 26, 1814, until January 20, 1815, and was a lifelong resident of Philadelphia, where he was engaged in the mercantile business, handling leather goods and accessories.

Joseph Stern George, the father of Henry Lewis George, was born in the City of Philadelphia, January 21, 1827, and was a natural mechanic, working at one of the skilled trades as a young man and later becoming prominent as a city official of Philadelphia, where he spent his entire life, dying at the age of seventy-seven years. He married Harriet Elizabeth Mulford, who was born of English parents, and she died at the early age of twenty-five years, Henry L. and Harriet being their only children.

Henry Lewis George was reared and educated in Philadelphia and New York, and commenced his active career as a grocer's clerk at the age of fourteen years, when he received a salary of $2 per week. After one year he became employed with a firm engaged in the manufacture of patent medicines, but when about fifteen years of age commenced business with wholesale dealers in hosiery, underwear and gloves, and continued with them for more than five years. At that time Mr. George came to St. Joseph, Missouri, in which city he arrived on the 9th day of September, 1869, and immediately entered the employ of R. L. McDonald & Co., with whom he continued for a period of twenty-seven years. In 1896 he engaged in the business of representing different mills in the sale of their products, and this has continued to be his line of endeavor to the present time. The industry, purpose and ideals of Mr. George have tended to the most substantial in commercial, industrial and business life, as well as to the most elevating in ethical, educational and civic growth. He belongs to the constructive class of men, and to the non-visionary conservatives who hold fast to old truths until the excellence of new ones has been demonstrated. On the other hand, he is progressive and enterprising, keeps in close touch with the progress of the world, and has the courage to grasp opportunities and the ability to make the most of them.

Mr. George was married January 23, 1884, to Miss Maggie Beattie McDonald, who was born in St. Joseph, daughter of Rufus L. and Mary (Wilson) McDonald, and to this union there have come three children: Mary Marjorie, who is the wife of Frazer L. Ford; Rufus Lewis, who died in infancy; and Harriet Louise, who is attending school. Mr. George is a member of Charity Lodge, F. & A. M.; Mitchell Chapter No. 89, R. A. M.; Hugh de Payne Commandery No. 51, K. T.; St. Joseph Council No. 9, R. & S. M.; St. Joseph Lodge of Perfection No. 6; Moila Temple, A. A. O. N. M. S., St. Joseph; St. Joseph Chapter Rose Croix No. 4, A. A. S. R.; Albert Pike Council of Kadosh No. 4, A. A. S. R.; St. Joseph Consistory No. 4, A. A. S. R. He is the oldest past master of his lodge, and is past high priest of Mitchell Chapter. Mr. George is a member of the Commercial Club, of which he was for four years president, is a member of the Sons of the Revolution, the Good Government League, and is also connected with the Benton and Country

Clubs, in all of which he has been chief executive. He is an official member of the First Presbyterian Church, which he has served as deacon and elder for many years.

Mr. George is the owner of the most valuable collection of Indian relics privately owned in the United States, an account of which recently appeared in the Kansas City Star, from which we quote the following: "Because a small basket, purchased ten years ago from an Indian reservation, merely as a souvenir of his Western trip, turned out to be a rare specimen, Harry L. George, of St. Joseph, Missouri, realized that the original Indian types of industry and art were rapidly passing and he began his collection of specimens of the North American tribes' handiwork, which is recognized as one of the most complete private collections in the United States. Mr. George places no price upon it. 'I could only estimate the sum of money I have spent in obtaining my specimens,' he says, 'and that gives no idea of the real value. Many of the pieces were made by tribes now extinct, and of course all of them will increase in value with time. In starting my collection I found that fifty-eight different tongues were spoken among the North American Indians, and my original intention was to get representative baskets from each of these families. But several of these are now extinct and among the fifty-three now in existence some, owing to their geographical location, are not now basketmakers. Thus, in order to get relics from each tribe, I have been forced to add pottery and bead-work to my collection. I have picked up many of my specimens during my travels through the West and Southwest, but most of them I have bought through agents and friends. I have obtained my specimens from every reservation in the United States and Alaska.' St. Joseph has no public museum and Mr. George has had a part of his collection placed in cases in the main public library. One of the central public schools has another portion of it, and the remainder Mr. George has in his home. The collection shows clearly to what almost unlimited uses the basket was put by uncivilized man. It was used for holding water, food and other precious objects in use in everyday life, for gathering articles of commerce and transporting them, for furniture and clothing. The woven receptacles played an important part in the love affairs of the dusky people, in their religion, in their family life, and in the weird ceremonials they produced. Before the coming of the white man, basketry supplied nearly every necessity. The wealth of an Indian family was reckoned by the number and the beauty of the baskets they owned, and the highest virtue of woman was in her ability to make them. It was the most expert woman in basketry who brought the highest price when sold in marriage.

"Among the ceremonial baskets in Mr. George's collection, perhaps the most interesting are his twenty-four tiny witch baskets, the largest of which, feather trimmed and greatly ornamented, measures two and one-half inches in diameter, and the smallest one, woven with a black and white design, is five thirty-seconds of an inch. It is indeed marvelous basketwork when one realizes what short, fat fingers have woven the intricate and smoothly perfect little models. These special baskets were made by the Pomo tribe of Northern California. In the collection are a number of their religious baskets which show the care and painstaking labor which must have been expended upon their construction. There are several specimens used by the Hopi Indians of Northeastern Arizona in their famous dances. There are several ceremonials made by the Hupa Indians of California, of which there are no duplicates and which are therefore very valuable. There is a basket with peach-stones carved and marked for dice. The game was played exclusively by the women. For a dice tray they used a large fine basket tray. Baskets played an important role in the etiquette of the red men. The Choctaw girls, in sending a gift of fruit or flowers, used a heart-shaped or double basket to convey a sentiment of sincerity. Mr. George has love baskets from several tribes and an exquisite specimen of the wedding basket of the Pomos. Specimens of cooking baskets no longer obtainable are found in the collection. They were of course not put over a fire. The food was placed in them and then clean, hot stones were put in. The heat from these stones, combined with constant stirring, cooked the food. These baskets are made of split cedar roots. Among the most fantastic specimens are baskets trimmed with shells, and other hard substances. The feather seems to have been one of the most used basket decorations. The plant materials used vary with the geographical location of the tribes. Dyes used in basket making were made from roots and pigments of the earth. Among the most beautiful and interesting of the carrying baskets are the pappoose baskets. There are nineteen cradles and several miniature cradles which the Indian children used to carry their dolls in. Two Pima carrying baskets, one for a child and one for an adult, are beautiful examples of lace work among the Indians. These burden-bearing baskets consist of a framework of poles, about which a bag or bowl is woven of Yucca palm strings. The sticks are carefully wrapped with hair. These baskets are fastened to the forehead when carried by a beautifully beaded band.

"Mr. George's object in the beginning was the collection of only baskets, but he found so many rare and beautiful Indian specimens of other articles, that his collection of these is as large or larger than that of the baskets. He has specimens of every sort of ornament, implement and dish used by the Alaska Indians. His collection of Indian necklaces, each with a history of its own, some of them known, is almost complete in itself. The claws and bones of animals and birds, beads and bits of abalone pearl and bright feathers, are the materials used in the making of these."

JOHN E. SMITH. The career of John E. Smith in Harrison County covers the period between the era of the log cabin and the undeveloped prairie, and the present day of the most modern improvements and fine fertile farms. Mr. Smith is now engaged in successful agricultural pursuits in White Oak Township, his home being located in section 11, township 63, range 29, Harrison County, and was born in a log cabin in the same community, December 30, 1866, his parents being Edward and Frances R. (Claytor) Smith.

Edward Smith was born in 1826, in the State of Missouri, and acquired a scant education in the country schools. He came to Harrison County prior to the outbreak of the war between the North and the South, but did not serve in that struggle, although he had previously had military experience as a soldier during the Mexican war. Mr. Smith came to Harrison County from one of the counties of this Northwest Missouri section, perhaps Daviess County, where he had been brought up from a child, and where he had entered land which he exchanged with his brother for his first home in section 11, White Oak Township. His final home was in section 2, and he came to be one of the large landholders of his township, was chiefly engaged in stockraising and feeding and was an occasional shipper to market. In politics he was a democrat, but never sought public office. His religious affiliation was with the Methodist Episcopal Church, South, and he took an active part in religious affairs, being an officer in the Shady Grove Church. Edward Smith was united in marriage with Miss Frances R. Claytor, a daughter of Henry Claytor, and she is now seventy-three years of age and lives at New Hampton, Missouri. Mr. Smith died in 1900, the father of the following children: Adaline, who married James Coleman, and died at Saint Joseph, Missouri; Price, who is a farmer of Bethany Township, Harrison County; Sarah, who died single; John E., of this notice; Thomas V., a resident of New Hampton; Martha, also of New Hampton; Samuel A., a farmer of White Oak Township; Mary and May, twins, the latter of whom lives in New Hampton, while the former died unmarried.

Edward Smith was a son of Vincent Smith, who passed away in Harrison County prior to the Civil war. He married Miss Sarah Wright, who died at Blue Ridge, Harrison County, when nearly eighty years of age, and they became the parents of the following children: Vincent, who died in Harrison County and left a family; Thompson, who passed away in Greene County, Missouri, leaving one child; Edward, the father of John E.; John W., a resident of Harrison County; Oregon, who married Andrew Graybill and lives near Hatfield, Missouri; Isabel, who married Alfred Thomas, and died at Blue Ridge; Benjamin, a resident of Greene County; Sarelda, who married Noah Dotson and died in Harrison County; Solomon, who is also deceased; Columbus, who lives at Saint Joseph; Susan, who married Thomas Shackelton, of Excelsior Springs, Missouri; Marcus, of Springfield, Missouri; and George, who died near Springfield, the next to the youngest child.

John E. Smith received his education in the schools adjacent to his childhood home, and as he grew up performed the services of a sort of cowboy in caring for the family herds. When he entered upon his own career he was past his majority and began life as a farmer, and so ably have his affairs been conducted that he is now the owner of 238 acres of fine land in section 11 and 285 acres in section 12, and it is practically all in cultivation. His buildings are modern, commodious and substantial, his machinery of the latest manufacture, and the entire appearance of the farm is a reflection of its owner's enterprise and excellent management. Mr. Smith handles stock quite largely as a feeder and occasional shipper, and is known as a good judge of cattle. He has a number of business interests, these including holdings in the stock of the Bank of New Hampton and of a mail order house in Minneapolis. Politically he is a democrat, but his activities in this line have been confined to voicing his preferences through his vote. With his family he belongs to the Methodist Episcopal Church, South.

Mr. Smith was married April 5, 1904, to Miss Hattie Bender, a daughter of John W. and Margaret (Funk) Bender. Mr. Bender came to Missouri from Indiana, and is of German stock, as was also his wife. Of his twelve children, Mrs. Smith is the fifth in order of birth. Three children have been born to Mr. and Mrs. Smith, namely: Clifton, Frances and Kenneth.

WILLIAM VAN LEAZENBY. A resident of Harrison County since 1880, and now a farmer near Ridgeway, William Van Leazenby came to this part of Northwest Missouri from Pickaway County, Ohio, his native place, he having been born near the town of Mount Sterling, Ohio, in the same house in which his father's birth occurred, July 29, 1857. He is the eldest son of Isaac Leazenby, who married Mary Tanner, a daughter of David Tanner, an agriculturist of Ohio. Isaac Leazenby was a son of Joshua Leazenby, mentioned elsewhere in this work, in the history of the old, well-known and honored family.

Isaac Leazenby was an agriculturist by vocation, and was an exhorter and class leader of the Methodist Church. He was decidedly a man of peace, and did much toward the prevention of trouble or animosity in his neighborhood. An extravagant instance of his endeavor to accommodate a neighbor is shown in his loaning of his own wagon—when he was really using it—to a neighbor and then sending his sons off to borrow one elsewhere that his own work might be completed. He came to Missouri in 1881 and lived near Ridgeway during the rest of his life, dying January 21, 1887. His children were as follows: William Van, of this review; Amanda, who married Jacob Frost and died at Grant City, Missouri; John W., of Ridgeway, who has served as county representative to the Missouri General Assembly twice; Charles C., of near Cainsville, who is accounted one of the leading auctioneers of Harrison County; and George, who is a resident and business man of Idaho.

William Van Leazenby grew up in his native locality and was educated in the district schools, and learned the vocation of his father, that of farming. After his marriage, as long as he remained in Ohio, he lived on the property adjoining his old home, but, in 1880, having friends and relatives in Missouri, he came West as a means of improving his condition and located first near Cainsville, in Harrison County. He had a wife and child and money enough to make a payment on an eighty-acre farm that he purchased in that locality, buying an eighty-acre tract which was partly improved. He remained on this land and farmed it until it became worth double what he had paid for it, and he then disposed of his interest therein and bought 280 acres in Marion Township, section 24, township 65, range 27. This farm was likewise started by settler Reyburn, an Illinois man, but Mr. Leazenby purchased it of the Hall estate. In this locality Mr. Leazenby lived continuously for sixteen years, and when he left it it was a well-ordered place. Mr. Leazenby made deals and changes in land, disposing of some and buying other during the time, and still owns 240 acres there. He also erected barns, built fences and cross-fenced it, and made numerous other intelligent improvements, and left it as one of the handsome and valuable country places of that community.

From the Marion Township farm, Mr. Leazenby came to his father's old home, which he purchased, within a mile of Ridgeway. It contains eighty-one acres and he has restored it to a splendid state of cultivation and substantial improvement. Here he provided a separate home for his mother and cared for her during her last years, she dying March 6, 1912. Here he is continuing his general farming in addition to carrying on the other farm. In a modest way he has been growing Short Horn cattle and his Norman horses have scattered themselves, through his sire, about over a wide territory adjacent to Ridgeway. His exhibits of stock for prizes have occurred at local fairs and stock shows and he also holds annual farm sales to dispose of his surplus stock, which have become quite a yearly event and are largely attended.

Mr. Leazenby is a Methodist. He was converted at the age of twenty years and is a trustee of the Ridgeway Methodist Church, and has ever given his strength to the work of the Sabbath school, which he has led in the capacity of superintendent and class leader. He was born a republican, and while on several occasions he has scratched his ticket it has been in the interest of good men for local offices always. He has been a justice of the peace in both Marion and Grant townships, serving eleven years in that capacity, and entered thus officially into the regulation of public morals. Mr. Leazenby is one of the stockholders of the Harrison

County Fair Association of Ridgeway, and for twenty years has been a Master Mason.

Mr. Leazenby was married in February, 1879, his first wife being Sallie Keys, a daughter of Thomas Keys and Elizabeth (Beatty) Keys. They were farming people of Ohio and early settlers of Pickaway County, that state. Their children were as follows: Mrs. Leazenby; Jane, who died single; Amanda, who married Albert Miller, of Columbus, Ohio; and Ida, who married Mr. Smith and resides near that city. Mrs. Leazenby passed away as a resident of Marion Township, having been the mother of the following children: Lizzie, who became the wife of Ed Girdner, and resides in the vicinity of Cainesville, Missouri; Ethel, who became the wife of William Norwood, and resides at Ridgeway; Minnie, who became the wife of Mack Burgin, is a resident of Marysville, Missouri; Wilda, who became the wife of Herman Wasso, and is also a resident of Ridgeway; and Miss Laura, who is a student of the normal school at Marysville, Missouri.

Mr. Leazenby was married the second time, August 26, 1900, to Miss Mary Harrison, a daughter of Henry and Catharine J. (Milligan) Harrison, who came to the State of Missouri in December, 1871, from their native East Tennessee and were farmers in Harrison County. Two children have been born to Mr. and Mrs. Leazenby, Truman and Ray. The boys are being educated in Ridgeway High School. Mr. Leazenby has educated his daughters liberally, graduating them from the Ridgeway High School and preparing them for effective spheres of usefulness in church and society where they live.

Grove E. Kelso. A newspaper which has had a fine and vitalizing influence in its community is the Hardin News in Ray County. Its editor and proprietor, Grove E. Kelso, is a newspaper man with ten years of successful experience, was for a number of years identified with educational affairs in Chariton County, and is one of the prominent citizens of his section of the state.

A native of Chariton County, Grove E. Kelso was born near Mussellfork, December 8, 1868. His father, Samuel S. Kelso, who is now living retired and one of the venerable citizens of Chariton County, was born in Richland County, Ohio, October 8, 1841. The mother's maiden name was Luella Frayer, who was born in Huron County, Ohio, August 15, 1848, and died January 2, 1907. They were the parents of nine children, and there are seven now living, in widely diverse portions of the country, who are named as follows: Grove E.; Mary, wife of William G. Pfeiffer, of Hugo, Colorado; Olive A., wife of Cornelius DeWese of Huntsville, Missouri; L. E. A. of Madison, Wisconsin; Warner E. of Missouri; Miss Meryl, of Hugo, Colorado; and Isaac E., of Quincy, Illinois.

Samuel S. Kelso, the father, grew up on an Ohio farm, attended the public schools and was educated perhaps more liberally than the average boy of his time. His career was identified with his home locality until the outbreak of the war. His record as a Union soldier was one of exceptional experiences, hardship and length. He assisted in raising a company and enlisted in Battery D of the First Ohio Artillery. During a campaign in Kentucky he was captured, but was soon paroled and returned to his command. Later after the fall of Atlanta he was one of fourteen men who were captured on the morning that Sherman started his march to the sea. Then followed thirteen months of imprisonment and the endurance of almost unspeakable conditions at Libby and Andersonville, and when he was released in August, 1865, he was the only one of the fourteen prisoners captured with him who survived the terrible hardships and exposures of those notorious prisons. When he was released he was naked and too weak to walk. Returning to Ohio, he soon left that state and came west and located in Chariton County, Missouri. Having made some money and unsatisfied with his experience in this state, he then went back to Ohio, was married on December 26, 1867, and brought his bride to Chariton County, where he bought land and engaged in the substantial business of agriculture. Subsequently he was identified with merchandising at Mussellfork, and for several years held the office of postmaster there. He is now living retired and enjoying the fruits of a long and well-spent career.

Grove E. Kelso, the first child of his parents, and born soon after the establishment of the home in Chariton County, grew up in his native locality, attended the country district schools, and early became ambitious for an education and for a larger life than could be found on a farm. At the age of sixteen he left home, and spent one year in attendance at the Stanberry Normal School, and then found work as a teacher and as a farm laborer. With the means thus acquired he paid his way for two years in Central College at Fayette, leaving there in June, 1893. Then followed a period of work on the farm, and beginning with July, 1894, he entered upon a long and successful experience as an educator, being identified with school work for eleven years in Ray County, and much of the time at Hardin with one year in Rayville.

Finally Mr. Kelso's energies were directed from education to journalism, and on January 2, 1904, he bought the Hardin News from Walter L. Bales. Since then he has given all his time to the publication of one of the livest papers of Ray County. Mr. Kelso as a result of his own experience and his broad outlook on life is in a position to afford a fine influence on local opinion through the columns of his paper, and maintains a journal which not only publishes the news but exercises a high standard of civic and public morality. Politically his paper maintains a neutral position, though personally Mr. Kelso is republican. He has an active part in the improvement of commercial and civic conditions in his home town, and is a member of the trade extension committee of the Hardin Commercial Club, a director of the Hardin Building & Loan Company, and besides his newspaper he has the agency for several fire insurance companies and writes a large amount of business in and around Hardin.

Mr. Kelso has fraternal affiliations with the Masonic order, the Independent Order of Odd Fellows and the Modern Woodmen of America, and belongs to the Methodist Episcopal Church South. On August 14, 1901, he married Mrs. Pernie Swinney, a widow, who died August 10, 1904. By her first marriage she had one son, Oliver K. Swinney, who now has his home in Ray County. On August 1, 1907, Mr. Kelso married for his present wife Miss Ida Kellenberger, who was born in Ray County, a daughter of George W. and Bertha (Hileman) Kellenberger. Her parents were both natives of Germany and now live at Hardin. Mr. Kelso and wife have one child, Bertha Luella, who was born November 27, 1909.

WILLIS G. HINE. Senior member of the law firm of Hine, Cross & Wells and vice president of the Wells-Hine Trust Company at Savannah, Willis G. Hine has had a long and successful career, beginning in the restricted sphere of farmer, student, teacher, and for more than twenty years as a lawyer of increasing distinction and business duties and civic responsibilities. Mr. Hine has a secure place in professional and business circles in Andrew County, and has done much for their advancement.

Willis G. Hine was born at Garden Grove, in Decatur County, Iowa, April 8, 1861, a son of Hiram and Evaline (Bradley) Hine. On both

Willis G. Hine

sides Mr. Hine comes of old and distinguished American citizenship. He
holds membership, by right of ancestry, in the Missouri Chapter of the
Sons of the American Revolution, and there were soldiers on both the
paternal and maternal side in that war. His mother was born in Woodford County, Kentucky, May 6, 1840, a daughter of William Bradley,
who in turn was a son of John Bradley, who was born in North Carolina
in 1780, and emigrated with his father to Kentucky about 1784. Kentucky was then a wilderness and the Bradleys were pioneers in the
"dark and bloody ground" and assisted in wresting that fair state from
the dominion of the wilderness and the Indians. The founders of the
Bradley family were John and William, brothers, who emigrated from
England in 1740 and located in Yadkin County, North Carolina. Senator Bradley of Kentucky, one of the most prominent figures in American public life for a number of years, was a cousin of Mr. Hine's maternal
grandfather. Three of Mr. Hine's ancestors served on the American side
during the War of the Revolution—Colonel Webb of Maryland, Ebenezer
Hine of Connecticut, and William Bradley, just mentioned. (Although
William Bradley never enlisted, he was, however, at the battle of King's
Mountain and served with Colonel Sumter.) William T. Bradley, the
maternal grandfather, after his marriage brought his family out of Kentucky to Illinois in 1842, went to Iowa in 1843, when that state was
still a territory, and in the following year entered Government land in
Marion County, lived there until 1853, and then transferred his residence
to Decatur County, Iowa, where he lived until death. Hiram Hine,
father of the Savannah lawyer and banker, was born at Milford, Connecticut, in 1840, and in the same year his parents went to Iowa, where
they were likewise among the pioneers. His death occurred in 1880 at
Garden Grove, and his wife passed away in 1886 at Fillmore, Missouri.
His father was a farmer in early life, and later a merchant and brick
manufacturer. In the family were three sons and three daughters who
reached maturity, and three are now living. Willis G. is the oldest;
Florence is the widow of Franz S. Cole, of Rea, Missouri; and Harry
E. lives in Seattle, Washington.

Willis G. Hine spent the first twenty years of his life in Decatur
County, Iowa, and starting life with the inheritance of good qualities
from his parents, has had to fashion his career largely through his own
efforts. He was graduated from the Garden Grove High School in 1876,
attended the Shenandoah Normal School of Iowa, and was in the State
University for one year until the death of his father called him home.
His first efforts in earning a living were as a teacher, and for two years
he was principal of the schools at Humeston, Iowa, and for five years
was principal of the schools at Fillmore, Missouri. During his residence
at Fillmore Mr. Hine was admitted to the bar in 1887, and in 1888 was
elected county surveyor of Andrew County, the duties of which office
kept him employed about two years. Since 1891 Mr. Hine has been established as one of the lawyers at the county seat of Savannah. In association with William B. Allen he organized the Allen & Hine Land and
Loan Company, which subsequently became the Hine Land & Loan
Company, and this business in 1914 was merged with the State Bank of
Savannah and incorporated as the Wells-Hine Trust Company, of which
Mr. Hine is vice president. As a lawyer he practiced alone until 1908,
except a year or two with Judge James M. Rea, and in that year formed
a partnership with Kipp D. Cross under the name of Hine & Cross, and
on September 1, 1914, Walter B. Wells was admitted, making the firm
style Hine, Cross & Wells. For several years Mr. Hine was vice president
of the First National Bank of Savannah, and though he still retains his
stock, resigned the office on September 1, 1914. For twenty-three years

in addition to his law practice he has been engaged in the land, loan and abstract business.

Mr. Hine has been identified with the republican party since casting his first vote, has served as mayor of Savannah, and was on the school board twelve years. Since his nineteenth year his membership has been with the Methodist Episcopal Church. He is affiliated with the Independent Order of Odd Fellows, enjoys associations with both the Chapter and Consistory branches of Masonry, was past chancellor of the Knights of Pythias during his residence in Iowa, and belongs to the Elks Club in St. Joseph.

On August 15, 1887, Mr. Hine married Mary Gregory, who was born at Fillmore, Missouri, a daughter of Rufus K. and Mary (Crawford) Gregory. Her parents were married in Kentucky about 1847, came to Missouri in 1854, and spent the rest of their lives in this state. Mr. Hine and wife have three children: Raphael G., who was educated in the University of Missouri, now has charge of the insurance department of the Wells-Hine Trust Company; Marjorie E., graduated B. A. from the Northwestern University at Evanston, Illinois, in the class of 1913, receiving the Phi Beta Kappa degree; Ruth is still in the Savannah High School.

WALTER T. LINGLE. At different places in Northwest Missouri the name Lingle has for many years had familiar associations, especially with the grain and milling business. For the past ten years Bethany has been the center of operations, where the late Elmore Lingle located in 1904, after returning from Salt Lake City, and where he leased the Bethany mill and operated it as the Bethany Mill and Elevator Company until his death in 1911, The business has since been conducted by his son, Walter T. Lingle, who is one of the stirring young business men of Bethany.

Elmore Lingle was born in Wauseon, Ohio, in 1842, the son of a farmer who spent his active life there, and was of German stock. Elmore was the third in a family of children, and one of his brothers is O. B. Lingle, long a prominent business man of Cameron, Missouri. Elmore Lingle had a limited education so far as books and schools were concerned, but was a thoroughly competent man of affairs. During the war, when a young man, he entered the volunteer service in an Ohio regiment, was in the Atlanta campaign and then with Sherman on the march to the sea. He served as a private and the only serious injury he sustained was a sunstroke. He was a pensioner in later years, and always an interested participant in Grand Army circles. While a stanch republican, he was never a practical politician. During his residence in Pattonsburg he was active in the Odd Fellows order, and his church was the Congregational. After leaving the army Elmore Lingle came out to Missouri and joined a number of Ohio people in Cameron, where he found employment in a flour mill conducted by Mr. Cline, a veteran miller, whose enterprise has since been continued by his son and grandsons and is now one of the oldest mills under one continuous ownership in that section of the state. Mr. Lingle eventually became associated with the Cline brothers, and many of the older residents remember the flour manufactured by the firm of Cline and Lingle. On leaving Cameron Mr. Lingle located at Concordia, Kansas, where with one of his former associates he bought a mill and continued its operation for seven years. Selling out, he moved further west, to Salt Lake City, and there bought the plant of the Salt Lake Mill and Elevator, which was operated under his ownership five years. During that time he won the medal for the best flour on exhibition at the Utah state fair in 1899. After selling this mill Mr. Lingle returned to Missouri and took up business at Bethany. At Came-

ron Mr. Lingle married Miss Mary C. Cline, who was born in Williamsport, Pennsylvania, in 1850, a daughter of the pioneer miller in Cameron, who was of Pennsylvania German stock.

Walter T. Lingle, the only son and child of his parents, was born at
Cameron, Missouri, June 13, 1877, and learned the milling business under
the eye of his father, and is a thoroughly practical man in all its details.
He attended the public schools of Cameron and made his education count
toward a practical training for business. He was a student in the Missouri Wesleyan College at Cameron, and while there helped to dig out
the trees for the athletic grounds. He also attended the Wesleyan School
at Salina, Kansas. He was with his father in all the changes of business and locations, and became manager of the Bethany mill when his
father died. He is also interested in the grain and feed business, owns
a fourth interest in the Schmid Drug Company of Bethany, and a half
interest in the elevator at Garden Grove, Iowa.

Mr. Lingle was married at Bethany in October, 1904, to Miss Emma
Jennings, a daughter of John and Mary Jennings, who came to Missouri
from Virginia, and spent their last days in Bethany. Besides Mrs.
Lingle the Jennings children were Verne, Oma, Lillie and Jacob. Mrs.
Lingle was born in Harrison County, Missouri, December 16, 1880. To
their marriage have been born two children, Bedonna and Elmore. Mr.
Lingle is a member of Lodge No. 204, Knights of Pythias. His wife is
a member of the Presbyterian Church.

HARVEY NALLY, M. D. A resident of Cainesville for a period of
twenty-eight years, Dr. Harvey Nally has been one of the most important
factors in the development of this thriving community of Northwest
Missouri. While he has won distinguished eminence in the ranks of the
medical profession, his activities have by no means been confined to his
labors therein, for in the fields of finance and business, in the promotion
of education and good citizenship and in the encouragement and support
of movements which have contributed to the city's prestige in various
ways, he has taken a most active and prominent part, and at all times
his name has been synonymous with the maintenance of high principles
and ideals.

Doctor Nally was born in November, 1854, on a farm in Jackson
County, Ohio, a member of a family which originated in England. His
father, William Nally, was born in Westmoreland, Virginia, and when
eleven years of age accompanied his parents to Jackson County, Ohio,
where he engaged in agricultural pursuits. In the fall of 1865 he came
to Missouri and settled temporarily four miles north of Chillicothe, Livingston County, but in 1869 moved to Harrison County and settled seven
miles southeast of Bethany. There he died December 31, 1888, at the
age of eighty-two years. He was a republican in politics, but had no
political aspirations, nor did he have a military record. He married in
Jackson County, Ohio, Miss Patsy Gillespie, who died at the old homestead, and their children were as follows: Mrs. Lucinda Barlow, of
Bethany, Missouri; Mrs. Sarah Gibbons, of Chillicothe, Missouri; Susie,
who is the wife of Edward Poor, of Jackson County, Ohio; W. J., of
Saint Louis; W. S., a resident of Southwest Kansas; Moses, who died in
Harrison County, Missouri, at the age of thirty-one years, leaving a
family; O. H., of Blue Ridge, Harrison County; Dr. Harvey, of this
review; and Frank H., who died in 1914, in Harrison County, leaving a
family.

Harvey Nally was eleven years of age when he accompanied his parents to Missouri, and his education was largely secured in the public
schools here. Having chosen medicine as a profession, at the age of

nineteen years he went to the university and entered the medical department, which was then located at Columbia, and graduated with the class of 1876. On January 1, 1877, he came to Cainesville, applied himself faithfully to his practice, and has continued to do so to the present time. He is a member of the Harrison County Medical Society, the Missouri State Medical Society and the American Medical Association, and is local surgeon of the Burlington Railway, as well as city physician and health officer of Cainesville.

In the business affairs of Cainesville, Doctor Nally has taken a prominent part. He was one of the organizers of the Cainesville Bank, in 1883, and save a year or two has been a director during all these years, having seen the institution grow from a capital of $13,000, to one of $20,000, then to $30,000, and finally, in 1914, to $50,000. Its surplus is $12,000, and its officers are J. H. Burrows, president; G. R. Wilson, vice-president; H. T. Rogers, cashier, and Dr. Harvey Nally and T. O. Wickersham, assistant cashiers, the official board being composed of J. H. Burrows, S. N. Glaze, M. F. Oxford, G. R. Wilson, C. H. Woodward, H. T. Rogers and Harvey Nally. The stockholders are scattered about over Harrison and Mercer counties and a few shares are held in Des Moines, Iowa. When the Cainesville Bank opened its doors for business, Mr. C. B. Woodward was cashier and bookkeeper and did all of the work of the bank for years, filling these positions until his death twenty years later. The first bank occupied an old frame building where the present new edifice stands, the latter being erected in 1897, and now a force of three in the institution is required to do the work, while another bank in Cainesville, with a capital of $25,000, requires the work of two. In 1913 the whole bank inside was refitted and furnished in marble, giving it a metropolitan appearance.

Doctor Nally was identified with the drug business at Cainesville for twenty-five years as a partner of I. B. Woodward. He was also engaged in the dry goods business here as one of the firm of the Shaw-Nally Dry Goods Company, and in addition has been interested in the promotion of enterprises which promised something for the town, but which have since gone out of existence. Among the latter were the Enterprise Manufacturing Company and the handle factory. He was one of the factors in securing the right-of-way for the Narrow-Gauge Railway here, and in company with J. H. Burrows brought the first railroad surveyor to Cainesville to look over the route. As they came down from Iowa the three mapped out in a general way the route of the new road, which was built, but later went into the hands of a receiver and was sold to the Keokuk & Western, which made a standard road of it and finally sold it to the Burlington System.

Doctor Nally is a republican, having been brought up in that political faith. He has served as a school director here for twenty-seven years, and has seen the Cainesville system grow from a little frame building with two teachers to a high school of the first class, this being affiliated with the state educational institutions, while the equipment compares favorably with that of any school in this part of the state. He is a member of the Baptist Church, is a Master Mason, and also holds membership in the Odd Fellows and the Knights of Pythias. His life has been a busy and useful one, his labors have been of the greatest importance, and his activities are by no means over. His tall, erect and energetic figure is a familiar sight on the streets of Cainesville, and his frank and open countenance shows all the characteristics of the man who was born to be a leader.

Doctor Nally was married at Cainesville, November 29, 1881, to Miss Charlotte E. Pickens, daughter of Enos Pickens, an early-day farmer who came from New York State, and Charlotte Ann (Earle) Pickens, of New Jersey. To Doctor and Mrs. Nally there have been born the following children: Dr. Enos Clifton, a graduate of the Cainesville High School and of the Northwestern Dental School, Chicago, who is engaged in practice at Rockford, Illinois; Hortense, the wife of F. D. Lawhead, of Cainesville; Bronna, who married Dr. H. A. Scott, of Cainesville; William H., engaged in farming near this place; and Eugene Field, a high school student at Cainesville.

REV. JOSEPH H. BURROWS. The various and diversified activities which have enlisted the attention and talents of Rev. Joseph H. Burrows, of Cainesville, president of the Cainesville Bank and one of his community's most prominent and progressive men, have extended over a long period of years, and in each of his fields of endeavor he has displayed fidelity to high principles. Coming to Missouri in 1862, and settling in Harrison County, he established himself in business among the few small stores then located in Cainesville, and for forty years was identified as a member of different firms. His business was opened and conducted for many years as J. H. Burrows, and during that same period he was interested in a harness shop and collar factory conducted as Burrows & Truax. Burrows & Webb succeeded J. H. Burrows & Company, which was formed by the admission of J. B. Woodward into the house, and following Burrows & Webb came the firm of Burrows & Shaw. Burrows & Oden and Burrows & Neal did business together after that, and Mr. Burrows retired from the latter firm about 1904. In 1885 he formed a partnership with W. C. McKiddy, as a hardware and implement concern, and Burrows & McKiddy did business for twenty years.

Rev. Mr. Burrows participated in the organization of the Cainesville Bank and has been a director thereof since, the organization being effected in 1883, and for the past three years has been president of this institution. In 1884 the Enterprise Manufacturing Company was formed at Cainesville by the citizens and Rev. Mr. Burrows became president of the concern. The object of the factory was to manufacture cheap furniture, but the expensive building of brick, 40x100 feet, two stories in height, absorbed most of the paid in capital, and the venture entered upon its career cramped for ready money. This feature, added to the fact that no cost price for manufacturing stuff was kept and the goods were being sold unconsciously for a time for less than cost, caused the concern finally to give up the struggle, and the building subsequently went into the hands of the coal company here.

In procuring the railroad connection for Cainesville with the outside world, Rev. Mr. Burrows, associated with Doctor Nally, brought a surveyor over the route selected to demonstrate that it was practical, and they succeeded in raising the $10,000 bonus required, Rev. Mr. Burrows giving his private obligation for nearly twelve miles of right-of-way for the road. The station of Burrows on the road is one of the lasting monuments to him that has come to Rev. Mr. Burrows. This was a narrow-gauge road at first, but it was later standardized and is now a part of the Burlington System and the terminus of the Des Moines branch. Rev. Mr. Burrows moved to his present home, on the farm in Mercer County, in 1865 and has been here since. Here he became a stockman and a feeder, and bought and shipped stock extensively while he was merchandising.

Rev. Mr. Burrows entered politics as a republican and his first campaign for office was for the Twenty-sixth General Assembly for Mercer County, in 1870, serving in that body and being reelected to the Twenty-seventh Session, the first man to ever achieve the honor of reelection from this county. In the Twenty-seventh Assembly he, in connection with Captain Harmon of Nodaway County, wrote the present township organization law twice, introduced it in the house and pushed it through as a law. He also introduced a number of temperance measures, and although none of these bills was acted upon, this was the earliest effort toward temperance legislation in the state. The body was democratic and elected Senator Bogee to the United States Senate, while the republicans supported Gen. John B. Henderson. Rev. Mr. Burrows' next election to the general assembly was in 1878, at which time he was the candidate of the "greenback" party. In 1880 he was nominated as the "greenback" and "union labor" candidate for congress from the old Tenth District, which included the counties of Harrison, Mercer, Daviess, Grundy, Livingston, Linn, Chariton and Randolph. He opposed Col. Charles H. Mansur, the democratic candidate and defeated him by sixty-five votes, and entered the house of the Forty-seventh Congress, being the last man elected from the Tenth District as then composed. In this congress he introduced the bill which reduced letter postage from three to two cents an ounce, and was on the Pension Committee, the department of the interior and the improvement of the Mississippi River. Gen. J. Warren Keifer was speaker of that house. His service in Congress concluded his public labors in politics, although he was renominated to succeed himself in the new congressional district, but the democratic majority of several thousand could not be overcome and he only made a skeleton canvass of the district.

For the past twenty years Rev. Mr. Burrows has voted the prohibition ticket and his campaigning has been purely local. He throws his influence toward the local option fights and has been a factor in winning a dry town at home. Rev. Mr. Burrows made a profession of faith in Christ February 14, 1867, at Cainesville, under the teaching of Elder John Woodward and was induced to take the floor and start preaching the next night. He was ordained three months later and served the Cainesville Baptist Church for more than thirty years. His knowledge of the Bible was only such as he had acquired as a Sunday school pupil, and he therefore became a student at the same time that he assumed responsibilities as a minister. He has been pastor of the churches at Mount Moriah, Eaglesville, Blythedale, Mount Pleasant No. 2, Freedom Church, Pleasant Valley, Zion, Princeton, River View (Iowa), Jamesport, Jameson and Gilman City. He built the church at Freedom and organized and built the church and house at Pleasant Valley. Rev. Mr. Burrows has been clerk of the West for the Baptist Association for twenty-five years and moderator twelve years, and is at present acting in the latter capacity.

Rev. Joseph H. Burrows was born in the City of Manchester, England, May 15, 1840, and came to the United States in 1842 with his parents, his mother passing away en route on a Mississippi River boat and being buried at Wellington's Landing, Louisiana, near New Orleans. The family settled at Keokuk, Iowa, and there made the brick and built the first brick house of that city. The father, who was a brickmaker and

He began his mercantile experience as a clerk at that place at a salary of four dollars a month, but subsequently secured ·employment at sixteen dollars a month, and remained with his employer until his salary had been raised to thirty dollars a month. When he left Keokuk he went to Centerville, Iowa, and clerked for his father-in-law, lived there about two years, and was married in January, 1860. Leaving Iowa, Reverend Burrows went to St. John, Missouri, and opened a store with his brother-in-law, and the firm of Young & Burrows did business two years, following which the stock was moved to Cainesville, where Rev. Mr. Burrows began his permanent career.

Rev. Mr. Burrows first married Miss Louisa A. Whittenmyer, a daughter of William Whittenmyer, and she died in February, 1862, without living issue. On November 16, 1862, he married in Appanoose County, Iowa, Miss Mary A. Shaw, a daughter of Lorenzo Shaw, who was a native of Orleans County, New York. Mr. Shaw married Cornelia Lewis, also of Orleans County, and their children were as follows: Charles, of Carrollton, Missouri; George W., of Cainesville; Albert, who passed away at Cainesville; Ernest, a resident of this place; Martha A., who married Lyman D. Westgate and resides at Wichita, Kansas; and Mrs. Burrows. The children of Rev. and Mrs. Burrows have been as follows: Alva Lewis, who died at the age of fourteen years; Gara M., who is the wife of S. P. Davisson, of Bethany, Missouri; Maggie C., who is the wife of Herbert T. Rogers, of Cainesville; Minnie M., who is the wife of Charles E. Oden, of Cainesville; Bertha G., who married William Lewis, of the firm of Lyster & Lewis, grocers of Cainesville; and William J., who married Cora Oxford and resides at Cainesville.

Rev. Mr. Burrows has been a Mason for almost fifty years. He joined Mercer Lodge at Princeton during the Civil war and belongs to the chapter there, as well as to the commandery at Bethany. He has also had an experience as a newspaper man, having helped to start the old Mercer County Advance, at Princeton, in association with A. O. Binkley; aided in establishing the People's Press, a "greenback" paper at Princeton, and afterward merged into the Princeton Post; acted as editor of the Cainesville News for some six months, and also published The Searchlight, a religious paper issued at Cainesville, monthly, for two years.

Rev. Mr. Burrows' talents as a preacher place him in demand for funerals, and he has preached more of them, far and wide, than any other minister of his section of the state. He also delivers addresses at celebrations, patriotic gatherings, Fourth of July meetings and old soldiers' reunions, and at all of them acquits himself with much credit. Rev. Mr. Burrows is the possessor of a most interesting "den," filled with books, geological specimens of rocks and woods gathered from different regions, stacks of old sermons he preached when young in the ministry, curios of historic interest, and walking sticks associated with the life of General Washington, together with other objects to which attach the greatest interest. This workshop he makes his sanctuary, where he loses himself in communion with the thoughts of men who now rest under passionless mounds.

His father was the late Edgar L. Hubbard, who settled in Harrison County more than sixty years ago. He was born in the state of Connecticut, October 3, 1816, and gained his education in the country schools at Higganum. As a young man he started out as a book salesman, beginning in Alabama and traveled over the country, finally reaching Barton County in southern Missouri in 1846. There he bought horses and drove them through to Connecticut. Soon afterward he returned to Missouri and established himself at old Pattonsburg, where he was a merchant several years. While there he acquired a reputation for staking California goldfield emigrants who were passing through, and finally made the trip across the plains himself. He went the southern route, taking teams, his destination being San Diego, but he finally reached Sacramento and engaged in mining in that district. It is a fact of some significance that of all the men he "grubstaked" for the mining venture, he never heard from more than ten per cent of them, though the common report is that frontiersmen of that time were strictly on the square and lived up to their obligations scrupu-lously. He was absent in the west about two years, returning home by the Panama route. At Panama he laid out his money in Panama hats, shipped them to New Orleans, and there sold at a good profit. From that city he came up the Mississippi, and on reaching Pattonsburg resumed merchandising.

From Pattonsburg he moved to Harrison County in 1853, and conducted one of the pioneer stores in Adams Township. On his farm he opened a stock of goods, and also established a postoffice called Pleasant Ridge, of which he was postmaster as long as it existed. He lived there, improving his government claim, selling merchandise, and erected one of the best farm residences in northwest Missouri. This farm is now the property of his son Edward S.

Edgar L. Hubbard was a man of small means when he moved to Harrison County, and his slow and continued progress brought the prosperity which he finally achieved. He became one of the principal stockmen of the county, and was one of the first in this vicinity to feed and fatten stock for the outside markets. In the beginning he drove his cattle across country to Springfield and Bloomington, Illinois, and later marketed in Chicago, where he became one of the familiar figures among the commission men at "the yards." He not only took his own cattle but bought extensively from his neighbors, and his experience enabled him to profit himself and help his friends get better prices. In 1868 he moved to Bethany and engaged in merchandising as one of the firm of Hubbard & Price. This was a general store, and was continued until 1880, when W. H. Hillman succeeded to it by purchase. The remaining active years of his career Mr. Hubbard devoted to his farming interests. His death at Bethany on July 21, 1910, took away one of the most interesting and useful of the old-time citizens of Harrison County.

During the war he was noted for his strong Union sympathies, but at that time was near fifty years of age, and gave no service except through moral support. His large country home was a sort of rendezvous for the "war widows," and his substantial aid went out to them as he discovered its need. He was not a leader in politics, though a republican, and his only public position was as merchant and postmaster. His store was the central meeting point for the community, and much wisdom was expended there in the discussion of all manner of public questions. The merchant himself was not noted as a talker, though his convictions were well known and positive, and he was never known to essay speechmaking. He was identified with no church, though his leanings were toward the old school of Presbyterians. He was a Mason.

Edgar L. Hubbard was married at old Pattonsburg, Missouri, to Miss Elizabeth Brown, who died April 1, 1903, at the age of seventy-seven. She was a daughter of Major John B. Brown, a pioneer of Daviess County in 1843, and a granddaughter of John Brown. The latter was a revolutionary soldier, enlisting from New Jersey and serving with the Jersey Line. He was wounded at the battle of Cowpens, and afterwards drew a pension. After the war he moved out to Mt. Sterling, Kentucky, and died there. His wife was a Miss Bridges, and among their several children, Major Brown, who bore the name John Bridges, was the only one who lived for any length of time in Missouri. Major Brown was born in 1794 at Mt. Sterling, Kentucky, had little education, and was a soldier in the War of 1812. He was married in that portion of Virginia now West Virginia, and from there came to Missouri. He brought a raft of salt down the Ohio and sold it at St. Louis. In Kentucky he had worked as a blacksmith, but after coming to Missouri was a farmer. During the war he was major of a regiment in the Union army, and saw some active service, and was ever afterwards known as Major Brown. He was interested in public matters, and was a republican, and his death occurred at Coffey, Missouri. His ten children were: Sarah A., wife of Boone Ballard; William, who lives near Springfield, Missouri; Eliza A., who married Elijah Hubbard, of Jameson, Missouri; Austin, who died at Chadron, Nebraska; Elizabeth J., who married Edgar L. Hubbard; Napoleon B., who died at Gallatin, Missouri; James, who died in the state of Nevada; Marion, who died at Coffey, Missouri; Mary, who married H. M. Cuddy and died in Bethany; and Eveline, who married James Ellis, of Liberal, Kansas.

The children of Edgar L. and Elizabeth J. Hubbard were: Wallace, who died in Chicago, leaving a family; Emily, who died in infancy; Henrietta, who died unmarried; Ann, wife of George W. Barry, of Bethany; Charles, who died unmarried in 1881; Edward S.; and Emma, wife of W. S. Walker, of Bethany.

Edward S. Hubbard was born on the old homestead in Adams Township of Harrison County October 23, 1861. His boyhood home was close to town and he attended the Bethany schools, and for three years was a student in the University of Missouri. In a small matter of hazing he and others were detected, and on that account left school before graduating. He then located at Albany and associated with his brother Wallace made a set of abstract books for Gentry County. Failing health took him away from the activities of office and store, and he applied his productive years to farming in Harrison County, until his retirement in March, 1914. Mr. Hubbard owns the homestead, a fine place of seven hundred acres, devoted to stock farming. He has been an extensive feeder as well as a dealer in stock. Outside of the farm his interests have been few. He is a stockholder in the Harrison County and the First National banks of Bethany. Politically he is a republican, and is affiliated with the lodge, Royal Arch chapter and Knight Templar commandery of Masonry at Bethany.

Mr. Hubbard was married in Harrison County in 1903 to Miss Hallie McDaniel. Her grandfather, Horatio McDaniel, was one of the early settlers of Harrison County. Her father, Josephus C. McDaniel, married Anna Matthews, and their children are: Harry, of Nodaway County; Hallie Hubbard; Lawrence, of Elba, Colorado; Hazel, of Akron, Colorado; and Marguerite, of Elba, Colorado. Mr. and Mrs. Hubbard have a son, Edward Leander, born in 1908.

JOHN M. DUNSMORE, M. D. Having early familiarized himself with the rudiments of medicine and surgery, John M. Dunsmore, M. D., of Saint Joseph, is constantly adding to his knowledge by study and earnest application, and sterling merit has gained a position of note among the more skilful and successful physicians of Buchanan County. A son of John McArthur Dunsmore, M. D., he was born in Mitchell, Perth County, Province of Ontario, Canada, coming from Scotch-Irish ancestry.

His great-great-grandfather on the paternal side was born in Scotland, but as a young man settled in Londonderry, Ireland, where he spent his remaining days, and where his son John, the next in line of descent, was a lifelong resident.

John Dunsmore, Jr., the doctor's grandfather, was born and reared in Londonderry, Ireland. Immigrating to America when young, he lived for awhile in Huntington, Province of Quebec, Canada. Subsequently removing to Perth County, Province of Ontario, he purchased a large tract of land, the improvement of which he superintended until his death, at the age of four score years. He married Mary McArthur, who was born in Scotland, a member of the well-known McArthur clan, and of their union eight children were born and reared. .

John McArthur Dunsmore was born at Huntington, Province of Quebec, in 1835. An apt student in his youthful days, with a decided preference for the medical profession, he was given excellent educational advantages, and was graduated from the McGill University, in Montreal. He was subsequently successfully engaged in the practice of medicine in Perth County for a full half century, continuing thus engaged until his death, at the age of seventy-eight years. The maiden name of his wife was Julia Hill. She was born at Mitchell, Perth County, a daughter of James Hill, who was born in Yorkshire, England, and on coming to America settled in Perth County, Province of Ontario, where he continued in business the remainder of his life. Mrs. Hill was born at Stirling Castle, Scotland, and with her parents came to Perth County, Province of Ontario, Canada, when a child. Mrs. Julia (Hill) Dunsmore died when but forty years of age, leaving five daughters and one son.

Brought up in Mitchell, his native city, John M. Dunsmore there attended the public schools and the Collegiate Institute, after which he entered the Medical Department of Trinity University, in Toronto, where he was graduated with the class of 1898, and was admitted as a fellow of the Toronto College of Physicians and Surgeons. In 1901 Dr. Dunsmore located in Saint Joseph, where he has since been actively engaged in the practice of his chosen profession, making a specialty of the treatment of nervous diseases in which he has achieved marked success.

Dr. Dunsmore married, in 1900, Frances Louise Gayfer, who was born in Ingersoll, Province of Ontario, Oxford County, Canada, a daughter of John and Mary (Clarke) Gayfer, both natives of the same county. The doctor and Mrs. Dunsmore have three children, Ruth, Jean, and Frances. The doctor is a member of the Buchanan County Medical Society; of the Missouri State Medical Society; and of the American Medical Association. Both he and his wife are members of Christ Episcopal Church.

HON. RUFUS A. HANKINS. No man in Colfax Township is more substantially and honorably identified with the agricultural growth of his part of De Kalb County than is the Hon. Rufus A. Hankins, ex-associate judge. Opportunity in the conditions of the life of this progressive and enterprising agriculturist has never been allowed to knock more than once at the door, but has been turned to the best possible account both from a personal and community standpoint, and from modest beginnings and without the encouragement of financial assistance, he has come to be the owner of a handsome estate, which, in its tillage and general improvement, compares favorably with any in this part of the township. Judge Hankins was born in Monroe County, East Tennessee, January 19, 1856, and is a son of Edward E. and Julia A. (Stephens) Hankins, the latter the daughter of Absalom Stephens. His parents were born in the same state and county, where they were reared and married. At the outbreak of the war between the North and the South, Edward E. Hankins enlisted in a Tennessee regiment for service in the Confederate army, and served until nearly the close of hostilities, winning a captaincy by brave and faithful services, and finally meeting a soldier's death on the field of battle. In December, 1872, the mother brought her family to De Kalb County, Missouri, and here she passed the remaining years of her life. There were nine children in the family, of whom six still survive: Rufus A., of this review; John A., who is engaged in agricultural pursuits in Colfax Township; Sophronia, who is the wife of N. J. Hunnicutt, of Texas; Martha C., who is the wife of John C. Marr, of Texas; Alice W., who is the wife of Vernon Rumsey, also a resident of the Lone Star state; Cordelia, who is the wife of Thomas H. Sparks, of Osborn, Clinton County, Missouri; Amelia A., who became the wife of Lloyd Grubb, and is now deceased; Edward, who died in De Kalb County, and one other child who died in infancy.

Rufus A. Hankins was sixteen years of age when he accompanied his mother, brothers and sisters to De Kalb County. Here he completed his education which he had commenced in the public schools of his native state, and as a youth took up farming as his life work, remaining at home until he reached the age of twenty-four years. When he started out upon a career of his own, he was just even with the world as to his finances, as his capital consisted of his ambition, his determination to succeed and his inherent ability. At first he became a renter, and carefully saved his earnings so that by 1907 he made his first purchase of eighty acres of land in Colfax Township, on which he now resides, having put in numerous improvements of a modern and handsome character, including his new residence, built in 1910, his commodious and substantial barn, erected in the fall of the same year, and his well-built outbuildings. In addition to general farming, he has successfully handled hogs, cattle and mules, which he buys and feeds and ships to the various markets. As a business man, Judge Hankins is held in the highest esteem by all who have had transactions with him, and throughout this section he bears the reputation of a man of the highest integrity.

In 1880 Judge Hankins was married to Miss Emma A. Squires, of De Kalb County, Missouri, and they have had the following children: Fred, who was given good educational advantages, was a telegraph operator for three years, and is now successfully engaged in farming in Colfax Township; Lee, who is a graduate of the Chillicothe Business College, and now bookkeeper with the packing firm of Swift & Company, at Kansas City, Missouri; Bryan E., who resides at home and is assisting his father in the operations of the homestead; Nova B., who is the wife of William M. Roberts, a farmer and stockman of Colfax Township; Lulu Grace, who is the wife of Andrew R. Seaton, of Grand River Township; and Florence and Bessie, who are unmarried and reside with their parents.

The members of this family are affiliated with the Methodist Episcopal Church, and Judge Hankins is a member of the official board and has been active in church work. Fraternally, he is connected with Osborn Lodge No. 317, Free and Accepted Masons. A democrat in politics, he served capably for one term as associate judge of De Kalb County, has been assessor of his township on several occasions, and at all times has been influential in local affairs.

COL. THOMAS E. DEEM. To become an expert in any line of business, and attain the full measure of success, demands special study, training and experience, all of which Col. Thomas E. Deem, of Cameron, has had in mastering the art, or profession, of auctioneering. A young man, yet in manhood's prime, he has become widely known in many parts of Nebraska, Missouri, Iowa, and Illinois, where he has been identified with large and important stock sales, his genealogical knowledge of pedigreed horses, cattle and hogs being of great value to him as an auctioneer. He was born on a farm in Daviess County, Missouri, and is a birthright auctioneer, his father, Col. D. D. Deem, having been an auctioneer for thirty-two years, and being one of the best known men in that line of business in Northwestern Missouri.

Brought up on the home farm, Thomas E. Deem received excellent educational advantages, and as a youth developed a strong liking for his father's occupation, and at the same time cultivated a clear, strong voice, which can be plainly heard a long distance, and is very effective. In addition to taking lessons from his father in auctioneering, Col. Deem made a special study of the different breeds of cattle, horses and hogs, becoming familiar with all the different pedigrees, and obtaining practical information in regard to stock of all kinds. Thus equipped by study and training, he is considered one of the best judges of stock in the county, while his fair and square dealing as a crier of sales has made him one of the most efficient and popular auctioneers of this section of the country. He has made sales in many states adjoining Missouri, one of the largest having been at Peoria, Illinois. Col. Deem is only twenty-nine years of age, being one of the youngest men in his line of business, and one of the most successful, having already acquired an enviable reputation as a salesman of stock.

Fraternally the colonel is a member of the Ancient Free and Accepted Order of Masons; of the chapter, Royal Arch Masons; of the commandery, Knights Templar; and of Moila Temple, of Saint Joseph. He also belongs to the Knights of Pythias.

ISAAC R. WILLIAMS has been a member of the Savannah bar forty years. Combined with the strict interests of his profession, he has been engaged in business affairs, particularly in real estate, and a common saying among his associates that throws light on his activities is that he has earned more money than any man in Savannah, and yet has less than many whose success has been on a moderate scale. Mr. Williams has always spent liberally, has entered heartily into many projects and plans proposed for business and civic improvements, and enjoys a reputation based on integrity and the best qualities of citizenship.

Isaac R. Williams was born in DeKalb County, Missouri, October 1, 1852, and thus represents a family of old settlers in Northwest Missouri. His parents were Thomas and Callista (Reece) Williams. They were both natives of Yadkin County, North Carolina. The father came to Northwest Missouri in 1845, and for several years was foreman of a hemp farm. The cultivation of hemp was in the early days one of the chief agricultural industries of this section of the state. In 1850 he returned to North Carolina, was married, and brought his bride to DeKalb County, locating near the Andrew County line, where he lived

until his death on May 1, 1906, at the advanced age of eighty-three. His first wife, the mother of Isaac R., died when the latter was an infant. The father spent most of his life in farming, and was also prominently identified with public affairs. He served as a member of the County Court from 1851 until the outbreak of the war, and held the same office after the war, and throughout his career was active in behalf of the democratic party. In religion he was a Universalist.

Isaac R. Williams is the only one living of the four children by his mother, and has two half-brothers. His early life was spent on the home farm, midway between Savannah and Maryville, and his education was acquired partly in the country schools with the freshman year at McGee's College. At the age of twenty-one he entered the law office of David Rea at Savannah, and was admitted to the bar in 1874. Since then he has been in very active general practice of the law, and is now one of the oldest members of the Andrew County bar. On March 1, 1887, he formed a partnership with Charles F. Booher, and for more than a quarter of a century the firm of Booher & Williams has had a recognized standing among the old and successful law firms of Northwest Missouri. Since the election of Mr. Booher to Congress eight years ago, his son, L. W. Booher, has assumed most of his responsibilities and work in the firm, but the title of the partnership remains the same as formerly. For the past twenty-eight years Mr. Williams has been financial correspondent for a number of eastern investors, and much of his time has been taken up with his extensive transactions in real estate and as an abstractor. He is a member of the St. Joseph Commercial Club, and in 1888 was one of the promoters of a street railway in that city. He has been identified with many business interests at Savannah and vicinity, and has always accepted the responsibilities of citizenship. For nearly a quarter of a century Mr. Williams served as mayor of Savannah. He has been a democrat since casting his first vote, and though his party was in a hopeless minority in Andrew County for many years, he accepted a place on the ticket in 1878 as candidate for prosecuting attorney and in 1892 for the Legislature, making the campaigns in order to keep up the party organization. For many years he has been an active member of the Christian Church.

On December 24, 1876, Mr. Williams married Miss Emma Frances, who died May 16, 1913. Their daughter, Lily, is the wife of Dr. C. E. Rainwater, Ph. D., who is identified with the University of Chicago, and both he and his wife hold the degree A. M. from Drake University of Iowa.

GEORGE T. NEFF. With the live stock business on a large scale, meaning thereby the feeding of large herds of beef cattle, hogs and other stock, the ownership of land in quantities that would make a big ranch even in the semi-arid districts of the Southwest, and in dealing and shipping stock by the carloads, perhaps no name in Harrison County is more closely associated than that of Neff. George T. Neff, of Bethany, has been in the business for years, but his father, who lives retired in California, is the real veteran of the industry.

George T. Neff is a native of Harrison County, born in Fox Creek Township, August 2, 1866, and has had his home in Bethany since 1912. His father is Daniel B. Neff, a brother of Isaac Neff, of whom a sketch appears on other pages. Daniel B. Neff was born in Ohio in September, 1842, and came out to Missouri some years before the war. Among his early experiences were his service in the volunteer army during the war. In 1862 he served in the Missouri State Militia in Captain Howe's company, and in 1863 enlisted in Company I of the First Missouri Militia, a cavalry organization. Although he had never learned the trade he was detailed as blacksmith, and worked for two years in that branch of the army. When his company was consolidated with Company M of the First Regiment, he was promoted to first sergeant. Most of his service was in Missouri, he took part in the fight at Marshall, and was in the pursuit of Price's army after its final raid into Missouri. At the close of the war he was mustered out.

His life as a soldier was unmarked with wounds or capture, and on returning to civil pursuits he became a farmer and teacher, though as the latter his career was brief. He married and then established his home in Fox Creek Township, where year after year marked accumulating and increasing interests as a farmer and stockman. His location was in section 12, township 63, range 26, and that was the center of his substantial achievements. For a number of years he excelled in the raising of grain, but more and more turned his attention to feeding and dealing in cattle, and ranked as one of the largest shippers in Harrison County. He provided a market for other people's stock, and it is asserted that for a time about half the live stock, of all kinds, shipped out of Harrison County went through his agency as a buyer and shipper. He never gave any particular attention to pedigreed stock. When he retired it was with a rating as one of the most substantial men of the county, measured in part by his ownership of 3,000 acres of fine land. He left the farm at the age of sixty, and somewhat later held a sale and disposed of one of the biggest bunches of stock ever offered at a public sale in the county. In November, 1912, Daniel B. Neff moved out to San Diego, California, where he has a comfortable and pleasant home for his declining years.

More in business than in politics have all his activities been directed, and though a republican he has never sought nor held office. He is a Methodist, but a member of no fraternal order. In his prime he possessed rather remarkable physical vigor, and even in his retirement his ambition for trading and money-making remains as keen as ever. He carries into age one valuable resource, and that is an interest in books and general affairs, and he has always been a wide reader, and has always retained an unprejudiced and impartial mind. Soon after his return from the army, November 2, 1865, he married in Harrison County Miss Nancy Ellen Wiley, who was born in Indiana December 2, 1844, and died November 4, 1911. She was a daughter of Wilfred Wiley, who lived in Johnson County, Indiana, and she came with her widowed mother in 1860 and located in Fox Creek Township of Harrison County. She was noted as an active Methodist, possessed a splendid voice in singing, and was a woman of strong and useful influence in home, church and community, and it was her efforts which brought her husband into the church. Mr. and Mrs. Daniel B. Neff had the following children: George T.; Landa P., who married Dora Harvey and at his death in Bethany left two children; Minta O., who married Robert Kinkade of Coffey, Missouri; Emma M., who married Albert Springer and died in Harrison County; Joseph S., who married Ella Babymeyer, and who is a farmer on the old homestead; Addie O., the wife of William Kinkade of Sherman Township; Eva L., wife of Frank Miller, near Harrisonville; Essie M., of San Diego, California; and Ona Ree, wife of Ross Tilley.

George T. Neff, the oldest of the children, grew up on his father's large stock farm in Harrison County, and received his education in the Stephens district school. At the same time he was given a thorough drilling in farming and stock raising, and was a pupil and disciple of his father. Leaving home at the age of twenty-one he became an independent farmer in Fox Creek Township, and later in Sherman Township, and in his developing career followed somewhat closely along the lines in which his father was so successful. He has fed stock in large numbers on his land, and shipped in carload lots to the principal markets. Although he still retains large interests as a farmer, Mr. Neff moved his family into Bethany two years ago in order to secure school advantages for his children. At Bethany he now conducts a meat and grocery business. Mr. Neff has taken no special active part in politics, and has never joined a secret order.

He is the head of a happy family. In Harrison County on December 17, 1889, he married Miss Cora B. Nighthart. Her father was Philip Nighthart, who was born in Hesse, Germany, October 10, 1833, and in 1838 the family emigrated to America and settled among the pioneers in Sherman Township of Harrison County. Philip Nighthart went out to California when he was still a boy, following the gold discoveries of the days of 1849, but the most of his active years were spent in farming. He married Elizabeth Smith, who is still living at the Nighthart homestead. Their children were thirteen in number, eleven of whom reached maturity, namely: Mary, wife of William Taggart; Mrs. Neff, who was born July 9, 1869; Ida M., wife of Willard Bolar; Calm G., of Sugar Creek Township in this county; Flora A., who died in Oklahoma as the wife of John Miller; John H., of Cypress Township, Harrison County; Bess M., wife of Oscar Sanders, of Sherman Township; Pearl E., wife of Pearl Puls; Miss Velma; Harrison; and Goldie, wife of Roy Fordyce.

The children of Mr. and Mrs. Neff are: Gladys Ona, a student in the University of Missouri; Kathleen, a senior in the Bethany High School; Daniel Barnett; and Maxine, who died at the age of four years.

JOHN H. CARPENTER. One of the old and honored family names of Harrison County is represented in the courthouse at Bethany by the present county treasurer, John H. Carpenter. Mr. Carpenter has the ability, not in common with most men, of combining politics and business successfully, and was a successful Harrison County farmer before he became generally recognized as a factor in public affairs.

He comes by this ability naturally, since his father, the late Judge Alfred Carpenter, is well remembered by all the older generation as one of the ablest men of his time, while the grandfather, Cephus Carpenter, back in Vermont, was a country lawyer and more especially distinguished for the ability of his sons. Cephus Carpenter died in Vermont, and was the father of Ira, whose son, Senator Matt H. Carpenter. was one of the ablest public leaders from the state of Wisconsin; John H.; Bradford; Alfred; Stephen and Curtis, besides two daughters.

Judge Alfred Carpenter was born in Washington County, Vermont, March 13, 1810, and lived there until 1837. His was a fair education, but much reading and a keen interest in all public questions broadened his intelligence far beyond that of the ordinary man. When he left Vermont and started west, he stopped a time in Galena, Illinois, and then on to Jackson County, Iowa. From Iowa he went west to California following the discovery of gold, encountering the Indians of the plains, later was a victim of the scourge of cholera, and after prospecting in California and being absent from home a year, returned by the Isthmus route. After nearly nineteen years of residence in Iowa, he moved to Missouri in 1856, locating and entering land on Yankee Ridge in Harrison County. His claim was in section 2, township 64, range 27. He broke the land, fenced it and lived there ten years. His next place was in section 28, township 64, range 26, Trail Creek Township, where he lived until his death. He was a successful farmer, owned half a section of land, and in material circumstances as well as in public affairs was one of the most substantial men of the locality. He died March 23, 1880, at the age of seventy.

Judge Carpenter became a proponent of the abolition movement before he left New England, and everyone knew his convictions on the matter. He was a whig and then a strong republican, and a fervid admirer of William Lloyd Garrison and Wendell Phillips, the abolition orators of slavery times, and during the existence of that institution was one of the conductors on "the underground railroad," assisting many fugitive slaves to get beyond the jurisdiction of their masters. His first public service in Harrison County was as justice of the peace, and during the war, though past fifty, he enlisted in the Sixth Missouri State Militia, and remained about thirteen months, until discharged for physical disability "over age." His service was all as a private and confined to the state.

After the war he was chosen one of the county judges, and drew the lot which made him presiding judge, in which capacity he administered the fiscal affairs of the county eight years. It was during his administration that the first county farm was bought and the first county home built. At the same time the municipal townships were established and named. His term as judge began in 1864 and continued until 1872. An important result of his official term was the placing of Harrison County on a sound financial basis, and the influence of that business-like term has continued and is said to be largely responsible for the freedom from indebtedness which the county now enjoys. After retiring from the office, he took little part in politics during the eight remaining years of his life. He assisted in the organization of the republican party in Harrison County, always attended county conventions, and was frequently honored as their chairman.

Judge Carpenter had no special gift as a public speaker, though able to hold his own in any conversation or private debate. He was noted for his independence in both thought and action. There was never a time when he did not have a conviction on questions of importance, and he uttered his sentiments without reservation. His pro-slavery enemies referred to him as the "old abolitionist of Yankee Ridge." In matters of religion he was considered by many an agnostic, though a believer in the immortality of the soul, and later in life he is said to have embraced the doctrines of spiritualism. While not opposed to the principles of secret orders, he never had a membership in one.

Judge Carpenter was married in Jackson County, Iowa, October 5, 1840, to Miss Mary K. Cheney. Her father, Carmel C. Cheney, was a shoemaker in Milford, Massachusetts, but after coming west was a farmer. He was prominent in Masonry, belonging to the chapter and commandery long before such organizations were effected in Harrison County, and had his affiliation with a lodge in Boston, Massachusetts. Mary K. Cheney, who died July 20, 1904, at the age of eighty-one, was born in Milford, Massachusetts, and was reared in a home of education and refinement. She possessed the intellectual and physical vigor of New England, was exceedingly industrious, and always retained her poise in whatever environment. When close to the age of four score, she was subpoenaed as a witness in court, and gave her testimony as composedly as if by her own fireside and in perfect English.

Judge Carpenter and wife were the parents of thirteen children, and those reaching mature life were: Winfield S., who died while in Company G of the Twenty-third Missouri Infantry; Annie U., who married Charles F. Fransham, and died in Harrison County; Carmel C., who was in the same regiment with his brother, and now lives at Moscow,

Idaho; Ruth P., who married Alexander Cochran, and died at Pawnee, Kansas; Martha W., who married Warren N. Stevens, and now lives at Iola, Kansas; John H.; Mary A., deceased, who was the wife of Carl Wilson; Ida E., wife of Thomas Renfro, of Bethany; Alfred, of Fort Scott, Kansas; Esther K., wife of John J. Ellis, and now lives in Idaho; Sarah E., who married Thomas E. Bridge, deceased, and now lives at Chandler, Oklahoma; Eldora, wife of George Wooderson, of Harrison County; and Schuyler C., of Mt. Moriah, Missouri.

Mr. John H. Carpenter was born in Jackson County, Iowa, December 14, 1851, and was about five years old when his father settled in the Yankee Ridge community of Harrison County. His education came from the country schools in Ridgeway and Mt. Moriah localities, and from his majority engaged in farming as his life work. His possessions in material goods were those of a poor man when he married, and near Mt. Moriah he bought forty acres on time, and paid for it by industry and frugality. His present farm, to which he moved in 1890, is located in section 34, township 64, range 26. His election in 1908 caused him to remove to Bethany.

In view of his father's activities in a political way, he grew up in an atmosphere where public questions and politics were in constant discussion, and since casting his first presidential vote for Rutherford B. Hayes he has never missed a general election. For twenty-one years he served his home township, Trail Creek, as clerk and assessor, and was the representative of Harrison County in the convention of assessors held at Jefferson City in 1894. He was in the township office when elected county treasurer in 1908. At that time he won out in the primaries in competition with five opponents, but had the primaries of 1912 all to himself. Mr. Carpenter is a Methodist, and a member of the Knights of Pythias.

July 27, 1879, he married Miss Mary Silby Prater, a daughter of William J. and Margaret E. (Bailey) Prater. Her father came from near Vandalia, Illinois, to Missouri in the fifties, and was a farmer and blacksmith at Mt. Moriah. Mrs. Carpenter was the first of six children by his first wife. Mr. and Mrs. Carpenter have two children, William A. and Edith, who died when four years old.

CHARLES W. LEAZENBY, who belongs to the pioneer settlers of the Mount Moriah community of Northwest Missouri, and whose life has been passed as a farmer and stockman almost within the atmosphere of his bringing-up, is a native of Pickaway County, Ohio, and was born July 22, 1853. His father was William Leazenby, one of the heads of this somewhat numerous pioneer family, and was born March 1, 1827, in the same county and under the environment of a Methodist preacher's home, his father being the Rev. Joshua Leazenby, who moved into Ohio among its pioneers and was born March 18, 1797.

Following back to the original of the Leazenby forefathers, we find Thomas, the father of Rev. Joshua Leazenby, born July 1, 1751, in Dublin, Ireland, of Scotch-Irish blood and an only child, and who seems to have run away from home, according to tradition, at the age of twelve years. Making his way to America, we find from the best records accessible that he located in the Pennsylvania colony and there married Miss Elizabeth Bailey, they rearing a family of four children, among whom were Thomas and Joshua. In later years the old folks moved to Ohio, and their last years were passed in Pickaway County.

Rev. Joshua Leazenby spent his life in the ministry, having much to do with the effective work of the pioneer Methodists of Pickaway County. He was an excellent type of the pioneer preachers of that day, wore his

"plug" hat, carried on his work on horseback, and possessed a greatly
treasured library which contained among other books, Flavius Josephus'
"History of the Jews," the works of Doctor Dick, and Baxter's "Saints'
Rest." Like most pioneer preachers his emoluments were few, and as
a result he left no large material estate, but the universal respect of
his community went out to his memory when he was laid to rest, July
29, 1836. Rev. Joshua Leazenby married Lucinda Toothaker, a member
of a family of rugged, virile, thrifty people, of English stock. Lucinda
Toothaker was born August 1, 1803, and died July 4, 1881. She was
the mother of these children: James, born July 27, 1823, who died in
Miami County, Kansas, leaving a family; William, the father of Charles
W., who died in Harrison County, Missouri, February 23, 1908; Rachel,
who died in infancy; Alexandria, who died in childhood; Wesley, who
spent three years as a soldier in the Union army during the Civil war,
returned to farming and died as one of the successful agriculturists of
Harrison County; and Isaac, born May 9, 1835, who died January 21,
1887, leaving a family of several children.

William Leazenby's wife was Nancy Jane Coffman, who bore her
husband two sons, Charles Wesley, of this review; and William Henry,
whose career is sketched on another page of this work.

Charles W. Leazenby was a child of three years when his parents
made their journey by wagon from Ohio and settled on Yankee Ridge,
near Ridgeway, Missouri, in August, 1856. The family lived in their
covered wagon until their primitive log cabin was built, having the
usual puncheon floor and clapboard door that were to be found on
Northwest Missouri pioneer homes. After a few years, however, the
family moved from this location and located at the Fransham farm,
east of Ridgeway, and there resided about five years. Mr. Leazenby
acquired his education from the country and in the Paola (Kansas)
Normal School, and at the age of eighteen years began his career on his
own account as a teacher. His first school was the "Stoner," now the
"Banner," school, a district which was three by six miles and which
sent to school then the well known Doctor Stoner, Rev. U. G. Leazenby,
the superintendent of the Crawfordsville (Indiana) district of the
Methodist conference, and Anthony Skroh, one of the leading Bohemian
farmers of Madison Township. Mr. Leazenby was paid twenty-five dollars a month for the first term, which pleased him much, and his board
cost him two dollars a week. On Saturdays he usually worked for the
farmer he boarded with and was allowed a dollar for his work, and
when he had finished his school he had saved enough money to buy him
a good mule. He rode this animal to and from his school for two or
three years. Mr. Leazenby's services were such as to be demanded again
by the board at an increase of five dollars a month and he continued to
teach in the country about Mount Moriah and in the schools of that
village, spending his summers as a farmer, and teaching his last school
at Melbourn in 1901.

Mr. Leazenby bought his first farm in 1880, in Madison Township,
and was married that year, and his first home was made where he now
lives. This place was a virgin farm, without evidence of having been
touched by the hand of man, and here Mr. Leazenby erected a small
frame house, 16x24 feet, a story and one-half high, this serving him
until the erection of his more substantial residence some years later.
He engaged in improving, breaking out and raising stock successfully
and some ten years ago became seriously interested in Short Horn cattle
and Poland-China hogs, a stock which he has continued to exploit on
his farm and in his community to the present time. He believes in the
best blood for his stock, and his success with it has been so marked that

his judgment would seem to be correct. Following the death of his parents Mr. Leazenby purchased his brother's interest in the old parental home and owns it now, this farm lying adjacent to his own pioneer home, his parents having moved to it in 1871.

Mr. Leazenby is of republican stock. His father voted that ticket, and he himself cast his first presidential vote for Rutherford B. Hayes and has voted for every republican presidential candidate since, save in 1888 when Grover Cleveland ran the second time, when he voted for him. He was sadly disappointed in the defeat of James G. Blaine and of President Taft. Mr. Leazenby attended the republican state convention at Jefferson City when Chauncey I. Filley was the acknowledged leader of the republican forces in Missouri.

On May 2, 1880, Mr. Leazenby was married to Miss Ella M. Forbes, a daughter of J. H. and Fannie (Griswold) Forbes, who came to Missouri at the close of the Civil war from Elkhart County, Indiana. Mrs. Leazenby was born at Port Huron, Michigan, October 27, 1855, and was the third of seven children: Maurice, now a resident of Arkansas, who at the age of fifteen years answered the call for "100-day men" during the Civil war, in 1861, and, re-enlisting, served for three years in the Union army; Iola, who became the wife of Eli Graves and now lives at Palisades, Nebraska; Ella M., who is the wife of Mr. Leazenby of this review; Louise, who married Bedford Graves, of Eureka, Nebraska; Cora M., who is the widow of Hick Price, of Longmont, Colorado; Franklin, of Harrison County, Missouri; and George W., of Marshalltown, Iowa.

Mr. and Mrs. Leazenby have the following children: Miss Bessie Ruth, born March 6, 1881, graduated at the head of her class at Bethany High School, in 1900, finished a course in the Kirksville Normal with the degree of B. P., in 1904, in 1910 did special work in English in the summer school of the state university, began teaching after she had finished at Bethany, taught in the New London High School, two years in the graded schools of Joplin, one year in Cainesville High School and a year in New Hampton, and at Kirksville and Joplin was active in the work of the Young Women's Christian Association; Homer Wadsworth, born June 16, 1882, took his education from the country schools, has spent his life as a farmer, living adjoining the old homestead, and married Rhoda M. Trotter, their children being Charles Edwin, Mary Fern, Forrest Wayne and Richard Thurman; Miss Amy Jane, born August 28, 1886, graduated from Bethany High School in 1904, spent two summer terms in the state university, taught in the rural schools and in the Mount Moriah graded schools two years, holds a state certificate and finished first in her class at Bethany, and is now (1914 and 1915) taking special work in the university; Miss Gladys Fern, born April 24, 1891, graduated from Bethany High School in 1910, began teaching then in the rural schools, spent a term in the Maryville Normal school, and has also taken a year's work in the University of Missouri.

Mr. Leazenby is a Mason, with a master's degree, and with his family is affiliated with the Methodist Church. He has given an impetus to the good roads movement, and was a deciding force in locating the Coal Valley Trail past his farm, having donated money and labor heavily on this road, far beyond the requirements of the law. He is a man of wide and varied information, entertaining and instructive in his conversa-

made themselves useful in a public way is John Brown Bryant, a son of Joseph F. Bryant, a prominent Northwest Missourian whose career is sketched at length on other pages of this work.

John Brown Bryant was born in Bethany August 20, 1870, and has spent most of his life either in the town or the close vicinity. His education came from the city schools, supplemented by attendance at Woodland College in Independence, Missouri, and a commercial course in the old Stanberry Normal. His practical business career began at the age of twenty in the Cottonwood Valley National Bank at Marion, Kansas, where he remained two years. He returned to Harrison County to take up farming, and it was as a substantial farmer that he was known in this community for fifteen years.

While on the farm, in 1904, he was elected a member of the county court from the south district as successor to Judge Taggart, and was re-elected in 1906. Judge Miller was presiding judge and his associates in the administration of county affairs were Judges Alley and Tucker. During those four years the board busied itself besides the routine affairs with repairing the bridges of the county destroyed or damaged in the notable flood of that time. They also improved the county farm, adding more land and constructing a substantial barn. Mr. Bryant's successor on the county board was Olin Kies. Besides his work as a county official Mr. Bryant also was a member of the Bethany school board a number of years.

Having given up farming in the meantime and moved into Bethany, Mr. Bryant became interested in merchandising as a grocer three years, and then became a partner in the firm of Walker, Bryant & Company until they sold out to Chambers & Davis. Since then his business has been real estate and insurance, and he is also secretary and a director of the Bethany Savings Bank. Since leaving the county board he has taken only a nominal interest in politics, but still classifies as a republican, the political faith in which he was reared. His fraternities are the Masonic, Independent Order of Odd Fellows and the Knights of Pythias.

In Harrison County on December 23, 1891, Mr. Bryant married Miss Carrie E. Howell. Her father was the late Judge John C. Howell, who died while on the circuit bench including Harrison County. Judge Howell was born in Morgan County, Illinois, August 18, 1833, and died at Bethany, September 29, 1882, and had been identified with Northwest Missouri since childhood and for many years was a notable figure in law and politics. He was one of two children, his sister being Mrs. Carrie Carson. His father was a Kentuckian, but settled in Illinois, and on moving to Missouri first lived in Clinton County, but in 1847 went to Gentry County, where Judge Howell grew up. He completed his education at old Bethany College in what is now West Virginia, an institution founded by Alexander Campbell. After entering law, he found himself rapidly promoted in favor and success, and as a democrat was elected to the circuit bench before the formation of the district in which Harrison County is now included. He was a Mason and a member of the Christian Church. Mrs. Bryant is the only child of Judge Howell's marriage to Belle Brown, who was born near Monroe, Wisconsin, and died at Bethany. Mr. and Mrs. Bryant have two children: Marie, who graduated from the Bethany High School in 1913; and Helen, now in one of the grades of the Bethany public schools.

JAMES HENRY MORROWAY, M. D. A resident of Ridgeway since 1900, where he is now in the possession of a large and profitable practice, Dr. Morroway is an excellent type of the modern and successful physician. Through his practice he has contributed a large amount of individual service, has taken a part in the organized activities of the profession and with his thorough knowledge of public affairs and capacity for civic leadership has come into prominence in Northwest Missouri politics.

James Henry Morroway was born in Tama County, Iowa, September 23, 1879. His father is James Morroway, a railway contractor, who for many years has been identified with that line of business. James Morroway was born near New York City, of German-Austrian parentage, the family having come to the United States about sixty years ago and settled in the vicinity of New York. James Morroway found his life work early in his career, began as foreman in construction work, and one of his early employments was as foreman in the construction of the New York postoffice. Coming west, he has since been identified with railroad contracting in Iowa. He still lives in Tama County. In politics he is a republican. James Morroway was married in Tama County to Mary Black, who came from Maryland. Their children are: James H.; John, of Tama County; Frank, of Tama County; Mrs. George Kinney, of Iowa; Mrs. James Lamer of Belleplaine, Iowa; and Mrs. Philip Sevcik of Iowa.

Dr. Morroway grew up in Tama County, finished his high school course in the county seat, and continued his education in a local academy for two years. After a year of medical reading with Dr. H. H. Sievers at Tama, Dr. Morroway entered the Milwaukee Medical College, was there for one year, took a year of laboratory work in Chicago, and finished his course at the Creighton University in Omaha, where he was graduated M. D. in 1900. Dr. Morroway received the first prize in general surgery at Creighton, and in 1904 took postgraduate studies in the same institution.

Dr. Morroway began practice at Ridgeway, and has since been steadily climbing into the first rank of Harrison County physicians and to influence as a citizen. He is a member and has served as secretary and treasurer, vice president and for two years as president of the Harrison County Medical Society. For a number of years he has been city physician of Ridgeway and also sanitary inspector of the town.

In politics Dr. Morroway is a stanch republican, and from that position has never been led astray by the arguments of so-called progressiveism. While he would perhaps claim no distinction as an originator, he has kept himself thoroughly posted on matters of current politics, and besides his capacity for leadership among men has competent views on state and national issues. He has attended various county, congressional and state conventions, and was a member of the famous Excelsior Springs convention of 1912 for the selection of presidential delegates to the National convention. In that campaign his party nominated him for Congress from the Third District, and he was renominated in 1914.

Dr. Morroway is affiliated with the Masonic Order and the Knights of Pythias. In Tama County, Iowa, October 22, 1902, he married Miss Emily, daughter of John and Agnes Kozisek.

LAKE BREWER, M. D. The success and efficiency of women in the field of medicine are too well established to require any comment. While women physicians are not numerous in any one county, they are usually regarded as among the ablest and most successful in the field of local practice, and the few who are identified with the profession in Northwest Missouri are no exception to the rule. At Ridgeway in Harrison County, Dr. Lake Brewer is enjoying a large and growing practice and competes on equal terms with her brothers in the profession. Dr. Brewer represents one of the first families at Ridgeway, and was the first child born in that new town.

Dr. Brewer's ancestors were Ohio people, who lived about Zanesville in Muskingum County. The grandfather was William Brewer, whose widow, Nancy Brewer, is still living at Springfield, Missouri. They had a family of five sons and a daughter. George W. Brewer, father of Dr. Brewer, was born in Muskingum County, Ohio, May 12, 1840, and was educated in the country schools. He came out to Missouri before the Civil war, and lived for a time near Independence. While there he entered Company H of the Thirteenth Missouri Cavalry, and subsequently transferred from the militia to the regular volunteer army. He was a member of Colonel Sigel's regiment, and spent more than four years in the army, spending one year on the plains after the close of the war. He was bugler in his company. After the war George W. Brewer returned to Illinois, finished his education in the University of that state, and was a teacher in the public schools both in Illinois and in Missouri. Mr. Brewer finally returned to Missouri, and located at Ridgeway when the town was founded, and followed merchandising there for a number of years. He was never identified with politics except as a republican voter.

George W. Brewer was married in Champaign County, Illinois, January 22, 1868, to Miss Delia Warner. She was born in Ohio, a daughter of Amasa Warner, also a native of that state. Amasa Warner was a son of Nathan Warner, who saw service as a soldier in the Revolutionary army. Amasa Warner married a Miss Lowery, a daughter of James Lowery, who was likewise a Continental soldier during the Revolution. The Warner family were farming people in Wayne County, Ohio. Mrs. George Brewer was reared in Champaign County, Illinois, was liberally educated, taught school in Vermilion County, and while there frequently saw Joe Cannon, then and afterwards one of the foremost leaders in the republican party. George W. Brewer and wife had one child, Dr. Brewer.

Dr. Lake Brewer was graduated from the Ridgeway public schools in 1899 as valedictorian of her class. The same fall saw her entrance into the University of Missouri, from which she was graduated with her A. B. degree in 1903, and at the same time received a life certificate to teach. She continued her work in the medical department of the university, and during her junior year was assistant in the department of physiology. Dr. Brewer finished her medical course and was given the degree of M. D. in 1908. With this thorough training, Dr. Brewer returned to her native village, and opened an office for practice in the fall of 1908. Her work as a physician has been steadily growing in this community for the past six years and her ability in diagnosis and treatment is beyond question. Dr. Brewer is a member of the County Medical Society and its vice president, and is also a member of the Missouri State Medical Society and American Medical Association. Dr. Brewer recently erected one of the brick business blocks in Ridgeway and has her offices there.

ALBERT OSCAR LAIR. One of the most earnest and enthusiastic promoters of the stock business as a buyer and shipper, and of agricultural pursuits at Ridgeway, Harrison County, is Albert Oscar Lair, who, aside from any prestige he may have received from connection with a fine old family, has mapped out his own fortunes with a certainty of intent and purpose which could have no other result than substantial success. He has lived in the state and county since 1892, when he came here from Illinois, where his birth occurred in Macoupin County, near Carlinville, March 9, 1860.

The Lair family is of German descent and is frequently found in different parts of the country and in various spellings, one of the most popular of which is "Lehr." The grandfather of Albert Oscar Lair was Charles Lair, a Tennessee man by birth, who came to Macoupin County, Illinois, as a pioneer, took up agricultural pursuits, and passed his remaining years in the same vicinity where he is buried. He married Miss Louisa Morris, and their family comprised sixteen children, twelve of whom reared families, namely: John, the father of Albert O.; Elizabeth, who married James McGinnis; Rebecca, who married Richard Nedrow; Jeremiah; Betsy, who became the wife of Mr. Murray; Thomas; Richard; Polly, the eldest daughter, who became the wife of George Bridges; Charles, who fought as a Union soldier during the Civil war; Marion; and James Buchanan. Jeremiah Lair of this family was also a wearer of the Union blue during the war between the forces of the North and South.

John Lair, the father of Albert Oscar Lair, was born in Macoupin County, Illinois, July 3, 1832, passed his life as a farmer, and died in the community of his birth, December 28, 1911. He married Miss Margaret Hart, a daughter of Nathan Hart, who was also a farmer, as well as a teacher and preacher of the Christian Church. He came from Kentucky to Missouri and passed his last years in the latter state. The children born to John and Margaret Lair were as follows: Jane, who became the wife of William Golding, of Portland, Oregon; and Albert Oscar. The mother passed away at Portland, Oregon, at the home of her daughter and son-in-law, in June, 1912. John Lair was a good, industrious and steady-going agriculturist, keeping steadfastly after what he started out to accomplish and winning success through persistence rather than by any brilliant coups. He had the reputation of being a man of strict integrity, and as a citizen was known to be a supporter of good men and progressive measures.

Albert Oscar Lair spent his childhood and youth on a farm and acquired his education from the country district school. His home was under the parental roof until he was past his majority and at the time of his marriage he entered upon a career of his own as a farmer. About this time he moved from Macoupin County, Illinois, to the fertile farming region of Sangamon County, in the same state, and there maintained his home on a tract in the vicinity of Virden, where he continued to carry on operations until he came to Missouri in 1892.

When he reached Missouri, Mr. Lair purchased the Judge Reeves farm of 200 acres, the first farm sold in Harrison County at forty dollars an acre. This was generally thought to be the limit of land prices, and his neighbors declared he would never be able to sell it at that value, although Mr. Lair felt confident that he had not made a bad bargain. This was a well improved tract at that time, and is now one of the most beautiful properties in Grant Township. There he resumed his career as a general farmer and stockman, and entered upon a career in stock feeding. While he was on the farm he entered the business of stock shipping, his first experience in the business, and began it by shipping the stock from his own farm. This experience was of a nature calculated to encourage him in extending his business and he subsequently entered this venture exclusively. In addition he added to his acreage, purchasing 195 acres adjoining his farm, known as the David Allen farm, and 395 acres now constitute his holdings in a body there. For the Allen farm he was forced to pay almost fifty dollars an acre. Mr. Lair left the farm in 1907 and moved to Ridgeway, where he has since continued to buy and ship stock as a business, having taken but two vacation trips during these years, one to Canada and one into our Northwest Pacific Coast country.

Mr. Lair's connection with Ridgeway, aside from his regular industry, has been as a butcher and market man, and as a contributor to the social and material affairs of the place which must, of necessity, have public support. He was reared a democrat and this ticket he has voted for as a man. He has filled the office of township trustee of Grant Township, served his country school district as a director, and in each of his offices has displayed excellent executive ability and an earnest desire to aid his community's interests and those of its people. Like his wife, he is a member of the Methodist Church, and at this time is a member of the official board of the church at Ridgeway.

Mr. Lair was married October 1, 1884, to Miss Mary Jessamine Johnston, a daughter of Henry and Emeline (Adkins) Johnston. Mr. Johnston was a native of Virginia, born May 13, 1815, near Natural Bridge, while Mrs. Johnston was born March 11, 1835. The father's death occurred in Macoupin County, Illinois, in December, 1912, while Mrs. Johnston passed away there in October, 1902. Their children were as follows: Elvira, a resident of Chicago, Illinois, and the wife of Ferd Richards; George, who died in Macoupin County, Illinois, without issue; Nancy, who became the wife of Oliver Lorton and resides at Virden, Illinois; Mary Jessamine, who became Mrs. Lair, and who was born November 5, 1859; Andrew, a resident of Springfield, Illinois; and Sophia, who is the wife of William Fenstermaker, also of Springfield.

To Mr. and Mrs. Lair there have been born the following children: Nathan Earl, who is his father's assistant in cultivating the old homestead farm, married Bessie Carson and has a daughter, Avis; Cyrus Albert, also carrying on farming on the homestead place, married Lela Taylor, and has one son, Forest Leroy; Sophie Emeline, who is the wife of Earl Sanford, of East End, Saskatchewan, Canada, and has one son, Oscar Kenneth; and John Frederick, the youngest, a lad of twelve years, who is attending the Ridgeway public schools.

REV. FIELDING MARVIN, D. D. One of the prominent ministers of the Methodist Church, South, Conference in Northwest Missouri is Rev. Fielding Marvin, now pastor at Savannah. Reverend Marvin is a son of the late Bishop Marvin, who for many years was regarded with peculiar veneration and respect by all members of the Southern Methodist Church and by his faith and works was a tremendous power for good in Missouri and all over the South.

Rev. Fielding Marvin was born at LaGrange, Missouri, November 1, 1849. His parents were Enoch M. and Harriet Brotherton (Clark) Marvin. The late Bishop Marvin was born in Warren County, Missouri, June 12, 1823, and his wife was born in St. Louis County of this state August 13, 1820. The Marvin family was established by two brothers who emigrated from England in 1635 and located in Connecticut. The grandparents on both sides came to Missouri about 1820 when Missouri was admitted to the Union and were prominent early settlers in St. Louis County and Warren County. The grandfather Marvin was a native of Connecticut, and left that state and lived in New York a short time before coming out to Missouri. The late Bishop Marvin was reared in Warren County and when about seventeen years of age began preaching in the Methodist Church and afterwards affiliated with the southern branch of that denomination. He had charge of a church in St. Louis and while there met Miss Clark, who had been reared in that vicinity, and they were married September 23, 1845. Many years of the active

Fielding Marvin
and family.

career of Bishop Marvin were devoted to the ministry. He was an itinerant worker and during the war was a chaplain in the southern army. In 1866 at the general conference at New Orleans he was elected a bishop, and gave his time to the duties of that office in various parts of the South and West until his death at St. Louis, November 26, 1877. His widow survived him and died at Fredericktown, Missouri, March 16, 1882. Rev. Fielding Marvin was the only son, and the four daughters of the parents are now deceased.

Fielding Marvin was educated in the noted Pritchett Institute at Glasgow, Missouri, graduating A. B. in 1870, and afterwards receiving the degree of Master of Arts from the same institution. Mr. Marvin first prepared for the profession of law, studying law in the University of Virginia, and was admitted to the bar at St. Louis about 1875. After a few years' practice at St. Louis he joined the Missouri Conference of the Methodist Church, South, in 1889, and has filled many pulpits and appointments in the Missouri Conference during the past twenty-five years. Reverend Mr. Marvin came to the church at Savannah in the fall of 1913 and has done an effective work in building up his congregation and organizing all departments of church activity. While Rev. Willis Carlisle was pastor here a Bible Class was organized about two years ago, and this has been one of the best features of the church and a power for good in the community. At the present time it has about ninety members, composed of many of the prominent men in the town, and the teacher is Mrs. Sam W. Wells.

Reverend Mr. Marvin is affiliated with the Masonic order. On October 31, 1895, he was married by Rev. Charles H. Briggs at Franklin, Missouri, to Miss Georgia Casey. They are the parents of two sons: Mather Casey and Edwin L.

JAMES WALTER SCOTT. Throughout his life James Walter Scott has been a resident of Gentry County, and for many years has been accounted one of its leading, influential and progressive agriculturists, financiers and business men. Among the great forces that bring success in life, one of the principal is unyielding tenacity of purpose. Action may be created for a time by dash and audacity and superficial cleverness, but these generally achieve no lasting success. Those who achieve the most satisfactory results are they who have gained their position through diligence and thoroughness in all things, and of this class Mr. Scott is an excellent type. He was born on the farm on which he now makes his home, September 22, 1870, and is a son of William Marshall and Catherine M. (Combs) Scott.

The late William Marshall Scott, who passed away near Ford City, Missouri, August 17, 1889, was one of the ante-bellum settlers of Gentry County, coming hither in 1866 from the mountain regions of the far West, whence he had gone in 1859 and spent some seven years in California and Nevada in mining operations. On his return to Missouri, he followed the trade of blacksmith as well as being engaged in agricultural operations, and in both lines was able to achieve success because of his persevering industry. Mr. Scott was born in Belmont County, Ohio, April 26, 1833, a son of Robert Scott, born in Ireland, and Mary (Stansberry) Scott, a native of Frederick County, Maryland. Among the issue of this old couple were: James B., who died near Ford City,

shall Scott came to manhood with a common school education and learned the trade of blacksmith in Belmont County, receiving twenty dollars for his first year's work, forty dollars during the second, and sixty dollars for the work of the third year. In the spring of 1855 he went to Muscatine, Iowa, and in 1856 came to Missouri, stopping at Weston, Platte County, where he worked at his trade. In May of that same year Mr. Scott first visited Gentry County and remained. here three years, and then proceeded to the gold regions of the West, as heretofore stated. In 1866, on his return to Missouri, he located on the farm which his son now owns, and here the remaining years of his life were passed. He confined his blacksmithing largely to his own work after locating near Ford City, and was numbered among the extensive farmers of his time, having 440 acres two miles east of the town.

In his political beliefs William M. Scott was a republican. He was identified with no church, although he was a believer in the benefits of church work, but failed to ally himself with any religious denomination. Mr. Scott was married in Belmont County, Ohio, to Miss Catherine M. Combs, a daughter of Elijah Combs, July 3, 1866. Mr. Combs was a Missouri farmer and came from Ohio, but was originally from Fleming County, Kentucky, where Mrs. Scott was born, as was also her mother, who bore the maiden name of Deborah Muncy. Mrs. Scott died in 1901, having been the mother of the following children: Mary L., a resident of Ford City; James Walter, of this review, and the owner and occupant of the old homestead; Frank L., a resident of Fredonia, Kansas; and Maude, who is the wife of Benjamin Newman, of Whitesville, Missouri.

James Walter Scott has spent his entire career in the Ford City community. Following his course in the public schools of this vicinity, he entered the Stanberry Normal School, and when he laid aside his studies he began farming in earnest. While she lived he managed his mother's place, and since the death of his father he has done a vast amount of substantial improving. His generous home is of twelve rooms, is modernly heated and equipped, and its immaculate white exterior makes it a conspicuous mark for miles around, the residence standing on an eminence. Mr. Scott received his early lessons in cattle raising from his father, and he has been a growing factor as a feeder for years, shipping his own stock and securing excellent prices in the markets. He is also widely known in financial circles of Gentry County, being president of the Ford City Bank, which was organized in 1914, with a capital of $10,000, its vice president being Ben Boley and its cashier Don C. Dougan. In politics, Mr. Scott has always been a republican, and fraternally he is a member of the Knights of Pythias, in which he has filled all the chairs in his lodge. In his community he is held in the highest regard by those who have had occasion to come into contact with him in any way, and as a citizen he has done much to advance the interests of Ford City and Gentry County.

Mr. Scott was married in Gentry County, February 27, 1895, to Miss Ethel E. Easterly, a daughter of Philip and Alpha (Pennington) Easterly. Mr. Easterly came to Missouri from Tennessee, and was the father of the following children: Ida, who is the wife of Lewis Butler of Lewiston, Montana; Maggie, who is the wife of Marion Burke, of the same city; Ethel E., who is the wife of James W. Scott; Grace, who is the wife of S. R. McConkey, of Albany, Missouri; Donna, who is the wife of Alexander Barger, of New Hampton, Missouri; John R., a resident of Gentry County; Hugh, a resident of the State of Idaho; and Philip, Jr., a resident of Lewiston, Montana. Five children have been born to Mr. and Mrs. Scott, namely: Stella K., Blanche E., Mildred, Marshall and Marion.

REV. ALFRED NOAH CAVE. As a minister of the Methodist Church and a farmer the Rev. Mr. Cave has been actively identified with Harrison County since 1858, most of the time in Daviess and Harrison counties. His father located on Sugar Creek in Harrison County in the spring of 1860. Rev. Mr. Cave was a soldier during the war, and comes of a family with a notable military record, beginning back in the days of the Indian wars in the colonies.

Alfred Noah Cave was born in Fairfield County, Ohio, October 25, 1840. His father, Alfred Noah, Sr., was born in Harrison County, Kentucky, April 25, 1814, and when a child his parents took him to Ohio and in 1833 settled in Fairfield County. In that state he grew up, with limited educational advantages, but with a superior intelligence and a gift for influencing people which he early employed in the work of the Methodist ministry. He was ordained by Bishop Waugh at Delphi, Indiana, and was soon in the ranks of the circuit riders who carried the message of Christianity to so many isolated communities in the early days. He rode circuits in Tippecanoe, Clinton, Montgomery and Jasper counties, Indiana, and attended many of the Indiana conferences. His work as a preacher continued almost to the month of his death. He was a man of talent, and gifted beyond the ordinary preacher. His sermons showed exact familiarity with the scriptures, and his knowledge of the old testament was almost as great as of the new. It is said that he could instantly name the verse and chapter of almost any quotation he heard from the Bible.

It was in 1847 that he located with his family in Tippecanoe County, and later in Clinton County, Indiana, and from there some years later set out for Missouri. The journey was made by wagon, the caravan consisting of a horse team and a yoke of cattle, and during a season of hot rainy weather. Central Illinois, through which they passed, was almost as thinly settled as Missouri, and offered good opportunities for settlement, but the family came on to the fringes of civilization in Northwest Missouri. The Mississippi was crossed at Quincy, and the first permanent location was a farm in Daviess County. The senior Cave, though living on a farm, practically devoted all his life to the ministry. He was a factor in the erection of several Methodist churches in Harrison County, particularly that at Bethany, and was pastor there while it was in his circuit. His work was mainly in the rural churches of Daviess, Harrison and Gentry counties.

As a young man Rev. Mr. Cave, Sr., was a whig, but joined the republicans at the organization of the party, gave his vote to Mr. Lincoln in 1860, and regularly supported other nominees until his death. He was rather prominent in public affairs, served as county treasurer of Harrison County from 1868 to 1870, was defeated in the latter year, but in 1872 was the successful candidate and served four years more. During the Civil war he joined the Twenty-third Missouri Regiment at Rolla in the capacity of chaplain, and was with Sherman's army until the fall of Atlanta, when he resigned on account of ill health and returned home.

Alfred N. Cave, Sr., was married in Fairfield County, Ohio, March 1, 1833, to Miss Rebecca Anderson, who died in Clinton County, Indiana, in 1849. Her family has many interesting relations with American history. Her great-grandfather was William Anderson, who was born in the Scotch Highlands in 1693, and because of his connection with the uprising in behalf of the Pretender, Prince James, son of James II, had to flee from Scotland about 1715. He passed through England and emigrated to Virginia, joining other refugees from the wrath of the English sovereign. With remittances from Scotland he was able to purchase lands in Virginia and Maryland, and the records state that in 1738 he owned in Prince George County, Maryland, several plantations on Conegovhiege Manor, one of which, "Anderson's Delights," he later sold to Dr. George Stewart of Annapolis, Maryland. Soon after his arrival in America, William Anderson, discovered far up the Potomac River a beautiful valley, in which he built a hunting lodge, and which has since been known as the Anderson Bottom. When Hampshire County, Virginia, was established, it included this bottom, which was only five miles from Fort Cumberland. William Anderson was a born soldier, had many conflicts with the Indians and was prominent in Virginia military affairs. Soon after the beginning of the French and Indian war, he recruited a company for Braddock's army, and was part of the ill-esteemed colonials who at the disastrous Braddock's Fields in Western Pennsylvania helped in a measure to retrieve the terrible defeat administered by the French and Indians to the trained British regulars. William Anderson died at Anderson Bottom in Hampshire County in 1797, having been a devout member of the Episcopal Church. He was the father of four children, and his daughter Agnes married Capt. William Henshaw.

Capt. Thomas Anderson, a son of the above and the grandfather of Mrs. Cave, was born in Berkeley County, Virginia, in 1733, and also added to the lustre of his family name in military annals. He took part in several Indian campaigns, and was with Governor Dunmore on his expedition into the Ohio Valley for the subjugation of the Indians. When the Revolution came on, he entered enthusiastically into the Colonial service, and was in command of a company at Yorktown when the surrender of General Cornwallis ended the war and made independence a fact. He married a Miss Bruce of Virginia, and all their four children were born at Anderson Bottom. Of their sons, William, Joseph and Abner took up arms against Great Britain in the war of 1812, serving under Colonel Sanderson.

Capt. James Anderson, a son of Captain Thomas and father of Mrs. Cave, was born in Hampshire County, Virginia, February 17, 1768, and although very young served for three months toward the close of the Revolution. After the war he located in Berkeley County, and became a merchant. While there Gen. Anthony Wayne was put in command of the army for the western Indian campaign, after two generals had suffered disastrous defeats at the hands of the red men. Captain Anderson left his business, recruited a troop of horse, and joined Wayne's army, probably at Fort Cumberland, and was made an ensign. He was a great admirer of his strenuous and impetuous commander, and supported him with daring and usefulness. Having some skill in mathematics and drafting, he superintended the construction of most of the forts erected by General Wayne in the old Northwest Territory, now the states of Ohio and Indiana. He continued with the army until the final overthrow of the western Indians, and was present at the treaty of Greenville in August, 1795. At the engagement known as Fallen Timbers his gallantry won him promotion, and he was eventually commissioned a lieutenant and finally a captain. Late in life he joined several of his children in Clinton County, Indiana, and died there October 24, 1844. Capt. James Anderson married Priscilla House, and Rebecca (Anderson) Cave was one of their ten children, five sons and five daughters.

The children born to Rev. A. N. Cave and wife were: James E., who was in an Indiana regiment during the Civil war, and died at Crawfordsville, Indiana; Hiram L., who also was with an Indiana regiment, and died near Darlington, Indiana; Priscilla J., who married Joseph Bounser and died at Cerro Gordo, Illinois; Alfred N., Jr.; and Elizabeth, who died at Chillicothe, Missouri, as Mrs. George Estep. Rev. Mr. Cave, Sr., after the death of his first wife married Elizabeth M. Loveless, daughter of Benjamin Loveless. She died without children at Bethany in April, 1887.

With such an inheritance, it would have been surprising if Alfred N. Cave, Jr., had not made his career one of useful service to his fellow men. Owing to the pioneer environment in which he was reared, he had limited educational advantages, and has depended largely on his own studies and reading and practical experience. His first serious work was when he became a Union soldier. He entered the army in 1861 in Company F of Merrill's Horse, the Second Missouri Cavalry, Captain Hanna being in command of the company. During the first and second years the command was in different parts of Missouri, and in the fall of 1862 went into Arkansas, participating in the engagements at Brownsville and Arkadelphia. Returning to St. Louis, the regiment was sent to Nashville, but arrived too late to take part in Sherman's campaign to the sea. The command did guard duty in Tennessee, and at the close of the war received the surrender of part of Gen. Joe Wheeler's cavalry. Mr. Cave escaped without wounds. He was sergeant of his company, and when mustered out at Chattanooga had in his possession Governor Fletcher's commission as second lieutenant.

In August, 1865, on his return home Mr. Cave began farming in Harrison County, and continued this business in Harrison County until 1878, when he moved out to Kansas and spent two years in Republic County. On returning to Missouri he located in the vicinity of Bethany, and has had his home permanently in this community for over thirty years. Like his father, he has identified himself with church work, and has been known in this part of Missouri as a local preacher and in circuit work for many years. Politically he is a republican, and while politics has never been a hobby with him, he was honored in 1900 with election to the office of county treasurer, and gave four years of capable administration of its affairs. He succeeded James Selby in the office. Since the war he has enjoyed many pleasing associations with old comrades, and about 1882 became a member of the Grand Army, has served as commander of T. D. Neal Post, No. 124, and attended one national Grand Army encampment, that at Chicago.

On January 1, 1866, Mr. Cave married Miss Martha E. Meek, who was born in Wabash County, Indiana, and came to Missouri in 1856. Her father, George W. Meek, married Mary E. Shockey, and they lived for many years on a farm in Sherman township, and both are buried in the Fairview Cemetery in same township. Mr. Meek was also a minister of the United Brethren Church. Their children were: Mrs. Cave, born October 31, 1846; Griffith, who died in Harrison County; Sarah A., who died unmarried; Malinda E., who married John L. Cole, of Bethany; Henry, who lives in Oklahoma; Abram, who died at Enid, Oklahoma, leaving a family; Reverend Paschal, of Blue Ridge, Missouri; Ruey M., wife of William Parnell, of Mountain View, Oklahoma; and Emma J., wife of David Joseph, of Elk City, Oklahoma.

The children of Mr. and Mrs. Cave are: Ollie M., who married William H. Swain, of Bethany, and is the mother of Marie; Rebecca Anna, who married David Bartlett of Harrison County, and is the mother of Alva and Kathryn; Miss Mary, a teacher; Eldora Lillie, wife of James Tippet, of Bethany, and the mother of Paul and Louis; and Etta May, who married Edwin Woodlin, of Kent, Washington, and has one child, Retta.

WILLIAM AVERY MINER. Conspicuously identified with the lumber and banking interests of Harrison County, William Avery Miner has grown into this situation and a condition of independence during a period of thirty years and as a result of his earnest efforts and the sheer weight and force of his characteristics. He has ever belonged to that class of men who accomplish something worth while each day of their lives and this always tells forcibly in the sum total of a finished career. Mr. Miner has been a Missourian since his advent to the state in 1881. He followed his brother, Edgar S. Miner, here, to engage in the lumber business, and did so as a subaltern where salaries were not large or robust. While he had no capital, it was really the opportunity he was most in need of and he began right where the finger board of circumstances pointed out the highway of opportunity. Notwithstanding there was no tangible evidence indicating large results at the end of a long career where he started, yet the student of conditions saw clearly the outcome for one in control of a given territory to be provided with the building material necessary to improve and develop it in accord with the modern method of homemaking. Seeing this situation as the Miner brothers did, and being favored by the presence of a "friend at court" with the capital, in the person of B. M. Frees, of Chicago, Illinois, the application of their abundant industry was easily and readily encouraged to enter a combination for business which has ramifications over much of Northwest Missouri.

Mr. Miner is a contribution to Missouri from the State of Wisconsin, having been born at Brodhead, Green County, May 8, 1861. He was reared at Monroe and educated in the high school there, and grew up in the home of a scholarly and intellectual father, and this fact had its influence in shaping the intellectual training of the son. When the guiding spirit of the home converted its professional atmosphere into a business one, the young man again profited in lessons of trade which capitalized his life, as it were, for an independent career.

The Miners belong to one of the old New England families. Rev. Samuel Elbert Miner, father of William Avery Miner of this review, went into Wisconsin during its pioneer days, well equipped with educational and other qualities which rendered his labors effective among the early builders of that commonwealth. Being a minister, he set about preparing the way for an effective campaign in the spreading of the Gospel, with establishing congregations and building churches, having caused the erection of the First Congregational Church, at Madison, the capital of the state. He was chaplain of the first constitutional convention of the state and his pastoral work was carried on for a period of many years. During his long and effective labors, he had at various times charge of the Congregational churches at Madison, Elkhorn, Wyocena, Brodhead and Monroe, but in his later years he gave up his ministerial work and engaged in the retail lumber business. Reverend Miner was known not only in the affairs of the church and in business in his state, but in politics as well. His Yankee birth and rearing set his heart unalterably opposed to human bondage and when the question of the abolishment of slavery came to be agitated his radicalism placed him with the Abolitionists of his state. During the period of the Civil war he was appointed a member of the Sanitary Commission, and his duties took him into the South where Wisconsin troops were fighting the battles of the Union, and when the Emancipation Proclamation was issued and the war entered upon a campaign to free the slaves he consented for his two sons, not yet of military age, to take their places in the ranks, and one of them lost his young life on the bloody field of Gettysburg.

Rev. Mr. Miner was born at West Halifax, Vermont, in December, 1815, and had a long line of New England ancestors who were factors in the colonial life of Stonington and Groton, Connecticut. His father was Samuel Holman Miner and his mother was Anna Avery, both born while the colonies were struggling for independence. The latter was a daughter of Capt. Thomas Avery, a first lieutenant in the First Connecticut Regiment of Revolutionary troops. Samuel Holman and Anna (Avery) Miner were the parents of nine children, several of whom lived beyond the years of "three score and ten," and one of them passed the century mark of time. Rev. Samuel Elbert Miner married Maria C. Kelley, who died in July, 1861, and their children were as follows: Charles E., who died in the uniform of his country at Gettysburg, as a member of Colonel Custer's famous Seventh Michigan Cavalry, and is buried in the National Cemetery there; Edgar S., of Bethany, Missouri; Mrs. Richardson, of Gilman City, Missouri; Mrs. B. F. Baker, a resident of Clear Lake, Iowa; Mrs. F. W. Stump, of Redfield, South Dakota; and William Avery, of this review.

William Avery Miner began his life in Missouri as a clerk in the Bethany yard of the Miner-Frees Lumber Company. This was the first unit of this concern's system of yards and was established there just ahead of the advent of the railroad to the county seat. When the road passed on to New Hampton, Mr. Miner followed and opened a yard for the company there, remaining until 1885 when the company purchased the yard at Ridgeway and he established himself at the latter point. Although the community had passed its fifth birthday it was still a "wooden town" and had some 260 people and the pioneer of them, S. D. Rardin, is still a factor in the social life of the place.

Upon coming to Ridgeway Mr. Miner embraced the opportunity to share in the profits of the Miner-Frees concern and invested what capital he had accumulated on salary and thus secured a foothold which made the results of his labor more effective to himself. It is due to the persistent efforts of the Miner brothers that the Miner-Frees Company has forged ahead and is supplying the building demand in their line over a large area of this part of the State of Missouri. Their ten yards are located in Harrison, Gentry, Grundy and Daviess counties and each of the brothers has brought up his family in Harrison County and builded substantially and participated forcefully in the towns in which they reside. Besides his commodious house at Ridgeway, William A. Miner has been the builder of two brick structures among the substantial business houses here and his contributions otherwise in the life of the town have been liberal and frequent, including the platting of Miner's Addition, the Fairview Addition and the Sunnyside Addition to the town.

In the field of banking, Mr. Miner has been almost a pioneer in Harrison County. In June following his advent to Ridgeway, Miner Brothers & B. M. Frees started a private bank at Ridgeway known as the Ridgeway Exchange Bank. It was capitalized at $5,000 and William A. Miner was the cashier, with Ellis F. Hopkins, who subsequently became cashier, as bookkeeper. The institution started with a fire and burglar proof safe located in the lumber office, where it remained until 1902 and in that year the brick building which houses its successor was erected. In December, 1902, the Ridgeway Exchange Bank had a paid up capital of $15,000, and a surplus of $3,000, at which time it was converted into the First National Bank of Ridgeway, with a paid up capital of $30,000, and a list of more than thirty stockholders. In June, 1914, the bank increased its capital to $60,000 from earned surplus. When the bank was nationalized, Mr. C. C. Fordyce was chosen its president, and when he retired from that position in March, 1914, William A. Miner became his successor and still retains that office. Mr. Hopkins was succeeded as cashier by H. Ray Tull, and Mr. M. F. Neff has been vice president since its organization, while Mr. J. L. Chambers is assistant cashier and Mr. G. R. Bridges is bookkeeper. Mr. Miner is a stockholder of the Bank of Coffey, Missouri, and of the Bank of Mount Moriah, this state. Fraternally he has taken the York Rite degrees in Masonry, and is a member of Moila Temple, A. A. O. N. M. S., St. Joseph.

Mr. Miner was married in Harrison County, Missouri, in March, 1883, to Miss Martha A. Spencer, who was one of the county teachers of that day. She was born in Harrison County and her father was John Spencer, one of the early settlers of Bethany and one of the officers of a pioneer log church of the town. Mr. Spencer came to Missouri from Muskingum County, Ohio, as a child and grew up around Pattonsburg where his parents had settled. He married Rachel Alley, whose father came to Harrison County in 1844 from Indiana, when this was still a part of Daviess County and when she was a child of nine years. The Spencer children were as follows: Mrs. Sarah E. Young, of Kansas City, Kansas; Mrs. Martha A. Miner; Mrs. Susan A. Tull, of Ridgeway, Missouri; and G. William, a resident of the town of Bethany.

The children of Mr. and Mrs. Miner have been as follows: Charles F., who resides at Ridgeway; Elbert S., who is associated with the Miner-Frees Company, a graduate of the law department of the University of Missouri, class of 1907, married Miss Clella Bunch and has a son, William A., Jr.; and Erwin Avery, who was educated at Missouri Valley College and in the State University, and is an aid in the business of his father.

HON. BENJAMIN MOORE ROSS. Through a long, eventful and active career, Hon. Benjamin Moore Ross, presiding judge of the district court of Gentry County, has been engaged in a variety of pursuits, all connected with the growing mercantile, agricultural and financial interests of this part of Northwest Missouri, where his signal services in public life have made him one of the conspicuous figures of his community. Born December 18, 1859, near Stanberry, Gentry County, Missouri, he is a son of John Adam and Margaret (Bradford) Ross, the former of whom was born in Nova Scotia, June 27, 1830.

John James Ross, the grandfather of Judge Ross, was a deep sea fisherman of Nova Scotia until his removal in 1839 to Ohio, where he worked for wages for one year and then made his way west with his family by boat to St. Louis, thence to St. Joseph, and on inland to Gentry County, Missouri, at that time a territory partly covered with timber. By reason of his Canadian training, Mr. Ross sought timber lands for his locality, as a protection from the winter cold, and thus he was able to raise a crop the first year. He continued to develop and cultivate his farm until the outbreak of the Civil war, when he secured a lieutenant's commission in the Union army, serving under Captain Stockton until receiving his honorable discharge at the close of hostilities, and at that time returning to his rural home, where he resided until 1872. In that year he erected a residence on the property of his son, Samuel C. Ross, and there passed the remaining years of his life.

John Adam Ross was a lad of ten years when he came to Missouri, and his education was secured in an early public school in Albany, Missouri. He was married in 1853 to Margaret Bradford, who died in 1861, at the age of thirty-four years, and they became the parents of these children: Mrs. Savannah J. Floyd, of Oklahoma City, Oklahoma;

John B., of Baldwin, Kansas; Judge Benjamin Moore, of this review; and Mrs. Mary F. Witten, of Washington, D. C. Mr. Ross took for his second wife Martha Howell, who resided near Albany, Missouri, and they became the parents of children as follows: James H., of St. Joseph, Missouri; George A., of Washington, D. C.; William Francis, of St. Joseph; Mrs. Ella Coffey, of Stanberry; Mrs. Myrtle Williams, of Marshall, Missouri; Mrs. Martha R. Garman, of Denver, Colorado; Mrs. Ollie R. Bray, of Denver, Colorado; Mrs. Esther Harlin, of Moberly, Missouri; and Thomas A., of Stanberry.

Benjamin Moore Ross attended the country schools until 1879, in which year he entered Grand River College, which institution he attended five years, taking a complete academic course. This was supplemented by a course in the Stanberry Normal School, and thus excellently equipped, in 1884 he entered upon his career when he purchased the stock and good will of Thomas Peery, of Albany, forming a partnership. This partnership was continued until 1886, when Mr. Ross entered the Farmers and Mechanics Bank, as bookkeeper, and continued to be thus engaged until 1888, when he turned his attention to agricultural pursuits, and moved to his father's farm, there remaining for eleven years. In 1899 Mr. Ross purchased an interest in the live stock commission business of Johnson & Sage, and was actively engaged with this St. Joseph firm until May, 1901, when he returned to Stanberry and began to operate the farm close to this town, land which he had acquired jointly with his father. Here he has carried on extensive general farming operations and has also been a leading breeder of and dealer in live stock, shipping several carloads each year to the markets. Mr. Ross is interested in financial matters as president of the Farmers and Mechanics Bank of Stanberry, one of the substantial institutions of Northwest Missouri, and is known as a banker of good judgment, foresight and acumen. He bears an excellent reputation in commercial circles, and is held in the highest confidence by his business associates. Long a prominent and active democrat, Judge Ross became his party's candidate for the district judgeship in 1908, to which office he was elected, and in 1910 took his present place on the bench as presiding judge. As a jurist he has been conscientious and impartial, greatly adding to the reputation secured by him in business circles. He has always been found at the forefront in movements which have been proposed to benefit the community in any way, and has given freely of his time, influence and means in their support. Fraternally, Judge Ross is connected with the Masonic Order. being a valued member of Stanberry Blue Lodge No. 34.

Judge Ross was married at Albany, Missouri, January 27, 1886, to Miss Callie B. Hunter, daughter of John J. and Margaret (Moke) Hunter, of Paris, Illinois, who came to Gentry County, Missouri, in 1850, and became the owners of a large tract of valuable farming land. Mr. Hunter was well known as a public-spirited and patriotic citizen, and during the Civil war served gallantly as captain of a company of Missouri volunteers in the Union army. The following children comprised the Hunter family: George W., Mrs. Emma Culp, Albert L., Mrs. Annie D. Jones, Mrs. Nettie Wood, Mrs. Lura Storey, Mrs. Ida Gardner and Mrs. Callie D. Ross. To Judge and Mrs. Ross there have been born the following children: John P., a resident of Laramie, Wyoming, who married Grace Martin; Clarence D., who is engaged in a general merchandise business at Cushing, Oklahoma; Margaret B., who married Melvin S. McEldowney, of Oklahoma City, Oklahoma; and Marion, who resides with her parents.

DANIEL W. MARTIN, M. D. Few men are better known and have been more actively identified with affairs at Bethany and in Harrison County during the last forty years than Dr. Daniel W. Martin. Doctor Martin came to Northwest Missouri in 1871, and his home has been in Harrison County since February, 1874. While he is well known as a physician, and particularly as a specialist in the treatment of cancer, he was in early manhood a Union soldier with almost a unique record, later a minister of the gospel, a vocation which he has also followed in Missouri, and an active business man, especially as a dealer in real estate.

Daniel W. Martin was born in Putnam County, Ohio, May 16, 1840, and has some interesting family history behind him. His grandfather, Dan Martin, was a native of Vermont, became a pioneer in Ohio, and died in Putnam County before Doctor Martin was born. He was a boy back in the Green Mountain State when the war for independence began, and saw some active service in that struggle as an American soldier. He married Elizabeth Tougee, and among their ten sons and three daughters the following are given brief mention: Obediah, who spent his life in Ohio; Uriah, whose life was passed in the same state; Thomas, who lived in east central Ohio; Robert, whose home was near Columbus; William, of Hancock County, Ohio; Dan, who became an early settler in Missouri and died in Sullivan County; Calvin, who died in Allen County, Ohio; Maurice, who lived in Ohio; Lucretia Conklin; Mrs. Sprague; Mrs. Vaughn; and Jared A.

Jared A. Martin, father of Doctor Martin, was never graduated from a school of medicine, but for many years was called Doctor Martin, was of a family of doctors and preachers, and perhaps the associations and traditions of the family had something to do with his discovering, late in life, a special method of treating cancer, a discovery that is now utilized by his son at Bethany. The father spent some ten years at Saybrook, Illinois, as a specialist in treating cancer. He was born in 1820 on the same farm in Ohio on which his son Daniel W. first saw the light. His early career was without special incident, was spent as a farmer, and after the war he moved to Saybrook, Illinois, and farmed until taking up the special work in the field opened for him by his discovery. Politically he was first a whig and then a republican, and voted the first republican ticket placed in the field in 1856. He was a strong friend of Horace Greeley before and during the war. He was a layman in the Christian Church. His death occurred at Saybrook, near the close of 1894. He married Electa Scoville, whose father was a native of Vermont and died in Shelbyville, Illinois. She died in February, 1851, and her children were: Daniel W.; Mrs. Lucy Chamberlain of Cincinnati; Martha, who died unmarried; Mary, who became the wife of Newton Nungesster and died at Cridersville, Ohio; Gilbert, who died in Southern Missouri; Clark R., of Saybrook, Illinois; Mrs. Nancy Bains, who lives near Bloomington, Illinois; Jared, of Chicago; and Amanda, who married and died in Iowa.

Dr. Daniel W. Martin grew up on an Ohio farm, and got most of his education from the common schools, and really prepared for his career after he had come home from the army. After reaching his majority he attended the seminary at St. Marys, Ohio, and pursued his medical studies in the Eclectic Institute of Cincinnati and the American Medical College of St. Louis, where he finished his course in 1877.

In 1862 he volunteered for service in the Union army. He was in Company A of the Fifty-seventh Ohio Infantry, under Capt. William McClure and Col. Clark Rice, the regiment being in the Second Brigade, Second Division of the Fourth Army Corps. Most of his service was detached duty until May, 1864, when he was appointed chaplain of the regiment. On July 22 of the same year, during the siege of Atlanta, he was taken prisoner and sent to the infamous Andersonville stockade. After being kept there a few months, he was sent to the prison at Florence, South Carolina, and toward the end of the war was moved to Goldsboro, and when Sherman's army came through that region he was moved about until the prisoners were turned into the union lines at Wilmington, North Carolina. While in the rebel prisons, Doctor Martin was exposed to outrageous treatment, from physical abuse by the notorious Wurz, to actual starvation, scurvy and gangrene. When he finally was released he weighed only ninety pounds, though his weight at enlistment was 170. After he had been in Andersonville he was put in line for exchange. While standing there it occurred to him as improper for him to accept liberty when about seven thousand of his comrades were lying about on the ground in the stockade scarcely able to get themselves a drink of water. With this prompting of sympathy, he stepped from the line and made a speech, reviewing the situation briefly, and asking for volunteers to stay with him in the stockade and accept the fortunes of the rest. One of his old schoolmates stepped to the front. This is perhaps the only case on record when prisoners, with the opportunity at hand to gain freedom, chose the harder lot to remain prisoners of war. They both remained until they and all their comrades were liberated, and his companion, Ernest Timbers, lived till a few years ago and died in Minnesota. After his release Doctor Martin was sent to Columbus, Ohio, where he was auditor in the paymaster's office until the business of the department was wound up, when he was discharged at Camp Chase and returned home.

After the war and before entering medical school at Cincinnati he read medicine for two years in the office of Doctor Prince at Freiburg, Ohio. His first two years of active practice were spent in Monroeville, Indiana, and then for three years at Monterey, Ohio. On coming to Missouri in 1871 Doctor Martin had an office at Jameson in Daviess County until moving to Harrison County. For the past forty years he has practiced either in Bethany or with headquarters on his farm near the county seat. About twenty years ago he took up the special work of cancer treatment, as taught him by his father, and this and his office practice comprise his professional activity.

Doctor Martin has taken no action in politics except as a voter of the republican ticket. For about thirty years he preached as a pastor of the Christian Church in Missouri, and practiced medicine at the same time. He began church work in Ohio soon after the war, and has thus combined the two most important vocations of human service—the care of both the soul and the body. Also for five years he owned a store at Blue Ridge in Harrison County, and previously a year in Bethany. For a quarter of a century he has been in the real estate business, buying and selling farms. During this period he bought extensively in Logan County, Kansas, and made a large profit out of those transactions. Near Bethany he owns several farms, aggregating a section, and all well improved. Dr. Martin began buying land with nothing but his credit, and the results have shown his judgment to have been little short of unerring.

In December, 1860, Doctor Martin married Lucinda Harris. She became the mother of: Mrs. Josephine Wooley, of Kansas City; Charles, of Oklahoma; Mrs. Flora Ford, of Bethany; Hattie, wife of John Looman of Kansas; James, who died in Wichita, Kansas; and Mrs. Fannie Conwell, of Bethany. Doctor Martin married for his second wife Mrs. Ruth F. (Hammons) Miller, born at Hillsboro, Illinois, daughter of John Hammons, Sr., deceased. They have a daughter, Neima, wife of William Johnson, of New Hampton, Missouri.

JAMES A. SCAMMAHORN. A resident of Canden Township in DeKalb County, the enterprise of James A. Scammahorn as an agriculturist has given him a high business standing in that community, and through many years of honest and persevering activity as a farmer and stock raiser he has acquired that material success which is the ambition of every right-minded man. At the same time he is known for his sterling citizenship and is a man of integrity in all his relations. Mr. Scammahorn has been a lifelong resident of this section of Northwest Missouri, and has advanced himself from modest circumstances to a position of prominence among DeKalb county farmers, and at the present time is successfully engaged in the cultivation of 280 acres of productive land.

James A. Scammahorn was born in DeKalb County, June 15, 1860, a son of Peter N. and Mary A. (Bacon) Scammahorn. Peter N. Scammahorn was born in Kentucky, and in 1850 he came to Missouri and joined the agricultural community and a tiller of the soil until his death December 16, 1913. He was a charter member of the Odd Fellows Lodge at Winston in Daviess County, and took an active part in public affairs at Maysville, of which town he was marshal for several years. His life was one of activity and industry, and he was held in high esteem with those who knew him because of his integrity, and honorable business record. In 1851 he married Mary A. Bacon. She was a native of Kentucky and came to Missouri in girlhood; she died May 12, 1880. She was the mother of nine children, of whom five survive, namely: Elizabeth J., widow of Ben England and living in Breckenridge, Missouri; Liefa D., widow of John Kendrick, of Kansas City; Mary B., wife of Thomas Phelan, of St. Louis; Seth L. Scammahorn, yardmaster for Southern Pacific Railroad at San Antonio, Texas, and James A.

James A. Scammahorn was reared in DeKalb County and spent his entire life in one locality. The district school of Hickory Grove furnished him with his education during the winter terms of his boyhood, while his summer months were devoted to acquiring the fundamental principles of farming. On February 1, 1880, he married Mary J. Thompson, daughter of Bradford and Mary A. (Redman) Thompson. Mr. Bradford Thompson was born in Tennessee and came to Missouri when he was a small boy. He was a tiller of the soil until he died in 1889. His wife, Mary A. Redman, was born in Kentucky and came to Missouri in girlhood. She died in 1907. She was the mother of nine children, of whom seven survive, namely: Emeline, widow of Robert Bird; Cindia, widow of Thomas Reed; Sam Thompson, of Oklahoma; Dave Thompson, of Oklahoma; William Thompson; America, wife of Oliver Ollson, and Mary.

Mrs. Scammahorn was born in Adams Township, November 5, 1860, and was educated in what was known as the old Cope School. She had known her husband from childhood. After their marriage they moved to Daviess County, where Mr. Scammahorn bought forty acres of land in the bottom of Grand River, which overflowed continuously for four years. This left him in such bad circumstances that he moved to Caldwell County, living there one year. He then moved to DeKalb County and has since been a permanent resident. For several years he and his wife lived in a small one-room house, the frame of which had been hewed out and used as a barn, but by continuing industry and earnest it has eventually placed them in a position where they could afford a more commodious home, and from that time to the present Mr. Scammahorn has forged rapidly to the front, his position among his community's substantial men now being assured. For a number of years he was engaged in general farming almost exclusively, but in 1902 started to raise Brown Swiss cattle, registered for dairy purposes, and continued to devote a large part of his attention to this enterprise until selling them in 1910. Since that time his operations in stock have been of a general nature. Mr. Scammahorn's association with the township has been for its betterment and a lesson in industry and patient application during the years of his adversity should be far reaching in their influence for good.

Mr. and Mrs. Scammahorn have had six children, of whom four survive: Peter B., who was a student in the Quincy Business College, lost his wife, and has a child seventeen months old; Cora A. is the wife of Burton J. Ryan; Iona J. is the wife of Arthur Ryan; and Myrtle M., unmarried and living at home. For several years Mr. Scammahorn was a member of the Maysville Lodge of the Independent Order of Odd Fellows.

A. M. BATES. In the business and civic activities of Excelsior Springs during the past twenty years A. M. Bates has performed a more than ordinary successful and influential part. Mr. Bates came to the city a young man without capital, embarked in merchandising, laid the foundation for a business career, and is now one of the leading real estate men of Northwest Missouri. His administration as mayor of Excelsior Springs is remembered gratefully by the citizens, and as executive of the city he inaugurated many improvements which have helped to increase the fair fame of Excelsior Springs.

Mr. Bates represents one of the old families in Clay County. The family has lived here through three generations, the first having come as pioneers, the second having carried on the development through the later decades of the last century, and Mr. Bates himself represents the third, and his position in the community adds to the reputation for progressiveness and enterprise which have long characterized the name.

A. M. Bates was born in Washington Township of Clay County, June 12, 1876. He was a son of Charles F. Bates, who was born in Ray County, Missouri, October 30, 1845, and is now living on his homestead two and a half miles north of Excelsior Springs. Charles F. Bates was a son of William and Serilda (Nowland) Bates, the former of Virginia and the latter of Tennessee, who came as early settlers into Ray County, where the former died in 1884 at the age of sixty-five, while the grandmother is now living at Excelsior Springs at the advanced age of ninety years. Charles F. Bates married Elizabeth Miller. She was born in Ray County, three miles northeast of Excelsior Springs, March 24, 1849, and is still living. Her parents were William Andrew and Sallie (McKee) Miller, the former of North Carolina and the latter of Kentucky. They came to Ray County about the same time as the Bates family. Charles F. Bates and wife were the parents of ten children, all of whom are living as follows: Robert L., of Excelsior Springs; A. M. and Ava E., twins, the latter the wife of Freeman Furman, of Excelsior Springs; L. E., of Excelsior Springs; Lucy, at home; Sallie Shoemaker, a widow living at Excelsior Springs; William, of Excelsior Springs; Ella, at home; and Frank, of Oklahoma. Charles F. Bates grew up in Ray County, was married there, and then moved to a farm five miles north of Excelsior Springs, and in 1873 came to his present location, which is the old Miller homestead. That home has been occupied by the family for more than forty years, and was originally entered directly from the Government by the great-grandfather of A. M. Bates, Frederick Miller, who died on the farm in May, 1872, at the age of seventy-eight.

A. M. Bates grew up on a farm, received his early education in the country schools, and lived at home until twenty-one. With money supplied him by his grandfather Bates, he then came to Excelsior Springs and made his first business venture in the purchase of a meat market, which he conducted for some time, and thus paved the way for a larger career. He and his brother R. L. Bates then bought a grocery store, and conducted a successful partnership for six years, at the end of which time the brother acquired the entire stock. Since 1900 Mr. Bates has been successfully engaged in the real estate business. He has platted and sold three additions to Excelsior Springs, and also owns a large amount of farm land in both Kansas and Oklahoma, and operates a large stock feeding farm in Oklahoma. Mr. Bates was one of the organizers of the First National Bank of Excelsior Springs, served as its first president, and is still a member of its board of directors.

In 1898 Mr. Bates was first elected to the office of mayor of Excelsior Springs, served for two years, and after that term was in the office as alderman for four years. In 1912 Mr. Bates was again the choice of the citizens for the office of mayor, and has led the city government and cooperating associations of citizens in the movement for the making of Excelsior Springs a greater and better city. His service as mayor was concluded in the spring of 1914. Mr. Bates is affiliated with the Masonic Order, the Independent Order of Odd Fellows, the Modern Woodmen of America, the Knights of Pythias and the Benevolent and Protective Order of Elks. In politics he has always allied himself with the democratic party.

On January 16, 1895, he married Sarabe McGlathlin, who was born at Brookfield, Missouri, in 1871, a daughter of John and Irene (Crisfield) McGlathlin, who came to Excelsior Springs in 1881, where her father was in the monument business and later real estate dealer. He died July 8, 1914, at the age of seventy-eight, while her mother passed away in 1906. To the marriage of Mr. Bates and wife have been born four children: Grace, Eugene, Harry and Donald.

JOSEPH REA. No publication purporting to touch consistently the history of Andrew County could justify its functions were there failure to pay a tribute of honor to the late Judge Joseph Rea, farmer, banker, lawyer and probate judge, for he left a deep and benignant impress upon the annals of this county, which represented his home from his boyhood days until his death, which occurred on the 28th of February, 1914. The judge was a scion of one of the most honored and influential pioneer families of Northwest Missouri, and in his sturdy physical and mental makeup he represented the best of the fine Scotch and Welsh strains of ancestry.

Judge Rea claimed the old Hoosier State as the place of his nativity, but was a lad of six years at the time of his parents' immigration to Missouri. He was born in Ripley County, Indiana, on the 13th of November, 1837, the second in order of nativity of the two sons and eight daughters of Jonathan and Lurana (Breden) Rea, the former of whom was born in North Carolina on the 26th of October, 1805, and the latter of whom was born in Kentucky, on the 7th of August, 1813, their marriage having been solemnized in Indiana. Of the ten children, all attained to years of maturity and reared children of their own, with the exception of one daughter, who died in infancy. The first to die of those who thus reached mature age was not summoned to the life eternal until thirty-seven years after the death of the parents, each of whom was forty-seven years at the time of death and both having expired from attacks of

Joseph Rea

pneumonia. That the second generation gave prolific progeny to the family line is evidenced by the statement that Judge Rea had nieces and nephews to the number of sixty-four. Jonathan Rea was one of the sterling pioneers of Andrew County, Missouri, where he developed a farm from the primitive wilds and where both he and his wife continued to reside on their homestead until the close of their lives.

Judge Joseph Rea was reared to the sturdy discipline of the home farm and while assisting in its work and management during the years of his youth he attended the district schools during the winter terms and thus laid the foundation for the substantial superstructure of knowledge which made him in his mature years a man of strong intellectuality and distinctive judgment. After the death of his father, in February, 1854, he continued to remain on the old homestead with his mother and sisters until the devoted mother likewise passed away, in February, 1861, the family having become scattered after that time. Thereafter Judge Rea remained on the old home farm with William Pettyjohn, who had rented the property, and while actively concerned with the work and management of the place, he devoted as much time as possible to the study of law, the reading of which he had previously prosecuted under the able preceptorship of Judge William Heren, of Savannah, judicial center of the county, this ambitious work having been prosecuted when he was also attending the school conducted by Prof. George W. Turner.

At the inception of the Civil war Judge Rea took a decided stand for the Union and became a member of the state militia, and after his marriage, in 1862, he soon subordinated his personal interests to enlist in the Fifty-first Missouri Volunteer Infantry, in which he rose from the position of private to the office of first lieutenant of Company B. He also served as assistant quartermaster and for a period of about two months was in charge of the Gratiot Street military prison, in the City of St. Louis. He continued in service until the close of the war, and thereafter he continued to be identified with agricultural pursuits and stock-growing in Andrew County during the remainder of his active career, besides which he was engaged in the practice of law for a long period of years and gained prestige as one of the well fortified members of the bar of this part of the state. For twenty-four years he was the popular candidate presented by the democratic party for the office of probate judge, for which he was nominated for six consecutive times and to which he was elected three times. In each instance of election he had anticipated defeat, and the anomalous condition was that at the time of each defeat he had anticipated victory. He served, and with characteristic loyalty and ability, three terms as judge of the Probate Court. Judge Rea was a man of forceful personality, inflexible integrity in all of the relations of life, and generous and considerate in his intercourse with his fellowmen, his strong mind and resolute purpose making him well equipped for leadership in public thought and action and his very nobility of character gaining and retaining to him the confidence and high regard of all with whom he came in contact. He was a man of dignified presence, more than six feet in height and weighing about two hundred and twenty-five pounds in the prime of his life. Sincere with himself and others, he demanded a reason for the faith that was to be adopted by him, and though he ordered his life on the highest plane of integrity and honor he did not become formally a member of any religious organization until about fifteen years prior to his demise, when he united with the Christian Church, of which he ever afterward continued a zealous and earnest member, his widow being one of the venerable and revered pioneer women of the City of Savannah. Judge Rea was a brother of Hon.

David Rea, who was elected a member of Congress from the then Ninth District of Missouri in 1872, as candidate on the democratic ticket, and who was twice re-elected. Hon. David Rea entered the Union army at the beginning of the Civil war and rose to the rank of lieutenant-colonel of a Missouri regiment.

In October, 1862, was solemnized the marriage of Judge Rea to Miss Sarah A. Muse, who was born in Fleming County, Kentucky, on the 27th of July, 1844, and who was five years of age at the time when her parents, the late Henry and Mahala Muse, came to Missouri and established their permanent home in Andrew County, within whose borders she has continued to reside to the present time. Judge and Mrs. Rea became the parents of nine children, of whom the eldest is Judge James M., who is now serving as judge of the Probate Court of Andrew County, a position in which he is admirably upholding the high prestige of the name which he bears, individual mention of him being made on other pages of this work; Jonathan H. remains with his widowed mother in Savannah; Thomas B., who resides at South Omaha, is United States livestock inspector of Nebraska; Claude is a resident of Edmonton, British Columbia, where he is identified with the wholesale grocery business; Ida is the wife of Henry S. Rector, a successful farmer near Tonganoxie, Leavenworth County, Kansas; Earl is a farmer and representative citizen of Saline County, Missouri, his homestead farm being situated two miles north of Marshall; Ellen, under the administration of her eldest brother, is the efficient and popular clerk of the Probate Court of Andrew County; Bettie died in 1903, at the age of twenty-five years; and Frank H. is special agent at Kansas City, Missouri, for the Home Insurance Company of New York.

JAMES M. REA. In an office that was signally dignified and honored by the services of his father, Judge Rea is maintaining the same high standard of efficiency and is one of the able and popular executives of the government of his native county. He is a son of the late Judge Joseph Rea, to whom a memoir is dedicated on other pages of this work, so that in the present article it is unnecessary to offer further review of the family history, though it may consistently be said that few names have been more prominent and represented greater influence in this history of Andrew County than that borne by him who is now serving as judge of the Probate Court of the county and who is known as a citizen of high civic ideals, as well as a man of broad mental ken, well fortified convictions and unquestioned integrity of purpose.

In what is now known as the Fisher farm, about two miles northeast of the Village of Rea, named in honor of the family, Judge James Muse Rea was born on the 26th of August, 1863, a scion of one of the sterling pioneer families of Andrew County. He is the oldest of the children of Judge Joseph Rea and Sarah A. (Muse) Rea, the latter of whom maintains her home at Savannah, the judicial center of the county, the death of her husband having occurred on the 28th of February, 1914. He whose name initiates this article has been a resident of Andrew County continuously from the time of his birth, save for an interval of one year, during which he was identified with the cattle business in Oklahoma and Indian Territory, in 1881. He attended the public schools of his native county until he had completed the curriculum of the Savannah High School, and in fitting himself for the profession in which his father achieved distinctive success, he entered the law department of Cornell University, at Ithaca, New York, in which he was graduated as a member of the class of 1892 and with the degree of Bachelor of Laws, his admission to the Missouri bar having been recorded in the year prior to his graduation. He engaged in the practice of his profession at Savannah and built up a substantial and representative law business, to which he continued to devote his undivided attention until his election to the office of Judge of the Probate Court, in 1910. His father held this important office for three terms and for the same was virtually the "perpetual candidate" of the democratic party, and he himself has given an administration marked by great circumspection and care, so that the many important interests presented for adjudication in his court have been handled most efficiently and to the satisfaction of those concerned.

Judge Rea has been unswerving in his allegiance to the democratic party and has been one of its influential figures in his home county. He has been a student of economic and governmental affairs, both local and generic, and has never lacked the courage of his convictions. In 1912 he circulated in Andrew County a petition in support of the initiative policy, to enable the people to adopt by vote or to defeat by the same process the single-tax policy, of which he is a stalwart advocate. He realized fully that the idea was one that was distinctly unpopular among the farmers and that his advocacy would possibly lose to him the political support of many of the sterling husbandmen of the county, but he held principle above personal advancement and lived up to his convictions. In the election of 1914 he was defeated at the polls on account of his convictions as to single taxes, but throughout the campaign no other than high encomium as a man and an officer were heard against him.

On the 2d of June, 1910, was solemnized the marriage of Judge Rea to Miss Nellie Barr, daughter of Boyd and Mary Jane (Jenkins) Barr, honored pioneers of Andrew County, and the one child of this union is a winsome little daughter, Blanche, who was born on the 2d of January, 1913.

JEREMIAH H. BRYAN. The remuneration of an active, useful and helpful career is an honorable retirement from labor and a season of rest in which to enjoy the fruits of former toil. The individual who through consecutive endeavor, resolute purpose, sound judgment and unfaltering energy achieves success in the active affairs of life is eminently entitled to a period of leisure in which to carry out his individual desires and indulge those tastes from which he has been formerly withheld by the strenuous duties of business life. For more than forty years Jeremiah H. Bryan was prominently identified with the agricultural interests of Northwest Missouri, and his career was an honorable one, in which his indefatigable labor brought him a handsome competence that now enables him to put aside the heavier burdens and find pleasurable recreation in his home and among his numerous friends.

Mr. Bryan was born in Greene County, Virginia, December 18, 1840, and is a son of Robert and Lavina (Ganes) Bryan. The family originated in Scotland and its founders in America settled in Culpeper County, Virginia, from whence Allen Bryan, the great-grandfather of Jeremiah H., enlisted for service in the American army during the Revolutionary war. Allen Bryan married a Miss Kendall, who was of English birth, and among their children was Jerry Bryan, the grandfather of Jeremiah H., who served valiantly as a soldier during the War of 1812 as a lieutenant. Robert Bryan was born in 1817, in Greene County, Virginia, grew to manhood in that vicinity, and in that county he married Lavina Ganes, who was born at Dayton, Rockingham County, in 1814. He then went across the line into Rockingham

County and there engaged in farming during the remainder of his life, and passed away at Dayton, aged sixty-five years, while the mother reached the advanced age of ninety-three years. They were faithful members of the old Baptist Church which was built in 1802, of chestnut logs and afterwards weatherboarded, and which is still standing as one of the old historical landmarks near Culpeper Courthouse. Of the eight children in their family, seven grew to man and womanhood, and four are living at this time: Jeremiah H.; Robert, a resident of Roanoke, Virginia; George, who resides at Dayton, Virginia; and Joe M., who lives at Warrensburg, Missouri.

Jeremiah H. Bryan was reared in Rockingham County, Virginia, and received his education in the public schools, upon his completion of the curriculum of which he learned the trade of carpenter. He was thus engaged and in his twenty-first year when the war between the South and North broke across the country in all its fury, and young Bryan, casting his sympathies with his state, offered his services to the Confederacy and was accepted as a member of Company I, Seventh Regiment, Virginia Cavalry. His subsequent services in the ranks of the Gray covered a period of three years, three months and twenty days, and ended only when he was paroled at the time of General Lee's surrender at Appomattox. Mr. Bryan's military record is one of which any soldier might well be proud, his engagements including such famous and sanguinary battles as Gettysburg, Second Manassas, Harpers Ferry, and all the engagements in which the greatly beloved "Stonewall" Jackson took part; the battle of·Sharpsburg, where he acted in the capacity of courier for "Marse" Lee, Port Republic, where he acted in the same position for General Jackson, Brandy Station, Spottsylvania, Cedar Mountain and Petersburg, surely names to thrill the hearts of the brave boys who fought under the Bonnie Blue Flag. Mr. Bryan's service was filled with escapades and exciting adventures, and during his service around Washington he swam the Potomac River five times. He was also a member of the party which slipped around in Grant's rear, at Sabona Church, capturing and running off 2,489 head of cattle, in spite of the Union general's 250,000 men. He was twice wounded by saber cuts, one across the back of his hand and the other across his forehead.

When the fortunes of war resulted in the fall of the Confederacy, Mr. Bryan returned to his home, and for three months was engaged in teaching subscription school. Following this he resumed the trade of carpenter, at which he worked until 1868, but the stirring experiences of army life had bred in him the desire for more activity and excitement than could be furnished amid the environments of his home, and he finally left the parental roof and started for Barton and Saline counties, Missouri, working at his trade and looking for a suitable place to locate permanently. He returned home for Christmas, 1868, but in the following spring returned to Missouri, and April 11, 1869, arrived at Richmond, Ray County, where he purchased eighty acres of land just to the north. He continued to work at his trade and to cultivate this land until 1874, when he traded this property for eighty acres of raw land, which is his present home. Here he settled down permanently to farming, although he continued to work at his trade until some fifteen years ago, and it is doubtful if there is a farm in Ray County that does not bear some evidence of his skill as a builder. From time to time he has added to his holdings, and with each purchase has cleared and improved the land, even to the planting of shade and fruit trees, and at present his holdings include 500 acres in Ray County, 100 acres in Carroll County, Missouri, and 500 acres in Texas. His buildings are of the most modern architecture and substantial construction, his improvements are the best to be obtained, and on his Texas property he has recently erected a pumping station worth $7,000. Everything he owns has been accumulated through the medium of his own efforts, and it is reasonable to believe that a better example of self-made manhood could not be found. Of recent years he has retired from the active work of the farm, which he has turned over to his sons and son-in-law, although he still takes a keen and active interest in the operation of his land and through his experience and good judgment aids in making it one of the most productive tracts in this part of the state. In business and social circles Mr. Bryan is held in the highest esteem; his name is an honored one in the commercial and financial world, and his word is considered as good as any parchment. He has taken a wholesome pride in the advancements which have marked his community's progress and development, to which he has contributed by his activities in the business world and as a co-worker in movements for the public welfare. A life-long democrat, he has had no desire for public life, but is always ready to bear his share of the responsibilities of good citizenship. He is a close relative of William Jennings Bryan. The family is connected religiously with the Baptist Church.

On April 24, 1867, Mr. Bryan was united in marriage with Miss Mary Frances Fridley, who was born in Rockingham County, Virginia, July 26, 1847, and to this union there have been born five children, of whom three are living: Jerry N., born March 1, 1877, who is carrying on farming in Ray County, Missouri; John Robert, born October 15, 1881, a graduate of the University of Missouri civil engineering department, who is now county surveyor for Jackson County, Texas; and Mary Ida, born August 20, 1884, who is the wife of William S. Mayers, living on the home farm in Ray County, and has one child.

IRVING MILLER. Although the well-directed activities of Irving Miller in Northwest Missouri belong to the past rather than the present, for he is now a resident of Kansas, they were such as to make his name well known and highly esteemed in business circles of Richmond and Brookfield, where for some fourteen years he was the proprietor of a clothing establishment. A man of excellent business ability, he bears a high reputation both in his old and new localities, and as a citizen has at all times shown himself helpful and public-spirited. Mr. Miller is a native son of Clay County, born at Liberty, November 26, 1864, his father being the Hon. Robert Hise Miller, Platte County's "grand old man," a review of whose career will be found on another page of this work.

Mr. Miller was reared at Liberty, and received his primary education in the graded schools, following which he became a student at William Jewell College. He did not graduate from this institution, however, but entered upon his business career when still in his 'teens in the newspaper office with his father, who was the founder of the Liberty Tribune and its publisher for about forty years. After a short time Irving Miller left the field of journalism for that of commercial activity, his father assisting him to establish himself in the clothing business at Liberty, and later at Pleasant Hill, where he remained until 1891. At that time, seeking a wider field for his abilities, he went to Richmond, to which place he transferred his business, there passing a successful twelve years in the same line of business. He then disposed of his interests there and went to Brookfield, but after two years sold and went to his present location, the town of Junction City, Kansas. Here for nine years his operations have met with satisfactory results and he is justly accounted one of the substantial merchants of that flourishing locality.

Mr. Miller was married to Miss Ola M. Lowery, who was born at Clinton, Henry County, Missouri, September 16, 1871, and is a daughter of James R. and Elizabeth R. (McEltheny) Lowery, natives of Harrodsburg, Kentucky, who in young married life came to Missouri and located at Clinton. In 1861 Mr. Lowery enlisted in the Confederate army for service in the Civil war under the noted southern General Price, and served until 1864, participating in a number of engagements. He was finally honorably discharged because of disability, having contracted a serious illness during his service. One daughter has been born to Mr. and Mrs. Miller: Miss Ozelle, of Liberty, who is well known in this city, where she has many friends, and is a popular member of the local chapter of the Daughters of the American Revolution.

CHARLES W. DALE. In the county that has been his place of abode from the time of his nativity Mr. Dale is now a representative agriculturist and stock grower, his well improved farm being eligibly situated in Knoxville Township, Ray County, and his being an assured place in the confidence and respect of the people of his native county. He is a scion of a sterling old family of this section of Missouri and is a son of Moses G. Dale, of whom specific mention is made on other pages of this history, so that repetition of the family data is not demanded in the sketch here presented.

Charles W. Dale was born on a farm near Swanwick, in Richmond Township, Ray County, Missouri, on the 25th of September, 1857, and his early associations were those of the old homestead farm on which he was reared to adult age, the while he duly availed himself of the advantages of the district schools, as well as of the high school at Richmond, the county seat. He continued to be associated in the work and management of his father's farm until he had attained to the age of twenty-three years, and in the following year he assumed connubial responsibilities, besides initiating independent effort in connection with the great basic industry under the influences of which he had been reared. In 1884 he removed to his present farm, situated north of the little village of Dockery, and upon the place he has made excellent improvements of permanent order, besides which he reclaimed a considerable portion of the land and under personal supervision brought the same under effective cultivation. His farm comprises eighty-five acres of fertile land and he gives his attention to diversified agriculture and the raising of excellent grades of live stock. He has made no dramatic exploits in his career, but in a quiet and unassuming way has pressed forward to the mark of large and worthy achievement and has never wavered in his allegiance to the staunch industry which is the recognized basis of all generic prosperity. He is unwavering in his allegiance to the democratic party. He is affiliated with the Independent Order of Odd Fellows and his wife is a member of the Methodist Episcopal Church, South, and a Rebekah

Mr. Magill died on the 12th of December, 1905, and his widow still maintains her home in Ray County. Of their five children three are living: Sallie is the widow of Thomas Lusk and resides in Kansas City, Missouri; Olivia is the wife of Mr. Dale of this review; and Fannie is the wife of Rev. J. L. Joyner, of Whitney, Texas. William Magill was a son of William and Polly (Baughman) Magill, and the family came to Missouri in 1832, remaining for a few months in Saline County and, in the spring of 1833, removing to Ray County, where settlement was made near Swanwick, in Richmond Township. William Magill, Sr., one of the sterling pioneers of Ray County, was born February 27, 1777, and his death occurred in Ray County, Missouri, on the 27th of March, 1847. His wife was born November 7, 1780, and was summoned to the life eternal on the 23d of January, 1843, their marriage having been solemnized January 3, 1803. This worthy couple became the parents of seven children: Mrs. Olivia Hodges, the eldest of the children, was born November 20, 1803, and died November 22, 1897; Henderson Magill was born August 26, 1805, and died September 4, 1864; Baughman Magill was born April 27, 1807, and died September 14, 1833; Samuel P. Magill was born November 21, 1809, and died in 1894; Lorenzo Magill was born January 30, 1812, and died July 3, 1887; John F. Magill was born November 20, 1814, and died within the same year; William Magill, Jr., father of Mrs. Dale, was born January 3, 1816, and died December 12, 1905, as has been previously noted in this context. The family is one that has been prominent in connection with the development and upbuilding of Northwestern Missouri and the name has ever stood exponent of the highest integrity as well as of productive industry. William Magill, Jr., first wedded Matilda Hamilton, who was born January 18, 1827, and whose death occurred August 14, 1855, their marriage having been celebrated September 12, 1844. Of the six children of this union five are living—Baughman, of Triplett, Chariton County, Missouri; Thomas and Henry, who still reside in Ray County, this state; Margaret R., who is the widow of Benjamin F. Baber and resides at Richmond, Ray County; Mollie, who is the widow of John L. Harrison, of Ray County; and John, who is deceased. On the 3d of February, 1856, William Magill wedded Miss Mary C. Haynes, and she still survives him, as has been stated in a preceding paragraph. Mrs. Mary C. (Haynes) Magill was reared and educated in Ray County and is a daughter of Joseph Haynes, who was a native of Murry County, Tennessee, and whose parents were born in North Carolina. William Magill was affiliated with the Masonic fraternity and both he and his wife were zealous members of the Cumberland Presbyterian Church. Mr. and Mrs. Dale have three children,—Nellie, who is the wife of Thomas M. Shelton, of Ray County; Glen married Maud Watkins and is identified with agricultural pursuits in this county; and Grover, who remains at the parental home. There are two grandchildren, Robert and Eudora Dale.

JOSEPH L. ASHBY. For nearly sixty years a resident of Clinton County, Joseph L. Ashby is one of the citizens whose name and a brief record of whose career should be permanently recorded in any history of Northwest Missouri. He had his part in the pioneer development of Clinton County, and has ably discharged his obligations in making a living and providing for home and family, and has also discharged his duties to the general community with an efficiency which brings him honor. The Ashby homestead is one of the most interesting as well as most valuable farms in Platte Township, comprising 540 acres of land, an old and attractive residence grounds, and not least among the picturesque features is the presence of thirty-nine different varieties of timber. One of the giant oaks on the farm is perhaps the largest tree of its kind in Clinton County. Mr. Ashby has lived in Clinton County since 1855.

Joseph L. Ashby was born November 25, 1831, in Kentucky, and has passed the age of four score years. His father was Manzey Quincy Ashby, and of notable American ancestry. His grandfather was Nathaniel Ashby, a son of Capt. Jack Ashby, who held a commission in the American army during the Revolutionary war and had previously gone with the Virginia troops under Washington with the British regulars against the French and Indians in western Pennsylvania, on the 19th of July, 1753, and was present at Braddock's defeat. He was selected by Washington to carry a message containing the awful results of the battle to Lord Fairfax, and the latter in turn was to send forward a messenger to Governor Dinwiddie. This Capt. Jack Ashby lived to be ninety-two years of age. The first of the family to come to America arrived on these shores in 1702. He was descended from Sir Edward Ashby, a Huguenot. In a later generation of the same family was Gen. T. Ashby, who held high rank in the Confederate army during the Civil war. Manzey Q. Ashby married Margaret Logan, who was of a Scotch-Irish family that settled in Kentucky. Of the children who reached maturity the following brothers and sisters of Joseph L. should be mentioned: Margaret, deceased wife of Samuel Woodson; Mary McKee, deceased; Ellen, wife of George Hamilton; Archibald L., a writer and editor, who died in 1891. The father of this family died at the age of eighty-six. At one time he owned as much as 25,000 acres of Missouri land, and was a man of unusual business judgment and ability. Physically he stood six feet and weighed 225 pounds. His wife died at the age of fifty-six years.

Joseph L. Ashby was reared in Kentucky, acquired his education there, and in his early manhood found the opportunities for a long and useful career in Northwest Missouri. His first wife was Mary Evans, a daughter of Dr. Peter Evans, a pioneer physician of Kentucky. After her death Mr. Ashby married Olivia Dunham, and they became the parents of seven children: Adull; Alden, of Clinton County; Erskine Birch, of Excelsior Springs, Missouri; Martha; Margaret; Olivia Beery, of Lawrence, Kansas; and Jassamine. All the children received the best of educational advantages. Mr. Ashby is a democrat in politics, is affiliated with the Independent Order of Odd Fellows, and for forty years has been a teacher in the Sunday school. His own life has been successful from every point of view, and he has always maintained a breadth of judgment and of observation, and has kept well informed concerning the great issues of life and world's affairs.

S. S. PORTER. Prosperity in all its meanings belongs to S. S. Porter, of Clinton County, where everyone knows him and he knows everybody. He has spent all his life there, and is first of all a very successful farmer and stockman, and according to the Quaker method of phrasing it is a birthright follower of that business. His father was prominent in the stock business in Northwest Missouri, and the name stands for successful operations in that line and for thorough public spirit in citizenship.

S. S. Porter was born December 21, 1879, on his father's homestead in Clinton County, a son of Benjamin F. Porter. Benjamin F. Porter was a son of Samuel S. Porter, of Clay County, Missouri. James Porter, a brother of Benjamin F., now living in Plattsburg, was a soldier in the Confederate army and lost a leg during the service. The wife of Benjamin F. Porter died when her son S. S. was fourteen years of age.

There were four children: Dr. Allen Porter, a prominent physician in Kansas City; the second child is deceased; S. S. is the third; and Frank B. is a resident of Shoal Township, Clinton County. Benjamin F. Porter died at Osborn in 1911, at the age of seventy. He was one of the extensive cattle feeders, and at times had as many as 500 cattle and 1,000 hogs.

S. S. Porter was married November 19, 1902, to Florence Duncan. Her father, P. S. Duncan, was born in Clay County, Missouri, April 22, 1844, a son of Stephen Duncan, a native of Bourbon County, Kentucky, and an early settler and stockman in Northwest Missouri. P. S. Duncan was married in Taylor County, Iowa, to Mary Severns, and they had five children: Florence, now Mrs. S. S. Porter; S. Stephen, who lives on the home farm; Leora, ·who married Wyatt Hord; Henry Clay; and Claud. Mr. and Mrs. Porter have four children: Mary Julia, Florence Hazel, Virginia Lula and Ben S. S.

Mr. Porter and family reside in one of the comfortable residences of Clinton County, a fine house of twelve rooms with all modern conveniences. His farm is thoroughly equipped for stock raising, has many acres of blue grass pasture, a fine barn 40x60 feet, and each year he turns off a large number of cattle. He makes a specialty of Hereford cattle. Mrs. Porter is a member of the Christian Church. In politics Mr. S. S. Porter is a democrat.

AARON B. CONROW, proprietor of a flourishing hardware business at Richmond, is numbered among the selfmade men of Ray County. No fortunate family or pecuniary advantages aided him at the outset of his career. On the contrary, the close of the Civil war found him fatherless, his education was necessarily limited, and from his boyhood he has been dependent upon his own resources. Obstacles and difficulties have confronted him, but these he has overcome by determined effort, and as the years have passed he has advanced steadily to a position of prominence in the business world. Mr. Conrow was born in Richmond, October 28, 1858, and here has spent his entire life.

Aaron H. Conrow, father of Aaron B., was born June 19, 1824, near Cincinnati, Ohio. He spent a part of his boyhood days at, or near, Pekin, Illinois, and from that place removed with his parents to Missouri and settled in Ray County. Here, through his own energy, he obtained a pretty thorough education, teaching school a part of the time in order to complete the same, and in this being very successful. He then chose the law as a profession and by rigid economy and persistent labor succeeded in making himself an eminent legist. On May 17, 1828, he was married to Mary Ann Quesenberry, daughter of David H. and Lucinda Quesenberry, natives of Kentucky and early settlers of Ray County, and to this union there were born four children, of whom three are living: William S., rural mail carrier at Richmond; Aaron B.; and Mamie, who is the wife of J. L. Farris, of Richmond, Missouri. The mother of these children passed away February 20, 1901.

Aaron H. Conrow was appointed by the governor judge of the first probate court established in Ray County. From January, 1857, to January, 1861, he was circuit attorney of the Fifth Judicial Circuit of Missouri, an office that had been previously filled by some of the most brilliant lawyers of the state. He was an astute and successful advocate, a fine judge of law, and a man who never descended to the slightest artifice to gain the advantage over an opponent; although ingenious he was open and candid, and above all littleness. Judge Conrow was the preceptor of several young men who afterward became able and prominent lawyers, was ever the fast friend of education, and no man ever contributed more liberally to the support of institutions of learning.

A democrat eminently worthy to be trusted, in 1860 he was elected to the general assembly of the state, and was serving as a member of that august body at the outbreak of the war between the South and the North. Casting his fortunes with the Confederacy, he was instrumental in recruiting and equipping the first company organized in Ray County for the defense of the cause which he believed right, and ranked as colonel of the Murrain State Guards, an organization he had helped to create by his vote in the legislature. He was by a majority of his comrades elected to represent his district (the Fourth Missouri) in the Confederate congress, and in that capacity, as in all others, served with zeal and promptness. He was at the first meeting and at the final adjournment of that body. At the close of the war the amnesty agreed upon did not include the members of the Confederate congress and, fearing that if he fell into the hands of the successful party his life would be forfeited, he went to Mexico, where, soon afterward, he was brutally murdered by a band of Mexican soldiers, on, or about, August 25, 1865. The last seen of this brave and distinguished man by his family was after the battle of Lexington, in which he had taken part, following which he visited his home for a short time.

Aaron B. Conrow was reared in Richmond, where he attended the public schools, but on account of the war his education was limited, although in later years his observation, wide experience and much reading have made him a very well-educated man with a broad knowledge of men and affairs. When eighteen years of age he began his business career as a clerk in the store of his uncle, John Quesenberry, and in 1878 began to carry on operations on his own account as the proprietor of a hardware store. This he continued to carry on successfully until, 1893, when under President Cleveland's second administration he was appointed postmaster of Richmond, an office which he held until 1897. In that year he was elected on the democratic ticket to the office of county recorder, and after his first term was re-elected, serving in all eight years to the satisfaction of the people of his community. When his public service was completed, Mr. Conrow returned to business life, purchasing the hardware stock of Jesse Child, at Richmond, and here he has since become one of the substantial business men of the city. He now has his own two-story building, where he carries a full and up-to-date line of hardware, stoves, harness and furniture, and through energetic effort and the intelligent use of modern methods has attracted a large and representative trade. Mr. Conrow is known as a public-spirited citizen who has ever had the best interests of his community at heart, and who is foremost in promoting movements for its welfare. In business circles his name is an honored one on commercial paper, and whether in business, public or private life, he has always merited the high esteem and confidence in which he has been held.

On November 17, 1881, Mr. Conrow was united in marriage at Richmond to Miss Ellen Menefee, who was born January 27, 1862, in Ray County, Missouri, a daughter of L. S. Menefee, a prominent attorney of Ray County who died during the Civil war. To Mr. and Mrs. Conrow there has been born one daughter: Forrestine, who resides with her parents.

JOHN H. ESTES. During the eighteen years in which John H. Estes has been connected with the business interests of Richmond his career has been one of advancement. Coming to this city with many hundred dollars less than nothing, a practical stranger, with no influential friends or connections, he has so ably conducted his operations and so well directed his efforts that today he is the owner of the largest retail business in Ray County—the Estes Department Store. His life has been one of constant industry and indomitable perseverance, and forms another chapter in the story of selfmade American manhood.

Mr. Estes was born on a farm in Caldwell County, Missouri, October 19, 1860, and is a son of James and Mary C. (Ribelin) Estes. His grandfather, William Estes, was born in Kentucky in 1802 and in 1820 came to Missouri, first locating in Saline County, although shortly thereafter he came to Ray County and located near Excelsior Springs. Following this he moved to Platte County, and in 1840 located in Caldwell County. Mr. Estes was a slave owner and a successful farmer, and one of the fine old characters found among the sturdy pioneers of that day, a progressive, enterprising and observant citizen. In 1850 he went to California in quest of gold, but was only moderately successful, and his trip was saddened by the death of two sons on the plains. Shortly after coming to Missouri Mr. Estes was married to Miss Susanna Hiatt, who died in April, 1865; while he survived until 1894, and passed away at the advanced age of ninety-two years.

James Estes, father of John H. Estes, was born in Ray County, December 23, 1828, and was reared in Caldwell County, where he attended the rural schools. He has spent his entire life in agricultural pursuits and has been successful in his ventures, being known as one of the substantial citizens of Polo, where he is living in quiet retirement. He married Mary C. Ribelin, who was born in Kentucky, October 30, 1835, and died in 1902; and they became the parents of seven children, of whom five are living; William M., a resident of Polo; Louisa, the wife of D. W. Hill, of Polo; Laura C., the wife of Silas Conway, of Liberty; Cora L., the wife of A. J. Smoot, of Polo; and John H.

John H. Estes was reared on his father's farm in Caldwell County, and there attended the rural schools, subsequently being a student of the graded schools of Kingston. In 1882 and 1883 he attended the University of Missouri at Columbia, and then returned to his home and farmed until 1884, when he went to Lathrop, Missouri, and obtained a position as clerk, which he held for three months. Following this he went to Turney, Clinton County, Missouri, and purchased a one-half interest in the store at that point belonging to his employers, the firm then becoming Bohart, Goff and Estes; but after eight months at that place they moved the stock to Kingston, Missouri. In 1887 Mr. Estes formed a partnership with W. H. B. Carter under the firm style of Carter & Estes, and in 1889 they moved the stock to Polo. The business was conducted at that point until 1895, when through hard times and a loose credit business the firm was forced to cease operations. This would have been enough to totally discourage the majority of men, but Mr. Estes was made of sterner stuff; and January 20, 1896, he arrived in Richmond with several wagon loads of merchandise which he had moved overland from Polo. At this time he was far in debt and the goods were not even paid for, but he courageously settled down to rehabilitate his fortune and to restore his good name in the business world. His first place of business was a small room on West Main Street, two doors east of his present location, where he started under his father's name. In two years time, so faithfully had he labored, that he had cleared himself of debt and purchased the John C. Brown mercantile stock. His original quarters he found much too small for his rapidly increasing business, and he moved to his present establishment, where he occupies a double storeroom, 40x150 feet, with a basement 40x90 feet, and a balcony in the rear of the main floor 31x40 feet. He carries a stock valued at $50,000, including dry goods, men's furnishings, children's clothing, ladies' ready-to-wear, shoes, hardware, graniteware, china, crockery, paints, wallpaper and millinery, the latter in the balcony. Twenty skilled clerks are regularly employed in this large enterprise, and at rush times many more are added. Mr. Estes is a well-read, broadminded man and a booster for his city, his county and his state, being amply capable and ever ready to convince even the most skeptical why this is the best community in the world. He is a member of the board of trustees of the Association of Missouri Municipalities, which has been since its organization a state-wide association for the bettering of conditions in the smaller towns and cities and to give publicity to the great advantages of the State of Missouri. He has various outside interests and is the owner of valuable farming property in Colorado.

On January 1, 1890, Mr. Estes was married to Miss Sophronia Isabelle Madden, who was born in Clinton County, Missouri, a daughter of James C. and Nancy (Hardwick) Madden. To this union there has been born one son, Earl C., a graduate of the University of Missouri, class 1913, and now engaged in business with his father.

JOHN MOUNT. A former soldier of the great Civil war, John Mount has lived in Northwest Missouri since 1871, when he located in Ray County, but for many years has been a practical farmer of Davis Township, in Caldwell County, and is now living retired at a comfortable home in Braymer. The same fidelity which marked his career as a soldier has characterized his later years of citizenship, and he is one of the highly esteemed men of Caldwell County.

John Mount is a Tennesseean by birth, grew up in that state, but when the integrity of the nation was submitted to the fortunes of war he took the Union side, and in 1862 enlisted in Company K of the Second Tennessee Infantry, under Capt. J. D. Underdown and Col. James Carter. He saw his first active service at Cumberland Gap on April 25, 1862, and continued with the regiment until his honorable discharge on June 15, 1865. For part of the time he was in the army of General Burnsides. On November 5, 1864, Mr. Mount was taken prisoner, and for several months suffered all the horrors and destitutions of Northern men in Southern prisons. He was confined for a time at Belle Isle, was in the Andersonville Stockade, and later at Florence, South Carolina. When he went into the army he weighed 160 pounds, but starvation, exposure and other sufferings reduced his weight to 90 pounds before he was released and rejoined his comrades. At Andersonville he saw dozens of his comrades die of starvation and exposure, and he was a prisoner there when the commander was Major Wurtz, who was afterwards, because of his brutal treatment of the prisoners, tried and hanged by the United States Government. After his honorable discharge Mr. Mount returned to his Tennessee home.

John Mount was born in Tennessee in 1840, a son of Samuel and Isabel (Underwood) Mount. His father was a native of North Carolina, but the family came from Pennsylvania, and the mother was a daughter of George Underwood, who saw active service in the War of 1812. Samuel Mount died at the age of seventy-six. The children were: John; Ella McKnight, whose husband was a soldier; Mary Petty; Humphrey; Martha Estes; Henderson; I. P., now deceased; George, deceased; Margaret; Napoleon B.; and Rebecca.

John Mount, a few years after the close of the Civil war, in 1871, located in Ray County, Missouri. In 1867 he had married, in Tennessee, Ella Thornburgh. She was born in Tennessee in 1842, a daughter of Samuel and Sarah (Moody) Thornburgh. Her father died at the age

MR. AND MRS. JOHN MOUNT

of eighty-four years. He was a farmer, and a member of the Methodist Church. After living in Ray County for a time Mr. and Mrs. Mount moved into Caldwell County, where he acquired a good farm four miles from Braymer, comprising 130 acres. He still owns this farm, but now rents it and has retired to a comfortable residence in Braymer. His farm is well improved, with good house and barn, and its cultivation gave him the prosperity which has enabled him to pass his later years in retirement. Mr. Mount is an active member of the Grand Army Post at Braymer, and is a strong republican in politics. His church home is the Methodist Episcopal.

Of the children born to Mr. and Mrs. Mount only two are now living. A daughter, Clara Phillips, died in Oklahoma, leaving one child, William Earl. The son now living is Doctor Mount, a successful physician at Polo, Missouri. The daughter is Almeda Phillips, who lives in Caldwell County. Doctor Mount has one son, while Mrs. Phillips has three children, Roscoe, Velma and Ira.

WILLIAM G. CARTER. A pioneer of Northwest Missouri and a farmer near Martinsville, William G. Carter has resided on the hill where is located his home since 1867. He came here from Gentry County, Missouri, where, near Lone Star, he was born October 23, 1841. His father was Vinson Carter, who settled in that county in the spring of 1841 and after the land was surveyed and sectionized he entered a tract and there spent the remaining years of his life in the peaceful pursuits of the soil, devoting himself to mixed farming. Vinson Carter died at the age of seventy-five years, in 1889, having been born January 4, 1814, and was buried in the Carter Cemetery, near his old home, his wife lying beside him. Before her marriage she was Patience Glendenning, a daughter of William Glendenning, who came to Missouri from Ohio in 1841, and died about 1851, leaving two sons and four daughters.

Vinson Carter was a native of Tennessee, born near White River, in which vicinity he resided until a young man. He married his wife in Putnam County, Indiana, for Greencastle was one of the Indiana towns of which he spoke familiarly. He was a man of fair farmer's education and the nearest he came to having a military experience was when he assisted in scaring the Indians out of Gentry County. When the republican party was organized he became an adherent of its principles and continued to support its candidates until his death. His only public service as an official was in the capacity of school teacher, but he is remembered as a citizen always ready to bear his share of responsibilities. In his religious faith, Mr. Carter was a Methodist and did his part in erecting the place of worship in his locality, in those times the community schoolhouse. He had no fraternal connections and was opposed to secret orders, which were contrary to his belief.

The children born to Vinson and Patience Carter were as follows: Elizabeth, born June 9, 1840, became the wife of Wesley Mock, and now resides near the home of her brother William G., in Harrison County, Missouri; William G., of this review; Susanna, born January 27, 1844, who became the wife of Jackson Dye and died in the vicinity of Grant City, Missouri; Elijah Albert, born January 13, 1846, who is now a resident of New Hampton, Missouri; John Lewis, born July 7, 1849, who resides near Lone Star, Missouri; a twin brother of John Lewis, who died in infancy; Martha, born September 28, 1852, who became the wife of William Clellon, engaged in agricultural operations in the vicinity of Martinsville, Missouri; Milton Riley, born October 16, 1854, who is now a resident near New Hampton, Missouri; Hiram Frank, born April 27, 1857, who is carrying on farming on the old Carter homestead near

Lone Star, Missouri; Jane, born September 1, 1861, who became the wife of Filmore Needles, and died in Gentry County.

Vinson Carter was a son of Elijah Carter, who came to Missouri with his son, by way of ox-teams, and settled near the Carter Cemetery, in Gentry County, one of his daughters being the first person to be buried in that graveyard, the grave being made by her brother, Joseph. Among the children of Elijah Carter were: Betsy, who became the wife of John Glendenning; Vinson, the father of William G.; Leta, who married Richard Glendenning, a brother of John; Joseph; Nancy; who became the wife of John Glendenning, a brother of the mother of William G. Carter; Katie, who married Hugh Ross; a daughter who became the wife of Cubbige Needles; Lewis; Nathan, and Martha, who was first the wife of George Ross and after his death married Mr. Swank.

William G. Carter received his education in the district school near Lone Star, his only schoolhouse being one of logs. During his first term in search of educational training he was forced to travel through the timber for a mile and one-half, following a "blazed" path, and as there were many wild hogs and other menaces to children roaming in the woods at that time, the neighbors were wont to accompany the children to and fro. Mr. Carter's first call from under the parental roof was when he entered the army for service during the Civil war, in 1861. He first enlisted for six months in Colonel Cragnor's regiment, which rendezvoused at St. Joseph, and after his time had expired he spent a few months on the home farm and then entered the three-years service. His company was B, belonging to the Thirty-fifth Regiment, Missouri Volunter Infantry, and his first captain was Captain Scott, who, however, proved so incompetent that he resigned and the company was without a captain until near the close of the war. The first colonel of the Thirty-fifth was Kimball, and the second a West Point man named Foster, but the boys of the regiment did not like Foster's red tape and they succeeded in getting rid of him without an investigation, he being succeeded by Lieutenant-Colonel Fitch.

The Thirty-fifth Missouri Infantry was organized at St. Joseph, and was sent to St. Louis for drill at Benton Barracks. The regiment went from there to Jefferson City for thirty days, then returning to St. Louis, and going thence down the Mississippi River to Columbus, Kentucky, and on to Helena, Arkansas. At the latter point it did guard duty for a long time, or until an expedition was formed to go down on the Yazoo River, in Mississippi, but was there but a few days when ordered back to Helena. It made next a trip to DuVall's Bluff and on its return was sent up the Red River from Helena, was mustered out at Little Rock, Arkansas, and was finally discharged at St. Louis, in 1865. Mr. Carter participated in the battle of Helena under General Prentiss, and there, as elsewhere, proved himself a brave and faithful soldier.

When his military career was finished, Mr. Carter returned to his home and resumed his agricultural pursuits, becoming a farmer and stockman. At the time of his marriage he was possessed of $400 in money, a team of horses, two cows and a heifer. He lived on a rented farm the first year, in Gentry County, and in the spring following began his career as a farmer in Harrison County. Mr. Carter paid $3 an acre for 100 acres in section 5, township 64, range 29, and built a loghouse, twelve feet square, just opposite his present dwelling, and to this cabin he brought his wife, it continuing to be their place of dwelling for perhaps ten years. This primitive home was succeeded by a frame structure, in keeping with the progress of the times, and just before his youngest child married, Mr. Carter erected his present commodious and extensive home, this now being accounted one of the splendid residences of the county.

When Mr. Carter started farming in Harrison County, he broke the sod and planted corn, and about the only way he had of getting cash was from hogs and cattle, although even then little was secured as only meager prices were obtainable. He was energetic, thrifty and persevering, however, and came to be the owner of 1,000 acres of land, and as his sons married, he helped them substantially to a start in life. Mr. Carter was one of the organizers of the Bank of Martinsville, of which he has been a director since its inception, and of which he is now president, managing its affairs with an ability which has done much to make it one of the strong financial institutions of Harrison County. He has also other business interests, and is a stockholder of the New Hampton Lumber Company.

In political matters Mr. Carter is a republican, but has confined his activities in politics to casting his vote. He is a member of the Methodist Episcopal Church, in which he is active, and has served his congregation at Martinsville as an official.

Mr. Carter was married February 22, 1866, to Miss Martha Wilson, a daughter of Adam and Matilda (McDonald) Wilson. Mr. Wilson came from Albany, Kentucky, to Missouri and settled first in Gentry County, but passed his final years in Harrison County, and died September 12, 1897, at seventy-eight years of age, having been born May 30, 1819. Mrs. Wilson passed away April 24, 1914, when almost ninety-two years of age. Their children were as follows: Elizabeth, who married William Clopton and lives at Jefferson, Iowa; Mary Ann, who died in childhood; Mrs. Carter, born February 3, 1846; James, a resident of Carlyle, Kansas; Harriet, who married Silas Ebersole, of Big Springs, Kansas; John, of St. Joseph, Missouri; Catherine, who married Sam Meredith, of Martinsville, Missouri; Ellen, who died as Mrs. Harvey Spillman; and Phebe, who became the wife of Tobe Coleman and died while a resident of Harrison County.

The children born to Mr. and Mrs. Carter have been as follows: Lewis P., born July 11, 1868, a resident of Lake City, Iowa, married Carrie Thailor, and has six children, Dean, Edith, Frank, Gertrude, Sam and Fay; Adam H., born September 26, 1870, a farmer near Martinsville, married Fannie Young, and has five children, William Y., Raymond, Thomas, Edgar and Velma; Vinson A., born February 6, 1873, a farmer near Washington Center, Missouri, married Maud Scott, and has four children, Ray, Gladys, Alice and Mildred; Charles O., born November 23, 1876, is a farmer near the homestead of his father, married for his first wife Rebecca Adair and for his second Myrtle VanHoozier, and had four children by his first wife, Clarence, deceased, Marie, Cora and Jessie, and one child by his second wife, Wayne; John R., born July 31, 1879, a farmer of Harrison County, married Femma Young, and has three children, Roy, Loren and Vondalena; and Silas Franklin, born November 5, 1881, a farmer on the property adjoining that of his father, married Fannie Creekmore, and has five children, Goldie, Lloyd, Lois, Gracie and Leslie.

WILLIAM DAVIDSON. For more than forty years William Davidson has been identified with the splendid country about Worth. His earlier years were spent in the strenuous activities of the Middle West and Far West, and always as a busy and industrious citizen. Mr. Davidson has passed the age of three score and ten, and has a retrospect over the years that have gone that can be contemplated only with satisfaction, since in that time he has gained those prizes which are the dearest ambition of mankind—ample material prosperity, provision for home and family, and the respect and esteem of a community.

William Davidson was born in Putnam County, Indiana, February 22, 1841. His birthplace was near Mount Meridian, situated on the old National Road, a noted thoroughfare constructed before the time of railroads, from the eastern side of the Alleghenies across the states of Ohio, Indiana and Illinois to the Mississippi River and surveyed even as far as Jefferson City, Missouri. His grandfather was William Davidson, of Scotch-Irish stock, who was perhaps a native of Ireland and came to America prior to the Revolutionary war. He afterwards settled in Erie County, Pennsylvania. He was an uncle of Captain Lewis, noted in American history as one of the Lewis and Clark Expedition to the Pacific Coast in the early part of the eighteenth century. Among the children of William Davidson were: William, Thomas, Polly and Joseph. Some of his children lived near Zanesville, Ohio.

Joseph Davidson, father of William, was born in Erie County, Pennsylvania, grew up there, and was educated in the schools of that section. When a young man he started West, locating in Illinois, and was identified with the early survey in that section of the country. While there he was first married. The children of this marriage were: Simon, who spent his life as a farmer and died at Boulder, Colorado, leaving a family; Ann, who married a railroad man and is believed to have died in Nodaway County, Missouri; Medina, who married Robert Mann and spent most of her years in Iowa, but died at Boulder, Colorado; Joseph, who went out to California and died at Sonoma; Allen, who also went west and died at Willis, California, leaving a family. Joseph Davidson removed from Illinois to Putnam County, Indiana, about 1838, and there married, after the death of his first wife, Elizabeth Albin. She was at that time the widow of John Collins. Her father, William Albin, came from Pennsylvania after living there many years to Kentucky, was one of the pioneers, and then settled in Putnam County, Indiana. The second Mrs. Davidson died in Worth County, Missouri, in 1885 at the age of seventy-six. Her children by Mr. Collins were: Thomas H.; Sarah J., who married Jesse Wright and lives in the Province of Alberta, Canada; T. H. Collins, who practiced law in Missouri twenty years and at Denver, Colorado, sixteen years, died in the State of Washington, leaving a family. The children of Joseph and Elizabeth Davidson were: William; Angeline, who died in Gentry County, Missouri, as Mrs. Warren Hill; Frances, who married Fred Cassins and died at Cisco, California, leaving two sons; and Laura, who died unmarried. Joseph Davidson and family removed from Indiana in 1851 to Iowa, locating in Fremont, eight miles south of Sidney, where he spent the rest of his years, passing away in 1854, when about seventy years of age.

William Davidson, who was ten years of age when the family came to Iowa, spent most of his early years on the frontier, where civilization had established few institutions, and his schooling was extremely limited owing to the absence of regular instruction in most of the neighborhood where his youth was spent. He lived for some years both in Iowa and Nebraska, but became of age in Missouri. He was in Gentry County, Missouri, at the beginning of the Civil war and in 1862 joined Company E of the First Missouri Cavalry of the Missouri State Militia under Captain Joseph H. Little and Colonel McFarran. This regiment acted under special orders for the guarding of the state after the Confederates had been driven off, and for a time it was stationed along the St. Joseph and Hannibal Railway, and had one small skirmish at Kirksville. They were then south of the Missouri River, and remained at Lexington or in that vicinity until Mr. Davidson was discharged after having served eleven months.

After his military experience Mr. Davidson sought entirely new fields of adventure. With an ox team and wagon he joined a caravan in Nebraska bound for Montana. His mother and sister accompanied him on this eventful journey. They were part of a train consisting of about sixty wagons, and followed the Platte River route, through Wyoming, through Bridger Pass until reaching the road leading from Utah to Virginia City, and arrived in the latter place without delay or special incident. While there Mr. Davidson engaged in mining, but his prospecting brought him little substantial results. Dissatisfied with that section of the West, he left after a year and in the fall of 1864 arrived in Humboldt County, California. He engaged in stock raising with a location near the Eel River, and spent about nine years in that location with considerable profit.

In 1873 Mr. Davidson returned to Missouri, his mother making the trip over the railroad, which had been constructed since they made their overland journey. On returning to Missouri Mr. Davidson bought land, a partly improved tract of 160 acres, in Section 18, including the old Smithton Village in Worth County. There he began his industrious career as a Missouri farmer. His home has been in that vicinity with the exception of eight years spent on the Kansas frontier in Sheridan County. He located there in 1890, bought a claim and engaged in both farming and stock raising. The decade of the '90s was a somewhat disastrous period for the farmers of Western Kansas, and in all the eight years spent there Mr. Davidson succeeded in raising only two crops, and was finally compelled to leave owing to the persistent drought. The chief advantage of his residence there was that it enabled him to keep his children in school at Hoxie, near his home, and in the State Normal School. Returning to Worth County in 1898, Mr. Davidson moved to his present farm in Section 18, and his residence stands not far from the old townsite of Smithton, the former county seat, the site of which is included in his land. It is a matter of interest to note that Smithton was named in honor of Mrs. Davidson's father, Eli Smith, some facts concerning whose interesting career as a pioneer in this section of Missouri are found in succeeding paragraphs. At the present time Mr. Davidson owns and operates 500 acres in this part of the state, raising grain and stock.

Mr. Davidson throughout his career has endeavored to perform those duties and obligations which are the part of good citizenship. His first presidential vote was cast for Abraham Lincoln in 1864, and he has never wavered from that political allegiance and has taken little stock in either the populist or free silver movements or the still later progressive propaganda. As to religious matters, one of his parents was a Baptist and the other a Christian, and he has compromised by choice of the Presbyterian faith, in which he has long held membership. Fraternally he is a Mason.

Mr. Davidson was married at Independence, in Jackson County, Missouri, March 15, 1871, to Miss Esther Mary Smith, eldest daughter of Eli Smith, who came from New Lexington, Ohio, May 7, 1857.

Eli Smith was of English descent, his father, James Smith, having come to America in an early day and settled in Washington County, Ohio, where he was married. Eli Smith was one of nine children. In 1842 he married Sarah Stewart. The only child, Arthur Smith, born to this marriage, died in 1879, at Omaha, Nebraska. Sarah (Stewart) Smith died in 1846. In 1847 Eli Smith married Miss Julia Ann Skinner. The four children of this marriage were: Esther Mary, Mrs. William Davidson, who was born in 1847 and died in 1910; Sarah Leanna, who is Mrs. H. C. Miller and lives at Seneca, Missouri; Julia Amanda, who is Mrs. T. A. Chase and lives at Pasadena, California; and James Jefferson, who died in infancy.

In 1857 Eli Smith moved from New Lexington, Ohio, and built a home on the Middle Fork branch of Grand River, situated in Worth County, Missouri. The site of this home later became the first county seat of Worth County. It was called Smithton in honor of its founder. Smithton remained the county seat of Worth County until about the close of the Civil war, when the county offices were removed to a more central location, at the site of the present Grant City. During the strenuous days that preceded the Civil war Smithton was the principal trading point in Worth County. The closest railroad was at St. Joseph, and all supplies were freighted overland from that point. Eli Smith was prominent in the pioneer affairs of North Missouri, both in its political and civil life. In the early part of the Civil war he enlisted in Colonel Cranor's regiment and held the office of quartermaster. Every movement for the betterment of North Missouri found Mr. Smith in the front ranks. As a temperance man he was uncompromising in his belief. After the close of the Civil war Mr. Smith was made a member of the assembly which drafted the new constitution of Missouri.

In 1863 Mrs. William Davidson, then fifteen years of age, moved with her father to Lexington, Missouri, where Eli Smith engaged in the mercantile business. There Mrs. Davidson received a high school education, subsequently supplemented by a course in a private institution of learning. Esther Mary Smith, whose death, as noted, occurred in 1910, possessed in a high degree the sterling qualities of her father. No mother ever showed a more unselfish devotion to her family and felt more keenly the responsibilities of home. Unselfish to a fault, ever ready to assist in the relief of human suffering, she lived a life of beauty and love that only her family and friends could appreciate. She was a member of the Presbyterian faith, in early life took an active interest in church affairs, but with the increasing cares and responsibilities of her home exemplified there her beautiful Christian spirit and lived always a life of high ideals and beauty of character.

While Mr. Davidson may regard with considerable satisfaction his experiences and accomplishments in the world of material effort, he is justified in taking special pride in his children, all of whom are now useful members of society and employed as workers and home makers in different parts of the country. The children are: Arthur D., Chase E., Phebe E., Clarence, Grace L., Frank L., Elmer S., Muriel and Kathryn.

Arthur D. Davidson, the oldest, was born in Worth County, Missouri, July 30, 1873, and died August 18, 1905, at the age of thirty-two. His boyhood days were spent in Missouri and Kansas, and in the latter state he attended high school and at the age of twenty took a commercial course in a Denver business college, graduating, and then returning to Hoxie, Kansas, and was employed for two or three years as bookkeeper in a bank, finally went to Oklahoma and was manager of a company store at that place, and the last year of his life was spent as cashier of a bank in Oklahoma. Phebe E. Davidson, who is the wife of Russell Green, of Midfields, Texas, was born in Worth County, spent her early life there, attended school at Hoxie, Kansas, and at Omaha, and after graduating from the normal school at Emporia, Kansas, engaged in teaching until her marriage. Chase E. Davidson, who is now a merchant at Worth and married Lucy Wilson, spent his boyhod days in Missouri and Kansas, attended a Kansas high school, later acquired a commercial training, and after returning to Worth was employed for a time as manager of a lumber company and finally engaged in the hardware trade. The son William C. Davidson is now a civil engineer with R. J. Windrow, of Waco, Texas, engaged in the building of public highways. He was graduated from the University of Missouri in 1905 in the civil engineering course, took post-graduate studies in the same department, and was an instructor in the engineering department and was finally offered an assistant professorship. For two years he was connected with the office of the state highway engineer at Columbia (as deputy highway engineer) and from there went to Fort Worth, engaged in highway construction, and finally to Waco. The daughter Grace L. Davidson was born in Missouri, graduated from the Hoxie High School in Kansas, attended the Emporia Normal School, and for several years was a successful teacher. September 10, 1914, she married Mr. M. P. Hudson, of Grant City, Missouri. Frank L. Davidson, also a native of Missouri, received his education in Kansas and Missouri, graduating from the commercial college at St. Joseph, and is now identified with farming and stock raising. Elmer S. graduated from the St. Joseph Veterinary College and is now engaged in his profession and also in farming. Muriel Davidson, who is now the wife of Fred Burnham, of Jourdanton, Texas, was born in Kansas, graduated from the Grant City High School, attended the normal at Warrensburg, Missouri, and after her return home taught school until her marriage. The youngest child, Kathryn, was born in Kansas, is a graduate of the Grand City High School, attended Christian College at Columbia, and is now at home. The sons Frank L. and William C. are both members of the Masonic order, while Elmer and Chase are affiliated with the Independent Order of Odd Fellows. The daughters, Phebe E., Grace L., Muriel and Kathryn, are members of the Eastern Star.

D. HARFIELD DAVIS. One of the builders of Gallatin from the time it was a village sixty years ago, D. Harfield Davis is best known as a successful druggist, and has sold goods to a widening circle of patronage in this locality for nearly six decades. A merchant who stays in one community and succeeds through such a period of time necessarily possesses the best qualities of the business man—integrity, a settled policy of square dealing, and the ability to win and keep the confidence of his custom. The "good will" of such an establishment as the D. H. Davis Drug Company is worth more than capital and stock of many concerns. Along with the responsibilities of private business affairs, Mr. Davis has borne many of the burdens of citizenship and in the early days held such important offices as county treasurer and postmaster at Gallatin.

D. Harfield Davis was born in Clark County, Virginia, one mile from the famous Lord Fairfax estate and near the city of Winchester, April 26, 1836. His parents were Baalis and Eliza (Timberlake) Davis, both natives of Virginia, where the mother died. The Davis family is of English and Welsh extraction. Baalis Davis was a merchant in Virginia and in 1855, accompanied by his son, D. Harfield, came out to Missouri. There are comparatively few men still living who have an accurate recollection of conditions in this state sixty years ago. All of Northwest Missouri was then isolated from railway communication and the only methods of transportation were by river and by the crude overland wagon or horseback travel. In leaving Virginia the father and son traveled along the old Baltimore & Ohio Railway, the pioneer line, as far as Wheeling, West Virginia, and there embarked on a river boat, descending the Ohio River to Louisville, thence to St. Louis, and came up the Missouri by boat as far as the old river port of Waverly. At that point The New Lucy, on which they had traveled from St. Louis, lost her rudder and the rest of the trip to Gallatin was made with horse and wagon. On reaching Gallatin Baalis Davis and his son, D. Harfield, engaged in the drug trade, and with that line the son has been almost

continuously identified every subsequent year. Such a record in merchandising is rare in Missouri.

In 1855, when they arrived, Gallatin had less than three hundred
population, had one brick house and three stores. The entire county had
only one other center of population boasting a name, and the inhabitants
were very thinly scattered over this section. Most of the land was still
owned by the Government. There were as yet no railroads, and Daviess
County had no railroad, properly speaking, until 1878. About the time of
the Civil war the old Hannibal & St. Joseph Railway was constructed
across the northern part of the state, but that was some twenty miles
or more south of Gallatin. In the early days all goods brought to Gallatin were hauled in wagons drawn by oxen from Camden, on the Missouri
River, a distance of seventy-five miles.

In politics Mr. Davis has been a democrat, with continuous affiliation
through nearly fifteen presidential campaign periods. While his party
allegiance has been the same in fundamental principles, Mr. Davis was
always a strong Union man and a supporter of the Federal Government
during the time before, and during and after the Civil war, when differences of opinion were very marked in this locality. During the war Mr.
Davis served as treasurer of Daviess County. At one time more than
forty-six thousand dollars were in his keeping. A report came to him
that bushwhackers were liable to make a raid on the town at any time,
and in anticipation of such a raid he took the money from the treasurer's
vault and concealed it in the county jail, where it remained until all
danger had passed. It is interesting to recall the times of Mr. Davis'
service as postmaster of Gallatin. His first commission in that office
was given by President Buchanan, who, it will be remembered, was
elected President in 1856. During Lincoln's term Mr. Davis was continued in office, and also held office for a part of Grant's administration.
Mr. Davis was a member of the first Gallatin Common Council and
for many years served as a member of that body and also of the school
board. Another means of important service to the community was his
purchase in 1869 of the local newspaper known as the Torchlight, the
name of which he changed to the Gallatin Democrat. That journal is
now one of the oldest publications in Northwest Missouri, has been continuously under the name of the Democrat for forty-five years, and is
perhaps as widely read and as influential as any weekly paper in Northwest Missouri. Mr. Davis conducted the paper for three or four years,
and then sold it and returned to the drug trade, with which he has been
identified to the present time. His company is now the D. H. Davis
Drug Company, but its management he has turned over practically to
others.

There is no merchant in Daviess County who has so long continuously
been identified with business as Mr. Davis. His business record covers
fifty-nine years, and his acquaintance is probably more extensive than
that of any other man living in the county. He knows not only the
greater part of the people, both young and old, who are now active, but
his recollections teem with memories of men and women long since called
to their reward and who were conspicuous actors in the early days.
Practically every important change in the transformation of this country
from a wilderness has been witnessed by Mr. Davis, and he may properly
be referred to as one of the human landmarks of the county. Mr. Davis
is a bank director and owns considerable real estate in Gallatin.

In 1858 Mr. Davis married Miss America Osborne, of Gallatin, a
native of Covington, Indiana. She came to Daviess County, Missouri,
with her father, Jesse Osborne, who was one of the pioneers. The five

children of Mr. and Mrs. Davis were: Robert and William, now deceased; Madora, Frank and Virgie.

JOHN C. LEOPARD. When the institutions of law and order were all fresh and new in Daviess County, the name Leopard became identified with the local bar at Gallatin, and for practically sixty years the name has been associated with the best ability and achievements of the profession. Father and son, the men of this name have practiced law, and during his time the older Leopard was considered from many quarters to be the ablest legal figure in this part of the state. The present John C. Leopard has spent all his life in Gallatin, and for many years has represented the best in his profession, both so far as private success and accomplishment in the broader fields of citizenship are concerned.

John C. Leopard was born in Gallatin July 20, 1862, a son of John A. and Caroline (Cravens) Leopard. His father was born in Morgan County, Virginia, December 25, 1828, a son of Jacob Leopard, who spent all his life as a Virginia farmer. John A. Leopard died at Gallatin July 30, 1905. Caroline Cravens was born in Rockingham County, Virginia, November 24, 1824, and died at Gallatin February 13, 1913. Both branches, both the Leopards and Cravens, were people of foremost ability and of distinguished influence in Northwest Missouri.

The late John A. Leopard was graduated in law from Princeton University in 1850 and was one of the few college-bred men in the ranks of the early bar in Missouri. For two years following his graduation he was associated professionally with a member of the Schley family, related to Admiral Schley, at Frederickstown, Maryland. In 1852 John A. Leopard set out for the West, having chosen Missouri as the state in which he would gain the honors and perform the services connected with his profession. By river boat chiefly he made his way to Lexington, Missouri, and thence crossed the country to Gallatin, which was then a small village chiefly conspicuous as a county seat. He established a law practice in the same year and followed his profession very actively until after the war. He finally retired to a tract of land two and a half miles northeast of Gallatin, built a log house in the woods, improved the land and continued to live there until his death.

Fortunately it is not necessary to dismiss the character and career of this pioneer lawyer without a more adequate recognition of his attainments. At the time of his death in 1905 many tributes were paid to his memory by old friends and associates, and one that perhaps best estimates his position as a lawyer and his general character was that contained in a letter written by Judge H. C. McDougal of Kansas City, but formerly probate judge and one of the distinguished lawyers of Gallatin, and the essential paragraphs of this communication to the son of the late Mr. Leopard are herewith quoted:

"The beautiful and touching tribute to his memory by his old friend and mine, D. Harfield Davis, printed in the Gallatin papers, inadvertently omitted the mention of your father's splendid scholarship, iron logic and rare powers as an eloquent, forceful, persuasive speaker before courts, juries and people.

"When I came West and located in Gallatin nearly forty years ago, John A. Leopard was the ripest scholar, the widest, deepest, and best read member of the North Missouri bar. His diction, whether in private talk or speech, was always couched in strongest and clearest English, while his iron logic in its irresistible force and power was like unto that of John C. Calhoun. Then there was a musically rhythmic ring and swing to his lofty eloquence and pathos, his classical and poetical reference, that charmed every thoughtful listener.

"I have since heard many able lawyers, in many courts, but have always believed that the most pleasing, eloquent and instructive law argument to which I ever listened was one made by your father in a land case before Judge Robert L. Dodge, then presiding in the old Common Pleas Court at Gallatin, back in '69. To me the marvel of it all was that his subject was that dryest of all dry legal questions, 'covenants running with the land,' and I do not yet understand how his wisdom, learning and logic enabled him to make so much out of it, but I can never forget the effect of that argument on court and bar.

"The last public address I heard your father deliver was on the 4th of July, '71, in front of the old court house at Gallatin. The bitterness of the Civil war still rankled in the hearts of the people, but by his charming personality, musical eloquence and fervent, patriotic appeal for peace and good will, he won the hearts of all and made each hearer feel that he was a better citizen. Soon after this he retired from the activities of life, quit the town, went to the farm and there amid the quiet of the home and family, the books, the magazines, the woods, flowers and birds he loved so well, like the sage and philosopher that he was, he calmly and fearlessly awaited the closing scene.

"His heart and his manners were as simple and unaffected as those of a little child, yet he was a most unconscious and unambitious intellectual giant whose like has seldom come to gladden the soul and brighten the pathway of his friends."

In September, 1854, the late John A. Leopard married Caroline Cravens. She was a daughter of Dr. John and Ruhama (Douden) Cravens, both natives of Virginia, where they were married. From Virginia they emigrated with their eight children in 1836 to the Far West. In a covered wagon they arrived in Saline County, Missouri, in the vicinity of Marshall, and Doctor Cravens lived there for two years, farming and practicing medicine. In 1838 he brought his family to Daviess County and entered land formerly occupied by the Mormons, 2½ miles northwest of Gallatin, in the beautiful Grand River Valley. A part of that land is still owned by his descendants. It was then a wilderness, a scene of great natural beauty, with wild game in the woods in superabundance, and with Indians still common and familiar visitors. Doctor Cravens lived at a little locality where he established a village known as Cravensville. He was the prominent figure there, and in the early days Cravensville was a rival with Gallatin for the honors of the county seat. The question was settled in favor of Gallatin, and Cravensville has long been only a memory. In 1850 Doctor Cravens himself moved to Gallatin, and built there the first brick dwelling, and the only one in the little village for several years. That house stood on the corner where the Farmers Exchange Bank is now located. Doctor Cravens practiced medicine until the close of the Civil war and then moved to a farm north of town, where his son, E. H. Cravens, now lives, and resided there until his death in March, 1882. His wife died in November of the same year. Doctor Cravens was a whig in politics and active as long as that party existed. During the '40s he served as a member of the Daviess County Court.

John C. Leopard was fifth in a family of seven children. Oscar is now deceased, also Frank B., while Charles W. and Holmes D. are both bachelors living on the old home farm, and two died in infancy. John C Leopard received his early education in the country and in the Gallatin schools and for three years was a student in the Normal College at Kirksville. Under the distinguished direction of his father he took up the study of law, and in 1883 continued his studies with J. F. Hicklin. In October, 1885, he was admitted to practice after examination before a committee appointed by the judge of the local courts, and in 1886 entered a law office at Pattonsburg. Mr. Leopard practiced with growing success at Pattonsburg for ten years, and in 1896 his election to the office of prosecuting attorney of Daviess County caused him to remove to Gallatin, where he has since lived and practiced. He was reelected prosecuting attorney in 1898 and again in 1902 and served three terms. From 1908 to 1912 he gave a capable administration of the office of mayor of Gallatin, through two terms. In politics he has always been aligned with the democratic party. Mr. Leopard is affiliated with the Independent Order of Odd Fellows and is a member of the Gallatin Commercial Club.

On December 10, 1891, Mr. Leopard married Miss Mary E. May, of Pattonsburg, a daughter of Gabe May. Mr. and Mrs. Leopard have two children: Buel is now a teacher in the Jamesport High School, and Dean, who completed the classical course at the University of Missouri, is now in his second year in the law department of the State University, and has stood at the head of his class each year and is one of the editorial staff of the Missouri University Law Bulletin.

WESLEY L. ROBERTSON. In Daviess County not to know "Wes" Robertson, the able and popular editor of the Gallatin Democrat, is virtually to argue one's self unknown. Mr. Robertson has been identified with the newspaper business from his boyhood days, when he gained admission to the fraternity through dignified and indulgently arbitrary incumbency of the exalted post of "printer's devil," in which capacity he doubtless manifested the usual independence and unconscious malevolence ever associated with the office. He is familiar with all practical and executive details of the business and as a publisher and editor has been concerned with the issuing of newspapers in various Missouri towns and cities, and few representatives of the "art preservative" have a wider acquaintanceship in this state. Mr. Robertson has been engaged in the newspaper business for more than forty years and is consistently to be designated at the present time as one of its most progressive and effective exponents in Northwest Missouri, the while his attitude is significantly that of a loyal and public-spirited citizen who is every ready to exploit local interests and to lend his influence in the support of measures and enterprises tending to advance the general welfare of the community.

Mr. Robertson is a scion of staunch old American ancestry, and though his parents were natives of the State of New York he himself claims New England, that cradle of much of our national history, as the place of his nativity. He was born at South Coventry, Tolland County, Connecticut, on the 30th of June, 1850, and is a son of David and Caroline (Mitchell) Robertson. He was but seven years of age at the time of the death of his father, who was a farmer by vocation, and his early education was acquired in the country schools of his native state, this being supplemented by effective individual application and by the discipline of the newspaper office,—a training that has consistently been termed the equivalent of a liberal education. In 1865, at the age of fifteen years, Mr. Robertson accompanied his widowed mother on her removal to Missouri, and after passing one year on a farm in Putnam County they removed to Centerville, the judicial center of Appanoose County, Iowa, where, in 1868, Mr. Robertson gained his initial experience in connection with the mysteries of the "art preservative of all arts" by assuming the position of "devil" in the office of the Centerville Citizen. He became a skilled compositor and general workman, and in 1872 he gave inception to his independent career as a newspaper editor and publisher, by purchasing the plant and business of the Princeton

Advance, at Princeton, the county seat of Mercer County, Missouri. There he remained until 1881, when he sold the business and removed to Bethany, Harrison County, and became editor and publisher of the Bethany Broadaxe. In 1884 he disposed of his interests at that place and purchased the New Century, at Unionville, Putnam County. Of this property and business he later disposed and in 1886 he established his residence at Gallatin, Daviess County, where he purchased the Gallatin Democrat, of which he continued editor and publisher until 1894, when he sold out and again indulged his itinerant journalistic proclivities by removing to Plattsburg, Clinton County, where he appeared as editor and publisher of the Plattsburg Jeffersonian until 1897, when another sale and change was made by him. He purchased the West Plains Gazette, at the judicial center of Howell County, but only three weeks later he retired from this association, and in 1898 he returned to Gallatin, where he formed a partnership with Robert J. Ball, the present postmaster of this city, and effected the purchase of the Gallatin Democrat, of which he had previously been editor and publisher, as already noted in this context. With this paper he has since been identified as editor and publisher and he has brought the same up to high standard as an exponent of the interests of the city and county and of the principles of the democratic party, of which he has long been a prominent and influential representative in Missouri, each of the papers with which he has been identified having been published at a county seat, and no publisher of weekly newspapers in the state having been more zealous in the effective advocacy of the party cause. The Gallatin Democrat is one of the leading organs of the party in Northwest Missouri, is modern in letterpress and general makeup, is ably edited and receives a consistent advertising patronage, the value of which is fortified by its circulation, which is now fully three thousand copies. The news and job departments of the plant have an excellent and up-to-date equipment, including a recently installed typesetting machine, and the business has been made distinctly prosperous and profitable under the able management of Mr. Robertson, whose personal success and advancement have been won entirely through his own ability and efforts, as he has been dependent upon his own resources from boyhood. In this connection it should be noted that his mother passed the closing years of her life at Centerville, Iowa, and was about sixty years of age when she was summoned to eternal rest.

Mr. Robertson has been an appreciative and valued member of the Missouri State Historical Society from the time of its organization and is at the present time a member of its executive committee. He is specially prominent and popular among the representatives of the newspaper fraternity in his home state, this being indicated by his service as president of the Northwest Missouri Press Association and as president of the Missouri Press Association, in each of which bodies he is still an active and influential figure. For five years Mr. Robertson was secretary of the Missouri State Board of Charities, as a member of which he was appointed by Governor A. M. Dockery. He is sincere, earnest, broadminded and genial, resolute in the upholding of his convictions, and tolerant in his judgment, so that he naturally has gained and retained a host of friends in the state that has so long represented his home. Mr. Robertson is a prominent member of the Gallatin Commercial Club, is affiliated with the Independent Order of Odd Fellows, and both he and his wife hold membership in the Methodist Episcopal Church South.

In 1872 Mr. Robertson wedded Miss Martha Mitchell, who died in 1880. They became the parents of three sons, one of whom died in infancy; Albert M. is editor of the Capital Democrat, at Tishomingo,

Oklahoma, and Gay R., who was graduated at the University of Missouri, is a mechanical engineer by profession and is now in the employ of the Atlanta Ice & Coal Company, of Atlanta, Georgia. In 1883 was solemnized the marriage of Mr. Robertson to Miss Eppie Davidson, of Gainesville, Texas. They have no children.

ROBERT J. BALL. In his rise from the position of "devil" in a printing shop to that of postmaster of Gallatin, Daviess County, to the half-ownership of the Gallatin Democrat, the presidency of the Commercial Club of this city, and various other positions of trust and importance, Robert J. Ball has given a notable illustration of the exercise of American energy, ability, integrity and superior mental attainments. While it has been his fortune to be identified with Gallatin during the period of its greatest growth and development, much of this development has come as a result of his contributions to its interests. At any rate, he fills a large and influential place in the community.

Mr. Ball was born at Gallatin, Daviess County, Missouri, May 25, 1873, and is a son of Alonzo Conrad and Elizabeth Frances (Boggs) Ball, natives of Kentucky. Alonzo Conrad Ball was born March 8, 1823, at Lexington, Kentucky, and in 1854 came to Missouri, settling in Boone County, where he resided one year, his advent in Gallatin occurring in May, 1855. His ancestors on his father's side were of Irish descent, while his mother was of German descent and bore the maiden name of Sheeley. Mr. Ball's grandfather, the great-grandfather of Robert J. Ball, was a Revolutionary soldier, enlisted under Washington in Virginia, and General Washington's mother was a Ball and of Irish ancestry. Alonzo C. Ball was married at Richmond, Kentucky, in 1849, to Elizabeth Frances Boggs, and the trip to Missouri was made partly by boat and partly overland. Mr. Ball was a carpenter and contractor, and one of the first of his vocation to come to Daviess County, his shop for many years being located on the southwest corner of the square, where the Fitterer grocery now stands. That he was highly esteemed in the community in which his home was made for many years is evidenced by a tribute by one of his friends, which appeared in the newspapers of Gallatin, and which said, in part, as follows: "Our friend Ball, with the impetuosity of the Celtic race and breathing the chivalric air of the blue grass of Kentucky, could not be anything else than a unique character. Whilst Mr. Ball has occupied no public positions of trust, in his sphere of action he has been an independent, fearless character, having ideas and views of his own, a strong will and inflexible purpose to do and say what he believes to be right, regardless of all consequences. For us to know a man we must meet him upon a common plane and get in close communion with him and in touch with his aspirations and trend of mind. We have known A. C. Ball forty-nine years, always found him to be frank and outspoken. If a friend, a true one, and always ready to punish an enemy and had no compromise to make. A typical Kentuckian, strong in his likes and dislikes." Mr. Ball died May 1, 1908, and interment was made at the Brown Cemetery, his comrades of Surgeon John Cravens Camp, U. C. V., acting as honorary pallbearers. Mrs. Ball passed away October 19, 1901, having been the mother of nine children, as follows: Mollie, Sallie, Frank C. and Willie, who are deceased; John H., who is engaged in contracting and building at Bridgewater, Massachusetts; Mrs. Lydia Thomas, a resident of Gallatin; Mrs. Maggie B. Edwards of Quincy, Illinois; L. D., who is proprietor of the hotel at Trenton, Missouri; and Robert J.

Robert J. Ball received his education in the graded and high schools of Gallatin and in 1887 entered upon his career as "devil" in the office of the Gallatin Democrat, of which Wes L. Robertson was owner and editor. From the time of his first connection with this paper a warm regard between employer and employe has been maintained. Mr. Ball rose to be foreman on the paper, then superintendent of the plant, and in 1898 bought a half-interest. As his partner, Uncle Wes Robertson, expresses it: "Mr. Ball reached the point in salary where he (Mr. Robertson) figured it would be better for him to sell a half interest and let Ball help foot the bills." With the exception of a short period when Mr. Robertson was identified with other ventures, the partnership has continued uninterruptedly to the present.

Long an active worker in democratic politics, in 1913 Mr. Ball was chosen postmaster of Gallatin by Hon. J. W. Alexander, and since May 1st of that year has ably discharged the duties of that office. His administration has been marked by much improvement in the service, and he is proving one of the most efficient and popular officials that Gallatin has known. For some years Mr. Ball was secretary of the Democratic County Committee. Fraternally he belongs to the Royal Arch Masons, the Independent Order of Odd Fellows, the Modern Woodmen of America and the Woodmen of the World. He is a member of the Northwest Missouri Press Association and its first vice president, and in January, 1915, will become its president by succession. He also holds membership in the Young Men's Christian Association and the Gallatin Commercial Club, and in 1914 was appointed president of the latter organization. The following is quoted from the Gallatin North Missourian, issue of November 19, 1914: "From the 'devil' in a print shop to the presidency of the Gallatin Commercial Club. That is what we call making good, and such was the sentiment of every member of the club at the 6:30 luncheon on Tuesday evening, when Robert J. Ball, postmaster and junior editor of the Gallatin Democrat, was chosen the active head of the Gallatin Commercial Club, succeeding C. M. Harrison. The committee is to be congratulated upon their selection, as a better man could not have been chosen. Ball is a live wire, energetic, a tireless worker and a splendid fellow. The club can rest assured that their interests will be carefully safeguarded and that the organization will move along with plenty of the right kind of enthusiasm and spirit. Mr. Ball is a 'gingery' man and whatever he undertakes he puts 'ginger' into it and makes it a success. Then, too, he is self made and has come up the line through his own efforts."

On March 5, 1896, Mr. Ball was married to Miss Theo M. Welden, of Gallatin, a daughter of C. H. Welden, a pioneer, ex-county official and prominent citizen of Daviess County. Four children have been born to Mr. and Mrs. Ball: Marjorie, Eleanor, Robert Welden and Conrad Luckey. Mr. Ball is a member of the Methodist Episcopal Church South.

Too much credit cannot be given to Mr. Ball. He started at the bottom, without means, and through thrift, intelligence, perseverance and clean living has risen to a place high in the esteem of his fellow citizens. It is to such men that the community must look for its further development.

JOHN W. McCLASKEY. In the spring of 1914 the citizens of Gallatin chose to the office of mayor a local business man who for upwards of thirty years had been known for his integrity and energy in pushing his individual enterprises, and it was on the basis of his thorough fitness for the office rather than any activity in politics that he was chosen to give Gallatin a thoroughly businesslike administration of its municipal affairs. Mayor McClaskey has spent practically all his life in Daviess County, represents families that were associated with pioneer things in this locality, and his own career has added some important particulars to the family record.

John W. McClaskey was born at Auldberry Grove, in Daviess County, October 4, 1851, a son of Albert and Martha (Koger) McClaskey. Both his parents were natives of Kentucky. When Daviess County was still a wilderness, in 1838, there arrived as one of the pioneers James Koger, grandfather of the Gallatin mayor. He stopped at a place five miles north of Gallatin, in the midst of the woods, and made entry to and purchased 160 acres of land from the Government. Then followed the building of a log house in the midst of the timber, the felling of countless trees to make an area for his plow, and gradual improvement along one line and another until he had perfected a homestead sufficient to provide all the material wants of the family. James Koger was a good business man, increased his land holdings, and lived in that locality until his death about 1859, his wife having died in 1856. The old Koger homestead is now owned and occupied by a grandson. All the twelve children in the Koger family are now deceased except Joseph Koger, of Gallatin, and Mrs. Martha McClaskey died November 30, 1906. The McClaskey family has an interesting origin. Two brothers came from Scotland and crossed from the Atlantic seaboard over the mountains into Kentucky about the time Daniel Boone led the emigration into the western wilderness. It is believed that nearly all the McClaskeys in America are descended from either one or the other of these two brothers. Students of genealogy have come to the conclusion that the original name was Claskey, who were established in the lowlands of Scotland, and later a branch of the stock went into the Scotch highlands and in order to distinguish themselves from the lowlanders took the prefix "Mc" and thus the American McClaskeys are descended from a highland clan of Scotland. It was about 1845 that Albert McClaskey, with his brother, Joseph, emigrated from Kentucky to Daviess County, Missouri. These McClaskey brothers were millers rather than farmers, and they added to the pioneer industry of Daviess County by establishing a sawmill at Auldberry, while later Albert operated a mill in Livingston County and lived there several years. In 1853 he went out to California as a gold seeker, making the trip overland, and died there about eighteen months after he left Missouri. Albert McClaskey and Martha Koger were married in Daviess County, and the latter lived continuously in this county from the arrival of her parents in 1838 until her death in 1906. The Gallatin mayor was the second of three children. His sister, Eliza Jane, first married Mr. Duskin and is now the wife of Joseph Lee, of Gallatin. His brother is James M. McClaskey, of Gallatin.

John W. McClaskey grew up in the country district of Daviess County, and has some interesting memories of the first schoolhouses that he attended. The first temple of learning in which he was a pupil was a log cabin, at one end of which was a broad fireplace, and at the other end a log was left out of the wall to admit light and air. The floor was covered with puncheons, and the boys and girls sat on benches which were heavy slabs supported by pins driven into the under side. All the furnishing was crude, and he wrote his first copy lesson with an old-fashioned quill pen. During his school days and early youth he lived at home with his mother, who owned a farm, and when not in school was active in performing the chores and doing the work in the fields and at planting and harvest times. When he had learned all the local schools could supply in the way of education, he secured a certificate and took up the work of teacher, which he followed during the winter seasons, and continued to lend a hand at the farm during the summers.

Mr. McClaskey established a home of his own by his marriage on

August 22, 1876, to.Miss Virginia A. Smith. She was a daughter of George A. Smith, a resident of West Virginia, and was visiting relatives in Daviess County when she met and married Mr. McClaskey. After his marriage Mr. McClaskey began farming as a renter, and for several years continued to combine the vocations of agriculturist and school teacher. In 1881 he bought a farm four miles northwest of Gallatin, and conducted his own place until 1886. In that year he sold out, moved to Gallatin, and after one year in the lumber business, began buying and shipping live stock. In 1893 he established a bus and transfer line and was in that business until 1910. For the past five years Mr. McClaskey has been in the grain, feed and milling business.

Mrs. McClaskey died September 20, 1888. She was the mother of four children: Forest D., Holly, Everett C. and Cloris. Holly and Cloris are now deceased. On January 8, 1909, Mr. McClaskey married Mrs. Fannie Estis Smith. By this marriage there is a daughter, Martha Y., born in January, 1910. Mr. McClaskey is a member of the Methodist Church, while his wife is a Baptist. He has been associated with the Masonic fraternity since 1883.

While in politics his support has been regularly given to the democratic party since casting his first vote forty years ago, Mr. McClaskey has never in any way indicated a desire for office, and it was only at the solicitation of his many friends that he consented to become a candidate for mayor, and all citizens have reason for congratulation on his election for a term of two years.

SAMUEL RATHBUN. Almost a lifelong resident of Caldwell County and for many years a progressive farmer in Davis Township, Samuel Rathbun has enjoyed the best elements of success, having acquired a good home, having given his family the comforts of living and education, and having steered an honorable and straightforward course throughout his own career. Mr. Rathbun owns and occupies a fine homestead of 222 acres in Davis Township, and it is land on which he was born, and which his father entered from the Government, paying 12½ cents an acre. A fair valuation of the land at the present time would be over a hundred dollars an acre. Mr. Rathbun has the distinction of having been born in a log cabin, and that was the typical home in Caldwell County sixty or seventy years ago. The log cabin has long since disappeared, and in its place is now found a handsome modern country home of six rooms, furnished and equipped with taste and comfort. A beautiful lawn, with shade and evergreen trees and flowers are among the attractive features which are at once noted by the passing traveler. Other features of the equipment are commodious barns and sheds, and the farm is divided between pasture, meadow and grain fields, with thirty acres of good native timber, furnishing abundance of fuel. It is a model rural home, and there Mr. Rathbun and his good wife enjoy the comforts of life. As a farmer he has paid much attention to the raising of high grade hogs and cattle, and his success illustrates what can be done by the agriculturist in Northwest Missouri.

Samuel Rathbun was born in Caldwell County, October 20, 1847. His father, Allen Rathbun, was one of the earliest pioneers, having come to Caldwell County in 1837, about the time the Mormons were driven out of this section of Missouri. He took up a tract of Government land, and the title to that farm has never been changed in name since it was deeded direct from the Government.. Allen Rathbun was born in Cayuga County, New York, and comes of a family of mingled Scotch and English descent. Members of the Rathbun family have participated in practically all the wars of the American nation, beginning with the Indian troubles

MR. AND MRS. SAMUEL RATHBUN AND DAUGHTER, MRS. LULU HUDSON

and in the Revolution, the War of 1812, the Mexican war, and the Civil war. From New York the family moved to Ohio spent some years there, where the father of Allen Rathbun died and is buried. Allen Rathbun married in Ohio for his first wife Mary Ann Edmonds, and the four children of that union are all now deceased. His second wife was Elizabeth Anderson, a woman of much strength and nobility of character, who became the mother of five children. The son, John, was a soldier in the Thirty-third Missouri Infantry, and gave up his life for his country in 1863, when only eighteen years of age. The daughter, Martha Phillips, is now deceased. The son, Robert, is also deceased, leaving Samuel the only survivor. Allen Rathbun was born in 1805 and died on May 17, 1862, and his second wife, Elizabeth, was born in 1819. Allen Rathbun's third marriage was to Mary Mann, on August 16, 1855. The one daughter of this union, Sarah L. Phares, is still living, and twin boys died in infancy. Allen Rathbun was a man of intelligence and good judgment; his word was regarded as sacred as his bond, and in the early community of Caldwell County, where he lived, he enjoyed the highest esteem of all who knew him.

Samuel Rathbun grew up on the old homestead, was taught the value of hard work, and has always been a useful and independent member of the community. Mr. Rathbun recalls the first school he attended, which was kept in an old log house, with slab benches, a puncheon floor, and a fireplace at one end. There he received instruction in the three R's, and has since advanced his education by generous reading and by dealings with men and affairs. Mr. Rathbun has been frequently honored with positions of trust and responsibility in his community, and served for several years as a justice of the peace and kept a court before which all men were equal and treated with absolute impartiality and fairness. In 1866 Mr. Rathbun left Caldwell County and spent a couple of years in farming in Dallas County, Iowa, but with that exception his residence has been practically uninterrupted in Caldwell County.

In 1871 Mr. Rathbun married Miss Martha F. Thompson. Her father was Samuel Thompson, who came to Missouri from Indiana and made a fighting record as a soldier of the Mexican war. He also had two sons who were soldiers in the Civil war, named Samuel and William A. Mr. and Mrs. Rathbun are the parents of a daughter, Lulu, who was married October 29, 1914, to Ernest Hudson, and they now reside at the Rathbun homestead. A son, William Albert, was born September 1, 1873, and died November 20, 1878.

Mr. Rathbun cast his first presidential vote for General Grant in 1868, and has never deviated from the strict party lines maintained by the grand old party. He has throughout his life believed in and practiced the golden rule, and his home has always been a center of attractive hospitality. He is a member of the Methodist Church, while his wife and daughter belong to the Christian denomination.

GEORGE W. LOCKRIDGE. Probably no man in official service has done more for Daviess County during the last fifteen or twenty years than George W. Lockridge, who is the county surveyor and highway engineer. From early youth he showed a genius for mathematics, and is a thoroughly grounded and practical engineer, and is able not only to plan but to execute the construction of any work from a modern highway to a complex river bridge. He is a past master in his profession, and through it has contributed much to public improvement, especially in that important department, first-class highways. His home is at Gallatin.

His family has been identified with Northwest Missouri from the time when Daviess County was a wilderness except in the few localities improved by the vanguard of settlers. George W. Lockridge was born November 26, 1871, on his father's old farm three miles north of Jamesport, in Jamesport Township. His parents were John and Caroline Poage (Miller) Lockridge, both now living retired in Jamesport. The former was born in Jamesport Township in 1846 and the latter in Rappahannock County, Virginia, in 1845. The paternal great-grandfather, Lancelot Lockridge, was a native of Virginia and of an old family of that province, where he owned many slaves and employed them to work his extensive plantation. Grandfather Andrew Lockridge, who was born and married in Rappahannock County, about seventy years ago put his possessions in a covered wagon and made the long migration over the mountains and through the valleys and across the plains of the Central West to Daviess County. The land he located and secured from the Government in section 15 of Jamesport Township, is still owned by his descendants. There the grandparents spent their remaining years, and both died in the same year, in 1854.

At that time John Lockridge was eight years old, and during the following years the orphan boy lived at different times with Judge Robert C. Williams, whose wife was an aunt, and also with his uncle, Nathan Gillilan. To escape the turmoil and discord of the Civil war he accompanied his sister and brother-in-law to Des Moines, returning to Missouri when the war was over. He had then nearly reached his majority, and while living with his sister made plans to take possession of the 100 acres which he had inherited from his father. The lumber for his first house, a story and a half structure, 16 by 32 feet, he hauled by wagon from Chillicothe, a distance of thirty-two miles. He possessed the industry and business judgment required for success in farming, and his prosperity is measured in part by the fact that he increased his original 100 acres to 600, comprising one of the best country estates in Daviess County. A large part of this he has since distributed among his children, and is now enjoying the fruits of a well spent career in ease.

John Lockridge married a Daviess County girl whose family is likewise of pioneer stock and old Virginia ancestry. Her parents, James W. and Harriet P. (Allen) Miller, were born in Rappahannock County, Virginia, and some years after their marriage came out to Daviess County, where their settlement was made subsequent to the Lockridges. Their location was on wild land in Jamesport Township, but after several years James W. Miller removed to Jamesport and became a clerk in the old Etter store. From there he went to Gallatin, and was for years the trusted and right-hand man in Etter's One Price Cash Store. The only important break in his long mercantile experience was during the years from 1883 to 1886, when he devoted himself to the careful handling of the county clerk's office.

Both the Lockridge and Miller families were of the old school Presbyterian faith, and in politics all the men adhered to the democratic party. The seven children of John Lockridge and wife are: Charles Sidney, a farmer in Jamesport Township; George W.; Harry Tate, a farmer in Jamesport Township; Homer, farming in the same locality; Mrs. Hattie Hill, of Grand River Township; Walter, who occupies the old homestead; and John Franklin, who is chief train dispatcher with one of the Northwestern railroads, his headquarters being at Pocatello, Idaho.

On the old homestead in Jamesport Township stood a schoolhouse attended by all the Lockridge children. The first teacher whom George W. knew was John C. Leopard. He took the usual curriculum of a country school, being noted for proficiency in arithmetic, and later was a student in the Gallatin High School. At the age of nineteen he took an examination and was granted a teacher's certificate, with which qualification he soon afterward appeared as the master at the Cole Springs School, and later had charge of the Griffith and Smith schools. His experience was then varied with employment in a drug store at Bancroft. In pursuit of more knowledge, he next entered the Grand River College at Gallatin, then under Rev. Dr. Pope Yeman, a noted Baptist clergyman. In the middle of his first term he definitely determined upon civil engineering as his career, and at once entered the State School of Mines, at Rolla, where he was a student 2½ years, completing the general mathematical course.

With this training, on his return to Daviess County he at once fitted into an unexpired term of county surveyor, was elected at the next regular election and continued in the office for eight consecutive years. As a side line, during two years of that time, he taught mathematics in Grand River College. His early experience in a drug store may have influenced his next move. After passing the examination before the state board and being qualified as a registered pharmacist, he formed a partnership with Dr. M. A. Smith, and for about eight years conducted a drug business in Gallatin, finally selling his interests in 1906. Going to Cameron he remodeled and opened a drug store for other parties, and was getting $20 a week for his work. In April, 1908, he resigned the position to begin work with the Dildine Bridge & Construction Company of Hannibal, which also had offices in Cameron. His first employment with this firm was in the capacity of a common laborer, but in a very short time he was promoted to foreman, and then went to Hannibal as superintendent of construction in the steel mills. He resigned this to become superintendent of construction on the rock road then being built between Hannibal and Palmyra. When this work was finished, he returned to Daviess County and resided at Pattonsburg until again elected to the office of county surveyor in 1912, with a majority of over nine hundred votes. Mr. Lockridge has saved the county thousands of dollars each year as a result of his expert knowledge, which enables him to do his own designing, purchasing of materials, and supervising of construction. He draws all plans for bridges constructed in Daviess County.

By marriage Mr. Lockridge is also connected with an early Daviess County family. His wife before her marriage, which was celebrated June 20, 1900, was Miss Minnie Frances Koger, of Pattonsburg. William G. Koger, her father, was born in Marion Township of Daviess County in 1851, and was the grandson on his mother's side of David Groomer. David Groomer, who came from Pennsylvania to Daviess County in pioneer times, is said to have had on his arrival only an old pony and $10 in cash. That was the beginning of a career which made him one of the wealthiest men in this part of Missouri, and at the time of his death he had 8,000 acres in Daviess County. Of this handsome estate 1,800 acres were bequeathed to his two grandsons, who had lived with him from early childhood, one of them being William G. Koger. The latter, who is now living retired in Pattonsburg, is a director of the Daviess County Savings Bank there. Mr. and Mrs. Lockridge are the parents of two children: John William, born in 1903, and Mary Frances, born in 1908.

Politically Mr. Lockridge has kept the same faith as his family, and has worked and voted with the democratic party. Originally a Presbyterian, he is now a Baptist, which is the church of his wife. He is a member of the Gallatin Commercial Club, of the Association of Highway Engineers, of the National Association of Retail Druggists, and affiliates with the lodge and chapter and Eastern Star of Masonry, with the Knights of Pythias and the Order of Yeomen.

Mr. Lockridge is a member and secretary of the highway commission on the county seat highway, a sub-member of the committee of the Omaha and St. Louis trail, a state highway. His position of highway engineer is by appointment from the county board, and its duties fit in well with those of county surveyor.

ELWOOD D. MANN. As a Gallatin business man Elwood D. Mann's career covers more than thirty years, and in that time he rose from the position of a clerk to president of a bank, and is now an active member of the firm of Cruzen & Mann, handling loans, abstracts and insurance. He represents the pioneer families of Mann and Drummond in Daviess County, and their residence in this section of Northwest Missouri covers nearly seventy years.

Elwood D. Mann was born in Union Township of Daviess County, December 2, 1861. He is a son of Matthew R. and Margaret A. (Drummond) Mann, and his two grandfathers were Jonathan R. Mann and James P. Drummond. All these older members of the respective families were natives of Virginia. Both the Manns and Drummonds came to Daviess County about the same time, James P. Drummond having brought his family out to this section about 1847 or 1848, and in Union Township he took up a tract of Government land, but subsequently removed to Jackson Township, where for nearly fifty years he was an honored and useful citizen. His death occurred at Jamesport. On coming to Daviess County both these families settled in the midst of the woods and while transforming a forest into cultivated fields they endured and experienced the numberless incidents of pioneer life. Matthew R. Mann came to Missouri when about twenty-four years of age. His wife was brought to Missouri as a child of ten years and grew up in Daviess County, and was married there. Matthew R. Mann was an active farmer, and after his marriage continued to live in Union Township for many years, and finally retired and lived in Gallatin until his death on December 13, 1903. His widow is still living. Elwood D. Mann was the second of three children, the other two being Joseph A. of Gallatin and James W., who died October 10, 1903.

It was on a Daviess County farm in the district schools that Elwood D. Mann had his early training, and on May 1, 1883, he began his real business career as clerk in a grocery store at Gallatin. On January 1, 1886, nearly three years later, he became associated with Oliver P. Walters in the hardware business, and it was as a successful merchant that he was best known in that city until 1893. In that year he turned his attention to banking, being elected cashier of the Farmers Exchange Bank, and subsequently was promoted first to the office of vice president and later to president, and altogether his banking experience covered seventeen years. In 1910 Mr. Mann engaged in the loan, abstract and insurance business, and that is the line along which he now concentrates his energies. On January 1, 1912, he formed his present partnership with N. G. Cruzen, a lawyer, under the firm name of Cruzen & Mann. Mr. Mann looks after the business end of the concern while his partner attends to the legal matters.

In 1883 Mr. Mann married Miss May Miller. One child was born of this union, named Robert. Mrs. Mann died in February, 1902, and in the following year he married Miss Bessie Gillilan, a daughter of W. J. Gillilan, of Jamesport, who was a pioneer in that locality.

Mr. Mann is a member of the Methodist Episcopal Church South, and has fraternal affiliations with the Masons and the Independent Order of

Odd Fellows. At the present time he is one of the executive committee of the Gallatin Commercial Club. In political matters he supports the democratic party, and has given some valuable service to his home city as a member of the council. He is one of the leading and reliable business men of Daviess County, and highly respected as a citizen.

JOHN SEBASTIAN BROOKSHIER. The present postmaster at Lock Springs, John S. Brookshier has lived in this part of Missouri all his life, represents two families that were among the pioneers of Livingston County, and in his business career has been identified with farming and with the management of a factory in Lock Springs, and in public affairs he has a number of times been honored with places of trust and responsibility.

John Sebastian Brookshier was born on a farm in Livingston County, Missouri, January 26, 1860. His father, Leander Green Brookshier was born in Missouri February 22, 1839, and his mother whose maiden name was Mary Louisa Minnick was born in Virginia in 1839. Both the Brookshiers and the Minnicks came into Northwest Missouri during the early days and founded homes in Livingston and Daviess counties.

John Sebastian Brookshier grew up on a farm in Livingston county, obtained an education in the country schools, and after the close of school days engaged in farming with his father until the age of twenty-one. He then started out for himself, first as a farm hand, and after four years, in 1883, began working for Francis Cook in Lock Springs. There he learned the trade of handle maker, and in 1888 bought the shop of Mr. Cook, and for the succeeding ten years made that an important local industry, and manufactured many thousand handles of all kinds each year. In 1898 Mr. Brookshier resumed farming, and continued actively along that line until 1913, and still has farming interests to which he gives his attention. In 1913 Mr. Brookshier was appointed postmaster of Lock Springs, and is now handling that office in a thorough and systematic manner.

As a democrat, his first local office was constable, to which he was elected about 1894 and served four years. In 1898 Mr. Brookshier was elected a justice of the peace, and was reelected for two terms, serving until 1904. He is a member of the Cumberland Presbyterian Church and fraternally is affiliated with the Blue Lodge in Masonry and with the Modern Woodmen of America.

On December 24, 1885, Mr. Brookshier married Miss Julia R. Yeager. Her parents were Minor W. and Emma (Woodward) Yeager. Mr. and Mrs. Brookshier have four sons, named Robert E., Harry Lee, Ralph O. and Walter F. The son Robert married Stella Doak of Texas, while the rest of the sons live at home with their parents.

ISAAC LUTHER WADE. Since 1903 cashier of the Bank of Lock Springs, Mr. Wade is a public spirited and successful business man of that community, with which he has been identified excepting for about two years since 1889. He began life as a telegraph operator, was in the railway service for a number of years, and he has had a steady progress from small beginnings to a degree of accomplishment which put him in the list with the leading men of Southern Daviess County.

Isaac Luther Wade was born in Clinton County, Illinois, March 18, 1860, and his family are a combination of Irish and German stocks, and their early place of residence was Pennsylvania. His father, John Wade, was born in Pennsylvania in 1838, a son of John and Mary (Eshelman) Wade. both natives of Pennsylvania. John Wade, the grandfather, learned the shoemaking trade in Pennsylvania, and then moved out to

Illinois, where he followed his occupation in Clinton County. Mr. Wade's mother was Martha Mary (Yingst) Wade. She was born in Ohio in 1837, a daughter of John and Mary (Ogle) Yingst, both natives of Pennsylvania. John Yingst learned the trade of blacksmith in Pennsylvania, and finally moved to Clinton County, Illinois.

Isaac L. Wade grew up in Clinton County, Illinois, acquired an education in the country schools, and in 1887 went to St. Louis and took a course in telegraphy. In the following year in 1888 the Wabash Railroad made him station agent and operator at Sampsel in Livingston County, and in 1889 he was transferred to Lock Springs, where he took charge of the station. In 1897 he was sent to Pattonsburg, Missouri, as assistant station agent, but in 1899 returned to Lock Springs, and has since been out of the railroad service and engaged in business lines. For three years he was engaged in merchandising and also held the position of postmaster. In 1903 he was elected cashier of the Bank of Lock Springs, and has had the practical management of that substantial institution up to the present time. The Bank of Lock Springs has a capital stock of $10,000, and enjoys the confidence and patronage of a large community in and about that town. Besides his work as a banker Mr. Wade is dealing in insurance and also has a commission as notary public.

Politically he has been identified with the republican party, and for a number of years has held a position as a member of the school board of Lock Springs. He belongs to the Methodist Episcopal Church, is a Blue Lodge Mason, and also affiliates with the Eastern Star, the Modern Woodmen of America and the Independent Order of Odd Fellows.

In 1891 Mr. Wade married Miss Margaret Matilda Brookshier, a daughter of Thomas Benton and Elizabeth (Brooks) Brookshier. Mr. and Mrs. Wade are the parents of four children, all of whom have been well educated and are being trained for careers of usefulness. Their names are Raymond Brooks, Clarence Coleman, Ashley Brookshier and Miss Easter May.

REV. WALTER FRANKLIN BRADLEY. One of the ablest young ministers of the Presbyterian Church in Northwest Missouri is Rev. Walter Franklin Bradley, now stationed at Lock Springs in the southern part of Daviess County. He has been very active in church affairs during the past five years, and in October, 1912, was elected superintendent of the Quiet Hour of the Missouri Christian Endeavor Union and in October, 1914, was chosen to the office of pastor adviser. In May, 1914, as a commissioner from the McGee Presbytery he sat in the general assembly of the Presbyterian Church in Chicago.

One of a family of twelve children, eight of whom are still living, Rev. Mr. Bradley was born at Onaga, Kansas, February 20, 1884. His parents were George Samuel and Elizabeth (Thomas) Bradley. His father was born in Virginia April 11, 1846, and his mother in Indiana October 5, 1853, and both are still living, their homes being in Bethany, Missouri. The Bradley family is of English ancestry, and has been established in the United States for a century and a quarter. George S. Bradley was a soldier during the Civil war. He first enlisted at Pine Village, Indiana, for six months term, and was stationed principally on the Great Lakes. On receiving his honorable discharge he reenlisted, and was in the South fighting the battles of the Union for about three years. His services included participation in the great battle at Pittsburg Landing, or Shiloh, and for a time he was stationed at Cumberland Gap and also at Nashville under General Thomas. In order to take advantage of the offer by the Federal Government of homesteads to the old veterans, the father moved out to Onaga, Kansas, in 1872 and there acquired a quarter section of land. The family were among the first settlers at Onaga. George S. Bradley was a blacksmith by trade, and followed that work in connection with farming. In 1890 the family moved to Bethany, Missouri, where the father was active in his trade until 1914, and has since lived retired.

Rev. Mr. Bradley acquired his early education at Bethany, graduating from the high school in 1903, and then entered the Missouri Valley College at Marshall, Missouri, and graduated A. B. His professional studies were pursued in the Lebanon Theological Seminary, where he graduated in 1910 B. D. and in the same year was ordained a minister of the Presbyterian Church. For the past four years he has had charge of the church at Lock Springs and has been very successful in upbuilding the various church activities. His interests extend to many affairs outside of his immediate responsibilities, and he is very enthusiastic on the subject of athletics. He affiliates with the Independent Order of Odd Fellows. Rev. Mr. Bradley was married May 5, 1910, at Iago, Texas, to Miss Iva Gertrude Chapman, daughter of James Madison and Josephine (O'Brien) Chapman of Illinois. They have one child, James Chapman Bradley, born May 23, 1912.

PHILIP A. ABBETT. Now recognized as the leading merchant of Lock Springs, Philip A. Abbett has been engaged in business affairs in Daviess County upwards of thirty years, and the greater part of the time was an active member of the business community at Jamesport. His dealings as a merchant have commended him to the confidence of all people in his locality, and when the leading citizens are mentioned the name of Philip A. Abbett is sure to be in the list.

Philip A. Abbett was born in Bartholomew County, Indiana, April 15, 1855, and both his parents were natives of the same county. His father, William A. Abbett, was born March 26, 1832, while his mother, Mary (Barnhart) Abbett was born February 10, 1833. The parental grandparents, James M. and Lucy (Abbett) Abbett were natives of Kentucky, but became pioneers in Bartholomew County, Indiana, locating there about 1828 and securing land direct from the Government at a cost of $1.25 per acre. The maternal grandparents were Philip A. and Sylva Barnhart. The former a native of Pennsylvania and the latter of Indiana.

Philip A. Abbett grew up in Bartholomew County, acquired his early education in the country schools, and took a course of instruction in the Hartsville College in Bartholomew County. While Mr. Abbett has prospered as a merchant and has long been identified with business affairs, his early career was devoted to educational work, and he taught many terms of school. For eleven years he was engaged as a teacher in his native state, and in 1885 moved to Missouri and spent a year in teaching in Harris County. Since then all his time has been devoted to business affairs. At Jamesport in Daviess County Mr. Abbett was known as a grocery and hardware merchant for nineteen years, but finally disposed of his interests there and in 1906 moved to Lock Springs, where he opened a general store and has since enjoyed an extensive trade. At the same time he has a farm, and combines both activities.

Mr. Abbett is a democrat in politics, and a member of the Methodist Episcopal Church. Fraternally his relations are with the Masonic Lodge and the Knights of Pythias.

On March 9, 1876, Mr. Abbett married for his first wife Anna Leeson, a daughter of James and Sarah (Young) Leeson. There are two daughters: Mrs. Eugene B. Russell and Mrs. Jean M. Wells, both of whom are now living in St. Joseph, Missouri. On October 9, 1901, Mr.

Abbett married Mrs. Jennie B. Knotts, a daughter of Robert and Romanza (Carter) Brown. There are also two children by the second marriage, Robert W. being eleven years of age and Philip A. was born in 1913.

GEORGE WASHINGTON LITTON. One of the oldest merchants and business men of Lock Springs, George W. Litton has spent a lifetime of more than three score and ten years in this section of Missouri, is the son of a pioneer in Livingston County, and the activities of his own career include a service in the Civil war, many years of relationship with farming, until about thirty-five yers ago he established himself in business at Lock Springs.

George Washington Litton was born in Livingston County, Missouri, May 16, 1842. His parents were Thomas and Mary Ann (Brookshier) Litton. His mother was born in Tennessee, and his father was born in Kentucky in 1822, and when a very young man established his home as a pioneer in Livingston County, Missouri, in 1840, and he was married after coming to Missouri. On coming to Livingston County he took up a tract of eighty acres of Government land. It was situated in the midst of the timber, and his first task was cutting down trees to use in the construction of a log house. In that humble but characteristic home for the time all his children were born. In the early days supplies had to be freighted in by wagon from Spring Hill, Missouri, and he went through all the usual experiences, the hardships and the incidents of pioneering in a new country. Thomas Litton was a man of much enterprise and used his keen business judgment to acquire large holdings of land in Livingston County and that vicinity. In 1850 he paid $1,500 for 160 acres adjoining his original homestead, and extended his work of improvement to the new land. Later another tract was added, of 240 acres, for which he paid $10 an acre. In 1863 he bought 160 acres in Daviess County, and that cost him $7 an acre. He was a stockraiser and besides a large estate left an honored name in his community. Thomas Litton was twice married. The children of his first wife, who died in 1847, are: George W., Elizabeth and Mary Ann. Later he married a Miss Myrier, a native of Kentucky, and there were nine children by the second union, those living being named: Eliza, Alexander, John S., Thomas, Sarah Ann.

George W. Litton grew up in Livingston County on the old farm, attended the district schools, which offered a very limited curriculum of instruction, and in 1861, when nineteen years of age, at the beginning of the war, enlisted in the Confederate State Militia under General Slack. His service as a soldier lasted nine months, and he was in four of the Missouri engagements during the first year of the war. These were at Carthage, Wilson Creek, Dry Wood and Lexington. In the battle of Wilson Creek, one of the most decisive in the western theater of the war, he was wounded. He was discharged in 1861, returned home, and after the war took up an active career as a farmer in Livingston County.

On May 21, 1865, Mr. Litton married Nancy Minnick, a daughter of John and Susan (Offield) Minnick, who emigrated from Virginia to Livingston County, Missouri, in 1842, and were also among the early settlers in that section. Mr. Litton has four living children, Mary, Jasper, Isaac F. and Dora. The daughter Mary is the wife of John Bray of Lock Springs. Jasper married Allie Bray, and is an Idaho farmer. Isaac F. married Adda Jones, daughter of Benjamin Franklin and Marinda C. (Connor) Jones of Mooresville, Missouri. Dora is the wife of Edward Tye of Livingston County.

From 1865 to 1880 Mr. Litton was one of Livingston County's rep-

FAMILY GROUP OF MR. AND MRS. JOHN KELLY

resentative farmers, and in the latter year moved to Lock Springs, and established a store for the sale of general merchandise. His store was burned out in 1909, but was soon afterwards replaced with a substantial brick building, which is now one of the best in the town. Besides his operations as a merchant, Mr. Litton has a good farm east of Lock Springs, and leases his land. Politically he is a democrat, and is a member of the Presbyterian Church, and in 1872, joined the Masonic Order and is also a member of the Independent Order of Odd Fellows. Though past the limit assigned by the Psalmist to human life, Mr. Litton is still in the best of health and his present vigor gives promise of many more years of usefulness.

MARY JOSEPHINE LANE KELLY. In Davis Township of Caldwell County are to be found many homesteads that are not only valuable and attractive places from the standpoint of farming, but represent many of the most substantial families in this community. One of them, two miles out of Braymer, is the Kelly estate, now owned and occupied by Mrs. Kelly, whose husband was the late John Kelly, for many years actively identified with farming interests in this section. Mrs. Kelly occupies a home with 110 acres of land, and the original farm comprised 250 acres, but it has been divided, and Mrs. Kelly now occupies about half of the original acreage, with the old home. The Kelly homestead is a residence of seven rooms, attractively situated, and surrounded with barns, fields of grain, meadows and pastures, and all of it comprising almost an ideal rural residence.

The late John Kelly was born in Fulton County, Illinois, September 23, 1846. His father was Joseph Kelly, a native of Ohio, and the grandfather came from Ireland and was an early settler in Ohio. John Kelly was reared in Schuyler County, Illinois, was educated in the local schools, and was only seventeen years old when he volunteered for service in the Union army. He made an excellent record as a soldier, and then returned home to take up the practical duties of civil life, in which his record was not less noteworthy for the prosperity he won.

Mr. Kelly married, in 1868, Mary Josephine Lane, who was born January 22, 1847, and was reared and educated in Illinois. Her father was Alfred Lane, an Illinois farmer, born in Kentucky, and a man who exemplified the best manners of the old-fashioned Kentucky gentleman. Alfred Lane married Lydia Stambaugh, who was of Pennsylvania German stock. Mr. Lane was a democrat in politics, and in religion affiliated with the German Baptist Church or the Dunkards. Mrs. Kelly's mother died at the age of forty-four. The children in the Lane family were: Adren; Mary Josephine Kelly; James C.; Napoleon Bonaparte; John C. B.; Rosa; Amanda; Elizabeth; and Robert Lee, now deceased.

After their marriage Mr. and Mrs. Kelly lived for several years on an eighty acre farm in Illinois, and then sold out and came to Caldwell County, where he acquired 250 acres. He was a successful farmer and stockman and also operated during the season a threshing outfit. The improvements now seen on the farm are largely the result of his labors and enterprise. When he died, on April 5, 1908, he left a family of seven children, named as follows: Joseph, who is a capable young farmer operating a place adjoining his mother's; Alfred E., who owns a valuable farm of 100 acres in Davis Township; James, now deceased; Iva McFee, who lives southeast of her mother; Cora M. Deam, who lives near Breckenridge, Missouri; Walter L., who is a young man in his twenties and a vigorous and successful farmer, assisting his mother in the management of the home estate; and Lou, who lives at Canton, Illinois.

The late John Kelly prospered during his residence in Caldwell

County, and deserved the high esteem in which he was held, since he made it a rule of conduct that his promised word should be as binding as a bond, and practiced the golden rule in all his relations with his fellow men.

NEVIN M. WETZEL, M. D. The president of the Daviess County Medical Society, Doctor Wetzel has been engaged in a large practice · as physician and surgeon at Jameson and vicinity since 1903. His natural qualifications, his thorough training, and successful work have given him the high standing among the county's medical fraternity, so that his official position is an honor well deserved.

Doctor Wetzel comes of a prominent old Pennsylvania family. Many of the name are mentioned for prominent activities in the Pennsylvania annals of colonial and revolutionary times as well as in the affairs of the state. Some years before the Revolution four Wetzel brothers, John, Henry, Lewis and Jacob, emigrated from Germany and found homes in the new world, and a large number of their descendants have been identified with Pennsylvania. Doctor Wetzel's grandfather was Joseph Wetzel, his great-grandfather, Philip Wetzel, and his great-great-grandfather, Peter Wetzel. Peter's grave in Pennsylvania is marked by a large boulder, on which is cut the enigmatic characters—"I II 17." Doctor Wetzel interprets this to refer to Isaiah II, 17, a passage that reads—"And the loftiness of men shall be bowed down and the haughtiness of men shall be made low, and the Lord alone shall be exalted in that day."

Dr. Nevin M. Wetzel was born November 9, 1869, in what is known as Nitney Valley, near Lamar, Union County, Pennsylvania, a son of Reuben and Matilda (Poorman) Wetzel. Both parents were born in the same locality, and the father was a farmer and stockraiser. In 1870 he brought his family from Pennsylvania, and after spending a year in Iowa settled in Daviess County, Missouri, in 1871, buying a farm two miles south of Jamesport. That was his home until about 1901, when he sold and bought another place three miles west of Jamesport, where he is still living, now in advanced years, at the age of eighty-three, having been born in 1831. The mother died in 1883. Her eleven children are named as follows: Alice, Mary, Olivia, Eva, Dr. Nevin, Cordelia, Reuben M., Ella and Etta, all of whom are living, while Lydia and Everett are deceased. The father is a republican and a member of the Presbyterian Church.

It was probably from his sturdy line of ancestors that Doctor Wetzel inherited his faculty of persistent and sustained effort which has been an important factor in his progress and success. His education has been exceedingly liberal and thorough, but it was acquired by hard work, and he earned nearly all the means used to take him through his various courses. He was educated in the country schools and the Jamesport High School, had a two years normal and business course at Grand River College in Edinburg, and in 1893 finished a special teacher's course at the Chillicothe Normal. Then followed several years of successful teaching, six months in Livingston County and the remainder of the time in Daviess County. In 1896 he entered the Barnes Medical College at St. Louis, now known as the National University of Science and Arts, took the full course of four years, and was graduated M. D. April 12, 1900. It has been the ambition of Doctor Wetzel to secure the highest qualifications in his service as a physician and surgeon, and following his graduation he spent several years in further preparation, attending post-graduate course and doing hospital work at Johns Hopkins in Baltimore, the Bellevue Hospital and Medical College of New York, the University of Pennsylvania at Philadelphia, and at Pittsburg. In the fall of 1903 he located for active practice at Jameson, and almost from the beginning has had full demands upon his time and ability. In 1908 he attended clinics in Chicago, and so far as his busy career allows is a constant student.

Doctor Wetzel has been honored for the past five years with the presidency of the Daviess County Medical Society, and is also a member of the Missouri State Medical Society and the American Medical Association. Politically he was formerly a republican, but is now aligned with the progressive movement. He and his wife are members of the Presbyterian Church. Doctor Wetzel was married October 4, 1910, to Miss Lillie Joachimi, of Versailles, Morgan County, Missouri.

JOHN EARL SCOTT. The Bank of Jameson, in which Mr. Scott has been cashier for the past five years, is the central financial institution of that prosperous and thrifty community served by it in Grand River Township of Daviess County. The names of the men associated with it during the quarter century of its existence would quite fairly represent the list of solid and substantial citizens of this community. The Bank of Jameson was organized in 1889, and started out with a capital of $10,000, but since 1892 the capital has been $15,000. An index of its strength is its present surplus and undivided profits, totaling over twenty thousand dollars. The first officers and directors were: M. G. Netheron, president; A. J. Selsor, vice president; L. M. Brown, cashier; R. J. Lownie, secretary; and Z. A. Kimball and E. J. Walls. Several changes in the personnel were made in 1910, and since then the officers have been: J. F. Brown, president; J. H. Gillespie, secretary and vice president; J. E. Scott, cashier; R. E. Irwin, assistant cashier.

The Scott family has long and influentially been identified with Daviess County, John Earl Scott was born on his father's farm near Jameson, November 15, 1880, a son of A. D. and Matilda J. (Brown) Scott, both of whom are still living, the former a native of DeWitt County, Illinois, and the latter of Harrison County, Missouri. The grandfather was Dr. Alexander K. Scott, who came to Daviess County many years ago and settled on a farm east of Jameson. Beside the improvement and cultivation of this land, which is still owned by his descendants, he also served the community through his profession as a physician. Up to 1892 Mr. A. D. Scott owned and operated a farm east of Jameson and adjoining the old homestead in Grand River Township, but then moved into town and began merchandising. The firm has since become the A. D. Scott & Sons, handling a large general merchandise stock, with a custom that has been steadily growing for years. Mr. A. D. Scott has been one of the very successful men, and besides his large farm east of Jameson owns 600 acres in Kansas and another tract in Oklahoma, and has stock in the Bank of Jameson. The father and sons have cooperated in their enterprise, and their success serves to illustrate the truth of the Maxim, "in union there is strength." The active management of affairs has been turned over to the sons, who are all capable business men. The six children in the family are: Cordie; John Earl; Jesse R.; Ray; Albert, who died in 1912; and Laura.

John Earl Scott had a thoroughly practical training for business, with an education from the public schools of Grand River Township. He gained a knowledge of merchandising in the Scott store at Jameson, and followed that with a business course in Chillicothe. For more than ten years most of his time has been given to banking. In 1903 he was elected assistant cashier of the Bank of Jameson, but in 1906 resigned to accept the place of assistant cashier in the First National Bank of Gallatin and a few months later was promoted to cashier of that institution. He remained with the Gallatin Bank until 1908, and after that assisted in the management of the Scott family interests at Jameson until January 18, 1910, since which date he has filled the post of cashier in the Bank of Jameson. He is also a member of the firm of A. D. Scott & Sons.

In 1905 Mr. Scott married Lulu J. Graham, a daughter of Charles J. Graham of Jameson. Their two children are Richard Earl and Martha Lee. Mr. Scott is the present chancellor commander of Jameson Lodge, Knights of Pythias, and while a republican has never mingled in politics with any ambition for office.

BEN A. YATES. Since the year 1878, when he established himself in business at Pattonsburg, Ben A. Yates has associated his name with every movement which has marked the city's growth and development. Primarily a business man, the needs of his adopted community found in him a liberal contributor of time, ability and energy, and his public-spirited services in office of importance have been such as to hasten his locality's growth, elevate its ideals and add to its prestige.

Mr. Yates was born in Rappahannock County, Virginia, August 21, 1855, and is a son of James A. and Louisa (Kibler) Yates. The Yates family is of English extraction, its founder in America having emigrated to this country prior to the War of the Revolution, and several families settled in New York and Virginia, Richard Yates, the war governor of Illinois, having come from the latter branch. The Kiblers originated in Germany, from whence Ben A. Yates' maternal grandfather came to the United States. The parents of Mr. Yates were both natives of Rappahannock County, Virginia, and there his father passed his entire life, teaching school in that and Page County. He died when Ben A. was still a small child, but the mother is still living, and since 1913 has made her home with her son, although previous to that time she lived in her native county.

Ben A. Yates received his education under the instruction of his uncle, Charles W. Yates, who was for fifty-two years a teacher and died in the schoolroom. After completing his studies, Mr. Yates secured employment with the blind millionaire, Charles Broadway Rousse, who operated a chain of stores in Virginia, and with whom Mr. Yates remained for three years. In 1876, desiring to see something of the West, and believing that here better opportunities awaited the man of ambition and energy, Mr. Yates came to Gallatin, Daviess County, Missouri, and in partnership with his cousin, R. G. Yates, began a grocery business. This association continued for two years, when Ben A. Yates disposed of his interests at Gallatin and came to Pattonsburg, here purchasing the Isaac McCulley hardware stock. Here he was successful in building up a large and representative business, through good management and hard and industrious labor, and continued to operate the enterprise alone until 1898, when he admitted to partnership his brother, W. Byrd Yates, and the firm adopted its present style of Yates Brothers. It is probable that this firm will be soon dissolved, however, as W. B. Yates has recently been appointed postmaster of Pattonsburg and will undoubtedly dispose of his business holdings that he may give his entire attention to his official duties. A large, up-to-date stock is carried by this store, including all kinds of shelf and heavy hardware, stoves and agricultural implements and machinery, and the various other articles which are to be found in a modern hardware establishment. On two occasions Mr. Yates has suffered severe losses by fire, but in spite of these setbacks has prospered satisfactorily, and his standing in business circles is that of a substantial man at the head of a paying business. His many years of honorable and upright dealing have also gained him the name of a man of the utmost integrity, and his signature is an honored one on commercial paper.

Mr. Yates was reared in the faith of the Methodist Episcopal Church, South, and has been generous in his support of its movements. Fraternally, he is connected with the Independent Order of Odd Fellows, in which he is the oldest in point of membership at Pattonsburg, and with the Knights of Pythias, in which he has been for years and is at present district deputy. Politically Mr. Yates is a democrat, and at various times has been called upon to fill such important offices as mayor, alderman and member of the school board, and for the past twenty years has held his present position of city treasurer. His public service has been characterized by a display of conscientious fidelity to duty and an interest in his community which has put personal ambitions aside. Personally, Mr. Yates is a polished, courteous gentleman, a credit to the name he bears and to the community in which he has spent so many years.

In 1880 Mr. Yates was united in marriage with Miss Minnie Gabel, of Kansas, who was born in Ohio, and to this union there have come two daughters: Helen G., who is the wife of Gilbert Gromer, of Pattonsburg; and Lee, who is the wife of Charles Agee, of Mount Ayr, Iowa.

W. Byrd Yates, recently appointed postmaster at Pattonsburg, and a brother of Ben A. Yates, was born in Rappahannock County, Virginia, January 19, 1852, and like his brother received his education under the instruction of his uncle, Charles W. Yates. When he was ready to enter upon a career of his own, he chose railroading as his sphere of activity, and until 1885 was employed on a run between Wilmington and Philadelphia. In the year mentioned Mr. Yates was appointed to the United States Mail Service, under the administration of President Cleveland, and in this connection came to Missouri, continuing to act in the same capacity until 1898, in which year he turned his attention to mercantile pursuits. With his brother, Ben A. Yates, he founded the firm of Yates Brothers, hardware dealers, a venture that succeeded and prospered, and which will only terminate because of Mr. Yates' appointment to the postmastership by President Wilson. Mr. Yates is a stalwart and uncompromising democrat and has long been an active and influential worker in the interests of his party. He is a Mason fraternally, and a member of the Christian Church.

In 1893, while a resident of Clinton County, Missouri, Mr. Yates was united in marriage with Miss Anna Wright, and four children have been born to this union: Mary, who is attending school at Lexington, Missouri; and Dorothy, Virginia and Elizabeth, all residing at home.

JOHN DAVIS DUNHAM, M. D. Holding the distinction of being the oldest practicing physician of Pattonsburg, in point of continuous service, Dr. John Davis Dunham has ministered to the physical wants and needs of the people of this place since July 14, 1881, and during this time has also taken an active and helpful part in the movements which have contributed to the community's growth and development. His skill in his profession and his sympathetic nature have attracted to him a large professional business and given him high position in his calling, but his increasing duties have not deterred him from participation in affairs aside from his vocation.

Doctor Dunham was born in Pike County, Ohio, February 28, 1855, a son of Dr. W. H. and Henrietta (Odell) Dunham, and a member of an old and honored family on both the paternal and maternal sides. The Dunham family originated in England, from whence two brothers came to the United States, one going to Michigan and one to Alabama, it being from the latter that Doctor Dunham is descended. His grandfather, Michael Dunham, emigrated from Alabama to Ohio. The Odell family came originally from Castle, Town and Church of Odell, Derbyshire, England, and possessed a coat-of-arms. The Castle of Odell was one of the strongest in the world at the time of its erection and was presented to Walter the Fleming by William the Conqueror. From Walter the Fleming descended the entire family, and the name has been variously spelled in the public records as Wahul, Woodhul, Wodhul, Wodell, Odle and Odell. The Castle of Odell passed out of the family name about the year 1575, when Agnes Odell, the owner, married Richard Chetwodes. The Ashtons, about two hundred years ago, purchased the property and erected a house of modern style (French Chateau) within the west wall; the wall they preserved, owing to its great antiquity and strength. The interior of the house contains some of the rooms that formed part of the ancient stronghold, and the River Ouse flows on the east side, while the Village of Odell surrounds it. The foregoing record, being taken from the British Museum, is correct and authentic.

The Odell family was founded in America by three Odell brothers, who emigrated to Baltimore, Maryland, in 1760, and one of these migrated to New York State, ex-Governor Odell being one of his descendants. The maternal great-grandfather of Dr. John D. Dunham was Maj. James Odell, who married and settled near Baltimore, Maryland, but in 1800 migrated to Fairfield County, Ohio, and later went to Highland County, Ohio, where he is found raising a company of volunteers for service during the War of 1812. At the close of that struggle he went to the Territory of Michigan and later was elected a member of the first Constitutional Convention of that state. He died in 1845.

William Odell, son of Maj. James Odell, and maternal grandfather of Dr. John Davis Dunham, was born at Hillsboro, Ohio, in 1806, and was seventeen years of age when he went to Virginia, in which state he engaged in teaching school. He served as a member of the Virginia Legislature in 1827 and 1828 and was a prominent man in his community, but in 1841 went to Pike County, Ohio, making the journey of 450 miles by wagon. There he passed the remaining years of his life. Among his children was a son, James F. Odell, who was land appraiser for Seal and Scotia townships, Pike County, Ohio, sheriff of Pike County, United States marshal, deputy sheriff and United States pension agent, and still a resident of Pike County.

While in Virginia, William Odell was married to Sarah Caudy, who belonged to a Scotch-Irish family that came to America from Ireland. Her father, Capt. James Caudy, emigrated to this country in 1751, built a blockhouse, and with a company of volunteers protected the first settlers of Hampshire and Jefferson counties, Virginia. Caudy Castle, an inaccessible retreat in the mountains, 887 feet high, is always pointed out to sightseers who visit that part of Virginia. Another family connection of distinction enjoyed by Doctor Dunham is through his father's mother, who was a Pickerel, and whose father, Thomas Pickerel, served as a drummer-boy during the War of the Revolution. The Pickerels were likewise known for their religious fervor, and were the builders of the first Campbellite (Christian) Church in Ohio.

Dr. W. H. Dunham, father of Dr. John Davis Dunham, was born in Brown County, Ohio, and for many years practiced medicine in Pike and Jackson counties, Ohio. During the Civil war he raised and commanded as captain a company of volunteers, known as Company I, Thirty-sixth Regiment, Ohio Volunteer Infantry, with which he served for two years, his principal services being at Summerville and Gauley Bridge, Virginia. In 1864 he graduated from the Cleveland Medical College, although he had been practicing for many years previous, and in 1865 came to Cypress Township, Harrison County, Missouri, and purchased land, his family joining him here in the following year, June 9, 1866. For many years Doctor Dunham continued to be engaged in the practice of his calling in connection with farming operations, but later removed to Kansas, where he remained for one year, and then made removal to Bentonville, Arkansas, where his death occurred, August 14, 1900, aged seventy-seven years, three months, twenty days. Mrs. Dunham is still living at Bentonville. She is now eighty years of age, having been born in Virginia, September 14, 1834. The five children of Doctor and Mrs. Dunham still survive: Mary, Dr. John Davis, W. O., Frank and G. A.

Dr. John Davis Dunham first attended the public schools of Harrison County, Missouri, and later became a student in Grand River College, at old Edinburg. In 1872 he attended the high school at Bethany, Missouri, but in the following year left his studies in order to engage in freighting between Wichita, Kansas, and Fort Sill, Oklahoma. During the winter of 1874 he entered the Keokuk College of Physicians and Surgeons, Keokuk, Iowa, and was graduated from that institution with his degree of Doctor of Medicine, March 16, 1879, at that time beginning practice in Harrison County. He remained there, at Happy Valley, for two years, and something less than one year at Blue Ridge, and July 14, 1881, came to Pattonsburg, which he chose as his permanent field of endeavor. He has never had reason to regret his decision, for here he has won success and standing in his profession, the esteem and respect of his fellow-citizens, and the reputation of being a helpful and stirring man in a progressive community. Aside from his calling, he has been engaged successfully in the drug business, having purchased a pharmacy December 15, 1907, and since 1892 has been a registered pharmacist.

Doctor and Mrs. Dunham are of the Presbyterian faith, but are not members of any church. Fraternally, he is connected with the Knights of Pythias, the Modern Woodmen of America and the Yeomen. Politically a republican, he served one term as mayor of Pattonsburg, is now and has been for years health examiner of the city, and under the administration of President Benjamin Harrison was United States pension examiner. He is surgeon for the Quincy, Omaha & Kansas City and Wabash railroads, and of the latter is the oldest in point of service along the line. He has continued as a close and careful student and keeps fully abreast of the advances constantly being made in his calling, holding membership in the Daviess County Medical Society, the Grand River Valley Medical Society, the Missouri State Medical Society, the Wabash Railroad Surgeons Association and the American Medical Association.

On July 14, 1884, Doctor Dunham was united in marriage with Miss Sophia Niewvahner, of Jackson County, Ohio, and to this union there have been born two sons: Leslie H., who is now taking a medical course at the University of Missouri, Columbia; and John Dunham, Jr., who graduated from the high school at Pattonsburg in 1914 and is now taking post-graduate work there.

Mrs. Dunham's ancestors were natives of Germany, and both her grandfathers, Niewvahner and Prior, were soldiers in the German army at Waterloo, the former being killed and the latter so seriously wounded that he died a few years later. Mrs. Dunham's parents, Henry and Mary (Prior) Niewvahner, were born in Hanover, Germany, the former emigrating to the United States about the year 1840, and landing at Baltimore, Maryland. For two years he followed steamboating and was then married and moved to Jackson Furnace, Ohio, where he was employed at the iron furnace, but later moved to Jackson Courthouse, Ohio, and the̊re lived retired until his wife's death in 1902. At that time he came to Pattonsburg to make his home with Mrs. and Doctor Dunham, but in the following year met his death when struck by a passenger train.

Hon. Jacob M. Poage. One of the worthy pioneer residents of Pattonsburg, who by reason of a long carer of industry, careful management, patient endurance and upright dealing, has earned the respite from labor which he is now enjoying in circumstances of ease and comfort, is Judge Jacob M. Poage. Now that the period of his life in Daviess County reaches back over a period of forty-eight years, he is fortunate indeed in being able to review the past with the happy consciousness that he has discharged faithfully his duties in public and private relations, and that he has borne his full share in building up the most important interests and promoting the highest welfare of the locality among whose people he has lived so long.

Judge Poage was born in Greenup (now Boyd) County, Kentucky, August 23, 1835, and is a son of Hugh Allen and Eliza (Murphy) Poage, the former born in Virginia and the latter in Pennsylvania. The mother died when Jacob M. was about three weeks old, the only child of his parents, while the father passed away at the home of his son in Daviess County, having come here about ten years after the advent of Jacob M.

Judge Poage's boyhood was passed in the mountainous, eastern part of Kentucky, where the soil was unproductive, the people poor, and the children forced to go to work at a tender age. The scene of his youth was the Ohio River, four miles from the Virginia state line, where the subscription schools were few and far between, his educational advantages being therefore very limited, although he has since been a reader and student and has added to his information by observation. He remained at home with his father until reaching the age of seventeen years, at which time he began to learn the carpenter's trade and served a two-year apprenticeship thereto. He subsequently began to work at his trade, and was thus engaged when the Civil war came on. His sympathies being with the Union cause he enlisted in Company E, Fourteenth Kentucky Volunteer Infantry, and with that organization saw three years and four months of service in Kentucky, West Virginia, Tennessee, Georgia and Alabama, during which time he participated in numerous hard-fought engagements, including Cumberland Gap and the Atlanta campaign. As a soldier he proved himself courageous in battle and faithful to duty, and January 31, 1865, was honorably discharged with an excellent record.

For the two years following his military service, Mr. Poage was employed at his trade in his native state, and there, in March, 1865, was united in marriage with Miss Margaret E. Savage, of Greenup County, Kentucky, a daughter of Nicholas and Mary (McCroskey) Savage, natives of the Blue Grass State. Mr. Savage was an extensive farmer and owned 400 acres of land in Greenup County, but during his later years disposed of his property and came to Daviess County, Missouri, with his wife, and here they passed their last days with their children, the father dying at the home of his daughter, Mrs. Fulwider, west of Pattonsburg, while Mrs. Savage died at the home of Mr. Poage.

In the spring of 1867 Judge and Mrs. Poage came to Daviess County, Missouri, and spent the first summer in Benton Township, with William Savage, Mrs. Poage's brother, whose wife had recently died, and for whom Mrs. Poage kept house. In the fall of the same year Judge Poage bought 160 acres of his present farm, that part on which the buildings are now located, but at that time there were only eight acres cleared, the balance being in brush and timber. There was a small log cabin on the place, with one door, one window and a six-foot fireplace, and in this primitive home Judge and Mrs. Poage began their life in Daviess County, moving to the place March 4, 1868. Judge Poage immediately began to improve the property—as he says: "I first cleared all on top of the ground, and then underneath." From that time to the present he has labored faithfully to make this one of the finest properties in the county. Many improvements have been made and he has added to the farm until it now contains 300 acres, all of which he has improved and put under cultivation. His first land cost him $6.25 per acre, some of which he could now sell for $300 an acre; one 80-acre tract, purchased subsequent to his first property, cost him but $2.50, while for other land he has paid as high as $20 an acre. All of his land could now easily bring $100 an acre.

In 1871 Judge Poage built his present frame house, the lumber for which he brought to his farm from the City of Chicago, just previous to the great fire, and this was the first carload of pine lumber shipped into the Town of Pattonsburg. He also displayed his progressive spirit by buying and bringing here the first reaper and dropper.

When Judge Poage bought his present farm, Pattonsburg had not been started, his nearest railroad being at Stewartsville, Missouri, thirty miles distant. The railroad did not come to Pattonsburg until 1871, at which time the present site of the city was covered with timber from Judge Poage's east line to Main Street. East of Main Street the land had been broken and this the judge farmed until he could get his other land cleared. The timber was so heavy, in fact, and the roads so scarce, that it was customary, when starting on a journey, for the settlers to take along an axe, with which to cut their way through. After Pattonsburg was started, Judge Poage purchased ten acres of land across the road from his farm east of Poage Street, named in his honor, for $20 per acre, and this property he laid off in lots and sold as such. Judge Poage now has four large barns on his farm, besides numberless outbuildings, as he has always been a firm believer in taking care of what he has raised. He has an outside wash house, an acetylene gas plant, tool sheds, stock sheds, feed grinding building, a large chicken house and a tenant house, and all are in the best of repair and condition. He also has five houses in the City of Pattonsburg, which he rents, and is a stockholder in the Daviess County Savings Bank of Pattonsburg, and a member of the directing board of that institution. For many years past he has been an extensive feeder of cattle, and at the present time is feeding sixty head of spring calves.

Judge and Mrs. Poage have been the parents of four children, namely: Mary Eliza, who was born in Kentucky and died in 1872 in Daviess County, Missouri; Carrie Luella, who is the wife of Ollie Weller and resides at Sherman, Texas; Daisy J., who is the wife of Alonzo Bridges, of Bedford, Iowa; and Nicholas L., who lives with his parents and is his father's assistant in his farming operations. Judge and Mrs. Poage and all of their children are consistent members of the Methodist Episcopal Church, South. Judge Poage is a Mason. In politics he is a democrat, and before the country school was consolidated with the city school, he served as director of the former for nine years. During the '80s he was elected and served four years capably in the capacity of county judge of Daviess County.

It is Judge Poage's opinion that it takes three classes of men to develop a country. The first class hunts, fishes and traps; the second class hunts, fishes, traps and clears out a little land; the third class, finding the game largely gone, clears and puts the land under cultivation and makes a home for his old age. Judge Poage belongs to the latter class. He has always been a hard worker and is still disposed to carry on his share of the work. Being a carpenter by trade, he has been able to furnish a large part of the labor required in the construction of every building on the place, and there are at least twenty good, substantial structures, much of the timber for which he has taken from his own woods, cut, hauled to the sawmill and put in place in the building. Judge Poage represents a type of pioneer now fast disappearing. In his eightieth year he is still active in mind and body, and his recollection of early events makes him an interesting conversationalist. He is well provided for in his declining years, and is passing them in peace and comfort, with the respect and esteem of all men as an additional reward for a life of honest and well-meaning effort.

GEORGE T. NETHERTON, M. D. The Netherton family was established in the wilds of Daviess County four score years ago, and Dr. George T. Netherton, now successfully practicing medicine in Gallatin, was himself born in this section of Northwest Missouri more than seventy years ago, and there are few men still living who have so close and accurate a recollection of early times and conditions. Doctor Netherton is an old soldier, for many years followed the business of farmer, and later in life took up the study and practice of medicine and has since enjoyed an extensive general practice.

Dr. George T. Netherton was born in Daviess County August 23, 1841, a son of James N. and Nancy (Thomas) Netherton. The parents were natives of Eastern Tennessee and were married there, and in 1834, with three children and with the parents of James Netherton, they all emigrated to Northwest Missouri, making the entire trip by wagon. Their destination was the Grand River Valley in Daviess County, and they laboriously proceeded through the wilderness until they arrived at a point eight miles north of the present City of Gallatin. At that time only one other family lived north of them as far as the Iowa boundary, and this extreme settlement was only a mile and a half north of the Netherton place. The land in Daviess County had not yet been put on the market by the Government, and the Nethertons and the other pioneers who came about the same time were ''squatters'' and occupied the land without legal leave until the Government opened it for entry through the land office at Lexington, Missouri, where the Nethertons secured and paid for their claims. Their settlement occurred several years before the Platte Purchase, and there were as many Indians as white settlers in Northwest Missouri. In a country that is now a smiling landscape of farms and cities it is difficult, if not impossible, to conceive the conditions which existed when the Nethertons came. The country was divided between prairie and dense primeval forest, and for a number of years it was possible to shoot deer without going more than a quarter of a mile beyond the homestead. Doctor Netherton's father built for the first habitation of the family a log house, which was covered with clapboards, split out of the native timber. This preliminary task having been accomplished, there remained before him the still heavier work of clearing a farm from the midst of the woods, and that work occupied him for many years, and he died on the old home place in 1868. His widow survived many years, passing away in 1894. Both were members of the Baptist Church, and the father was originally a democrat, but subsequently joined the republican party. In their family were fourteen children, named briefly as follows: Catherine, deceased; Elizabeth J., deceased; Rev. John L., who was the first male white child born in Daviess County and now lives at Montrose, California; Henry, deceased;

Sarah A. Coffey; Dr. George T.; James C., of Clinton, Henry County, Missouri; M. G., now deceased, who was at one time treasurer of Daviess County; William B., who enlisted in the Forty-third Missouri Volunteer Infantry, was taken prisoner at Glasgow, Missouri, and subsequently died during service as a result of disease near Kansas City; Adelbert L., who lives at Gilman; Iciphena Z., deceased; Caroline, deceased; and two that died in infancy.

Doctor Netherton was born on the old home farm in Grand River Township, and his earliest recollections are of log cabin homes, a comparatively limited area of cultivation, most of the fields being thickly set with stumps, and practically all his education was acquired in school houses that had puncheon floors, split log benches, with instruction almost as crude as the furnishings. He lived at home and attended school until the outbreak of the war, and at that time was about twenty years of age. He was in the first command raised for service in Northwest Missouri, enlisting for a term of six months in a battalion organized by Major Cox. All his service was in this section of the state. In February, 1862, Doctor Netherton enlisted in the First Missouri State Militia Cavalry, being assigned to Company A, his commanding officers being Capt. Joseph H. McGee, Major Cox and Colonel McFarren. He saw a great deal of active service, and at the Battle of Mine Creek was shot through the left arm, and has never entirely recovered from that wound. He remained with his regiment until mustered out in February, 1865, being at that time a non-commissioned officer.

With his return to Northwest Missouri Dr. Netherton bought a small tract of unimproved land, and in order to earn a living taught school while clearing up and getting his farm into a productive condition. He went on with his work until a hundred acres had been cleared, and his occupation was as a progressive and successful farmer for twenty-five years. Towards the close of his farming experience he attended one year of medical lectures at St. Joseph, and took two years in the Kansas City Medical College, from which he was graduated M. D. in 1897. He at once began practice at Gallatin, remained there until 1901, and then went to the Southwest and was in practice in one of the comparatively new counties of North Texas, Archer County, until 1908. Returning to Missouri, Doctor Netherton has since had his offices in Gallatin and still attends to large professional business.

On August 2, 1866, Doctor Netherton married Miss Hannah Everly, of Daviess County. Her parents were John J. and Iciphena (Seat) Everly, the former a native of Pennsylvania and the latter of Missouri. The Seat family came from Tennessee to Morgan County, Missouri, among the pioneers, while the Everly family located in the same county in 1838 and in the fall of the same year moved on to Daviess County, where they were among the early settlers. Doctor Netherton and wife have two children: The son Charles O. is now practicing as a veterinary surgeon at Gallatin. E. J. Netherton now has charge of the hog cholera serum preparation in the laboratory at St. Joseph.

Doctor Netherton is a member of the Baptist Church, keeps up his associations with the old veterans as a member of the Grand Army of the Republic, and is affiliated with the Masonic and Odd Fellow fraternities. As a young man his political sympathies were with the democratic party, but after the war he became an active republican, and continued that affiliation until the Chicago convention of 1912. He broke away from the party in that year, served as delegate to the state progressive convention, and later was in the convention at Chicago which nominated Roosevelt and Johnson as progressive candidates for President and vice president. He is a thorough believer in progressive principles and hopes for the ultimate success of the progressive party. Just following the war Doctor Netherton served for a time as supervisor of registration in Daviess County.

MELVIN A. GODMAN was one of the most venerable and interesting survivors of that group of early settlers whose gamut of experience ran back to the time when Daviess County was only emerging from the dominion of the wilderness. Considering his early lack of opportunity and the hard necessity which imposed continuous toil upon the shoulders of a child, he had a career of remarkable accomplishment and deserved all the honors paid him in his declining age.

The birth of Melvin A. Godman occurred in Monroe County, Missouri, March 17, 1836. He was a son of John and Tabitha (Jones) Godman, both of whom were natives of Virginia, were married in Bourbon County, Kentucky, and about 1830 emigrated and established homes in the new country of Monroe County, Missouri. They made the trip in a covered wagon drawn by four horses. Two families comprised the party and most of them rode in the one wagon. They located near the old Town of Palmyra, where John Godman took up Government land in the midst of the woods, built a log house, and cleared off many acres and prepared them for cultivation. John Godman was a hard worker all his active career, but circumstances were conflicting, and he lived in a time when life was largely heavy toil and hardship, with few comforts and advantages. In 1844 he brought his family to Livingston County, Missouri, and again took up Government land a mile and a half east of Spring Hill. On that place was a small log cabin, and during the four years he lived there he did a large amount of improvement. In 1848 he came to Daviess County and five years later entered 200 acres of Government land located eleven miles north of Jamesport. That was his home until his death in 1875, while his wife passed away in 1872. Melvin A. Godman was the eighth in a family of nine children, and all the others are now deceased, their names having been Ann, Eliza, Jane, Nancy, Allen, William, Caroline, Lucy and Mary Boone.

Melvin A. Godman had no school advantages when a boy, owing to the fact that his home was first in Monroe County, then in Livingston County and then in Daviess County, all of which at the time were on the frontier. His entire attendance at any sort of school was limited to about three months, and his training for life was the result of practical effort, swinging the axe in the woods, plowing the heavy virgin soil, and planting and harvesting crops. He lived at home with his parents until thirty years of age, having been married when twenty-two. In the spring of 1865 Mr. Godman bought of his father-in-law, Thomas Michals, 320 acres of partly improved land twelve miles north of Jamesport in Lincoln Township. There was a log cabin, and seventy acres had been broken, while ten acres were in pasture. All the rest of the heavy work of clearing and improvement was performed by Mr. Godman, who in time erected a substantial residence and barns, built line and cross fences, and with the steady industry which was his lifelong characteristic continued to accumulate and add to his estate until he was the owner of 810 acres of well improved land, divided into three farms, with three separate dwellings and other buildings. For many years he was a large cattle and hog raiser, and shipped extensively from his farm to the markets of Chicago, Kansas City and St. Joseph. Mr. Godman remained on that farm until February, 1891, when he moved to Jamesport and lived retired, and there he died November 27, 1914.

On September 3, 1857, Mr. Godman married Miss Clara Michals. She was born in Montgomery County, Indiana, in 1840, a daughter of

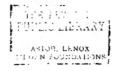

Roscoe. A. Morris

Thomas H. and Deborah (Cravens) Michals. Her father was born in Tennessee and went as a child to Kentucky, while her mother was a native of Kentucky, where they were married, and moved to Montgomery County, Indiana, about 1830, and thence in the fall of 1856 took the interesting journey which established them in a new home in Lincoln Township of Daviess County. They came to Missouri with two teams, one of horses and the other of oxen. Mr. Michals bought 320 acres, paying $5 an acre to its owner, who had secured the land direct from the Government. Only twenty acres had been broken by the plow, and after Mr. Michals had lived there some years he sold the place to his son-in-law, Mr. Godman, for $10 an acre and then returned to Indiana, lived there three years, and on coming back to Missouri located in Saline County and a few years later returned to Lincoln Township, in Daviess County, where he died in 1879. His wife passed away at the home of Mr. and Mrs. Godman in 1882. Mrs. Godman was one of a large family of children, mentioned briefly as follows: Nancy Williams; Solomon, who died while a soldier in the Mexican war; Joel W., who also saw service in the war with Mexico; Cassie; Ann Endicott; Thomas B., Mrs. Godman, and several others that died in infancy. Mrs. Godman, like her husband, is the only survivor of her immediate family.

The long companionship of Mr. and Mrs. Godman was blessed by the birth of eleven children, five of whom died in infancy, and the other six are: Perry A., of Jamesport; Palmer F., of Lees Summit; Cassie, wife of P. V. Neighswenger, of Jamesport; Atlanta A., wife of John K. Everly, of Jameson; Belle, wife of John Meserva, of Trenton; Amanda A., wife of Harry B. McCluskey, of Jamesport.

From the time he located in Jamesport Mr. Godman divided half of his farm among his children, and sold the balance, and has invested to a considerable extent in Jamesport City real estate. He was a member of the Baptist Church, as is his widow, and in politics he was a democrat, but never sought office. It was the fortune of Mr. Godman to have seen Daviess County grow from an almost uninhabited section to a thickly populated district. After his marriage he did his trading largely at Chillicothe and Spring Hill, thirty miles away, and it required two days to make a trip to and from mill to get meal and flour. For many years after he came to Daviess County Jamesport was unoccupied Government land. There were no public schools, and the settlers supported schools by paying $1 a month per pupil, while the teacher boarded around. In spite of the deficiencies of his early training, Mr. Godman was thoroughly successful, largely due to his native intelligence and an experience which developed keen business faculties.

Roscoe A. Morris. A resident of Savannah for a period of forty-three years, Roscoe A. Morris has been a witness to and a participant in the era of this city's greatest commercial growth. For thirty-four years he was engaged in the sale of agricultural implements, and is widely known to the trade all over this part of the state, but at the present time is living in retirement. Mr. Morris was born at Petersburg, Illinois, August 6, 1852, and is a son of Martin S. and Elizabeth (Wagoner) Morris.

Martin S. Morris was born at Richmond, Kentucky, in 1817, and as a young man went to Illinois, becoming the owner of a large plow manufactory at Petersburg, a business of which he was the directing head for a period of twenty-five years, or until coming to Savannah, in 1871. Here also he was engaged in making agricultural machinery, but finally retired from business, and died May 6, 1884. A lifelong republican, Mr. Morris took a particularly active participation in the movements of his party, and was personally acquainted with many of. the leaders of the organization in Illinois. One of these was War Governor Richard Yates, who was his intimate friend, and Roscoe A. Morris now has in his possession a letter from the governor, written to his father in 1850, and sent through the mails with a five-cent stamp and without envelope. Mr. Morris was also an intimate fried of Abraham Lincoln, and his son has also a letter from the martyred President, and well remembers accompanying his father to the Lincoln home to congratulate the President upon his election. Mr. Morris was offered a number of high positions by Mr. Lincoln, but followed his fixed rule in declining office, and his only public service of importance was as revenue collector of the port of New Orleans, an office in which he served three years. While in Illinois Mr. Morris was an extensive land owner, and at one time was known as one of his community's most substantial men. He was fraternally connected with the Masons. Mr. Morris was married at Springfield, Illinois, to Miss Elizabeth Wagoner, who was born in Pennsylvania, and she died January 24, 1900, at Savannah, at the age of eighty years. There were six sons and six daughters in the family, of whom Mr. Morris is the only son living, while three daughters also survive.

Roscoe A. Morris attended the public schools of Petersburg, Illinois, until reaching the age of fifteen years, at which time he received his introduction to business methods in his father's plow works. He had just reached his majority when he came to Savannah, and here also was associated with his father for a time, but subsequently turned his attention to the sale of agricultural implements, in which he was engaged for thirty-four years. This long period of unabated industry and well-directed effort culminated in the accumulation of a handsome competency, and in 1909 he retired from business cares, and since that time has lived quietly, enjoying the fruits of his labors. His name in commercial circles is an honored one, for he achieved his success through no underhand dealings, but ever maintained a high standard of business ideals. He is a public-spirited citizen, ever ready to give his support to progressive movements and enterprises, but his political activity has been confined to casting his vote for the candidates of the republican party. Like his father, he is a Mason.

Mr. Morris was married in 1881 to Miss Emmazella Stark, who was born at Dowagiac, Michigan, July 11, 1858, and was ten years of age when she came to Savannah, Missouri, with her widowed mother. She is a daughter of Erastus and Anna (Riggin) Stark, the former born in New York and died December 19, 1863. He was a grandson of Gen. John Stark. Mr. Stark was a farmer and mechanic, and spent the active years of his life on his property in Michigan. Mrs. Stark was born in Virginia, November 25, 1817, and died at Savannah. Of the five sons and five daughters in the Stark family, three sons and four daughters still survive. Two children have been born to Mr. and Mrs. Morris, namely: Mrs. Josephine Dailing, who resides with her parents and has a son—Roscoe Morris; and Martin S., residing on a farm four miles north of Savannah, who married Miss Laura Burns, of Andrew County.

HOMER L. FAULKNER. As vice president of the Peoples Exchange Bank of Jamesport, and one of the best known and most extensive breeders of the old original Big Boned Spotted Poland-China hogs in America, Homer L. Faulkner, proprietor of Highview Breeding Farms, occupies an important position in the business, agricultural and financial life of Daviess County, Missouri. His interests are large and of a valuable character, yet his activities have not been confined to participation in affairs merely for his own benefit, but have branched out into matters concerning the public and community welfare, in the advancement of which he has always been ready to enlist his time, his energies and his means.

Mr. Faulkner was born on the old homestead farm located south of Jamesport, in Daviess County, Missouri, September 1, 1876, and is a son of Lewis M. and Salatha Jane (Siler) Faulkner. His father was born in Campbell County, Tennessee, and his mother in Whitney County, Kentucky, counties which adjoined, being on the border of their respective states. They were married in the latter county in 1854, and during the same year started on their long and tedious jurney in a covered wagon, drawn by an old mule and a blind horse, to Jackson Township, Daviess County, Missouri, where the family located on unimproved land in the timber, and near a spring of water. There was plenty of good prairie land to be secured near at hand, but like most of the pioneers they feared the cold winters on the prairie and the least desirable land was taken first. Springs of water and material for rail fences were to be found in the rough timber country, and there also were secured the logs with which Mr. Faulkner built the little family home. After this he cleared, fenced and broke the land, and added to his original holdings until he had 400 acres, part secured from the United States Government, part from the old Hannibal & St. Joseph Railroad, and the balance from individual owners, all in Jackson Township. In addition to doing general farming, Mr. Faulkner was a raiser and breeder of thoroughbred Short Horn cattle. He and Mrs. Faulkner were devout members of the Methodist Episcopal Church, South, and in politics the father was a democrat. He died in 1878, and Mrs. Faulkner survived him until 1905, being seventy years of age at the time of her demise. Homer L. Faulkner was the youngest·of a family of twelve children, of whom eleven are still living: Lucinda, the one deceased, passed away in infancy; Marion, who is a resident of Gray County, Texas; Mattie, the wife of George D. Burge, of El Reno, Oklahoma; Ferdinand, a resident of Swisher County, Texas; Samantha, who is the wife of Dr. J. G. Wingo, of Swisher County, Texas; King, a resident of Hood County, Texas; Mollie, who is the wife of J. T. McClure, of Jamesport, Missouri; Robert, of Swisher County, Texas; Siler, of Gray County, Texas; Marvin and George, both resident of Swisher County, Texas; and Homer L., of this notice.

From his birth Homer L. Faulkner has been compelled to struggle against disadvantages, for he was born of exceedingly small stature, yet in spite of this he has succeeded far better than the majority of men. He received his education at the Jamesport public schools and the Gallatin High School, this being followed by a course at Grand River College, Gallatin, and after his graduation returned to the home farm, where his mother resided, and engaged in general farming and the raising of thoroughbred Short Horn cattle. In the latter line he continued until 1907, when he had a disposal sale, preparing to devote his entire time to his thoroughbred hogs, this business having increased so enormously as to demand his entire time and attention. He had begun, in 1893, his now famous herd with three thoroughbred old original Big Boned Spotted Poland-China sows. Since that time his business along this line has increased until he now owns the largest herd of this particular breed of hogs in the world, selling hundreds of hogs. principally boars, all over the United States, Canada and Mexico. through mail orders, and also holding an annual sale of sows, at which the price per animal averages about $100. At his 1915 sale he sold sixty thoroughbred sows.

Among the many famous boars which have come from Highview Breeding Farms may be mentioned "Budweiser," an animal owned by Mr. Faulkner for ten years, and the best advertised Poland-China boar in the world, and "Brandywine," one of the largest of the breed, weighing 1,060 pounds. Among the sows may be mentioned such famous animals as "Carrie Canton," "Miss Carrie," "Lady Perfection" and "Tecumseh Girl."

Mr. Faulkner has an excellent location for handling animals and sending them to various shipping points, Jamesport being located on the Rock Island Railroad, eighty-five miles northeast of Kansas City, and sixty miles northeast of St. Joseph, Missouri. His foundation stock came from the old spotted Poland breeders of Illinois and Ohio; his hogs are all recorded with the Standard Poland-China Record, Maryville, Missouri, of which he is a director, and he furnishes a certified pedigree with every hog he sells. Of the more than four hundred hogs he sells annually, not over half of them are seen by their buyers prior to their purchase, for his hogs are so well known that they are largely sold by mail order. He sends out only first-class stock, guarantees everything as represented, and every hog a breeder, and as he has always been faithful to his obligations he has an honored name in commercial circles. Mr. Faulkner is the owner of 160 acres of land in Jackson Township, forty acres of which was a part of his father's home place and purchased from the old Hannibal & St. Joseph Railroad.

In March, 1904, Mr. Faulkner was married to Miss Ocie Owens, of Coffeyburg, Missouri, a daughter of John S. Owens, now a farmer in Iowa. Three children have been born to this union: Hazel Ray, Richard and Thomas Benton. In 1908 Mr. Faulkner took up his residence at Jamesport, which has since continued to be his home. In January, 1912, he was one of the organizers of the Peoples Exchange Bank of Jamesport, and at its organization was elected active vice president, a position which he has continued to hold to the present time. The growth of this bank may be realized by a glimpse of the following figures: Resources January 10, 1912, $25,337.33; October 21, 1913, $80,680.32; March 4, 1914, $115,102.23. On the last named date the following statement was issued: Resources, loans and discounts, $80,164.45; overdrafts, $348.72; furniture and fixtures, $2,600; cash and sight exchange, $31,-989.06; total, $115,102.23. Liabilities, capital stock, $20,000; surplus, $3,500; undivided profits, $586.62; deposits, $91,015.61. The officers are as follows: John W. Thompson, president; H. L. Faulkner, vice president; George B. Koch, cashier; and these gentlemen and the following as directors: John Gildow, J. A. Smith, W. F. Burge and J. F. Kesler. Their new building, which they have recently occupied, is one of the most commodious and handily arranged bank homes in this part of the state, a feature of which is a large farmers' room, provided with an old-fashioned fireplace, library tables, comfortable seats and every other convenience which is found in all up-to-date banking institutions.

Politically, Mr. Faulkner is a democrat, but he has never sought or accepted public office. He is a member of the Commercial Club of Jamesport, of which he has served one year as secretary; is fraternally connected with the Royal Arch chapter of the Masonic order and the Odd Fellow lodge and encampment, and is also a member of the Standard Poland-China Record Association of America, and has for the past three years been a member of the board of directors, a most important position. During the sixty years that the Faulkner family has resided in Daviess County, its members have made an enviable record for straightforward and honorable participation in those things which have made its agricultural and business history, and Homer L. Faulkner is proving

himself a worthy representative of a name that has always been held
in the highest esteem.

ROBERT V. THOMPSON, M. D.   Though a native of New York State,
Doctor Thompson spent most of his youth on a small farm in Livingston
County, Missouri, and is a successful physician and business man whose
ambition and energy guided him in his early search for opportunity.
Doctor Thompson now occupies a prominent position in business affairs
at Jamesport as president of the Commercial Bank of that city, and
except as business interests have interfered has been in active practice
as a physician and surgeon for twenty-five years.

The Commercial Bank of Jamesport, of which Doctor Thompson is
now the president, was organized in 1892 as the Farmers and Merchants
Bank. It began with a capital stock of $30,000, and the first officers were:
T. B. Yates, president; W. F. Phipps, cashier, and W. I. Jones, assistant
cashier. Doctor Thompson was one of the original board of directors.
In 1904 the capital stock was increased to $50,000, and in 1911 there
was a consolidation of this with the First National Bank of Jamesport,
at which time the name was changed to its present form. The capital
stock was then increased to $80,000. It is one of the soundest banks of
Northwest Missouri, as a brief glance at some items from an official statement in October, 1914, will indicate. The total resources aggregated
$417,514.64, and besides the capital of $80,000 the bank's surplus and
profits aggregated nearly twenty thousand dollars. An important feature
of the general statement is the amount of deposits, which at that time
totaled upwards of $290,000. The personnel of the officials and directory
include many of the best known men in Daviess County. Besides Doctor
Thompson as president, the vice president is Ben F. Wood, a banker of
long experience; James Guerin, secretary, and W. T. McClure, cashier.
Other names from the list of directors are C. G. McKinley, H. J. Kesler,
T. K. Hays and W. C. Pogue.

Robert V. Thompson was born February 27, 1864, in Chemung
County, New York, a son of Richard and Hester (Booth) Thompson.
His father was a native New Yorker and of English descent, while his
mother was born in England and was brought to America by her parents
when one year of age. Richard Thompson was a miller by trade, followed his vocation in New York State, but died when Doctor Thompson
was but four years of age. In 1868 the widowed mother brought her
children out to Livingston County, Missouri, and bought a small slightly
improved farm, which with the assistance of her older sons she broke up
and improved, and that little homestead was the place where she ended
her days, her last years being spent in comfort and plenty, passing away
in 1898. Doctor Thompson was the ninth among ten children, and one
daughter and three sons are still living.

Doctor Thompson grew up on the little Livingston County farm,
attended the common schools in the country districts, and for a time
was a student at Avalon College. His early medical studies were carried on under the direction of Dr. T. W. Foster, with whom he remained
two years, and then entered the Missouri Medical College at St. Louis,
graduating M. D. in March, 1889. Doctor Thompson began his practice
of medicine at Jamesport and has been one of the favorite physicians
of the city the greater part of a quarter of a century. Three years after
beginning practice he took a post-graduate course at the Chicago Poli-
clinic, and then returned and practiced regularly until 1897. In that
year he was elected cashier of the old Farmers and Merchants Bank of
Jamesport and took an active part in the bank's affairs for two years.
He then resigned to resume his practice, but after three years again

acquired an interest in the bank and was again its cashier for seven years. In 1909 he was elected president, and devoted all his time to the active management of the institution for three years, and since 1911, though still retaining his post as president, has continued the work of his profession. At one time Doctor Thompson owned a large amount of Missouri farm lands, but his investments in recent years have been turned to the irrigated district of Colorado, where he now has some valuable interests.

In his professional associations he is a member of the Daviess County Medical Society, Grand River Valley Medical Society, the North Missouri Medical Society and the Missouri State Medical Society. While never active in politics for the sake of an office, Doctor Thompson has never avoided the responsibilities of citizenship, and has filled elective offices as coroner of Daviess County two terms, mayor of Jamesport one term, and as a member of the city council several terms. He is now and for seventeen years has filled the office of director and treasurer of the Jamesport School Board. In politics he is a democrat, and is affiliated with the Knights of Pythias.

Doctor Thompson was married February 11, 1891, to Miss Jennie Nickell. Her father, Rev. W. N. Nickell, who has been identified with the Missouri Presbytery throughout a long career as a minister, is now Presbyterian clergyman at Lowry City, Missouri. To the marriage of Doctor Thompson and wife have been born three children: Blanche, wife of J. Frank Smith, of Colorado; Victor, who also lives in Colorado; and Mary Frances, still attending school.

GEORGE DOWE HARRIS, M. D. While he is one of the younger physi- cians of Daviess County, Doctor Harris has had unusual success since beginning practice at Jamesport about four years ago, and in 1914 was honored by election to the office of vice president of the Missouri Eclectic Medical Society. Through his grandparents on both sides Doctor Harris is identified with pioneer times in Northwest Missouri, since the familiies have lived here seventy years or more, and the first to come had to hew homes out of the wilderness.

George Dowe Harris was born in Grundy County, Missouri, January 1, 1884, a son of James P. and Jennie (Anderson) Harris, his father a native of Grundy County and his mother of Livingston County. The paternal grandparents, Jesse and Mary (Embrey) Harris, natives of Kentucky, where they were married, left that state more than three quarters of a century ago, drove overland with wagon and ox team to Grundy County, Missouri, where Jesse Harris was one of the very early arrivals, and entered a section of Government land in Jefferson Town- ship. This land, it is interesting to note, is now owned by Doctor Harris' father, who inherited it from its first settler. A log house was the first home of the Harris family in Missouri, and it was built by Jesse Harris, assisted by his neighbors. The old house is still standing, an interesting relic of bygone days, and in a good state of preservation. Jesse Harris was a hard working farmer, improved his land, and remained on the old place until he died. The Harris family have been members of the Baptist Church for generations.

The doctor's maternal grandparents were George Washington and Jean (Leeper) Anderson, who were also from Kentucky, the state which furnished so many early settlers to Northwest Missouri. They were mar- ried there and not long after the Harrises made their journey also came to Northwest Missouri, locating in Livingston County. The family and many of their household goods were conveyed in a covered wagon. During the excitement over the California gold discoveries George W.

Anderson made two trips across the plains with wagon and ox team. Before coming to Missouri he had been a teacher in Kentucky, and in Livingston County served for more than twenty years as justice of the peace. Although a farmer by occupation, he never owned any land. His death occurred in Grundy County, just a mile from the Livingston County line, having moved to that locality a short time before his death. He was a stanch member of the Methodist Episcopal Church, a class leader, and would travel many miles to attend the early camp meetings and revivals.

James P. Harris, father of Doctor Harris, was born on the old farm in Grundy County July 22, 1839, and has spent practically his entire lifetime, covering three-quarters of a century, on the same place. As a boy he attended a school supported by subscription and kept in a log cabin, which had a fireplace at one end, split slab benches, puncheon floors, and the open space that by courtesy was called a window was covered with greased paper. It was the custom for the family of each pupil in school to furnish one load of wood, and that wood was prepared and placed in the fireplace by the boy pupils. James P. Harris lived at home with his parents throughout their lives, and inherited the farm. His first wife was Elizabeth Crockett, and the two daughters by that marriage were: Alice Ann, now deceased, who was the wife of Lewis Saltzman, and was the mother of thirteen children, eleven of whom are living, and among them are two sets of twin girls and triplet boys; and Polly, wife of Silas Chumley, of Grundy County. After the death of his first wife he married Jennie Anderson, who died shortly after the birth of her son, now Doctor Harris. The father then married Miss Ella Anderson, a sister of his second wife.

Doctor Harris, while a member of a substantial family and reared in comforts far superior to those enjoyed by his father, has had to work out his own salvation, and paid his own expenses for his higher professional training. He attended the country schools of Grundy County, and in 1902 entered the normal school at Chillicothe, remained there one year, and the next four years were spent in earning money as a country school teacher during the winter months and as a farmer in the summer. In 1907 he again entered the normal at Chillicothe and graduated the same year. The following fall saw him a student at the Eclectic Medical School of Cincinnati, Ohio, and after two years there he entered a regular school of medicine, the Bennett Medical College of Chicago, where he was graduated M. D. in 1911. Prior to his graduation and for some following months he served as an interne in Jefferson Park Hospital at Chicago, his service in that connection altogether being about six months. In July, 1911, Doctor Harris returned to Missouri and located at Jamesport, where he became associated in practice with Dr. Charles Gordon McKinley, under whom he had received his first instruction in medicine. This is one of the best known firms of physicians and surgeons in Daviess County, and they have a large general practice both in Jamesport and in the surrounding country.

Doctor Harris has professional associations with the Daviess County Medical Society, the Missouri State Medical Society, the Missouri Eclectic Society, of which he was elected vice president in June, 1914, and the National Eclectic Society. He is also serving as a member of the Jamesport Board of Health, and is an examiner for several life insurance companies. His church is the Baptist, while in politics he is a republican, and affiliated with the Knights of Pythias. On December 24, 1911, Doctor Harris married Miss Myrtle Sebastian, of Jamesport, a daughter of James E. and Marticia Sebastian, her father being a Daviess County farmer.

GEORGE W. HILL. In the election of George W. Hill to the office of mayor in 1914, the citizens of Jamesport honored a man who has been identified with this part of Daviess County nearly sixty years, and who has always shown public spirit in community affairs and marked efficiency as a business man. His prosperity came from long continued operations as a farmer near Jamesport, and being now retired with an ample competence he has had the leisure and experience to give Jamesport an able administration of municipal affairs.

George W. Hill was born in Pocahontas County, West Virginia, November 11, 1843, and the same county was the birthplace of his parents, William P. and Elizabeth (Poage) Hill. His father was a blacksmith by trade, and followed that occupation during his career in West Virginia. It was in the year 1855, when the present Jamesport mayor was about twelve years of age, that the Hill family left West Virginia, made part of the trip by wagon, part of it down the course of the Ohio River, and finally arrived by these combined methods of water and overland transportation in Daviess County, Missouri. William P. Hill had the vigor and enterprise of the true pioneer. He preempted 160 acres and bought another 160 acres lying west and south of the present site of Jamesport. That was only the beginning of his accumulations as a landholder, and at the time of his death his estate aggregated 1,300 acres, and was worth many times what he paid for his first land in this section. He was the builder of the first home occupied by the family. It was a house small in dimensions and with few comforts, and was constructed of round logs. The fall after his arrival he built a hewed log house, and then with these provisions for his family he proceeded to clear up the land, fence and improve it, and in the course of years the log buildings gave way to a substantial frame residence and barn, and there were few men in Daviess County more prosperous. William P. Hill was born in 1818 and died at the old homestead in Daviess County in 1882, while his wife was born in 1816 and died at Jamesport in 1906, when in her ninety-first year, being active and clear-minded to the last. George W. Hill was the second in a family of eight children, the others being mentioned briefly as follows: John, who died on the home farm; Nancy, deceased, who was the wife of G. B. Kimball; Jane, who died of cholera shortly after the family came to Missouri; Sampson L., deceased; Mary, wife of Samuel Leonard, of Jackson Township; Jennie, deceased; and Davis, of Gallatin.

George W. Hill has depended upon his native intelligence and a keen faculty of observation for his education, since all his regular schooling was compressed within the first eleven years of his life. He attended the schools for several winters in West Virginia, but after the family came out to Daviess County, owing to limited school facilities, he applied himself to the more practical duties of clearing up a new farm. He continued with his father until twenty-six years of age, and was then married and started for himself. Mr. Hill was married August 26, 1868, to Mrs. Addie (Leonard) Moore. He then began farming for himself on a place three miles southwest of Jamesport, on 160 acres of partly improved land. That was the scene of his activities until his final retirement from farming as a business, though the prosperity that grew with his continued efforts resulted in additions to his original ownership until he had 400 acres. Nearly all of this land has been well improved, and it has a group of good substantial buildings. However, it is interesting to note that as Mr. Hill spent his first years in Daviess County in a log house, he also started housekeeping for himself in a similar home.

In 1891 his wife died, and in 1893 he left the farm and moved to Jamesport, and about that time married Mrs. Ella M. (Jones) Tonkrey.

Her death occurred in 1898, and in the following year he married her sister, Mrs. Lizzie (Jones) Power. Mr. Hill has two children, both by his first wife: William L., who owns a portion of his father's old farm and is active manager of the entire estate; and Fondie E., wife of Orphus Critten, of Gilmer, Texas. Mr. Hill is a member of the Methodist Episcopal Church, South, and has fraternal associations with the Independent Order of Odd Fellows.

Politically he is a democrat, and until recently the only office he consented to hold was that of school director in his home district in the country. He was prevailed upon to become a candidate for the office of mayor of Jamesport and was elected in April, 1914, for a term of two years.

When Mr. Hill came to Missouri Jamesport was still in the future, and he has witnessed practically every improvement from the erection of the first buildings through the various changes which have developed a thriving and prosperous little city. When he was a boy very little of the land was improved, and the settlers carried their grist sixteen miles to mill, that being an undertaking that required a day each way, coming and going. There were no railroads within 100 miles, and all the country was a paradise for hunters, abounding in wild game, including deer, turkey, prairie chicken, etc. Mr. Hill himself has experienced practically all the inconveniences, discomforts, pleasures and incidents of pioneer times, and is one of the intelligent, prosperous and public-spirited citizens of this community.

WILLIAM CARSON ELDER. In the service of the Burlington Railway as its agent at Albany since January 12, 1886, Mr. Elder has had personal supervision of nearly all the merchandise shipped in and out of that thriving Northwest Missouri community during the past thirty years. For a number of years he performed his official duties almost unaided and with his own hands handled most of the freight that came in or went out over that road. While his relations with the community have thus been of an interesting and important nature, he has also been a constructive business man, and is interested in several of the local enterprises that constitute the business activities of Albany.

William Carson Elder was born in Warren County, Illinois, December 18, 1860. His boyhood was passed in the manner of boys at that time, with school attendance, recreation in baseball and other outdoor games, and with a practical experience as clerk in his father's store at Gerlaw. In 1879 he began his career as railroader with the Burlington Company as an extra man on the St. Louis division of the road. At Gerlaw he acquired the art of telegraphy, and his first regular station was at Alsey, Illinois. He was transferred to Mount Ayr, Iowa, on a letter from W. C. Brown, now president of the New York Central Lines. From there he was transferred to Hummeston as agent, subsequently in the same capacity to Ridgeway, Missouri, and in 1886 to Albany. This station had had several agents before Mr. Elder came, but he now has one of the longest continuous records in one place with this division of the Burlington system.

On coming to Albany Mr. Elder worked in a small office about 8 by 10 feet, and only at times was given a helper. Still though the business of the station grew with the general development of the town and surrounding district, the adequacy of the station and its facilities was not materially improved until 1911, when two new rooms were built. Albany at that time was a division point. During the early years traffic was light and the train often came in with only an engine and two or three merchandise cars, and very frequently Mr. Elder did all the work of handling the freight, at the same time looking after the duties of the telegraph room and the clerical matters. Since then his responsibilities have increased and he now has five aids on the payroll and all of them are kept busy.

Mr. Elder has the distinction of having shipped the first carload of coal into Albany for the retail trade in 1887. He has been in the coal business ever since, and subsequently added grain. Five years ago he began putting up natural ice, and is now at the head of the Artesian Ice Company, while his grain and coal business is conducted under the name Elder Grain and Coal Company. His company and the Albany Milling Company ship all the grain marketed at this point.

While these duties and activities have made him a useful factor in the community, Mr. Elder has also been a leader in local affairs. When the aldermanic body was doubled he was elected an alderman and served two terms. During that time the electric light committee had him as chairman four years, and many important extensions to the plant were made. While a citizen who endeavored to do his full share in community improvements, Mr. Elder is not a politician, and confines his interest along that line to voting with the republican party.

Mr. Elder is a member of the Methodist Church and of the Order of Railway Telegraphers. At Albany on April 25, 1888, he married Miss Lola C. Twist. Her father, Frank Twist, was a Union soldier, a carpenter by trade, and came to Missouri from Ohio, though born in New York State. Mr. and Mrs. Elder had the following children: Frank Cleo, who died at the age of three years. Frederick Alonzo, who married Bernice E. Jones and has a son Donald Franklin, and a daughter, Anna Kathlyn; Harry T., of Seattle, Washington; Morris D., his father's assistant in the railroad office; Paul Shamblin; Clarice May; Margaret Frances; and Alice Kathryn.

Mr. Elder has an interesting ancestry. His paternal grandfather, David Elder, who died at Mount Ayr, Iowa, at the age of seventy-two, was a native of Ohio, and spent all his active career as a farmer. He was a member of the United Presbyterian Church, and of Scotch stock, his father having been born in Scotland. David Elder married Isabel Wray. Their children were: John; William; Clark; A. Alonzo; James, who was killed in the battle of Stone River during the Civil war; Rebecca, who married William Campbell, of Kenton, Ohio; and Margaret, who married R. J. Lawhead of Mount Ayr, Iowa.

The maternal grandfather of Mr. Elder was John Hogue, a son of James Hogue. James Hogue was born in Ireland in 1754, came to America at the age of fifteen, and a year later found work at Carlisle, Pennsylvania. From that community a few years later he enlisted for service during the American Revolution in Captain Henrick's Rifle Company, and in three days was on his way to Boston. At that city his company was assigned to the Quebec expedition under General Benedict Arnold, made the arduous campaign to the St. Lawrence, participated in the battle and the storming of the heights, and was taken a prisoner after General Montgomery was killed. The British threatened to send all the English, Irish and Scotch back to England to be hanged as traitors unless they enlisted and fought against the Americans. Before the prisoners were sent off James Hogue and Thomas Walker escaped, were recaptured, again escaped, and while living among the French the British authorities again apprehended him, and tried him by court martial and sent him to England. While being taken to prison in England he got loose from his captors, hid for a time in a cellar, and then traveled overland towards London. While on the way he met the king's brother, the Duke of Gloucester, who asked him and his companions what ship they belonged to. They explained to the duke that they had permission to go by land to London. In London they were once more captured, made their escape and James Hogue was finally put aboard a British ship bound for Halifax, subsequently sent to Charleston, South Carolina, then back to Halifax, and there was put on board an English privateer which fell in with an American vessel and in the engagement the British ship was captured. Mr. Hogue quickly made friends with the captain of the American ship, finally reached Baltimore, and was assigned to service on the American frigate Trumbull. After about five and a half years of service in the many vicissitudes between the English and Americans, he reached Philadelphia, and was granted as pay for his work in the patriot cause a ticket for forty shillings. In 1784 James Hogue moved from Pennsylvania to Kentucky and in 1788 to Butler County, Ohio, which was his home until 1826. One of his children was John Hogue, maternal grandfather of William C. Elder.

Mr. Elder's father was A. Alonzo Elder, who died in Albany, Missouri, December 31, 1895, at the age of fifty-seven. He had come to Albany a few years previously, and was associated with his son in the coal and grain business. He was born in Canton, Ohio, in 1838, came to Illinois in childhood, took up a career as a farmer, and in that state married Sarah Hogue, daughter of John and granddaughter of James Hogue. She died in Tarkio, Missouri. The children of A. Alonzo Elder and wife were: William C.; Margaret I., wife of Clark McConnell of Fairfax, Missouri; Anna Lee, wife of William H. Kendall of Tarkio, Missouri.

WILLIAM SAMUEL WALKER. More than threescore years and ten have passed since the Walker family became identified with Harrison County. In this Middle West country that is a long time to be resident of one locality, and the associations with the name are as honorable as they are long continued. Almost exactly seventy years after William S. Walker was brought to the county as an infant he became postmaster of Bethany by appointment from President Wilson on June 6, 1913. The date of his first arrival in the county was July 4, 1843, and with the exception of his army service and several years during the war decade he has lived in Northwest Missouri ever since.

William Samuel Walker was born in North Carolina October 16, 1842. His grandfather, William Walker, was a native of Ireland and founded the family in America, locating in North Carolina, where he died a number of years before the Civil war. He owned slaves and operated a plantation in Rockingham County. His children were: James, who spent his life in North Carolina; John, who died in North Carolina; Daniel; and Jesse, who was last heard of in Indiana.

Daniel Walker was born in Rockingham County, North Carolina, in 1810, and died in 1864 at the age of fifty-four. He had perhaps the ordinary education of men of the time, and was trained to farm pursuits. Soon after the birth of his son William he started with wagons and teams for Missouri, where he entered a tract of government land in Butler Township of Harrison County, and for the next twenty years was successfully identified with agriculture and the improving of his land. The old homestead is situated in section 9, township 63, range 29. Daniel Walker was a quiet unassuming farmer citizen, and had no military or political record, though a regular supporter of the democratic party and decidedly in sympathy with the southern cause and during the war furnished a son to the Confederate army. More of his time and attention were given to church matters. He was an active Presbyterian and helped erect the Matkins Church in Harrison County, and was one of its elders. He was likewise positively committed to the advancement of education.

and as a trustee of his district helped to provide school facilities in a pioneer country. He died from a bronchial affection when he should have been in the prime of his life.

Daniel Walker married Mary M. Edminston, a daughter of Samuel and Mary (Gilson) Edminston, both of whom were of North Carolina. Mrs. Walker died in Andrew County, Missouri, at the age of sixty-four. Her children were: William S.; John G., a farmer in Butler Township, Harrison County; James, who died unmarried; and Newton, who died in West Haven, Connecticut, leaving a family.

William Samuel Walker grew up in the new country of Harrison County, and the outbreak of the war between the states found him just coming into manhood. His education had been finished in the country district near home, and soon after leaving his books he enlisted in Company G of the First Missouri Cavalry, in the Confederate army. The company was raised in Harrison County and its first commander was Captain Patterson and the second Captain Enyart, while the regiment was first commanded by Colonel Childs and subsequently by Colonel Elijah Gates. From the rendezvous at Gentryville the regiment went to the front at Lexington where it did its first fighting as part of the army of General Sterling Price. From Lexington the army fell back into Arkansas, and Mr. Walker participated in the battle of Cross Hollows, better known in history as Pea Ridge or Elkhorn. The entire army then was transferred to Memphis, but arrived too late for the battle of Shiloh, though it took part in the battle at Corinth, and then moved to the vicinity of Vicksburg, where Mr. Walker was in the Baker's Creek or Champion Hills fight. At that point, May 16, 1863, he was with a squad of his comrades who were captured by the Third Kentucky Regiment. The prisoners were taken to Camp Morton, Indianapolis, and thence started for Point Lookout, Maryland. At Harrisburg, Pennsylvania, Mr. Walker made his escape just a month after his capture. The box-car in which he was riding was waiting in the yards for another train to pass, when an Irishman came by and asked if the boys wanted water. He took Walker's hand and gave it a squeeze and whispered that if he made his escape the Irishman would be on hand to do all he could for him. It was dusk, and while the car-doors were locked, the prisoners had cut holes to let in air, and these apertures were large enough to crawl through. Walker and a companion made the passage without being discovered, and, following directions, on reaching a little hedge gave a cough, which was answered by the Irish friend. The latter took them to his own home, put them upstairs in a double tenement house, the other side of which was occupied by Union people, and there Mr. Walker discarded his Confederate uniform and was given a hat and trousers instead. After spending the night there Mr. Walker went to the iron furnace in the city, and was given work. That was June 17th, and he remained in the furnace two months, and then worked in the harvest fields until September 1st, and then went south to Kentucky. Near Maysville he hired out to a farmer named Henry Jeffries, and became so much one of the family and so intimate that when Mr. Jeffries accused him of being a Confederate he admitted the truth of the suspicion on the assurance that the fact would not get beyond the knowledge of the family circle. After that he was treated in the same kindly manner by this Union friend, and lived in Kentucky, was married, and in 1867 left the state with his young wife and returned to Missouri.

On reaching the community where he had spent his boyhood Mr. Walker took up farming and followed it actively for five years. He then went to Andrew County to a farm, and later for ten years was a merchant at King City. During his residence there he served as a member of the council, and was otherwise active in local affairs. In 1898 Mr. Walker returned to Harrison County and at Bethany became a member of the firm of Slemmons & Walker Brothers, the principals of which were his sons and his son-in-law. Mr. Walker was bookkeeper of the concern until he retired to accept the duties of the local post-office.

Politically Mr. Walker has always been a democrat, and cast his first presidential vote for Horatio Seymour, later voted for Horace Greeley, and for every democratic candidate since. He is an original Wilson man, and had two competitors for the postmastership, and succeeded B. P. Sigler in that office. He has given an excellent administration of the local office. He is a past grand of the Independent Order of Odd Fellows, and has sat in the grand lodge. His church home is the Presbyterian. He owns one of the substantial homes of Bethany, located in front of the Christian Church, and his family are located in the same neighborhood.

Mr. Walker was married in Kentucky about war times to Kate Calvert, who died at Bethany in 1900. Their children were: Mary, wife of J. B. Slemmons, of Bethany; Robert L., who married Elizabeth Walker, is a member of the firm of Slemmons & Walker Brothers; James M., who married Nancy Clark, is also of the same firm; George P., who married Lois Barnes, also a partner in the firm. For his second wife Mr. Walker married Miss Emma Hubbard, a daughter of Edgar L. Hubbard and a sister of Edward S. Hubbard, an old and prominent family elsewhere mentioned in this work. Mr. and Mrs. Walker had two children, Ralph L. and Walter, the latter dying at the age of seven.

RILEY NAPOLEON FUNK, of New Hampton, is one of the successful agriculturists of Harrison County and a native of the locality. He was born on his present farm, December 13, 1869, and has spent his entire life on this property. Here he lived as a schoolboy, here he passed his youth and secured his first impressions of work and here he began life when he married. His farm, which his father purchased at the close of the Civil war and on which he spent his last years and died, is situated in section 17, township 63, range 29, where Mr. Funk is the owner of 190 acres of good land, and forty acres in section 11.

Martin Funk, the paternal grandfather of Riley N. Funk, was born December 25, 1800, and was of German descent of Rockingham County, Virginia, his remote ancestor being one of four brothers who came to America from Germany and probably settled in the Old Dominion State. There is no record of their having owned slaves and few of them deviated from the beaten path of agriculture. They were Mennonites originally, and one Henry Funk, of the earlier members of the family, published an almanac in Virginia, and was one of the few who became a scholarly man. Martin Funk was a man of fair education and a democrat in politics, but was not a confessed member of any church nor did he have any military or political history. His life was passed amid the peaceful pursuits of the soil, and his death occurred in June, 1881, when he was eighty years of age.

Nathaniel Funk, the father of Riley N. Funk, was born August 25, 1826, and as a child went with his parents to Henry County, Indiana, where he was reared, educated and married. He did not serve in the army during the Civil war, as the township in which he resided made up the money necessary to provide the troops called for by the Government, and in 1865 came to Harrison County, Missouri. Mr. Funk was a democrat, but in no sense was a politician and ran for no office, although he held that of postmaster, when the office was located in his house, before the location of the Town of "Hamptonville," now New Hampton, which latter place was laid out the same month Riley N. Funk was born. Nathaniel Funk was one of the substantial men of his community and was called upon to aid in the erection of the first churches of the locality. He aided in the building of the Foster Church, being one of its chief contributors, and never failed to donate to such worthy objects. He was a Universalist in religious belief, and having no such organization here he divided his church labors. Mr. Funk belonged to no secret order; his friendship for education was shown by his capable and faithful service as a member of the district school board.

Nathaniel Funk lived a long and active life, and died December 23, 1909. He married the first time Eliza J. Courtney, a daughter of John Courtney, of Indiana, and to them there were born three children: Joseph, a leading farmer of Harrison County; Mart, of El Paso County, Colorado; and Margaret, who became the wife of J. W. Sevier, of Portland, Oregon. Mr. Funk's second marriage was to Miss Catherine Huffman, who was born August 15, 1832, and died in June, 1890, daughter of Jonathan Huffman, a Virginia man who passed away in Rockingham County, that state. Three children were born to Mr. and Mrs. Funk: Riley N., of this notice; Gillie A., who is the wife of Sam Claytor, of Harrison County; and Sam T., a farmer of New Hampton.

Riley N. Funk has passed his life as a farmer, and has been successful in his ventures, having also identified himself with a number of business ventures, including the public or farmers scales of New Hampton and the farmers lumber yard, in both of which he is a stockholder. He has taken enough interest in public affairs to gain the name of being a good citizen, and gives his political support to the democratic party. A Methodist in his religious belief, he is one of the trustees of Shady Grove Church. Mr. Funk was married February 14, 1894, to Miss Margaret A. Smith, a daughter of Edward Smith and a sister of John E. Smith, a sketch of whose career and family will be found in this work. To Mr. and Mrs. Funk there have been born the following children: Kathryn Frances, born November 26, 1894, was educated in the New Hampton High School and the Maryville Normal School, and is now a teacher in the public schools of Harrison County; and Estella Alice, born September 6, 1897; Nora Thelma, born October 16, 1899; Hazel Agnes, born March 14, 1901; Roberta Moe, born September 17, 1902; Garland Edward, born June 3, 1904; Marie Pearl, born August 15, 1906. All these children except the two youngest, Garland and Marie, are members of the South Methodist Church with their parents. Mr. Funk is a member of the Knights of Pythias, Lodge No. 285, of New Hampton.

GEN. ROBERT WILSON. Among the stalwart men who helped to shape the destinies of the state, few have played a more important part than Gen. Robert Wilson, who spent the latter years of his life on his farm in Andrew County, a short distance north of St. Joseph. Sympathetic with the needs and aspirations of the people, clear and fixed in his own ideas of expediency and right, and giving expression to his ideals both by precept and example with force and dignity, his was a character of inestimable usefulness during the formative and tempestuous years of the state's first half century.

Born near Staunton, Virginia, November, 1800, Robert Wilson lived there until he came to Missouri in 1820. Settling in Howard County, he taught school for a time and later found employment in the office of the Circuit Clerk. Subsequently he was appointed postmaster of Fayette and in 1823 was elected Judge of the Probate Court. In 1828 he was elected clerk of the Circuit and County Court, which office he continued

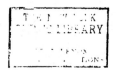

DR. NICHOLS' SANATORIUM, SAVANNAH

to hold until 1840. Meantime he had studied law under his brother General John Wilson and had been admitted to the bar. In 1837 on the outbreak of the so-called Mormon war, he was appointed brigadier general of the state forces by Governor Boggs and was instrumental, by his firm and judicious conduct of affairs, in ridding the state of a population so generally obnoxious to its citizens. In 1844, Randolph County having been formed and he having removed to Huntsville, he was sent therefrom to the State Legislature. Removing thence to Andrew County in 1852, he was elected in 1854 to represent that district in the Senate and re-elected in 1858, although he was a whig and the district strongly democratic.

In the early part of 1861, General Wilson was chosen as a union delegate to the convention called by the state to determine its attitude regarding secession and at its first session, February 28th, he was elected vice-president with Sterling Price as president. Subsequently Price having fled to join the Confederacy, General Wilson succeeded to the presidency and presided over the convention's deliberations until its close. In January, 1862, he was appointed by Acting Governor Hall to the United States Senate to fill the unexpired term of Waldo P. Johnson expelled, and discharged the duties of that office for two sessions until the election of B. Gratz Brown.

After retiring from the Senate, General Wilson though keeping in close touch with public affairs devoted himself to agriculture, in which his interest was intense. While on a visit to his old surroundings in Central Missouri, he was stricken with pneumonia and passed away May 10, 1870, at the home of his nephew, Capt. Ben Wilson, at Marshall, leaving behind a record that was unblemished as to both public and private life and one that was unusually rich in evidences of the highest usefulness to his fellow-men.

In 1825 General Wilson was married to Margaret Snoddy who died in 1836, leaving him three children, John, who was graduated from Yale in 1847 and who died in St. Joseph in 1858; James, who was educated at Centre College, Danville, Kentucky, and who died in St. Joseph in 1906, and Mary Ann who in 1855 was married to Rufus L. McDonald of St. Joseph and who still survives.

PERRY NICHOLS, M. D. As one scans the progress of medical science during past ages and more particularly during the present and preceding century, amazement and admiration are aroused and faith grows where doubt once prevailed. While marvelous things have been accomplished in the domain of medicine there have been a few ills that afflict mankind that, until recently, have seemed entirely resistent to every treatment and perhaps none have been more dreaded and fatal than cancer. The general reader is not unacquainted with the progress of research along the line of cure for this cruel disease, which attacks every class, irrespective of wealth or station, and, if humane and sympathetic, must feel keenly regret and disappointment when one heralded cure after the other has been swept aside as entirely inadequate. Hence great interest all over the country has been aroused by the astounding success which has attended the scientific treatment and cure of cancer by one who has made the study of this scourge of mankind his life work, Dr. Perry Nichols, founder of the Nichols' Sanatorium, located at Savannah, Missouri.

Perry Nichols was born at Shellsburg, Benton County, Iowa, March 20, 1863, and is a son of Ira S. and Anna (Carrier) Nichols. The father was born in New York and the mother in Vermont. They were married in Wisconsin and then moved to Benton County, Iowa, and there spent the rest of their lives. They had two sons, Frederick and Perry, both residents of Savannah.

The duties pertaining to the cultivation of the home farm claimed Perry Nichols until he was about twenty years of age. He had, however, excellent educational opportunities, attending school at Iowa City, afterward spending two years in the Iowa State University, in the meanwhile pursuing his medical studies and in 1901 was graduated from the medical department of the University of the South. He immediately entered into practice at Watertown, South Dakota, three years later removing to Hot Springs and three years afterward came to Savannah. For the past eighteen years he has devoted his attention almost entirely to the treatment and cure of cancer and maintains his sanatorium at Savannah, Missouri. The sanatorium was incorporated June 25, 1914, with a capital stock of $500,000. It is under the management of the following staff: Perry Nichols, B. S., M. D., formerly professor of malignant diseases in the Lincoln Medical College, Lincoln, Nebraska, president; W. A. Stearns, vice president; J. H. Reaugh, treasurer; Edith Eason, secretary. The board of directors is made up of the above officials and also W. H. Bailey, M. D., Ella Nichols and Lydia Reaugh. Dr. W. H. Bailey is medical director.

Doctor Nichols lives a busy life, but will never complain as long as he sees the beneficent results arising from his enterprise and his scientific discoveries. It was only after many years of research and diligent study that he discovered a safe and sane cure for the malignant disease of cancer without the use of the surgeon's knife and the miraculous cures that he has performed entitle him to the gratitude of thousands of patients and should give him eminent standing among the benefactors of mankind. His institution is modern in every way, with skilled medical practitioners and corps of trained nurses, and the location of the building is in a section where may be found every requirement of health. Although Doctor Nichols has built up this enormous business in but a few years and has comfortable accommodations for many patients, coming from every section of the country, at the present writing (1915) he is contemplating further extension, which means still further humanitarian usefulness.

Doctor Nichols has three children and all are pupils in the high school. They are George, Helen and John.

HARRY PHILIP WOODSON has been a constant factor in the upbuilding of the City of Richmond for more than thirty years. As the directing head of important mercantile enterprises bearing his name, and later in the management of his father's estate and the manifold interests of his own, he has given employment to many men and has directed their energies into channels that have brought adequate rewards to themselves, to their employers and to the city in which they have lived and labored. Mr. Woodson belongs to an old and honored family, whose members have been prominent in various walks of life, and a short review of its members follows.

H. P. Woodson was born March 23, 1859, and is a son of Thomas D. Woodson, the latter a son of Robert S. and Hulda Ann (Young) Woodson. Thomas D. Woodson was born at Woodsonville, Hart County, Kentucky, March 10, 1828, and died at Richmond, Missouri, August 28, 1902. His father was born in Goochland County, Virginia, November 26, 1796, and moved with his parents to the present site of Woodsonville, then in Barren County, Kentucky, in 1804. The great-grandfather, Thomas Woodson, was born in Goochland County, Virginia, on the River James, twenty miles above the City of Richmond, Virginia, December 2, 1772, and died in Woodsonville, Kentucky, February 14, 1857. He was the founder of Woodsonville, once a bright and attractive village situated on a high plateau overlooking the surrounding country, on the south bank of Green River, in Hart County, Kentucky. The great-grandmother of H. P. Woodson was also a native of Virginia, born May 2, 1776, and died in the same village in Kentucky, July 21, 1844. His grandmother was born in Rockingham County, Virginia, and died at Richmond, Missouri. Matthew Woodson, the great-great-grandfather of H. P. Woodson, was born in 1731, and married Elizabeth Levilian, the only child of John Peter Levilian. Jesse Saunders, the great-great-grandfather through his maternal grandmother, married Mary Levilian, the only child of Anthony Levilian. The paternal great-great-grandparents, the great-grandparents and the grandparents were all members of the old school Baptist Church. Mr. Woodson's grandparents had a family of nine children, of whom three died in infancy, the others being: Jane Ann, who married John H. Ardinger, a merchant of Woodsonville, Kentucky, who later moved to Lexington, Missouri, and there became a prominent citizen; Philip J.; Martha A., who became the wife of Austin A. King, governor of Missouri from 1848 to 1852; Elizabeth L., who became the wife of Dr. Shelby A. Jackson, of Ohio County, Kentucky; Robert Hyde, who joined the Confederate army at the outbreak of the Civil war, was wounded at the battle of Champion Hills, Mississippi, fell into the hands of the enemy and died; and Thomas D.

Thomas D. Woodson volunteered for service in 1847 in the Mexican war, joining the Fourth Kentucky Infantry, in the company of which first Pat Gardner and afterwards Thomas Mayfield were captains. At the close of his service he received his honorable discharge and came to Missouri, locating at Kingston, Caldwell County, where he established himself in the mercantile business. In the spring of 1852 he left Kingston and crossed the plains with a train of ox-wagons to the gold fields of California, but in January, 1854, returned to his Missouri home and again entered mercantile pursuits at Kingston. Like many other formerly successful men of his day, Mr. Woodson was ruined by the Civil war, and he accordingly disposed of what small interests he still had at Kingston and in 1863 came to Richmond, which city continued to be the scene of his activities during the greater part of the balance of his life. For one year he clerked for the firm of Wasson & Hughes, and then went into business on his own account, conducting a store until 1878, in which year he sold out to Holt & Hughes. In 1868 he assisted in the organization of the Ray County Savings Bank, of which he became president, a position which he continued to retain for ten years, and in 1878, when he decided to concentrate his entire energies upon the banking business, he was made president of the institution and continued as such up to the time of his death. He was also actively engaged in farming and stock raising and was the owner of large tracts of land in Ray and adjoining counties. A man of excellent business abilities, he bore a sterling reputation for honesty, uprightness and honorable dealing. On December 5, 1854, Mr. Woodson was married to Miss Sabina L. Hughes, a native of Clark County, Kentucky, who was born in 1830 and died April 11, 1871, and to this union there were born three children: Lydia A., who was born September 27, 1855, single and a resident of Richmond; Harry Philip; and Virginia Elizabeth, born September 11, 1870, and now the wife of Dr. Robert Sevier, a prominent physician and surgeon of Richmond. Thomas D. Woodson was a devout and constant worker in the Methodist Church, South, attended all general conferences and annual conferences for years, and was a power in the upbuilding of the church at Richmond, being a member of the board of curators for years. He donated $12,000 for the purpose of building Woodson Institute, succeeded in firmly establishing it by untiring effort, and it was finally named in his honor. He was one of Ray

County's grandest men, his name was untarnished, his friends were legion and his life was not lived in vain.

H. P. Woodson was reared in Richmond, where he secured his early education in the common schools. He then went for one year to the University of Missouri, following which he entered his father's store as a clerk, having determined to learn the business from the bottom. In 1879 he went to Carrollton, Missouri, and purchased an interest in a store with John Guitar, but after one year, on account of failing health, was compelled to go to Texas. After one year spent in the Lone Star State, Mr. Woodson returned to Richmond and purchased the interest of Mr. Hughes of the firm of Holt & Hughes, and about twelve months later Mr. Holt sold his interest to W. H. Darneal, the firm then becoming Darneal & Woodson. Subsequently, three years later, Mr. Woodson bought Mr. Darneal's interest, but still later this was sold back to him, and the firm of Woodson & Darneal continued in active business until 1905. Mr. Woodson then disposed of his share to Mr. Darneal, who still conducts the business, and since that time Mr. Woodson has devoted his attention to looking after his father's estate and his own large interests.

On November 16, 1881, Mr. Woodson was married to Miss Stella H. Galtney, a native of Mississippi, who at her parents' death came to Missouri to make her home with her sister, who was the wife of Capt. James L. Farris. She died June 6, 1912, at the age of fifty-two years. Four children were born to this union, namely: Thomas D., a graduate of Richmond High School, Woodson Institute, the University of Missouri and the medical department of Washington University, St. Louis, spent one year at Washington, D. C., taking a medical course of one year to fit himself for army work, and is now stationed at Washington, D. C.; James R. and Harry P., Jr., who are successfully engaged in the lumber business in Texas; and Clara G., who resides with her father.

Mr. Woodson is a member of the Methodist Episcopal Church, South, is a member of the church board of trustees and stewards, and has attended several general conferences. He is a member of the board of curators of Central College, and in every movement for the advancement of education, religion, morality and good citizenship takes an active and helpful part. His entire career has been marked by constant advancement, and he is proving himself a worthy representative of the honored name he bears.

Roy E. Powell. A man of less than forty years, yet with fully twenty-five of them spent in the trade and profession of newspaper work, Roy E. Powell has a high standing among the press fraternity of Northwest Missouri. He is editor of the Holt Rustler, and has been connected with various papers in this section of the state and in Nebraska.

Roy E. Powell was born at Fillmore, Andrew County, Missouri, May 21, 1875. His father Job Powell was born in Massachusetts, July 29, 1829, of good New England stock, and is now living at the venerable age of eighty-five in Fillmore, Missouri. A blacksmith by trade, he had a career filled with the vicissitudes of the world. When eleven years old he was apprenticed or bound out to his uncle, a blacksmith. In a few years the boy was a capable workman, but the uncle, who was somewhat of the avaricious type, withheld from his apprentice his small wages, and the youth rebelled at the age of seventeen and ran away from his master. In 1858 he came west to St. Louis, and thence came by boat into Northwest Missouri, locating in Andrew County. He responded to the first call for three-year men in the Civil war, and enlisted on August 21, 1861, in the engineer corps of the Twenty-fifth Missouri. Later he was transferred to the regimental band, and served until honorably discharged shortly before the close of the war at Atlanta, Georgia. He was offered $150 to re-enlist as a substitute, but refused and came home to resume his business as a blacksmith. For many years that trade continued his source of livelihood, and he was located at Fillmore, Maryville, Cameron and again at Fillmore, where he finally retired in 1899, but at this writing is still hale and hearty. Many years ago he served as a justice of the peace in Andrew County, has been a republican since the party came into existence, and is a member of the Presbyterian Church. His first wife was a Miss Hart, a Massachusetts girl, who left one child, Laura E., wife of W. W. Spicer, of Fillmore, Missouri. By his second marriage there was also one daughter, Rosa A., wife of B. F. Middaugh, of St. Joseph, Missouri. His third wife was Elizabeth Nodie, who was born in Maryland September 9, 1839, and is still living. Her five children are: Ursula A., wife of James E. Bell, of Maryville; Bessie L., wife of Elmer Calhoun of Richmond, Oklahoma; Roy E.; John E., of Kearny; and Lucy, widow of George Thompson, of Kansas City.

When Roy E. Powell was five years old his parents moved to Cameron, Missouri, in 1883 to Gallatin, and from there to Maysville. In these places he acquired his common schooling, which terminated when he was thirteen, and he then began working for himself. Five years of practical apprenticeship with D. F. Jones of the DeKalb County Herald gave him a foundation equipment as a printer and newspaper man. He then went to Nebraska and for five years was connected with the Pawnee City Republican, then spent a year on the Daily Call at Excelsior Springs, and on June 20, 1907, came to Holt and leased the Rustler. At the end of nine months he bought the plant, and has since continued this well known Clay County journal, which has been established about twenty-five years and is now more prosperous and influential than ever.

On April 12, 1899, Mr. Powell married Kate Good. She died December 10, 1911, aged thirty-six, leaving two children: Lena and Catherine. On August 11, 1912, Mr. Powell married Miss Jeanette Reece, who was born at Lathrop, Missouri, daughter of Thomas J. and Alice (Eby) Reece. Her parents are now living in Holt. Fraternally Mr. Powell is affiliated with the Masonic order, the Independent Order of Odd Fellows and the Modern Woodmen of America. In politics he is a Democrat and he and wife are members of the Christian Union Church.

HON. FRANK REILEY. Of so forcible and stirring a personality as Hon. Frank Reiley, the biographer speaks the most who says the least. An outline of his career needs no furbishments or extravagant embellishments, his life having worked itself out simply and harmoniously and being a record of opportunities recognized, grasped and made the most of. Entering upon his career when but a lad, through his own efforts, he has worked himself to a position where he plays an important part in the commercial and agricultural life of his community and to the enviable office of presiding judge of De Kalb County.

Judge Reiley was born in Johnson County, Iowa, February 18, 1869, and is a son of William and Ann M. (Ellenberger) Reiley, natives of Pennsylvania. They were reared in their native state, and after their marriage, during the early '60s migrated to Iowa, where they passed the remaining years of their lives in the pursuits of the soil. Judge Reiley was twelve years of age at the time of his father's death, and his educational advantages were limited to attendance at the public schools up to that age, when he entered upon his struggles with the world.

As a youth he learned the trade of machinist and became a stationary engineer, a capacity in which he was working at the time of his marriage to Miss Mary C. Miller, of Andrew County, Missouri. In 1901 Judge Reiley came to De Kalb County and invested his capital of $150 in a mercantile business, but two years later came to Clarksville, where he bought out an established business, and has continued to conduct it to the present time. In addition to this he is the owner of 120 acres of farming land in De Kalb County, and all of his earnings have been accumulated through his own individual effort. In politics he has ever been a stalwart republican, and has taken an active part in the public affairs of this part of the state. ' He was elected judge of the District Court, and after serving as such two years was elected presiding judge of De Kalb County, a position he has continued to retain. In his judicial capacity Judge Reiley has shown himself a fair, impartial and thoroughly informed jurist, whose services upon the bench have been of a nature such as to commend him to his fellow-townspeople and to firmly establish him in general confidence. He has been foremost in the support of all measures and movements which have contributed to the welfare of his adopted locality, and education and religion have found in him an active co-worker. With his family, he attends the Methodist Episcopal Church. He has been interested in fraternal affairs for some years, and at present is a valued member of Lodge No. 476, Independent Order of Odd Fellows. Widely known throughout De Kalb County, he has friends in every locality, and as official and citizen is held in the highest esteem.

Judge and Mrs. Reiley have three children: William A., Violette and Mamie, all of whom are students in the Clarksdale public schools.

NOAH R. SPILLMAN. Not only is Noah R. Spillman the architect of a substantial fortune, acquired through enterprise and earnest endeavor in the field of agriculture, but in its acquisition he has maintained the reputation for industry and reliability established in Worth County by his pioneer father, Charles W. Spillman, who journeyed Missouriward from Kentucky about 1845, since which time the family has been well and favorably known in this locality. Noah R. Spillman was born in Worth County, Missouri, January 11, 1861, and is a son of Charles W. and Susan (Walker) Spillman.

Henry Spillman, the grandfather of Noah R. Spillman, was born in Culpeper County, Virginia, where he passed his entire life, being engaged in the pursuits of the soil. He was the son of Henry Spillman, who emigrated to Virginia with his two brothers, George and William. The grandfather married Annie Tapp, the daughter of a soldier of the War of 1812 who was given a land warrant by the Government for 5,500 acres, which has never been adjusted in the interest of his posterity, although it is believed that the grant was laid near Lexington, Kentucky, and that a part of that city now covers the ground. Henry and Annie (Tapp) Spillman were the parents of the following children: William, who died single; Robert, who married a Satterwhite; George, who married Catherine Abbott; John, who married Nancy Harris; James, who married Nancy Shepherd; Henry, who married Nancy Webb; Thomas, who married Elizabeth Whiteside; Francis, who married Eliza Abbott; Charles, who married for his second wife Susan Walker; Nancy, who married Elisha Robertson; Mary, who married William Satterwhite; and Annie, who married Jackson Fletcher.

Charles W. Spillman was born in Virginia, in 1824, and at the age of five years was taken to Trimble County, Kentucky, where he grew to manhood, securing a somewhat limited education and learning the trade of stone mason. About 1845 he came to Worth County, Missouri, to devote himself to agricultural pursuits, settling on a property located in section 25, township 65, range 30. He was a democrat on his political views, but did not hold office nor take an active part in public life, nor did he have any military record. He was just a plain, unassuming, hard-working citizen, a man of intense loyalty to his friends and a devout member of the Missionary Baptist Church. His death occurred in March, 1907. He was married to a Miss Rowlett, who died leaving five children, of whom the first born was Newton, who became the father of William P. Spillman, a review of whose career will be found on another page of this work. Mr. Spillman's second wife was Mrs. Susan (Walker) Murphy, the widow of Joseph Murphy, by whom she had two children: Amanda, who married, and died at Hominy, Oklahoma; and Martha, who married Henry Franklin and resides at that place. Mrs. Spillman was a daughter of Harris Walker, who came from Kentucky as a pioneer to Worth County, where he was engaged in agricultural pursuits until his death at the age of seventy-six years. Mrs. Spillman passed away in April, 1891, being the mother of the following children: Noah R., of this review; Cordelia, the wife of Ransom Stormer, of Harrison County, Missouri; Elizabeth, who married George Webb, also of that county; Harris, who is engaged in farming in Worth County; Alice, who is the wife of James Owens of Worth County; Kittie, who is the wife of John Owens, also of this section; Missouri, who married Frank Stufflebean, of Worth County; Gertrude, who married William Van Hoozer, of Martinsville, Missouri; Arabella, who married Jacob Stormer, of Harrison County; and Melissa, who became the wife of Charles Bowen and died in 1911.

Noah R. Spillman grew up on the old homestead where his father had settled upon coming to Worth County, and his education was secured in the district school. A lad of industry and ambition, during the long summer months he worked faithfully on the home place, and before reaching his majority began to make his own way in the world, first accepting employment as a farm hand at $15 per month, and later earning promotion to $20 for the same period. While thus working he added to his meagre income by trading in stock, and so successful was he in this line that he was able to purchase his first tract of land in section 36, on which he made a number of improvements and there resided for several years. At the time of his father's death he purchased the interests of the other heirs of the estate and moved to his old home, but later went to New Hampton, Missouri, where he was associated with his brother in the business of shipping and dealing in stock. Finally, in 1910, he came to his present farm, in section 36, Allen Township, where he has improved a handsome and valuable property. His hard and persistent labors have been rewarded with a full measure of success, and today he is recognized as one of the substantial men of his community, a title honestly earned.

Mr. Spillman was married in Gentry County, Missouri, October 9, 1880, to Miss Matilda Adams, a daughter of William and Delila (Wood) Adams, who came to Missouri from Illinois. The children in the Adams family were: Mary, who is the wife of William Hunter, of Harrison

Joseph North of Worth County, has a son—Wilbur; Charles C., a farmer of Worth County, married Miss Lou Wilson, and has three children— Jellene, Velma and Clifford; William W., who married Maggie McNeace and has three children—Ruth, Verdie and Merl; Emmet, a farmer in Worth County, married Jennie Zimmerman and has a son—Garnard; Vernie, the wife of Benjamin Lykins; Laura, the wife of Jesse Allen, of Gentry County; and Lawrence C. A democrat in politics, Mr. Spillman began his political activities as a young man in the county conventions of the earlier times, and is now an influential factor in his party's activities in Worth County. He is a devout member of the Missionary Baptist Church of New Harmony, and takes a helpful part in its association work.

CHARLES MILTON ADAMS. Among the citizens of enterprise and progressive spirit who are ably representing Worth County's agricultural interests Charles Milton Adams holds deservedly high place. A resident of Northwest Missouri for a long period of years, he has become the owner of a handsome property in the vicinity of Worth, and his long and useful career has been characterized by industry, integrity and public spirit, qualities which commend him to his fellow-citizens. He is a native of Edgar County, Illinois, and was born March 23, 1852, a son of Joseph and Sarah (White) Adams.

Joseph Adams was born in Kentucky, and was there engaged in farming until 1832, in which year he went to Illinois with his parents, the family settling on the grandfather's homestead in Edgar County. A graduate of the common schools, he was reared amid agricultural surroundings, and after his first marriage, to a Miss Moore, engaged in farming on his own account. After the death of his first wife, Mr. Adams was married to Miss Sarah White, the daughter of a Revolutionary soldier and pioneer of Coles County, Illinois, where he owned a farm of 160 acres. In 1856 Mr. Adams took his family by ox-team to Missouri, and there rented land from his brother Samuel, a tract in Worth County which is now owned by L. G. Elliott. Here he remained until 1862, when, because of the Civil war, he left his crops and stock and returned to Coles County, Illinois, where he rented land. This trip was made from Worth, the family traveling north through Iowa, crossing the Mississippi River at Fort Madison, and thus avoiding the "bushwhackers," who were numerous in Northwest Missouri, although the trip consumed three weeks. Mr. Adams was an invalid and was not able for service in the army. His sympathies were with the South, but because of his family he took the oath of allegiance and thus secured a pass from the Government. In the fall of 1869 he disposed of his Coles County interests and returned with his family to Worth County in the same manner, and again took up his residence in the house which he had left. In later years he purchased a small farm close by, and there passed the remaining years of his life, dying February 8, 1895, while Mrs. Adams survived him only one year. Joseph Adams served during the '50s as constable, but was not a seeker after public office. In his early years he was a member of the Missionary Baptist Church, but after coming to Missouri joined the Presbyterian faith. He and his wife were the parents of four children: Charles Milton, Thomas J., Lillie and Lewis Monroe.

On returning from Illinois the second time, Charles Milton Adams attended the public schools until 1869, and then turned his attention to farming, beginning to work for wages in 1878. He was married on November 22d of that year to Miss Rachel Ellen McCord, daughter of William and Eliza Jane (Carmichael) McCord, of Greenville. Mercer

County, Pennsylvania. William McCord was a native of Pennsylvania, and came to Missouri with his father, Robert McCord, making the trip by team to St. Louis, and then by steamer on the Missouri River. He purchased 320 acres of land, located in township 62, section 32, range 32, at that time all prairie land and known as the Thomas Jacks farm, and in addition to this subsequently purchased three eighty-acre tracts and one forty-acre tract of land. He cleared and fenced his property, and there continued to be engaged in farming during the remainder of his life, passing away in 1898. Mrs. Adams' mother was born in Mercer County, Pennsylvania, a daughter of John and Maggie (Garvin) Carmichael, the former a native of Scotland and the latter of Ireland. There were six children in the McCord family: Maggie, Lizzie, Rachel Ellen, Cora, Olive and John.

Mr. Adams has continued to follow farming and stock raising in Worth County and has been substantially successful in all of his operations, being possessed of thrift, industry and a comprehensive knowledge of the principles of agricultural work. He is a valued member of Oxford Lodge, of the Independent Order of Odd Fellows, of which he is past noble grand. In political matters he is a democrat, but public life has held out but few attractions to him, he being content to devote himself to his soil cultivating activities. He has been the father of the following children: William J., who married Mattie B. Moore, of Gentry, Missouri, and has three children, Goldie and Gladys, twins, and Mildred; Elizabeth, who has been for some years a popular school teacher of Worth County; Edson, who married Daisy Laing, of Worth County, and has two children, Doyle and Charles Blaine; Jessie, who married Wilbur Wilhite, a farmer of Worth County, and has one child, Cecil; John L., who is engaged in farming operations with his father; Katherine, who resides at home; and Vittoria, who graduated from St. Joseph Central High School, class of 1914, and is now engaged in teaching school.

CHARLES G. MCKINLEY, M. D. While his chief work during a residence in Jamesport since 1891 has been as a successful physician and surgeon, Doctor McKinley is also the owner of a fine farm and gives attention to its supervision and is a banker. Throughout a professional career of more than thirty years he has rendered a skillful and kindly service to a generation of patients, and has been a factor in the useful citizenship of each community which has represented his home.

Charles Gordon McKinley was born on a farm near Clarksburg, West Virginia, August 29, 1852. He comes of that fine Scotch-Irish stock that did so much to people and give vitality to the institutions and society of the Allegheny frontier before the beginning of western expansion. One of his ancestors was Colonel McKinley, who commanded a regiment during the Indian border wars about the time of the Revolution, and was captured and beheaded by the Indians, who in order to strike further terror to the settlers put his head on the end of a pole and exhibited it during their raids. Doctor McKinley's uncle was William McKinley, a soldier in the War of 1812, and the doctor has a cousin relationship with the late President William McKinley. Doctor McKinley's parents were Edmund and Caroline (Reed) McKinley, who had a farm near Clarksburg, West Virginia, and during the boyhood of Charles G. moved to another farm in Lewis County of the same state, where the parents lived until their death.

Doctor McKinley acquired his early education in the common schools of Lewis County, following which he attended the Alfred Center College at Alfred Center, New York, and from that entered the Eclectic Medical Institute of Cincinnati, graduating M. D. in 1883. Doctor McKinley began his practice of medicine at French Creek, West Virginia, remained there until 1891, and in that year established his office in Jamesport, where he has since been permanently identified with his profession. Some years ago he took post-graduate work in orificial surgery in Chicago, and although his practice is of a general nature both he and his associate, Dr. G. D. Harris, who has been his partner since 1911, specialize more or less along the line of orificial surgery.

After coming to Jamesport Doctor McKinley bought two farms, comprising 240 acres. He gives a general supervision to this property, and besides the staple crops raises a good deal of stock. Doctor McKinley is a stockholder and director of the Bank of Jamesport, and has been interested in that institution a number of years.

Doctor McKinley is an active member of the Jamesport Commercial Club, is affiliated with the Knights of Pythias, and in politics is a republican. For sixteen years he served as United States Pension Examiner at Jamesport. He is a member of the Missouri State Eclectic Society, of which he is an ex-president, and of the National Eclectic Society.

On February 12, 1885, he married Miss Martha M. Thorpe, of French Creek, Upshur County, West Virginia. To their marriage have been born three daughters, Georgie E., at home; Vesta, wife of Harold Lewis of Grundy County; and Letha, wife of Walter Scott of Jamesport.

· JAMES SCOTT. A resident of Martinsville or its vicinity since 1867, James Scott came to this locality in that year from Lanarkshire, Scotland, where for many generations the Scotts had resided, being, in the main, farming people, although James was identified with mercantile pursuits as foreman at Glasgow for ten years prior to coming to the United States. He was born in the Parish of Stonehouse, July 22, 1835, and is a son of James Scott, who died in the Martinsville community in 1881, at the age of eighty-four years. The father was born in Lanarkshire, Scotland, and in active life was a farmer, but in the United States was little more active than a retired citizen. He married Lucy Campbell, a descendant of the Campbells of Argyle, Scotland, and she died at Martinsville in 1886, at the age of eighty-six years. The children born to James and Lucy Scott were as follows: Miss Jeanie, a resident of New Hampton, Missouri; Janet, who married Robert Stone, of Harrison County; James, of this review; Archibald, a resident of Bethany; Elizabeth, who is the widow of Michael Cochrane, of New Hampton, Missouri; and Thomas, who is engaged in agricultural pursuits near Martinsville.

James Scott acquired a liberal education after going to Glasgow, in which city he attended the lectures at the Mechanics Institute. Succeeding this, he connected himself with a grain and provision establishment and went from a menial position to the foremanship of the house, and when he was thirty-two years of age left his native land, sailing from Glasgow aboard the steamer St. Andrews, bound for Quebec. He was accompanied by his parents and the journey was made without untoward incident, and from the Canadian city he crossed over to the United States at Port Levi and went then on to St. Joseph, Missouri.

could not, so he just retained it and made himself a permanent part of the county. Mr. Scott farmed the place until six years ago, and during this time made many substantial improvements, also secured other lands as the years went by, and added another quarter section, making him the owner of a half a section in section 9, township 64, range 29, the tract lying one and one-half miles north of Martinsville. In his operations, Mr. Scott first entered the stock business in a small way with young cattle, and his success, coming slow but surely, enabled him to advance from them to "feeders," and he finally became a feeder of stock, a line in which his prosperity continued.

Mr. Scott took out citizenship papers after five years of residence at Martinsville, soon assumed an interest in educational matters, and was for many years a member of his district board. He united himself politically with the republican party and voted first for General Grant for President in 1872 and has not missed a presidential election since, always supporting republican candidates. He has never become confused by blatant politicians and their theories, but has gone along in a modest way, making a success both of his citizenship and of his private affairs. In church matters Mr. Scott is a Presbyterian, having been brought up under that influence in Scotland. He has served the Martinsville Church as an officer since the congregation was organized, and is an elder therein at this time.

Mr. Scott was married in Harrison County, Missouri, in June, 1868, to Miss Elizabeth Murray, a Scotch woman, who was born in the same shire as her husband, and came to America during the year she was married. Her father was Alexander Murray, a merchant and her mother was formerly Elizabeth Baird, and of their children two sons and two daughters came to America. To Mr. and Mrs. Scott there have been born the following children: Elizabeth Baird, who graduated from Park College, Missouri, taught then in Bethany school, was elected county school commissioner of Harrison and served two years, was then employed in the public schools of Kansas City as a teacher in the grades, and was finally transferred to the manual training high school as teacher of English literature and now acts in that capacity; Jeanie, who married Elmer Baldwin, a farmer near Martinsville, and has three children, Margaret, Truman and Eleanor; Lucy Campbell, who is the wife of Hinton Van Hoozier, a farmer, and has two children, Elizabeth and Eldon. The children were all given excellent educational advantages, were reared in an atmosphere of culture and refinement, and were carefully and thoroughly trained to accept and dignify the honorable positions in life to which they have been called.

HON. JOSEPH L. BENNETT. In 1856 there arrived at Savannah, Missouri, one who was destined to take an important part in the development and upbuilding of Andrew County. There was nothing in his appearance, however, to justify the belief that such was the case, for he had just completed a long and arduous journey from Louisville, Kentucky, having traveled from that city to St. Louis, Missouri, then on to Weston by boat, and because of the shallowness of the river had been compelled to complete his trip by stage. Moreover, he was practically at the end of his resources, his cash capital being in the neighborhood of twenty-five dollars. This was the modest and unassuming advent of Judge Joseph L. Bennett in Savannah; but in the fifty-eight years that have intervened happenings have occurred that have developed the poor and untried youth even as they have developed the wild and unproductive county. While the latter has become one of the most fertile, stirring and progressive sections of Northwest Missouri, the former has taken his place as one of his community's most substantial men, a successful agriculturist, a capable financier and business man, and a citizen who has been repeatedly called upon to represent his fellow men in public positions of trust.

Judge Joseph L. Bennett was born in Spencer County, about twenty-five miles south of the City of Louisville, Kentucky, February 29, 1836, and is a son of Joseph H. and Susan W. (Overton) Bennett, and a grandson of John and Charlotte (Drake) Bennett, members of a family which originated in New Jersey. Joseph H. Bennett was born in the Jersey Blue State, February 24, 1799, and as a young man went to Kentucky, where he was married August 29, 1821, to Miss Susan W. Overton, who was born in Kentucky, October 8, 1798. Mr. Bennett was a carpenter and cabinetmaker, and in addition owned a small farm in Spencer County, which he cultivated for a number of years. He was an industrious, capable and persevering man, and through a life of earnest endeavor accumulated a competence. He was also a man of some importance in public affairs, and for thirty years served in the capacity of assessor of his county. He was a democrat in his political affiliations, and both he and his wife were members of the Baptist Church. The father died at Louisville, Kentucky, November 22, 1888, while the mother passed away at Spencer, that state, October 22, 1872. They were the parents of twelve children, as follows: John E., born in 1822, when sixteen years of age went to Baton Rouge, Louisiana, there taught school for some years while reading law, was admitted to the bar and engaged in practice until his death in 1849; Fannie C., born November 20, 1823, married Gideon G. Jewell, who is now deceased; Sarah Ann, born April 13, 1825, died August 15, 1847; Joseph D., who died in infancy, October 1, 1826; Samuel C., born September 6, 1828, who died December 18, 1875; Susan M., born August 18, 1829, married James Tansill, and is now a widow and resides in Chicago; Charlotte A., born January 27, 1831, died July 28, 1847; Julia A., born May 12, 1833, died October 2, 1857; Judge Joseph L., of this review; Nancy J., born July 14, 1839, married James H. Bennett, deceased, and is now a resident of Savannah; James H., born November 24, 1841; and Bernard, born January 24, 1844.

Joseph L. Bennett received his early education in the public schools of his native place, was reared to young manhood on the home farm, and as a youth carefully saved his earnings that he might secure a start for himself in some new and undeveloped region where land was cheap. Accordingly, in 1856, he left the parental roof and journeyed to St. Louis, as before related, where he boarded the boat and paid his fare as far as St. Joseph. The river was found to be too low for navigation, however, and the steamship company sent its passengers on to their destination by way of stage coach, and it was thus that Mr. Bennett came to his new home. From that time to the present, with the exception of one year, 1857, in Kansas, he has been a resident of Andrew County, and this has been the scene of his labors and of his success. From the time that he secured his first tract of land farming and stockraising have continued to be his chief occupations, and for several years he devoted his attention to the raising of Short Horn cattle, in addition to which he was for eighteen years hog buyer for a large St. Joseph packing company, although he resided during this time on his farm adjoining the City of Savannah. He was for many years a partner with his brother-in-law, S. R. Seleeman, in farming on Seleeman Heights, Savannah, but Mr. Bennett disposed of twenty-one acres of his interests in 1897 in this property, which was platted by W. G. Hine. While residing in the country Mr. Bennett was the owner of a beautiful home, but this was destroyed by fire in 1905, and he now resides in his present modern residence, at the corner of Third and West Bennett avenues, in Bennett's

HISTORY OF NORTHWEST MISSOURI   1475

Addition, a residence district of Savannah which he platted himself. In
the line of finance Mr. Bennett was the original organizer of the State
Bank of Savannah, in 1887, and was its president for a number of years.
In various ways he has assisted in the development and growth of his
community, and as a citizen he is known to be progressive and public-
spirited. A lifelong democrat, in 1887 and 1888 he served very capably
in the capacity of collector of revenue of Andrew County, and in 1881
was appointed county judge to fill a vacancy and served ably for two
years. Judge Bennett, however, is primarily a business man, and while
he has always shown fidelity in discharging the duties of citizenship, he
has not been a seeker for public favors.

Judge Bennett was married August 1, 1857, to Miss Martha S. Selecman, who was born in Kentucky, February 8, 1841, and came to this
county with her parents, Henry and Mary Selecman, in 1844. She died
March 15, 1894, without issue. Judge Bennett has reared and educated
three children of his relatives, and now has three more under his charge
who are being trained to man and womanhood under his wise direction
and being given the advantages of superior mental training. Judge
Bennett was married the second time, October 9, 1895, to Miss Elizabeth
E. Gore, a native of Andrew County, and a daughter of Green L. and
Emeline Gore, both of whom are deceased.

Mr. Bennett was converted, in 1854, in Spencer County, Kentucky,
and is a member of the First Baptist Church of Savannah, which was
organized in 1902. And of this church Mrs. Bennett is also a member.
Mr. Bennett is one of the trustees of the church, and he and other trustees
selected and paid for the present site. In this connection it is with
pleasure that we state: "Mr. Bennett has been one of the most liberal
contributors to the Baptist Society."

LEE J. EADS, M. D. By a career of kindly and capable service to the
community in his profession as physician and surgeon, Dr. Lee J. Eads
has become known all over the country about Hamilton, and is a man
who, once known, is not easily forgotten. He combines with a thorough
ability in his chosen calling a striking physical presence, stands six feet
four inches, and weighs more than two hundred pounds. He is a man
of powerful build, of great energy, and his splendid physique has stood
him in good stead in his untiring devotion to the welfare of his patients.
Doctor Eads located at Hamilton in 1901. He is a graduate of the
Louisville Medical College with the class of 1889.

Doctor Eads was born at Monticello, Kentucky, March 18, 1868, a
son of William T. Eads. William T. Eads was a brother of the well-
known Colonel Eads, who built the great Eads Bridge, the first structure
to span the Mississippi River at St. Louis. The Eads family came originally from Virginia, and furnished many men prominent both in peace
and in war. The first ancestors in America were three brothers who
came from England before the Revolutionary war. Doctor Eads' grandfather, Jacob E. Eads, was a native of Virginia, and moved from there
to Louisville, Kentucky. He married Ada Norman, who was of a Protestant Irish family. Jacob B. Eads and wife had sixteen children, nine sons
and seven daughters. Doctor Eads' grandmother was Esther G. Stevenson, a cousin to Hon. Adlai Stevenson, who was vice president of the
United States with Grover Cleveland as President, and was also a cousin
to the Hon. L. J. Stevenson, a Kentucky congressman living at Mount
Sterling in that state. Doctor Eads was one of a family of eleven children, and one of three brothers still living. His brother J. B. Eads is a
well-known physician at Paris, Kentucky, while William is living in
Lexington, Kentucky. A sister Sallie P. Rexroat lives in Kentucky;

another sister, Ann E. Eads, lives at Lexington; Bettie P. Dugan is a
resident of Shafter, Kentucky; Fern lives in Earlville, Kentucky, and the
last of the daughters is Fannie P. The father of this family was a farmer,
a democrat in politics, and a member of the Baptist Church. His death
occurred at the age of fifty-two, while his wife is still living at the age
of seventy-four.

Doctor Eads grew up in Kentucky, was a farmer boy in that state,
and when he reached his majority he stood six feet four inches in height
and weighed 220 pounds. He was as athletic as he was large and powerful, and excelled in many forms of sport, particularly in boxing. Such
was his skill in this work that he was at one time urged by the champion
of the world, John L. Sullivan, to take up the sport as a profession.
However, his ambitions kept him in a different line, and one more serviceable to the country. He attended high school, also a college at Monticello, Kentucky, and afterwards graduated from the Louisville Medical
College.

Doctor Eads married Mantie Richardson, a daughter of Rev. Samuel
Richardson and Edith (Thompson) Richardson. Mrs. Eads died in
1895 at the age of twenty-six, and left one son, Lee S. Eads, who was
born in 1894 and is now in his third year at the University of Missouri
in Columbia. In 1900 Doctor Eads married his present wife, Sula E.
Dunagan, of Brownstown, Kentucky. She was a daughter of Jefferson
and Mary (Simpson) Dunagan. By his second marriage Doctor Eads has
one son, Elton C., born April 14, 1902. Doctor Eads is a democrat in
politics, and has taken much part in Masonic affairs, having served as
high priest of the Royal Arch chapter. He is also affiliated with the
Independent Order of Odd Fellows, and with his wife belongs to the
Eastern Star. They are members of the Methodist Church.

FRANK N. BROWNLEE. One of the popular young citizens of Mound
City is Frank N. Brownlee, whom the people of Holt County have known
for several years in his capacity as an auctioneer. Mr. Brownlee is a
man of wide and varied experience, has traveled over many states, both
east and west, and from an early age it has been his ambition to render
a service of value, and in his chosen work he is one of the most successful
judges of livestock and general auctioneers in this part of Missouri.

Frank N. Brownlee was born at Peoria, Wyoming County, New York,
December 16, 1883. His parents are David and Mary (Noble) Brownlee,
and his father has for many years been engaged in farming in Wyoming
County, New York. The old homestead comprised 120 acres of land,
and in its improvements and general character was a typical New York
farm. There was one other child in the family, Edna, now the wife of
John D. Greenleaf.

Frank N. Brownlee remained with his parents until the age of twenty-
one years, grew up on a farm, and has close practical familiarity with
all branches of farming, and that experience has been valuable to him
in his profession. As a boy he attended the country schools, and received
as good an education as could be had. Though reared on a farm, his
inclinations were for a more active and broader career, and his first position after leaving the farm was with the Lock Insulator Company, with
which concern he remained a year. For the following year he traveled
as a representative of the International Harvester Company, and in that
time he broadened his acquaintance among farmers and gained a thorough knowledge of agricultural implements. It was while engaged in
this work that he conceived the idea of taking up auctioneering as a
profession, having been influenced in this direction through his acquaintance with a number of the largest livestock breeders in the country. He

took a course in the Missouri Auction School, graduating and receiving a diploma, and his services were soon in demand as a judge of stock, and as an auctioneer he has since traveled over all the country, making sales for some of the largest breeders in the country.

In 1911 Mr. Brownlee came to Oregon, in Holt County, and while there conducted a number of important sales for livestock men. Ill health compelled him to leave his vocation, and he acted on the advice of his physician and went to California, where he at once found work in crying sales for a number of large breeders. While in California he was also in the commission business. After recovering his health he spent some time in Oklahoma, as an auctioneer, and then returned to Holt County and located in Mound City, his headquarters being in the Gladstone Hotel. His prepossessing manner, his thorough knowledge of his business, and a successful record have ingratiated him in the confidence of Holt County people, and he has conducted a number of sales with satisfaction to all parties. His recommendations are of the best, and in his field of work has professional engagements both in Holt County and surrounding district.

Mr. Brownlee is a thorough booster and has shown the same qualities of enterprise in Mound City and Holt County that have made him a factor in other communities. While in California he was an active member of the Chamber of Commerce of San Bernardino, and he has many friends in that state. Mr. Brownlee was reared in the Presbyterian Church, and in politics is independent, voting for the man rather than for the party.

R. L. CASON. An ever increasing prosperity has rewarded the efforts of R. L. Cason since he embarked in agricultural pursuits in young manhood. To his agricultural labors at that time he brought an earnest purpose and a strong physical equipment, which counteracted in large degree the disadvantages of a poor education and the lack of capital, and through the years which have passed he has advanced himself, step by step, to a position of substantiality among the men who have maintained the high agricultural standards of Holt County. At the present time he is the owner of a handsome property comprising 338½ acres, in which are to be found improvements of the most modern character.

R. L. Cason was born in Howard County, Missouri, September 2, 1863, and is a son of J. M. and Melvina (Cropp) Cason. The parents were natives of Virginia and were married in Missouri, becoming the parents of six children, of whom four still survive. The first settlement of the Casons in Howard County was in Sheridan Township, where the father purchased a tract of land comprising 250 acres, upon which some improvements had been made, from a man named Liggett. Here the father was engaged in cultivating the soil when the Civil war broke out and he enlisted for service, becoming captain of an infantry company in a regiment of Missouri volunteers. He met a soldier's death in 1865, when he was drowned in the Red River. The widow was thus left alone with her little family, but her troubles were not over, for in some manner she incurred the enmity of a band of guerrillas known as the Kansas Jayhawkers, who burned her home, and R. L. Cason, then being a baby, was nearly burned to death, being rescued at the last moment. He grew

later she sold to W. C. Andes, later moving to the John Martin farm, in Lewis Township, where she died. R. L. Cason left that property to go and live with his father-in-law, and finally settled on his present land, a tract of 144 acres in South Benton Township, in the cultivation of which he has met with very satisfying success. He has made various improvements of a most substantial character, and his buildings are among the most modern to be found in this section. He is now accounted a well-to-do man, and the abundant means he has acquired are the result of the energy, sound judgment, tenacity of purpose and wise management with which he has conducted his operations.

Mr. Cason was married to Miss Minnie F. Hutton, daughter of Wash Hutton and Caroline Hutton, and they have had the following children: Daphene, who married Professor Rock; Mildred, who married George Kuhn; Ruby; Russell, deceased; Marjorie; John, and one who died in infancy. Mr. and Mrs. Cason are members of the Christian Church. He has always been a friend of education, realizing the handicaps under which he labored by a lack of training in this direction, and has consistently supported movements which have bettered the school system of his community. Largely through his encouragement and efforts, the new schoolhouse was erected in South Benton Township, and for seven years he served as an active and helpful member of the school board. Mr. Cason is the owner of property aggregating 338½ acres, and he has been the largest taxpayer of his township. Fraternally, he is connected with the Odd Fellows and the Masons, in both of which he has warm friends.

ROBERT L. MINTON. At no time, perhaps, in the history of the world, has there been more call than at present for the use of the qualifications and the exercise of the talents of the practitioner of the law. Putting aside the great national problems that at present are being fought out in foreign lands, and which, it is reasonable to suppose, will finally have to be settled in courts of arbitration and largely through eminent jurists, the changing conditions of industrial and social life in America bring new questions to the courts such as were once unthought of. To meet such conditions the lawyer must be well equipped indeed, not only in the fundamentals of the law, but in every line to which the activities of life penetrate. It means a great deal, therefore, when a young man is acknowledged to be a leading member of the bar of his county, and such is the position of Robert L. Minton, attorney-at-law at Mound City. He was born in Minton Township, Holt County, Missouri, December 15, 1883, and is the son of Dr. I. M. and Mary E. (Shepherd) Minton.

Both the Mintons and Shepherds were very early settlers in Holt County. The paternal grandfather, Henry Minton, was born in the Village of Mintonville, Casey County, Kentucky, and from there, in 1847, moved to Holt County, Missouri, and settled at a point on the Missouri River, called Minton's Bend. There he entered land and spent the remainder of his life. He took part in the Mexican and later the Civil war. The Shepherds belonged to the Old North State and the maternal grandfather of Mr. Minton left North Carolina at the age of eighteen to become a resident of Holt County, Missouri, where members of the family still reside. The following children were born to Dr. I. M. and Mary E. (Shepherd) Minton: Zoe M., who married Dr. Charles H. Thomas; William H., physician and surgeon, who married Mayme L. Catron, daughter of J. G. Catron, of Bigelow Township, Holt County; Robert L., and George A., who still resides on the old home place in Minton Township.

Robert L. Minton was afforded excellent educational advantages, first attending the local schools and afterward the high school at Oregon, the

county seat of Holt County, and from that institution he entered the
Missouri State Normal School at Kirksville, from which he was graduated in 1903. Following 1903 he taught school and farmed, studied law
in the office of Senator Wilson, of Platte City, in 1906, then entered the
law department at Ann Arbor of the University of Michigan, where,
after two years of application, he was graduated in June, 1908, and in
the following year was admitted to the bar, locating for practice at Mound
City. He has built up a substantial practice and has secured a number
of important clients through his sound knowledge of the law and close
attention to their interests.

Mr. Minton was united in marriage with Miss Eleanor G. Breier, a
daughter of John B. Breier, of St. Louis County, Missouri, who for twelve
years was superintendent of schools of that county. They have one child,
a son, Marion J., who was born October 16, 1913. Mrs. Minton is a
thoroughly educated and highly accomplished lady, a graduate of the
Ferguson schools, of the Kirksville Normal School in 1903, and of
Chicago University in 1908. She is interested in many of the questions
that concern the women of today and both she and her husband take
part in the pleasant social life of Mound City.

In politics Mr. Minton could be nothing but a democrat, for he was,
as it were, reared in the cradle of democracy, the family belonging to
that political party as far back as he can trace. His fraternal connections include membership in the W. O. W., at Fortescue, Missouri; the
Odd Fellows and local Masonic Lodge at Mound City, of which lodge he
has been several times master. He is also a member of Moila Temple,
A. A. O. N. M. S., of St. Joseph, Missouri.

WILLIAM ERWIN. For many years the Erwin family have been substantial farming people, good citizens, kindly neighbors, and representatives of morality and religion in Holt County.

William Erwin, whose record is that of a successful young farmer
in Benton Township, was born in Holt County on the farm that is still
his home on February 8, 1874. His parents are Goldman and Margaret
Erwin. They were married in Holt County, and became the parents of
eight children, six of whom still survive, and all were born on the old
homestead. The father on locating in Holt County first settled on land
adjoining the present farm, now known as the Jim McNulty farm. This
estate comprises eighty acres of land, all of which has been well improved
under the united labors of both Goldman Erwin and his son, and under
the present management of William Erwin is one of the most profitable
farms, considering its size, in Holt County. Both parents are still
living and in good health. The father's people originally were Kentuckians, and during the war lost all their property, and had to begin
over again. The mother was born in Jackson County, Missouri. William
Erwin is the only son left on the old farm, and realizing his duty to his
parents has never married.

The Erwins were originally members of the Methodist Episcopal
Church, South, but now affiliate with the Christian Church. The politics
of the family has always been democratic. Both Goldman and William
Erwin are citizens who have worked for the good of the community, and
both have served on the local school board, the son being now clerk of the
board. The father in the early days was a teacher, and kept school in
Holt County. The father is a Mason and the son affiliates with the Odd
Fellows at Mound City. The parents and the son have all the comforts
of a good country home, and the only other member of the family living
with them is a niece, who has been a member of the household since
childhood.

JACOB BOHART. Apart from the piling up of great wealth or conquering high position in the public view, there are distinctions of a quieter and more satisfying kind that are none the less difficult of attainment, and yet are possible to a long and well ordered life such as has been that of Jacob Bohart, for many years a resident of Holt County. Mr. Bohart represents a family that came into Northwest Missouri before the country was legally open to settlers, and he is himself one of the older native sons of this section. His young manhood fell during the Civil war, in which he served, and he has been the witness of many remarkable changes. He had already reached the summit of life and had his children grown or growing up about him when the modern twentieth century was ushered into Northwest Missouri.

Jacob Bohart was born on a farm sixteen miles east of St. Joseph on July 25, 1845. His parents were Phillip and Martha (Russell) Bohart, who were married in Buchanan County, Missouri. Both the Boharts and Russells were pioneers. Grandfather Elijah Russell, who was a native of Scotland, came into the country surrounding the old trading post at St. Joseph as early as 1833. He put up a building and lived as a squatter for a time. That was before the opening of the Platte Purchase, and the soldiers of the United States tore down his first dwelling in an endeavor to drive him from the country. He remained, and restored the building, and spent the best part of his life in this section. Phillip Bohart was also a pioneer settler in Buchanan County, moved from there to Andrew County, and after a few years sold out and bought a new home in Holt County. Phillip Bohart was a native of Germany, and a member of the Lutheran faith. He was in many ways an exemplary character, and is said to have never used a profane word in all his life. On coming to Holt County he first settled on what is known as the Beaver farm, and later bought land of his own, improved it with buildings, cleared up the fields, and lived there quietly and industriously until his death on February 17, 1866. During his residence in Holt County he served on the school board. There were seven sons and two daughters in the family.

Jacob Bohart grew up in these different localities of Northwest Missouri, and as the schools at that time had limited sessions and the duties of home were considered more important than literary instruction, his early training was limited. He was still a boy when the great Civil war threw the entire nation into confusion, and for three months towards the close of the struggle he served with the State Reserves. Mr. Bohart lived at home until his marriage to Martha A. Gibson. She was born two miles north of the Village of Oregon, a daughter of John C. Gibson, a native of England, and Sarah Noland, who was a native of Kentucky. Mr. Gibson was a prominent citizen, served as county judge and was active in the republican party.

After his marriage Mr. Bohart settled on his present farm, which now comprises 120 acres. However, he at one time owned much more land, but has divided his possessions among his children. Mr. Bohart and wife have two daughters: Anna Lizzie married F. C. Burnett, and they have three sons, Russell B., Dwight B. and Jay; the daughter Orrie May married Marion F. Wilson, and they have a son, Kenneth. Jacob Bohart has long been regarded as one of the substantial men of Holt County, and while his material prosperity has been represented by a large farm with improvements all of his own construction, he has likewise been public spirited in his relations with the community. In politics he is a democrat, and he and his family are active in the Christian Church. Mr. Bohart is still a resident of the old homestead, but has retired from active business.

GEORGE KAUFMAN. Now owner of a well improved farm estate, and a prosperous and contented agriculturist in the vicinity of Mound City, George Kaufman has had a career of varied activity, has lived in many localities in Northwest Missouri and in adjoining states, and has had to work out his own prosperity. While he has enjoyed many kindly friendships in his progress through the world, Mr. Kaufman had practically nothing given him, and his own industry has constituted his best capital.

George Kaufman was born at the little community known as Irish Grove, near Milton, in Atchison County, Missouri, November 3, 1870. His parents were Joseph Ruel and Hanna S. (Baker) Kaufman, who were married in Morrow County, Ohio, and were of Pennsylvania Dutch stock. They moved out from Ohio to Atchison County, Missouri, about 1869, locating near Milton. Joseph R. Kaufman for a long time conducted a sawmill. While he owned a small farm, his favorite activities were in mechanical lines and especially in work which kept him much outside and away from home, and it was his idea that more money could be made that way than by the quiet, persistent, stay-at-home farming. He finally lost his life by being struck with a piece of machinery while digging a well. He was a man who provided generously for his large family, which comprised eleven children, nine of whom still survive. He never used liquor, was a member of the Dunkard Church, and at one time taught school, served as road overseer, and was also a justice of the peace. His widow now lives at Guide Rock, in Nebraska.

George Kaufman was educated in Atchison County, and had some higher schooling for a brief term. With the conclusion of his school days he lived with his mother on several different farms. On the advice of a cousin at Maitland, Mr. Kaufman found a job that gave him employment on a farm for a year, after which he returned and engaged in farming and stock raising with his mother a year, and then resumed employment with his former employer. At the end of two years Mr. Kaufman made a purchase of thirty-three acres near Newpoint, but after a year, during which he had made a little money, he sold out and began working by the year for about two years with William Kneal at Newpoint.

On December 31, 1905, Mr. Kaufman married Miss Anna Schull, daughter of William Schull. After his marriage he continued to work for William Kneal for one year, after which he was employed by Phillip Schull, his wife's uncle. Mr. Kaufman then moved to Barton County, Missouri, bought a farm there, and cultivated it for two years. Being dissatisfied with that locality he returned to Mound City, lived there from March to August, and then located with his brother-in-law, Frank Schull, on the farm just opposite the old Schull homestead. That was his location for two years, after which he bought his present place of seventy-five acres, all of it improved land, and he is now well situated, has good land and good improvements, and is one of the contented and prospering farmers of Holt County.

Mr. and Mrs. Kaufman have two children: Avis May, born April 6, 1907; and Hazel Grace, born August 5, 1911, both natives of Holt County. Mr. Kaufman is a member of the Presbyterian Church and in politics a republican, while his father was a democrat.

ORLIFF V. SELLS. As manager of the Mutual Telephone Company of Andrew County Mr. Sells has proved essentially to be "the right man in the right place," and his well ordered executive policies have been potent in bringing the telephone system up to a high standard of efficiency. Mr. Sells was born on a farm in Clay Township, Andrew County, on the 22d of October, 1871, and is one of the well known citizens of this section of the state, where his circle of friends is coincident with that of his acquaint-

ances. He is a son of James P. and Mary (Joy) Sells, both natives of
Ohio and both of whom came to Missouri about the year 1865, their
marriage having been solemnized in this state, where the father was long
a substantial and representative farmer and stock grower. His devoted
wife was summoned to the life eternal in 1908, at the age of seventy years,
and after years of earnest and fruitful endeavor he is now living retired
in the City of Los Angeles, California. Of the three children, Orliff V. is
the eldest; Frank is now a resident of Colorado; and Lee maintains his
home at Laclede, Linn County, Missouri.

Orliff V. Sells has never faltered in his loyalty and allegiance to the
county of his birth and has been a resident within its borders all his life,
his early years having been compassed by the conditions and influence
of the home farm and his educational advantages having included those
of the high school in Savannah, judicial center of the county. That he
made good use of the opportunities thus afforded is shown by the fact
that for some time he was found numbered among the successful and
popular teachers in the district schools of his home county. Thereafter
he engaged in the insurance business, and for nine years he has been
actively identified with the telephone business. He has been the progressive and valued manager of the Mutual Telephone Company since 1907
and the service of the system has been brought up to its present admirable
status not less through its excellent physical equipment than through his
efficient management.

Mr. Sells is a staunch democrat in a county that has long been a
republican stronghold, and thus it was but a normal political exigency
that he met defeat at the polls when he appeared as his party's candidate
for the office of county clerk. He served six years as city collector of
Savannah, which has been his place of residence from the time he retired
from the pedagogic profession, and he was for eight years a member of
the board of education. He and his wife are zealous and valued members
of the Baptist Church at Savannah, and he is serving both as clerk and
treasurer of the same.

In 1898 was solemnized the marriage of Mr. Sells to Miss Alice Cobb,
who likewise was born and reared in Andrew County, a daughter of Amos
Cobb, and the four children of this union are Vincent, Harold, Raymond
and Margaret.

BENJAMIN SHAFER.   Enterprise, thrift and industry are the characteristics of Benjamin Shafer's career as a farmer in Northwest Missouri.
He now has one of the well improved farms in Benton Township, and
he and other members of the family throughout their residence in this
section have identified themselves with the things that mean better life
and general improvement of the community.

Benjamin Shafer was born in Berks County, Pennsylvania, March
22, 1849, a son of John and Ellen (Smith) Shafer. His parents were
married in that state, and there were ten children, three of whom are
now deceased. John Shafer during his residence in Pennsylvania was
engaged in the manufacturing of brick. On coming West, he first settled
in Iowa, subsequently entered land from the Government in Nebraska,
and finally traded that land for unimproved acreage in Holt County,
Missouri. All this land was in the timber, and it was left to the labors
of his sons to clear it up. Altogether the estate comprised 466 acres.
The buildings were erected by the sons, and the greater part of the lands
put in cultivation.

That was the home of Benjamin Shafer for eight years, and he then
traded for 130 acres in his present farm. Here again he has gone through
the task of improving new land, erecting good and substantial buildings,

and thus all his property represents the substantial efforts of his own career.

Benjamin Shafer married Mary Hahn, daughter of Richard Hahn. The children are: Anna Bell, who married Bert Mead, and they are the parents of five children; Frank married Nellie Lester and has two children; Estella, who married Mose Keefer, and has four children, one of whom is deceased; David Allen is unmarried; Minnie Nora is the wife of Charles Fields and the mother of three children. The family are members of the Christian Church, while Mr. Shafer's father was a Lutheran. In politics they are democrats. Benjamin Shafer has served as school director, and has always shown a willingness to work with his neighbors for those things which are the result of organized effort in a community.

ROBERT BAGBY. A native son of Holt County, one of the progressive young farmers of Hickory Township, Robert Bagby has made considerable progress along the road to success, is able to compete on terms of equality with other farmers in his section, and while looking after his private interests also lent his aid to community improvements and betterment.

Robert Bagby was born in Holt County May 13, 1881, a son of Joseph Paxton and Nancy (Rogers) Bagby. The parents were married in Iowa and had a family of eight children, four of whom are now living. Robert Bagby married Daisy McKenney, daughter of Thomas and Jane (Williams) McKenney. Mr. and Mrs. Bagby have two children, Helen and Harry, both of whom were born in Holt County.

Robert Bagby grew up on his father's farm, received a fair education in the local schools, and learned farming under his father's direction. The farm he now occupies in Benton Township was one bought by his father a number of years ago, and most of the improvement were placed here by the elder Bagby, though Robert has also done his part. Robert Bagby is a member of the school board, and in politics a democrat, the same party with which his father affiliated.

W. W. MURRAY. One of the successful farmers of Holt County, Mr. Murray came to this section a few years ago after a varied experience, spent partly back East, where he was born and reared, and after work in the City of St. Joseph. Mr. Murray is a practical farmer, a thorough business man, and has a position of influence and usefulness in his community.

W. W. Murray was born in Holt County May 30, 1872, a son of Charles and Hannah (Taylor) Murray. Both families came originally from Pennsylvania, and the maternal grandfather settled in Holt County near Forbes in the very early days. Charles Murray was born in Pennsylvania, spent his life as a farmer, and he and his wife died within eleven days of each other. They left six children.

W. W. Murray was nine years old when he lost his parents, and then lived with different relatives, who expected him to pay his own way by practical work, and in consequence he found himself face to face with the serious responsibilities of life at an early day and his education was much neglected. Since early youth he has been a worker, always self-reliant, and among other experiences was employed for three years with the street car company in St. Joseph.

Mr. Murray married Ida M. Andes, of the old family of that name in Holt County. He and his wife now occupy the old Andes homestead, and have 280 acres, located in Hickory Township. Mr. Murray raises a good deal of stock, and keeps his farm improved up to the standards set by Northwest Missouri agriculturists. He and his wife have four children:

Marie, Harold, Willard and Lila, all of whom were born in Holt County except Marie, who was born in St. Joseph. The family are members of the Methodist Episcopal Church, and at the present time Mr. Murray is serving on the local school board. In politics he is a democrat.

DR. E. M. MILLER. While Doctor Miller is regarded as one of the ablest physicians at Mound City, his varied business interests in that locality have obliged him in recent years to give up much of his practice, except such as he can attend to in his office, and he is now one of the leaders in progressive affairs in Holt County.

Dr. E. M. Miller was born at Troy, Ohio, October 6, 1869, a son of H. H. and Hesther (Enyart) Miller. His father was a farmer, and was also engaged in the milling business, and handled large quantities of walnut timber. Doctor Miller spent the first fifteen years of his life on a farm, and in that time attended country schools. After that he was reared in the City of Troy, and attended the high school there. His higher education was acquired in the West, and he has both the bachelor's and master's degrees from Baker University of Kansas. Doctor Miller is a graduate M. D. from the Ensworth Medical College at St. Joseph, having taken his degree in 1897. He was also connected with that institution for seven years as one of the lecturers.

Since coming to Mound City Doctor Miller has built up a large practice as a physician, but soon became closely identified with business affairs. He organized the Holt County Telephone Company, and was associated with George W. Meyer, R. E. Decker, R. W. Neill and others in the reorganization of the Mound City Electric Light Company, and has been president of the company for the past ten years. He has been identified with the Mound City Commercial Club since its organization, and was one of the leaders in the Commercial Club campaign which brought about the paving of the business section of Mound City. Since coming to Mound City Doctor Miller has been surgeon for the Chicago, Burlington & Quincy Railroad.

Doctor Miller was married in Mound City to Anna L. McCoy, daughter of Thomas W. and Laura (Keedy) McCoy. Their three children were all born in Mound City and are named Margaret, Edwin and Robert. Doctor Miller is at the present time serving as a member of the school board, and is deserving of much credit for his work in securing the erection of the present handsome school building, which is to cost about fifty thousand dollars and will be completed and ready for occupancy in the spring of 1915. Doctor Miller served as one of the trustees of the Methodist Episcopal Church, and has been quite active in democratic politics, having been a member of the board of managers of Hospital No. 2 under Governor Joseph W. Folk. Fraternally his associations are with the Masonic Lodge No. 294 at Mound City, with Scottish Rite Masonry up to and including the thirty-second degree, and with the Temple of the Mystic Shrine at St. Joseph. He is also a member of the Woodmen of the World.

WILLIAM CANADAY. It is difficult to realize the epochs of the nation's history covered by the span of William Canaday's long life. This venerable resident of Harrison County, now living retired at Ridgeway, was born more than ninety-two years ago, when James Monroe was president of the United States. During his young manhood in Illinois he heard Abraham Lincoln plead cases at the bar, at that time hardly known beyond the limits of that state. William Canaday cast his first presidential vote about the time of the invention of the telegraph, and whereas in these later days of his life he is able to read news of the

European war only a day after the event, during his youth it required some six weeks to two months to transmit news from the Old World to the New. William Canaday was one of the first settlers in Northwest Missouri, has lived in Harrison County for sixty years, and has witnessed practically every phase of development here. During his activity his identity with Harrison County was both extensive and substantial. As a farmer he was in command of large interests, and was equally successful as a financier. When the evening of life brought him the feebleness of old age he laid down the implements of toil, and is now living in the spirit and among his remaining friends of a vigorous past. William Canaday was born in Ohio on April 15, 1823. The family for three generations have been pioneers, building homes and improving land along the frontier. His grandparents were Walter and Annie (Hussey) Canaday, who were of Southern stock and Quakers in religion. From Alabama they moved north into Ohio, making the journey with a two-wheeled cart, in which were their two children Mary and John, the parents walking behind this vehicle. After they settled in Highland County, Ohio, other children were born, namely: Nathan, who became a physician and spent his active career at Pekin, Illinois; Christopher, who moved out to Lowell Mills, Iowa, and in 1845 started over the Oregon trail to the Northwest and nothing more was ever heard of him. The daughter Mary above mentioned married Frederick Barnard, and they spent their lives at Bloomington, Illinois.

John Canaday, father of the venerable Ridgeway citizen, was born in Alabama in 1801, and was a baby when the family moved north to Highland County, Ohio. He grew up in Highland County, was there married to Sary Purteet and established a home, and during the later '20s made plans for removal to the frontier State of Illinois. He explored that country on horseback, and for six weeks was away from home, his whereabouts being unknown. He finally decided to bring his family to Illinois, and in 1828 started West, with three yoke of cattle and a carriage. The wagon drawn by the oxen was of the old prairie schooner type, and behind came the carriage drawn by the family horse, and bringing up the procession at the rear was the family cow. They crossed Indiana during the winter of 1829, stopped for a time at Georgetown, Illinois, and while there a daughter was born. At Georgetown the carriage was sold to a widower who wanted the vehicle in order to satisfy a widow, who had promised him her hand provided he could purchase a carriage. The money received for the carriage was invested in part in a sod plow, mounted on wheels. Thus when the family again took up its line of march for the chosen location in South Central Illinois, a plow took the place of the carriage behind the wagon, and "old brindle" was tied behind the plow. The family became practically the first settlers at Short Point, then in Tazewell County, but later McLean County, twelve miles south of where Bloomington now stands. With his oxen John Canaday plowed the first furrow of sod ever turned over in that county, and was also the first white man to use his ax in felling a tree in the same locality. The family were settled in the midst of the Kickapoo Indians, who were their only neighbors. John Canaday sought out Government corners, and entered 160 acres of half timber and half prairie land in the vicinity of the present village of Heyworth. He constructed a rude log house, and while farming was his basic activity, he also set up as a merchant, starting the first store in that whole country, with goods purchased at St. Louis. Pekin, forty miles away, was the nearest postoffice, and when a letter came to the family they had to pay 25 cents postage. Soon after getting his household and business affairs fairly started, John Canaday was stricken

Vol. III—12

with illness, and was given medicine, prescribed by a traveling doctor, which undoubtedly hastened his end. He died on June 3, 1835, and after that his widow capably carried on the family affairs.

John Canaday, Sr., married Sarah Purteet, a daughter of George Purteet, who lived in Kentucky when his daughter was born. The children of John and Sarah Canaday were: William Canaday, the subject of this sketch; Phebe, who married Robert Turner, and who died in Daviess County, Missouri; and Nancy, who married Allen Turner, a brother of Robert, and died in Blythedale, Missouri. After the death of her first husband Sarah Canaday married Benjamin Slatten, who subsequently became one of the early settlers of Harrison County, Missouri, and died at Bethany, Missouri, in 1868, where his descendants became prominent as farmers. The Slatten children were: Martha, who died in childhood; Joseph P., who spent his life in Harrison County, and though a man without an education acquired an immense landed estate at Bethany, Missouri, and died February 27, 1914; Hester, who married Samuel Travis and who died in Oklahoma, September 25, 1914. Mrs. Slatten, the mother of William Canaday, died in her eighty-sixth year.

Thus William Canaday grew up in a frontier community in Illinois, being six years of age when his father and mother moved from Ohio to that state, and all his early associations were with the type of civilization which the present generation knows only from books. His first experience in school was a week spent some six miles from home, his mother calling for him at the end of the time. He prayed not to be sent back, and his mother consented and kept him at home. William Canaday as a boy and youth read the Bible for three purposes, first to learn his letters, second as a text book to learn to read, and finally to learn his duty to man and to God. He was something of a student, desired an education, but was forced to get it largely by self-study. In spite of these deficiencies, he was qualified to teach school one winter, and through his varied experience became a man of wisdom if not of book learning.

On March 24, 1842, he was united in matrimony to Miss Elizabeth Leeper, of McLain County, Illinois. She was born in Flemming County, Kentucky, September 17, 1824, the daughter of Samuel and Nancy (Prine) Leeper, who moved to Muskingum County, Ohio, in the fall of 1830, and in the fall of 1834 to the State of Illinois. Her father's family consisted of nine children, Charles, Elizabeth Leeper Canaday, the subject of this sketch, William, Thomas, Huston, Nancy Jane Buck, Margaret, Mary Gossard and Martha Gossard, all of whom are deceased except Mrs. Nancy Jane Buck and Mrs. Mary Gossard. Elizabeth Canaday was the mother of seven children, namely: John Canaday, Eagleville, Missouri, born in McLain County, Illinois, December 17, 1842, married to Martha M. Dale, May 4, 1862, and they are the parents of ten children: Anna, Joseph A., William A., Stella Vanzant, Charles, Samuel, Elmer, Clara Heckenlively, Hattie Johnston (deceased), and Laura Drew. Christopher Canaday, Blythedale, Missouri, born in McLain County, Illinois, October 26, 1847, married to Angeline Brower, July 3, 1870, and they are the parents of four children: John T., Harvey P., Mabel Baldwin, and Myrtle Richardson. Phoebe A. Poynter (deceased), born January 6, 1853, in McLain County, Illinois, married William A. Poynter. Joseph W., born July 29, 1856, in Harrison County, Missouri, married A. V. Willis in 1880 and they are the parents of three children:

Lolita, and Maxine, all of Columbia, Missouri. Charles, and Benjamin, who died in infancy.

William Canaday, after his marriage began farming, and in 1854 came out to Missouri and prepared the way for his later settlement by purchasing and entering fourteen forties of land in Colfax Township. He brought his family from Illinois the following year, and thus began his permanent relations with Harrison County. His success as a farmer was encouraging, and he proved his foresight by investing his surplus in cheap lands, and as his children came of age he was able to give each one a farm. When he finally decided to quit business, he converted a magnificent estate into cash, a large part of which was distributed among his children with enough reserved for his own use to the end. For a number of years William Canaday was engaged in the banking business at Bythedale, was a charter member of the bank, and his family also had large interests in the institution for a number of years. Since 1909 Mr. Canaday has spent his years in quiet retirement at Ridgeway.

In public affairs his stand has been conspicuous in behalf of temperance, and he has always been an opponent of tobacco in all its forms. As a citizen he is first a patriot, and of secondary consideration have been party ties. William Canaday cast his first vote for President for James K. Polk in 1844, and in 1860 voted for Douglas for President. Although he made the acquaintance of Abraham Lincoln as a young man and heard him try cases at the bar, and while the great war President was entertained in the Canaday home in Illinois, he never received the ballot of William Canaday. He also knew Mr. Lincoln's wife and played with her as a child at the home of her father, Doctor Todd.

When the war came on Mr. Canaday in 1861 entered military service in behalf of the Union and assisted in the protection of his state, though without regular enlistment, until 1864, when he was commissioned first lieutenant of Company E in the Forty-third Missouri Infantry, under Colonel Hardin. The regiment was sent to duty at Chillicothe, and a portion of it was subsequently captured by General Price's Confederate troops at Glasgow, Missouri. Mr. Canaday received his discharge with the rank of quartermaster as the close of the war, and had never participated in a real engagement.

About the year 1856, two years after he came to Harrison County, William Canaday was elected justice of the peace and served continuously until 1862, when he was elected county judge. In August, 1864, he enlisted in Company E, Forty-third Missouri Volunteer Infantry, being first lieutenant in said company. He has been more or less active in Grand Army matters and attends the local meetings of his old comrades whenever convenient. He has participated in the programs, often making talks and singing songs for their entertainment. Mr. Canaday was one of the organizers of the Taylor Grove Christian Church on February 19, 1859, and has been identified with that church ever since. His means have been liberally bestowed on religious activities in Harrison County, and it is said that he has helped build more churches than any other resident, and his donations for that purpose have always been liberal.

On July 10, 1907, Elizabeth Canaday died at her home in Blythedale, Missouri, aged eighty-two years and now lies interred in the Blythedale cemetery. She was a pioneer in every sense of the word and to her carefulness and efficiency is to a large extent, due the prosperity of William Canaday of whom this sketch speaks.

On January 6, 1909, Mr. Canaday married Mrs. Jennie Reed, who is a daughter of John and Margaret (Brooks) Shirts, who came to Missouri before the war.

William Canaday is now spending his declining years at his home in Ridgeway, Missouri, where he is faithfully and devotedly cared for by his wife and is happy and contented in his old age.

W. J. CLARK. For more than forty years the Clark family enterprise and influence have been active factors in business, public affairs and the social activities of Hamilton. W. J. Clark is postmaster of that city, a well-known business man, who has capably administered the local postoffice for the past six years. His brother, E. E. Clark is equally prominent as a banker, though educated for the law, and other members of the family have contributed their share of useful work to the community.

Mr. W. J. Clark was first apointed to the office of postmaster May 27, 1908, by President Roosevelt. At the end of the first four years, to the complete satisfaction of all patrons of the office, he was reappointed by President Taft in May, 1912, and still has two years to serve. The Hamilton postoffice has been brought into a high state of efficiency, having two assistant clerks, besides five rural carriers. The postoffice at Kingston, the county seat of Caldwell County, is served as a star route by the Hamilton postoffice. The postoffice now is housed in a building on which more than two thousand dollars were spent in fixtures, and it is one of the best equipped offices in Northwest Missouri in a town of its size.

W. J. Clark, who has lived in Hamilton since 1870, was born in the State of Connecticut, and comes of an old New England family. He was born December 2, 1865, a son of Henry Clark, who was a miller. The first American of the family was Abraham Clark, one of the signers of the Declaration of Independence in 1776, but the family had been identified with this country during the Colonial era. Henry Clark moved to Northwest Missouri in 1870, and was prominently known at Hamilton as proprietor of a flour mill for a number of years. He married Aurelia Eldridge, also of Connecticut. She was born in the same house in which her son W. J. first saw the light of day. Henry Clark died at the age of seventy-two. During the war he had performed important service in raising two companies of recruits for the Union army. He was a republican in politics,* and lived a long and useful life. Of the family four children grew up: Charles H., who died at the age of twenty years; Frank, who died February 19, 1913, at Hamilton; Elmer E.; and W. J.

W. J. Clark was reared in Hamilton, received his education in the local schools, and for about twenty years was engaged in the newspaper business. He has long been regarded as one of the wheel horses of the republican party in Caldwell County, and has assisted a number of men to public office. Fraternally his affiliations are with Blue Lodge, No. 224, A. F. & A. M.; Royal Arch Chapter, No. 45; and also with Lodge No. 212 of the Knights of Pythias.

Mr. W. J. Clark was married May 5, 1891, at Hamilton, to Miss Anna Rogers, of an old and well-known family of Caldwell County, daughter of David C. Rogers. They have one son, Francis E., who graduated from the Hamilton High School in 1911, attended the Missouri School of Mines at Rolla for one year and is now a student in the State Agricultural College at Manhattan, Kansas.

Elmer E. Clark, who is cashier of the Hamilton Savings Bank, has for more than twenty-five years been identified either with his profession as a lawyer or in banking. The Hamilton Savings Bank was organized in 1877, and the present officers are: S. L. Wonsettler, president; John

N. Morton, vice president; J. R. Cheshier, second vice president; and E. E. Clark, cashier. The capital of the institution is $60,000, and its surplus and undivided profits of nearly $50,000 indicates the conservative management which has always been characteristic of this institution.

Mr. Clark was born October 29, 1862, in Connecticut, a son of the late Henry Clark, for many years engaged in the milling business at Hamilton. Mr. Clark has lived in Hamilton since he was eight years of age, and after finishing the public schools graduated from the Ann Arbor High School in 1884, took two years literary course in the University of Michigan, then entered the law department of the University of Michigan and was graduated with the class of 1888. Locating at Arkansas City, Kansas, he opened a law office with H. D. Cummings, and remained there about a year. Though prepared for the law, he found banking a field of work more to his inclination, and returning to Hamilton, Missouri, he accepted a position with the Hamilton Savings Bank, and of which institution he is now cashier.

Mr. Clark was married in 1892, to Nellie Austin, daughter of Oliver Austin, an old and well-known citizen of Caldwell County. Mr. Clark is a republican, is affiliated with Knights of Pythias Lodge, No. 212, and has always exerted himself for the benefit of the community when any enterprise was undertaken in that direction.

FRANK CLARK. No historical sketch of Hamilton, Missouri, covering recent years would be complete without mention of Frank Clark—a man who left his impress upon all Hamilton's business, political and social life for more than forty years. He came to Hamilton with his father, Henry Clark, in 1870. He was then a young man of eighteen but very soon thereafter became actively associated with his father in the milling business. He mastered the minutest details of this business and in 1874 bought out his father's interest in the mill. Four years later, September 28, 1878, his mill burned to the ground and without a dollar of insurance. Then it was that his true mettle appeared for within six months he had a new three-story and basement brick mill fully equipped and in running order. Four years later it was completely changed over to the roller process, which was then just coming in vogue. This mill and the accompanying elevator he continued to operate with signal success for many years.

In 1893 he turned his attention to the electric light business and, securing a twenty-year franchise from the City of Hamilton, erected what was at that time a thoroughly modern and up-to-date electric light plant. This business he kept fully abreast of the times and continued to conduct it up to the time of his death.

He was one of the original organizing stockholders of the Hamilton Savings Bank, which institution was organized in 1877, and of which he had been vice president for a number of years prior to his death.

Politically, Mr. Clark was an ardent republican and always took an active part in matters political although he never held nor was even a candidate for political office. Fraternally, he was a member of Blue Lodge, No. 224, A. F. & A. M.; Royal Arch Chapter, No. 45; and Kadosh Commandery No. 21. He was also a member of Hamilton Lodge No. 212 Knights of Pythias.

Warmhearted, kindly dispositioned, generous to a fault, his friends were limited only by his acquaintance and in his passing Hamilton lost a splendid citizen who had spent practically his whole life with her and striven ever for her advancement.

Frank Clark was born in Vernon, Tolland County, Connecticut, October 22, 1852; was married in Willington, Connecticut, October 22, 1874, to Miss Netta L. Eldredge; and died at Hamilton, Missouri, February 19, 1913.

WALTER C. MYERS, M. D. No other profession is of such ancient dignity as is that of medicine and it invites to its service men of learning and ability, often returning but few rewards in material things for the preparation and self sacrifice it demands, and not always bestowing the honors fairly won. Nevertheless the call to this profession is insistent and it seems, sometimes, as if the call might be an inherited one, for in many families other and more promising careers are presented only to be turned aside by several generations for that of the healing art. Of such ancestry is Dr. Walter C. Myers, an eminent physician and surgeon of Savannah, whose medical knowledge and achievements reflect credit upon his ancestors.

Walter C. Myers was born January 26, 1876, at Uhrichsville, Tuscarawas County, Ohio, and is a son of J. C. and Martha A. (Campbell) Myers, the latter of whom was born at Allegheny City, Pennsylvania, and died at Troy, Kansas, in 1910. The father of Doctor Myers was born at Uhrichsville, Ohio, and is now a leading practitioner of dentistry at Troy, Kansas. He began the study of his profession with Doctor McKinley, who was a resident of Uhrichsville and an uncle of the late President William McKinley, and afterward completed his course at Columbus, Ohio. His brother, Dr. James Myers, is a retired physician of Hutchinson, Kansas, and his uncle, Dr. John Myers, was an eminent early physician and surgeon near New Philadelphia, Ohio. He married into a medical family, four of his wife's brothers being physicians, two of whom, Doctor William and Dr. O. B. Campbell, resided in St. Joseph, Missouri, but the latter is now deceased. Of the three children born to his parents, Walter C. is the only son. He has two sisters: Mary Elberta, who is the wife of R. B. Castle, of Kansas City; and Adaline E., who is the wife of Oscar Dubasch, of Troy, Kansas.

Walter C. Myers was two years old when his parents, in 1878, moved to Highland, Kansas, two years later settling permanently at Troy, where he passed his boyhood and educational training, completing the high school course. From childhood he believed that his mission was to become a physician, this impression being so strong that his boyish comrades dubbed him "doctor" in their play. He was happy in having a tender, devoted and ambitious mother, and it was at her knee he learned his first lessons in anatomy and physiology and through her encouragement decided to become a medical student under his uncle, Dr. O. B. Campbell, at St. Joseph, Missouri, and in 1898 was graduated from the Central Medical College of that city, and for ten years was engaged in a general practice at Rea, Andrew County, Missouri, during that time continuing his studies and scientific investigations and taking post graduate courses as opportunity offered. In 1906 he spent the summer in special laboratory work, in Chicago, and after he came to Savannah, took a regular post graduate course in the New York Post Graduate College in 1906, also took a clinical course under Doctors Mayo, at Rochester, Minnesota, subsequently taking a special course on tuberculosis, at Chicago, under Doctor McMichael. In fact, whenever friends miss him or patients clamor for him during certain portions of the summer, when many of both think of recreation in some chosen restful place, they may easily guess that he is hard at work in some famous distant clinic or, in their interest, spending days and nights in study with his test tubes and microscopes. The effect of this constant investigation and close study

at first hand has given him qualifications that have proven far reaching in his ministrations to the sick of Savannah and probably Andrew County has never had a more competent health officer. He has served one term also as county coroner, elected on the republican ticket, but has never been very active in the political field.

Doctor Myers was united in marriage in September, 1913, to Miss Georgia Newman, who was born at Savannah, Missouri, and is a daughter of William Newman. Doctor and Mrs. Myers have one son, Victor Campbell Myers. Doctor Myers is a valued member of the Buchanan County, the Missouri State and the American Medical associations. A man of cultivated tastes he enjoys congenial companionship in many circles and has the pleasing personality that wins friends. Fraternally he is identified with the Masons, the Odd Fellows at Savannah, and the Elks at St. Joseph.

JUDGE JAMES RILEY CHESHIER. When James Riley Cheshier was elected presiding judge of the Caldwell County Court, he overturned a precedent that had stood for nearly half a century, ever since the Civil war. He was the first democrat to be honored with that important office in all that time, and his election is a splendid tribute to his individual character as well as to his leadership in the party. Judge Cheshier has been a resident of Caldwell County, prominent as a farmer, stock man and banker for many years, and came to this section of Northwest Missouri on October 17, 1857.

He was born January 3, 1847, in Jefferson County, Tennessee. His father, William E. Cheshier, was a native of Ohio, of Scotch and English ancestry. He married Susan Spencer who was born in Jefferson County, Tennessee, of an old Tennessee family of Irish and Scotch ancestry. Judge Cheshier was ten years of age when the family came overland from Tennessee to Northwest Missouri. They made that journey with wagon and teams, and were seven weeks before finally coming to a halt in Caldwell County. This section of Missouri at that time was almost a wilderness, and wild game was more plentiful than domestic animals are at the present time. There were six children in the family. Judge Cheshier's brother, J. M. Cheshier, lives at Glendale, Washington. A sister, Mary Jackson, lives in Caldwell County. The father died at the age of sixty-three. The Cheshier family during the early days in Caldwell County was noted for its hospitality, and there was welcome for everyone who opened the door of that generous home. The father was a man of extraordinary physical energy, and had probably no equal in this part of the country as a rail splitter. He stood 6 feet 2 inches, weighed 185 pounds, and the same strength and endurance which made him conspicuous in the handling of the ax were displayed in his other activities. He spent his last years in the home of his son, Judge Cheshier. The mother died at the age of thirty-seven.

Judge Cheshier was reared on a farm, and trained his muscles and his mind at the same time, alternating between the work of the homestead and attendance at the country schools. Like his father, he became adept in the handling of an ax, and has split many hundreds of rails. At the age of twenty-eight he established a home of his own by his marriage to Harriet A. Hill, who was born in Montgomery County, Missouri, a daughter of Rev. Arthur Hill, a missionary Baptist minister who did work all over Central Missouri. After his marriage Judge Cheshier lived northwest of Cowgill on forty acres of land, having bought that on time, and after paying out on it, sold and bought other land until he had developed a fine farm of 240 acres. That farm is still in his possession. and is one of the best kept places and one of the most comfortable country estates in Caldwell County. In 1911 he turned its management over to his son-in-law, and has since been busied with his banking and official affairs. He has served as a stockholder and director in the Cowgill Bank, and also in the Hamilton Savings Bank, of which he is vice president. As a judge he has made an admirable record, is a man of steadfast convictions as to correct principles of individual and social conduct and entered upon his office with the complete confidence of the county, and nothing in his record has dispelled the trust which was thus manifested in his ability. Judge Cheshier was formerly affiliated with the Masonic Lodge at Polo, and later became a member of the Cowgill Lodge.

Judge Cheshier and wife have two daughters: Pearl L. is the wife of Clarence Brown, and they live on Judge Cheshier's fine farm near Cowgill. The daughter Camora is at home, and has been a successful teacher. Both the daughters were educated at Stevens College in Columbia, the older graduating in 1910 and the younger in 1911.

NEILL D. JOHNSON, M. D. Representing the first class ability and skill of his profession and enjoying a large general practice at Hamilton and vicinity, Doctor Johnson is a physician and surgeon who since graduating from the Chicago Homeopathic College of Medicine in 1903 has taken front rank in his profession. He located at Hamilton in 1912, and has since built up a large practice. He began his work with an excellent equipment, and the test of real practice found him qualified for this important service among the social professions.

Dr. Neill D. Johnson was born at Leroy, McLean County, Illinois. His father, Rev. Archibald Johnson, was a prominent minister of the Presbyterian Church. He was born in Dickson County, Tennessee, of an old Tennessee family, and married Sallie Davis, daughter of Rev. James E. Davis. The Davis family located in Southern Illinois at Mount Vernon during the Black Hawk war. Rev. Archibald Johnson subsequently moved out to Ottawa, Kansas, and died in that state in 1872 at the age of sixty-four years. He spent many years in the work of his Master, and his name is gratefully remembered in a number of localities in different states. He was a republican in politics, and one of his sons, William T., served during the Civil war with the Chicago Light Artillery, and died in service. The mother of the family died at the age of eighty-seven years. There were five sons and three daughters in the family.

Doctor Johnson was thirteen years of age when his parents moved out to Kansas, and finished his education in Missouri and in Indiana. He was ordained as a minister of the Presbyterian Church, and spent about twenty-five years in its service, being located for several years at Topeka, Kansas. He later turned his attention to the study of medicine, was graduated in 1903, and has thus been a contributor to the world's work through two great professions.

Doctor Johnson was married in 1880 to Jane R. Chase, a daughter of Rev. Moody Chase, a cousin of Hon. Salmon Chase, who was a member of Lincoln's cabinet during the Civil war. Doctor Johnson has one son, Archie.

Doctor Johnson at Hamilton has one of the best equipped medical offices in Northwest Missouri, with half a dozen rooms employed for specific purposes, and with a thorough equipment of medical and surgical appliances. He is a specialist in the treatment of the eye, and it is for his skill as an oculist that many patients resort to him from remote parts of the country.

D. M. CLAGETT, M. D. Though Doctor Clagett has been through the toils and hardships of an arduous medical practice at Winston for more than forty years, he is still hale and hearty and looks after a large practice and is held in high esteem by everyone in that section of Missouri. When Doctor Clagett located at Winston it was a settlement not far removed from pioneer conditions, and in the early days he had to travel over all sorts of roads, and was the kindly family physician who brought professional service and cheer and comfort to many an isolated home. For many years he carried on his practice without the aid of the telephone and other modern facilities which have lightened the burdens of the doctor, and he is now one of the oldest members of his profession in Daviess County.

Dr. D. M. Clagett was born at Natchez, Mississippi, March 24, 1846, a son of Hezekiah and Elizabeth (Shipp) Clagett. His father was born in Fredericton, Maryland, and his mother at Lexington, Kentucky, and the grandparents on both sides were Virginians. Doctor Clagett acquired his early education at St. Louis, Missouri, where he attended the public schools, and is a graduate of the St. Louis Medical College. In 1872 he moved to Winston, and has been in practice there ever since. When he located in Winston the Rock Island Railroad had been constructed through the village only about a year, and many of the homes in the town were built of logs. The surrounding country was largely a wilderness of bald prairie, and the whole country was just emerging from the conditions which had prevailed for untold centuries.

Doctor Clagett is a democrat in politics, and was one of the early coroners of Daviess County, having held that office until 1876. He is a member of the Methodist Episcopal Church, and is a Blue Lodge Mason.

On January 1, 1873, Doctor Clagett married Miss Mary A. Wood, a daughter of James and Martha (Osborn) Wood, who lived in Colfax Township in Daviess County. Of the four children born to the doctor and his wife, James, Virgil and Mattie died in childhood. The son is Dr. Oscar F. Clagett, now engaged in the successful practice of medicine at Carbondale, Colorado. Doctor Oscar married Miss Effie E. Stevens, and both were born at Winston, Missouri. She is a daughter of John S. and Bettie (Burch) Stevens.

WILLIAM LAFAYETTE HOUPT. Following are the more important scenes and phases in the life of one of Harrison County's finest old-time citizens, a pioneer of Fox Creek Township and the oldest living settler in that section of Harrison County and the only settler living on the land he entered and patented from the Government. Though nearly eighty, Mr. Houpt looks ten years younger, and both mind and body are active and he still keeps himself in the harness, though prosperity and comfort were assured to him many years ago.

William Lafayette Houpt was born in Sullivan County, Indiana, within four miles of the Wabash River, about half way between Terre Haute and old Vincennes, on September 11, 1835. That was a picturesque landscape of heavy woods and prairies during his youth, and he was well trained in woodcraft and pioneer economy, though of formal schooling he had almost none. At the age of seven his father took him a mile and a half through the woods, blazing a trail for his following, and entered him in the first subscription school taught in that locality. An old hunter's cabin at the head of a small branch was the temple of learning, and even this he was not permitted to attend the full term taught by Professor Moore. His father was injured, and all hands were needed at home, including the young pupil who became practically head of the household in the absence of his father. Though his school days were a small portion of his youth, Mr. Houpt retains an accurate and interesting impression of the old school. The benches were of white walnut or poplar logs, with holes bored on the underside for the wooden pins or legs with the tops smoothed off, but no backs. He was seated on a bench so high that his feet could not touch the floor. One day he went to sleep and dropped his book, and though he jumped down and quickly recovered the property his fault was observed and the teacher punished him by splitting a quill and hanging one on each ear. These remained until removed by the teacher, and Mr. Houpt testifies that such punishment will not fail to keep a child awake. The only book he ever took to school, save for four days, was an old speller, and at the age of eight was able to spell every word between its covers. He never owned an arithmetic in his life.

With the responsibilities thrust upon him by his father's injury, he remained at home, grubbed land and farmed, and had only a few of the intermissions of toil that relieved the monotony of Indiana pioneer days. At the age of eighteen he was given a horse by his father, and went with his Grandfather Correll to another frontier bounded by the great Missouri. In 1854 they left Indiana in a wagon and camped by the roadside every night during the ten days they traveled until reaching Harrison County, Missouri. His mother's brother having written how the old "bucks" would approach a cabin and stamp their feet, Mr. Houpt was keenly excited over the prospect and came out to Missouri to hunt deer. The journey had only one incident of specially good or bad fortune, and that was the loss of the horse given him by his father. Up to January, 1855, he did nothing but hunt through the splendid game preserves then existing everywhere in Northwest Missouri. After this he took a job of making 5,000 rails. This was a work for which he had no experience. In Indiana all the work he had done in the timber was clearing away the tree tops where railmakers had felled the trees, but in Missouri finances were such as to introduce him through practical necessity to this new and untried field of labor. His aggregate experience as railmaker covered about fifteen years, and he believes that he made in this time about thirty-five thousand rails. He cut and split all the rails for the fencing of the eighty acres he entered from the Government. This labor and corn cutting and mowing hay with a scythe were about the only kind of work in the new country that offered profit to man with only his hands as capital. In those early times in Northwest Missouri Mr. Houpt mowed hay and put it in the shock at 50 cents an acre. He had a fork with tines made of ash wood, and in that way earned the money by which he bought a spinning wheel for his home. With the increasing growing of grain, he found still another means of earning money, by swinging the cradle. When only twelve years of age, back in Indiana, he had taken his first lessons with the cradle, and was an expert in the handling of that implement. The first one he used had been brought by his father from North Carolina, and his own old cradle, used forty years ago, now hangs in the shop at his home.

Where Mr. Houpt now resides he entered an 80-acre tract in section 6 of range 63, town 26, and had to borrow every cent of the preemption fee. He had occupied this land before entering it, and erected his cabin on Trail Creek. It was made of small white oak logs, 14 by 16 feet, and he carried the logs himself and put in his own puncheons. That was his home for twenty-five years before he felt able to build a better residence. His first team was one that he watched grow from bull calves, and they proved their value by breaking his land, which accomplished he sold the oxen to finish payments on the land. When the store of grains and crops ran low, he supplemented his food supply with meat from the forest, and the first four winters in Missouri he hunted deer almost constantly for their hams and hides, for which there was a ready sale. The hams brought from fifty to seventy-five cents per pair and dry hides 12 cents per pound.

After overcoming the first obstacles and proving his ability to live by service in this new country, Mr. Houpt entered two other forties, and subsequently bought 160, and altogether these comprise his farm estate today. All his buildings were put up on Trail Creek, and the center of his farm industry is a beautiful dell, the banks of the creek being studded with splendid walnuts and oaks. All these trees have grown up since 1863, in which year a fire devastated all the timber in this region and destroyed the building improvements on the Houpt Farm, making its owner poor.

During the war Mr. Houpt was in the Missouri State Militia, entering the state forces under the arrangement for "armed neutrality." He was with the Fifty-seventh Mounted Infantry, in Company E, under Captain Prather and Col. James Neville. His service was all over the state, but much of the time in Southern Missouri engaged in a sort of guerrilla warfare with Quantrell's men. In politics Mr. Houpt cast his first vote for Stephen A. Douglas for President in 1860, but his opposition to slavery and his admiration for Abraham Lincoln caused him to vote for the latter in 1864, and he has regularly supported the republican presidential nominees ever since. In a modest way he assisted in making Harrison County the banner Republican County it is, but has never felt able to assume the responsibilities of office himself, and has declined various honors of this kind. He was never a strong Roosevelt man, and his own principles of action were unchanged in the party split of 1912. To quote his own language, "He has never permitted any Bull Moose to kick up its heels in his pasture." In the days of convention work following the war he had a regular function, and was always in the county meetings when his influence was needed.

Almost since he came to Missouri Mr. Houpt has enjoyed the relations of his own household and fireside. He was married August 26, 1856, to Miss Jincy Morgan, whose parents were Kentuckians. To this marriage the following children were born: John, who was robbed and killed in Colorado, being unmarried; Miss Susan, of Joplin, Missouri; Arch A., a farmer in Cherokee County, Kansas; Mary, wife of Philip Usrey, of Redondo Beach, California; Rhoda, who married David Elder, of Oklahoma; Charles S., whose home is at Castle Rock, Washington; Mrs. Vira Elsmer, of Joplin; and Clara, wife of Charles Rankin, of Joplin. In January, 1889, Mr. Houpt married for his second wife Mrs. Rosa Keech, and of their union is one daughter, Miss Altha, living at home. Mrs. Houpt, who was a daughter of John and Maggie (Morris) Kinzie, was born near Berne, Switzerland, October 16, 1846, and by her first marriage her children were: Alice, wife of Edgar Ross, of Mammoth Springs, Arkansas; Mary, wife of Emil Linstrum, of Tarkio, Missouri; and Katie, wife of John Gates, of Harrison County.

To conclude this sketch some reference should be made to Mr. Houpt's family in its earlier generations. His grandfather was a native of Germany, and on coming to America settled in Pennsylvania, where he married a Scotch girl named Albright. They moved to South Carolina, and later to Indiana, where both died. Their children were: John W., father of the Harrison County citizen; Jacob, who died in Sullivan County, Indiana; Henry, who also died in that county; Thomas, who died in early life leaving a family; Sarah, who married John Correll and spent her life in Indiana; Adaline, who married Maurice Miles and died in Indiana; and Angeline, who died unmarried.

John W. Houpt, the father, was born in North Carolina before the Carolinas were separated into states. He grew up in Roane County, and in pioneer times came to Indiana, and lived there until most of his family moved on west to Kansas, and he then followed and died in Graham County in 1902. He was married in North Carolina to Margaret Correll, a daughter of Samuel Correll. The latter's father was from Scotland and a farmer, while Samuel was a wagon-maker in Indiana. Mrs. John W. Houpt died in Sullivan County, Indiana. Her children were: William W.; Mary, who married William Adkisson and died in Gove County, Kansas; Eliza, who married P. G. Adkisson, of Oklahoma; James F., who died in young manhood in Indiana; Thomas S., who lives in Graham County, Kansas; Harvey, of Nebraska; and Alvin, who lives near his brother Harvey.

HARRY M. DAVIS. Four generations of the Davis family have added to the development of those communities wherein they had their residence, in so far as authentic record is available, and a fifth generation is being reared to take its place in public and private life. That representative of the family with which this review is most deeply concerned is Harry M. Davis, a son of James A. Davis and grandson of Nathaniel Davis. He was born in Richmond, Missouri, on a spot now occupied by the Richmond Hotel, on July 25, 1857, and there was reared to the age of twenty. His father, James A. Davis, was born in Ray County, Missouri, on November 27, 1837, himself a son of Nathaniel Davis, born July 31, 1807, in Washington County, Tennessee, where the family was long established.

When Nathaniel Davis was five years old he removed with his parents to Knox County, Tennessee, and there he spent his youth and was reared to manhood. When he was twenty-two years old he entered the University of East Tennessee and was graduated with honors from that college in 1832. He then came to Ray County, Missouri. At that time Ray County, and, indeed, the whole State of Missouri, was then regarded as the far West, and by many the wild West. He was prepared for hardship and his intention was to carve out his destiny in a new land. How well he succeeded, the affection of his old friends and the respect and esteem in which he was held by the people of the entire county will bear eloquent testimony. His character was without taint and his very name was a synonym for integrity, honor, hospitality and charity. He was an eminently successful physician, skillful, prompt and always to be depended upon. He was here through the exciting period of the Mormon war, as the excitement of the time was designated, and was compelled to seek safety, for a time leaving his home.

In the fall of 1837 Nathaniel Davis married Miss Maria A. Allen, a native of Pennsylvania, and she died in the year 1878, aged seventy-six years. Of her six children, all are living, James A. being the father of the subject of this review.

James A. Davis attended the common schools of his native community and finished his training in Richland College. In 1862 he engaged in the mercantile business, in company with James F. Hudgus and Thomas H. Bayliss, continuing until 1864, when he withdrew from the firm and went to Salt Lake City, Utah. He remained there for a year, then returned to Richmond and resumed business for five years. At the end of that time he began to devote himself to farming activities, and he was thus occupied for three years, when he was appointed to the post of deputy county collector under Thomas Fowler. He also served through the administration of A. M. Fowler, successor to Thomas Fowler, so that his service in the office covered a period of five years.

In 1878 Mr. Davis was elected on the Democratic ticket to the office of county collector, in which he had shown his capability as deputy, and he was reelected in 1880, in 1882 and in 1884, discharging the duties of his office in a manner highly creditable to himself and to the county.

In 1887, following the expiration of his last term, Mr. Davis organized the Exchange Bank of Richmond, whereupon he was elected cashier and served in that office until 1900, at which time he retired from active business. He has since lived a life of practical retirement in Richmond.

In 1890 Mr. Davis built the Eagle Mill at Richmond, and he and his son, Harry M. Davis, operated the plant for two years, when they sold it to its present owner, O. N. Hamsaler.

Mr. Davis married on May 15, 1861, Miss Mary Tripplett, a native of Rappahannock County, Virginia. She died on November 26, 1864, leaving one child, Carrie, now the wife of Frank Clark and living in Ray County, Missouri.

On May 15, 1866, he again married, Miss Allen M. Hughes, of Howard County, Missouri, becoming his wife. She was born in 1843, and still lives. To them were born seven children: Harry M., whose name heads this review; Frank, also a resident of Richmond, Missouri; Katy, deceased; Lucy N., the wife of F. M. Hyffaker, of Chicago; Allie, who married C. W. Harrison, of New York City; James A., Jr., of Richmond; and Estelle, the wife of Dr. E. M. Cameron, of Richmond.

When Harry M. Davis was twenty years old he went to Chicago to add something to his education, and there he took a rigid course in business training in the Bryant & Stratton Business College. Returning home when he had completed his commercial studies, he soon after went to Kansas City, and there he took a position as traveling salesman for Barton Brothers, a wholesale shoe house, and for five years thereafter he worked for that concern. He then returned to Richmond and during the next two years he was engaged in the milling business with his father. In 1892 he joined a Mr. Bates in the purchase of a lumber yard, and for the next seven years operated the yard under the firm name of Bates & Davis. In 1899 Mr. Bates disposed of his share to L. T. Child, and then Mr. Davis and Mr. Child incorporated the business under the firm name of Davis & Child, with a capital of $10,000. Mr. Davis became president of the firm, and they have since continued in operation, increasing the capitalization as the demands of the business grew. The business is now capitalized at $30,000, and the establishment is making steady progress. Everything in the building line is carried by Davis & Child, the yard itself being under the personal supervision and management of Mr. Child.

In 1906 Mr. Davis was elected to the office of county collector and he served for four years. At the end of his term of office he turned his attention to farming, and he is now operating a farm comprising a full section of land, 380 acres of which he owns. He makes a specialty of jacks, mules and hogs, and has been very successful in his breeding enterprise.

It is not too much to say that Mr. Davis is a man who has the genuine confidence and esteem of the public, and that he is one of the most prominent and popular men in these parts. He proved an excellent public official, and if he could be induced to enter the lists in political conflict, it is morally certain that he would find continued favor with the people as an official. Fraternally he is a member of the A. F. and A. M. and of the Benevolent and Protective Order of Elks.

On December 30, 1891, Mr. Davis married Miss Edwina Menefee, who was born in the house where she now lives in the year 1874. She is a daughter of Berrien J. Menefee, a native of Culpeper County, Virginia, born there on January 22, 1832, and who died on December 30, 1890, at Richmond. His parents were early settlers in Missouri. Mr. Menefee was twice married. His first wife was Cynthia Cole, who died and left two children, Kate, the wife of James S. Lightner, and Henry R., of St. Louis, Missouri. His second wife was Miss Elizabeth Newland, a native of Pike County, Missouri. She is living and for the past eighteen years has been housekeeper at Central College, this state. There were five children of this second marriage: Newland lives in the West; Mrs. Davis was the second born; Emma is the wife of R. L. Tracy, of Albany, Oregon; Susie married M. W. Little, of Oklahoma City, Oklahoma; and Berrien is the wife of H. F. Blackwell, of Lexington, Missouri.

Berrien J. Menefee was a soldier of the Confederacy, serving as lieutenant in Company D, First Missouri Cavalry. In 1864 he went across the plains in company with James A. Davis, father of the subject, returning, together with Mr. Davis, in the following year. For twenty-five years he was a merchant in Richmond, operating a hardware and implement store. He dropped dead of heart disease while busy about the store one day.

Mr. and Mrs. Davis have no children, but they have reared the child of a sister, Catherine Allen, now fifteen years of age, and attending school at Lexington, Missouri.

JODIA A. MAGRAW, M. D. Owning a name that has been honorably identified with Harrison County for sixty years, Doctor Magraw was long known as an educator, but since 1902 has been a successful physician at Gilman City. Most of his life has been spent in the service of others, and as a physician he is kindly, even tempered, and a skillful counselor and friend to his widening circle of patients.

Doctor Magraw was born on a farm in Adams Township, Harrison County, November 22, 1859. There he grew up, had a farm training and environment, an education from the district schools, later supplemented from the Kirksville State Normal and the old Stanberry Normal, where he was graduated in 1892. He had been teaching for some years, and that was his regular profession for twelve years thereafter. His country school work was done in his native county, and his last teaching in a graded school was at Valparaiso, Nebraska, where he located in 1894. He took up the study of medicine at Cotner University in Lincoln, Nebraska, and was graduated M. D. in 1899. In that school he was demonstrator of anatomy one year and during 1901-02 filled the chair of diseases of children. After three years of practice at Pleasant Hill, Nebraska, Doctor Magraw returned to Missouri, and located in the same locality in which he had been reared. His office and home have been in Gilman City since 1902. He has membership in the Harrison County and the State Medical societies.

Doctor Magraw's grandfather was John Magraw, who was born at Germantown, Pennsylvania, the son of a Scotch father and of an Irish mother. When he was seven years old these parents died of yellow fever, being victims of the only epidemic of that scourge which ever reached as far north as Philadelphia. The three orphan children were reared in different homes. The daughter married a Mr. Latta and spent her life in Ohio. The other son became a resident of West Virginia, and among his well known descendants still in that state is former Governor Magraw, a grandson. John Magraw was reared in the East, served as a soldier in the War of 1812, and afterwards moved west and died in Fayette County, Illinois, at the age of eighty-five. He married an orphan girl, Elizabeth McGuire, and their children were: Eleanor, who married Samuel Sidener, of Fayette County, Illinois; James, who died in Fayette County; John D., father of Doctor Magraw; Joseph, who died in Fayette County, leaving a family; and David, who died in Macomb, Illinois.

John D. Magraw, who was born in Knox County, Ohio, May 9, 1830, began active life with only a country schooling, but all his life was a studious reader. In 1855 he came to Missouri and entered land in Adams Township of Harrison County, and improved it and made the home where his children grew up. He died in Gilman City March 31, 1905. In politics he belonged to the old know-nothing party that existed before the war, and was one of 'the two men in his township to cast votes for Abraham Lincoln in 1860. He volunteered for service in the Union army, being rejected on account of a crippled arm, but had a place in Company G of the Fifty-seventh Missouri Militia, being called out for brief periods only. He was one of the party leaders among the republicans of his locality, never aspired to office, and for about a dozen years served as justice of the peace. He was an active Methodist.

John D. Magraw was married in Harrison County, March 13, 1857, to Miss Matilda J. Miller. Her father, Dr. Benjamin C. Miller, was a native of Ohio, and from the vicinity of Kokomo, Indiana, came to Missouri in 1855. He had practiced medicine in Indiana, but in Harrison County became a farmer until his death in 1876. His wife was Elvira DeVore, and of their eight children the following are mentioned: Jackson Greene, who was named in honor of Gen. Nathaniel Greene; Matilda J.; Rebecca A., deceased, who married John T. Price and left a family in Harrison County; Samantha E., who married John H. Myers; Alice, the wife of Mandrid Hart, lives at Carlsbad, New Mexico; John A., of DeKalb County, Missouri; and Samuel J., of Arickaree, Colorado. The children of John D. Magraw and wife were: Walter G., a farmer in Adams Township, Harrison County; Dr. J. A.; Altha, a teacher in the high school at Maysville; Naomi, wife of Charles McClary, a Gilman City merchant. There are no grandchildren by any of these.

Doctor Magraw was married at Albany, Missouri, December 28, 1899, to Rose M. Selby, a daughter of Joshua J. and Mary E. Selby and a sister of Columbus O. Selby, mentioned on other pages of this work. Doctor Magraw is affiliated with the Independent Order of Odd Fellows, having filled all chairs in the lodge, and is past chancellor in the Knights of Pythias. He is a member of the Christian Church. Besides his profitable practice, he owns property in Gilman City and a farm near by. Doctor Magraw is a man of excellent physical presence, is alert, and full of life and hope.

WALTER CLEMENT CHILDERS. While Walter Clement Childers, of Grant City, is a newcomer in the ranks of Northwest Missouri journalism, his accomplishments in other lines of business endeavor, and as a public official, may be taken as an assurance that in his new venture he will meet with a full measure of success. He has been a resident of Grant City since his first election to the office of county clerk in 1906, a position which he still retains, and has been owner and editor of the Worth County Times since January, 1914, and is, all in all, considered one of his community's stirring and helpful citizens. Mr. Childers is not a native of Worth County, but has resided here since his infancy, having been brought here from Jay County, Indiana, where he was born November 8, 1876, a son of James H. and Hannah (VanSkyock) Childers.

The paternal grandfather of Walter C. Childers spent his final years in Jay County, Indiana, to which locality he had gone from Adams

County, Ohio. He was of English stock, the first of the name in this country having come from England early in our national history, and while it is not definitely known where the progenitor settled, it is established that his posterity early located in Ohio. James H. Childers was born in Adams County, Ohio, and received a somewhat limited education in the public schools. He was brought up in the same manner as the majority of Ohio farmers' sons, and although a cripple spent a busy life and achieved some success through his energy and perseverance. Coming to Missouri in 1877, he located two miles and a quarter north of Isadora, in Worth County, where he established himself in the nursery business and later also spent some years as a salesman. Mr. Childers held no political office, although he was a staunch and lifelong democrat. He was identified with no religious denomination, although he firmly believed in churches and contributed his share to their movements. Mr. Childers' fraternal connection was with the Odd Fellows. He died in Worth County in February, 1902. Mr. Childers married Miss Hannah Van Skyock, daughter of Jonathan VanSkyock, a member of a Dutch family of Jay County, Indiana, and sister of Washington VanSkyock, who was one of the early pioneers of that county. She is still living, making her home among her children, and is seventy-eight years of age. The children born to Mr. and Mrs. Childers were as follows: Dr. Allen G. T., a practicing physician of Mullhall, Oklahoma; John Calvin, who is engaged in agricultural pursuits in Worth County; Stephen M., who is carrying on operations on the old homestead farm in this county; and Walter Clement, of this review.

Walter Clement Childers lived in the country until attaining his majority, and acquired an ordinary education in the rural schools. Later he attended the Stanberry Normal School, where he prepared himself for the vocation of educator, and engaged in work in the rural districts, his first school being the Platt Dell School. After three years passed in the country, Mr. Childers became principal of the school at Athelstan, Iowa, a position which he retained for a like period, and then deciding upon a career in a profession, entered the Highland Park Law School, at Des Moines, Iowa. After one year, however, Mr. Childers gave up his legal studies and engaged with his brother in the general merchandise business at Athelstan, Iowa, but in 1906 made the race for county clerk of Worth County, and was elected to that office in November of the same year, as the successor of W. P. Spillman. His energetic, capable and faithful services during his first term earned him repeated reelections and he has continued to serve his county in this capacity to the present time, much to the satisfaction of his fellow citizens. He has handled the affairs of his office conscientiously and well, and his record is one deserving high commendation.

In January, 1914, Mr. Childers purchased the Worth County Times, a democratic weekly and the only democratic paper in Worth county. During the forty years of its life it has had several owners, chief and oldest among whom is E. S. Garver, from whom Mr. Childers purchased the plant. This is equipped with linotype, good imposing stones, modern press and all utensils and appurtenances to be found in an up-to-date plant, and is operated by gasoline power. Mr. Childers is endeavoring to give to the people of Worth County a clean, reliable newspaper, and to mold public opinion along the lines of advancement and helpfulness in education and good citizenship.

Mr. Childers cast his first presidential vote in 1900 for William Jennings Bryan and has since consistently supported democratic principles. His convention work has been confined to local matters, and he has served as chairman of the democratic central committee, during the

campaign of 1908, and has been also a member of the congressional committee. Fraternally, he is connected with the Independent Order of Odd Fellows, and is a Master Mason and a member of the Modern Woodmen of America. His religious connection is with the Missionary Baptist Church. He has been connected with a number of business interests which have contributed to the growth of Grant City's importance, and at the present time is one of the owners of the city electric light and power plant.

On August 4, 1901, Mr. Childers was united in marriage with Miss Emma Weese, a daughter of Leonard and Nancy J. (Martin) Weese, whose children were as follows: Edith, who is the wife of P. S. Round, of Hanson, Idaho; Dr. W. W., a practicing physician of Ontario, Oregon; Emma, who is now Mrs. Childers; Elmyra, who became the wife of R. B. Hill, and is a resident of Nampa, Idaho; and Guy, who resides at Hanson, that state. Two children have been born to Mr. and Mrs. Childers, namely: Tessie Helen and Vilas Evan.

B. L. RALPH. Now living quietly on his farm, which is partly within the city limits of Savannah, B. L. Ralph has had a varied business career which has taken him into all the states west of the Mississippi River, as far north as Alaska, during the Klondike mining excitement, and as far south as Old Mexico. He has done a great deal of work in a constructive way, has prospered as a business man, and is a good substantial citizen.

B. L. Ralph was born near Albany in Gentry County, Missouri, January 1, 1863, a son of George S. and Mary J. (Twedell) Ralph. His father was born in Ohio, June 30, 1824, and his mother in Illinois, February 15, 1829. Left an orphan, his father came out to the Platte Purchase in Northwest Missouri in 1846, while his wife came with her parents to St. Joseph, Missouri, in 1848, and they were married in Gentry County, where the father spent his active career as a farmer. The mother is still living at Albany. Their three children are B. L. Ralph; William, of Gentry County; and Ida, wife of J. W. Worden of Gentry County.

B. L. Ralph spent the first twenty-three years of his life in Gentry County, lived on the old farm with his parents, and in the meantime had gained the fundamentals of an education in country schools. Among other experiences of his lifetime he has done a considerable amount of school teaching, teaching for two winters in his home district, and after moving to Andrew County in 1884 taught a country school one winter.

In 1886 Mr. Ralph was married in Savannah to Amy M. Cobb. She was born in England, August 25, 1870, and at the age of four years came with her parents, Amos and Harriet (Brand) Cobb, who settled in Savannah. After their marriage Mr. Ralph moved west, locating in San Luis Park, Colorado, took up a homestead, and assisted in the building of irrigation ditches. After a year spent there he returned to Missouri, and became foreman on mason work during the construction of the Chicago Great Western Railroad through Savannah. His next venture was in the wholesale and retail oil business at Maryville, and subsequently he was connected with the Standard Oil Company, and went out to Kansas and was located at Salina for nine years. He was interested there in the Lee Mercantile Company, a wholesale grocery firm. After selling out, Mr. Ralph was one of the men attracted to the far North by the gold discoveries in Alaska in 1897. He went over the Dyea Trail and down the Yukon River to Dawson City. This was a trip fraught with many difficulties and dangers. The party had to whipsaw the lumber used for the construction of boats, and there were times when provisions were scanty and when all manner of difficulties threatened them. Mr.

Ralph spent fifteen months in prospecting in the Yukon Territory, and returned to Skagway, a distance of seven hundred miles, by dog team, making that trip in twenty days. He arrived home in the spring of 1898. With his brother-in-law, Charles B. Cobb, he engaged in masonry contracting along the line of the Chicago Great Western, and did all the masonry contracting on that system. Since giving up his contracting business Mr. Ralph has looked after his farming business. He has twenty-two acres with his home partially in the corporate limits, and another place of 220 acres outside.

Mr. Ralph is a democrat in politics, and is affiliated with both the York and Scottish Rite branches of Masonry, including the thirty-second degree and the Shrine. He and his wife are the parents of two children: Mildred and Elizabeth.

WILLIAM H. RICHTER. Here is a name which, introduced into Harrison County in 1855, has for sixty years been identified with some of the most substantial improvements and activities in agriculture and stock raising. Many people recall the old pioneer, James Richter, whose equal as a hunter and trapper never lived in this section of the country. The Richter Stock Farm near Gilman City has for a number of years been the home of some of the finest Shorthorn cattle raised anywhere in the country, and many farms not only in this state but elsewhere have received the nucleus of their high-grade stock from this place.

James Richter was the son of German parents, and was born aboard a sailing vessel while en route from a German port to the United States in 1813. His parents located in Maryland, and while he was still a child moved out to Wayne County, Indiana, where they were among the earliest settlers in that old Quaker community. His father died there in 1819, and the widowed mother, whose name was Melcher, lived at Hagerstown, Indiana, until her death. Among their children were: John, William, Leonard, James and two daughters whose names are not now recalled. All these children lived in Wayne County, Indiana, with the exception of James.

James Richter grew up in the new country of Eastern Indiana, and had his education in the country schools. When a young man he moved to Fulton County, in Northern Indiana, and took up government land among the Miami and Pottawatomie Indians. He lived among these Indians as a neighbor, and when as a tribe they were removed to White Cloud, Kansas, he was appointed by the United States Government as commissary sergeant of the commission that moved them west. While in Fulton County James Richter cleared up an 80-acre farm and followed and became expert in the woodcraft of his Indian neighbors. In that section of Indiana his home was in a low, swampy country, characterized by heavy malarial fogs and swarms of mosquitoes. All the animals of the primeval forest could be found, including wild hogs, and his life there was spiced with hunting and other outdoor sports. From his Indian friends in Fulton County James Richter learned to trail game with the same exquisite art employed by the red men of the forest, and after he came to Harrison County he proved his skill by trailing wolves even without tracks for six miles to their den, a feat that no man could accomplish without Indian training and instinct. During the last years of his life in Harrison County he was a trapper and hunter, and his piles of skins showed his prowess. In the month of November after his seventy-fifth birthday he caught furs to the value of $130 in one month.

When James Richter came to Missouri in 1855 he entered land in Sherman Township of Harrison County, in section 29, township 63, range 27. This he improved from the prairie sod, and his log house, sixteen feet square, was the first one built standing on the prairie between Bethany, in Harrison County, and Bancroft, in Daviess County. During the first year spent there he hired men to break fifty acres, the work being done with great sod plows, drawn by seven yoke of cattle to each plow. He produced from that virgin soil fifty bushels of corn to the acre. His work as a farmer was confined to grain raising, since the handling of stock would have interfered with his hunting pursuits. In the early days, as proof of the cheapness of land in this vicinity, it was customary for him to give an 80-acre tract of land to a man for a year's work. His home in Sherman Township was a headquarters for early hospitality, and every older resident of Harrison County is familiar with the place. James Richter lived there from the time he came to Harrison County with the exception of a time spent at Edinburg in order to give his daughters an education.

Politically James Richter was an old line whig and then a republican. He had firm convictions on currency questions; took a good citizen's interest in politics, and voted for only one democrat in all his life. In 1860 he cast his ballot for Abraham Lincoln at a time when it required considerable courage and independence to openly support such a candidate in Missouri. He was a loyal Union man during the war and had previously been counted as a sympathizer with the conductors of the "underground railroad." When quizzed as to what he would do if he saw a fugitive negro, he replied that he would say "Go it, darkey, get away if you can." And when asked what he would do if he saw the master come along hunting the darkey and was asked as to his whereabouts, he replied that he would say: "Catch him if you can." He was never in public office, and though not a member of a church, was a moral man and never failed to give aid, in the construction of pioneer churches, was a generous contributor to the poor and needy, and is remembered for his charitable character.

James Richter died February 25, 1894, when past eighty years of age, and he and his wife sleep side by side in the Odd Fellows Cemetery at Bethany. He was first married in Fulton County, Indiana, to Eleanor Gordon. Her father, Robert Gordon, was of the well known Gordon clan of Scotland, was a school teacher, and died in Fulton County, Indiana. Among other children one is the mother of Doctor Walker, of Bethany. James Richter and his first wife had the following children: Marie E., wife of S. A. Pettit, of Steamboat Springs, Colorado; and William H. James Richter married for his second wife Belinda Chambers, who died at Bethany, and is buried in the Odd Fellows Cemetery. She died in March, 1899. Of this marriage the children were: Ella, who spent her life in Harrison County and married William McCollum; Dr. Louisa M., of Los Angeles, California; and Sarah Etta, who married John Smith, of Los Angeles.

William H. Richter was born in Fulton County, Indiana, September 9, 1848, but from the age of seven grew up on his father's farm in Harrison County. His father had walked all the distance from Indiana to Missouri to enter his land, and then in 1855 the entire family started out to take possession of the new home. They made the journey with a covered wagon, which was the primitive method of travel, and on arriving found the country almost destitute of social advantages. There were no schoolhouses, and William H. Richter first attended a select school kept in a private home by Mrs. Hannah Boyce. He was also a pupil in the old Ground Hog schoolhouse, a log cabin located on Polecat Creek, and in 1858 became a pupil in the newly organized Spring Hill school district. There he attended school in a frame house built for the purpose, the first frame schoolhouse of Harrison County. As an illustration of the backwardness of educational facilities in this county at the time, Mr. Richter recalls having witnessed the spectacle of two young men, one nineteen and the other twenty-one, both learning their A B C's in this school. Mr. Richter for three years attended the old Grand River College at Edinburg, and had his home with his parents until the age of twenty-one. At the age of twelve years he commenced transacting business for his father and under his instructions, such as paying the taxes, buying stock and collecting small debts, which was a great help in after years. At the age of fourteen he was sent by his father to the State of Nebraska alone, with team and wagon, a distance of 100 miles across a wild country, in places twenty miles without a house in sight, a trip which he made, there and back, in safety.

Part of his early career was devoted to teaching, and he taught in country schools for seven winters, occupying himself with farming in the summer. He then turned his attention exclusively to farming, and has lived on his present place since June, 1871. His land lies in sections 11 and 12, and forty years ago it was all raw prairie. For the eighty acres which comprised his first home he paid by raising corn at 15 cents a bushel, the first crop paying for the land. He broke up the sod and fenced his fields, and there he and his wife spent their first years in a log house with a puncheon floor. In that humble cabin their first child was born. Later the cabin gave way to a more comfortable frame house, and that was the home while the children were growing up and being educated. In 1910 the farm was improved by the construction of an attractive farm residence, one of the conspicuous places now in that locality. From time to time as needed barns and other buildings and conveniences for stock have been added, and his equipment for the handling and housing of his blooded cattle is now complete. His farm, or ranch, as it may properly be termed, has grown from an 80-acre tract to 490 acres, and has for many years been noted as a thoroughbred stock farm.

Mr. Richter began handling Shorthorn cattle in 1896, starting his herd with "Gold Standard" and "Minnie's Eagle," of the George Neff herd. He has also added strains from the Duncan and Bellows herds, and his stock is now exclusively made up of the "Choice Goods" strain of the Bellows herd. Mr. Richter's fine stock has found its way into other states, into Nebraska and as far west as Washington, and in Missouri he has furnished the nucleus for many herds. His active management of the farm and the stock continued until he reached the age of sixty, and at that time he turned over the business to his sons, and they continue it under their father's name.

Mr. Richter is a republican, having voted for only one democrat in his life, and has served as township collector. Although a man of Christian principles, he has never affiliated with any one denomination. On June 1, 1871, Mr. Richter married Mrs. Jennie Elwell, widow of Capt. George W. Elwell, and a daughter of David B. Manville. Mr. Manville, who now lives at Gallatin, Missouri, at the venerable age of ninety-three, was born in Morrow County, Ohio, July 3, 1821. His father, Fleming Manville, settled near Valparaiso, Indiana, about 1855, and died there in 1863. Fleming Manville married Sallie Steward, and they became the parents of eleven children. David B. Manville came out to Missouri in the fall of 1859. He was a teacher in early life, but later followed farming, and was a republican in politics. He married Mary B. Lounsberry, who was born in New York State and died in Harrison County. Her children were: Mrs. Richter, who was born July 18, 1845; and James Harvey, who died at Bethany, leaving two sons. Mrs. Richter by her marriage to Captain Elwell has a daughter, Mary E., wife of William H. Hockridge. The children of Mr. and Mrs. Richter are: Frank M., who was born June 8, 1872, was educated in the public schools and in the Chillicothe Business College, and for several years has been actively associated with his brother as a farmer and stock man. Frank Richter married Hattie Carr, and they have a son, William Edward. James George, the second son, was born August 24, 1884, is one of the firm of stock men and farmers of which his father is the head, and by his marriage to Ruth Vosburg has a daughter, Edna Jane.

HON. DAVID J. HEASTON. In the death of Judge David J. Heaston, which occurred July 21, 1902, at Bethany, there passed from life's activities one of the unique and forceful characters of Harrison County and one who had been a resident here from the year 1859. He was an eastern man, having been born in Champaign County, Ohio, March 22, 1835, and in 1839 was taken by his parents to near Winchester, Indiana, where he grew to manhood and received his education in the public schools. In addition to the elementary schools, he attended Asbury University, at Greencastle, Indiana, and owing to his limited means was obliged to teach school to secure the funds with which to pursue his higher education. In 1857 he entered college at Oxford, Ohio, and spent a year there, and prior to this time had read law for about a year with Judge Jeremiah Smith, of Winchester, Indiana, continuing his legal studies while he taught school. In 1858 he was admitted to the bar in the Circuit Court at Winchester and was prepared to enter his profession with credit and confidence of success.

It was in the spring of 1859 that Judge Heaston decided to come into the great valley of the Mississippi, and accordingly, in that year, established himself at Bethany, where he was shortly afterward licensed by Judge McFerran. During the Civil war he was commissioned colonel of the state militia, having always been a great Union man and wielding great influence for the flag. In 1861 he took editorial charge of the Weekly Union, of Bethany, at the request of its owners, and through this connection his influence 'for the Government was made felt. He was a clear, terse and energetic writer and soon placed the paper at the head of journalistic efforts in this section. Judge Heaston was elected captain of the first company organized in response to the call of the governor, and when the enrolled militia of the county was formed into the Fifty-seventh Regiment he was commissioned colonel of the same.

In politics Judge Heaston was always a democrat, and died in the faith. He canvassed the County of Harrison in 1860 in behalf of Stephen A. Douglas for President and did a like service for every democratic candidate for that office until he died. He was a delegate to nearly all the democratic state conventions from the war on, and in 1872 was a delegate to the national democratic convention at Baltimore, assisting in the nomination of Greeley and Brown, the standard-bearers of that year. In 1876 he was the elector for his congressional district on the democratic ticket and, being elected, he attended the electoral college and aided in casting the electoral vote of Missouri for Tilden and Hendricks for President and vice president.

In 1870 Judge Heaston started a democratic paper at Bethany, known as The Watchman, and conducted it with success for three years. In 1877, in connection with B. F. Meyer, he started a democratic paper in Harrison County—the county being without such a paper at that time—known as The Broad-Axe. This he edited with his accustomed vigor until 1884, and under his editorial management the paper acquired a state reputation as a fearless and able exponent of democratic doctrines and principles.

In 1878 Judge Heaston was elected a member of the state senate from the fourth district by a large majority, his counties being Ray, Caldwell, Daviess and Harrison, and served as chairman of the committees on Public Printing and Federal Relations, in addition to doing other important committee work. His qualifications as an able attorney brought him forward prominently as one of the revisionists of the state statutes in 1879, and in the special session of 1882 he presented a bill for the redistricting of the state into congressional districts which, after a warm struggle, was adopted in the democratic caucus decisively and became a law as he introduced it. He became a candidate for congress upon his record in the senate and his other public work, and after a lively and interesting campaign came within a very few votes of the nomination.

During all this time, notwithstanding his heavy and important editorial labors, his official duties and political work and aspirations, he read law assiduously and practiced his profession vigorously. He was longer in the practice than any other member of the profession when he left it, and was honored with the title of "The Father of the Bar."

Judge Heaston was made a Mason at Winchester, Indiana, where he grew up, taking the master's degree in June, 1857. He received the Royal Arch degree at Gallatin, Missouri, in 1866, and the order of Knight Templar at Trenton in 1882, while the Council degree was conferred upon him at St. Louis in 1885. He served as worshipful master, as high priest and as eminent commander, and frequently represented the lodges in the grand bodies of the state as a delegate. He was for many years district deputy grand master for his Masonic district and spent much time delivering lectures and building up the order.

In September, 1866, Judge Heaston joined the Christian Church at Bethany, and became a member of the committee which was in charge of the building of the new church. In all walks of life he was always an exemplary citizen and did much to build up the religious, educational, moral and industrial phases of his county and town. No man was held in higher esteem than he and when he passed away his sterling advice and kindly counsel were greatly missed by those who had benefited thereby and who knew the man, his great mind and his earnest heart.

On January 17, 1861, Judge Heaston was united in marriage with Miss Margaret E. Monson, a daughter of Thomas Monson, then sheriff of Harrison County, Missouri. Of the six children of this union who grew to mature years, Sarah Catherine is the wife of Ed L. Dunn, of Oklahoma City, Oklahoma, and has one child, Ed L. Dunn, in the real estate and loan business in Oklahoma City; Truman; Heaston; Leonard who is a resident of Oklahoma City and register of deeds there, married May McClure in 1888, and has two children, Bert, a dealer in automobiles, and Victor, in high school; George W. died unmarried, February 14, 1902; and Warren L. married Allie Crickett and died December 27, 1900.

For over forty-three years Judge Heaston was a resident of Bethany and in all that time his honesty and probity of character were never questioned. In all matters pertaining to the material prosperity of his city and county his assistance, financially and otherwise, could always be counted upon and he was also an earnest advocate of all movements tending to elevate humanity and make society and home better and happier.

HON. ALEXANDER M. DOCKERY. During the past thirty years there has hardly been a man, woman or child in Northwest Missouri who has not been familiar by constant repetition with the name of Alexander M. Dockery, whose career of public service has kept him almost constantly active in district, state and national affairs through an entire generation. For sixteen years Mr. Dockery represented the Third Missouri District in congress, and since the beginning of the present administration has held the post of third assistant postmaster-general.

His active public service has obscured the fact, except in his home town of Gallatin and among his more intimate friends, that Mr. Dockery began his career as a physician, and besides several other degrees is entitled to the letters M. D. Alexander M. Dockery was born in Daviess County, Missouri, February 11, 1845. His parents were Rev. Willis E. and Sarah E. (McHaney) Dockery, his father having been a distinguished minister of the Methodist Episcopal Church, South. Mr. Dockery, who is the only survivor of three children, was liberally educated in Macon Academy at Macon, Missouri, and in 1863 entered the St. Louis Medical College and was graduated in March, 1865, M. D. He later attended lectures at Bellevue College in New York and the Jefferson Medical College at Philadelphia, and did his first practice at Linneus, Missouri, and from 1867 to 1874 practiced at Chillicothe. He was recognized as a thoroughly equipped and skillful physician, and might have attained distinction in the profession had he not chosen other lines of endeavor.

In March, 1874, having abandoned practice, Mr. Dockery removed to Gallatin and became associated with Thomas B. Yates in the establishment of the Farmers Exchange Bank, an institution which has had a solid career of forty years. He served as its cashier until 1882. Prior to his election to Congress Mr. Dockery served as county physician of Livingston County from 1870 to 1874, was president of the board of education at Chillicothe in 1870-72, was a member of the board of curators of the University of Missouri from 1872 to 1882, and at Gallatin was a member of the city council 1878-81, and mayor during 1881-83.

From 1878 until his election to Congress Mr. Dockery was chairman of the democratic congressional committee of the Tenth District, in 1880 was chairman of the congressional convention at Brunswick, and in 1882 at the convention in Cameron was nominated for representative in Congress. Altogether there were six men in the field for the nomination, and it was one of the most exciting conventions held in that district for many years. The deciding ballot was twenty-eight. The opposition had been unable to unite, since Mr. Dockery was the second choice in all the counties. His election from the Third District came in November, 1882, and he continued as representative in Congress from March 4, 1883, to March 4, 1899. In the successive seven conventions Mr. Dockery was renominated without opposition. During his career in Congress Mr. Dockery was a member of the Committee on Claims, Committee on Accounts, Committee on Postoffices and Post Roads four years, and for the last ten years of his service in the house was a member of the Committee on Appropriations and had charge of the District of Columbia and the legislative, executive and judicial appropriation bills. From 1893 to 1895 he was chairman of what is known as the "Dockery Commission," which, among other notable achievements, devised the present accounting system of the national treasury. This system has been in successful operation since October 1, 1894. During the World's Fair at Chicago he was chairman of a special committee appointed by the house to investigate and simplify methods of business. This committee's elaborate report served as a basis for the work of organization of the Louisiana Purchase Exposition at St. Louis. While a member of the Committee on Postoffices and Post Roads Mr. Dockery was instrumental in securing the installation of the second fast mail train service in the United States, from New York to Kansas City by way of St. Louis. In 1886 Mr. Dockery was chosen permanent chairman of the democratic state convention of St. Louis.

At the conclusion of his eighth term Mr. Dockery declined a renomination in order to enter the race for governor in 1900. He was nominated by acclamation in June of that year in the convention held in a large tent at Kansas City, the nominating speech being made by Hon. W. S. Cowherd, of Kansas City. In the following November he was elected Governor of Missouri against his republican opponent, Joseph Flory, of Moberly. Taking his oath as governor January 14, 1901, Mr. Dockery was chief executive of his native state four years. After retiring from the governor's chair in 1905 he continued active in democratic politics, being chairman of the state convention in 1906, and in 1912 was elected treasurer of the democratic state committee and reelected in 1914. At the beginning of President Wilson's administration Mr. Dockery was appointed third assistant postmaster-general, his appointment being confirmed by the senate March 13, 1913, and he entered upon his duties March 17th. As third assistant postmaster-general he has supervision and control of all the fiscal affairs of the postal service, including the postal savings system, amounting in volume to more than three hundred and sixty million dollars yearly.

In 1906 Governor Dockery was awarded the degree LL.D. by the University of Missouri. In the interval between his term as governor and his recent promotion to the postoffice department, Mr. Dockery proved himself a citizen of force and influence in his home city of Gallatin. He served as a member and president of the board of education from 1908 to 1912, was president of the Gallatin Commercial Club from its organization in 1908 to 1914, and has been president of the Daviess County Chautauqua Association since its organization in 1909. He was also chairman of the building committee which supervised construction of the new courthouse, and of the committee which supervised construction of the new Gallatin schoolhouse. Of his local civic activities Governor Dockery probably takes most pride in his work as ex-officio road overseer in his county, a service which he has performed gratuitously but none the less effectively at various times during the past thirty years. Governor Dockery was married April 14, 1869, to Miss Mary E. Bird, daughter of Greenup Bird. All of the seven children of their marriage died in infancy. His wife died at the executive mansion, Jefferson City, January 1, 1903.

Governor Dockery has some interesting fraternal relations. In 1880 he was elected eminent commander of Kadosh Commandery No. 21, Knights Templar, at Cameron; in 1881 was elected grand master of Missouri Masons; in May, 1883, was chosen grand high priest of the Royal Arch Masons of Missouri, and since 1886 has been a member of the board of directors of the Masonic Home of Missouri, being chairman of the executive committee the greater part of the time. In May, 1910, he was elected grand master of the Missouri Odd Fellows, and this gives him the unusual distinction of being the only person in the state who has been grand master of both Missouri Masons and Missouri Odd Fellows. Since May, 1910, he has been president of the Odd Fellows Home Board of Liberty.

COLUMBUS L. KUNKEL. Among the steadfast, upright and highly honored citizens of Nodaway Township, Holt County, is the representative farmer and stock grower whose name initiates this paragraph and whose well-improved farm gives ample voucher for the industry and well-directed energy which he has brought to bear in its improvement and various operation. Mr. Kunkel is a native of Holt County, which has been his home from the time of his birth to the present, and he is a representative of one of the sterling pioneer families of this favored division of the state.

Columbus L. Kunkel was born on the old homestead farm of his father in Nodaway Township, Holt County, and the date of his nativity was February 2, 1857. He is a son of William M. and Elizabeth A. (Robinson) Kunkel, of whose eight children—four sons and four daughters—five are living. William M. Kunkel was born near Galion, Crawford County, Ohio, on the 20th of June, 1832, and about the year 1845 he accompanied his parents on their removal from the old Buckeye State to Missouri, the journey having been made with team and wagon to the Mississippi River, and from St. Louis to St. Joseph by boat, the latter place being the point from which they made their way to their destination in Holt County. Jacob Kunkel, grandfather of the subject of this sketch, purchased a relinquishment claim to land that had been entered from the Government by the original owner, and he there instituted the reclamation of a farm in the midst of a virtual wilderness. Both he and his wife passed the residue of their lives on this old homestead and there their son William M. became, with the passing of years, one of the substantial and successful farmers and stock raisers of the county. He made excellent improvements on the place and there continued to reside until 1880, when he removed to the Village of Newport, this county, where he has since followed the shoemaker's trade, though he has reached the age of more than eighty years, this trade having been learned by him under the direction of his father. He is one of the well known pioneer citizens of Holt County and his circle of friends is coincident with that of his acquaintances. He is a republican in politics and both he and his wife, who likewise is of venerable age, are zealous members of the Evangelical Church.

Columbus L. Kunkel was reared to adult age on the old homestead farm which was the place of his birth and his early educational advantages were those afforded in the public schools of the locality and period. As a boy he began to assist in the work of the farm, and during the long intervening years he has found both satisfaction and profit in his continued identification with the basic industries of agriculture and stock growing. His present homestead, which comprises 178½ acres, is under excellent cultivation and he has here maintained his residence since January 2, 1879. The land was obtained from the Government by his great-uncle, Henry Kunkel, a brother of the grandfather of the present owner, and by him was sold to Joseph Anselman, who was the father of Mrs. Kunkel, wife of him to whom this review is dedicated. Mr. Anselman became the owner of the property in the autumn of 1865, and of the buildings now on the place the only one that was not erected by the present proprietor is the old house that was built by Mr. Anselman and which stands to the rear of the newer and essentially modern residence. On this old homestead Mr. Anselman continued to reside until his death, in December, 1882, and here also his devoted wife passed the closing years of her life. In the winter of 1866 Mr. Anselman was associated with others in the founding of the Evangelical Church near his old home, and of this church Mr. Kunkel and his wife are zealous and valued members. Mr. Kunkel has served as a member of its board of trustees and as superintendent of its Sunday school, in which department he now holds the office of assistant superintendent. He is a staunch republican in politics but has had no ambition for the honors or emoluments of public office. In a fraternal way he is affiliated with the Woodmen of the World.

In the year 1878 was solemnized the marriage of Mr. Kunkel to Miss Eliza Anselman, who was born and reared in Holt County, her father, Joseph Anselman, having been a native of Germany, whence he emigrated to the United States when he was twenty years old. In about 1866 he came to Missouri and settled on the farm now owned by his son-in-law, Mr. Kunkel, as previously noted in this sketch. He became the father of three sons and seven daughters, and of the number four are deceased. Mr. and Mrs. Kunkel became the parents of ten children, all of whom are living except one, Norman, who died at the age of fourteen months. The names of the surviving children are here entered in the respective order of birth: Adolph E., Beryl S., Mabel A., Julia, Jesta M., Harrison, Dale D., Ruby and Charlene. Mabel A. is the wife of Roy Hardman and Charlene is the wife of Wesley Mart.

B. F. PRAISWATER. Northwest Missouri has been the home of Mr. Praiswater all his life, and from a farmer boy he graduated into independent activities as an agriculturist, and for many years has been one of the most substantially situated citizens of Hickory Township, in Holt County.

B. F. Praiswater was born in Andrew County, Missouri, December 30, 1856, a son of Samuel and Susan (Nease) Praiswater. He was one of seven children, of whom five are still living. His father was born and reared in Tennessee, moved from there to Indiana, and then came to Missouri. His first land was an unimproved place, and for some time before buying he worked as a renter. He lived in Andrew County about ten years, and the first place he came to in Holt County was down near Newpoint on the Nodaway River. That farm stands today as a monument to his active labors in clearing up and developing a farm. Both parents were members of the Presbyterian Church, and in politics he was independent, a man of excellent character, and never sought the honors of public office. He saw some active service in the state militia.

B. F. Praiswater married May Ludema Trimmer, daughter of John Q. and Elizabeth Marian Trimmer. There were twelve children in the Trimmer family, six of whom are still living. Mr. and Mrs. Praiswater are the parents of four children: Lula May, wife of W. A. Richardson, and has two children, Wayne A. and Wilma R.; John married Iva Drehen, and has one child, Leroy L.; Joseph B.; and Francis. All the children were born in Holt County.

Mr. Praiswater is one of the most extensive land holders in Holt County, and in his career has shown unusual capacity and judgment as a business man. He is the owner of 326 acres altogether in Missouri, and has 960 acres in Chase County, Nebraska. Mr. Praiswater has perfected the improvements on his home farm, and now has one of the most attractive homesteads in this section of Holt County. He is a member of the Presbyterian Church, and has served his district on the school board. In politics he is independent. In his church he has worked actively and has been a deacon and is now an elder.

JAMES BUCHER. One of the best known residents of Lewis Township in Holt County was the late James Bucher, who died at his home there September 1, 1913. He was an industrious and thrifty farmer, a man who had lived in Holt County nearly half a century, and while winning a competence for himself and family had also played the part of a good citizen and was a father and husband and friend to those immediately dependent upon him. Mrs. Bucher still survives and resides at the old farm, and represents one of the oldest and most prominent pioneer families of Holt County.

The late James Bucher was born at South Bend, Indiana, April 4, 1860, and was about five years of age when he came to Holt County. He and Mrs. Bucher were married in this county, and before her marriage she was Ione Curtis, daughter of John Curtis, a pioneer settler in Holt County. Mr. and Mrs. Bucher became the parents of four children: Earl, died at the age of nineteen; Bessie, died when one year of age; Hazel is still living; and Paul is a young farmer and married Grace Dooley.

The late Mr. Bucher during his many years of residence and farming activities acquired a fine estate, the home farm now comprising 320 acres. He improved it extensively, and for a number of years the family resided in the large square farmhouse, which is now the home of the widow. It is a modern structure, situated in the midst of a big lawn, enclosed with an iron fence. All the buildings are substantial, and kept in fine repair.

The late Mr. Bucher was a member of the Christian Church, and for twenty-two years acted as superintendent of the Sunday School. Mrs. Bucher's father was also one of the active members of the church in his community, and her mother is still living. Mr. Bucher was a man of excellent habits, and left an honored name to his family. For several years he served on the school board, in politics was a republican, and was affiliated with the Independent Order of Odd Fellows and the Modern Woodmen of America.

DANIEL FUHRMAN. Representing the substantial German-American citizenship which has done so much to improve and develop the agricultural resources of this country, Daniel Fuhrman has spent nearly all his life in Holt County, the family having come here about forty-five years ago. As a farmer he is regarded as one of the most efficient and prosperous in Lewis Township, and has also done his part in affairs of public importance.

Daniel Fuhrman was born in Adams County, Indiana, October 24, 1861. His father, Christopher Fuhrman, was born in Germany. There were seven children in the family. In 1868 the parents located in Holt County, and came to the farm now occupied by Daniel Fuhrman. At that time the land was almost unimproved, and a log house was the first habitation. After living there a few years the father put up a frame house that is still standing, located some distance from the present residence of Daniel Fuhrman, standing on the North Road in the hollow. This farm was the scene of the activities and the home of both parents until late in life when they moved to Oregon and spent their last years in that town. The father was a man of good habits, and though beginning his career in Northwest Missouri a poor man, he left a property which was good evidence of his industry and successful management. All the fields in the farm were broken up as a result of his own labor at the plow.

Daniel Fuhrman grew up in Holt County, and acquired his education in such schools as existed at that time. He trained himself by practical work for the career which has brought him a satisfying degree of prosperity, and is now the owner of 160 acres and has done much to improve the place and increase its value. His business is that of general farming and stock raising, and he is sharing in the general prosperity which Northwest Missouri farmers have enjoyed in recent years.

Mr. Fuhrman married for his first wife Jesta Price, daughter of H. R.

Price. By this union there were three children: Edith, wife of Albert Noellsch; Florence; and Edna. After the death of his first wife Mr. Fuhrman married Mary Noellsch, daughter of John Noellsch. By this marriage there is one son, Roy. All the children were born in Holt County and either have homes of their own or are preparing themselves for useful places in the world. Mr. Fuhrman is a member of the Evangelical Church, has served for three years on the school board, and in politics is a republican.

JOSIAH ELLINGSWORTH. One of the well-known and highly respected residents of Andrew County is Josiah Ellingsworth, now living retired in Rochester Township, for many years after completing his honorable service as a soldier in the Civil war, having been a farmer in Missouri. He is a native of this state, born on his father's homestead on Shoal Creek, near Mirabile, in Caldwell County, July 1, 1841. His parents were James and Elizabeth (Estis) Ellingsworth.

James Ellingsworth and wife were natives of Maryland and married in that state. In 1833 they moved to Quincy, Illinois, and from there, in 1837, to Caldwell County, Missouri, where Mr. Ellingsworth secured a homestead on Shoal Creek, and there his first wife died when their son Josiah was ten years old. His second marriage was to a Mrs. Green, a widow, and in 1852 they moved to DeKalb County near Maysville, and in 1867 he died on his farm near Stewartsville. He was a man of solid worth and was widely known, was a stanch democrat in politics and a consistent member of the Christian Church. To his first marriage the following children were born: Margaret, who is deceased, was the wife of Thomas Williams; Josiah; Martha, who is deceased, was the wife of W. N. Tucker; James, who is deceased, served almost four years in the Civil war as a member of the Twenty-fifth Missouri Regiment; Elizabeth, who died at the age of four years; and William, who now lives in Washington, served three years of the Civil war as a member of the Twelfth Missouri Volunteer Cavalry. One daughter, Lucy, was born to the second marriage. She was the wife of Louis Davis and is now deceased.

Josiah Ellingsworth was reared on the home farm and went to school in boyhood as opportunity offered. At the outbreak of the Civil war he was at Sardis, in Mason County, Kentucky, on a visit and great excitement prevailed there, people taking sides as is usual in such cases, no one being permitted to be neutral. At once companies were raised for both the Federal and Confederate armies and Mr. Ellingsworth enlisted in the former, in Company A, Sixteenth Kentucky Volunteer Infantry, in which he served out a first enlistment of ninety days. On September 23, 1861, he enlisted for three years, in the same company and regiment, and the first battle in which he participated was that of Ivory Mountain in Kentucky, on November 8, 1861. Then followed others thick and fast, including the siege of Knoxville, all the engagements of the Atlantic campaign in which his regiment, as a member of the Twenty-third Army Corps, took part, following which came Nashville with two days of fighting, and the fierce battle of Franklin. He fought in two engagements after his time of enlistment expired, serving until February 28, 1865. In some ways he and his brothers were very fortunate. They served in different regiments and faced thousands of dangers but all lived to return home without suffering wounds, and Mr. Ellingsworth was not once posted on the sick list. On two occasions he was knocked down by the explosion of shells in his vicinity and at

Josiah Ellingsworth

the time was blinded and deafened, suffering loss of hearing in his right ear.

After his military life was over Mr. Ellingsworth returned home and for forty years engaged in farming, residing on one farm, in Sherman Township, DeKalb County, one-half mile from the Andrew County line, where he owned 170 acres. After selling his farm property he moved to St. Joseph, where he resided for two years, in 1912 coming to the home of his son, Hugh O., at Helena, where he has since resided, surrounded with all the comforts dear to his age.

Mr. Ellingsworth was married in October, 1867, to Miss Missouri Graham, who was born in Andrew County in February, 1840, and died on the farm in October, 1896. Her parents were Alexander and Elizabeth (Miller) Graham, the former of whom was born in Scotland and came first to Canada and then to Andrew County, Missouri. Mr. and Mrs. Ellingsworth had two sons: Hugh O., who is in business at Helena, Missouri; and Charles, who died when aged eight months. Hugh O. Ellingsworth married Miss Belle Dixon, and they have one son, Everett.

In politics Mr. Ellingsworth has always been a republican but has never consented to hold a public office. For many years he has been an Odd Fellow. His interest in the Grand Army of the Republic has never failed since he united with this noble organization, and it is but reasonable to suppose that these old soldiers find much of interest to quietly discuss as they, from the peaceful country their valor and patriotism won, watch another generation on the battlefields across the ocean. Knowing well what a soldier's life is, they can give a kind of sympathy that no others can. Mr. Ellingsworth is a member of the Baptist Church. He has a fund of recollections of early days that are interesting and instructive to those permitted to listen to their recital.

WESLEY ZACHMAN. In connection with the presentation in this history of individual records concerning many of the representative farmers of Northwest Missouri, it is specially gratifying to note that there is a very appreciable percentage of this class who can claim as their native places the counties in which they are successfully pursuing their agricultural and live-stock enterprises and carrying forward the admirable work that had been instituted by their fathers. Such application is to be made in connection with the career of Wesley Zachman, who is one of the substantial farmers and popular citizens of Holt County, where he was born on the farm which is now his place of residence, in Nodaway Township, the date of his nativity having been April 25, 1868, and the same indicating definitely that he is a representative of a pioneer family of this county. He is a son of Henry and Mary (Anselman) Zachman, who came from Ohio to Holt County about the year 1864 and who now reside in Oregon, the county seat, the father having retired after long years of earnest and productive application to agricultural pursuits. Upon coming to Holt County Henry Zachman purchased a portion of the present homestead farm of his son Wesley, a considerable portion of the land having previously been brought under cultivation, though the permanent improvements on the place were otherwise of inferior order, as may be realized when it is stated that the only barn on the farm was a primitive log structure. He made excellent improvements on the homestead, upon which he erected the present substantial and commodious house and barn, and with the passing years he added to his farm until he accumulated a valuable estate of 271 acres,—the present area of the place. Since the farm came into the possession of Wesley Zachman he has manifested the same progressive spirit and mature judgment that characterized the course of his father and has made numerous improvements, including the erection of a silo of the best modern type. He is wideawake and energetic as an agriculturist and stock-grower and well merits recognition as one of the essentially successful and representative farmers of Northwest Missouri.

Henry Zachman has ever been found enrolled as a stalwart advocate of the principles of the republican party, and both he and his wife are earnest members of the Evangelical Church. Of their nine children, the first two of whom were born prior to the removal from Ohio to Missouri, six are now living.

In his political allegiance Wesley Zachman is a republican and he has shown a lively interest in public affairs of a local order, though he has had no ambition for political preferment. He has served at several different times as a member of the school board of his district, and of the Evangelical Church in their home community both he and his wife are most zealous and valued members, he having served as a member of its board of trustees and as superintendent of the Sunday school for fifteen years, besides having held the position of classleader for several years.

On November 15, 1894, was solemnized the marriage of Mr. Zachman to Miss Effia A. Hardman, who was born in Ohio, October 31, 1876, but who was a child at the time of the family removal to Holt County. She is the only daughter of Daniel and Jane (Bissel) Hardman, the former of whom died in 1903, after having been for many years one of the substantial farmers and honored citizens of Holt County, where his widow still resides. Mr. Hardman was a consistent member of the Christian Church in which his widow likewise holds membership. They became the parents of three children, but one of the two sons is deceased. Mr. and Mrs. Zachman have three children, whose names, with respective dates of birth, are here recorded: Dwight, April 26, 1897; Harland, November 15, 1900; and Rhonald, August 28, 1903.

GEORGE KURTZ. A representative of one of the well known and highly honored pioneer families of Holt County, Mr. Kurtz has been a resident of the county from the time of his birth, has had the good judgment to avail himself of its natural resources and advantages and stands today as one of its popular citizens and substantial farmers. His well improved homestead comprises 100 acres of most fertile and productive land and is eligibly situated in Nodaway Township.

Mr. Kurtz was born on his father's pioneer farm in this county, on the 1st of February, 1859, and is one in a family of thirteen children, all of whom are living except two. He is a son of Isaac and Mary (Seeman) Kurtz, all of whose children were born in this county, with whose civic and industrial development and upbuilding the family name has been closely and worthily identified. Isaac Kurtz came to Holt County in an early day and settled on a tract of wild land about one mile east of the present homestead of his son George, of this review. His original domicile was a primitive house of only two rooms, but with the passing of the years his ability and energy became manifest in the very appearance of his farm, which he reclaimed to cultivation and upon which he erected good buildings, this place continuing to be his home until his death, as was it also that of his wife. He eventually accumulated a valuable landed estate of 320 acres and was one of the substantial farmers and influential citizens of the county at the time of his death. His success was the result of close application and good judgment, as he started his independent career as a youth without financial resources or other fortuitous influences. He reared a large family of children and gave to them the best possible educational advantages, while his sterling integrity of purpose gained and retained to him the good will and confidence of his fellow men. His political allegiance was given to the republican party but he had no desire for public office of any description.

George Kurtz was reared to maturity on the home farm and is indebted to the public schools of his native county for his early educational advantages. He has never wavered in his allegiance to the basic industry of agriculture and has become one of its successful and progressive representatives in Holt County. He purchased his present farm in 1887, and has made all of the improvements now in evidence on the place, the farm having had only a small dwelling of primitive type when he purchased the property. He gives his attention to diversified agriculture and raises live stock upon a minor scale, as an effective supplement to other departments of the farm enterprise. He is a stalwart supporter of the principles of the republican party, takes a lively interest in public and general civic affairs of a local order and has served as a member of the school board of his district.

The maiden name of Mr. Kurtz's wife was Emma Derr, and she was born in Cumberland County, Pennsylvania, being a daughter of the late Ferdinand and Sarah (Kissinger) Derr. Mr. and Mrs. Kurtz became the parents of six children,—of whom three are living,—Ida, born September 28, 1880; Ernest, born April 22, 1888; and Esamiah May, born February 24, 1890.

JAMES E. BUNTZ is one of the representative farmers of the younger generation in his native county, where he is associated with his father in the management of their fine homestead farm of 160 acres, in Holt County. His father was a carpenter by trade and erected the present attractive and commodious residence building on the farm before the property came into the possession of the son, who has since made many other substantial improvements on the place.

James E. Buntz was born at Mound City, Holt County, on the 10th of August, 1879, and is a son of Andrew J. and Mary (Bucher) Buntz, both of whom still reside on the home farm. He is indebted to the public schools of the county for his early educational advantages and as a farmer he has displayed marked progressiveness and enterprise, besides which he has deep appreciation of the attractions and advantages of his native county and finds pleasure in his association with its civic and industrial interests. He is a republican in his political proclivities and has served as road overseer of his district. Both he and his wife are members of the Evangelical Church and he is affiliated with the Independent Order of Odd Fellows.

At the age of twenty-four years Mr. Buntz was united in marriage to Miss Blanche Stephenson, daughter of George Stephenson, concerning whom individual mention is made on other pages of this work. The one child of this union is a winsome little daughter, Marjorie. Mr. and Mrs. Buntz are popular factors in the social life of their home community and have a wide circle of friends in the county which has been their home from the time of their birth.

CHRISTIAN MEYER. Born on the fine farmstead which is now his place of residence, in Nodaway Township, Mr. Meyer has gained secure status as one of the enterprising and successful agriculturists and stockgrowers of Holt County, and is a scion of one of the well known and highly honored pioneer families of this county. He was born on the 12th of February, 1875, and is a son of Gottlieb and Anna (Mart) Meyer. The father came to Holt County about the year 1846 and settled on the farm now owned by his son Wesley. On the place at the time it came into his possession was a primitive log house of the type common to the pioneer days, and the land was virtually in its wild state. Indefatigable industry and well regulated policies brought to Gottlieb Meyer a generous measure of success as the year passed by, and he became eventually the owner of a valuable landed estate of 310 acres, the while he was known as one of the representative farmers and sterling citizens of the county in which he long maintained his home and in which he continued to reside on his farm until his death. He erected excellent buildings and made other substantial improvements that indicated his progressiveness and·thrift, and he was about seventy years of age at the time of his death. His wife still survives him and is more than eighty years of age,—known and revered as one of the noble pioneer women of Holt County. Mr. Meyer was a stalwart adherent of the republican party and was a consistent member of the Evangelical Church, of which his widow has been a devoted communicant for many years.

Christian Meyer was reared to manhood on the old homestead occupied by his brother Wesley, and in connection with its work he early gained benignant fellowship with honest toil, the while he duly availed himself of the advantages of the public schools. He has continuously been identified with agricultural pursuits on the old homestead and is one of the energetic and successful farmers of his native county, his landed estate comprising 155 acres of excellent land and his attention being given to diversified agriculture and stock-growing. His farm came into his possession in 1900 and he is fully appreciative of the advantages that have been afforded him for productive effort in his native county, where he is recognized as a loyal and public-spirited citizen. Mr. Meyer gives his alliegiance to the republican party, is affiliated with the Modern Woodmen of America, and both he and his wife are zealous members of the Evangelical Church of their neighborhood, he being a trustee of the same.

In 1902 Mr. Meyer wedded Miss Estelle Belle Miller, who was born and reared in Andrew County, Missouri, and who is a daughter of Elmer Miller. Mr. and Mrs. Meyer have three children.—Paul A., Beatrice M. and Elmer Ray.

WESLEY MEYER.   One of the well improved and eligibly situated farms of Holt County is that which figures as the birthplace and present residence of Wesley Meyer, who is a scion of a family that has been one of prominence in the industrial and civic development of this county, his father having settled on the present homestead fully fifty years ago and having achieved success through earnest and honest endeavor.

Wesley Meyer was born on his present homestead, on the 8th of July, 1872, and is a son of Gottlieb and Mary (Mart) Meyer, the former of whom was born in Ohio, of German parentage, and the latter of whom was born in Germany. The marriage of the parents was solemnized in Holt County and here were born their four children,—Grant, Albert, Wesley, and Christian. Gottlieb Meyer was reared and educated in the old Buckeye State and about the year 1844 he came to Holt County, Missouri, the long overland journey having been made with a wagon and ox team. He was fortified with ambition and resolute purpose; but his financial resources when he came to this county were merely nominal. He purchased from a man named Nichols the present homestead farm of his son Wesley, erected on the same a log cabin and then essayed the arduous task of reclaiming a farm from the wild state. Industry and good management brought to him with the passing years definite and well merited success, and at the time of his death he was the owner of a valuable landed estate of 310 acres. He erected on his farm the present house and barn, and the son has since made other excellent building improvements on the place, which gives evidence of thrift and prosperity. Wesley Meyer has 160 acres of the landed estate accumulated by his father and he gives his attention principally to the raising of excellent grades of live stock, though the agricultural department of his farm enterprise likewise is given the careful supervision that entails due returns. He is indebted to the public schools for his early educational discipline and his progressiveness and energy have given him place as one of the substantial and representative farmers and stock-growers of his native county. He is a republican in his political allegiance, as was also his father, and for several years past he has served as a member of the school board of his district. He and his wife are members of the Evangelical Church. His mother still remains with him in the old homestead and to whom he accords the deepest filial affection and solicitude. She is a member of the German Methodist Episcopal Church.

In 1900 Mr. Meyer wedded Miss Daisy Hershner, who likewise was born and reared in Holt County, where her father was a pioneer settler. Mr. and Mrs. Meyer have five daughters: Hazel, Frances, Maudene, Alice and Ruth, and the family is one of marked popularity in the social activities of the home community.

JAMES CURTIS. For three score and ten years the Curtis family has had homes in Holt County in Lewis Township. In the pioneer times the family did its part with an industry which resulted in the clearing up and improvement of many acres in this fertile section, and in all the years that have elapsed the name has been associated with honorable activity in business, with material prosperity and good citizenship.

James Curtis, a son of the pioneer settler, was a child when the family came into his part of Northwest Missouri, and his range of recollection extends as far back as perhaps any other living resident in Lewis Township. James Curtis was born in Marion County, Indiana, not far from Indianapolis, on August 25, 1839. His parents were James and Jane (Beelen) Curtis, his father a native of Kentucky and his mother of Marion County, Indiana. They were the parents of seven children: Thomas, John and James; Mary, wife of Robert Kane; Minerva, widow of Jake Meyer; Hannah, widow of Napoleon Irwin; and Rebecca, widow of Clark Proud.

In 1845 the father and his family sold their interests in Indiana, put their household goods in wagons, and made the long overland journey to Holt County, Missouri. The entire trip was accomplished with wagons and teams, they settled on land that is now included in the fine farm of James Curtis. The father on arriving at once applied himself to the heavy task of creating a pioneer home. He built a log cabin, and that was the habitation until a better residence could be erected. There were no railroads in that part of Missouri for a number of years, and the only high roads were little more than Indian trails. In fact, the Indians still lived in that section and around the settlers' cabins the wolves howled at night and there was plenty of wild game that could be stalked and killed by the expert riflemen. On coming to the county the father first bought eighty acres, paying about six dollars an acre. All the land was prairie, but it was a heavy task to turn over the virgin sod and prepare the fields for planting. In that vicinity the parents continued to live through the rest of their years, and the mother died when about sixty-six years of age and the father at the advanced age of eighty-three. At the time of his death he was the owner of 150 acres of land, and all of it was well

improved and represented a valuable homestead. The father was a man
of exemplary habits and for many years an active worker in the Christian
Church. Politically in early days he had followed the fortunes of the
whig party, and from that went into the republican organization.,

James Curtis spent his boyhood on the old home farm, had schooling
from such schools as were maintained in this part of Holt County during
the '40s and '50s, and on reaching manhood applied himself industriously
to the work of farming, which has been the basis of his prosperity. He
married Elizabeth Cottier, daughter of John Cottier, and Catherine Callow, born on the Isle of Man. Mrs. Curtis was also born on the Isle of
Man. They are the parents of four children: Seth, who married Elizabeth Markt; Catherine, wife of E. T. McFarlan and the mother of Eugene
and Catherine; Maud, wife of Fred Campbell, and the mother of a
daughter Kathleen; and Clarence, who died in infancy.

Mr. Curtis now has a splendid homestead, built up around the nucleus
of the old estate owned by his father. All the improvements in buildings have been put here by his own efforts and management, and he is
now the owner of 360 acres, constituting a splendid farm, devoted to general agriculture. Mr. Curtis is a member of the Christian Church, is a
republican in politics, and has served as a director on the home school
board.

SCOTT CARSON. Of the men who have participated actively in the
great growth and development of Holt County during the past four decades, none are better or more favorably known than Scott Carson, the
owner of 160 acres of good land, secured through the medium of individual effort. It has been Mr. Carson's fortune to have realized many of
his worthy ambitions and to secure a standing in the community that
makes him one of its representative men, not alone as a farmer who has
always supported progressive methods and high standards, but as a citizen who has the welfare of his township and county at heart.

Scott Carson was born at Kokomo, Howard County, Indiana, November 7, 1858, and is a son of Henry S. and Elizabeth (Markland) Carson.
He had one brother, two sisters and one half-brother, the mother having
been twice married. Henry S. Carson was a farmer throughout a long
and reasonably successful career, and spent his early life in Howard
County, Indiana, where he was the owner of a small property. In November, 1864, he came to Northwest Missouri in search of a new home on
which to locate, it being said at that time that it cost more to improve a
farm than it did to purchase it. Finally he decided upon an eighty-acre
tract, totally unimproved, which lay a little to the west of the present
home of Scott Carson. The original house, built of logs, and boasting of
but one room, continued to be the family home for five years, but the passing time brought about a decided change, and new and substantial buildings succeeded the straw sheds, while a commodious, modern home was
erected as the family residence. Here Henry S. Carson continued to follow agricultural pursuits for twenty years, or until within a short time of
his death, when he retired from active labor, retired to his home at
Maitland, and there passed away. Both he and Mrs. Carson were devout
members of the Christian Church, and in political matters he was a
republican.

Scott Carson was about six years of age when he came with the
family to Holt County, and here he grew to manhood on the home place,
being thoroughly and effectively trained in the various pursuits with
which the successful farmer must be familiar. When he was ready to
enter upon a career of his own he was well prepared for his chosen
calling, and as the years have passed he has well demonstrated the bene-

PEOPLES EXCHANGE BANK, JAMESPORT

fits of an early training, when combined with industry, energetic labor and well-directed management. During his career he has accumulated a tract of 160 acres of fertile land, which he devotes to general farming and the raising of a good grade of stock, and here he has erected a set of good buildings, attractive in appearance, well arranged, and thoroughly equipped with comforts and conveniences. A life of honorable dealing has made Mr. Carson's name an honored one in commercial circles. In political matters he is a republican, and as such has been elected a member of the district school board of Hickory Township. Fraternally, he holds membership in the lodge of the Independent Order of Odd Fellows, at Newpoint. Mr. Carson was formerly a member of the Christian Church.

Mr. Carson was married to Miss Mahala C. Howard, who was born in Kentucky, daughter of Benjamin Howard, and to this union there have come five children: Elwin Edwards, Roxie May, Fred Blaine, Sarah Grace and Ruth, all born in Holt County, with the exception of Roxie, who was born in Southwest Nebraska.

GEORGE B. KOCH. As the popular Jamesport banker, George B. Koch requires no introduction to banking circles of Northwest Missouri. For a young man who has not yet passed his thirtieth birthday Mr. Koch has accomplished considerably more than the range of his years would lead one to expect. He was the organizer, is the chief stockholder, and practically the head of the Peoples Exchange Bank of Jamesport, an institution which in service and equipment has few superiors among the country banks of this state. Mr. Koch is a young man of broad outlook, of untiring industry, and his work shows him possessed of unusual ability as an organizer. With all this he possesses the genial manner which makes friends and holds them in bonds of steel.

George B. Koch was born October 22, 1885, in Clinton County, Missouri, a son of Jeremiah and Mary (Ward) Koch. His father was a native of Pennsylvania and his mother of Illinois. The former spent most of his life as a farmer. Some years ago he removed to Hample, Missouri, engaged in merchandising, served as a justice of the peace, and under the administrations of McKinley and Roosevelt was postmaster of that village, although his own party affiliations were with the democrats. He possessed many admirable qualities of character, was successful in business and provided generously for his home and family. He and his wife were the parents of two children, and the other son, Alvin, lives in Kansas City.

George B. Koch received his education in the public schools of Clinton County, in William Jewell College at Liberty, where he was graduated in 1906, and from the Gem City Business College at Quincy, Illinois. He had already chosen banking as his profession, and his success therein is largely due to the fact that he has pursued the object of his ambition without pause since entering active life. He was first in banking at King City, Missouri, where he was cashier of the First National Bank. He filled that position until the fall of 1911, and then came to Jamesport and took the lead in organizing the Peoples Exchange Bank, of which he has since been cashier and is now the largest stockholder. Besides his banking interests Mr. Koch owns considerable improved real estate in Jamesport.

The Peoples Exchange Bank has a building which in point of equipment may properly deserve some consideration in this brief article. There are few bankers anywhere in Missouri that have a banking house equal to this, and it would do credit to a city of large population. The building stands on a foundation 30 by 80 feet, is built practically fire-proof, and besides its exterior attractions as one of the notable business blocks of the little city, its interior arrangement is of special note. The finishing is in Circassian walnut. Among other features one of the first to attract the casual visitor is the "farmers' corner," a particularly cosy place for the patrons to rest and discuss business, politics and other current matters, while sitting before the open fire in the old-fashioned fireplace. There is also a rest room for the benefit of the ladies who are patrons of the bank. The building is fitted with lavatories for the guests, a private water supply and sewer system, with hot water, heat, electric light, and the safety devices comprise the latest standard equipment of burglar proof safes and vaults.

Mr. Koch was married July 27, 1910, at King City to Miss Anna Claxton, who was born in Missouri. They have twin children, born October 23, 1914, named George B., Jr., and Mary Anna. Politically Mr. Koch is a democrat. Of a social nature, he finds time to belong to the following fraternities: The Scottish Rite Masons, the Mystic Shrine, the Independent Order of Odd Fellows, the Knights of Pythias, the Modern Woodmen of America, with his wife has membership in the Eastern Star and the Pythian Sisters, and he is also state treasurer of the Order of Yeomen. Mr. and Mrs. Koch are members of the Methodist Episcopal Church at Jamesport, and he is president and treasurer of the board of trustees. He has a large acquaintance with men in banking circles, and his varied experience has given him a thorough insight into all the details of the business. At his age he has much to work for and attain, and those who know him predict that he is far from having reached the climax of his career.

G. W. GLENN experienced numerous hardships and discouragements, and it would be hard to find an individual who is more deserving of credit for lifting himself above the limitations of a responsible and cheerless youth. Early thrown upon his own resources, with his only advantage a somewhat limited education of the district school kind, he applied himself so earnestly and ambitiously to the securing of a competence that he was able to rise, step by step, to a position of independence, and today he is numbered among the substantial men of his locality.

G. W. Glenn was born in Highland County, Ohio, April 1, 1857, and is a son of James W. and Mary A. (Garrett) Glenn. The father, an agriculturist all his life, brought the family from the Buckeye State to Missouri in 1868, settling first in Holt County, about one and one-half miles south of Maitland, on a tract of 160 acres, which had been partly improved. Such improvements as there were, however, were of the most primitive kind, the house consisting of two rooms, while the other buildings included a few straw sheds. The father settled down here to make a comfortable home for his family, but did not live to see his labors bear fruit, as he passed away about four or five years after his arrival. Later the farm was disposed of to William Shields, the mother married William Calloway, and the boys branched out for themselves. The children, all born in Ohio, were as follows: Emma, who married George Haigh; G. W., of this notice; Elwood, who married Ella Hinton; Elmer Ellsworth, who married Lillie Lowper; and Mattie, who married James Carlile.

G. W. Glenn was eleven years of age at the time the family came to Missouri, and he had already received an indifferent public school training. For several years he attended the district school here, but the illness and subsequent death of his father made it necessary that he go to work, and his education was thus neglected. In later years, however, he has added to his mental training by reading and observation, and is today considered a very well informed man. On taking his place among the world's workers, Mr. Glenn first was employed by a farmer, Freeman Libbie, for about four years, then becoming a renter on his own account. He lived on several properties at various times after his marriage, and then became a land owner. He has charge of 480 acres of good land, all devoted to general farming and stock-raising, in both of which enterprises Mr. Glenn has met with well-earned success. He is known as a man of intelligence, both in his farming work and as a citizen, and can be depended upon to support good and progressive movements. In political matters he is allied with the republican party, but has not found time to enter actively into politics, or to seek public preferment.

Mr. Glenn was united in marriage with Miss Augusta Liddy, and to this union there have been born four children, all in Holt County: Florence, who became the wife of Emmett Hodgins, a farmer of Holt County; and Charles W., Mattie and Freeman, who are single and reside with their parents.

J. T. NOLAN. In the fine rural community of Lewis Township in Holt County the Nolan family have been residents for more than three-quarters of a century. Mr. J. T. Nolan was born in this section and has spent a long and active career here as a farmer and useful citizen. It was his father who was the pioneer, and whose name appears on the records as an official actor in the first governmental activities of this county. As a family the Nolans have been close to the soil, enjoyed peace and prosperity, and their lives have been led along the paths of quiet industry and they have helped to make the community what it is today.

J. T. Nolan was born on the farm that he now occupies and which was his father's homestead on October 4, 1849. His parents were Harmon G. and Emilie (Hensley) Nolan. His father came to Holt County about 1838, soon after the Platt Purchase and before the land had been surveyed. Indians were numerous, wild game abundant on the prairies and in the forests, and his early experiences were full of pioneer incidents and hardships. He put up a log cabin in the midst of the woods, entered his land direct from the Government, and lived to see a wilderness transformed into a landscape of smiling farms. He and his wife came to Northwest Missouri from Jackson County, this state, and the parents were married in Independence, Missouri. In the early days all the grain raised on their farm and those of the neighbors was taken to market at Independence, and later to river ports higher up the Missouri. Nearly thirty years passed away before the first railroad was built, in 1868, through Forrest City, and by that time markets had been well established in different sections and the country very much changed from the time Harmon Nolan had first seen it. There were twelve children in the family, of whom ten grew to maturity. Both parents were of Irish descent and died on the farm now occupied by their son J. T.

Mr. J. T. Nolan grew up in Holt County, was educated in the local schools, and after reaching manhood married Fannie Cooper, daughter of George Cooper. To their marriage were born three daughters, Elma, Stella and Lela, all born on the home farm. After the death of his first wife Mr. Nolan married Frances Alkire, who at that time was the widow of West Dorsey. Mr. and Mrs. Nolan have two boys, Nelson and Guy, who were also born on the home farm.

Mr. Nolan has eighty acres of land, has made many improvements, and has an attractive farmstead, with comfortable means of living. Mr. Nolan's father was one of the early county judges of Holt County, and had the distinction of being foreman of the first grand jury ever empaneled in this county. During the Civil war he was captain of a company recruited to the strength of 115 men known as the Silver Grays. While they did not get into active service, they were well drilled and always ready to guard the peace and security of the homes in this section of the state. Harmon Nolan was a man of fine character, and while he started life with nothing except willing hands, he at one time owned 320 acres in the home place, eighty acres in section 16, another eighty northwest of the home, and some forty acres besides that. He also at one time owned 160 acres in Kansas. Politically Harmon Nolan was an active democrat, and his son affiliated with that party until his recent change, as a result of his mature judgment, to the republican ranks. Mr. Nolan has done his part in public affairs, and for forty years has served as a member of the local school board. He is a member of the Christian Church. Both parents now rest in the Nolan graveyard, on the opposite side of the road from the son's home, and altogether there are about a hundred interments in that cemetery.

RICHARD WORNALL. Few names have been longer, more prominently and more worthily identified with the annals of Missouri's history, than that of Wornall, and the earliest pioneer of that name came to Missouri in 1844, landing at the foot of Main Street on the 12th of April, at what was then known as Westport Landing.

For many years previous Richard Wornall had been a successful farmer in Shelby County, Kentucky, and was looked upon as one of the leading representatives of this all-important and basic industry. It was but laudable ambition that prompted in him the desire to achieve affluence and a position of social and commercial priority, but the speculative enterprises in which he embarked resulted disastrously and entailed such pecuniary loss and financial embarrassment that he found it necessary to dispose of his fine landed estate in order to pay his indebtedness and preserve his unsullied reputation for integrity and honesty, his character having eminently justified his reputation. With undaunted courage, he came to Missouri and set to himself the work of retrieving his fortunes in a new community and under conditions that typified the pioneer epoch in the history of this commonwealth.

On the confines of what is now Kansas City he purchased land at five dollars an acre, and this property is now appraised at almost fabulous valuation, as may well be understood. At the time of his removal to this state his family consisted of his wife and their two sons, John B. and Thomas, a daughter, Sarah E., having died at the age of fourteen years. Both Richard Wornall and his wife continued to reside on their Jackson County homestead until her death; he then returned to Kentucky and two years later remarried and continued to reside here, Winchester, Clark County, until his death in 1864.

Of his two sons who came to Missouri, his youngest son, Thomas, did not long survive his mother, dying with pneumonia only a few years after their landing at Kansas City.

JOHN B. WORNALL was born in Clark County, Kentucky, on the 12th day of October, 1822, and was a son of Richard and Judith Wornall. Richard Wornall removed with his family from Clark to Shelby County, Kentucky, in 1824, and purchased a farm four miles north of the historic old town of Shelbyville. This fine old homestead was near the old Burke Baptist Church, and in the services conducted in this somewhat primitive edifice John B. Wornall gained his early impressions of the spiritual verities and planted the seed of that deep Christian faith that guided and governed his entire life thereafter. He was further fortified for character building through the counsel and admonition of parents of deep religious convictions and high sense of duty and responsibility, the gentle consideration and intrinsic piety of the devoted mother having left a gracious and abiding influence upon the lives of her children who ever accorded to her the utmost filial love and solicitude while she was living and revered her memory after she had passed forward to the "land of the leal." John B. Wornall became a man of broad information, wide intellectual ken and mature judgment, but his education was gained largely through self-discipline and active association with men and affairs, for in the days of his boyhood and youth the scholastic advantages afforded in the vicinity of his home were very meager, there having been no academy or other institution of higher learning within many miles of the old homestead plantation in Kentucky, where conditions were still to a large extent those of the pioneer days. After having resided for nineteen years on the Shelby county farm, John B. Wornall came with the family to Missouri and established a home in Jackson County, within whose limits is situated Kansas City, which metropolitan community was then represented by an obscure village known as "Westport Landing."

On the 12th of June, 1850, Jno. B. Wornall, who was a young man at the time of the family removal to Missouri, was united in marriage to Miss Matilda Polk, daughter of William Polk, of Kentucky, and she died within a year after their marriage, leaving no issue. On the 20th of September, 1854, was solemnized the marriage of Mr. Wornall to Miss Eliza S. Johnson, daughter of Rev. Thomas Johnson, and of the six children of this union two are living, Frank C. and Thomas J. Mrs. Wornall was summoned to the life eternal July 5, 1865, within a short time after the birth of her son Thomas J. Wornall, to whom a later sketch is dedicated, and later John B. Wornall wedded Miss Roma Johnson, a daughter of Reuben Johnson, of Howard County, Missouri. Of the three sons born of this union, one died in infancy, and the two surviving are John B., Jr., and Charles Hardin. Mrs. Wornall survives her honored husband and still resided in the beautiful old family homestead, at Sixty-first Street and Wornall Road, Kansas City.

John B. Wornall was ever the zealous supporter of the cause of popular education and his influence in all the relations of life was benignant and pervasive. He was a patron of the arts and sciences and he held the highest of civic ideals, the while his inspiring faith was one of liberality in both action and financial co-operation. He was for more than a quarter of a century a member of the board of trustees of William Jewell College, at Liberty, the judicial center of Clay County, and for more than twenty-eight years of this period he was president of the board, besides which he contributed $10,000 as an endowment fund for the institution. Neither from choice or inherent predilection was Mr. Wornall a practical politician, but his ability and many sterling qualities so commended him to his fellow citizens that he was not permitted to escape official preferment. In 1869 at the democratic convention for the Fourteenth senatorial district, then comprising Cass, Bates and Jackson counties, he was nominated by acclamation for representative of the district in the state senate, to which he was elected by a large and gratifying majority and in which he served four years, his record having been in every respect admirable and marked by evidences of his earnest wish to foster the best interests of the state and its people. He was not a brilliant speaker but was looked upon as one of the most reliable, substantial and far-sighted members of the deliberative body of the legislature. In his speeches on the floor of the senate and his utterances in the councils of the committee room he was invariably direct and sincere, resolute in his upholding the principles and measures which his judgment approved, and never compromising with a signally acute conscience for the sake of expediency. About the time of the close of his senatorial career, Mr. Wornall's name was prominently brought forward in connection with the candidacy for governor of the state and though the overtures made in this direction came from strong and influential sources he insisted upon withdrawing in favor of another candidate, Charles Hardin, his bosom friend, for the distinguished office.

In 1872 Mr. Wornall was elected president of the Kansas City National Bank, and he retained this post until the institution resigned its charter and closed its business. He was instrumental in organizing the Bank of Kansas City, now incorporated as the National Bank of Kansas City, and of this institution he was president for many years prior to his death. In 1872 and 1873, as a mark of respect and as indication of his influence and high standing in the Baptist Church, he was twice and successively elected moderator of the Missouri General Association of this denomination, this being the highest honor conferred by that body. For eleven years he served as moderator of the Blue River Association of his church, in which he was ever a zealous and devoted member. Within the climacteric period of the Civil war Gennison and 1,400 of his men took possession of the home of Mr. Wornall, both the farm and the residence, and in this occupation by military forces the family were deprived of the use of all save one room of the house. Mr. Wornall was informed that on Saturday morning he would be shot, and the intervening four days he and his devoted wife passed in prayer to the Throne of Grace. Gennison finally sent for Mr. Wornall, on Saturday morning, and after cursing him with noteworthy fluency said to him: "I came to kill you but why in hell I can't, I don't know. Pray your God for me," following with the statement that if Mr. Wornall would go with him and figure up the damages done by the invader and his men everything would be paid for in gold. This generous recompense was made and Mr. Wornall even had to intervene, and beg clemency for a private who had shot a pig the same morning and whom Gennison had threatened to execute.

Secure in the high regard of all who knew him, a man of lofty ideals and noble character and one whose career was marked by large and worthy achievement, Hon. John B. Wornall passed to his reward on the 24th of March, 1892, shortly after he had passed the psalmist's allotted span of three score years and ten.

THOMAS JOHNSON WORNALL, the subject of this sketch, was born at Ninth and Main Streets, Kansas City, Missouri, on the 28th day of June, 1865. He was a son of John B. Wornall and Eliza Johnson Wornall, and in 1869 his parents moved to where the Densmore Hotel now stands, between Ninth and Tenth on Locust Street, so far out that their friends talked of their then being in the country. In 1876 the family moved to what was known as the Stockdale Farm, or more generally known as the Wornall Farm. He was reared on this farm, educated at the country school nearby, and after having attended high school at Eleventh and Locust, in Kansas City, for a year and a half, started into William Jewell College in 1882.

After four years at William Jewell College, he was married on the 19th of May, 1886, to Miss Emma Lee Petty, only child of L. T. Petty, a widower living eight miles northeast of Liberty, and half way between that and Excelsior Springs.

Mr. Petty came from that sturdy Virginia stock, and immigrated by land with his mother, two brothers and three sisters—two brothers having preceded him. Mr. Petty having lost his wife some eight years previous, and having but one child, it was deemed best for all concerned that Mr. Wornall quit the old home and move over here, which he did.

Out of the union of this family were born four children, but Lindsay P. died in infancy. Thomas J. Jr., attended school in the country, also the high school in Liberty, and graduated from William Jewell College in 1910. He was married on October 30, 1911, to Miss Floy Crews of Liberty, Missouri, and they have a girl and boy, Sue Melva and Lindsay Petty, and are residing at present on part of the old farm, known as the "George Petty Farm." A daughter, Lucy Lee Wornall, was born on the 4th of September, 1891, and died in January, 1906, passing away in her fifteenth year. She was by nature one of the sweetest children that ever lived, uniting with the Baptist Church when she was nine years of age, and through her sweetness of character, leading both her brothers to Christ before she was called to her Heavenly Home. She was a natural musician, and while never taking lessons, had composed over forty pieces before her death. Their next child, Richard Bristow Wornall, was born the 26th day of November, 1893. He attended Liberty High School, two years at William Jewell, one year at Culver, and one year of mining engineering at Rolla, and is now taking a four year course in agriculture at the University of Missouri at Columbia.

Mr. Wornall naturally loving agricultural pursuits, and especially the raising of fine stock, and showing the same, has spent the greater part of his life in these pursuits.

In 1897, having disposed of his cheaper cattle, he started in to build a herd of Shorthorn cattle, the equal to any in the world. As a steer feeder, previous to '96, he had topped Chicago market nine years out of ten, and using the same judgment in picking his breeding herd, he entered the show ring in 1899. And in 1899 and 1900 won first in herd over Shorthorns and all other beef breeds, Grand Champions for two years at Iowa, Minnesota, Milwaukee, Indiana, Illinois, St. Louis, and American Royal, without a single defeat in a two years' unbroken record that has never been equaled before or since.

He continued in the show ring until he dispersed his herd in 1906, winning more than his share of the premiums wherever shown. In 1897 he helped form the Association of Fair Managers, he having in 1902 been chosen secretary and general manager of the American Royal Live Stock Show. This association of fair managers is composed of representatives from every state fair and national exposition, including five in foreign countries. Mr. Wornall has held the position of chairman of the executive committee two years, vice president two years, and president two years.

While not caring especially for politics, except to help his friends, yet in 1905 he was unanimously nominated, and the republicans refusing to nominate anyone against him, was unanimously elected to the senate from the Fifth district.

He was appointed, by Governor Dockery, chairman of the Junketing Committee, and afterwards appointed chairman of Appropriations Committee, a distinguished honor, since the same had never before been held by a new member. He was chairman of the Inauguration Committee of the induction of Governor Folk to his seat. He was the author of the Wornall Demurrage Bill, which sought to give the farmers and grain men more time to unload their grain, but at the same time prohibiting them from using railroad cars as warehouses. This bill was the hardest fought of any in the three sessions of the Legislature by Senator Wornall, and was the first anti-railroad bill passing the Missouri state senate in sixteen years. His interest in agriculture led him to look after the needs of the experiment station at Columbia, and he increased their appropriation from $45,000, the session previous, to $187,000, and through his efforts both the agriculture building at Columbia, costing $100,000, and the college gymnasium, costing $70,000, were the direct results.

His ability as an organizer was shown in the passage of the appropriation bills in the senate, with but one dissenting voice, and that on a clause of militia, in forty-five minutes, appropriating over nine million dollars. But the absolute fairness to each institution was the cause.

After his term in the senate had expired, and refusing to again stand for election, he was importuned by friends all over the state to permit the use of his name for that of governor, but having served, as he considered, his duty to his state, and having had the extreme pleasure of occupying the same seat as his father, he desired no further honors. However, Governor Hadley honored him by appointing him one of the curators of the Missouri State University. He was chosen on the Executive Committee at the School of Mines, Rolla, and served as chairman and was chosen a member of and chairman of the Executive Board at Columbia, and served in that capacity until the close of his term.

The most signal honor that has been paid him was being chosen unanimously as member of the Executive Committee, and then as chairman of the Conference on Education in Missouri, Secretary of Agriculture Houston being one of the vice presidents, and Dr. A. Ross Hill, of Columbia, another.

Mr. Wornall has been one of four delegates-at-large for sixteen years to the National Association of Stockmen, the most powerful organization of its kind in existence.

These honors have come to him unsought, but he has put forth his best efforts in every way to serve at the best of his ability, and the results can show for themselves.

In 1901, with two friends he visited Europe and brought all the champion Shorthorns home with them, which sold in the sale ring in Chicago on November 7th of that year, making an average of $1,122.00, being the highest average of any breed since the New York Mill Sale of 1872.

He is at the present time living in Liberty, Missouri, where they moved in 1901 for the education of their children.

JOHN RICHARD WEBB. In the person of John Richard Webb is found a sample of that material which has brought Harrison County into the limelight as a prosperous agricultural center. Endowed with more than average ability and backed by shrewd business judgment and determination, this progressive farmer has worked his way to the ownership of a handsome property, located two miles south of Mount Moriah, which he is devoting to cattle feeding and the growing of horses, mules and hogs.

John R. Webb is a son of the late Joseph Webb, and now occupies the old Webb homestead on which he was born March 8, 1866. He received his early education in the district schools and this was supplemented by attendance at Grand River College, now Gallatin College, which was then situated at Edinburg. When he finished school he returned to the homestead, and soon thereafter embarked upon a career of his own on a quarter-section of his father's estate, his subsequent success in life having been made as a cattle feeder and a grower of horses, mules and hogs. As a shipper he has used the railroad to some extent, and as a trader he is known widely all over the county. He has added some twelve hundred acres of land to his original holdings, the chief of which tract or tracts is a grass farm, his plan being to grow and buy young stock that will become ready for shipment off his pasture land. In 1914

Mr. Webb replaced the old home which had been erected by his father with a more pretentious and modern structure, suggestive of the bungalow, with six rooms and closets, and including bath and running water, with all other modern improvements.

Mr. Webb was married in Harrison County, Missouri, April 22, 1893, to Miss Dora Weathers, a daughter of William H. and Ellen (McKinley) Weathers, the latter the daughter of an Illinois family. Mr. Weathers came from Toledo, Illinois, where he was born, to Missouri prior to the outbreak of the Civil war. His family comprised the following children: Mollie, who became the wife of James S. Graham, of Bedford, Iowa; Hannah, who became the wife of Bud Ferguson, of Gilman City, Missouri; Dora, born November 30, 1869, and now the wife of John R. Webb; Ida, who became the wife of D. Plank, of Bolton, Missouri; Etta, who became the wife of Anderson Foster, of Bolton, where her parents now reside; Alonzo, also of Bolton; and Frank, who is a resident of Blue Ridge, Missouri. To Mr. and Mrs. Webb there has been born one daughter, Catherine Marie, born September 23, 1897, who is now the wife of Clay Criger.

Mr. Webb's political affiliation is with the democracy, his father having belonged to that party, but his only activities are as a voter at elections. He has, however, taken an interest in those things which have affected his community, and may always be depended upon to support beneficial movements and enterprises. His long residence in this vicinity and his wide business connections have given him an extensive acquaintance, and he is universally known as a man of integrity and high principles. With his family, he is identified with the Baptist Church.

RICHARD FRANKLIN CRAVEN. Forty-two years ago, when he first came to Gentry County, Richard Franklin Craven was the happy possessor of $24 in cash and a two-year-old colt. These were his material possessions, but far more valuable than either were his ambition, his determination, his indomitable spirit and his intense energy, characteristics which have since combined to form the medium through which he has worked out his success. Today he is one of the most substantial of Albany's residents, possessed of a handsome competency and the esteem and respect of his fellow-citizens, and a short review of his career should be of interest to every admirer of American self-made manhood.

Mr. Craven was born October 16, 1854, in Ray County, Missouri, and is a son of Dr. Franklin and Annie (Campbell) Craven, and a grandson of Richard Franklin Craven, who reared a large family. Franklin Craven was born at Knoxville, Tennessee, April 19, 1817, and died in Missouri, November 23, 1901. He was not an educated man, being unable to either read or write, came to Missouri in young manhood and devoted himself to agricultural pursuits throughout his career. His title of "Doctor" was given him merely because he was the seventh son of his parents. He and his brother Wyatt were soldiers in the Mexican war, while Joel and John Craven were other brothers who reared families in Ray County, Missouri. "Dr." Franklin Craven was married in Tennessee to Miss Annie Campbell, who was born in Indiana, and she died in 1857, leaving the following children: James, who died in Ray County, Missouri, leaving a family; Nancy, who became the wife of John Craven; Wyatt, who spent his life in Ray County; Clementine, who became the wife of John Metcalf and lives at Syracuse, Kansas; Jerre, a resident of Bates County, Missouri; Elizabeth, who became the wife of A. W. Wyman and spent her life in Ray County, owning Excelsior Springs, which was opened up on their farm; Jackson, who died as a young man; Henley,

who passed away in early life; Hulda, who married James Grace and
died in Gentry County, Missouri; Julia, who married Doctor Kelley and
died in Kansas City, Missouri; and Richard Franklin, of this review.
Franklin Craven was married the second time to Mrs. Narcisis Wilson,
and they became the parents of three children, namely: John F. Craven,
O. W. Craven and Anna Craven.

Richard Franklin Craven grew up at Excelsior Springs where he
resided until about nineteen years of age, when he came to Gentry
County. His education was of the ordinary kind, finishing at a four-
months' term in Gentry County, the best he ever had. He was brought
up on a farm and that vocation he took up when a man, and has continued
to be engaged in tilling the soil to the present time. When Mr. Craven
began life independently he settled at Siloam Springs. He had worked
for an uncle to secure the cash and colt before mentioned, and these constituted his capital when he faced life on his own accord. Mr. Craven
had made up his mind to leave the old home where some turmoil and
discord had resulted from the coming of a stepmother and subsequent
children, and also because he had awakened to the fact that his social
companions at home were not the most desirable. He came to Gentry
County because his brother and sister lived here, and with the latter he
located for a time, and in that locality was married. With his young wife
he started to keep house in the most primitive manner, aided by good
friends, and for several years was a renter, but soon gained a place of
his own and his substantial building toward the top continued from year
to year. Hard work stared Mr. and Mrs. Craven in the face from the
start, but they accepted the challenge, fought hard and held fast until a
condition of financial independence came to them. Mr. Craven bought
his first land, a tract of forty acres, near Siloam Springs, and to this he
added until he had gathered 160 acres of timbered bottom, as fine soil
as there is in the county. It was at first covered with a heavy growth of
timber, and hazel brush ten feet high, and the grubbing and clearing of
this formed the real labor of his early life. It was all cleared in time and
the fertility of the soil has responded to the touch of the plowman and
yielded abundantly, never failing Mr. Craven until the big flood on
Muddy Creek overran it, took the crop and seeded it somewhat to burrs.
His wife was the great factor in the economy of the household and Mr.
Craven attributes to her the credit for their combined success. Mr.
Craven stayed with his farm actively until overtaken by the afflictions
of sciatica when his physical troubles began. He was occupied for the
next two years trying to rid himself of the disease through the medium
of medicine, doctors and medical springs, but finally decided to leave
the farm exposures and take up his residence at Albany, a course which
he followed, now being the owner of a small tract adjoining the town,
where he has a comfortable home.

In his political life, as he expresses it, Mr. Craven has been "just a
voter." His political training was of the democratic faith, his people
having espoused that cause for generations back. He is liberal with his
ballot, or franchise, in the matter of selecting men for public office and
reforms his ticket to suit the best interests of the county before he votes
it. His only political service, if it may be termed as such, was as an
alderman of Albany. It devolved upon the council of which he was a
member to take care of the load placed upon the town as a result of
whisky prosecutions and the burden of the water tower, and these services it ably discharged. In church matters Mr. Craven was brought up
under a righteous influence, so far as morality went, but his father
never allied himself with the church until sixty-five years old. His teachings, however, were of the right kind in the matter of instilling principle

Rev. Henry F. Saurgass D.D. and Family.

into his children. Mr. Craven and his wife joined the Missionary Baptist Church at Siloam Springs, and he officiated with it from that time until he left the locality. They are now members of the Albany Baptist Church.

Mr. Craven was united in marriage in September, 1875, with Miss Mary Ann McGill, daughter of Frank M. and Catherine (Davis) McGill, farming people of Gentry County who are well known here. Frank M. McGill died April 2, 1909, being seventy-seven years, seven months and twenty-seven days old. Catherine Davis McGill died at the age of eighty-one years, seven months and five days. There were eight children in the McGill family, those growing to maturity being: Nancy, who became the wife of Mat Chilton; Mrs. Craven; John W.; William; Martha, who married Giles Parman; James F.; and Rilla, who married Charles McNees. Five children have been born to Mr. and Mrs. Cravens: Katie Lee, who is the wife of Bert Williams, of Kansas City, Missouri; James, a resident of Conard, Montana; William V., who resides at McFall, Missouri; Charles F., engaged in farming at Siloam Springs; and John F., who resides at the old home place.

REV. HENRY A. SAWYERS, D. D. During the last quarter of a century one of the leading figures in the Presbyterian Church of Northwest Missouri has been Rev. Henry A. Sawyers, now pastor of the First Presbyterian Church at Savannah. Reverend Sawyers began his pastorate work in Missouri at Cameron in July, 1890, was pastor of the church there about four and one-half years, in November, 1894, took charge of the church at Oregon, in February, 1903, became pastor of Hope Presbyterian Church in St. Joseph, and in May, 1912, left that charge to accept his present pastorate in Savannah. Along with the duties of active pastoral work Reverend Sawyers has served as moderator of the Presbytery of St. Joseph and the Synod of Missouri, and represented the St. Joseph Presbytery in the general assembly of the Presbyterian Church, United States of America, four different times, at Saratoga, New York, in 1894; at St. Louis, Missouri, in 1900; at Columbus, Ohio, in 1907; and at Atlanta, Georgia, in 1913; also with his wife was a delegate to the International Christian Endeavor Convention in New York City in 1892, and again in San Francisco in 1897. For more than twenty years he has served as chairman by regular annual election of the home mission work in the Presbytery of St. Joseph, and is also chairman of the Vacancy and Supply Committee, which exercises a general supervision over vacant churches and provides them with ministers.

Henry A. Sawyers was born near Woodsfield in Monroe County, Ohio, February 22, 1859. He was born on a farm and was the son of a farmer, the late William Orr Sawyers, and his wife, Agnes (Kirker) Sawyers. His father, who spent his last years in Missouri, died at his home three miles west of Maryville October 1, 1914, when past eighty-five years of age. His life was as useful as it was long. He was born on a farm near Bellaire, Ohio, November 22, 1828, the son of parents who were of Scotch stock and natives of the north of Ireland. William O. Sawyers spent most of his life in Eastern Ohio in the valley of the Ohio River, and when three years of age his parents moved to Monroe County not far from the site of Woodsfield, the county seat, and as a boy he could stand on the hills of his home farm and see the smokestacks of steamboats passing up and down the Ohio. He attended a log schoolhouse in that community, settled down on a farm after his marriage, reared all his family there, and in December, 1894, when already advanced in years, moved to Northwest Missouri in order to be near his children. All his education had come from attendance at a subscription school, and what he lacked of book knowledge was made up by keen observation and experience in dealing with men and affairs. Of his character it has been said: "His sense of fairness and justice was strong and although fearless and of a positive temperament he never sued anyone or was sued in his life and was often called upon to adjust differences between people. He lived a clean, religious, moral and temperate life. These qualities, joined to a witty, social nature, surrounded him always with a host of friends." His ancestors had for generations been Presbyterians, and early in life he united with the Pleasant Ridge United Presbyterian Church in Ohio, and later with the Presbyterian Church at New Castle in that state, and subsequently became identified with the Maryville Presbyterian Church. In all these different congregations he was made a ruling elder. On April 22, 1858, William' O. Sawyers married Agnes Kirker, and they became the parents of ten children, two of whom were twins. Agnes (Kirker) Sawyers, who died at her home near Maryville on Thanksgiving Day, November 26, 1908, was born on an old family homestead near Belfast in County Antrim, Ireland, June 26, 1837, and was a child of three years when her parents came to America and settled in Ohio. She was reared partly in a brother's home in Baltimore, Maryland, and married Mr. Sawyers in Belmont County, Ohio. William O. Sawyers and wife lived together as man and wife for more than half a century, and in April preceding the death of Mrs. Sawyers celebrated their golden wedding anniversary among their children, grandchildren and friends. The surviving children of this fine old couple are: Rev. Henry A.; John K. and William G., both of Maryville, the latter a prominent lawyer; Robert J., a farmer west of Maryville; Lulu M., wife of T. M. Neff; Jennie B., wife of Wilbur Snyder; Christina S., wife of Lawrence Gault; and Miss Elizabeth A. When William O. Sawyers died he was survived by nineteen grandchildren.

Rev. Henry A. Sawyers grew up as a farmer boy in Eastern Ohio, attended country schools, and at the age of sixteen became a teacher, continuing that work for three years and was in one school for five terms. He entered as a student of Franklin College, New Athens, Ohio, in 1879, and was graduated B. A. in 1883, and later received the degrees Master of Arts and Doctor of Divinity from the same institution. In the fall of 1883 Doctor Sawyers entered Lane Theological Seminary of Cincinnati, and was graduated in 1886. After leaving college he had served as a supply and in evangelistic work until graduating from the seminary, and his first pastoral charge was at Auburn, Indiana, where he remained from May, 1886, until July, 1890, when he came to Missouri and began the activities which have already been outlined. Reverend Sawyers has long been esteemed for his talent as a pulpit orator and ability as pastor. A large number of his sermons have appeared in periodicals and their publication in book form in the near future will prove a welcome addition to religious literature. Reverend Sawyers and his wife have some valuable interests in St. Joseph, consisting of some pieces of real estate, and also considerable farming land. Reverend Sawyers is independent in politics.

On September 2, 1886, he married Miss Martha Elizabeth Scott. She was born in the same section of Ohio where some of his early days were spent, near Cadiz in Harrison County. Her mother after becoming a widow moved to New Athens in the same county in order to educate her children, and while Mrs. Sawyers was attending college at Franklin College she met her future husband. She was graduated there in .1885, two years after Mr. Sawyers took his degree, and they were members of the same literary society. Mrs. Sawyers is a daughter of Alexander Foster and Eleanor (Barnes) Scott, natives of Ohio and Pennsylvania, respectively. Her father was the son of a Presbyterian minister, was an active church worker and also an extensive land owner with large estate in Ohio, Iowa, Missouri and Nebraska. He died in Ohio when Mrs. Sawyers was a babe. Her mother was born September 1, 1826, and died September 10, 1894, as a result of a railroad accident. Mrs. Sawyers is of Scotch-Irish Presbyterian ancestry on both sides of her parentage. On her father's side she belongs to the sixth generation born in this country, many of whom have attained distinction in both church and state. Her own grandfather, Rev. Abraham Scott, and his brother, Rev. James Scott, were among the first and most successful pioneer preachers of Eastern Ohio. The same is true of her mother's people. Her mother's grandfather, Isaac McKissic, was a soldier of the Revolutionary war under Washington. Rev. Samuel Davis, D. D., an uncle of her mother, succeeded Dr. Jonathan Edwards as president of Princeton University.

Reverend Sawyers and wife are the parents of six children, mentioned briefly as follows: Lucile, born December 30, 1887, is a graduate of the Central High School at St. Joseph, of the Normal Training Class in that school, was for three years a student in Park College, Parkville, Missouri, and for several years has been teaching in St. Joseph. Paul Henry, born September 5, 1889, spent two years in Park College, now holds a responsible position with the Standard Oil Company at St. Joseph, and on September 18, 1912, married Miss Litta Roelfson of Maryville. Eleanor Marie, born September 20, 1893, is a graduate of the Savannah High School, and on November 18, 1914, became the wife of Karl Emil Zimmerman of Amazonia, Missouri, and they now reside on a farm near Maryville. William Orr, born April 7, 1898, is a junior in high school. Agnes, born October 4, 1901, and Scott Kirker, born August 6, 1903, and are both students in the grade schools.

REV. ABNER NORMAN. A loved and revered clergyman of the United Brethren Church in Northwest Missouri, Mr. Norman has been a resident of this state for nearly forty years and he labored with much of zeal and consecrated devotion in the ministry until impaired health compelled his retirement, in 1911. He has in the meanwhile been actively concerned with the great basic industry of agriculture in this section of the state and now resides upon and gives supervision to his excellent farm property, in Worth County, his home being on Route No. 3, of the rural free mail delivery from the Village of Gentry, in Gentry County. Honored alike for his sterling character and worthy accomplishment, Mr. Norman has the further distinction of having served as a loyal soldier of the Union in the Civil war. His life has been one of earnest and worthy achievement and it is gratifying to present in this history a brief review of his career.

Mr. Norman was born in Vermilion County, Indiana, on the 3d of February, 1830, and in 1834 his parents removed to Henry County, Illinois, where he was reared on a pioneer farm in the midst of a virtual wilderness and where his early educational advantages were those afforded in the primitive country schools of the period. His father was one of the early settlers of Henry County, where neighbors were few and widely separated and where Indians and wild game were much in evidence. In a reminiscent way Mr. Norman recalls the fact that when his father essayed the construction of his rude log house on the embryonic farm in Henry County he was assisted by kindly and considerate neighbors, if so they may be designated, who came from Henderson Grove, a place twenty-five miles distant, and aided him in building his humble abode.

Mr. Norman is a son of Charles and Parthenia (Arrowsmith) Norman, the former of whom was born in Virginia, at the foot of the Blue Ridge Mountains, in January, 1801, and the latter of whom was a daughter of Wesley Arrowsmith, of Bourbon County, Kentucky. Wesley Arrowsmith was born in North Carolina, and was a farmer by vocation, though never a slaveholder. He finally removed from Kentucky to Illinois, and he passed the closing years of his life in Mercer County of the latter state. Charles Norman accompanied his father, Moses Norman, from Virginia to Bourbon County, Kentucky, where his marriage was solemnized. As Lincoln said of his own ancestral record, it was composed of the "short and simple annals of the poor," and this was essentially true in the case of Charles Norman, who received most limited educational advantages and who passed his mature life as a hard-working farmer. He was a man of sterling character and excellent judgment and did his part in connection with the development and progress of the State of Illinois, prior to removing to which he had been a pioneer in Vermilion County, Indiana, lying along the Illinois line. He reclaimed a farm in Henry County, Illinois, near the Mercer County line, and there he continued to reside until his death, which occurred in 1892, after he had attained to the patriarchal age of ninety-one years, his wife, Parthenia, who had been a devoted helpmeet, having died in 1871. Of their children the eldest was Wesley, who was a farmer and carpenter by vocation and who was a resident of Nodaway County, Missouri, at the time of his death, several children surviving him; Sarah became the wife of Alden Pearce and her death occurred in the State of Ohio; Moses removed from Illinois to Iowa and finally established his residence in Worth County, Missouri, where his death occurred and where he left a number of children; Abner, of this review, was the next in order of birth; Elizabeth, who became the wife of Horace McMullen, died at Farragut, Iowa, as did also her sister Mary, who was the wife of William McMullen; Perlina, next older than Mary, became the wife of Solomon Sayre and her death occurred in Hardin County, Iowa; Melissa, the wife of Charles Richmond, died in Mercer County, Illinois; Charles served as a soldier in the Civil war, as a member of the One Hundred and Second Illinois Volunteer Infantry, and he passed the closing years of his life as a farmer in Mercer County, Illinois, where he died a bachelor; Parthenia is the wife of John McElheiny, of Rock Island, Illinois; Andrew Jackson died in infancy; and Aaron, a bachelor, died in Mercer County, Illinois.

As previously intimated, the early associations of Rev. Abner Norman were those of the pioneer farm of his father in Henry County, Illinois, and he has maintained during the long intervening years a deep appreciation of and allegiance to the great basic industry of agriculture, the foundation on which has ever rested much of our national prosperity. Mr. Norman was about thirty-one years of age at the inception of the Civil war and he soon made all other associations and interests secondary to the call of patriotism. In Henry County, Illinois, in 1862, he enlisted as a private in Company H, One Hundred and Twelfth Illinois Volunteer Infantry, Col. Thomas Henderson having been in command of the regiment and Capt. George W. Shrof, the commander of Company H. The

General Longstreet, and where Mr. Norman was wounded, by being shot
in the mouth, the injury involving the loss of his front teeth. After being
confined for a time in the hospital at Knoxville he was sent back to Illinois, as a nurse with a number of wounded men, and after an incidental
visit of sixteen days at his home he rejoined his regiment at Lexington,
Kentucky. In the spring of 1864 the command again crossed the mountains and at this time it joined Sherman's army at Buzzard's Roost,
from which point it participated in the further operations of the Atlanta
campaign until the fall of Atlanta. When Hood made his flank movement the Twenty-third Corps, of which Mr. Norman's regiment was a
part, was cut off from the main body of the army, encountered Hood's
forces at a point about seventy miles distant from Atlanta and thence
fought him all the way to Nashville. Mr. Norman took part in the battles
of Franklin and Nashville, and when Hood had been driven back across
the Tennessee River the Twenty-third Corps was again separated from
the main army and proceeded to Alexandria, Virginia, whence it went on
transports to Fort Fisher, North Carolina, to assist in bringing into full
Union control the Cape Fear River. In this connection it participated in
the taking of Fort Anderson and Wilmington. From the latter point the
command started across to Goldsboro, and it finally met Sherman's army,
with which it was consolidated and marched to Raleigh and Greensboro,
the latter place being the stage on which General Johnston surrendered
his army and at which the troops under General Sherman were discharged. Some of the gallant soldiers returned by rail to their native
states and others by water, as the surrender of Generals Lee and Johnston
marked the close of the great fratricidal conflict. Mr. Norman made his
way to the City of Chicago, where he received his pay and he then
rejoined his family, on the 8th of July, 1865, after nearly three years
of valiant and loyal service in behalf of the cause of the Union.

Prior to his enlistment Mr. Norman had been in active service as a
preacher of the United Brethren Church, his conversion having occurred
when he was twenty-seven years of age, under the zealous exhortation of
Rev. Joshua Dunham. Immediately after thus expressing his Christian
faith, Mr. Norman began to give close attention to Bible study and his
initial work in the ministry was that of a local preacher with a license
from the quarterly conference, his first sermon having been delivered in
the Hermitage schoolhouse in Henry County, Illinois. He was active in
work of this order at the time when he went forth to battle for the
integrity of the nation, and his final ordination as a clergyman of the
United Brethren Church occurred at Shields' Chapel, in Fulton County,
Illinois, under the direction of Bishop Edwards. His first regular charge
was at Tylerville Mission, and while the incumbent of this pastorate he
gave his attention also to the work of his farm.

In 1876 Mr. Norman came from Illinois to Nodaway County, Missouri,
where he purchased land near Gaynor, but in 1879 he removed to Worth
County and established his home in the Village of Sheridan. He has been
the owner of his present farm since 1883, the same being known as the old
Joe Hall farm and comprising 120 acres of excellent land. Prior to coming to Missouri he had been for four years a resident of Fulton County,
Illinois. The first ministerial work done by Mr. Norman in Missouri was
that of traveling for two years through the district virtually represented
by the activities of the United Brethren Church organization at Hopkins,
Nodaway County, and for the two succeeding years the headquarters of
his zealous and effective labors were at Grant City and its circuit. He
later was in the Albany circuit, and his last regular work in the pulpit
was on the Grant City circuit, with which he was identified at four
different periods. He was serving as presiding elder of his district when

he received a stroke of paralysis, the incidental infirmity compelling his virtual retirement from the active work of the ministry soon afterward, in 1911.

Mr. Norman has never had any desire to enter the turbulence of practical politics and has held himself measurably independent of strict partisan lines, though his convictions in a general way have been indicated by his support of the republican party in national elections. On one occasion he was thus questioned by a church brother: "Brother Norman, I have heard you preach many a time and you have stayed at my house many times, but you have never told me your political views. Now tonight when you preach I want you to tell us what your politics are." When he had finished his sermon that evening Mr. Norman said to his congregation that he had nearly forgotten one thing. A brother had asked him to state his politics before he dismissed the congregation and he would respond to this request by saying that his politics were: "Christ first, Christ second, and Christ all the time."

While he has passed by far the three score years and ten marked in the span of life allotted by the psalmist of the Old Scriptures, Mr. Norman in appearance and mental and physical vigor gives denial to the years that have passed over his head—this showing that his has been a career of right living and right thinking. Though his naturally vigorous constitution was impaired to some extent by the hardships of his army life and certain physical disorders marked his course as a result, the ailments finally disappeared and in the gracious twilight of his long and useful life he is enjoying excellent health. Mr. Norman has shown much business acumen and circumspection and has made judicious investments in consonance with the means at his command. In 1893 he removed to Oklahoma, where he took up a homestead claim of land in Garfield County, eleven miles south of Enid. He perfected his title to this homestead and purchased another quarter section adjoining, so that he became the owner of a valuable tract of 320 acres, the property being now in the hands of his younger children.

In Rock Island County, Illinois, on the 18th of January, 1855, Mr. Norman wedded Miss Mary J. Crist, daughter of William Crist, who was a gallant soldier in the war of 1812 and also in the Black Hawk Indian war and who carried in his body seven bullets as perpetual mementos of his military service. Mrs. Norman was summoned to the life eternal on the 4th of May, 1899, and concerning the children of this union the following brief data are entered: Arminda is the wife of Abram Cox, of Chanute, Kansas; John M. died at Sheridan, Missouri, and is survived by one child; Ella is the wife of John Mantonya, of Fairview, Illinois; and George maintains his home at Eldorado Springs, Missouri. On the 8th of March, 1900, was solemnized the marriage of Rev. Abner Norman to Miss Mary E. Glick, daughter of Frederick Glick, whose father, Theobald Glick, immigrated to America from Germany. Frederick Glick wedded Miss Bettie Cole, and Mrs. Norman was one of their seven children. Mr. and Mrs. Norman have three children—Nellie, Abner Clarence, and Cecil Catherine.

JAMES FRANKLIN SCOTT. The president of the Scott Mercantile Company at Blythedale is a Northwest Missouri citizen whose career has illustrated the best elements of substantial accomplishment. The man who has a willing industry and some readiness and versatility in adapting himself to the changing circumstances of life is always sure of success. The world always has something for such a man to do, and he will be certain to use each successive position as a stepping stone to better things.

James F. Scott was born in Floyd County, Indiana, April 18, 1852.

His childhood was spent in the country and his education such as the country school gave him. His father had a farm and country blacksmith shop, and in the latter this son learned a trade, and for about three years ran the shop. Just before twenty years old he married, and supported his life household chiefly by his trade. In 1876 he came west, landing in Davis City, Iowa, worked as a journeyman for a time, and then did a draying business between Davis City and Leon. Without capital, he bought the line on time, and at the end of two years was induced by its former owner to turn his attention to merchandising. This substantial benefactor in his business career was J. E. Teale, a merchant and man of wealth in Davis City. He had acquired a very favorable impression of young Scott, and one day told the latter it was to his interest to take up the line for which he was best fitted by nature, since he would undoubtedly succeed. His offer was accepted by Mr. Scott, who worked four years on a salary and in that time gained a thorough knowledge of merchandising. Then a working interest in the store was given him, and he managed the firm of J. F. Scott & Company two years.

In the meantime his acquaintance in the county had brought him a popularity that caused the democrats to nominate him for the office of auditor of Decatur County. Entering the race in the face of a normal republican majority of 600, he justified the faith of his friends and supporters and was elected in 1883 and made an excellent record in the courthouse for the next two years.

Leaving Davis City after about ten years, he for four years was in the real estate business at Independence, Missouri, and next enjoyed the keen competition of business in a big city, and for about four years was identified with the Metropolitan Hotel Company of Kansas City, Missouri, as its manager. During the last thirty-five years, with few interruptions, he has been in active business affairs. On leaving Kansas City and identifying himself with the Blythedale country, his first work was as a farmer. For three years he conducted a farm three miles south of town, and then in 1897 became a hardware merchant. The scope of his enterprise as a merchant has been greatly expanded since he started here seventeen years ago. The beginning was with a stock valued at $1,500 on the site of the corner building of his present headquarters. Mr. C. B. Neville subsequently became associated with him, but after a few years his interests were acquired by Mr. Scott and sons, and they also bought out W. H. Scott, a brother, who had previously been one of Blythedale's leading dry goods merchants. There were several separate enterprises under joint management at first, but gradually the proprietors have worked a consolidation, and now have a single store building of two rooms with a frontage of seventy-five feet, besides another large room which is occupied by the furniture store. Under its present title of Scott Mercantile Company it is in every sense of the word a department store and carries the largest stock of any department store in Harrison County, and the only one of its kind in Blythedale. Everything in general merchandise is handled, including dry goods, clothing, shoes, furniture, hardware, automobiles, groceries, etc.

Besides the upbuilding of this enterprise, Mr. Scott has in other ways identified himself with the substantial improvement of the town, notably in the erection of the best home, a twelve-room modern residence, constructed in 1909. For a number of years a member of the school board, it was largely his aggressive fight for better school facilities that gave the town its present school edifice. Twice he led the progressive citizens in elections and twice was defeated, but the third time his cause won, and now the four-room brick building is one of the attractive features of the town. During his residence in Harrison County, he has been comparatively inactive in politics except so far as local interests could be served. He is a past noble grand of the Independent Order of Odd Fellows, and his family have long been identified with the Christian Church.

Mr. Scott's grandfather was John A. Scott, a native of Virginia and a minister of the Christian Church. In young manhood he located in Kentucky, and married Annie Reasor, whose people lived about Shelbyville. From Kentucky he became a pioneer in Indiana, and died near New Albany. His children were: Reasor, who spent his life in Indiana; James G., who lived and died in Indiana; Robert, whose career was lived in the same state; Rev. Harbert, mentioned below; Vardeman, who lived in Indiana; John, of the same state; David, a cooper, whose work was all done in the same state; Moses R., also a cooper, and a resident of one county all his life; Emily, who married Samuel McCutcheon and died in Pawnee, Missouri; Elizabeth, who married Thomas Akers and died in Indiana.

Rev. Harbert Scott, father of the Blythedale merchant, was one of seven brothers, all of whom were preachers except one, who was a deacon in the family denomination. As already indicated, Harbert Scott was also a farmer and blacksmith, and was born near New Albany, Indiana, January 25, 1829. His life was one of great industry and with a sense of responsibility to his fellow men which he fulfilled by devoted service to the ministry while providing for the material wants of his family by hard labor. He lived on one farm half a century, until his death in 1911. He was a democrat in politics. He married Nancy McKinley, who died in 1911, just thirty days after her husband. Her father, James McKinley, who married a Miss Packwood, came from Virginia, and was a farmer and tanner at Borden, Indiana. Reverend and Mrs. Scott had the following children: James F.; Jincy, wife of T. J. Bell, of Pawnee, Missouri; Miss Eliza, of Jeffersonville, Indiana; William W., of St. Joseph, Missouri; Carter, of Davis City, Iowa; Winfield H., of Eufaula, Oklahoma; John R., now treasurer of Clark County, Indiana; Samuel L., superintendent of schools in Clark County; Emma and Lizzie, twins, the former Mrs. Henry Temple of Jeffersonville, Indiana, and the latter Mrs. Charles Emery, of New Albany; Zenas E., principal of schools at Asbury Park, New Jersey; Eva, wife of Harry E. Pickens, of New Albany; and Glenn E., superintendent of schools in Floyd County, Indiana.

Mr. James F. Scott has a fine family of his own. He was married April 14, 1872, to Miss Olivia Taylor, daughter of Jonathan Taylor, whose wife was a Miss Horner. Mr. Taylor was a boat carpenter on the Ohio River. His children were: Goodrich, of Bloomington, Indiana; Laura E., wife of Albert Scott, of Greenville, Indiana; Olivia, wife of James F. Scott, born September 30, 1852; Susie, who married Joseph Scott, of Kansas City; and Henry, of Blackwell, Oklahoma.

Mr. and Mrs. Scott's children are: Cortez A., who married Norah Morgans, is general salesman for Kansas for the Wheeler & Motler Mercantile Company, of St. Joseph, Missouri, and a stockholder in the above concern and also a stockholder in the Scott Mercantile Company of Blythedale, Missouri, his home being in Topeka, Kansas; Archie E., who is a member of the Scott Mercantile Company and president of the Farmers and Merchants Bank of Blythedale, married Bessie Canady; Winnie E. is the wife of Elza Jones of Blythedale, a prosperous farmer; Miss Dee Etta, of Kansas City; Ralph F., of the Scott Mercantile Company, married Winnie Craig; and Susie E. is the wife of Glenn H. Dale, a practicing lawyer at DeQueen, Arkansas. Mr. and Mrs. Scott have seven grandsons and four granddaughters.

EZRA H. FRISBY. The entire career of Ezra H. Frisby, one of the substantial business men and public-spirited citizens of Bethany, and one who has taken an active part in the upbuilding of this locality, has been spent in the community in which he now lives, he having been born near Bethany, in Harrison County, October 17, 1862, a son of Capt. Jonathan C. and Sarah J. (Briggs) Frisby.

The grandfather of Ezra H. Frisby was born in Pennsylvania, where the family was located in the Pennsylvania Dutch settlement, and during the pioneer days, prior to the War of 1812, moved to Muskingum County, Ohio. In his latter years he was a Baptist minister, and his death occurred near Bloomington, Illinois, the grandmother passing away in 1871, in Harrison County, Missouri. They were the parents of two children: Jonathan C. and Russell. By a former marriage the grandfather was the father of a son, James M., who died at Centerville, Iowa, and a daughter, Sarah, who married a Mr. Smith and died near Oskaloosa, Iowa.

Capt. Jonathan C. Frisby was born in Muskingum County, Ohio, April 19, 1817, and was given but little schooling, attending the district schools two terms of four months each, and walking six miles for that meager training. From Zanesville, Ohio, he went to Bloomington, Illinois, and in 1858 came to Harrison County, Missouri, where he engaged in farming and established a place for himself among the modestly substantial agriculturists of his locality. During the Civil war he was a captain in the Missouri militia, being identified with the Home Guards, and furnished a son for the Union army, James O. Frisby, who served three and one-half years and was honorably discharged after a valiant service, without wounds or capture. Captain Frisby was once county judge of Harrison County, from 1868 to 1870, and was a member of the republican party from the time of its organization. Fraternally he was a Master Mason. He was widely known throughout Harrison County, and was particularly noted for his strong physique. In addition to general farming, he was engaged in buying and shipping stock at an early day, driving it to Chillicothe, Missouri, and Burlington, Iowa, for shipment. Captain Frisby married Sarah J. Briggs, a daughter of John Bowles and Catherine (Eveland) Briggs, natives of Muskingum County, Ohio, and she died August 4, 1894, Captain Frisby surviving her until June 20, 1903. They were the parents of the following children: James O., who died at Bethany, Missouri, December 25, 1894, leaving a widow and two sons; Adnah H., of Supply, Oklahoma; Catherine, who became the wife of Dr. Jackson Walker, of Bethany; Perry, who died in New Mexico; and Frank, who died at Bismarck, North Dakota, both leaving families; Jennie, who married Asa M. Wood, of Overland Park, Kansas; and Ezra H.

The boyhood of Ezra H. Frisby was passed in the vicinity of Bethany, where he secured his early education in the public schools, following which he graduated from Bethany High School and entered the law department of the University of Michigan, where he was graduated with his degree of Bachelor of Laws in 1883. Having completed his education, he was admitted to the bar of Michigan in the fall of 1882, and to the bar of Missouri in 1883, the latter upon examination before Judge Goodman. He was admitted to the bar in Marion County, Kansas, in 1886, but never practiced his calling except in Missouri. Mr. Frisby associated himself with Judge S. W. Vandivert, as Vandivert & Frisby, which combination was dissolved by the judge's removal to Kansas, and for some years Mr. Frisby practiced alone. His second partnership was with Judge Daniel S. Alvord, as Alvord & Frisby, which covered a period of twelve years and was dissolved by the death of Judge Alvord, and

Mr. Frisby's present partnership with his son, Frank M., was formed in 1911.

· Mr. Frisby's first important law case was his prosecution and conviction of Freeman J. Cochran for the murder of Stanbrough, the prisoner being convicted and sent to the gallows. Another murder case which he prosecuted was that of Mrs. Frances M. Linthicum for the killing of her child, but the jury brought in an acquittal. In his political life Mr. Frisby is a republican, and his first presidential vote was cast for James G. Blane, since which time he has never lost an opportunity of voting for presidential candidates of his party. He was secretary of the county central committee for several years and his campaign work comprises speeches in local campaigns. He attended the national republican convention at Chicago in 1908, when Taft was nominated, and was present as a spectator at the St. Louis convention in 1904, when Colonel Roosevelt was nominated for President. Mr. Frisby was elected county attorney of Harrison County in 1888 and again in 1890, and succeeded in office George W. Barlow. He was elected to the State Senate in November, 1904, at a special election to fill the term of Lieutenant-Governor McKinley, and filled this term with one session of the Legislature, his district comprising the counties of Harrison, Mercer, Grundy, Putnam and Livingston. His entry of the Senate marked his service in a democratic body and a republican house, and he served just the one term and then retired. Mr. Frisby was made a member of the Committee on Education, the Committee on Penitentiary and Reform, which started the work on the new buildings at Jefferson City, and the investigating committee which was sent to St. Louis to investigate the Kerns-Niedringhaus senatorial contest.

Mr. Frisby was one of the organizers of the Harrison County Bank and has been a director thereof since its inception, acting in a like capacity with the Bethany Savings Bank, was one of the incorporaters of the Bethany Hardware Company, and president of the Bethany Printing Company, also holding large shares of stock in various other corporations of the town. He has had farming interests all of his life and at the present time has six different properties in Harrison County, being also extensively interested in wheat raising near Regina, Saskatchewan, Canada, where he is cultivating some 4,000 acres of land. As a builder of Bethany he erected his residence on the corner of Brush and East streets, and also is the owner of eight business houses here. In various ways and in numerous positions he has assisted in the material, industrial and civic development of this town. During four years he was city attorney, and from 1886 until 1890 he served in the capacity of mayor, but during this time nothing more was done beyond the routine business, although his administration was an exceptionally able and prosperous one. Fraternally Mr. Frisby is a Knight Templar Mason and belongs to the Knights of Pythias. His boyhood was passed under the influence of Christian parents of the Presbyterian faith.

On April 20, 1885, Mr. Frisby was married at Eureka Springs, Arkansas, to Miss Eva M. Tucker, a daughter of James G. Tucker, formerly of Harrison County, Missouri, and a native of Bethany. Mr. ·Tucker married Rhoda J. Howell, and both now reside at St. Joseph. Mr. Tucker is a native of Virginia and passed the active years of his life as a farmer. His children were four in number: George M., Thomas O., Mrs. Frisby and Lee. Three children have been born to Mr. and Mrs. Frisby, namely: Miss Lane, a graduate of the New England Conservatory of Music, attended Northwestern University, Chicago, and Randolph-Macon College, Macon, Virginia; Frank M., schooled in Missouri University, where he took a literary course, and the University of Michigan, where he graduated from the law department in 1898, since which time he has been engaged in practice, with his father since 1911; and Miss Lottie, who died in 1912, while attending the Bethany High School.

JAMES KENNISH.   One of the successful farmers of Holt County and a citizen always held in high esteem is James Kennish, who has spent most of his life in the vicinity of Mound City. Mr. Kennish is a man of thorough industry, has applied his energies to the complicated tasks of farming with the best results, and in all his relations stands honorably toward his community.

Mr. Kennish is a Manxman, that is, a native of the Isle of Man, where he was born June 8, 1862. His parents were William and Catherine (Kello) Kennish, and their family comprised thirteen children, one of whom died young. When James was a child they emigrated to America, and first lived near Oregon, Missouri. They possessed exceedingly modest means, and in 1872 acquired a tract of 240 acres about six miles northwest of Mound City. It was unimproved land, excepting a small acreage under plow, and the father showed great enterprise and determination against obstacles in providing for his family and improving his farm. That was the home of the parents as long as they lived.

James Kennish acquired a country school education, and worked for his father a number of years. Finally he and his brother, Thomas, rented the home place on shares, and finally Mr. Kennish bought a quarter section of land east of Mound City. In 1897 he married Gertrude Stratford Saunders. They have two children, Lois and Johnnie, both of whom were born in Holt County.

Mr. Kennish lived on his first farm until 1900, and then rented a half section for two years and then bought 240 acres of this half section. He now has a farm of 240 acres, all in a body, and he is one of the representative and prosperous farmers of Holt County. His work has been along general farming lines, and there are few men in Holt County who have surpassed him as a producer of regular staples, and as a breeder of Poland China hogs he stands in the front rank. He has also handled Shorthorn cattle, and makes a practice of breeding and raising only the best grade stock. Mrs. Kennish is a member of the Methodist Episcopal Church. In politics Mr. Kennish is a republican. Of Mr. Kennish's family, his brother, John, is a member of the Utilities Commission, having been appointed by the governor, and lives in Jefferson City, Robert is deceased, Thomas lives on a part of the home farm, Edward is a farmer in Arkansas, Anna and Maggie live in California, Christian is a resident of Colorado, Catharine lives in Mound City, Ellen resides near Mound City, Jennie resides on a part of the home farm, and Alice lives with her brother, Edward, in Arkansas.

WILLIAM LORIN WEBB.   In Harrison County, on the road between Bethany and Cainsville known as the Coal Valley Trail, is a farm home that suggests the solid comforts of country life and the enterprise of a successful citizen. For the past six decades there has been no family whose general position and activities have been more useful in the community than the Webbs. The farm just referred to belongs to William L. Webb, who has lived in this section all his life, having been born on the old Webb homestead two miles south of Mount Moriah, December 19, 1856.

His father was the late pioneer Joseph Webb, who came into Missouri in 1844 and a dozen years later settled in Harrison County. The grandfather was Jonathan Webb, who was born in Connecticut while the Revolutionary war was in progress, and whose activities were identified with the tilling and management of the soil. After his marriage he was crippled by a fall from a loft onto a cook stove, and remained so for life. His career was spent in several states of the Middle West, and from Iowa he moved to Harrison County not long before the war and lived there with his wife until his death at the age of eighty-nine. He married Elizabeth Henisey, of English stock, and she lived to eighty-two, and both are buried at Mount Moriah. Of their children one daughter married a Mr. Smith and lived in Iowa; Catherine married Henry Levan and lived in Nevada; Mrs. Millie Warnock had her home in Iowa; Ephraim, whose home was in Columbus, Ohio, was a preacher and for many years in the employ of the railroads at the union station there, and was so well thought of that the company built him an overhead room for holding his preaching services; Jonathan was a farmer whose life was spent about Mount Moriah; and Edward, who lived and died on a farm at Warren, Missouri.

Later generations in Harrison County will do well to remember and honor the memory of such men as the late Joseph Webb. He was born in Wayne County, Pennsylvania, June 24, 1820, and during his youth, which was spent partly in his native state and partly in Ohio, all his schooling was compressed in not more than three months. He came to know several states and many localities along the frontier, and was living in Iowa when he became of age. There he bought twenty acres of land, paid for it from his wages of $8 a month as farm hand, and after locating his parents there and thus giving them the means of providing for themselves, he set out to make his independent fortune. Working here awhile and there awhile, he finally reached the vicinity of St. Louis. Out of his earnings he bought a horse to transport himself from place to place, and when near St. Louis loaned this animal to a stranger to drive cattle and as he was sick at the time that was the last he saw of his horse. When he recovered he began chopping cordwood at 25 cents a cord, and in this way began working back to financial independence. He remained for some time in St. Louis County, working for farmers, and eventually acquiring a team and some other property. An interest in a threshing outfit proved the most profitable venture so far. During the several years he operated the machine he showed such industry and application that even his marriage called him away from his duties only one evening, when he drove to St. Charles and was back in the following morning.

His first visit to Harrison County was made on horseback, and during an inspection of the country about Mount Moriah he discovered the knoll upon which he subsequently settled, and then rode to Bethany to enter the land. Collins Hamilton, a carpenter on the river nearby, was hired to build his first house, a log building, with a very few comforts and conveniences, and with only a dirt floor the first winter. Most of his children, if not all of them, were born in that home. On moving from St. Charles County, he headed a considerable cavalcade, consisting of two yoke of cattle, a horse team and an extra horse pulling a phaeton, with a darky and an Irishman as drivers of the teams. He also had $500 in money, and during the first winter Mr. Webb and the Irishman split out rails and hauled them sufficient to fence in 100 acres. This land having been enclosed and broken up the following spring, he planted his first crop of corn and began a successful career of farming in the new country of Northwest Missouri. The range was then open and a large part of his profits came from the cattle and other livestock that he kept in increasing numbers on the pastures. He employed system and conservatism in the management of his business affairs, but usually bought any kind of stock that his neighbors offered for sale, and in this way his dealings became extensive. His first important venture was the buying of

100 head of work steers, which he fattened and drove to Osceola, Iowa, as the shipping point. He continued feeding and shipping his own stock, and buying and fattening others, and was a regular and large shipper to the Chicago market for a number of years. The profits which came to him he invested in land, and as fast as he added a farm to his holdings he rented it. He loaned a large amount of money, and some land came to him through mortgages. On the whole, he was a buyer more frequently than a seller. One of his policies was to buy all the corn offered by his neighbors, and he frequently had rows of rail pens piled high with corn that cost him 10 cents a bushel, and this he either kept until better prices could be secured or fed to his hogs and cattle. In his granary was always a supply of wheat for his bread, and so far as known there was never a time when he did not have an ample margin of corn beyond the needs of his stock. Apparently everything he touched turned to money under his management, and his land holdings at one time comprised 2,000 acres nearly in one body.

As a citizen he was patriotic and at the outbreak of the Civil war tried to enlist. Sometime before during an illness he had been salivated and his teeth came out, a condition which rendered him incapable of duty as a soldier. His physician at Princeton, to whom he reported for examination, told him to go home and not think of enlisting because he could not eat, let alone bite a cartridge and do other things required of a soldier. Failing to go himself, he sent a substitute, Robert Baker, and also provided seven mounts from his stock for the militiamen of the state. Politically he confined his interest to casting a vote for democratic candidates, while his father and brothers were all republicans, the former. originally a whig. He was a Missionary Baptist in church affairs, and also a Knight Templar Mason.

A few years after the war Joseph Webb engaged in merchandising at Cainsville with J. H. Burrows, and that was a successful partnership for several years, and later was at Mount Moriah for several years. Still later he became identified with banking, first at Lyons, Kansas, where his son-in-law, Mr. Deupree, organized a bank. Later he joined another son-in-law, J. W. Pulliam, at Little River, Kansas, in the organization of a bank, and when his youngest daughter married G. W. Hanna his assistance was extended to the latter in the establishment of a bank at Galvia, Kansas. Mr. Deupree, Jo Slatten, Joseph Bryant and Mr. Webb organized banks at other points in Kansas, and they were successful institutions until the panic of 1893 and the crash of small banks all over the West, when their "second loans" brought bankruptcy, and Joseph Webb was a heavy loser. Joseph Webb was a man of strenuous activity all his life. While not of large physique, he weighed 180 pounds, was stout as a mule and could lift 900 pounds, only one man in Missouri having ever proved his superior in this feat of strength. He was always in the lead when work was to be done, and he could never bear to see anyone idle. His own children were put into the harness of practical work at an early age, and he impressed them with the value of time. If a rain drove his workers to shelter, he always had some task ready to hand until the weather cleared. If nothing else, there was wood to chop or stable to clean.

Joseph Webb married his first wife in St. Charles, Missouri, but she died in nineteen months without children. His second wife, whom he married in 1854, died in seven months. In February, 1856, in St. Charles County he married Elizabeth Cockrell. She became the mother of eleven children, and the eight who grew up are mentioned: William L.; Martha L., wife of E. A. Deupree, of Dora, Missouri; Charles T., a farmer of Mount Moriah; Mary C., wife of J. W. Pulliam of Lyons, Kansas; Joseph

E., of San Diego, California; J. Richard, a farmer at Mount Moriah; Sarah E., wife of George W. Hanna, of Kansas City; and James A., of Bethany, Missouri.

The extensive business relations of Joseph Webb furnished a scene of action already prepared for his son, William L. Webb. He obtained an education from the country schools, but began farming when eight years old. Plowing was about his first important service, and by the age of fifteen he was counted as a full hand in the harvest field. His father used him a great deal in his stock operations, and he often went to Princeton for the thousands of dollars needed to pay for the stock when it was assembled at such points as Clinkinbeard's, at Cheney's near Ridgeway, and also at Mount Moriah where Joseph Webb put in the first scales. Until the railroad came the shipping was done through Osceola, Iowa, and later from Princeton. Among other experiences Mr. Webb became acquainted with merchandising and spent two years of his early manhood in running a store at Mount Moriah, and this was a practical addition to his general education.

When Mr. William Webb married he located on one of the tenant places of the family homestead, and the next year came to his present farm. At the time there was a fairly good house, but it burned and was replaced by the present residence. Much of his 260 acres Mr. Webb rents, but in the course of thirty years all the improvements represent his practical work and judgment. He is a stockholder in the Bank of Mount Moriah, to which his father stood in a similar relation. Mr. Webb was the pioneer in using the road drag along his own highway, known as the Coal Valley Trail. He is a democrat in state and national questions, but supports the man who will give service on local matters. He has served as secretary of Mount Moriah Lodge of Odd Fellows, and his household is represented through his wife and daughter, Zoe Louise, in the Methodist Church.

April 24, 1881, Mr. Webb married Miss Carrie Mumma, the youngest child of John and Mary (Blount) Mumma. Her father died at Winchester, Indiana, and was buried at his birthplace, Middletown, Ohio. His wife was a daughter of Ambrose Blount, who was a doctor and who had a son, a famous dentist at Springfield, Ohio. After the death of John Mumma his widow came to Missouri in 1869 and married George Stewart of Mount Moriah, where she spent her last days. The other children besides Mrs. Webb were: Charles, of St. Joseph; Ambrose, who was killed while a soldier in the Union army; Eliza, who married Daniel Kent and died in Harrison County; John, of Kansas City; Mary, who married Elias M. Riley and died in Harrison County, leaving a daughter, Mrs. Doctor Stoughton, of Ridgeway. The children of Mr. and Mrs. Webb are mentioned briefly as follows: James Edwin, who was killed by a horse when four and a half years old; William Earl, a farmer, who married Grace Coffman and has two children, Joseph Paul and Freida Elizabeth; and Miss Zoe Louise, who graduated from the Bethany High School and attended the University of Missouri at Columbia, and is now teaching in the Mount Moriah schools.

WILL C. BALDWIN. Harrison County has profited by the stable citizenship and unfaltering industry of the Baldwin family since 1857. Practically all bearing the name have been interested in agriculture, but their services have been extended also to business, finance, politics, education, religion and society. Will C. Baldwin, a resident of Martinsville, president of the Farmers' Insurance Company, and widely known as a farmer, is the representative of the third generation of Baldwins in Harrison County. He was born in his present locality in Dallas

Township, October 4, 1860, and his old home is still in the family, it having been entered from the United States Government by his father in 1857.

Ezra Baldwin, the grandfather of Will C. Baldwin, entered the land upon which Martinsville is now situated and made that his home until he passed away in 1884. He was a New York man, born in that state in 1800, and was there given good educational advantages, eventually adopting the profession of law, at Detroit and in other cities of Michigan. At one time he was a member of the Michigan Legislature, and prior to the organization of the republican party gave his support to the whigs. Mr. Baldwin came West to secure homes for his children from the public domain, and what little he had to do with affairs in Harrison County was as a farmer. Mr. Baldwin was a good business man and died leaving a landed estate. He married Mary McClung, an Irish girl, born in County Armagh, Ireland, who came to the United States in 1819, when she was twenty years of age, and she passed away in 1886. Their children were as follows: Ezra T., the father of Will C. Baldwin; Edward, who was a resident of Texas when the Civil war came on, served in that struggle as captain of a company of Texas troops in the Confederate service, returned successfully to his home and took up the practice of law, and spent his latter years in Harrison County, Missouri, where he died; Sarah, who gave many years of her life to school teaching, married George Raines, and died near Mount Ayr, Iowa; and Alexander, who died unmarried.

Ezra T. Baldwin, father of Will C. Baldwin, was born at Birmingham, Michigan, March 24, 1837, and spent his boyhood in that city and at Detroit, where his father practiced law. He was given the privileges of a liberal education, and this assisted him greatly in after years, when it enabled him to surpass the business qualifications of the average of his fellowmen in Missouri. He was early able to see the future of Missouri lands, and acquired a great amount of other land adjacent to his original entry, mentioned before, becoming one of the leading farmers of his part of Harrison County, and at his death deeding his property to his children in common, in which form it still stands. Mr. Baldwin was residing in this county when the great struggle between the North and the South swept across the country, and he gave his support to the Union, not only morally, but as a soldier. For several years of the war he held the rank of lieutenant, and his service was principally in Missouri, but although evidence has it that he was at all times a brave and faithful soldier, in later years he would say little about his service, and he seldom took part in the meetings or activities of the Grand Army of the Republic. In political matters he was a republican, and was an active man in that sphere, attending numerous conventions and state meetings, particularly in early days. In 1872 he was elected to the office of county treasurer of Harrison County, but with the expiration of his four-year term his public services ceased. As a business man, Mr. Baldwin was one of the main factors in the organization of the Bank of Martinsville, and at the time of his death was its chief executive. Fraternally, his connection was with the Independent Order of Odd Fellows, assisted to organize the lodge at Martinsville, and filled its chief chair for a long period. A man of determination and initiative, he always had his plans ready and complete and followed them to the letter, while he left behind him a record worthy to be studied by posterity, for his great success was built up on nothing more than his disposition to achieve.

Mr. Baldwin was united in marriage with Miss Margaret Clark, a daughter of Thomas Clark, who lived and died in Ohio, and who was engaged in agricultural pursuits. Mrs. Baldwin passed away in 1878, at the age of forty-two years, having been the mother of four children, as follows: Will C., of this review; Elmer, who is a successful farmer and owns a property in the vicinity of Martinsville; Miss Lucile, who is engaged in teaching public school in Harrison County; and Miss Hattie May.

William C. Baldwin had access to the Stanberry Normal after the public schools, and after his graduation therefrom, in 1884, entered upon his career as a public school teacher. This he followed for some eight years, doing work at Martinsville and became popularly known, but during this time did not discard the vocation of farmer, an occupation in which he had been reared. At the time of his marriage he located at his present home, where he has continued to reside to the present time and to be successfully engaged in farming and stock raising, pursuits for which he has demonstrated great adaptability.

Mr. Baldwin was married May 20, 1886, to Miss Hattie Robins, a daughter of John Robins, an old pioneer of Linn County, Iowa, where Mrs. Baldwin was born in 1868. There were four children in the Robins family, namely: Mrs. Baldwin; Will; Libbie, the wife of Bert Pletcher; and Ella, the wife of L. Roberts. Mr. and Mrs. Baldwin have one child: Marie, who is the wife of Will Ross, the latter the active farmer of the Will C. Baldwin homestead.

Mr. Baldwin is a republican in politics, but has held no public office. He is a valued and popular member of the local lodge of the Independent Order of Odd Fellows, in which he is past grand. His religious connection is with the Martinsville Presbyterian Church, and for several years has served as elder. The Farmers Insurance Company of Harrison County, of which Mr. Baldwin is president, was organized in 1897, at which time he became a member of the board of directors. He was made president of this institution in 1912, and has represented it in the conventions of the Farmers' Mutual Insurance Association of Missouri on various annual occasions. He has written business for this company for the west half of Harrison County since the time of its organization.

ROBERT RUSSELL. A Holt County citizen whose enterprise is exhibited in the ownership of a fine farm in Liberty Township, which represents the accumulations of his active experience, Robert Russell is a native of Holt County, and represents one of the pioneers of this section of Missouri.

He was born at Oregon, Missouri, December 9, 1858, a son of R. H. and Mary (Crowley) Russell. He was one of a family of seven children, and after the death of his mother, his father married Susan Bishop, and there were three children by that union. R. H. Russell came to Missouri from Miami County, Ohio, and founded a home in Holt County when it was just emerging from the wilderness.

Robert Russell married Bettie Cottrell. They were married in Oregon, where Mrs. Russell was born, a daughter of John and Matilda (Kennedy) Cottrell. Mrs. Russell had one sister and one brother, and after her mother's death her father was again married and had a child by the second wife. Mr. and Mrs. Russell are the parents of two children, both of whom were born in Holt County. Their names are Leila and Cleve. The son married Ruth Vance, and has one child, Marcell.

After his marriage Mr. Russell began to provide a living for his family by working for others, and some years later settled on a farm of his own two miles east of Oregon. He cleared it up and did some improvement, then sold at an advantage, and continued buying and selling and improving land until he located on his present farm in 1901. Previously

W, H, Winningham

he and his family had spent two years in California. The present Russell farm in Liberty Township comprises 120 acres, and practically all its improvements represent the management of Mr. Russell. Mr. Russell has served on the school board of Holt County, and in politics is a democrat.

WILLIAM HENRY WINNINGHAM, M. D. Many of the men in the medical profession today are devoting themselves in a large measure to the prevention of disease as well as its cure. In this way their efficiency as benefactors has extended much beyond the scope of the old-fashioned practice when the doctor was related to his patients only as an individual. One of the ablest representatives of this type of modern physician, who has enjoyed special prestige as a physician and surgeon, is Dr. William H. Winningham of Trenton. Doctor Winningham for the past two years has served as city and county physician, and is a man of broad attainments and has given much practical service to the community through his professional work. He comes of an old Northwest Missouri family, and its members have been prominent in the professions and in business and public affairs.

William Henry Winningham was born in Harrison County, Missouri. His father, Isam Winningham, was born in the same county in 1844. Grandfather John Winningham was a native of Kentucky, came to Missouri and after a short residence in Boone County moved to Harrison County, where he was one of the pioneers. He entered land from the Government about two miles northeast of the present site of Bethany. Possessing means and exceptional enterprise, in 1849 he fitted out a train of ox teams and made the overland journey to California. In that state he disposed of his teams and other merchandise, and returned east by sea around Cape Horn. Subsequently he ventured twice more into the wilds of the West. On the third trip he loaded his wagons with bacon and boots, much in demand among the mining population of California. Arriving there he disposed of his goods at a profit, but lost his life while returning home. His wife, whose maiden name was Melinda Boyd, was left a widow with seven young children, and had considerable trouble to keep them all together and give each a substantial education and training for life. She spent her last days in Gentry County. Her children were: Charles, Isam, Frank, Sharpe, Julia, May and Sarah. Charles lost his life while a soldier in the Confederate army; Frank embraced the profession of medicine and for upwards of half a century practiced in Harrison County. Sharpe is still a substantial farmer of Harrison County. Julia married William Buzzard and lives at Cedar Edge, Colorado. Sarah died unmarried, and Mary married Dr. F. M. Burgin, who for about fifty years was a physician in Harrison County.

Isam Winningham grew up in Harrison County, was a young man when the war broke out, and at the age of seventeen enlisted for service in the Confederate army, his and his family's sympathies having been with the South. He fought under General Price in the important campaign in Southwestern Missouri and Northwestern Arkansas and was severely wounded at Pea Ridge, the culminating battle of that campaign. After a few weeks he recovered and with that exception fought with his command through all its campaigns and battles until the close of the war. Returning home he resumed farming at the old homestead, and in 1880 moved to Albany, where he was engaged in the hardware trade until 1900. Selling out, he then continued his business enterprise, although at a good old age, and at Edinburg operated a feed mill until his death in 1904. His life was terminated through the explosion of a boiler in his mill, and thus both grandfather and father of Doctor Winningham lost their lives while in the active work of their careers. Isam Winningham was married in Benton County, Arkansas, to Nannie Neill. She was born at Nashville, Tennessee, and her father, John Neill, moved to Arkansas in 1851. He brought his family with him and with teams and wagons penetrated the wilds of Northwest Arkansas and established a pioneer home in Benton County. Benton County was then and for many years afterwards located on the frontier, there was no railroad within a hundred miles, and Nannie Neill was thus reared in the midst of pioneer surroundings. Benton County was in the direct path of the important campaign of the early Civil war which terminated in the battle of Pea Ridge, and Nannie Neill met her future husband while he was fighting under General Price, and they were married some time during the progress of the war. She is still living, her home at Edinburg, and has reared four children: William Henry, May, wife of C. S. Horr, of Kansas City; Katie, wife of David Witten; and Amie, wife of Charles Warner.

Doctor Winningham received his early education in the country schools and subsequently attended the Albany High School and the Stanberry Normal. When he was nineteen years old he taught his first term, and had already determined upon medicine as his profession. He began the study of medicine with Dr. G. F. Peery of Albany, and subsequently entered Marion Sims Medical College, now the medical department of the St. Louis University. He graduated M. D. March 23, 1893. His initial practice was in Albany, and in 1893 he moved to Edinburg and in 1905 established his office at Trenton. Doctor Winningham has never been content to fall into a rut in practice, and has been a constant student and a close observer ever since beginning practice. In 1901 he took postgraduate work in the Chicago Polyclinic, and in 1904 did further work in St. Louis and several times since then has absented himself from his local business long enough to enjoy the opportunities of the larger cities and hospitals.

In August, 1895, Doctor Winningham married Miss Nannie Floyd Witten, who was born in Daviess County, Missouri, a daughter of William and Pamelia Witten. Mrs. Winningham died in 1899, and left two daughters, Elizabeth and Helen. Elizabeth died when fourteen years old, and Helen is now a student in the Trenton High School. Doctor Winningham has membership in the Grundy County and Missouri State Medical societies and the American Medical Association. Fraternally he is affiliated with Trenton Lodge No. 111, A. F. & A. M.; Royal Arch Chapter No. 66 at Trenton; and Godfrey de Bouillon Commandery No. 24, Knights Templars. He is also affiliated with Lodge No. 801 of the Benevolent and Protective Order of Elks, with the Knights of the Maccabees and with Edinburg Lodge No. 394, I. O. O. F. Doctor Winningham has served as city and county physician for the past two years, and has done much to safeguard public health and improve the public knowledge and practice of sanitation in this community.

GODFREY MARTI. A resident of Holt County for thirty years, Godfrey Marti is the owner of a large and finely improved farm near Mound City. His career has encouragement for young men who start without resources except those contained in themselves. Mr. Marti was foreign born, came to this country in young manhood, had no capital, and began his career as a renter, steadily prospered and thriftily turned his surplus into more land, until he now finds himself independent and with ample provision for the future of himself and family.

Godfrey Marti was born in Switzerland May 15, 1864, a son of John and Rose (Schorer) Marti. The parents were born and married in Switzerland, and after seven children were born to them, six daughters and one son, they all emigrated to America in 1883. They came directly to Northwest Missouri, settling in Holt County. The father died in Holt County in 1909, and the mother is now seventy-two years of age and living with a daughter in Wisconsin. Both parents were members of the German Methodist Church, and the father now rests in Mount Hope Cemetery.

Godfrey Marti had a limited education, and learned the English language after coming to America. Hard work constituted the lever by which he elevated himself into prosperity. For several months after reaching Northwest Missouri he worked as a laborer for others, and then for two years was a renter. With such means and credit as he could acquire, he bought a small piece of land, and has kept adding in small amounts until his present farm comprises 300 acres. His original purchase consisted of 120 acres in section 6 of Liberty Township. It was considered an improved farm, though the improvements were poor as compared with those at present. The old house burned down, and Mr. Marti has replaced it with a comfortable modern dwelling, and has also erected a good barn.

Mr. Marti married Mary Schneider, daughter of George Schneider. They are the parents of five children: John, Frances, Anna, Herman and Lester, all of whom were born on the Marti farm. Mr. Marti and family are members of the German Methodist Church, and in politics he is a republican, the same party with which his father affiliated.

J. E. WARD. Long known as an enterprising and successful farmer in Holt County, J. E. Ward came to this section of Northwest Missouri about thirty-five years ago, and has since been identified with the community about Mound City and vicinity. Mr. Ward in early life had to struggle hard for what he got, and since coming to Northwest Missouri has found ample reward for his industry, and is one of the men of substantial influence in Holt County.

J. E. Ward was born in Parke County, Indiana, September 24, 1848, a son of John E. and Margaret (Mulhallen) Ward. The parents were married in Western Indiana, where the father was a blacksmith. Seven children comprised the family, and three of them are now deceased. When J. E. Ward was nine years of age the father died, and the family was thus left without a head, and the children had to bear an important share in the supporting activities. They had previously moved to Pervia and from there went to Marshall County, Illinois, where the father died. The family then moved out on the prairie thirteen miles east of Lacon, Illinois, the county seat of Marshall County, and remained there until 1879. J. E. Ward began work there as soon as his strength permitted. His education came from the local schools, and as a boy he was hired out to others and had a thorough experience as a farm workman. The little homestead in Illinois on which the family lived comprised eighty acres. Mr. Ward lived there until about 1879 and after selling the Illinois land came to Northwest Missouri.

Mr. Ward has 240 acres in Holt County, and when he first settled on it, it had no improvements. His mother lived with him until her death. Mr. Ward married Catherine Cottier, daughter of Thomas Cottier, one of the oldest and best known early settlers of Holt County. To their union have been born five children: Walter D., born January 5, 1883; Thomas C., born February 8, 1885; Minerva, born July 25, 1890; Clifford G., born October 18, 1893; and Harold C., born January 12, 1896. All the children were born in Holt County, received their education in the local schools, and are now useful members of society. At the time of their marriage Mrs. Ward's father gave them 120 acres of land, unimproved, on which they located and improved the same, also adding to it another 120 acres. All the improvements have been made by Mr. Ward. In 1913 his house of seven rooms and contents burned to the ground, causing a loss of about four thousand dollars, with small insurance. But the same year he rebuilt his present residence at a cost of about thirty-five hundred dollars, a modern house of nine rooms.

The family worship in the Christian Church. Mr. Ward has taken an active part in local affairs, for a number of years has served on the school board, and while originally a republican in politics, with his father a whig voter before him, has recently become a democrat.

JOHN G. FRIES. The great Empire State has contributed in large degree to the citizenship of Northwest Missouri, and those who claim New York as the place of their birth have, as a rule, been found to be men of industry, ability and energetic nature. All, however, have not met with the success that has attended the efforts of John G. Fries, who is accounted one of the leading farmers of Holt County, and the owner of 250 acres of land in Benton Township. When he first came to Northwest Missouri, Mr. Fries was possessed of little save his native industry and determination, but through intelligent and well-directed effort he has steadily advanced himself to a position of substantiality among the men of his adopted community.

John G. Fries was born November 14, 1850, at Callicoon, Sullivan County, New York, and is a son of George and Minnie Fries, natives of Germany. The parents of Mr. Fries emigrated to the United States and were married in New York. They settled at Callicoon, New York, where the rest of their lives was passed in the pursuits of the soil. One of a family of eleven children, John G. Fries secured a common school education in his native state and grew up amid agricultural surroundings, so that it was but natural that he should adopt farming as his life work. He was still a young man when, with his brothers, he sought the broader opportunities of the West, coming to Northwest Missouri and settling in Holt County, near the Village of Oregon. The brothers settled on a tract of 250 acres of raw land, on which there had been made no improvements, and through hard and industrious labor converted it into a valuable and productive property. Later their interests were divided and John G. Fries went to Atchison County, Missouri, where he purchased a modest property and as the years passed added to it from time to time until he had a large and valuable farm, on which he made many improvements. He eventually became satisfied that Holt County offered a better field for his labors, and in 1913 he returned to this county, taking up his residence in Benton Township, not far from Mound City. Here he has continued to be engaged in general farming and feeding stock, and through good management, a thorough knowledge of modern agricultural methods and tireless perseverance, has put 250 acres of land under a high state of cultivation and is accounted one of his community's substantial men. He has made many improvements of an up-to-date character and his farm reflects his industry and ability, his buildings are commodious and substantial, and his stock well fed and content. He has 340 acres of land in Dale Township, Atchison County, Missouri, in addition to his 250 in Holt County, and is a general farmer and stock raiser. His business ability has enabled Mr. Fries to secure the best of prices in the local markets for his product, and those who have had business transactions with him know him as a strictly reliable and honorable man of business. While he is not a politician, he takes a keen interest in those things which affect the welfare of his community, and may be counted upon to support good and beneficial movements.

Mr. Fries was married to Miss Rosa Brown, who was born in Henry County, Indiana, a daughter of Isaac Brown, their union being solemnized October 11, 1884. Mr. Brown was one of Henry County's prominent citizens, serving as justice of the peace and township trustee for a number of years, and was the father of three daughters and four sons. Four children have been born to Mr. and Mrs. Fries, all in Atchison County, namely: Sarah Sylvia, Mammie N., John J. and Lawrence. Mrs. Fries is a member of the Methodist Episcopal Church, and, like her husband, is widely and favorably known in Benton Township.

DAVID F. ROMINE. A worthy representative of a sturdy pioneer family of Holt County, Missouri, is found in the person of David F. Romine, who is now carrying on successful agricultural operations on the old homestead place in Bigelow (now Minton) Township. Here he has spent his entire career, and while he is still in the prime of manhood, he has witnessed some remarkable changes and developments in this agricultural region. Mr. Romine was born on the farm on which he now resides, February 20, 1872, and is a son of George and Marguerite (Martin) Romine.

George Romine was born of honorable parents who were in modest financial circumstances, and during his boyhood was forced to undergo numerous hardships and to give up many of the pleasures which the average American youth considers his birthright. Reared in a farming community, he labored in the fields and secured such educational advantages as the district schools afforded in the winter months, and thus continued until the outbreak of the Civil war aroused his patriotism and he enlisted for service as a private in an Indiana regiment of volunteers. When the war had closed, spent with his long and arduous service, Mr. Romine looked for a field in which his labors might bear fruit, and eventually deciding upon Missouri as a promising locality, came to this state in 1866 and settled on an unimproved farm in Holt County. Here, with his young wife, he resolutely set to work to conquer the unpromising conditions. The first shelter for the family was a one-room cabin, the one room serving as dining-room, living-room and bedroom, to which a small lean-to kitchen was later added, which, to the mind of the young mother, made this a most wonderful home. The energetic and industrious labors of the couple soon were rewarded, however, and a more pretentious residence was built, this being followed by various other buildings, each erected according to the increase in the owner's prosperity. A man of exceptional native talent, George Romine was not alone able to improve and cultivate his farm and to place himself as a substantial citizen among the farmers of Bigelow Township, but found the time and the inclination to assist in movements for the public welfare, and never refused his support to those enterprises which his judgment told him were for the general good. During his lifetime he accumulated 320 acres of valuable land, all through his own unaided efforts, and this was gained through the most honorable dealing, so that no person of his community had aught but well to say of him. When he died, at the age of fifty-six years, Bigelow Township lost one of its best and most public-spirited men. A republican in politics, he was not a seeker for public preferment, but for twenty years rendered most valuable service as a member of the school board. He had put in his application for entrance into Masonry, but died just prior to taking his degree. Mr. Romine was married in Washington County, Missouri, to Miss Marguerite Martin, who survives him, and they became the parents of four children: Cora, who became the wife of John Scott; Charley, who is deceased; one child who died in infancy; and David F.

David F. Romine attended the public schools of Bigelow Township, and has passed his entire career on the property which he now occupies. He has continued the work commenced by his father, and through an intelligent use of modern methods has been able to achieve a gratifying success. His farm presents an attractive appearance, the house being painted white, while the barns and outbuildings are red, and everything about the place denotes the presence of able management. Mr. Romine is a republican, but is a modest and unassuming man and has not sought the doubtful honors to be found in the political arena.

Mr. Romine married Miss Ida Hutchinson, daughter of A. C. Hutchinson, of Holt County. They have no children.

R. C. BROWNLEE. The Bank of Fortescue, though recently established, has already made a record for the successful handling of finances and through the personnel of its officers and directors has furnished a substantial service to the business community in that section of Holt County. The bank opened its doors for business in July, 1914, and occupies a small frame building near the depot. The executive officers and directors of the institution are as follows: A. W. Van Camp, president; John E. Slater, vice president; R. C. Brownlee, cashier; George W. Hinkle, J. F. Iden, George H. Minton, J. E. Alkire. Mr. Van Camp, the president, has long been one of the substantial business men in the vicinity of Fortescue, is a large owner of farm property, and was actively engaged in farming, and has served as county judge. The bank was organized under a state charter, with a capital of $10,000. It offers a general banking service to the community.

R. C. Brownlee, the cashier, has active charge of the institution, and has lived in Fortescue since the bank started. Mr. Brownlee comes from Horton, Kansas, where he was born and educated, and was a student for a time in the University of Kansas. Mr. Brownlee gained his experience as a banker at the Bank of Horton, and his father, John W. Brownlee, is a farmer and president of the Horton Bank. R. C. Brownlee married Maud L. Clem, daughter of Daniel Clem of Horton. Mr. Brownlee is affiliated with the Masonic order at Horton, Kansas.

JOHN F. IDEN. A resident of Holt County nearly fifty years since early childhood, John F. Iden has the material accumulations and interests of the thoroughly successful man of affairs. In his early years he went through all the arduous toil necessary to clear off the forest and prepare the land for cultivation, and from his success as a farmer has broadened his interests to include extensive land holdings and relations with banking and other business enterprises.

John F. Iden was born in Platte County, Missouri, near the City of Atchison, Kansas, May 24, 1862. His parents were George W. and Nancy L. (Yocum) Iden, who were married in Platte County. One of the seven children is now deceased. In 1866 the family moved to Holt County, and the father died here when the son, John F., was twelve years of age. The first location was on the farm now owned by John F. Iden. Some time after George W. Iden had taken possession, it turned out that the previous occupant's possession was based upon "a squatter's right," and that title had never been properly acquired from the Government. Thus George W. Iden had to buy the farm a second time, and its title now is directly validated by the Government. The land was entirely unimproved when the family located there, and the greater part was covered with heavy timber, some of the trees measuring from six to seven feet in diameter. There were a few rude buildings on the farm, but the commodious and well arranged structures now found there are the result of Mr. John F. Iden's enterprise.

Mr. Iden was married to Sarah R. Edwards, daughter of Hayden Edwards. They have one child, Zetha Maud, who was born October 28, 1896.

In his home place Mr. Iden has ninety-six acres, besides 110 acres west of Bigelow and twenty acres next to the river. Some years ago he was one of the organizers of the bank at Fortescue and is still serving as one of its directors, and later bought the grain elevator at Fortescue, and is now engaged in the grain business and coal and implement trade at Fortescue. Mr. Iden was formerly a member of the Methodist Episcopal Church, and his mother was a devout adherent of that church. Fraternally he is affiliated with the Independent Order of Odd Fellows at Mound City and the Modern Woodmen of America. He has served as road overseer and director of the school board. His politics is democratic, though his father was a republican.

GUY JONES is one of the reliable and industrious farmers and stockraisers of Holt County, classed with the rising generation of agriculturists, who are acknowledged to be as broad and scientific in their methods and as fruitful in valuable results to the community as the workers in any other branch of modern industry. At the present time Mr. Jones is engaged in the cultivation of 640 acres of fine land in Bigelow Township, a large part of which is devoted to pasture, where he raises large herds of thoroughbred cattle, in addition to which he feeds and ships hogs. He is well known to the people of his community as a progressive and energetic citizen, who can at all times be depended upon to support beneficial measures.

Mr. Jones was born in the vicinity of Big Lake, Holt County, Missouri, May 30, 1882, and is a son of Henry and Julia (Chaney) Jones, who are living on an adjoining farm to that occupied by their son. Henry Jones came to Missouri from the East at an early date, and here for many years has followed the pursuits of the soil, being accounted a substantial farmer and helpful citizen of this progressive section of Northwest Missouri. Guy Jones was given a good education in the public schools, and this was supplemented by attendance at a business college, where he took a commercial course. He is the only child of his parents, although by his father's previous marriage, to Lucinda Green, he has two half-sisters, Minnie and Addie. Mr. Jones was brought up on the farm and thoroughly trained by his father in the various methods of successfully conducting agricultural operations, so that he arrived at man's estate well fitted to enter upon a career of his own. He remained, however, under the parental roof until the time of his marriage, in 1907, when he moved to his present farm of 640 acres, where he has continued to make his home, having developed it into one of the most valuable and attractive country places in this part of the county. The improvements have all been made under his supervision, the barns and sheds are of modern construction, well equipped within and without, roofed with tin and furnishing excellent facilities for the feeding of cattle, and the home, while not large, is well kept up and attractive. The buildings are well arranged, and everything about the place suggests the presence of able and intelligent management. While Mr. Jones has done some general farming, the greater part of his attention has been devoted to feeding and shipping stock, chiefly Hereford cattle and Duroc-Jersey hogs. His efforts have met with a most gratifying success, and he is justly named as a business man of more than ordinarily keen perceptions. In political matters he is a democrat, but his activities in public life have not extended beyond that interest which is felt by every good citizen in the welfare of his community. Fraternally he is connected with the Woodmen of the World, and also is prominent in Masonry, having attained the Shriner degree and being a member of the Temple at St. Joseph. Mrs. Jones is a member of the Methodist Episcopal Church.

Mr. Jones was married in 1907 to Miss Hazel Spellman, of Mound City, Missouri, daughter of Mathew and Elizabeth (McRoberts) Spellman, who came to Missouri from Canada. Mrs. Jones has one brother and one sister: Earl, who married Anna Evans and is a resident of St. Joseph; and Grace, who is single.

PLATT HUBBELL, the senior member of the firm of Hubbel Brothers, at Trenton, Missouri, was born in Myers Township of Grundy County on January 12, 1870.

His father was the late Loring W. Hubbell, who was born in Trenton Township of Grundy County, December 18, 1845.

The Hubbell family in America has a continuous record of lineage going back to Richard Hubbell, who was born in England in 1627, and on coming to America settled at Fairfield, Connecticut. There is a book entitled "History of the Hubbell Family," showing that men of that name have had a modest part in the work of developing this nation.

The late Loring W. Hubbell was educated in the public schools of Grundy County, and when he was a young man commenced teaching, a vocation to which he devoted the best years of his life, although at the same time he was a farmer. Finally he located in the City of Trenton, and operated in real estate and insurance until his death on August 18, 1913. The position he held in the community can best be described in the words of a review which appeared in the Trenton Daily Republican at the time of his death:

"Loring W. Hubbell lacked little of living the allotted period of three score and ten, being just sixty-seven years and eight months of age on August 18, the day of his death. Born and reared in Grundy County, he never sought to change his place of residence. He died within a quarter of a mile of the spot where he was born. During his latter years his bodily infirmities kept him from taking part in the active affairs of life. As the world views it, he never sought position, place or power. He chose to cultivate the modest yet endearing graces of mind and heart, rather than to attempt the achievements which men applaud. His most pronounced trait of character was his advocacy of the importance of education. He believed that the mind and soul are so inseparably intertwined that the cultivation of the mind is one step in the direction of cultivating the soul in the immortality of which he firmly believed. He has often quoted the words of Plato, 'A house that has a library in it has a soul.' This trait of his character is illustrated by the fact that when a young man he taught school and for several terms taught a Bible class in the Christian Church, of which he was a member. He helped his own children to get a practical education, thus benefitting them more than if he had left them a vast estate without an education. In the active part of his life he did what he could to increase the efficiency of the public schools. Until his eyesight failed he was a habitual reader, and thus kept in touch with current events. In his early life he was an industrious student and received a liberal education. In his student days he saw the leading artists of the opera and the drama on whose attainments he was pleased to dwell. He advocated fraternity among men, as witnessed by his membership in the Knights of Pythias. He made his life useful by doing the plain, un-

MR. AND MRS. PLATT HUBBELL AND FAMILY

pretentious things which helped others. For instance, he took a leading part in preserving the burial places of the dead. He said, 'If we love the living we will provide a suitable resting place for their earthly remains.' 'If we love the dead we will preserve their graves as sacred shrines.' His ever patient and cheerful disposition endeared him to all who knew him. To his immediate family earth cannot replace the loss of him.''

The late Loring W. Hubbell married Nannie M. Browning. Her father, John M. Browning, was born in Kentucky, and from that state in 1858 came to Missouri accompanied by his family, their journey being made across the country with teams and wagons. He located in what is now Myers Township of Grundy County, and bought land six miles east of Spickard. He there built a log house, which served his family as a home for several years. He was successful as a farmer, added to his land and improved his home, planted a good many fruit trees and surrounded himself with all the comforts of rural life. He served as a soldier in the Union army during the Civil war. Mr. Browning married Jane McBride Ewing, who was born in Kentucky and who survived her husband some years. They reared several children. Nannie M. Hubbell died March 19, 1905, and a brief estimate of her life was given in a Trenton paper, which will be appropriately quoted herewith:

"Nannie M. Hubbell was born on February 2, 1853, near Sherburne, in Fleming County, Kentucky. Her maiden name was Nannie Metcalf Browning. With her parents she came to Grundy County, Missouri, when she was a little girl. Though only a child when she removed from Kentucky, she vividly recalled and fondly cherished the men and memories of her native state. She became a member of the Christian Church when quite young, and ever afterward remained an earnest toiler in the vineyard of righteousness. In addition to her regular church work, she made many private individual appeals for a higher life. Many personal, yet unpretentious, acts of charity attest the sincerity of her purposes. She became a member of several fraternal orders, to which she was closely attached, and in which she was an industrious worker. Among these are the Knights and Ladies of Security, the Rathbone Sisters and the Eastern Star. She was married to L. W. Hubbell on November 20, 1867. She leaves four children, named Platt, George, Hallie and Alida, together with their father. . . . She had a wide circle of personal, lifelong friends. Devotion to the duties that lay nearest to her was a distinguishing trait of her character. Her highest pleasure was in humbly rendering service. To render self-sacrificing, simple service to the persons and the causes she loved was to her a perpetual joy. The cares of her home and family and others she chose to serve kept her from using any system in her reading. Yet in the midst of her toil and cares she read much of the best literature and highly appreciated good thought, in whatever form it might be expressed. She had a natural aptitude for music. Her originality in arranging and combining the moderate means and small influences within her reach for the accomplishing of generous purposes was an impressive quality of her mind. She did not climb the Heights of Earth, but, walking with her Savior as her guide, she trudged along in the lowly valley path. On Sunday, March 19, 1905, after a lingering illness, she wearied of her many burdens and, reclining upon them for a couch to rest a while, passed into that silent slumber from which she shall not be awakened until the resurrection morn. To those by whom she was known and loved, earth cannot replace the loss of her.''

Admitted to the bar in 1891, Platt Hubbell began practice at Trenton. For some years he and his brother George have been in partnership, and they occupy a good suite of offices on Main Street. Theirs is considered one of the most complete law libraries in the north part of the state, and it includes many special works on railroads and other specialties. The Hubbell Brothers are not corporation lawyers, and most of their cases originate among the plain people. They have fought many important cases to a successful conclusion, and have a reputation for serving the best interests of their clients. A brief examination of court calendars shows that the Hubbell Brothers practice not only in Grundy County, but in many adjacent courts and even in the states of Iowa and Kansas. A number of cases in which they have been employed have been adjudicated in the Appellate Court and have set valuable precedents in Missouri law.

Platt Hubbell was married at St. Joseph, Missouri, March 4, 1909, to Maude Irene Ray. They are the parents of three sons, Ray, Paul and Ernest. Mr. Hubbell and wife are members of the Christian Church, and he is affiliated with Trenton Lodge No. 111, A. F. and' A. M., and with other fraternal orders.

GEORGE H. HUBBELL. Junior member of the firm of Hubbell Brothers, attorneys, at Trenton, George H. Hubbell was for several years a successful educator in Northwest Missouri, and since turning his attention to the law has gained a secure position in the profession.

He was born on a farm in Jackson Township, Grundy County, May 24, 1878, a son of Loring W. and Nannie Browning Hubbell, the details of which prominent family in Northwest Missouri are to be found in a preceding article. George H. Hubbell attended country school as a boy, and in 1897 graduated from Avalon College. Three years were spent in the work of teaching in the country districts, and for two years he was principal at the Third Ward School at Trenton. He also did a great deal of private tutoring in preparing pupils for advanced schools, and was particularly successful in this work. Walter E. Reno, who later graduated from the Annapolis Naval Academy, was one of the young men who came under his supervision at that time. At Avalon College Mr. Hubbell took a course in stenography with a view to becoming a court stenographer. While teaching he devoted much time to the study of law, and eventually determined upon that as his chosen profession. He was examined and admitted to practice on November 12, 1902, and in 1904 formed his present association with his brother Platt under the firm name of Hubbell Brothers. They have in the last ten years built up a large and prosperous legal business.

On October 20, 1907, Mr. Hubbell married Essie Pearl Barnes of Trenton. Mrs. Hubbell is a member of the Methodist Episcopal Church, while her husband affiliates with the Christian denomination. He is well known in fraternal circles, having affiliation with Lodge No. 801, B. P. O. E.; with Aerie No. 721, Fraternal Order of Eagles; with Modern Woodmen of America; and with Lodge No. 38, Knights of Pythias. From April 19, 1912, to May 28, 1913, Mr. Hubbell was president of the Second District Pythias Association, comprising the counties of Grundy, Mercer, Putnam, Schuyler, Sullivan and Adair. Mr. Hubbell has made a careful study of the ritual in the Knights of Pythias and is a constant advocate of its teachings and principles as one of the best mediums to attain better citizenship and stronger manhood. He is a republican, having cast his first vote for William McKinley. In November, 1906, Mr. Hubbell was elected prosecuting attorney, and by re-election in 1908 served two terms in that office.

LOT BROWN. One of the most valuable and beautiful of the many valuable and handsome properties of Holt County, is the property of Lot Brown and son, an 800-acre tract lying in Bigelow Township, known as Walnut Meadow Farm. Here is to be found every improvement which makes country life attractive; its owner has spared no pains in developing and beautifying it, and the result of his labors is a country home that probably equals any in point of beauty in Northwest Missouri. Mr. Brown is a member of that class of individuals whom nature has endowed with versatile talents. Primarily a railroad man, with little previous experience in agricultural pursuits, when he came to his present problem he at once entered upon a career of success that equalled his achievements in his former field of endeavor, and from that time to the present has continued to be known as one of Bigelow Township's most substantial farmer-citizens.

Lot Brown was born at Rockford, Nebraska, and is a son of William and Abigail (Waite) Brown. His parents, both members of old and prominent New England families, were married at Providence, Rhode Island, and as a young married couple came to the West, taking up their residence in Nebraska, where they spent the remaining years of their lives and both passed away. Educated in the public schools of his native state, Lot Brown early adopted railroad work as his line of endeavor, and worked his way from position to position in this field to a place of prominence with the Burlington System. He had a large force of men under his employ, and continued as a railroad man until 1906, when he turned his attention to the management of his farm, and from that time to the present has steadily developed into a skilled and progressive agriculturist. Walnut Meadow Farm, Mr. Brown's 800-acre tract, was formerly a part of the estate of Mr. Brown's uncle, E. A. Brown, who was widely known in Northwest Missouri as "Parson" Brown. He came to this part of the state in 1870 as a poor man, and through wise investment and continued successes became the owner of some ten thousand acres of land, a large part of which he put under cultivation.

Since his arrival here, Lot Brown has erected an entirely new set of buildings, which are accounted among the best in the township, if not in the county, substantial and commodious in character, attractive in appearance, handsomely furnished, and with every modern equipment known for comfort and convenience. The residence is set well back, with a well-kept grove to one side, and this is one of the show places of the county. Mr. Brown's agricultural operations have been largely confined to the raising of alfalfa, and each year he gets out about five crops. He is a republican in politics, but has taken little save a good citizen's part in public affairs. Mrs. Brown is a consistent member of the Baptist Church.

Mr. Brown was married to Miss Anna Wilcox Payne, of Nebraska City, Nebraska, daughter of Robert Payne, and to this union there have been born two children: Robert, born at Nebraska City, who is prominent in Masonic circles, having attained the Shriner degree; and Miss Lucy Ellen, who was born at Chicago. Both children reside with their parents.

C. S. McKEE. One of the men active in commercial affairs at Bigelow is C. S. McKee, now at the head of a large general merchandise establishment which has made a progressive growth since it was founded here about fourteen years ago. Mr. McKee has spent most of his life in this section, represents an honored family, his father having been long prominent in business affairs, and through his own career has done much to increase the business facilities of Bigelow. It was in 1900 that Mr. McKee engaged in merchandising on a small and modest scale at Bigelow. His first location was in an old frame building just across the street from where his now large store stands. He subsequently moved his stock to the W. O. W. Building, and was located there about six years, and in July, 1913, moved to his present quarters. His store is larger and more modern in every respect than his previous location, and consequently he is better prepared to handle the trade which has been steadily growing since he began business.

C. S. McKee was born at Savannah, Missouri, November 22, 1875. His father, H. N. McKee, has lived in Holt County since 1877. He established a grain elevator and began the buying and selling of grain at Bigelow when that was one of the most important railway stations in this part of Missouri. Previous to the building of the branch road to Skidmore and Mound City, all the farmers in that vicinity hauled grain from a radius of twenty-five miles to Bigelow. H. N. McKee thus had important relations with the producing community and at times handled as much as thirty-five cars of grain in a single week. H. N. McKee married Sarah Scott. They were married in Iowa, and she was born in Pennsylvania. There were eight children in the family, all of whom were born in Northwest Missouri.

Mr. C. S. McKee married Edna E. Bridgman, daughter of J. F. Bridgman. They are the parents of four daughters. Mr. McKee is affiliated with Camp No. 35 of the Woodmen of the World, and with Holt Lodge No. 34 I. O. O. F. Mr. McKee has served on the local school board and was mayor of the town, and he and his family are members of the Christian Church.

GEORGE W. POYNTER. The Bank of Bigelow for thirteen years has given ample facilities to the town and surrounding country at Bigelow. . The officers and directors have all been men of substantial position in the community, and the bank has been the medium for a large share of the general commercial transactions of the community, has offered a safe service in the conservation of surplus funds, and has been conducted throughout on stable and conservative lines. The bank was organized November 22, 1901, by W. H. Poynter, W. M. Poynter and A. W. Chuning. Mr. Chuning was its first president. The original directors included John C. Hinkle, C. C. Catron, and T. O. Davis. The capitalization was $10,000 from the beginning. J. F. Bridgman succeeded Mr. Chuning as president and still holds that office. John C. Hinkle has been vice president since the organization of the bank, and the position of cashier has been held by George W. Poynter since the bank opened its doors for business thirteen years ago.

The Poynter family has long been prominent in affairs in this section of Northwest Missouri. George W. Poynter's father was born in Hart County, Kentucky, and also the grandfather was born in the same state. George W. Poynter's mother was Margaret C. Stanton. There were seven sons and one daughter in the family, all of whom are living. George W. Poynter first married Mabel Graham, who died at Kansas City in April, 1912, leaving a son and a daughter. Mr. Poynter subsequently married Jennie McKee of Craig, Missouri. Mr. Poynter and his father are both affiliated with Masonry, the father at Avalon, Missouri, and the son belongs to the Blue Lodge at Oregon, the Royal Arch Chapter at Rockport, and the Lodge of Perfection at St. Joseph. In politics Mr. Poynter is a democrat.

J. R. KRUSOR. The community of Bigelow has been well served through the general merchandise and hardware and implement house of J. R. Krusor & Company. The head of this firm is a thorough merchant, understands his business and the needs of the people, and has energetically and successfully endeavored to supply those needs, not only by handling reliable goods but by affording his own judgment and integrity in all his relations as a merchant. The present business of J. R. Krusor & Company was established at Bigelow by R. W. Graham on November 1, 1912, and on June 1, 1913, Mr. Krusor bought out the stock and has since continued under the firm name of J. R. Krusor & Company.

Mr. Krusor began business as a general merchant at Craig, Missouri, in 1909, and sold out his interests there on moving to Bigelow. Mr. Krusor was born four miles northeast of Craig on a farm, a son of Michael and Emerald (Gallaway) Krusor, and was one of three children. As a boy he grew up on a farm, received a training in the country schools, and lived the life of a farmer until twenty-two years of age, when he engaged in selling merchandise. Mr. Krusor's father was one of the early settlers in the vicinity of Craig, and both parents are now deceased having passed away on the old homestead. Mr. Krusor married for his first wife Elva Cook, daughter of P. G. Cook. To that union were born two children: J. R., Jr., and Vera, both of whom were born at Craig. Mr. Krusor's present wife is Florence, daughter of W. G. Sping. They have in their home five children, named as follows: Gomez Garcia, Joubert, Mattie, Fredia and Louis Sping. In politics Mr. Krusor is a democrat.

JOHN COUGHLIN. Few men have contributed more practical encouragement to the farmers of Holt County than has John Coughlin. whose hay and grain establishment has been one of the chief commercial factors of the Town of Bigelow since his arrival here in 1909. With a variety of experience to back him in his project, Mr. Coughlin came to this community, and within the short space of five years has advanced so rapidly in business circles that he is now known far and wide as the "Hay King," and is doing business with farmers in every part of the county. His career is another instance of the strong call of the soil and its varied interests rising superior to other callings, for Mr. Coughlin resumed his connection with agriculturists and agricultural products after some years spent in other pursuits. He has had no reason to regret his decision, for he has not only succeeded in a material way, but has also gained and held the respect and entire confidence of those with whom he has had business dealings.

By birth Mr. Coughlin is a Kansan, and comes of a family which originated in Ireland. His birthplace was the Town of Silver Lake, in the Jayhawker State, his natal date June 12, 1870, and his parents John and Mary (Collopy) Coughlin. The parents were married at Warrensburg, Missouri, but shortly after their marriage removed to Kansas, and there the father took up land, on which he established a home for his family. He, however, never followed agricultural pursuits, being throughout his life a railroad man. Both he and his wife are now deceased. They were honest and hard-working people, lifelong members of the Roman Catholic Church, in which they reared their family of six children, and in the faith of which they themselves died.

John Coughlin was reared on the home farm in the vicinity of Silver Lake, Kansas, and secured his education in the public schools of that community. His early activities were devoted to tilling the soil, but subsequently he went to Kansas City, Missouri, where he secured employment as a member of the police department, and continued as an officer for three years and eight months. In 1909, Mr. Coughlin came to Bigelow and established himself in business under his own name as a dealer in hay and grain, although from the first he has made a specialty of the former. He rapidly became one of the prominent factors in this line of endeavor here, and soon his reputation extended all over this part of Northwest Missouri, winning for him the sobriquet of "the Hay King." He not only does a large business in handling the product of the agriculturists of this county and adjoining ones, but is himself a large raiser of the product, his fine farm of 810 acres, in Bigelow Township, being devoted exclusively to raising hay. Primarily a business man, with large interests to demand his attention, Mr. Coughlin has had little time to devote to public matters, although he takes a good citizen's interest in the welfare of his community. He was reared in a republican atmosphere, but is himself a democratic voter. Mr. Coughlin has never married.

W. H. WILSON. Prominent among the old and honored families of Holt County, one which has been identified with the growth and development of Bigelow Township, and particularly with the agricultural interests, is that bearing the name of Wilson. A worthy representative of the family is found in the person of W. H. Wilson, the owner of fifty-five acres of well cultivated land, and a citizen who at all times has taken an active part in the movements which have made for progress and advancement. Mr. Wilson was born in Bigelow Township, Holt County, Missouri, December 25, 1878, and is a son of John R. and Serilda (Eastridge) Wilson.

The paternal grandparents of Mr. Wilson, Daniel A. and Lydia Wilson, were among the very earliest settlers of this county, and were honored and respected people of their community, where their lives were passed in the cultivation of the wild soil. Among their children was John R. Wilson, who was born in Holt County, here received his education in the primitive schools which marked the pioneer period, and grew up amid the surroundings of that day, becoming accustomed to the hard and unceasing toil through which this section was developed into one of the most fertile in Northwest Missouri. A man of excellent habits, industrious, energetic and persevering, he was able to accumulate a satisfying competence, his homestead consisting of eighty acres of land, in addition to which he had other interests. While achieving a personal success, he gained also the esteem and respect of his fellow citizens, and retained their regard to the last. The substantial set of buildings which he erected on his property was destroyed by fire, but has since been replaced by a new set. Fraternally, Mr. Wilson was connected with the Odd Fellows, in which he had numerous friends. He was a republican, although not active, and in his religious views belonged to the Methodist Episcopal Church, to which Mrs. Wilson also belongs. She still survives at the age of fifty-three years, but at this time is not in the best of health. There were three children in the family, all born in Holt County: Anna, who died in infancy; Lydia E., who became the wife of Oliver J. Nolan, and has three children, Clarence, Glenn and Orville; and W. H., of this review.

W. H. Wilson was educated in the district schools, and has always resided on the old homestead, where he now has fifty-five of the original eighty acres. He is carrying on general farming operations, and is considered one of the practical and intelligent farmers of his locality, ready to embrace innovations and new methods and at all times capable of recognizing opportunities and carrying them through to a successful conclusion. He is a republican in politics, and has served his community capably in the capacity of school director, a position which he now holds. Fraternally he is affiliated with the Woodmen of the World, the Yeomen and the Modern Woodmen of America, and his religious belief is that of the Methodist Episcopal Church. His many friends throughout this section testify to his popularity.

Mr. Wilson was married in 1902 to Miss Estelle Lease, daughter of L. L. and Katherine (Wagner) Lease, early settlers of Holt County. Three children have been born to Mr. and Mrs. Wilson on the old Wilson homestead in Bigelow Township, namely: Daisy, Oscar and Beatrice.

L. A. MEADOWS. The Meadows family has been identified with Holt County since pioneer times, and L. A. Meadows, of the second generation, has for the past quarter of a century or more been a prosperous farmer in the vicinity of Maitland. His good citizenship is indicated by the fact of his service in connection with local affairs and movements for the benefit of the community, and his enterprise is reflected in the attractive and valuable farm of which he is proprietor.

L. A. Meadows was born as one of a family of nine children, in Appanoose County, Iowa, March 11, 1857, a son of Sidney S. Meadows, and Elizabeth Ann (Scarborough) Meadows, who were of German ancestry. His father was born in Kentucky, February 27, 1818, and died in Holt County, January 6, 1892. His mother was born in Tennessee, December 5, 1826, and died January 8, 1911.

The father came to Holt County at an early day, 1865, was a poor man at that time, had a very limited education, and as one of the pioneers through hard work and overcoming of obstacles developed a fine farm and provided generously for his large family of children. His first place of settlement was six miles north of Oregon. He was a member of the Baptist Church. Mr. L. A. Meadows has lived on his present homestead since 1887. It comprises 240 acres of land, and is improved with good modern buildings. The chief feature of his industry is stock raising, which he carries on in connection with general farming. For the past fourteen years he has been a member of the Maitland Independent School Board, and has done much to improve the schools in his community, and is always ready to cooperate with any movement that means better living conditions.

Mr. L. A. Meadows was married to Mary Lydia Weller, daughter of Jacob and Katharina Weller, January 26, 1887. Their family consists of three children, Marvin P., Cassius and Lillie, all being born in Holt County.

ALONZO MEADOWS. More than forty-five years ago the Meadows family became identified with Holt County, settling on lands that had been little touched with the ax and plow of white men, and since that time many hundreds of acres have been transformed into cultivated fields by their labors. Alonzo Meadows represents the second generation in residence in Holt County, having come here when a boy, and is now one of the leading citizens of Clay Township.

Alonzo Meadows was born in Appanoose County, Iowa, April 10, 1854, a son of Sidney S. and Elizabeth (Scarborough) Meadows. His father was born in Estill County, Kentucky, and was married there. There were nine children in the family. The father was a carpenter in earlier years but subsequently took up farming. On moving to Iowa he acquired some prairie land, broke it up and cultivated it for several years, and in 1867 moved to Holt County. His first location was a farm five miles north of Oregon, comprising 200 acres. Some improvements had been made, but the father went ahead with characteristic energy and in time placed it entirely under cultivation with the exception of forty acres of native timber. The farm had a house which at that time was one of the most substantial in the neighborhood, but the father erected the barn and did a great deal to increase the general value of the property. His next home was another farm about two miles farther north, and containing a quarter section of land. His chief improvement there was the building of a barn. After those two experiences in farm development, the father bought the northeast quarter of section 14 in Clay township, paying $10 an acre for land that could hardly be classed as improved. He continued his enterprising labors, erecting buildings, cultivating the land, and lived there until his death at the age of seventy-two. While a believer in religion, he was a member of no church, and in politics a republican. Starting life poor, through his native thrift and industry and good habits he acquired a competence and did well by his children.

Alonzo Meadows was thirteen years of age when the family moved to Holt County, acquired his education in the district schools, and was well trained by his father for the practical career of farming which he has followed. He married Anna Riley, daughter of William Riley. By this marriage there were two children: Dillard, who married Ida Younger, and has one child, Wilma Marion; and Sydney, who married Nellie Landon. After the death of his first wife Mr. Meadows married Hettie Riley, daughter of Sanford and Louise (Keetley) Riley. By this union there is a large family of ten children, as follows: Cortez, who married Linda Campbell; Lelah, unmarried; Lemuel J., who married Edna Borring; Ninah; Dwight; Lester; Clyde; Freeman; Donald; and Fredah May. All the children were born on Mr. Meadows' fine homestead of 160 acres. This land represents his individual success as a farmer, and all the improvements have come from his hands. Besides this estate he owns 162 acres in DeKalb County. His occupation is that of general farming and stock raising, and all the facilities on his place, including barns and domestic structures, are modern and equipped with excellent conveniences. In politics Mr. Meadows is a republican.

JAMES B. WRIGHT, M. D. Through his work and attainments Doctor Wright has earned a place as one of the eminent physicians of Northwest Missouri. The Wright Hospital at Trenton, of which he was the founder and which has been conducted under his supervision for some years, has afforded facilities to the profession and to the general public which have been greatly appreciated, and it is one of the most valuable institutions of its kind in the state. Through his hospital and by his large private practice Doctor Wright has contributed a valuable public service both to Trenton and to Grundy County. The hospital occupies a commodious and handsome brick building, and has every equipment and appliance needed for the modern hospital, and its establishment filled a long-felt want in the city.

James Buchanan Wright was born at Xenia, Greene County, Ohio, a son of Albert Wright, who was born on a farm in Loudon County, Virginia, in 1808. Grandfather William Wright was born in Pennsylvania, moving from that state to Loudon County, Virginia, where he spent the rest of his life. Albert Wright moved west and located at Xenia, Ohio, and was employed there as a contractor and builder for many years. In 1873 he came out to Grundy County, Missouri, and established his home on a farm in Washington Township. He lived there until his death in 1895. Albert Wright married Elizabeth Ann Davis. She was born in Pennsylvania in 1810 and died in 1890. Her

WRIGHT HOSPITAL, TRENTON

WRIGHT HOSPITAL, TRENTO.

five children were: John A., a farmer in the State of Washington; Sarah A., widow of Charles H. Snyder; William H., deceased; Maggie E., deceased, and James B.

Doctor Wright received his early training in the public schools of Ohio, and like many successful members of the profession entered and prepared for his chosen vocation after some years spent as a teacher. While teaching he began the study of medicine, and finally entered the Missouri Medical College, where he was graduated doctor of medicine in the class of 1883. For a number of years Doctor Wright had a large country practice at Spickard, and in 1896 moved to Trenton. In 1903, in order to afford his own practice the much-needed hospital facilities, and as a result of his long experience, he established the Wright Hospital at Trenton. Doctor Wright is a member of the Grundy County Medical Society, is a councilor to the fourth district in the Missouri State Medical Society, a member of the Mississippi Valley Medical Society and the American Medical Association. Outside of his profession he is also a director in the Farmers Exchange Bank at Trenton. Fraternally his affiliations are with Trenton Lodge No. 111, A. F. and A. M.; Godfrey de Bouillon Commandery No. 24, Knights Templars; has taken thirty-two degrees of the Scottish rites, belongs to the consistory, and also to the mystic shrine. His wife was an active member in the Eastern Star.

On November 30, 1880, Doctor Wright married Eva Fox. She was born in Wisconsin, a daughter of Myron and Lamira Fox. Mrs. Wright, who died in September, 1913, was a very talented woman, a leader in social circles, and in many ways set high standards of culture. She was skilled in the use of brush and pencil, and the walls of her home was decorated with her own paintings, and she also did much work in the painting of china. With a large knowledge of general literature, she was a fluent writer, and her place in Trenton society has not been filled.

CHARLES C. LIMPP is member of a prominent family in Holt County, and he and his brothers and sisters make up a large and useful relationship in the country community about Mound City. The father of the family was the late John G., and his career deserves some special mention in any account of Holt County.

His career was one of success. Many things constitute success, and it was not only in his material possessions, ample though they were, that the success of John G. Limpp was measured. He was born in Germany, December 29, 1829, and came to America in 1854, without the knowledge of the English language and with only $2 in his pocket when he reached St. Louis. In order to get money to carry him to St. Joseph, which was his destination, he worked for a time on a railroad. Arriving in St. Joseph he found work with a German farmer in Buchanan County at wages of $15 per month. While this position enabled him to make a living, it did not present opportunites to learn the English language, which was a first and important step toward a larger career of usefulness. After a year, accordingly, he found employment with an American named Boone, who had a large plantation, most of the work being performed by slaves. The German hand learned to speak English from these slaves. During the two years of his employment on the Boone plantation, John G. Limpp was assigned the duties of "breaking hemp," which, as all familiar with the cultivation and working up of that crop know, was a task requiring unusual strength and skill. It was difficult to get men to perform that kind of labor, and John G. Limpp served a full apprenticeship.

At the age of thirty Mr. Limpp married Helen Lee Hinman. She was of Scotch parentage and of Canadian birth, and at the time of her marriage was employed in Buchanan County, where she met the young German whom she subsequently married. After his marriage John G. Limpp took up farming, but in a short time the war broke out, and he was one of many Germans who fought for their adopted country, enlisting in the Twenty-ninth Kansas Infantry and serving till mustered out at St. Louis.

At the close of the war John G. Limpp came to Holt County and bought eighty acres of land, to which he soon added another eighty. After a period as a farmer he engaged in the brewery business at Forrest City for a time, but soon returned to agriculture. Selling his original farm, he bought eighty acres that is still included in the large Limpp homestead. The price paid for that land at that time was $15 per acre. It was in this vicinity that John G. Limpp spent the rest of his days, a prosperous farmer, and with growing accumulations that made him one of the large land owners and substantial men of the county. While getting material prosperity he discharged the obligations of citizenship, and dealt squarely with all men, so that none could begrudge him his well won prosperity. . John G. Limpp was brought up in the faith of the German Lutheran Church, was a man of excellent habits, and though a hard worker attained the good old age of eighty-three. He was useful in his community, and for many years served on the school board. For a long time the three directors of the Blair neighborhood school were John G. Limpp, Andrew Meyer and Uriah Blair. John G. Limpp had nine children, and six of them attended that school. In politics he was an ardent republican.

John G. Limpp and wife had nine children in all, mentioned briefly as follows: Fannie, the only one now deceased, was the wife of Charles Patterson; Mary, who married James Poynter; Rosena, who married Alexander Swope; Emma, the wife of S. Stevenson; Laura, the wife of Walter Smith; John R., who married Irma Durrett; Anna, wife of George Chriswell; Grace, who married Bert Patterson; and Charles, who married Maud Gillis.

Charles C. Limpp, who has now taken his place among the productive workers in Holt County, was born here August 6, 1882. At the present time he is engaged in farming 200 acres of land, a portion of the original estate acquired and largely improved by his father. Mr. Limpp has three children: Helen, Earl and Wilma. Mr. and Mrs. Limpp are members of the United Brethren Church, and he is at the present time serving on the school board and is a republican in politics.

O. D. HARDMAN. What may be accomplished when one is young, strong, clear of brain and studiously inclined, in this twentieth century, is being demonstrated by O. D. Hardman, who is engaged in cultivating 120 acres of land in Hickory Township, Holt County. The agricultural community of Northwest Missouri has undergone a wonderful transformation in the past several decades, but methods and returns have not yet reached their ultimately high standard, and it is to such progressive, energetic and industrious young farmers as Mr. Hardman that Holt and the surrounding counties must look for the advancement which will bring about improved conditions. In the meantime he is steadfastly carrying on his labors in tilling the soil and in building up his substantial position in the community.

Mr. Hardman was born in Ottawa County, Kansas, March 17, 1884, and is a son of Albert and Mattie (Goodwin) Hardman. The family was founded in Holt County about the year 1880 or 1881, and a short time later went on to Ottawa County, Kansas. However, the father had become so favorably impressed with Northwest Missouri, that after a short time in Kansas he returned to Holt County, settling on a farm located north of the Town of Newpoint. There he continued to be engaged in farming and stockraising until failing health caused his retirement and removal to Idaho, where his death occurred. He was a man of industry and enterprise, of fidelity to engagements and of strict integrity in all dealings, and won a reputation that made his name an honored one in business circles. The mother, who still survives, is a woman of many excellencies, both of mind and heart. There were three children in the family: Laura, who became the wife of W. H. Huntsman; Ola, who married Charles Conn; and O. D., of this review.

O. D. Hartman was brought up amid the farming locality of Holt County, and here, during the winter months, attended the district schools. Being the only son in his father's family, he was early called upon to share in the duties and labors of the farm's management, and thus received a training in his youth that has since proved invaluable to him. He was married in Holt County, to Miss Pansy Kunkel, a daughter of Benjamin Franklin Kunkel, who was a well-known farmer and pioneer settler of Hickory Township. Mr. Kunkel was married several times, as was also his wife, and they had a number of children, but Pansy was the only one by their union. Mrs. Hardman was born and reared on the farm which she and her husband occupy, and which is known as the Kunkel homestead. This is one of the old properties of this township, the first buildings thereon having been erected some forty years ago by one Huntsman. When Mr. Hardman first located on this land, the tract consisted of but forty acres, but to this original acreage he has added from time to time until he now has 120 acres, all under a good state of cultivation. His improvements consist of a modern residence, substantial barn and good outbuildings, the farm is well fenced and drained, the live stock is of a high grade and everything about the property denotes good management and well-directed industry.

Mr. Hardman is a republican in his political views, and is fraternally an Odd Fellow. His religious connection is with the Christian Church, while Mrs. Hardman is a Presbyterian.

W. N. HODGIN. An energetic, purposeful and intelligent participation in the affairs which have made up the history of Holt County since the occupation of this part of Northwest Missouri by the Indians, entitles W. N. Hodgin, of Hickory Township, to a place among the representative citizens of his community. A member of a pioneer family of agriculturists, the greater part of his career has been devoted to the pursuits of the soil, and his careful management and discriminating use of modern methods have eventuated in crowning his labors with a measure of success that should be as gratifying as it is well earned.

W. N. Hodgin is a product of Holt County, Missouri, born in the vicinity in which he now resides, August 20, 1857, a son of John and Mary Ann (Hill) Hodgin. His father came to Northwest Missouri from Washington County, Indiana, about the year 1854, and settled in Holt County, pre-empting a tract of 160 acres of uncultivated land on which there had been made no improvements. There has been only one deed to this property, this being the original one which bears the signature of President Buchanan. John Hodgin was a poor man when he came to Missouri, and his early life here was replete with the hardest kind of struggles, but he possessed an abundant force of energy and ambition, which he directed in such a manner that he was able, before he died, to justly account himself a substantial man, both in a material way and in the esteem of the people of his locality. In order to erect his first log cabin, he was compelled to haul logs from the Missouri River bottoms, and this humble residence continued to be his home for a long number of years, his other buildings being correspondingly primitive. Here, frequently, the Indians would visit, and the brave little mother prepared them many a meal, thus using diplomacy in keeping them friendly. With the father she labored faithfully and energetically, and finally they came into the possession of 400 acres of good land, on which they had been able to make many improvements. Mr. Hodgin has been dead for a number of years, and Mrs. Hodgin passed away in 1889. They were the parents of five sons: W. N., of this review; W. S., engaged in the mercantile business at Forbes, Holt County, who married Ida Donovan; W. H., who married Lillie Allen; W. B., deceased; and J. S., who died in infancy. Reared in the faith of the Quakers, John Hodgin continued as a Friend until coming to Missouri, and here joined the Christian Church. His political belief was that of the republican party.

W. N. Hodgin grew up amid pioneer surroundings and still remembers the visits of the red men to the crude little home in which he was born. He received his education in the district school and in the public school at Oregon, Missouri, the latter of which he attended for about two terms, and thus prepared himself for employment as a teacher. He had several charges in Holt County and continued as an educator until his marriage, at which time he purchased an interest in a livery business at Craig, Missouri, but after about two years thus engaged returned to the farm, in 1883, and has continued to devote himself to agricultural pursuits to the present. He is now the owner of 240 acres of fertile, well-cultivated land located in Hickory Township, which has been brought under his management to a state of development which makes it really one of the valuable tracts of this part of the county. Modern, substantial buildings, kept in excellent repair, give it a decidedly attractive appearance, and in every way Mr. Hodgin lives up to his reputation as a progressive and energetic agriculturist. As a man who has always been faithful to his obligations, he holds a high standing in commercial circles, while his good citizenship has been proved on many occasions and his friendship for the cause of education has been demonstrated by a number of years of efficient service as a member of the school board. He was formerly an Odd Fellow for an extended period, and at this time his fraternal affiliation is represented by membership in the Woodmen of the World and the Masons, both lodges being located at Maitland.

Mr. Hodgin was married, November 27, 1879, to Miss Maggie Heskett, daughter of Curtis Heskett, and five children have been born to them: J. L., who is engaged in the clothing business with his brother at Maitland, married Emma Marti and has one daughter, Caryl; W. E., who is his brother's partner in the clothing business, married Laura Brownlee; Grace, who is the wife of C. D. Fulton, of Trenton, has two children, Morris and Harold V.; J. L. and L. R. All the children were born in Holt County.

LAFE KUNKEL. Among the substantial farmers of Holt County who have made an especially creditable record in agriculture and in citizenship, is the gentleman whose name is found at the head of this biographical record, and whose valuable and attractive farm and residence are located in Hickory Township. Mr. Kunkel is a native of Holt County, and during his long residence here has seen the development of the county as well as the numerous changes which have revolutionized the vocation of agriculture, and, while contributing to the advancement of his community's interest, has kept himself fully abreast of modern inventions and new innovations.

Lafe Kunkel was born July 28, 1867, on the family homestead in Liberty Township, Holt County, and is a son of Benjamin Franklin and Hannah (Chester) Kunkel. His father, a native of Ohio, became one of the very earliest settlers of Holt County, traveling overland to this locality as a poor man and taking up his abode in the midst of a practical wilderness. In the years that followed he experienced the hardships and discouraging experiences that are incidental to the first settlers in any new part of the country, but his untiring perseverance, steady application and good management of his affairs enabled him to overcome all obstacles which appeared in his path, and he was eventually able to retire from business activities with a handsome competence, now being a member of the retired colony at Forest City, Missouri. During his career in Holt County Mr. Kunkel established a reputation for honesty and integrity in his dealings and for public-spirited citizenship. He was married four times, and by his union with Hannah Chester was the father of four children: Lafe, Alvah, James and Willie, of whom the last named died at the age of eighteen months. Benjamin F. Kunkel was a republican in his political views, but during his residence in Holt County never sought political honors. He is a member of the Methodist Episcopal Church, in the faith of which his children have been reared. Mrs. Kunkel passed away on the homestead place in Holt County.

Lafe Kunkel passed his boyhood and youth in alternately assisting his father in the work of the home place and attending the district schools of Hickory Township, where he obtained a good ordinary education. When he was reared to enter upon his own career, he secured a part of the old homestead, and in association with his brother, James, started operations, they now having 240 acres, all under a good state of cultivation and devoted to stock raising and general farming operations. Some of the present buildings were started by Mr. Kunkel's father and completed by him and his brother, and they are now well arranged, in a good state of repair, furnished with good equipment, and present an attractive appearance. Nothing that goes to make up a modern twentieth-century farm has been neglected or left out of this property, and in every way it is a credit to its progressive and enterprising owners.

Lafe Kunkel married Miss Anna Jackson, who was born in Page County, Iowa, daughter of John and Catherine (Parsons) Jackson, who had three other daughters and four sons. These were: George, James, Charles, Mattie, Alma, Blanche and Frank. Mr. and Mrs. Jackson, farming people, were early settlers of Page County, Iowa, subsequently moved to Kansas, and finally came to Holt County, Missouri. The father is deceased but the mother is still living. Eight children have been born to Mr. and Mrs. Kunkel: Nettie, Harold, Mark, Mildred, Raymond, Carl and Hugh, twins, and one who died in infancy. Mr. and Mrs. Kunkel are members of the Presbyterian Church. Mr. Kunkel, like his brother, is a republican, and is fraternally connected with the Woodmen of the World and the Independent Order of Odd Fellows, of which latter order James is also a member.

RALPH M. MEYER. One of the fine farm homes near Maitland is owned and occupied by Ralph M. Meyer and his family. Mr. Meyer is the grandson of one of the pioneer settlers in this section of Northwest Missouri, and is a young man of much enterprise, has shown industry and intelligence in the management of his affairs, and stands as an influence for morality and progress in his community.

Ralph M. Meyer was born on the old homestead in Holt County, February 1, 1878. His parents were J. H. and Fannie (Pointer) Meyer, and all their six children are still living. J. H. Meyer was also born in Holt County, and his father settled here when nearly all the county was a wilderness.

Ralph M. Meyer married, December 27, 1899, Mabel Terry of Forrest City, a daughter of W. H. Terry. They are the parents of four children: Galen, Ralph, Jr., Lucy S. and Clinton R. The present farm of Mr. Meyer has been occupied by him since 1902. In spite of misfortune he has prospered. He lost both his barn and his house by fire, the barn having been burned October 13, 1908, and the house on April 15, 1914. Both have been replaced by substantial structures. Mr. Meyer cultivates 187 acres of fine land, has improved it and does general farming and stock raising.

He was reared in the Christian Church, and has been assistant superintendent of its Sunday school. Fraternally he is affiliated with Lodge No. 473 of the Independent Order of Odd Fellows at Newpoint. He is now serving his third term as a member of the school board, and politically is a democrat.

LOGAN MEYER. Prominent among the younger generation of agriculturists of Hickory Township, one who has spent his entire career here and through progressive ideas and a thorough knowledge of farming has gained a substantial position is Logan Meyer. Mr. Meyer was born in Hickory Township, Holt County, Missouri, one-half mile from his present home, May 12, 1880, and is a son of James Henry and Fannie L. (Pointer) Meyer.

Mr. Meyer belongs to a family which has been long and favorably known in this part of the county. It was founded here by his grandfather, Andrew Meyer, who emigrated from his native Germany to the United States in 1834 and worked in the City of St. Joseph, Missouri, when there were but two white men at that place. During the gold excitement of 1849 he crossed the plains by ox-team to California, and returned in 1850 with $6,000 in gold, which he invested in farming lands in Holt County. He became one of his community's substantial men, the owner of 2,300 acres of land, and served for a time as county judge. Andrew Meyer married Mary Secriut, and they became the parents of thirteen children: Anna E., James H., Mary M., Alfred A., an infant, Willard P., Annilda, George, Robert E., Charles, Emma J., Marvin E. and Don C. James H. Meyer, the father of Logan Meyer, was born in Holt County, December 31, 1853, and secured an ordinary education in the district schools of his day. As he grew to manhood, he adopted the vocation of farming, in which he has continued to be engaged to the present time with much success, and at one time was the owner of 400 acres of land, but has since disposed of 200 acres of this property. He is a democrat in politics and has served for twelve years as a member of the school board, and is widely and favorably known throughout this section. He married Fannie L. Pointer, and six children were born to this union: William H., who married Cora Trimmer; Ralph M., who married Mabel Terry; Logan A., of this review; James H., Jr., who married Floy Sieper; Edgar R., who married Miriam Hayhurst; and Frances P., who is the wife of Virgil Carter. All the children were born, reared and educated in Holt County, all are married, and all have children.

Logan Meyer was given his education in the district school and grew up on his father's homestead, on which he resided until embarking upon a career of his own. He is now the owner of 120 acres of good land, all under a state of cultivation, and with good improvements, all of which, with the exception of the barn which he built himself, having been here at the time of his arrival. Mr. Meyer is an energetic and persevering agriculturist, and his good business judgment, foresight and ability have enabled him to make a success of his operations. He is a well known and popular young farmer of this locality, and belongs to that class to which the county must look for its future improvement.

Mr. Meyer married Miss Hattie Wakely, who had three sisters and two brothers, of whom one sister died in infancy. Her father, William Wakely, has been a prominent republican, and served for some years as road overseer. To Mr. and Mrs. Meyer there have come four children, as follows: Ellen, born December 12, 1903; Mary, born September 23, 1905; Hazel, born July 6, 1907; and William Henry, born February 12, 1914, all in Holt County. Mr. and Mrs. Meyer are members of the United Brethren Church.

BARNEY HODGIN. Among the representatives of the younger generation of agriculturists in Northwest Missouri, there are found a number who have spent their entire lives on the properties which they now own and cultivate, and this class may be said to have an advantage of some nature, for a lifetime of residence on one tract naturally gives the resident a thorough knowledge of its needs and peculiarities. In this category may be numbered Barney Hodgin, of Hickory Township, an energetic and enterprising young farmer who is obtaining excellent results from his labors in the cultivation of a farm that has been in the family name for fifty-eight years.

Mr. Hodgin was born on his present property, March 23, 1887, and is a son of Joseph and Susan E. (Denny) Hodgin. The father was born near Salem, Washington County, Indiana, October 5, 1835, and was nineteen years of age when he first came to Northwest Missouri. At that time he was possessed of no means, and his first employment was that of breaking up the virgin prairie on the farm of a pioneer family of Holt County named Ish. Thus he secured the money to buy his first tract of land, located in what is now the City of Omaha, Nebraska, but at that time only a little settlement of sod houses. He had, however, during his former short residence in Holt County, become so favorably impressed with the opportunities here, that in 1857 he returned to this locality and invested his earnings in Hickory Township land, paying therefor $4 an acre. There had been no improvements of any kind made on this property, and Mr. Hodgin first put up a small log cabin, which was followed by several other structures also composed of logs. His were the experiences which attended the efforts of the majority of pioneers who settled in this fertile region with little to aid them save their native intelligence and boundless ambition. The first ten or more years following his arrival were ones filled with the hardest kind of work, countless disheartening incidents and constant self-sacrifice, but his perseverance won out in the end, his original log shacks were succeeded by substantial frame structures which still stand, and when he died he was the owner of 720 acres of valuable land, 600 acres being located in one body in Hickory Township. He died January 29, 1913, one of the substantial and highly respected men of his community. Mr. Hodgin was married first to Harriet Lawrence, and by that union there are two children living—Jennie Kline and T. E. In 1874 he was united with Miss Susan E. Denny, and they became the parents of three children: Barney, of this review; Emmett, a graduate of Drake University; and Nellie, who is the wife of Mr. J. I. Williams. Mrs. Hodgin, who survives the father, still makes her home with her sons on the old family place.

Barney Hodgin secured his early education in the district schools of Hickory Township, but was given better advantages than many youths, in an educational way, being sent to the high school at Oregon, and the State University at Columbia. When he laid aside his school books he returned to the duties of the homestead farm, and has continued to occupy himself in agricultural pursuits to the present time. He is thoroughly familiar with modern methods and machinery, which he uses constantly in his work, and through his accomplishments has earned the right to be accounted one of Hickory Township's able farming representatives. Mr. Hodgin was reared in the faith of the Christian Church, of which his parents were both members.

Mr. Hodgin was married to Miss Maud L. McNutt, one of the eight children of W. F. McNutt, who is a traveling salesman and resides at Columbia, Missouri.

COL. WILLIAM B. ROGERS. A veteran editor of Northwest Missouri, it has been given to Colonel Rogers to attain many distinctions both in and out of his profession. His career is a somewhat remarkable one, both for its length of service in the newspaper field, and for its experience as a citizen, and official, a soldier, and a hard and conscientious worker for the right in whatever sphere duty has called him. He has been at the head of the Trenton Republican for forty-five years, and in his eightieth year is still an active figure in Grundy County affairs.

William B. Rogers was born February 8, 1835. His birth occurred in a portion of Greene Township now included in Perry Township of Fayette County, Ohio. His father was Joel Rogers, born in Pennsylvania in 1808, a son of Joel Rogers, a native of New Jersey, and the great-grandfather was named Thomas. The grandfather lived a time in Pennsylvania, moved thence to Ohio, and settling early in Fayette County, bought a tract of land in Greene Township, to the clearing of which he devoted all his spare time. By profession he was a Baptist minister of the old school, but like many pioneers in the faith gained most of his livelihood by tilling the soil. He continued his life as a preacher and farmer of Fayette County until his death. His first wife, grandmother of the Trenton editor, was Milcah Young, who died in early life. He was afterward twice married and had children by each wife.

Joel Rogers, father of Colonel Rogers, grew up in Fayette county, was trained in pioneer surroundings, and after reaching manhood bought a piece of timbered land in Perry Township. The mother of Colonel Rogers was Priscilla Beals, who was born in Greene Township, Fayette County. William Beals, her father, was born in North Carolina, moved to Tennessee, later to Ohio, where he early settled in Fayette County, and cleared a farm from the wilderness of what was later Perry Township. He died there at a good old age. He married Nancy Caldwell, a native of the North of Ireland and of Scotch stock. Her oldest brother inherited the family estate, sold out and brought other members of the family to America, settling in Highland County, Ohio. Priscilla Beals Rogers died at the age of twenty-nine, leaving four sons and two daughters, the latter then spending several years in the home of their grandparents before returning to their father. The latter did not marry again until his children were nearly all grown.

With this ancestry and early environment, William B. Rogers was reared to habits of industry and as soon as old enough took his share in the duties of the household and farm. The school he first attended

was kept in a house of logs. There was a typical fireplace and mud-and-stick chimney, and all the furniture had been roughly made by the home community. He sat on a slab seat, with no back and supported from the ground by wooden pins. For the older pupils in their writing exercises with the old quill pen a broad board was fastened at an angle to the side wall, and the boys and girls stood while at this rude desk.

Colonel Rogers first came to Missouri in 1856. At Burlington he left the railroad and crossed the Mississippi, and made his way on foot to Mercer County. None of that country had a railroad, a few of the streams were bridged, and civilization had taken an only insecure foot-hold. At fifteen dollars a month he labored as a farm hand, and that was his first business in this state. Having a pretty good training in the fundamentals, he was then selected as teacher of a district school, and was paid twenty-five dollars a month for looking after the intel-lectual and corporeal welfare of some country boys and girls who at-tended a log school such as he himself had known back in Ohio. With his earnings he advanced his own education through the Grand River College at Edinburg, and was a student there when the war broke out.

One of the instructors of the college resigned and young Rogers for a time supplied her position and also continued his own studies. Returning to Mercer County in the fall of 1861, he enlisted in the Mercer Battalion for six months, and remained in the service until the end of his enlistment. Some while after his return home he was elected in the fall of 1862 sheriff of Mercer County. A little later came the general order from Governor Gamble that all able-bodied men should join the state militia, and in response to that order twelve companies were formed in Mercer County, with Sheriff Rogers holding a commis-sion of colonel from the governor and in nominal command of all the county troops. Before the expiration of his term as sheriff he raised a company of volunteers for active service, which was designated as Company D and attached to the Forty-fourth Regiment of Missouri Infantry, commanded by Col. R. C. Bradshaw, and himself as captain of the company. From Rolla, the first rendezvous, the regiment went into Tennessee and joined the Sixteenth Army Corps. Colonel Rogers was on the firing line at the great battles of Franklin and Nashville, and was with the federals who pursued the shattered troops of Hood toward Shiloh, and for a time was encamped on the Tennessee River. From there he went to New Orleans, was at the operations about Mobile Bay, including the siege and capture of Spanish Fort and Fort Blakely. The regiment then went to Montgomery and went into camp on the site now occupied by the famous Tuskegee Institute. While on the march from Mobile to Montgomery the first news came of Lee's sur-render. Colonel Rogers received his honorable discharge after a long and creditable record in August, 1865.

Returning to Missouri, he was engaged in the mercantile business at Ravenna four years. In 1869 he bought the Grand River Republican at Trenton, and thus entered upon his long career as newspaper pub-lisher and residence at Trenton. The Republican was established in 1864, under the name of Grand River News, and will soon complete its fiftieth volume. A. C. Bentley and G. W. Buckingham were the first proprietors and editors. The ownership soon changed, and the name became Republican-News. When Colonel Rogers bought, the paper was a small weekly issue, four pages and seven columns to the page. Many improvements have been introduced. It has always progressed with its news service in keeping with the advancement of the community, and through its editorial columns has exercised a leadership and influ-ence over the moral and civic affairs of Grundy County which could

not be omitted in any comprehensive survey of the last half century in
that portion of Northwest Missouri. Some years ago a daily issue was
begun and has successfully continued. The Republican has the distinction of being the only country paper in Northwest Missouri having the Associated Press service.

Colonel Rogers was married April 14, 1863, to Cynthia A. Buren.
They had been students together at Grand River Institute, and the
acquaintance there ripened into marriage. Theirs was an unusually
long and happy companionship. On April 14, 1913, family and friends
celebrated with them their golden wedding anniversary, and a few
months later, on August 21, Mrs. Rogers passed away. She was a member of the Ninety-nine, a woman's club, and was reared a Methodist,
but joined the Baptist Church after marriage, and she and husband
were both devout worshipers in that faith.

Cynthia A. Buren was born in Daviess County, Missouri. Her
father, Rev. John Johanneus Buren, was born near Rogersville, in Hawkins County, Tennessee, a son of Henry Buren, who in turn was a son
. of Simon Boerum. The latter, probably of Holland Dutch stock, lived
in New Jersey, was a member of the first Continental Congress, and
later fought for independence in Captain Brinkerhoff's company of
New York volunteers. Grandfather Henry Buren went to Hawkins
County, Tennessee, where he was granted a large tract of land, part
of which is still owned by his descendants, and died there at the age
of one hundred and five years. He married Mary Miller. Rev. John
J. Buren early joined the Methodist Church, was licensed to preach,
and about 1833 migrated to Missouri, and after residence in Jefferson
County became one of the pioneer ministers of Northwest Missouri in
Daviess County and vicinity. Later he was appointed presiding elder
for the South St. Louis district, and lived in St. Louis four years. He
then settled near Edinburg, where he entered government land, and
lived until his death in 1852. Rev. John J. Buren was married in
Tazewell County, Virginia, in 1809, to Cosby Peery, a daughter of William and Sarah (Evans) Peery, and granddaughter of Thomas and
Mary Peery of Augusta County, Virginia. William Peery, who fought
in both the War of the Revolution and the War of 1812, as is proved
by Virginia records, subsequently became a planter and slaveholder in
Tazewell County, where he and his wife died. Both Rev. John Buren
and his wife received a present of slaves at their wedding, but the
blacks were freed, and Reverend Buren was an original abolitionist
and active in the cause. Cosby Peery Buren survived her husband
until 1884, and her ten children were named: Paschal, Sarah M., Fielding P., Wilbur F., Melville C., Emily, Cullen E., Cynthia A., John O.
and Alvin B.

Colonel and Mrs. Rogers had three children, Carrie, Noble Giotto
and William B., Jr. Carrie, the widow of Frank Louis Clark, was for
thirteen years librarian of the Jewett Norris Free Public Library until
she resigned in November, 1913. Noble Giotto Rogers, whose lamented
death occurred July 21, 1912, was liberally educated, first in the Trenton schools and then in De Pauw University at Greencastle, Indiana.
For two years he taught Latin in the Trenton High School, and for
some years prior to his death was associated with his father in newspaper work. He was the compiler and publisher of a handsomely illustrated booklet setting forth the advantages and resources of Trenton,
and in 1911 published a history of Mercer County, a work of great
merit and a contribution to local annals in that section of the state.
By his marriage to Minnie Isabelle McGuire were born three children,

namely: Alice Marion, William B. and Robert M. William B. Rogers, Jr., died when fifteen years old.

Colonel Rogers cast his first vote with the republican party, and has been a stanch upholder of the policies and candidates of that great political organization. Besides the office of sheriff, he was also honored while in Mercer County with election to the state senate, representing the fourth senatorial district. He has affiliation with Col. Jacob Smith Post No. 72, Grand Army of the Republic, and with Trenton Lodge No. 111, Ancient, Free and Accepted Masons. Among other interests he is president of the Trenton Building and Loan Association.

ALBERT J. LOUCKS. One of the young men of progressive enterprise whose energies are contributed to the welfare of the community as well as to the accumulation of material prosperity for himself is Albert J. Loucks of Holt County. Mr. Loucks owns a fine farm, and has introduced modern improvements instead of the old fashioned buildings and conveniences which satisfied an earlier generation. He carries on the solid industry which in Northwest Missouri brings good crops and a satisfying degree of prosperity, and is not only providing well for his family but is a man of influence in his community.

Albert J. Loucks was born in Holt County, July 28, 1883, a son of John F. and Mary (Kunkel) Loucks. The parents were married in Holt County, and all their five children were born here, namely: David F., Charles E., Samuel G., Albert J., and Emma, wife of Louis Meyers. The paternal grandfather, Peter M. Loucks, came to Northwest Missouri from Ohio, settling here about 1851. Mary Kunkel was born in Holt County, and her father was a very early settler. The son Samuel G. is a graduate of the University of Missouri as a mechanical engineer, having been a member of the class of 1904.

Albert J. Loucks married Ethel Gibson, daughter of Theodore and Nancy J. (Hanks) Gibson, a family that has been identified with Holt County since the period of early settlement. Mr. and Mrs. Loucks have the following children: Edna, Franklin and Iris, all of whom were born in Holt County. Mr. Loucks several years ago bought his present farm, and it was already improved and equipped with buildings, but he has since modernized the entire place, and among other improvements has introduced a system of waterworks to supply the house and grounds with running water. Mr. Loucks is the owner of 160 acres of land, all of it cultivated, and he has made considerable success as a raiser of Red Duroc hogs and Shorthorn cattle. His wife is a member of the United Brethren Church. Mr. Loucks has served as justice of the peace and at the present time is a member of the school board.

JOSEPH HENRY. Liberal ideas, self-acquired independence, ambitions expressed in promoting agriculture, education and simplicity of living, as well as unquestioned public and private integrity, constitute the fundamentals upon which rest the enviable reputation of Joseph Henry, one of the substantial farmers and representative citizens of Clay Township. Mr. Henry is one of those who have been the architects of their own fortunes, for he entered upon his career as a renter and subsequently took up undeveloped land, which he has brought to a high state of cultivation through the labor of his own hands. He was born in Howard County, Indiana, March 10, 1855, and is a son of George and Maria (Gouldsberry) Henry.

The parents of Mr. Henry were natives of Ohio, where they were married, and shortly thereafter removed to the Hoosier State, where their children were born. In 1863 they again turned their faces toward the West, making their way to Missouri, where they located on the old Alexander farm of 100 acres, about one mile southwest of the court-house at Oregon. This tract was largely covered with timber, and the only improvement in the way of buildings was a small frame house, which is still to be seen standing on the property, one of the landmarks of the locality. The father did not live long to carry on operations on the new home, as he passed away in 1864, but the mother and children continued to reside there, and in some manner managed to keep her little family together. She survived her husband many years, and died in 1889, when eighty-seven years of age. There were eight children in the family, of whom but three now survive.

Joseph Henry was but eight years of age when he came to Missouri with his parents, and was nine years old when his father died. He secured his education in the district schools of the locality, but this was necessarily somewhat limited, as a large part of his time was expected to be devoted to work in assisting in the support of the family. How-ever, he made the most of his opportunities, and acquired a good, prac-tical training, which has since been supplemented by observation and reading, so that today he is well informed on important subjects. When he was ready to establish a home of his own, Mr. Henry was married to Miss Eliza A. Huiatt, daughter of Daniel Huiatt, and for the six years that followed rented his father-in-law's farm. Working faith-fully and perseveringly during this period, he was successful in accumu-lating enough means to purchase, in 1887, his present farm of eighty acres, to which he has since added an additional eighty to the north. When he located on this land it was destitute of improvements, but under his skilled and energetic management the property has grown and developed into one of the handsome country places of Clay Town-ship. He has devoted his attention chiefly to general farming, in which he has met with a satisfying measure of success, and his ability as a business man is evidenced by the profitable transactions which he carries on in the markets. His implements and general improvements have been selected with rare discretion, and suggest the man who is willing to profit by the experience of others, rather than one who recklessly bows to the novelty of invention.

Four children have been born to Mr. and Mrs. Henry, all in Clay Township, where they have been educated: Mattie, Pansy and Pearl, twins, and Homer.

JOHN LONG. Holt County has no better-developed or more attractive agricultural property than that known as Pine Hill Farm, a tract of 320 acres lying in Clay Township. This tract has been developed under the supervision and capable management of John Long, who has spent nearly the entire period of his active career in developing its resources, and who is known as a thoroughly progressive and up-to-date agricul-turist. Mr. Long was born March 12, 1867, in Franklin County, Pennsyl-vania, and is a son of Adam and Mary Ellen (Bradley) Long.

Adam Long went to Iowa prior to the Civil war, and during the period of that struggle served in the capacity of postmaster at Bedford. He then returned to Pennsylvania for a time, but in 1871 came to Holt County, Missouri, and here purchased an improved farm of sixty acres, for which he paid $40 per acre. Subsequently, after some years, he dis-posed of this property and moved to Russell County, Kansas, and there continued to reside until his death in 1890. Mr. Long was a democrat in his political views, and always took an active interest in the success of his party. He held various offices within the gift of the people and at one time was mayor of the town in which his last years were spent. While it is not remembered that he was a man of any professed religious faith, it is known that he was a firm believer in Christianity and that he was a generous supporter of movements making for morality, education and good citizenship. Mrs. Long died in 1909, the mother of nine children, of whom two are now deceased.

John Long received his education in the country schools and was brought up as a farmer's son, so that when he started upon his own career he chose the pursuits of the soil as his life's vocation. He was married in 1890 to Miss Capitola Artt, daughter of James Artt, and at that time settled on his present property, at that time a farm of 160 acres, which had been purchased by Mr. Artt from the original settler, one Hitchcock. To the original property Mr. Long has added from time to time, until he is now the owner of 400 acres, all under a good state of cultivation, and fully equipped with substantial buildings of Mr. Long's own erection. Because of the beautiful hills and groves of pine trees in this vicinity, Mr. Long has named this Pine Hill Farm, and the district school here has taken its name from this property. Mr. Long has devoted his energies to general farming, and has also been a successful breeder of livestock. He is an excellent agriculturist, and in business circles has won the reputation of being a man of strict integrity and honorable dealing.

In politics a democrat, Mr. Long has taken some active part in local affairs, and at the present time is serving capably as a member of the school board. His fraternal connection is with the Knights of Pythias. While not a member of any religious denomination, he has done his full share in supporting movements of the church. Two children have been born to Mr. and Mrs. Long: Helen and Lorene.

BERT E. PATTERSON. The most satisfying rewards of rural experience have compensated the untiring labors and well-directed efforts of Bert E. Patterson, who is known as one of Holt County's progressive and enterprising farmers, and the owner of 200 acres of well developed land. A resident of his present property since 1890, it has grown and developed under his management, and while he has been an extremely busy man with his private interests, he has still found the time and inclination to devote to community affairs, having thus gained the deserved reputation of being a public-spirited, stirring and helpful citizen.

Mr. Patterson was born on a farm located east of Oregon, Andrew County, Missouri, December 16, 1875, and is a son of George T. and Lizzie (Brady) Patterson. Henry Patterson, the grandfather of Bert E. Patterson, was born in Ireland, and as a young man emigrated to the United States. After a short time passed in the East, he turned his face Missouriward, and became one of the first thirteen citizens to settle in this part of Northwest Missouri. He was a rugged, sturdy and energetic pioneer, capable of bearing his share of work in the wild, rough days of the frontier, and through a life of industry was able to accumulate a competency. He outlived all of those who had accompanied him to Andrew County, and died at the ripe old age of eighty-three years. Mr. Patterson married Miss Canada Cobb, and among their children was George T. Patterson, who was born at Savannah, Andrew County, Missouri, July 6, 1848. He grew to manhood in his native community, and when he embarked upon his own career adopted the vocation of his father and became a farmer. For some years he was the owner of a property in Andrew County, east of Oregon, but in 1890 moved to Holt County, and here rounded out his long and industrious career. He was a skilled agriculturist, and as a citizen was held in the highest esteem in his community.

Bert E. Patterson was educated in the district schools of his native locality, and was reared to agricultural pursuits, which he adopted as his life work when he entered upon his own career. He was about twenty-two years of age when he came to his present property in Holt County, to which he has added from time to time until at present he is the owner of 200 acres of land, the greater part of which is under cultivation and very productive. He has a fine set of buildings, uses modern machinery in his work, and is daily demonstrating his right to be known as a member of that class of farmers who maintain a high agricultural standard in any community. While general farming has received the greater part of his attention, he is also an excellent judge of cattle, and his yearly shipments are large. Mr. Patterson has been somewhat interested in fraternal matters, being a member of the Woodmen of the World and the Independent Order of Odd Fellows, in the lodges of both of which orders he has numerous friends. With his family, he attends the United Brethren Church and heartily and generously supports its various movements. In political matters he is, like his father, a democrat, and has shown his ability as an official in the capacity of member of the school board, an office which he has held for a number of years.

Mr. Patterson married Miss Grace Limpp, daughter of John G. Limpp, and to this union there has been born one daughter: Marie.

H. A. ARMACK. Material prosperity has long been in the possession of H. A. Armack, whose home is a fine farm near Mound City. Mr. Armack has earned all that he has ever acquired. At the time of his marriage he possessed nothing more than courage and determination to give a good account of himself, and had many years of hard work before getting a foundation under his feet. He now owns what may be considered a competence, in a first-class farm, improved with good dwelling house and barn, and the well cultivated fields, the well kept stock, all indicate thrifty and efficient character of the proprietor.

H. A. Armack was born in Butler County, Ohio, on August 24, 1857, a son of August and Agnes (Holle) Armack. His parents were married in the State of Ohio, and their family comprised eleven children, two of whom are now deceased. From Ohio the family moved to Welch County, Indiana, and a number of years later made the journey by covered wagon across the states of Illinois and Missouri to the northwestern section of this state, first settling at Nichols Grove. August Armack, though providing fairly well for his family, was a man of modest circumstances, and spent his years in Northwest Missouri as a renter. He died about ten years ago.

Mr. H. A. Armack got his early education in the Indiana public schools and also attended school for a time after coming to Missouri. He was about fourteen years of age when he arrived in Northwest Missouri. In 1884, in Bolt County, Mr. Armack married Alice Blair, daughter of Uriah and Evaline (Mackey) Blair. Her father died in 1907. Mrs. Armack was one of a family of seven brothers and sisters, of whom two are deceased. Her mother is now living at Mound City. Mr. Armack and wife are the parents of three children: Arthur, who died in infancy; Alfred, who was born March 17, 1886, and married Ida Clark, daughter of Worth Clark of Holt County; and Prudie, born in October, 1887, a graduate of the Mound City High School, and a successful and popular teacher for four years until her marriage to Frank Fleming, daughter of James and Margaret Fleming. There is one grandchild, Durbin Fleming.

Mr. Armack on coming to Northwest Missouri spent several years as a shoemaker, but finally drifted into farming, and after his marriage spent about eight or ten years as a renter before getting his present estate. He and his wife had only a team and a cow after their marriage, and worked hard to get the nucleus which they invested in their present place of eighty acres. At that time there were no improvements but a fence, and Mr. Armack has since placed good buildings, has cultivated the fields without impoverishing the soil, and is now in a position where he can take farm life somewhat leisurely, having a hired hand to do much of the labor. As to his relations with the community, Mr. Armack is a member of the Evangelical Church in which his father served as a trustee. He has himself served for a number of years as a director of the school board. Mr. Armack is affiliated with the Modern Woodmen of America.

Mrs. Armack represents one of the oldest families in Northwest Missouri. Her grandfather, John Blair, is usually credited as being the first white settler in Holt County. He came in 1839, and settled on a farm that is now owned by Jim Collins. When the gold discoveries on the Pacific Coast started the California exodus of 1849, he joined in the rush for the fields, and died while on the journey across the plains. Mrs. Armack's father was also a California forty-niner, but returned to Holt County, and lived on a farm here until his removal to Kansas in 1885. Mrs. Armack's father was married in Pike County, Missouri. She and her brothers and sisters were all born in Holt County, and she is now the only one of her generation left in this section. Her father was a member of the Christian Church and one time served as school director.

W. M. GIBSON. A family that has been identified with Holt County since pioneer times is represented by W. M. Gibson, whose own career has been worked out in this county, and who is one of the substantial farmers and young men of influence who are carrying on the progressive movement which was initiated by their forefathers during pioneer times.

W. M. Gibson was born March 5, 1870, in Holt County. His parents were Theodore and Nancy J. (Hanks) Gibson. Theodore Gibson was born also in Holt County. It was the grandfather who established the family name and fortune in Holt County, and he was a man of unusual prominence and influence, and had the distinction of serving as the first county judge in Holt County. Grandfather Gibson died in Missouri and was laid to rest in Holt County. Theodore Gibson also spent his career in this section of Northwest Missouri, and during the war was a soldier in the Thirty-third Missouri Regiment. He died November 21, 1888. He was an active member of the Christian Church. The farm now occupied by W. M. Gibson was largely improved and brought into its present condition by Theodore Gibson. The widow of Theodore Gibson is still living.

The children of these parents are named briefly as follows: W. M., born March 5, 1870; Frank E., born November 7, 1871; Edgar A., born December 26, 1873; James T., born September 25, 1878; Cora A., born July 27, 1881; and Lurthel, born January 11, 1886. All were born in Holt County. In politics the male members of the family have usually voted as republicans.

WILLIAM HUIATT. During the entire fifty years of his life, William Huiatt has been a resident of Holt County, and of that part of this prosperous community in the vicinity of Oregon and Maitland. He has witnessed its development from an uncultivated, unproductive and unattractive stretch of country into a fertile, prosperous and handsome farm-

ing community, a center of agricultural activity and the home of some
of the most substantial men in Northwest Missouri, and has borne his
full share in the work of development which has brought this change
about. Mr. Huiatt was born on a farm in Holt County, located southeast of Oregon, November 20, 1864, and is a son of Daniel and Martha
(Ashworth) Huiatt.

The Huiatt family is one of the old and honored pioneer organizations of Holt County, having been founded here some time during the
early '40s by John Huiatt, the paternal grandfather of William, who
brought his children, including Daniel, from the home in Kokomo,
Indiana. The paternal grandfather, William Ashworth, came about this
time with his family from Kentucky, settling in the same vicinity.
Daniel Huiatt, who was born July 1, 1830, at Kokomo, Indiana, was
still a lad when he accompanied his parents on the long overland journey,
and here he has passed his entire life in the pursuits of the soil, and
still survives at the advanced age of eighty-four years. Mrs. Huiatt
died January 3, 1912, in Holt County, having been the mother of thirteen
children, all born here. Mr. Huiatt was formerly a member of the Independent Order of Odd Fellows, but as he reached his later years resigned
his membership.

William Huiatt grew up on the old homestead and received his
education in the public schools. At the time of his marriage, in 1889,
he settled on his present property, on which the buildings had all been
erected, although the land to the north and east was all still unimproved
and in prairie. The tract just to the north, a property of 120 acres in
section 29, owned by Judge Leeper, was the last property to be purchased and improved. While he found a number of improvements here,
Mr. Huiatt broke the greater part of this land, and from time to time
has added to the equipment and buildings, so that he has today a
thoroughly up-to-date farm in every respect. He owns in all about five
hundred and twenty acres, all under cultivation, and devotes his land to
the raising of general produce and the growing of stock. While new
innovations appeal to him, as they do to every progressive, thinking
man, he has a strain of practicality that causes him to be thoroughly
assured of the value of a method before he adopts it. Mr. Huiatt is a
member of the Knights of Pythias and the Modern Woodmen of America
at Maitland, and has numerous friends in both orders. He has taken
some interest in republican politics, and the high esteem in which he is
held by his fellow-citizens is evidenced by the fact that he has been frequently elected to offices of public trust, serving as a member of the
school board for a number of years, and being clerk of his district for
sixteen years.

On March 3, 1889, Mr. Huiatt was united in marriage with Miss
Julia Noellsch, of Holt County, daughter of John and Anna (Damman)
Noellsch, well known and highly esteemed residents of this county, where
they have carried on agricultural pursuits for many years. To Mr. and
Mrs. Huiatt there have come two children: Chauncey, born March 21,
1893; and Daniel, born April 5, 1897, both on the present farm. The
sons have been well educated and thoroughly trained in farming, and
are now capably assisting their father in his labors on the homestead
place.

WILLIAM CAWOOD. The late William Cawood was for many years
a resident of Andrew County, and when he died, May 18, 1912, the
community lost one of the most charitable and honored of its citizens.
During his long and busy life he had been successful in the accumulation
of a large estate, being known as one of the most prominent farmers and

Wm Cawood

heavy landowners of Northwest Missouri, but he left behind him also something more desirable—a name beyond reproach and to be remembered, as an inspiration, by his surviving children and widow.

William Cawood was born at Whitesville, Andrew County, Missouri, in October, 1842, and was a son of Berry and Lucy (Bailey) Cawood. His parents, natives of Kentucky, came to Northwest Missouri at an early date, settling in the vicinity of Whitesville, where the father was engaged in agricultural pursuits during the remainder of his life. Of the children of Berry and Lucy Cawood four grew to maturity: Mary, deceased, who was the wife of Young Howard; William, of this review; John, who died young; and George, a resident of Nebraska.

The public schools of Whitesville furnished William Cawood with his education, and he grew up amid rural surroundings, remaining on the home farm until reaching the age of nineteen years. At that time he set forth on a journey across the plains to the West, a journey fraught with much danger, and spent eight or nine years in the mountain states, when he returned to the vicinity of his birth. The remainder of his life was devoted to farming and stockraising in Andrew County, he making a specialty of raising cattle and hogs. Through good business management, foresight and judgment, he was able to accumulate a large property, and at the time of his death owned 1,219 acres of good land, well cultivated, fertile, and boasting of modern improvements of the most substantial character. When the Great Western Railroad put its tracks through this section, they passed over section 5, Platte Township, where was located a part of Mr. Cawood's farm, and when the station was erected here it was named Cawood in his honor, this having been the start of what is now a thriving little village of 100 people. Mr. Cawood never received any money by inheritance, and what he accomplished was through his own efforts, aided by those of his faithful wife and children, to whom he was ever a kind and indulgent husband and father. Among his neighbors and fellow-townsmen he was known as a generous-hearted wholesouled man, ever ready with his charity and always willing to contribute to the welfare of individual or community. His numerous friends mourned his loss, and he is still remembered as one whom the county could ill afford to spare. His political affiliations were with the democratic party. On Saturday evening, May 18, 1912, Mr. Cawood left home not feeling well, to drive an animal from his meadow, lying east of Cawood, that belonged to one of his neighbors. Some parties from Cawood were watching him from the stockyards, and presently saw him dismount, an unusual thing for him to do, as he was a splendid rider for a man of his age and seldom left the saddle even when conversing with friends. The parties from town, suspecting that something was wrong, waited for a reasonable time and then started for the spot, where they found Mr. Cawood dead, the physician who was called pronouncing the cause of death as hemorrhage of the lungs.

Mr. Cawood was married January 25, 1872, to Miss Flora Hunt, who was born at Whitesville, Missouri, in 1854, a daughter of Orlando and Lettis (Poppliwell) Hunt. Mr. Hunt was born in Ohio and as a young man accompanied his parents to Missouri, the remainder of his life being passed on a farm in Gentry County, where he died in 1901, at the age of eighty years. Mrs. Hunt was born in Kentucky, and came to Missouri as a young woman, and still survives her husband, her home being at Stanbury, Missouri, where she still lives, hale and hearty at the age of eighty-one years. Mr. and Mrs. Hunt had three children: Flora, who is Mrs. Cawood; Cora, who is the widow of James Hamaker, of Stanbury; and Lyman, a resident of Oklahoma. To Mr. and Mrs.

Cawood there were born ten children, namely: Franklin O., of Hull, Iowa; C. Alice, of Ravenswood, Missouri; Ovid L., who lives at Cawood, Missouri; Annie, who is the wife of William House, of Cawood, Missouri; Albia C., who is the wife of Thomas House, of Cawood, Missouri; Minnie, who lives at home; Myrtle, who is the wife of V. C. Taylor, and lives with her mother, Myrtle and Minnie being twins; Clara, who is the wife of J. D. Hannah, of Cawood, Missouri; and twin sons, who died in infancy.

THOMAS KENNISH. The Kennish family has been well known in Holt County for more than forty years, and in the old home in Liberty Township Thomas Kennish as a son of the original settlers still lives. Farming has been the chief line of business activity of this family, and in that community the name signifies material prosperity, honorable business and civic relations, and they are good neighbors and workers for the community welfare.

Thomas Kennish was born in the Isle of Man on September 14, 1869, a son of William and Catherine (Callow) Kennish. The family came to America and settled in Holt County in 1870, where William Kennish acquired and developed a fine farm of 240 acres. This homestead has since been divided, and Thomas Kennish has 120 acres, and occupies the house in which his parents lived until their death. The Kennish farm was originally. all prairie, and the breaking of the virgin sod and the cultivation of fields and the other material improvements are all the result of the work of father and sons.

Thomas Kennish was married in Holt County, June 11, 1902, to Jessie Lawrence, daughter of H. B. and Mary (Curry) Lawrence. They have one child, Thomas, born April 27, 1909. Mr. Kennish is affiliated with the Independent Order of Odd Fellows at Mound City and in politics is a republican.

ALFRED W. COLLISON. The career of Alfred W. Collison reflects practical and useful ideals and its range of activities has included farming, merchandising and the promotion of education. In the achievement of his personal success, he has not been unmindful of the duties of citizenship, and his assistance has never been refused to movements which have promised the betterment of his community in any way. Mr. Collison has been a life-long resident of Holt County, having been born on a farm one mile east of his present property, July 25, 1864, a son of Richard and Mary Ann (Rollings) Collison.

About the year 1855 or 1856, Richard Collison came to Holt County, and engaged in the boot and shoe business at Forrest City prior to removing to the vicinity of Maitland, at that time known as Whig Valley. The first farm on which he located was to some extent under cultivation, but subsequently he bought several unimproved farms, and brought them to a state of cultivation. This country at that time was but thinly populated, and the few roads which crossed the country were designated as "ridge" roads. Since that time, however, Mr. Collison has witnessed changes that have completely transformed this region, and has himself borne a full share in bringing about this development. He still survives, in hearty old age, now retired from active life, being eighty-four years of age, while Mrs. Collison, who also survives, is seventy-nine years old. They have lived on their present farm since 1876, and are widely and favorably known throughout this part of the county, being universally esteemed for their many excellences of mind and heart. There were nine children in their family, of whom five are now living: Joseph R.;

Edwin; Nellie, who became the wife of Charles Botley; Alice, who became the wife of Edward Kinnish; and Alfred W.

The early education of Alfred W. Collison was secured in the public schools of his native vicinity, this being supplemented by a course in the agricultural college at Manhattan, Kansas. He spent his boyhood days in agricultural pursuits, but at the age of about twenty-three turned his attention to mercantile business, being associated in partnership with his brother, Joseph R., as merchants at Maitland. In this line Mr. Collison continued to be engaged from 1888 until 1895, in the latter year selling out to his brother and his nephew, Ralph. Later, associated with Mr. Graves, Mr. Collison built the broad-gauge store at Maitland, with which he was identified until 1906, and in that year returned to agricultural interests, taking over the management of the homestead farm. The residence now standing on this property was built prior to Mr. Collison's taking charge, but all the other buildings have been erected under his management. The property now contains 160 acres of well-cultivated land, of which the greater part is given over to general farming, although Mr. Collison has also met with much success as a cattle raiser. He has succeeded in firmly establishing himself in the confidence of his fellow citizens as a thoroughly reliable business man, and those who have had dealings with him will vouch for his integrity and honorable dealing. Mr. Collison has made no profession of religious faith. He is a member of the Maitland Lodge of the Modern Woodmen of America. In political matters, he was a republican until 1912, when at the birth of the progressive party he transferred his support to the new organization. At the present time he is capably serving as a member of the school board.

Mr. Collison married Miss Blanche DeBord, daughter of William DeBord, and they have three children: Erma, who was born in 1899; William, born in 1902; and Mary, born in 1905, all on the present farm.

JERRY DUNKELBERGER. In Holt County, Mr. Dunkelberger is one of the men who have witnessed and assisted in the transformation of a wilderness into a landscape of splendid farms, connected with improved highways, with schools, churches, and all the facilities of the twentieth century civilization. Mr. Dunkelberger has resided in Liberty Township of Holt County for forty-five years, and his neighbors pay him a high tribute for his industry and good citizenship.

Jerry Dunkelberger was born in Northumberland County, Pennsylvania, August 16, 1844, a son of John and Lydia (Bysel) Dunkelberger, who spent their lives in Pennsylvania. Jerry Dunkelberger was one of fifteen children, and was reared and educated in Pennsylvania. He later moved to Michigan, and was married in Berrien Springs of that state to Lydia Shunkwiler, a daughter of Henry.

The date of Mr. Dunkelberger's arrival in Holt County was 1869, and in that year he located on a portion of the land which is his present farm. It was entirely wild, no plow had been set in the ground, and there was a heavy task confronting him in clearing off the woods and brush and converting the soil to a productive state. Mr. Dunkelberger now owns 100 acres, and all the improvements in buildings, cultivation and farm facilities are the result of his long continued labors.

Mr. and Mrs. Dunkelberger have six children: G. W., Cora E., William F., Iuda May, C. F., and Earl, all of whom were born on the old homestead in Holt County. Mr. Dunkelberger is a member of the Independent Order of Odd Fellows Lodge at Mound City, and in politics is a republican. His active and serviceable citizenship is indicated in his work as a member of the school board, and he has always been found on the side of progressive movements.

J. M. W. CANNON, M. D. For more than thirty years Doctor Cannon has quietly performed his round of professional service and duties at Kidder and vicinity, and is not only one of the oldest but one of the most highly esteemed practitioners in that section of the state. A physician cannot live and practice his calling for thirty years or more in one locality without possessing a faithful character and a high ability and skill, qualities which have contributed to make the splendid type of family physician known both in literature and in actual life.

Dr. J. M. W. Cannon is a Pennsylvanian by birth, born in Westmoreland County January 21, 1851. He comes of a Scotch-Irish family, the stock which was so prominent in the early settlement and later development of that section of Pennsylvania. His father, Robert B. Cannon, was also a native of Pennsylvania, and his wife was Juliet Willson, born in Pennsylvania, a daughter of Rev. J. A. Willson, a minister of the Reformed Presbyterian Church, a faith to which practically all the members of these families subscribed while in Pennsylvania. Robert B. Cannon and wife had four children. One of the sons is a successful school man.

When Doctor Cannon was a child his parents moved out to Louisa County, Iowa, in 1854, and settled in a community which was still on the frontier of civilization. The father was a preacher, and died at the age of seventy-nine years in Chicago. He was an abolitionist and though active as a republican was a great admirer of Horace Greeley. The mother died at the age of thirty-five.

Doctor Cannon grew up in Iowa, lived on a farm for a number of years, and was educated in the public schools, and subsequently taught in Wisconsin. In 1878 he was graduated from the Hahnemann College of Medicine and Surgery in Philadelphia, and in the same year came out to Northwest Missouri and located at Kidder. In the course of a few years Doctor Cannon had a well established reputation over all that section of country, and his buggy was regularly seen driving over the roads for a radius of many miles. Doctor Cannon has kept in touch with the modern advancement of medical science and practice, and in recent years has enjoyed a large office practice and that together with the improvement of highways and other facilities for traveling have relieved him of the heavier burdens which he carried during his first year of practice.

Doctor Cannon married in Lorain County, Ohio, Mary Foote, daughter of Rev. W. W. Foote, of Ohio. Their children are Eunice, a music teacher living in Kidder; Mary, a graduate of Kidder Institute; Willson Brookes, who finished the course in the Kidder Institute in 1914 and is now in Chicago; Harold R., aged thirteen; and Robert M., aged eleven. The children have all been given the best of educational advantages and opportunities. Doctor Cannon has been active in church affairs, and for twenty-five years has served as superintendent of the Sunday School.

JOHN ALFRED LILLY. This particular branch of the Lilly family has a country home, which once visited is not soon forgotten, in Grant Township of Harrison County, on rural delivery route No. 2 out of Ridgeway. The name has been identified with this section since before the war. It has been associated with some of the most progressive features of farming enterprise, and as home-makers and people of intrinsic culture and upholders of morality and high ideals few families in Northwest Missouri have a better record.

John Alfred Lilly was born in Livingston County, Missouri, April 15, 1860, but has lived in Harrison County since 1861, and his present farm contains land that was entered by his grandfather as early as 1856. The family came to Missouri about 1850 and first located in Livingston County. Grandfather John Lilly had lived in several states before he came to Missouri. He was born in Maryland in 1796, was reared in Virginia, and when a young man moved to Park County, Indiana, where he married Rebecca Storms, moving later to Ross County, Ohio, and they subsequently, after the birth of some children, moved to Illinois, where she died in Hancock County. In that state he married for his second wife Rebecca Matthews, and in moving out to Missouri they came by wagon and team to Livingston County. The grandfather died in 1863, and his second wife died in Jamesport. The children of the first union were: Joseph M., who died in Livingston County; Elizabeth, who married John T. Carns and died in Jasper County, Missouri; Mary A., who married John Browning and died in Hancock County, Illinois; and John, who is sketched in the following paragraphs. The second wife became the mother of: Perry H., of Jamesport; Theophilus, who died as a Union soldier in the Civil war; Milton, who died in McDonald County near Indian Springs, Missouri; and Florence, who married Henry Lee and lives at Hutchinson, Kansas.

One of the venerable and highly esteemed old citizens of Harrison County is John Lilly, son of the above John and father of John Alfred. He was born December 14, 1833, in Ross County, Ohio, and has passed the age of four score. Most of his youth was spent in Hancock County, Illinois, where he attended country schools. In early life he became a farmer, and followed it all through his vigorous career. He came to manhood in Northwest Missouri, and in 1861 enlisted in the army at Bethany in Capt. John A. Page's company of the Sixth Missouri, under Col. E. C. Catherwood. His command saw service in Arkansas, Missouri, and Indian Territory, was at Fort Smith when it was captured from the enemy, and was in the fight at Newtonia, Arkansas. He was mustered out at the close of the war, and escaped wounds and capture.

While he has spent the last nineteen years retired at Ridgeway, John Lilly has achievements to his credit as a farmer such as few other men can parallel. He had a knack of succeeding often where others failed, and came to own and control 600 acres of land and at one time was the largest fruit grower in Harrison County. He set out extensive orchards of apples, pears, peaches, plums and cherries, and also derived revenues from stock raising. His father before him had whig affiliations, and his own support was given regularly to the republican candidates, though in 1912 he followed many other republicans to the support of the progressive leader, and has since reconsidered the action and is now faithful to fundamental republican doctrines.

John Lilly married Artemissa Westfall, who was born at Quincy, Illinois, a daughter of Alfred Westfall. She died on the old Lilly homestead in Harrison County October 21, 1892. Her children are: Angeline, now the wife of Lycurgus Edwards of Howell County, Missouri, first married Newton Beeson, who was the father of her children; Jane married Joel Harrold, of Blythedale, Missouri; Elizabeth is the wife of Alfred C. Sellers of Ridgeway; John Alfred is sketched in following paragraphs; Joseph Milton died at Ridgeway, leaving a family; Clara R. married Caleb Young of Ridgeway; Catherine married Woodson Baber of Jamesport; Rose is the wife of Norman Johnson on the old Lilly homestead of Harrison County; and Charles died in childhood. For his second wife John Lilly married Alice Burwell, who is the mother of Vesper Ann, a teacher in Harrison County.

John Alfred Lilly grew up on the farm that he still owns, and his education came from the neighboring district school. Among the pupils in that school then was Theophilus Carns, later a prominent lawyer of Kansas City, but most of them became farmers and several of them are still living in Harrison County. Mr. Lilly was with his parents until of age, and the day after his marriage in Ridgeway moved out to his present farm, with which all the memories and associations of his mature life are identified. The land, when first occupied by himself and Mrs. Lilly, was a piece of wild prairie. It had never produced a crop under cultivation, and the house they lived in for several years was a single room 14 by 15 feet. During the eight years they called that home all their children but one were born.

As a farmer Mr. Lilly has been both a grain and stock man. By purchase and additions he now owns 460 acres in this community. Twenty-five acres are planted in all varieties of fruit, and in some respects that is the most interesting feature of the farmstead. They have the much talked of Himalaya berry, which in 1914 bore its first crop in this country. This fruit resembles the blackberry, it grows on a trellis like a grape, is perfectly hardy, and bears in clusters from June to October, the fruit always coming through the leaves to the light. In spite of the extreme drought of 1914 it surprised its owners by its prolific fruiting and bearing. The family has made a specialty of flowers, annuals and perennials, and their home is a bower of beauty and delight to those who know the flowers, shrubs and trees which grow in profusion. The lawn is shaded with maple, elm and box elder, while in the garden are found both the chestnut and the white walnut, the latter a disappointment so far as fruiting is concerned. One valuable item of their experience is that by using salt in the treatment of pear trees every year, they bear better, smoother and larger fruit, and with less blight on the tree trunk.

As a stock man Mr. Lilly has been breeding Herefords for fifteen years. He keeps up his register and is a member of the Hereford Association of the United States. "Old Defender" of the Comstock herd was the sire of much of his stock, and he has kept the blood of prize winners circulating through his own stock. The poultry yard of the Lilly homestead contains the Toulouse goose, the Hamburg chicken and also the pure Plymouth Rock and White Orpington, Pekin ducks, Pearl guineas, Bourbon red and slate turkeys. It is a fact that will interest many that the revenues from eggs and chickens average about four hundred dollars annually.

In his civic and social relations Mr. Lilly has been consistently a republican, though voting for Roosevelt in 1912. He declined the nomination for representative of his county in the Legislature, and for many years served on the school board. For twenty-two years he has been an elder in the Christian Church, and with the aid of his good wife has trained his children in the same faith. Their home has always been the home of the ministers and the orphan and no one is ever turned from their door who needs their help.

Mr. and Mrs. Lilly began their united careers a little more than thirty years ago, after their marriage in Ridgeway on November 25, 1883. In addition to the cares of a home and family, Mrs. Lilly has shown her ability and energy in acquiring a more than local reputation as a journalist. After her marriage she took to writing for the county papers, and finally became more ambitious and skillful and has contributed to such magazines as McClure's, McCall's, the Century, the

Brown Book, church papers like the Christian Evangelist and the Christian Standard, and the Sunday school journal, Front Rank. Mrs. Lilly was formerly a public school teacher, and for many years has been a deaconess in her church. She is also a graduate of the White Cross School of Nursing at. Jamestown, New York.

Mrs. Lilly was born December 25, 1862, at LaFayette, Wisconsin, her maiden name being Emma Burwell. Her parents were Jedediah and Lucinda (Wilcox) Burwell. The former was born in Westmoreland County, Pennsylvania, September 1, 1826, in 1859 went to LaFayette County, Wisconsin, where he married, and ten years later moved to Missouri, locating in Daviess County and in 1872 moving to Harrison County. A cooper by trade, he followed farming in Missouri, and died January 25, 1891. His first wife was a Miss Haver, and her children were: Sarah, who married John Ethridge of Monroe, Wisconsin; Anna, wife of Edmond Opdyke of Ridgeway; Henry C. of Reynolds, Nebraska; Ella, who married J. T. Travis, of Bethany; James H., of Loup City, Nebraska. Lucinda Wilcox, the second wife, was born in September, 1832, in Pittston, Pennsylvania, and died at the home of Mr. and Mrs. Lilly December 22, 1912. By her marriage to Mr. Burwell she had the following children: John, who died in infancy; Mrs. Lilly; Aaron G., of Lane, Kansas; Melissa, wife of George Jones, of May, Oklahoma; Ira B., of Civil Bend, Missouri; Lewis, who died in infancy; and Charles H., of Shattuck, Oklahoma; also an infant son who died at birth.

The children of Mr. and Mrs. Lilly are: John Ralph, a farmer near the old home, married Ida Reeder and their children are Clarence Leroy and Ernest Raymond; Nellie is the wife of Charles M. Reeder of Ridgeway, a Baptist minister, and their children are Esther Charlotte, Esta Claire and Charles Washington; Charles Burwell married Lelie Henry, lives on the home farm; and Jeanne and Joseph Westfall are also at home. The daughter, Mrs. Reeder, was educated in the Bethany High School and was a teacher in the public schools until her marriage. Miss Jeanne finished the four-year course in the Ridgeway High School at the age of fifteen, and stood second in a class of ten, later attended the Warrensburg Normal, and for three years has held a first grade certificate and is now working rapidly to the goal of obtaining a life certificate in Missouri. The two sons, Charles and Joseph, both quit school after the course in the Ridgeway high, and all the sons are enterprising young farmers.

E. FRANK DARBY. Anyone familiar with the business and community life of the City of Cameron during the last thirty years will recognize the name of E. Frank Darby, who was one of Cameron's most substantial men. His death on July 9, 1909, took away one of the strongest and influential figures from the community. For many years he was a merchant and his business habits were so methodical that it is difficult to think of the business community without his active presence. Outside of business he took a keen interest in civic affairs, but was especially devoted to his home and family. The fine Darby residence in the south end of town has been a conspicuous landmark in the little city for many years and the family have always been among the leaders in social affairs.

E. Frank Darby came to Cameron in 1880, and for twenty-five years was a member of the harness firm of Ford & Darby, which did the largest business of its kind in Cameron. Mr. Darby was a native of New York State and was born in Oneida County September 27, 1852. His family were of substantial Quaker stock, of English origin, and furnished soldiers to the war of the Revolution, the War of 1812 and good citizens in every generation. Mr. Darby was the son of Edward and Helen Darby. The parents moved from New York to Maryland in 1865, and in 1892 came to Missouri, where they spent the rest of their lives. The late Mr. Darby had two brothers who are living in the Northwest, owners of fruit ranches, another whose home is in Mendota, Illinois, and is a railway mail clerk, while a sister lives in St. Joseph.

E. Frank Darby was married October 18, 1883, to Ella P. Newberry, a daughter of Hon. Oliver P. Newberry, who died in 1874 at the age of forty-three. He was a prominent and successful lawyer at Cameron, and was a brother of the late Hon. Walter C. Newberry, of a family long prominent in commercial and public affairs in this county. Walter C. Newberry gained the rank of brigadier general by service in the Civil war, became identified with Chicago business affairs in 1876, had the management of the extensive Newberry estate in that city, held the office of postmaster at Chicago and was also a member of Congress. Mrs. Darby's mother was Lydia McCorkle, who was born in Clay County, Missouri, in 1834, and belongs to the prominent McCorkle family, one of whose members, Judge McCorkle, laid out the town of Cameron.

Mr. and Mrs. Darby were the parents of four children: Helen, who finished her education at Monticello College, Godfrey, Illinois; Walter Newberry, one of Cameron's most popular younger business men, who was educated in the local high school, in the University of Missouri at Columbia and in the University of Michigan at Ann Arbor; Cornelia and Amasa Franklin, deceased. Mrs. Darby and her family still occupy the old homestead in Cameron, and the son, Walter, is now the active head of the family.

RALPH O. WOODWARD. In the community of Cainsville in Harrison County, one of the oldest citizens is Ralph O. Woodward, whose home has been there since childhood for more than sixty years. Both his father and grandfather were early settlers in this vicinity, and as several of his own children are residents here, the activities and influences of four generations of the Woodward family have contributed to the growth and betterment of this locality. Ralph O. Woodward was a soldier during the war, had considerable experience following that struggle in the life of the Western plains, but the greater part of his life has been identified with the quieter vocations of teaching, milling and farming. His grandfather was Rev. Chesley Woodward, a Baptist minister, who moved from Kentucky and was one of the frontiersmen in the wooded country of Decatur County, Indiana. After his son had gone to Missouri in 1852 he followed on and spent about twenty years of his life in this state until his death when more than seventy years of age. Besides farming he did religious work, and preached for the Cainsville congregation and other churches in this part of Missouri. While a man of no education, he was a ready speaker and a thorough student of the Bible. Chesley Woodward married Elizabeth Blankenship, and both are buried in the Cainsville Cemetery. She was a devout woman, had the Christian graces, and exemplified them in her relations with her own family and her neighbors. Their children were: Reverend John, father of Ralph O.; Nellie, who married a Mr. Fuqua; Margaret, who married Peleg Baker; Dolly, who married a Mr. Fuqua and died at Mercer County, Missouri; Chesley, who died at Fullerton, California; Susan, who married James T. Cooper; James M., who spent his life as a farmer and preacher in the vicinity of Cainsville.

Rev. John Woodward, of the second generation, was born in Indiana January 11, 1821. He had few opportunities when a youth, and made

himself what he was from sheer force of will. He had the gift above
the average man without training preparatory to appearing in public,
and during his period of church work had missions in different sections
of the country, and rode about on horseback to preach and instruct in
the word of God. He was moderator of the West Fork Baptist Association for many years. It was in 1852 that he left Decatur County, Indiana, crossed the intervening states by wagon and joined a small colony
of Indiana people who had settled near the edge of Harrison County.
Rev. John Woodward was one of the men who helped to clear the forest
and brush and cultivate the land of Harrison County, and carried on his
work as a minister in the Missionary Baptist faith in addition to his
labors as a home-maker. At the opening of the war he was a Union
democrat, and subsequently became republican. During the war he
served as chaplain in the Third Missouri State Militia, but before his
regular enlistment had been among those called out to secure the peace
of the country. He took part in the battle of Springfield on January
8, 1863, and his regiment was so much reduced by losses that it was
distributed among the Sixth and Seventh regiments of the militia, and
after that the Third Regiment ceased to exist. Rev. John Woodward
passed through his military experiences without wounds or capture.
Always a man of strong temperance views, he was one of the early
organizers of the Good Templars movement in this section of Missouri.
He had no aspirations for office, and before his death left the republican
party, and again joined the democrats, whom he had supported until
after the Douglas campaign of 1860. For many years he was identified
with the Masonic order, having joined the lodge at Princeton, Missouri.

Rev. John Woodward married Julia A. Kennedy, daughter of a
New York man who settled in Decatur County, Indiana. Mrs. Woodward died February 16, 1893, and her husband December 17, 1898. Their
children were: Ralph O.; Mary Elizabeth, who married T. E. Salee and
died at Cainsville; Chesley B., who spent many years as a banker and
died at Cainsville; Rhoda B., who married G. R. Wilson of Cainsville;
Susan J., who married Lewis M. Wickersham and lives at Cainsville;
Eliza Catherine, who became the wife of John W. Burton of Gallatin;
Nancy E., who married Thomas Harris and lives in Tacoma, Washington.

Ralph O. Woodward was born in Decatur County, Indiana, December 3, 1842, and was about ten years of age when the family located at
the edge of Harrison County in 1852. His formal instruction in schools
came largely from the institutions of learning supported in the vicinity
of Cainsville during the decade of the '50s. The longest term of school
he ever attended was one of six months, and like both father and grandfather, he suffered from lack of opportunities. These difficulties only
spurred him to greater efforts, and in spite of early embarrassments in
the matter of education he qualified as a teacher, and for sixteen years
taught in country schools and at the same time kept up his farming.
In 1877 he taught one of the two departments of the Cainsville school,
and his last work in that line was at the Ross Schoolhouse in Harrison
County. On his marriage he established a home in Mercer County, just
northeast of Cainsville, and in 1867 moved from there to Daviess County
and lived near old Bancroft for ten years. After returning to Harrison
County he spent a few years in Cainsville, where he bought an interest
in the old Peter Cain mill. He finally left milling, trading his interests
for a farm, and resumed that industry six miles southwest of Cainsville. His last move was to a portion of the old Woodward homestead, where he lives today.

On May 25, 1863, when twenty-one years of age, Mr. Woodward
entered the army in Company M of the Sixth Missouri State Militia,

under Captain McAfee and Colonel King. Most of his service was in Missouri, and in October, 1863, he was captured at Neosho, when his entire company was taken by Jo Shelby's troops, but he was paroled the same day, October 4th, and left at Neosho. He and his comrades found their way back to Springfield, camped there during the winter, and were then rearmed and reenlisted as veterans on July 20, 1864, in Company D of the Thirteenth Missouri Cavalry under Captain Mayo and Colonel Catherwood. After his second enlistment Mr. Woodward was quartermaster sergeant of his company and was mustered out as sergeant-major of the regiment at Leavenworth, Kansas, January 11, 1866. When the great war between the North and South had ended his regiment was ordered west to join an Indian expedition, but after reaching Denver it was found their services were not required. On their return they crossed the plains in the dead of winter on horseback and in wagons, and met no resistance either going or coming. They saw some of the evidences of Indian massacre and destruction of property in the ashes of a stage coach, but had no actual encounters with the red men. The company was discharged as soon as papers could be made out and Mr. Woodward was paid off at St. Louis.

His political record covers almost the entire period of the existence of the republican party. While in the war he cast his first presidential vote for Abraham Lincoln, second election, and has ever since affiliated with the republican party. He has filled township office as assessor and trustee, and during one term as justice of the peace. Since thirteen years of age he has been a member of the Baptist Church, has served as church clerk and for two terms was clerk of the West Fork Baptist Association. He is a past grand of the Independent Order of Odd Fellows and was a Good Templar during the existence of that organization at Cainsville. On October 17, 1884, when the Cainsville Post, No. 216, G. A. R., was organized, he became one of its members, and has always kept up his interest among his old comrades.

Mr. Woodward has been three times married. On July 7, 1864, Nancy E. Moss became his wife. Her father, Marcellus Moss, was a pioneer of Mercer County. The children of that marriage were: Leona A., wife of J. W. Welden of Gilman, Missouri; Edgar E. of Arkoe, Missouri; William H., of Denver, Colorado; and Maud, wife of Mr. Feltz. The second wife was Jeanette Girdner, who had no children. Mr. Woodward afterwards married Christina Pontius, daughter of Joseph and M. M. Pontius. Mrs. Woodward died November 2, 1907, leaving: Avis, who graduated from the Kirksville Normal School and is the wife of L. L. St. Clair of Caruthersville, Missouri, where both are teachers; Miss Olive B., who was educated in the Cainsville schools, the University of Missouri and the State Normal at Kirksville, from which she holds a life certificate to teach, and is now a teacher in the Cainsville schools; and Miss Ruth O., who is a member of the class of 1916 in the Cainsville High School.

ROBERT WILEY ALLARDICE. One of the best known business men of Trenton is Robert W. Allardice. A Scotchman born and bred, reared in an industrial community noted for its coal mines and iron works, he came to the United States in youth, and after some years spent in the coal industry of the East came to Trenton to take a hand in the development and working of the coal deposits here. For a number of years he was a practical mine operator, but his chief business at present is as a coal, grain and hay merchant.

Robert Wiley Allardice was born October 12, 1862, at Kilwinning,

Scotland, a place famous for its iron works. His parents were William and Mary (Wiley) Allardice, both natives of Scotland, where his father was long identified with the coal industry. The maternal grandfather was a structural engineer, and acquired considerable wealth and prominence. The family home is Irvin, situated four miles west of Kilwinning. Mr. Allardice had an uncle, John Allardice, who was an officer in the British army and saw active service during the Indian mutiny.

Mr. Allardice grew up in his native land, attended the common schools and after graduating from the Naper high school of Kilwinning emigrated to the United States in 1881. He found employment in the coal mines at Midway, Pennsylvania, and in 1882 engaged in mining at Montgomery, West Virginia. Mr. Allardice came out to Trenton in 1883, and gave his experience to the Grundy County Coal Mining Company, which made him foreman in 1889, and in 1894 he was promoted to superintendent, a position he held until the mines were worked out. In 1905, when the Trenton Mining Company was organized, Mr. Allardice became manager of the company, and began sinking shafts for the development of a new mine. Under his supervision the company developed a good producing property.

December 1, 1911, Mr. Allardice resigned from the company to become inspector of fuel for the Rock Island Railway, a position he held one year. In 1912, having left the railroad service, he came to Trenton and organized the Allardice & Baker Coal Company, and since 1913 has been engaged for himself in the coal, grain and hay business.

Politically he is a democrat. An active worker in the Presbyterian Church, he is an elder and for ten years was superintendent of the Sunday school. His fraternal associations are with the Independent Order of Odd Fellows, the Knights of Pythias and the Benevolent and Protective Order of Elks, and the Woodmen of the World. He has a large following of stanch friends, and enjoys a fine business. Mr. Allardice married Miss Minnie W. Myers, daughter of Michael and Mary Myers, of Trenton. They have two children. Minnie lives at home, and William A. married Miss Edna French, daughter of James A. French of Trenton.

SAMUEL RICE. The residence of Samuel Rice in Gentry County dates back to the year 1842, and since that time he has continued to make his home here, at this time living retired at Bethany. At the period of his arrival Albany was called Athens and contained a little log courthouse and a few straggling log cabins; John B. Hundley was the proprietor of a small store, but there was no doctor located here then and Bethany seems to have furnished medical attention through its doctor, although Dr. George Fallis, on Sampson Creek, also peddled pills and "practiced physic" in this region.

Mr. Rice came to the Northwest Missouri country from Trimble County, Kentucky. He walked the entire distance, a boy of less than sixteen years, and came to his uncle, Martin Fallis, near New Castle, after a journey that could have not been made much more rapidly on horseback, for on many days he covered forty miles. The Mississippi River he forded at Hannibal, and all that he brought along were the clothes upon his back. Here he was a farm aid to his uncle until the Mexican war came on, when he enlisted at Albany in Captain Denver's company of the Twelfth Missouri Infantry. He began his military career at St. Louis, where his regiment rendezvoused, following which it passed down the river to New Orleans and there shipped to Vera Cruz. General Scott had already occupied the city, and in a few days the army advanced toward the City of Mexico. Mr. Rice participated in the battles of Cerro Gordo, Chapultepec and Contreras and saw the city capitulate. Mr. Rice remembers that General Scott had one cannon with him "that would shoot as far as the road was cut out," and when he ordered his cannoneer to knock two holes in the walls surrounding the city, he did so. There was a temple standing high above the other buildings of the city, in which an immense bell was located, and which seemed to hold Mexican officers watching the proceedings of the Americans. General Scott ordered his big gun trained on this temple, but before it could be discharged "as many white flags as a cat has hairs" were raised, and the City of Mexico belonged to the American troops. Mr. Rice's regiment returned by water, as it had gone out, he received his honorable discharge at New Orleans, and he came back to St. Louis and by boat to the landing on the Missouri River. After a year passed in Gentry County, he made a trip across the plains to the Pacific coast.

It was in 1850 that Mr. Rice started as a teamster with six yoke of oxen and a train of twenty loads of canvased hams for the miners of the West. The caravan was six months on the road, went up the Platte River, through Utah north of Salt Lake and down the Humboldt River and arrived at Sacramento, where Mr. Rice left the wagons and struck out for himself. He worked for a time at Hangtown in the mines and with his earnings bought mules for packing his goods and started north. He finally landed in Shasta Valley and there resumed mining, digging out gold enough to buy a farm or two and set himself up in business when he returned home. He had been absent four years when he and his partner, Samuel Bell, who died in Harrison County, Missouri, a few years back, returned to this state, the journey being made by boat to the Isthmus of Panama and then on to New York and by rail back to St. Louis. He carried his gold in belts around his body and in New York it was exchanged for coin and brought home thus.

On his return from the coast Mr. Rice bought land in Harrison County and engaged in farming, but soon disposed of this property and bought another tract six miles east of Albany, where he spent the rest of his active life and reared his family. In the substantial improvement of his farm, he hauled his lumber from St. Joseph, and his business, aside from growing grain, was the raising of cattle and hogs.

Mr. Rice lived in peaceable possession of his farm save during the period of the Civil war. It was known that his sympathies were with the South and he was annoyed by the Federal authorities more or less on this account. Finally, to escape some persecution, he moved his family to Iowa, where the draft was served upon him from Missouri and he appeared before a corps of doctors for examination. He declared to them that they could force him into the army, but that they could not force him to shoot a man and the doctors then, after a consultation, offered to let him off for $100. He "had the money in his breeches" and handed it to them with the declaration "that he wouldn't have to answer for that in the day of judgment," regarding the whole procedure in the light of a graft.

The fact that Mr. Rice had failed to secure an education hampered him much as a citizen. He never went to school a day in his life and passed through his career without the ability to either read or write. He trusted to the honesty of others largely and when he married took a wife who had an education. He married, in November, 1854, Victoria Duncan, a daughter of Frank Duncan, one of the first settlers of Gentry County, and also a Kentuckian. Mrs. Rice lived until 1882 and was the mother of these children: Laura, who died here; Frank, of Oregon; John, of Kansas; Rojene, wife of M. S. Anslyn, of Albany; Patience, who married William Hill, of Gentry County; Nancy, who married P. I.

Gibony, of Roswell, New Mexico; Julia, who married George Dunlap, of Harrison County, Missouri; Maggie, the wife of Alvin Whitten, of Gentry County; and Lucy, who married J. W. Hunter, of Kansas City. Mr. Rice was married a second time to Mrs. Boyd, and had one son, Dan, a resident of Pratt County, Kansas.

Mr. Rice was born in Trimble County, Kentucky, August 5, 1825, a son of Daniel Rice, a farmer who was, perhaps, a native of that county. His people were from Virginia. Daniel Rice married Susan Fallis, and they had ten children who grew to maturity. The parents came to Missouri about 1848 and their children subsequently moved to various parts of Missouri and the West. Daniel and Susan Rice are buried at Jones Chapel, in Harrison County. Samuel Rice has been a member of the church since 1861, and has at all times endeavored to live up to its teachings.

GEORGE KEIFFER. The Keiffer family has lived in Holt County since before the war. Hard working farmers, public-spirited citizens, and people who have taken hold of every enterprise with a vigor characteristic of the name, they have long been identified usefully and worthily with this section of Northwest Missouri.

George Keiffer was born in Mercer County, Missouri, October 25, 1845. His parents were Martin and Jane (Mullen) Keiffer, who were married in the State of Missouri, the mother born in Cooper County, Missouri, and the father in Rockingham County, Virginia. There were ten children in the family, seven of whom reached maturity. Martin Keiffer was a farmer and brought his family to Holt County in 1857, settling on a farm about two miles southeast of Oregon. The father bought eighty acres there, and its chief improvement was a two-room log house. A large part of the land was covered with a heavy growth of timber, and the Keiffer family cleared a large field, and left some of the timber when they sold the farm in 1865. The next purchase was a farm near the one owned now by George Keiffer in Hickory Township. It was all wild land, and George Keiffer put the first plow into the soil and was the first to turn over a furrow in land that had lain virgin to the sun and wind for centuries. That land, comprising 160 acres, was where the Lincoln Schoolhouse now stands. It had no buildings, and all the improvements were erected by the father and son. Previous to that time the father had bought 120 acres now owned by the widow Jackson, but kept it only one year. The father also owned forty acres of timber land. That was his home until the last year of his life, and he died in Mound City. Having come to Northwest Missouri a poor man, though possessed of a good education, by means of his hard labor and thorough-going habits he acquired more than a competence. He and his wife were devout Baptists, and his moral principles are indicated by the fact that he never entered a saloon in all his years.

George Keiffer lived at home until his marriage in 1865, and after that farmed on his father's place for a year, and then bought a farm from Andrew Meyers. Since then, for more than forty years, his home has been in one locality. He originally owned 160 acres, but has since reduced that to eighty. In 1865 Mr. Keiffer married Elizabeth Beeler, daughter of Israel and Mary (Darhl) Beeler. Her people were early settlers in Holt County and were natives of Indiana. Mrs. Keiffer had eleven brothers and sisters. Mr. and Mrs. Keiffer are the parents of ten children, one of whom died in infancy, and the others are mentioned as follows: Anna Belle, who first married Charles Beckner and second Robert Clopton and became the mother of seven children; Rose, who died at the age of fourteen; Elmer, who first married Bryna Connor, and had three children, and for his second wife married Nell Johnson; Marus, who married Stella Shafer, and has four children; Lew, who married Dollie Clark, and has three living children and two deceased; Laura May, who married Wilson Kaufman; Guy, who lives at home; Inez, who married L. B. Hollenbeck, and has one son; Alma, who married Arch Patterson, and has two children. All the children were born in Holt County, and all in Hickory Township except two.

The Keiffer farm is one of the model places in Hickory Township, and every improvement, the buildings, the plowed fields, the fences, are all the direct result of Mr. Keiffer's management and labors. The land was only a pasture when he bought it, and he has gone ahead steadily in its improvement and at the same time has prospered as one of the progressive farmers of this section. Mrs. Keiffer is a member of the Christian Church, and he was brought up in that faith. He has served as school director and road supervisor, and in politics is a republican, while his father was a democrat.

CHRISTOPHER CANADAY was born in McLean County, Illinois, on October 26, 1847. He is a son of William and Elizabeth Canaday, whose biography appears in this volume.

He came to Missouri with his parents in the year 1855; he attended district school about four months of each year and worked on his father's farm the balance of the time until he reached the age of twenty-two; he also attended a graded school at Leon, Iowa, for nine months, thus finishing his school work; however, his education did not stop, but really only began, as he had a keen and active mind and was capable of grasping opportunity and turning it into gold.

On July 3, 1870, he was united in matrimony to Miss Angelina Brower. She was the daughter of James B. and Elizabeth (Bailiff) Brower and was born in Jennings County, Ohio, on July 16, 1852.

Her father, James B. Brower, who traces his lineage back to Holland, was born in Clermont County, Ohio, September 15, 1824.

In the year 1828, Mr. Brower moved with his father's family to Jennings County, Indiana, on September 3, 1846; he was united in marriage to Miss Elizabeth Bailiff, who was born in Ohio November 14, 1828. To this union ten children were born, viz.: Benjamin R., Leonora, Angelina, Sylvania, James L., Charles H., Millard F., Ellis M., Mary and Jasper.

In the year 1854, James B. Brower moved with his family to Harrison County, Missouri, and settled on a farm, where he helped to blaze the way for his posterity in a new country. In 1856 he engaged in the mercantile business in Eagleville, Missouri, under the firm name of Brower & Gilkey and also helped to lay out what are now known as the Brower and Gilkey surveys to the Town of Eagleville. In 1859 he quit business and moved to a farm four miles northwest of Eagleville.

In 1863 he enlisted in Company A, Thirty-fifth Regiment, Missouri Volunteer Infantry, and was first lieutenant of said company during his entire service, commanding the company. He was mustered out on July 10, 1865, never having had a furlough and never being wounded or taken captive and he had the distinction of never having applied for a pension, something very rare, indeed, among the soldiers of our Civil War.

Mr. Brower, who is so well known to all of our older citizens, was a remarkable man for the times in which he lived, and stood for temperance and right living. As a little side light into his character as well as that of the early history of Eagleville, the following instance is related: Mr. Brower did teaming with cattle between Eagleville and

St. Joseph, and the merchants would give him sealed orders to have filled by the wholesale merchants at St. Joseph, and he would then bring the goods ordered back with him. On one occasion when loading, a barrel of whisky was rolled out ready to load. Mr. Brower objected to taking it, saying that his cattle would not haul whisky. They insisted that he should, saying that the order said they were out and needed it. Mr. Brower said, ''They may want it, but they do not need it.'' That settled the matter and the whisky was left in St. Joseph. Mr. Brower was elected and served four years as county judge, from 1872 to 1876. He was then elected to represent the county in the State Legislature and was reelected in 1878, serving two terms.

To Christopher and Angelina Canaday were born four children and their names appear in regular order, together with the names of descendants born to the time of this history.

John T. Canaday, born April 21, 1871, married to Miss Eva Klopenstein July 23, 1894, their descendants being Ray V., Lavare J., and Nelva A.

Harvey P. Canaday, born August 15, 1872, married to Miss Nellie Carlton September 15, 1895, their descendants being Pauline, Marguerite, John, George, Togo and Marvin.

Mabel Canaday, born February 5, 1878, married to Charles Baldwin June 19, 1900. Their descendants are Winifred, Susie and Gladstone.

Myrtle Canaday, born July 25, 1879, married to Pascal J. Richardson October 24, 1897. Their descendants are Nellie T., Phil (deceased), Ruby A., Hugh and Helen.

Returning to the history of Christopher Canaday, he has always been interested in farming and stock raising, even though he did business along other lines. For seven years after his marriage he followed this business exclusively. In 1878 he engaged in the mercantile business in Eagleville, Missouri, with R. H. Wren, with whom he remained in partnership for a year, then going back to the farm for a time. In 1896 he again went into business, this time in Blythedale, Missouri, under the firm name of Canaday & Son. He was also one of the charter members of the Blythedale Savings Bank, which, to a large extent he financed. In 1910 he helped to organize the Citizens Bank of Blythedale and was its president for two years. He is a careful business man and has amassed a considerable fortune.

Mr. Canaday is a democrat in politics and in religious belief his faith is allied with that of the Christian Church, of which both he and his wife are members; he is a total abstainer from intoxicants and has never had a chew of tobacco or a pipe in his mouth. He has witnessed the evolution of the ox cart into the automobile and flying machine and drives a car of the latest make; he has seen the hut or cabin of the early settler give way to modern homes and the land which produced timber, brush, wild grass and weeds bearing the golden sheaf of grain.

He has always been progressive, has lived a clean and honorable life and holds the respect of the community in which he lives. He has also traveled considerable, having made three trips to California and is at present planning another and a visit to the exposition.

Mr. Canaday lives at Blythedale, Missouri, is still active in mind and body and personally attends to his business, that of loaning private money.

His life, with that of his father's family, is intertwined with the early history of Harrison County and it is fitting that his record be kept in this volume.

URI HALLOCK. Although not a native of Missouri, Uri Hallock, one of the early farmers of the Bethany locality of Harrison County, has passed nearly a half a century here, having attached himself to the community in 1867. He is a native of Jefferson County, Ohio, born August 2, 1840, and a son of John Wesley and Mary (Stone) Hallock.

The grandfather of Uri Hallock was Joseph D. Hallock, a native of Vermont, who was brought up among humble surroundings and thus was able to acquire only a meager education. At the outbreak of the War of 1812 he enlisted for service in the American army, and for this was granted at the close of the war a land grant, which he laid at Centerville, Iowa, or that vicinity. There he passed away about the close of the Civil war, aged eighty-four years, after a life spent in agricultural pursuits. He married Susanna Birch.

John Wesley Hallock, the father of Uri Hallock, was born at Vergennes, Addison County, Vermont, and was little more than a lad when he accompanied his parents to near Columbus, Ohio, where he grew to manhood. He acquired a fair education and adopted the vocation of farming as his life work. In politics he was an ardent whig and his religious faith was that of the Methodist Church, in which he served as an exhorter and leader. When he first went to Iowa he was engaged in teaching singing, but in later years devoted his entire attention to his farming interests in Jefferson County, where he died in 1852, Mrs. Hallock surviving for some time. Their children were as follows: Joseph, who was a Missouri soldier of the Eighteenth Volunteer Infantry during the Civil war and spent his last years at Leadville, Colorado, being the father of a son; Emily, who married Samuel McGill, spent much of her life in Van Buren County, Iowa, and died at Norman, Oklahoma, where her husband owned a claim; Uri, of this notice; Hymen, who died as a member of the Seventh Iowa Infantry, during the Civil war, at St. Louis; and Irene, who became the wife of Jonathan Harris, and died at Olathe, Kansas.

Uri Hallock was nine years of age when he accompanied his parents to Iowa, and near Centerville he grew to manhood, his youthful environment being that of the farm and his education coming from the district schools. He had barely begun life on his own account when he responded to President Lincoln's call for 75,000 volunteers to defend the Union, and he enlisted at Centerville, Iowa, in Company D, Sixth Regiment, Iowa Volunteer Infantry, his captain being M. M. Waldon and his colonel, McDowell. The regiment rendezvoused at Burlington, Iowa, and was ordered to Jefferson Barracks, St. Louis, subsequently taking part in the Springfield campaign after the engagement at Wilson Creek, and spending the following winter at Sedalia. In the spring of 1862 the Fifteenth Army Corps went to Shiloh to assist General Grant, and Mr. Hallock took part in the battle at that place and was taken prisoner by the enemy. He was sent to Montgomery, Alabama, where he was confined for a short time, as well as at Griffin and Macon, Georgia, and in the prison at Atlanta. At Macon he remained during the summer and was finally exchanged, being sent, with about fifteen hundred others, to Richmond, Virginia, and walking to the flag of truce boat bound for Annapolis, Maryland. There he was turned over to the Federal authorities and after about a month was sent to St. Louis.

At St. Louis the former prisoners were sent each to his own command, Mr. Hallock finding his regiment at Memphis, Tennessee. The winter of 1862-3 the command spent at Grand Junction, Tennessee, and the next spring went to the investment of Vicksburg where General Sherman's troops kept Gen. Joseph E. Johnston's army from going to the relief of Vicksburg. After the fall of the city the Fifteenth Corps

fought Johnston at Jackson, Mississippi, and then went back to Vicksburg and up the river to Memphis and across to Chattanooga, taking
part in the battle of Missionary Ridge. There Mr. Hallock was wounded
and left the regiment. He was hit with a musket ball in the right arm
and was in the hospital there and at Nashville until he became able to
go home, when he was paroled, staying home until the spring of 1864.
At that time he rejoined his regiment, then at Chattanooga, and started
with Sherman's command on the Atlanta campaign. He only accompanied his regiment a few days when it was discovered that lying on
the ground had set up inflammation in his injured ribs and he was
sent back to the hospital and when he rejoined his command it was on
the Chattahoochie River, July 16th. The next day his term of enlistment
expired and he was discharged and sent back to Davenport, Iowa.

Mr. Hallock then returned to his home, recuperated from his wound,
was married, and in 1867 came to Missouri. When he came here he was
without capital and accordingly moved to an eighty-acre tract of land
which was owned by his wife, in section 12, and which formed the
nucleus for his present home. He has done all the substantial improving
necessary to make a comfortable and attractive home and has been
identified with diversified farming all his life. For a time he was a
breeder of English Shire horses, which he carried on in a small way, and '
this business is still being conducted in a modest manner by his sons.
Mr. Hallock's home farm of 250 acres is located in section 7, township
63, range 7.

In politics Mr. Hallock has identified himself with the democratic
party and has served as justice of the peace of his township two years,
his locality being ordinarily a republican stronghold by the odds of
three to one. He has been in the Christian Church ever since coming to
the county, as a member of the Bethany congregation, and while he
resided in Bethany served as elder.

Mr. Hallock was married September 16, 1866, to Mrs. Electa A.
Dale, a daughter of Shubal and Rhoda A. (Withington) Fuller, she being
born at Beekmantown, Connecticut, where she was a school teacher.
Mr. Fuller was born in Ohio, a son of Isaac Fuller, of New York. Mrs.
Hallock's first husband was Thomas J. Dale, who died of typhoid fever
in the Union army and left the following children: Shubal A., a
farmer of Harrison County; Victoria A., the wife of John L. Foster, of
Ridgeway, Missouri; and Sarah E., the wife of B. O. Coleman, of
Clinton, Oklahoma. The children born to Mr. and Mrs. Hallock have
been as follows: Hymen J., a farmer of Harrison County, married Dora
Frencham; Barton C., engaged in farming near his brother, married
Maggie Harrison; John W., a farmer near his father, married Rose
Spencher; and Ora M., who is the wife of J. M. Bender, a farmer of
Harrison County.

MRS. ROBERT KENNISH. In Liberty Township of Holt County one
of the homes which suggest comfort and enterprise and the best standards
of Northwest Missouri agriculture is that now occupied by Mrs. Robert
Kennish, and has been her home for the past thirty years. It was here
that her late husband, Robert Kennish, who died July 29, 1909, spent
his active career, developed a good farm, and while providing for his
family also accumulated the honors of good citizenship and kindly and
helpful relations with the community.

Mrs. Robert Kennish was the mother of eight children, and the
seven still living are: William, who married Martha Harshman; Nettie,
wife of William Cantlin; Grace, unmarried; Emma, wife of B. E. Hed-

rick; Robert, who lives at home; Catherine, unmarried; and Myrtle. All the children were born on the home farm.

Mrs. Kennish before her marriage was Dora Skeels, a daughter of George and Serelda (Caton) Skeels. Mrs. Kennish had five brothers and sisters named Frank, Floyd, Myrtle, May and George.

Mr. and Mrs. Kennish were married in Holt County, March 11, 1883, and at once settled on the farm which has been the family home for more than thirty years. The land had no improvements at the time, and they lived in the first buildings erected there. The homestead comprises 120 acres, and Mrs. Kennish and her son, Robert, are now active managers of the farm. Mrs. Kennish is a member of the Presbyterian Church, and her husband was a republican in politics. Though he had begun life a poor man and with very little schooling, having gained his education by self study and observation, his thorough industry and good habits put him among the successful men of Holt County. He was from a family that originated on the Isle of Man.

Mrs. Kennish was born in Fulton County, Ohio, and came to Holt County with her parents about 1864. Her father was a prominent man in Holt County, taught school here for several years, later was postmaster at Mound City, and for a number of years served as judge of the County Court from the upper district of Holt County. He was an active republican, and cast his first vote for John C. Fremont in 1856. After some years as a Holt County farmer he moved out to Parsons, Kansas, and lived there until his death. Mrs. Kennish's mother is still living, with her home in Mound City.

CHARLES JOSEPH DOPKINS, of Bethany, has passed his life as a farmer and has lived in the County of Harrison since 1866, in which year he came hither with his parents from Cattaraugus County, New York, where his birth occurred August 16, 1859. His father was Joseph C. Dopkins, born at Hoosac, Rensselaer County, New York, June 18, 1820, and on his father's side was of German descent, while his mother was of Irish stock. Joseph C. Dopkins was one of several children, among whom were: Ann J., who married Mr. Havens and spent her life in the City of Buffalo, New York; Matilda, who married William Madison and died also at Buffalo; Daniel, who died at Woodland, California; Joseph Case, the father of Charles Joseph; and Elizabeth, who became the wife of Mr. Miles and spent her life at Randolph, New York.

Joseph Case Dopkins was orphaned as a child and grew up in the home of relatives, his sister, Mrs. Madison, having much of his care. He was fortunate in securing a collegiate education and started out in life for himself at a rather early age, taking to the Lakes as a sailor and soon drifting into the whaling business, which he followed for many years, visiting many ports and various parts of the world. He completed his life on the water as a sailor on the Great Lakes, and when he abandoned that career became attached to the Pennsylvania Railway shops, at Corry, Pennsylvania, as a carbuilder, leaving that vocation to come to Missouri. He missed active service during the Civil war, having suffered a broken arm, but was an ardent Union man and several of his relatives served in the volunteer forces throughout the struggle.

Mr. Dopkins brought his family of six children to Missouri by railroad to Chillicothe and by wagon to his destination in Harrison County. He had made a prospecting tour of this country which had favorably impressed him with the opportunities and advantages here, and settled in Jefferson Township on land which he had previously purchased. This was nearly all wild and uncultivated and presented many discouraging problems to a man whose former life had been connected with vocations in no way allied with the soil, but he possessed energy and perseverance, and during the fifteen years that he resided on this property he was able to bring it under a good state of cultivation, only leaving it because of encroaching years and attending feebleness. In 1886 he located at Bethany, and here he was largely occupied with his duties as public administrator of Harrison County.

Mr. Dopkins was a republican in his political views, and was elected public administrator of the county some time during the '70s, his services being so acceptable in that capacity that he served therein for a period of sixteen years. Among the many estates he administered was one of peculiar interest, that of a miser named Barker, who lived and died southeast of Bethany. He lived in a miserable hovel or shack and was supposed to be poor, aside from his realty possessions, which were in sight. In searching for property, however, Mr. Dopkins found several thousand dollars in gold coin and currency, hidden in an old trunk and in other junk about the premises, and while there seemed to be no relatives at first, when the money was found and advertised a daughter appeared on the scene, proved her identity, and secured the estate. Mr. Dopkins passed away while still in office, July 10, 1894. Mr. Dopkins' early experience as a sailor, his early ones as an educated youth and his wide travels made him a personage of wide information, when to this is added his course of historical reading throughout life, but he never essayed to public speaking. He belonged to the Methodist Church and served it faithfully as a trustee.

Joseph Case Dopkins was married to Miss Sarepta Barnum, who was born at Collins, Erie County, New York, November 21, 1822, the daughter of natives of the Empire State. She still survives her husband and resides at Sanger, Fresno County, California. The children born to Joseph Case and Sarepta Dopkins were as follows: Florence S., who is the wife of Z. T. Rose, of Dinuba, California; DeWitt H., who is a resident of the same place; Mary E., who became the wife of N. L. Durgin, of Sanger, California; George M., of Dinuba, California; William H., who married Harriet Browning and died in Harrison County, Missouri, leaving a family; and Charles Joseph, of this review.

Charles Joseph Dopkins received his education in Jefferson Township, Harrison County, and engaged in farming in that locality at the time he reached his majority. He had thoroughly learned this vocation from his father, and met with a fair measure of success in his operations, but in 1877 crossed the plains to Denver, Colorado, and located at Longmont, where he worked on a ranch and was also connected with railroad construction work as a section boss. After two years spent in Denver, Mr. Dopkins returned to Missouri, and was engaged in farming until 1883, when he again turned his face westward, this time making a trip to California. He was still a single man, and at the end of one year returned to take charge of matters at home, his brother having died. He resumed farming in Jefferson Township until 1902, when he again went to California, this time with his family, and after spending 2½ years largely in sight-seeing among the big trees, the orange and fruit country, the mountains and the big observatory, returned to his home. At that time he located at Bethany, which has been his place of residence to the present time.

In political matters a republican, Mr. Dopkins cast his first presidential vote for James A. Garfield and has continued to vote for every candidate of his party for that office, casting a vote for Colonel Roosevelt while in California, at that time being yard boss for a sawmill in Fresno County. He has served as township assessor two terms and as township trustee one term. A Methodist in his religious faith, Mr.

Dopkins has been both class leader and trustee of his church at Bethany, and for three years was superintendent of the Sunday School there. His fraternal connection is with the Yeomen.

On October 26, 1887, Mr. Dopkins was united in marriage with Miss Emma May Weary, a daughter of Franklin and Mollie (Grim) Weary, natives of Union County, Pennsylvania, from whence they moved to Illinois prior to the outbreak of the Civil war. They resided in Stephenson County for several years, and there Mrs. Dopkins was born July 14, 1865, one of seven children. Mr. Weary was a widower when he married Mollie Grim, his first wife having been a Miss Stover, by whom he had a son, Millard, who is now a resident of Lanark, Illinois. Mrs. Weary was a widow at the time of her marriage to Mr. Weary, her first husband having been Philip Shaffer, by whom she had two children—Chesty, who died in Jefferson Township, Harrison County, as Mrs. Sharp Winningham; and Clementine, who married Edward Hicks, of Fort Scott, Kansas. The brothers of Mrs. Dopkins are: Thronton, of St. Joseph; Franklin G., also of that city; and Lewis, of Wetmore, Kansas.

Two daughters, Iva May and Florence S., have been born to Mr. and Mrs. Dopkins. The former was educated at Bethany and graduated in music at Cameron, Missouri, taught one season in the Missionary Training School, Chicago, and then completed her education by a course of one year at Northwestern University, Evanston. Miss Florence S., who obtained her early education in the Bethany public schools, is now a student of Northwestern University.

ALEXANDER GREENWELL. The distinction of being the oldest settler now living in Gentry County, Missouri, belongs to Alexander Greenwell, one of the successful farmers in the locality tributary to Darlington, who came hither in 1840 from Schuyler County, Illinois, with an ox-team, in company with his parents, Robert and Dorcas (Frakes) Greenwell.

Robert Greenwell was born in Maryland, and as a young man moved to Kentucky, where he was residing at the time of the commencing of the War 'of 1812. He enlisted for service in the army of the United States, went down the Mississippi River on a flatboat to engage in his duties as a soldier, saw active and heavy service, including the decisive battle of New Orleans, and when he received his honorable discharge made his way home on foot. From his Kentucky home he migrated as a pioneer to the State of Illinois, there residing in Schuyler County until 1840, when he gathered his family about him and sought a new location in the promising and newly-opened country west of the Mississippi, making the journey with an ox-team and carrying his family belongings with him. The Father of Waters was crossed at Quincy, Illinois, and the family then wended their way westward toward their destination in the County of Clinton, Missouri, Gentry County at that time having not yet been laid out. Robert Greenwell entered 160 acres of land on Grand River and patented it, and here for seven years made his home and engaged in agricultural pursuits, then returning to his former home in Schuyler County, Illinois, where he passed away when about sixty years of age, in 1860. His wife, whom he married in Kentucky, died in Cowley County, Kansas, as a pensioner of the War of 1812. The children of Robert and Dorcas (Frakes) Greenwell were as follows: James, who died while a resident of California, leaving a son who is still a resident of Cloverdale, that state; William, whose death occurred in Cowley County, Kansas, with his mother; Henry, who died at Wichita, Kansas; Robert, who died at Kansas City, Missouri;

Alexander, of this review; Stephen, who died in Cowley County, Kansas; Marion, who passed away in Colorado; Hardin, who died in Schuyler County, Illinois; and Jane, who married James Chick and resides in Palo Pinto County, Texas.

When Alexander Greenwell came to Missouri he was a lad of but thirteen years and from that time he has spent his life within the limits of Gentry County. His early recollections are of Indians, a wild community filled with game, deer, turkeys, a few elk and wild bees beyond description. This made living a matter of conquest over Nature. The trading place was St. Joseph, the boat-landing was on the river, and there were but two stores there, these being kept by Jo Roubidoux and a Mr. Patch, while the few people who were living along the Grand River and could be called neighbors devoted themselves to farming. Corn was the chief product, no wheat being grown at that time, and the market products comprised hickory and hazel nuts, while occasionally they drove a few hogs to market. Each did his own work, making the clothing they wore, and the roads were little more than paths across the country, not a bridge being found in the entire county.

Mr. Greenwell purchased the old homestead his father entered from the heirs, and of the timber lands he has acquired he cleared up forty acres. He has added to the farm, and it is now rated among the best bottom properties in the county. While he was making a farm and raising stock, he ran a ferry on Grand River, at the place called Greenwell's Ford, establishing the first ferry there years previous to the Civil war. This institution proved to be a money-maker and aided him materially in the building and improving of his farm. His ferry rates for a two-horse wagon was 50 cents, for a footman 10 cents and for a single horseman 20 cents, although he received nothing from the soldiers whom he ferried across during the Civil war. His whole career as a ferryman was spent without an accident or untoward incident, although many times the water covered the wide bottoms adjacent to the stream. When the bridge was built the ferry was abandoned. Mr. Greenwell was in the Union army a short time, being under Colonel Cranor and stationed at St. Joseph for a period. His duties were as a guard, and he finally left the state service, securing a substitute in his place.

Mr. Greenwell is a democrat. His life has been practically without political activity, save as a voter, and he has never held office. It was his privilege to see Abraham Lincoln when he was wont to plead law cases in Schuyler County, Illinois, and has always regarded the Martyred President as one of the best and greatest men the Nation has known. Mr. Greenwell is something of a philosopher in his way and it is his observation that there is only one way of making a success of life and that is in a straightforward, honorable career. He has always been a temperance man, and favored giving the ballot to women in 1914, in Missouri, believing that such a course of action would soon seal the doom of the liquor interests. He belongs to the Christian Church, of which he has been a member for a long time, and has helped build many churches, his last contribution being toward the new edifice of the Christian congregation at Albany. He has distributed charity in a practical, unassuming and quiet way, giving freely of his means to all worthy appeals.

Mr. Greenwell was married in 1846, in this community, to Miss Bathena Gossett, a daughter of Joseph Gossett, and she died in 1864, having been the mother of three children, namely: John, who was murdered by robbers in 1889; Stephen, who lives on the homestead place; Mary, who married Lee Stone, of Jackson County, Missouri. Mr. Greenwell was married the second time, in September, 1865, to Mary J. Matney, a daughter of John Matney, who came from Kentucky to Missouri, engaged in agricultural pursuits, and died in Platte County. Mr. and Mrs. Greenwell have had five children: Jasper, a resident of Wyoming; Thomas, who resides on the homestead farm, married Blanche Edwards; · Alexander S., a resident of Wyoming; Charley, a resident of Nebraska, married Tot Rhodecker; and Nellie, who is the wife of Harry Johnson, of Albany. Mr. Greenwell is one of the old Masons of Gentry County, and belongs to the lodge at Darlington.

RICHARD C. NORTON. The late Richard C. Norton, who died at his home in Trenton, Missouri, May 18, 1908, was one of Missouri's distinguished educators, and for upwards of forty years was engaged in his chosen work as a teacher, an educational executive and in the effective exercise of his influence in behalf of better schools and other moral and intellectual agencies in this state. Mrs. Norton, who survives him, is still living at her home in Trenton.

Richard C. Norton was of old and distinguished lineage and was born near Hiram, Portage County, Ohio, June 16, 1840. The genealogy of the Norton family which has been compiled by one of its members, shows an unbroken line of twenty generations from the late Richard C. Norton. In the twentieth generation the head of the family was a Lord Norville, of France, who was an officer under William the Conqueror, and went with that Norman invader into England in 1066. For many generations the family home was in England. Richard Norton, who was in the eighth generation before Richard C. Norton, came to America in 1635, having been preceded by some of his brothers. He was a New England settler, and from him the line of descent is traced through the following heads of generations: John Norton, who owned landed estates at Branford, Connecticut, in which colony he died November 5, 1709; John Norton, II, born at Branford, October 16, 1657, and died April 25, 1725; Ebenezer Norton, born at Farmington, Connecticut, and died March 21, 1750; Bethuel Norton, born at Farmington, subsequently removed. to Oneida County, New York, served as a soldier in the Revolutionary war, and participated in an exploring expedition over the western country towards the Mississippi River; Peter Norton, born May 11, 1770, at New Hartford, New York, was grandfather of the late Richard C. Norton. Peter Norton married Elthina Thompson. About 1807 he came out to the new State of Ohio, living for two years in Trumbull County, and then locating in what is now Summit County.

Among Peter Norton's children was Thuel, who was born March 10, 1801, in Oneida County, New York, and died at Hiram, Ohio, April 2, 1880. He was about six years of age when the family moved to Ohio, and grew up to manhood among pioneer surroundings. He lived the quiet and unostentatious life of the farmer, was devoted to church and was a neighbor whose many acts of practical charity have not yet been forgotten in that part of Ohio. While this article does not call for an extended sketch of his career, a few sentences concerning some of the prominent attributes of his mind and character should be quoted from a memorial address delivered after his death: "Unobtrusive, quiet, conservative, attending strictly to his own affairs, he was respected of all, lived at peace with his neighbors and without an enemy in the world. He was known in the community as the one man in a hundred who has something of his own to do and does it. When he passed along the streets you knew that he was on no mission of evil gossip. When he knocked at your door you knew that Father Norton was on no·errand but of peace. Too timid to enter into or enjoy general society, he still loved his friends with a fervor and a constancy of a great heart and was

R. C. Norton.

happy in the society of a limited circle. He naturally shrank from doing business, and could never think of speculation. Everything, he thought, should be worked out or grow up. He knew of no other methods of making money. His life has been one of great toil and he could not give it up even in old age. With him honest work was good company. Often imposed upon because he thought everyone honest and truthful, he still trudged on, slowly but honestly making his living and serving those dependent upon him. While the noisy, busy world rushed past him and men now and then arose in his sight to higher points of wealth and fame, he ate bread the world knew not of, and amassed wealth where moths and rust do not corrupt, and where no cheat can wrong him.''

Thuel Norton was married August 4, 1822, to Harriet Rebecca Harrington. Their children were: Anna; Seth D.; Edwin; Amelia C.; Julia M.; James; Lois E.; Emily E.; Richard C.; Harriet R.

The late Richard C. Norton thus came of some of the best American stock. His family was closely associated with the sterling pioneers that made up the community about Hiram, Ohio, a society possessed of the high ideals of New England culture, thrift and sobriety, and centered about the educational institution which has long made Hiram known to the outside world, Hiram College, an institution of higher learning conducted under the auspices of the Christian Church, of which James A. Garfield was at one time president. Richard C. Norton grew up in that community, spending his early life on the farm, and supplementing the training of the public schools with a course in Hiram College while Mr. Garfield was president. From early life he came into contact with scholarly men and Christian gentlemen and along with broad culture acquired the true courtesy of the heart and the fundamentals of Christian character. At the age of sixteen he had begun his career as a teacher in the public schools near his old home. While still a boy he united with the Christian Church, and was always a faithful member of that denomination.

He had hardly reached his majority when the Civil war broke out and was one of the youthful soldiers who volunteered and served with the Forty-second Ohio Regiment of Infantry, with James A. Garfield as its commander. After serving for more than two years he was discharged on account of ill health March 18, 1863.

Soon afterwards Mr. Norton determined to give his life services as an educator to the newer country of the Middle West, and in the spring of 1865 came to Trenton to take the position of principal of the public schools. He remained at the head of the Trenton schools for ten years, and many of his old pupils are still living in this section of Missouri. From Trenton he became vice president of the State Normal School at Warrensburg, resigning that position to become president of the Cape Girardeau Normal, and was at the head of that institution for thirteen years, until ill health compelled him to resign. Later he took a chair of instruction in the Kirksville Normal, and was also a member of the board of regents and was connected with the Kirksville schools for six years. Again ill health compelled him to give up his regular duties as an educator, and after that he kept his residence at Trenton, a city which he had considered his home practically ever since coming to Missouri. During his residence at Cape Girardeau Mr. Norton was given the degree LL. D. for distinguished services in the cause of education and for his great learning. He was affiliated with Trenton Lodge, A. F. & A. M., and was laid to rest under the rites of Masonry, and was also a member of Col. Jacob Smith's Post, G. A. R.

On March 17, 1864, the late Richard C. Norton married Miss Mariah Lucretia Mason. They had no children, and Mrs. Norton is now living at Trenton in the old home. Mrs. Norton is likewise a representative of one of the pioneer families of Eastern Ohio. She is a descendant from Elijah Mason, who was born in Lebanon, Connecticut, in 1756. Elijah Mason belonged to a prominent New England family, one of whose members was Capt. John Mason of the Pequot Indian war, and another was Jeremiah Mason, prominent in national affairs and an associate of Daniel Webster. Elijah Mason married for his first wife Mary Marsh and for his second Lucretia Green, who was a relative of Gen. Nathaniel Green, one of the conspicuous leaders in the Revolutionary war. Elijah Mason first came out to Ohio in the spring of 1802, buying several tracts of land near Hiram, and with the aid of his sons cleared up some of the first land put in cultivation in that region. However, he did not become a permanent settler of Portage County until 1816, when quite an old man, and lived there until his death in June, 1833, at the age of seventy-seven.

HIRAM M. TRAVIS. One of the few remaining pioneers of Harrison County who came here prior to the county's organization is Hiram M. Travis who is now living in quiet retirement at Albany after many years passed in agricultural operations. Mr. Travis came here in 1840, with his father, Beverly Travis, a full-blooded Irishman and a son of David Travis, who came to America prior to the War of the Revolution, in which he served as a soldier of the patriot army. He settled in Tennessee and died there in Overton County. Whom he married is not now a matter of attainable record, and of his sons and daughters the only ones whose names are remembered are Beverly and Isaac.

Beverly Travis emigrated to Missouri from Illinois, but had formerly left the State of Tennessee for the West, winding up his wanderings in Missouri. He lived for a brief time in McLean County, Illinois, and his inclination to get out on the frontier where land was cheaper and where opportunites for his growing and numerous family were greater, caused him to make his way to where plenty of room could be found. He came by way of ox-wagon and crossed the Mississippi River at Quincy, Illinois, the journey being made without special incident save the night camp and the study of the wilds as the little party threaded the sparsely settled counties toward the frontier.

Beverly Travis located five miles southeast of Bethany, before that town was thought of and when the present County of Harrison was still included in the territory of Daviess County. The public domain had not yet been surveyed, nor was it on the market for entry, but as soon as it was advertised for homestead entry Mr. Travis filed on land near where the present town of Blythedale stands, a tract which he proved up and patented and on which he had his home during the remainder of his life. He was identified with his county purely as a farmer, but although a man somewhat handicapped by lack of educational advantages demonstrated his ability as a business man and agriculturist and at his death left his family well provided for. He died in the faith of the Christian Church, of which he had long been a member. He did not aspire to public life, but had a creditable military record as a soldier during the War of 1812, during which he served under Gen. William H. ("Old Tippecanoe") Harrison. His death occurred in August, 1845, when he was about fifty-two years of age.

Beverly Travis married Miss Lydia Allen, a daughter of William Allen, of Overton County, Tennessee, and a sister of Rev. John S. Allen, the well-known business man and pioneer of Bethany, and the Christian gentleman and worthy citizen who filled many places of trust in Harrison County. Mrs. Travis died in 1872, at the age of seventy-five years, being the mother of the following children: Mary, who became the wife of Mathew Taylor and spent her life in Harrison County; David, who remained around Bethany as a farmer and died here leaving a family; Elizabeth, who married Joseph Gillespie and still lives in Harrison County at the advanced age of ninety-four years; William, who spent the greater part of his life in Harrison County as a farmer but died in the Town of Bethany, leaving a family; Nancy, who became Mrs. William Alexander and died in Harrison County; Julia, who married Gibson Ansley and died in Alton, Kansas; Hiram M., of this review, who through life has been familiarly known as ''Mac'' Travis; Thomas, who died on the Sacramento River in California, without issue; Rachel, who married Elkanah Timmons and passed her life in Harrison County; and Samuel, who died in Hennessey, Oklahoma, and left a family there.

Hiram McGinnis Travis was born in Overton County, Tennessee, February 3, 1829, and was a lad of eight or nine years when the family emigrated to the State of Illinois. The schooling of any value which he received was obtained in Harrison County, Missouri, and was of a subscription character, of course, and there is no doubt as to the log-cabin appearance of the house in which he studied. He learned his father's vocation, farming, and at the age of fifteen years began making his own living thereat, his first home being established in the community in which he was reared. He entered land and enjoyed the presence of prosperity, continued to reside in that township for fifty-three years, and when he left the farm disposed of it, and in 1909 came to Bethany, where he has since lived quietly, enjoying the fruits of his long years of toil. His old home is now owned by Charles Dobkins. While he belonged to no church himself, Mr. Travis believed in church work and the elevating effects of religious movements, had faith in its good influence and aided substantially in the erection of Morris Chapel.

During the war between the North and the South, Mr. Travis was a member of the Sixth Missouri Cavalry, Captain Page, Colonel Catherwood, he enlisting in 1862 in Company G of that organization. His service was given altogether in Missouri and he took part in skirmishing at different points, had a horse shot under him, and before his time expired was taken ill with typhoid fever and lay in the Sedalia Hospital until recovery, soon after which he was discharged. In politics, Mr. Travis is a republican, although his brothers and father were democrats. He cast his first ballot for President for Buchanan, he having been reared a democrat, and in 1860 voted for Stephen A. Douglas. When Fort Sumter was fired upon all his democracy left him, however, and in 1864 he voted for President Lincoln. He has continued to vote regularly for the nominees of his party ever since, and has no apologies to make for his record. He has never filled a public office save when he was a member of the school board while living in the country.

In 1849 Mr. Travis went to California by the usual route, across the plains, being a member of a small company, of which he is the sole survivor, and went up the Platte River to Fort Laramie, down the Humboldt River, and on to Sacramento, then going to the diggings east of Stockton, where he spent the winter in mining. The following spring he went up on Trinity River and worked all summer, and his trip proved to be of some profit to him in the way of ''dust,'' he returning home after an absence of four years, by water, crossing the Isthmus of Nicaraugua, going then by boat to New Orleans, up the Mississippi River to St. Louis and by way of the Missouri River to Camden, from whence he made his way to his home.

The marriage of Mr. Travis occurred January 30, 1848, when he was united with Miss Mary Gillespie, a daughter of Moses Gillespie, who came to Missouri from Ohio and was a farmer. Mrs. Travis died in, 1868, the mother of these children: Amanda Jane, who married Samuel Speer, of Trenton, Missouri; Lydia, who became the wife of Jacob Cannon, of Lock Springs, Missouri; Susan, who married Jackson Smith and died at Meriden, Kansas; Beverly, who died at Jamesport, Missouri, leaving a family; Eliza, who married Andrew Hornbeck, of Des Moines, Iowa; Butler, a resident of Seattle, Washington; and George, whose home is at Ridgeway, Missouri.

Mr. Travis was married a second time, March 30, 1870, when he was united with Miss Elizabeth Jacobus, a daughter of James and Eliza Jacobus. Mr. Jacobus came originally from the State of New York, but left his home in the Empire State for the West and passed away in Fulton County, Illinois. He was the father of five children, as follows: Jackson, who passed his life as an agriculturist in Fulton County, Illinois, and there passed away; Jefferson, who enlisted in the Union army at the outbreak of the Civil war, was wounded in battle, and returned to his home, where he died from the effects of his wound; Elizabeth, who became Mrs. Travis; John, who also entered the volunteer service during the Civil war, was wounded in battle and died in an army hospital; and David, who died at Peoria, Illinois. Mrs. Travis was born November 3, 1835, in Decatur County, Indiana, and went to Illinois with her parents when a child of ten years. She was married first to Andrew Taylor, and they were the parents of two children: Alice, who is the wife of Jehu Gillespie and has six children, Joseph, Myrtle, Christina, Amy, Belva and Robert; and Frances, who married Thomas Thurman, and died in Knox County, Illinois, leaving three children.

Four children have been born to Mr. and Mrs. Travis: Carrie, who died unmarried as a young woman of nineteen years; David, who is a resident of Bethany, Missouri; Leona, who became the wife of Edward Melvin and died at Bethany, leaving two children, Jewell and Bessie; and James, a resident of Bethany, who married Effie Williams and has five children, Garland, Carrie, Mary, Madaline and Maxine.

JOHN W. HAIGHT. Wide-awake, energetic and progressive, John W. Haight, of St. Joseph, was clearly destined to be the architect of his own fortune. Having begun on a low rung of the ladder of attainments, he has made diligent use of his faculties and opportunities, and by untiring energy and wise management has proved himself an eminently useful and worthy citizen, and an important factor of the business and social life of the city. A son of Isaac Haight, and grandson of David B. Haight, he was born in St. Joseph, Missouri, in 1873, of pioneer ancestry.

His great-grandfather, Caleb Haight, was born in New York State, of Welsh ancestors. He chose the independent occupation of a farmer, during his earlier life being engaged in agricultural pursuits in his native state. He subsequently migrated to Illinois, and after living there a few years removed to Utah, and spent his last days in Salt Lake City.

David B. Haight was born in the Empire State, near the Catskill Mountains, and was there reared and educated. He began his career as a farmer in Cayuga County, New York, remaining there a number of years. In 1840, following the march of civilization westward, he made an overland journey to Illinois, where he lived two years. Crossing then the Territory of Iowa, he lived for two years in the vicinity of Council Bluffs, but not pleased with the prospects in that region came from there to Missouri, locating in Platte County at a time when nearly all of the land in Iowa and Missouri was owned by the Government. Wild animals of all kinds were plentiful, even the buffalo were still roaming at large. Taking up land, he carried on general farming for a time, and then removed to Jefferson County, Kansas, where he spent the remainder of his days. His wife, whose maiden name was Clarissa Reckmeyer, was born in New York State, and died in Platte County, Missouri. They were the parents of eight children, as follows: Frances, Isaac, Julia, Nora, Martha, Annie, David B., and Benjamin.

A native of New York, Isaac Haight was born in Venice, Cayuga County, September 18, 1836. Four years of age when his parents started westward, he was eight years old when they settled in Platte County, Missouri, where he attended the district schools for a time. At the age of eleven years he was sent to Weston to learn the blacksmith's trade, but not liking the work he ran away at the end of four weeks in search of more congenial labor. He found employment on a farm at $10 a month, and from that time was self-supporting, earning his living at various employments until reaching the age of eighteen years. Then, in 1854, he entered the employ of Ben Halliday as a driver, and started westward with an emigrant train, driving a team of mules attached to the wagon in which Mr. Halliday's family were traveling. The train, which consisted of about twelve wagons, with four mules to each wagon, started in the spring of the year for San Francisco. Denver had then no place on the map, and Salt Lake City was but a small village.

Arriving on the present site of San Francisco after several months travel, Mr. Isaac Haight remained in camp a number of weeks, and then accompanied the Hallidays back to Missouri, coming by way of the Isthmus, and the Mississippi and Missouri rivers. Then, in the employ of Major & Russell, he again crossed the plains to Salt Lake City, and was afterwards employed by others in teaming to the far West, making in all eighteen trips across the plains. He was but four years old when he began trekking towards the West with his parents, and he is now one of the living men that have covered the entire distance from New York to the Pacific Coast by team, and is also one of the few living that teamed across the plains in the employ of Ben Halliday and Major & Russell, and one of the very few that ever rode the "pony express," which was too heavy for continuous service.

In 1861, at the breaking out of the Civil war, Isaac Haight was in Denver, which was a mere hamlet at that time. He returned home intending to enlist in the Confederate army, but his family demurred, and he entered the employ of the United States Government as a teamster and wagon master, and served until the close of the conflict, seeing service in Missouri, Kansas and Arkansas. Returning then to Denver, he spent a year there, and then came back to St. Joseph, where, with the exception of one year in Montana, and two years in Platte County, he has since been a resident, the greater part of the time being employed in teaming.

On September 3, 1871, Isaac Haight married Elizabeth Jane Woady, who was born in St. Joseph, Missouri, November 11, 1857. Her father, Elisha Woady, was born near Louisville, Kentucky, and as a young man came to St. Joseph, Missouri, where he spent the remainder of his life, passing away in 1859. The maiden name of the wife of Mr. Woady was Jane McIntosh. She was born in Kentucky, near Barbourville, a daughter of Jesse McIntosh, who left his native state, Tennessee, when young, and until 1850 resided in Kentucky. Starting westward then with his family, Mr. McIntosh stopped first in Indiana, then in Illinois, from whence, in 1852, he came by boat to St. Joseph, Missouri. Locating then in Andrew County, he carried on general farming until his death, which occurred a few months later. He married Jean Smith, who was born in Virginia, of Scotch ancestry, and died in St. Joseph in

1878, at an advanced age. Mrs. Jane (McIntosh) Woady, Mr. Haight's maternal grandmother, was left a widow in early womanhood, and subsequently married for her second husband Mr. Abraham Lytle. She lived to the good old age of four score years, passing away February 15, 1913. Mr. and Mrs. Isaac Haight are the parents of seven children, namely: John W., Clara J., Jessie G., Samuel H., Nora C., Hazel H., and Elsie E.

Gleaning his elementary education in the public schools, John W. Haight began his active career when a boy by working in a blacksmith's shop for $1.50 a week. At the end of two months he gave up his job, and soon after began learning the trade of a lozenger maker with the National Biscuit Company, with whom he served an apprenticeship of three years. He subsequently continued with that company for five years, when he resigned and went to Chicago, where he remained two months. Coming back to St. Joseph, Mr. Haight was solicitor and collector for the American Wringer Company until 1902. During those years he enjoyed life as young men do by spending liberally, when he left that company having but $38 with which to engage in business. With that limited capital, Mr. Haight started in the furniture business, having no store, but soliciting trade for eighteen months. Succeeding in his undertakings, he subsequently opened a store on St. Joseph Avenue, where he has since carried on a prosperous business, being now rated among the popular and substantial business men of the city.

Mr. Haight married, November 21, 1894, Katie Ford, a daughter of Henry and Bridget Ford, of St. Joseph, and they have two children, Gertrude and Dorothea. Mr. Haight cast his first presidential vote for William J. Bryan, and has since been a consistent supporter of the principles of the democratic party. He is active in local affairs, and has served as a member of the executive committee for both the city and the county.

Fraternally Mr. Haight is a member of the Benevolent and Protective Order of Elks; of the Improved Order of Red Men; of the Fraternal Order of Eagles; of the Modern Woodmen of America; of the L. O. O. M.; and of the K. and L. of S. He is also a member of the Commerce and Monroe clubs; of the Missouri and Amazonian Gun clubs; and of the North St. Joseph Hunting Club.

JAMES BARNETT GRAHAM, M. D. A Jameson physician of seventeen years residence, Doctor Graham represents old family stocks in Northern Missouri, and men and women of the name have lived worthy and useful lives in the Grand River Valley since almost the beginning of development there. Doctor Graham is the son of a physician and practical business man, and in his own career has increased the favorable associations of the name in this part of Missouri.

James Barnett Graham was born at Gentryville, Missouri, October 18, 1874, a son of Dr. George and Martha Jane (Dobbins) Graham. His father was born in Ohio, but was brought when a child to Missouri, where grandfather John Graham was a pioneer of Grundy County. The latter was a miller, and during his lifetime operated mills at various points along the Grand River, and at one time or another had associated with him all of his six sons. These six sons were Doctor George, James, John, William, Alfred and Oliver, and there was one daughter, Emeline, who married Henry Whitten.

Dr. George Graham was well educated, and after attending the Grand River College at Edinburg entered the Missouri Medical College at St. Louis. After graduating he located for practice at Lindley, in Sullivan County. While there he met and married Martha Jane Dobbins. She was of a prominent family in Sullivan County, where she was born. Her parents were Thomas and Sarah (Kirkpatrick) Dobbins, who not long after their marriage in their native county of Sangamon, Illinois, set out with a wagon and ox-team for Missouri. The first year was spent in Livingston County, and Thomas Dobbins then moved to Sullivan County and became the first settler at and founded the Town of Lindley. His home was in the midst of an almost untouched wilderness, abounding in wild game. In order to pay for the land which he entered from the Government he split 30,000 rails, and the industry with which he began the task of home-making was the sure foundation of a bountiful success, measured afterward by the ownership of 1,500 acres and a position as one of the most influential citizens. He lived at Lindley until his death in 1896 at the age of eighty-two, his wife having passed away at the age of seventy-two. They were the parents of the following family: Mrs. Polly Ann Humphreys, George, John, Charles, Mrs. Elizabeth Cook, Mrs. Margaret Bailey, Mrs. Martha J. Graham, William, Mrs. Kittie Moberly, Mrs. Linda Lane, Mrs. Hattie Doolin and Timothy. Politically the Dobbins family was usually found supporting the republican ticket, and all were good church people.

After his marriage Dr. George Graham moved from Lindley to Gentryville, where he engaged in the grist and woolen mill business. This was a large and important enterprise, with a patronage drawn from a large territory. In 1879 the mills were destroyed by fire, causing a loss of many thousand dollars to the owners. After this misfortune Doctor Graham bought the City Mills and the Grand River Mills in Trenton, and resumed business. During the cyclone of July, 1883, the mills were blown into the river and destroyed. Doctor Graham practiced to some extent while looking after his business, and in 1887 moved to McFall with the intention of taking up the regular work of his profession in that community, but died three weeks after his arrival, being then hardly in the prime of life, aged forty-seven. He was a member of the Christian Church and a democrat, and others of the family have usually followed the same lines in religion and politics. Mrs. George Graham died in March, 1913, at the home of her daughter, Mrs. Emma J. Carson, of St. Louis. Her five children are: David T., in the manufacturing business at St. Louis; Mrs. Emma J. Carson, of St. Louis; Mrs. Sarah M. Asher, of Trenton; Leota Lee, deceased; and Dr. James B.

Dr. James B. Graham spent part of his boyhood in Trenton, where he attended the public schools, later was in the McFall High School and also a student of Avalon College. In 1893 he began to prepare for his profession in the Barnes Medical College, now the National University of Arts and Sciences, at St. Louis, where he completed the regular course and was graduated M. D. in 1897. The subsequent seventeen years have been devoted to a general practice at Jameson, where his success and standing in the profession give him first rank. In 1912 he returned to his alma mater for post-graduate work, and at its conclusion received an ad eundem degree.

August 21, 1895, Doctor Graham married Miss Maud C. Miller, of Jamesport, daughter of Mack Miller, a well known farmer in that locality. To their marriage have been born four children: James B., Jr., who died at the age of one year, Martha Lois, Jack Sutcliff and Mary Elizabeth.

Doctor Graham is a democrat, fraternally is a member of the Masonic Lodge, the Independent Order of Odd Fellows, the Knights of Pythias and the Woodmen of the World, while his professional associations are with the Tri-State Medical Society, comprising Missouri, Iowa and Illinois, the Grand River Valley Medical Society and the Missouri Valley Medical Society.

E. W. SMITH. The business of general farming, under the favorable conditions offered in Hickory Township, Holt County, has an enthusiastic and altogether successful follower in the person of E. W. Smith, the owner of a fine farm of 240 acres. He has not only won material success in the time of his residence here, but has contributed to the progress and welfare of his community by years of efficient public service, as justice of the peace and in other capacities, and is also widely known in religious work.

" 'Squire'' E. W. Smith was born in Vernon County, Missouri, January 23, 1864, and is a son of Elijah W. and Annon K. Dunnigan Smith, the former a native of Indiana and the latter of Missouri. The children, all born in Vernon County, were as follows: Gaddson, Vincent C., E. W., Seamore, Dr. A. S. J. and James E. E. W. Smith, the third child, was reared in the vicinity of his birth and there received his education in the district schools, which he attended during the winter months. He remained under the parental roof, assisting his father with the duties of the homestead, until his marriage, at which time he went to live on the farm of his father-in-law, but subsequently bought a farm in Andrew County, Missouri, and there lived for about six years. When he first located upon that tract, it was still in its wild state, but Mr. Smith improved and cultivated the ground, and erected a number of substantial buildings. When he disposed of his interest in this property, Mr. Smith came to Holt County, and in Hickory Township bought the 120-acre farm which formerly belonged to the original settler, D. P. Smallwood, to which he later added by purchase another tract of 120 acres. He now has all his land under a good state of cultivation, engaging in general farming and stockraising and securing excellent results from his labors. As a farmer he is classed among the progressive tillers of the soil in his part of the county, and has always shown a willingness to try new inventions and methods, while he always uses the most highly improved machinery in his work. His buildings are commodious, attractive and in a good state of repair, and the whole appearance of the farm is one which stamps its owner as a man of good judgment and careful management.

A democrat in politics, Mr. Smith has taken some active part in public affairs, and has been called to fill several offices of local importance. He has for ten years been justice of the peace, being three times elected and once appointed and is now on his last four-year term. He was a member of the school board at Newpoint shortly after his arrival in Holt County, and was district clerk at Shiloh for a number of years. His public services have been characterized by faithful performance of duty and capable handling of the affairs of office. Fraternally he is connected with the Masonic Order, belonging to the Blue Lodge at Mound City. Mr. Smith has been very active in religious affairs, being elder in the Christian Church at Newpoint, township president of the Sunday School Organization, and secretary and treasurer of the Christian Church Sunday School Organization for Holt County.

In the spring of 1886 Mr. Smith was united in marriage with Miss Frances A. Praisewater, daughter of Samuel and Susan A. (Neas) Praisewater, early settlers of Andrew and Holt counties, who came here in the early '50s and are now deceased and buried in Holt County. They were farming people, and the parents of six sons and four daughters. Ten children have been born to Mr. and Mrs. Smith, namely: Harry, who died at the age of eighteen years; Nellie; Susan, who married J. Ralph

Myer; Samuel, who married Rosie McIntyre, and has one child, Louise; Myrtle L., who married Chauncey W. Huiatt; William H., who married Cleo Proud; Mabel S.; Vera Fay; Opal Temple and Emil A.

HUSTON WYETH. The careers and activities of many citizens enter into the solid structure of a city like St. Joseph. But the solid prosperity which distinguishes this commercial and industrial center can be traced to the enterprise of a group of men who have chosen this center as the scene of their business careers, and who through their leadership, their executive abilities, and their splendid capacity for business organization, have created and maintained a greater proportion of what is prominent and flourishing in local commerce. As a name that is both familiar in its associations with the wholesale and manufacturing activities of the Upper Missouri Valley, probably none is better known, and none is more distinctive of success and broad accomplishments, than that of Wyeth. Two generations of business builders have been identified with the growth and development of the great Wyeth Hardware and Manufacturing Company, and Mr. Huston Wyeth, president of the corporation, is the son of its founder, the late Mr. William Maxwell Wyeth.

In 1909, just fifty years after the business was established at St. Joseph, the outward evidences of its growth were substantially illustrated in the completion of the magnificent seven-story building which now serves as the business offices, the packing rooms and the general headquarters of the entire concern, in addition to the factories located in the same vicinity. This building occupies a half block of ground, 240x 140 feet, on the east side of Second Street, between Jule and Faraon streets, and on adjoining ground are located the harness and saddle factories and the collar factory, connected with the main building by tunnels. In November, 1908, the foundation of the new building was laid, and the entire structure completed ready for occupancy on July 24, 1909. Six and a half acres of floor space are provided by the seven stories and the basement, and including the floor space in the factories there are 10½ acres, now devoted to the great business under the name of Wyeth. So far as possible the building has been made fireproof, and has been equipped not only with all the mechanical facilities for the expeditious handling of goods, but also with many comforts and conveniences for the employees and the official staff.

While this modern commercial building is in itself an illustration of the magnitude of the business transacted by the Wyeth Hardware and Manufacturing Company, perhaps a more graphic evidence is found in the fact that the pay roll of the company comprises more than five hundred persons. Two hundred and twenty-five men are in the harness, collar and saddlery departments, and 152 are in the hardware department, ninety-three of these being in the general office. The trade of the Wyeth Company is with retail dealers from the Mississippi River to the Pacific coast, and a corps of seventy-six traveling men represent the company in all the states from the Canadian boundary line to Mexico, and from the Mississippi to the Pacific.

When the late William Maxwell Wyeth came to St. Joseph in 1859, he began selling hardware in a little three-story building, twenty feet in front, on the south side of Market Square. St. Joseph was then a thriving river town of about seven thousand people, and had recently come into prominence as an advantageous point for business through the completion of the Hannibal and St. Joseph railways, the first road to reach the Missouri River on its north and south course. To the west were the plains of Nebraska and Kansas territories, and over all the vast intervening country between the Pacific and the Missouri River the only routes of transportation were the Santa Fe, the Overland and the Salt Lake .trails. Thus St. Joseph became naturally the distributing point for all the West, and there the Pony Express and the Overland stage met the freight and passenger coach. Though the late Mr. Wyeth began business with a limited capital and on a moderate scale, and was soon overtaken by the unsettled conditions of the Civil war, he exercised such energy as to cause a steady progress in his undertaking, and there has never been a time when the business was not on a substantial basis. Soon after the war, in 1866, fire destroyed all the block in which the business was conducted, but there was little interruption, since other quarters were temporarily obtained, and a new building, with three times the floor space of the first, was completed in 1867 at 105-107 South Third Street. During the first dozen years the business was confined to general lines of hardware, but in 1872 the manufacture of harness and saddles was begun on a large scale, and the goods turned out under the Wyeth brand have for forty years held an unrivaled place in the trade. That extension caused the building of additional facilities, and every few years some improvement of quarters has been made. The firm up to 1881 was conducted under the name of W. M. Wyeth & Company, and in that year was incorporated as the Wyeth Hardware and Manufacturing Company. At that time the business occupied three store rooms on Third Street, one on Fourth Street, a factory for collars on North Second Street, and a building. just completed, for a harness and saddle factory, on Second Street next to the collar factory. In course of the next twenty-five years at least half a dozen important building additions and remodelings were undertaken to provide needed quarters for the enlarging scope of the trade and manufacture. When the company in 1892 erected its five-story building, 130x140 feet, on North Second Street, that was one of the most conspicuous additions to the wholesale district, and was hailed as a great step in advance for St. Joseph commerce, though in comparison with the new building above described, that was a comparatively insignificant structure.

The Wyeth family which has been so conspicuous in St. Joseph business and civic life has a long and interesting American history. The founder of the name, and the direct lineal ancestor of the St. Joseph Wyeths was Nicholas Wyeth, who was born in England in 1595, came to América about 1630, settled at Newton, Massachusetts, and spent his last days in Cambridge, where he died January 19, 1680. He was twice married, and the second wife and the mother of the children was Rebecca Andrew, who survived him and married Thomas Fox: (2) John Wyeth, next in line. was born July 15, 1655, and on January 29, 1682, married Deborah Ward. He added to the military distinctions of the family by service in King Philip's war in Major Goodkin's company, and was also at one time constable in Cambridge. His business was that of stone and brick mason, and he died December 13, 1706. His wife was the daughter of John Ward. (3) Ebenezer Wyeth, who was born in 1698. was a custom shoemaker, and died April 3, 1754. He married in 1726, Susanna Hancock, who was born in 1707 and died January 29, 1789. (4) Ebenezer Wyeth, Jr., was born April 8, 1727, followed farming as a vocation, and held the office of selectman in Cambridge from 1781 to 1790. He and his son Joshua were members of

the age of twenty-two, moved to Harrisburg, Pennsylvania. He became a prominent business man and citizen of the state capital, and with John Allen published the paper called the Oracle of Dauphin until 1827. From 1793 to 1798 he was also postmaster at Harrisburg. In connection with his other business he opened a book store and conducted a general publishing house. One of the publications was a music book compiled by himself and of which about one hundred and twenty thousand copies were sold. He served as president of the board of trustees of the Harrisburg Academy, and had a long and useful career. His death occurred at Philadelphia January 23, 1858. He was twice married. On June 6, 1793, he married Louise Weiss, a daughter of Lewis and Mary Weiss of Philadelphia. She died June 1, 1822, and on May 7, 1826, he married Lydia Allen. (6) Francis Wyeth, who was born at Harrisburg, Pennsylvania, April 5, 1806, was educated in the Harrisburg Academy, graduated from Jefferson College in 1827, and later succeeded his father as editor of the Oracle of Dauphin, and also was in business as a book seller and publisher and followed the example of his father in his relation to public affairs. He served as president of the board of trustees of Harrisburg Academy, and during the Civil war did much patriotic work as a member of the United States Sanitary Commission. On May 29, 1829, he married Susan Maxwell, a daughter of William and Ann Maxwell, natives of Pennsylvania. She died December 24, 1841.

(7) The late William Maxwell Wyeth, the St. Joseph business pioneer and founder of the great company above described, was born in Harrisburg, Pennsylvania, February 17, 1832. While he was active in business at St. Joseph for more than forty years and a vigorous worker from youth up, he attained almost the psalmist's span of life, and at his death in 1901 left a splendid record of material accomplishments and individual character. He received an academic education in his youth, and early in his manhood moved to Chillicothe, Ohio, where for a time he was employed as clerk in a dry goods store and for a short time worked in a hardware establishment. Thus he was early destined to leave the paths traversed by his father and grandfather, and all his career was devoted to merchandising on a large scale. He soon bought an interest in the hardware business at Chillicothe, and became junior member of the firm of Lewis & Wyeth. In 1858 he left Ohio and visited several western cities in order to investigate the possibilities and prospects for a location. As a result of this tour in 1859 he sold his interest in the hardware business at Chillicothe and moved to St. Joseph. The situation of that city with respect to the trade of the great western territory and its transportation by the new railroad and by the old river route has been set forth in a preceding paragraph, and Mr. Wyeth was a man capable by experience and natural ability of making the most of the opportunities which he found. Thereafter for years he was the guiding spirit in the successful growth of the W. M. Wyeth & Company and later of the Wyeth Hardware and Manufacturing Company, and when he died one of St. Joseph's most eminent merchants was taken from the community.

William Maxwell Wyeth on September 28, 1858, married Eliza Renick. She was born near Bainbridge, Ohio, August 25, 1837. Her father, Thomas Renick, was born January 11, 1804, and died in 1844, and married Elizabeth Morris. Thomas Renick's father, Felix Renick, was born November 5, 1770, and died in January, 1848. He was a farmer and stock raiser in Ohio, and one of the first men to import blooded stock from England. His father in turn was William Renick, who was reared in Hardy County, Virginia, now West Virginia, and moved to the new State of Ohio about 1806, where he spent the rest of his days. William Renick married Ann Heath.

(8) Huston Wyeth, who was born in St. Joseph, Missouri, July 8, 1863, the only son of William Maxwell Wyeth, was in the eighth generation from the founder of the Wyeth name in America, and there are few families in Northwest Missouri whose genealogy can be traced in such an unbroken line through so many generations in American history. He received his early education in the public schools of St. Joseph, and was also a student in St. Paul's Academy at Racine, Wisconsin. Aside from the time devoted to schooling, he has spent practically all of his active career in the business founded by his father, grew up in the offices, the warehouses, and the factories, and has long had a responsible place in the management of the enterprise. On completing his education he spent several years in the retail hardware trade, and then in 1880, in recognition of his interest and ability, was elected a director and vice president of the Wyeth Hardware and Manufacturing Company. On April 13, 1901, following the death of his father, he was elected president of the company. While the Wyeth name has deservedly stood foremost in the history of the development of this great business, there has also been capable associates, and Mr. Wyeth has always been quick to recognize and appreciate what these associates have done toward the success of the business. After the death of William M. Wyeth, the oldest official in the business was Charles F. Steinacker, who joined the company in 1861, and has been continuously associated with its progress, and for a number of years has been treasurer. George M. Johnson, vice president of the company, entered its employ in 1883, thirty years ago, and there are several others who have been continuously in the service of the firm for thirty years or more. Mr. Huston Wyeth is also president of the St. Joseph Artesian Ice and Cold Storage Company, and has stock and is officially connected with a number of other corporations. While he has been a business man closely absorbed in his work, he recognizes the value of a vacation, and has traveled extensively in both the United States and Europe.

On April 4, 1883, Huston Wyeth married Leila Ballinger. She was born in St. Joseph, a daughter of Isaac and Elizabeth (Kuechle) Ballinger. The four children of their marriage are named as follows: William Maxwell, Maud, Alison, and John. The daughter, Maud, married Kenyon V. Painter. Alison is the wife of Forrest C. Campbell, and has a daughter named Elizabeth. John married Margaret Mitchell. The oldest son, William M., who was born in St. Joseph May 12, 1884, and following the example of his father, grew up in the business, was elected second vice president February 2, 1909.

Huston Wyeth has a number of fraternal and social relations: Charity Lodge, No. 331, A. F. & A. M.; Mitchell Chapter, No. 89, R. A. M.; Hugh de Payne Commandery, No. 51, K. T.; St. Joseph Lodge Perfection, No. 6, Scottish Rite; Moila Temple of the Mystic Shrine; St. Joseph Lodge, No. 22, Knights of Pythias; St. Joseph Lodge, No. 40, B. P. O. E.; and is a member of the St. Joseph Country Club, the New York Yacht Club, and the Atlantic Yacht Club.

WESLEY HODGIN. Holt County has been the home of Wesley Hodgin all his life, and his father was one of the pioneers of this community, having located here sixty years ago. Since then the Hodgin family name has stood for the best qualities not only in the life of an individual and community but in that of the nation—industry, improvement, home making, and a steady influence in behalf of education, religion and morality.

Wesley Hodgin was born in Holt County, April 16, 1860, a son of John and Mary Ann (Hill) Hodgin. There were five children in the family, named William, Walter, Wesley, Scott and Sherman, all of whom were born on the old homestead in Holt County. John Hodgin, the father, came from Washington County, Indiana, to Northwest Missouri in 1855, bringing with him his wife, whom he had married in Indiana. His first year was spent as a renter, but he then bought and entered land, which became the nucleus of his large homestead, and on which he lived until about ten years ago. His original farm comprised 160 acres, and a part of it was entered direct from the Government. The deed to this property was signed by James Buchanan, who was then President of the United States. The deed is now prized as a family relic. All the land was prairie, and was in the condition which had prevailed for centuries, no plow ever having turned over a foot of the soil. The first home was one of the typical log cabins which were so numerous in Northwest Missouri at that time, and in the early days neighbors were few and far between. In this community the father spent his active career, and passed away an honored old settler on November 5, 1912. The mother is also deceased.

Wesley Hodgin married Lillie Allen, daughter of Edgar and Eliza (Risk) Allen, who lived in Holt County, where Mrs. Hodgin's mother was born. Mrs. Hodgin was one of eleven children, of whom four are now deceased. Without children of their own, Mr. and Mrs. Hodgin have taken into their home three children to rear, and two of them are now deceased. They now have a foster daughter aged ten, and she came to live with them about two years ago. Mr. Hodgin has occupied his present farm since 1903, and it comprises 300 acres all told. This is the first farm that ever sold in Holt County for $100 an acre. Politically Mr. Hodgin votes with the republican party.

JASPER NEWTON RICE. The general course of action displayed in the life of Jasper Newton Rice, by whose stable citizenship the Town of Martinsville has profited greatly, has been an expression of practical and diversified activity, and in its range has invaded the realms of finance, education, agriculture, politics and society, all of which have gained by the breadth and conscientiousness which are distinctive features of his work and character.

Mr. Rice belongs to one of the old and highly esteemed families of this part of Missouri, having been born in Jefferson Township, Harrison County, March 13, 1872, a son of Jasper Newton Rice. The father was born near Ridgeway, Missouri, in 1837, had a limited education, and was a son of Henry Rice, who came to Missouri as one of Harrison County's pioneers, at a time when this whole North Missouri country was a wilderness frequented by game. He came from near Frankfort, Kentucky, and his leaving home was as a runaway lad, he going to New Orleans by boat, and, following his disposition as a hunter, drifting up into this part of Missouri. He was a crack shot with his rifle and his marksmanship gained him great reputation through the community. He married in this section and settled down in the Ridgeway locality, finally moving to near the old Town of Brooklyn, Missouri, and in the '80s moved to Kansas, where he died about 1890, aged eighty-two years. He was a modest farmer, inclined largely to the pioneer sports of the country, participated little in politics and was a confessed member of no church. He married Catherine Taylor and their children were: Jasper Newton; Richard, a resident of Allendale, Missouri; Phoebe, who married Douglas Noseman; and Kate, who died unmarried.

Jasper Newton Rice, the elder, died before the birth of his son, Jasper N., of this review. His death occurred in August, 1871, as a result of injuries received and sickness contracted during the Civil war, through which he served as a private of the Twenty-third Regiment, Missouri

Volunteer Infantry. While his service was confined chiefly to Southern Missouri, he also took part in the battle of Pea Ridge, Arkansas, and was in the fight at Wilson Creek just before that engagement. Mr. Rice was in the army until after the surrender of General Lee. As a citizen he was a man of quiet demeanor, without any public career, and was a member of the Christian Church. In political matters he was a stalwart and uncompromising republican.

Jasper Newton Rice, Sr., married Joanna Dale, a daughter of Edward and Sarah Dale. The Dales came to Missouri from Kentucky prior to the outbreak of the Civil war and were farming people. Mrs. Rice is now a resident of St. Joseph, Missouri. She and Mr. Rice had three children: John H., of St. Joseph, assistant engineer of the public schools of that city; Ira W., who is a resident of Martinsville; and Jasper Newton, of this review. Mrs. Rice was married a second time, her husband being the late W. W. Wiatt, and to this union there were born two children: Claud F., a resident of St. Joseph; and Edward, who lives at Lakin, Kansas.

Jasper Newton Rice passed his boyhood on a farm within five miles of the Village of Martinsville, and his education was secured from the country schools and through a year's work at Stanberry Normal School. Qualifying as an educator, he adopted that line of work, and during the next twelve years taught country school in Harrison County, in the meantime spending the summer months in farming. He left the schoolroom to enter his present position as cashier of the Bank of Martinsville, coming into this institution in 1909 as its third cashier and succeeding John H. Ross. This bank was organized in 1903 and capitalized at $10,000, and its first officers were W. L. Magee, president; E. T. Baldwin, vice president, and T. J. Wayman, cashier. Its president at this time is W. G. Carter and its vice president W. R. Clelland. The bank's earnings have gone into the surplus fund, which is now $15,000, while the undivided profits are $2,500.

Mr. Rice's interest in farming has continued undisturbed, and his landed connections with this locality are extensive, aggregating 755 acres. The farms are well improved, one of those recently acquired by him being the best improved property in this section of the state. Mr. Rice has been connected with one of the local telephone companies since its organization, and at present is treasurer of the Harrison County Mutual Telephone Company. He is also treasurer of the Bethany and Mount Ayr Trail Association, a public highway organization founded for the purpose of donating toward the upkeep of a main thoroughfare north and south, to which movement he is himself a liberal contributor. He is president of the Martinsville school board, takes a keen, active and helpful interest in all that promises to advance the welfare of his community, and is justly accounted one of Martinsville's representative men. Mr. Rice's political affiliation is with the republican party, but his activities in political matters have been principally as a voter.

Mr. Rice was married in Harrison County, Missouri, in May, 1896, to Miss Estelle Porter, a daughter of Charles E. and Mary A. (Edgar) Porter. The Porters originated in Ohio, from whence they migrated West to Kansas, spending a few years in that state and then coming to Missouri during the '80s. Mr. Porter was a farmer by vocation and an industrious and enterprising citizen. His children were: Carey; Laura, who is the wife of H. E. Bird, of Denver, Colorado; Ada, who is the wife of C. R. Long, of Harrison County; Jennie, who married John Nichols, of Martinsville, Missouri; Estelle, who is Mrs. Rice; Maud, who married George Jones, of Hinton, Oklahoma; Veva, who is the wife of Orley Hefner, of Lakin, Kansas; and Claud, of Nevada, Missouri. Three children have been born to Mr. and Mrs. Rice, namely: Eunice, Dwight and Delia, the latter two twins.

Mr. Rice has shown some interest in fraternal work and is connected with the local lodge of the Independent Order of Odd Fellows, in which he has numerous friends, as he has in the various walks of life which he frequents. He has always supported the denomination of the Methodist Episcopal Church, although not wholly in accord with all the doctrines of any orthodox church.

JOHN WESLEY KENYON. Active in business and in county affairs, John W. Kenyon has been a resident of Harrison County since July, 1868. His life has been distinguished by none of those abnormal events that make a man notorious, but by steady, persevering performances of duties that lay close at hand, by rendering faithful service whether as a soldier or in his civil duties, and by an integrity and honorableness that are permanent assets of his character.

Coming of a Methodist family as his name indicates, and of good old American stock, John Wesley Kenyon was born in Warren County, New York, March 3, 1845. Nearly half a century before the triumphant conclusion of the Revolutionary war two Kenyon brothers came from England and in 1734 settled in Rhode Island. One of these brothers, the direct ancestor of John W., had seven sons and two daughters, and these children and their cousins scattered through New England and New York, and in a later generation the name was transplanted in the West. John S. Kenyon, one of the seven sons just mentioned, was a native of Rhode Island, gave his services to the colonies in their struggle for independence and soon after that war settled in Warren County, New York, where he acquired some extensive tracts of land. He died in Warren County and had for several years been getting a pension from the Government for his services as a Revolutionary soldier. He married a Miss Cameron, of Scotch family, and among their children were Clayton Y., David S., Anna, who also married a Cameron, Phineas and Ebenezer.

Phineas Kenyon, father of John W., who is thus the grandson of a Revolutionary soldier, was born in Warren County, New York, December 3, 1792, at a time that made him old enough to serve as a soldier in the War of 1812. He participated in the campaign, the chief battle of which was fought at Plattsburgh, New York. For this service a land warrant was given him, and he laid it in Minnesota, but subsequently exchanged it for property in Illinois. In 1855 he moved to Illinois, settling in Henry County, where his years were spent in farming until his death on September 29, 1863. In his home community he was affectionately known as "Uncle Fin," and was a man of wonderful physical vigor, having few equals in chopping wood, handling logs, running the river, lifting loads, and in a rough and tumble scuffle or wrestling match. Originally a whig, he was ardent in his support of the abolition cause, and in 1860 he and his son and two sons-in-law cast their votes at Erie in Whiteside County, Illinois, for Mr. Lincoln. He was a faithful, quiet Christian, being a member of the Methodist Church.

The first wife of Phineas Kenyon was Emily J. Cameron, and their children were: Emily, who married Charles J. Clark, of Bennington, Vermont; Jane and Margaret, who both died unmarried; Rev. Randall J., a minister of Methodist Episcopal Church in Illinois, who moved to Grinnell, Iowa, belonged to the Iowa Conference, but later went to Jetmore, Kansas, where his remains are now interred; and Ruhama, who married Oren Ingram and died in Henry County, Illinois. After the death of his first wife Phineas Kenyon married Mrs. Elizabeth J. (Ross) Bullock, whose father was Samuel Ross, also a soldier of the Revolution, as one of the Green Mountain boys, thus making John W. a grandson of two Revolutionary soldiers. Samuel Ross was also a pensioner of the Revolutionary war. Mrs. Kenyon was born at Bennington, Vermont, June 10, 1808, being eighteen years younger than Mr. Kenyon. She died at Bazine, Kansas, in March, 1879. Her only child by her second marriage is John W. Kenyon. Her first husband was Reuben Bullock, and of the children of that union the only one to grow up was Lucy, who married Richard Reynolds, and both died at Meeker, Colorado.

John W. Kenyon went with his parents to Henry County, Illinois, at the age of ten, and lived there uninterruptedly until the beginning of his military experience. His education came from the common schools, and he was seventeen when he volunteered to defend the Union of states. He enlisted August 15, 1862, in Company K of the One Hundred and Twelfth Illinois Infantry. His captain was Joseph Wesley and his colonel Thomas J. Henderson, who afterwards was promoted to brigadier general, represented Illinois in Congress, and died only a few years ago. The regiment was part of the fourteenth corps in Kentucky and Tennessee, of the sixteenth corps in Tennessee and Georgia, and finally in the fifteenth corps in the campaigns back through Georgia and Tennessee after the fall of Atlanta. His first engagement came a few weeks after enlistment at Perryville, Kentucky, and he was in some skirmishes around Franklin and Nashville, fought at Lookout Mountain, and at Resaca during the Atlanta campaign received a wound in the foot and a rupture. He was in the hospital at Nashville until his recovery, and then was honorably discharged and returned home.

He was still a boy in years when the war closed, and after a short time spent on the home farm he set out to join his brother in Iowa, who was in ministerial work in Jasper County, and at Newton found employment with a marble and monument man. It never occurred to him at the time that he was entering the field of his permanent life work, but such proved to be the case, and for nearly half a century he has been more or less active in the marble and granite business. He was attracted to Bethany in 1868 by a desire to become a salesman and see the country. He was a salesman of marble at St. Joseph and Chillicothe and other places in Northwest Missouri, but his headquarters have been for the greater part of the time at Bethany. He represented the Bethany yard established in 1880 by Mr. Sykes, but soon afterward acquired control of the business, and for many years was the sole proprietor. He now has an associate in the business, Mr. S. D. Stanley.

While the above explains the chief fact in his business career, Mr. Kenyon has been more or less an active figure in county affairs, and many people know him best through his official duties. The first fall he spent in Harrison County he was employed in the sheriff and collector's office, and was deputy sheriff and collector and deputy county clerk until his election in 1874 as county clerk. He has subsequently served in the offices of the circuit clerk, the county clerk, probate judge and sheriff, as deputy, and altogether spent twenty-five years in the court-house, looking after his business interests at the same time. Politically he has always been found supporting the republican party, and was elected county clerk and to various township offices on that ticket. As deputy or chief assessor he has assessed Bethany Township thirteen times, and has at different times been deputy county treasurer. Perhaps no one citizen has a more exact knowledge of the details of the various public offices of Harrison County than Mr. Kenyon. In earlier years he was in the habit of attending congressional and state conventions, and was in the convention which nominated B. Gratz Brown for governor

of Missouri, and also supported the candidacy of Reverend Mr. Burroughs, who was sent from this district to Congress as a greenbacker.

As a Grand Army man Mr. Kenyon is a charter member of Neal
Post No. 124, which was organized in 1882, and is one of the forty-five
who now compose its active membership. He has always held some
position in the post, and is its present adjutant. The National encamp-
ments he has attended have been five, those at Columbus, St. Louis, Milwaukee, Chicago and Salt Lake City. His Masonic affiliations are with
the lodge, chapter and commandery and the Order of the Eastern Star,
and in the first three he is respectively past master, past high priest
and past eminent commander, and at the present time is recorder in all
three branches. He is also identified with the subordinate and encampment degrees of Odd Fellowship, is a past grand, and has sat in the grand
lodges of Missouri both in Masonry and the Odd Fellows. He was at one
time a member of the old "87th" lodge of the Knights of Pythias. As a
layman he has done honor to his Methodist name, has been an official
member, has taught the Bible class of Sunday School thirty-four years,
and in all that time has been absent only twenty-three Sundays, due to
sickness or unavoidable absence from home.

Mr. Kenyon has been twice married, both times in Harrison County.
His first wife was Mary E. Howell and they were married November 17,
1870. Her father, Marshall K. Howell, was a native of Kentucky, a
pioneer Northwest Missourian, lived in Daviess County through the
Mormon war, and very early established a home in Harrison County.
Mrs. Kenyon was one of the four children of her father's marriage to
Mary Young, and there were three children by his first marriage. Mrs.
Kenyon died December 12, 1875. Her two children are: Maud, wife of
Charles H. Cole, of Pueblo, Colorado, who has five children, Ernest,
Edna, Edward, Robert and Virgil; and Guy M., who lives in Glenwood
Springs, Colorado.

On October 11, 1876, Mr. Kenyon married Miss Hetta J. Burns.
Her father, Thomas Burns, who now lives at McFall, Missouri, was
born in Cattaraugus County, New York, has spent his life as a farmer,
and by his marriage to Jane Doane, also of Cattaraugus County, New
York, has the following children: Mrs. Kenyon; Emma, wife of Price
Taylor, of Pattonsburg, Missouri; Rose, wife of David Burton, of McFall,
Missouri; Ella, wife of William Meyers, of McFall; Ida, wife of Charles
A. Stewart, of McFall; and Thomas, of Craig, Missouri. Mr. and Mrs.
Kenyon are the parents of four children: Omer J., who lives in St.
Joseph, married Margaret Jenkins, of Denver, Colorado, and they have
a daughter, Annetta; Lucy R., wife of A. C. Flint, the present sheriff
of Harrison County; Irma and Charles W., both attending high school
at Bethany.

JOHN A. BURTCH, M. D. Among those qualities which have contributed to the professional success and standing of Dr. John A. Burtch,
of Coffey, Daviess County, are good birth and breeding, an excellent
training in advanced institutions, and a devotion to his calling that has
frequently caused him to sacrifice his own interests in its behalf. He
came to this community as a young man of twenty-five years, with an
earnest and clearly defined purpose, and from the time of his arrival
has been an active factor in the things that have developed the community.

Dr. John A. Burtch was born at Mapleton, Bourbon County, Kansas,
August 17, 1871, and is a son of George W. and Theresa M. (Greer)
Burtch, the former a native of Ohio and the latter of Missouri. During
the Civil war, George W. Burtch served in the Union army as a member
of the Missouri Volunteer Cavalry, and was wounded by bushwhackers

near Jefferson City. After several months passed in the hospital he received his honorable discharge because of disability. He was married to Theresa M. Greer at Lindley, Missouri, and subsequently moved to Bourbon County, Kansas, where Mr. Burtch was engaged in agricultural pursuits for eleven years, at the end of which time they returned to Lindley. They went thence to Grundy County, Missouri, where they resided from 1889 to 1906, later went to Kansas City, Kansas, where the father died January 13, 1913, while the mother still makes her home there.

John A. Burtch attended a public school in Bourbon County, Kansas, for one term and after accompanying his parents to Linn County, Missouri, was a student in the country log schoolhouse, there completing his primary education. He next attended the high school at Laredo for two terms, this being supplemented by one year in the normal school at Chillicothe. In 1892 Mr. Burtch entered the College of Physicians and Surgeons, at Keokuk, Iowa, after teaching school for one year, and March 5, 1895, was graduated from that institution with the degree of Doctor of Medicine. He immediately entered upon the practice of his profession at Lucerne, Missouri, where he remained for ten months, and in February, 1896, came to Coffey, Missouri, where he opened an office. Doctor Burtch has been in continuous practice here to the present time, and in point of service is the oldest physician at Coffey. From the time of his arrival his practice has steadily grown, and he is now recognized as one of the representative members of his calling in this part of the county. His inherent skill is constantly being supplemented by study and research, and he keeps fully abreast of the advancements which science is making in the medical profession. He holds membership in the Daviess County Medical Society and the Missouri State Pharmaceutical Association. In 1909 Doctor Burtch bought from the widow of J. W. Pennebacker the drug stock formerly owned by her husband, and since that time has carried on the business in connection with his practice. He has been a registered pharmacist since August 31, 1900.

On July 11, 1895, Doctor Burtch was united in marriage with Miss Melissa E. Kilburn, of Gallatin, Missouri, a daughter of David Kilburn, of Laredo, Missouri. They have had no children, but have reared an adopted niece, Opal Warren.

Fraternally, Doctor Burtch is connected with the Royal Arch Masons, the Woodmen of the World and the Modern Woodmen of America. Politically a ''stand-pat'' republican, he is one of the leaders of his party in Daviess County, and has been called upon to fill various offices in the community. He was a member of the school board for six years, was township trustee of Salem Township for two terms, and health officer during the siege of small-pox at Coffey, when he showed his bravery and skill in many ways and personally attended fifty-four cases. During the past twelve years he has been a member of the United States Board of Pension Examiners for Daviess County. In every respect, Doctor Burtch is a stirring, valuable and valued citizen, and his contributions to his community's welfare have gained and retained for him the respect and esteem of the people among whom he has made his home for eighteen years.

RALPH COTTIER. Three generations of the Cottier family have contributed to the material advancement of Holt County, and more particularly to the agricultural interests of this community. Those bearing the name have always been accounted men of industry, initiative and energy, doing whatever they have found to do in an intelligent and thoroughly capable manner, and in this connection it may be said that Ralph Cottier, one of the enterprising young agriculturists of Benton

Township, is no exception to the rule. He has followed in the footsteps of his father and grandfather, devoting his energies to the cultivation of the soil, and at the present time is the owner of a handsome and well-cultivated property of 110 acres.

Thomas Cottier, the grandfather of Ralph Cottier, and founder of the family in Holt County, Missouri, was born on the Isle of Man, and had not long passed his majority when he took up his residence in Northwest Missouri, settling first about two and one-half miles north of Oregon. There he put up a log cabin and several other buildings and cultivated his land with slave labor, but four or five years after his arrival removed to Forest City, Holt County, by way of the river, this being before the time that the course of the stream was changed. He was the father of seven children, all born in Holt County, and all except one still reside here. Mr. Cottier was known as one of the earliest pioneers of this locality, where he erected the first frame house, and is still remembered by some of the older generation as a sturdy, self-reliant and reliable citizen.

James Cottier, son of the pioneer, and father of Ralph, was born in Holt County, Missouri, here grew to manhood, and adopted farming as his life's vocation, in which he still continues to be engaged. He has made a success of his operations and is now comfortably situated on a nice property located about eight miles north of Mound City. Mr. Cottier is a republican but has taken only a good citizen's interest in matters of a public nature. He married Flora Alice King, who was born in Indiana, and who as a child accompanied her parents to Missouri, the family driving through in a wagon in true pioneer style. She still survives and has been the mother of six children, as follows: Ralph, Fred, Frank, Ira, Edith and Earl.

Ralph Cottier was born in Holt County, Missouri, August 31, 1884, and grew up on the homestead, on which he worked during the summer months, while attending the district schools in the winter terms. This educational training was subsequently supplemented by a course in a business college, at St. Joseph, and when he had completed his education he settled down to farming on his present property in Benton Township. He is possessed of modern ideas, is a firm believer in the use of modern machinery and utensils, and has done much improving on his land, the farm's appearance testifying to the presence of good management. Still a young man, he has already won a substantial position in his community and is justly accounted a member of the element upon which the county must depend for its future progress and advancement. Like his father, Mr. Cottier is a republican. He belongs, fraternally to the Independent Order of Odd Fellows and the A. F. & A. M., and with his family attends the Christian Church.

Mr. Cottier married Miss Gotha Long, the daughter of Dr. W. A. Long, of Holt County, and to this union there has been born one daughter: Elizabeth.

WILLIAM KURTZ. A member of a family that has many sterling representatives in Holt County, Mr. Kurtz is numbered among the enterprising and substantial farmers and popular citizens of Noday Township, where he has a well improved farm of 102 acres, the same lying on the opposite side of the road from the old homestead place on which he was born, on the 11th of June, 1863, a son of Isaac and Mary (Suman) Kurtz, the former of whom is deceased and the latter of whom is now venerable in years and one of the noble pioneer women of Holt County. Of the thirteen children all are living except two and all are well established in life and in independent circumstances, with character and achievement that have honored the family name, which has been long and worthily identified with the history of this county. The parents were born in Germany and came to Holt County in the pioneer era of its history. The father had virtually no financial resources at the time when he came to Holt County, but he was imbued with self-reliance and ambition, and through his industry and good management he became one of the prosperous farmers of the county, his old homestead comprising 160 acres and the same having been by him reclaimed from its wild state. When he obtained the property its only definite improvement was a small frame house of only two rooms, in which the home was established. He eventually was able to erect the substantial buildings that now mark the farm as being well improved and on this old homestead he continued to reside until his death. He reared his children to lives of usefulness and honor and gave to them the best educational advantages it was possible for him to provide. He had the industry and energy typical of the race from which he sprung, and his career was marked by earnest and fruitful endeavor as well as by impregnable integrity in thought, word and deed, so that he ever commanded the confidence and good will of all who knew him and his name merits enduring place on the roll of the sterling pioneers who aided in the development and upbuilding of Holt County. His political support was given to the republican party and he became a church member prior to his emigration from his native land, his widow being a devout member of the Presbyterian Church at the present time.

William Kurtz has been actively concerned with agricultural enterprise in Holt County from the time of his early youth and is indebted to the schools of the county for the educational training which he received. He purchased his present farm in 1890, the buildings on the place having at the time been old and dilapidated, so that he was not long content to permit them to remain, as his spirit of thrift demanded better accommodations and provisions. Thus it comes that the excellent buildings that are now on the farm have been erected by him, the while he has made many other improvements and has brought the land into a high condition of productiveness, besides giving considerable attention to the raising of approved grades of live stock.

Mr. Kurtz is liberal in the support of measures and enterprises projected for the general good of the community, is a republican in politics, has served with zeal and efficiency as a member of the school board of his district, is affiliated with the lodge of Independent Order of Odd Fellows at Oregon, the county seat, and both he and his wife hold membership in the Presbyterian Church.

In 1891 Mr. Kurtz was united in marriage to Miss Anna Gelvin, who likewise was born and reared in Holt County and who is a daughter of the late Matthew Gelvin. Of the five children of this union, Roy, Lewis, Russell and Lester are living, and Mabel died at the age of six months.

THEODORE NEWBURN. During a residence at Bethany of fully forty-five years, Theodore Newburn has not only identified himself in a successful manner with the cares and responsibilities of private business, but has possessed and exercised that public spirit which looks after the welfare of the community, and supports institutions and movements that have a broader significance than the well being of the individual.

Theodore Newburn was born in Jefferson County, Ohio, October 26, 1845, and was reared in that vicinity. He comes of a family of quiet and industrious people, and his grandfather Mahlon Newburn was a farmer in Pennsylvania and Ohio and died in Jefferson County of the latter state during the early '50s. He was born in Bucks County, Pennsylvania, and by his marriage to Miss Puntney had children, John, Mahlon, Jane, Sarah and Eliza.

William Newburn, the Bethany citizen above named was born in Fayette County, Pennsylvania, July 11, 1818, was brought up on a farm, had a limited education, and learned the trade of bricklayer and stone cutter, an occupation followed by him for many years. When a boy he went with his parents to Ohio, and in 1844 was married in Wellsburg, West Virginia, to Miss Elizabeth Crayton. Her father was a farmer near Wellsburg and had been born in London, England. William Newburn died in 1896, and his wife in 1909 at the age of ninety. Their only child was Theodore Newburn.

Theodore Newburn during his youth spent on a farm acquired a somewhat limited education in the district schools of Eastern Ohio, and besides his training as a farmer was also taught the trade of stone cutter and brick layer. He spent seven years as a farmer and in work at his trade at Vandalia, Illinois, and in 1869 came to Northwest Missouri, making the trip by railroad as far as Chillicothe and reaching Bethany by means of the stage coach. He continued work at his trade in Harrison County until 1874, and in the following year took up merchandising in Bethany, as a partner of Andrew J. Fuller, succeeding W. H. Hillman in the drug business. From 1875 for about fifteen years this firm was the leading drug firm at Bethany, and Mr. Newburn was then in business alone until his retirement in 1896. In the meantime he had acquired numerous interests, has been identified with the Harrison County Bank for many years, and for several years was a director. He has always contributed to propositions that were designed to develop new resources about Bethany, and also to the corporations which promised larger activities and greater benefit to the town. Mr. Newburn has invested in local real estate, and now has one of the good homes of the city.

As to his political activity, Mr. Newburn was reared a democrat and continued to vote with that party until, as he explains, "Mr. Bryan tried to make the people believe that fifty cents was worth as much as a dollar," and in that campaign voted for McKinley, and has since been allied as a voter with the republican party. He was formerly quite active in the democratic party in Harrison County, served for ten years as chairman of the democratic committee, was frequently in the state conventions, and as a public officer was at one time city treasurer of Bethany. Fraternally Mr. Newburn has been affiliated with the Masonic Order since 1872, and has passed the chairs in the Blue Lodge, Chapter and Commandery, and has gone to the Grand Lodge as a delegate. He is a supporter of the Methodist Church, which he calls his church home, and with which his family are identified as members.

On September 10, 1868, Mr. Newburn was married in Vandalia, Illinois, to Miss Clarinda Weidner. Her father, Isaiah Weidner, married a Miss Schmidt, both of Pennsylvania German farming people. Mrs. Newburn died in Bethany, September 2, 1910, leaving two children: Mrs. W. C. Barlow and Mrs. W. W. Myers, both of Bethany. On December 1, 1913, Mr. Newburn married Mrs. Alice Browning, of Danville, Illinois. She was a sister of his first wife. Besides the two wives of Mr. Newburn, the children in the Weidner family comprised: Mrs. Mary Browning, of Burlington Junction, Missouri; Mrs. D. Browning, of Vandalia, Illinois; Mrs. Florence Freeland, now deceased, of Hagarstown, Illinois; and I. J. Weidner, of Sapulpa, Oklahoma. By his first marriage Mr. Newburn has four grandchildren, as follows: James T. Barlow, a senior student in the agricultural department of the State

University, and Harry M. Barlow; Zola Myers, a student in the University of Missouri; and Charles W. Myers.

LEE H. BUSSELL. The career of Lee H. Bussell, of Mount Moriah, reflects practical and useful ideals, and its range of activities has included merchandising, farming and banking, in each of which he has met with well-merited success. Mr. Bussell is a native of Mercer, Missouri, born near the line of Mercer and Harrison counties, March 24, 1864, and is a son of Elihu and Sarah J. (Milner) Bussell.

William Bussell, the grandfather of Lee H. Bussell, was born in Tennessee, from whence he removed to Kentucky and there carried on agricultural pursuits until the time of his death. His children were as follows: Martin, who spent his life at Indianapolis, Indiana; Eliza, who married Rankin Dinwiddie, and passed away at Albia, Iowa; Elihu; John T., of Nebraska City, Nebraska; and Will, who was killed as a Union soldier during the Civil war. Elihu Bussell, the father of Lee H. Bussell, was born in Kentucky, January 15, 1836, and was brought up on the home farm, his education being secured in the country public schools. As a youth he was taken by his parents to Hancock County, Indiana, and there he grew to manhood and was married, and in 1856 brought his family by way of wagon to a point seven miles southeast of Mount Moriah, which he patented and improved, and on which he made his home until the close of the Civil war. He then moved to a locality east of Mount Moriah, where he resided until 1884 and then moved to the village, where for a time he was interested in mercantile pursuits, and where he died April 22, 1887. During the Civil war he served for six months in the Missouri State Militia, as a member of Captain Hensleys' company, but was out in the field only upon the call of his colonel. In politics he was a republican and never held office nor did he attend conventions. Although not a member of any religious denomination, he attended the Baptist Church. Mr. Bussell was married in Indiana to Miss Sarah J. Milner, a daughter of James Milner, a farmer who went from Indiana to Kansas, and died at Madison in the latter state. Mrs. Bussell died June 23, 1909, having been the mother of the following children: James W., who is a resident of Osawatomie, Kansas; Mary A., who became the wife of Marshal Mullins, of Mercer County, Missouri; Julia E., who is the wife of C. B. Johnson, of the same county; Lee H., of this review; Jasper M., a resident of Osawatomie, Kansas, and Samuel R., of Kansas City, Missouri.

Lee H. Bussell grew up in the community in which he was born, received his education in the district schools of that vicinity, and lived there until nearly reaching his majority. His business career was commenced as a clerk in his father's mercantile establishment at Mount Moriah, the firm being Shoemaker & Bussell until the young man became a partner, when it was changed to Bussell & Son. This style continued until the death of the father, when the stock was sold to J. H. Myers, and Lee H. Bussell subsequently purchased an interest in the business, which became known as Myers & Bussell and continued as such for two years, when Mr. Bussell disposed of his interest to purchase a stock of dry goods at Princeton, at which point he engaged in merchandising. Mr. Bussell remained in Princeton as a merchant for one year, but at the end of that time, not feeling satisfied with his location, moved his stock to Mount Moriah and conducted a thriving business for two years. At that time his stock was destroyed by a fire, but he immediately secured another line of good, resumed business, and has continued to be engaged therein at Mount Moriah practically ever since. He is a partner in the dry goods concern of E. B. Johnson & Company, and in the firm of

C. S. Carpenter Hardware Company, of Mount Moriah, and his farming interests are extensive and important near this place. He is a wheat, corn and grass raiser, and grows from 350 acres of corn up and as much wheat. In addition, he handles stock as a feeder and shipper, and his own stock as well as a dealer and shipper.

Mr. Bussell was one of the organizers of the Bank of Mount Moriah, an institution which was formed in 1898 with a stock of $10,000, with Mr. Bussell as vice president, Mrs. N. M. Stoughton as president and W. P. Chambers as cashier. The bank has a $5,000 certified surplus, which is treated as capital stock, and a total surplus of $10,000. In 1906 Mr. Bussell became president of the bank as the successor of T. F. Gray, who had succeeded Mrs. Stoughton. The vice president at this time is E. L. Stoughton, and the cashier remains the same, while the official board comprises Mr. Chambers, John S. Twadell, E. L. Stoughton and Mr. Bussell.

Mr. Bussell cast his first presidential vote for Benjamin Harrison, and has supported all the republican nominees since that time. He was a delegate to the St. Louis State Republican Convention, in 1912, and helped name the delegate-at-large to the National Republican Convention at Chicago. He has also held various local offices, including those of trustee and member of the school board. Fraternally he is connected with the Independent Order of Odd Fellows, being past grand of Mount Moriah Lodge.

Mr. Bussell was married first March 16, 1892, at Modena, Missouri, to Miss Hattie B. Rock, a daughter of Joshua Rock, a pioneer to Missouri who first lived at Macon, his forefathers being from Kentucky. Mrs. Rock was formerly Amanda Scott. Mr. Rock was a farmer and merchant and his family comprised Walter F., of Denver, Colorado; Mrs. Bussell; and Stella, the wife of James S. Arnett, of McAlester, Oklahoma. To Mr. and Mrs. Bussell there have been born the following children: Walter I., who is a student at the Ottawa (Kansas) University; and Vivian, who is attending the public schools of McAlester, Oklahoma. Mrs. Bussell died January 13, 1905, and Mr. Bussell was married again, his wife being Zelpha Ross, a daughter of James and Margaret (Lloyd) Ross, who were early settlers of this section from Virginia and Ohio, respectively. Mr. Ross, who is a farmer, has been the father of the following children: Alice, who is the wife of W. P. Chambers; Jennie, who married Robert Frazee and died at Gilman City, Missouri; Mattie, who married Daniel Landes, and died in Oklahoma; Jacob W., of Mount Moriah; and Mrs. Bussell. Mr. and Mrs. Bussell have one son: Arthur Ross.

As a builder of Mount Moriah, Mr. Bussell erected the largest home of the town, and built also the store building where his enterprises do business. He was identified with the school board when the new brick schoolhouse was erected here, and has encouraged all worthy and progressive movements.

W. H. KELLER. In noting the qualities which have advanced W. H. Keller from the drudgery of a small rented farm to his present standing as one of the foremost citizens of Clay Township, Holt County, one is forced to renewed appreciation of courage, moral strength, perseverance and industry, for these have been the qualities which have formed the medium through which his rise has been made. Mr. Keller was born at Oregon, Holt County, Missouri, January 13, 1853, and is a son of Charles and Mary (Harmon) Keller, natives of Germany.

Charles Keller grew up in the Fatherland, and there received his education, learning also the trades of carpenter and furniture maker.

Deciding that there were better opportunities for advancement in the United States, he emigrated to this country in young manhood, and after traveling around for some time took up his residence in Oregon, Missouri, where not long afterward he was married. After following his trade for several years, Mr. Keller turned his attention to agricultural pursuits, settling on a small property four miles east of Oregon, which he developed from the raw prairie, and to which he added from time to time until he became the owner of 240 acres of good land, all under cultivation. He was a good business man and a reliable citizen, and when he died, November 2, 1894, left many friends to mourn him. The mother survived him ten years, dying in 1904, and like her husband was widely esteemed. They were the parents of four children, all born at Oregon, and of whom one is now deceased. A daughter is living in Andrew County and a son in Axtell, Kansas.

W. H. Keller was given only those educational advantages which are furnished by the public schools, and when ready to enter upon his own career was forced to do so on a rented property of eighty acres. Through hard and persevering work and economy he managed to accumulate enough to purchase his first eighty acres of land, the houses on which were fastened together with a plaster preparation containing straw and hair. As the years passed, and his finances permitted, Mr. Keller added to his holdings and gradually began to make improvements, so that today he is the owner of 808 acres of good land, on which are to be found fine, modern improvements. A part of this property has been inherited, but the greater portion has come to Mr. Keller as a result of his untiring, industrious labor. He is not a politician in the accepted sense of the word, having been too busily engaged with his own enterprises to seek the doubtful honors of the political arena, but has been willing to do his share in bearing the responsibilities of citizenship, and during the past three years has served very acceptably as a member of the school board. He supports republican candidates and policies, and both Mr. and Mrs. Keller belong to the Christian Church, but their children all belong to the Methodist Church. During the forty years of his residence in Clay Township, he has formed a wide acquaintance, and his general popularity is evidenced by his wide circle of friends.

Mr. Keller was married to Miss Mattie Hodge, one of the eight children of Steven and Martha Ann (Howell) Hodge, the former of New Jersey who is now a merchant of Oklahoma, while the latter was born in Mason County, Illinois, where they were married, and where Mrs. Keller was also born. Five children have been born to Mr. and Mrs. Keller, all on the present farm: Charles, who married Della Rowlett; Bertha, who is single and resides with her parents; Maud, who is the wife of Walter Rowlett; and Steven Henry and William Hobart, who are engaged in farming with their father, as is also Charles. Father and sons are looked upon as most progressive and energetic men, able representatives of the farming class that is maintaining such a high standard of agricultural supremacy in Holt County.

FRANCIS MARION SPRAGG. One of the public spirited men of Ridgeway in Harrison County is Francis Marion Spragg, successful as a real estate dealer, and a man who has devoted considerable attention to the civic, educational, moral and religious interests of that community

Francis Marion Spragg was born in Greene County, Pennsylvania, October 29, 1854, and comes of an old Pennsylvania family. The first American settler of the name is said to have come from Whitehall, England, and some of his descendants served in the Patriot Army of the United States in aid of independence. The great-grandfather of the Ridgeway citizen was Caleb Spragg. The grandfather, David Spragg, was born in Greene County, Pennsylvania, and spent his life as a farmer there. The family has been represented in Greene County since colonial times, and through their activities and their membership in one community there originated the town known as Spragg's Postoffice. Grandfather David Spragg married Nancy Gordon, and both spent their lives in Greene County. He was the owner of a large amount of land, was a favorite socially among his neighbors, entertained much company in the old home, and they were both active workers in the Methodist Protestant Church. He was a democrat, and all the family have affiliated with the same party. His death occurred at the age of eighty-one, followed about five years later by his wife. Their children were: Polly, who married Jesse Phillips, and died in Pennsylvania; Caleb A., who was born in December, 1829; William G., who died in Greene County; Adam, who spent his life in that Pennsylvania community; and Debbie, who married Joel Strawn of Greene County.

Caleb A. Spragg, father of Francis M., was born in Greene County, as already stated, in 1829, was active as a farmer and stock man, and for many years postmaster at Spragg's. He was a regular worker in church, and though never a speaker took active part in democratic politics and held several local offices. His death occurred in July, 1913. His wife was Sarah Johnson, daughter of William and Nancy (Lantz) Johnson. Their children were: Sylvanus L., a prominent surgeon and graduate of Jefferson Medical College at Philadelphia and now practicing at Wheeling, West Virginia; Francis M.; William F., who died in Greene County in 1913; David G., who died at Ridgeway, Missouri; and Clara N., who became the wife of C. K. Spragg of Waynesburg, Pennsylvania.

Francis M. Spragg was reared on the old farm at Spragg's Postoffice, was educated in the local schools and the high school, and qualified as a teacher, holding a permanent certificate in that state. For two years Mr. Spragg served as deputy sheriff, and for three years was in the newspaper business, managing the Greene County Democrat. During that time the circulation of the paper was increased from a thousand to more than three thousand. It was a democratic paper, published at Waynesburg, the county seat, and Mr. Spragg as editor pursued a vigorous policy in his editorials for good government and for temperance, and placed the paper in hundreds of homes where it had not been previously read. In Greene County at that time the dominant party was the democrats, and Mr. Spragg was one of its active leaders, though he declined to become a candidate for the office of sheriff, though urged in that course by his friends.

From Pennsylvania Mr. Spragg came west and located at St. Joseph, Missouri, where he was engaged in the real estate and mercantile business, and from there investigated the country about Ridgeway in 1888. After five years in St. Joseph he returned to Ridgeway and became a local merchant, a business he followed at intervals for a number of years. With his son Lloyd Mr. Spragg was for three years identified with the publication of the Ridgeway Journal, but since selling that paper he has given all his attention to real estate.

Mr. Spragg was married in Greene County, Pennsylvania, August 3, 1879, to Jane Yeater, daughter of Joseph and Mary Ann (Phillips) Yeater. Joseph Yeater was a son of John Yeater, and a grandson of

Andrew, who served.as a Revolutionary soldier from Pennsylvania. Joseph Yeater was a farmer and miller at Waynesburg, Pennsylvania, a man of wide acquaintance and eminent public spirit, and toward the close of his life came out to Missouri and died in Ridgeway in 1903 at the age of seventy-six. His children were: Mrs. Spragg; Harry L.; Joseph F.; Edwin R.; Albert W.; and Robert. Mrs. Spragg was graduated from the Waynesburg College in Pennsylvania and from the Millersville Normal in that state, and like her husband was for several years engaged as a teacher. Mr. and Mrs. Spragg had the following children: Earl G., a graduate of the law department of the University of Missouri and now living at Ridgeway; Lloyd Yeater, who took a course in journalism in the State University and is associated with his brother and is also engaged in the real estate business at Ridgeway; Frances M., a graduate of the Warrensburg Normal School, for several years a teacher and now the wife of Hamlin R. Tull, cashier of the First National Bank of Ridgeway.

During his residence at Ridgeway Mr. Spragg has served on the town board, was at one time mayor, and during a number of years as president of the school board the present brick schoolhouse was erected. Both he and his wife are active Methodists, and he has been identified with that church all his life, served as superintendent of the Sunday school in his native county, and at Ridgeway was a member of the building committee when the home church was erected. He has in a similar manner been interested in practically all the public enterprises that have appealed to the Ridgeway patronage. Mr. Spragg is affiliated with the Woodmen of the World, the Modern Woodmen of America, the Yeomen, the Knights of Pythias, is a past consul of the Modern Woodmen, and has been chief officer of the Yeomen for a number of years.

WILL R. VANHOOZER. In none of the activities of life to which men bend their energies do individuals become so widely known as in journalism, not always, perhaps, as personalities, but surely as influences, their printed thoughts reaching thousands while their spoken words could be heard by comparatively few. Hence the responsibility of a journalist is of exceeding weight and in the molding of public opinion the editor of a newspaper plays an important part in securing reformatory legislation and in changing public policies. Prominent among the newspaper men of Northwest Missouri is found Will R. Vanhoozer, editor of the Orrick Times, which he has published at Orrick since 1891, always with an increasing circulation and greater popularity. Mr. Vanhoozer entered the journalistic field in 1889, and during the quarter of a century he has been engaged therein has made his name widely known in this section of the state.

Will R. Vanhoozer was born at Elkhorn, Ray County, Missouri, July 12, 1864, and is a son of Alfred and Catherine (Odell) Vanhoozer. His father, born in Eastern Tennessee, May 24, 1843, was a son of Hugh and Rebecca (Callahan) Vanhoozer, natives of that state who came to Missouri in 1855 and located in Buchanan County, in 1859 removed to Gentry County, and in 1862 came to Ray County and settled at Elkhorn, north of what is now the City of Hardin. Alfred Vanhoozer was twelve years of age when the family came to Missouri, and here he was

May 24, 1880, when forty years of age. Mr. Vanhoozer was a popular member of the Blue Lodge of the Masonic Order, and he and Mrs. Vanhoozer were affiliated with the Baptist Church. Of their four children three are living: Will R., of this review; Mary J., who is the wife of L. G. Smith, of Ray County; and Lucy A., the wife of J. O. Billings, of Clay County.

Will R. Vanhoozer's schooling lasted barely until he reached the eighth grade, when he became self-supporting, and from that time to the present he has led a life of constant activity. He received his introduction to the newspaper business in 1889, when at Sedalia, Missouri, he was given employment by J. West Goodman, editor of the Sedalia Bazoo. In the fall of 1890 he went to Richmond, where he worked on the Richmond Democrat, and in April, 1891, came to Orrick and established the Orrick Times, the pioneer newspaper of this place, which he has successfully continued to publish up to the present. The Times is a democratic organ, but it is the aim of its editor to present to its readers a fair, unbiased opinion on all questions of public importance. A neat, well-printed sheet, its pages are devoted to the interesting national news of the day, all the local happenings and terse, well-written editorials. It is its policy to educate the reading public into discouraging sensational "yellow" matter, the publisher believing that a clean, reliable newspaper will be the means of ultimately developing the best interests of the community. Politically Mr. Vanhoozer is a democrat, and during three terms served as mayor of Orrick, a capacity in which he was able to do much to bring about reformatory movements. His fraternal connection is with the local lodge of the Modern Woodmen of America.

On November 28, 1894, Mr. Vanhoozer was married to Miss Emma Kirkham, who was born in Ray County, Missouri, daughter of W. N. and Susan Kirkham, prominent farming people near Orrick. One son has been born to this union: Cecil M., who resides with his parents.

GEORGE HENTON MAGEE. In George Henton Magee is found a sample of that material which has brought Gentry County to the forefront as a prosperous agricultural center. Endowed with natural ability and backed by shrewd business judgment and determination, this sterling citizen so ably conducted his activities that in September, 1907, he was able to step aside from the path of labor to let pass the younger generation with their clear-cut hopes and unrealized ambitions. Although now living a somewhat retired life at Albany, Mr. Magee continues to retain his interest in the affairs of his community, and although not an office-seeker or politician is a supporter of all worthy and beneficial movements.

Mr. Magee was born in Henry County, Kentucky, March 19, 1851, and is a son of Tolbert and Mary J. (Gibbany) Magee. During the winter of 1852-3 the father brought his family from the South to St. Joseph, Missouri, and wintered close to the present site of New Hampton, but in February came to Gentry County and bought 240 acres of land. This he continued to cultivate with industry and perseverance until his retirement, in 1893, and in February, 1897, his death occurred when he was eighty-two years of age. The mother died several years before, there having been the following children in the family: Mrs. Elizabeth Marrs, now deceased; Perlina, who died in 1861, at the age of sixteen years; James W., a resident of Marshfield, Missouri; Thomas R., a resident of Albany; George Henton, of this review; Mrs. Susan A. Tockey, of Boelus, Howard County, Nebraska; and Mrs. Mary C. McCord, a resident of Bartley, Nebraska.

The education of George Henton Magee was obtained in a log cabin schoolhouse in the Glendenning District, which he attended until reaching the age of nineteen years, during which time he assisted his father in the duties of the homestead during the summer months. Following the completion of his education he continued to work on the home place until his marriage, then purchasing 120 acres of partly-improved land, in section 10, township 63, range 30, and to this he added from time to time until he now has 375 acres, all in a good state of cultivation, a farm which he has improved with modern buildings and the latest equipment in the way of machinery. He carried on general farming and also met with much success in the raising of stock, and at all times maintained an excellent reputation for integrity in his business dealings and fidelity to his engagements. Always a progressive and enterprising citizen, Mr. Magee was the owner of the first registered red hogs in the county, and was always ready to give a trial to new methods, with the result that he did much to assist the development of his community and to raise the standard of agricultural work. In 1907 he retired from active pursuits and removed to Albany, where he resides in his comfortable, modern home. Mr. Magee is a democrat, and while he has not been very active in public affairs, has been ready to share the responsibilities of citizenship, serving on the first board of township trustees. His religious connection is with the Christian Church, of which he has served as an elder for a number of years.

On November 14, 1872, Mr. Magee was united in marriage in Gentry County, Missouri, with Miss Sarah E. Madden, daughter of William T. and Frances (Wayman) Madden, natives of Tennessee, from which state they came to Gentry County, Missouri, in the spring of 1853, Mr. Madden entering a considerable tract of land. He was engaged in general farming until the outbreak of the Civil war, when he enlisted in Company E, Captain Little, Missouri Volunteer Cavalry, and served two years with this organization, when he was honorably discharged and returned to his home. In 1893 he retired from active pursuits, and lived quietly until his death in June, 1913, at the age of eighty-nine years. He was a son of George and Delilah Madden, natives of Tennessee, who came to Clay County, Missouri, with their son and here died. Mr. and Mrs. Madden were the parents of the following children: William M., who is now deceased; Mrs. Margaret Sullenger, of Albany; Mrs. Victoria Sellers, of that place; George M., of Albany, and Mrs. Magee. To Mr. and Mrs. Magee there have been born the following children: Franklin L., a farmer in the vicinity of Albany, married Carrie Menger, and has one son, Carl; James W., also a farmer of Albany, married Julia Nicholson, and has four children, Ray, Wayne, Victor and Beatrice; Thomas A., engaged in farming at Albany, married Mary Clabough, and has four children, Zola, William, Mary and Lena May; Stella, married Joseph V. Bentley, engaged in the produce business in Albany, and has one daughter, Georgia; Fleetie, married John J. Sweeney, engaged in farming at Albany, and has two children, Donald and Francis; Curtis, engaged in farming at Albany; and Goldie, who is single and resides with her parents.

ANDREW THOMPSON. The farming interests of the community of Hatfield, Harrison County, are ably represented by Andrew Thompson, who is widely known in his field of operations, is also a stock breeder with extensive interests, and is equally well known as a business man and a citizen who has rendered his community excellent services of a public character. He is a native of Harrison County, having been born in Lincoln Township, December 29, 1864, and is a son of David and Rebecca C. (Knox) Thompson.

David Thompson is now an octogenarian and a man of considerable vigor who has witnessed the wonderful changes which have marked the development of Northwest Missouri. Whereas he was a young man himself when he cast his lot with Harrison County and occupied the frontiersman's cabin with sod chimney, now his posterity is among the numerous families of the county and in the evening of life and full of life's activity and achievements, he is retired and finishing his course in the home of his son, William F. Thompson. David Thompson is a native of Dumfriesshire, Scotland, born near the Town of Ayr, in 1831. His father was a farmer, and the family had lived for generations in that locality. The children were: Robert, William, James, David, Samuel, Agnes, Mary and Jane. Of these children, William and David came to the United States, and the former spent his life at Canton, Ohio, where he passed away and left a family.

David Thompson left his native land at the age of twenty years, and finally made port at New York after a voyage of forty days in a disabled sailing vessel. Locating in Pennsylvania, he secured employment at railroad work on the Pennsylvania Central, about Johnstown and Ligonier, and subsequently came West and joined the force constructing the Hannibal & St. Joseph Railway in the '50s, and was a day laborer for at least a time on this road, while in Pennsylvania he was a section foreman. His approach to St. Joseph with the construction of the railroad caused him to prospect Harrison County for a location and this resulted in his locating here. Although he was married, his wife remained in Pennsylvania until the family cabin was erected on section 4, township 66, range 29, then known as the John Hacker Farm, but now owned by G. F. Emerson. He made a farm of that tract, which he entered, and later on purchased the James Marshall Tract and here his most successful achievements took place. For some twenty years of his later life he lived in Worth County, and there he reached the limit of his active life, retiring after he reached more than eighty years of age. He was one of the few men who took the lead in the cattle business in Lincoln Township, and he acquired considerable of the cheap land of this community. He gave each of his children a tract of 160 acres out of what was, when he came here, threaded with Indian trails, while some of the tribe were yet camped here during the war between the North and the South. David Thompson took out his naturalization papers late in life, and from that time forward he identified himself with civic affairs, his vote going to the support of the republican party in politics. He has never been a member of any church or of any fraternity, and was a subject of England during the Civil war, thereby missing service.

While a resident of Westmoreland County, Pennsylvania, David Thompson was united in marriage with Miss Rebecca C. Knox, who was born in that county, in 1838, and who still survives. She is a daughter of John Knox, who was of Scotch and English ancestry and a lifelong farmer by vocation. Mrs. Thompson followed her husband to Missouri and occupied the cabin home with him, and was a strong factor in assisting him to achieve the substantial things done by him. Six children were born to Mr. and Mrs. Thompson: William F., who is the largest cattle feeder of the Township of Lincoln, Harrison County, and a man widely and favorably known in his community; Jane, who is the wife of Harry Hern, of Worth County, Missouri; Andrew, of this review; Alexander, a resident of Hatfield, Missouri; Miss Jeannette, of the W. F. Thompson Ranch; and Robert, who is a resident of Grant City, Missouri.

Andrew Thompson secured his schooling in a log cabin northwest and in the vicinity of his present home, and started out for himself at the age of twenty-one years. His first home was established south of Grant

City, he having married in Worth County, and he lived there two years and then returned to the locality of his birth, starting on a tract of land given him by his father in section 3. Subsequently Mr. Thompson bought another quarter of the same section which contains all his substantial improvements and which has been the scene of practically all his material success. He purchased other land adjoining until he holds above four hundred acres and has been devoting it to cattle, horses and hogs, besides the matter of grain raising. While Mr. Thompson breeds pedigreed stock, particularly hogs, he does so for the betterment of his own farm and herd, and not for any profit which he might derive in that line as a breeder. While he has grown many fine cattle he has practiced selling them from the grass rather than to feed and ship them to the markets.

In politics Mr. Thompson is a democrat but was brought up under republican influences. He has filled local offices at various times, and has made an excellent official, being president of the township board of Lincoln Township, a justice of the peace and a director and clerk of the school district for twenty-eight years. His attention has been given more to his own interests, however, than to public or political activities. He is a well known figure in business circles and secretary of the local telephone company.

While residing in Worth County, Missouri, Mr. Thompson was married in February, 1886, to Miss Louisa Wardlaw, a daughter of William Wardlaw, who was of Irish extraction, was a farmer, and died in Kansas. His wife was formerly Hannah Mow, and Mrs. Thompson is one of six children of their union. Mr. and Mrs. Thompson's children are as follows: Eugene Howard, a traveling man for the Hanlin Supply Company, married Miss Helena Thomason, of Columbus, Georgia; Francis Grover, like his elder brother a graduate of Highland Park College, Des Moines, Iowa, is bookkeeper and bill clerk for the Hoffman Music Company, married Miss Grace Clepper, of Kansas City, Mo.; Horace Roswell, a resident of Iowa, married Edith Campbell, who died without issue; Carl Guy, who is associated in business with his father; and Isabel and Clarence Bryan, who reside at home with their parents.

WILLIAM J. BRINIGAR. One of the foremost breeders of blooded cattle and hogs in Harrison County, William J. Brinigar, entered the field of Hampshire hog breeding ten years ago and during the past six years has been a leading exhibitor at many state fairs in the West, and has shipped his animals all over the Union. About nine years ago he began breeding cattle, and so great has been the demand for his stock that it has far exceeded the supply. Mr. Brinigar has long been a resident of the Blythedale neighborhood, and is living on the farm on which his father settled as early as 1870, and through his own efforts and steady industry has steadily worked himself to a position of prominence among the agriculturists and business men of this locality. He was born at Darlington, Lafayette County, Wisconsin, August 29, 1863, and is a son of Michael and Emily (Kreamer) Brinigar.

Thomas Brinigar, the grandfather of William J. Brinigar, was born in Kentucky, fought as a soldier during the war between the United States and Mexico, and died in Illinois, when about eighty years of age. His children were as follows: Michael, Jackson, William, Minerva who married a Mr. Cross, and Amanda who married a Mr. McIntosh. Michael Brinigar, who was a farmer all of his life, was born in Polk County, Indiana, in 1819, and there received his education in the public schools. He went to Wisconsin as a young man, and there resided at the time of the Civil war, but did not enlist as a soldier. In political matters a democrat, he served as justice of the peace in Wisconsin and in other local offices, and although he had no particular gift as a speaker was an interesting conversationalist. He was a good business man and showed a conservatism in his affairs that was marked. At one time he was a member of the Methodist Church, and although a member of no religious organization at the time of his death, was always a good Christian. Mr. Brinigar married Emily Kreamer, who was born in 1831, in Lancaster County, Pennsylvania, daughter of Michael Kreamer. Their children were as follows: Ellen, who married Wallace W. Hurd, of Arkansas; Thomas, who married Lucindy Bandy, and is engaged in farming in the vicinity of Blythedale, Missouri; William J., of this review; Louella, who became the wife of Will Wilson, of Blythedale.

William J. Brinigar secured a country school education, and began his active life on the farm when a lad of less than twelve years. During the summer months he worked as a hand on the homestead, while in the winter he attended the district schools, and thus continued until he had reached his 'teens, securing much valuable experience in the raising of grain and the breeding of hogs and cattle. He was induced to engage in blooded stock raising by what he witnessed at the St. Louis Exposition, where he saw his first Hampshire hog, and this caused him to cease experiments with Chester White and to experiment with the new strain. He saw "Shady Brook Gerben" there, of the Holsteins, became much attracted to her strain, and desired to add them to his farm. Mr. Brinigar's first exhibit of a state character was at Des Moines—a full herd—and during the five years showing at such fairs he has carried off more than five hundred ribbons and fully half have been first, including champions and grand champions. He bred the sire of "Messenger Boy," owned at Keswick, Iowa, and also the sire of "Lookout," which is owned by John E. Robbins, of Greensburg, Indiana, and which sold for $750, while "Messenger Boy" has brought an offer to his owner of $1,500. He has bred many grand champion sows, among them "Princess," which took the first ribbon at the state fair at Sedalia many times. He bred also "Missouri's Best," who was never beaten at the many shows attended, either as a yearling or a senior, and who is still owned by Mr. Brinigar. He still owns "Blythedale Jim," the sire of "Lookout." Mr. Brinigar's annual sale of hogs in 1913 brought buyers from Illinois, Indiana, Ohio, Iowa, Kansas, and all over Missouri, and his sales averaged him $57.50 a head.

Mr. Brinigar began the breeding of Holstein cattle in 1905 and has not been able to supply what he can sell at private sales. His cows have shown wonderful records as milkers, and one of them, while on the grass and without feed, has a record of nine gallons of milk daily. He started his herd with a "Shady Brook Gerben," and a nephew of the cow that made the most butter of any cow exhibited at the St. Louis Exposition in 1904. The heifers Mr. Brinigar got from his first sire he has now and is breeding them to "Orchard Hill Hengerveld DeKol," a bull which he secured from Davis Brothers, Fulton, New York, and the heifers of this new family are proving better than their ancestors as milkers. The White Wyandotte chicken is also a feature of Mr. Brinigar's farm. As a farmer Mr. Brinigar has 360 acres in his home and owns a quarter section of land in Harper County, Oklahoma. He is president and a director of the Blythedale Telephone Company, president of the American Hampshire Hog Association, and president and a stockholder of the Citizens Bank of Blythedale. In politics Mr. Brinigar votes the democratic ticket, and supports the man he considers best qualified in local office. His fraternal connection is with the Independent Order of Odd Fellows, he being past grand of Blythedale Lodge. He is not identified with any religious organization.

Mr. Brinigar was married in Harrison County, Missouri, in December, 1886, to Miss Mary Scott, a daughter of Moses and Mary (Graham) Scott. Mr. Scott was a pioneer of Harrison County and entered land here, passing his life in the pursuits of the soil. He reared a large family, the children being: Graham; Elzumer; Oliver; Sadie, who married Frank Loy; Allie, who married John Jones; Mrs. Brinigar; and Carrie, the wife of Porter Reeves. Mr. and Mrs. Brinigar have two children: Hugh F. and William Bryan.

The Brinigar sons here have the only considerable skunk farm in Harrison County. The enterprise was commenced in 1912, and is creating some interest and securing satisfactory profit. A tract of five acres of land is fenced off, with sheets of galvanized iron set several inches below the surface to prevent digging out, and the old orchard plat provides brush chunks and other retreats for the animals. They domesticate readily and thrive on milk, chopped rabbits and other game offered them.

ALEXANDER VAN BUSKIRK. One of the most honored names in Holt County citizenship has been that of Van Buskirk. It has been known and has been associated with various honors in official and professional affairs and also in business, at Oregon, for more than sixty-three years. Alexander Van Buskirk is a son of a prominent pioneer citizen, and for nearly a quarter of a century has been successfully engaged in the practice of law at Oregon.

Alexander Van Buskirk was born in Andrew County, Missouri, November 17, 1849. His parents were Ellzey and Eliza Jane (Hart) Van Buskirk. His father was a native of Mansfield, Ohio, and his mother of Morrow County, Ohio, and they came to Northwest Missouri at an early day and were married in Andrew County, December 25, 1844. Other children in their family were: Priscilla, now deceased, who married Martin Whitmer (and their daughter Jennie married George S. Loucks); Lawrence, who died young; John, who died in 1885; Mary, who died in 1884; and Eliza Jane, who also died in youth.

Ellzey Van Buskirk was prominent both in Andrew County and in Holt County, and in the early days conducted a paper for a few years at Savannah, the county seat of the former county, and also conducted a paper at Weston, Platte County, Missouri. In March, 1852, he moved to Holt County and in 1853 was elected circuit court clerk on the democratic ticket, an office he continued to fill until 1865. At that time he took up the practice of law and was regarded as one of the ablest members of the bar until 1890. In that year he was stricken with paralysis and died August 15, 1895. His wife passed away in Oregon in 1906. The two-story brick building in which Alexander Van Buskirk now has his offices as a lawyer was erected by his father, and that was one of many ways by which he was closely identified with the growth and development of this community. He was a Union democrat in politics, a member of the Missouri State Convention in 1861, and a member of the State Committee of the democratic party many years ago. He served on the first board of directors of the Citizens Bank of Oregon.

Alexander Van Buskirk received his education in the Oregon public schools, and his first regular vocation was that of farmer in Holt County. Later he took up the study of law, was admitted to the bar in 1890, and has since given his time to his clients and also to his private interests. He owns considerable property both in Oregon and in Holt County, and has made himself a factor in business affairs.

Mr. Van Buskirk is an active member of the Presbyterian Church, and is now and has been for a number of years a ruling elder in that denomination. His father was a Primitive Baptist in religion. Both he

and his father were Masons, and members of Lodge No. 189, A. F. & A. M. at Oregon. Mr. Van Buskirk married Charlotte V. Cummins, who was born near Shelby, Ohio. They were married October 12, 1871, and are the parents of two daughters. Caroline, the first, is now the wife of George Lehmer of Oregon. Rebecca is the wife of Frank C. Allen, also a resident of Oregon. A son of Mr. and Mrs. Van Buskirk died in infancy. The grandchildren are: Lawrence V. Lehmer and Paul V. Allen, Ruth Allen and Charlotte Allen.

AARON GRAHAM SCOTT, one of the ante-bellum settlers of Harrison County, Missouri, came hither in September, 1858, with his father, Moses Scott. He is a native of Jefferson County, Indiana, born near the City of Madison, July 18, 1850, and his father was born just across the Ohio River from Indiana, December 3, 1817, and died on his farm near Blythedale, Missouri, February 3, 1888, aged seventy years and two months.

Aaron T. Scott, the grandfather of Aaron G., was a Scotch-Irishman and a soldier during the War of 1812, and spent the greater part of his life near Madison, Jefferson County, Indiana. He died near Galesburg, Illinois. Mr. Scott's wife's maiden name was Anna Aja Scott, and they had the following children: Moses, the father of Aaron G.; Elizabeth, who married Oliver Graham; Sarah, who married Colonel Amix; Jerome; Benjamin F., who went through the Civil war for four years as a soldier and died in Oklahoma; Harriet, who was one of the older children and married Lewis Traupel, and Rachel, the youngest daughter, who lives at Hoyt, Kansas, and is the widow of William Robb.

Moses Scott spent his boyhood in Jefferson County, Indiana, and there was educated sparingly, so that he was able to do little more than to read and write. He was a brickmaker by trade and made the brick from which was built the first college at Hanover, Indiana, and worked at that and farming both in his native state and Missouri. Finally, however, in the latter state, he abandoned his trade that he might give his entire attention to the pursuits of the soil. His settlement was a mile southwest of Blythedale, and that farm he improved and made his final home, most of this property now being owned by William J. Brinigar. His old brick kiln was on Big Creek, west of Eagleville, on the William place. Moses Scott came to Missouri in company with several families from Knox County, Illinois, where he had spent some three years as a farmer. His outfit for the transportation of the family and effects comprised an ox-team and a yoke of cows, and the journey occupied from June to September. Among the families forming the caravan were those of James Graham, his father-in-law; Oliver Graham, and family; and John R. and William Graham, the latter of whom lives at Ridgeway, Missouri. All of these settled in the same neighborhood and their posterity is numbered among the citizenship here now. Moses Scott's participation in politics was as a democrat, but he never held public office. He was a Baptist of the Missionary faith who lived up to the teachings of his church, was known to be strictly reliable in his dealings, paid his way as he went, and never allowed himself to go into debt. The period of the Civil war did not materially affect him save as his son, Elzumer, entered the Twenty-third Regiment, Missouri Volunteer Infantry, Company D, and went with General Sherman to the sea. Moses Scott married Mary A. Graham, daughter of James and Jemimah (Talbert) Graham, and of English descent on her mother's side. Mr. Graham was a native of Bardstown, Bullitt County, Kentucky, and moved first to Indiana and then to Knox County, Illinois. He was a carpenter by trade and his home in Harrison County was 3½ miles north of Blythedale. He died at about seventy years of age, about 1872, and his wife passed away a few years later, and both were buried at Eagleville. Their children were as follows: Arthur, a Mexican war soldier who died at Eagleville, Missouri; Elizabeth, who married Joseph Horn and died in Texas; John R., who was a teacher and died in Mercer County, Missouri; Calvin, who was a teacher and died in Harrison County, Missouri; Sarah, who married Harry Barnes and died in Southern Illinois; Mary A., who became the wife of Mr. Scott; and William, of Ridgeway, Missouri, the youngest, who became a Union soldier during the Civil war.

The children born to Moses and Mary A. (Graham) Scott were as follows: Elzumer, who as before stated was a soldier during the Civil war, and afterwards engaged in farming in Harrison County, Missouri; Aaron Graham, of this review; Sarah J., who married Frank Loy, of Ridgeway, Missouri; Oliver, a resident of that place; Alzira, who married John A. Jones, and died in Mitchell County, Kansas; Mary, who married William Brinigar, a farmer and well-known breeder of blooded stock, near Blythedale; and Carrie, who became the wife of Porter Reeves, and now resides at Cainsville, Missouri.

Aaron Graham Scott was a child when brought to the vicinity in which he now makes his home and here he secured a somewhat limited education in the district schools. Starting out as a farmer just before reaching his majority, he worked for a time as a hand at a salary of $15 per month, his employer being Mr. Bandy, whose daughter he married after several years. He first rented a small property known as the Guist Farm for several years, located near Eagleville, and later rented the Lundy place, on which he spent a short time. Next he purchased 100 acres of raw land, now the Loveless place, and this he improved and exchanged for his present farm in section 14, township 65, range 27. This was a settled place and he succeeded William Kincaid here in 1888. He owns 260 acres and has been engaged in stock and grain farming. Recently he has embarked in the Short Horn and Poland-China hog breeding, his Short Horn cattle coming from the Kansas Bellows herd and his first exhibit for prizes being made in the fall of 1914. In politics Mr. Scott is a republican, and for two years was assessor of Marion Township.

· Mr. Scott was married the first time, August 24, 1871, to Miss Ann Eliza Bandy, a daughter of Pascal and Lovica Bandy, who came to Missouri from Knox County, Illinois, and here were farmers. Mrs. Scott died August 22, 1897, leaving the following children: Elzumer, cashier of the Commercial Bank of Ridgeway and one of its organizers, married Carrie Sallee, and has three children, Kenneth, Winogene and Roland; Charles, traffic manager for the Pioneer Cooperage Company, of Chicago, Illinois, married Annie Hughey, and has four children, Beulah, Aaron Graham, Jr., Geraldine and Annie Hughey; W. Ota, of Towner, Colorado, married Mary Morris, and has three children, Ronald, Morris and Estalene; Oscar, a farmer of this county, married Myrtle Israel, and has three children, Vera, Truman and Lucile; Minnie, the wife of Ruthy Jacobs, of St. Anthony, Idaho, has four children, Olin, Evelyn, Hazel and Charline; Zene, associated with the Interstate Commerce Commission, at Washington, D. C., married and has a child, Mildred; Edna and Eva, twins, the former unmarried and a resident of Indianapolis, Indiana, while the latter is the wife of Ernest Grubb, of Maryville, Missouri, and has two children, Roberta and Marion; Ruth, who is the wife

Alice Eyerly, daughter of George W. Eyerly and Martha A. (Howell) Eyerly. Mr. Eyerly came to Missouri from Ohio, but now resides at Winterset, Iowa, while his wife is deceased. He is a veteran of the Civil war, and has passed his life in the pursuits of farming. Of his thirteen children, eleven have grown to maturity, but only two, Mrs. Scott and Mrs. Louella Cocklin, reside in Missouri. Five children have been born to Mr. and Mrs. Scott: Howard, Russell, Raymond, Fern and Ione. Mr. Scott is the father of sixteen children, all living, and is the grandfather of twenty.

FRED HARTLEY. For thirty-eight years Fred Hartley has been identified with the monument business, and for twelve of these has been in business for himself at Savannah, Missouri, where he is one of the representative and enterprising men in other lines and is numbered with the most useful citizens of the county seat of Andrew County. He was born in Putnam County, Indiana, May 31, 1861, and is a son of Rufus and Jennie (Beard) Hartley. Both parents were natives of Indiana and resided there until 1865 when they moved to Ringgold County, Iowa, and from there in 1872, to Worth County, Missouri, settling permanently in Andrew County, Missouri, in 1877. The father was engaged in the monument business at Savannah during the rest of his active life. His death occurred in 1907, at the age of seventy-seven years. The mother survives and lives at Savannah. They had five children: John, who is a resident of New Mexico; Charles, who is in business at St. Joseph, Missouri; Fred; Samuel, who is associated with his brother Fred at Savannah; and Minnie, for the past fifteen years a teacher in the public schools at Savannah, who is now the wife of Samuel Cline.

Fred Hartley obtained his education in the public schools and began to learn marble cutting in his father's shop in boyhood and later mastered every detail of the business. For twelve years he was superintendent for the Des Moines Marble and Mantel Company, a large concern doing business in several states, but for twelve years he has conducted his own monument works at Savannah, which city he has claimed as his home since 1877. He has large yards and employs skilled workmen, conducting his business according to his ideas of a business man's responsibility. His public spirit was manifested in the establishing here of the Globe Theater, a moving picture house and the first of its class in the place. The building was opened April 20, 1914, and he operates it himself. It is proving a very successful venture. In politics Mr. Hartley is a republican and is serving as one of the city's aldermen and is credited with looking after the interests of his own ward with the same care that he gives to his private affairs.

In 1888 Mr. Hartley was united in marriage with Miss Anna M. Smith, who is a daughter of Henry M. and Katherine Smith. Mrs. Hartley was born in Pennsylvania but was reared in Andrew County, Missouri. Mr. and Mrs. Hartley have one son, Harry S., who is a very talented young man and is a graduate of the class of 1913, of the Art Institute, Chicago. At present he is a popular cartoonist, working under Cartoonist Darling, on the Register and Leader, of Des Moines, Iowa. Mr. Hartley belongs to the Modern Woodmen of America and to the Knights of Pythias.

O. N. THOMPSON, M. D. More than twenty years of practice as a physician and surgeon have brought Doctor Thompson special distinction and success as an able and skillful doctor and as a man who devotes himself conscientiously to the duties of professional life. Doctor Thompson has been located at Breckinridge as one of the leading physicians and surgeons since 1908, and previous to that for a number of years practiced at Lock Spring in Daviess County. Doctor Thompson is a graduate of the College of Physicians and Surgeons at Keokuk, Iowa, in the class of 1891, and his wife, a graduate of the same institution, is also a successful physician and an able coadjutor to his own efforts, and through their cooperation they have performed a large amount of capable service in this section of Northwest Missouri.

Dr. O. N. Thompson was born near Chillicothe in Livingston County, Missouri, on a farm, December 23, 1866. His father was Archibald Thompson, who was born in Tazewell County, Virginia, a son of Archibald Thompson, Sr., a native of the same state, of Scotch-Irish ancestry, and of Presbyterian stock. Archibald, Jr., with two brothers served in the Confederate army during the Civil war. He married Millie Perry, who was born in Virginia. Archibald Thompson, who died at the age of seventy-seven in Livingston County, was one of the leading men of his section and served as judge of the county court. He was an active member of the Methodist Episcopal Church South, and was affiliated with Lodge No. 408 of the Masons of Lock Spring. His widow passed away at the age of fifty-six. In their family were five sons and five daughters, seven of whom are still living: Mrs. L. S. Dorsey; Mary R. Thompson; Oscar N.; Archibald, a dentist at Gallatin, Missouri; C. E., a physician at Enid, Oklahoma; and W. P., a farmer and stockman at Lock Spring, Missouri.

Dr. Oscar N. Thompson was reared in the country on a farm, attended the public schools, and began the study of medicine under Doctor Dorsey. At the age of twenty-three he married Miss Emma Boyington, who had been a successful teacher and as already stated was a graduate of the College of Physicians and Surgeons at Keokuk, Iowa. Since her marriage she has been particularly helpful in actual practice and consultation work on diseases of women and children. Her father was Robert Boyington, now living in Oklahoma. Doctor Thompson and wife have four children: Leaffa, who is a graduate of high school and is now in her second year at the Howard Payne College at Fayette, Missouri; Mary M., also a graduate of the high school and in her first year at Howard Payne College; Helen, a high school student; and Mildred Catherine, still in the grade schools. The two older daughters have taken special musical instruction in instrumental and voice, and all the family are more or less talented musically. Doctor Thompson is affiliated with the Masonic Lodge at Lock Spring, and also with the Independent Order of Odd Fellows. His church is the Methodist Episcopal South. Doctor Thompson has served five years as a member of the public school board, and besides his work as a physician has also performed much public spirited labor in behalf of the community where his home has been.

C. E. GRAFF. Farming and stock raising naturally engage the attention of well informed, practical men in Andrew County, nature having here provided rich pasturage and fertile soil, and one who has profited by these advantages is C. E. Graff, a well known grower and dealer of Nodaway Township. He has also proven that this section is particularly well adapted to the growing of fruit and the yield of his orchards brings him a satisfactory income.

C. E. Graff was born in Clay Township, Andrew County, Missouri, September 30, 1860. His parents were Peter and Catherine (McElroy) Graff. His father was born May 26, 1825, at Bingen on the Rhine, Germany, and died on the farm now owned by his son, C. E., December 5, 1907. The mother was born in North Carolina and came to Andrew County with her people in 1848. She died on the home farm, September

12, 1884, at the age of fifty-eight years, six months and one day. They were parents of the following children: Sarah Jane, who is the widow of Walter B. Tolle, lives at Savannah; J. H., who died in April, 1914, at the age of fifty-five years; C. E.; Clara Agnes, who is the widow of William H. Heren, lives at Savannah; and William Luther, who was born in 1869, died in 1892.

Peter Graff, the father, remained in his own land until he was twenty-one years of age and then came to the United States and direct to Andrew County and three years later his father followed him and together they bought a farm in Lincoln Township. On that farm Peter Graff spent a short time of his life and all the rest of it in Andrew County with the exception of about six years, during which he lived on a homestead he had taken up in Kansas.

C. E. Graff has been a lifelong resident of Andrew County, with the exception of seven years, during which time he lived in Logan County, Kansas. Farming, fruit growing and stock and cattle raising have occupied his attention ever since he has been in business and he has made them all profitable. When he started out for himself he invested in Norman horses, Shorthorn cattle and Poland China hogs, but experience taught him that for his purposes the Chester White variety of hogs was superior. He has been an extensive breeder of Percheron horses and has probably sold more high-priced horses than any other man in the county. Mr. Graff has thirty-nine acres in his home place, in the suburbs of Savannah, northwest of the town, and fifty-three acres adjoining the corporation of Savannah on the north. His residence stands on an elevation that gives an extended view of the country and at all times of the year is attractive, with a background of orchards and an evergreen grove of sixty trees. He has hundreds of trees in his orchards and they yield bountifully of cherries, peaches, apples, plums and pears, while berries of all kinds do equally well. Mr. Graff has shown excellent judgment in the laying out of his grounds and has every reason to take pride in his surroundings.

Mr. Graff was married March 3, 1887, to Miss Lucy L. Gee, who was born in Andrew County, Missouri, January 30, 1863, and is a daughter of C. C. and Elizabeth (Bayne) Gee. The mother was born in Indiana and came to Andrew County with her parents, in childhood, and died in Logan County, Kansas, June 29, 1897, at the age of fifty-nine years, one month and one day. The father of Mrs. Graff was born in Carroll County, Tennessee, February 22, 1835, and was brought to Andrew County by his parents in 1837. In 1886 he moved from this county to Kansas and now owns 480 acres in Logan County. Mr. and Mrs. Graff have no children of their own, but they are rearing James H. and Nora F. Cruse, a brother and sister, who are second cousins of Mr. Graff. He has always given his political support to the republican party, but has led too busy a life to ever entertain a desire for public office. Nevertheless he is just the type of citizen that a community often needs in public life, good judgment, sound common sense and honesty and business foresight being very desirable qualifications in those who make and those who desire a chance to carry out laws. Mr. Graff and family belong to the Methodist Episcopal Church.

J. S. PETERS. One of the old and honored citizens of Savannah, who at the age of eighty years is now living in comfortable retirement from life's activities, is J. S. Peters, who for forty years was engaged in agricultural pursuits in Andrew County. Mr. Peters has led an active and useful career, which has taken him into various pursuits and strange localities, and has been an eye-witness to happenings that have made history in several parts of the country. Born in Preble County, Ohio, April 29, 1834, Mr. Peters is a son of John and Elizabeth (Gossett) Peters, natives of Franklin County, Virginia, where they were married. The paternal grandparents were natives of Pennsylvania, where the family was known from Colonial times. In the fall of 1822, John and Elizabeth Peters loaded their family effects into a wagon, and started from their Virginia home on the long and hazardous journey overland to the undeveloped country of Ohio. Locating on a virgin farm, they cleared a property and established a home, and there passed the rest of their existence in pastoral pursuits. They were the parents of six daughters and three sons, and two children of this family now survive: Mrs. Susanna Swihart, of Dayton, Ohio; and J. S.

J. S. Peters was reared on his father's farm, and secured such educational advantages as were afforded the pupils by the early Ohio schools. He continued to assist his father in cultivating the old homestead until April of 1860, when he started on an overland journey to Colorado, with an ox-team, going through Kansas and Nebraska and on to Colorado on the old military trail, finally arriving at Denver, May 23d. During the years 1860 and 1861 he remained in the mining country, being engaged in prospecting, but in the fall of the latter year started on his way back to th East with ox-teams, going down the course of the Platte River, crossing the Missouri and on to Chariton, Iowa, at that point taking a coach which brought him to Eddyville; the nearest railroad point. He went thence to Ohio. As a comparison of the methods of the early '60s and those of today, and to illustrate the wonderful progress that has been attained under Mr. Peters' observation, it is interesting to note that in September, 1914, he covered the Iowa part of this journey, but instead of traversing the country with an ox-team, made the trip in his high-powered automobile.

Mr. Peters remained in Ohio until 1874, and in that year came to Andrew County and settled down to agricultural pursuits. Through industry, perseverance and good management, he accumulated 200 acres of good land in Kansas and Missouri, but since his retirement this has been divided among his children. At the present time he is one of the valued residents of the retired colony at Savannah, and his long life of honorable dealing eminently entitles him to the respect and esteem so universally accorded him. On his return from the West, in the late fall of 1861, Mr. Peters became a member of the Ohio Militia, and May 2, 1864, went into the United States service for 100 days, as a member of Company E, One Hundred and Fifty-sixth Regiment, Ohio National Guards, under General Kelley. One of his most highly prized possessions is a certificate of thanks from President Lincoln, given him for his valuable war services. In political matters Mr. Peters has been a lifelong republican, but at no time in his career has he been an office seeker. He was a member of the Union League during the days of the Civil war, and still holds membership in the Grand Army of the Republic.

In 1862 Mr. Peters was married to Miss Sarah C. Swihart, who was born in Preble County, Ohio, March 29, 1836, and died May 3, 1905, at Rea, Missouri. Two sons were born to this union: O. E., who is rural free delivery mail carrier out of Bolckow Missouri; and F. R. who is

perience as an educator, for his entire career has been devoted to his profession, upon which he determined in early youth. He has been the incumbent of his present office for four years, and his well-directed labors have resulted in gaining for his county an efficient and comprehensive school system which compares favorably with that of any county in Northwest Missouri. He has been earnest and energetic, bringing to his work an enthusiasm which, combined with his natural adaptation for his calling, has accomplished remarkable results in advancing the cause of education.

Mr. Dobbs was born on a farm five miles north of Savannah, Andrew County, Missouri, May 21, 1884, and is a son of William F. and Elva (Spohn) Dobbs. He is descended from distinguished ancestry, for his great-great-grandfather, Arthur Dobbs, was commissioned by King George III of England as royal governor of the colony of North Carolina, and served in that capacity for four years. He was also at the head of fifty families of Scotch and Irish who came to America during Colonial days. Arthur Dobbs had two sons, Wesley and Chester, the latter of whom went to New York and founded the town of Dobbs Ferry, while Wesley made his way to the West, and the Missouri members of the family have all descended from him. On the maternal side, Mr. Dobbs is a grandson of a minister of the German Reformed Church, who established the first congregation of that faith in the vicinity of Hillsboro, Ohio.

William F. Dobbs was born in Illinois, July 25, 1855, and as a child came with his parents to Nodaway County, Missouri, where he met and married Elva Spohn, who had been born at Hillsboro, Ohio, March 21, 1851, and had come to Missouri at the age of eighteen years. After their marriage they settled on a farm in Andrew County, on which they continued their labors until their retirement, and at the present time are living quietly in their comfortable home at Savannah. They have had four children: Inez, who is the wife of Joseph Jenkins, of Balckow, Missouri; Cyrus C., pastor of the Christian Church at Denver, Colorado; Cleo, the wife of Samuel Sears, living north of Savannah; and Leslie M.

Leslie M. Dobbs has resided in Andrew County all of his life. He was reared on the home farm and in his boyhood attended the rural schools of his native locality, subsequently supplementing this training by two years of attendance at the Warrensburg Normal School and two summers at the State University. In the meantime, he had started teaching in the rural districts, his services in this direction covering a period of ten years and attracting such favorable attention that in 1910 he was appointed county superintendent of schools of Andrew County. The people have had no reason to regret their choice, for his labors have been conscientious and persevering, and he has been able to achieve many of his commendable ideals. Professor Dobbs is unmarried. He is a republican in politics, although not a politician. Fraternally, he is affiliated with the Independent Order of Odd Fellows and the Modern Woodmen of America, and his religious faith is that of the Presbyterian Church.

WILLIAM FULKERSON. A life of quiet effectiveness, marked by a record of many duties well done and many responsibilities faithfully fulfilled, was that of the late William Fulkerson, who was a pioneer of Andrew County and was one of the men who developed and made that county what it is. In the round of everyday duties and in the faithful and intelligent performance of every task that was allotted to him during his long life, he left a record which may well be admired by the generations that follow him. His venerable widow is still living at

Savannah, surrounded by children and grandchildren, and is now well past the age of fourscore.

William Fulkerson was born in Rhea County of East Tennessee April 3, 1819, a son of Frederick and Sarah (Bradley) Fulkerson. Both parents were natives of Virginia, where they were married, and soon afterwards settled in East Tennessee. About 1829 they moved out to Missouri, and located on the frontier in Lafayette County. The father was a merchant and farmer, and died in advanced years in 1841, followed by his wife in 1845. Their large family of children were: Eliza F.; Dr. James M.; Reuben Bradley; Isaac; Dr. Peter Perry; William; Mary Hannah Davis; Caroline; Margaret Gordon; Frederick D.; Catherine Gordon; Emmet Bradley; and Susan Rebecca—thirteen in all, and death has claimed the entire family.

William Fulkerson was about ten years of age when the family moved to Lafayette County, Missouri, where he was reared on his father's farm, and had only the limited advantages offered by the country schools of that early day. In 1850 he joined in the great exodus from Missouri to the Pacific Coast, and spent about twelve months in California, in the mining districts. In the spring of 1851 he returned to Missouri, and thereafter was content to follow the quiet vocation of farming. In 1846 he had bought a farm in Jefferson Township of Andrew County, and was one of the early settlers in this section of Northwest Missouri. He became the owner of 335 acres, improved and cultivated it, and was steadily prosperous in his varied activities. In 1892 he retired to Savannah, and died in that city December 11, 1894, when seventy-five years of age. He was a stanch democrat in politics, and a member of the Presbyterian Church.

On October 5, 1848, Mr. Fulkerson married Miss Sallie Brackenridge. She was born in St. Louis County, Missouri, April 1, 1830, and was fourteen years of age when her family moved to Northwest Missouri and located in Andrew County. Her parents were John and Eliza (Post) Brackenridge, the former a native of Kentucky and the latter of Vermont. Her mother died in Andrew County when about eighty-seven years of age, and her father passed away in Troy, Kansas, at the age of about eighty years. Mr. and Mrs. Fulkerson were the parents of nine children, namely: Eliza, wife of Robert Catron of Butler, Missouri, and she is the mother of four children; Monroe, who died at the age of twenty-one; John, who died in infancy; Frederick, who died at the age of forty-seven, leaving a widow and seven children; Elizabeth, who died in infancy; Margaret, who died aged two years; Ruth, who died in infancy; Florence, who lives with her mother in Savannah; and William, who died at the age of twenty-one. Mrs. Sallie Fulkerson now lives in Savannah and is eighty-four years of age. She has eleven grandchildren and one great-grandchild. For more than forty years she had membership in the Primitive Baptist Church, but after her removal to Savannah united with the Christian Church, and both she and her daughter, Florence, are regular attendants at the services of that denomination.

HARVEY VAN BUSKIRK. One of the oldest citizens of Savannah in point of residence is Harvey Van Buskirk, who came here in 1852 when this was still a struggling village with 300 inhabitants. During his boyhood he passed through experiences that would hardly be believed by the members of the younger generation, who, seeing the thriving and progressive city, with its large business and financial institutions, its modern schools and churches, and its distinguishing marks of advanced civilization, would find it hard to realize that but sixty years ago slaves were sold and publicly whipped here; that it was a nightly occurrence to hear the great black timber wolves howling in the near vicinity; that rags soaked in grease and tallow candles were used for lighting purposes, and that, having never heard of screens, the inhabitants were forced to burn great smudges to keep off the mosquitoes. All these things Mr. Van Buskirk has witnessed and more. His career has been an exceptionally active one and has included a variety of pursuits, and at the present time he is engaged in the photographic business, in which he has gained much popularity and success.

Harvey Van Buskirk was born in Morrow County, Ohio, July 22, 1846, and is a son of John and Eliza (Cook) Van Buskirk. The father was of old Holland Dutch stock, and belonged to a family that was connected by marriage with Lord Lawrence of England. The grandfather of Harvey Van Buskirk, John Van Buskirk, removed from New York to Pennsylvania at an early day, and in Greene County, the latter state, John Van Buskirk, the father of Harvey, was born in 1800. He was still a youth when the family moved to Richland County, Ohio, where they settled in the heavy timber and cleared a farm, and when he grew to manhood moved to Morrow County, where he was married to Eliza Cook, who had been born in that county in 1805. In 1852 the parents came to Savannah, Missouri, and located on a farm seven miles west of the town, and there the mother died during the fall of the same year. The father, who was a farmer, cabinetmaker and carpenter, survived for many years, and died in March, 1894, on his farm adjoining the town of Savannah. He and his wife were devout members of the Baptist Church, and he was originally a democrat in politics, but cast his last democratic vote for Stephen A. Douglas, following which he always voted the republican ticket. There were ten children in the family: Stephen, who died in infancy; Asher, who served in the Missouri State Militia during the Civil war and later went to Camas, State of Washington, where he died; John, who served in the Indian wars in Oregon, and died at Tacoma, Washington; Rhoda, who died at Savannah, in 1908, was the wife of Capt. Simon Evans, who was captain of Company B, Twenty-fifth Regiment, Missouri Volunteer Infantry, during the Civil war; Mary, who died at Savannah as the wife of Milas Wilson; Ida, deceased, who was the wife of John Roberts; Rufus, who served during the last six months of the Civil war as a member of Company B, Fifty-first Regiment, Missouri Volunteer Infantry, and died at Savannah in 1908; William, who served in the Fourth Missouri State Militia for three years during the Civil war and is now a resident of Tacoma, Washington; Eliza, who married David Mendenhall, and resides 2½ miles west of Savannah; and Harvey, of this review.

Harvey Van Buskirk remained on the home farm until he was twelve years of age, at which time his father moved to Savannah. He was only fifteen years old when he began his active and varied career as the driver of teams across the plains for John Hobson, freighting to Denver, Colorado, and subsequently making a trip for the United States Government to Fort Union, New Mexico. He also followed the printer's trade to some extent as a youth, having learned the trade as a boy in the office of the Plain Dealer, under Charles Whitaker. On February 25, 1865, Mr. Van Buskirk enlisted in Company B, Fifty-first Regiment, Missouri Volunteer Infantry, with which he served until the close of the war; having a very creditable military record. In 1866 he went to White Cloud, Kansas, where he secured employment as a printer on the White Cloud Kansas Chief, with which he remained until 1883, and after two years spent at Ouray, Colorado, in the same capacity, returned to the White Cloud paper for a short time. Returning to Savannah, he succeeded his brother, Rufus, as the proprietor of the photograph gallery here, and with this business he has continued to be identified to the present time. He has attracted to his studio an excellent patronage, and the excellence of his work has made him favorably known throughout the county. Politically Mr. Van Buskirk is a republican, but he has had no political aspirations. He has accepted his share of the responsibilities of good citizenship, and may be depended upon to give his support to good men and beneficial measures.

Mr. Van Buskirk was married in 1876 to Miss Cora Spaulding, a native of Kansas, and she was the mother of two children: Anna, who is the wife of T. E. McFarlin, of Belleville, Kansas; and Edith, now Mrs. Howard, of Oklahoma City, Oklahoma. In 1889 Mr. Van Buskirk was married a second time, being united with Mrs. Jennie June Rusing. They have had no children.

J. C. GILMORE. The career of J. C. Gilmore, a venerable citizen and retired farmer of Savannah, is one that is remarkable for the interesting incidents and experiences that have marked its course, and for the breadth of country and diversified occupations that it has covered. An Irish emigrant lad at the age of eleven, a gold seeker during the ''days of old, the days of gold, the days of '49,'' a marshal in the mining camps when pay was exceptionally good because the men who would accept such dangerous office were few and far between, a business man in Savannah when this city was in its infancy, and for many years a successful tiller of the soil—his life has been one of constant activity, and his eyes have been witnesses to wonderful transformations and developments. If the span of human life be measured by ideas, by new sensations, then the life of Mr. Gilmore may be said to be longer than that of the patriarchs who drew out centuries amid the monotony of the deserts in the dull round of pastoral pursuits.

J. C. Gilmore was born in County Down, Ireland, June 24, 1822, and is a son of Patrick and Susan (Logan) Gilmore, also natives of that part of Erin, where they passed their entire lives. They were the parents of seven sons and two daughters, but besides J. C., only two came to the United States, Henry and Anna. J. C. Gilmore received only an indifferent public school training in his native land, and in 1833 was brought in a sailing vessel to the United States by neighbors who were making the trip, the youth joining his brother Henry, who had preceded him about six years, at St. Louis. There he was given further educational opportunities, attending school for about six years, and then following whatever honorable employment presented itself until the discovery of gold in California was announced and people from all over the country set forth, in a mad hunt for the yellow metal. An adventuresome young man, with no particular family ties to bind him, Mr. Gilmore joined the courageous throng which wended its hazardous and wearisome way across the broad burning plains. His experiences during that journey will ever live with him, and culminated in his capture, with another teamster, by the famous bandit Jewell who detained them for three days and then released them and sent them on to their destination with two scouts. Arriving in the Golden State, Mr. Gilmore found, with others, that all was not so bright as it had been painted, but he immediately settled down to mining, at which he was principally engaged during the following twelve years with some degree of success. During this time he was in both California and Idaho, and in the latter state served as marshal of Idaho City, a position the danger of which was shown by the enormous wages paid the incumbent.

Returning from the West, in 1866, Mr. Gilmore established himself in business as the owner of a saloon and billiard hall, on the present site of the Methodist Episcopal Church, but when he turned his attention to farming disposed of this business and became a charter member of the Bible class of the new congregation. He still continues as a member of this organization. When he became a tiller of the soil, Mr. Gilmore purchased a farm six miles west of Savannah, which he cultivated until his retirement, January 6, 1912. Long years of faithful and well-applied labor eventuated in the accumulation of a handsome competence, and he is now living at his comfortable home at Savannah, content in the knowledge of a useful life. In political matters Mr. Gilmore is a democrat, but public life has not appealed to him. He is willing at all times to assist movements which will make for the betterment 'of his community, and is known.as a good citizen. With the carriage and appearance of a man thirty years his junior, his life of activity and out-door exercise is shown at its face value.

On March 6, 1870, Mr. Gilmore was united in marriage with Miss Elizabeth Blair, who was born in County Donegal, Ireland, December 25, 1850, and came to the United States with her parents in May, 1866, they being Thomas and Eliza (Patterson) Blair, both of whom passed away at Savannah. Eight children have been born to Mr. and Mrs. Gilmore, namely: Mary, who is the widow of Wood Cobb, of Savannah, and has three daughters; Susan, who is the wife of.Clyde Fralikill, of St. Joseph, and has three sons; William, who is a farmer of Andrew County and has one son and two daughters; Robert, of St. Joseph, who has two sons and three daughters; Grace, who is the wife of Lee Fralikill, of St. Joseph, and has no children; Anna, who is the wife of William Benningfield, of Chicago, and has one daughter; Harry, of St. Joseph, who is single; and Effie, who died at the age of nine years. Mr. Gilmore has fifteen grandchildren and one great-granddaughter.

JOHN D. KERR. While Mr. Kerr was for one term the efficient incumbent of the postoffice at Savannah, he is probably best known over Andrew County for his many years of active connection with newspaper work, as editor and publisher of the Savannah Republican. His family is one that has been identified with Andrew County the greater part of forty years, and his father, Dr. William M. Kerr, is one of the oldest and most prominent physicians of Savannah.

Dr. William Morrison Kerr was born in Woodsfield, Monroe County, Ohio, February 28, 1840, a son of John and Janet (Davidson) Kerr. The parents were both natives of Dumfriesshire, Scotland, and in 1836 emigrated to America, bringing with them two children, John, who died in Wheeling, West Virginia, and Mary, also deceased. The parents died at Woodsfield, Ohio. The father was a carpenter by trade, having learned that business in Scotland, but after locating in Ohio was a farmer. His death occurred at the age of seventy-nine and his wife was past eighty. Altogether there were thirteen children, and five sons and four daughters reached maturity. Two of the daughters and one son died in Scotland from the scourge of cholera.

Doctor Kerr grew up in Ohio, learned the duties of a farm and acquired a common school education, and when about twenty-two years of age, in August, 1862, was commissioned second lieutenant in Company A of the One Hundred and Sixteenth Ohio Volunteer Infantry. He continued in active service until November, 1864, when discharged from the hospital following a severe attack of typhoid fever. In the meantime he had been promoted to first lieutenant and was commissioned captain in September, 1864, but was never mustered in with that rank. After the war Doctor Kerr studied medicine in Miami Medical College at Cincinnati, graduating M. D. in 1868. He has been actively identified with his profession now more than forty-five years. He began practice at Fairfield, Illinois, but in 1876 moved to Northwest Missouri, locating at Fillmore in Andrew County. He later spent a year in Kansas, returned to Missouri, and in 1887 again moved to Jewell County, Kansas, and lived there about three years. Since his return in the fall of 1890 his home has been at Savannah, and he has a high standing among the physicians of the county.

Doctor Kerr's brother, John D., was a soldier in the same company and died on the Antietam battlefield, while his youngest brother, George, now a resident of Woodsfield, Ohio, was a member of the noted organization known as the "Squirrel Hunters" during the war. Doctor Kerr has been a republican almost since the organization of the party, and is an active member of Peabody Post, No. 41, of the Grand Army of the Republic. He has been a Mason for more than half a century and is affiliated with Savannah Lodge, No. 71, A. F. & A. M. His ancestors in Scotland were covenanters, and he is an elder in the Presbyterian Church in Savannah. Doctor Kerr was married in Illinois in 1871 to Mary I. Trousdale, who was born in Wayne County, Illinois, daughter of John and Ellen (Wilson) Trousdale, the former a native of Tennessee and the latter of England. Doctor Kerr and wife were the parents of the following children: Anna, who died at the age of eight years; John D.; William R., of St. Joseph; and Alice, who was assistant postmaster at Savannah.

John D. Kerr was born in Fairfield, Illinois, August 1, 1873. That was the home of his mother at the time she married Doctor Kerr. He was three years of age when his parents located at Fillmore, and has spent most of his life in Andrew County. Mr. Kerr graduated from the Savannah high school in 1892, and in the following year entered the office of the Andrew County Republican, and was in active newspaper work for twenty years. In 1896 he bought a half interest in the paper, and in 1905 became sole proprietor and successfully managed that influential news organ until he sold out in August, 1913. On February 23, 1911, Mr. Kerr received appointment as postmaster at Savannah, and during his incumbency did much to improve service to patrons.

Mr. Kerr has been a republican all his mature life, and is a member of the Presbyterian Church and of the Modern Woodmen of America. In 1896 he married Mattie Buis, who was born in Andrew County, and they were graduated from the high school in the same class. Her parents, both deceased, were Perry and Mary Buis. Mr. Kerr and wife have eight children: Eleanor, John, Jr., Morris, Janet, Catherine, Gertrude, Helen and Charlotte.

GEORGE W. RODECKER. The retirement of George W. Rodecker from active life, in 1900, was justified by the accomplishment of success in its broadest sense, by many years of devotion to the vocation of farming, by a brave and active service in the ranks of the Union army during the great Civil war, and by faithfulness to public and private duties and conscientious regard for the perpetuation of his name and labor in the bringing up of his children. His life has been a singularly active one, and the end of his labors finds him financially prosperous and rich in the esteem of a wide circle of appreciative friends.

Mr. Rodecker was born in Fayette County, Pennsylvania, August 29, 1840, and is a son of Samuel and Ann (Best) Rodecker, the former a native of Fayette County, Pennsylvania, and the latter of Chambersburg, that state. The family was founded in America during Colonial days by the great-great-grandfather of Mr. Rodecker, who emigrated to this country from Germany, while his great-grandfather was born in the

Keystone state, where the family has been known for many years. Samuel Rodecker resided on the farm on which he was born until 1854, in which year he migrated with his family to Illinois as a pioneer, and there passed his life in the pursuits of the soil, dying in Knox County. The mother passed away in Andrew County, Missouri. They were the parents of eight children, of whom six grew to maturity: George W., of this review; Mrs. Nancy Andrews; Frederick, deceased, who was a resident of Southern Missouri; Alice Hensley, a widow, who resides at Lincoln, Nebraska; Mrs. Kate Bell, a widow of Chicago, Illinois; and William, a resident of Nebraska.

George W. Rodecker was fourteen years of age when he accompanied his parents to Illinois, and in that state he completed his education in the public schools. He remained at home assisting his father on the farm until the fall of 1861, when his country's need for defenders of the flag caused him, with other patriotic young men of his neighborhood, to enlist in the Union army. He became a member of Company K, Fifty-fifth Regiment, Illinois Volunteer Infantry, attached to the Fifteenth Army Corps, First Brigade, Second Division, with which organization he served for three years. During this service he participated in nine great battles, in addition to numerous smaller engagements and skirmishes, and at all times bore himself as a courageous, faithful and cheerful soldier, winning the respect of his comrades and the confidence of his officers. He took part in the great battles of Shiloh and Hollow Springs, Mississippi, the advance on Corinth, Sherman's march to and past Vicksburg, where he helped dig the canal approaching the fortifications and was on guard duty when the Indianola ran the blockade, and the battles of Missionary Ridge and Black River, and was then disabled by sickness and taken to the hospital at Memphis, Tennessee, where he was confined for two months. He was finally mustered out of the service with an excellent record, receiving his honorable discharge at Springfield, Illinois, in the fall of 1864.

When his military service was completed, Mr. Rodecker returned to farming in Knox County, Illinois, and there remained until the spring of 1882, when he came to Andrew County, Missouri. Here he successfully followed agricultural pursuits until 1900, when he rented his property and moved to King City, in order that his children might secure better educational advantages. In 1904 he took up his residence at Savannah, where he has a comfortable home and is surrounded by all the comforts that a life of industry and honorable dealing may bring.

Mr. Rodecker was married in 1865 to Miss Louise Marks, a native of Kentucky, who died five years later without issue. In 1872 Mr. Rodecker contracted a second marriage, being united with Miss Eliza Cooper, who was born in Kentucky, in 1847, and died at Savannah, in February, 1907, the mother of five children, as follows: Frank, who is a resident of Durango, Colorado, and has six children; Nera, who is the wife of Morris McColley, of St. Louis, Missouri; Irma, who resides at home with her father; Mrs. Alice Sealey, who died in April, 1913, leaving two children, Maxine Elliott and Leon, who make their home with their grandfather; and George C., who is a shoe merchant at Savannah, and the father of two children.

Mr. Rodecker has been a lifelong democrat. He heard the great joint debate between Stephen A. Douglas and Abraham Lincoln, at Galesburg, Illinois, and subsequently, while in the army, cast his ballot for George A. McClellan. He has continued to support democratic candidates to the present time and has been an active worker in the party, although he has not sought personal preferment. While a resident of Illinois, however, he acted capably for a number of years in the capacity

of justice of the peace. Mr. Rodecker is a member of the Presbyterian
Church, and has served as elder and trustee for a number of years,
holding the latter position at the present time. He has continued to
maintain an interest in his old army comrades, and is a popular member
of the local post of the Grand Army of the Republic.

LLOYD W. BOOHER. The son of Congressman Charles F. Booher,
Lloyd W. Booher, took his father's place in the old established and
prominent law firm of Booher & Williams in 1909, and has been one of
the active lawyers of Andrew County for the past fifteen years. As his
father began practice at Savannah in 1871, the name has been continuously identified with the law and with public affairs in this city
over forty years, and is one of the most prominent and best known in
Northwest Missouri.

Charles F. Booher, who has represented the Fourth Missouri District
in Congress since the Sixtieth Congress, was born at East Groveland,
New York, January 21, 1848, a son of Henry and Catherine Booher.
The family came out to Northwest Missouri many years ago, and Charles
F. Booher was educated in district schools and in 1871 was admitted
to the bar and at once began practice at Savannah. In 1887 he formed
a partnership with Isaac R. Williams, and the firm of Booher & Williams
has been continuously in practice at Savannah since that time. Mr.
Booher's career as a lawyer has been marked by numerous political
distinctions. He served six years in the office of prosecuting attorney,
was democratic presidential elector in 1880, for six years held the office
of mayor of Savannah, and in 1906 was elected to represent the Fourth
District in Congress. He took his seat in 1907, and is now concluding his
fourth term. Congressman Booher was married at Rochester, Missouri,
January 11, 1877, to Sallie D. Shanks.

Lloyd W. Booher was born at Savannah, November 12, 1877, and
this city has been his home all his life. He was graduated from the high
school in 1895, entered the University of Missouri in the same year,
and after one year in the Academic Department took up the study of
law and was graduated LL. B. in the class of 1898. Admitted to the bar
in the same fall, on reaching his majority, he began active practice, and
in 1909 became a member of the firm of Booher & Williams. Mr. Booher
had the distinction in 1900 of being the only democrat elected to a county
office in Andrew County. He was elected prosecuting attorney and
served one term. Mr. Booher was a member of the Beta Theta Pi college
fraternity during his university career, and is affiliated with the Masonic
lodge at Savannah, the Benevolent and Protective Order of Elks at St.
Joseph, the Knights of Pythias at Rochester, and is a member of the
St. Joseph Country Club. On January 15, 1902, he married Josephine
E. Hurley, who was born in Andrew County. Her father, O. J. Hurley,
was for a number of years editor of the Savannah Democrat.

SAMUEL B. STEWART. One of the best known resident of Andrew
County is Samuel B. Stewart, who has lived in the vicinity of Savannah
nearly all his life, and is now a resident of the county seat and semi-
retired. Mr. Stewart is a man of extensive interests, and has had an
interesting career.

He was born about six miles south of Savannah near the Buchanan

In the early days he knew Joseph Robidoux, the founder and pioneer of St. Joseph. His death occurred when Samuel B. was five years of age and the mother died about the same time. There were four children: Frances Gillespie; Martha Sherman, deceased; Robert, of Reserve, Kansas; and Samuel B.

After the death of the parents Samuel and his brother were adopted by the late David Moran, a wealthy farmer and land owner whose home was about eight miles east of Savannah. Mr. Stewart lived with Mr. Moran until the latter's death. He had an average education in the country schools and learned to work on his foster father's farm, and at the death of his benefactor inherited a farm of 500 acres which he still owns. In the fall of 1905 Mr. Stewart moved to Savannah, and his son, Robert, now operates the place. Mr. Stewart was active manager of Mr. Moran's large land holdings and in all his business operations has proved himself a capable and energetic worker. Since moving to Savannah he has engaged in the buying and shipping of live stock and for a time had a livery establishment.

Mr. Stewart is a 'democrat in politics, and at one time was candidate for the office of sheriff, but otherwise has not sought any public honors. Mr. Stewart was a party to the most famous lawsuit ever tried in Andrew County, and it is a case with which lawyers all over Missouri are familiar. This case, entitled Moran vs. Stewart, was a long drawn out piece of litigation, and was in the courts from 1891 to 1913. The Supreme Court reviewed the judgments of the lower courts five different times, and it will probably stand for many years as one of the record cases tried in Missouri. A complete account of this case is found in the Missouri Reports of the Supreme Court and was also published in the Southwestern Reporter of January 1, 1913.

In 1876 Mr. Stewart married Hettie Carson, who was born in Andrew County, October 5, 1852, daughter of Joseph Carson. Mr. and Mrs. Stewart are the parents of three children: David M., who lives in San Francisco, California; Robert, who is active manager of his father's farm; and Eva, wife of Carl Lambright of Hot Springs, South Dakota.

Joseph Carson, father of Mrs. Stewart, was born in Rockcastle County, Kentucky, December 12, 1812. When a child he lost his father, had only limited opportunities for gaining an education, but eventually succeeded in life. He learned the trade of stone mason, and came to Missouri in the latter '40s with wife and two children. He entered land along the Platte River in Andrew County, sold that, and finally bought 160 acres of some of the finest land in this vicinity. He lived on that farm, eight miles east of Savannah, until seventy-five years of age, and spent his latter years in King City, where he died in December, 1892. He was a member of the Christian Church from boyhood and in politics a democrat. Joseph Carson was married in Kentucky to Margaret Montgomery, a native of that state. She died in 1855, and her five children were: Elizabeth, who died young; Joseph R., a farmer in Gentry County; Mary J., deceased wife of Luther Carter; Margaret, deceased wife of John Bedford; and Mrs. Stewart, who was the fourth in order of birth. In 1860 Joseph Carson married Mrs. Sophia Mitchell, widow of Charles Mitchell, and a sister of the late David Moran. By this marriage there were five children: David M. Carson of Jackson, Tennessee; Kate M., of King City; William, who died at the age of one year; Charles B., who lives near Guthrie, Oklahoma; and James H., of Gentry County, Missouri.

WOODFORD MARTIN, M. D. There is comparative little interest for the general reader in the history of lives that have been without

HISTORY OF NORTHWEST MISSOURI

struggle, and it is because of this that romances enthrall because they tell of difficulties met and overcome and of the consequent development of character. In every community, doubtless, there are many now quietly pursuing their daily avocations, into whose lives have come struggles and achievements, the telling of which may be of encouragement to others and cannot fail to excite universal interest. Among the prominent citizens of Savannah, Missouri, who has achieved success in the practice of medicine, winning his way through sheer determination, is Dr. Woodford Martin, whose practice, in point of years, covers a longer period than any other physician in Andrew County.

Woodford Martin was born in Lincoln Township, Andrew County, Missouri, November 30, 1843. He is a son of Elijah and Sarah Elizabeth (Goodloe) Martin, the former of whom was born in 1811, at Woodford, Kentucky, and the latter near Richmond, Virginia. They were married in Kentucky and came to Andrew County in 1836, waiting for the opening of the Platte purchase, when they secured a homestead, in Lincoln Township, on which they lived until within five years of their decease, when they moved to the home of their' son, Woodford, at Savannah, and died there, the mother at the age of seventy-nine years, and the father in his eightieth year. They were real pioneers and faced hardships without number, bravely bearing their part in the developing of their section. They were devout Presbyterians and their faith was a strong anchor when the troubles of life fell upon them. Elijah Martin was first a whig in his political sentiments, but later became a democrat and his sons adopted the same political faith. Five children were born to Elijah and Sarah Elizabeth Martin: James E., who is now deceased, served all through the war between the states under General Price and was a member of his body guard at the time of that officer's surrender; Robert H., who is engaged in farming in Lincoln Township; John S., who was also a soldier and participated in the battle of Blue Mills, Missouri, escaping death on the field, but shortly afterward died of measles; Woodford; and Eliza V., who is also deceased. The first store in Andrew County was located on the Martin homestead and conducted by Robert Elliott, a relative, with John Samuels, Mr. Elliott's son-in-law, under the name of Elliott & Samuels, they having secured permission from the United States Government to operate a trading post in 1835. Later they moved the store to Whitehall and then to Savannah, being the earliest merchants in the last named place.

Woodford Martin had but meager educational opportunities in boyhood, school sessions being short and irregular, as in all newly settled sections, nevertheless he had an ambition to excel and a determination to become a practitioner of medicine. When he reached manhood it was during the troubled days of Civil war and the future looked anything but bright, and he concluded to remain still longer on the home farm, and, while his brothers were in the army, still further assist his father. In the hope of finally attaining his ambition he secured medical books and for two years carried on his studies alone, but in 1868 became a student under the direction of Dr. J. B. G. Ferguson, of Savannah, proving diligent as a student and so reliable that his preceptor permitted him to practice in the local regions to some extent. It was with high hopes that in 1873 he set out for a medical school at St. Louis and there applied himself so assiduously to study for six months, denying himself comforts and recreation, that he fell so dangerously ill that he was sent to his home in the expectation that death would surely soon follow. Home care, however, so restored him to normal condition that in 1874 he insisted on again leaving home for a medical school at Louisville, Kentucky, and there remained until he was graduated in 1876. With

little intermission, Doctor Martin has been in medical practice ever since. For about ten years he was in partnership with Dr. M. F. Wakefield, who was one of the first practitioners at Savannah, a well known man and at the time of death accounted one of the wealthiest men of Andrew County. Another of the early physicians of the county was Doctor Smith, a cousin of Doctor Martin by marriage. The profession was not greatly crowded at that time and its emoluments in those days in no way recompensed the physicians for the hardships they endured. Doctor Martin built up a very substantial practice and acquired a reputation for medical skill that carried his name to other counties. He has practiced under three different registers and was the first health officer appointed in Andrew County, this precaution being taken by the authorities after an epidemic of smallpox. He is identified with several medical bodies, including the St. Joseph Medical Society and the Missouri State Medical Society. His acquaintance is wide over the county and in many households his name is held in affectionate regard because of his faithfulness in times of dire illness.

In 1866 Doctor Martin was married to Miss Louisa Goodloe, who died in 1869, survived by two sons: J. L., who resides on the old Martin homestead in Lincoln Township; and Joseph, who is a resident of Nodaway Township, Andrew County. In 1890 Doctor Martin married Miss Sarah Elizabeth Compton, a native of Iowa. For many years Doctor Martin has been a Master Mason, but otherwise has not identified himself with secret organizations. His life has been a busy one, happy in the fulfillment of his early ambition, and useful and beneficial to his fellowmen.

A. S. KEEVES. During the period from 1866 until 1899, the late A. S. Keeves was one of the most prominent business men of Savannah, and it is doubtful if any other man played a more important part in establishing this thriving city's commercial stability. His was a career notable for success achieved through honorable effort, for prosperity gained fairly and without questionable dealing and for constant adherence to high ideals of business integrity. Fifteen years have passed since his death, yet the business which he founded, and to the development of which his best years were given, still flourishes and continues, a monument to the ability and sterling judgment of its originator.

Mr. Keeves was born in Berkeley County, Virginia (now West Virginia), December 19, 1820, and there as a young man received his introduction to the dry goods business with a merchant named Wysong, in whose employ he remained about five years, serving a complete apprenticeship. Following this he went to Newark, Ohio, where he remained for four years, and in 1854 returned to Virginia, where he was married to Miss Virginia Wilson, a native of that state. In the same year they came to St. Joseph, Missouri, by way of boat, and traveled on to Oregon, Holt County, where they lived on a farm for about a year. At that time Mr. Keeves returned to mercantile pursuits as an employe of William Zook, who conducted a dry goods establishment at Oregon. Mr. Zook subsequently sent Mr. Keeves to Forest City to manage his branch store there, which he continued to do successfully for three or four years. At that time, desiring to enter business on his own account, Mr. Keeves went to Nebraska City, Nebraska, and put in a stock of furniture, but after about two years was induced by Mr. Zook to enter a partnership in a venture at Kansas City, Mr. Keeves going to St. Louis where he purchased a stock of goods worth $15,000. The store at Kansas City was conducted for about two years, and the stock was then divided, part being sent to Forest City and part to Savannah, although the partnership was still continued, Mr. Zook remaining at Forest City and Mr. Keeves coming, in 1866, to Savannah. In March, 1876, Mr. Zook died and Mr. Keeves bought the interest from the heirs, and from that time until his death, May 11, 1899, continued in full charge of the business. Since then it has been conducted by his son and two daughters and is known as Keeves' Dry Goods Company. Mrs. Keeves survived her husband several years and died at Savannah, May 11, 1903. Throughout his career Mr. Keeves was known as a man of the most sterling integrity, and at all times had the full confidence of his associates and the respect of his competitors. He did much to advance the civic interests of Savannah, gave freely of his time and means toward the forwarding of education and religion, and through his own example and precept encouraged good citizenship. He and his wife were the parents of four children: M. T.; C. F., who died in 1898; and Misses Zua and Carrie, who are associated with their brother in the management of the business.

M. T. Keeves was born at Oregon, Holt County, Missouri, November 5, 1857. Here he received his education, and for thirty-eight years has been associated with the business of which he is now the manager. Through his good business judgment and acumen and the following out of his father's policies he has made the enterprise continue to flourish, and his name is a respected one in commercial circles. He is a member of the Independent Order of Odd Fellows, and in political matters is, like his father, a democrat. On October 26, 1897, Mr. Keeves was married to Miss Kate Henderson, and they have one son, Stuart.

WALLACE A. CROCKETT. Of the men who have participated actively in the agricultural, commercial and financial development of the City of Savannah, none are better or more favorably known than Wallace A. Crockett, who now belongs to the retired colony. Mr. Crockett was born in Henry County, Ohio, March 28, 1850, and is a son of Milton and Sarah (West) Crockett, the former born in Seneca County, Ohio, January 11, 1825, and the latter in the State of Vermont, April 26, 1830. Mrs. Crockett was nine years of age when she moved with her parents to Seneca County, Ohio, and there met and married Mr. Crockett, shortly following which they moved to Henry County, in the same state, and settled in the heavy timber of the Black Swamps, on Turkey Foot Creek. There Mr. Crockett had about fifty acres cleared, when in 1857 he left for Andrew County, Missouri, with a twin brother, Nelson Crockett, who was his partner. They purchased 320 acres of land four miles northeast of Whitesville, Andrew County, and there settled down to the pursuits of the soil. In 1860 the brothers cast their votes for Abraham Lincoln for President, theirs being two out of fifteen ballots so cast in the county, and owing to the unpleasantness that marked the beginning of the Civil war the brothers took their families back to Ohio. There Nelson Crockett enlisted for service in the Fifty-fifth Regiment, Ohio Volunteer Infantry, and was wounded at the battle of Bull Run (second), and never fully recovered from the effects of his injury, from which he died in 1892. Ten months after his brother's enlistment, Milton Crockett joined the same regiment, with which he fought until the close of hostilities. In 1865 the brothers returned to Andrew County, and here continued in partnership until 1870, when they divided

over the county. He was also a man of prominence in civic and political affairs, and in 1872 was sent to the State Legislature as representative, being elected on the ticket of the liberal party and serving two terms. He was a member of the Grand Army of the Republic, at Whitesville, and a member of the Universalist Church, as was also his wife, who died in December, 1896. They were the parents of six children, as follows: Wallace A., of this review; Ezra, who died at the age of 1½ years; Homer, a resident of Whitesville; Emily M., who is the wife of David Gebhart, of Whitesville; Nathan W., of Whitesville; and L. R., who is the owner of the old homestead property.

Wallace A. Crockett received his education in the public schools of Andrew County, and was reared on the home farm, on which he remained until twenty-nine years of age, when he was stricken with rheumatism and obliged to change his mode of living and employment. Accordingly, he left his 120-acre farm near Bolckow, Missouri, and went to Whitesville, where he secured a position as clerk in the dry goods store of M. K. Manning for one year and was then with Watson & Cline one year. Subsequently, he and his brother-in-law, Newton Thompson, purchased the store and successfully conducted the establishment until 1892, when he disposed of his interests therein. In the meantime, in 1890, the bank at Rea had been started, known as the Rea Banking Company, and Mr. Crockett was made its cashier, a position which he held for eleven years. He was then elected president of this institution and continued to serve as such until 1909, when he retired from active participation in business affairs. Since December, 1912, he has been a resident of Savannah, where he erected his beautiful home at No. 202 East Pearl Street. Mr. and Mrs. Crockett are members of the Christian Church at Whitesville. He is a Master Mason and a member of the Eastern Star, to which Mrs. Crockett also belongs. Politically, he has always supported republican principles. Mr. Crockett has led an active and useful life, and his standing in his community is that of a man of sterling integrity and public-spirited citizenship.

On November 23, 1871, Mr. Crockett was married to Miss Florence E. Thompson, who was born at Duncanville, Pennsylvania, February 26, 1851, a daughter of Michael and Susan J. C. (Rodkey) Thompson, natives of Pennsylvania. Mr. Thompson first came to Missouri in 1856 and bought a farm four miles north of Whitesville, on Hickory Creek, returning to Pennsylvania for his family in 1859. He continued to be engaged in agricultural pursuits until his death in 1877, and Mrs. Thompson, in 1880, came to the home of her daughter and son-in-law, Mr. and Mrs. Crockett, with whom she resided until her death at the age of ninety-two years. There were nine children in the Thompson family: Newton and Wirt, who are both deceased; Ney, a resident of Andrew County; Hortense Eugenia, deceased, who was the wife of Job Pierce; Irene, who is the widow of W. H. Bulla, of Empire Prairie; Mrs. Crockett; Tell, who is deceased; Solon M., who still resides on the old Thompson homestead; and Grace Anna Lee, who died at the age of 1½ years. Mr. and Mrs. Crockett have one child, Emily L., the wife of S. R. Murphy, of Savannah, and they have one daughter, Florence Jane, who is the wife' of Warren W. Gee, of Whitesville.

JOHN K. WHITE. Many of the pioneer families that were the first to settle in Andrew County have long since ceased to be connected with this section by living representatives. John K. White, now an active business man, and for many years identified with public affairs, represents in the second generation a family which was established here more than seventy years ago, and which by its honorable activities has well upheld and honored the position of pioneer.

John K. White was born at Flag Springs, in Andrew County, April 8, 1856. His parents were John and Asenath (Farrington) White. His father was born in Muskingum County, Ohio, August 30, 1817, while the mother was born in Guilford County, North Carolina, March 22, 1822. Both families were among the very early pioneers of Iowa Territory, the Farringtons having moved to that section about 1837, and the Whites in 1838. John and Asenath White were married in Iowa, March 28, 1839, and in the following year came to Northwest Missouri and settled on a tract of wild land, a quarter section, southeast of Helena in Andrew County. John White had all the hardy virtues of a pioneer, cleared away the forests, made his land tillable, and was a useful member of the community. He lived on his first homestead until 1853 and then moved to the village of Flag Springs, buying a farm there and remaining a resident of that community until his death on March 17, 1901. His widow died August 15, 1902, and both of them had reached venerable years, past fourscore. John White voted for John C. Fremont, the first standard bearer of the republican party, in 1856, and continued faithful to the cause of the republican party all his life, having cast his last vote for William McKinley in 1900. He and his family were members of the Baptist Church. There were three children: R. G., who died in April, 1914, in Colorado and whose body was laid to rest at the old cemetery at Flag Springs; L. T., who died in 1900 at St. Joseph; and John K.

John K. White has lived in Andrew County and has been identified with its agricultural, business and civic interests all his life, grew up in the rural districts, acquired a substantial education, and for a number of years combined farming and teaching. Fifteen years were spent as a teacher in the district schools of this county. During 1874-76 he was a student in the State Normal School at Kirksville. In this way his career went steadily forward as a farmer and educator until 1894, in that year he was elected county assessor, served two years and was then reelected for a four-year term. Following this term of office Mr. White engaged in general merchandising at Flag Springs about three years, in 1904 moved to Savannah, and for three years was deputy county clerk, then returned to his farm for three years, and has since been engaged in the insurance business at Savannah. He is now manager of the Savannah Insurance Agency with offices over the First National Bank.

Mr. White has been affiliated with the republican party since reaching his majority, and was twenty-one years of age when given his first office, as township clerk. He is a member of the Baptist Church, is affiliated with the Masonic Order, the Independent Order of Odd Fellows, the Knights of Pythias and as a citizen his support can always be counted upon to help forward any movement that means the advantage of the community.

On May 1, 1878, Mr. White married Mary W. Combest, who was born in Andrew County July 12, 1863, a daughter of Wyatt and Mary (Shepherd) Combest. Her parents were early settlers on Empire

Missouri, and he is also the postmaster at Savannah. To his profession he has brought an industry and ability which would have enabled him to succeed in lines of business much more remunerative, and since he was fourteen years of age has been through all the grades of service in the fourth estate, from printer's apprentice to foreman, from reporter to editor, and from a salaried position to independent publisher.

A native of England, William S. Dray was born at Swansbrook in Sussex County, August 20, 1861, a son of Alfred Henry and Susan (Smith) Dray, who were natives of the same county. When William S. was a boy of five years the family emigrated to America, landing in New York City, January 1, 1865, and five days later arrived at Nebraska City. In 1876 they found a home in Page County, Iowa, in 1885 moved to Northern Kansas, and in 1889 to Mound City, Missouri. The father became a resident of Nebraska in 1891, and died in that state in 1901. The mother is still living, and resides in Northern Idaho. The father was a blacksmith and machinist by trade, and an industrious worker and made all the provisions possible for his family. Of fifteen children, the parents reared ten, and nine of them are still living.

William S. Dray, who was the fifth in order of birth, had his home with his parents until they moved to Mound City, but since attaining his fourteenth year he has been identified with the printing and newspaper business. He worked in various offices, learning the art of composition and all mechanical details in the printing trade, and in 1890 came to Savannah and became foreman in the Democrat office. In June, 1895, he moved to Mound City and was engaged in the newspaper business there three years, after which he returned to Savannah and became editor and business manager of the Democrat. In 1901 Mr. Dray bought the Democrat printing office and paper, and for thirteen years has employed his energies in maintaining a first-class newspaper, one of the best mediums for news and general publicity in Andrew County. He has been interested in the success of the democratic party since casting his first vote, and has done much to build up the party organization and assist his friends to office. On December 29, 1914, he was appointed postmaster at Savannah.

Outside of his profession and business situations Mr. Dray finds his chief interests in church work as a member of the Christian Church, and is especially prominent in the Christian Endeavor Society. Fraternally he is affiliated with the Modern Woodmen of America.

In 1894 Mr. Dray married Belle Garner, of a pioneer family. They are the parents of four children: Francis Earl, Ernest Alfred, Mary Margaret and Robert Garner.

Oren Heth Clark. During the nine years that he has been connected with the circuit court clerk's office, Oren Heth Clark has established an excellent record for faithful public service, a record that has commended him to the people of Andrew County whose interests he has served so long and so well. Entering the office in the capacity of assistant, after four years of capable work, he was elected circuit court clerk, and since that time he has continued to vindicate the faith placed in his integrity and his ability.

Mr. Clark is a native of Andrew County, having been born at Flag Springs, June 2, 1879, a son of Logan A. and Ellen Elizabeth (Clark) Clark, who, although bearing the same name prior to their marriage, were not related. With the exception of two years in Lawrence County, Arkansas, the parents passed their entire lives in Andrew County, where the father was at various times engaged in farming, in sawmilling and in mechanical work, and here he died March 7, 1893, the mother passing away June 12th of the same year. They were married by Capt. J. B. Majors, in this county, March 30, 1878, prior to which time Mrs. Clark had been engaged in teaching school in the vicinity of Flag Springs. They were faithful members of the Methodist Episcopal Church, and in politics Mr. Clark was a republican. There were three children in the family: Oren Heth, of this review; Herbert Alonzo, a resident of Fort Collins, Colorado; and Ormie Wilson, of St. Joseph, Missouri.

Oren Heth Clark was but fourteen years of age when he lost his parents, and at that time went to make his home with his uncle, John A. Clark, at Bolckow, Andrew County. He was given a common school education, and during his vacation periods displayed his industry and ambition by working in his uncle's sawmill, and his time continued to be thus occupied until he reached his majority. In 1900 he entered upon his career as a teacher in the district schools of Andrew County, and continued as an educator for 5½ years, making a record as an efficient and popular teacher. On January 1, 1906, Mr. Clark was appointed deputy circuit court clerk of Andrew County, under E. E. Townsend, and his services in this capacity were so appreciated during the next four years that in 1910 he became the candidate of the democratic party for the office of circuit clerk, and was elected. In 1914 he was again the candidate of his party for circuit clerk and was re-elected and is the present incumbent of that office.

On January 20, 1909, Mr. Clark was married to Miss May Louise Kelly, a native of Andrew County, and the eldest child of B. F. and Rosa (Schneider) Kelly. They have no children. Mrs. Clark is a graduate of Savannah High School, and attended Stephens College one term, taking a musical course. She and her husband are members of the First Baptist Church, in which Mr. Clark is a deacon, and is also actively interested in the work of the Sunday school, of which he is superintendent. His fraternal connections are with the local lodges of the Masons and the Independent Order of Odd Fellows, in both of which he has numerous friends.

MRS. JULIA GLAZIER. In a list of the prominent citizens of any community today, mention is made of women as well as men, for whether they are actively in the business world or not, the high position of woman as a factor in civilization is being recognized as it has never been before. Of the venerable and high-minded womanhood of Andrew County, Mrs. Julia Glazier is one of the best representatives. She has lived in this community upwards of half a century and besides her service in making and maintaining a home, has been a leader in those social organizations in which women have so conspicuous a part, and which do so much real good as charitable and benevolent forces. While Mrs. Glazier has a winter home with her son in California, she feels too much attached to Savannah and her various interests there to leave the community which she has called home for so many years.

Her husband, the late George W. Glazier, who was for a number of years an active merchant in Savannah, was born in Athens County, Ohio, April 10, 1828. His parents were John and Mary (Henry)

and continued active in business affairs until his death in July, 1873. His father had been a soldier in the Civil war, although at the time he was advanced in years. He entered as a captain of a company, and was brought home stricken with camp fever and died in 1861, a few months after the war began.

George W. Glazier was married in 1862 to Julia A. Joy. She was born on a farm in Morgan County, Ohio, in 1837, and lived there until her marriage. When they came to Savannah in 1867 they bought the homestead which has been her home now for nearly half a century, and it is one of the oldest homes and a real landmark in the county seat. Mrs. Glazier has been an active worker in the Methodist Episcopal Church since 1869, and has been particularly prominent in the work of the Woman's Foreign Missionary Society since its organization, having served as its first president. She is one of the noble women of Northwest Missouri who have given all the influence of their characters to the cause of temperance, has been a member of the Woman's Christian Temperance Union since its organization in Savannah in 1882, and was its president for a number of years. Until resigning she was for twenty years state treasurer of the W. C. T. U.

Mrs. Glazier is a daughter of James and Mary (Law) Joy, both of whom were born in Wheeling, West Virginia, but were brought to Ohio by their respective parents, and grew up on a farm and lived in Morgan County. Mrs. Glazier was one of a family of one son and eight daughters. She herself has two children: Frank O., who lives in Los Angeles, California, and Charles L., who died at Boston, Massachusetts, in 1911, being then forty-one years of age.

JOSEPH BIELMAN. From the year 1874 until his retirement in 1912, Joseph Bielman was identified prominently with the business life of Savannah, and during this time built up a reputation as a substantial and capable man of affairs. His entrance into commercial life was as a blacksmith, but as the community grew and developed he branched out into broader lines, and during the last eighteen years of his connection with industrial matters he was engaged in the manufacture of vehicles. Mr. Bielman is a native of Baden, Germany, and was born February 19, 1845, a son of Philip and Helena (Buchholtz) Bielman, who passed their entire lives in the Fatherland, where the father was a blacksmith and a hard-working and energetic man. There were three sons and one daughter in the family.

Joseph Bielman was educated in the public schools of his native land, and under the preceptorship of his father learned the blacksmith trade. Desiring broader opportunities, in 1868 he left Germany with his brother Philip, and, coming to the United States, located at St. Joseph, Missouri, where for six years he followed his vocation with a fair measure of success. His advent in Savannah occurred in 1874, which is remembered as "the year of the grasshoppers," and established a blacksmith shop on the north side of the square, in partnership with John Bitzer. The business grew under the partners' good management, but they finally decided that one could find more profit than two, and two years later Mr. Bielman bought Mr. Bitzer's interest. Later, however, he took as a partner Gottlieb Mack, and they continued together for two years, Mr. Bielman then again assuming entire charge of the business. This he conducted as a blacksmith and general repair shop until 1894, when he began the manufacture of carriages and wagons, and in this line continued successfully until his retirement in 1912. While the greater part of his attention was given to the enterprise which his hands had founded and which had grown so steadily under his able direction,

Mr. Bielman was also interested in other ventures, serving as a director of the Commercial Bank from the time of its organization until it was merged with the Exchange Bank. He has always been accounted by his associates a man of sterling integrity and great capacity, and one to whom they looked in matters of importance. A republican in political matters, he served Savannah capably for twelve years as alderman, during which he demonstrated more than ordinary official ability in securing improvements of a civic nature, and his time was given whole-heartedly to the best interests of his home locality. In the campaign of 1912, because of the issues involved, he supported the presidential aspira-tions of Woodrow Wilson. He belongs to the Knights of Columbus and a number of German fraternal organizations, and, with his family, attends the Catholic Church, of which he has been a lifelong member. His good citizenship has never been questioned, and during his long residence at Savannah he has formed a wide circle of sincere and appre-ciative friends.

While a resident of St. Joseph, Missouri, Mr. Bielman was united in marriage with Miss Barbara Probst, a native of Bavaria, Germany, who died at Savannah, December 31, 1907, at the age of sixty years, having been born April 23, 1847. To this union there were born five children: Mary, who is a Catholic Sister in the Benedictine Convent, at Clyde, Missouri; Joseph, a resident of Philadelphia, Pennsylvania; Emma, who is also a Catholic Sister in the Benedictine Convent at Clyde; Rosa, who died at the age of fourteen years; and Clara, who is a Catholic Sister in the Mount St. Scholastica Convent, at Atchison, Kansas. On July 20, 1910, Mr. Bielman was married to Miss Myrtle Donovan, who was born at Chicago, Illinois, July 20, 1884, daughter of John and Jennie (Foley) Donovan, natives of Illinois. Mr. Donovan was for eighteen years a member of the Chicago Police Department, and died while still an officer of that organization in 1909.

Mr. Bielman is fond of travel, and in 1908 took an extended trip through Germany with his daughter Clara, also visiting various points of interest in other European countries.

JOHN A. MILLER. The present efficient and popular county clerk of Andrew County is a scion in the third generation of one of the sterling pioneer families of this county, with whose history the name of Miller has been intimately and worthily linked for nearly seventy years, the maternal ancestors of Mr. Miller likewise having been early settlers of the county and his parents having been children at the time of the removal of the respective families from Indiana to this state. In addition to serving as county clerk, to which office he was reelected, for his second term, in the autumn of 1914, Mr. Miller is numbered among the most progressive and enterprising business men of the thriving little city of Savannah, judicial headquarters and metropolis of his native county. He is here engaged in the buying and shipping of grain and is the owner of a well equipped grain elevator. That he is not like the prophet of scriptural aphorism and "without honor in his own country," needs no further voucher than his official preferment, but it may further be said that on his "native heath" he finds the coterie of his friends to be equal in number to his acquaintances.

John A. Miller was born on what is now known as the Bennett Farm, four miles northwest of Savannah, and the date of his nativity was August 6, 1862. He is a son of William T. and Charity (Burns) Miller, both of whom were born in Indiana and both of whom were children at the time of the removal of the respective families to Missouri, as has been previously stated. The paternal great-grandfather of Mr. Miller was a patriot soldier in the War of the Revolution. The Burns family was early founded in North Carolina, and was represented in the pioneer settlement of Indiana, as was also the Miller family.

William T. Miller was a lad of ten years when he came with his parents to Andrew County, where he was reared to maturity on the pioneer farm that continued to be the home of his parents until their death. With the passing years he gained prominence as one of the substantial agriculturists and stock-growers of the county and he continued to reside on his well improved homestead farm until three years prior to his death, the closing period of his life having been passed in well earned retirement, in Savannah, where he died on the 30th of May, 1912, at the venerable age of seventy-six years, his widow still maintaining her home in this city and being a devoted member of the Methodist Episcopal Church, of which her husband likewise was a zealous adherent, his political allegiance having been given to the republican party. Of the five children, John A., of this review, is the eldest; Chester A. resides in Savannah; Benjamin R. is identified successfully with farming enterprise in this county; Roy A. is engaged in the grocery business at Savannah; and Mary is the wife of Wirt Ball, of Savannah.

John A. Miller was reared to adult age on the homestead farm and acquired his early education in the public schools of his native county. In 1888, at the age of twenty-six years, Mr. Miller removed to Holt County, where he remained thirteen years, at the expiration of which, in 1900, he established his business at Fillmore, Andrew County, where he became actively identified with the milling business, both as an executive and a practical miller. For three years he was engaged in the same line of enterprise at Whitesville, this county, and in 1910, upon his election to the office of county clerk, he established his home at Savannah, the county seat, where he has since continued the incumbent of this important office, to which he was reelected in the fall of 1914, for a second term of four years. Here also he has been engaged actively and successfully in the grain business since 1907, and, with his elevator facilities of excellent order, he controls a substantial and profitable business.

Mr. Miller is an ardent supporter of the cause of the republican party and is one of its influential workers in his native county. He is a Master Mason and affiliated also with the Independent Order of Odd Fellows, and both he and his wife hold membership in the Methodist Episcopal Church.

In 1885 was solemnized the marriage of Mr. Miller to Miss Sadie E. Sayers, who was born in Pennsylvania, a daughter of John Sayers, and who was a child of six years at the time of the family removal to Andrew County, Missouri, where she was reared and educated. Mr. and Mrs. Miller became the parents of three children, of whom the second in order of birth was Jessie C., the only daughter. She was born February 24, 1891, and was summoned to the life eternal on the 20th of November, 1906. William S., elder of the two sons, was a student in the electrical engineering department of the University of Missouri for one and a half years and is now one of the progressive young farmers of his native county. On the 20th of December, 1911, he wedded Miss Ella Caldwell, and they have one child—Jessie Bernice. Ray, the younger son, served three years as his father's deputy in the office of county clerk and is now taking a course in the agricultural department of the University of Missouri.

HON. PETER C. BREIT. To the professional success which has attended the practice of Peter C. Breit as a lawyer at Savannah for twenty years, have come also the honors and distinctions of public office, and his record throughout has been one of faithful devotion to the interests of his clients and competent discharge of the duties of citizenship.

Peter C. Breit is a native of Andrew County, born on a farm April 26, 1866, and his family on both sides have been identified with this section of Northwest Missouri since pioneer times. His parents were Christian and Margaret (Jenkins) Breit. His father, a native of Switzerland, was brought to America when a child, located in Ohio in 1842, and not long after moved out to Northwest Missouri, grew up and became a farmer in Andrew County, and spent the rest of his life actively engaged in that location. He died in Andrew County in 1875 at the age of fifty-seven. The mother was born in Tennessee, and her family came from Kentucky to Missouri during the early '40s. She died in 1887 at the age of sixty-one. There were four sons and four daughters in the family, and the Savannah lawyer is next to the youngest.

His boyhood and youth were spent on a farm, with a country school education, and for the most part he had to work out his own destiny, ambition and self-reliance having been the actuating principles in his successful career. He attended a business college at Savannah, took up the study of law on his own account, and later spent one year in the law department of the University of Missouri, graduating in 1894 LL. B. Admitted to the bar in the same year, he began practice at Savannah, and in the past twenty years has been connected with much of the important litigation tried in the local courts. Mr. Breit's offices are in the First National Bank Building.

As a republican, he has long been active in local affairs. In 1890, four years before his admission to the bar, he was elected county assessor, and held that office two years. In 1894 Mr. Breit was elected a member of the Legislature and was returned to the office in 1896. On November 3, 1914, he was elected probate judge of Andrew County.

Mr. Breit is affiliated with the Masonic Order and the Knights of Pythias. In April, 1906, he married Miss Mary E. Doersam, who was born in Andrew County, a daughter of Adam Doersam.

CAPT. WILLIAM HENRY BULLA. The late Capt. William Henry Bulla was one of Andrew County's distinguished citizens from the time of his arrival here in 1867, until his death, which occurred October 9, 1902. As a soldier of the Union, he earned promotion by his fearless exploits upon the field of battle during the Civil war; in the pursuits of agriculture he subsequently showed himself a man of industry and energy, and as a private citizen and public legislator he gave to his community his best energies. A work of this nature would be decidedly incomplete did it not contain the records of such representative men.

Capt. William Henry Bulla was born at Richmond, Indiana, October 29, 1836, and was a son of David H. and Sarah (Cox) Bulla. His grandfather was William Bulla, a native of North Carolina, who came of French-German lineage. David H. Bulla was born at Richmond, Indiana, January 14, 1812, and in early life followed farming, but subsequently became a wholesale dealer in tobacco, having an establishment at the corner of Seventh and Main streets, Louisville, Kentucky. He

William Henry, of this review; and David, born July 28, 1838, died February 1, 1839.

William Henry Bulla was given a public school education and grew up amid rural surroundings, continuing to farm in the vicinity of Richmond, Indiana, until reaching the age of fifteen years. At that time, with an uncle, he immigrated to Iowa, where he was engaged in farming, and in the spring of 1857 went to Kansas and entered 160 acres of land on the Neosho River, in the vicinity of Emporia. While there he assisted in surveying the City of Emporia, carrying the chain. After a short experience as a farmer in that vicinity, he entered the employ of the Santa Fe Mail, but in the spring of 1859 resigned his position to join a great immigrant train the destination of which was the famed gold fields of Cripple Creek and Pike's Peak, Colorado, and there continued with more or less success in mining and prospecting. The outbreak of the Civil war drew Captain Bulla to Omaha, Nebraska, and thence to St. Joseph, Missouri, where he joined a cavalry organization known as the "Stewart Horse." Shortly thereafter this regiment disbanded, and Captain Bulla enlisted in Company F, Second Regiment, Iowa Volunteer Cavalry, November 9, 1861, as a private. His subsequent service was one of constant activity. He participated in the great battle of Shiloh, was wounded at Corinth, May 9, 1862, fought at Iuka, Second Corinth, Siege of Vicksburg, Raymond, Champion Hill, Jackson, Stone River and Tupelo, and at the sanguine engagement at Franklin, declared by many authorities to have been the bloodiest of all the great conflict, was again wounded and was captured by the enemy, November 30, 1864. Captain Bulla experienced the horrors of Andersonville Prison, for he was confined in that stockade until April 14, 1865, when he was released, sent to St. Louis, via Vicksburg, and there mustered out of the service, May 15, 1865. In the meantime he had won repeated promotion, and was serving as second lieutenant at the time of his capture by the Confederates, and while held prisoner by them his captain's commission was granted him, but this did not reach him until he had reached home, although he had been receiving a captain's pay for some time. His entire record was one of the greatest bravery and faithful performance of duty, and in after years those who had fought side by side with him through the war related many tales of his prowess in action.

Captain Bulla returned to his native place after the close of his military service, but in 1866 went to Omaha, Nebraska, where he fitted out a wagon train with general merchandise and made a trip to Virginia City. With a number of others he then constructed a fleet of seventeen flatboats at the foot of Yellowstone Falls, this being freighted with passengers and taken to Sioux City, Iowa. Captain Bulla located on his farm on Empire Prairie, Andrew County, Missouri, in the spring of 1867, and there began a career in agriculture which only terminated with his death. His original purchase was 180 acres of land, on which he carried on operations of a general farming nature, and to this he subsequently added eighty acres, his widow still being the owner of the entire tract. Since her husband's death, however, she has resided in her handsome home at Savannah. As an agriculturist, Captain Bulla did much to popularize the use of progressive and modern methods. While he realized the value and practicability of time-proved methods, he was ever ready to experiment with innovations and inventions, and when his judgment told him they were serviceable, he did much to advance their interests. His business associates knew him as a man to be relied upon implicitly, and no blemish mars his record in commercial circles. A life-long republican, he held various minor offices within the gift of the people, and was sent twice to the Legislature of the state from Andrew County, being also a member of the special session called at the time of the burning of the State University. His labors as an official in behalf of his community and his constituents were at all times conscientious and commendable. Fraternally, Captain Bulla was connected with the Masons, and until his death he held membership and took a lively interest in the Grand Army of the Republic and the Andersonville Veterans Association.

Captain Bulla was married January 11, 1870, to Miss Irene Thompson, who came to Andrew County, Missouri, from Blair County, Pennsylvania, in 1859, her father, Michael Thompson, having come here three years previously to prepare a home for his family. She had been given a country school education, and as a young woman taught school at Narrows, Nodaway County, Missouri. She was still a young girl when the Civil war broke out, but rendered her country invaluable service in carrying messages of importance for the Government, but finally her activities were discovered, and her life was so threatened that her parents forbade her continuing this work. She has been very prominent and active in the work of the Women's Relief Corps, at King City, and for three years has served as senior vice president thereof. Various other social activities have attracted her attention, she being treasurer of the Women's Missionary Society and past matron of the Eastern Star, at Whitesville, and for years she has been a generous and helpful factor in the work of the Methodist Episcopal Church South. Two children were born to Mr. and Mrs. Bulla: Julian, born December 11, 1870, residing on a farm in Gentry County, Missouri, married Sarah Hensen, of King City, and has four children—Louise, Maude, Glenn and Clyde; and William H., born May 6, 1872, residing on the home farm in Andrew County, married Clara C. Peters, and has two children—Alice Virginia and William Henry.

GILBERT McDANIEL. A career of business efficiency and success that marked him out as one of the ablest men of Andrew County was terminated with the death of Gilbert McDaniel at his home in Savannah, December 6, 1912. A man of sterling character, he was honorable in business, stanch in his friendship, sincere in his religious profession and true to every trust, and with his passing an entire community was bereaved.

Gilbert McDaniel was born on a farm near Whitesville in Andrew County, February 26, 1857, and was in his fifty-sixth year when death called him. His parents were John and Mary (McClanahan) McDaniel, natives of Tennessee. His father moved from Tennessee to Cooper County, Missouri, and married there, and later moved to Andrew County, one of the early farmer settlers of this section. Gilbert McDaniel lost his mother when he was about three years of age, and was reared by a stepmother who was in every sense a true mother to him. In 1865 the McDaniel family moved to a farm south of Savannah.

Gilbert McDaniel spent all his career in Andrew County, attended the district schools as a boy, and completed his education in the State Normal School at Kirksville. For several years he was active as a teacher. In all his varied relations and activities he displayed a personality, a genius for making friends, and an integrity which entitled him to the thorough confidence of all who knew him. In 1905 Mr. McDaniel became cashier of the Exchange Bank at Savannah, an institution which had been organized in 1902. Within the few years that covered Mr. McDaniel's connection with the institution it rose from a place among the smaller financial establishments of Andrew County to first place among the county's banks, and it is said that the efficient management of Mr. McDaniel and his popular qualities and standing in the community had more to do with the prosperity of the bank than any other one factor.

Gilbert McDaniel was affiliated with the Masonic Order. There were many tributes, sincere and admiring, paid to his memory at the time of his death, and a brief characterization that sums up some of his especial qualities is contained in the following resolution from an order of which he was a member: "His genial personality and superior ability in business relations and his optimistic and comforting greetings to acquaintances and friends will be treasured by each and the memory of him will never perish nor the results of his good deeds diminish. He always kept his own troubles to himself, for those about him were never asked to share them, but he was ever ready to help and disperse the burdens of others and was generous to a fault to his friends and his family."

In 1879 the late Mr. McDaniel married Jennie Ham. She was born in the Province of Ontario, Canada, eighteen miles north of Kingston, August 21, 1852, a daughter of Simeon and Eliza (Scott) Ham, both natives of Ontario. When she was fourteen years of age her parents moved to Missouri in 1866, locating near Mexico, and she finished her education in the Kirksville Normal School. For ten years she was a successful teacher in the schools of Andrew County, where her father spent his last years as a farmer. Mrs. McDaniel survived her husband. She was the mother of eight children, and two of them, Paul and Mabel, died in infancy. The surviving children are: Lawrence, Mrs. W. T. Fling, Mrs. Carl Gee, John, Mary and Allen. The son Lawrence was educated at Savannah and in the law department of the University of Missouri, and is now a successful attorney at St. Louis, having been recently honored by selection as one of the assistants to the circuit attorney of St. Louis County. He has been active in democratic politics, and his professional work gives promise of a brilliant career. The daughter Clara, now the wife of Walter T. Fling, a Savannah jeweler, was graduated from the Savannah High School and from Howard Payne College, and also took a business course in Drake University at Des Moines. Mildred G., the wife of Carl Gee, a well known farmer north of Savannah, is also a graduate of the Savannah High School. The son John graduated from the Savannah High School, took a course in agriculture at the University of Missouri, and is now a successful and scientific farmer on the old homestead, comprising 100 acres, six miles south of Savannah. The daughter Mary is a graduate of the Savannah High School, of the Scarrett Bible and Training School at Kansas City, and is now taking the medical course in the State University, preparatory to a career as a missionary. The son Allen is a boy of exceptional talent in music and is a student at the American Conservatory in Chicago.

GROVER C. SPARKS. That a young man should be elected to the important office of prosecuting attorney of Andrew County when but twenty-seven years of age argues forcibly for his possession of ability in his profession and for the confidence in which he is held by his fellow-citizens. Such is the record of Grover C. Sparks, who was the incumbent of this office from 1912 to 1914 and whose services have firmly established him as one of his county's most efficient and popular officials. Mr. Sparks is a native of this county, having been born on his father's farm in Jackson Township, five miles northwest of Savannah, November 27, 1885, and is a son of William and Sarah A. (Bohart) Sparks.

William Sparks was born near Covington, Kentucky, and about the year 1860 migrated to Platte County, Missouri, from whence he came to Andrew County six years later. He was engaged in agricultural pursuits in Jackson Township throughout the remainder of his career, and died in 1890, when about thirty-eight years of age. Mrs. Sparks was born on a farm five miles northwest of Savannah, Missouri, a daughter of William Bohart, a pioneer of Missouri, who came from Indiana to Holt County in 1856, and in 1860 removed to Andrew County, where both he and Mrs. Bohart passed away. Mrs. Sparks still survives her husband and makes her home seven miles east of Savannah. She has been the mother of two children: Lulu, who is the wife of Charles Beaty, of Helena, Andrew County; and Grover C.

Grover C. Sparks was reared on a farm until sixteen years of age, in the meantime securing his primary education in the district schools of Empire Township. Following this, he attended the academy at Hiawatha, Kansas, from which institution he was graduated with the class of 1907, and at once took up the study of law. After some preparation he entered the State University of Missouri, and in 1911 graduated and was given his degree of Bachelor of Law. Being admitted to practice in May of that year, he at once opened an office at St. Joseph, but subsequently removed to Savannah, and this city has since been his field of activity and the scene of his success. His ability was soon recognized, and in November, 1912, he became the candidate of the democratic party for the office of prosecuting attorney. In spite of the fact that Andrew County ordinarily goes republican by a majority of 400, Mr. Sparks secured the election by a plurality of 310 votes. His services in this capacity have entirely vindicated the faith reposed in him by the people. He is a member of various organizations of his profession, and stands high in the esteem of his fellow-practitioners. Fraternally, Mr. Sparks is connected with the local lodges of the Masons and the Independent Order of Odd Fellows. Aside from the duties of his profession and his office, he has taken much interest in the cause of temperance, and has been active in movements promising its advancement.

On December 20, 1913, Mr. Sparks was married to Miss Lillian Danforth, of Warrensburg, Missouri, daughter of J. S. Danforth. Mr. and Mrs. Sparks are consistent members of the Baptist Church.

GEORGE GRANT TEDRICK. One of the newer towns of Daviess County is Altamont, which measured by progress and not by years is one of the live and prosperous communities of Northwest Missouri. From the time the village was a collection of homes around a couple of stores and general shops to the present George G. Tedrick has been a factor in local enterprise. Mr. Tedrick is now proprietor and editor of the Altamont Times and a large dealer in and shipper of produce, and in the latter relation has been known to the farmers and citizens of this locality for twenty years.

George Grant Tedrick was born on a farm one mile southwest of Gallatin in Daviess County, October 6, 1869, a son of John H. and Rebecca (Shaffer) Tedrick. His father was born in Maryland, April 10, 1839, a son of Jacob Tedrick, a native of Germany, who in 1839 moved from Maryland to Ohio, where he followed farming. Rebecca Shaffer, who was born in Ohio, was the daughter of Colonel George Shaffer, a native of Germany, who commanded a regiment in the American army during the war with Mexico, but whose permanent vocation was a minister of the German Lutheran Church. He attained the age of ninety-four, while his wife lived to be ninety-two. John H. Tedrick also made a military record. He was with the Union army during the Civil war for about three years, being a member of the Forty-eighth Ohio Infantry. After the war he spent a year in Daviess County, Missouri, then went back to Ohio and married, after which he returned to this

HISTORY OF NORTHWEST MISSOURI 1661

county as his permanent home. He first bought an improved farm a
mile southwest of Gallatin, where his son George was born, but later
sold it and bought eighty acres still further southwest of town. There
he and his good wife have lived for thirty-eight years, and the original
farm has been materially increased in acreage and general improvement.
He is a republican, and with his wife a member of the Christian Church.
They are the parents of four children: George G.; Eva, a teacher in the
Maysville High School; Jessie, wife of Wood Snyder, of Altamont;
and Winniefred, now a student in the State Normal School at Warrensburg.

George G. Tedrick was well educated, first in the country schools, then
in the Gallatin High School, and completed a commercial course in
Kidder Institute. His first vocation after leaving school was to teach
for three years in the country districts of Daviess County, and there are
a number of men and women in this part of Missouri who recall his work
with them as an instructor.

In February, 1894, Mr. Tedrick joined his fortunes with the new
Town of Altamont, which had begun to grow around the station of the
Rock Island Railroad, but still had only two stores and a few dwellings.
There he opened a meat market and began handling local produce, buying from the farmers and shipping to the city markets. He has since
disposed of his market, but his place is the headquarters for produce, and
in the past twenty years he has shipped many hundred carloads out of
Altamont. In 1912 Mr. Tedrick bought the plant of the Altamont Times,
and has since given much of his attention to making that a successful
and influential journal, telling the news of this locality and working as
a medium for the improvement of all local interests. It has a weekly
issue, and a wide reading public. At the present time Mr. Tedrick is
ably assisted by his son, who is becoming proficient as a compositor and
in the general management.

In April, 1895, Mr. Tedrick married Miss Addie Martin, a daughter
of Thomas A. Martin, one of the Daviess County pioneers. They have
two children: Orson, now with the Altamont Times; and Orlo, in school.
Mrs. Tedrick and the older son are members of the Christian Church.
Mr. Tedrick is an Odd Fellow and a republican, and has served as a
school director and a member of the town board. He is a quiet, modest,
unassuming citizen, a good business man, and has many loyal friends
in this part of Missouri.

PROF. W. F. NULL. Missouri Wesleyan College, at Cameron, Clinton
County, has been exceptionally fortunate in securing for its teaching
force men of unquestioned talent and capability, prominent among its
present corps of instructors being Prof. W. F. Null, who for the past
seventeen years has rendered this institution most efficient service. A
Missourian by birth, he was born, October 3, 1871, in Maryville, Nodaway
County, and was there brought up and educated.

His father, George W. Null, was born in Pennsylvania, but came
when young to Missouri to live, locating at Maryville. He subsequently
purchased land, and for many years was extensively and successfully
engaged in agricultural pursuits, including general farming and stockraising. In 1861, at the outbreak of the Civil war, he enlisted in the
Union army, and having reenlisted at the expiration of his term served
until 1866. He took part in many engagements, at Fort Donelson
being severely wounded. He married, at Maryville, Lydia More, a native
of Iowa, and to them nine children were born, four sons and five
daughters. One of the sons, Rev. Charles W. Null, is pastor of the
Methodist Episcopal Church at San Jose, California, and another son is
Vol. III—24

connected with the Government service. The parents were both active members of the Methodist Episcopal Church.

After leaving the public schools of his native town, W. F. Null completed the literary course at the Maryville College, and later entered the University of Chicago, from which he was graduated with honors, receiving also the degree of A. B. Professor Null spent the next two years as a teacher in the public schools, and then, in 1897, accepted his present position with the Missouri Wesleyan College, his long service as a member of its faculty bearing evidence of his genuine worth as an educator.

On October 14, 1901, Professor Null was united in marriage with Miss Chloe Herrick, a daughter of C. I. and Frances (Lyon) Herrick, and a relative of General Lyon, commander of a Michigan regiment, who was killed in the engagement at Willow Creek, Missouri, in 1861. Fraternally the professor is a member of the Independent Order of Odd Fellows. Religiously he is a valued member of the Methodist Episcopal Church, in which he has held most of the official positions, and has likewise served as superintendent of its Sunday school. Professor and Mrs. Null are very genial, pleasant people, and at their hospitable home, No. 423 South Church Street, take much pleasure in entertaining their many friends.

W. H. WEIGHTMAN. Active manager at Mound City for the Farmers Mutual Insurance Company of Holt County, W. H. Weightman has been for several years successfully engaged in the real estate and insurance business at Mound City, and is one of the substantial business men of the county. Mr. Weightman has been identified with public affairs, has had a varied but generally successful career, has been a farmer and stock raiser, and was also one of the county's teachers.

W. H. Weightman was born near Mound City in Holt County, Missouri, September 7, 1871, a son of William and Henrietta (Noland) Weightman. Mr. Weightman grew up in the country about Mound City, attended the public schools there, and finished his education in Avalon College at Avalon in Livingston County. With the conclusion of his formal education Mr. Weightman returned to the farm, and combined farming and teaching for a number of years. With the exception of a few years spent in the West, Mr. Weightman has had his home in Holt County all his life. After retiring from the farm Mr. Weightman engaged in the real estate business at Mound City, and has made a specialty of placing loans on country real estate, and represents several insurance companies, and has executive control of the Farmers Mutual of Holt County.

Mr. Weightman married Eliza Anna Aude, daughter of William C. Aude. Her father was one of the early settlers of Holt County, and prominent as one of the organizers of the Mound City Bank. Her mother was a native of Holt County. Mr. and Mrs. Weightman have three children: Lorna, Esther and William R., all of whom were born in Holt County.

Mr. Weightman's public carer has included some important service. From 1901 to 1905 he was assessor in Mound City, and is now a member and treasurer of the school board. Politically he is identified with the progressive movement in national politics. Mr. Weightman has taken thirty-two degrees in Scottish Rite Masonry and is also affiliated with the Independent Order of Odd Fellows and the Modern Woodmen of America. His church, where he and his family worship, is the Methodist Episcopal.

CHARLES M. CHILDERS. The community about Maitland knows Charles M. Childers, not only as a man who from small beginnings has subdued to cultivation many acres of fine farm land in that vicinity, but also a progressive citizen and factor in public improvements. He has spent more than thirty years in this locality, and while gaining a comfortable share of material prosperity has won the confidence of his friends and neighbors.

Charles M. Childers was born in Gallia County, Ohio, October 18, 1861, a son of John H. and Sarah A. (White) Childers. The mother died in Gentry County in September, 1907. There were in the family seven sons and one daughter, named as follows: Clara, who married George Crawford; Charles M.; John W.; William A.; James J.; Joseph F.; Louis E.; and Luke F., who is an instructor in the Agricultural School of the University of Missouri.

The family moved from Ohio to Missouri in 1865, when Charles M. was about four years of age. They first settled in Gentry County on a farm, and lived as renters for two years until the father bought the eighty acres which comprised the homestead in which the children grew to maturity. It was unimproved land, and the first habitation of the Childers family in Gentry County was a log house, erected by the father. The land was unfenced, and there was practically nothing in the way of improvements. It was prairie land, and after he had broken and cultivated it for several years the father replaced the original buildings with more modern and comfortable structures, and by additions had in time a large and valuable farm.

Charles M. Childers grew up in Gentry County, attended the country schools for his education, and at the age of seventeen left home and struck out for himself. He came to Holt County, and found his first employment with John Foster, for whom he split rails and chopped wood for his board. In the following spring he went to work for N. F. Murray, and was with that employer for about three years. Later he worked for Bob Patterson and Freeman Libbie.

About 1882 Mr. Childers married Jessie J. Murray, a daughter of his former employer, N. F. Murray. He came with his bride in March, 1882, to his present farm, which at that time comprised eighty ‛acres. It was all prairie land without a stick of timber on it, and as his first home he put up a rude two-room frame house, constructed of plain boards without any paint, and at one side he had a small shed covered with straw for his stock. He faced a situation that would discourage many of the young men of the present generation, but he went ahead with the spirit of the true pioneer, broke up his land, fenced it, and in a short time his neighbors began to speak of him as a prosperous young farmer. During his early years there his first wife died, and their only child Effie lived less than a year. About six years later Mr. Childers married Elizabeth Hamm, a daughter of Andrew J. Hamm. By this marriage there are four children: Hazel A., Esther C., Bryan O. and Robert C., all of whom were born on the present farm.

Mr. Childers is now the owner of a fine estate, all improved, of 220 acres, and the land and its group of substantial buildings are the chief measure of his labors and prosperity during the past thirty years. He is affiliated with the Masonic fraternity at Maitland. Active in politics, he is the present chairman of the democratic committee, and has been especially prominent in the matter of educational affairs, having served on the district school board for sixteen years. His home district is made up of four former districts, and the fight for consolidation of these small districts into one central school was led by Mr. Childers about sixteen years ago.

WILLIAM H. HOCKRIDGE. Six decades have passed since the Hock-ridge family found a home in the new country of Harrison County. They took up land from the Government, contributed their share to material progress and betterment in this locality, and have always been identified with the good citizenship of the community. William H. Hock-ridge is a native of the county, a member of the second generation of the family, and is well known both in Bethany and in Adams Township, where he has his farm on rural route No. 7.

William H. Hockridge was born in Adams Township, March 8, 1864, and spent his youth on land that had been entered by his father from the Government, in township 62, range 27. He is of English descent, his grandfather having been an English sea captain.

Nelson A. Hockridge, his father, was born in Oneida County, New York, January 1, 1830, and is now living retired at a venerable age in Bethany. In the early '50s he joined a caravan at Detroit whose destina-tion was Missouri, and in the course of the journey became acquainted with the Hart family, also of the party. They came through Iowa, and while in that state he married Maretta G. Hart, daughter of James Hart and a native of Jefferson County, New York. On reaching Harrison County he entered land, improved it, and made it his home until moving to Bethany. His life was one of quiet industry and success in business, as a farmer and stockman. He always fed his grain to his own stock, and in the early days drove his cattle across country to distant markets, and with the building of the Rock Island Railroad sent them to Chicago. His prosperity enabled him to buy other lands, and his home farm com-prised 240 acres. His first house was of frame, in which his children were born, but in the course of years many better buildings have taken the place of those in use during his active career.

Nelson A. Hockridge had gained nearly all his education by attend-ing a night school. He has been a great reader, and is informed on topics that do not usually come within the range of most men. His industry was noteworthy, and his knowledge and practice of the stock business thorough, and it is said that no one in this section marketed better cattle than his and made a better success of the industry. He was a frugal liver, and kept his accounts as strictly as a merchant. He retired from the farm to Bethany in 1888. Politically his course has been as a voter in the republican ranks. During the war he was in the militia, being out three months, first in Captain Howe's company and then in Captain Frisbey's company. He was one of the charter members of the Fairview Church. His wife died in May, 1900, and their children were: Lizzie, wife of George W. Barlow, of Bethany; Emma, who died in Harrison County as the wife of Frank Nally; and William H.

William H. Hockridge was reared on the farm where he was born, received his education in a country school, and has spent all the years of manhood in farming, though other interests have come into his life. He is now a stockholder in the Bethany Printing Company and of the Citizens Bank of Gilman City. After his marriage he located on a farm in Sherman Township, but subsequently removed to his present place in Adams Township, where he is one of the cattle feeders.

December 23, 1884, Mr. Hockridge married Mary Elwell, of a promi-nent Harrison County family. Her father was the late Capt. George W. Elwell, a pioneer, a captain in the Union army during the war, and at the time of his death serving as state senator. He was a captain in Merrill's Horse, and saw much hard service east of the Mississippi. He came to Missouri from Macomb, Illinois. After the war he became a Methodist minister, and died in Bethany in 1869. Captain Elwell mar-ried Eliza Jane Manville, whose father was David B. Manville, who came to Harrison County in 1859, and concerning his family more. will be found in the Richter sketch on other pages. Mrs. Captain Elwell now lives in Adams Township as Mrs. William H. Richter.

The children of Mr. and Mrs. Hockridge are: George Leslie, a farmer of Adams Township, married Sarah E. Ford, daughter of William Ford, and they have one son, Charles Elwell; David Nelson, a farmer in the same township, married Mary Rose Hall, daughter of William H. Hall; Glenn L., the youngest, is attending the country schools. Mr. Hockridge as a republican cast his first vote for Benjamin Harrison, and has voted for every presidential candidate of that party since. For several years he served as school director, and is a trustee of the Methodist Church.

BENJAMIN F. KIDWELL. The activities of Benjamin F. Kidwell, who has long been a resident of Martinsville, have included successful operations in merchandise, carpentry and agriculture, as well as a stirring participation in the civic life of this thriving community. He belongs to one of the well known families of Harrison County, his father, the late Thomas D. P. Kidwell, being one of the pioneers of Northwest Missouri and a potent factor in the early and later affairs of Harrison County.

Thomas D. P. Kidwell was a son of Benjamin W. and Rebecca (Taylor) Kidwell, the former born June 13, 1801, and the latter October 1, 1804, and he died in Harrison County. The father of Benjamin W. Kidwell was Thomas Kidwell, and his father was Jonathan Kidwell, a veteran of the Revolutionary war. The latter was of Welsh origin and the family originated in this country in either Maryland or Virginia. The advent of Thomas D. P. Kidwell in Missouri dates from 1854, when he settled in Gentry County, but in 1858 he came over into Harrison County and established himself near Martinsville and here the chief events in his life as a citizen took place and the leading achievements of that life as a man were consummated.

Mr. Kidwell entered land in the Martinsville locality in 1854 and this he set about improving and converting into a home, he continuing to be engaged in farming during the period of his lifetime. He did valuable service locally during the dark days of the Civil war in aiding those who met misfortune by having relatives in the army of the Union. A member of the Christian Church, which he joined at the age of seventeen years, he remained true to its teachings throughout his life and reared his children to honorable and upright lives. In politics Mr. Kidwell was a republican, and at various times was honored by election to local offices, serving efficiently and faithfully as assessor, surveyor and justice of the peace, while in his church life he was also looked up to as a leader, and at different times for a long period of years acted as deacon and elder. He manifested an active interest in the development of the school system, believed firmly in public education of an advanced order, and four of his children taught school, while one of them is now a practicing osteopath physician. As a farmer, Mr. Kidwell was successful in his general operations, and also carried much stock. His farm was in section 22, township 64, range 29, and there he continued his active labors until his retirement some time before his death, an event that occurred June 5, 1910.

Mr. Kidwell was married to Miss Rebecca E. Magee, who was born October 20, 1829, daughter of John and Elizabeth Magee, of Henry County, Kentucky, and died March 18, 1905; both are buried in the old cemetery. The children born to Mr. and Mrs. Kidwell were as follows: Livonia, who died in childhood; Jemimah B., born July 16, 1851, who died in 1858; Josephine, born October 13, 1853, married E. P.

Jessee, and lives in Loveland, Colorado; Benjamin F., of this review; Emma F., born February 4, 1858, married John Barnes and lives near Martinsville, Missouri; Julia A., born December 27, 1860, married Dr. George Eberhart, and both are deceased, she being buried at Benkleman, Nebraska; John F., born November 18, 1862, and now living at Loveland, Colorado; Rebecca E., born March 18, 1864, married Tol Anderson and lives near Martinsville, Missouri; Alvin P., born January 6, 1868, lives at Ottawa, Kansas; and Ollie Jane, born December 20, 1870, married Doctor Quigley, and lives at Mound City, Missouri.

Benjamin F. Kidwell was born November 12, 1855, and was reared near Martinsville, where his education was secured in the country schools, although this was of a limited character, as he did not start going to school until he reached the age of thirteen years. As a youth he gave his attention to assisting his father on the homestead place, and in the meantime learned the trade of carpenter, a vocation which he has followed with some degree of success in connection with his other enterprises. In 1891 he embarked in the mercantile line at Martinsville, and in this vocation has continued to be engaged ever since, being at present the proprietor of a business which attracts a trade extending all over this part of the county. In addition he has carried on farming, and has shown himself a capable man of affairs in whatever venture he has found himself engaged. As a developer of Martinsville, Mr. Kidwell has erected the best residence in the village, two store buildings and other substantial structures here, and helped promote the Martinsville Bank as a stockholder, being also a stockholder in one of the New Hampton banks. In political matters he is a democrat, but frequently exercises his right of franchise independently, and has never taken enough interest in politics to endeavor to secure public preferment, although always ready to give of his time, his influence or his means in supporting good and progressive civic movements. His religious connection is with the Christian Church.

On November 25, 1877, Mr. Kidwell was married to Miss Laura E. Edson, a daughter of Alonzo and Arloa (Ferguson) Edson. Mr. Edson came to Missouri from Coles County, Illinois, about the time of the close of the Civil war, and here both he and his wife passed their remaining years in the pursuits of the soil. The children of Mr. and Mrs. Edson were as follows: William A., a resident of Kendall, Kansas; Daniel Leroy, who died in infancy in Illinois; Isaac Millard, a resident of Harrison County, Missouri; Mrs. Kidwell, who was born February 13, 1860; James Martin, who is a farmer of the New Hampton locality; Ulysses Grant, who died in childhood; and Ira Ellsworth, a resident of Great Bend, Kansas.

The children and grandchildren of Mr. and Mrs. Kidwell are as follows: Nellie Arloa, born January 27, 1879, married September 28, 1898, Henry Atwood, who died May 31, 1903, leaving two children, Ione K. and Goebel Dean, and she married again a Mr. Sylvey, lives at Martinsville, and by this union has one daughter—Laveska Maud; Lemon Leroy, born December 2, 1880, married April 8, 1912, Maud Deason, and has four children—Laberta Margarite, Lilburn Worth, Grace Mildred and Catherine Elaine; William Gustavus, born October 12, 1882, married March 26, 1905, Jennie Bartlett and has three children—Mary Etta, Berdina Ruth and Paul William; Alvin Elsworth, born February 2, 1885, married March 11, 1906, Fannie Lambert and has two children— Eunice Luella and Bernice Lavaughn; Mary Bertha, born August 8, 1888, married October 17, 1906, Lloyd England, and has a son—Harold D.; Alta Gladys, born December 3, 1890, married November 17, 1909, Charles Walters, and has one child—Opal Madaline; and Robert Wilber, born September 6, 1893, Ola Edith, born September 21, 1896, Lucy Dorothy, born June 17, 1899, and Lula Ruth, born January 21, 1902, all living at home with their parents.

PROF. A. E. TAYLOR. Cameron, Clinton County, has a full corps of painstaking, efficient school teachers, noteworthy among whom is Prof. A. E. Taylor, principal of the high school, one of the best schools of the kind in the county. Well educated, wide-awake and progressive, Professor Taylor holds a position of note among the successful educators of Northwestern Missouri, the satisfactory results that he obtains from his chosen work proving that he is in reality the right man for the right place. A son of Rev. T. C. Taylor, he was born, December 12, 1883, on a farm in Sullivan County, Missouri, not far from Green City.

Rev. T. C. Taylor was born in Ohio, of English ancestry, and was there reared to agricultural pursuits. A man of deep religious convictions, he became a minister of the gospel, and as a preacher in the Methodist Episcopal denomination was for many years a circuit rider. He is now living in West Plains, Missouri, an honored and respected citizen. The maiden name of his wife was Edson.

The son of a circuit rider, A. E. Taylor attended school in many different localities as a boy and youth, also receiving instruction in books at home. He subsequently attended high school and college, and after a brief experience in teaching completed the course of study at the Wesleyan College. In 1908 Professor Taylor accepted his present position as principal of the Cameron High School, and has since performed the duties devolving upon him in this capacity with rare ability and wisdom, winning the praise and approval of parents and pupils. He is fond of athletics, playing base ball and foot ball easily and enthusiastically, and is especially popular with the boys under his charge.

Professor Taylor married, July 18, 1907, Bertha Snyder, and they are the proud parents of two sons, K. Wetzel and Murlin. The professor and Mrs. Taylor are faithful and valued members of the Methodist Episcopal Church.

J. EMMETT HODGIN. Sixty years have passed since the Hodgin family first established its home in Holt County, and through these years the name has been associated with successful enterprise in the handling of land and live stock, with progressive activity in community affairs, and with those substantial virtues which give character to any community.

A son of the pioneer settler and one of the leading farmers in the vicinity of Maitland, J. Emmett Hodgin was born in Holt County, August 28, 1879. His parents were Joseph and Susan E. (Denny) Hodgin. His father, who came to Holt County in 1854, arrived with only $30 in his pocket, having driven by wagon across the country to this then wilderness community. He broke hemp ten days for Mr. Ish for his first log cabin, his habitation for a number of years, until he was able to construct a more modern dwelling. His first settlement was on the place where he spent the remainder of his life. In spite of the small capital with which he started, he eventually acquired ownership of 725 acres in Holt County, all of it improved with the exception of forty-five acres of timber land. The land was put in cultivation and managed through his labors, and in time he erected several substantial buildings. When Joseph Hodgin passed away in Holt County in January, 1914, the community lost one of its finest old settlers. He was an active republican, a member of the Christian Church, and one fact in particular that should long be remembered is that he was instrumental in starting the first school and the first church in his community. Joseph Hodgin married for his first wife Harriett Lawrence, and the two children living of that marriage are Jennie and Ellsworth. His second wife, Susan E. (Denny) Hodgin, is still living, and is the mother of three children: Nellie, the wife of Dyke Williams; J. Emmett; and Barney.

J. Emmett Hodgin married Florence Glenn, a daughter of William Glenn. To their marriage have been born three children: Glenn, and twins, Hazel and Helen. These children were born on Mr. Hodgin's present homestead, which is a portion of his father's estate. Mr. Hodgin is now farming 288 acres of land, and is the individual owner of 200 acres. When he located here the house in which he still lives was on the farm, but all the other improvements and buildings have been the result of his own efforts. For the past two years he has taken an active interest in good roads. In the capacity of overseer he put the roads in good condition and obtained the county seat road past his farm. Mr. Hodgin is affiliated with the Woodmen of the World, and has served as clerk on his school board. In politics he is a republican.

STEPHEN C. ROGERS. The gentleman whose name heads this review is one of the best known citizens of Kingston, as well as one of the most familiar figures on its busy streets. He may not have earned the distinction of being one of the earliest settlers, but fifty-eight years of residence in Missouri will at least entitle him to a place among its representative citizens. An early teacher, for many years a leading member of the bar, a successful operator in the line of agricultural endeavor, and a public-spirited citizen who has contributed to his community's welfare in various ways, Stephen C. Rogers in each of these varied capacities has shown himself a man of resource and ability, and is entitled to the esteem and respect in which he is universally held.

Born in Claiborne County, Tennessee, March 20, 1848, Mr. Rogers is a son of Hugh L. W. Rogers. His great-grandfather, John Rogers, was a soldier under General Washington during the Revolutionary war, while Maj. David Rogers, the grandfather of Stephen C. Rogers, was an officer during the War of 1812, and fought under the redoubtable General Jackson at the battle of New Orleans. Hugh L. W. Rogers was a farmer by vocation, and in his native State of Tennessee married Miss Barbara Cawood, a daughter of Stephen Cawood, a son of a Revolutionary officer and a member of an old and honored Virginia family. In 1856 Hugh L. W. Rogers migrated to Missouri, settling in Clinton County, and engaging in farming until the Civil war, when he took the Union side and had a brilliant record as a soldier and officer. Returning to his farm at the close of hostilities, he continued as a tiller of the soil until his death in 1875. Their children were as follows: Albert G., Stephen C., Rhoda J., David H., Hugh L., Mary and Alice.

Stephen C. Rogers was reared a farmer and his early education was secured in the public schools, following which he became a student in the University of Missouri, from which he was graduated in 1873, with a good record as a student. At that time he accepted a call to take charge of the Kingston school, which had just been established in its new brick building, and entered upon his duties in 1874 as superintendent, a position in which he secured the approbation of the people of the community and in which he remained until increasing interests in other directions demanded his undivided attention. He studied law while engaged in this capacity, and in 1875 was admitted to the bar, since which time he has continued in practice as one of his community's leading lawyers. In recent years Mr. Rogers has been engaged in farming and real estate operations, and at this time is one of Kingston's large land holders and heaviest taxpayers. He is also widely interested in business interests of varied character, including the proposed interurban railroad, of which he has made the survey from Excelsior Springs to Kingston. A man of intense public spirit, he has served in various positions of trust and responsibility, giving of his best efforts in behalf of the community welfare. He served as county prosecuting attorney, as mayor of Kingston, as school commissioner and was president of the school board, and county surveyor and highway engineer. In 1914, at the solicitation of friends, accepted the superintendency of the public schools of Kingston, of which he has since had charge. Under his able direction, the school system of this thriving city is being developed into one of the finest in this part of the state. As is evident, even from this brief sketch, thoroughness is one of Mr. Rogers' most prominent characteristics. No rolling stone, he has evinced exceptional perseverance and patience, as well as talent, in every position which he has been called upon to fill. His support is given to the republican party in affairs of a political character.

In 1876 Mr. Rogers was married to Miss Mattie Edwards, of Boon County, Missouri, and to this union there has been born one child: Miss L. R., a graduate of the University of Missouri, and a well-known Government educator, who has spent some time teaching in the schools of the Philippine Islands, and is now stationed at Ponce, Porto Rico.

JOHN E. SLATER. Practically everyone in Holt County knows this prominent resident of Bigelow Township. Mr. Slater has lived in this locality thirty-five years, and his experiences and achievements, both before that time and since, have been such as to furnish data for interesting reading.

John E. Slater was born June 14, 1854, in Yorkshire, England, at the town of Wakefield, a place made famous in literature as the scene of the story, "The Vicar of Wakefield," by Oliver Goldsmith. His parents were Abraham and Sarah (Emerson) Slater. Of the seven children, five grew to maturity. John E. was fifteen years of age when his parents emigrated to America. His father had spent seven years as a mechanic's apprentice in England, and was a product of the thorough and systematic training which prevails in old country industrial lines. He worked as machinist and engineer in England, and it was the custom in his time for an apprentice to know every detail in the construction and operation of an engine before getting a certificate entitling him to perform the duties of engineer. After coming to America he located in Pittsburg, found work as a machinist, and later was sent to South St. Louis, a suburb of the city better known as Carondelet. Some years later he assisted in the construction of three of the largest locomotive engines ever operated west of the Mississippi River. Work as engineer and machinist employed him during most of his remaining years, and he died at St. Louis, while his wife passed away in the same house a few years later.

John E. Slater is a man who has made his way with few of the advantages of education and training so liberally supplied to boys of the present generation. His schooling was at an end by the time he reached the age of thirteen, and at that time he began firing an engine of which his father was foreman. It has been his lasting regret that his opportunities for schooling were so limited, and though his own success has been all the more noteworthy for these early deficiencies, he does not take the view that many practical self-made men do, but believes thoroughly in the right of every boy and girl to thorough training at public expense. On leaving home Mr. Slater first located at Lockport in Will County, Illinois, and engaged to work for $100 a year. His labors were almost incessant from 4 o'clock in the morning until 8 o'clock at night. He remained there about eighteen months, then returned home to South St. Louis, and got employment in the same plant with his father. He continued at work in rolling mills until 1876, and then began farming a little west of St. Louis, renting a place.

In 1878 Mr. Slater married Ella Stuart, daughter of Samuel and Adeline (Shepard) Stuart. She was one of a family of eleven children, nine of whom survive. Her father came from Kentucky and her mother from Pennsylvania, and they were married in St. Louis County. In the spring of 1879 Mr. Slater and his bride arrived in Holt County, and, almost strangers and with few possessions, began the long struggle to make themselves a home and a competence. Mr. Slater rented about sixty acres, comprising a portion of his present fine estate. The house was a log building, and the first settler on the farm owned by A. B. Welton, arrived in 1849, an early period in the history of Holt County, when a horse and buggy was as unusual and rare a sight as an aeroplane at the present time. The roads then were mere paths through the woods, and had many devious turnings in order to follow the high ridges of ground. Mr. Slater's career as a Holt County farmer was spent on rented land for some twelve or fifteen years, but prosperity was gradually coming to him, and his first purchase was forty acres at $25 an acre. Since then he has steadily increased the area of his land holdings, and now has 485 acres, all situated in the bottom and regarded as some of the finest and most productive soil in Holt County. Year after year has witnessed extended improvements in buildings, fencing and better adaptation of the land to advanced farming, and his homestead now represents almost the last word in its facilities and comforts.

Mr. and Mrs. Slater became the parents of three children: Irl R. died at the age of eighteen, while attending the Kirkwood High School, and it was the cherished ambition of his father to give him all the advantages which had been lacking in his own career. The other two boys, Cecil Stuart and Ralph Emerson, died in infancy. They were twins, and died about four months after their birth.

Mr. and Mrs. Slater are members of the Methodist Episcopal Church South. He is a Scottish Rite Mason, has membership in the lodge at Mound City and in the Temple of the Mystic Shrine at St. Joseph. For a number of years he has been active in local affairs, has served on the school board, and is a member of the committee supervising the big drainage ditch through his land, and also on the board in what is known as the Tarkio Drainage District. He has been a member of the board since it was organized about seventeen years ago.

JOHN RICHARD SIMPSON. Farming, in all its branches, has been considered a good line of business since the beginning of the world, and particularly in the rich farming districts of Northwest Missouri it is possible to find in that business many of the most competent and successful citizens. Among the men of Worth County who have long been identified with this industry, and in such a manner as to reach substantial places in the general business consideration of the district is John Richard Simpson. He is a son of Joseph Simpson, who came as a pioneer to Worth County in 1859, and settled on the west fork of Grand River, where he still lives, after more than fifty years as an active and successful farmer.

John Richard Simpson is a native of Northwest Missouri, and has spent practically all his life in the community where he was known as a child and youth. He was born January 1, 1861, grew up in the country districts about Grand River, and was educated in the district schools.

While still living at home, he started for himself at the age of twenty-one, and finally moved to a farm rented from his father, located in Union Township in section 35, township 67, and range 32. In that one locality Mr. Simpson has had his home since 1886. After a few years as a renter, he bought the 114 acres comprising the place, and began a vigorous campaign of improvement, both of the land and of his own material resources. When he moved to that farm its improvements were of a somewhat primitive character, consisting of a box house of one story on a foundation 14 by 16 feet, and a stable for four horses. For several years Mr. Simpson boarded as a bachelor until he was thirty-three. The years of successive industry and good management have told their tale, and his success is now measured by a splendid farm of 286 acres, besides a half interest in 160 acres in Butler County. His home tract lies in several different sections and in adjoining townships, though only a public highway separates the various fields. As a farmer, Mr. Simpson has found his chief success as a stock raiser. He has an ideal farm for cattle and hogs, with splendid natural windbreaks, an abundant supply of water, and an equipment in buildings which it has been his pride to keep thoroughly up to date and in line with the most advanced ideas of farm and stock management. For a number of years he has been one of the large feeders in that locality, and has shipped both to Chicago and St. Joseph markets.

Politically a republican, Mr. Simpson cast his first presidential ballot for James G. Blaine, and has never missed a presidential vote since. He has held no office, except as a member of his home school board. On September 27, 1893, in Worth County, Mr. Simpson married Miss Sarah Angeline Strachan. Her father, William Strachan, a native of Scotland, was a veteran of the Civil war, having twice enlisted and beginning as a private, was discharged at the end of the war as fife major. William Strachan married Mary J. Hagans, a daughter of Mason Hagans, one of the old settlers of Missouri. Mr. Strachan died August 28, 1893, and his wife ten months later. Their children were: Nellie, wife of B. F. Wall of Worth County; Mrs. Simpson; Stella J., who married Ralph Moore of Jerome, Idaho; and Mrs. Dr. B. H. Miller of Blockton, Iowa. While Mr. and Mrs. Simpson have no children of their own, Mr. Simpson has a paternal pride in his nephew, Silas T. Simpson, who has distinguished himself. After graduating from the State University in 1912, owing to his splendid record in the agricultural department, was at once assigned to a position as assistant professor of animal husbandry. At his home farm Mr. Simpson has one of the beautiful country residences which give character to the rural districts of Worth County, and it was erected in 1900, and is surrounded by substantial barns and other buildings for stock and grain purposes. Mr. Simpson is a member of the Cumberland Presbyterian Church, while his wife is identified with the Christian denomination.

J. E. GARTSIDE, M. D. The present efficient county recorder of Caldwell County needs no introduction to the county's people. Doctor Gartside has lived in Caldwell County for thirty-one years, is one of the most successful practitioners of medicine, and while there are hundreds of people who place implicit faith in his ability as a physician, there is a still wider range of his followers who esteem him for his ability and influence as a public leader. Doctor Gartside has for a number of years been one of the leaders in the republican party of Caldwell County, has acted as delegate in county, congressional, state and national conventions, and was a delegate to the convention of 1908 at Chicago. He was elected to his present office as county recorder in 1910, and has handled its affairs in a manner to justify the action of the people in electing him.

Doctor Gartside was born at O'Fallon, St. Clair County, Illinois, June 22, 1860. His father, Job Gartside, who was a coal contractor engaged in the development of coal mines, was a native of England, came to America in his youth, and was in the midst of a successful business career when called away for service in the Union army to defend the integrity of his adopted country. He went South in Company D of the One Hundred and Twenty-fourth Illinois Infantry. His services included duty during the siege of Vicksburg, at Champion Hill, Black River Bridge, and his army career was terminated by ill health. He was brought back to St. Louis and died from the results of his service as a soldier in 1864. He was at that time in the prime of life. He left a widow and an only son, Doctor Gartside. The mother of Doctor Gartside was Alice D. Blackshaw, who was also born in England and is now living in Montgomery County, Missouri.

Doctor Gartside was reared in Illinois, attended the public schools, and was a student in the Jacksonville Business College at Jacksonville and had as a classmate William Jennings Bryan. Doctor Gartside graduated in medicine at the Physio-Medical College of Indianapolis in 1883, and since that year has practiced continuously with rising reputation in Caldwell County.

In 1883, the year he located for practice in this community, Doctor Gartside married Ella F. Cadman, who was born in Mercer County, Illinois, and educated in the public schools of Illinois and Missouri. They are the parents of two sons and a daughter: Ralph E., who was educated in the State University at Columbia, is now connected with the Drovers National Bank in Kansas City; Harold H. is now getting started in business in St. Louis; Gayle Hamilton, the daughter, was educated in the Woman's College at Lexington, Missouri, and is now the wife of Tinsley Brown, Jr. Doctor Gartside has membership in Lodge No. 118, A. F. & A. M.; in the Independent Order of Odd Fellows, belongs to different medical societies, and whether as a physician or as a private citizen is one of the most genial of men and has hosts of friends in Caldwell County.

O. J. ADAMS. The achievement of such a position as O. J. Adams has attained in the legal circles of Caldwell County while still so young in years is typical of American grit and the true western spirit of enterprise. His only resource when he began active life was natural ability, but he possessed immense will power, and has been able to make the most of every opportunity which has arisen. Setting himself a high ideal, in a practical, common sense way he has directed his every effort towards its attainment, with the result that now in the strength and vigor of young manhood he has achieved a most gratifying success in his profession and is justly accounted one who will go far in his chosen line.

Mr. Adams was born at Macon, Missouri, August 26, 1888, and is a son of D. E. and Louisa (Bush) Adams. His father, one of the prominent and well-known attorneys of Hamilton, is known as one of the leaders of the Caldwell County bar, is a graduate of the Missouri State University, class of 1895, has been prosecuting attorney of Caldwell County for two terms and has represented his county one term in the Legislature. He married Louisa Bush, who was born here, a member of an old and honored family of Caldwell County, and three children have been born to them: O. J., of this review; Bernard, who is an assistant instructor and student of the Rolla School of Mines, at Rolla, Missouri; and Leland, a student of the public schools.

O. J. Adams grew up in Caldwell County and secured his early education in the public and high schools, following which he decided upon a career in the law and received a thorough preparation in the Missouri State University, completing the course in June, 1912. This training was largely gained through his own close study and close application, and he successfully passed the examination of the State Board of Examiners. He was admitted to the bar January 27, 1912, and in that year came to Kingston, where he has since continued in the enjoyment of a constantly increasing practice. Although Mr. Adams has been a general practitioner, he has given much attention to abstract and title law, and in addition to his professional duties carries on a successful abstract and title business, proving himself as able a business man as he is a lawyer. He has not ceased to be a student, and has at his command the large and valuable law library of 800 volumes which was formerly the property of the late C. S. McLaughlin, of Kingston. He is an able, well-read attorney, an eloquent advocate, and a reliable counsellor. In his professional advice he is honorable and honest, consulting in every way possible the interests of his clients, and is noted for the care and attention he devotes to every detail of whatever business may be entrusted to him. For some time he has been spoken of favorably for judicial position and in 1914 was a candidate for the office of probate judge of Caldwell County, being defeated by a small majority.

Mr. Adams was married July 2, 1913, to Miss Otie M. Frazier, a lady of excellent education and family, and daughter of the late Joseph Frazier of Caldwell County. Mr. and Mrs. Adams are consistent members of the Christian and Presbyterian churches, respectively. He is associated fraternally with the Masons at Kingston and the Knights of Pythias at Hamilton.

PERRY W. HAMPTON. Owner and editor of Hampton's Mercury at Kingston, Perry W. Hampton is one of the successful newspaper men of Northwest Missouri. To journalism he has brought talent which would enable him to succeed in lines of business much more remunerative, and during the last forty years has been through all the grades of service in the fourth estate, from printer's devil to editor and proprietor. Mr. Hampton is also one of the foremost republicans of Northwest Missouri, and for nineteen years held the office of postmaster at Kingston, having been first appointed by McKinley and serving through his administration, under Roosevelt and Taft until January 1, 1914, when relieved of office by the present administration. Hampton's Mercury is an influential journal in Caldwell County, and is probably as frequently quoted by the other papers of the state for its editorial opinions as any other country journal. Mr. Hampton was formerly engaged in the newspaper business and founded the Mercury at Mirabile in Caldwell County, and in 1895 moved it to Kingston. The Mercury is independent republican in politics, and follows the policy of treating all parties fairly. Its motto is "Home first and the world afterwards."

Perry W. Hampton was born in the city of St. Joseph, Missouri, February 1, 1856. His father was one of the pioneers of Northwest Missouri. In the early days he was employed at St. Joseph by the Studebakers, making wagons that were used in the overland freighting business from the Missouri River west to Denver and Salt Lake. Later for a time he was agent for the Studebaker Brothers at St. Joseph, handling their line of wagons, carriages and supplies, and was a carriage maker by trade. He later moved to Cameron, and remained one of the highly respected men of that city until his death. He was born in Barron County, Kentucky, of an old family of that state, and was eighty-four years of age at the time of his death. He located at Cameron in 1868. His wife was of an old Virginia family, and also died at Cameron. There were two sons and three daughters in the family.

Perry W. Hampton was two years of age when the family moved to Cameron, was educated in the public schools there, learned the printing trade as an office boy and all around worker, and it was as an expert in handling type and a competent printer that he made his start toward independent journalism. In 1884 Mr. Hampton moved to Lincoln, Nebraska, and was engaged in business there five years, returned to Cameron, and from there moved to Mirabile in Caldwell County, and in 1895 established the Kingston Mercury, of which he is editor and proprietor.

Mr. Hampton has always been a hard worker, knows his business thoroughly, and his competence has been joined with a genial personality that has brought him hosts of friends. He was married in Atchison, Kansas, in 1886 to Sarah Taylor, daughter of A. S. Taylor of Cameron. The Taylor family came from Missouri to New York State. Mr. Hampton has a son, Chester, at Lincoln, Nebraska, and Paul, a schoolboy of fourteen years of age. Mr. Hampton is affiliated with the lodge and Royal Arch Chapter of Masonry and the Independent Order of Odd Fellows.

JAMES TAIT. The incumbent of the office of postmaster at Polo, Missouri, since 1903, James Tait is one of the best known of Caldwell County's old residents, and has had a long and honorable career in business, in which he has won success through the possession of the qualities of industry, honesty and integrity. He was born in Scotland, in 1829, a member of a family noted for its sterling characteristics, and is a son of James and Mary (Davis) Tait.

The parents of Mr. Tait, accompanied by their seven children, emigrated to the United States in 1840, and after a voyage of six weeks on the sailing vessel Sardus, landed at New York. Subsequently they removed to Syracuse, where they resided for three years and then went to Waterdown, County Wentworth, Ontario, Canada. At Duart, Kent County, the father built a mill for the manufacture of rakes, scythe swathes and cradles. His death took place at St. Thomas, Ontario, at the age of eighty-four years. James Tait received his education in the schools of Ontario, and grew up with his father's milling business, learning every detail thereof, and continuing to be connected with the Canada mill for a long period of years. He came to Missouri in 1890, when he located in Ray County, there building a mill at the town named in his honor, Taitville. Later Mr. Tait came to Polo, where he also built a mill and operated it with some success, then went to Mulhall, Oklahoma. At the latter place he built a mill and established a business which was conducted by his son, James Tait, Jr., but has since been sold. In 1902, during President Roosevelt's administration, Mr. Tait was appointed postmaster at Polo, and took charge of the duties of that office in February of that year. Originally a fourth-class office, under Mr. Tait's administration it has been advanced to third class, and now has four rural delivery routes, covering a territory of twenty-seven miles each. The present carriers are: E. L. Thomas, J. M. Clevenger, H. H. Hauser and William F. Achenbach. Mr. Tait's record as postmaster is an excellent one, and he has done much to improve the service. He is careful, painstaking and accommodating, patient and pleasant with those who have business at the office, and is naturally very popular with his fellow townspeople. A stalwart republican, he wields a distinct influence in his community. A well-preserved man, both in body and mind, he continues to take an intelligent interest in all that affects the welfare of his

community, and no movement is considered complete that does not have
his name upon its list of supporters.

Mr. Tait was married at Chatham, Ontario, to Miss Mary A. Mc-
Intyre, a member of a Highland Scotch family, and four children have
been born to this union: James, Jr., of Blackwell, Oklahoma, who
holds a responsible position with a flouring mill company; Martin, of
Herrington, Kansas, a railroad man and train despatcher; Duncan M.,
connected with the State Department at Jefferson City, Missouri; and
Miss Nan Tait.

DR. R. L. MOUNT. Among the medical fraternity of Northwest Missouri, Doctor Mount deserves a place of prominence on account of more
than twenty years of active practice, in which time he has devoted himself unselfishly and untiringly to the interests of a large patronage, both
in town and country. Doctor Mount is now located at Polo, but for a
number of years practiced at Mirabile.

Doctor Mount was born near Knoxville, Tennessee, July 21, 1867.
His father, J. Mount, was a Tennessee farmer, during the Civil war
saw active service in the Union army, and subsequently moved to North-
west Missouri and continued an active and successful career as a farmer.
He is now living at Braymer at the age of seventy-five. His wife's
maiden name was Ellen E. Thornburgh, also of an old Tennessee family,
a daughter of Samuel Thornburgh, who was of Scotch-Irish ancestry.
J. Mount and wife were the parents of three sons and five daughters.
The father in politics is a republican and a member of the Methodist
Church, and has long been affiliated with the Grand Army Post.

Doctor Mount was four years of age when the family came to
Northwest Missouri, grew up on a farm, developed his muscle by farm
labor, and after securing his education in the public schools and in the
Missouri Wesleyan College at Cameron, took up the study of medicine
with Doctor Leeper at Braymer, and in 1891 graduated with honors
from medical college. Doctor Mount practiced for eleven years at
Mirabile, among the people who had known him from childhood, and has
since enjoyed a large practice at Polo and vicinity. Doctor Mount is a
student, keeps up with the advances in his profession, and is easily in
the first rank of physicians and surgeons in Caldwell County.

Doctor Mount was married December 24, 1890, at Cowgill, Missouri,
to Mary Hudson, a daughter of G. Hudson, now deceased, who came
to Missouri from Indiana. Doctor Mount and wife have one son, Otto
C., who is now twenty-one years of age and a graduate of the high
school and a student in Columbia University. Doctor Mount is a
republican in politics, and both in his profession and as a citizen is one
of the popular men of Caldwell County. He has a modern home in
Polo, a nine-room residence, and also a well-equipped office.

DR. F. H. HEALY. DR. ESTELLE D. HEALY. In the practice of
osteopathy at Braymer, Dr. and Mrs. Healy, both of whom are graduates
of the Still School of Osteopathy at Kirksville, have enjoyed unusual
professional success, and have a large practice, both in the town and in
a large tract of country surrounding Braymer.

Dr. F. H. Healy was born at Britt, Hancock County, Iowa. His
father, E. P. Healy, who was born at Dayton, Ohio, lived for a time
at Milton, Wisconsin, and thence came to Britt, Iowa, and is one of the
prominent bankers of his state, being head of the Commercial State Bank
of Britt. E. P. Healy married Lillie E. Hoxie, and they are the
parents of two children, and the son, Walter H., lives in Duluth, Minne-

sota. The father is a republican in politics, and a sterling business man and influential citizen.

Doctor F. H. Healy grew up in his native town of Britt, was educated in the public schools, finishing at the high school, was a student for a time in Racine, Wisconsin, spent two years in the University of Chicago, and was prepared for his profession by a thorough course lasting three years in the Still School of Osteopathy at Kirksville. During his college days Doctor Healy was noted in Missouri as a foot ball player, and played the position of fullback on his team, and won premier honors in the Missouri Valley Association.

Doctor Healy was married October 17, 1913, at New Hampton, Iowa, to Estelle D. Powell. Mrs. Healy is a graduate with the class of 1914 from the Still School of Osteopathy at Kirksville, and has proved a valuable assistant to her husband in their combined practice. Doctor Healy is affiliated with the Masonic order, both he and his wife having membership in the Eastern Star, and he has taken the Knight Templar degrees in the York Rite and belongs to the Temple of the Mystic Shrine at St. Joseph. He is also a member of the Theta Psi, and affiliates with Lodge No. 464, B. P. O. E.

IRA JAMES. Assistant cashier of the First National Bank of Braymer, Ira James has united with a capacity for commercial and financial service a genial personality and a thorough public spirit, and having applied his efforts to one line his concentration has placed him among the leading young business men of Caldwell County. The position of Mr. James in his community is further illustrated by the fact that in 1912 he was elected on the Citizens ticket mayor of his city, and since taking office has performed his duties with an energy that has meant much to this community in progressive improvements. Mr. James has been identified with the First National Bank for the past eleven years, and is one of the popular young bankers of Northwest Missouri.

Ira James was born at Dawn, in Livingston County, Missouri, April 9, 1881. His birthplace was a farm, where his father, J. J. James, is still living. The mother's maiden name was Mary Jones, a daughter of Robert Jones. She died in 1907. There were nine children, three sons and six daughters. One son, J. J. James, lives in Kansas City, and Will James is in the postal service.

Ira James was reared on a farm and a considerable part of his early experience was the varied duties of farm life. His education came from the country schools and from the Chillicothe Commercial College, and before taking up his work as a banker he taught school a time. Mr. James is careful and methodical, looks after his business at the bank with scrupulous care and diligence, and in the last seven or eight years has done much to build up the institution, in which he occupies an official position.

In 1911 Mr. James married Catherine E. Herndon, daughter of Joseph Herndon. Mr. James is affiliated with the Masonic Lodge, No. 135, and with Lodge No. 203 of the Knights of Pythias, and his wife is a member of the Baptist Church. He has taken an active part for a number of years in the affairs of the republican party in Caldwell County, and is one of its spirited young leaders.

tunities along these lines. He is proprietor of the leading garage of the town, and one of the best in its facilities and service in Northwest Missouri. The garage occupies a substantial brick block, 50 by 60 feet, with ample floor space and large quarters for fixtures and supplies. The principal machine handled through Mr. Wetzel's agency is the Buick, undoubtedly one of the best machines on the market at the present time. The garage building was erected in 1913, and is an addition to the business district of Braymer. Mr. Wetzel knows the automobile business in all its details, is a natural mechanic, and having grown up and spent all his life in this community, has made it his ambition to serve the people with garage equipment and facilities equal to the best found in metropolitan centers.

J. W. Wetzel was born on a farm near Braymer in Carroll County, Missouri, a son of E. E. Wetzel. The father was a native of Germany, came to America, and after living at Dawn a time, moved to Carroll County, where he has been a successful and substantial farmer. E. E. Wetzel married Rachel Baxter, who was born in Missouri. They became the parents of six children, one son and five daughters.

J. W. Wetzel grew up on a farm, where he developed his muscle and got a hardy training for a broader career, was educated in the public schools, and graduated from the Braymer public schools with the class of 1906. He was in the hardware business for several years, and in that line got the training which has served him so well in his present profession. Mr. Wetzel was married May 9, 1914, at Ludlow, Missouri, to Ora Lane, who was born at Black Oak, Missouri, a daughter of Charles Lane. Mr. Wetzel in politics is a republican.

GEORGE S. DOWELL, M. D. With residence at Braymer since 1900, Doctor Dowell has built up a substantial practice and is known as one of the able, earnest and popular representatives of the medical profession in this section of Northwest Missouri. Partly to accommodate his own private practice and partly as a public institution of the town, Doctor Dowell has established a hospital at Braymer, has excellent equipment and trained assistants, and through his individual skill and these facilities has become one of the most successful physicians and surgeons in Caldwell County. Doctor Dowell graduated from the Kansas City College of Medicine in 1900, and at once began practice in Braymer.

George S. Dowell was born in Livingston County, Missouri, on a farm, March 23, 1876. His father, John H. Dowell, was a farmer and stock man, a native of Meade County, Kentucky, and during the war between the states served as a Confederate soldier in the splendid cavalry organization commanded by Gen. Joe Wheeler. The father is still living, a resident of Chillicothe, Missouri. He married Elizabeth Simpson, a daughter of John Simpson, who came from Tennessee. She died in Chillicothe, Missouri, in 1909, at the age of sixty-eight. She was an active member of the Methodist Episcopal Church South. In the family were five sons and one daughter. The daughter is Lora Wingo of Chillicothe, Missouri. Two of the other sons are physicians, Doctor Robert, now living retired at Los Angeles, California, and H. S., a physician in Nodaway County, Missouri. The father was an active democrat and a member of the Baptist Church.

Dr. George S. Dowell was reared on the home farm, was taught the value of earnest toil at an early age, and acquired an education partly in the public schools and partly in college. He took up the study of medicine under a brother, and in 1896 entered the Medical College at Kansas City and remained until graduating M. D. in 1900. A few years after locating at Braymer Doctor Dowell constructed a building particularly adapted for offices and a hospital, and now keeps a trained nurse and has accommodations for service in surgical cases much above those usually found in towns of this size. Doctor Dowell is an active member of the County and State Medical Society, affiliates with the Masonic and Knights of Pythias orders, and has been quite active in fraternal matters. For several years he served as a member of the Braymer school board.

In 1901 Doctor Dowell married Miss Bessie Moorman, a daughter of Laban F. Moorman, former citizen of Braymer, where her mother is still living. Doctor Dowell and wife have one child, Donald M., now eleven years of age. Doctor Dowell and wife are active members of the Baptist Church, while his wife is prominent in club work and in the Eastern Star. They occupy one of the comfortable homes of Braymer and are both willing workers for the improvement of Braymer as a good town in which to live.

H. A. SCHROEDER, M. D. One of the younger members of the medical fraternity in Caldwell County, Doctor Schroeder, in ability and in the extent of his patronage, ranks second to none of his competitors. He has brought to the active work of medicine and surgery an exceptional equipment, gained both from the schools and from the resources of his own mind and adaptability for his chosen vocation. Doctor Schroeder has practiced medicine and surgery at Braymer since 1900, having graduated in medicine the previous year.

Doctor Schroeder was born February 1, 1873, in Toledo, Tama County, Iowa, a son of Peter Schroeder, a prosperous land owner and merchant of Tama County. Peter Schroeder was a native of Germany, reared and educated in that country, served three years in the German army, was under the command of the famous Von Moltke, and in his native land married Antjie Reimers. Peter Schroeder is now living retired at the age of seventy-five. In politics he is a democrat and his church is the Lutheran. There were five children, three sons and two daughters. One son, Peter, is a graduate of the University of Iowa and a physician at Davenport.

Dr. H. A. Schroeder was educated in the public schools, finishing with the high school, and took up the study of medicine at Davenport under Dr. L. Hagenbach. Doctor Schroeder is proficient, both in the English and German languages, is a man of thorough scholarship, has followed out a broad line of reading and research, and is exceptionally equipped for his practice. Besides his general practice as a physician, Doctor Schroeder is local surgeon at Braymer for the Chicago, Milwaukee & St. Paul Railroad.

Doctor Schroeder is a member of the county and state medical societies, has affiliations with the Masonic order, and represents in his profession a number of leading life insurance companies. He is a member of the United States Pension Examining Board.

LOUIS F. BLACKETER. As postmaster of Braymer since 1912, Mr. Blacketer has performed a large amount of useful public service for his home town and has managed the affairs of the office to the best advantage and convenience of the citizens. Mr. Blacketer has for a number of years been known to this section of Missouri as a merchant, and his family came to Missouri nearly sixty years ago. His appointment as postmaster came in April, 1912, by President Taft. The office at Braymer is a third class office, but has business which places it as the second largest office in the County of Caldwell. There are six rural mail routes radiating from Braymer, and the carriers cover each day in the week 150 miles of highway leading out from Braymer. The mail is delivered into four counties, Caldwell, Ray, Carroll, and Livingston. Braymer postoffice occupies a well arranged building, 25 by 75 feet, with ample quarters for the local postoffice and the rural carriers. Mr. Blacketer has as his assistant postmaster Flora T. Blacketer, while Ralph F. Blacketer is clerk.

Louis F. Blacketer was born at Unionville, Missouri, December 20, 1873, son of Thomas B. Blacketer. His father was a carpenter and contractor, was born in Indiana in 1854, and was the son of an Englishman, who was born in Sheffield, England, and after coming to America located in Indiana. The family in 1856 emigrated to Missouri and settled in Putnam County. There were six sons and six daughters in the grandfather's family, and three of the sons saw active service in the Union army during the Civil war. Thomas B. Blacketer was reared in Putnam County, and married Mary E. Davis, who was born in Wayne County, Kentucky, daughter of C. J. Davis, a native of the same state. Louis F. Blacketer has one sister, Bessie Lee, wife of J. W. Walker, a railroad man. The father died in 1886 at the age of thirty-two, and his widow is still living at Unionville.

Louis F. Blacketer was reared in Putnam County, acquired an education in the public schools, and in 1892 graduated from the Chicago College of Pharmacy. With this preparation for a business career he engaged in the drug business at Tina in Carroll County, subsequently moved to Dawn in Livingston County, and from there to Braymer. He has a large and successful business, one of the best stores of the kind in Caldwell County. Mr. Blacketer married Flora T. Callaway, a daughter of Joseph Callaway, who was born in Tennessee. Mr. Blacketer has two sons: Ralph F., who was born March 17, 1895, and in 1914 graduated from high school, where he was manager of the baseball team and captain of the football team; Roy B., was born May 29, 1897, and is in the second year of the Braymer High School. Mr. Blacketer is an active republican, is past master of Masonic Lodge No. 135, affiliates with Lodge No. 656 of the Benevolent and Protective Order of Elks at Chillicothe, and is a member of Braymer Lodge No. 203 of the Knights of Pythias.

JAMES E. NICHOLS. As postmaster of Breckenridge since June, 1912, James E. Nichols has performed a large amount of useful public service for his home city and has managed the affairs of his office to the best advantage and convenience of the citizens. Mr. Nichols has spent many years in Caldwell County, is a veteran of the war in the Philippines, and is a popular man among all classes. The Breckenridge postoffice employs three clerks and has four rural carriers. Mr. Nichols is a methodical and careful worker, and has conducted his office so as to afford perfect service to every patron, whether adult or child.

James E. Nichols was born April 10, 1872, in Coshocton County, Ohio, on a farm. His father, Willard Nichols, was a native of New York, of a family noted for honesty and industry. He was a miller by trade and an excellent workman. In 1849 he joined the exodus to California, went across the plains with ox teams and wagons, and spent ten years on the Pacific Coast, digging gold and in other employment. He then returned to the United States by way of the Isthmus of Panama. He was married in Ohio to Nancy A. Henderson. Willard Nichols died at the age of seventy-two. In politics he was a republican, and he and his wife, who is still living in good health at the age of seventy-three, were members of the Methodist Church. There were eight children, seven sons and one daughter, the sons being named as follows: Charles F., Ed, Willard, Jr., James E., Frank, L. A., and Howard, and the daughter, Iva.

When James E. Nichols was twelve years of age the family came out to Missouri and settled in Caldwell County near Hamilton on a farm. He acquired his education in district schools and at Kidder Institute, and by work on a farm developed his muscle and was prepared for a career of usefulness. He began life as a farmer, also teaching school for one year, and was one of the young men of Northwest Missouri who volunteered for service during the Spanish-American and .Philippine wars, enlisting in the Twenty-third Regiment of the United States Army. He was sent out to the Philippines, was at Manila and in other parts of the islands under the command of General Merritt and General Otis, and saw much active and dangerous service. Later he was at Tokio, Japan, and in other ports of the Orient, and finally returned by a transport steamer to San Francisco and received an honorable discharge. After returning to Caldwell County, Mr. Nichols engaged in farming, and was also in business at Kidder and Breckenridge until he was appointed postmaster.

In 1901 occurred his marriage to Laura E. Adams, daughter of Dr. Tyler Adams, of an English family. Mr. and Mrs. Nichols have three children: Nadine, Mary and Ethel, while their son, Roy E., died at the age of eight years. Mr. Nichols is a prominent republican in Caldwell County, and is affiliated with the Knights of Pythias and the Independent Order of Odd Fellows. He is one of the solid men and good citizens of Northern Caldwell County.

J. E. PLUMMER. One of the strongest combinations of legal talent in Caldwell County is the firm of Reed & Plummer at Breckenridge. J. E. Plummer, the junior member, was admitted to the bar in 1909, and became a partner of Mr. Reed in September, 1913. They enjoy a large practice, and their individual records commend them as leading young lawyers in this part of Northwest Missouri. Mr. Plummer was admitted to the bar in 1909 and began his practice in the State of Washington near Spokane, but after three years returned to Missouri and has since been a member of the Caldwell County bar.

J. E. Plummer was born in Carroll County, Missouri, September 12, 1876. His father, Enoch Plummer, was born in Mercer County, Ohio, and for three years fought in the Union army as an Ohio soldier. He married in Ohio Susan Dean. Besides the Breckenridge lawyer there is a brother, Elmer, and two daughters, Emma Plummer and Ada Higgins.

J. E. Plummer was reared and educated in Caldwell County, attended the public schools, and finished his studies in the University of Missouri at Columbia. For three years, from 1903 to 1906, he was connected with the Breckenridge Savings Bank as bookkeeper and assistant cashier.

Mr. Plummer was married in March, 1910, at Marceline, Missouri, to Stella Caldwell, who was born and reared in Kansas, attending high school at Breckenridge and Western College at Oxford, Ohio. Her father, Rev. Dennis Caldwell, was a prominent minister of the Presbyterian Church. Both Mr. and Mrs. Plummer are active in church affairs and have taken an interest in Sunday school and in the various social and benevolent work of their home town. Mr. Plummer is a close student of the law, is a frank-spoken, genial gentleman, and is already firmly established in the practice of his chosen calling.

A. B. CLEAVELAND. The Caldwell County bar has one of its able advocates in A. B. Cleaveland of Breckenridge, and his position in this community as a rising young attorney is already well established. His work has given much promise of distinctive achievements at no far distant time, and he has all the qualifications needed for success in this most exacting profession. Mr. Cleaveland was admitted to the bar in 1909, and has since been in practice at Breckenridge.

He was born in the State of Iowa, in Osceola County, October 2, 1883. He was the only child of his parents. His father, F. M. Cleaveland, is a successful farmer and stockman, a son of Q. E. Cleaveland, who was a native of Pennsylvania, a soldier during the Civil war and was with General Sherman on his march to the sea, and after the war came west and settled in Iowa in 1870. F. M. Cleaveland married Anna Pell, who was born at Burlington, Iowa, a daughter of Reverend Pell, prominent as a minister in Iowa. Both parents are members of the Methodist Church, and the father is a republican.

A. B. Cleaveland was reared on a farm, was taught the value of industry at an early age, and by hard work has reached his present position in the law. He was educated in the district schools, in high school and college, and has been one of Caldwell County's rising attorneys since 1909. Mr. Cleaveland was married at Boulder, Colorado, in August, 1911, to Miss Elizabeth Clark, a daughter of J. C. F. Clark, a prominent citizen of Denver, Colorado. Mrs. Cleaveland was educated at Lawrence, Kansas. They have one child, Lois. Mr. Cleaveland is a republican in politics, and has been active in his party in Caldwell County. He is affiliated with the Masonic order and he and his wife are both members of the Methodist Church. Since taking up the practice of law he has distinguished himself for his fidelity to his clients, and has been an eager and ambitious student, possessing forceful powers in advocating cases before court or jury, and at the same time is active in the local affairs of his home town.

S. D. SMITH, M. D. For nearly twenty years Doctor Smith has been performing the duties of the physician and surgeon, and is regarded as one of the ablest men in practice at Cowgill or vicinity. Doctor Smith began practice at Cowgill in 1896, and after some years of absence in other fields returned to the town in 1906, and has since built up a large general practice, his business taking him all over the country about Cowgill.

Doctor Smith is a graduate of the medical department of Washington University at St. Louis. He was born in 1867 on the old homestead of his father near Lawson in Ray County. His father, Joseph A. Smith, who is now ninety-three years of age, is one of the very few living veterans in Northwest Missouri who saw active service during the Mexican war. He was born in North Carolina, and married Kate Miller, a native of Ohio. Mr. Smith went out to war with Mexico with the troops under General Davidson, and marched a total distance of 5,000 miles before returning to Missouri. Doctor Smith is a member of a family of seven sons and five daughters, ten of whom are living.

Doctor Smith grew up on a farm, was trained in the duties of country life, attended the public schools, and began the study of medicine under Dr. W. C. James at Lawson. He began the practice of medicine at Cowgill in 1896, and then for five years was in his profession at Colorado Springs, Colorado. Returning to Cowgill in 1906 he has since given all his time and attention to his large practice.

Doctor Smith was married April 29, 1895, to Anna Waites, daughter of Henry Waites. They have one daughter, Margaret. Doctor Smith is affiliated with the Masonic order, his wife is active in the Methodist Church, and they reside in one of the modern homes of Cowgill.

HON. JOSHUA W. ALEXANDER. In the forty years since he entered the practice of law at Gallatin, few Missourians have enjoyed more of the honors of distinctive public service than Joshua W. Alexander, now member of Congress from the Third Congressional District. His record as a congressman is familiar to all the people of the Third District and more or less to those of the state, while a great many times during the epoch-making years in the development of American public policies since he took his seat at Washington his direct action and collaboration have been marked with favor by the general political correspondents.

While his own youth was one of comparatively humble circumstances, Judge Alexander comes of fine family stock. The Alexanders were Scotch-Irish, having located along about Revolutionary times in the rugged district of Southwestern Pennsylvania, in the thrifty, independent and Presbyterian neighborhood of Washington County. His paternal grandparents were both natives of Washington County, were married there in 1796, and then moved north of Pittsburg to Mercer County, where Grandfather Alexander improved a pioneer farm. In that county the name still remains, associated with all that is old and substantial.

Thomas W. Alexander, father of the congressman, was born in Mercer County, was reared on a farm, and learned the trade of carpenter and builder, which he afterwards followed in Cincinnati. While in that city he married Jane Robinson, who was born in England and brought when a child by her parents to Cincinnati. Joshua W. was the only child of his father and mother, and was born in Cincinnati, January 22, 1852. In 1856 his father went out to the new Territory of Minnesota, hoping to recover his health, and was joined by his wife and child in 1857. The father died in Minnesota October 12, 1859.

Judge Alexander's mother then lived a brief time at Canton, Lewis County, Missouri, returned to Cincinnati and remained there until 1863, coming back to Canton in that year. As a boy he had three years of schooling in his native city, and after completing the course of the public schools at Canton, Missouri, entered Christian University of that city in 1868 and was graduated A. B. in June, 1872. In June of the following year he came to Gallatin to visit William N., James A. and George W. Richardson, classmates in Christian University, the sons of Judge Samuel A. Richardson. That was one of the incidents which so often become turning points in the human destiny. Young Alexander was then twenty-one, with a definite ambition for the law, but with his future course otherwise unplatted. He intended to continue his journey to California, and teach for a time, and later study law in that state. Judge Richardson induced him to remain in Gallatin and study in the Richardson law office. Later the families became united by the marriage of Mr. Alexander with a daughter of Judge Richardson.

In 1875 Mr. Alexander was admitted to the bar at Gallatin, which city has been his home since 1873. In 1876 he was elected public administrator of Daviess County, and reelected in 1880. In 1882 he became a member of the Gallatin Board of Education, and served first as president and later as secretary for a period of twenty-one years. Also in 1882 he was elected to the General Assembly of Missouri from Daviess County, and by two successive reelections served in the thirty-second, thirty-third and thirty-fourth assemblies, being chairman of the committee on appropriations in the sixty-third and speaker of the house in the sixty-fourth. For two terms he was mayor of Gallatin. In 1894,

Governor, now Senator William J. Stone appointed him a member of the Board of Managers of the State Asylum for the Insane at St. Joseph, and in that capacity he served a number of years. In the meantime he had been practicing law with increasing success, and eventually was elected to the bench, serving as judge of the Seventh Judicial Circuit from January, 1901, to February, 1907. He retired from the bench a short time before being sworn in as a member of the Sixtieth Congress, to which he was elected by the Third Congressional District in November, 1906. Judge Alexander served in the House of Representatives in the sixtieth, sixty-first, sixty-second and sixty-third congresses, and in November, 1914, was elected to the Sixty-fourth Congress. He has been chairman of the committee on the merchant marine and fisheries, one of the most important committees of the house, since the democrats gained control of the House of Representatives in the Sixty-first Congress and has taken a specially influential part in national legislation, and is now one of the leading democrats of the house. As chairman of the committee on the merchant marine and fisheries, Judge Alexander conducted the investigation of steamship combinations, provided for by House Resolution 587, adopted by the Sixty-second Congress. His work in this connection, his report to the house and the bill introduced by him to carry out the recommendations of the committee, are his greatest achievements during his comparatively brief service in Congress. Following the sinking of the steamship Titanic in April, 1912, Judge Alexander introduced the joint resolution, which became a law in June, 1912, authorizing the President of the United States to call or participate in an international conference on the subject of greater safety of life at sea. Great Britain called the conference. President Wilson appointed Judge Alexander chairman of the United States Commission to this conference, which met in London from November 12, 1913, to January 20, 1914. Fourteen other nations and Canada, Australia and New Zealand participated in the conference. The convention agreed to in the conference has been ratified by the United States Senate, and Judge Alexander was personally congratulated by President Wilson for his distinguished service in the conference which framed it. In June, 1907, Christian University at Canton, his alma mater, conferred on Judge Alexander the degree of Master of Arts.

Judge Alexander was married in February, 1876, to Miss Roe Ann Richardson, daughter of Judge Samuel A. Richardson, a sketch of whom follows. Mr. and Mrs. Alexander have had a large family, nine sons and three daughters, four of whom died in infancy. Those living are: Samuel T., educated in the Gallatin schools and the University of Missouri, was for ten years Missouri grain inspector at St. Louis under the State Railroad and Warehouse Commission, married Miss Campbell of Columbia, and is now associated with her father, J. R. Campbell, in the book and stationery business at Columbia. Julia, who was educated in the public schools and Grand River College, is the wife of Dr. N. R. Jenner, of Washington, D. C. Frances, who was educated in the public schools, Grand River College, and studied 3½ years in the St. Louis School of Fine Arts, is now the wife of A. G. Ficklin of Gallatin. George F., who finished his education in the academic and law departments of the University of Missouri, receiving the degree of LL. B. from the latter, is now practicing law at Portland, Oregon. Rowena, at home, was educated in the public schools and the William Wood College at Fulton, Missouri. Preston Carter, who graduated from both the academic and law departments of the University of Missouri, is now associated with his brother, George, in the practice of law at Portland, Oregon. Walter Richardson, was educated in the public schools, studied two years at the

University of Missouri and one year in George Washington University in the academic departments of those schools, is now a student in the law school of the latter, and was secretary of the United States Commission to the International Conference on Safety of Life at Sea, of which his father was chairman. The youngest son, Laurence Woodward, is now attending school at Washington, D. C.

JUDGE SAMUEL A. RICHARDSON. A former judge of the judicial circuit, including Daviess County, Judge Richardson was a resident of Gallatin from 1859 until his death, December 11, 1882. He was one of the distinguished men of his generation in Northwest Missouri, where he spent nearly all his life. Though his life was comparatively short, he possessed extraordinary energy and great physical and mental endurance, and as a lawyer for years ranked with the best talent of the Missouri bar, enjoying a large practice in all the courts. As a citizen he was unswerving in his devotion to what he believed was right, was public-spirited and liberal, but unostentatious, and was devotedly attached to his family and friends.

Samuel A. Richardson was born in Anderson County, Kentucky, July 6, 1826, and was fifty-six years old when he died. His father, Col. John C. Richardson, was a native of Virginia, and of a prominent family of that state and Kentucky. The paternal grandfather was Judge Nathaniel Richardson, who moved out from Kentucky and became a pioneer in Lewis County, Missouri. The maternal grandfather, Samuel Arbuckle, was also from Kentucky, and one of the pioneers in Ray County, Missouri. Both grandfathers lived to advanced age, and left large families. Col. John C. Richardson grew up in Anderson County, Kentucky, and in the spring of 1831 moved his family to the Missouri River bottoms above Camden, in Ray County, and later went south of the river to Lexington.

Judge Samuel A. Richardson was reared on the Ray County homestead at a time when that part of the state was just being developed. He helped his father in opening up and improving three farms, and as a young man was proficient in prairie-breaking, as an ox driver, and also had his experience in breaking hemp and splitting rails. Schools were of meager equipment during his boyhood, and as his services were needed at home he had little instruction up to his fifteenth year. Later he attended the high school in Richmond, getting a good foundation in the elements of English, Latin, Greek and mathematics. In the early part of 1845 he entered the University of Missouri at Columbia, and completed a course of study in two years. Afterward he was engaged in trading for a time, and then took up the study of law under Judge Philip L. Edwards. His studies were continued under Hon. Edward A. Lewis, at that time presiding judge of the St. Louis Court of Appeals and afterwards a member of the Missouri Supreme Court. He was admitted to the bar in September, 1852, before Judge George W. Dunn, for many years judge of the circuit including Daviess County, and afterwards of the Fifth Judicial Circuit.

For the twenty years following his admission, Judge Richardson practiced law over a large circuit, including Ray, Clinton, Carroll, Livingston, Caldwell, Daviess, DeKalb, Gentry, Harrison, Grundy and Worth counties—most of Northwest Missouri—after 1859 having his residence in Gallatin. On the formation of the Twenty-eighth Judicial Circuit in 1872 after a short but spirited canvass, he was elected judge of the circuit as a non-partisan, defeating the republican candidate, Isaac P. Caldwell. In 1874 he was elected for the regular term of six years, and at its expiration, January 1, 1881, declined reelection. He then resumed private practice at Gallatin until his death, less than two years later.

Judge Richardson was county school commissioner of Ray County several years, and was county attorney of Daviess County almost continuously from the time he came to Gallatin until his election to the bench. He was also extensively interested in real estate, farming and stock raising. He was a member of the Christian Church.

In 1850 Judge Richardson married Miss Julia A. Woodward, a daughter of Maj. George W. and Nancy (Whitney) Woodward, of Richmond. Her father was born in Ireland and her mother in Lexington, Kentucky. Major Woodward for many years was circuit clerk of Ray County, serving at a time when Ray County extended north to the Iowa line. Judge Richardson had eight children, three of whom died in infancy. The others were: James A., deceased; George W., deceased; Samuel P., deceased; Roe Ann, wife of Congressman J. W. Alexander; and William N., who now resides in Gallatin, Missouri.

DANIEL BRAYMER. One of the best towns of its size in Northwest Missouri is the little city of Braymer in Caldwell County, which was named in honor of the prominent farmer, stockman and capitalist, Daniel Braymer, who is one of the largest land owners in Northwest Missouri, and whose stock farms were the most conspicuous features of the locality before the Chicago, Milwaukee & St. Paul Railroad laid out the townsite in 1887. Braymer is now a place of about twelve hundred population, with good schools, churches, banks, stores, and is the home of a high class citizenship. Mr. Braymer first began investing in Caldwell County lands in 1869, and has ever since been a prominent factor in the upbuilding of this community. He owns more than two thousand acres, including some of the best land in the county, and there are few men in Northwest Missouri whose success along the general lines of farming, stock raising and the ownership and control of lands has been greater than Daniel Braymer's.

Daniel Braymer was born in Washington County, New York, on a farm, March 17, 1844. His father was Daniel Braymer, and his grandfather, Jacob Braymer, was of German ancestry and gave active service to the American colonies during the Revolutionary war. Daniel Braymer, Sr., married a Miss Woodward, who was born and reared in Washington County, a daughter of a Revolutionary soldier. The children of Daniel Braymer, Sr., and wife were: Jacob, who died in 1902 in New York State; Jennett, who died at the age of twenty-three; Alfred, who lives in Washington County, New York; Daniel and Rosalinda. The father was first a whig in politics and later a republican, and a member of the Baptist Church. He died in Washington County, New York, at the age of eighty-four, and his wife passed away aged eighty-five.

Daniel Braymer, Jr., grew up on a farm in New York State, and while his education came from the public schools, his best training for life was in the habits of industry and thrift which he acquired when still a boy. At the age of twenty-three he left his home state, and since then has traveled and acquired interests in many parts of this country and also of Mexico. He spent some time in Georgia, then in Tennessee and Kentucky, and for several years was located in Leavenworth County, Kansas. Afterwards he lived one summer in Buchanan County, near St. Joseph, and from there came to Caldwell County, where he bought a section of land, all of it raw and unimproved. It has been genius and enterprise as a farmer and stockman which have transformed these barren acres into a splendid country estate, with corn fields and pastures, and thousands of dollars invested in permanent improvements. Mr.

Braymer's large landed acreage in the vicinity of Braymer is divided among several farms, each improved with good houses, barns and all the facilities for successful stock farming. He keeps from a hundred to three hundred head of cattle on his Caldwell County places, also about five hundred hogs, and as a measure of his enterprise it can be stated that few of the larger business men and manufacturers of the cities of Missouri control more extensive interests than Mr. Braymer.

His interests extend to various other states. There are 800 acres of land under his ownership near Fort Sill in Oklahoma, a large tract of valuable land near Ellensburg, Washington, and another fine farm in South Dakota. Mr. Braymer has always followed the practice of investing his surplus capital in land, and his skillful knowledge of how to make land productive and profitable is a full justification of this practice. He is also owner of about thirteen thousand acres in South Mexico, one of the most beautiful tracts of land anywhere in North America, with almost untold wealth in timber and other resources.

Since 1896 Mr. Braymer has lived in the City of Braymer, where he has a fine home. He was married in 1869 in Washington County, New York, to Miss Nancy Woodward. She was born in Washington County, a daughter of John and Fanny (McCarter) Woodward, both New York State people. The other Woodward children were: John, now deceased; Alexander, deceased; Mary Jane, who lives in Washington County, New York. Her father died at the age of sixty-seven and her mother at seventy-nine. Her father was a democrat in politics and a member of the Baptist Church.

Mr. and Mrs. Braymer have children as follows: George V., who is following in the footsteps of his father and is one of the prominent stockmen of Caldwell County, was married first to Stella Feese, who died three years after marriage, leaving one child, Pauline. He married second Alice Morris, and to this union three children were born, Daniel Richard, George V., and Mildred; Frank, who died at the age of fifteen; and Lulu, who is married to Dr. Boone Woolsey and lives at Braymer, and they have one child, Randall B. Mr. Braymer and his family are members of the Methodist Church. He is a republican in politics, and served as county judge of Caldwell County in 1881 and 1882. He is content to perform his share of public service through the management of his extensive interests, which are not only a source of profit to himself but have resulted in the upbuilding and improvement of the community, and are a source of wealth to a number of men in this section and elsewhere. Mr. Braymer has always proved himself a strong supporter of good roads, schools and churches and law and order, and when public undertakings are proposed he is one of the first men whose endorsement and practical cooperation are required.

SID F. THOMSON. Cashier of the First National Bank of Cowgill, Sid F. Thomson has been identified with banking in this town for the past six years, was formerly in business as a merchant and is a Cowgill County citizen whose career has been passed here from birth, and has always been honorably and influentially identified with the welfare of the community. Mr. Thomson in 1914 was honored by the citizens of Cowgill with election to the office of mayor, and since the beginning of his administration has done much to improve the town as a business and home center. The First National Bank of Cowgill was established in 1887, at first as a private institution, and took out a National charter about fifteen years ago. Its officers are: A. M. Delany, president; W. H. Lile, vice president; C. L. Wells, vice president; Sid F. Thomson, assistant cashier. The bank has a capital of $35,000, and its surplus is now $15,000. Mr. Thomson has a large acquaintance both in Caldwell and in Ray counties, has spent his youth and manhood in this section, and possesses the esteem paid to honest ability in all his relations, whether in business or with civic affairs.

Sid F. Thomson was born on the old home farm in this vicinity, August 14, 1873. His father, Frederick Thomson, was a farmer and stock man, and died in 1897 at the age of fifty-three. He was born and reared in Caldwell County, and his parents came to this section from Kentucky. He was married in Lincoln Township to Mary Thomson, a cousin, who is now living at the age of seventy on the old homestead. There were five children: Sid F. Thomson; Samuel, in Excelsior Springs, Missouri; Ella, wife of E. M. McCray of Cowgill; Crosby, of Cowgill; and R. A., a farmer and stock man operating the old homestead. The father of these children was a prominent citizen, served as county commissioner, was an elder in the Christian Church, and in politics a democrat.

Sid F. Thomson grew up on the home farm, learned its duties and developed a good physique, and was educated in the public schools, finishing with a business course. His father was postmaster at Cowgill during the second Cleveland administration, and Sid Thomson during that time served as assistant postmaster. In 1900 Mr. Thomson married Linnie May, a daughter of C. A. May, now deceased, while her mother is living in Grand Junction, Colorado. Mrs. Thomson was before her marriage a popular teacher, and is a graduate of the Breckenridge High School. Mr. and Mrs. Thomson have three children: Frederick A., Dorothy May and Robert H. Mr. Thomson affiliates with Lodge No. 561 of the Masonic Order, he and his wife are active in the Christian Church and for a number of years they have made themselves useful and influential members of local society.

MICHAEL R. FOWLER. It is by no means an empty distinction to have lived actively and usefully for a period of fourscore years. At this writing Michael R. Fowler has passed his eightieth birthday. He was born in Missouri during pioneer times, and has been both a witness and an actor in the changing development of this state since he was a boy. Mr. Fowler is now retired, but still more or less active in supervising his extensive interests. As a farmer and stock man he is regarded as one of the wealthiest and most successful, and is known in all the region about Polo, both in Caldwell and Ray counties, where most of his active career has been spent.

Michael R. Fowler was born May 4, 1834, in Howard County, Missouri. His birthplace was a log cabin, the type of home which was more frequently found in Missouri eighty years ago than any other kind. His parents at that time lived north of Fayette. His father, Elijah Fowler, was an early settler in Missouri, and came from the vicinity of Boston, Massachusetts, and was of English descent. Elijah married Matilda Burton, who was a native of Kentucky and of an old family in that state. The family moved from Howard County to the vicinity of Huntsville in Randolph County, and from there came to Clinton County. The father improved a large tract of land in Ray County, and followed farming until his death at the age of seventy-seven. He was a democrat in politics. The mother passed away at the age of seventy. They were the parents of a large family of children, named as follows: William, who went out as a volunteer to the Mexican war in 1846, and is now deceased; John, deceased; Stephen, deceased; Jesse, deceased; Moses R.; Elizabeth; Michael R.; James, who lives in

Randolph County; Matilda, whose home is in Cooper County, Missouri; and Ellen, who lives in Randolph County.

Michael R. Fowler grew up on a farm, and hard work was his portion as a boy, and all his education came from one of the primitive schools kept in Missouri during the '40s and '50s. It was in a log cabin, with a puncheon floor, with slab benches, a mud and stick chimney, and the crude furnishings matched the old fashioned methods of instruction, which included only the fundamentals of reading, writing and arithmetic.

Mr. Fowler was married in Ray County, Missouri, in 1864 to Elvira Moss. She was reared and educated in Ray County, a daughter of Archibald Moss, who was born in Kentucky, of an old French family. Archibald Moss married Lucy Boston, also a native of Kentucky. Their children were: William, Reuben, Elizabeth Jane, Thomas, Archibald, Nancy, Irene, Susan, John, Elvira Fowler, and one that died in childhood. Mrs. Fowler's father died at the age of eighty-five. He had served in the Confederate State Militia during the war. The mother died at the age of seventy-two and both were members of the Christian Church.

Mr. Fowler began his career as a farmer and stock raiser more than half a century ago, and his operations have always been carried on on an extensive scale, as a raiser, feeder and dealer in cattle, hogs and other live stock. He has handled many hundreds of acres of land, both as a farmer and a dealer, and at one time owned 2,000 acres in Ray and Caldwell counties. This was divided among several farms, and he has long been one of the heavy tax payers in this section. Mr. Fowler was formerly a stockholder in the Farmers Bank of Polo, and though he has given liberally to his children still has large interests to supervise. His home in Polo is a substantial and comfortable eight-room house, and he has all those material good things which make old age pleasant.

Mr. and Mrs. Fowler became the parents of seven children. Their son Archibald is one of the prominent farmers and cattle men in the vicinity of Polo and operates over eleven hundred acres of land. He has a son named M. R. Thomas, the next child, is a stockman in Ray County, with 1,000 acres of well improved land, and has a home and family. The son Charles is likewise a farmer and cattleman, occupying 350 acres in Ray County. Fred B. is proprietor of a farm of 400 acres in Caldwell and Ray counties. Lulu is now deceased. Carrie is the wife of J. G. Withers, the popular cashier of the Farmers Bank of Polo. Mr. and Mrs. Fowler have reared their children to lives of honorable usefulness, and take great pleasure in their grandchildren and in the successful careers of the sons and daughters. Mr. Fowler and wife are both members of the Christian Church. Mr. Fowler is a democrat in politics but has never sought office.

JOSEPH S. LEAMER. When Joseph S. Leamer came into Caldwell County in 1866, he brought with him one horse and a set of harness. He had no money, and the first winter was spent in cutting cord wood at the rate of $1 per cord, and he also split several thousand rails. That was the means by which he was started on a successful career. It is needless to say that he possessed industry and a vigorous physique, and these resources with a faculty of good business judgment have put him in a position through the succeeding years where he is now regarded as one of the most influential and prosperous men of Polo. He is one of the most extensive land owners in the county, and his farms aggregate 635 acres. His home place comprises seventy-five acres and adjoins the Town of Polo, being situated in section 21 of Grant Township. His own residence is a large and commodious house of ten rooms, surrounded with large barns, feed lots, and all the facilities for conducting his industry as a stock farmer. He keeps cattle and hogs, and makes a specialty of the breeding of mules and horses. On his place can be found some of the best thoroughbred Duroc swine in Caldwell County. Mr. Leamer understands his business, is a thoroughly practical man, and his success is based on thorough business qualifications and an integrity which has stood without question for nearly half a century.

Joseph S. Leamer comes of good old Pennsylvania stock of German ancestry on the maternal side and of Scotch Irish on the paternal, and he was born in Blair County, Pennsylvania, in 1847. His parents were Jacob and Rebecca (Stevens) Leamer. In 1850 the family left Pennsylvania and embarked on a river steamboat on which they descended the Ohio River and then came up the Mississippi and found a home in Benton County, Iowa, where for several years they lived surrounded by pioneer conditions. The father died at the age of forty-seven, leaving a widow and nine children. The mother attained the advanced age of ninety-three years. The parents were members of the United Brethren Church.

Joseph S. Leamer grew up in Iowa, had the surroundings of a pioneer farm and a new country, and all his education came from the public schools. In 1867, about a year after his arrival in Caldwell County, he married Elizabeth Webb, a daughter of Isaac Webb. Mr. and Mrs. Leamer have a fine family of sons and daughters, mentioned briefly as follows: Elma, wife of George Dixon of Polo; Lenora, deceased; Richard R., who is married and has two children; Hiram, who died at the age of nineteen; Nellie Minger; Mattie Minger; Maude Stone; Blanche Stone; and Frank, who is married and has two children. Mr. Leamer's sons are all active farmers and cattle men. Mrs. Leamer is a member of the Baptist Church. Though his own success has come from hard work and in spite of obstacles and lack of advantages, Mr. Leamer has always shown a friendly interest in schools and other provisions for the education of the young, and is a man of public spirit in all movements affecting the improvement of his community.

WILLIAM C. STONE. While the foundation of his business career and prosperity has been in farming and stock raising, William C. Stone has for several years been best known to the business community of Polo and vicinity as president of the Farmers Bank. The Farmers Bank of Polo is one of the strong institutions of Caldwell County, and has a capital stock of $35,000 and surplus of over $17,000. The institution represents the resources and personal character of a group of substantial citizens, and under his management Mr. Stone has done much to increase the solidity and service of the bank.

While Mr. Stone now makes his home in Polo, he still gives active supervision to the interests of his fine farm of 500 acres located 2½ miles east of town. In many of its features it is a model farm estate. It has a large comfortable residence of nine rooms, and a large barn and cattle sheds indicate that the primary industry is stock raising. The land is divided among blue grass pastures and grain fields, and one conspicuous feature is a fine pond, furnishing water sufficient for 500 head of cattle, and well stocked with fish. The farm is located in Grant Township. Mr. Stone moved into Polo in 1909, and his town home is a substantial residence of eight rooms, all well furnished and making one of the best residences of Polo.

William C. Stone was born in Ray County, Missouri, at the old Stone Homestead March 10, 1857. His father, William Stone, a native of

Kentucky, was a soldier in the Civil war, and his business was that of farming and stock raising. He married Mary F. Baker, a sister of James and John W. Baker, well known citizens whose careers are sketched on other pages of this work. William Stone died at the home in Caldwell County at the age of forty-seven, leaving a widow and nine children. The mother is now living at Polo. The names of the children were William C., James, Sarah, Addie, Martha, Minnie, Lillie, Eva and John. Politically the father was a democrat, and his church was the Baptist.

William C. Stone grew up on a farm and as his years increased and his strength likewise he aided actively in its cultivation, and when not employed on the farm attended the country schools. Mr. Stone was married March 29, 1876, to Rachel Flint, who has been his faithful companion and helpmate for thirty-six years. She was born in Caldwell County, a daughter of Jesse K. and Asenath (Owens) Flint. Her father was born in Illinois, but was reared in Iowa, and his wife was a native of the latter state. Mrs. Stone's father died at the age of seventy, and there were five children in the Flint family: John, Henry, George, Elizabeth and Rachel. Mr. and Mrs. Stone are the parents of nine children, five sons and four daughters, namely: Nellie, wife of R. H. Baker, and the mother of two children; Pearl; Fred H.; Frank; Samuel; Ellis; Jesse; Verne; and Nettie. The sons are all prosperous farmers and stock men.

COLUMBUS OWEN SELBY. Only few families of Harrison County have had three active generations identified with the management and cultivation of the farms in this district. One such family is the Selbys, and Columbus O. has spent twenty-five years or more in active and influential citizenship, and has a farm near Bethany in the same community in which his grandfather Selby founded the family about the year Harrison County was organized.

His grandfather was William Selby, a native of Kentucky, from which state he moved to Rush County, Indiana, and from there came to Harrison County more than seventy years ago. In Rush County he married Martha Flint, a relative of Thomas J. Flint, mentioned elsewhere in this work. Their children were: George W., a farmer in Harrison County; Joshua J., father of Columbus O.; John F., who spent his life in Harrison County and left a family; Thomas, who died when young; James P., of Harrison County; Jesse B., who was the head of a family when he died; and Rachel, widow of Leonard Nichols of Harrison County. John F. Selby served Harrison County two terms as associate judge of the county court and James P. Selby was elected county treasurer two terms and county collector one term.

Joshua J. Selby, of the second generation in this particular history, was born in May, 1843, soon after the advent of the family into Harrison County. He grew up in a pioneer locality, spent his life as a farmer and stock man, and died on the old farm in April, 1900. With limited schooling, he later acquired a general fund of information, and always maintained a lively interest in public affairs. During his early manhood the Civil war was in progress, and he served about two years with the Forty-third Missouri being corporal of his company. All his service was in the home state, and he was never wounded or captured. His home was in Sherman Township, adjoining the homestead of his father, and there he acquired more than half a section of land, and had a local reputation for growing and feeding stock. He was a republican and a member of the Christian Church.

Joshua J. Selby married Mary Fail, who was born in Illinois. Her father, Isaac Fail, of German family, moved to Harrison County when it was new, and was a farmer and merchant at different times, spending the rest of his life in Harrison County. He married a Miss Rathbone, of New England family. Their children were: Bolivar Fail, who died in Rice County, Kansas, leaving a family; Webster Fail, of Hodgeman County, Kansas; Samuel Fail, who died as a Union soldier at Atlanta, Georgia, leaving a family in Iowa; George Fail, who died at St. Joseph; Mrs. Joshua Selby, who now lives in Gilman City; Jane, who married John Brown of Oklahoma; Elizabeth, who died near Bethany as the wife of James Buck. Mr. and Mrs. Joshua Selby had the following children: Rose, wife of Dr. J. A. Magraw, of Gilman City; Columbus O.; Percy, a farmer in Harrison County; and Clifford, who occupies the old farm.

In Sherman Township Columbus O. Selby was born September 20, 1867, and since reaching manhood a quarter century ago has done much to prove his ability as a home maker and a good citizen. His education in the country schools was supplemented by the old Stanberry Normal, and for twelve years he was actively engaged in educational work. His first school was the Pin Oak District near Bethany, and his last was at High Point, his home district. For two years he was principal of the Blue Ridge schools. During the summer seasons while teaching he either farmed or attended school. While a teacher he was a member of one of the old boards of commissioners appointed to aid the county superintendent in selecting instructors for the county institute. Since leaving the school room his career has been one of increasing activity as a farmer. His attractive and well improved estate comprises 210 acres, in sections 17 and 7, township 63, range 27, being a part of the George Selby Farm. His business may be described as mixed farming and stock raising.

More or less ever since reaching manhood Mr. Selby has mingled in local and national politics. As a republican, he was in the County Central Committee sixteen years, its secretary and treasurer six years, and his voice was influential in making candidates and party management. He campaigned in Harrison and Daviess counties in 1896 and 1900 in opposition to free silver and imperialism. In 1912 he became interested in the progressive movement, supported Roosevelt for President, and is now chairman of the Progressive County Committee. He is a director in his home school district, and his church is the Christian.

September 3, 1899, Mr. Selby married Miss Ethel Miller, a teacher in the schools of Harrison County. She is a daughter of John A. and Adella (Collins) Miller and a granddaughter of Dr. Ben Miller, who was at one time county superintendent of schools of Harrison County. He came from Indiana to Harrison County before the war, locating in Sugar Creek Township, where he practiced medicine and lived until his death. Doctor Miller's children were: Green Miller, Mrs. Matilda Magraw, Mrs. Alice Hart, Mrs. Ann Price, Mrs. Samantha Myers, John A. and Jasper, the last named being a resident of Colorado. John A. Miller now lives at Maysville, and is a mechanic. His children are: Mrs. Selby, who was born September 3, 1876; Herbert, of Maysville; Ben H., deceased, who was a teacher in Harrison County; Percy A., of Daviess County; John, of Harrison County; and Merl, a teacher in Harrison County. Mr. and Mrs. Selby have one son, Eugene, who was born July 23, 1903.

HON. EDWARD M. McLEOD has maintained his residence in the district near the dividing line between Gentry and Worth counties for more than forty years, and though his splendid landed estate is situated in Gentry County, the Village of Denver, Worth County, represents his postoffice address. His has been a life of signal achievement and sterling principles, and he has ever commanded the confidence and esteem of his fellow men, his title of judge being conferred by reason of his service as judge of the county court of Gentry County. To him also is the honor of having been one of the patriotic and loyal young men who gave gallant service in preserving the integrity of the Nation in the climacteric conflict of the Civil war, and in the more mature years of his long and useful life the same spirit of faithfulness has characterized him.

Edward Miles McLeod was born in Delaware County, Ohio, on the 6th of September, 1846, and is a son of Ingles and Hettie (Roberts) McLeod, the former of whom was born in the State of Kentucky, in 1822, of stanch Scotch-Irish lineage, and the latter of whom was born in Delaware County, Ohio, her entire life having there been passed, and her death having occurred in 1898. Ingles McLeod's father was a native of Pennsylvania, born near the City of Philadelphia, and in his earlier life this worthy ancestor was a sea-faring man, later learning the trade of rope making. He finally removed to Kentucky, for the purpose of manufacturing rope in a district where adequate supplies of hemp were grown, but when he found it virtually impossible to compete with slave labor in the old Bluegrass Commonwealth, he removed with his family to Delaware County, Ohio, where he entered claim to a section of wild land and developed a fine farm, besides continuing to give more or less attention to the work of his trade. He attained to the age of sixty-five years, and his wife, who was born in Pennsylvania and whose maiden name was Ingles, preceded him in death by a few years. They became the parents of eleven sons and two daughters, namely: John, Reynolds, Lewis, Turner, George, Edward, Ingles, Charles, Alfred, Walter, Leonard, Margaret and Eliza. Margaret married Jacob Wicks and the name of Eliza's husband was Amlin. The sons were reared to manhood in the old Buckeye State, and it may be noted that of the number John died in Shelby County, Missouri; Reynolds established his home in Iowa; Turner passed the closing years of his life in Southern Missouri; and Lewis and Edward were residents of Indiana at the time of their death.

Ingles McLeod learned the trade of ropemaking under the direction of his father, but when machines were invented for the manufacturing of rope the tradesmen who still utilized the old-time hand method found it impossible to compete with the modern system. Mr. McLeod became one of the substantial and prosperous farmers of Delaware County, Ohio, where he served also as a member of the state militia in the early days, his son, Judge McLeod, having clear memory of the insignia of patriotic colors which the father was entitled to and wore upon his hat, though he was never called into active war service. He died in 1860, at the age of forty-two years. His wife was a daughter of John Roberts, a Pennsylvania man who settled on "Yankee Street" in Delaware County, Ohio, and, like all other residents of that colloquially designated thoroughfare, he became a wealthy and independent farmer. Mrs. Hettie (Roberts) McLeod survived the husband of her youth by nearly forty years and continued to reside in the county of her birth until she too was summoned to eternal rest, in 1898, at a venerable age. Of the children the eldest is Emory, now a resident of Westerville, Franklin County, Ohio; Judge Edward M., of this review, was the second in order of birth; and Caroline is the widow of Henry M. Williams, of Westerville, Ohio.

Judge McLeod gained his rudimentary education under the conditions and influences marking the pioneer epoch in the history of Ohio, and though he was but fifteen years of age at the time of the inception of the Civil war he gave prompt evidence of his intrinsic and youthful patriotism, by tendering his services in defense of the Union. In response to President Lincoln's first call for 300,000 men, he enlisted, on the 27th of August, 1861, as a private in Company I, Thirty-second Ohio Volunteer Infantry—Capt. J. Dyer and Col. Thomas Ford. The regiment was mobilized at Camp Denison, Ohio, and thence proceeded to West Virginia, where it met with genuine hardships in its first camp, at Cheat Mountain. In crossing the Allegany Mountains the forces of General Lee were in front of the Union command in which Judge McLeod was aligned, but the gallant soldiers of the Union pushed forward to aid in the capture of the City of Richmond, the capital of the Confederacy. At Staunton, Virginia, the command was opposed by the forces under Gen. Stonewall Jackson, and on the 9th of June, 1862, the battle of Port Republic was fought. In the following September Judge McLeod arrived with his command at Harper's Ferry, and here they were captured by the Confederate forces under Jackson, Longstreet and Hill. The captives were taken to a point near Baltimore, Maryland and upon receiving paroles were sent to the prison camp in the City of Chicago. In February, 1863, their exchange was effected and the Thirty-second Ohio Regiment came into rendezvous at Cleveland, Ohio, where it was armed and otherwise equipped for further field service. The regiment joined Grant's army at Memphis, Tennessee, and took part in the Vicksburg campaign. Judge McLeod participated in the valiant charge on the works and fortifications surrounding the City of Vicksburg, and with others of his command assisted in carrying the ladders used in climbing the Confederate breastworks at Fort Hill. Prior to this he had taken part in the preliminary battle of Champion's Hill, Mississippi. In this battle, his regiment, which was a part of Logan's division, in Stephenson's brigade, captured a battery of six guns. The command remained at Vicksburg and performed its part in the siege until the capitulation of the city, July 4, 1863, and there the most of the members of the Thirty-second Ohio Regiment re-enlisted, as veterans, after which the command accompanied General Sherman in the ever memorable Atlanta campaign, taking part in the battle of Kenesaw Mountain and later in that of Atlanta, July 22d and July 28th at Ezra Church, and at Jonesboro, which virtually marked the close of that campaign. The regiment then followed Hood back toward Tennessee and kept that able Confederate commander under surveillance until he had crossed the Tennessee River, after which it returned South and accompanied Sherman's forces on the march from Atlanta to the sea. At Savannah General Sherman embarked most of his troops on transports which proceeded to Buford, South Carolina, and the Thirty-second Ohio was one of the regiments for which this provision was made. It took active part in the campaign through South Carolina, scattering the straggling Confederate commands that were attempting to make their way to North Carolina, to join Johnston's army. The last battle in which Judge McLeod took part was that of Bentonville, and about this time word was received of the surrender of General Lee. Judge McLeod was at Raleigh at the time when General Sherman and Johnston arranged their historic meeting and conference at Goldsboro. Sherman's army marched on to Washington to take part in the Grand Review of the victorious Union forces. The whole army of the Tennessee was ordered to the western department, to aid in the subjugation of the forces under Gen. Richard Taylor in Arkansas, Louisiana and Texas, and was at Louisville at the time when the terms of his surrender were arranged. There also the troops of the corps received their pay and the Ohio command in which Judge McLeod had proved so loyal and valiant a young soldier, was among those shipped back to Columbus, Ohio, where his regiment was disbanded on the 27th of July, 1865, and where he received his honorable

discharge—three years and eleven months after the date of his enlistment. He had participated in battles and skirmishes to the number of
more than thirty-two, but was never wounded. He celebrated his nineteenth birthday anniversary one month and eleven days after his discharge from the army. It is hardly necessary to state that Judge
McLeod perpetuates the more gracious memories and associations of his
youthful military career by active affiliation with the Grand Army of the
Republic.

After the close of the war Judge McLeod set to himself the task of
supplementing the meager education which had been his when he subordinated all other interests to go forth in defense of the Nation's integrity.
He finally became a student in an academy in his native county, and while
thus applying himself he also taught a class in geometry in the same
school. He knew and could recite by number every one of the 180
propositions in the nine books of geometry, and otherwise gave evidence
of his specially receptive memory and close application to study. After
his first year in the academy he was licensed to teach school, and he
taught two terms in his native state before coming to Missouri, in 1869.
In 1870 he established his home in the neighborhood in which he has
resided during the long intervening years and in which he has a circle
of friends that is circumscribed only by that of his acquaintances. The
judge is a man of liberal education and fine intellectuality, his maturity
of judgment and broad views representing the result of years of long and
practical experience. For fully a quarter of a century Judge McLeod
continued to teach in the schools of Missouri during the winter terms,
and as soon as his accumulations justified the action he began to make
investments in land, his first purchase having been ninety-eight acres of
his present estate, this land having been unreclaimed and he having paid
$1,000 for the property. In connection with his operations as a farmer
and stock-grower progress and distinctive success have followed the well
ordered endeavors of Judge McLeod, as he is now the owner of a well
improved and valuable landed estate of 540 acres, divided into two
farms.

Judge McLeod has been a stalwart in the camp of the republican
party, which has ever been much in the minority in his home county and
district, so that he naturally failed of election when he appeared as
republican candidate for sheriff on one occasion and for that of circuit
clerk on another. His eligibility and personal popularity overcame the
partisan handicap, however, when he was elected county judge of Gentry
County, and he carried his own township by a vote of nearly two to one
over his opponent, likewise a resident of the same township. He served
one term, and notwithstanding the fact that this republican court did its
duty to the taxpayers, the letting of the county printing to the lowest
responsible bidder caused the defeat of the two republican judges before
the next caucus of the party. Judge McLeod is president of the Bank
of Denver, a substantial and popular financial institution of this section
of the state, and he is one of the local and progressive citizens of the
state that has long represented his home. Both he and his wife are active
members of the Christian Church.

On the 17th of June, 1869, was solemnized the marriage of Judge
McLeod to Miss Caroline Green, who was born and reared in Gentry
County and who is a daughter of William and Mary (Rambo) Green

Charles died at the age of nineteen years, Lovina at the age of twenty-one, and Onis W. at the age of thirteen months; Cora M. is the wife of William Henderson, of Gentryville; Hattie is the wife of Edward Todd, of Gentry County; Dr. Walter McLeod was graduated in a medical college in the City of Chicago and is now engaged in the practice of his profession in Illinois; Miles E. is a progressive farmer of his native county; Elizabeth is the wife of Dr. Ira S. Abplanalp, engaged in the practice of medicine in the State of North Dakota, Mrs. Abplanalp being a graduate of the Missouri Normal School at Maryville; Albert is a representative farmer of Gentry County; Bessie is the wife of Christopher C. Spainhow, of Gentry County; and Carrie is the wife of Henry Seat, of this county.

GEORGE A. RICHARDSON. Manager of the Miner & Frees Lumber Company at Gilman City, George A. Richardson is one of the enterprising business men of Harrison County, and has been a resident of Missouri since 1890. For the first ten years he was engaged in farming between Ridgeway and Cainsville in Madison Township, and then engaged in the lumber business as an assistant to the Miner & Frees Company at Cainsville. Three months later he moved to Gilman City, and as local manager has done much to build up and extend the trade of this company over a large section of country.

George A. Richardson was born at Monroe, Wisconsin, May 28, 1852. His father Asa Richardson, who was born in New Hampshire, came west to Wisconsin as a young man, and spent much of his life as a banker. He was connected with the firm of Ludlow, Bingham & Company at Monroe, Wisconsin, and later the bank was carried on under the firm name of the Bank of Monroe, and still later was organized as the First National Bank. In 1870 Asa Richardson moved to Lawrence, Kansas, where for a number of years he was identified with the Second National Bank, and died on his farm near that city in 1886 at the age of seventy-five. Politically he was a republican. Asa Richardson was married at Monroe, Wisconsin, to Phebe A. Watson, who died at Lawrence, Kansas, December 13, 1912. She was a daughter of George Watson, who moved to Illinois from Pennsylvania, and spent the rest of his life as a farmer in the former state. George Watson married Miss Sarah Sutton, who also died in Illinois. Asa Richardson had four brothers: Frank, of Minnesota; John, of New York; Josiah, of Wisconsin; and Seth, of Iowa; and four sisters: Hepibah, Mrs. Becker, of Wisconsin; Mary, Mrs. Patchin, of New York; Nancy, Mrs. Norton, of Ohio; and Sarah, of Iowa. The children of Asa Richardson and wife were: Sarah A., of Lawrence, Kansas; Flora, wife of O. A. Colman, of Lawrence; George A.; Miss May E., of Lawrence; Alma, widow of Joseph Wallace, who lives near Hermosa, Colorado; Don Albert, of Lawrence; Fred O., of Lawrence; Herman O., of Lawrence; Mabel, wife of Arthur Pontius of Chase County, Kansas; Ernest A., of Lawrence; and Olla, Mrs. Guy Bigsby, who died in Douglas County, Kansas, in 1905.

George A. Richardson was eighteen years of age when his father moved to Kansas, and previously he had attended the public schools of Monroe and also spent one year at the Wisconsin State University. He began life as a farmer, was occupied in that business for about twelve years near Lawrence, and then came to Harrison County, where he is now one of the substantial business men.

George A. Richardson was married at New Hampton, Missouri, October 29, 1883, to Miss Frances M. Miner, a sister of William A. Miner, a sketch of whom is found on other pages of this work. Mr. and Mrs. Richardson have the following children: Asa Verne, a merchant at Broadwater, Nebraska, who married Beatrice Proper; Etta M., wife of

Eugene Ham, of Chaney, Oklahoma; Fannie M., wife of Haver Bruner of Broadwater, Nebraska, and they have two children, Marjorie and Miner; Flora A., lives at home in Gilman City; and Edwyl E., assisting his father in the lumber business. Mr. Richardson has identified himself with the republican party, though never in office, and has been content to do his civic duty as a business man and through his personal influence. He is past master of Gilman Lodge, A. F. & A. M., and has represented the lodge in the Grand Lodge at Kansas City and St. Joseph.° He is also a past noble grand in the Independent Order of Odd Fellows.

CHARLES F. WELLER.   The material circumstances that indicate thrift, wise provision for the future, and long continued and wisely directed industry, are the possession of Charles F. Weller, one of the most substantial residents of Clay Township and Holt County. The Weller family has been identified with this section of Missouri for forty-five years or more, and the name has always been associated with integrity and substantial position in the community.

Charles F. Weller was born in Clark County, Indiana, September 21, 1856, a son of Jacob and Catherine Margaret Weller. Both parents were natives of Germany, and his father followed school teaching in the fatherland for about eighteen years before emigrating to America. Out of a family of seven children, four are now living. When Jacob Weller arrived in America, his first destination was Louisville, Kentucky, and from there he went to Clark County, Indiana, and bought some land and took up farming. In 1870, one year after the arrival of Charles F. Weller in Holt County, the father came on to the same section, and located on land about a mile from where Charles F. now lives. He improved that property and made a valuable farm of 160 acres. Jacob Weller was a Missionary Baptist and for a number of years was a preacher in that faith. He died in Holt County on his seventieth birthday, August 22, 1888. He was a democrat in politics after becoming an American citizen, a man of exemplary habits, and both because of what he was and of what he had accomplished from narrow circumstances in youth was thoroughly esteemed.

Charles F. Weller grew up in Indiana, was educated in the common schools, and in 1869 arrived in Holt County. Another member of the family who should be mentioned is his brother Ernest, who is president of the Farmers Bank at Maitland. Mr. Weller located on his present farm about 1882, and is responsible for all the improvements that now constitute it one of the best estates in Clay Township.

Mr. Weller married Maggie A. Carroll, a daughter of James and Elnora Carroll, who were early settlers in Carroll County, Illinois, a county that was named for the family. Mrs. Weller was one of eleven children, and when she died in December, 1904, she left the following living children: Charles F., James Robert, Paul Andre, Mark Anthony, Charles Carroll, and Nellie Rosina, the wife of William Fedder. On August 16, 1907, Mr. Weller married Mary D. Munk. She was born in Germany, a daughter of Fred and Dora Johanna Munk, both of whom are now deceased. Mr. Weller is a member of the Christian Church, while his wife belongs to the United Brethren. He is a republican in politics and has interested himself in all progressive movements for the advancement of Clay Township and Holt County.

JOHN R. THOMPSON.   One of the well improved estates of Holt County is occupied by John R. Thompson, where he is successfully engaged in diversified agriculture and the raising of high grade stock. Mr. Thompson has lived in Holt County practically all his life, and commands the confidence and esteem of all who have known him from earliest youth.

John R. Thompson was born in Benton Township of Holt County, as was also his sister Helen, now the wife of Richard Gillis. The other children of his parents were born in Buchanan County, namely: Corda, wife of Frank Decker; and James D., who married Fannie Smith. Those children are likewise residents of Holt County. William Landon Thompson, their father, was also born in Buchanan County, a son of Frank Thompson, one of the prominent pioneer settlers in Buchanan County. Virginia Dysart, the mother of John R. Thompson, was a daughter of James Dysart, who settled about seven miles southeast of the present site of St. Joseph, but long before St. Joseph came into existence as a town. Most of the inhabitants of the region were at that time Indians, and wild game was so plentiful that the pioneer could keep his family supplied with meat. Virginia Dysart had six full sisters and six half-sisters and two half-brothers. After the marriage of William L. Thompson and Virginia Dysart they lived about six years in Buchanan County, and then moved to Holt County, settling in Benton Township. He bought land that cost him about ten dollars an acre, part of it being improved, and unimproved land being worth at that time only about two and a half dollars per acre. During the first years of their residence in Holt County corn, though produced with almost as much labor as at the present time, sold at from eight to ten cents a bushel, when delivered in cars at Bigelow. Bigelow was then the main grain shipping station and market for all the surrounding country, since Mound City had not yet come into existence except as a small cross roads hamlet known as Jackson Point. The first home of the Thompson family in Holt County was a small frame house, and it is still standing as a landmark of the early days and the center of many associations for the Thompsons. The original part of the old homestead is now owned by Dick Decker. William L. Thompson began life a poor young man, was industrious, and combined business ability and diligence with morality and strict religious practices, as a member of the Christian Church. He deserves the greatest credit for what he has accomplished, and at the present time owns 200 acres of well improved land. During the war he served about a year in the state militia, but did not get into any important battles, though one of his brothers, Robert, was for four years a soldier in the Southern army, and also lived in Holt County for a number of years.

John R. Thompson attended school in Holt County, along with his brothers and sisters, and finished his education in the Mound City High School. Mr. Thompson married Ila Roseberry, daughter of Thomas Roseberry, who came to Holt County from Illinois. Mr. Thompson and wife have one child, Frances, born December 29, 1909, in Holt County. Mr. Thompson has lived on his present estate since his marriage, and his farm comprises 120 acres, besides 200 acres located in the bottoms in Benton Township. Mr. Thompson is affiliated with the Masonic Lodge at Mound City, and at the present time is performing useful service to his community as president of the local school board.

F. O. MITCHELL. In Mound City the Mitchell Mercantile Company is one of the largest and most prosperous commercial institutions, and every year handles many thousand dollars worth of general merchandise. The customers of the store live in a country with a wide radius about Mound City, and the management of the store has been such as to establish confidence in every patron. The business is one of the oldest in Mound City, having been first organized by Groves & Ferguson. Later Mr. Joseph Groves bought the Ferguson interests, conducted the store under his individual name for some time, and for three years he had as one of his employes Mr. F. O. Mitchell, who has been a well known citizen of Mound City for the past thirty years, and in 1900 bought out the store. His partner in the transaction was Paul R. Davis from Kirksville, Missouri. The business was conducted under the name Davis & Mitchell, until the two brothers, F. Q. and Robert G., and the son of F. Q. Mitchell, James W. Mitchell, bought the entire establishment. Since then they have conducted it as the Mitchell Mercantile Company.

F. Q. Mitchell came to Mound City on January 1, 1884, from Hillsboro in Highland County, Ohio, where he was born. The house in which he was born was the only residence his father occupied from the time of his marriage until his death, it having been built at the time of his marriage. His father died at the age of sixty-nine, and the mother then came to Mound City and lived with her sons for twenty-two years. She died June 16, 1913, and was laid to rest by the side of her husband in Ohio. The family consisted of ten children, as follows: John H. of Ottumwa, Iowa; William S. of Mount Pleasant, Iowa, who died in 1912; T. G. Mitchell, of Paris, Missouri; J. A., F. Q. and Robert G., all of Mound City; Charles, who died at the age of three years; Arabella, who was married in Ohio to R. C. Glenn of Mound City, his home having originally been in Ohio until he was seven years of age; Jennie, who died at the age of fourteen; and Sarah Elizabeth, wife of Prof. J. U. Croson of Mound City.

F. Q. Mitchell married Miriam U. Davis, a daughter of Senator Llewellyn Davis, of Lexington, Missouri. Mr. and Mrs. Mitchell are the parents of three children, all of whom were born in Mound City. The son, Earle McDowell, in September, 1906, at the age of sixteen entered the University of Missouri at Columbia being the youngest student in a body of 2,800, and at the age of seventeen, on May 22, 1907, was accidentally drowned in Columbia. The living children are James W., Jr., and Merrie Boyd.

Mr. Mitchell has been deacon and elder in the Christian Church and Sunday school superintendent, although he was reared in the Methodist Church and subsequently joined the Christian Church and served as a member of its official board. He is active in the Mound City Commercial Club, which he served as treasurer, and is president of the library board and is a member of the lecture board, having assisted in its organization. During Cleveland's administration Mr. Mitchell served as postmaster at Mound City four years, and this indicates his political affiliation. Fraternally he has membership in the Yeomen, the Knights and Ladies of Security, the Woodmen of the World and the Modern Woodmen of America. Mr. Mitchell's father was a contractor and builder and also a farmer in Ohio. The son feels a lasting debt of gratitude to his parents, who were good Christian people, and his father was a man who not only kept busy himself but believed that the sons should be trained to industry and should be given something practical to do as soon as old enough.

JOHN W. LEAZENBY. In a number of localities in Northwest Missouri farming is the big business, conducted on a scale and with facilities similar to those which are found in the management of large industrial and commercial concerns. The careers of a number of such big farmers are noted on different pages in this work, and attention is here called to John W. Leazenby, whose farm is situated on the Cainsville Mount Moriah Road, four miles south of Cainsville in Harrison County. His farm is the old Leazenby homestead where he was born, and to which he succeeded by purchase some years ago. His landed possessions comprise 925 acres, and more than eight hundred of these acres have been employed in the production of crops. It is a large estate, well managed, and in the course of his active career Mr. Leazenby has sent many carloads of hogs and cattle to market. He evinces a fondness for the Norman horse and the Durham cattle.

John W. Leazenby was born on the farm that is now his home, April 15, 1875. His father was Wesley Leazenby, a pioneer in this section of Missouri, having come to the state some years before the Civil war and settled land that had never known the plow, and his individual efforts were responsible for the clearing up and cultivation of a large tract.

The remote ancestor of the Leazenby family in the United States was an Irish pioneer in the mountains of Virginia prior to the Revolutionary war. His name was Thomas Leazenby. He was born in the City of Dublin, and left Ireland to escape the political and economic burdens which harassed that country. He settled in the vicinity of Harper's Ferry in Virginia, at once became patriotically devoted to the cause of the colonists, and when the struggle with Great Britain broke out he joined a company and served as a soldier. A son of Thomas Leazenby was Joshua Leazenby, who was born in Harper's Ferry in Virginia, and when a child moved out with his parents to Pickaway County, Ohio. There he was a farmer and Methodist minister. He married Lucinda Toothacker, and both spent their lives in Pickaway County. Among their children were William and Wesley Leazenby, both of whom came into Harrison County, Missouri, and were followed by their brothers James and Isaac, Isaac also settling in Harrison County while James went on to Kansas. These brothers began work of improvement and development which their posterity has since carried on. Wesley Leazenby had left Pickaway County and for a time identified himself with the State of Iowa. In 1856 William Leazenby brought his family to the West, joined Wesley in Iowa, and from there the two families drove into Missouri together. Wesley Leazenby married Celia Lima, daughter of Harrison Lima a native of Pickaway County and a farmer. Mrs. Leazenby still lives, while her husband died in 1904 at the age of seventy-three. On coming to Harrison County Wesley Leazenby entered land in the vicinity of Ridgeway, but soon after the war moved to Madison Township and remained there the rest of his life. He became an extensive farmer, owning 570 acres of land, and about five hundred of that was under cultivation before he retired from active affairs. He conducted his farm on a generous scale, raised corn, hogs and cattle, and occasionally shipped his own stock to market. Wesley Leazenby built the pioneer house on his farm, and was living in the second and more commodious dwelling at the time of his death. Though a man of little education, having been reared in a time when opportunties were meager, he had a broad experience and a practical industry which carried him further than most men. His forefathers were whig partisans, and he voted with the republican cause. He had no inclinations for office, and was a member of no church nor society. During the war he served as a Federal soldier in the Third Missouri State Militia as a private, but was always very modest about his military career and said little about it. The children of Wesley Leazenby and wife were: Mary, who married Andrew Bush and died in Harrison County; Jincy, wife of W. M. Wamoth of Kansas City; Grant, of South Bend, Indiana; and John W.

John W. Leazenby grew up on the old homestead, and has spent practically all his life within its limits. His education was supplied by the country schools, but his vigorous body and craving for outdoor life made him somewhat restless of the restraints of a school room. He lived with his parents until his majority, was married and then continued to reside on the farm and assist in its management. Subsequently by purchase he succeeded to the ownership of the homestead, and has spent his life along lines similar to those of his father.

Mr. Leazenby was married February 2, 1895, to Miss Lillie Vanderpool. Her father, James Vanderpool, was a native of Tennessee and an early settler of Mercer County, Missouri, where he was a farmer and a man who commanded the entire respect of the community. Mrs. Leazenby was the youngest of three daughters and a son. Mr. and Mrs. Leazenby's children are: Alma, a student in the Warrensburg State Normal; Loucile, in the Cainsville High School; Ruth; John Wesley, Jr.; and James Eugene. Mr. Leazenby outside of farming has been one of the promoters of the First National Bank of Cainsville and is a stockholder in that institution. He takes little interest in politics and his contributions to the welfare of the community have been through the large results of his farming enterprise.

JOSEPH W. BARMANN. Having taken an intelligent and purposeful participation in the happenings which have made up the history of Andrew County between the time of his arrival in 1876 and the present, Joseph W. Barmann, of Nodaway Township, claims place also among the agricultural promoters and well-known and financially strong citizens of the county. He is a native of Ross County, Ohio, and was born November 20, 1853, a son of George and Josephine (Gertisen) Barmann.

The Barmann family was founded in the United States in 1816, when George Barmann, the paternal grandfather of Joseph W. Barmann, left his native Baden, Germany, and with his little family boarded a sailing vessel for this country. Owing to storms which took the vessel far out of its course it required eight months to make the journey across the waters, and during this trip one of the children died, but port was finally made, and the grandfather took his family to what is now Cincinnati, Ohio, he there being the owner of ten acres of land on the present site of the customs house, where he spent the remaining years of his life. In addition to the one that was lost at 'sea, the grandparents had a family of six children.

George Barmann, son of George the emigrant, was eight years of age when he accompanied his parents to the United States, and his boyhood and youth were passed in the vicinity of Cincinnati, where he was given ordinary educational advantages. When he embarked upon a career of his own he chose farming for his work, and in this continued to be engaged during the remainder of his life in Ross County, Ohio, where he died in 1888. He was married in Ohio to Josephine Gertisen, who was also born in Baden, Germany, in 1811, and whose father, John Gertisen, was likewise an early settler in the vicinity of Cincinnati. She died in 1882, having been the mother of twelve children, of whom ten grew to maturity, while six are still living.

Joseph W. Barmann was educated in the public schools of Ross County, Ohio, and grew to manhood on his father's farm, being well reared to habits of industry and thrift and thoroughly trained in farm labor by his father. In 1876, seeking a broader and newer field for his activities, he came to Missouri, and at once located in Andrew County, where he purchased a farm of 159 acres in Jefferson Township, 4½ miles south of Savannah. That continued to be his home for thirteen years, at the end of which time he bought his present farm in section 16, Nodaway Township, one mile south of Savannah, a tract of 165 acres which he has brought to a high state of cultivation; in addition he owns his father's farm, as well as a tract of 160 acres lying five miles north of Savannah. These properties total 484 acres and make Mr. Barmann one of the substantial men of his part of the county. In addition to general farming operations, he has been successfully engaged in the raising of blooded Holstein cattle and high grade horses and hogs, and as a stockman is known far and wide in Andrew County.

Mr. Barmann was married in 1883 to Miss Mary Jane Barr, who was born two miles south of Savannah, Missouri, April 26, 1862, a daughter of Boyd and Mary Jane (Jenkins) Barr, the former born in Ireland the latter in Kentucky, and early settlers in Missouri where they located in 1848. Four children have been born to Mr. and Mrs. Barmann: George, who died at the age of twenty-nine years; Nellie, who is the wife of A. H. Zimmerman, of Southern Florida; and Pearl and Charley, who reside with their parents.

Mr. Barmann has a number of interests outside those of an agricultural nature, and for the past ten years has been a member of the directing board of the First National Bank of Savannah, of which he has been vice president for five years. He is a republican, but has taken only a good citizen's part in politics, although he has always been ready to assist in movements for the public good. With his family, he attends the Catholic Church.

C. C. SCHMITT. A former county treasurer of Andrew County, C. C. Schmitt has lived in this county forty years, and while looking after his individual fortunes and proper provision for his family has also accepted the responsibilities of citizenship and has been public spirited in all his relations.

C. C. Schmitt was born in Newton County, Missouri, December 7, 1870. His father, Charles Schmitt, was born in Bavaria, Germany, April 13, 1832, and when seven years of age was brought to this country by his parents, George Jacob and Anna Elizabeth (Librach) Schmitt, who located in Illinois and spent their last years in that state. Charles Schmitt grew up in Illinois and was married in Washington County of that state to Catherine Hackett. She was born in Jefferson County, Illinois, January 28, 1841. In 1868 the family moved to Newton County, Missouri, and in 1875 to Andrew County, locating near Bolckow, where the father is still living. He has been a farmer all his active career, and though he has not been active for the past ten or twelve years still resides on a farm and retains about a hundred acres of his original estate in this section. In politics he is a republican, is a member of the Methodist Episcopal Church, in which church his wife was also a member until her death on July 29, 1914. By a previous marriage Charles Schmitt had three children: Reuben, deceased; Charles J., deceased; and William B., who lives in the State of Washington. By the second marriage there were seven children, four of whom died in infancy, the others being: J. W., who lives near Bolckow; C. C.; Mary M., wife of Asa Pettyjohn of Rea, Missouri; and Oliver E. of Oskaloosa, Iowa.

Mr. C. C. Schmitt was about five years old when his parents established a home in Andrew County, and he lived on the home farm until his marriage. Besides the training afforded by the local schools he took a course in the Northwestern Normal School at Stanberry, Missouri, and for two years was engaged in teaching country schools in Andrew County. After his marriage he bought a farm near that of his father, began to prosper in agricultural lines, and his wide acquaintance over the county and popularity as a citizen brought him into prominence in public affairs. In 1902 Mr. Schmitt was elected county treasurer and by reelection in 1904 served two terms or four years. He was elected on the republican ticket, and for a number of years has been active in that party. After retiring from office Mr. Schmitt bought his present farm, located two miles north of the courthouse in Savannah. It contains 126 acres, all well improved, and is known in that vicinity as the Plainview Farm. He is classed as a general farmer, but has made somewhat of a specialty of Poland China hogs.

Mr. Schmitt is an active member of the Baptist Church of Savannah, is a deacon and assistant superintendent of the Sunday school, and fraternally is affiliated with the Modern Woodmen of America. In 1896 he married Sarah Ann Townsend. She was born three miles north of Fillmore March 29, 1874, a daughter of J. F. and Emily (Farris) Townsend. Her father, who was born in Andrew County February 28, 1848, was the son of Elison and Catherine (Zimmerman) Townsend, who were among the pioneers in this section of Northwest Missouri. With the exception of three years, J. F. Townsend spent all his life in this county, and on the farm where he died August 27, 1900, and where Mr. and Mrs. Schmitt now reside. He was an active republican, and for one term served as county collector. Mrs. Schmitt's mother was born in Ohio in 1845, and came to Andrew County with her parents when she was a child, and died here March 26, 1905. Mr. and Mrs. Schmitt are the parents of six children: Franklin O., Warren L., Loma Marie, Floyd, and Luetta and Luella, twins.

CHARLES SCHMITT is now past the age of four-score years, and has spent nearly half his life in Andrew County. While living somewhat retired, he still occupies his farm in Benton Township near Bolckow and with ample material comforts enjoys a most pleasing retrospect over his past life.

Charles Schmitt was born in Bavaria, Germany, April 13, 1833, a son of George Jacob and Anna Elizabeth (Librach) Schmitt, both also natives of Bavaria. His father was born November 28, 1798, and his mother March 6, 1800, and the father died August 8, 1844, and the mother on September 8, 1852. In 1840 the family left Germany and emigrating to the United States located in Washington County, Illinois, where both the parents died. George J. Schmitt followed the trade of butcher in the old country, but occupied a small farm in Illinois. The children were: George, who enlisted in an Illinois regiment for service in the Mexican war and died of fever while in the army; Mary Holler of Illinois; Christina Middleton, who died in Illinois in 1913; Charles; William, who died in 1913 in Southwest Missouri, was for three years a soldier in the 111th Illinois Infantry during the Civil war; Elizabeth Williams, who died at Bolckow in Andrew County; Margaret Merick of Illinois; and one child that died in infancy.

Charles Schmitt grew to manhood in Illinois, and about 1869 moved to Newton County, Missouri. After a residence there of about eight years he came on to Andrew County in 1877, and has lived here and enjoyed a measurable degree of prosperity as a farmer ever since. He originally owned 166 acres of land in Benton Township, but sold about sixty acres to his son, and though he has not been active for the past ten or twelve years still resides on the farm and retains about one hundred acres of his original estate. He has followed the general lines of grain and stock farming, and in view of the present average price of corn at seventy cents a bushel it is interesting to recall a bit of his experience in buying corn at fourteen cents a bushel. He has also bought land in Andrew County at a price as low as twenty dollars per acre, though the general average of real estate values in the county is now several times that amount.

Mr. Charles Schmitt, while following the quiet and industrious vocation of farmer, has never sought to escape public responsibility, and has been quite active in the republican party. He served as a delegate to a number of county conventions. In early life he had no opportunities whatever for gaining an education, and only learned to read after he had a family of his own. He has long been identified with the Prairie Temple of the Methodist Episcopal Church, and served as class leader and steward twenty-five years.

Charles Schmitt was first married in Illinois in 1852 to Celia M. Parker, who was born January 1, 1835, and died November 6, 1861. Their three children were: Reuben, who died at the age of twenty years; Charles J., who died leaving a widow and six children; and William B., who lives near Seattle, Washington. Charles Schmitt was married in 1863 in Washington County, Illinois, to Catherine Hackett. She was born in Jefferson County, Illinois, January 28, 1841, and died at Bolckow, Missouri, July 29, 1914. By the second marriage there were eight children, but four of them died in infancy or early childhood. The other four are: John W., who is a farmer and neighbor to his father near Bolckow; C. C., whose sketch has been given above; Mary M., wife of A. C. Pettyjohn of Rea, Missouri; and Oliver E., a merchant of Oskaloosa, Iowa.

SAMUEL COFFMAN. Many people of Andrew County will recall this venerable citizen, who was one of the real pioneers of Northwest Missouri, became a settler on government land in Andrew County more than three-quarters of a century ago, and lived there until his death on September 27, 1897, when in his eightieth year. His descendants are numerously represented in this state and elsewhere, and for his own children he not only made ample provision during their childhood and youth, but left to them the heritage of an honored name.

Samuel Coffman was born near Frankfort, Kentucky, April 21, 1818, when James Madison was President of the United States. When he was an infant his father died, and his widowed mother brought him to Missouri in 1822, locating in Clinton County, which was then a wilderness. Missouri had been admitted as a state only about a year, and out on the frontier he spent his boyhood and received such instruction as could be obtained at home and in the primitive schools. In 1837 Samuel Coffman came to Andrew County, and soon afterward entered in the United States Land Office a quarter section of land in section 27 of Nodaway Township. That has for nearly three generations been known as the Coffman Farm, and is still occupied by one of his sons, Pleasant Coffman. To the first quarter section he afterwards added 160 acres more, and at the time of his death still owned 320 acres. In Andrew County his life was passed in the quiet vocation of farming, and there were few men who worked with steadier industry and accomplished more in clearing away the wilderness than this well remembered citizen. With his own hands by continuous labor day after day he cleared up most of his own farm and placed it under cultivation. In politics he was always affiliated with the democratic party, and was an active member in the Christian Church.

Samuel Coffman first married Susan Richardson, and of the six children born to that union two lived to maturity, namely: Benjamin F. of Andrew County, and Missouri Ann Butts, now deceased. Mr.

Coffman married for his second wife Elizabeth Richards. She became the mother of eight children, mentioned briefly as follows: Newton of Andrew County; John of Oklahoma; Sigel of Oregon; George of Wisconsin; Susan, Alice and Dora, all of whom married brothers named Davidson, and the two first are now deceased; Lucy J., the eighth child, died in infancy.

In 1872 Mr. Samuel Coffman married Mrs. Christina (Nix) Turner. She was born in Whitley County, Kentucky, March 5, 1850, and when two years of age came to Andrew County with her parents, John and Mary (Raines) Nix, who were natives of Kentucky and spent their last days in Missouri. Mrs. Coffman by her marriage to Silas Turner had two children, who are Bell Holland of Savannah and Lucinda Rhoads of the same place. Mrs. Coffman has three children by her marriage to Samuel Coffman: Martha Holland of Helena, Missouri; Bertha Ferguson, deceased; and Pleasant. Mrs. Coffman is still living, and has the unusual distinction of having twenty-four grandchildren and four great-grandchildren.

Pleasant Coffman was born on his father's farm in Nodaway Township January 23, 1878, and grew up and has lived here with his mother since his father's death. He operates 166 acres of the old homestead, and owns a part of this farm. It is well known throughout Andrew County as the Old Homestead Farm, and most of the land has been in continuous ownership under one name for more than three-quarters of a century. Pleasant Coffman has been very successful and has a reputation in this part of Missouri as a breeder of saddle and draft horses and mules. Politically he is a republican, and is a member of the Methodist Episcopal Church. His fraternal affiliations are with the Masonic Order and the Independent Order of Odd Fellows.

JOHN N. SCHREIER. Not only is John N. Schreier the architect of a substantial fortune, acquired through agricultural enterprise, but in its acquisition he has maintained the reputation for industry and reliability established in Andrew County by his pioneer father, the late Nicholas Schreier. Mr. Schreier belongs to that class of Northwest Missouri farmers who have passed their entire lives in the vicinities in which they now live, and who for this reason have an intimate knowledge of conditions here. His life has been devoted to agricultural work, and at the present time he is the owner of an excellent tract of 240 acres, located in section 28, Jefferson Township.

John N. Schreier was born in the vicinity of the Village of Amazonia, Andrew County, Missouri, June 13, 1859, and is a son of Nicholas and Annie (Zimmerman) Schreier. His father, a native of Switzerland, emigrated to the United States as a young man with little capital save his zealous ambition to succeed, and located in the State of Ohio, where he met and married his wife. Together they came to Andrew County, Missouri, taking up their residence amid pioneer surroundings and experiencing all the hardships and discouraging experiences incident to such an existence. Together they labored faithfully and industriously, and through their untiring toil succeeded in winning an independent position and accumulating two good farms, so that their declining years were passed in ease and comfort. Both are now deceased. Five children were born to them, as follows: Jacob, who is engaged in farming enterprises in Andrew County; John N., of this notice; Emma, who is the widow of John Wiedner of Savannah; Carrie, who is the wife of Henry C. Schneider of Avenue City, Missouri; and L. W., who is a resident of Savannah.

John N. Schreier received his education in the district schools of Andrew County, and passed his boyhood and youth much the same as other farmers' sons of this locality. He assisted his father in the work of the homestead, was thoroughly trained in farming and raising stock, and remained under the parental roof until the time of his marriage, when he located on his present land. This is a tract of 240 acres, lying three miles south of Savannah, and is now one of the really valuable farms of Jefferson Township. There were but few improvements on the property when Mr. Schreier first became its owner, but as the years have passed he has put in new equipment and machinery and has erected buildings of attractive design, modern architecture and substantial character. In his general farming operations, he grows the staple grains and produce, for which he finds a ready market, and he has also been successful in raising all kinds of high grade stock. Modern methods have always appealed to him and he keeps fully abreast of the advancing times, so that his labors yield him a full measure of prosperity. Mr. Schreier is a republican, but his activities in politics have been confined to performing the responsibilities of good citizenship. He has shown himself to be fully in accord with the progressive movements which are advancing the community's welfare, and lends them his hearty support and cooperation.

On June 13, 1889, Mr. Schreier was united in marriage with Miss Anna Mosser, who was born in Andrew County, Missouri, February 21, 1854, a daughter of Peter Mosser. She died October 2, 1912, the mother of two children: Alva M. and Warren, both residents of Andrew County. Mr. Schreier is a consistent member of the German Reformed Church.

JUDGE THOMAS A. REECE is one of the upstanding and forceful figures in the citizenship of Andrew County. For the past four years he has served as presiding judge of the County Court, and the people recently set the seal of approval on his administration by electing him for a second term. His chief reputation, however, is as a breeder and raiser of fine Hereford stock, and the Oakhurst Farm, six miles north of Savannah, is a model place of its kind and its improvements and adaptation to the uses of modern stock raising are the results of an exceptional degree of enterprise on the part of Judge Reece.

Thomas A. Reece was born in Rochester Township of Andrew County December 6, 1867. His parents were William A. and Obedience A. (Hobson) Reece. His father was born in North Carolina and came to Andrew County about 1848, being then eighteen years of age. He lived for a number of years with the family of Stephen H. Hobson.

Obedience Hobson, whose parents were Thomas and Rebecca Hobson, was born in Indiana and came to Missouri with her parents during the '40s. She is now living at Bolckow in Andrew County. William A. Reece and wife were married on the place now occupied by the county farm. Her parents were natives of North Carolina, settled first in Indiana, and on coming to Missouri bought the farm now occupied by Judge Reece. Mr. Hobson bought the land from the original entrant. The house, which was built in 1848, is still standing, and Mr. Hobson subsequently acquired the land now contained in the county farm. He died in Rochester Township July 21, 1889, in his ninety-fourth year. He was the owner of four good farms at one time, comprising an aggregate of nearly a thousand acres. Judge Reece's father died on the farm in Rochester Township January 25, 1881, at the age of fifty-three. Prior to his marriage he had followed his trade as a bricklayer, and was afterwards a farmer. The children were five in number, as follows:

Mary Jane, wife of Isaac Neely of Bolckow; Louisa Alice, the deceased wife of William E. Brown; Rebecca M., wife of G. W. Neely, who lives near Bolckow; Thomas A.; and Estella Elizabeth, wife of George Buck, who lives near Bolckow.

Judge Reece was reared on the home farm in Rochester Township, and two years after his marriage in 1891 moved to his present place. The Oakhurst Farm comprises 300 acres, lying partly in section 25 of Nodaway Township and partly in section 30 of Empire Township. When Judge Reece took possession 240 acres of the farm was in the heavy timbers, and he has done more than the individual share in clearing off and putting the land of Andrew County under cultivation. All of his land except twenty acres is now cleared and under the plow, is well fenced, has a modern home and substantial outbuildings, and is excellently equipped for its purposes as a stock breeding farm. Judge Reece set out the flourishing apple orchard which is also a feature of the place. Since 1905 Judge Reece has been engaged in the breeding of Hereford cattle, and keeps about a hundred head. He also raises hogs and horses, and none of the grain and grass raised on his farm is ever sold, all of it being fed to his stock, while he buys a lot more. The Oakhurst Farm is conducted under the business title of Thomas A. Reece & Son, and the firm are extensive advertisers in the American Hereford Journal and their stock has a recognized reputation among Hereford cattle men all over the country. Several of the registered bulls from Oakhurst have been regarded as among the best specimens of this stock in America.

A lifelong republican, Judge Reece in 1910 was elected county judge of Andrew County, and was reelected in 1914. Since January 1, 1911, he has been presiding judge. By an interesting coincidence Judge Reece received 1,958 votes at both elections, and in 1910 his majority was 351, and in 1914 it was 329. In all the four years of his incumbency of the judicial office he has never missed a day from court. Several times when the roads were blocked with snow so that a horse could not get through he has walked the entire distance of six miles from his home to the courthouse.

Judge Reece is an active member of Mount Vernon Baptist Church, and was elected a deacon in the church at the age of twenty years and has held the office ever since. On December 23, 1888, Judge Reece married Rosa B. Elliott, who was born in Nodaway Township of Andrew County October 18, 1867. Her parents were M. M. and Elizabeth (Townsend) Elliott. Her father was born in Nashville, Tennessee, and died in 1900 at the age of eighty-four. During the Mexican war he went out from Missouri with the troops under Gen. A. W. Doniphan and was a teamster in the long march to New Mexico and Old Mexico, while later he saw service in the Missouri State Militia during the Civil war. He was a farmer by occupation, and owned a place of 224 acres. The Mount Vernon Baptist Church stands on a part of his original farm, and he donated the land for the site. Both he and his wife were active members of this church. Mrs. Reece's mother was born in Monroe County, Indiana, February 9, 1831, and came with her parents to Savannah, Missouri, in 1847. She was married February 14, 1850, and died September 28, 1914. She was the mother of eleven children, eight of whom grew to maturity. Judge Reece and wife are the parents of three children: Verna Maud, who died at the age of six months; Virgil Thomas, who lives at home and is associated with his father in the management of Oakhurst Farm; and Mary Obedience, the wife of D. C. Middleton of Andrew County, and they have a son, William Thomas.

HON. JACOB WALL. When Judge Jacob Wall first came to Missouri, thirty-nine years ago, his possessions included the clothes which he wore, $1.50 in money, and a limitless stock of ambition and determination. With these he resolutely set about to make a place for himself in a growing community, and, once established, he directed his labors in such an able manner that today he is the owner of the beautiful Elm Grove Dairy Farm, a tract of 221 acres, located in section 33, Rochester Township, and is known as one of the substantial men of his locality. His career is one that should be encouraging to the youth dependent upon his own resources, for all that he now owns has been accumulated through his own efforts, always directed by the closest adherence to honorable and upright principles.

Judge Jacob Wall was born April 11, 1854, in Casey County, Kentucky, and is a son of W. H. and Mary J. (Lucas) Wall. His father was born May 3, 1825, and his mother February 18, 1836, both in Kentucky, where the father in his earlier years was engaged in the trade of blacksmith. In the fall of 1881 they came to Andrew County, Missouri, where W. H. Wall engaged in farming, and his death occurred in 1900 in Gentry County, Missouri, where he had resided for a few years, the mother passing away in 1913 at the home of a daughter in Lafayette County, this state. Both died in the faith of the Christian Church, in the work of which they had been prominent in Kentucky. They were the parents of twelve children, as follows: Jacob, of this notice; Hezekiah, born February 15, 1856, a resident of Hayes County, Nebraska; Francis M., born April 11, 1858, who lives in Nodaway County, Missouri; Randolph C., born January 13, 1861, a resident of Phelps County, Nebraska; Coleman L., born March 13, 1863, who also lives in that state; Ann, born March 23, 1865, who died at the age of two years; Mollie, born January 2, 1870, who is the wife of Thomas E. Wade, of Lafayette County, Missouri; Laura E., born April 27, 1867, who is the wife of William E. Sheeley, of Clinton, Oklahoma; William S., born September 7, 1872, who is a resident of Harlan County, Nebraska; Henry C., born August 19, 1874, who lives in Atchison County, Kansas; Ramon C., born July 9, 1877, also a resident of that county and state; and Arthur S., born January 15, 1881, who lives in Phelps County, Nebraska.

Jacob Wall was reared on his father's farm in Casey County, Kentucky, and there was given his education in the common schools. He remained under the parental roof until 1876, at which time, embarking upon a career of his own, he made his way overland to Andrew County, Missouri, and here soon secured employment as a farm hand, working four years for agriculturists in the county. With his carefully saved earnings he next rented a small property for two years, at the end of which time he felt ready to start operations for himself, and accordingly bought sixty-five acres in the northern part of the county, which he improved and subsequently traded for eighty acres in Rochester Township, this tract forming the nucleus for his present beautiful farm, a tract of 221 acres, the greater part of which is under a high state of improvement. Here Mr. Wall has made many improvements and erected numerous substantial buildings, including a commodious residence, a large and well-built barn and a modern silo. A nice grove of white elm trees suggested the name which he has given to the property, Elm Grove Dairy Farm, and this is one of the best watered properties in the county, having three fine springs and two good wells. Mr. Wall has engaged in general farming and has extended his operations to agriculture in all its branches, shipping several carloads of hogs annually, as well as some horses, keeping about twenty cows, manufacturing butter, and operating a butter wagon, he having a large patronage in the latter line among the private families of St. Joseph. He is known as a good business man, and in commercial circles has an excellent reputation for integrity and honorable dealing. A democrat in politics, in 1909 Mr. Wall was elected county judge from the eastern district of Andrew County, and served in that capacity from January 1, 1910, until January 1, 1912. He has made two other races for this office, but has been unable to overcome the large republican majority, there being about 300 of that party in the district. Judge Wall is a member of the Christian Church at Long Branch, Missouri, and for the past ten years has served in the capacity of deacon.

On December 25, 1879, Judge Wall was married to Miss Eliza J. Reece, who was born in North Carolina, February 26, 1862, and came to Missouri in 1867 with her parents, Joel M. and Mary M. (Fleming) Reece, natives of the Old North State. The father was born February 15, 1833, and the mother about one year later, and he met his death by a stroke of lightning in 1874, while the mother passed away in 1871. Ten children have been born to Judge and Mrs. Wall, as follows: William, born January 1, 1881, who died January 10, 1881; Maggie, born November 24, 1881, who died September 29, 1903; Mary, born February 23, 1884, who is the wife of Elmer Bowlin, of Rochester; Maude, born December 24, 1885, who resides with her parents; Loren, born November 27, 1887, who resides at home; Laura, born February 23, 1891, who is a schoolteacher; Lula, born November 6, 1893; Arthur, born May 12, 1896; Archie, born July 23, 1898; and Jacob, born July 23, 1902.

HENRY B. McDONALD AND DUDLEY S. McDONALD. One of the long established and prominent families in Andrew County in the vicinity of Savannah is the McDonalds, and their home farm, known as Elm Place, south of the county seat, is a well-known landmark in that section. The McDonalds through three generations have had many interesting experiences in Missouri and the western country, and the more important facts in the family history are appropriately related in the following paragraphs.

Henry Buford McDonald was born near Harrodsburg, Mercer County, Kentucky, May 23, 1844. His parents were Daniel and Martha (McMurtry) McDonald, both of whom were natives of the adjoining county of Washington in the same state. Daniel McDonald was born August 13, 1803, and died at what is known as the Jimtown Farm in Andrew County, October 24, 1876. His wife was born May 21, 1804, and died June 3, 1873, also at the Jimtown place.

Henry B. McDonald was educated in the common schools of Kentucky, and during the terms of 1859 and 1860 attended the Kentucky University, then situated at Harrodsburg. The battle of Perryville in the fall of 1862 was fought within ten miles of his father's home. About a year after that battle Henry B. McDonald moved from Kentucky to St. Joseph, Missouri, arriving in the latter part of September, 1863. The winter of 1863-64 he spent clerking in the store of his brother, R. L. McDonald, at St. Joseph. His brother had collected a large drove of mules which he designed to send overland and market in California, and Henry B. McDonald gladly accepted the commission to take these mules across the plains. Leaving St. Joseph, May 16, 1864, he crossed the Missouri River on a ferry boat, having a hundred head of mules and six wagons. The wagons were loaded with goods designed for the Salt Lake market. Others of his immediate family who accompanied him on this trip were his uncle Dr. Silas McDonald and son Daniel. They. had two wagons loaded with drug supplies for the same market. In 1864 there was an immense emigration to the West, and the McDonald party was never out of sight of covered wagons throughout the journey along the Platte River. For about one week they were delayed at Julesburg by the high waters of the South Platte River, which at that point was nearly two miles wide. It was possible to swim the mules across, but it cost ten dollars for each wagon, which was taken over on a flat boat. Salt Lake City was reached July 16th, and they remained there three weeks awaiting the arrival of Henry's brother, R. L. The goods were sold in Salt Lake, and the wagons were likewise disposed of with the exception of two. From Salt Lake Mr. McDonald went on west, accompanied by his brother to Austin, Nevada. There Dr. Silas McDonald and son and R. L. took a stage for California, while Henry B. remained about six weeks in Nevada. This delay was to take advantage of the abundant grasses found in Nevada, on which the mules were recruited. In the latter part of October he started for California, and after a hard trip over the Sierra Nevada mountains, on account of scarcity of feed, he arrived in Sacramento the day of the presidential election of 1864. For several preceding years most of the California country had suffered from drought, and feed was very scarce. Consequently he drove his mules down in Sonoma County, where they were fed during the winter on straw from the good crops of oats and barley made possible by the fogs from the ocean. In the spring the mules, being in fine condition, were sold and delivered to the Government at the Presidio in San Francisco.

On June 5, 1865, Henry B. McDonald left San Francisco, and after a hard stage trip arrived in St. Joseph, July 1. On the 7th of April, 1865, his father had come from Kentucky to Missouri and bought a farm south of Birds Mill in Andrew County. The son remained with his father on this farm until 1872, in which year they all moved to what is known as the Jimtown Farm north of St. Joseph, now owned by R. L. McDonald, a brother of Henry. As already stated, it was on the Jimtown Farm that the parents died in 1873.

On June 20, 1877, Mr. McDonald married Sarah Emily Rogers. She was the daughter of Edward Payne and Joanna (Steele) Rogers, both of whom were natives of Woodford County, Kentucky, where they were married. The Rogers children were: Mary Bowman Wilson and Sarah Emily McDonald, both natives of Mercer County, Kentucky, Sarah Emily having been born December 25, 1853, and after the Rogers family moved to Andrew County a son, John Bowman, was born. Mr. Rogers bought a farm in Andrew County near the old Rochester Road, but subsequently sold that and moved to St. Joseph. Edward Payne Rogers died at the home of his daughter, Mrs. McDonald, August 18, 1895, while Joanna Steele Rogers died July 12, 1900. Mrs. McDonald was married at the home of D. M. Steele in St. Joseph.

In the spring of 1880 Mr. and Mrs. McDonald, with their two children, and with Mr. Edward Rogers and a colored girl named Louisa Mosley, started for Montana. From St. Joseph they went as far as Yankton by railway, taking with them thirty head of Shorthorn cattle, a span of mules and one riding mare. They arrived at Fort Benton, the head of navigation on the Missouri River, about June 30th, having traveled by boat from Yankton. From Fort Benton Mr. McDonald started with his family in a spring wagon, looking for a location for a home. After a few days he found a ranch, known as the Rock Creek Ranch, which pleased him very much and which he afterwards purchased. Rock

Creek Ranch was the McDonald home in Montana for almost five years. During that time the family made a trip in a covered wagon to Yellowstone Park, and spent six weeks enjoying the delights of that great natural park. In 1881 Mr. McDonald bought over four hundred head of cattle to run on his range, and three years later, the price of cattle having advanced and the range having become short, he sold out and also disposed of the ranch. He then returned to Missouri, arriving February 22, 1885. For almost two years he was again located on the Jimtown Farm, but in the fall of 1886 purchased a farm in Andrew County, one mile south of Savannah, known as the China Clark Place, and the family took possession the same fall. Mrs. Henry McDonald named this farm Elm Place, and not only the trees but many other surroundings and improvements give it an attractiveness which marks it out among the country homes of Andrew County. Mrs. Henry McDonald died August 24, 1890.

To their union had been born four sons and two daughters: Dudley Steele and Mary Lydia, who were both born on the Jimtown Farm; Rufus Lee and Joanna Steele, who were born on the Rock Creek Ranch in Montana; Henry Buford, born after the family returned to the Jimtown place; and William Wallace, who was born at Elm Place. The youngest child died at Elm Place March 29, 1895. Mr. Henry B. McDonald was converted at a meeting held in Jimtown by Rev. T. M. Miller and Rev. Jesse Bird in the year 1865, and joined and helped to build the church at Fairview. From there his membership was transferred to the Presbyterian Church at Savannah, where it has since remained.

In the fullness of his three score years and ten and after comfort, peace and plenty had succeeded to the varied experiences and vicissitudes of the career which has just been sketched, Henry B. McDonald was called away by death on December 1, 1914. Both during his active lifetime and at his death there were many substantial evidences of his high standing as a man and citizen. His useful career has ended, and its influences are now transmitted through his children.

Of the children, Dudley S. is now operating the Elm Place Farm, and has gained a more than local reptuation as a successful stock raiser, especially in cattle and hogs. Dudley is a democrat, and married Grace Maxwell. The daughter, Mary Lydia, is the widow of Charles I. Rowe of Omaha. Rufus married Miss Jessie Laney, lives in Itasca County, Minnesota, and has four children named William Dudley, Virginia Lee, Wallace M. and Roger L. The daughter, Joanna S., is the wife of Dr. R. L. Laney of Virginia, Minnesota. Henry B., Jr., lives in Rocky Ford, Colorado.

JACKSON VAN SCHOIACK, who has been a resident of Jefferson Township, Andrew County, throughout his life, and who for thirty-three years has been carrying on operations on his present property in section 34, is one of the native sons of this locality who have taken a helpful part in advancing the community's interests while gaining success on his own account. His career is expressive of the possibilities of country life when directed by an intelligent purpose, earnest industry and persevering effort.

Mr. Van Schoiack was born in Jefferson Township, Andrew County, Missouri, February 16, 1847, and is a son of Machiga and Luella (Jackson) Van Schoiack, natives of Kentucky, who were married in that state and moved to Indiana, remaining there three years and came to Missouri in 1839, locating on land in Jefferson Township, where the father entered a tract from the Government. In 1852 Machiga Van Schoiack purchased the farm of his father, Josiah Van Schoiack, who started across the plains in that year for Oregon, but never reached his destination, dying on the way of the numerous hardships encountered. Machiga Van Schoiack died on the farm which his father had entered, one mile south of the present home of his son Jackson, in November, 1906, and would have been ninety-three years old in the following April. He was at that time one of the substantial men of his community, being the owner of 200 acres of land, and stood high in the esteem of his fellow-citizens. Mrs. Van Schoiack died in 1895, at the age of seventy-seven years, having been the mother of eleven children, as follows: William, who is deceased; Thomas, who is engaged in agricultural pursuits in Jefferson Township; Joseph, who died at the age of nine years; Rachel, who married Lee Hall and resides on the home place; Rebecca, who married Healby White, deceased, and resides in Arizona; Jackson, of this review; Martin, who is deceased; Holland, who married Thomas Ridgeway, and is now deceased; George, who died in Los Angeles, California; Laura, who is deceased; and Mary, who married George Rockwood of St. Joseph.

Jackson Van Schoiack received his education in the subscription schools of his native locality, as at that time there were no free schools, and as an illustration of the advancement of the times it may be here noted that today he pays a school tax of $140. He was brought up a farmer boy and remained under the parental roof until the time of his marriage, when he purchased a farm of 120 acres in Gentry County, Missouri, residing there for nine years and meeting with moderate success. Selling out at the end of that time he returned to his native township and bought his present home, on which he has lived for thirty-three years and where he has met with a full share of prosperity. At this time he is the owner of 162 acres, although he formerly had a larger tract, but sold off fifty-four acres. The greater part of this land has been cleared by Mr. Van Schoiack, and all the improvements have been made by him, his present buildings being of substantial character and attractive appearance. In his general farming and stock raising operations he has shown himself a skilled and practical farmer, and uses the most modern methods and machinery in his work.

On November 14, 1869, Mr. Van Schoiack was united in marriage with Miss Missouri Ann Turpin, who was born in Andrew County, Missouri, June 15, 1848, a daughter of Edward and Lavina (Abbott) Turpin, natives of Indiana, where they were married. Mr. and Mrs. Turpin came to Missouri in 1844 and located in Jefferson Township, where they continued to be engaged in agricultural pursuits during the remainder of their lives. The mother, who was born December 25, 1804, died October 20, 1887, while the father, born in 1806, died April 25, 1873. They were the parents of seven children, as follows: Margaret, the widow of William Colburn, a resident of Oklahoma; Jane, the widow of Sam Duncan, a resident of Mound City, Missouri; James, who died in childhood; Celestine, the widow of Frederick Breit, residing in Jefferson Township; William Isaac, a resident of Empire City, Oregon; Mary Ann, deceased, who was the wife of Nelson Graves, who is also deceased; and Missouri Ann, who married Mr. Van Schoiack.

Mr. and Mrs. Van Schoiack have had two children: Addie, who is the wife of Elias Wrigley of Jefferson Township, has two sons, George Dewey and Alva; and Laura, who died at the age of ten years. Mr. and Mrs. Van Schoiack are consistent members of the Christian Church, in the movements of which they have taken an active part. He has not been a seeker for public preferment at the polls, but at all times has supported good men and measures and is accounted one of the public-spirited men of his township.

EDWARD R. GIBBINS. A companion of the wilderness of Andrew County and a sharer in the prosperity unfolded by the zeal and enterprise of its tireless workers, Edward R. Gibbins, of Jefferson Township, has been a witness to and a participant in the wonderful changes which have transformed this part of Northwest Missouri from an unproductive, valueless waste into one of the most fertile and valuable sections of the country. A resident of this county and township for more than seventy years, no one has better maintained the personal honor and public-spirited characteristics of the best class of pioneers, or more forcibly and persistently projected the usefulness of his family into a later and more progressive period than has this highly esteemed agriculturist of section 35.

Edward R. Gibbins was born in Washington County, Kentucky, March 10, 1842, and is a son of Edward R. and Sarah (Noel) Gibbins, natives of the Blue Grass State, the former born June 19, 1805, and the latter June 13, 1811. The grandfather was William Gibbins, probably a native of Kentucky, who was the son of an emigrant from Scotland. In the year 1843 the parents of Mr. Gibbins came direct to Andrew County with their eight children and located on a farm one and one-quarter miles south of the present home of Edward R. Gibbins. There they secured a quarter section of land from the United States Government and continued to make it their home until 1865, when they sold out and moved to Illinois. Three years later they disposed of their Illinois property and went to Boone County, Missouri, and the father spent his last years with his son, Rev. Beeler Gibbins, in Harvey County, Kansas, at whose home he died at the age of ninety years. The mother had died in 1843 soon after the family came to Andrew County, and the father was later married to Mary Van Schoiack, who also died in Kansas. Edward R. and Sarah Gibbins had a family of eight children, as follows: Mary, who married Sam Miller, went to Oregon in 1852 and there died; William, a preacher, who crossed the plains in 1852 and died in Washington; Rebecca Ann, who married Sebastian Nordyke and died in 1881 in Andrew County; James Noel, a resident of Highland, Kansas; Samuel David, a resident of Oregon; George Washington, who makes his home with Edward R.; Thomas Houston, who resides in Montana; and Edward R., of this review. To the union of Edward R. and Mary (Van Schoiack) Gibbins there were born four children: Martin, a resident of Audrain County, Missouri; John, a Methodist circuit rider who died in Boone County, Missouri; B. Levi, who lives in Oklahoma; and Beeler, a missionary Baptist preacher, whose home is in Harvey County, Kansas.

Edward R. Gibbins was a child of one year when brought by his parents to Andrew County, and here his education was secured in the primitive district schools. He grew up on the home farm and has always lived in this community, his activities being devoted to general farming and the raising of stock. His present home property is a nicely cultivated tract of sixty acres, and here he is spending the evening of life surrounded by the comforts and ease which his many years of labor have brought. He has seen the changes that have occurred since he cut many acres of grain with the primitive implements of the pioneers, plowed his land with an ox team and used the same ox team in going to church on Sundays. His life has been a very full and satisfying one, and through it all he has retained the respect and esteem of his fellow citizens. A democrat in his political views, Mr. Gibbins has served his community as justice of the peace for thirty-two years, and in 1914 was the candidate of his party for representative to the Legislature. He is a consistent member of the Baptist Church, and has served for many years as deacon.

In 1863 Mr. Gibbins was married to Miss Elizabeth Ridgeway, who was born in Calloway County, Missouri, February 10, 1843, a daughter of Thomas and Elizabeth (Stephens) Ridgeway, natives of Kentucky and pioneers of Missouri. They were the parents of six children: Sarah, who died at the age of five years; John William, deceased; Martha Ellen Armstrong, deceased; Nicholas, deceased; Thomas, deceased; and Elizabeth, Mrs. Gibbins. Mrs. Gibbins lost her mother when she was an infant, and her father died when she was five years of age. In 1849 she was brought to Buchanan County, Missouri, and was here reared and educated in the family of her mother's sister and the latter's husband, John K. and Mary Ellen (Stephens) Johnson. Mr. Gibbins has reared a remarkable family, and one of which any man might well feel proud. Seventeen children were born to him and Mrs. Gibbins, there being four sets of twins, and of these children five are deceased: Mary Ellen and Martha Ellen, twins, who died aged five and eleven months, respectively; Elisha, a twin of Elijah, died at six months; Nicholas died at the age of two and one-half years; and Elizabeth died at the age of three months. The other children are as follows: John Thomas, a farmer of Jefferson Township; Rebecca Ann, who resides with her parents; Ida Jane; Charles Edward, a resident of DeKalb County, Missouri; Samuel David and Roger Lee, twins, both residing in Andrew County; Sebastian Ellis, of this county; William Arthur, who also lives in Andrew County; Elijah, of DeKalb County, Missouri; Alice Belle and Sarah, twins, the former of whom is the wife of Sam Redman, of Andrew County, and the latter of whom resides with her parents; and Nancy Elizabeth, who also resides at home. Mr. Gibbins' eldest son's son, John Edward, has a daughter, Ethel Marie, Mr. Gibbins' only great-grandchild. All the children who are married own their own homes. The children were carefully reared, well educated and thoroughly fitted to become good citizens, and to honor the name which they bear, as well as to lend dignity to the positions in life which they have been called upon to fill.

AMOS MEYER. Many of the successful agriculturists of Holt County are carrying on operations on farms upon which they were born and on which they have resided all their lives. In this class is found Amos Meyer, who has a tract of 124 acres lying in East Lewis Township, and who is known as a progressive and enterprising farmer. He has devoted his career to the pursuits of the soil, and his energetic labors have resulted in the accumulation of a valuable property and a position among the substantial men of his locality. Mr. Meyer was born on the farm on which he now lives, June 20, 1874, and is a son of Martin and Catherine (Miller) Meyer.

Martin Meyer was born in Germany, and in young manhood, seeking the greater opportunities offered by the United States, emigrated to this country. After some search for a suitable locality, he finally decided to locate in the fertile region of Northwest Missouri, establishing himself in Holt County. A man of industry and energetic habits, he was successful in making a comfortable home for his family, and when he died, in 1886 or 1887, was the owner of 666 acres, of which eighty were under cultivation. A good citizen and generous neighbor, true to his obligations and his friendships, he was held in high esteem among the people with whom his life was passed, and when he died left many to mourn his loss. Mrs. Meyer, who was a worthy helpmate to her husband, survived him several years, dying about the year 1895. Both were laid to rest in Holt County. Among their ten children three are deceased, while the survivors are: John, George, Mary Ann, Alex, Eliza, Sophronia and Amos, all being born in Holt County. They were given good educational advantages, reared to habits of industry and honesty, and trained to occupy the places in life to which they were called.

The public schools of Holt County furnished Amos Meyer with his education, and during his boyhood and youth he spent his vacations industriously by assisting his father in the work of the home farm. He has continued to reside on this property to the present time, and now has 100 of his 124 acres under cultivation, although he has not been actively engaged in farming recently as he has suffered a spell of ill health. The buildings on this land are practically the same as when his father lived here, except that they have been rearranged, and in several instances have been remodeled, while numerous improvements have been made and new equipment installed. Mr. Meyer has always been a believer in the use of modern methods and machinery, and the success which has attended his efforts would seem to indicate that his is the proper idea. Like his father, he is an adherent of republican principles, but has not sought nor desired public office. As a citizen he has encouraged and supported good movements in his community, the best interests of which he has always had at heart.

Mr. Meyer was married to Miss Goldie Hamilton, daughter of John and Mary (Smith) Hamilton. To their union have been born three children: Mary, Opal and Luther, the last two being twins, and all born in Holt County.

WILLIAM LINNEAUS WRIGHT. There are only a few country estates which compare in extent, productiveness and general value with that of W. L. Wright in Benton Township of Andrew County. Mr. Wright has lived a long and useful life, his early years in particular were filled with many interesting experiences, and his home has been in Andrew County for half a century. While it has been characteristic of him to give strict attention to his own affairs, and while there is little that lends itself to fluent description in the life of a progressive, prosperous and diligent farmer and stock man, Mr. Wright has never in all his years sought to avoid the responsibilties that go with capable and substantial citizenship. He has been a factor in the development and life of Andrew County.

William Linneaus Wright was born in Des Moines County, Iowa, February 20, 1837, a son of John D. and Celia (Hanks) Wright. His father was of a New England family, was born February 8, 1807, was liberally educated, and for five years was a teacher in New Jersey. He had the spirit of the true pioneer, early became discontented with the settled and staid life of the East, came out to the then frontier, and from that time forward lived pretty close to the edge of western civilization, moving further west as the country around him became settled up. His wife was a native of Kentucky, and it is a fact of interest to note that she was a cousin of Abraham Lincoln. She was a daughter of William Hanks, and it will be recalled that Mr. Lincoln's mother was Nancy Hanks. John D. Wright moved to Illinois in the early days, locating in Macon County, where he served as sheriff and surveyor.

While holding those offices the Black Hawk war broke out, and he was an orderly sergeant in the company commanded by Abraham Lincoln. John D. Wright had many interesting reminiscences of Mr. Lincoln, whom he frequently met in early days in Illinois, and of whose career and character he was always a great admirer. About 1834 John D. Wright became one of the pioneers in Des Moines County, Iowa. That was a number of years before Iowa was organized as a state, and in his capacity as a surveyor he did some valuable work in laying out the wilderness and many of the lines he established are still in existence. He platted the townsite of Burlington, Iowa, and for four terms represented Des Moines County in the Iowa Territorial Legislature, while the territorial capital was at Iowa City. He made the trips to the capital by stage or horseback. Mr. W. L. Wright recalls that his father once brought home a pair of overshoes made of buffalo hide, the hair being left on the inside, and they made a very serviceable article of footwear. When W. L. Wright was about six years old his mother died. After he reached the age of eighteen his father moved to Union County, Iowa, thus again transferring his home to the western margin of settlement. Very few pieces of land had been entered in Union County at that time, and the father preempted a homestead two and a half miles southeast of the Town of Afton, and secured a house that had formerly been occupied by the Mormons. While in Union County he continued his work as a surveyor and laid off the Town of Afton, his son William helping in the survey by carrying the chain. John D. Wright became one of the big factors in Union County, bought land extensively around Afton, and at one time owned about nine hundred acres. While he was engaged in his duties in locating settlers and making surveys, he had his sons and hired other men to break up the prairie.

About 1863 John D. Wright sold his Iowa interests and came to Andrew County, Missouri, locating two miles north of Savannah. Later he bought a place near Rosendale, and lived there until his death at the good old age of eighty-five. He was three times married. His first wife was a Miss Robison, and their only child died in infancy. By his marriage to Miss Celia Hanks there were the following children: Marvin, who died in infancy; Elizabeth, who died in infancy; William L.; J. D., of Oregon; Priscilla, who died in infancy; Elisha and Electa, twins, the former of Kansas, and the latter the wife of Mr. Ward of Spokane, Washington. His third wife was named Simmons. Her children were: Charles of Savannah, Missouri; Emily Parker of Oregon; Justus of Utah; Lyman of Oregon; George of Baker City, Oregon; and Mary Jamison of Union, Oregon.

William L. Wright is the owner of a fine estate of 640 acres. This includes the north half of section 13 in Benton Township, the southeast quarter of section 12, eighty acres in section 11 and another eighty acres in section 12. The place is about four miles from Rosendale. As his early life was spent largely on the frontier with his father he had little opportunity to gain an education, but by association with his father and by his own reading and observation and experience with men he has always passed as a man of intelligence and of more than the average attainments. Until he was about twenty-five years of age he went barefoot and drove an ox team for the breaking of prairie land in Iowa, that comprising the major part of his early experience. In early years he met with some vicissitudes in getting established, but finally began making money and really owes all his prosperity to his individual efforts. Mr. Wright is a democrat, and at one time was defeated by only seventeen votes for the office of presiding judge of the County Court. His party was in the minority, and while he accepted the nomination he made no effort to be elected, and the close margin by which he was defeated was really a high tribute to his popularity and his qualifications as a citizen.

On August 12, 1855, Mr. Wright married Sarah Clemmons, who died May 16, 1860. On December 5, 1860, he married Matilda A. Bonifield, who died January 8, 1871. The third marriage occurred November 2, 1871, when Fannie G. Gillam became his wife. The two children of the first marriage were: Elizabeth Jane, who died in the State of Oregon as the wife of Joe Wilson, leaving two children; John D., who married Alice Carter, and both died in Oregon, leaving four children. By the second marriage there were three children: Ellsworth, who died in childhood; Albert, also deceased; and Virginia, who married Milton Holt, and she died in Oregon October 18, 1902, leaving four daughters and one son. Mr. Wright by his present wife had three children: Canby Allen, who lives on a farm adjoining his father; Martha, wife of John Coffman of Oklahoma; and W. L., Jr., on one of the farms owned by his father.

HON. W. A. PYLE. In the peaceful pursuits of agriculture, more than one veteran of the great Civil war has tried to forget the inevitable horrors of that conflict, in which, from a sense of duty he participated and gave years of his young manhood to his country's service, but not all of them have later been called from farm and orchard to assume such public responsibilities as was W. A. Pyle, one of Andrew County's most representative men. Judge Pyle has been a resident of Andrew County for forty-seven years and his stability in every phase of life, his business judgment, his public spirit and his personal integrity have long been recognized by those who have known him in every day affairs, in commercial relations and in the responsible office of presiding judge of the county. He served on the county bench with honor, efficiency and usefulness for eight years.

In the ancestry of Judge Pyle some distinguished names are found. His paternal grandmother, Sabina Marshall, was a daughter of Samuel Marshall, who was a brother of Hon. John Marshall, who held the office of chief justice of the United States for thirty-four years, during which his decisions on constitutional questions established precedents in the interpretation of the Constitution that have been accepted ever since. Another member of this branch of the Marshall family is found in Indiana's most distinguished citizen, the present vice president of the United States.

W. A. Pyle was born in Scioto County, Ohio, January 3, 1844, and is a son of G. W. and Susannah (Rankin) Pyle. The father was born also in Scioto County, in 1815, a son of Absalom Pyle, who was of English extraction but was born in Roanoke County, Virginia, from which state he moved to Ohio and there became a farmer. In 1847 the parents of Judge Pyle came to Andrew County, Missouri, the father purchasing the farm on which his son W. A., the only living member of his family, now resides, both he and wife dying in the same year. He married Susannah Rankin, who was born in 1817, a daughter of William Rankin.

W. A. Pyle was reared on his grandfather's farm in Ohio and was given educational advantages, attending an academy at Jackson at the time of the outbreak of the war between the states. Although only seventeen years old at that time he enlisted for army service, entering Company E, Thirty-third Ohio Volunteer Infantry. His service was long and severe, testing not only the physical strength of the boy but proving that a man's courage is not always measured by years. He accompanied his regiment through Kentucky, Tennessee and Alabama, fought in the battle of Perryville when twenty-four of his comrades in his company fell, later participated in the battle of Stone River, the Tullahoma campaign, and in the fall of 1863 in the battle of Chickamauga. On the last day of this battle the brave young soldier was wounded and then taken prisoner and in danger and suffering was later transferred to Atlanta, where he was held a prisoner until February 17, 1864, when he was exchanged, under a flag of truce. His condition was such at this time as to make necessary his removal to a hospital and he was a patient at Nashville until a furlough home was secured and after he reached Ohio he reported at Cincinnati and was again placed in a hospital, from which place, in August, 1864, he was sent to Todd Barracks at Columbus, and on October 4, 1864, he was mustered out. His long period of suffering and the serious character of his injuries made his recuperation slow and for the next three years he remained on the old home place in Ohio.

In 1867 Mr. Pyle came to Andrew County and took possession of his present farm, on which the only improvement was a one-room log house. He now owns 195 acres in Jefferson Township, three miles south of Savannah, and has refused an offer of $250 per acre because of the improvements here and the fine condition of his land. He gave the right of way through his property to the St. Joe & Savannah Interurban Electric Railroad. General farming according to modern methods is carried on here and a specialty is made of fruit growing.

Judge Pyle has always been a man of enterprise and has been intelligently interested in public matters at home and abroad. Until 1896 he was identified with the republican party but the issues brought forward in that year changed his views and since then his allegiance has been given to the democratic party. It was in 1890 that he was first elected presiding judge of Andrew County and his administration was publicly justified by his reelection in 1894. Important matters came before him during his eight years of public service and the fruits of his good judgment, his business capacity and his adjustment of affairs in county finances, still are remembered as admirable results of his terms of office. It was during his administration that the contract was let for the erection of the present courthouse, which cost, including its furniture, the sum of $43,000. This handsome building is conceded the best structure of its kind as to cost and stability in the state. Almost all the county's indebtedness also was cleared off during Judge Pyle's term as presiding judge, county obligations which were selling at a discount when he took charge, selling at par when he retired.

In 1867 Judge Pyle was united in marriage with Mary J. Bennett, who was born in Ohio, December 26, 1847, a daughter of James Bennett, and they have had four children: William Rankin, who died at the age of five years; David Emery, who operates a farm adjoining that of his father, married Ora Breit, and they have three daughters, Mamie, Annie and Gladys, the eldest being the wife of Walter Oliver and the mother of a son, Harold; Judge Pyle's third child, Herbert Bennett, a well-known attorney of St. Joseph, acting for the Burlington Railroad as claim agent, married Octavia Cann and they have four children: Ruth M., Herbert Bennett, Harold and Mary E.; and Edna is the wife of Otto Alburn, who cultivates a portion of Judge Pyle's farm, and they have two children, Carl Raymond and Mary Edith.

Judge Pyle and family belong to the Presbyterian Church, in which he is a trustee. He is a member of the organization known as the Central Protective Association.

HON. CHARLES E. CALDWELL. Among the old and honorable families of Andrew County must be mentioned the Caldwells. They have been identified with agricultural and industrial development for many years and in numerous ways have made their influence felt to the advantage of this section. A prominent representative of this family in Rochester Township is Hon. Charles E. Caldwell, who is serving in his second term as county judge. He has extensive farm and stock interests and is one of the county's leading men along many lines.

Charles E. Caldwell was born in Rochester Township, Andrew County, Missouri, July 27, 1867, and is a son of David G. and Josephine (Searles) Caldwell, and a grandson of John and Margaret (Clouse) Caldwell, the latter natives of Ohio and Pennsylvania, respectively. David G. Caldwell was born in Ross County, Ohio, March 7, 1847, and was brought to Andrew County by his parents in 1851 and now lives retired at Rochester. After serving three pears as a private soldier during the Civil war he turned to the peaceful pursuit of agriculture and his subsequent life until retirement was spent as a farmer. He married Josephine Searles, who was born in Rochester Township, Andrew County, May 17, 1846, and of their nine children, Charles E. was the first born.

Charles E. Caldwell was educated in the public schools of Rochester Township and remained on the home farm assisting his father until he was twenty-two years of age. A few years later he was married and then moved to Denver, Colorado, where he entered into an entirely different line of work, entering the employ of the Denver City Railway Company, as a street car conductor, in which capacity he served for six years. In 1896 he returned to Rochester Township where he now owns a fine farm of 200 acres, on which he has made many improvements, erecting substantial buildings for stock and other purposes and in 1911 erecting his handsome 10-room residence. Judge Caldwell does an extensive stock business, raising mules, cattle and hogs for market and still largely looks after this industry himself notwithstanding public life has claimed much of his attention for some years.

In his political views, Judge Caldwell has always been a republican and it was on the ticket of that party that he was first elected county judge in 1912. In no way could public approbation of his administration have been better shown than by his reelection to this important office, in 1914. On the bench he has shown impartiality and fairness in all his decisions and that his knowledge of law is sound and thorough.

Judge Caldwell was married on March 26, 1890, to Miss Cora E. Sigrist, who was born in Rochester Township, Andrew County, September 15, 1871. She belongs to an old and prominent county family and is a daughter of Philip and Mary Sigrist, both now deceased. For many years her father was a leading business man and a public official at Rochester. Judge and Mrs. Caldwell have four children: Marie, Hazel, Ada and Philip. The family belongs to the Cumberland Presbyterian Church at Rochetesr. Judge Caldwell finds but little time to devote to what is termed recreation, but he enjoys genial companionship and highly values his membership with the Knights of Pythias at Rochester.

CAPT. FRANK KNICKERBOOKER. A gentleman who, coming to Savannah after reaching his forty-third year and mingling in the city's busy life for forty years, and was among its active men, giving daily attention to the management of his interests and the duties of an official position, is an anomaly. Most men who have reached their eighty-fourth year, especially if fortune has crowned their life's labor, feel like retiring from the strife and enjoying the ease and dignity which they have earned. Not so did Capt. Frank Knickerbocker feel. With intellect unclouded, and with manly strength but slightly abated, with an erect form, firm step and undimmed vision, he went about his daily round of affairs as in the days when struggle seemed necessary. It was an inheritance from a vigorous ancestry, strengthened by a life of activity and healthful labor.

Capt. Frank Knickerbocker, who was an incumbent of public office during the entire forty years of his residence at Savannah, was born near Rochester, New York, January 22, 1831, a son of Richard W. and Patience (Smith) Knickerbocker, the former being a native of the Mohawk Valley, New York, a member of the famous old Empire State family so prominent in history, and a nephew of Diedrich Knickerbocker. The captain's parents came West to Michigan in 1836, traveling considerably over the state in searching a suitable location to take up the 160-acre land grant which Richard W. Knickerbocker had received from the Government as a reward for his faithful services as a soldier during the War of 1812. Eventually they decided upon a tract fifteen miles west of Detroit, eighty acres being located on each side of the Village of Wayne, in Wayne County. The father cleared forty acres from the heavy timber, erected a log cabin, and there experienced all the hardships and privations incident to settling in a new country. When the Michigan Central Railroad was built through that part of the country it crossed the two eighties, and these accordingly increased greatly in value. There the parents spent the remaining years of their lives in the peaceful pursuits of farming, passed away at the homestead, and were buried in the Wayne Cemetery. They were devout members of the Methodist Episcopal Church, and in political matters the father was a whig. They were the parents of nine children, as follows: Samuel, who is deceased; Mrs. Mary Tyler, deceased, one of whose sons, Richard W., enlisted in the Union army during the Civil war, rose to the rank of major, subsequently became a well-known officer in the regular army, and died at Washington, D. C.; Chauncey W., who became one of the most prominent Universalist preachers of Michigan, had charge of the parish at Lansing, and there erected a church and organized a large congregation; Daniel, who was a farmer and died at the age of thirty five years; Ursula, who married Henry Fargo, who served in the Seminole war and subsequently met a soldier's death during the Civil war, and she is also deceased; Capt. Frank, of this review; Smith, who entered the ministry, became prominent in the Upper Iowa Conference of the Methodist Episcopal Church, and died at Cedar Falls, Iowa, at the age of seventy years; Phoebe Ann, who died at the age of nine years; and Richard, who died in infancy and was buried with his mother, who passed away a few days later.

Capt. Frank Knickerbocker was given an ordinary public school education in Michigan, where he was taken by his parents as a lad, and in his youth learned the trades of carpenter and wheelwright. These he followed for some years in Michigan, in the meantime remaining under the parental roof until his marriage in 1851, at Ypsilanti, Michigan, to Miss Eunice E. Durkee, who was born at Utica, New York, in 1833, and died at Fillmore, Andrew County, Missouri, 1867. After his marriage Captain Knickerbocker removed to Delaware County, Iowa, where he followed his trades for a short time and then returned to

Michigan. In 1859 Captain Knickerbocker came to Andrew County, Missouri, and settled in the vicinity of Fillmore, where he at once began to be engaged in the carpenter trade and the contracting business, erecting many buildings and bridges in this and adjoining counties, his operations in this line extending over a period of thirty years and being rewarded by the greatest success.

It was while living at Fillmore that the Civil war broke out and Captain Knickerbocker secured his title. Entering the Missouri State Militia, the state being under martial law, he rose from the rank of private to that of orderly sergeant, and then was promoted to captain of Company G, a rank which he held throughout the remainder of the war. He made an excellent record as a soldier, his services being confined to guard duty, although at times he was called upon to act with the United States troops.

Prior to the outbreak of the war, Captain Knickerbocker had taken up the study of law, and in 1862 took the examination before Judge Parker at Savannah, and was admitted to the bar. He continued to be engaged in practice at Fillmore until 1874, in which year he was elected state's attorney, and was from that time a resident of Savannah. He served one term as state's attorney, was subsequently employed by the county to build bridges for several years, and in 1888 was appointed postmaster of Savannah, under the administration of President Benjamin Harrison, and held that office four years. He has also been mayor of Savannah eight years, having been elected to that office on four different occasions, served as justice of the peace for five years and as city attorney for five years, and also served four years in the capacity of public administrator of Andrew County. Such a long service, unmarked by stain or blemish of any kind, denotes the possession of superior abilities. He was a lifelong republican and consistently supported the presidential candidates of his party ever since his first vote was cast for Taylor. He was a Presbyterian in his religious faith, and fraternally a Master Mason, a Mason for fifty years, was master of Round Prairie Lodge at Fillmore during the greater part of his residence there, and an "Ancient Member" of the Independent Order of Odd Fellows.

Captain Knickerbocker was the last one of his parents' children to pass away. His death occurred January 27, 1915, and with the exception of his own children and those of his brothers he knew of no other Knickerbockers. By his first union Captain Knickerbocker was the father of six children: Lewis, who is a resident of Fall City, Nebraska; Florence May, who married L. M. Woodcock and is a resident of Seattle, Washington; Cora, who married M. S. Ingersoll of Seattle, Washington; June, who is a resident of Savannah; Charles, who died at the age of two years; and Peter, who died when eighteen months of age.

Captain Knickerbocker was married a second time in 1868 to Sarah Jane Warner, who was born in the City of Philadelphia, Pennsylvania, December 25, 1833, and came from that state to Illinois with her parents. To this marriage there were no children born.

As an expression of the high esteem in which Captain Knickerbocker was held by his fellow citizens, it may not be inappropriate to quote the following, which appeared in a local publication, in closing this all too brief review of one of Northwest Missouri's most representative citizens: "Among those who have been active in commercial and political affairs of Andrew County for the past half century, there are none more worthy than Capt. F. Knickerbocker, whose office is in the courthouse of Savannah. At an advanced age he is still active and strong, mentally and physically, now serving a term as justice of the peace, having been elected after finishing the term of the late Captain Mercer by appointment. Captain Knickerbocker is a lawyer of ability, is a notary public and has an insurance agency representing six old-line companies. He was a captain in the State Militia service during the entire Civil war. While a resident of Fillmore he was elected county attorney several years, was appointed postmaster by President Harrison, serving four years, including two years of Cleveland's administration. He is known as a pioneer citizen of ability and integrity, reliable in all business dealings, and is held in high esteem by his fellow citizens here, purely upon his merit as a citizen, thoroughly capable and deserving. His life is worthy of emulation by the younger set.''

R. E. GIBSON. The Farmers and Merchants Bank of Hamilton, of which R. E. Gibson is cashier, is one of the strong and conservatively managed financial institutions in Northwest Missouri. Its officials and stockholders are in the main farmers and stock men and among the most substantial citizens of Caldwell County. The present officials of the bank are: I. M. Hemry, president; J. C. Haynie, vice president; Henry Gee, vice president; and R. E. Gibson, cashier. The capital stock of the bank is $25,000, and it offers complete banking service to the community.

R. E. Gibson was born at Browning, Missouri, on a farm, May 8, 1887. His father, S. L. Gibson, is one of the most prominent bankers and business men in Linn County, Missouri. He has assisted in the organization of a number of banks, has been a stockholder and bank official, and acquired his early capital by a successful career of farming and stock raising. He is president of the Bank of Sumner and has influential relations with a number of other institutions in that section of the state. He has three sons, all of whom are bankers: A. E. Gibson is cashier of the Bank of Livingston County; L. E. Gibson is teller in the Night and Day Bank of St. Louis; while R. E. Gibson is cashier of the Farmers and Merchants Bank of Hamilton.

R. E. Gibson was reared in Linn County, educated in the high school at Browning, and took a course in the Country Business College in Illinois. He got his early training in banking in one of the St. Louis institutions before he was twenty-one years of age, and for five years was connected with the Kansas City Bank. In 1912 Mr. Gibson came to Hamilton, and has since occupied the post of cashier. He knows banking in all its details, and his thorough experience in large metropolitan banks has given him exceptional qualifications for handling the business of the Hamilton institution.

Mr. Gibson was married in Kansas City, Missouri, to Miss Hazel L. Billingsley, a daughter of D. F. Billingsley, a well-known citizen of Kansas City. Mr. Gibson and wife have one son, R. E., Jr., now three years of age. Mr. Gibson is a democrat in politics, is affiliated with the Masonic Order, and his wife is a member of the Methodist Church.

ERNST OPPENLANDER. Industry and laudable ambition have characterized the course of this energetic and progressive representative of the agricultural industry in Holt County. He has depended entirely upon his own exertions in making his way to the goal of independence and worthy success and is now the owner of an excellent farm of 165 acres, eligibly situated in Nodaway Township. Mr. Oppenlander came from his native land to the United States when a lad of thirteen years and was accompanied by his brother John, who was at the time fifteen years of age. They severed the home ties in Germany and thus set forth to win for themselves such success as was possible in the land of their adoption, neither of the adventurous youths having had cause to regret the decision that brought them as strangers to a strange land.

Mr. Oppenlander was born in Germany on the 13th of July, 1872, and is a son of John and Louisa (Gebhardt) Oppenlander, neither of whom ever came to America. In his Fatherland Mr. Oppenlander acquired his early education and at the age of thirteen years, as already noted, he came with his older brother to the United States. Soon after landing in New York City they made their way to Missouri, and in Holt County they found employment, principally in connection with farm work. After being in the service of others for seven years Ernst Oppenlander decided to initiate an independent career as a farmer, and from that time forward his advancement has been substantial and productive. He had carefully saved his earnings and the year after his marriage he and his young wife established their home on their present farm, which comprises most fertile and productive land and upon which he has made, within the comparatively short period during which the property has been in his possession, greater improvements than have been accomplished by many farmers who have held their properties for long periods. Energy and progressive policies significantly dominate the course of Mr. Oppenlander, and his farm gives every evidence of thrift and prosperity, with all things in good order and with buildings that are substantial and modern, these having been erected by the present owner of the property. Mr. Oppenlander is not self-centered in his activities but is always ready to do his part in the furtherance of measures tending to advance the best interests of the community, the while he is deeply appreciative of the advantages and opportunities that have been afforded him in the state of his adoption. He is a republican in politics and both he and his wife hold membership in the German Methodist Episcopal Church.

At the age of twenty-eight years Mr. Oppenlander married Miss Lillie Hoffmann, daughter of Frederick Hoffmann, of Holt County, and they have two children: Hazel, born August 16, 1903; and Leone, born February 4, 1912.

REV. EDWARD HENRY ECKEL, B. D., for upward of nine years and until May 1, 1914, rector of Christ Church parish (Episcopal), was born in New Orleans, Louisiana, on November 5, 1862. He was graduated from Rugby Academy, Wilmington, Delaware, in 1880; received his A. B. degree from Delaware College, Newark, Delaware, in 1886; and B. D. from the General Theological Seminary of the Episcopal Church, in New York City, in 1889. During a portion of the time in which he carried on his studies he gave music lessons and taught in private schools, also engaging in missionary work as a layworker. He was ordained deacon by Bishop Coleman, of Delaware, in Holy Trinity ("Old Swedes") Church, in Wilmington, on June 16, 1889, and priest in St. James Church, near Stanton, Delaware, on May 28, 1890.

Rev. Mr. Eckel was rector of St. James' Church, near Stanton, St. James' Church, Newport, and St. Barnabas' Church, Marshallton, Delaware (the last named being organized by him), from 1889-91; rector of Trinity Church, West Pittson, Pennsylvania, from 1891-96; rector of Christ Church parish, Williamsport, Pennsylvania, 1896-1905, resigning the last to become rector of Christ Church parish, St. Joseph.

Missouri, March 1, 1905. Elected field secretary of the Province of the Southwest at the primary synod of the province in Muskogee, Oklahoma, in January, 1914, he took up the duties of this office May 1st.

He was the founder and first president of the Church Students' Missionary Association of the Episcopal Church in 1888, while a student in the seminary, an organization which has had a continued existence since then and has been instrumental in directing the energies of a large number of young people of both sexes towards the mission fields of the church. He has been a member of the advisory board of this association for a number of years. He has been a member of the Joint Diocesan Lesson Committee for Sunday Schools since about 1895; a member of the General Committee of the Church Congress since about 1902; a provisional deputy to the General Convention of the Episcopal Church from the Diocese of Central Pennsylvania in 1897 and 1901; a deputy from the Diocese of Kansas City (now called West Missouri) in 1907 and 1910, in both of which he was a member of the Committee on the State of the Church, and in the latter convention the vice chairman of this committee, as well as a member of the Committee on the Admission of New Dioceses. He has been a delegate from the Diocese of Kansas City to the Missionary Council of the Sixth Department and to the Missionary Council of the Department of the Southwest (Seventh), in 1908, 1909, 1913, 1914 and 1915. He was offered the position of field secretary of this missionary department in 1909, but declined. When elected to the same position under the new provincial organization in 1914, he accepted, as stated above, and is now engaged in this work, which requires almost constant travel and public speaking in Missouri, Kansas, Arkansas, Oklahoma, Texas and New Mexico. He was also appointed a delegate to the Pan-Anglican Congress in England from the Diocese of Kansas City in 1908, but was unable to attend.

Rev. Mr. Eckel was examining chaplain to the Bishop of Central Pennsylvania from 1898 to 1905; a member of the committee on the increase of the Episcopal endowment fund, 1901-04, and chairman of the committee on the same and on the organization of the new Diocese of Harrisburg in 1904; a member of the committee on diocesan apportionment in 1902-03, a member of the board of missions of that diocese, 1904, and dean of the northern convocation of the Diocese of West Missouri from 1905-14; a member of the standing committee (the Bishop's council of advice) from 1906 to 1914; a member of the diocesan missionary board from 1909 to 1914; a member of the diocesan committee on constitution and canons since 1906, and chairman of the same since 1909. Rev. Mr. Eckel was nominated for the Bishopric of Harrisburg in 1904 and for that of the Diocese of Kansas City in 1911.

Rev. Mr. Eckel organized the Pittston Library, making it a popular public institution; he organized the Williamsport Bureau of Associated Charities, now defunct; he was a deputy representing the City of Williamsport in the National Conference of Charities and Correction in New York City, in 1898; a trustee of the James V. Brown Public Library, Williamsport, in 1904; one of the organizers and a director of the Buchanan County (Mo.) Society for the Relief and Prevention of Tuberculosis, 1910-11; and a director of the St. Joseph Art Society, 1911-13. He was for several years a member of the Commerce Club of St. Joseph and a member of some of its committees. He organized St. Luke's Mission, South St. Joseph, in 1906. His fraternal relations are with the Masons, in which he is a thirty-second degree Mason and a member of the Royal Arch, and with the Benevolent and Protective Order of Elks. He was a member of the Benton Club and the Country Club of St. Joseph, and from October, 1912, to May, 1914, he was chaplain of the Fourth Regiment Infantry of the National Guard of Missouri. Since resigning the rectorship of Christ Church Parish, St. Joseph, he has removed with his family to Warrensburg, Missouri, where his son, the Rev. Edward Henry Eckel, Jr., is rector of Christ Church.

On June 27, 1889, Rev. Mr. Eckel was married to Miss Anna Todd Reynolds, the ceremony taking place in St. Andrew's Church, Wilmington, Delaware. Three children were born to them. Edward Henry; Elizabeth; and Albert Reynolds; the last named died in 1913. The first named took his B. A. degree in the second class of the honor school in theology in Oxford University, England, in 1913, having won a Rhodes scholarship while a student in the University of Missouri, and a year later he graduated with the degree of B. D. from the General Theological Seminary in New York City. He has since been ordained a deacon and priest by Bishop Partridge. Miss Eckel, after filling positions in public libraries of Cincinnati, Ohio, is at present living at home.

E. POWELL. Because of the extent and quality of his achievements, his financial soundness and acumen, his public spirit and integrity, and his generally excellent record as agriculturist and citizen, E. Powell, of Clay Township, Holt County, furnishes an encouraging example of success gained through the proper use of everyday ability and opportunities. Of him it may be said that his life work is a response both to his early teaching and the needs of his positions as he has reached them. He has laboriously climbed every round of the agricultural ladder, and now, in his declining years, he may look back contentedly over a career characterized by steadfast perseverance and unquestioned integrity, satisfied in the knowledge that his handiwork has been good.

Mr. Powell was born in Kentucky, October 10, 1838, one of the five children of David and Jane (Riddle) Powell, the others being John, Mary, Nancy and Lucy. He early met with handicaps in life, for when his mother died he was placed in the hands of strangers to rear, who were so mercenary that they kept the lad almost constantly at work, leaving him but little time to acquire an education. Thus he grew to manhood, and when the war between the South and the North broke out, his southern sympathies caused him to enlist in the Confederate army, with which he served for two years during the latter part of the struggle, but received his honorable discharge prior to its close. He was married in his native state to Miss Charlotte Elizabeth Nute, and they subsequently became the parents of two children, both born in Holt County, Missouri: Charles W., who married Maud Duncan, and has two children, Homer K. and Mary Catherine; and Sallie A., who married Frank Gibson, and has two daughters, Hazel and Irene.

In 1869 Mr. Powell left the state of his birth and with his young wife traveled by rail to Forest City, Missouri, from whence they drove through by team to Holt County. For the first year they lived on a rented farm, but in 1870 Mr. Powell bought the present home place, erecting the house in that same year. Subsequently as the years passed he put up other buildings and installed other improvements, all the present structures having been built by him with the exception of the barn, which the son built. This tract of 160 acres is now one of the fertile, productive and well-managed properties of Clay Township, and yields large and valuable crops of grain, which are fed to the cattle, Mr. Powell having for some years been extensively interested in stock raising. He also carries on general farming, and in each of the branches of his vocation has met with success. Mr. Powell is now somewhat retired from active life, having reached the age of seventy-six years, but supervises the operations on his property, which are being carried on by his son.

Mrs. Powell died September 24, 1911, at Maitland, in the faith of the Presbyterian Church. She was a devout Christian woman and an excellent helpmate to her husband, while in the community she was beloved and respected for her many qualities of heart and mind. Mr. Powell and his children are members of the Christian Church, and he and his son have always been firm and unwavering democrats. While he has not sought office for the emoluments or honors thereof, Mr. Powell has been always ready to serve his community, and for a number of years was a director and member of the school board. His upright and public spirited life has attracted to him the confidence and esteem of the community, as well as the warm friendship of many who, like himself, have developed with the forces within rather than without.

Hon. Charles F. Booher. When the Fourth Missouri District reelected Charles F. Booher to Congress in November, 1914, it insured the retention in the House of Representatives of a faithful and able public servant, a man who has already spent eight years in Congress, and whose long career as a lawyer in Northwest Missouri and whose ripe experience and judgment insure the wisdom of his choice as a popular representative.

Charles F. Booher was born at East Groveland, Livingston County, New York, January 31, 1847, a son of Henry and Catherine (Updegraff) Booher. His father was a native of Switzerland and his mother of Germany, and both were brought to America in early childhood by their respective parents. They were reared in New York State and married in Livingston County, where they spent the rest of their lives on a farm. The mother died in 1859 at the age of forty-four, and the father in 1886, aged seventy-four. Congressman Booher's father was a great reader, and was well posted in political history. Throughout his career he voted with the democratic party. Both parents were members of the Methodist Episcopal Church. They reared ten sons and one daughter, and three of the sons and the daughter are now deceased. The sons, Henry, Samuel and James, were all soldiers in a New York regiment during the Civil war, and Sam was killed at Blackwater River, Virginia, and is buried in the National Cemetery at Hampton. James died several years after the war as a result of wounds. The son Henry now lives at Geneseo, New York.

Charles F. Booher was reared on a farm in Livingston County, New York, and lived in that vicinity until 1870, when he came west and located in Andrew County. Here he taught school, worked on a farm, studied law and was admitted to the bar at Savannah in 1871. Altogether he taught school for about seven years. Mr. Booher practiced alone until 1888, and in that year formed a partnership with I. R. Williams, a firm that is now one of the oldest in the Andrew County Bar, and Booher & Williams have since controlled a large amount of the best legal practice in the Savannah courts. Since Mr. Booher's election to Congress his son Lloyd has been the active member of the firm, though its title still remains Booher & Williams.

Mr. Booher has always affiliated with the democratic party, and in his earlier public career served as prosecuting attorney of Andrew County and as mayor of Savannah. He was elected to Congress to fill the vacancy caused by the death of Hon. James N. Burris, and in 1906 was elected a member of the Sixtieth Congress and has been regularly reelected, his recent election in 1914 qualifying him for his fifth successive term. Mr. Booher is affiliated with the Masonic fraternity and the Benevolent and Protective Order of Elks.

In 1877 he married Sallie D. Shanks of Rochester, Missouri. To their marriage have been born four children: Lloyd W., a young attorney and partner of his father; Prince L., who is his father's private secretary at Washington; Nellie, at hôme; and Helen W., wife of G. E. Hines of Kansas City, Missouri.

EDWARD L. WATSON. Of the native sons of Holt County who are carrying forward the work commenced by their fathers, many years ago, mention is due Edward L. Watson, whose well cultivated farm is found in Clay township. Born September 11, 1871, he is a son of John W. and Selah (Offutt) Watson, who were married at Oregon, Missouri, to which place John W. Watson was taken by his father when a lad. In 1869 John W. Watson moved to Holt County and located on the old homestead in Clay Township, on which he has continued to reside to the present time, and which now consists of 443 acres. At that time this section was a raw prairie, with no promises of the civilization that was to develop it into one of the most fertile parts of Northwest Missouri. Roads there were none, save the Indian trails, for the Indians were still numerous here at that time and were frequently fed at the home of the Watsons, with whom they were on the best of terms. The wild game at that time was so plentiful that the hunters would not think of going after such small game as ducks, and on a number of occasions Mr. Watson brought home four deer as the result of one day's shooting. The house that he put up not long after his arrival is still standing and was erected on a corn field, as is evidenced by the fact that the withered stalks still stand under the house. John W. Watson still survives, one of the oldest pioneers of his locality. Primarily a farmer, he has never been a seeker after political honors, but has served his community faithfully as a member of the school board. The mother passed away in May, 1914, leaving four children, all of whom were born on the old homestead in Clay township: Edward L., of this review; L. H., who married Lena Lutz; C. N., who married Gertrude Foster; and Elmira, who married F. A. King.

Edward L. Watson was reared amid the rural surroundings of his father's home and acquired an ordinary education in the district schools. He was reared to the pursuits of the farm, and has continued to devote himself thereto throughout his life. At this time he is the possessor of eighty acres of well-cultivated land, on which he has made the greater number of improvements, his present home having been enlarged from the original two-room house that was built on this property as early as 1865. His operations in general farming and stockraising have been uniformly successful, and his success has come to him through the medium of his own efforts and perseverance. Fraternally, Mr. Watson is a member of the Woodmen of the World. He has not engaged to any considerable extent in public affairs, but has always been ready to lend his aid to beneficial and progressive movements, and has the entire confidence of his community as a man of the strictest integrity.

Mr. Watson was married in Holt County, to Miss Clara Goodhart, who was reared in this county, although born in Ohio, a daughter of John A. and Minerva (Buckingham) Goodhart, the former born in Cumberland County, Pennsylvania, and the latter at Richmond, Ohio. The parents of Mrs. Watson came to Missouri in 1874, settling in Holt County, where they have spent their remaining years in the pursuits of the soil. The mother is of the old school Baptist and the father of the Methodist Episcopal faith. They had two children: Clara, who became Mrs. Watson; and Oliver C., a member of the Independent Order of Odd Fellows and the Woodmen of the World, who is engaged in farming in Holt county, and who married Laura Shield, by whom he has three children, all born in this county: Ethel, Theodore and Bryan. Three children have come to Mr. and Mrs. Watson, all born on the present farm: Dale, born January 9, 1895; Imogene, born August 16, 1896; and Velma, born October 3, 1903. They have been given good educational advantages, and well trained for the places in life which they will be called upon to fill.

SETH H. WHITE. Elected sheriff of Clay County in 1912, Seth H. White represents the progressive farming element and the substantial rural citizenship of his section of Northwest Missouri. Mr. White is a practical and successful farmer, has a large acquaintance and is very popular in his home county, and by experience and native ability is well fitted to discharge the important duties with which his fellow citizens have intrusted him. Mr. White, besides his official connections with one of the most important counties in this quarter of the state, is further identified with the region through his pioneer family relationships, since the Whites were among the first settlers and did their share in developing the country from the wilderness.

Seth H. White was born near Missouri City November 26, 1867. His grandfather, Jeremiah White, was born in Fayette County, Kentucky, September 15, 1812, emigrated to Missouri in 1834, and acquired his first land from the Mormons, who at that time comprised a large part of the population in this section of Missouri. His land was situated near Missouri City. In 1836 Jeremiah White married Elizabeth McQuiddy. He was a man of unusual enterprise, and possessed the adventurous spirit of early settlers. In 1850 he made the journey overland to California, as a gold seeker, and found employment on the coast with a surveying gang, carrying a chain at a wage of five dollars a day. Subsequently he managed a livery stable in Sonoma, California. His return home was made by way of the Isthmus of Panama, to New Orleans, and thence up the river to Clay County, where he remained quietly engaged in farming until his death. Jeremiah White was a whig in politics, but all members of the subsequent generations have been democrats.

Benjamin White, father of Seth H. White, was born in Missouri City June 21, 1839. He married Sallie Marlatte, who was born in the northeastern part of Clay County May 4, 1844. Her parents, Thomas and Mahala (Munkers) Marlatte, were from Kentucky and among the earliest of Clay County's pioneers. As to religion, all the early members of these families were Hard-shell Baptists. Benjamin White and wife are both still living on a farm in Clay County. They were the parents of three children: Seth H., James, of Clay County, and Carrie, wife of Charles Hart, of Clay County. Benjamin White at the beginning of the Civil war enlisted in the Confederate service in Scott County, and served until illness obliged him to leave the ranks in 1863. After that he lived in the West, in Colorado, until after the close of the war, and has since been identified with farming pursuits in Clay County.

Seth H. White was reared on a farm, attended the common schools, entered the State Normal School at Warrensburg, and in 1888 took up work as a teacher, and was successfully engaged in teaching rural schools for five years. Following this came an active period of farming in Missouri City, and in 1903 he engaged in the hardware business at Missouri City. Selling out his mercantile business in 1908, Mr. White retired to the farm, and was employed with its management until his election in the fall of 1912 to the office of sheriff on the democratic ticket. Mr. White on January 1, 1913, took up the duties of his office and has since had his home in Liberty.

Mr. White is affiliated with the Masonic Order, the Independent Order of Odd Fellows and the Knights of Pythias. On November 6, 1905, he married Mary C. Calvert, who was born in Clay County June 7, 1869, daughter of F. H. Calvert, who is still living in this county. Mr. and Mrs. White have one child, Ford, still at home.

OSCAR M. PETERS for the last twelve years has been associated with a group of men who are active as officers and directors of the Cosby State Bank, in the capacity of cashier of that institution, which is one of the strong and well conducted country banks of Northwest Missouri. For a number of years before taking up banking Mr. Peters was known in Andrew County as a teacher, and is a thoroughly educated, progressive and public spirited citizen in all his activities and relations with the community.

His home has been in Andrew County nearly fifty years, but he was born in Preble County, Ohio, October 22, 1864, a son of Joseph and Rebecca (Reddick) Peters. His father was born in Preble County near the birthplace of his son, while the mother was born across the state line in Indiana. In 1865 the family left Ohio and came to Northwest Missouri. They drove across the country in a wagon and there were seven families who comprised the party. Joseph Peters located on a farm three miles northwest of Cosby in Rochester Township, and spent the rest of his life in that vicinity as an active farmer. He retired to Cosby in 1891. He was born April 10, 1827, and died at Cosby January 25, 1911, when past eighty years of age. His wife was born January 16, 1831, and is now living in her eighty-fifth year in Cosby. Besides farming the father also did much business as an auctioneer, and for one term served as a judge of the County Court. Politically he was a republican. During the Civil war, while living in Ohio, he was drafted for service, but paid the salary of a man who was working for him to go as a substitute. At that time help was very scarce, and almost all the burdens of farming fell upon his shoulders. After swinging a cradle in the harvest fields all day long, he would spend half the night binding up the grain. In Andrew County he and his family were members of the Long Branch Christian Church. The children were: Frances Ellen, who died May 10, 1913, married T. J. Fox, also deceased, who was for a number of years a merchant at Cosby; Mary H., who now lives with her mother in Cosby, married the late William A. Brooks, who was an auctioneer; Edward M. is in the lumber and hardware business at Rushville, Missouri, but lived at Cosby a number of years and established the Cosby State Bank, and later was in banking at Rushville; Clara B. is the wife of T. E. Maughmer, a retired farmer at Union Star.

Oscar M. Peters has spent all his life in Andrew County since he was one year of age, with the exception of the time he was away at college. He attended the public schools, and for two years was a student in the Stanberry Normal School. After that his services were employed as a teacher, being principal of the schools at Rosendale two years. From 1895 to 1900 Mr. Peters was a student in Drake University at Des Moines, Iowa, and has the degree bachelor of didactic science from that institution, spending one year in the university in the study of the sciences after his graduation. He later became principal of the schools at Union Star, and then spent a year in the same line of work at King City. In 1903 Mr. Peters took his present post as cashier of the Cosby State Bank, and for the past twelve years has devoted his entire attention to banking. While it is the nature of bankers to take a conservative attitude in business affairs, Mr. Peters has a genial personality which won him and the bank many friends and patrons, and he can be depended upon to support movements undertaken for the general welfare of this community.

Politically he is a republican, is a member of the Long Branch Christion Church and has fraternal affiliations with the Independent Order of Odd Fellows, and the Modern Woodmen of America. In 1893 Mr. Peters married Carrie E. Strock. She was born three miles west of Cosby November 14, 1865, a daughter of Judge James F. and Minerva (Spence) Strock, who were natives of Kentucky and early settlers in Andrew County, and both are now deceased. Mrs. Peters before her marriage was also a teacher in Andrew County, and was in the Rosendale schools at the same time with her husband. While he was a student in Drake University she took work in the music and department of expression in the same college. Mr. and Mrs. Peters have three children: Lucile Majorie Peters, born November 27, 1899; Virgil Leland Peters, August 4, 1906; and Mae Evalyn Peters, May 31, 1908.

JACOB HEINZ. The Town of Cosby in Andrew County is built largely on land originally comprised within the farm of Jacob Heinz, who since the railroad was built and the town started has been one of the most active factors in its development. Mr. Heinz is no longer engaged in active farming, having turned over the responsibilities of his land to his sons, and is now chiefly engaged as president of the Cosby State Bank. The other officers of the bank are: F. E. Kline, vice president; O. M. Peters, cashier; and P. E. Newburn, assistant cashier. The Cosby State Bank has had a successful and prosperous record for a number of years, and a statement of business in November, 1914, showed its total resources to be nearly one hundred and thirty thousand dollars. It has capital stock of ten thousand dollars, with a surplus fund of a like amount. and undivided profits of nearly two thousand dollars. Its standing and popularity in the community is well indicated by its total deposits, which amount to considerably more than a hundred thousand dollars.

Jacob Heinz has spent about sixty years of his long and active life in Missouri, and is the example of a poor German boy who came to this country with no capital or resources except willing hands and for many years has been one of the prosperous and influential citizens. He was born in Wuertemberg, Germany, February 7, 1836, a son of Louis and Catherine (Meck) Heinz. His parents spent all their lives in the old country, but most of the children came to America. The five children were: Jacob; Kate, widow of George Haas of St. Joseph; Anna, widow of William Fick of Colorado Springs; Barbara, widow of Joseph Zimmerman of St. Joseph; and Louis, who lives near Cosby.

Jacob Heinz left the old country, where he had been reared on his father's farm and had acquired a substantial education, at the age of eighteen, being the first of the children to leave Germany and find a home in the New World. His first location was at Weston in Platt County, Missouri, and he was employed in a blacksmith shop during the fall, and spent part of his time in the winter in work on a farm. He then moved to the country near Rushville, and was employed at different places in Platt and Buchanan counties as a farm hand until 1860. He then worked two years in various lines of employment, and during the war times served for three years in the Missouri State Militia. In 1863 Mr. Heinz bought a small piece of land near Rushville, and that was the start of his independent career which has been accumulating success ever since.

In 1864 Mr. Heinz married Mary Mereoff, who was born in Germany, and died at Cosby in 1894. After his marriage Mr. Heinz continued farming near Rushville, and about 1875 came to Andrew County, and bought eighty acres of land lying across the line in DeKalb County. Later he bought ninety-six acres, comprising a portion of the present site of Cosby. At that time the railroad had not been constructed through this part of the country and when it was built the Town of Cosby was laid out around a station on the route. All that portion of the town lying north of Main Street is built upon land platted from Mr. Heinz's farm. When he bought this land he paid $30 an acre and it was considered a rather fancy price at the time. For the past ten years he has been retired from active farming, allowing his sons to conduct the seventy acres which still remain of the old homestead. Mr. Heinz has been president of the Cosby State Bank since its organization.

Politically he has been a republican since he became an American citizen, and has been identified with that party since Mr. Lincoln was first elected to the presidency. His church is the Methodist Episcopal. To his marriage were born four children: Louis, who is a farmer conducting the eighty acres bought by Mr. Heinz about forty years ago, situated in DeKalb County half a mile east of Cosby; Mollie, wife of Calvin Wild of St. Joseph; Gustav, a farmer in Monroe Township; and one that died in infancy.

FRANK E. KLINE. When Frank E. Kline began business as a merchant at Cosby twenty years ago he had only a thousand dollars in capital, half of which was borrowed, and his chief guaranty for success was a record of industry and integrity, and a thorough confidence on his own part in his ability to meet obstacles as they should come up. This confidence has been well justified by his record of accomplishment since that time. Mr. Kline is a general merchant, handling hardware, implements, dry goods, groceries and other general merchandise. At the present time he carries a stock of goods valued at about fifteen thousand dollars, and also owns the building in which his store is conducted. He has been one of the leading factors in the development of this thriving little village of Andrew County. In 1913 he conducted the Kline Opera House, 36x60 feet, a two-story frame building, covered with galvanized sheeting. In 1913 he also built and has since operated the electric light plant, which supplies lighting current for most of the town. He is vice president of the Cosby State Bank and is one of the first group of half a dozen men who controlled most of the affairs in that locality.

Franklin Elliott Kline was born in Madison County, Illinois, December 27, 1868. His father, Godlove Kline, was born in Maryland in 1824, a son of Godlove and Nancy (Byerly) Kline. Both parents were native of Saubia, Germany, were married in the old country, and soon afterwards set out for the United States. The vessel on which they were passengers was shipwrecked, and only they and one passenger were rescued. On arriving in Maryland all their possessions were sold to pay for the passage. Later the family moved from Maryland to Ohio, and the grandfather died there, while his wife passed away at Madisonville, Illinois. Their children were August, John, Stephen, Godlove, Elizabeth and Mary.

Godlove Kline, father of the Cosby merchant, was married in Vinton County, Ohio, to Nancy Byerly, who was born in Vinton County in 1827. In 1856 they moved to Madison County, Illinois, lived there and at Quincy until they moved out to Bates County, Missouri, in 1877, and in the fall of the same year located at Rochester in Andrew County. There

the father passed away in 1897 at the age of sixty-six, and his wife died in February, 1907, at the age of seventy-nine. Godlove Kline spent his life as a farmer, and had a large estate in Illinois. There were eleven children, namely: Mary Elizabeth, wife of John Kurth of Cosby; Isabelle, who died when about twenty-one years of age; Melsina, who died in infancy; Jacob I., of Springfield; Margaret, wife of G. Roper of Stubblefield, Illinois; Elijah, who died in Bates County, Missouri, when about forty years of age, leaving a widow and four children; Kate, wife of A. L. Nash of St. Joseph; John W., who lives in Savannah; Daniel, who died at the age of two and a half years; Mazie, who died in 1902 as the wife of Robert Hawk; and Franklin Elliott.

Frank E. Kline has been a resident of Andrew County since 1877, when he was nine years old, and received most of his education in the local schools here. For ten years he was employed in a store at Rochester for his brother, J. W. Kline, and there gained a thorough training and experience in merchandising. For two years he was employed in the Artesian Ice Plant at St. Joseph. It was on April 9, 1895, that Mr. Kline started in his present business with the limited capital and facilities already noted. Politically Mr. Kline is a republican, and for eighteen years served as postmaster at Cosby, from April 22, 1897, to January 1, 1914. Fraternally he is affiliated with the Modern Woodmen of America.

On May 2, 1894, he married Mary Snowden, who was born in Andrew County, a daughter of Judge Jonathan and Mary Elizabeth (Carson) Snowden, now deceased, and early settlers of Andrew County. Mr. and Mrs. Kline have five children: Maggie May, who died at the age of eight years; Fred B., who is now attending high school at Savannah; Harold, Frank and Marion.

WALTER SCOTT HUDSON. Few names are more widely or favorably known in Northwest Missouri than that of Hudson, which family has contributed men of worth and substance to professional and business circles, and to military and public life.

The name Hudson, since the first progenitor came over from England, has always been associated with pioneer work and pioneer developments. Nearly all of them have been pioneers, pushing westward with the early stages of civilization.

Walter Scott Hudson, the subject of this sketch, was a descendant of William Hudson, about whose history, at this time, but little is known. The records in the family show that in 1702 William Hudson purchased from William Penn 1,600 acres of land in Lancaster County, Pennsylvania, for sixteen pounds. This land is about twenty miles north of Lancaster City. Penn had a provision in the deed that eight acres of the land should be deeded by Hudson to the church, the reservation being in the following words: "Eight acres of land as a site for a house in which to worship Almighty God." This land is still held by the church, and as one building wore out with age, another and better one has taken its place, and today there is a fine large Presbyterian Church on this same site, known as the "Blue Bell Church."

George Hudson was the son of William Hudson, and like his father

the Delaware River with his army in three divisions. The night was cold, dark and stormy; the river was crowded with broken ice sweeping down its rapid current, making the crossing so difficult that only the division commanded by Washington in person succeeded in getting over. Hudson had preceded the army by several hours, had selected the landing place on the Trenton side, and, standing on the bank of the river with his clothes frozen to his back, pointed out the landing for the troops as they arrived. He was also engaged in the fight with the Hessians at Trenton at 8 o'clock the next morning.

On the 11th day of September, 1777, George Hudson took the oath of allegiance under the act of the General Assembly of Pennsylvania, passed June 13, 1777.

George Hudson was married to Isabella Buchanan, an aunt of President James Buchanan, on the 9th day of May, 1775, and had thirteen children, seven sons and six daughters. He purchased a large tract of land adjoining "Shade Gap," part of it having been granted by John Penn, Thomas Penn, and Richard Penn, presumably heirs of William Penn. He built his first house, which was a mere cabin, and later established a woolen and grist mill, which were of great value to the early community, and also built a Presbyterian Church. He was a justice of the peace appointed by the governor, and held the office many years; was a man of fine qualities and good judgment and great usefulness and influence. He was a Scotch Presbyterian, and a man of strong faith. The exact date of the death of George Hudson is not known, but he signed his will April 26, 1819, and it was proved March 12, 1821, in Huntington, Huntington County, Pennsylvania.

Walter Buchanan Hudson was a son of George Hudson and Isabella (Buchanan) Hudson, and was one of the pioneers in Western Pennsylvania, having located at Shirleysburg (at that time Fort Shirley), in Huntington County. He married Eliza Barton, daughter of Kimber A. Barton, of Shirleysburg, Pennsylvania. Mr. Barton was the first postmaster of Shirleysburg, appointed February 22, 1805, and served until February 13, 1824.

Walter Buchanan Hudson was a man of powerful physique and a man of scholarly attainments. He was very accurate and a practical lawyer, giving instructions in that science to young men of that day. He was a man of books, and spent much of his time in the study of philosophy, astronomy, and the languages, and without the aid of a teacher or the advantages of early education, made wonderful attainments in the knowledge of these branches. He died at the age of sixty-seven years. The exact date of his death is not now known, but it was about 1850-54. Eliza (Barton) Hudson died in the year 1857.

Walter Buchanan Hudson was a justice of the peace in his home town for many years, was a man widely known and of large influence in the community. He was a member of the Presbyterian Church, in which he had been reared, and like his father was a man of strong faith.

Walter Scott Hudson was a son of Walter Buchanan Hudson and Eliza (Barton) Hudson, of English ancestry on both sides. He left his native Town of Shirleysburg, Pennsylvania, in the early '20s, locating in Peoria, Illinois. Being a civil engineer, he was employed to assist in locating the first railroad that crossed the State of Iowa. This was in the early '50s and before the outbreak of the Civil war. He came from Huntington County, Pennsylvania, his birthplace, his natal date being May 4, 1831. He was liberally educated at Shirleysburg, Pennsylvania, where a reputable college was maintained, and for a time taught school in Pennsylvania. He gave instructions to pupils in surveying, a subject that was then regarded as of great importance.

Upon discontinuing his activities in railroad work, Mr. Hudson came directly to Worth County, which was then a part of Gentry County, and secured the appointment to the position of deputy surveyor. Subsequently he took up a homestead in the Worth end of the county, and took up teaching again in order to add to his meager income. Mr. Hudson surveyed off Worth County from Gentry County, and later surveyed the county seat, Grant City, and the original plat of Grant City is in his handwriting.

After the organization of Worth County, Walter S. Hudson was elected county surveyor, a position which he held for something like twenty years. In 1868 he was elected assessor of Worth County, holding the two offices, assessor and surveyor. In 1870 he was elected clerk of the Circuit Court of Worth County, Missouri, which office he held four years. He was elected justice of the peace several terms, was always loyal to democratic principles, and was identified with the political life of the county from the time of his advent here in the fall of 1856 until his death, which occurred July 9, 1882. He took an interest in all schools, their organization and their welfare, and in the bringing of the railroad to Grant City he played an important part. He proved up on a homestead which he took and part of which he held until his death, and all his investments were made in lands of the pioneer sort.

In his manner he was one who made his visitors feel at ease and comfortable, and never departed from that culture which he brought with him from the East.

Mr. Hudson was somewhat reserved as a conversationalist, seldom told his guests a story, had an unusual memory, and was a man who practiced accuracy in the little things of life. For instance, he insisted that his children should close the door in just such a manner, that they should never cross their legs in the presence of company, that they should be seen to laugh and not to be heard, that they must use their right hand in writing, and many other "straight-jacket" rules. His characteristics or the absence of them, however, were most pronounced. He was not a man of dress, allowing himself to wear an old hat or a pair of shoes until long after they were worn out, wearing a collar or going without one as the case happened, and never making an apology for his personal appearance. He retained friends always. He was rather slow to make them, but attachments once formed were invariably lasting. It is said of him that he made no enemies, and a reason for this lay in permitting his rights to be imposed upon frequently and suffering himself rather than make an enemy of some neighbor by rebuking him.

In the matter of legal forms, Walter S. Hudson was an adept. He possessed the requirements to draw up deeds, mortgages, and contracts according to law and was the only man in the county who was relied upon for those things before the days of printed forms. He was a splendid penman, and did his best in everything that he undertook. He had refined literary tastes and was an accomplished musician. Brought up in the faith of the Presbyterian church and always maintained an interest in church work and ministers. No man demonstrated more integrity than he did, and in every word and act was just what he pretended to be.

He occasionally delivered public utterances, although he did not pose as a speaker or orator, and his speeches were given reluctantly, and only when he was urgently pressed to do so, but his mastery of the vocabulary was sufficient for him always to have the right word at the right time and place. He became one of the early members of the first Masonic lodge organized in Worth County, at Allendale, and was one of the first secretaries of the lodge, and not since his regime has that body had a recording officer who has approached him in the nicety and care with which he kept the records of the order.

Mr. Hudson never visited his native place after he left it. He was a member of a numerous family of Huntington County, Pennsylvania. He had three brothers, George, Barton Augustus, and James; two sisters, Margaretta and Mary Isabella, all of whom are dead. The dates of their births cannot be given. Walter S. Hudson was the youngest member of his family. The family married into the Buchanan family, and President James Buchanan was an own cousin of Walter Scott Hudson. During the Civil war the latter remained neutral, as nearly as possible, although his own people were Unionists, and some of them were in the army of the North, including his brother, Barton Augustus, who is supposed to have been killed at the Battle of Gettysburg and sleeps in an unknown grave. He was in Captain Moore's company, who was also a cousin of Mr. Hudson. His wife's people were of the slave-holding class, and his father-in-law, Dr. Samuel S. Early, was a man of strong influence, a native of Tennessee and a pioneer of Worth County, where for years he was actively engaged in the practice of medicine. One of his sons, James Early, is still living in Grant City, now past eighty years old. During the campaign of 1860 Mr. Hudson supported Douglas for President. He was a man who loved to help others. In the early work of improving the county, to which he was always devoted, he gave time without stint and without pay in the aid of bridge building, old-time road making, schoolhouse construction, early courthouse construction, and was one of the owners and promoters of the first democratic news-paper (the Worth County Times) ever published in the county, and seemed to have none of the sordid money-making idea with him.

Mr. Hudson was a large man, standing six feet without his shoes, well proportioned, with no surplus flesh, had a fair complexion, blue eyes and black hair.

Walter Scott Hudson was married in April, 1858, in Gentry County (now Worth County), Missouri, prior to the Civil war, to Miss Ellen Early, a daughter of Dr. Samuel S. and Julia Ann (Botts) Early. Mrs. Early was a native of Kentucky. The Early family contained such a distinguished son as Gen. Jubal A. Early of the Confederate army. Mrs. Hudson was a small, neatly proportioned woman, active and grace-ful in her movements, with medium complexion, dark hair and small gray eyes. She was entirely devoted to her family, taking no interest in social affairs, was not inclined to travel or extend her acquaintances, and survived her husband twenty-three years. She was born on the 2d day of June, 1836, and died on the 1st day of May, 1905. She was the mother of ten children, seven of whom had the misfortune to survive her. Two of her children died in infancy, and a son, John, died February 3, 1883, unmarried, aged twenty-one years and one day. The following children of Walter Scott Hudson and Ellen (Early) Hudson are still living: Othniel Bruner, Ada B., Cora L., Kate, Peter, Mark P., and Walter Scott, all of Grant City. Othniel Bruner and Mark Pomeroy are the only members of the family that are married, Mark P. having been married to Grace L. Davidson on September 10, 1914.

The Hudson family is one which stands out prominently as one with few marriages. Walter Scott Hudson was the only son of his parents' family to marry, and the other members of the family among the older

part in public affairs, is a son of the author and planner of the county seat of Worth County (Grant City), Walter Scott Hudson and Ellen (Early) Hudson. He was born on a farm in Worth County, Missouri, February 16, 1860, remaining on a farm most of the time until he was sixteen years old. He secured his education in the country public schools and the Grant City High School. He taught one term of school in Worth County in the old Amity district. Securing some experience as a lad in a clerkship, at the age of nineteen, he engaged in merchandising on his own account at Redding, Iowa, where he remained for about five years. During that time, what time he could spare from his business, he devoted to the study and practice of law.

Having decided upon a career in law, Mr. Hudson secured a clerkship in a law office in Grant City, where he spent most of his time for three years, and followed this by a law course in the University of the City of New York, where he graduated on the 1st day of June, 1894, and received the degree of Bachelor of Laws. Prior to this time he had spent several years pettifogging before country justices of the peace and occasionally appearing before the Circuit Court. Mr. Hudson was admitted to the bar in Grant City, Missouri, on the 20th day of October, 1893. During much of this time he felt himself capable, and was, of practicing law as an admitted attorney, but seemed to fear the "starvation period," which comes to every young lawyer, and refrained from applying for admission to the bar for many years.

While a law student at the university, Mr. Hudson was elected, after a protracted triangular fight, president of his class, and as such presided at the graduation exercises, an honor which, coming to a resident of a rural community like Grant City, made Mr. Hudson feel very proud of his achievement. This also brought him much attention from important personages in New York City, who sent him invitations to social functions, and among these were Mrs. Russell Sage, Helen Gould, Dr. Austin Abbott, and Mrs. General Dodge. After his graduation, Mr. Hudson formed a law partnership with C. H. Lingenfelter, now Federal attorney for Idaho, and the firm of Lingenfelter & Hudson practiced law in Grant City for about ten years. For the past six years Mr. Hudson has practiced law alone, he and his brother Peter officing together. Mr. Hudson has some taste for traveling, and as a young man has visited nearly all of the states of the Union and nearly all of the principal cities of the United States and Canada; has made several trips over the southern states, spent several years in the eastern states, and in 1900, in company with Mrs. Hudson, made a trip to Europe, visiting the Paris Exposition.

In his political views Mr. Hudson is a democrat, and his first vote for President was cast for Grover Cleveland in 1884. His first office was that of coroner of his county in 1888. In November, 1900, he was elected to the Forty-first General Assembly of Missouri, and again in November, 1902, he was elected to the Forty-second General Assembly. In the latter year he was a prominent candidate for Congress, but was defeated at the Plattsburg convention of that year on the four hundred and fifteenth ballot, coming within four votes of the nomination. During the sitting of the Forty-first General Assembly, Mr. Hudson was a member of the railroad committee, and was one of three who made the minority report on the famous railroad two-cent fare bill, which finally carried through the House, but was defeated in the Senate. His second election resulted in Speaker Whitecotton appointing him chairman of the railroad committee of the House. His support of the two-cent fare bill and his open opposition to the legislation demanded by the railroads, put them against him for reelection, and their influence invaded his county and endeavored to defeat him. Failing in this, they took their fight on him into the Legislature. He was offered the chairmanship of the railroad committee by the speaker and accepted it because he believed it offered the opportunity to punish his enemies while aiding in some wholesome legislation on the subject of railroads. He found the railroad influence too powerful, and they were able to exert such an influence over his committee that he was able to do but little good for the state. Almost his entire committee was made up of men favorable to the railroads.

Mr. Hudson surprised his committee one morning by appearing before the House with an armload of bills which he proceeded to report out of his committee. This action soon brougfit the head of the lobby to his committee room with the complaint that the railroads had not been heard on these bills and that it would cost $10,000 to get the bills back to the committee room. Mr. Hudson did not believe that that move could be accomplished by even the powerful influence of the railroad lobby, but it was done through the influence of the lobby and the connivance of paid clerks, and all of Mr. Hudson's efforts were brought to naught.

Mr. Hudson has been a successful lawyer since his admission to the bar in 1893. All of his investments have been in real estate, which have paid very handsome returns.

Mr. Hudson was married April 21, 1897, to Miss Esther M. Loughlin of New York City, a daughter of Edmond and Almeda A. (Brooks) Loughlin. Mrs. Hudson prepared herself for music under the best masters in New York City, and is, perhaps, one of the most accomplished musicians of Northwest Missouri. She is an Episcopalian, and at the time of her marriage was a member of Doctor Rainsford's church. No children have been born to Mr. and Mrs. Hudson.

Mr. Hudson is a member of the Knights of Pythias, and is also connected with the Masonic fraternity and a member of the chapter. His acquaintance in professional, political, and social circles is wide, and his numerous friends in all walks of life have been attracted to him by his fearlessness, his direct honesty, and his loyalty to those who have expressed faith in him.

ERNEST H. CARPENTER, M.D. In the twelve years since Doctor Carpenter located at Helena in Andrew County his reputation as a capable young physician has been steadily growing, and he now enjoys the largest practice in that community. He is a thoroughly educated and experienced physician and surgeon, and at the same time is one of the leaders in local affairs and improvements.

Dr. Ernest H. Carpenter was born three miles north of Helena on a farm July 27, 1878, a son of Daniel E. and Mary C. (Utz) Carpenter. Both his parents were born in Virginia, his father July 9, 1847, and his mother in June, 1847. They were brought when children to Missouri, their respective parents locating in Buchanan County near St. Joseph. There they grew up, were married, and about 1874 moved to Andrew County. The mother died there September 16, 1896, and the father afterwards retired to Union Star, where he is now living. Their five children were: Ada E., wife of S. B. Kirtley of Union Star; Dr. Ernest H.;

Doctor Carpenter grew up on a farm, but when a boy resolved upon a professional career, and while enjoying the wholesome environment of the farm also utilized every opportunity to prepare himself for his chosen work. He attended the country schools, spent two and a half years in the Chillicothe Normal School, and then entered the Central Medical College at St. Joseph, where he remained three years, about half of which time was devoted to his duties as interne in St. Joseph Hospital. Doctor Carpenter took his concluding course in medicine and his degree as doctor of medicine from the Marion Sims-Beaumont Medical College at St. Louis, graduating April 25, 1903. Since his graduation he has been located at Helena, and in connection with his growing practice as a physician conducts a drug store. He owns his place of business, which is on the corner opposite the bank.

Doctor Carpenter is a democrat in politics, and has associated himself in a public spirited manner with local improvements since coming to Helena to live. He has his church membership in the First Christian Church at St. Joseph and is affiliated with the Masonic fraternity in the Scottish Rite degrees and also belongs to the Independent Order of Odd Fellows. Doctor Carpenter was married November 4, 1914, to Miss Ida May Kuenzi, who was born in Rochester Township, a daughter of Fred and Emma (Brand) Kuenzi. Her father is now deceased, and her mother lives on the old farm in Rochester Township. Mrs. Carpenter graduated with the class of 1911 from the Missouri Wesleyan College at Cameron, and was engaged in teaching for two years prior to her marriage.

JOSEPH E. ADCOCK. An honored veteran of the Civil war, with a record for brave service during the great struggle between the North and the South and for faithful citizenship during the days of peace which followed, Joseph E. Adcock is now living in comfortable retirement at his home at Helena, enjoying the fruits which his years of labor have brought him. He is a native of Trimble county, Kentucky, and was born August 3, 1846, a son of Elijah and Susan (Adcock) Adcock.

Mr. Adcock's parents, who were cousins, were both born near Spottsylvania Courthouse, Virginia, and after their marriage there removed to Kentucky, where the father died when Joseph E. was a lad of eight years, Mrs. Adcock surviving until 1856 and passing away at Macomb, Illinois. There were six children in the family, namely: Amanda, who is the widow of James Alberson and resides at Chicago; Mrs. Mary Salter White, who is deceased; Joseph E., of this review; George T., now a resident of Wyoming, who served 100 days in Company C, One Hundred and Thirty-seventh Regiment, Illinois Volunteer Infantry, during the Civil War, and then enlisted in Company L, Seventh Regiment, Illinois Volunteer Cavalry, with which he served one year; Mrs. Nancy Powell, who left a large family at the time of her death; and Sallie, who died at the age of six years.

Joseph E. Adcock received his early education in the public schools of Trimble County, Kentucky, but his education was interfered with by the occurrence of his father's death, and in 1855 he accompanied his widowed mother to Macomb, Illinois. Her death followed in 1856, and from that time forward Mr. Adcock was reared largely by strangers. He lived at the home and on the farm of A. C. Russell for several years, and was there at the time of the outbreak of the Civil war, and in August,

Mr. Adcock's service was crowded with active participation in some of the principal engagements of the long and bloody struggle. He fought at Corinth and Nashville, was with General Grant in all his campaigns in the West, and engaged in Grierson's Raid, from LaGrange, Tennessee, to Baton Rouge, Louisiana. Finally, Mr. Adcock celebrated Thanksgiving Day, 1864, by being captured by the Confederates, at Campbell, Tennessee, and was taken to the awful Andersonville Prison, where he was confined until the close of the war. At all times Mr. Adcock conducted himself as a brave, faithful and efficient soldier, cheerfully performing whatever duty he was called to discharge and winning the respect and esteem of his comrades and officers.

When he once more joined the workers in the ranks of peace, Mr. Adcock returned to Illinois, where he remained for one year, and then decided he was ready to establish a home of his own. He was married October 22, 1866, to Miss Lizzie Satterwhite, who was born in Oldham County, Kentucky, November 3, 1848, a daughter of Mortimer and Jane (Callis) Adcock, who spent their lives there. Mr. and Mrs. Adcock began housekeeping in Iroquois County, Illinois, where they resided for fourteen years on a farm, and in 1881 went to the West, locating on a ranch in Wyoming. That state continued to be their home until 1887, when they came to Missouri, Mr. Adcock establishing himself in the transfer business at St. Joseph. After thirteen years they returned to Wyoming, where for six years Mr. Adcock carried on ranching and railroading, and in 1910 retired from active pursuits after having spent a number of years in farming in Andrew County, Missouri. He has since made his home at Helena, and is in the enjoyment of a handsome competence. earned through long years of faithful and energetic labor. Mr. Adcock is known as one of the substantial and representative men of his community. He is a republican but not a politician. Mr. Adcock has never lost interest in his comrades of the war days, and is a valued member of the local post of the Grand Army of the Republic. With his family he attends the Methodist Episcopal Church.

Mr. and Mrs. Adcock have been the parents of five children, as follows: Susan J., who is the wife of Enos Thompson, of Helena; Anna M., wife of Daniel Thompson, of Rochester Township; Maggie, the wife of Samuel Driver, of Caliente, Nevada; Orin K., who resides also at Caliente; and Sallie, who died at the age of five years.

JOHN T. McELWAIN. Now living retired and quietly enjoying the fruits of a well spent life at Helena in Andrew County, John T. McElwain, who is a veteran of the great Civil war, was incapacitated for further service about the middle of the struggle by wounds, returned to his native State of Ohio, and a few years later, in 1871, came out to Northwest Missouri. Mr. McElwain for nearly forty years was one of the prosperous and active farmers of Rochester township in Andrew County, and long years of industry, honorable dealing with his fellow men, and strict observance of the principles of integrity have given him a high esteem in this community.

John T. McElwain was born near Washington Courthouse in Fayette County, Ohio, January 22, 1836. His parents were John T. and Eleanor (Todhunter) McElwain. His father a native of Kentucky when

County, Missouri; Robert Parker of New Mexico; John T.; Maria Jane, widow of Andrew Glasgow, of Osborn, Missouri; Eliza, widow of William Stone of Kansas; Euseba, who married William Hinkson, and both are now deceased; Sarah Minerva, who married Scott Orr of Florida; Samuel Q. of Newark, Ohio; Thomas Nesbit, who died at the age of eight years; and Alfred Jackson, who lives in Ohio.

John T. McElwain grew up on his father's farm in Ohio, lived with his parents until twenty-four, and soon after the outbreak of the war between the states enlisted October 17, 1861, in Company D of the Forty-eighth Ohio Volunteer Infantry, Capt. F. M. Posegate's company. He saw eighteen months of active service, and was twice wounded. He was in the great battle of Shiloh on the memorable Sunday, the first day of that struggle, and while fighting was struck by a bullet in the jaw, breaking the jaw bone. He carried that bullet for seven days before it was extracted. He was sent home on a thirty-day furlough, and then rejoined the army in time to take part in the siege of Corinth, marched through Tennessee to the city of Memphis, where he was stationed five months, and then followed Sherman on his first attack against Vicksburg. He fell back with the troops to Arkansas Post, and there was again wounded by the same kind of bullet which struck him at Shiloh, this time in the right hand. Mr. McElwain still keeps as relics of his military experience these two balls. On account of his wounds he received an honorable discharge in May, 1863, at Mound City, Illinois, and then returned home, being incapacitated for labor for nearly a year. Mr. McElwain for his services as a soldier received at first a pension of four dollars per month, and it has gradually been increased with increasing years until he now gets twenty-seven dollars a month.

His years were spent in farming in Ohio until he moved to Missouri, and in the fall of 1871 located in Rochester Township of Andrew County. His business interests have been gradually expanding, and at the present time he owns two fine farms, one comprising eighty acres and the other 125 acres, while his wife owns a place of 120 acres. All three of these farms are in Rochester Township. About five years ago Mr. McElwain and wife left the country and have since lived retired in the village of Helena, where they own and occupy an attractive and comfortable home.

Mr. McElwain has always affiliated with the republican party since the war, but has never sought nor held public office. He and his wife are members of the Long Branch Christian Church, in which he has served as deacon for many years. He was active in the Grand Army Post until it was disbanded.

On October 17, 1867, Mr. McElwain married Mary J. Harris. Mrs. McElwain was born in Clinton County, Ohio, March 14, 1838, a daughter of Lewis and Clarissa (Patten) Harris. Her father was born in Kentucky and her mother in Ohio, and both died in the latter state. Mr. and Mrs. McElwain are the parents of two children: Harry and Frank Martin. The latter was born April 1, 1877, and died January 12, 1896. The son Harry is now a merchant at Helena. He married Stella Zimmerman, and they are the parents of seven children, named Beulah, Lola, Pearl, Bernice, Thelma, Margaret and Opal Fern.

WILLIAM H. SHARP. In the prosperous little village of Helena, Andrew County, the chief factor in business enterprise is William H. Sharp, the vice president and cashier of the Exchange Bank of Helena. In 1900 Mr. W. M. Walker and Mr. Sharp established this bank as a private institution, each gentleman having half interest. Its ownership has remained the same and its management has been under the direction

of Mr. Sharp for the past fifteen years. Mr. Walker, the president,
resides at Atchison, Kansas. This is one of the accommodating private
banks of Northwest Missouri, has a large total of resources, and has been
an important factor in the business and agricultural community at which
it is the center. A recent statement shows the total resources to be more
than a hundred thousand dollars, and this is a fine showing for a town
the size of Helena. Its capital stock paid in is $5,000, its surplus
fund $10,000, and net undivided profits amount to more than ten thou-
sand dollars. The aggregate deposits amount to more than seventy-five
thousand dollars.

William H. Sharp was born in Doniphan County, Kansas, March 25,
1866, a son of Joseph D. and Elizabeth Sharp. His father' and
mother were both born in Tennessee and they were married at Knoxville,
Tennessee, and in 1863 settled in Northeastern Kansas. About 1888
they moved to Oklahoma, and spent the rest of their days near El Reno.
The father spent most of his life as a farmer, and for several years in
Tennessee was engaged in merchandising. Mr. William H. Sharp was
one of the youngest of ten children. Three are now living, the other two
being: Mrs. Martha Bunson of Elk City, Oklahoma; and Mrs. Alice T.
Cortelyou of Muscotah, Kansas.

William H. Sharp grew up on a farm in Kansas, and lived there until
he was married in 1884. His education came from the country schools,
and his early experience made him ready for his first venture after his
marriage as a farmer. After farming for about three years, he took
work under his uncle in a sawmill in Arkansas. On returning to Effingham, Kansas, he became assistant cashier in the State Bank of Effingham.
He began in that work in 1891 and remained eighteen months. The
cashier of the bank was Gilbert Campbell, regarded as one of the best
bankers in Eastern Kansas, and under his capable direction Mr. Sharp
secured an unusually thorough training in the banking business. W. M.
Walker, who is now president of the Exchange Bank of Helena, subsequently bought stock in the State Bank of Effingham, and took the
position of assistant cashier. After that he returned to the farm for
three years, and then engaged in the lumber, stock and grain business
at Muscotah in Atchison County. He was in that business five years,
and in 1900 came to Helena, Andrew County, and besides organizing
the bank opened up a lumber and hardware store. He continued this
mercantile business for several years, but now gives most of his time
to his duties as vice president and cashier of the bank. Since 1907, Mrs.
Sharp, his wife, has held the post of assistant cashier.

Mr. Sharp is one of the active members of the Methodist Episcopal
Church at Helena, and president of the official board. He is affiliated
with Rochester Lodge No. 248, A. F. & A. M. Outside of business he is
devoted to home and church, and takes much interest in music. In 1884
Mr. Sharp married Ella R. Best, who was born at Monrovia, Kansas,
in 1861, a daughter of Capt. A. S. and Malinda (Bricker) Best, both
natives of Pennsylvania. Mr. and Mrs. Sharp's children are mentioned
as follows: Bearl, who died at the age of ten months; Joseph Aaron,
who died at the age of three months; John Harvey, who died in infancy;
Ralph, who died at the age of three years; Albert, who is now fourteen
years of age; and Twila, aged twelve years.

JOSEPH P. GARRETT   Among the enterprising agriculturists of Holt

rett holds a place in the front ranks. Mr. Garrett comes of an agricultural family, and has made a place for himself among the substantial men of his community.

Joseph P. Garrett was born in Henry County, Illinois, April 20, 1867, a son of James and Jane (Skillekorne) Garrett. His parents were born on the Isle of Man. In 1870 the family, consisting of the parents and four children, moved from Illinois to Northwest Missouri. Three children were born after they came to Missouri. James Garrett located on a farm four miles east of Mound City in Holt County. The land comprised a hundred and sixty acres, unimproved, and was bought for about nine dollars per acre. James Garrett had all the enterprise of the average Illinois farmer, and went to work improving his land, which now consists of 560 acres and has excellent buildings and is in thorough cultivation. He has served his community as school director, and was reared in the faith of the Episcopal Church.

Joseph P. Garrett acquired his education in the local schools of Holt County and the State University at Columbia, Missouri. He taught school and lived at home with his parents until his marriage. Mr. Garrett married Clara Baer, daughter of Noah F. and Mary Baer. The Baer family came to Northwest Missouri from Virginia in 1880. After his marriage Mr. Garrett began farming three and a half miles east of Mound City, and from there moved to his present farm. Mr. Garrett now owns and operates 240 acres, all of which is well improved and the efficiency of superintendence is reflected in the farm buildings and the condition of the fields. Mr. and Mrs. Garrett are the parents of six children: Irlene, Cleon, Marjorie, Maxine, Byron and Melba. All the children were born in Holt County. Mr. Garrett is a member of the local school board, and had a place on the democratic ticket a few years ago as candidate for county surveyor. He is affiliated with the Masonic Lodge at Mound City and is a member of the Methodist Church.

STEPHEN BOND. The connection of Stephen Bond with the farming interests of Holt County has made him widely known among the citizens about Maitland, and he has contributed his share to the growth and development of that section, where by his industrious efforts and able management he has caused a fertile tract of land, originally an uncultivated prairie, to become a fine farm, and has generously provided both for his own needs and those dependent upon him. Mr. Bond has always been a busy man, and yet found time to devote to the needs of his locality, and is one of the public spirited citizens of Holt County.

Stephen Bond is a descendant of Joseph Bond, who emigrated to America in 1735. The family is of English origin, the English stock coming originally from Saxony to England about the time of William the Conqueror. Stephen Bond was born in Lake County, Indiana, September 8, 1843, a son of Jesse and Rachel (Hobson) Bond, who were among the pioneers of Lake County, in Northwest Indiana. The parents represented the substantial old Quaker stock of North Carolina, and came from that state in the very early days and settled in Henry County, Indiana, and from there moved to the northwestern section of the same state in Lake County. The mother came to Indiana, when about three years of age, and the father when about eighteen. In 1850 they

age. The father entered eighty acres of land from the Government, and by purchase had a hundred and fifty-seven acres, only twenty-five or thirty acres of which could be classified as improved land. The labors of Jesse Bond were not long continued in Northwest Missouri, and he died November 9, 1852, and his wife passed away August 6, 1855. Both died in Andrew County. There were four children: George, Maryann, John and Stephen. Those now living are John and Stephen, and John has his home in Texas.

Stephen Bond acquired an education partly in Indiana and partly in Northwest Missouri, and in 1855 came to Holt County to live with his uncle, John Hobson. In his uncle's home he continued to live until about sixteen years of age, and then struck out for himself, and has since hewed out his own career. For a time he was employed by his grandfather, Geo. Hobson, who was a Quaker, and who died December 24, 1864. After this he returned to Andrew County and improved his father's homestead. After four years there Mr. Bond returned to Holt County and bought eighty acres of raw prairie land, comprising half of his present fine farm. He later added another eighty acres and now has a quarter section, which in its improvements and fertility is classed as one of the best country estates about Maitland. Mr. Bond has placed all the improvements which now mark the land, and it stands as a monument to his long and earnest endeavor. Mr. Bond married Elizabeth Brinson, daughter of Louis Brinson, an old resident of Holt County. To their union were born nine children, three of whom are deceased. Those surviving are: Anna M., who married Albert D. Stafford; Frances N., who married David Hildebrand, a Dunkard minister; William S., who married Ada West; Rebecca, who married John Norvell; May, unmarried; and Loretta, also single. All the children were born in Holt County except Frances and William, who were born in Andrew County. Mr. Bond is a republican in politics but usually votes for the best fitted man for the office rather than as a partisan.

LYMAN S. WHITE. Four successive generations of the White family have been identified with Andrew County. The prosperous little Village of Whitesville originated with an enterprise conducted by a member of this family, and that is the origin of the name. As farmers, pioneer developers of the land, merchants and thoroughly progressive citizens the Whites have contributed a valuable part to the history and growth of this community.

The first generation represented in Andrew County was John White, who married Charlotte Hunt. Both were born in Ohio, and came to Northwest Missouri in the early days. John White established a small country store in Platte Township, while his wife's father built a mill close by, and these two enterprises were at the foundation of the village of Whitesville, which was named to honor John White. In 1849 John White moved out to California, and the rest of his life was spent there. His widow, a venerable woman of ninety-nine years at this writing, is still living in California, with her home at San Jose and is the oldest representative of the White family still alive.

Among the children of John and Charlotte White was the late Lyman A. White, who was born in Ohio and when ten years of age accompanied his parents to Andrew County. He spent the rest of his life here as a farmer, and died in February, 1883. He was a member of the Christian Church and in politics a democrat. Lyman A. White married Susan E. Clemmons, who is now living in Whitesville. Her five children were: Charlotte, wife of C. H. Allen of Oklahoma; John R.; Maggie, now Mrs. McCue of Gentry County, Missouri; George F. and Laura, twins, former residents of Whitesville and the latter the wife of Charles Petree of Rea.

John R. White, representing the third generation in Andrew County, was born near Whitesville August 5, 1859. He grew up near his birth-place, was educated in the common schools, and has lived in that one locality of Andrew County all his life excepting only three years spent in California. He was a boy of thirteen when he went west with his parents. John R. White has been generously prosperous in his efforts as a farmer, and owns 160 acres of land a mile south of Whitesville. For several years he had made a specialty of raising seed corn, and much of his corn has been exhibited at the Whitesville Corn Show. He also raises high grade stock of all kinds. John R. White is a democrat and a member of the Christian Church.

On April 2, 1884, John R. White married Miss Verdi Saunders. She was born in Andrew County November 4, 1865, a daughter of O. B. and Mary A. (Combest) Saunders, her father a native of Virginia and her mother of Kentucky. O. B. Saunders was brought to Northwest Missouri by his parents at a time when the City of St. Joseph was a village. The Saunders subsequently settled in Andrew County, and O. B. Saunders and wife were married at Whitesville. He died at Savannah April 13, 1907, at the age of seventy-six, and his widow since that time has lived in California. Mr. Saunders was an active farmer until he retired to Savannah, and was a public spirited leader in his community. Politically he was a democrat and his church was the Christian. He was also affiliated with the Masonic Order. In the Saunders family were three sons and eight daughters, and all are living except one son and one daughter.

John R. White and wife have three children, one of whom died in infancy. The son, Lyman S., is a Whitesville merchant and C. Paul lives in Platte Township.

Lyman S. White, one of the energetic young business men of Platte Township, and representing the fourth generation of the White family, was born in Platte Township May 9, 1885, and grew up in this locality, being educated in the local schools and living with his parents until the age of nineteen. In 1904 he entered the Kirksville Normal School, spent two years there, and then traveled for the New Press of St. Joseph for eighteen months. This was followed by a business experience of one year as clerk in a wholesale drygoods house in St. Joseph, and after farming for a time he engaged in the garage business and hardware trade at Whitesville. He is now active manager of a large hardware and implement house in Whitesville. Mr. White also operates a farm of 260 acres east of Whitesville. In everything that pertains to the betterment of his community he has been an active spirit, and has given special attention to the success and prosperity of the Whitesville Corn Show. His enterprise is also shown by his having established and owning the Acetylene Lighting Plant, which furnishes acetylene gas light to the business district. With other members of his family he is connected with the Christian Church and is affiliated with the Masonic Order and the Modern Woodmen of America.

On September 12, 1909, Mr. White married Lulu Cline, who was born in Platte Township February 23, 1885, a daughter of Harvey and Lucinda Cline.

Harvey Cline, one of the substantial farmers and business men of Andrew County, was born in Ohio November 25, 1841, spent several

years in his early youth in Wisconsin with his parents and then came
to Harrison County, Missouri. While in Missouri he enlisted for three
years' service in the Civil war. After the war he became a clerk to
William Weaver at Whitesville, and the Weaver store was the original
mercantile enterprise which under successive ownership has been continued, and is now under the active management of Lyman S. White.
Harvey Cline later bought this store and conducted it for many years.
The stock of goods was sold to W. A. Crockett. The family then spent
several years on a farm and then returned to Whitesville and acquired
the former business. Mr. Cline was identified with merchandising
most of the time from the close of the war until 1900, in which year
he moved to his farm east of town, and since the marriage of his daughter
Lulu to Mr. White has been a member of their household. He owns
the farm of 260 acres operated by Mr. White. Mr. Cline now spends
his winters in Florida. He is a republican in politics, a member of the
Grand Army of the Republic and of the Christian Church. Mrs. Cline
died in 1907. Their children are: Ada, wife of James F. Case of Largo,
Florida; Edgar H. of Platte Township; A. O. of St. Joseph; N. G.;
Curtis P. of Platte Township; Lulu, wife of L. S. White; and H.
Victor of St. Joseph.

J. F. ROBERTS. While Mr. Roberts represents one of the oldest families settled in Andrew County and has had success above the average
as a substantial farmer in the vicinity of Whitesville, special interest
attaches to his name through his active influence as one of the originators
of the famous Whitesville Corn Show, of which he has been president
since it was organized in 1907. The Whitesville Corn Show, though
starting as a local society, for the benefit of a small community of
farmers, has developed into an institution deserving of some particular
comment as one of the factors in the agricultural development of the
state. Twenty-one farmers in the vicinity of Whitesville may be called
the charter members, each contributing one dollar in order to hold a
small exhibition of the products of local corn fields. At the close of
the fair all the corn on exhibit was sold in order to pay the premiums,
which totaled about fifty dollars. From that somewhat humble beginning the show has been developed into the biggest of its kind in
Missouri. The value of the premium list in 1914 was about a thousand
dollars. While the first exhibitors and most of the patronage was
drawn from the immediate locality, the scope of the enterprise has
been continually broadened, until for the past two years it has received
exhibits from corn growers in six different states, and since 1912, owing
to this development, the name has been changed to the Whitesville
Interstate Corn and Poultry Show. Aside from the interest attaching
to the daily exhibits during the fair, a special feature is the banquet, and
at the last show about five hundred plates were laid. During 1913 the
association entered upon still further extension of its worthy influence.
A monthly bulletin will be issued under the auspices of the show, beginning in January, 1915. For the month of March a bulletin is in
course of preparation, which will be mailed to each of the members
of the association and will be distributed to about twenty-five thousand
corn growers in the corn belt. While this corn show started as a
modest affair with headquarters at the little Village of Whitesville,
which contains about 125 people, it has since outgrown the town, and
the village is now more an appendage of the corn show than the show
an institution of the town. To provide adequate quarters a hall costing
seven thousand dollars was built at Whitesville.

J. F. Roberts is a native of Buchanan County, Missouri, where he was born June 17, 1868, a son of J. P. and Jane (Richards) Roberts. Both his parents were natives of Andrew County, Missouri, and with the exception of about four years spent in Buchanan County lived in Andrew County practically all their lives. The father was born in 1842 and the mother in 1841. He died February 26, 1912, and since then the widowed mother has lived with her son J. F. The paternal grandparents were Thomas and Polly Roberts, both natives of Kentucky, where they married, and came to Missouri about 1840, securing Government land near Rosendale. About the time of the war they sold their property and moved to Clinton County, where both died when about eighty years of age. Grandfather Roberts in the early days gave considerable time and attention to the raising of horses. There were four sons and three daughters in his family: James, Thomas, Martha, John, Jane, Porter and Ella. The maternal grandparents of Mr. Roberts were Mr. and Mrs. Zachariah Richards, the former a native of Tennessee, from which state he removed to Illinois and was married there and came to Andrew County, Missouri, in 1841, locating four miles southwest of Whitesville. He died on the old homestead there after a residence of sixty-one years. He was likewise head of a large family of children.

The career of J. P. Roberts was spent as a farmer, but for a number of years he was a stock shipper, and at the time of his death was connected with the bank at Rea.

J. F. Roberts, the only son of his parents, was reared in Andrew County, attended the public schools, and turned his early training to advantage when he chose farming as his regular career. He now resides on the old home farm in section 28 of Platte Township. He owns 308 acres, divided into two farms. The home place, comprising about one hundred and forty acres, is situated a mile west of Whitesville, while the other farm is a mile and a half south of the home place. He operates both farms for the raising of grain and stock. His farm is known as the Cloverdale Farm, and has come into considerable note as the home of some fine Shorthorn cattle. He has made a specialty of planting and raising the Boone County white corn.

Mr. Roberts is a democrat, has taken considerable part in local affairs and though a member of the minority party was a prominent candidate a few years ago for the office of county judge, being defeated by only six votes out of a total of 1,900, the normal republican majority of the county being about three hundred. Mr. Roberts is affiliated with the Masonic Order and the Independent Order of Odd Fellows.

In 1894 he married Maude Wilson. She was born in Kansas June 24, 1871, a daughter of Henry and Sarah (Clark) Wilson, both natives of Illinois. Her father died in Andrew County in 1911, and her mother now resides at Bolckow in this county. Mr. Roberts takes much pride in his children, who are five in number and named Oscar, Chloe, Clarence, Forest and Clyde. The son Forest, aged twelve years, at the last Whitesville Corn Show delivered the address of welcome, and is called the boy orator, and gives promise of a brilliant career. In 1913 he also made a speech at the banquet, when about one hundred and fifty persons were present, fifty of them being members of the Commercial Club of St. Joseph. Among them was the vice president of the Chicago Great Western Railway, who had the boy's speech typewritten and published in the St. Joseph Gazette. All the children take much interest in corn growing, and they are showing the influence of that movement for agricultural uplift which has resulted in the formation of so many boys' corn clubs throughout this country, and is bringing about a training for the younger generation which will undoubtedly show some remarkable results in future years.

G. M. SCOTT. Some of the finest pedigreed stock in Northwest Missouri originates at the Quiet Glen Stock Farm in Andrew County, located on section 31 in Platte Township. According to all available information this farm furnishes a larger numerical breeding service than any other farm in America. The stud stables at different times have had as many as sixty jacks and stallions and the judgment and long experience of the proprietor, Mr. Scott, have given a reputation to his animals second to none in the Middle West. The Quiet Glen Farm is famous for its jacks and jennets, its high grade Percheron and also saddle and harness horses. Mr. Scott does business in a business-like way, and every year issues a large amount of literature concerning the animals kept on his farm. Every year or so one of the large engraving houses of St. Joseph gets out for him a handsomely illustrated booklet of twenty-five or thirty pages giving description of pedigrees and terms of breeding stock, illustrating half a dozen or more of his draft and saddle horses, and a large number of the jacks which have made his stables known all over the West. Every year in the month of September, Mr. Scott holds an annual colt show at his farm, a custom that has been observed for the past fifteen years, and which is of great benefit to his customers. This show brings from two thousand to four thousand people to the farm, and it is one of the celebrated one-day events in Northwest Missouri. As high as two hundred colts are usually shown at each show.

In improvements and equipment the Quiet Glen Farm is one of the most conspicuous in Northwest Missouri. The seventeen-room modern house would do credit to a big city, and at well placed intervals around stand the five substantial barns and enclosed lots, besides a variety of smaller buildings. The main breeding barn is 72 by 100 feet. The farm has a large acreage of as fine blue grass land as can be found in the famous blue grass districts of Kentucky, and underlaid with limestone, well drained, and especially suitable for stock farming. Besides the chief industry of the farm, Mr. Scott also breeds a few Jersey cattle and Poland China hogs.

Mr. Scott has the genial personality of the typical successful Missouri business man, and as his business has been built up on the basis of thorough integrity and exact representation and the strictest regard for all promises, he has had no need to resort to exaggeration in any of his claims concerning his achievements. It is therefore with the quiet humor characteristic of the man that in one of his circular letters he refers to the long standing of the business and the comparatively ancient relations of his family with the stock breeding enterprise. Seventy years or so past his great-grandfather, Robert Scott, kept a breeding stable on Scott's Ridge in Marion County, Kentucky. At his death George S., a son, continued the business, and in 1856 moved to Andrew County, Missouri, where he died soon afterward. Then came George's son, S. M. Scott, who took up the business and in 1866 commenced the breeding of jacks and jennets and continued it until his death in 1898. Mr. G. M. Scott began the same business for himself in 1873, and as he expresses it has not been "out of the sound of their gentle voice more than two weeks at a time since 1866." The records of the breeding and sale barn go back to the early '40s, and there has never been a case of litigation, the motto of the present and past proprietors having been "do to others as we would have them do to us."

G. M. Scott, to take up some of the further details of his career and his ancestry, was born in Platte Township of Andrew County November 20, 1861, a son of S. M. and Elizabeth C. (Abell) Scott, both of whom were born in Marion County, Kentucky. The great-grandfather, Robert Scott, was born and died in Kentucky, and was in business as a breeder of jacks and horses. The grandfather, George S. Scott, married Rachel Miller, both being natives of Kentucky, and George came to Northwest Missouri with his son in 1856, and died about six months after his arrival. His wife also passed away in this county. The late S. M. Scott was born in Marion County, Kentucky, in 1834, and died January 4, 1898, aged sixty-three years, six months and seven days. His wife was born March 21, 1835, and now lives on a farm adjoining that of her son, G. M. Scott. S. M. Scott, after first locating in Andrew County, returned to Kentucky in 1857 and was married in that state. On coming to Andrew County he entered land from the Government, and during the war sold out and lived in Illinois from 1862 to 1866. On coming back to Andrew County after the war he bought what is known as the old homestead on Rock Creek, and at one time owned about a thousand acres in this township. Besides his regular business as a breeder of jacks, jennets, mules and horses, he was for several years well known as a breeder of Durham cattle. S. M. Scott was a lifelong democrat, and a Baptist, and his widow is a member of the Baptist Church at Whitesville. Their five children were: G. M. Scott; Fannie M., living with her mother; Nannie E., who died in 1895, as the wife of W. E. Younger; Eliza Alice of St. Joseph; and Samuel P., with his mother.

Mr. G. M. Scott has lived on his present place, the Quiet Glen Farm, since his marriage on December 19, 1883, to Mary Bell Smith. Their children are: Bonnie Scott Garrett of Platte Township; Annie Scott Warrick of St. Joseph, Missouri; and Freeman Scott, attending high school at St. Joseph. Mrs. Scott was born in Platte Township September 3, 1864, a daughter of Thomas K. and Eliza (Allen) Smith. Her father was born in Missouri and her mother in Illinois, and both died on their old farm. The Quiet Glen Farm is an estate of 390 acres, and its nearest railroad station is Rea.

G. B. GILLIS. Of the men who have actively participated in the transformation of Benton Township during the past quarter of a century, none are better or more favorably known in Holt County than is G. B. Gillis, who is the owner of 500 acres of valuable land. That he has been one of the busy men of the community is apparent from the many changes which he has wrought upon his farm, and the excellent equipment which lightens labor and contributes to economic results. As a citizen he is held in high esteem by reason of the honorable manner in which he has conducted his dealings, and, all in all, his life has been a very useful and successful one.

Mr. Gillis was born in Mound City, Holt County, Missouri, May 2, 1866, and is a son of the late Edward and Amanda (Moore) Gillis. His father was born in Scioto County, Ohio, and as a young man, without capital or influential friends, came to Holt County in 1844, entering a tract of land. This he put under cultivation after a period of intense activity and hard labor, and subsequently secured 160 acres opposite this first property. On the latter land he built a brick house which stands, and the property still belongs to a member of the family. As the years passed and his finances permitted, Mr. Gillis added to his holdings through wise and judicious investment, and at one time was the owner of 1,800 acres, his home where he died being located 2½ miles north of Mound City. Mr. Gillis was a zealous friend of education, and his eight children were given every opportunity of acquiring a good mental training, the father even maintaining a private school for their use. He was interested in fraternal affairs, being a member of the local lodges of the Masons and the Knights of Pythias, and his political views corresponded to those of the democratic party.

Like his brothers and sisters, G. B. Gillis was granted good educational opportunities in his youth, and early decided upon a career in agriculture, in which he has gained such a noteworthy success. He was only eighteen years of age when he secured possession of the nucleus for his present property, and from that time to the present he has been adding continually to his holdings, which now aggregate 500 acres. This long period of time on one property has witnessed a realization of his most practical ambitions, and has placed him among the most scientific and progressive landsmen of Holt County. He is appreciated for his sterling traits of character, his genial manner, and his contributions to the well-being of the township in which his entire career has been passed. Like his father, he believes in the value of education, and has done his part in advancing it by a number of years of service on the school board of Benton Township. Politically he is a democrat, and his fraternal connection is with the local lodges of the Woodmen of the World and the Knights of Pythias.

Mr. Gillis married Miss Helen Thompson, daughter of W. L. Thompson, who came to Holt County from Buchanan County, Missouri, where he was an early settler. Five children have been born to this union, all in Holt County: Emmett, Clarence, Lloyd, Rollie and Ruth.

IRA CALDWELL. For forty years a resident of the Blythdale locality, Ira Caldwell has resided on the farm which he now owns for one year less than that time, having in 1875 purchased 120 acres of land in sections 11 and 12, at that time unimproved. During his first year here he built a shelter for his family and a place for the protection of his stock, proceeded to break the sod, and the second year obtained a crop. From that time to the present time he has been engaged in mixed farming and the raising of livestock, and his property is now one of the finest and most valuable in the community, while the little cabin that served him as a home during the first years of his stay here has been replaced by a commodious and handsome country residence. Mr. Caldwell was born in Fayette County, Indiana, May 12, 1839, and is a son of Train and Jane (McClure) Caldwell.

James Caldwell, the grandfather of Ira Caldwell, was descended from a South Carolina family, but was a Kentuckian by birth. Some time after his marriage he took his family from Kentucky up into Indiana, crossing the Ohio River at Cincinnati and following the boundary line of the states north to a point opposite Fayette County, and there awaited the conclusion of the treaty with the Indians which brought the region of Fayette County into the public domain. He then crossed over and entered land and spent the rest of his life in that county. When he crossed the Ohio River, Cincinnati had only four houses and the region of Western Ohio was barely touched with settlements. After he settled in Indiana, James Caldwell followed teaming to Cincinnati, and on one of his trips met with an accident that resulted in his death some time later. He married Mary Loder, who lived to a ripe old age, and they had the following children: Benjamin, who died in Wayne County, Indiana; Train, the father of Ira;

Lucinda, who married James Tiner; Jane, who married William Ross; Mrs. Daniel DeHaven; Jonathan, who died in Rush County, Indiana; James, who died at Lewisville, Indiana; and Frank, who died at Indianapolis. The above brothers were all farmers and stockmen, and worked together in the latter business during the greater part of their lives.

Train Caldwell was born in a block house on the edge of Ohio October 1, 1810, while the family waited for the opening of the lands in Fayette County, Indiana, and he died March 2, 1887, at Connorsville, Indiana. In Fayette County he spent all his life and within the very atmosphere of his birthplace. His education was of a practical nature and his career showed him to have been a man of business judgment. He raised, fed and shipped stock for many years and at one period of his life was a breeder of fine horses and cattle at Bentonville. He accumulated a splendid estate during his career. During his life he had no military record, nor did he serve his community in any official capacity, but always gave his support to the candidates and policies of the democratic party. He was reared as a Primitive Baptist, but in after life united with the Christian Church. He was a solid and substantial citizen, greatly interested in the affairs of his community, and was taken away at the end of a rather active career. Mr. Caldwell married Jane McClure, a daughter of Samuel McClure, of Irish descent, who settled in Fayette County, Indiana, from Adams County, Ohio. Mrs. Caldwell died in 1869, having been the mother of the following children: James, who spent his life in Fayette County, Indiana; John, who died in the same county; Benjamin, who died in Henry County, Indiana; Nathaniel, who died at Richmond, Indiana; Mary A., who married Lee Fox and died at Connorsville, Indiana; Ira, of this review; Jonathan, who lives at Cambridge City, Indiana; Sanford, of Fayette County, Indiana; Wilson, of Indianapolis, Indiana. Only one of these numerous sons served the Union during the Civil war.

Ira Caldwell was educated in the district schools at a time when the advantages to be secured in an educational way were of a primitive nature in his locality. He went into the Union army in 1862, enlisting at Lewisville, Indiana, in Company I, Eighty-fourth Regiment, Indiana Volunteer Infantry. His captain was A. W. Fellows and his colonel was Nelson Trussler, and the regiment crossed the Ohio River at Cincinnati and met Kirby Smith's troops at Covington, at which point they participated in a skirmish. The command then went to West Virginia and did guard duty along the Ohio River, and later, in the spring of 1863, the regiment joined General Thomas' army at Nashville, Tennessee, and participated in the fighting during the campaign under Thomas through to Atlanta, Georgia, participating in the engagements at Chickamauga, Chattanooga, Lookout Mountain, Resaca, Ringgold Gap, Kenesaw Mountain, Peach Tree Creek, Buzzard's Roost, Tunnell Hill. and the siege of Atlanta, and finally Goldsboro, where the southerners were defeated decisively. General Hood having retreated toward Nashville, Thomas' command, with others, followed him up and fought him at Franklin and Nashville, where they practically annihilated his army. The command of Mr. Caldwell next went to Huntsville, Alabama, and after there spending some time was ordered to Eastern Tennessee, his regiment being engaged in repairing the railroad near Greenville, Tennessee, when the war ended. Mr. Caldwell was mustered out of the service June 30, 1865, without having been wounded or without a hospital record. He went into the service as a duty sergeant, and was orderly sergeant when mustered out, his record having been a most excellent one.

Mr. Caldwell began life after the war as a farmer in Rush County. He lived there until he left the state for Missouri, and was married there October 11, 1866, to Miss Margaret J. Kelsey, a daughter of Joab and Sallie (Broadway) Kelsey. Mr. Kelsey was a Warren County, Ohio, man, where he was born and married, and by vocation was a farmer. He settled in Rush County, Indiana, as one of that section's pioneers, and there lived until advanced years reached him, when he moved to Missouri, and here died at his Caldwell County home in 1882, at the age of seventy-four years. His wife died in 1872 and their children were: Sarepta, who died at Blythedale as Mrs. Isaac Irvin; Ambrose, who died in childhood as did Amy; Mary, who married Francis Campbell and died in Jasper County, Iowa; Lewis, of Mattoon, Illinois; Margaret, born in March, 1841, and the wife of Mr. Caldwell; Samuel H., who died at Kansas City, Missouri, was wounded while serving in Company F, Eighty-fourth Regiment, Indiana Volunteer Infantry, with Mr. Caldwell; and Caroline, who married DeCamp Voorhees, her second husband being J. W. Moore, and she now resides at Ridgeway, Missouri. Mrs. Caldwell's grandfather, John Kelsey, was a son of James Kelsey, whose home was originally in old Virginia, near the Gettysburg battle-field. The family moved into Kentucky during the settlement of the state. John Kelsey married Miss Margaret Powell, and Joab Kelsey was one of their children.

Mr. and Mrs. Caldwell have one child: Hester, who is the wife of Coleman Harrison, who resides on the Caldwell farm. They have two children, Margaret and Harold. Mr. and Mrs. Caldwell are Missionary Baptists, and he is a member of the Blythedale Post of the Grand Army of the Republic. He is a democrat in politics, but has not been particularly active in public affairs, his only service of this character being as a member of the school board. He has won success in his chosen calling because of his industry and persevering effort, and has fairly established himself as one of his community's substantial men and representative citizens.

B. F. KINCAID. Few rural homes in Northwest Missouri represent more of the material comforts and practical business-like arrangements than the Grand View Farm of B. F. Kincaid in Lincoln Township of Caldwell County. As a home it represents those conveniences and comforts which are becoming more and more typical of country life in America, and which serve to raise the general standard of rural living. The home is only the central feature of a business or industry in the management of which Mr. Kincaid has proved himself a past master, and as a productive and profitable farm his is ranked as one of the best in the township. It comprises 240 acres of land, devoted to general farming and stock raising. The modern residence was built in 1914 at a cost of $5,000, and is regarded as one of the best in the entire county. It occupies a building site not far from the old homestead where Mr. Kincaid was born. The residence comprises nine rooms, and the basement has a cement floor and walls and is divided into three compartments, one of which is for a bathroom, another for the laundry, and the other for furnace and general supply room. Many compliments have been paid to both the convenience of arrangement and the general architectural plan of this home. It has such conveniences as hot and cold water in every room, while an acetylene gas plant furnishes light for both house and barn. The woodwork is of pine and hardwood, and the general furnishings are in keeping with the good taste and comfort displayed in the building itself. Around the south and east sides of the house extends a commodious and attractive porch, fifty-two feet in length. The home is set in the midst of a beautiful lawn, with large shade trees, and Mr. and Mrs. Kincaid take pride in making the sorroundings measure up to the high standard set by the home itself. The business part of the homestead comprises a large stock, hay and grain barn, 48x50 feet, with other outbuildings, including two windmills that pump water for both stock and domestic purposes. Stretching beyond the barns are seen the broad fields of corn, meadow, and pasture land. Grand View is happily named, since one of the finest views of landscape can be obtained here of any to be noted in this section of Northwest Missouri. Poultry raising is one of the profitable and important features of the Grand View industry, with the flock of Rhode Island chickens, of which there are no better specimens of this splendid breed to be found in Northwest Missouri.

Benjamin F. Kincaid was born on the old homestead in Caldwell County, May 5, 1871, a son of William Kincaid, now deceased, who was for many years one of the prominent and well known citizens in this locality. He died when about sixty-three years of age, after a career as a farmer and stock man, and his wife died a few years afterward. Of this union there were thirteen children, only four of whom are now living: Fred, who lives on the old homestead; William, who lives near Braymer, Missouri; Ben F.; and Mary C., who lives with her brother Fred in the old home. Both parents were members of the Methodist Episcopal Church South.

Benjamin F. Kincaid grew up on the old farm, developed his physique by farm labor while attending the local schools, and after finishing his education in the Chillicothe Normal engaged in work as a teacher and spent four years in instructing the youth of the country district. Since then he has given all his time and attention to the development of his farming interests, and his success is well measured in the splendid home above described.

On February 20, 1895, Mr. Kincaid married Susie Bates, who was born at Excelsior Springs, Missouri, and was reared and educated in Clay County. Her father, Charles Bates, was for many years a well known resident of Excelsior Springs. Mr. and Mrs. Kincaid are the parents of three children: Leslie Bryan, Russell Grady and Mary Elizabeth.

Mr. Kincaid affiliates with the democratic party, and has given some official service to his community. Whether as a farmer or in his relations as a public spirited citizen he has always shown a striking energy and an earnestness that give effectiveness and value to every undertaking. Mr. Kincaid is a Royal Arch Mason, being affiliated with the chapter at Hamilton, Missouri. Physically he is a large man, with a soldierly bearing, and has a frankness and geniality which enable him to mingle with all classes and count his friends by hundreds. He and his wife are both members of the Methodist Episcopal Church South, and he has served as an officer in the church for a number of years, and both are active in church affairs. Mr. Kincaid is also secretary of the Missouri Valley Fox Hunting Association, an organization of about three hundred members, which hold their annual hunt, and with their wives and friends, spend a week in camp at some suitable place. He also maintains a kennel of some of the best fox hounds in Missouri.

ISAAC L. McCALLON. As a representative of the agricultural interests of Andrew County, Missouri, Isaac L. McCallon has established a creditable record for industry, perseverance and integrity. With the exception of several years his entire life has been passed within the borders of this county, and during the past seven years he has lived on the farm which he now occupies, located in section 8, Nodaway Township. Mr. McCallon is a native son of Andrew County, born in Clay Township, January 29, 1850, a son of John C. and Mary Jane (Dunlap) McCallon.

John C. McCallon was born in the State of Tennessee, in 1818, and as a young man migrated to Andrew County, Missouri, where he was married in 1845 to Jane Dunlap, who had been born in Tennessee in 1825 and came to Missouri with an aunt at the age of eighteen years. After their marriage the parents located on a farm which Mr. McCallon had entered from the United States Government, a tract of 160 acres in Clay Township on which Isaac L. McCallon was born. During the time of the gold excitement, in 1850, Mr. McCallon made the long and dangerous trip overland to the gold fields of California, and there remained three years, but was only moderately successful in his search for the yellow metal, and in 1853 returned to his Missouri home. There he continued his agricultural labors for about eight years, but the outbreak of the Civil war and the attending unpleasantness between the rival factions in Missouri caused him to remove his family to Iowa, where they resided for four years. When peace was declared they returned to the homestead and Mr. McCallon continued his farming operations until his death, in 1889, the mother having passed away during the previous year. Mr. McCallon was a successful business man, won success through persevering industry, and at the time of his death was the owner of a half-section of valuable and productive land. He was a democrat in his political views, but not an office seeker. Both he and his wife are remembered as honest, God-fearing people and faithful members of the Presbyterian Church. They were the parents of twelve children, namely: Robert, who died at the age of five years; Sarah Vaughn, who is deceased; Isaac L., of this review; Phoebe Ousley, deceased; Wilson K. and Calvin, twins, both deceased, the latter in childhood; Annie Stephens, deceased; John, a resident of Clay Township, Andrew County; James, a resident of Oklahoma; Mary, who died in childhood; Walter of Clay Township; and Cora Gossett, of Holt County, Missouri.

Isaac L. McCallon received his early education in the little log subscription school in Clay Township, his first teacher being Jeff Mills and his second James Ewing. He later attended the "Institute," in Clay Township, erected by stockholders in the community, but the outbreak of the war caused him to give up his studies and go to Iowa with the family. On their return to Clay Township, he remained under the parental roof until his marriage, shortly after which he went to Kansas, and there spent four years in farming, but soon returned to Clay Township and continued farming there until 1907, when he came to his present farm of twenty-six acres located in section 8, Nodaway Township, one-half mile west of Savannah. He still, however, owns 275 acres of well-improved land in Clay Township. Mr. McCallon, in addition to carrying on general farming, has been interested in stock and has raised and fed high-grade cattle, hogs, mules and horses. His improvements cover a wide range of years and are of a thoroughly practical and dependable nature, his farms have profited by his wise application and untiring industry, and his present home reflects the qualities which have brought him success and standing among his fellow-men. Mr. McCallon is a democrat and has taken an interest in his party's success, although not as a candidate for official position. With his family, he attends the Presbyterian Church.

In 1877 Mr. McCallon was married to Miss Elizabeth Clare, who was born in Kentucky, January 17, 1858, and came to Missouri with her parents in childhood, she being a daughter of James and Sarah (Collier) Clare, natives of Kentucky. Mr. Clare, who is a retired farmer, resides at Bolckow, Missouri, while Mrs. Clare died on the farm in Andrew County, in 1898. Seven children have been born to Mr. and Mrs. McCallon: Emma, who is the wife of Norman Cole, both being graduates of the State University and now teachers in the public schools of Idaho; John W., who is engaged in farming in Clay Township; Rev. Frank C., a minister, in charge of the Christian Church at Lenox, Iowa; Lafayette, who died in 1908, at the age of twenty-two years; Clifford, a resident of Nebraska; and Grace and Walter, at home. All the children are graduates of the high school.

EUGENE MUELLER. An ever increasing prosperity has attended the well-directed efforts of Eugene Mueller since his arrival in Andrew County in 1889. To this community he brought an earnest purpose and worthy ambition, and he has not only been successful in the accumulation of a good farm of 160 acres, located in Jefferson Township, three miles south of Savannah, but has also taken an active part in the affairs of the community, so that he is known as a public-spirited and helpful citizen.

Mr. Mueller is a native of Germany, born in Böblingen, Württemberg, November 17, 1861, and is a son of Christian and Ernestine (Geschwindt) Mueller, natives of Nagold, Württemberg, the father born August 1, 1826, and the mother July 14, 1834. There both passed away, Mr. Mueller October 18, 1886, and his wife September 22, 1908. During his early life Christian Mueller received a good education and adopted the profession of architecture, but later became postmaster at Böblingen and also owned a farming property, on which he kept about twenty-five head of horses. Prior to the advent of the railroads he was engaged in carrying mail and passengers to different points, but when his father-in-law died he disposed of his own interests in order to look after those of Mr. Geschwindt, which included a hotel and post business at Nagold. He and his wife were the parents of three sons and three daughters, namely: Pauline, in Germany; Eugene, of this review; Ernestine, who married in Germany and still resides there; Carl Felix, a resident of Germany; Beatrice Elise Hettler, a widow with two children who came to the United States in 1913 and now makes her home with Mr. Mueller; and Wilhelm Heinrich, who is a soldier in the German army and is at present participating in the great European war.

Eugene Mueller grew up on big farms in Germany, attended agricultural college and secured a high school education, which entitled him to a one-year's service in the regular German army. In 1882 he came to the United States, a single man and alone, and for two years was employed at St. Joseph, Missouri, subsequently spending a like period as a hand on Missouri farms. The death of his father, in 1886, called him back to Germany, where he conducted the elder man's business for three years and closed up his interests, and then disposed of his business there and in 1889 returned to the United States. Choosing Andrew County as his field of labor, he bought his present farm in Jefferson Township, and here has continued to reside to the present time. Much of this 160-acre tract has been cleared by Mr. Mueller, who has erected good buildings and made many substantial improvements, which have added to the farm's value and appearance. He has devoted his attention to general farming and the raising of a good breed of stock, and in both lines has met with the prosperity that comes to men of intelligence, ability and industry. Mr. Mueller became a citizen of the United States as soon as he could secure his citizenship papers, and since then has generally supported republican candidates, although in local affairs he exercises his prerogative in giving his vote to the man he deems best fitted for office. For himself, he has not sought public honors, but has been a willing worker in movements which have promised to culminate in civic betterment. He was reared a Lutheran, but now attends the German Reformed Church at Amazonia. Mr. Mueller holds membership in the C. P. A.

In 1890 Mr. Mueller was married to Miss Anna Reichert, who was born in Württemberg, Germany, March 7, 1871, came to the United States in 1889, and died January 5, 1913. She was a third cousin of her husband, and they were the parents of six children, namely: Ernestine, who died at the age of twelve years; Herman F., who resides with his father and is his assistant in the work of the home place; Frank, who died at the age of six years; a child who died in infancy; and Albert C. and Bertha Anna, who reside at home.

MRS. MAUD FAIR CRECELIUS. The important duties of librarian of the beautiful Jewett Norris Library are entrusted to the capable hands of Mrs. Maud Fair Crecelius, at Trenton, and under her management the institution is filling the field and accomplishing the mission for which it was intended by its revered founder. Mrs. Crecelius is eminently fitted in every way for the position of trust and responsibility which she holds, being a lady of many graces and attainments, and is very popular in the social life of Trenton.

Mrs. Crecelius was born near Avalon, Livingston County, Missouri, and is a daughter of Thomas and Nannie (Shields) Fair. Her father was born in Pennsylvania, in 1844, a son of Simon and Catherine (Booher) Fair, and her mother was also a native of the Keystone State, having been born in 1848, a daughter of David and Mary (Craig) Shields. Thomas Fair grew to sturdy young manhood in his native Armstrong County, and July 12, 1862, enlisted in Company A, One Hundred and Twenty-first Regiment, Pennsylvania Volunteer Infantry, for service in the Civil war. He underwent his baptism of fire at the awful Fredericksburg, December 13, 1862, and following that battle participated in all the engagements fought by the Armies of the Potomac and the James until the close of the Civil war, with the exception of Gettysburg and Hatcher's Run. He proved a brave, faithful and courageous soldier, and was honorably discharged and mustered out of the service June 2, 1865, with an excellent record. Mr. Fair has been a resident of Missouri since 1868 and of Grundy County since 1892, being at this time assistant to his daughter at the library.

Mrs. Crecelius received her early education in the country schools of Livingston County, Missouri, and when eleven years of age accompanied her parents to Grundy County, here attending school three miles east of Trenton until 1896, going then to the Spickard High School and completing her education at Avalon College, Trenton, where she took a three-year course. On November 1, 1903, she was married to Charles Walter Crecelius, a son of David and Samantha (Curry) Crecelius, who are farming people residing seven miles north of Brookfield, Missouri, and one child, Geraldine Fair, was born to this union. Mr. Crecelius died March 14, 1913. On November 23d of that year Mrs. Crecelius was elected to the office of librarian of the Jewett Norris Library, and has continued in this capacity to the present time, her services having been of a singularly helpful and satisfying character. Mrs. Crecelius is a consistent member of the Methodist Episcopal Church, belongs to the Woodmen's Circle, and is widely and favorably known in social circles of Trenton.

In this connection it may not be inappropriate to briefly sketch a history of the library and of the life of its founder. Judge Jewett Norris was born at Dorchester, Grafton County, New Hampshire, June 11, 1809, and lived on the homestead farm until about his fifteenth year. His facilities for early education were meager, being only such as the district school during three months of the year afforded, but by economizing the spare hours from a busy life he came to be a ripe scholar of extensive and accurate information. About the fifteenth year of his age, he entered a country store as clerk, where he remained over a year, and succeeding this three years were spent in Boston and seven in New York, as a clerk. Failing health admonished him that he must seek employment in the open air. Another New Hampshire boy said: "Go West, young man," but young Norris had already gone. In 1835, he crossed the Father of Waters and located on unsurveyed land near where the City of Trenton, Grundy County, Missouri, was afterwards located.

In November, 1837, Judge Norris was married to Sarah E. Peery, a daughter of George Peery, one of the first settlers of the county. She was born in Tazewell County, Virginia, July 20, 1813. With his young wife, Judge Norris moved into the log cabin he had built on the Government land where for twenty years he was extensively and successfully engaged in farming and stock raising, and where his six children were born. About 1855 he moved to Trenton, where afterwards he engaged in merchandizing. On the farm three of his children had died, and soon after his removal, June 17, 1858, the mother followed them, and then his beloved eldest daughter, Rebecca, died also.

Judge Norris had actively participated in the organization of the new county, was one of the judges of the first County Court, and was afterwards elected state senator. From the very first agitation of the question of secession, he took a strong and unconditional position in favor of preserving the Union at all hazards and at any cost. The situation in Missouri early in 1861 was a peculiar one. The governor and every state officer, except possibly two—the Legislature, with almost unanimity —and probably more than two-thirds of all the county and other officers in the state were aggressively and avowedly for the South. It required courage to meet this tide and turn it back. The quiet farmer and merchant, however, and his compatriots in Missouri, were of the same stuff as those men who seventy-five years before had pledged "our lives, our fortunes and our sacred honor." Little known as a public speaker, Judge Norris surprised and electrified the country by his eloquence and earnestness. He canvassed most of North Missouri in behalf of the Union candidates for members of the convention called by the Legislature to consider the relations of Missouri to the Federal Government in the hope and expectation it would declare them dissolved. With the election machinery all in the hands of their enemies and before one United States soldier had been sent into the state, the Union candidates were elected by a majority of nearly two to one. That convention, in spite of the governor, Legislature, judges and officers, saved Missouri to the nation —and probably saved the nation to us all, for with Missouri allied to the South, the result might have been seriously jeopardized. From the time of his election to the presidency, Judge Norris was always a great admirer and warm supporter of Mr. Lincoln.

In 1862 he was again elected state senator—the district then comprising the counties of Grundy, Mercer, Harrison and Daviess, and served as such during the next four eventful years with marked credit and ability. He was one of the leading, if not the leading man in devising ways and means for maintaining the Provisional or Union Government and keeping the militia in the field. In 1863, Judge Norris introduced in the Senate strong resolutions taking advanced ground in favor of a vigorous prosecution of the war, the abolition of slavery and the punishment of the traitors. In support of these he made a clear, bold and able speech which was published throughout the state and did much to revive the hope and courage of the loyal people.

Judge Norris was captain and quartermaster of the Grundy County Battalion, Missouri Militia, in 1861 and 1862, and with his private means furnished supplies to them and the Mercer County Battalion to a large amount which was afterwards repaid in Missouri defense warrants— then worth, in greenbacks, only 75 cents on the dollar. In 1863, 1864 and 1865 he was lieutenant colonel of the Thirtieth Enrolled Missouri Militia, and in that capacity was detailed as a mustering officer for many counties in North Missouri and contributed largely towards maintaining the organization and efficiency of the Union militia.

After the expiration of his term as senator, in 1866, Judge Norris took no further part in public affairs, but devoted himself exclusively to the closing up of his large personal business. Meantime his health had become impaired, and believing that a change of residence would be beneficial, in 1870 he moved to St. Paul, and made some very profitable investments in land and city property, residing the most of the time in the city, although opening up a large farm some distance north of the city. The change proved beneficial and although not active in business pursuits he accumulated a comfortable fortune. However, he did not forget his old home and friends in Missouri, where he had spent thirty-five years of his active life. It was in Trenton that his wife and five of his children were buried, one, a daughter, having died after his removal to St. Paul. Here his first successes in life were obtained; here his public services were matters of record; here the prime of his life was spent and his active mind, broad culture and intellectual genius had made its impress in moulding and building up the institutions of the country. When Judge Norris left here he took with him about $50,000 accumulated capital. He returned the whole of it to the people among whom he had acquired it, in the founding of the Jewett Norris Library.

Judge Norris died at St. Paul, May 12, 1891. He never affiliated with any church or religious denomination. He was extremely liberal in all his views concerning religious affairs; but was a firm believer in a Supreme Being and a future existence. His belief was in the "Universal Fatherhood of God and Brotherhood of man." Strictly scrupulous and conscientious in all his duties to his fellow men, he lived a blameless and useful life.

The following is a draft of the proposition of Hon. Jewett Norris to the board of education of Trenton School District: "To the Board of Education of the City of Trenton, Grundy county, Missouri. Gentlemen:—I herewith offer to give to the Public Schools of the City of Trenton, fifty thousand dollars, in trust, for the purpose of establishing and maintaining a free Public Library and Reading Room in your city. I

Rooms in the city of Trenton, under such rules and regulations as your Board may from time to time adopt for its successful maintenance and support, having in view the use of said Library and Reading Room free to the people of Trenton and Grundy County forever, and that the same shall be kept open to the public every day from 9 A. M. until 9 P. M., Sundays and legal holidays excepted, and on such other days and hours as you may see fit, and that the said building shall be kept in good repair by your Board, and that a competent librarian and necessary assistants shall be employed to take charge of the property and serve the public, and that your Board shall annually provide for the defraying of all necessary expenses for the support of the aforesaid institution. And I further stipulate that your Board shall never sell nor convey the building or land upon which it is situated, but forever retain it for the use of the people of Grundy County. If the above conditions are accepted by your Board I will place the sum of thirty thousand dollars in the Union Bank, subject to your order, as fast as it.is required for the erection of the building, and whatever amount of the said sum is not required for the building, may be used for the equipment of said Library and Reading Room with furniture, books and literature. When the Library Building is completed and furnished with furniture, books and literature as far as the funds at your disposal will admit, and the institution is in successful operation, I propose to furnish twenty thousand dollars, five thousand of which shall be made available for its further equipment if your Board think it necessary, and the balance as a permanent endowment fund, to be invested in the same manner and under the same restrictions as the common school fund is now required to be invested by the school law of your state, the annual income from which to be used in the support of said institutions. Should your Board approve of all the above conditions, you will please give me your formal acceptance of the same, and have it recorded with the proceedings of your Board. Jewett Norris. Saint Paul, January 22nd, 1890.''

. The following is the acceptance of the proposition by the board of education: ''Whereas, The Hon. Jewett Norris of Saint Paul, Minnesota, having submitted to the Board of Education of the Trenton School District a formal proposition to donate the sum of ($50,000) fifty thousand dollars, for a free public library in the town of Trenton. Therefore be it Resolved, that we, the said Board of Education, acting for and on behalf of the Trenton school district, do hereby accept the said proposition upon the terms and conditions therein stated, and agree in all things to carry out the wishes of said Jewett Norris contained in said formal proposition in accordance with the laws of Missouri, and that said proposition, together with this preamble and resolution, be spread upon the minutes of the Board and made a part of the records of the Trenton School District. And in behalf of ourselves and of the inhabitants of said School District whom we represent, and of the people of Grundy County, we hereby tender to Judge Norris our thanks and gratitude for this munificent public benefaction, the influence of which, for enlightenment and refinement, should be felt by this and future generations for all time to come. H. C. Sykes, Pres., A. Chapman, Sec'y, G. W. Smith, Treas., William Gessler, Chancy Hall, H. F. Benson.''

REV. WILLIAM A. CHAPMAN. A resident of Rosendale, Andrew County, for thirty years, Rev. William A. Chapman is one of the most widely known and best.beloved ministers of the Christian Church in Northwest Missouri. He was born in Knox County, Ohio, June 29, 1850, and is a son of Benjamin and Margaret (Spry) Chapman.

Benjamin Chapman was also a native of Knox County, Ohio,

1758 HISTORY OF NORTHWEST MISSOURI

born in 1819, and was left an orphan when still a lad. As a young man he went to West Virginia, where he was married the first time, and had one daughter. His wife subsequently died and he returned to Ohio and married Margaret Spry, who was born in Knox County, that state, in 1821. In 1851 Mr. and Mrs. Chapman started for Missouri, locating in Holt County, but three years later moved to Brownsville, Nebraska, where Mr. Chapman assisted in the building of the first house. In 1859 he went to Texas, but in the following year returned to Nebraska, and a later trip was made in 1873, this extending until 1876. At that time the parents again came to Missouri, settling first in Nodaway County, and there the father passed away in 1880. The mother died at Savannah, at the home of her son, Judge J. H. Chapman, in 1904. In his younger life, Mr. Chapman was engaged in steamboating on the Ohio River, but after coming West devoted his entire attention to agricultural pursuits, in which he met with well-deserved success. He was a man of high principles and sterling citizenship, and was esteemed and respected among a wide circle of friends and acquaintances. There were four children born to Benjamin and Margaret Chapman, as follows: Rev. William A., of this notice; Mary E., who is the wife of T. J. Sonedley, of Monet, Missouri; Rebecca L., the wife of Josephus Edwards, of Anglin, Washington, and Judge J. H., a resident of Savannah.

From the time he was four years of age until he reached the age of twenty-three years, William A. Chapman resided on his father's farm in Nemaha County, Nebraska. While being reared to agricultural duties, he attended the district schools of that locality, as well as the State Normal School, at Peru. At the age of twenty years he entered upon a career as an educator, and for the next twenty years engaged in teaching, becoming widely and favorably known as an educator. Mr. Chapman was twenty-three years of age, in 1873, when he was married to Armilda T. Tharp, who was born in Jasper County, Iowa, February 25, 1854, and who at the age of eighteen years was taken to Nebraska by her parents, C. C. and Emmeline (Wolf) Tharp, natives of Indiana, the former of whom died in Nebraska at the age of eighty-four years, while the latter was sixty-nine years of age at the time of her death. They had spent their lives in the pursuits of the soil, and were known as honest, hard-working and God-fearing people. Three weeks after their marriage Mr. and Mrs. Chapman went to Blanco County, Texas, and later removed to Bell County, in the same state, but in 1876 returned to Nebraska, in 1878 came to Missouri and settled in Nodaway County, and in 1885 located at Rosendale, Andrew County, where he continued to be engaged as a school teacher until 1890.

In 1877 Doctor Chapman had preached his first sermon in the old home schoolhouse in Nebraska, and he continued to preach intermittently until 1890, when he gave up schoolteaching to devote his undivided time to and concentrate his energies upon the work of the ministry of the Christian Church. The first church he served was Fairview Christian Church, two and one-half miles south of Rosendale, and there he has spent the greater part of his time. He has preached longer than any other clergyman in Andrew County, has preached more funeral sermons, solemnized a greater number of marriages, and has baptized more people than any other. He is an earnest, zealous worker, always interested in the affairs of his people. who have given to him that affection which but few men can inspire. Doctor Chapman is a charter member of both the Masonic and Odd Fellow lodges at Rosendale.

Nine children have been born to Doctor and Mrs. Chapman, as follows: Nellie, who is the wife of W. A. Housman, of Andrew County; Edgar O., of Guthrie, Oklahoma, a traveling salesman; Cora, the wife of J. O.

Brown, of St. Joseph, Missouri; Charles B., of that city; Jessie, who is the wife of O. B. Smith, of Downs, Kansas; Robert K., of Denver, Colorado; Edna, the wife of O. H. Spicer, of Fillmore, Missouri; Edith, the wife of J. A. Shunk, of Fillmore, and William A., Jr., who resides with his parents.

JOSEPH H. CALDWELL. The progressive agriculturist of Northwest Missouri, after many years spent in tilling the soil of any one locality, is usually loath to turn over to other hands the property to which his life's labors have been devoted; but when he feels that advancing years entitle him to a rest from his activities, and he retires from active participation therein to the quietude of private residence in the adjoining town or village, he is welcomed as an addition to the community who, through his years of practical experience, cannot fail to contribute to his new home interests. Joseph H. Caldwell, who is now living in retirement at Rochester, Andrew County, was for many years engaged in agricultural pursuits in Rochester Township, and his energetic and well-directed labors have earned him a competency that assure him of all of life's comforts in his declining years.

Mr. Caldwell was born in Noble County, Indiana, May 17, 1841, and is a son of John and Margaret (Clouser) Caldwell. His father was born September 13, 1810, in Ohio, and was there married to Miss Margaret Clouser, who was born October 24, 1816, in Pennsylvania, and shortly after their marriage they moved to Noble County, Indiana, where they resided on a farm until 1848. In that year they removed to Schuyler County, Illinois, but in 1851 came on to Andrew County, Missouri, where the father secured a tract of land one-half mile south of Rochester. In addition to carrying on agricultural pursuits, Mr. Caldwell was a millwright, and in partnership with his brother, William, conducted the Rochester Mills for several years. He was faithful and energetic in his labors and was able to furnish a good home for his family before his death, which occurred December 27, 1857, the mother surviving him until April 9, 1872. They were the parents of six children, namely: Simon C., who is deceased; Joseph H., of this review; David G., who served in a Missouri Cavalry regiment during the Civil war and is now living retired at Rochester after many years spent in farming, and a sketch of whose life will be found elsewhere in this work; John, who is deceased; Eliza, who died at the age of twelve years; and Henry C., who makes his home with his brother, David G.

Joseph H. Caldwell was about ten years of age when the family came to Andrew County, and here he grew to manhood in the vicinity of Rochester, where he received his education in the public schools. The outbreak of the Civil war found him, with other young men of his community, ready to serve the Union, and March 14, 1862, he enlisted under Capt. H. B. Johnson, in an independent battery of light artillery. This organization, in the latter part of 1863, was converted into the First Missouri Cavalry, and Mr. Caldwell remained in active service until peace was declared in 1865, when he was mustered out at St. Louis. He had a good record as a soldier, and on his return home resumed his activities as a farmer, and for thirty years continued to be a tiller of the soil. Through industrious and persevering labor he succeeded in the accumulation of a handsome property, which he eventually sold, and since that time has been residing at Rochester, where he still takes an active interest in the affairs and movements which affect his community. He is a republican in his political views, but his chief connection with political matters has been as a voter and a stanch supporter of good men and measures.

Mr. Caldwell was married in 1866 to Miss Minerva Tomlinson, who was born December 8, 1844, in Indiana, and came to Missouri in 1854 with her parents, John and Delilah (Christie) Tomlinson, the former a native of Maryland and the latter of Ohio and both of whom died in Missouri at advanced ages. Eight children were born to Mr. and Mrs. Caldwell, four of whom died in infancy, the others being: F. L., who is a resident of Atchison, Kansas; Maude, who is the wife of Thomas N. Jaynes, a farmer of Rochester Township; Margaret, who is the wife of William Shrives, also a farmer of Rochester Township; and Mattie, the wife of George Miller, of the same township.

J. M. STOUT. Among the well known farmers and substantial citizens of Rochester Township, Andrew County, no one stands higher in public esteem than J. M. Stout, whose well improved farm of 159 acres is situated in section 29, the other acre of the quarter section having been donated for church purposes. Mr. Stout was born in Rochester Township, Andrew County, Missouri, November 10, 1854, and is a son of Thomas and Elizabeth (Walter) Stout. The father was born in Ohio in 1810 and the mother in Kentucky in 1815.

The parents of Mr. Stout resided for some time after marriage in Indiana and afterward on Skunk River, in Iowa, in 1837 moving to Andrew County, Missouri, and entering land near Savannah. After eight years, however, Thomas Stout decided to return to Indiana, but after two days on the journey turned back and bought the farm that C. K. Stout now owns. The mother survived until 1897, but the father died in 1888. He was a fine type of the old-time pioneer, courageous and resourceful, a good neighbor, an honorable man and a sincere Christian. He and wife were earnest members of the Christian Church. They left numerous descendants and in different parts of the western country they have made the name known and respected. Three of their sons, William, Joseph and John, all served as soldiers in the Civil war. The eldest son, George W. Stout, who still survives and lives near Farmington, in the State of Washington, left home in 1853, being then eighteen years old, and started out for himself, locating first in Oregon and removing from there to Washington. He has never returned to Missouri, and his brother, J. M., who was not born until the following year, has never seen him. The other members of the family in order of birth were as follows: John, who died in 1909, in Kansas; Nancy, who is the widow of W. Snowden, lives at Omaha; Joseph, who died in 1906, in Holt County, Missouri; Polly, who is the widow of Henry Hopkins, lives in Utah; William, who is a resident of St. Joseph; Martha, who was the wife of Jasper Huffman, died in Colorado at the age of twenty-eight years; Lizzie, who is the wife of E. M. Richey, of Howard, Colorado; Rebecca, who is the widow of Perry Snowden, lives in Rochester Township; J. M.; and Thomas, of Bolckow. At the time of writing there are thirty-four grand-children in the family.

J. M. Stout remained at home with his parents and assisted on the home farm until his marriage, when he moved to Kansas, where he entered a tract of land in Gove County and proved up within the year, returning then to his father's place, which he managed for three years and then bought fifty acres near the home place. Twelve years later he purchased his present property, and a general agricultural business is carried on, which formerly included a large dairying industry, Mr. Stout conducting a butter wagon for nine years, having customers all along the route as far as St. Joseph. This farm is very well improved and has two sets of farm buildings, Mr. Stout occupying one and his son Everett the other.

Mr. Stout was married in 1886 to Miss Addie Henderson, who was born in Andrew County, May 28, 1866, and is a daughter of Thomas and Mary Jane (Cooper) Henderson. Both parents of Mrs. Stout were born in Ohio, he in 1820 and she in 1829, and after their marriage in that state they came to Missouri, settling in Nodaway County prior to the Civil war. In 1865 Mr. Henderson came to Andrew County and settled on a farm near Savannah, where he died December 15, 1909, his wife having died August 22, 1888. Mr. and Mrs. Stout have had five children: Chester A., who was born December 15, 1886, died October 18, 1895; Everett and Elmer, twins, who were born June 4, 1890, the latter dying September 16, 1890; Irvin, who was born September 27, 1895, died August 22, 1897; and Mildred Elsie, who was born August 29, 1906. The second son, Everett, assists his father in the management of this farm. He married Blanche Nuckols and they have one son, Kenneth Meryl.

Mr. Stout and family belong to the Long Branch Christian Church. In politics he has always been a republican, as was his father after the defeat of Stephen A. Douglas for the presidency.

COL. CLYDE K. STOUT. Combining farming, stock raising and auctioneering, Col. Clyde K. Stout, a leading citizen of Rochester Township, Andrew County, finds little time hanging heavily on his hands. He was born on his present home farm, which is situated 4½ miles south of Savannah, lying in section 18, township 59, range 34, Rochester, on October 24, 1876. His parents were William and Affie (Lewis) Stout.

The Stout family was established in Andrew County by the grandfather, Thomas Stout, in 1837. He was born in Tennessee and in Indiana married Elizabeth Walter, who was born in Kentucky. When they came to Missouri he bought a farm just on the edge of the Village of Savannah, and there they lived until 1847, when he purchased the present home farm in Rochester Township, on which he continued to live until his death, in 1885, at the age of eighty-five years, his wife dying here in her eighty-third year. They reared eleven children, six sons and five daughters.

William Stout was born in Andrew County, Missouri, January 17, 1844, and remained with his parents and later bought the interests of the other heirs in the home farm and for many years continued large agricultural operations here, making a specialty of the buying and shipping of stock. He sold the farm to his son, Clyde K., in 1910, and he and wife then retired to St. Joseph, where they are passing the evening of life in the midst of comfort. He married Affie Lewis, who was born in Henry County, Indiana, March 3, 1838, and came to Andrew County with her widowed mother in 1870. They have four children: C. G., who is a resident of Paonia, Colorado; May, who is the wife of Ben Snowden, of Mount Pleasant, Washington; Clyde K.; and Carl L., who is a resident of Los Angeles, California. During the Civil war Mr. Stout served four years as a member of the Fifth Missouri Infantry. He is a member of the Grand Army of the Republic post at St. Joseph. In politics he has always been a republican, and both he and wife are members of the Christian Church. They are highly respected people and wherever they have lived have been sincerely esteemed for their estimable traits of character.

Clyde K. Stout spent his boyhood happily on the home farm, attending the neighborhood schools and under the wise direction of his father learning those practical details of an agricultural life that have helped in making his own career successful. Deferring to his father's judgment regarding cattle and stock, in his early working years, he thereby gained valuable first-hand information that many another young man entering the stock business has to learn through experience. Following his marriage, Mr. Stout bought and settled on a farm near Bethany, which he operated for two years, when he sold to advantage and returned then to the homestead, which he bought in 1910. He has over 118 acres, a well situated tract, one that has been creditable as to location, to the discriminating judgment of his grandfather. He finds the raising of shorthorn cattle a very profitable industry. Endowed with a pleasing personality, of genial disposition and possessed of a ready wit, Mr. Stout has become popular, during the past eight years, as an auctioneer, confining himself mainly to farm sales, in which line his work is without an equal in the county.

Mr. Stout has been twice married. He was first united with Miss Alice Misner, February 27, 1902, who died without issue on February 27, 1909. Mr. Stout's second marriage was celebrated November 15, 1911, to Miss Lucy Munkres. Mr. Stout is not particularly active in politics, but he recognizes every demand of good citizenship and his affiliation is with the republican party. He has accepted no political favors. For many years he has been a member of the Long Branch Christian Church, in which he is one of the elders. Not only is he a worthy representative of one of the stable old families of Andrew County, but he is a steadying citizen of the present day, busily concerned in reputable activities and lending his influence to the higher things of life.

WILLIAM N. CLAYTOR, who is favorably and prominently known as a farmer and stockman of the community of Shady Grove Church, and on Rural Free Delivery Route No. 2, out of Bethany, has his home in the vicinity in which his father settled when William N. was a child. He is a son of Samuel A. Claytor, who came to Harrison County in 1861 and settled on land in Bethany Township, which is now the property of Will Rogers, and here Mr. Claytor did the substantial work of his life as a farmer and successful and extensive stockman, also acquiring a large acreage and bringing a great deal of it under cultivation. He erected one of the best residences of that day, built barns for the accommodation of his livestock and remained on the farm until old age overtook him, when he retired with his wife and they passed their declining years in the homes of their children.

Samuel A. Claytor was a son of William Claytor, a Virginian by birth and a man of some education, having taught school in Harrison County, Missouri, for several years, to which locality he had preceded his son and being the means of inducing the latter to come here. In later life William Claytor returned to the Old Dominion State, and there died in advanced years. His first wife, whose name is not remembered, was the mother of Samuel A. Claytor and died early in life, her other children being: Milton; Harvey; Mary, who married George Thompson; Fannie, who married Edward Smith; Martha, who married Mr. Young and died in Texas; Adaline, who married John Smith; and Edward, who was the youngest. All the above children came to Missouri, and from here the family scattered to various points, Harvey going to Denver, Colorado, and Milton and Edward going to Texas, where they died, while the remainder spent their lives in Missouri.

Samuel A. Claytor came to Missouri in a wagon from Tazewell County, Virginia, where he was born about the year 1813. He passed through life with only a fair education, but showed rather extraordinary business acumen and splendid judgment, and through the possession of these faculties was able to achieve marked success. During the period of the Civil war Mr. Claytor was a member of the militia of the Confederacy, but saw little military service, and made only one trip to Saint Joseph. In political matters he was a democrat, but did not take any active part in political life, never held a public office, nor made a public speech, and seemed to care to be only what he was, a good and reliable citizen. In religious belief a Methodist, he took an active part in the work of the Shady Grove Church, which he assisted to build with his means and of which he was a member of the board of trustees at the time of his death, about 1897.

Mr. Claytor married Miss Margaret Sicks, a daughter of William Sicks, a Virginia planter. Mrs. Claytor, like her husband, acquired a common school education; she survived him some years, passing away in 1909, at the age of seventy-six years. Their children were as follows: Nancy, who married Marcus Smith and died near Springfield, Missouri; William N. and James W., twins, the latter a resident of Bethany; Edward, who also resides at Bethany; Mary, who married Will McCoy, a farmer of White Oak Township; and I. Samuel, the youngest, who occupies the old home—the Needles farm.

William N. Claytor, of this review, was born December 19, 1853, and was eight years old when the family came overland to Missouri, the migrating caravan comprising four wagons, all Claytors but Robert Rogers, who is now a resident of Bethany. The journey occupied several weeks and a portion of the trip was made by river, the party disembarking at St. Louis and continuing their journey by land. William N. Claytor received his education principally at home, for he was enabled to go to the district school very little. He continued as one of his father's able assistants on the home place until the time of his marriage, when he settled on his present property, building first a small shanty, which has been succeeded by the present splendid country home, located on an eminence in section 2, township 63, range 29, where he started life with 120 acres. He broke the sod, produced grain crops on it for some years, and has grown what cattle, hogs and sheep his grass would raise. Unlike his father, he has never been a feeder, but has succeeded from year to year, increasing the size of his farm as his means have allowed, and is now the owner of 240 acres in section 2. He is an adherent of and firm believer in modern methods, has at all times been ready to experiment with new inventions and discoveries, and is known as one of the most progressive of his community's agriculturists.

As a citizen Mr. Claytor has aided materially in the erection of the New Hampton Christian Church, the Shady Grove Church and the Union Chapel, comprising the union of three denominations. He helped build his home schoolhouse, and has served faithfully and efficiently as a member of the district board for many years. His religious affiliation is with the Christian Church, of which his wife is a member. Mr. Claytor is not connected with any fraternal organization, but has no objection to secret orders, merely preferring his home to outside entertainments or affiliations. Politically a democrat, he is without experience as a holder of public office, having not even been a delegate to conventions.

On May 28, 1876, Mr. Claytor was united in marriage with Miss Alice Stockwell, a daughter of Shelton M. Stockwell and a sister of S. Bob Stockwell, one of Harrison County's well-known agriculturists,

a review of whose life will be found in this work. Three children
have been born to Mr. and Mrs. Claytor: Ash, who is engaged in
farming near his father's home, married Fay Mears and has a daughter, Mildred; Eva, who married John Cuddy, has one daughter, Alice
Jean, and lives at Bethany; and Manley, who still resides with his
parents and is assisting his father.

DAVID G. CALDWELL. With the exception of three years, during
which time he was serving as a soldier in the Union army, at the time
of the Civil war, David G. Caldwell has been a resident of Andrew
County since 1851. His life has been devoted to the pursuits of agriculture, and his labors have been so well directed, that now, in his
declining years, he is living retired from activity, enjoying that peace
and comfort which only comes to the laborer who knows that his work
has been well and faithfully done.

Mr. Caldwell was born March 7, 1847, in Noble County, Indiana,
and is a son of John and Margaret (Clouser) Caldwell. His father
was born in Ohio, September 14, 1810, and as a young man engaged
in farming, a vocation in which he continued to be engaged throughout the remainder of his life. He was married in Ohio to Miss Margaret Clouser, who was born in Pennsylvania, October 24, 1816, and
not long thereafter they moved to Noble County, Indiana, where they
made their home on a farm until 1848. In that year they removed
to Schuyler County, Illinois, but after about three years in the prairie
state again turned their faces to the West and finally took up their
residence in Andrew County, Missouri, one-half mile south of Rochester. In addition to being a practical and energetic farmer, Mr. Caldwell was a millwright by trade, and for a number of years, in partnership with his brother William, conducted the Rochester Mills at that
place. He was an industrious workman, directed his labors in an intelligent manner and lived to see the modest holdings of his younger
years grow and develop into a substantial property, and to see his
children reared to sturdy man and womanhood, ready to take their
places among the world's workers. John Caldwell died December
27, 1857, while Mrs. Caldwell survived him for some years, passing
away April 4, 1893. They were the parents of six children, as follows: Simon C., who is deceased; Joseph H., a well-to-do retired
farmer of Rochester, who served three years in the Missouri Light
Artillery during the Civil war, and a sketch of whose career will be
found elsewhere in this work; David G., of this review; John, who is
deceased; Eliza, who died at the age of twelve years; and Henry C.,
who resides with his brother, David G.

David G. Caldwell was a child of one year when taken by his parents to Illinois, and but four years of age when the family made the
overland journey to Andrew County, Missouri. Here he grew to
sturdy young manhood as a farmer boy, and received his education
in the district schools, which he attended during the winter months.
On August 8, 1863, he enlisted in Company C, Twelfth Regiment,
Missouri Volunteer Cavalry, with which organization he served three
years, participating in engagements in Tennessee, Mississippi and Alabama, and being mustered out of the service at Fort Leavenworth,
Kansas, April 9, 1866. He proved a good and faithful soldier, and
when his military career was ended returned to the home farm, ready
to prove himself just as good and capable citizen in times of peace.
In the years that followed, Mr. Caldwell carried on extensive farming
operations, winning success through his industry and intelligent application of practical methods to his work, and when advancing years

came on disposed of his land and removed to Rochester, where he has since lived in quiet retirement. A republican in his political views, at various times he has been called upon to serve in public office, having acted at various times as constable, deputy sheriff and deputy revenue collector, in each of which capacities he has given evidence of the possession of executive ability and a conscientious wish to serve the best interests of his community. In 1890 he took the census in the west half of Monroe Township, Andrew County, Missouri.

Mr. Caldwell was married November 4, 1866, to Miss Josephine Surles, who was born at Rochester, Missouri, May 17, 1848, a daughter of John and Sarah (Yingst) Surles, the former a native of Kentucky and the latter of Ohio. Mr. Surles came to Missouri with his parents as early as 1832, securing land of the United States Government, three miles north of Rochester, where his wife's people located the same year. In 1852 Mr. Surles crossed the plains to California, and while in that state succumbed to sickness, while Mrs. Surles died in Missouri. Eight children have been born to Mr. and Mrs. Caldwell, namely: Judge Charles E., a sketch of whose career appears on another page of this work; Magdalena, who died at the age of two years; Claude O., a resident of Cosby, Andrew County; Ella, who is the wife of O. K. Barton, of Flag Spring, Missouri; Grace, deceased, who was the wife of Earl Dungan, of Rochester; May Bell, who is the wife of Clyde Belton, of Helena, Missouri; Lovina, who is the widow of Carl Kimerlin, and resides with her father; and Jesse, who resides near Cosby, Missouri.

HON. THOMAS J. KELLY. Among the old and honored families of Andrew County, none is held in higher esteem than that bearing the name Kelly, which has been located in Monroe Township since 1837, and a worthy representative of which is found in the person of Judge Thomas J. Kelly, whose many years of agricultural operations have given him a substantial position in a community which does not want for capable men.

The entire career of Judge Kelly has been passed within the borders of Monroe Township, and the greater part of this has been spent on the farm which he now occupies. Here he was born, February 9, 1849, in the old double-log home, which boasted a fireplace in each end. The family was founded in Missouri by Edward Kelly, the paternal grandfather of Judge Kelly, a native of North Carolina, who, in 1837, came to Andrew County with his wife and eleven children, the latter being as follows: Isaac, who went to Texas in 1856; John, who met his death in a runaway accident in Andrew County; Edward, the father of Thomas J.; Nehemiah; Andrew; Henry; Thompson; George; Mrs. Sally Black; Mrs. Celia Hoblett; and Mrs. Lamb. All the children are now deceased.

Edward Kelly, the father of Judge Kelly, was born in North Carolina in 1811, and was twenty-six years of age when he accompanied his parents to Missouri. He was twice married, and by his first union had one son: Nathan, now deceased, who served with the Missouri State Militia during the Civil war. Later Mr. Kelly was married to Mrs. Hepsibah (Deakin) Eslinger, the widow of Daniel Eslinger, by whom she had one daughter: Rachel, who is now the wife of William Parker, of Monroe Township. Six children were born to Mr. and Mrs. Kelly; Thomas J., of this review; A. J., a resident of Monroe Township; B. F., of Walla Walla, Washington; Lizzie, deceased, who was the wife of Willis McKowen; Lucinda, who is the wife of Daniel Isenhouer, of

Monroe Township, and one son who died in childhood. After their marriage, although Mr. Kelly had a farm of his own, Mr. and Mrs. Kelly settled on the farm in section 8, Monroe Township, which had been entered in 1837 by Mrs. Kelly's first husband, and there they continued to live and carry on agricultural operations during the remainder of their lives, the father dying in 1885. During the Civil war he was a stanch Union man, and in his community was known as a sterling citizen and a strictly honorable man of business.

Thomas J. Kelly was reared on the farm on which he now lives, and on which he has spent his entire life with the exception of six years on an adjoining property and sixteen years in the mercantile business at Avenue City, two miles west of this homestead, which is very appropriately known as the Homestead Farm. Mr. Kelly, during his long residence here, was successful in the accumulation of 224 acres, but sold twenty-four acres of the land, still retaining 200 acres. In addition to carrying on general farming, for many years he was engaged in the manufacture of butter for his customers at Saint Joseph, but of recent years has given up the latter business. He has always been a citizen ready to assist his community in any way, and at various times has been called upon by his fellow-townsmen to hold public offices of responsibility and importance. For sixteen years he served in the capacity of notary public, and in the fall of 1896 was elected judge of Andrew County, and served as such two terms, or four years. It is a curious and interesting coincidence that Judge Kelly was acting in the capacity of county judge when the present courthouse was built, while his maternal grandfather, Judge William Deakin, was county judge when the first courthouse was built in Andrew County. Judge Kelly has always been a stanch supporter of republican candidates, principles and policies. He is a devout member of the Baptist Church at High Prairie, and at present is acting as deacon and treasurer.

On April 4, 1874, Judge Kelly was married to Miss Sarah L. Gordon, who was born in North Carolina in 1852 and was six years of age when brought to the farm adjoining that of Judge Kelly by her parents, Eli and Elizabeth Gordon, both of whom passed away here, the father shortly after arrival. Six children have been born to Judge and Mrs. Kelly: Bessie M., the wife of Irvin Hartman, of Rochester Township, who has seven children, Lee, Allen and Alfred, twins, Lottie, Dorothy, Helen and an infant son; Will E., who resides at home and assists his father in the operation of the homestead; Addie, the wife of W. J. McBean, of Union Star, who has three children, W. K., J. H. and Agnes; J. Ed, engaged in merchandising in this township, who has one son, Jewell; Lottie, who makes her home with her parents; and Rachel, the wife of B. B. McGill, of Monroe Township, has two children, Ralph B. and Clarence James.

WILLIAM PARKER. Of the old pioneer families of Andrew County, none have stood higher as good and worthy people than the Parkers, a well-known representative being William Parker, one of the substantial farmers and stockmen of Monroe Township, who has been a continuous resident of this county since brought here by his parents in 1841. William Parker was born in Bartholomew County, Indiana, March 12, 1836. His parents were Daniel K. and Sarah (Davis) Parker, the former of whom was born in Brown County, Indiana, in 1813, and the latter in Bartholomew County in 1817. Late in the '30s they came to Missouri, locating first near Weston, in Platte County, and from there, in 1841, came to Andrew County, the family home from then until the present. Daniel K. Parker preempted 160 acres of land situated two miles north of Avenue City and on this place he died in 1889, having survived his

wife for one year. They had but two children: William and Elizabeth, the latter being the widow of Jesse F. Wright, of Rochester
Township, Andrew County.

William Parker had such school advantages as the neighborhood
afforded in his boyhood, but his life has been devoted to farming since
early youth, and long experience has taught him methods that bring
about the best results in this section of the country. His farm contains
210 acres, 160 of which came to his wife from her father's estate. When
Mr. Parker came here this property was all open fields, but he has greatly
improved it and now has substantial and adequate buildings for his
grain and stock and a comfortable farm residence.

Mr. Parker was married May 1, 1862, to Miss Rachel H. Esslinger,
who was born on a part of this farm, September 20, 1843. Her parents
were Daniel and Hepsibeth (Deakins) Esslinger, and her maternal
grandfather was Hon. William Deakins, who was one of the first judges
of Andrew County. Mr. and Mrs. Parker have had six children, all of
whom survive: Sarah E., who is the wife of Edward Feichter, resides
at Atchison, Kansas; Francis A., who is a resident of Colorado Springs,
Colorado; Mrs. Jennie Tebbs, who lives with her parents; Daniel E.,
who is in business at Boise, Idaho; May, who is the wife of E. E. Zimmerman, of Boise, Idaho; and Stella, who is the wife of Dr. C. L. Allen,
of Cosby, Missouri.

Mr. Parker has witnessed many changes take place in Andrew County
during the past seventy years and has always done his part in bringing
about those of which his judgment approved. In politics he is a republican, but has never accepted any public office except that of township assessor, in which he served for three years. He is one of the
best known men of this part of the county and has reared a creditable
family.

CHARLES C. SIGRIST.   One of the substantial men of Andrew County,
who has practically spent his entire life in Rochester Township, where
he owns an exceptionally fine farm, is Charles C. Sigrist, a member of
well-known old families of this section. He was born at Rochester, February 7, 1864, and is a son of Philip and Mary L. (Walter) Sigrist.
His father was born in France, February 27, 1834, and died at Denver,
Colorado, in 1893, having been a resident of the United States from
infancy, and for forty-five years of Missouri. In 1856 he was married
in Andrew County to Mary L. Walter, who was born in Ohio in 1836,
and died at Rochester when aged sixty-three years. Her parents were
David and Mary (Sherr) Walter, the birthplace of both having been
Strasburg, Germany. After emigrating to the United States they settled in Ohio and early in the '50s came to Andrew County, Missouri,
entering land near Rochester. Grandfather Walter was a baker by trade,
and he also engaged in farming and was one of the early money lenders,
his German thrift enabling him to accumulate the means which afterward preserved his neighbors from distress on many occasions. He and
wife were interred in the cemetery at Rochester. They reared a family
of six sons and seven daughters.

Charles C. Sigrist was educated in the public schools of Rochester.
He entered business first as a stock clerk for the Saint Joseph firm of
Tootle, Hosea & Co., where he continued about one year and then returned
to Rochester. In the meanwhile his father, a man of much business
enterprise, had founded the mercantile house which yet largely dom-
inates the trade in this section of the county, and with other interests
was a leading factor in business and in politics in Rochester Township.
In 1888, on account of an accident, he retired from business and turned

his mercantile interests over to his sons, Charles C. and R. E. Sigrist, and they continued as partners, under the firm name of Sigrist Brothers, for twenty years. In 1908 Charles C. Sigrist sold his interest to his brother and since then has devoted himself to agricultural pursuits. He bought the old Judge Snowden farm of 155 acres, which lies one-half mile north of Rochester, a finely improved property which numbers among its attractions a lake well stocked with fish and by Mr. Sigrist equipped with pleasure boats.

Mr. Sigrist was married February 23, 1890, to Miss Bettie Taylor, who was born 'at Rochester in 1871, and is a daughter of James and Margaret (Beers) Taylor, the former of whom is deceased. The mother of Mrs. Sigrist resides at Rochester. Mr. and Mrs. Sigrist have had nine children: Flossie Pearl, who is the wife of Leon Chaney of Rochester, and they have two children, Irene and Leona; Maggie May, who died when aged three years; and Anna Belle, Jennings Bryan, James Taylor, Edna, Charles Raybun, William Rufus and Catherine Mary, who reside with their parents. The children are being given educational and social advantages and all are numbered with the representative people of this part of the county. Mr. Sigrist follows in the footsteps of his father in being a stanch democrat, but he has never consented to hold public office. He belongs to the fraternal order of Odd Fellows, being identified with the lodge at Helena.

R. E. SIGRIST. As proprietor of one of the oldest mercantile houses in Rochester Township, Andrew County, and as postmaster of Rochester for the past twenty-one years, R. E. Sigrist may justly be mentioned as one of the best known men in this section. He is a native of Rochester, born June 7, 1861, and is a son of Philip and Mary L. (Walters) Sigrist.

Philip Sigrist, for many years a leading citizen of Andrew County, was born in France, February 27, 1834, and in infancy was brought to the United States by his parents. They settled in Pennsylvania and he continued to live in that state until 1855, when he came to Andrew County and established himself in the wagon-making business, a trade he had learned in Pennsylvania. Later he engaged also in undertaking and, being a man of great business enterprise, in 1885 started a general store, founding the business which has been continued ever since and which is now the sole property of his son, R. E. Sigrist. Philip Sigrist was made postmaster under the democratic administration, and was also a justice of the peace for fifteen years. He continued all his enterprises until an accident befell him which made it necessary to practically retire, and in 1888 he turned his mercantile interests over to his sons, R. E. and C. C. Sigrist. In 1890 he went to Denver, Colorado, and died there three years later. On February 28, 1856, he was married in Andrew County to Mary L. Walters, who was born in Ohio in 1836, and six children were born to them: Emma, who is the wife of J. A. Belton, resides at Helena, Missouri; Henry, who died when aged eleven years; R. E.; Charles C., who is a farmer in Rochester Township; Willie, who died when aged ten months; and Cora E., who is the wife of C. E. Caldwell, of Rochester Township. After the father of the above family died in Colorado the mother returned to Rochester, where her death occurred at the age of sixty-three years.

R. E. Sigrist was educated in the public schools and as soon as old enough gave his father assistance, and has been identified with the present store ever since it was started in 1885. For three years he was with his father, and afterward carried on the business in partnership with his brother, C. C. Sigrist, until 1908, when the brother retired to his farm after selling his interest to R. E., who has continued alone ever since. He carries a large and well selected stock, and as a business man enjoys the confidence of patrons all over this section of the county. Mr. Sigrist has always been a democrat in politics, but has never accepted any public office except that of postmaster, his appointment dating April 26, 1894. This office is one of considerable importance and Mr. Sigrist makes it his business to see that its service is entirely satisfactory.

Mr. Sigrist was married May 23, 1890, to Miss Ada Brown, who was born in Andrew County, Missouri, in September, 1870, and is a daughter of Gorman and Sarah Brown, the former of whom is deceased. The mother of Mrs. Sigrist makes her home with her daughter. Mr. and Mrs. Sigrist have five children: Elmer P., who is a resident of Saint Joseph, Missouri; G. Fred, who is a student in the Saint Louis University; Ralph E., who is attending school at Rochester; and Maude and Lester, who are twins.

Mr. Sigrist belongs to a number of the fraternal organizations of the country. He has been an Odd Fellow for many years, following the example of his father, and belongs also to Lodge No. 334, Knights of Pythias, at Rochester, and to Lodge No. 66, Elks, at Helena, Missouri.

D. A. REECE. That energy, prudence and industry are the leading elements of success in agricultural as well as in all other lines of endeavor has been very clearly proved by D. A. Reece, a prominent farmer and cattle raiser and shipper of Andrew County, who is the owner of the Kodiak Stock Farm, a tract of 298 acres situated in section 7, Rochester Township, one-half mile south of Kodiak. Left an orphan in childhood, Mr. Reece has had to make his own way in the world, and that he is now a substantial, prominent and respected citizen of his county proves that he is a man of character and enterprise, hard working and thrifty.

D. A. Reece was born in Yadkin County, North Carolina, March 8, 1866, and is a son of Joel and Malissa (Fleming) Reece. Both were natives of North Carolina, and in 1868 removed to Andrew County, Missouri, locating in Rochester Township. There the mother died in 1870, and the father in 1874, his death being caused by a stroke of lightning. They were the parents of four children: Louise, who is deceased; Eliza, who is the wife of Jacob Wall, of Rochester Township; D. A.; and John F., who is a resident of Oregon.

After the loss of his parents D. A. Reece became a member of the household of Samuel O. Daily, of Rochester Township, and remained with Mr. Daily until he reached manhood. When he started out for himself he went to Colorado, where he located a claim and remained in that state for eighteen months, working on an irrigation project the most of the time. After returning to Andrew County he rented land for three years and then bought fifty-eight acres in Rochester Township, on which he resided for seven years, when he sold to advantage and for three more years rented the adjoining farm of 187 acres, which he then bought and continued to operate for seven years. In the meanwhile he had gone extensively into the cattle business and bought his present farm of 298 acres, later selling his other farm. Mr. Reece has a fine property and has added to its value by making excellent improvements. He is one of the large cattle raisers of this section and feeds and buys for market and for several years has shipped annually four or five cars. He is an expert judge of cattle and the product of the Kodiak stock farm commands the highest market price.

Mr. Reece was married January 20, 1889, to Miss Emma V. Roberts. who was born near Jefferson City, Missouri, April 4, 1870, a daughter of

Andrew and Sarah (Williams) Roberts. They were natives of Kentucky and both died in Moniteau County, Missouri. The mother of Mrs. Reece died when she was one year old and in 1873 the father married a second time in Andrew County. Mr. and Mrs. Reece have five children: Joel A., who resides in York County, Nebraska, married Happy A. Graham; John M., who is a farmer in Rochester Township, married Ura M. Cortney; Mary D., who resides at home; Eliza S., who is the wife of Stanley G. Kelly, a farmer in Rochester Township; and Eddie Rosa, who resides at home.

Mr. Reece and family are members of the Christian Church at Long Branch. For many years he has been a Mason, as was his father before him, and belongs to the blue lodge and chapter at Savannah. He has never been an office seeker, but has always given his political support to the democratic party from principle. It is largely due to the sturdy good citizenship of such men as Mr. Reece that Andrew County has made such substantial progress in the last decade, and to this class the best interests of their home community will always appeal.

WILLIAM LILLIBRIDGE was born at Omaha, Nebraska, May 15, 1857, and is a son of I. B. and Martha (Swift) Lillibridge. The father was born at Stafford Springs, Connecticut, in 1827, and died on his homestead in Rochester Township, April 11, 1885, at the age of fifty-seven years. His ancestors were from Scotland, and they settled in Rhode Island in colonial days. His paternal grandmother was Bessie Ruby, who was a granddaughter of John Adams, once President of the United States. I. B. Lillibridge was married to Martha Swift, who was born at Watertown, New York, and died at Savannah, Missouri, in February, 1901, at the age of sixty-eight years. They had three children: William; Thomas, who followed farming on a part of the old homestead until he removed to Hot Springs, Arkansas, in 1912; and Walter K., who was born at Rochester, Missouri, February 5, 1870, and died at Savannah, June 28, 1877.

In early manhood I. B. Lillibridge learned the trade of painting and graining, and for eight years was employed in the cotton mills at Chicopee Falls, Massachusetts, where he became boss painter and grainer. After his marriage he moved to Ringgold County, Iowa, and from there to Omaha, Nebraska, where he followed the business of painting and decorating until the fall of 1857, when he came to Savannah, Missouri. He continued to work at his trade at Savannah and also at Saint Joseph and then went into the mercantile business in Gentry County and had a store at Mount Pleasant and another at Alanthus Grove. These enterprises he conducted from before the opening of the Civil war until 1867, when he came to Rochester and purchased the farm, a part of which his son William now owns. He bought about nine hundred acres of land in all, for which he paid $10 per acre. His last years were spent mainly at Savannah and at Pueblo, but he died, as above stated, on the old farm. He was an extensive stockman, raising many horses, mules, cattle and hogs. He was a member of the Masonic fraternity during a large part of his life. In many ways he was a man of unusual ability, possessing excellent judgment and business capacity, and wherever known he was regarded with respect.

William Lillibridge was given educational advantages and before entering into business life for himself took a course in the Nebraska State Normal School. He then embarked in the grocery line at Pueblo, Colorado, where he continued for three years, then was in the newspaper business in Kansas City, and afterward, for three years, followed newspaper illustrating in St. Joseph. After marriage, in 1885, he located on the home place and remained for six years and then went to Saint Joseph and resumed newspaper illustrating. For the next seven years he was in the mercantile business at Savannah, and then, for five years he was a merchandise broker at Saint Joseph. Mr. Lillibridge then returned to the old homestead, 370 acres of which he owns, and here has given a good account of himself as a farmer and stockman. This property is valuable, being favorably situated and well watered and lies on the west side of the Platte River, opposite Rochester. It is practically a stock farm.

Mr. Lillibridge was married December 1, 1885, to Miss Orlena F. Auble, who was born at New Michigan, Illinois, July 6, 1860, and came here in 1864 with her parents, H. C. and Hannah A. (Parmenter) Auble. They have had three children: Nellie S. and Bessie F., both of whom are at home; and Bennie, who died at the age of ten years.

During the Civil war Mr. Lillibridge's father was a strong supporter of the Union cause, and the first Union meeting held in Gentry County in the early days met at his house.

S. F. COFFMAN. In Braymer the leading dry goods store is operated by S. F. Coffman & Sons, general merchants, who have long had an established reputation for their goods and their standard methods of merchandising. The members of the firm understand merchandising in all its details, and have succeeded in building up a store which now supplies the most discriminating wants of patronage in Braymer and surrounding district.

The senior member of the firm, S. F. Coffman, was born in Fairfield County, Ohio, in 1856, on a farm, son of Martin Coffman, who was an honored and respected farmer in that county, and is now living retired at the age of eighty-four in Braymer, while his wife is aged eighty-one. He is a republican in politics and a member of the United Brethren Church. S. F. Coffman was reared in Ohio, was educated in the schools of that state, and prepared himself for a business career by practical experience in various lines. When twenty-one years of age he came out to Ray County, Missouri. In 1882 he married Miss Luella Alspaugh, who was also born in Fairfield County, Ohio. S. F. Coffman has long been identified with the business of contracting and building. For thirteen years he was manager of the M. D. Tait Lumber Yard and has erected many of the most substantial buildings in Braymer. He is a careful and thorough business man, has made a record for square dealing in every relation with the community, and has done much for his community. He and his wife are members of the Methodist Episcopal Church, and formerly he was active in the United Brethren Church. On the local school board he has served twelve years and is one of the active republicans in Braymer and vicinity.

The children of S. F. Coffman and wife are: Albert L. Coffman, a business man at Grand Rapids, Michigan; Laurence E. Coffman, who is now the active head of the firm of Coffman & Sons; Ada Coffman, who is cashier in the store; and Martin A. Coffman, who is a jeweler in Braymer. Laurence E. Coffman was born in Ray County, Missouri, April 14, 1886. He was reared in Ray County, and at Braymer received a good substantial education in the public schools, and got his early training for commercial pursuits in the M. D. Tait Lumber Company. For three years he was assistant cashier and bookkeeper of The Bank of Braymer. Mr. Coffman was married September 23, 1908, to Miss Myrtle Isom, daughter of J. M. Isom. They have one son, L. E., Jr. The Coffman & Sons store occupies a building 50 feet front by 105 feet in depth, furnished with all the modern fixtures and facilities for complete and adequate service to the customers, and stocked with a large line of dry goods and general merchandise. Up-to-date business methods have brought and retained an extensive trade, and in the success of the establishment personality of the owners and managers has been an important factor.

HUGH BURRIER. One of the fine homesteads in Lewis Township of Holt County is the property of Hugh Burrier, years of whose life have all been spent in Holt County, and whose individual enterprise and judgment as a business man have been chiefly responsible for his prosperity. He represents one of the old and honored family names in this section of Missouri.

Hugh Burrier was born at Oregon, April 30, 1857, a son of Andrew and Sarah (Reidenour) Burrier. Both parents came to Northwest Missouri from Pennsylvania in pioneer times, settled on land that was unimproved, developed a good farm and lived here until they were called away in death, the father preceding the mother. Hugh Burrier had seven brothers and sisters, and all were born in Holt County.

Mr. Hugh Burrier married Barbara Fry, daughter of Jacob Fry, and both her parents died in Holt County. Mr. and Mrs. Burrier have seven children: Ida; Edward, who married Grace Momine; Jesse, who died at the age of eighteen; Rosie, who married Earl Wastel; Fred; William; Johnnie. All the children were born in Holt County and were educated here, and have now found places of usefulness and honor.

Mr. Burrier is the owner of 400 acres in Lewis Township and practically all the improvements on his farm are the result of his individual labors. Mrs. Burrier's father and mother were active members of the German Methodist Church. Her people were all born in Germany, and she had five brothers and sisters, all of whom are living. Her father was a stonemason in Germany, and after coming to America and settling in Holt County combined that occupation with farming. Her father was a hard working and thrifty man, and having come to Missouri comparatively poor lived a life that brought a substantial home and ample provisions for his children, and he cleared up a large amount of land in Holt County. While Mrs. Burrier's father was a republican, Mr. Burrier's father was a democrat, but Mr. Burrier himself is a republican. He has also served on the school board and is a citizen always ready to help any community enterprise.

ABSALOM HARVEY. Brief mention in any history of Northwest Missouri should be given to Absalom Harvey, who was not only one of the early settlers in Grundy County, but has special distinction, owing to the fact that he had served during his early manhood as a soldier with the American forces during the second war with Great Britain, from 1812 to 1815. He was one of the noted characters of his time, and left many descendants.

Absalom Harvey was born in Randolph County, North Carolina, June 13, 1791. · When he was thirteen years old his parents joined in the tide of emigration which was flowing from the Carolinas into the Northwest Territory. In that country he grew to manhood, and when war broke out in 1812 joined the forces under General Harrison, and followed that leader in the various campaigns against the British throughout the Middle West. Following the war he became a permanent settler in Wayne County, Indiana, where he lived until 1820, and then removed to Henry County in the same state. In 1842, a year or two after the organization of Grundy County, he came out to Northwest Missouri and established himself on what was then the frontier of western civilization.

He was a pioneer by instinct and habit, and found a congenial situation in the new country. His home was established near the present site of Edinburg. While he was known and followed the vocation of farmer, he was also a noted hunter, and kept a pack of hounds and frequently accompanied Indians on their hunting expeditions. He continued to reside in Madison Township of Grundy County until his death, on September 17, 1872. His body was laid to rest in the City Cemetery in Trenton, and it is said to be the only remains of a soldier of the war of 1812 reposing in Grundy County.

Absalom Harvey was married October 5, 1813, to Eleanor Julian. She was born in Randolph County, North Carolina, October 9, 1796, a daughter of Isaac and Sarah Julian. She survived her husband and died at a good old age. There were eight children of their union, and at the time of her death she was survived by about forty grandchildren and thirty great-grandchildren.

JOHN M. TOWNSEND. Prominent among the agriculturists of Andrew County who through years of industrious labor have attained substantial fortunes and at the same time have acquired and held the respect and confidence of their fellow citizens is John M. Townsend, of Benton Township. Mr. Townsend, with the exception of two years, has been a resident of Andrew County all of his life, and has watched the growth and development of this part of Northwest Missouri with the eye of a proprietor, seeing the log-cabin days of his youth pass into the things that are gone and the modern, progressive age succeed that of the pioneer.

Mr. Townsend was born in a log house on his father's farm, located four miles northwest of Savannah, in Andrew County, Missouri, January 20, 1851, and is a son of William Calvin and Mary Ann (Judd) Townsend. His father was born in Indiana in 1821, and was there married May 26, 1842, to Mary Ann Judd, also a native of the Hoosier State, born in Dearborn County in 1825. About the year 1846 Mr. and Mrs. Townsend migrated to Missouri, settling on the farm four miles northwest of Savannah, on which their son was born, a raw tract of land on which there was a log house. The family made their home here until about the year 1861, when they went to Iowa and remained two years, returning to Missouri in 1863 and again locating in Andrew County, this time on a farm 2½ miles south of Bolckow. There William C. Townsend continued to be engaged in agricultural pursuits until the time of his death, which occurred July 12, 1882, Mrs. Townsend surviving him until August 29, 1907. Mr. Townsend was an industrious farmer and a capable man of business and during his active career amassed something more than three hundred acres of good land. He was engaged in general farming principally, but also met with a full measure in the raising of stock, to which he devoted much attention. Both he and his wife were charter members of the Bolckow Baptist Church, in which he was a deacon for many years, and there his children erected one of the largest memorial windows in the church to the memory of their beloved parents. In political matters Mr. Townsend was a republican. Ten children were born to William C. and Mary Ann Townsend: Sarah, who is the widow of George H. Sexton and resides in Oklahoma; Emeline, who married David W. Headley, and is now deceased; Nancy A., deceased, who was the wife of James C. Campbell; John M.; William Calvin, a resident of Benton Township; Thomas Jefferson, also of this township; Harriet F., who is the wife of G. F. Wilson, and resides at Warrensburg, Missouri; Charles G., of Benton Township; Elizabeth E., deceased, who was the wife of T. J. Officer; and Ida B., who died at the age of four years.

John M. Townsend attended the public schools of Andrew County until he was ten years of age, at which time the family removed to Iowa, and there he secured some further training, which was completed when he again located in Andrew County. He was reared to the pursuits of the farm, and remained on the home place until his marriage, at which time he took up his residence on his present property, a tract of 220 acres, two miles south of Bolckow, a part of it being the old homestead. This is located in section 23, Benton Township, and is one of the best-improved places in this part of the county, Mr. Townsend having made many additions to its buildings and equipment during the thirty-four years he has resided here. The small log house of his birth and youth has been replaced by a modern ten-room house, with all up-to-date conveniences and comforts, and substantial barns and other buildings have also been erected by Mr. Townsend. His attention is given mainly to grain and stock raising, and in both departments his judgment, ability and foresight, gained through a long and practical training, have enabled him to gain a full measure of profit from his intelligent labors. Politically a republican, Mr. Townsend has served at various times in school and road offices to the entire satisfaction of his fellow citizens. He is a member of the Baptist Church, in which he is at present serving as a deacon, and was treasurer of the building committee which erected the church at Bolckow in 1908. Mr. Townsend's fraternal connection is with Blue Lodge No. 413, Ancient, Free and Accepted Masons, at Bolckow.

On June 12, 1881, Mr. Townsend was united in marriage with Miss Lavina J. Wells, who was born in Andrew County, Missouri, February 18, 1863, a daughter of Judge F. M. Wells, a sketch of whose career will be found elsewhere in this work. Mr. and Mrs. Townsend have had two children. Their daughter, Miss Iola A., was born March 30, 1887, on the home farm, received her early education in the country schools, and subsequently attended the Maryville Normal School. She now resides at home. The only son of Mr. and Mrs. Townsend, Marion Calvin, was born August 14, 1883, and died August 10, 1886.

JAMES S. TOWNSEND. With the exception of two years, when in his young manhood he was engaged in clerking at Bolckow, James S. Townsend has passed his entire life on the farm and has devoted his entire energies to agricultural pursuits. For nearly thirty years he has resided on his present property, which is known as East View Stock Farm, located in section 8, Platte Township, Andrew County, a community in which he is known as a progressive and practical agriculturist and a public-spirited citizen who has ever been ready to assist his community's development.

Mr. Townsend was born in Andrew County, about two miles north of Savannah, May 5, 1855, and is a son of Jonathan and Kittie Ann (Landers) Townsend, a sketch of whose lives will be found in another part of this work. The third in order of birth of his parents' six children, James S. Townsend grew up amid rural surroundings, and passed his boyhood in much the same manner as other Missouri farmers' sons, assisting in the work of the homestead during the summer months, and securing his education in the country schools during the winter terms. He remained under the parental roof until 1880, in which year he went to Bolckow for an experience in merchandising, as a clerk, but after two years thus spent returned to the pursuits of the soil, first buying a farm west of Bolckow, from the Rev. Willis Sapp, one of the well-known properties of this locality. Mr. Townsend remained on this farm for four years, at the end of which period he sold out and bought his present tract, at that time known

as the Daniel Hildman farm, a property including 187 acres, on which
he has made his home since March, 1886. This has since been renamed
by Mr. Townsend, and is known now as the East View Stock Farm, Mr.
Townsend making a specialty of raising all kinds of high grade stock for
the market. He has made numerous substantial improvements on his
land, including two sets of modern buildings, and in every respect the
property reflects the enterprise, thrift and progressive ideas of its
owner. Mr. Townsend is well and favorably known in business circles
of Andrew County, and has various outside holdings and interests, at this
time being a stockholder in the Union State Bank, of Bolckow, with which
he has been identified since its organization. He has done much to
"boost" the agricultural interests of this part of the state, and is an
active and working member of the Whitesville Interstate Corn and Poultry Show. Politically a democrat, he has taken only a good citizen's
interests in matters of a political character. He has long been a
devout member of the Whitesville Baptist Church, and at this time is
serving in the capacity of deacon.

Mr. Townsend was married in 1882 to Miss Louisa Baum, who was
born in Benton Township, Andrew County, Missouri, March 10, 1859,
daughter of John and Christina (Frick) Baum, natives of Germany, who
came to the United States as young people. During the last fifteen years
of her life Mrs. Baum made her home with Mr. and Mrs. Townsend.
Two children have been born to this union: Prudie, who is the wife of
W. S. Miller of Platte Township, and had three children,—Eugene, who
died January 16, 1908, at the age of two years, four months, Reed and
Marjorie; and Vergie, who is the wife of Samuel Goforth, of Platte Township, and has had three children,—James Laverne, who died in infancy,
Virginia, and Winfred Dale.

JAMES FRANKLIN MUNKRES. The claim of James Franklin Munkres
upon the good will and confidence of the people of Andrew County rests
upon his long residence here, his high standing as a public-spirited and
stirring citizen, the success of his labors and the development of a good
agricultural property, and the straightforward manner in which all of his
dealings have been carried on. Mr. Munkres is now the owner of Brookdale Farm, a well-cultivated tract of land located in section 26, Benton
Township, which has been developed under his supervision into one of the
really valuable properties of this locality.

Born in Clay County, Missouri, October 12, 1854, Mr. Munkres is a
son of William and Frances Jane (Thorpe) Munkres, both of which
families were represented in Howard County, Missouri, as early as November, 1819, or two years before the admission of the state to the Union.
The Munkres family originated in Cornwall, England, and came to the
shores of America, settling at Jamestown, Virginia. The great-grandfather of James Franklin Munkres, William Munkres, was a native of
Virginia, served as a soldier throughout the War of the Revolution, and
in his declining years came to Clay County, Missouri, dying at the home
of one of his sons. The maternal grandparents of Mr. Munkres, John
and Elizabeth (Crowley) Thorpe, came from Tennessee to Missouri about
the same time as the Munkres, and the family history is practically the
same, the family having originated in England and gone thence to Virginia. Elizabeth (Crowley) Thorpe was a sister of Sam Crowley, a
sketch of whose life appears elsewhere in this work. The paternal grandparents of Mr. Munkres were Richard and Malinda (Lynch) Munkres,
natives respectively of Virginia and North Carolina and married in the
latter state. They came to Clay County, Missouri, as pioneers, Mr.
Munkres entering a large tract of land from the Government, and here

both he and the grandmother passed away. They reared a family of ten children, as follows: James, William, Redmond, John, David, Washington, Melvin, Mary, Louisa and Rachael. William Munkres, the father of James F. Munkres, was born in Tennessee in April, 1813, was six years of age when the family moved to Howard County, Missouri, and subsequently went to Clay County, where he continued to have interests throughout his life, although in 1858 he moved to Andrew County, where he was engaged in farming until his death, at the home of his son, in 1894. Mrs. Munkres, who was born in Holt County, Missouri, in 1828, died in Clay County in January, 1856, aged twenty-eight years.

James Franklin Munkres, the only child of his parents, was two years of age when his mother died, and for about three years thereafter resided with his grandparents. In 1860 he came to Andrew County, Missouri, and for about ten years boarded around at different houses, while he was securing his education in the public schools, and William Jewell College, at Liberty, Missouri, which he attended about two years. In 1868 Mr. Munkres and his father began "baching it" on the farm, and thus continued until the marriage of the younger man, when he set up an establishment of his own. Mr. Munkres has continued to be engaged in general farming and stockraising, and has met with good success in each department, raising large crops of grain annually and feeding large herds of stock. Brookdale Farm is a tract of 240 acres, the northwest quarter of section 26, and the south quarter of the southwest quarter of section 23, township 61, range 35, 1⅓ miles northwest of Rosendale. Here are located fine, substantial buildings, including a handsome residence, located on an elevation, sixty-eight rods from the highway, with a grove and creek to the south of the residence. Mr. Munkres is a skilled and practical farmer, ready at all times to experiment with new discoveries and inventions, and keeping fully abreast of his vocation. He is a democrat in his political views, and has served capably as justice of the peace for one term and as a member of the school board for twenty years.

On October 6, 1878, Mr. Munkres was married to Miss Mary A. Wilhelm, who was born in Andrew County, Missouri, March 19, 1860, a daughter of Ferdinand and Anna (Benner) Wilhelm, the former a native of Stotzen, and the latter of Hirschleheim, both towns in the Province of Hanover, Germany. They were married in St. Charles County, Missouri, December 24, 1847, and both died in Andrew County, the father in 1874, when fifty-nine years of age, and the mother June 24, 1909, when eighty-four years of age, at the home of her son-in-law, Mr. Munkres, with whom she had resided for fourteen years. They were the parents of one son and four daughters: J. L., a resident of Benton Township; Helen C., the wife of Jacob Schunck, of Benton Township; Henrietta D., who was the wife of Owen Deardoff and is now deceased; Elizabeth, deceased, who was the wife of J. B. Guinn; and Mrs. Munkres. Three children have been born to Mr. and Mrs. Munkres: Clara C., born July 11, 1879, a teacher in the public schools of Andrew County, educated at Gallatin (Missouri) College and the business college at Shenandoah, Iowa; Nellie C., born August 30, 1881, who graduated from Grand Business College, received instruction in instrumental music, and is now a teacher of music; and Anna Frances, born February 7, 1892, educated in the Savannah High School, married Frank E. Johnson, in February, 1910, resides at Bolckow, and has one daughter,—Mary Louise. Both Mr. and Mrs. Munkres are well educated, she being a graduate of Savannah High School, and he having been a school teacher in the rural schools of Andrew County, in 1875 and 1876 and the winter of 1877 and 1878.

LEONIDAS W. CRAIG. A resident of Andrew County for more than forty years, Leonidas W. Craig has during this time been engaged in farming pursuits, and is now the owner of Grass Hills Stock Farm, a magnificent tract of 653½ acres, located in section 7, Platte Township. Mr. Craig is a practical and progressive farmer and stockraiser, and has gained his present substantial position by the exercise of native ability and tireless industry, but at the same time, while gaining a personal competence, has contributed to the general welfare and advancement of his community. Mr. Craig is a Kentuckian, born at Ghent, Carroll County, January 13, 1850, a son of Walton and Lorinda (Peak) Craig.

Walton Craig was born at Ghent, Kentucky, in 1803, and as a lad was engaged in agricultural pursuits and continued to be interested in farming throughout his life, but also gave some attention to mercantile pursuits, and for a number of years was the proprietor of a store at Ghent. In 1856 he made a trip to Andrew County, preempting a farm in Platte Township, but soon returned to his native state, and there continued to make his home until his death, in 1886. Mr. Craig was a democrat in his political views, and his religious faith was that of the Baptist Church. He married Miss Lorinda Peak, who was born in Scott County, Kentucky, in 1809, and she died in 1869, having been the mother of seven children, as follows: Evelina Peak, deceased, who was the wife of the late James S. Frank; Bettie, deceased, who was the wife of the late James M. Fisher; Dudley Peak, a resident of Vevay, Indiana; Walton, a resident of Canton, Ohio; Albert G., who is deceased; Benjamin, a resident of Oklahoma; and Leonidas W.

Leonidas W. Craig received his education in the public schools of Ghent, Kentucky, and grew up as a farmer's boy, remaining on the homestead until 1874, in which year he came to Bolckow, Missouri, and settled on the farm which his father had preempted some eighteen years before. To the original property he has since added greatly, and at this time is the owner of 653½ acres, known as Grass Hills Stock Farm, one of the valuable and handsome tracts of Andrew County. Mr. Craig is a practical farmer, fully abreast of all modern methods and inventions, and carries on his operations in a progressive manner. Practically all the improvements made on the property have come under his supervision, and the substantial buildings, well-kept fields and prosperous appearance of the entire farm indicate that good management and thrift are not lacking. For many years Mr. Craig has been engaged in raising thoroughbred cattle, horses and hogs, for which he secures topnotch prices in the markets. He has a number of business connections aside from his farming operations, and at this time is a director of the Union State Bank of Bolckow, a position which he has held from the time of this institution's organization. Mr. Craig is a democrat in politics, but has strong temperance tendencies, and, other things being equal, is liable to give his vote to the candidate who has prohibition views. He is a member of the Baptist Church at Bolckow, in which he is serving as deacon.

Mr. Craig was married December 21, 1876, to Miss Mary Talbott, who was born in Minnesota, November 2, 1857, and who came to Missouri at the age of four years with her parents, R. H. and Elizabeth (Evans) Talbott, natives of Pennsylvania, who died at Baxter Springs, Kansas. Six children have been born to Mr. and Mrs. Craig, namely: Walton W., a resident of Bolckow; Frank J., a resident of Clay Township, Andrew County; Mary Elizabeth, who resides with her parents; Ulie P., who is engaged in cultivating a part of his father's farm; and Jane W. and Lorinda, who live with their parents.

THOMAS SLAWSON. Those economists and philosophers who have given the most thorough study to American problems and whose judgment deserves the highest consideration have frequently pointed out in recent years that the greatest and primary need of the country is more and better production from the land, rather than in the increase of commercial and industrial activities. For many years to come, say these scholars, American soil must produce not merely a sufficiency to supply the needs of our own country, but for the markets abroad. Since the area and resources of the United States are now thoroughly known, are not capable of continued expansion, the solution of the problem seems to rest upon more intensive cultivation, the making of one acre yield more than it has ever done before and the general improvement of the quality of the products, and this is exactly what the foremost agriculturists are doing and what the prominent agricultural associations are advocating. The slogan of the Missouri State Corn Growers' Association is "increase the yield, improve the quality."

In Northwest Missouri one of the best exponents of this new philosophy of intensive cultivation and of better quality is Thomas Slawson, of Rea, Andrew County. Mr. Slawson is one of the vice presidents of the Missouri State Corn Growers' Association, and is known over all the corn belt as the prize winner in the production of seed corn. His farm in section 28 of Platte Township is known as the Edgewood Seed Farm, and its products have been exhibited at hundreds of corn shows and agricultural fairs, have gained ribbons and prizes by the dozen and hundreds, and samples of the Slawson corn have been admired and inspected by thousands. While it is a most creditable occupation to grow the products of the field to supply the needs of direct consumption, it is a business many degrees higher in importance to supply the grain that can be used by hundreds of other farmers to plant their fields. That is the life work of Thomas Slawson, an Ohio man, who came into Andrew County a little over thirty years ago and has since made himself a factor in the development and progress of the great corn belt of the Middle West.

Thomas Slawson was born in Delaware County, Ohio, July 8, 1849, a son of Samuel and Ellen (Grant) Slawson. His father was born in New York and his mother in Rhode Island, grew up in Ohio and were married in that state. The mother died in Delaware County in 1900 at the age of sixty-four, and the father spent the last six years of his life with his son Thomas in Andrew County, dying in 1907 at the age of eighty-four. He was a farmer by general vocation, and also for a number of years dealt in lumber and walnut logs. He was also a great lover of horses and stock cattle, and in the early part of his career had bought and shipped stock from the Middle West to Buffalo and New York. There were just two children in the family, Thomas and Alice, the latter the wife of I. M. Spohn of Whitesville.

Thomas Slawson was reared in Ohio, received his education there, and in 1880 came out to Missouri and located at Rosendale. Two years later he established his home on his present farm, which comprises 585 acres, all of it in one body except 120 acres. The land is, as a matter of course, in the highest state of development, and Mr. Slawson has taken great care to conserve and improve the resources of the land and make them in the highest degree efficient for his purposes. While his business as a raiser of seed corn is perhaps of primary importance, he also keeps a large herd of stock, chiefly Shorthorn cattle. He is a man of original mind, and besides his activities in other directions patented a surface cul-

fairs and shows all over the Middle West that Mr. Slawson's name is most widely known. He has been one of the prominent exhibitors at the National Corn Show in Omaha for several years. In 1909 he won a prize of $100 on a single ear of corn at Des Moines, in a contest open to the world, and against about three thousand rivals for the prize. In 1908 he won first premium on yellow and white corn, and in 1909 his exhibit received the first premiums in the Missouri class at the National Corn Show in Omaha. He won two firsts at Columbia in the Missouri State Corn Show, one on the acre yield and the other on ten ears of white corn. At Dallas, Texas, in 1914, the first prize was given to the Slawson exhibit of oats. He also won two first premiums at the Sedalia State Fair, one each for yellow and white corn, in 1913, including the grand champion prize on corn. Also in 1913 he was given two first premiums and champion prize at the St. Joseph Interstate Fair. He has taken many other champion and sweepstake prizes, and has exhibited at more than two hundred fairs and shows. He has more than three hundred ribbons as proof of the honors won by his exhibits. Mr. Slawson sells seed corn all over the corn belt, and in this way disposes of about a thousand bushels annually, all of it raised in his own fields and commanding prices of from $2.50 to $5 per bushel. One year Mr. Slawson paid out more than three hundred dollars in order to buy back from the different fairs and shows his own exhibits, in order to carry them on to other fairs. During one year his cash premiums aggregated $350. Besides the numerous ribbons which have been bestowed on his exhibits, Mr. Slawson also has three trophy cups and two gold medals, the latter being awarded at Omaha, one in 1908 and the other in 1909. In order to hold the cups he had to win three consecutive times, and these cups are now in his permanent possession.

Mr. Slawson is a director of the Savannah Agricultural and Mechanical Society, and has been an assistant superintendent since its organization. He has been an important factor and one of the vice presidents for several years of the Missouri Corn Growers' Association. It is a matter of interest to note that some of the products from Mr. Slawson's fields were selected as part of the Missouri corn exhibit for the San Francisco Exposition of 1915. While he has done much along these lines to stimulate larger yields and better farming methods, he does not stop short of what he accomplishes through his own products, but lends his voice and argument wherever possible to better farming methods and especially to better stock. In his home community he has always been a public spirited worker for improvements. For three years he served as road overseer in his district, and the roads were kept in such excellent condition during that time that photographs were taken of them for exhibits in other places. Mr. Slawson has furnished grain from his farm for class work in the Maryville Normal, the Savannah High School and also the agricultural school at the State University.

In 1882 Mr. Slawson married Agnes Heaverlo. She was born in Delaware County, Ohio, July 13, 1853, a daughter of Jacob and Elizabeth (Eakelbery) Heaverlo. Both her parents were natives of Ohio and in the fall of 1880 came to Andrew County and spent the rest of their lives on a farm near Rosendale. Mr. and Mrs. Slawson are the parents of eight children: Wesley; Frederick, who died October 1, 1903, just at the entrance to a promising manhood, being then twenty-one years of age; Nellie, wife of Walter Worthington of Gravity, Iowa; Nettie; Bessie; Ruby; Harry; and Grover. All the children live at home except Nellie, and all were born in Andrew County.

HON. WILLIAM MARVIN DENSLOW. Representing one of the early families of Grundy County, Mr. Denslow has for a quarter of a century been an active newspaper man, a professional photographer and prominent in public affairs, having held several responsible positions in local and state government.

William M. Denslow was born in Grundy County, Missouri, August 9, 1858. His father was the late Judge William V. Denslow, who was born in Jennings County, Indiana, February 7, 1823. Grandfather Denslow lost his life from an attack of cholera while crossing the plains in 1849. Judge William V. Denslow moved from Indiana to Benton County, Iowa, settling near Shellsburg, and in 1856 became an early settler in Grundy County, Missouri, and remained in the same neighborhood until his death on April 25, 1882. His home was five miles east of Spickard. In August, 1861, he enlisted in the Union army in Company C of the Twenty-third Missouri Infantry. On April 6, 1862, in the great battle of Shiloh he was captured at 4 o'clock on that memorable Sunday and for six months and thirteen days endured the rigors of confinement in the notorious Libby prison and other Southern prisons. While at Libby he almost starved to death and as a result of that and exposure his constitution was nearly wrecked. After the war he took an active interest in politics, and in 1868 was elected a member of the Grundy County Court, and used his influence to build up the commercial interests of the county in every possible way. At that time Grundy County was without a railroad, and he was one of the leaders in promoting and advocating railroad construction, and finally in 1871 had the pleasure of seeing the completion of the Chicago and Southwestern branch of the Chicago, Rock Island & Pacific Railroad through Grundy County and on to the Southwest. Judge Denslow was an active republican in politics. Fraternally he was affiliated with the Masonic order, including the Royal Arch degree, and belonged to the Methodist Episcopal Church. A man of convictions, he never hesitated to make known his opinion on any public question without waiting to ascertain if such an opinion would be popular. In July, 1855, Judge W. V. Denslow was united in marriage with Miss Martha M. Coyburn, a native of Kentucky. To their union were born three children: Cornelius E., William M. and John A., all of whom are living. Martha M. Denslow, the mother, died at her home in Spickard April 10, 1899.

The early education of William M. Denslow was completed in the Trenton High School, and at the age of seventeen, at the request of the board of education in the Denslow district, where he had grown up and attended country school, he became a teacher in a locality where he knew all the boys and girls, and the fact that he taught a very successful term was in a high degree creditable to his capacity for leadership. He continued to teach there for three terms and elsewhere in the county for several years. Mr. Denslow, however, has for many years given most of his time to newspaper work, to photography, and public affairs. In 1888 he took charge of the Grundy County Gazette at Spickard. That paper had just been established and had less than twenty-five bona-fide subscribers. Under his management the paper grew until its sworn prepaid subscription list comprised more than one thousand readers. In 1898 he was elected president of the Northwest Missouri Press Association at St. Joseph.

In the meantime he had been drawn into public affairs. He represented Grundy County in the State Legislature from 1895 to 1899, and served in the thirty-eighth and thirty-ninth and the extraordinary sessions of the Legislature during that time. On July 1, 1898, he was appointed United States district deputy revenue collector with headquarters at Macon. In 1899 he moved his residence to Macon, and continued in the Government service until the repeal of the Spanish-American war tax law. He then became editor and business manager of the Macon Citizen, a newspaper then owned by the late Colonel Blees. In 1902 the four newspapers of Macon were consolidated into two plants, and Mr. Denslow then engaged in professional photography at Macon. Altogether he was in that profession at Macon for six years, and for one year had a studio at Kirksville and for two years at Trenton.

In 1908 the Trenton Daily News was organized with a capital stock of $10,000 and chartered as the News Publishing Company, with W. M. Denslow as editor. In less than three years this paper under his management had succeeded in building up the largest bona-fide daily subscription list of any daily paper in Grundy County. After nearly three years as editor and manager of the daily and weekly, Mr. Denslow resigned in order to take charge as secretary and manager of the Denslow History Company, which at that time was arranging for the publication of a voluminous history of Adair County, a publication which required two years' time to complete. After the successful issue of that publication Mr. Denslow concentrated his attention upon the business of photography at Trenton, until June, 1914, when he was called to take the position of local editor of the Trenton Daily and Weekly Times, a position in which he is still engaged.

Mr. Denslow has always been a republican in politics, but for the past several years the party has not shown sufficient progressiveness to justify his support, and in 1912 he entered the ranks of the progressives, and is still active in the support of their principles. Fraternally he is affiliated with the Masonic lodge, the Royal Arch chapter, is Past Eminent Commander of Godfrey de Bouillon Commandery No. 24, Knights Templar, at Trenton, and also has affiliation with the Woodmen of the World and the Brotherhood of American Yeomen.

On May 22, 1880, Mr. Denslow married Malinda Caroline Schooler, a daughter of William D. and Malinda (Nichols) Schooler. To their marriage has been born one son, Ray V., a prominent Northwest Missouri citizen whose career is briefly sketched elsewhere in this publication.

JUDGE HENRY MILLS. In the election of November, 1912, the only candidate on the progressive ticket in Caldwell County to be elected was Henry Mills, who had been nominated by the new party for the office of county judge for the eastern district of the county. The mere fact of his election against the candidates of the older parties demonstrates his popularity and wide acquaintance in the county, and his fitness for the responsibility and the honor on the basis of his subsequent administration is unquestioned and exceptional. Judge Mills has been a resident of Caldwell County most of his life, has been a practical and successful farmer, and has always been noted for his honesty and efficiency in every undertaking with which his name has been connected. He is an excellent business man, and in his private affairs as in his public duties has shown progressive views and is always ready to uphold what he believes to be right and his duty. His body has nominated him for a second term.

Judge Henry Mills was born on a farm April 26, 1872. His father, A. Mills, a native of Kentucky and of Kentucky and Virginia ancestors, saw service as a Union soldier during the Civil war. He was married in Kentucky to Miss Dicy Messer, also a native of Kentucky. They came into Missouri and settled in Ray County, where the father followed farming until his death at the age of seventy years. In politics he was a republican, a member of the Grand Army of the Republic, and both he and his wife were active in the Baptist Church. His wife died at the age of sixty-five. There were six children, two sons and four daughters.

Judge Henry Mills grew up on a farm and as soon as his strength permitted was made acquainted with the practical details of farm work, in which way he acquired a substantial training for the business which he has since followed, and was also given the advantages of the public schools. He began his career without means, and by industry, good management and close application has made a noteworthy success as a farmer and stockraiser. Judge Mills owns 255 acres of land eight miles northwest of Cowgill, and there has one of the best improved and most valuable estates in the county. His farm shows in its every detail the progressive character of its owner.

Judge Mills married Dora Parker, who was born in Iowa, but received her education in Clay County, Missouri. Her father was William Parker, who with his wife is now deceased.

CHARLES G. TOWNSEND. No name in the northern part of Andrew County bespeaks a larger family relationship and one whose members have been more actively and influentially identified with the community than that of Townsend. With only a brief reference to the history of older generations, which has been covered in other articles in this work, the following paragraph will be confined to the career of one representative of the family, Charles G. Townsend, who for a number of years has made a success as a farmer and stock man in section 23 of Benton Township.

Charles C. Townsend was born in Winterset, Iowa, September 19, 1861, and is the eighth of ten children of William Calvin and Mary Ann (Judd) Townsend. The residence of the family in Iowa was only temporary, and soon after Charles C. Townsend's birth they returned to Missouri and located in Andrew County.

Charles C. Townsend grew up in this section of Northwest Missouri, attended the local schools, and for more than thirty years has been one of the prosperous factors in the agricultural district of Benton Township. He is the owner of 142 acres, a portion of his father's estate, and is a farmer on the intensive plan, operating his property in the growing of grain and stock.

Aside from his industry as a farmer his name has been well known in the community through its relations with public affairs. For about twenty-five years Mr. Townsend served as judge of elections. He is president of the board of education, which position he has held for the past fifteen years, and is also a director in the Andrew County Agricultural and Mechanical Society. Politically he lines up his principles and actions with the republican party. Mr. and Mrs. Townsend are both members of the Baptist Church at Bolckow, and he was superintendent of the Sunday school six years and treasurer of the church seventeen years. Fraternally Mr. Townsend is affiliated with Lodge No. 413, A. F. & A. M., at Bolckow. On December 14, 1890, he married Alice Wells, who was born in Putnam County, Missouri, June 19, 1865, and died at her home in Andrew County, January 14, 1908. She was the daughter of Judge F. M. Wells. Mrs. Townsend was a woman of thorough culture both of mind and heart, and was noted for her many useful activities. She spent about ten years as a teacher in Andrew County, having begun that vocation at the age of sixteen. A part of her education came from the Stanberry Normal School. She was also an effective member of the Baptist Church and for many years a teacher in the Sunday school. Four children were born to Mr. and Mrs. Townsend: Grace, who lives at home; Mabel, who died at the age of six months; Ray L.; and Warren Reid.

J. G. MOHN. One of the most favored localities in Caldwell County is Lincoln Township, and among the excellent farm homes found in this locality is the Sunnyside Farm, the proprietor of which is Mr. J. G. Mohn. Mr. Mohn is a native of Germany, though nearly all his life has been spent in America, and has introduced some of the German characteristics of thrift and thorough industry and careful management into his work as a Northwest Missouri farmer and stock man. His farm is located 4½ miles southwest of Cowgill, and contains 160 acres of rich and productive land, farmed to the crops of corn, wheat, oats and grass, and his profits come largely through dairy and general stock raising. He keeps a good dairy with ten cows of high grade, and his other stock are cattle, hogs and poultry. The Mohn residence is a modern home of seven rooms, well furnished in good taste, and occupying a particularly attractive building site, overlooking a broad expanse of prairie and woodland, the view being one that is hardly excelled in this beautiful region of Caldwell County. Around the house are many large shade trees and a well kept and bearing orchard. Mr. Mohn has a large barn for his stock, 30x40 feet, besides sheds and granary, and keeps all his farming equipment in first-class condition, and even the casual observer can spell thrift and industry in every department of Sunnyside Farm.

Mr. J. G. Mohn was born in Germany in 1855, and his father was Fred Mohn, who had been reared on a German farm and was trained in the careful and thrifty manner of the German agriculturist. J. G. Mohn was a small boy when his parents emigrated to America and settled in Pennsylvania, where his father died when about twenty-eight years of age, leaving a widow and two sons, J. G. and William; the latter is now a resident of Colorado. The widow was again married and came out to Ray County, Missouri, and died there. Both the parents were Lutherans in religion, and were substantial, honest and honorable people, and those qualities have been exemplified in their children.

J. G. Mohn was educated in the public schools, and was taught as one of the first principles the value and need of industry and honest relations with his fellow men. In 1884 Mr. Mohn married Miss M. Zieseniss, a woman of intelligence and piety who has been his loyal helpmate for thirty years. She comes of a family who for many years lived near Hamilton, Missouri, and her father was Henry Zieseniss, a prosperous farmer of Ray County, who was born in Germany and died in Ray County in 1893, at the age of sixty-eight. Mrs. Mohn was one of a family of five children, and has three brothers and one sister still living in Ray County. Mr. and Mrs. Mohn are the parents of three children: Mildred, wife of Frank Lamer, who lives near Polo, and they have two small children, one son and one daughter; and Albert Oscar, both of whom are at home. The sons were well educated, and are now progressive young farmers and assist actively in the management of Sunnyside Farm. Mr. Mohn is a republican in politics, and his wife belongs to the Methodist Church, and all the family have done much to support and keep up church activities in their community.

J. EDWARD CLARY. The substantial occupation of farming has enlisted both the early and the later interests of J. Edward Clary, who for thirty years has been a resident of Worth County, and for twenty-two years of this period has been located on his present property, two miles southeast of Sheridan. Mr. Clary came to Missouri from Menard County, Illinois, where he was born December 29, 1857. His childhood was spent on the family homestead near the Village of Petersburg, and his education came from the country schools, his father, Hugh Clary, being an agriculturist. The latter was also born in that county, spent his entire life there as a modest farmer, and died in November, 1896. He was without political history, save as a supporter of the democratic party, and was a member of the Presbyterian Church.

The Clary family were among the very first to settle in Menard County, Illinois. Judge John Clary, grandfather of J. Edward, located at Clary's Grove, in that county, about 1818, the year that Illinois was admitted as a state. Judge Clary was a Tennesseean, and was one of the judicial officers of Menard County during pioneer days. He was one of the old-time judges, upon whom it devolved to enforce the Illinois statutes as then in force, and the old volume of statutes which he used in his office with his name inscribed on the fly leaf in his own hand with a quill pen is one of the valued heirlooms in the home of J. E. Clary. Judge Clary's settlement in Illinois was at a time when that region was still overrun with Indians, and at this time it seems rather strange that he should imperil the lives of his family by exiling them among the redmen of the forest and plains in order to take part in the initial work of bringing civilization to a wilderness locality. He made the trip from Tennessee by the usual mode of travel, horseback, and brought with him his wife and two children. After selecting his location he left his little family to the mercies of a kind Providence, while he returned to his native state on a business mission that could not be transacted without his presence. His absence necessarily covered a period of weeks, and his family sorely felt his absence and proportionately welcomed his return. He was a factor in the establishment of order and the enforcement of law of the primitive sort that prevailed. Judge Clary was a factor in Menard County public affairs when "Honest Abe Lincoln" with his mighty frame and homely face presented himself as a citizen of the Prairie State, and the Clary and Armstrong homes provided for brief periods a residence for the youth who was later to become the nation's preserver. The wife of Judge Clary was a Miss Armstrong, a sister of old "Jackie" Armstrong, Lincoln's old chum in Menard County, and whose son, Duffy Armstrong, Lincoln defended and cleared of a charge of murder. Two of Judge Clary's sons were in the Mexican war. One of them, Thomas, died while the troops were crossing the Gulf of Mexico, and his body was lowered over the side of the transport into the waters of the gulf. The other, Robert, returned to Illinois after the war and lived out his life there. Other children of Judge Clary were: Royal; John; William; Martha, who married James Bell; James; Hugh; and Abe L., who was the first white child ever named after Abraham Lincoln in that county, and who died in the spring of 1914.

Hugh Clary, father of J. Edward Clary, married Louisa Traylor, a daughter of Henry Traylor. She is still living in Menard County, Illinois. Their children were as follows: John H. of Petersburg, Illinois; J. Edward; Samantha, who married G. M. Hudspeth of Petersburg, Illinois; Leonidas, of Petersburg; William T., of Beason, Illinois; Frank of Petersburg; Warren P. of Grant City, Missouri; and Marion B. of Petersburg, Illinois.

J. Edward Clary has special distinction in Worth County through his business as a breeder of jacks for a quarter of a century, an industry which has developed into considerable proportions. He is one of the three men who have been most prominent in advertising Worth County in the stock business, and his products have been shipped to most of the states of the Union. Mr. Clary has also extensively engaged in feeding cattle for the market, and has through his enterprise in this direction afforded a market for thousands of bushels of corn in his neighborhood. He is also a sheep breeder, and for years handled the full bloods of the Shropshire strain. It is difficult to appreciate the full

extent of the influence that can be exerted by the presence of one enterprising citizen in such a rural community as Worth County. Mr. Clary,
as an instance of his progressiveness, built the first silo in Worth County,
and demonstrated to his own satisfaction and that of many farmers who
examined it the success of this container as a means of conserving and
modifying the food qualities of forage crops for all kinds of stock. He
subsequently, with the confidence bred of his own experience, took an
active part in introducing silos all over the county. When the good
roads movement was launched in this part of Northwest Missouri, it
found in Mr. Clary an earnest and enthusiastic advocate, and for twenty
years he has helped drag the road from his place to Sheridan. He
made the first road drag ever used in this county, taking his pattern
from an address delivered by Mr. King, the inventor of the road drag,
at Sheridan. He has well sustained in his community a reputation as
an energetic, enterprising, progressive and public-spirited citizen.

On first coming to Missouri, in 1884, Mr. Clary settled on a property
northwest of Sheridan, a short time later moved into town, and from
there came to his present place in 1892. He has been an ardent democrat all his life, but though attending county conventions has had no
aspirations to serve the public in an official way. Fraternally he is
connected with the Modern Woodmen of America and the Brotherhood
of American Yeomen. Though reared a Presbyterian, he affiliates chiefly
with the Christian Church.

On February 22, 1881, Mr. Clary was married at Petersburg, Illinois,
to Miss Louie E. Dowell, a daughter of Thomas F. Dowell. Mrs. Clary
died December 4, 1884, leaving one daughter, Bertha. The second marriage of Mr. Clary occurred April 1, 1886, when he married Miss Amy
E. Allison, the oldest daughter and fourth child in a family of nine born
to James Allison, a successful Missouri farmer. To Mr. and Mrs. Clary
the following children have been born: Luther L., who is engaged in
farming in the vicinity of Sheridan; and by his marriage to Ethel
Calkins has two children, James Edward and Marzella; Harvey E., also
a farmer who makes his home near that of his father, married Florence
Scott, a daughter of W. W. Scott, and has one daughter, Alline; Kyle A.,
a farmer in the locality of Sheridan, who married Selma Straight;
Norma R., who married Newton Burns of Sheridan, has two children,
Marvel and Max; Gertrude, who is a student in the Maryville State
Normal School; and Elsie Marie, who lives at home and attends the pub-
lic schools in Sheridan.

JOHN T. COTTIER. This name bespeaks a large family relationship
with pioneer settlers in Northwestern Missouri, and fully seventy years
have passed since the Cottiers first became identified with Holt County.
Agriculture has been the chief vocation of the family, and an examination of the records shows the Cottiers have been upholders of morality
and religion and people of kindly neighborliness and usefulness.

John T. Cottier was born in Holt County on the old Cottier homestead. That place was long one of the landmarks in Lewis Township,
and there was no change in its ownership from about 1847 until 1899.
Thomas Cottier, the father of John, was born on the Isle of Man in 1829.
He married Minerva Beeler. They were married on the old Beeler
homestead at Oregon, Missouri, February 7, 1850. Thomas Cottier came
to Northwest Missouri by boat up the Missouri River as far as St. Joseph,
and walked overland to Holt County as far as Oregon in 1847. He
bought a relinquishment on an old land claim comprising 315 acres, and
thus acquired the Cottier homestead, which was owned by him until
his death. When he first found the land it had no improvements, and

his first habitation was a log house, roofed with clapboards. His home was on this farm until 1891, when he moved to Forest City, Holt County, where he remained until his death in 1899. All his children, eight in number, were born on the farm. After his death the estate was divided and the homestead is now the property of Paul Elliott. Thomas Cottier was a sterling pioneer, and among his early experiences was as a soldier in the Mexican war, driving an ox team and wagon to Mexico.

John T. Cottier grew up among pioneer scenes, was educated in the district schools and also took a course in the high school at Oregon. At the age of twenty-seven Mr. Cottier established a home of his own by his marriage on September 5, 1882, to Cora Ferrin, daughter of Reuben Ferrin, who was one of the early settlers in Minnesota Valley. Mr. and Mrs. Cottier have six children: Hugh M., who married Flora Meyer, daughter of Judge George Meyer; Bettie, Helen, Thomas, Fay and Theodore.

Since his marriage Mr. Cottier has occupied his present home farm, and all his children were born there. He is the owner of 320 acres, all of it under cultivation, and his material progress and enterprise are illustrated by the improvements and commodious buildings which stand on the farm, all of which have been placed there since he took possession. Mr. Cottier and family are members of the Methodist Episcopal Church, and in politics he is a progressive.

R. K. Ross. Sixty or seventy years ago Holt County was still largely wilderness. The settlers about that time found a few village communities, numerous clearings and tilled fields, and some roads, but still the burden rested upon most newcomers of cutting down countless trees, uprooting the stumps and brush, and starting cultivation where never before had been the civilized activities of white men. That was the condition when the Ross family first became identified with this section of Northwest Missouri, and as its members did their share of pioneer toil, so a later generation has enjoyed the fruits of better days, and has carried forward the same thrift and independence which have always characterized the name.

Mr. R. K. Ross, one of the most substantial farmer citizens of the county, represents the second generation of the family's residence, and is himself one of the older native sons. He was born at Ross Grove, November 26, 1852. His parents were Robert K. and Jane (Bird) Ross. His father was born in North Carolina and reared in Tennessee, where he married Miss Bird, a native of the latter state. Nine of their children were born in Tennessee, and altogether the family comprised fifteen children, three of whom died in infancy. In 1846 or 1847 Robert K. Ross came out to Northwest Missouri. Railroads had not yet penetrated this section, and all transportation and carriage was either by boat or overland by wagon and pack horse. He made the journey with wagon and team, and arrived in this wilderness country without means. He worked for others for a time, and in 1851 settled on a small tract of land which he had acquired at Ross Grove. The first habitation erected for the shelter of his family was one of the typical log houses, and it was in that rude structure that R. K. Ross first saw the light of day. For a number of years wild game was plentiful, and even Indians were frequent visitors at the home of the settlers. The land was divided between prairie and timber, and in either case it was a difficult task to prepare it for cultivation. Robert K. Ross made his first acquisitions of land partly from the Government and partly from private owners, and paid from $2.50 to $3 an acre. He was a man of industry, of good habits, and of moral and religious character. He lived many years with

his son R. K., and died February 4, 1899, and was laid to rest at Mound City. As a result of his industry he left an estate of 200 acres. He was at one time the owner of 380 acres of land, but of this he sold a part to his three boys. His wife passed away in July, 1876,

R. K. Ross had the advantage of the district schools only, but no small part of his education was acquired in the home circle, by his own effort, through the advice of his teacher, and he therefore urges upon all young people not to neglect study at home. He lived at home with his father until March 1, 1877, and then started out on a farm of eighty acres. Mr. Ross married Mary Wehrli in 1877, a daughter of Peter and Mary (Vogel) Wehrli. Mrs. Ross was one of nine children, and the only daughter. To Mr. and Mrs. Ross have been born nine children, two of whom died in infancy: William T., who married Arletta Byergo; Robert, deceased; Isaac M., who married Elizabeth Jobe; Earl L., who married Emma Goodpasture; Roscoe P.; Varna May, who married E. L. McConnell; and Eva M. All the children were born on the home farm.

Mr. Ross' farm comprises the land on which he first settled after his marriage. All the improvements are the result of his management. He has owned as high as 618½ acres of Missouri land, but has divided it in part with his children.

For many years Mr. Ross has been an active member in the denomination known as the Reorganized Church of Jesus Christ of the Latter Day Saints. There has been a church of that denomination in this vicinity ever since 1870, and Mr. Ross has for the past thirty-six or thirty-seven years served as an elder. The church house at the present location has stood for about fifteen years. Its membership at the present time is fifty-eight. Mr. Ross' father was a prominent early settler who gave service to the community on the school board, and was one of the republicans in the early days. He was also a Mason. R. K. Ross has served as justice of the peace for eight years and served as one of the school board for several years. Like his father, he is a republican.

JOHN H. TOWNSEND. In the eightieth year of his age the venerable John H. Townsend still occupies his fine old homestead in section 21 of Benton Township, Andrew County. Mr. Townsend came to Andrew County when a boy, and imprinted on his life record and recollection are all the important phases of development, beginning with the pioneer period of log houses and primitive schools and crude means of cultivation, transportation and marketing, the beginning of the railroad era, and finally all those remarkable changes brought about in the age of electricity and modern machinery and industrialism. He is one of the splendid old citizens of Northwest Missouri, has spent his life in the quiet and unobtrusive vocation of the farmer, but in all his public relations has served his community well and is the head of a fine family.

John H. Townsend was born in Morgan County, Indiana, October 25, 1835. His parents were Ellison and Catherine (Zimmerman) Townsend. His father was born in Washington County, Indiana, during the pioneer period, January 2, 1817, about a year after Indiana became a state. Catherine Zimmerman was born in North Carolina June 2, 1816, a daughter of Joseph Zimmerman, a native of Germany. Her father married in North Carolina, Miss Fiscus, who died in Stokes County of that state. The father later followed his two married daughters to Indiana and spent the rest of his life in that state, having been a farmer by vocation. Ellison Townsend and wife were married in Morgan County, Indiana, January 3, 1833. In the paternal line Mr. Townsend is descended from good old American stock. His grandparents were William and Mary (Voiles) Townsend, the former a native of North Carolina and the latter of Washington County, Indiana. William Townsend died in Morgan County, Indiana, but had lived in Andrew County, Missouri, from 1847 to 1857. He was also a farmer, and farming has been the regular vocations of the Townsends from their early settlement in America. The great-grandfather of John H. Townsend was also named William Townsend, and was a soldier from North Carolina in the Revolutionary war, serving under Gen. Nathaniel Greene. He joined the army in 1776 and served seven years, going through Tennessee, South Carolina, and Georgia, and never receiving a wound. He was also a Baptist and was born in 1755, dying at the age of seventy-seven. He married Miss Mary McGraw, and had two brothers, Henry and Joseph.

Ellison Townsend and wife resided in Morgan County, Indiana, until they removed to Missouri in the fall of 1847. They came in covered wagons and saw their first railroad, which came no further West than Springfield, Illinois. They located a mile and half north of Savannah. This was then a new country, very little of the prairie land had been broken and only here and there had the axe been laid at the root of the trees in the great forests that covered so much of the fertile soil. Ellison Townsend lived on his farm near Savannah until his death on August 30, 1870. His wife passed away there June 12, 1877. He became a factor in community affairs and served in the office of public administrator, appointed under the provisional government on June 3, 1862, and was afterward elected, serving until January 1, 1869. As justice of the peace, he was appointed in August, 1856, when Nodaway Township was changed to include Jasper and part of Jackson, and was elected and re-elected, serving until 1866. He supported the republican party and was a member of the Masonic Order.

Ellison Townsend and wife had eleven children who reached maturity, four of them now living. These children are briefly mentioned as follows: Elizabeth Worth, deceased; John H.; Rebecca Fazee, deceased; Delilah Roberts, deceased; Mary Catherine Maxwell of Nodaway County; Joseph F., who served two years as county collector in Andrew County and is now deceased; William, who died in Indiana, but spent many years in Andrew County and enlisted from this state for service in the Civil war; Jesse A., of Wyoming; Jane Maxwell, who died in Iowa; Martha A. Alexander, deceased; and Louis A., of Savannah.

John H. Townsend has lived in Andrew County since 1847, being about twelve years of age when the family removed to this part of Northwest Missouri. Savannah was six years old then and he remembers it as a small hamlet with only a few frame houses, the others being of logs. He had attended country schools back in Indiana, and was also a student in one of the early schoolhouses of Andrew County, the first one being a log house on the south line of the Lander's homestead. Since early manhood his career has been consistently pursued along one line, that of farming. He lived at home with his parents until his marriage, then rented a farm about six years, until about 1864, and then invested his small capital in 120 acres south of Bolckow. There was no town there then, not until after the railroad came in 1868. Mr. Townsend had to move his log house off the right of way. He had moved this log house here from the last place he had rented. He sold that property in 1890, and later he bought his present place, which was formerly the property of his wife's father, who purchased it in 1857. The farm originally comprised 275 acres, but some of it has since been sold to his two sons. In the course of many years this farm has produced many crops and has returned much substantial revenue to its owners. The general business has been farming and stock raising. The place is well improved, and Mr. Townsend some years ago erected one of the most substantial country homes in this part of the county. Mr. Townsend is a republican and has taken some part in public affairs, having been elected in 1872 as the first justice of the peace of Benton Township and serving twelve years. He is a member of the Baptist Church, and is at the present time the oldest member in active standing in the Bolckow Lodge of Masons.

On April 13, 1858, John H. Townsend married Malinda Roberts. She was also born in Morgan County, Indiana, July 25, 1841. Her parents were Benjamin and Elizabeth (Roberts) Roberts, who came out to Missouri and settled in Andrew County in the spring of 1856. It was on the old Roberts homestead that Miss Roberts married Mr. Townsend and has lived there the greater part of her life. Her parents, though of the same name, were not related, and were both natives of Pulaski County, Kentucky, her father born in 1811 and her mother in 1810. They were married in Kentucky and about 1830 moved across the river into Indiana, and both died on the old farm in Andrew County, the mother at the age of eighty-four and the father at seventy-seven. They took an active part in the establishment of the pioneer schools and churches in their locality and were Baptists as were their parents before them. There were eleven children in the Roberts family, eight of whom reached maturity, as follows: Gideon, deceased; Margaret Stotts, deceased; Rebecca Best, deceased; John, who was killed in the battle of Shiloh in April, 1862; Malinda Townsend; Elizabeth Jane Stotts of Hill City, Kansas; James Mason, of St. Joseph; and Joseph, who died in 1911.

To the marriage of John H. Townsend and wife were born the following children: Elizabeth Jane, Joseph M., Benjamin Pierce and Delilah Olive. There are a number of grandchildren and even great-grandchildren. Elizabeth Jane married George Baum, and at her death on February 8, 1905, she left three children: Alma, wife of George T. Genther, and the mother of two children, Margaret E. and Christina Malinda; John, who married Pearl Genther, and their two children are Catherine L. and John, Jr.; Jacob Lenoir, who married Emma Shipley, and they have two children, George and Ellen Emma. The son, Joseph M., who lives on a farm near his father, married Lucy Wilson, and their three children are named Gladys L., George Joseph and Flint Wilson. Benjamin Pierce, who helps to manage the home farm for his father, married Matie Whitney, and their four children are Elvie Alice, John Paul, Linn Whitney and William Victor. Delilah Olive is the wife of Mr. S. E. Lee, the newspaper man of Savannah, and a brief sketch of Mr. and Mrs. Lee is found on other pages of this work.

FRANKLIN HUNT BROYLES, M. D., has been a resident of Bethany since the year 1900, and during this time has been engaged in the active practice of his profession, in which he has won an enviable standing among his fellow practitioners and in the confidence of the community. He came to Bethany from Pawnee County, Nebraska, where, at Table Rock, he was a professional man for ten years, but lived in the state thirteen years, being stationed at Beatrice for three years in the same vocation. Dr. Broyles came to Missouri from Tennessee, having been born near Jonesboro, that state, September 2, 1859. His childhood was spent on a farm, his early education being secured in the district schools. He furthered his training at Martin Academy, at Jonesboro, and began the study of medicine in 1883, reading with Dr. S. S. Todd, of Kansas City, Missouri, and following this took lectures in the Kansas City Medical College and graduated there in March, 1887, following which he went straight out to Nebraska, and there spent his first three years as a physician at Beatrice.

At Bethany Dr. Broyles has served both as secretary and president of the Harrison County Medical Society and as city and county physician, and has been a member and president of the board of education for a number of years. He is local surgeon for the Chicago, Burlington & Quincy Railroad Company, and is a member of the Burlington System Surgeons' Association; also a member of the Missouri State and American Medical associations. Fraternally Dr. Broyles is a member of the blue lodge, chapter and commandery of the Masonic fraternity here, is a Pythian Knight and belongs to several fraternal insurance orders. His religious connection is with the Christian Church, of which his wife and children are also members.

Doctor Broyles was married at Auburn, Nebraska, October 26, 1887, to Miss Leila Watkins, a daughter of David and Elizabeth (McGrew) Watkins of Ohio. David Watkins was born February 26, 1824, at Radnor, Ohio, and died November 13, 1912, at Auburn, Nebraska. Elizabeth McGrew, his wife, was born May 31, 1827, at Alexandersville, Ohio, and died June 7, 1908, at Auburn, Nebraska. David Watkins and Elizabeth McGrew were married December 24, 1851, at West Carrollton, Ohio. David Watkins located in Nebraska in 1857, when the nearest railroad to that locality was at Iowa City, Iowa. In Nemaha County he took up agricultural pursuits, and lived on the same farm until his death, when he was nearly eighty-nine years of age. His children were as follows: Arlington, who died at Bethany, Missouri, leaving a family which now resides at Medicine Lodge, Kansas; Mrs. Broyles, wife of the doctor; Mrs. Charlena Ramsey, wife of Dr. A. J. Ramsey, of Auburn, Nebraska; and William, a resident of North Yakima, Washington. To Doctor and Mrs. Broyles there have been born the following children: Glen H., a senior in the medical department of the University of Kansas; Watkins A., a senior at the Bethany High School; and Elizabeth L., a junior at the Bethany High School.

The father of Doctor Broyles is Andrew C. Broyles, a native of Tennessee, who resides in that state at Knoxville. He spent the active years of his life in agricultural pursuits, and is still in good health at the age of eighty-three years. Mr. Broyles was educated at Emory and Henry College, Virginia, and missed the Civil war as a soldier, was not in politics, save as a member of the county court of his county, and belonged to the Southern Methodist Church. He has passed a normal and rather unassuming life, but has been a man of sound vigor and earnest in his support of what he has considered beneficial measures.

The grandfather was Jacob F. Broyles, who was born December 10, 1804, in Chucky Valley, Tennessee, married Lucinda Broyles, a very distant relative, December 13, 1827, and died at Jonesboro, Tennessee, November 2, 1895. His wife, who was born September 11, 1804, died at Jonesboro, Tennessee, October 4, 1891. Jacob F. Broyles was a farmer, but also served as a boatman down the Tennessee River before the advent of railroads, and served as a magistrate in his district for many years, being a democrat, as were his sons, and a member of the Methodist Church, in which he served as a class leader for sixty years. His children were as follows: Andrew C., the father of Doctor Broyles; Margaret A. became the wife of John S. Henley, who died near Jonesboro, Tennessee; Adam H., of Chattanooga, Tennessee; James V., who met his death in battle as a Confederate soldier December 21, 1864; John S., of Erwin, Tennessee; Frances R., who married Joseph Hunter and died at Jonesboro, Tennessee; Mary A., who became the wife of William Sparks, of Johnson City, Tennessee; Malinda E., who died at Jonesboro, unmarried.

The father of Jacob F. Broyles was John Broyles, born in Culpeper County, Virginia, October 7, 1773. About the close of the Revolutionary war he went to Horse Creek, Greene County, Tennessee, and settled on a farm, and was there married in 1796 to Frances Bays, who was born in 1771 in Rutherford County, North Carolina. John Broyles died March 3, 1847, and his wife April 27, 1847. He was a son of Jacob Broyles, who was born in Culpepper County, Virginia, in 1743, and married Elizabeth Yowel of a noted Virginia family. The father of this Jacob Broyles was John Broyles, believed to have been born in 1710 and was one of two brothers who came to America from Germany and settled in Culpeper County, Virginia, about 1740, while his brother, George Broyles, located in Randolph County, North Carolina.

The children of John and Frances (Bays) Broyles were as follows: Mary, who married John Wilhoit, was born October 27, 1798, and died in February, 1877, in Tennessee; Elizabeth, born March 20, 1800, married Jacob Broyles, and was drowned in Nola Chucky River on Easter Sunday, March 28, 1829; Lucinda, born December 18, 1802, married James F. Broyles, and died in August, 1838; Jacob F., the grandfather of Doctor Broyles; Elender, born February 4, 1806, married Philip Broyles, and died in September, 1884; Nathaniel B., born June 2, 1808, married Elender Broyles, and died December 9, 1883, in Tennessee; Jack, born April 25, 1810, married Lucinda Broyles and died in 1854; Washington, born February 10, 1812, drowned at the same time his sister met her death; Amanda, born in 1815, married Jesse Broyles; Osey R., born in October, 1809, married Sarah Harman, and died January 19, 1907; and David N., born in 1821, married Elizabeth Harman and died in October, 1893.

Andrew C. Broyles married Louisa Anna Eliza Hunt, born at Elizabethton, Tennessee, May 23, 1838, and married, August 6, 1857. She died at Monmouth, Illinois, March 27, 1906, and was buried at Jonesboro, Tennessee. She was a daughter of Warrington C. Hunt, of Elizabethton, Tennessee, and his wife, Mary C. (DeVault) Hunt. Mr. Hunt was a son of Henson and Mary (Pope) Hunt, the latter of whom came from Greenbriar County, West Virginia. Warrington C. Hunt was a tailor by trade, was crippled, and died December 5, 1876, while his wife was born at Hanover, Pennsylvania, June 30, 1810, married June 10, 1833, and died February 15, 1895, at Jonesboro, Tennessee. There was only one child born to Mr. and Mrs. Hunt: Mrs. Broyles, the mother of the doctor.

To Andrew C. Broyles and wife the following children were born: Mary L., born in Carter County, Tennessee, May 26, 1858, married Samuel H. Ballard, January 20, 1885, and lives at Knoxville, Tennessee; Doctor Broyles, of this review; James H., born May 18, 1861, and died August 15, 1864; Robert S., born May 26, 1863, married Ella May Crumley, and lives at Pawnee City, Nebraska; William Milton, born August 26, 1865, married Julia Clements, at St. Louis, Missouri, November 28, 1900, and now lives at Denver, Colorado; Emily E., born August 25, 1867, married Jacob Hunt, January 20, 1885, and lives at Alexander, Oklahoma; Florence A., born January 10, 1870, married Rev. William R. King, June 21, 1892, and resides at Monmouth, Illinois; Rev. Edwin H., born April 18, 1873, married Ida Perryman, May 18, 1898, and is pastor of the Mount Baker Presbyterian Church at Seattle, Washington.

HENRY S. WOLFORD. Now living retired at Braymer in Davis Township of Caldwell County, Henry S. Wolford has been a resident of this section of Missouri for nearly half a century, having located here soon after the close of the Civil war, in which he bore a gallant part as a soldier with an Ohio regiment. Whether as a soldier, a teacher, or a farmer, Mr. Wolford has given a good account of himself in his varied relations with the world and with his fellow men, and now that he has passed the mark of three score and ten years he has a pleasant retrospect over a career that has been useful and honorable.

Henry S. Wolford was born in Knox County, Ohio, December 30, 1838, and his early life was spent on a farm. His father, Jacob Wolford, was a native of Pennsylvania and of German ancestry. The mother, whose maiden name was Elizabeth Welker, was born in Knox County, Ohio, but was likewise of Pennsylvania German stock. In the fall of 1865 Jacob Wolford and wife emigrated to Missouri, locating on a farm in Livingston County, where he died at the age of seventy-three. Politically he was a republican, and his wife was a member of the Methodist Episcopal Church. The mother died at the age of eighty-four. During the Civil war the father was employed for a time in the service of the Government. A number of their sons became soldiers, the family military record being as follows: William Elliott, who died at Braymer, was a member of the One Hundred and Twenty-first Ohio Infantry; P. W., also of the One Hundred and Twenty-first Ohio Regiment, died in 1907 in Nebraska; Marvin T., who was in the Eighty-sixth Ohio Infantry, died at Columbus, Ohio; John, who also was in the Eighty-sixth Ohio Infantry; and Henry S. The other children of the family were: Clarind, who lives in Kansas; Mrs. Sarah Proctor, who died at Braymer; and Elizabeth, who lives in Nebraska.

Henry S. Wolford grew up on a farm in Ohio, was educated in the country schools, and prepared himself for teaching, which he followed for several years in his native state. A young man of twenty-three when the war broke out, he answered the first call for volunteers for ninety days' service. He enlisted at Columbus, in Company B of the Thirteenth Ohio Infantry, and after serving his time was honorably discharged. In November, 1861, he again proffered his services to the Union, and this time entered Company D of the Fortieth Ohio Infantry under Capt. James Watson and Colonel Kramer. This time he got into some of the heaviest service of the war, in the Army of the Cumberland. He fought with the Union forces in Tennessee, Georgia, and other southern states, was present at Chickamauga and Chattanooga, was with General Sherman in the battles between Chickamauga and Atlanta, including Resaca, Kenesaw Mountain, Big Shanty, and was then sent back with the troops after General Hood, and fought that army at Franklin and later at Nashville. He then rejoined the army under Sherman, participated at Ringgold, where he was struck by a bullet, and for some time lay in a hospital. After his recovery he received his honorable discharge. He had served with the rank of a non-commissioned officer, and few men saw harder service, and none showed greater fidelity to the duties of a soldier.

Some time after his return to Ohio, Mr. Wolford determined to follow other members of the family to Missouri and arrived in Caldwell County in 1866. He did work as a teacher, but his principal business has been farming, and having provided an ample competence against the future is now living retired. Mr. Wolford first married Mary J. Bliss, who left one daughter, Mrs. John Rathbun of Braymer. In 1880 he married Mrs. Keller, a daughter of James Leslie. Her father was born in Kentucky of German stock, while Mrs. Wolford was born in Ohio, was reared and educated in that state, and came to Missouri in 1867, locating in Carroll County. Her father died at the age of seventy-three. Politically he was a republican, and a member of the Methodist Episcopal Church. Her mother died at the age of sixty-nine. Besides Mrs. Wolford, the other children in her family were: Mrs. Nancy Keller, of Hamilton, Missouri; Frank E., of Oklahoma; Almira

Eaton, who died at Plymouth, Missouri; J. W. Leslie, of Los Angeles, California. Mrs. Wolford was first married to E. Keller in 1872. He made a good record as a soldier of an Ohio regiment during the war, was captured, and spent some time in the notorious Libby Prison. Mr. Wolford has been a strong republican party man, has assisted his friends to office, and is a liberal, public-spirited citizen. He is affiliated with the Independent Order of Odd Fellows, and is well known in Grand Army circles. He and his wife are members of the Methodist Episcopal Church.

NEY THOMPSON. From the close of the great Civil war, in which he took an active and stirring part, Ney Thompson has been engaged in agricultural operations in Andrew County, and so well have his labors been directed that today he is the owner of a handsome property on the west side of the Platte River, 3½ miles north of Whitesville. His excellent record as a soldier has been duplicated by his sterling citizenship in times of peace, and a life of integrity and straightforward dealing has won for him the confidence and esteem of the people of the community in which he has passed so many years of his long and useful career.

Mr. Thompson was born at Duncansville, Blair County, Pennsylvania, November 25, 1838, and is a son of Michael and Susan J. C. (Radkey) Thompson, the former a native of Huntingdon County, and the latter of Blair County, Pennsylvania. In his native state Michael Thompson conducted a store and inn, and had a small farm at the foot of the Allegheny Mountains, and there resided with his family until 1857, when, with his son Ney, he made the journey overland to Andrew County, Missouri. Here he purchased a farm north of Whitesville, and when a home was prepared the rest of his family joined him, in 1861. Mr. Thompson continued to be engaged in the pursuits of agriculture during the remainder of his life, and through steady application and untiring industry was able to accumulate a good property. In politics he was at various times a whig, a "knownothing" and a republican. He died at the age of seventy-five years, while Mrs. Thompson survived him for a long time, and died at the advanced age of ninety-one years. They were the parents of nine children, as follows: Newton, who died as a bachelor; Wert, who met an accidental death while serving as a conductor on a railroad in Pennsylvania; Ney, of this review; Hortense Eugenia, deceased, who was the wife of Joseph Pierce; Irene, who became the wife of Capt. W. H. Bulla; Flora, who married W. A. Crockett, a sketch of whose career will be found on another page of this work; Tell, deceased, who was named after William Tell; Solon, who is residing on the old family homestead in Platte Township; and Gracie, who died at the age of two years.

Ney Thompson grew up as a farmer boy and received his education in the public schools of Pennsylvania, being nineteen years of age when he accompanied his father to Andrew County. He assisted his father in the preparation of the home, and worked on the farm until 1861, when the outbreak of the Civil war caused him to enlist in the state militia, with which he was connected for six months. Subsequently he entered Company M, of the Ninth Missouri Cavalry, a famous organization which was known as the "Bloody Ninth," owing to the fact that on two occasions, in terrific fighting, it was literally cut to pieces. Mr. Thompson served under Captain Hunter, known by his men as "Rough and Ready," and was chosen by that doughty soldier to carry messages through Western Missouri, and from St. Joseph to Macon City, a service which called for work of the most hazardous character. In this capacity he met with thrilling experiences and narrow escapes from death, on one occasion being compelled to swim the river at high tide with his horse in the dead of night. Eventually, while engaged in dangerous service, he threw his ankle out of place, and after being confined to the hospital for four or five months received his honorable discharge. For several years after the close of the war he was compelled to use a crutch.

With a brave and honorable military record, Mr. Thompson returned to the duties of peace, and resumed agricultural operations, in which he has continued to be engaged to the present time. He now has an excellent farm of 160 acres, located in Platte Township, on the west side of the Platte River, 3½ miles north of Whitesville, on which he has improvements of the most modern character. His land is well tilled and productive, growing all the products of this section, and Mr. Thompson has shown himself a good business man in his transactions. His methods have been such as to place him firmly in the confidence and esteem of his fellow citizens, and few men of the community are held in higher general regard. In spite of his seventy-six years, Mr. Thompson is still active and energetic and attends to the management of his farm in the same able way that he did when it was necessary for him to make each dollar count. He is an independent republican in his political views, but confines his interest in public affairs to casting his vote. Until its disbandment he was a member of the local post of the Grand Army of the Republic.

In 1870 Mr. Thompson was united in marriage with Miss Mary Sherman, who was born in 1848, and died in December, 1911, a daughter of John Sherman. Two daughters were born to Mr. and Mrs. Thompson: Elizabeth, who is the wife of Everett G. Fisher, of Knox City, Missouri; and Caroline, who lives with her father.

FRED E. GOODNOW. One of the most progressive men in Caldwell County, whether considered as a farmer and stockman, or as a citizen, is Fred E. Goodnow, who resides in Lincoln Township. He has been a resident of this locality for a quarter of a century, and everyone in that community can testify to his ability in getting profits from the soil and in the intelligent care and handling of livestock. He believes in and practices intensive farming, and finds the raising of cattle and hogs both a pleasant and profitable business. His farm comprises 120 acres of highly improved land.

Fred E. Goodnow is a native of Wisconsin and was born in Trempeleau County, July 23, 1866. The home farm in Wisconsin was located near the Mississippi River. His parents were L. E. and Louise (Bissell) Goodnow. His father was of old New England family, and it was in that part of the United States that he grew up and married. The parents lived in Trempeleau County, Wisconsin, until 1869, and then when their son Fred was three years of age moved to Caldwell County, Missouri, and located on a farm 1½ miles southwest of where Fred E. Goodnow now lives. The father died at the age of sixty-three. The mother passed away in 1912. Both were active members of the Baptist Church, and the father was a republican and held several local offices, and at one time was public administrator. There were eight children in the family, namely: Mrs. M. De Walt; Fred E.; Gertrude E. Spicer; Carrie Ure; Alice Spicer; L. H.; Ada Anderson; and Walter E. All the children were well educated, and four of them were successful and popular teachers before the responsibilities of home making larger interests called them from that profession.

Fred E. Goodnow was reared in Caldwell County and obtained a part of his education from the public schools. The training that has been of most value to him in later life was the practical experience on the farm while growing to manhood. On March 6, 1889, Mr. Goodnow married Lou Bays, who was born in Caldwell County, a daughter of Miles and Elizabeth Bays. Mrs. Goodnow died at the age of thirty-six years, and left two sons: Miles, who is connected with the railway service in Kansas City; and Laurence, who is in California. On August 9, 1907, Mr. Goodnow married for his present wife Malvina Blair. Mrs. Goodnow was born, reared and educated at Breckenridge, in Caldwell County, and is a daughter of the Hon. W. F. and Edith (Waldo) Blair, her father a well-known citizen of Breckenridge and a former member of the Missouri Legislature. Mrs. Goodnow was one of five children, the others being Angeline, Vashti, Olive and Willard. Mr. and Mrs. Goodnow have three children, Louise, Olive and Freddie B.

Mrs. Goodnow supplies a part of the enterprise which makes the home farm profitable through her special department in the raising of white Wyandot chickens, and her flock is one of the best in Caldwell County. Mr. and Mrs. Goodnow have an attractive country home, an eight-room modern dwelling, situated on a beautiful building site surrounded by an ample lawn and fine shade trees. Other features about the farm are a large barn, 40x60 feet, extensive fields of blue grass meadow and the staple crops of Northwest Missouri, and the water supply for the farm is pumped by windmill.

Mr. Goodnow has been a republican for years, and in 1914 was the nominee of the progressive party for the Legislature, and although defeated he ran ahead of his ticket and everyone, regardless of party ties, considered him thoroughly qualified for the office of representative. Mr. Goodnow affiliates with Cowgill Lodge of the Masonic order. He is a man of medium height, frank and courteous in manner, thoroughly business-like in everything he undertakes, and one of the valued and responsible citizens of Caldwell County.

WARREN E. DANLEY, M. D. Among the well-established medical practitioners of Avenue City is Dr. Warren E. Danley, who is also prominent in business circles as a member of the important firm of W. E. Danley & Co., conducting a large milling and mercantile enterprise, having substantial trade connections over a wide territory. Warren E. Danley was born at Red Bud, Randolph County, Illinois, December 25, 1865, and is the only child of Harley E. and Rosamond (Swift) Danley.

Harley E. Danley was born in Washington County, Ohio, November 28, 1842, the eldest son of J. W. and Elizabeth (Fairchild) Danley, the former of whom was born in Washington County, Ohio, in 1822. He was a son of John Danley, and a grandson of Benjamin Danley, who was a Revolutionary soldier, who was killed at the battle of the Brandywine, just before the birth of his son. The family preserves the old powder horn that he wore in his last battle. In the Civil war the grandfather of Doctor Danley proved that he possessed the same patriotic spirit that belonged to his grandfather, enlisting for service in Company I, One Hundred and Forty-eighth Ohio Volunteer Infantry, with his son, Harley E., and died in the long siege that preceded the capture of Petersburg, Virginia. The grandmother of Doctor Danley survived him many years, dying in Avenue City, Missouri, March 17, 1913. They had three sons: Harley E., Joseph W., and Chauncey, the last named dying at the age of five years.

Harley E. Danley grew to manhood on the home farm in Ohio and taught school for some years. When the Civil war became a fact he enlisted for service, entering the same company and regiment as his father, and was promoted to the rank of sergeant, and during his term of enlistment was stationed for four months in front of Petersburg, Virginia. He then returned to Ohio, and in 1865 moved to Illinois, and from there, in 1867, to Johnson County, Kansas, and for seventeen years was a traveling salesman in that state for the William Deering Harvester Company and was also in the milling and mercantile business for three years. In 1900 he came to Avenue City and is now a partner with his brother, Joseph W. Danley, and his son, Dr. Warren E. Danley, in the firm of W. E. Danley & Co. He was married in Washington County, Ohio, to Rosamond Swift, who was born there January 24, 1842.

Warren E. Danley was carefully reared and liberally educated. After his boyhood school days he spent two years in the Baptist University at Ottawa, Kansas, and two years more in the Kansas State University, where he was graduated with his medical degree in 1887, nevertheless he then entered the medical department of the Northwestern University at St. Joseph, where he was graduated two years later. He decided to locate at Avenue City, and came here on March 6, 1889, and is the only one of his class of twenty-five doctors who has never changed his field of practice since beginning. He has been very successful in his profession, has shown exceptional business capacity along other lines and personally stands high with his fellow citizens. A close attachment prevails between himself, his father and his uncle, and as they are united in a business relation they are equally so in many of their tastes. H. E. and W. E. Danley belong to the Masonic Blue Lodge at Saxton, in Buchanan County, and J. W. has his membership in Olathe, Kansas, and all are Shriners. Doctor Danley is a member of the county, state and of the American Medical Association.

JOSEPH W. DANLEY. Associated with his brother, Harley E. Danley, and his nephew, Dr. Warren E. Danley, in the milling and mercantile firm of W. E. Danley & Co., at Avenue City, Joseph W. Danley is one of the representative business men of this place. He was born in Washington County, Ohio, February 18, 1862, the third son of J. W. and Elizabeth (Fairchild) Danley. He resided with his widowed mother and his brother for a number of years, and up to the time of his marriage, December 16, 1886, to Miss Mattie Berryman. She was born at Hudson, Illinois, and died October 24, 1896, at Olathe, Kansas, survived by two children: Royal C. and Faye E. The former is a practicing physician at Hamburg, Iowa, having graduated at Bennett Medical College, Chicago, in the class of 1914. Mr. Danley was married June 7, 1899, at Fairfax, Virginia, to Miss Oneita G. Wakefield.

Mr. Danley is quite prominent in Masonic circles and is past commander of Olathe Commandery, Olathe, Kansas, and served four times as high priest of Olathe Chapter. Both he and brother are members of Sesostin Temple, Lincoln, Nebraska. The entire male membership of the family is affiliated with the republican party.

A. L. LEWELLEN. In some communities are found men hard to classify except as prominent and representative, because their activites are so numerous and useful, and they have achieved success·in all their undertakings. Such a man is A. L. Lewellen, merchant and banker and formerly mayor and assistant postmaster, who is also a well-known journalist, through editorial connection with the Rosendale Signal for a number of years. At present Mr. Lewellen is vice president of the Rosendale Bank and has high standing as a financier all over Andrew County. He was born in Preble County, Ohio, September 19, 1851, and is a son of Baford and Nancy (Peters) Lewellen.

Baford Lewellen was born in Kentucky in 1820 and died on his farm, near Rosendale, in February, 1899. He married Nancy Peters, who was born in Pennsylvania in 1821, and from Ohio they moved to Andrew County, Missouri, in 1866. They lived one year in Rochester Township and then located on the farm three miles from Rosendale, where they passed the rest of their lives, Mrs. Lewellen surviving until August, 1900. Baford Lewellen was a substantial farmer, owning 500 acres of land, and also was a lender of money before his neighbors could get bank accommodations. There were nine children in his family: Caroline, who is the wife of Z. T. Wells, of Springfield, Missouri; Elizabeth, who is the widow of R. P. Bell, of Rosendale; A. L.; Joseph, who is deceased; Andrew M., who is a resident of Florence, Alabama; Ambrose, who lives at Gaylord, Kansas; John, who is a resident of Rosendale; Sarah F., who is the wife of G. W. Wells, of Prineville, Oregon; and Charles, who lives at Shenandoah, Iowa.

The public schools of Preble County, Ohio, provided the early education of A. L. Lewellen, his training since then having been given by farm work and the business activities into which his energy and enterprise have led him. He accompanied his parents when they came to Andrew County and assisted his father on the farm until 1882, since when he has been a resident of Rosendale and a leader in its business and public affairs. For sixteen years he was associated with his brother, A. M. Lewellen, in a general mercantile business, under the firm name of Lewellen Brothers. Under the administration of President Harrison, A. M. Lewellen was appointed postmaster of Rosendale and A. L. Lewellen was made assistant and continued in that capacity under other postmasters for eighteen years. He has always been very active in republican politics and at one time, in the old convention days, before the adoption of the primary system, he was made his party's candidate for probate judge. Subsequently he was elected mayor of Rosendale and in that position served his fellow citizens ably, many improvements being undertaken and completed during his administration. He has always been a friend of education and has served on the school board with patience and wisdom. Mr. Lewellen is one of the original stockholders of the Rosendale Bank, one of the soundest institutions of the county, and for ten years served as vice president. For the last six years he has been very active in this connection.

In 1896 Mr. Lewellen was united in marriage with Miss Verna C. Holmes, who was born in Iowa, in February, 1866, and was reared in her native state. They have two sons: Maurice and Everett. Mr. Lewellen belongs to Lodge No. 414, Ancient, Free and Accepted Masons, Rosendale, and also to the Odd Fellows at Rosendale.

For about four years Mr. Lewellen was associated with J. I. Bennett as editor of the Rosendale Signal, and during this period became a member of the Missouri Press Association, being recommended for membership by Dean Walter Williams, at Warrensburg. Mr. Lewellen has not made journalism his career, but he recalls with lively pleasure the acquaintances he made while in harness and can never forget the enjoyment he found during numerous trips, including one down the Mississippi River, as a member of the above organization.

JOHN H. VAN BRUNT. Few cities may boast of a street railways system as complete and well operated as that which furnishes transportation for the citizens of St. Joseph. The second city in the United States to operate cars by electricity, and the first in the world to use the trolley pole under the wire, it has long been proud of the facilities granted to the public, and its example has been followed by the progressive municipalities in every state in the Union. It would be neither just nor correct to give the credit for the desirable state of affairs to any man or any gathering of men, but it is only equitable to place an appreciation upon the signal services of John H. Van Brunt, who has been connected with the management of this important enterprise since 1890. A man of wide experience and intricate knowledge of transportation, in the capacity of vice president and general manager he has brought to his work a wealth of enthusiasm, a multiformity of ideas and a conscientious regard of the public welfare that the people of St. Joseph have not been slow to appreciate.

Mr. Van Brunt is an easterner and came to Missouri only when his business called him here, but since that time St. Joseph has been his home. He was born at Red Bank, New Jersey, September 7, 1867, and is a son of Peter S. and Mary H. (Thomas) Van Brunt, natives of Perth Amboy, New Jersey, the father being a wholesale oyster dealer on the Shrewsbury River. Educated in the public schools, Mr. Van Brunt was graduated from the high school at Orange, New Jersey, and immediately entered upon his business career in the employ of I. B. Newton & Co., bankers, Wall Street, New York. He rapidly rose in this firm, and in 1887, when the concern purchased the St. Joseph Street Railways, he was given the responsibility of taking charge of the receipts of the business. The firm had acquired the Frederick Arc Line and the Citizens' Line, operating as the People's Street Railway, Electric Light and Power Company, and in 1888 built the Jule Street line and in 1889 the Messanie Street line. In 1890 the Union line was absorbed and subsequently the Wyatt Park line, and in 1895 the People's Street Railway, Electric Light and Power Company was reorganized, at that time becoming the St. Joseph Railway, Light, Heat and Power Company. This was owned by the Harriman interests until 1902, when it was purchased by E. W. Clark & Co., of Philadelphia, and in February, 1913, again changed ownership, the purchasers being Henry L. Doherty & Co., of New York, the present owners. William T. Van Brunt, a brother of John H. Van Brunt, was president and general manager of the company from 1890 until 1902, when he retired and went to New York. He had been brought to St. Joseph from Scranton, Pennsylvania, originally to manage the system at the time of its purchase and development. John H. Van Brunt became the superintendent of the system in 1890, and in 1902 was made vice president and general manager. Mr. Van Brunt's masterly management of the affairs of his company has made him widely known all over the state. He has made a close study of the science of transportation, has a broad knowledge of the principles governing the operation of railways and all the rules and regulations pertaining to traffic. The duties and responsibilities of the positions which he has held have demanded a large share of his attention, yet he has found time to give other enterprises the benefit of his broad knowledge and abilities and is president of the St. Joseph & Savannah Interurban Railway Company, running from St. Joseph to Savannah, and is a director in the Empire Trust Company and the Provident Building and Loan Association, both of St. Joseph. He has also found leisure to mingle with his fellow men, and is a popular and valued member of the St. Joseph Country Club, the Benton Club of this city, the St. Joseph Commerce Club and Elks Lodge No. 40. His pleasant residence is situated on Asylum Road.

On April 27, 1892, Mr. Van Brunt was married to Miss Pearl Dougherty, daughter of Alexander M. Dougherty, of St. Joseph, and they have three sons: John H., Jr., Frederick C. and Alexander D.

JOHN H. HURST. Born on the fine farmstead in the ownership and active management of which he is associated with his brother Absalom,

John H. Hurst is numbered among the progressive young agriculturists and stockgrowers of Holt County, the well-improved farm being situated southeast of Oregon, the judicial center of the county. Here Mr. Hurst was born on the 14th of November, 1884, a son of John Hurst, and both of his parents are now deceased, the two sons mentioned in this paragraph being the surviving children, and one having died in early childhood.

John Hurst was one of the early settlers of this section of Holt County, where he established his residence on the farm now owned by his sons and where he devoted himself earnestly and effectively to its reclamation and development, the homestead comprising 160 acres and the permanent improvements being of substantial order. John Hurst was a citizen of sterling character, was a republican in his political allegiance, as are also his sons, and he commanded the high regard of all who knew him, the while he achieved independence and prosperity through his own well-ordered efforts.

John H. Hurst was reared to the sturdy discipline of the home farm and is indebted to the public schools of Holt County for his early educational discipline. He has never faltered in his allegiance to the industrial enterprise under whose influence he was reared, and as a progressive farmer and loyal and public-spirited citizen he is well upholding the prestige of the name which he bears. He is a zealous supporter of the cause of the republican party, but has not been ambitious for public office, which was likewise true in the case of his honored father, whose civic loyalty, however, prompted him to serve in the early days as a member of the school board of his district. Mr. Hurst still permits his name to be enrolled on the list of eligible young bachelors in his native county.

JAMES COLLINS. Few men in Northwest Missouri have had a more interesting and instructive experience in the acquisition of the material fruits of prosperity, particularly in the buying and selling of land, than James Collins. A native of Holt County, where his people were early settlers, he had to work from the time of childhood, and by hard experience knows how to estimate the value of every dollar he has earned. Experience and honest toil taught him cool judgment in his transactions, and in the past thirty or forty years he has bought, improved and sold land all over this quarter of the state. His present position is one of well-established prosperity and esteem in the fine country community of Hickory Township.

Born in Holt County, March 10, 1855, James Collins was a son of J. Mason Collins, who came to Northwest Missouri at the pioneer year of 1833, and secured his first land from the Government. He was married in Missouri to Rebecca Stevenson, and their family consisted of eleven children altogether, five of them by a second marriage. His second wife was Achsah Robinson. The father died at the age of fifty years. His first location was near the Nodaway River, southeast of Oregon. He went out as a soldier to the Mexican war, and died in 1862, about a year after the outbreak of the Civil war. He was an industrious citizen, a man of good habits, and though beginning life poor was able to provide for his family and interest himself in the general welfare of the community. He served for a time as justice of the peace, when that office was the highest in the community, where practically all the difficulties and litigation of the neighborhood was tried. Though his schooling was limited, he had a hard, practical wisdom which availed him for good service in that office.

James Collins was about seven years of age when his father died, and he was reared in the home of his grandmother. With a common school education, he began work for his board and clothes at an early age, and in 1865 started out for himself. His first employer was a man named Price in Atchison County; in 1867 he went to Fremont County, Iowa, and worked for an uncle named Stevens, then returned to Holt County and did farming for himself as a renter. In 1872 Mr. Collins located nine miles north of Craig, in Atchison County, and in 1873 bought sixty acres at $7 an acre. His next important step in life was his marriage to Julia Chainer, daughter of Andrew. Mr. Collins lived on his first sixty acre until the death of his wife, about 1877. Their one child was Della, who married Peter Souer, and they became the parents of two children, Esther and Edith, who now live in Atchison County. After the death of his first wife Mr. Collins married Anna Noble. That was in 1879.

His home was on his first farm for about nineteen years, and in the meantime he had increased his land to about three hundred acres. When he sold the price secured for his property was $40 an acre, several times what he had paid for it. Mr. Collins next moved to the vicinity of Tarkio, bought half a section, and was the first man in that part of the country to pay as high as $40 an acre for land. It was a well-improved farm, and by the improvements he placed upon it and by the general increase in land values, when he sold in 1900 it brought $50 an acre. Mr. Collins then returned to Fairfax and bought two farms, paying about $45 an acre for one and for another paid $100 an acre. That purchase likewise set a high mark in real estate transactions, since it was the first time anyone had paid $100 an acre for land in that vicinity. Later Mr. Collins bought an adjoining quarter section for $62.50 an acre, but while his first purchase was thoroughly improved, with excellent buildings, the second lot of land had no buildings. It was on his farm at Fairfax that his second wife died. When Mr. Collins sold his land it brought $125 an acre. Mr. Collins then moved to Hickory Township, in Holt County, rented land for two years, and then bought the improved farm, comprising 200 acres, where his present home is situated. He married for his third wife Susan Miles. Both are members of the Christian Church, and Mr. Collins is a Mason at Fairfax. He has served on the school board, and is a democrat in politics. It will be of interest to recall some other land transactions, when Mr. Collins, about 1911, paid $104.50 an acre for a large tract of 480 acres. About 1879 Tom McCoy had bought the same land and paid only $5 an acre, and this remarkable increase indicates how Northwest Missouri has developed in the last thirty-five years. Mr. Collins also owned half a section of land in North Dakota, for which he paid $12 an acre, and three years later sold it for $25. Such are some of the more salient facts in the career of a man who began with no capital and has made his success entirely through his own energies.

DAVID CRIDER. Some of the most successful and progressive farmers of Holt County are carrying on operations at this time on the properties on which they were born and where they have passed their entire life. Thus, being thoroughly familiar with conditions, they are able to make their labors pay in full measure and have advanced beyond their fellows who have had to learn within a few short years the methods best adapted to the soil. In the former class stands David Crider, who is numbered among the younger generation of agriculturists, and is known as an energetic and thorough-going farmer of Hickory Township.

Mr. Crider was born May 19, 1880, on his present property, and is one of the nine children, of whom seven are living, of John and Hannah (Galvin) Crider. John Crider was born in Pennsylvania and there he grew to manhood in a farming community, early adopting agricultural work as his life's vocation. He was thus engaged in a modest way until the Civil war called him to the front in support of the Union, when he shouldered a musket and marched away as a member of Company F, Two Hundred and Ninety-seventh Regiment, Pennsylvania Volunteer Infantry, with which he served until the close of the war, having an honorable record. When his military experience was completed he returned to the pursuits and duties of peace, and for four years labored faithfully in his native state. His achievements, however, did not seem productive of great gains, and so, in 1869, he sought new fields, turning his face toward the West and finally locating in Holt County. Two years later he settled on the farm on which he spent the balance of his life, and where he died in February, 1906. When Mr. Crider arrived in Missouri he was possessed of a little capital, saved from his labors as a farm hand and his salary as a soldier, but he had unlimited ambition, determination and perseverance, and these led him to a well-won success, his accumulations comprising one-half section of land at the time of his death. A man of good habits and an exemplary citizen, he held a high place in the esteem of the people of his community, and when he passed away there were many to mourn his loss. He was a republican in politics and an influential man in his party, although not one to thrust himself forward for personal preferment. Early in life he joined the United Brethren Church, to which he belonged throughout his life, and Mrs. Crider, who survives, is also a member of that denomination. She is a native of Cumberland County, Pennsylvania, and was married to Mr. Crider in that state.

David Crider was educated in the public schools of Hickory Township, and following in his father's footsteps adopted the vocation of tilling the soil in his youth. He was thoroughly trained under the excellent preceptorship of his father in all matters necessary for the modern farmer to know, and has since been quick to adopt modern methods and ideas and to take advantage of the invention of labor-saving power machinery. His eighty-acre tract of land, on which he has carried on operations during the past five years, shows the beneficial results to be obtained by good management, and under its owner's direction yields golden harvests. Like his father, Mr. Crider is a republican, but his public activities have been confined to those taken by every good and helpful citizen. With his family he attends the United Brethren Church.

Mr. Crider married Miss Alice Nichols, one of the nine children, of whom seven are living, born to Fred Nichols, of Holt County. Three children have been born to Mr. and Mrs. Crider, all on the present farm in Hickory Township; Catherine Hannah, Nelson Lawrence and Virgil Fred.

W. L. ARMENTROUT. Success has been worthily attained in the field of agricultural effort by W. L. Armentrout, who is today accounted one of the energetic and progressive of the younger generation of farmers of Holt County, and this is attributable to his energy, enterprise and careful management. He started out in life as a farm hand, but soon attained a property of his own and now has eighty acres of desirable land located in Hickory Township.

Mr. Armentrout was born in Nodaway County, Missouri, October 25, 1880, and is a son of Remiger and Mary (Handley) Armentrout. The parents were natives of the State of Virginia, where they were married and began their life on a farm, but seeking better opportunities decided to come to the West and accordingly, about the year 1870, made their way to Nodaway County. Being in moderate circumstances, the father was at first compelled to accept such honorable employment as presented itself, but, being enterprising and industrious, soon saved enough means to purchase a tract of 160 acres of land, which he cultivated for a number of years. Later he disposed of this property and bought 120 acres in Holt County, seven miles northeast of Mound City, where he has continued to carry on operations to the present time. He is a republican in his political views, and has taken an active interest in the affairs which have affected his community, served for a time as a soldier during the Civil war, and is a member of the Woodmen of the World. A man of exemplary habits, he early joined the Christian Church, in which his family has been reared and to which Mrs. Armentrout, who survives, belongs. There were six children in the family: Thomas; John; Arthur I., who died in Virginia; Walter; Marvin and W. L.

W. L. Armentrout secured his education in the district schools of Holt County and grew up on his father's homestead, being reared to habits of honesty and integrity and thoroughly trained to know the value of industry. When he started upon his independent career he worked for ten months on farms in his locality, and then purchased his present land, a well-situated and well-cultivated tract of eighty acres. He has made a number of improvements on his property, which have added materially to its value, and through close attention to business has made his land pay him well for the labor he has expended upon it. Progressive in all things, he has taken kindly to modern ideas and methods and has assisted in movements which have advanced the community. At the present time he is a director of the local telephone company. A republican in politics, he stanchly supports the policies and candidates of his party, but has found no time to seek personal preferment. His fraternal connection is with the local lodge of the Modern Woodmen of America.

Mr. Armentrout was married to Miss Ella Mickels, the daughter of Fred Mickels, and to this union have come two children, both born in Holt County, Elvis and Opal May.

GEORGE W. GLICK. Among the native sons of Hope County who are not only maintaining the pioneer records of their fathers, but are establishing precedents for their successors, mention is due George W. Glick, the owner of a well-cultivated and productive farm in Benton Township and one of his community's energetic and progressive men. He was born about five miles southeast of Mound City, Missouri, March 14, 1873, and is a son of Samuel and Martina (Pearson) Glick, the latter of whom belonged to a family that originated in Tennessee.

Samuel Glick was born in Virginia, and during the late '50s came to Northwest Missouri with his father, it being believed that this journey was made by way of ox-team. They were not overburdened with capital in the way of money, but both were energetic and progressive men, willing to work hard if given the opportunity, and through the possession of these traits each carved out a satisfying success. The grandfather purchased land in Holt County, on Blair Hill, about two miles from the present farm of George W. Glick, put up substantial buildings and made other improvements, and there passed the remaining years of his life, winning the full confidence of his fellow men by his honorable dealing and many admirable traits of character. He died on this farm and in later years his remains, which had been buried there, were removed by his grandson, George W., to the cemetery. He was a faithful member of the German Baptist Church, lived up to his religious belief, and served his church in the capacity of deacon for a number of years. In politics he was a democrat. After his death the land was divided between his sons, Joseph and Samuel Glick, and the same farm was later inherited by George W. Glick, which he sold when he moved to his present property. The boyhood of Samuel Glick was passed in the hard, unrelenting work of cultivating the raw prairie, and he was given but little chance to acquire an education, although he later made the best of his opportunities and became a well-informed man. Throughout his life he was an ardent supporter of education, his own lack of advantages making him appreciate them the more, and he always encouraged his children to secure the best of training, offering them college careers should they so choose. Reared to habits of industry and economy, he was a faithful and energetic worker all of his life, and his straightforward dealings and strict honesty won him a high place in the confidence of the people of his locality. Like his father, he belonged to the German Baptist Church, served as deacon, and died in the faith in the fall of 1896, the mother following him to the grave in the fall of the following year. In politics Mr. Glick was a democrat. Samuel and Martina (Pearson) Glick were the parents of six children, of whom two died in infancy, the others being: Susan B., who married Jacob Kuhn; Anna B., who married Ira L. Drake; Emma May, who became the wife of John Christ; and George W., of this notice.

George W. Glick, like his brothers and sisters, went to the local school in the Blair district, and followed this by two years at the Mound City High School. At that time he embarked upon his independent career as an agriculturist, locating upon the original pioneer farm of his grandfather, upon which he put many improvements. This he sold in 1909 to James Collins and removed to the adjoining property, his present home, where he has one of the finest farms in the township, well cultivated, finely improved and with a substantial and attractive set of buildings and numerous up-to-date improvements. He has succeeded eminently in his life vocation and is worthily upholding the reputation of the honorable name he bears.

Mr. Glick was married to Grace B. Henning, and to this union there have been born five children: Edna May, Samuel Glenn, Edgar Lee, Russell Clayton and Mildred Marie, all born in Holt County. Mr. Glick was reared in the faith of the Baptist Church, and with the exception of one intervening year has been superintendent of the Blair Sunday school for the past six years. He is popular fraternally as a member of the Independent Order of Odd Fellows, the Woodmen of the World, the Modern Woodmen of America, the Royal Neighbors and the Order of the Eastern Star, and is well known in Masonry, in which he has attained to the fourteenth degree. A democrat in his political views, he has taken a deep interest in the success of his party and is one of its leaders in Holt County. Elected to the State Senate for a two-year term in 1906, Mr. Glick has the distinction of being the only man of his political inclinations so honored since 1876 in Holt County, and at the present time is the nominee of his party for senatorial honors from the Third Senatorial District. His acquaintance throughout the county is wide and includes a large number of sincere and appreciative friends.

Hon. W. R. Swope. A thoroughly representative member of the progressive element of Holt County which is maintaining high standards in this part of Northwest Missouri is found in the person of W. R. Swope, who is the owner of 120 acres of good land in Benton Township, on which he carries on successful general farming. He has spent his entire career in this county, and has not only contributed to its agricultural welfare and development, but has also found time to devote to the interests of his community, being at the present time the representative of his district in the State Legislature. Whether as a farmer, a citizen or a public official, Mr. Swope has shown himself energetic and progressive, and the high esteem in which he is held in his community has come to him as a reward for a strictly honorable career.

W. R. Swope was born in Holt County, Missouri, March 7, 1878, and is a son of D. H. and Malinda C. (McCoy) Swope. The father, a native of Kentucky, grew to manhood in the Blue Grass State, and then, in search of better opportunities for advancement, migrated to Northwest Missouri, settling in Hope County. His career has been an industrious and successful one, and he is now living in semi-retirement, having resided in his present home for a period of thirty-three years. He has taken a keen and intelligent interest in the affairs of his county, is a republican in his political views, and is a consistent member of the Methodist Episcopal Church. Mrs. Swope, who also survives, is a native of Northwest Missouri and a devout member of the Christian Church. Two children were born to them: Albert O., who married Alice Arnett and resides on the farm adjoining that of his brother; and W. R., of this notice.

W. R. Swope was given good educational advantages in his youth, first attending the district schools of Holt County, later the high school at Mound City, and finally Drake University, where he took a full course of four years. When he laid aside his school books he returned to the farm, and since that time has devoted himself to general agricultural operations. His well-developed tract of 120 acres in Benton Township gives evidence of Mr. Swope's industry and good management, yielding large and profitable crops, and among his associates he is considered a man of excellent judgment in matter relating to agriculture. The present buildings have all been erected under his supervision, and are well arranged, substantial in character, attractive and commodious. Fraternally, Mr. Swope is well known in the Masonic Order, belonging to the Lodge at Mound City, the Shrine at St. Joseph and the Eastern Star, and also is a member of the Modern Woodmen of America. In his political views Mr. Swope is a republican, and has served in various township offices, where his signal service commended him to the people for the office of representative of his district in the State Legislature, a capacity in which he is capably serving at the present time. He is conscientious in the discharge of his duties, and has been able to secure some favorable legislation for his constituents.

On February 14, 1905, Mr. Swope was united in marriage with Miss Mary Minshall, who was born in Holt County, Missouri, daughter of J. B. and Eva (Fields) Minshall. They have no children. Mrs. Swope is a consistent member of the Christian Church, in which she has numerous friends.

E. R. SHULL. The residence of E. R. Shull in Holt County has spanned a period of forty-six years, during which time he has been a witness of and a participant in the wonderful development which has marked this section's growth and prosperity. Mr. Shull has wrought well with the material at hand, and has established a reputation as a capable and successful agriculturist, while his good citizenship has been

though he was not able to read or write in English until after he had
passed his majority. He was sober, industrious and ambitious, and carefully saved his wages, so that in 1868 he was able to come to Missouri
and buy a Holt County farm. This was unimproved at that time, but
Mr. Shull broke up the land and erected a small log house, containing
three rooms, in which he and his family resided for some years. Later
other buildings were erected and various improvements were made, Mr.
Shull becoming known as one of the substantial men of his locality. Here
he died, respected and esteemed by all with whom he had had dealings.
In politics a republican, he did not seek public honors, but was content to
remain merely a useful and public-spirited citizen. Mr. Shull was a lifelong member of the United Brethren Church, always took an active interest in its movements, and was one of the organizers of the first congregation brought together in Holt County, subsequently becoming a
member of the board of trustees. In all of life's activities he was governed by a high sense of honor, and he is still remembered by the older
generation in Hickory Township as a man of the strictest integrity. Mrs.
Shull was a Pennsylvania German and also passed away on the homestead
place. They were the parents of five children, namely: Frank C., who is
single and is associated with his brother E. R. in the operation of the
present farm; Leah, deceased, who was the wife of W. M. Coffin; E. R.,
of this review; Hiram, who is deceased; and Anna F., who married
George Kunzman.

E. R. Shull was a child of three years when he came from Ohio with
his parents to Holt County, Missouri, and here he grew up on the homestead and received his education in the district schools. On attaining his
majority he engaged in agricultural pursuits, and when his father died
he and his brother Frank C. began operations in association on the homestead, which they have continued with success to the present time. They
have added materially to the improvements as well as to the acreage, and
now have a handsome and valuable farming property of 160 acres, with
a full set of attractive buildings and improvements of the very latest
character. E. R. Shull is a member of the Knights of Pythias, and is
popular with his fellow-members in the lodge. He has had his time
largely occupied by his farming interests, but has always been ready to
serve his community, and has acted very acceptably as a member of the
district school board. Both he and his brother are republicans.

Mr. Shull married Miss Mary Fancher, daughter of William and
Rosie (Stone) Fancher, and five children have been born to them: Fred;
Grace, who is the wife of Frank Bohardt; Worthy; Marion and Lloyd,
all born in Holt County.

GEORGE M. POLLOCK. A resident of Holt County since the days of his
boyhood, Mr. Pollock is a member of a family that was here founded
half a century ago and he personally is well entitled to consideration in
this history by reason of being one of the representative agriculturists
and stock-growers of this county, where his fine homestead farm was that
formerly owned by the father of Mrs. Pollock.

A member of a family of eight children, two of whom died in infancy,
Mr. Pollock claims the old Buckeye State as the place of his nativity.
He was born in Fayette County, Ohio, on the 20th of May, 1850, and is
a son of David M. and Julia (Kyle) Pollock, who came to Holt County in
March, 1864, and settled on a farm just west of that now occupied by
their grandson, Henry Pollock, son of him whose name introduces this
article. They established their home in a small frame house that had
been erected on the embryonic farm of 120 acres, of which only a part
had been broken for cultivation. David M. Pollock, with the assistance

of his sons, reclaimed the land and developed one of the excellent farms of the county, this old homestead continuing to be his place of abode until his death, in 1907. His wife survived him by two years and passed the closing period of her life in the home of her daughter, Mrs. Samuel J. King, of this county. Both were devoted members of the Methodist Episcopal Church and the father was inflexible in his allegiance to the republican party. These worthy pioneers contributed their quota to the civic and industrial progress of Holt County, where their memories shall be held in lasting honor.

George M. Pollock acquired his early education in the public schools of Ohio and was a lad of about fourteen years at the time of the family removal to Missouri. Here he attended school in Holt County for a time and he found ample requisition for his services in connection with the reclamation and cultivation of the home farm. In 1882 was solemnized his marriage to Miss Jannie Marian Mettler, who was born on the farm which is now their home and who is a daughter of Henry and Elizabeth Mettler, the parents having reared to maturity four sons and eight daughters. The parents of Mrs. Pollock were numbered among the early settlers of Holt County, the father having been a native of Ohio and the mother of the State of New York. Mr. Mettler made good improvements on his pioneer farm and this continued to be his place of residence until his death, his wife having survived him by several years and both having been well known and highly esteemed citizens of the county that was their home for many years. Mr. and Mrs. Pollock have only one child, Harry E., who was born January 11, 1886, and who wedded Miss Mary Alice Mitchell, daughter of Joseph Mitchell, a prosperous farmer of this county. The one child of this union is Corwin Mitchell Pollock.

Mr. Pollock and his son, who is one of the ambitious and progressive young farmers of his native county, are associated in the cultivation of 160 acres of land, and all of the present improvements upon the fine homestead place were made by Mr. Pollock, these including his erection of his large and attractive modern residence. He is a loyal and public-spirited citizen, taking a lively interest in all that concerns the general welfare of the community, and he has served as a member of the school board of his district, though never imbued with a desire for public office. He is aligned as a staunch supporter of the cause of the republican party, is affiliated with the Woodmen of the World, and both he and his wife hold membership in the Presbyterian Church.

L. B. SHELDON. For many years Lathrop has been regarded as one of the world's centers of the mule raising industry, and one of the farmers and stockmen in that township who gives special attention to that branch of industry is L. B. Sheldon, whose home is in Lathrop Township, comprising a stock farm of ninety acres. It is thoroughly equipped not only for general farming purposes, but also for the handling of stock, and its improvements consist of a comfortable residence, surrounded with barns, sheds, well arranged feed lots and with every convenience that makes stock raising both easy and profitable.

L. B. Sheldon has spent all his life in Clinton County, and was born

country boys in Northwest Missouri thirty or forty years ago, and the training from the local schools was supplemented with plenty of hard work on the farm. At the age of twenty-three Mr. Sheldon married Miss Lettie B. Holland, a daughter of L. Holland, of Clinton County, now deceased. Mr. and Mrs. Sheldon have one daughter, Ruth, wife of Carl Breckenridge, of Clinton County. They have a daughter, Vivian Ruth Breckenridge. Mr. Sheldon has found his best profits in farming in the raising of mules and horses, and is considered one of the most capable judges of this class of live stock in Clinton County. For six years he served as road supervisor of his district, and in that time had the satisfaction of producing some of the best roads found in Clinton County.

ALEX DORREL. As a breeder and raiser of horses, Alex Dorrel has a reputation even beyond the limits of his home County of Andrew. Mr. Dorrell has a well equipped horse farm in section 29 of Platte Township, near the Village of Rea, and through his enterprise has introduced the blood of some of the best imported Percheron stallions among the horses in Andrew County. Mr. Dorrel began his career as a renter and by an exceptional degree of enterprise has prospered, has owned and operated different farms at different times, and the confidence felt in his business judgment and his popularity as a citizen are indicated by the fact that he served a term as county judge.

Alex Dorrel was born in Harrison County, Missouri, March 2, 1858, a son of James and Eliza J. (Huffman) Dorrel. Both parents were natives of Morgan County, Indiana. They came to Missouri when young, and were married in Harrison County. About ten years later, in 1866, they located in Platte Township of Andrew County, and there spent the rest of their active days. The father died there November 23, 1871, at the age of forty-five. The mother, who was born January 8, 1838, is now living at a good old age in Bolckow. After the death of her first husband she married Moses Wilson, who is now deceased. Judge Dorrel was the second in a family of five children, the others being mentioned as follows: Sanford, deceased; Dora E., wife of T. J. Townsend, who lives near Bolckow; J. H. and George, twins, the former of Benton Township, and the latter deceased.

Judge Dorrel has lived in Andrew County since he was eight years of age. His education came from country schools, and with the training he received on a farm in early life has always been at home in the agricultural industry. His fondness for farm animals developed into an expertness in handling them, and that has been the chief feature of his career. In early life Mr. Dorrel was for three years in the livery business at Rosendale, spent two years in the hardware business, and the rest of the time has been active as a farmer. For the first two years he rented, and then bought land of his own, and at one time operated 300 acres under his individual ownership. He traded this land, bought and sold a number of farms, and his present place comprises forty acres, situated half a mile east of Rea. He has a well equipped stable, and keeps for breeding purposes two imported Percheron stallions and also one Jack.

Mr. Dorrel has always affiliated with the republican party and for two years represented his district of Andrew County as a member of the County Court. In April, 1882, Judge Dorrel married Sarah W. Wilson, who was born in Andrew County, in 1863, a daughter of Moses and Dema (Mann) Wilson. To their marriage have been born seven children, namely: Redmond B., at home; Clara, wife of R. R. Beattie of Platte Township; Edith; Lois; Loid; Clifford and Frances.

P. W. ZACHARY. Success consists in a steady betterment of one's material conditions and an increase of one's ability to render service to

others. Measured by this standard, one of the exceptionally successful men of Holt County is P. W. Zachary, who has spent nearly all his
life in Northwest Missouri, and who is now one of the largest landed
proprietors in the vicinity of Mound City, and the father of a large and
useful family. From the beginning of his independent career over thirty
years ago, when he started with a nucleus of eighty acres of land, Mr.
Zachary has been steadily advancing to independence, and is now considered one of the most substantial men in his section.

P. W. Zachary was born in Pulaski County, Kentucky, October 6,
1856, a son of Bourne and Nancy (Haskell) Zachary. The parents were
married in Kentucky, and there were nine children, five of whom are still
living. The father was a farmer, and from Kentucky brought his family
to Northwest Missouri, making the greater part of the journey by railway,
and then driving overland to a place in Andrew County, where they
spent one winter, and the following spring came to Holt County. The
father rented a farm in what is now Clay Township, but later moved to
Nodaway County, and lived for about five years in town, and ran the
mail route while his sons looked after the farm. He then bought a farm
adjoining the one occupied by P. W. Zachary, comprising 160 acres of
raw land, and he and his boys worked hard to improve and cultivate the
soil, and the father continued increasing his land holdings until at his
death his estate comprised 320 acres. He had also bought eighty acres
and had given it to his son Henry. Bourne Zachary died in September,
1883. He was affiliated with the Masonic Order and in politics a democrat, and in his personal characteristics was noted for his good habits,
his hard working ability and an absolute rectitude in all his relations with
his neighbors. When he came to Northwest Missouri he was practically
penniless, and became a fairly wealthy man according to the standards
of the time through hard industry. His widow is still living, at the
age of eighty-two, and enjoys the best of health. Her home is with her
son John. She is a member of the Christian Church.

P. W. Zachary acquired most of his education in Nodaway County.
There were a few months each year when work on the farm was slack, and
that was the term when school advantages could be enjoyed, but otherwise he was engaged from an early age in the practical responsibilities
of farm life. In 1883, after the death of his father, Mr. Zachary married
Nancy Browning, whose father Napoleon Browning was one of the
pioneers of Holt County. Mr. and Mrs. Zachary began their wedded life
on eighty acres of land, an improved farm, and that is the nucleus around
which has been accumulated their present large estate. Mr. Zachary has
kept adding to his holdings until at the present time they aggregate
560 acres, and all of it is in a condition of improvement and mostly
under the plow. Mr. Zachary is one of the large cattle raisers, and raises
and feeds great quantities of corn.

Mr. Zachary and wife are the parents of eleven children: Emmett,
deceased; Earl, who married Maud Lundy; Paul; Mabel, deceased;
Helen; Myron; Esther; Ralph B.; Ruth; Mary; and Dorothy. All the
children were born on the present farm, and those still living are either at
home or located within convenient distances of the old homestead. Mr.
Zachary is a member of the Christian Church and in politics a democrat.

R. C. GILLIS. This name bespeaks a large family relationship with
pioneer settlers in Holt County. The Gillis people through three generations have had their share in pioneer things; agriculture has been their
chief vocation, and in all their relations they have appeared as stanch
upholders of morality and religion and people of intrinsic neighborliness
and usefulness.

Robert C. Gillis, who represents the third generation of residents in Holt County, was born on the farm where he now makes his home February 4, 1876. His parents were Wayne and Rutha J. (Minton) Gillis. Wayne Gillis was born in Holt County and he and his wife married here. Grandfather George Gillis was the founder of the family name and fortune in this section of Northwest Missouri, having come from New York State, and entering land in Holt County as one of the pioneers. His first settlement was about a mile north of Mound City on the Bluff Road. That was at a time when Mound City as a village was not yet in existence, and there were no railroads through the country, and George Gillis and his neighbors had to combat the forces of the wilderness and primitive conditions on every hand. This pioneer spent the rest of his days in Holt County. Wayne Gillis was likewise a farmer, and a man possessed of industry and good judgment, and also of a thoroughly moral character which constituted him a man of standing and influence in the community. He was a member of the Christian Church and in politics a democrat.

Wayne Gillis and wife were the parents of nine children, all of whom are living, as follows: Mary Elizabeth, wife of J. C. Wilson; Robert C.; Ruth J., wife of W. L. Brown; Mabel; Maud, wife of Charles Limpp; Myrtle; Refta; Earl and Fred. All the children live in the vicinity of the old homestead, and Robert C. Gillis and his unmarried brothers and sisters have their home together on the old homestead. This is a fine farm of 360 acres, and the children also own forty acres north of Mound City. General farming and stock raising are the principal industries, and the children have maintained the same high standards of conduct and individual ability which characterized their father and grandfather before them. They were all reared as members of the church, and Robert C. Gillis is affiliated with the Independent Order of Odd Fellows, and like his father is a democratic voter.

ERNST GELVIN. Among the younger element of the agricultural community of Holt County, one who is winning success in his operations through good management and energetic labors, is Ernst Gelvin, whose well-cultivated property of 235 acres is located in the vicinity of Maitland. He belongs to a family of agriculturists, was reared on a farm, and by training and inclination is a true son of the soil. While still a young man he has demonstrated the possession of superior abilities in his chosen work, and has already achieved a success that might well be envied by men many years his senior.

Mr. Gelvin has the added distinction of being a native of Holt County, having been born at Maitland, Missouri, May 5, 1890, a son of D. A. and Lizzie R. (Hershner) Gelvin. There were nine children in his parents' family, and of these three sons are now deceased. After the death of Mr. Gelvin's mother, his father was married a second time, to Mary Meyers, and to this union there were born two children, of whom one is deceased.

The public schools of his native locality furnished Ernst Gelvin with his educational training, and when he laid aside his studies he began to assist his father with his farm work, remaining under the parental roof until his marriage, in 1911, to Miss Gladys E. Brumbaugh, the daughter of Al Brumbaugh. To this union there were no children. At the time of his marriage, Mr. Gelvin located on his present property, a cultivated tract on which there had been erected a full set of substantial buildings, with the exception of the residence, which was built by Mr. Gelvin. He has continued to be engaged in general farming, and has also met with deserved success in the line of cattle feeding, shipping a large amount of stock each season. Politically a republican, like his father, he has been content to discharge the duties of good citizenship, without seeking the doubtful honors of the public arena. He and Mrs. Gelvin are members of the Presbyterian Church, and are always ready to support good and beneficial movements in their community. Both are widely known and have many sincere friends.

ARCH SHARP. Capably representing the agricultural interests of Holt County in Union Township is found Arch Sharp, a progressive farmer and public-spirited citizen and a member of an old and honored family which has lived in Holt County for many years. Mr. Sharp was born in the locality in which he now resides, on his father's homestead place, September 3, 1853, a son of W. A. and Caroline (Elliott) Sharp.

W. A. Sharp was born in Kentucky and was a young man when he came to Missouri seeking his fortunes, the trip being made by boat. He had no capital save that represented by his ambition and determination, but he was willing and steady and straightway secured employment from others. While he was principally engaged in farming at that time, he also did whatever honorable work came to his hands, and he kept a stage station for a number of years, preceding the Civil war. Finally he accumulated enough to begin a career of his own, and at that time entered his first tract of land, which formed the nucleus for his later large holdings. He added to his property from time to time, made good investments, and when he died was considered one of the substantial men of his township. He was a man of high principles and a faithful member of the Presbyterian Church, and in his political views was a democrat. His son Asa was probably the first male white child born in Holt County. He married Emeline Taylor, and has two sons,—William and D. B. Another son was born to W. A. and Caroline Sharp, but he died in childhood.

Arch Sharp received only limited educational advantages in his youth, for the schools at that time in this part of the state left much to be desired. However, in later years Mr. Sharp has been a reader and somewhat of a student, particularly of human nature, and through observation has gained much information that the ordinary man misses. His entire life has been devoted to the pursuits of the soil, and as a developer of Holt County has cultivated several farms, he now being the owner of 990 acres. On each of these properties he has made modern improvements and erected good buildings, and thus has contributed to the community's interests while advancing his own. In business circles Mr. Sharp bears the name and reputation of being a man of strict integrity and fidelity .to engagements.

Mr. Sharp was married to Miss Isabelle Browning, daughter of E. W. Browning, and three children were born to this union: Asa, who married Belle Bowen; W. A., who married Golda Watson; and Minnie, who died at the age of four years. W. A. Sharp has three children, all born in Holt County: Wayne, Wilma and William. Mr. Sharp's first wife died, and he was married a second time, his bride being Cora Etta Davis, daughter of William Davis, and one child has come to them: Dorothy.

Mr. Sharp was reared in the faith of the Presbyterian Church and has continued to believe in its teachings. Like his father, he is a democrat, and has rendered very efficient public service as a member of the school board, on which he has served several times. On a number of occasions he has shown his public spirit in assisting movements for the benefit of his township and its people, and in every particular he may be named as one of his locality's representative men.

HENRY JUDSON HUGHES. The family represented by this well-known real-estate operator, land owner, and cattle breeder of Trenton, came to

Grundy County, Missouri, among the pioneers. During a long and active business career, which began in the capacity of delivery clerk for a local grocery store, Mr. Hughes has created for himself an excellent prosperity and at the same time has made his business work to the benefit of the community. In the last twenty years Mr. Hughes has handled many thousands of acres in this part of Northwest Missouri, and has done a great deal to exhibit to the rest of the world the resources and advantages of Grundy County soil. Naturally his business relations have brought him into contact with all classes of people, and it is noteworthy that he has never had any trouble, either through his personal relations or in anything that might result in lawsuits. He has been fair and honest and liberal, and his success has been worthily won.

Henry Judson Hughes was born on a farm in Trenton Township of Grundy County, January 30, 1858. He is a lineal descendant from Leander Hughes, who was born in Cumberland County, Virginia, and whose father migrated from Wales to Virginia, about 1700. The next in line was Leander's son Powell Hughes, great-grandfather of the Trenton business man. Powell Hughes, who was a soldier in the War of the Revolution, spent all his career in Virginia. Little Berry Hughes, the grandfather, was born in Prince Edward County, Virginia, October 15, 1770, and was reared and married in that vicinity. In 1810 with others he emigrated to Smith County, Tennessee, and this migration was accomplished with teams and wagons, and several women in the party rode horseback over the mountains to Tennessee. Grandfather Hughes bought land in Mulherrin Creek, seven miles southeast of Carthage, became prosperous and an extensive farmer, and was prominent in public affairs. He was in the State Legislature for nineteen years, was in the State Senate in 1825 and was a candidate for the senate at the time of his death in 1835. He married Mary Walker, who was born June 3, 1780, and was married June 3, 1798. She was the daughter of William and Lucy Walker, natives of Prince Edward County, Virginia. By their marriage they reared nine children.

Gedeliah Hughes, father of Henry J., was born in Smith County, Tennessee, January 30, 1816. His education was acquired before the introduction of the public school system, and largely through private tutors. He afterwards received a college training in Virginia. He was married in Muhlenburg County, Kentucky, May 9, 1839, to Jane Penn Walker, daughter of Thomas A. and Mary (Dillon) Walker. With his bride he returned to Smith County, Tennessee, making the journey on horseback. Subsequently they lived in Muhlenburg County, Kentucky, and in 1842 accompanied other pioneers overland to Grundy County, Missouri. It was a party of homeseekers quite typical of the times, and besides the men, women and children, there were wagons and teams, a drove of cattle, and all the household goods and tools which could be carried along. At night they camped by the wayside, and were several weeks in accomplishing the journey. Gedeliah Hughes located six miles from Trenton, and entered Government land in section 12, township 60, range 24, and at once built a log house in which Henry J. Hughes was born. Subsequently he devoted his time to the clearing of the land, the tilling of the soil, and lived in the country until his death in 1861 at the age of forty-five years. His widow survived him many years and kept their children together until each became self-supporting. She died at the venerable age of eighty-nine. Her father was Thomas Walker, who came to Grundy County as a land-looker in 1839, and traded a few slaves for 240 acres two miles from the Trenton courthouse. In 1842 he settled on that land, and lived there until his death in 1856. His widow survived him and died in her ninetieth year. Gedeliah Hughes and wife reared five children, namely: Susan, now the widow of Jacob Helwig; Thomas, who lives at Kingman, Kansas; James C. of Eldorado, Arkansas; Henry J.; and Lizzie Lea, who died at the age of twenty-one.

Henry J. Hughes was three years old when his father died, and he had only limited school advantages, but made the best of all his opportunities and from the time he was thirteen years of age has been earning his own way. At that time he found a place as delivery clerk with a Trenton grocery store. It was a time long before the modern mercantile delivery system was inaugurated, and he served in the capacity of horse, wagon and driver, carrying most of the goods on his shoulders or in his arms to the customers. Later he sold goods over the counter, and learned all the details of the business and gradually got into trade on his own account. Since 1891 Mr. Hughes has been engaged in real-estate. When he opened his office in that line all property values in this part of Missouri, as well as over the country generally, were at a low ebb. The average price at which farm land was sold in the surrounding country was $20 an acre. The same land now brings $100 an acre. Mr. Hughes has done a great deal to advertise Grundy County and recently issued a pamphlet beautifully illustrated with farm scenes and homes and containing an accurate summary description of the land and the opportunities to be found by the homeseeker in Grundy County. Mr. Hughes does not confine his operations to local real estate, but sells and buys in many states of the Union and also in Canada. On one day he sold a tract of land in the Panhandle of Texas and also in Saskatchewan, Canada. One farm sold recently through his office brought $62,500, and for one year his total sales aggregated $600,000. To one customer he sold property valued at $107,500, and this indicates how completely he has won the confidence of investors and the public generally through his well-known integrity as a business man. As a representative of eastern capital he has also loaned millions of dollars in this part of the state, and these transactions have been effected without a single foreclosure or the loss of a dollar in principal or interest.

The Hughesdale Stock Farm is his special pride. Three hundred and twenty acres of highly productive and well improved land, supplied with excellent buildings and farming equipment, afford a setting for the raising of high grade live stock. He specializes in his full-blooded registered shorthorn cattle and Duroc Jersey hogs. At the World's Fair in St. Louis in 1904 Mr. Hughes exhibited "Rowena II," the cow that was awarded championship as the best dual purpose cow. Rowena is still a cherished animal in the Hughes herd, and is now fifteen years old. The Hughes shorthorn herd comprises sixty head, and a number of them are descendants of Rowena.

Mr. Hughes was married December 30, 1879, to Alice Austin, daughter of James and Susan (Collier) Austin. To their marriage have been born two sons and one daughter: Ray A. is now associated with his father in business; Lela A. is the wife of E. D. Winslow, chief clerk to the general manager of the Rock Island Railway at Des Moines; James Blaine, the second son, died when thirteen years old. Mr. and Mrs. Hughes occupy a pleasant home at 314 West Fourteenth Street in Trenton. They are members of the First Baptist Church, and active in social and community affairs. Mr. Hughes cast his first vote for Garfield, and

W. D. Stepp

MAJ. WILLIAM DALE STEPP, a well-known attorney-at-law of Trenton, Grundy County, was born in that city September 12, 1873, a son of Hon. Paris C. D. Stepp. He comes of Revolutionary stock, his great grandfather, James Stepp, having served in the Revolutionary war under Gen. Francis Marion. James Stepp subsequently removed from North Carolina to Kentucky, settling on the· Cumberland River in pioneer days. Among his children were three sons, Golson, Reuben and Joshua, the latter being the Major's grandfather.

Joshua Stepp was born October· 19, 1800, in North Carolina and as a boy accompanied his parents to Kentucky. There, in 1827, he was united in marriage with Rebecca Owen, who was born in the vicinity of Sweet Briar Springs, Virginia, and as a small child was taken by her parents to Kentucky. Soon after his marriage he migrated with his bride to Indiana, becoming an early settler of Monroe County, where he bought land, and was engaged in farming until 1853. In the spring of that year, again seized with the wanderlust, he started for Oregon, an almost unknown country at that time. There were then no railways west of Bloomington, Indiana, and the removal was of necessity made with ox teams. He left Indiana with his entire family, consisting of himself, wife, and fifteen children, and took with him all of his worldly goods. He crossed the Mississippi River at Alton, the Missouri at Lexington, and while camping on Missouri ground was induced by the few settlers already established in that vicinity to locate there. Listening to their persuasions, he bought, in Grundy County, a tract of land·on Honey Creek, known as the Tadlock Farm, and also other tracts amounting in all to 320 acres, the greater part of which was in its primitive wildness. With the assistance of his children he cleared the larger portion of his land, erected a substantial set of buildings, and was there a resident until his death, in 1884. His wife also spent her last years on the homestead, dying in 1885. She had a brother, Greenberry Owen, who moved from his native state, Indiana, to Illinois, and a sister, Mrs. Blanche Ayers, who settled in Missouri, and another sister, Mrs. Irene Murphy, who became a resident of Ohio. The children reared by Joshua and Rebecca (Owen) Stepp were as follows: Jackson, Greenberry O., William L., Leonard, Thomas O., Paris C. D., George D., Louisa, Lourena, Minerva J., Arthusa, Sarah J., Sumilda, Perilda and Elvira.

Paris C. D. Stepp was a lad of eight years when he came with the family to Grundy County, Missouri. The country had then been settled twenty years, but there were neither railroads nor navigable streams, and but little of the land was improved, the lines of neighborhood being far extended. In the winter of 1853-54 he attended a school taught by one of his older sisters in a log cabin that was heated by a fireplace, while the rude slab seats had neither backs nor desks in front. For several years when not in school he assisted in clearing the land and tilling the soil. As soon as old enough, in 1864, he enlisted in the Tenth Kansas Regiment, and did guard duty at St. Louis for awhile, after which he was honorably discharged. On July 20, 1864, Paris C. D. Stepp enlisted in Company E, Twelfth Missouri Cavalry, and going South was soon in the thickest of the fight. On August 10, 1864, he was in battle on the Chattahoochie River, and later was with Smith's Division in the Oxford campaign. On September 30, 1864, he started with his command in pursuit of General Forrest's troops, but at Clifton, Tennessee, his command was ordered to Paducah to meet General Hood's troops, which were en route to Nashville, and from September 8th until September 19th was continuously engaged with the enemy. On the latter date, being far outnumbered by the enemy, he was forced, with his comrades, to retreat to Columbia. From that time he was with his command, and in one of the battles before

Nashville, Paris C. D. Stepp received his only wound while in service, a minnie ball piercing his arm. He was in a stooping posture when hit, and after piercing his arm the ball passed through seventeen letters that he had in his pocket, and then landed in his cap pouch without doing other harm than inflicting the flesh wound on Mr. Stepp's arm.

After the Battle of Nashville, Mr. Stepp was with his command in Alabama and Mississippi until the spring of 1866 when he went with his command to the Northwest to assist in looking after the Indians, who were then on the war path, going by way of Fort Leavenworth to Omaha, thence to the Powder River country, where his command had several engagements with the Indians. He spent the winter with his command at Forts Laramie and Sedgwick, guarding the United States overland mail, and in the spring of 1866 was honorably discharged.

Returning to Trenton, Paris C. D. Stepp farmed, taught school and attended school the next three years. In 1869 he entered the Indiana State University, at Bloomington, Indiana, where he remained a year. He then studied law in the office of Colonel Shanklin, and in 1871 was admitted to the bar before Circuit Court Judge R. A. DeBolt. The ensuing year he taught in the Trenton High School, and the following four years served as county surveyor. In 1876, he was elected as a representative to the State Legislature, and in 1878 was elected probate judge, serving so acceptably, that in 1884, and again in 1888, he was honored with a re-election to the same office, which he filled for twelve years. He was a member of Trenton School Board from 1880 until 1890. In 1892 he was elected judge of the Third Judicial Circuit of Missouri and re-elected to same office in 1898, serving twelve years, his last term expiring January 1, 1904. In the spring of 1907, he removed to Riverton, Wyoming, where he has since been actively and successfuly engaged in the practice of law.

On November 24, 1872, Paris C. D. Stepp was united in marriage with Mary Elizabeth Fleming, with whom he became acquainted while teaching school in Andrew County, Missouri, which was her birthplace. Her father, Elijah Franklin Fleming, was born in Flemingsburg, Kentucky, June 12, 1811, and died in Andrew County, Missouri, April 5, 1892. He was reared in Kentucky, and as a young man went to Indiana, where, in 1844, he married Sarah Jane Francis. In 1853, Mr. Fleming came with his family to Andrew County and bought land lying two miles west of the courthouse in Savannah. Subsequently disposing of that land, he bought another tract twelve miles north of Savannah, and was there engaged in farming and stock raising until his death. Mrs. Mary E. (Fleming) Stepp, mother of Major Stepp, died October 2, 1901, and his father, Paris C. D. Stepp, married for his second wife, Carrie Evans, a daughter of J. B. Evans, of Princeton, Missouri.

Acquiring his rudimentary education in the Trenton public schools, William Dale Stepp continued his studies at the Gem City Business College, in Quincy, Illinois, and at the University of Missouri, in Columbia. Admitted to the bar in 1895, Mr. Stepp began the practice of his profession in Trenton, being in company with his father until 1907, when the

Upon the organization of Company D, Fourth Regiment, Missouri National Guard, on May 2, 1902, Mr. Stepp was elected first lieutenant of the company, and commissioned by Governor Dockery, the commission bearing date of May 23, 1902. In December of the same year, the captain of the company having resigned, he was elected to fill the vacancy, receiving his commission as captain from Governor Dockery on December 12, 1902. On July 24, 1909, he was elected a major in the Fourth Regiment and received his major's commission August 21, 1909, ranking from July 24, 1909, and still holds that rank in his regiment, having been continuously and actively connected with the guard since May 2, 1902.

HENRY NEWTON KENNEDY. One of the valuable and attractive farming properties of Northwest Missouri is Merrievale Farm, a tract of 320 acres lying in Platte Township, section 5, which is devoted to the raising of grain and the breeding of thoroughbred cattle and mules by its owner, Henry Newton Kennedy. Mr. Kennedy is one of the progressive and substantial agriculturists of this locality, and has contributed greatly to the development of the community's farming interests, while as a citizen he has taken a full share in advancing the welfare of Platte Township and Andrew County.

Henry N. Kennedy was born in Polk Township, Nodaway County, Missouri, November 25, 1855, and is a son of the late Judge Samuel T. and Lucretia (Smith) Kennedy. Judge Kennedy was born on a farm in Fayette County, Indiana, September 29, 1830. His father, John Kennedy, by occupation a farmer, was a native of North Carolina, and his mother, whose maiden name was Charity McMichael, was also born in the Old North State. When Judge Kennedy was fourteen years of age the family came to Missouri, and settled in Platte County at a time when Indians were almost the sole inhabitants. In 1850 Judge Kennedy removed to Nodaway County, Missouri, and settled on a farm near Maryville. At that time there were no settlers between his property and Maryville, and only four families and one store in that town, while his parents and a nephew located on a property that subsequently became the county poor farm. The nearest supply point was St. Joseph and four days were necessary in which to make the trip. In 1897 Judge Kennedy moved to Maryville, and from that time resided with his daughter, Mrs. J. H. Booth, until his death, Saturday, September 4, 1909, at the age of seventy-eight years eleven months four days, death being caused by cancer, an illness with which he was afflicted for several months. The funeral services were held at the Methodist Episcopal Church, South, and were in charge of the Masons and White Cloud Lodge No. 92, Independent Order of Odd Fellows, of which Mr. Kennedy had been a member, also attended the services in a body. Burial took place at Miriam Cemetery. Judge Kennedy was a member of the Methodist Episcopal Church, the Odd Fellows and Maryville Lodge No. 165, Ancient, Free and Accepted Masons, of which he had been master for eight years, and district deputy grand master in 1873 and 1874. A democrat in politics, in 1873 Judge Kennedy was elected chairman of the County Court, filling the position for five years and six months in a most satisfying manner.

Judge Kennedy was married July 14, 1850, at the home of William

to Nodaway County, and at this time makes her home with her daughter at Maryville. On July 14, 1900, Judge and Mrs. Kennedy celebrated their golden wedding anniversary at the home of B. A. Willhoyte, their son-in-law, who resides west of town, and there attended their children, sixteen of their twenty-three grandchildren, and their four great-grandchildren. Judge and Mrs. Kennedy were the parents of ten children, of whom seven still survive: Mrs. M. J. Willhoyte, northwest of Maryville; John W., a resident of Parnell, Missouri; Henry N., of this review; Mrs. Ward Miller, of St. Petersburg, Florida; Mrs. F. M. Taylor, of Des Moines, Iowa; Mrs. B. H. Lingenfelter, of Seattle, Washington; and Mrs. J. H. Booth, of West Sixth Street, Maryville. The deceased children were: Austin S., Andrew W. and Archibald S. Judge Kennedy was appointed coal inspector by Governor Dockery and also held the same position under appointment by Governor Folk.

Henry Newton Kennedy received a country school education and grew up amid rural surroundings, early adopting the vocation of farmer as his life work. Until his marriage he resided with his father, and at that time established a home of his own, having 120 acres 1½ miles south of Wilcox. On January 18, 1901, he came to Andrew County, locating on his present property of 320 acres, in section 5, Platte Township, and this is now under a high state of cultivation, yielding large crops of grain and furnishing excellent pasturage for Mr. Kennedy's livestock. Merrievale Farm has been improved by the erection of a handsome set of buildings, including a modern residence, substantial barn, a large silo, and various outbuildings, in addition to which Mr. Kennedy has the most up-to-date machinery and equipment. For a number of years he raised about fifty mules annually for the market, and still breeds many jacks, although for the past several years he has devoted more attention to breeding thoroughbred white faced cattle. He has lent encouragement to the farming interests here, and is an active member of the Whitesville Interstate Corn and Poultry Association. Politically Mr. Kennedy is a democrat, and his fraternal affiliation is with the Masonic Lodge at Bolckow. Among those who have had business dealings with him, Mr. Kennedy bears the reputation of being a man of integrity, and is justly accounted one of the representative men of his community.

Mr. Kennedy was married September 23, 1876, to Sarah Nettie Ford, who was born in Nodaway County, Missouri, November 25, 1855, the same day as Mr. Kennedy was born. She died April 15, 1886, having been the mother of four children: Ida May, who is the wife of C. J. Duncan, and resides west of Wilcox; Lucy W., who married Frank Carter, and resides in Putnam County, Missouri; Harlan E., a resident of Andrew County; and Wallace, who lives near Parnell, Missouri.

On November 23, 1887, Mr. Kennedy was married to Mary Bell ("Minnie") Lindsay, who was born near Rainsboro, Highland County, Ohio, April 1, 1860, and came to Missouri with her parents in 1870, they being Jacob J. and Amanda M. (Hiatt) Lindsay. Jacob J. Lindsay was born July 24, 1823, in Pike County. Ohio, and there grew to manhood and was married to Amanda M. Hiatt, September 21. 1848. In 1870 they moved to a farm east of Bolckow. Missouri, where they resided until 1892, when they removed to Maryville, there living until the death of Mrs. Lindsay, January 24, 1900, having lived together for over fifty years. From the time of his wife's death until his own Mr. Lindsay made his home alternately with his daughters, Mrs. J. R. Carson, of Berlin, Missouri; Mrs. C. W. Talbot, of Haven, Kansas, and Mrs. H. N. Kennedy, of Bolckow. Mr. Lindsay was chosen captain of a company of volunteers in the Mexican war in 1846, when but twenty-three years of age, and was also a soldier during the Civil war, being lieutenant of a company in the Sixtieth Regiment, Ohio Volunteer Infantry, and participating in several battles. After four days of fighting at Harper's Ferry, he was captured by General Jackson's men. One sister survives him. Mr. Lindsay was converted and joined the Christian Union Church, of which he remained a faithful member. He died of pneumonia April 5, 1906. Amanda M. Hiatt was born at Leesburg, Ohio, June 11, 1830, and died January 24, 1900, at Maryville, Missouri. She was married at Cynthiana, Ohio, to J. J. Lindsay, and to this union there were born seven children. One, the youngest, died in infancy. The three oldest, Sarah Redkey, Dr. J. O. and J. H., all preceded their mother in death. Three daughters survive: Mr. J. R. Carson, of Berlin, Missouri; Mrs. C. W. Talbot, of Haven, Kansas; and Mrs. Kennedy. At the time of her demise Mrs. Lindsay had twenty-eight grandchildren and six great-grandchildren. Mrs. Lindsay was converted and joined the Methodist Episcopal Church in the year 1849, but after coming to Missouri united with the Baptist Church, and was always a faithful member, but on account of ill health was unable to attend during the last several years of her life. Mrs. Lindsay left a brother, J. J. Hiatt, of Carmel, Ohio, and one sister, Mrs. Eliza Warntz, of Rainsboro, Ohio. The funeral services were held at the Baptist Church, conducted by Dr. G. L. Black, the pastor, after which burial took place at Miriam Cemetery. Four children have been born to Mr. and Mrs. Kennedy: Wray L., who died at the age of thirteen years; Verna Marie, a graduate of Maryville Business College, who lives at home with her parents; and Eva C. and Martha, who are attending the home school.

Mrs. Kennedy is a lady of culture and education, having been graduated from Stanberry State Normal School, class of 1885, following which she was for about twenty years a teacher in the public schools of Andrew and Nodaway counties. Mr. and Mrs. Kennedy are Christian people, but have not been identified with any church since they moved from the old home place in Nodaway County. Mr. Kennedy has met with vicissitudes in his career, but has always overcome all obstacles and discouragements. On July 13, 1883, a windstorm visited his farm in Nodaway County, and stripped it completely of buildings and trees. Most of the members of the family had taken refuge in their cyclone cellar, but Mr. Kennedy and his daughter Lucy remained in the house, which was demolished, although they received no serious injury. Mr. Kennedy did not have one cent of insurance and his possessions were all taken from him, but he still retained his credit in the community, and with this as a basis started all over again, and eventually regained his lost fortunes.

WILLIAM CALVIN TOWNSEND. A farm that represents some of the best improvements and values in Northwest Missouri is the East Lawn Farm, located on the One Hundred and Two River, in section 16, Benton Township, Andrew County. It is a stock and grain farm, and its genial proprietor, William Calvin Townsend, knows farming as a business, and conducts it on the same principles that a manufacturer would run his factory or a merchant his store. Stock and grain are his staple products, and he has prospered both through the intelligent management of his place year after year, each successive twelve months period adding a little more to his enterprise, and also through the great increase in farm values, which are the result of the aggregate labors of many farmers in this section. Mr. Townsend some thirty years ago bought his first 200 acres of land at $20 an acre, and each succeeding purchase required more money per acre, and a general average of value on his land now would be about $150 an acre.

William Calvin Townsend was born four miles north of Savannah, in Andrew County, March 16, 1853, and is the fifth in a family of ten children, whose parents were William Calvin and Mary Ann (Judd) Townsend. The Townsends are numerously represented in Andrew County, have been identified with this section of Northwest Missouri since pioneer times, and more complete data concerning the family in general, and this immediate branch, will be found on other pages of this work.

William Calvin Townsend has spent all his life in Andrew County, except eighteen months, during which period his parents lived in Iowa in order to avoid the local troubles incident to the Civil war. Reared on a farm, he was educated in district schools and, like many other men, has found in agriculture the freest and most independent vocation open to man. He lived at home with his parents for the first twenty-nine years, and then was married and started for himself in 1880. On March 1, 1881, he came to the nucleus of his present place, which is situated three miles southwest of Bolckow. At the present time Mr. Townsend owns 345 acres, and has several sets of improvements, and most of the land in cultivation on the intensive plan. As a stock man he features the Hereford cattle, and all his stock are of good grades.

Besides his success as a farmer, Mr. Townsend has interested himself in local affairs in keeping with the ideals of good citizenship. He is a republican in politics, has served as school and road officer, and is always ready to give his support to enterprises which mean a better community, socially and otherwise. Mr. Townsend has served as a trustee in the Baptist Church at Bolckow.

While successful in a material way, he can perhaps take even more pride in the fine family which he has brought into the world and for whom he has provided home and means of training for useful citizenship. On April 28, 1880, Mr. Townsend married Amanda Elizabeth Neely. She was born in Andrew County, southeast of Bolckow, in 1861, a daughter of Franklin and Nancy (Wilds) Neely, who were among the pioneers of Andrew County. The family circle of children comprised fourteen in number, several of whom are now at the heads of their own homes, while several others are deceased. By name they are mentioned as follows: Charles Royal is a resident of Bolckow and married Cora White; Byron Franklin, of Benton Township, married Dora Hartman, and their three children are named Marvin, Loyd and Charles Royal; William Perry died at the age of twenty-three; Calvin, Jr., who lives on a part of his father's farm, married Eva Violet, and their five children are Calvin, Hallie, Phyllis, Helen and Vernie Alice; Russell, who lives at home; Logan, of Benton Township, married Emma Violet. and their three sons are Virgil Paul, Floyd Logan and William Harrison; Jessie, the only daughter, died in infancy; David, who married May Rowland; and Emery, Arlie and George, still under the family rooftree; Freemont, the twelfth child, died at the age of five years; and the two youngest are Timothy and Daniel.

LE ROY CROCKETT. On section 14 of Platte Township, Andrew County, is the home of Le Roy Crockett, known among farmers and stock men in this section of Northwest Missouri as the Prairie View Stock Farm. Four or five hundred acres of some of the finest land to be found in Andrew County are the basis of Mr. Crockett's industry as a farmer and stock man, and by his success he stands in the very front rank of producers of agricultural crops. His judgment in farming matters is regarded as almost infallible, and everything about his place attests the progressive and prosperous business man. The Prairie View Farm can be recognized by its commodious dwelling house, barns and silos, and the condition of the fields and the fences is one of the features which at once commend this farm to the casual observer. The Crockett family has been identified with Andrew County since early times, and the success of the earlier generation has been greatly increased by Mr. Le Roy Crockett.

The founders of this branch of the family in Andrew County were twin brothers, Milton and Nelson Crockett, of whom the former was the father of Le Roy Crockett. Milton Crockett was born near Tiffin, Seneca County, Ohio, January 11, 1825, a son of Asa and Miriam (Keating) Crockett. His father was born in Thomaston, Lincoln County, Maine, in 1790, and was of Scotch-English descent. He was a sailor in early life, but at the age of twenty-six settled in Ohio and engaged in business as a farmer. His wife was born at Ashpoint, Maine, in 1800, and had eight sons and four daughters. Milton Crockett was reared on a farm, had a common school education, and as a young man taught school several terms in the winter while employed on a farm in the summer. This was his vocation for about twelve years. His twin brother Nelson had a similar training, and in 1857 they both left Ohio and came out to Andrew County, Missouri, where Milton Crockett secured the land which is now a part of the estate of the Prairie View Stock Farm. During the Civil war both brothers returned to Ohio and enlisted in the Union army, Nelson enlisting September 28, 1861, in Company A, of the Fifty-fifth Ohio Volunteer Infantry, in which he was commissioned second lieutenant, and served until a wound in the second battle of Bull Run caused him to resign, while Milton enlisted August 2, 1862, in the same company and regiment, and continued in service until mustered out and given an honorable discharge on June 30, 1865. He fought at the battles of Chancellorsville, Gettysburg, Lookout Mountain, Missionary Ridge, Nashville, Tennessee, and for nearly three years was one of the faithful soldiers who upheld the integrity of the Union. Milton Crockett was married March 22, 1849, to Sarah E. West, a daughter of Ezra and Prudence (Culver) West. She was born near Arlington, Vermont, April 27, 1830. Milton Crockett and wife became the parents of five sons and one daughter: Wallace A., Ezra, Homer, Emeily M., Nathan N. and Le Roy. Milton Crockett was a man of prominence and influence in Andrew County, and in 1870 was elected as the liberal candidate for county representative, and served in the Legislature one term.

Le Roy Crockett was born on the farm that he now occupies, in Platte Township, June 24, 1869, and has never known any other permanent home. His education came from the local schools, and at the age of twenty-one he accepted an offer to become a partner with his father in conducting the farm, and from that time forward took the complete management of it. His father for a number of years had been very successful as a dairyman, running from fifty to seventy cows. It will be appropriate to recall an event which is well remembered by the older settlers in Andrew County and gave a new direction to the Crockett farm activities. On Sunday afternoon, May 13, 1883, a cyclone struck over this section of Missouri and almost completely destroyed all the improvements on the Crockett farm, blowing down nearly every tree and all the buildings and fences. The house was also crushed down, but the six members of the family in it were not seriously injured. As a result of this disaster Milton Crockett closed out his dairy business, and since that time the farm has been conducted on general lines, with general agricultural crops and stock raising.

Before his father's death Le Roy Crockett bought a part of the homestead, and has since acquired adjoining land until the Prairie View Farm now comprises 430 acres in one body. His father's first land comprised a quarter section, and he added to that until he owned a half section at one time. Mr. Crockett has had his farm registered under the name of the Prairie View Stock Farm, thus giving it a title by which it is becoming increasingly known, with a special reputation for its horses and mules. Mr. Crockett for a number of years has made a feature of the raising and shipping of this stock, and each year sells about twenty mules from his barn. He also keeps cattle and horses, and feeds every bushel of the grain raised in his fields, and buys large quantities for his stock besides. Since he acquired possession Mr. Crockett has remodeled the home, and has built new barns and silos, and has introduced such improvements as to make the Crockett home one measuring up to the best standards of comforts and conveniences found in the larger cities. Among other things he has introduced a water system, heating plant, and lights the house with an acetylene gas plant. It is a splendidly situated home, with well-kept grounds, and is really one of the model rural places of Andrew County.

Mr. Crockett is a republican in politics and with his family worships in the Methodist Church at Empire Prairie. On October 15, 1890, he married Kate Bradford, who was born at Whitesville, in Andrew County, August 21, 1869, a daughter of Duffield and Caroline (Worth) Bradford. The Bradford family in this branch is one of the oldest in American history. Duffield Bradford was born in Ohio, August 9, 1819, and his wife in Wilkesbarre, Pennsylvania, and at the age of twelve years went out to Iowa. Mr. and Mrs. Bradford were married at Mount Pleasant, Iowa, in 1864, and in 1865 located in Andrew County, where Mr. Bradford died at Whitesville in 1871, and his widow survived until April 24, 1909, at the age of seventy-five. Mrs. Crockett's family lineage is one that would do credit to any printed page. The Bradfords are not only among the oldest and most numerous in America, but have furnished many illustrious men to the nation, and have done their share in the upbuilding of the country as soldiers, patriots, business men and citizens. The family originated in Austerfield, England, where the first ancestry concerning whom information is available was William Bradford, and also his son William Bradford, both of whom lived in England during the sixteenth century. The second William Bradford was burned at the stake by order of Queen Mary. The third in line was Governor William Bradford, whose name is familiar to every reader of United States history. He was born at Austerfield, England, in 1588, at the age of nineteen was arrested and imprisoned on account of his religious beliefs, emigrated with many other non-conformists to Holland, was married there, and in 1620 made the famous voyage with other pilgrims in the Mayflower. For many years he was governor of Plymouth Colony, and his grave can now be seen in the old churchyard at Plymouth, Massachusetts. In his declining years his son, Maj. William Bradford, served as lieutenant governor and bore the chief responsibilities of the office. Maj. William Bradford was born at Plymouth, June 17, 1624. His son, Maj. John Bradford, was born February 20, 1653, and lived at Kingston, Massachusetts. Major John had several sons and daughters, and two of the sons, Joshua and Elijah, moved to the State of Maine. It is not accurately known whether Joshua or Elijah was the father of Joseph Bradford, who continues the line of descent. Joseph Bradford was the father of Moses Bradford, who was born in Maine in 1776, and in 1800 moved out to Ohio, which was then the Northwest Territory. Moses married Anna Ward, and was the father of several sons and daughters, including Joseph, Ward, Duffield, Moses and William. In this list of children is Duffield Bradford, father of Mrs. Crockett. In Revolutionary annals several of the Bradfords appear as soldiers, and it is said that one woman of the family dressed in men's attire, marched as a soldier all during the war, was wounded once or twice, and afterwards married and reared a family.

Mrs. Crockett is the only child living of the five born to her parents. Mr. and Mrs. Crockett have five children: Elbert M., who lives on part of the home farm and married Hazel Thompson; Eunice C., wife of Frank W. Edwards of Empire Township, Andrew County; Mabel Clementine; George D.; and Stanley B., all living at home.

HON. JAMES E. FORD. In November, 1914, the fourth district reelected James E. Ford to the State Senate. His return to the body in which he has served as representative and senator for eight years is an encouraging sign of the time to all citizens who believe in the essential wholesomeness of the modern progressive tendencies in politics and government. Senator Ford has given excellent and positive service to the cause of good government in Missouri, and by their votes at the recent election the people of the fourth district justified his record and thereby added a strong and experienced member to the next senate.

Senator Ford was elected to represent Grundy County in the lower house in 1906, and during his second term was speaker pro tem. In 1910 he was elected for his first term in the senate. In that year Governor Hadley appointed him a member and he was chosen chairman of the auditing committee to investigate state offices. About half of the forty bills he has introduced have become law. He was a joint author of the present county school supervision law. He was the author of the enabling act, now a law, defining and restricting the use of the initiative and referendum, by which the people of the state have authority to originate and also to approve or reject legislation. He was joint author of the bill establishing the present state poultry experiment station, and introduced a bill to prevent the importation of diseased live stock into the state, a bill that failed of passage, but the essential value of which has been emphasized by recent events. Among the measures introduced by Senator Ford in the session of 1915 is one providing for a system of township school districts, managed by one board of six with a uniform levy throughout the township, defining township districts as "town districts" with power to levy and collect taxes now allowed other town districts, and providing for the establishment of township high schools or joint township high schools. This plan Senator Ford thinks corrects the two fundamental weaknesses of the present country school system, the low tax levy required under the constitution, and the weak, isolated independent district, and he thinks it will soon place a high school within horseback distance of nearly every boy and girl in the state. Another bill is a system of building permanent country roads by convict labor, which is advocated by the state highway commission. His progressive tendencies are also shown by his introduction of bills to provide for a presidential preference primary and another for the popular election of United States senators, now provided by amendment to the Federal Constitution. He was the first man in Missouri to conceive and advocate the use of the initiative as a means of overcoming the practice of gerrymandering congressional and senatorial districts.

Senator Ford is a young man, but his career has stimulating interest to those who believe in the efficacy of hard work and ambition. He was born on a farm in Grundy County, April 5, 1880, a son of John B. and Sarah (Cooksey) Ford, the former a native of Shelby County, Missouri, and the latter of Illinois. His paternal grandparents, James H. and Amelia (Cockrum) Ford, were both born in Kentucky. The senator is descended on both sides from ancestors who took part in the Revolutionary war.

His first schooling was in the old Ford School in Myers Township of Grundy County, but most of his education has come from hard study at home. He graduated in the Kirksville Normal, also attended the Missouri State University, and took a course in logic and other subjects through the correspondence department of the University of Chicago. He has taught school, has owned and edited several newspapers, and besides his active public career has kept close to the farming vocation at which he was reared. His home is on his farm, Silverdawn, 2½ miles north of Trenton. In 1904, after leaving the Kirksville Normal, Senator Ford bought a newspaper at Gault, but sold it in 1906 and came to Trenton and for a time was in the real-estate business. For a short time he owned and edited a Trenton paper. He is also known as an author, having completed some very authentic county histories, now in book form, and is the author of a volume of humorous sketches entitled "Fact, Fun and Fiction," of which he sold the copyright. During 1911-12 he managed the home farm, then bought and conducted a newspaper at Hamilton, which he sold in 1913, and has since given his time to the operation of his own farm. In politics Mr. Ford is a republican.

In 1907 Senator Ford married Miss Grace Humphreys, a daughter of Wade H. and Nettie (Cooper) Humphreys, of Gault, her father being a large land owner in Grundy County. Mr. and Mrs. Ford are the parents of three children, Wade H., James E. and Allie Grace.

WILLIAM R. ANDERSON. A vigorous young Trenton business man who has shown much capacity to manage large responsibilities and build up business is William R. Anderson, local manager for the T. W. Ballew Lumber Company. Mr. Anderson has had much experience in the lumber trade, and though a young man still in his twenties has demonstrated both ability and success in his relations with business and with citizenship.

William R. Anderson was born in Montrose, Henry County, Missouri, February 22, 1888. His father, Jno. Q. Anderson, was born in Kentucky November 12, 1862, and all the Andersons came originally from Kentucky. The mother, whose maiden name was Sallie Wilson, was of an Illinois family, but was born in Ray County, Missouri, February 28, 1864. They were married at Kansas City in 1884. The father located in Polk County, Missouri, in 1874, taught country schools there for several years, and in 1891 became identified with the E. W. Blew Lumber Company at Montrose, Missouri. In 1898 he took over the business, making the firm the Anderson Lumber Company. His death occurred in 1902.

William R. Anderson acquired his early education in the public schools of Montrose, graduating from the high school in 1905, then in the fall of the same year entered the Western Commercial and Military School at Clinton, Missouri, was a student there until 1906, and during 1907 attended the Hill Business College at Sedalia. His practical business career began in the fall of 1907 at Excelsior Springs, where he was connected with the Roanoke Lumber Company until 1912. In that year he became local manager for the T. W. Ballew Lumber Company at Trenton, and has since been a resident of that city.

Mr. Anderson is a republican, is affiliated with the Lodge and Royal Arch Chapter of Masonry, and with the Benevolent and Protective Order of Elks, being a popular member of these different fraternities. December 26, 1912, he married Miss Bessie Peterson, a daughter of Peter and Viola (Schultz) Peterson of McCook, Nebraska. The Peterson family were pioneer settlers in Nebraska.

ROBERT A. COLLIER. One of the venerable citizens of Grundy County is Robert A. Collier, whose home has been in that locality for more than seventy years, and whose mind is filled with recollections of the early surroundings and events of Northwest Missouri. He is one of the honored veterans of the great Civil strife of the '60s, and has given many years to public in Grundy County.

Robert A. Collier was born at Fayette, in Howard County, Missouri, March 19, 1838, a son of William and Susan Collier. His father was a man whose enterprise did much for early Grundy County, and who was the contractor who constructed the first courthouse at Trenton. The family history is of much interest, and will be found somewhat in detail in the sketch of Hon. Luther Collier, a brother of Robert A.

Robert A. Collier was five years old when the family moved to Trenton, and grew up in that city. He has recollections of some of the early schools and early school teachers, and among those who directed his mental training as a boy he recalls Col. John H. Shanklin, George H. Hubbell, James Turner, Jacob T. Tindall, Rev. James Vincent, J. B. Allen and Joseph Ficklin. Later he attended school for a time at Bethany. For a practical vocation in life he learned the trade of bricklayer under his father's direction, and that has been his main business, although the greater part of his active years have been spent in other duties.

In 1861 Mr. Collier enlisted for service in the Union army, becoming a member of Company B, of the Twenty-third Regiment of Missouri Infantry. He was made orderly sergeant, and in 1863 was commissioned lieutenant by Governor Gamble. Soon afterwards by order of President Lincoln he was appointed a mustering officer, and thus became a member of the general staff. He served on the staff of Gen. Thomas A. Davies, General Guitar and General McNeil. After three years and four months in the army he returned home and was appointed mustering officer for Grundy County, a position which he retained for about one year. Soon after the close of the war Mr. Collier continued his public work as deputy county clerk, and finally resigned that position to engage in merchandising. In 1870 he was elected county clerk, and gave twelve years to that office.

In 1863 Mr. Collier married Miss Ann E. Cooper, a daughter of Dr. James and Mary A. E. Cooper. They are the parents of four children: William C., Robert E., Leon E. and Mary E., the last being the wife of W. E. Pierson. Mr. Collier has affiliated with the Masonic Order for half a century, and is one of the oldest Masons in Northwest Missouri.

LESLEY P. ROBINSON. Prosecuting attorney of Grundy County, to which position he was elected in 1912, Lesley P. Robinson is one of the most popular officials of the county, and for nearly ten years has practiced law with growing success at Trenton.

Mr. Robinson was born on a farm four miles from Corydon, Wayne County, Iowa, October 17, 1881. His father was Peter Lunsford Robinson, who was born in Greencastle, Indiana, June 1, 1832. The grandfather was Addison Newton Robinson, a native of Kentucky, whose father moved to Indiana during the territorial period, and who lost his life while defending the old fort at Vincennes against Indian attack. Grandfather Robinson was a pioneer of Putnam County, Indiana, and had his home near Greencastle. In 1843 he went West and found a home in the Territory of Iowa. He entered land four miles northwest of the present site of Corydon, and was one of the early settlers who cleared the wilderness and prepared the way for modern civilization in that part of the state. He improved his land and lived upon it until his death when about seventy years of age. He married Elizabeth O'Neil Lunsford, who was born in 1812, and whose parents were probably natives of Ireland and early settlers in the State of Indiana. Grandmother Robinson died at the age of eighty-seven years.

Peter Lunsford Robinson, father of the prosecuting attorney, was eleven years old when the family located in Iowa, was reared amid pioneer surroundings in that state, and during his later life he often recalled many circumstances which characterized the country in that day. He knew Iowa when wild turkey, prairie chicken and all kinds of game roamed and could be found by the hunter in abundance on every quarter section. There were no railroads for a number of years after the Robinson family located there, and the farmers of Wayne County in the early days took their grain to Alexandria on the Mississippi River, there loading with goods needed for domestic consumption at home. When ready to start in life on his own account Peter L. Robinson bought land near the homestead and finally succeeded to ownership of the old place, where he lived until 1896. Selling out his Iowa home, he then moved to Grundy County, Missouri, and bought land in Madison Township. He became one of the well known farmers and stock raisers and lived there until his death a few years ago. Peter L. Robinson married Mary Atkinson, who was born in Lee County, Iowa, December 13, 1849. Her father, James Atkinson, was one of the early settlers of Grundy County, and had the distinction of operating a grist mill for the benefit of the settlers in the early days. About 1863 he went out to Denver, Colorado, and was one of the early residents of that western city. Later he returned to Missouri, and spent his last days in Boone County. He was by profession a Primitive Baptist preacher and was quite successful as a trader. The maiden name of his wife was Margaret Mendenhall, who was born in Illinois and died at Trenton before her husband went out to Colorado. Mrs. Peter L. Robinson died December 22, 1910, and she reared eleven children, namely: Willett, Ida, Edwin, Stephen, Lizzie, Lida, Lesley P., Nellie, Maggie, Newton and William. Of these children Willett and Lizzie are now deceased.

Lesley P. Robinson received his early education in the rural schools of Wayne County and as he was about fifteen when the family came to Grundy County he had some schooling here, and later entered the University of Kansas and studied law in the Kansas City Law School. Admitted to practice in the fall of 1904, he has since been steadily advancing in professional attainments, and in 1905 formed a partnership with the veteran lawyer, Luther Collier, a partnership which has continued with mutual profit and satisfaction to the present time.

In 1908 Mr. Robinson married Nellie May Songer. She was born in Grundy County, a daughter of John R. Songer, who was born in Trenton Township November 9, 1847, and was the son of Giles Songer and grandson of Abraham Songer. The last named was a native of Pennsylvania and of German stock, later removing from Pennsylvania to Washington County, Indiana, and finally to Clay County, Illinois, where he died. Abraham Songer married Catherine Sawyer, who was born in Pennsylvania and also died in Clay County, Illinois. Giles Songer came to Grundy County in 1846, only five years after this county was organized, and got a tract of land direct from the Government six miles northeast of Trenton. He was a man of much industry and enterprise, and after developing his first tract of land sold out at a profit and bought more land three miles east of his previous location where he resided until his death in 1884. Giles Songer married Nancy Childress, who died in 1907, at the good old age of eighty-seven years. John R. Songer, Mrs. Robinson's father, has spent his entire life in Grundy County, and now lives

retired in the City of Trenton. He married Nannie V. Shanklin, who
was born in Trenton, a daughter of Andrew and Rachel (Sharpe) Shanklin, and the granddaughter of Absalom and Nancy (Leester) Shanklin. Mr. and Mrs. Robinson have one daughter, named Mary Virginia.

In public affairs Mr. Robinson has enacted a considerable role, and is
regarded as one of the leaders of the local democracy. He cast his first
vote for W. J. Bryan, and has served as a member of the Grundy County
democratic central committee and as delegate to county and state conventions. In the campaign of 1912 he was candidate on the democratic
ticket for the office of prosecuting attorney, and his name contributed to
the strength of that ticket, and since taking up his duties he has well
justified the confidence of his friends and political supporters.

LEVI M. HICKEY. From the close of the Civil war until his retirement a few years ago to the Village of Whitesville, Levi M. Hickey was
one of the industrious and hard-working farmer citizens of Andrew
County. Mr. Hickey won his competence under conditions which would
be deemed hardships by the present generation of agriculturists. Persistent toil, early and late, vigilant attention to all details of his business, and observance of all the old-fashioned rules of honesty and fair
dealing, have been the cornerstones on which his career has been based.
He is one of the highly honored citizens of Andrew County.

Levi M. Hickey was born in Carter County, Tennessee, December 21,
1838, and belonged to a large family of that plainspoken and hardy class
of people known as East Tennesseeans. His father was a whig, during the
war was a Union man, and the son Levi was one of the family who
fought for the cause of the Union. The parents were James M. and
Nancy (Millard) Hickey. His father was born in Washington County,
Virginia, in 1797, and his mother in Sullivan County in East Tennessee
in 1803. They were married in Sullivan County, and spent their lives
in that state on a farm. The mother died in 1862 while her son Levi was
in a Confederate prison at Richmond, Virginia. The father died at the
age of seventy-two. There were fourteen children, all of whom lived to
maturity, and all were reared in a hewed loghouse, one of the typical
homes of Eastern Tennessee, where there was an abundance of the
necessities, but very few of the luxuries and in that time and place
schools were held in less esteem as a means of discipline than the work
and experience of the home farm. The children are briefly named as
follows: Charlotta White, who died in Tennessee in December, 1912,
at the age of ninety; Elizabeth Lacey, Matilda Miller, Timothy, James,
William and Nathaniel, all deceased; Ann, who married Thomas Crumley and is now deceased; Levi M.; Mary, deceased wife of Jack Crumley;
Martha; Emma, wife of George Crumley of Knoxville, Tennessee; and
Paulina Dinwiddie of Knoxville, Tennessee.

Levi M. Hickey lived at home until his marriage in 1859, and then
moved to Washington County, Tennessee, and lived in that vicinity until
the outbreak of the war. He early determined to enlist in the Union
army, and while trying to get through the Southern lines to the Union
forces was made a prisoner, and for three months kept at Richmond,
Virginia. Having been exchanged, and sent through the lines, he
reached Louisville, Kentucky, where the regiment which he was to join
was then stationed. Thus his formal enlistment was delayed until December 26, 1862, when he became a member of Company B of the Fourth
Tennessee Infantry, and remained with that organization until August
2, 1865, being mustered out at Nashville with the rank of sergeant.
In the fall of 1865 Mr. Hickey came to Andrew County, Missouri, locating 2½ miles north of Whitesville. His chief possessions at that time

were a willingness to work hard for a living, and by steady industry he prospered as a farmer and acquired a valuable estate. His home was burned in 1907, and owing to his advanced age he decided to sell his land, and has since lived in Whitesville, in a home he built on coming to that village.

Mr. Hickey has a record of exceptional length as a republican voter. Owing to the fact that there was no Lincoln ticket in Tennessee in 1860, he gave his ballot to John Bell, the free soil candidate, but while in the army voted for Lincoln the second time, and has supported every presidential candidate of that party down to date. In state and county elections he splits his ticket. Mr. Hickey was a member of the Dunkard Church until removing to town, and now attends worship in the Christian Church.

In 1859 he married Mary Bashor, who died in Andrew County in 1892. Their children were: Nancy, wife of Charles Daggett of Kansas; Thomas, of Idaho; Louisa, wife of G. W. Gebhart of Platte Township; Paulina, wife of Bert Riddlesbarger of Idaho; Wallace of Wright County, Missouri; and Henry Milton, who died in infancy. In 1896 Mr. Hickey married Mrs. Malinda (McNatt) West, who was born in Gentry County, Missouri, a daughter of William McNatt and widow of Joseph West. By her first marriage her children are: Esther, wife of George Hardwick of Los Angeles, California; and Elmer, of Ravenswood, Missouri.

JAMES GIBSON. Scotch persistence, thrift and industry, qualities which he brought over from the old country, have enabled James Gibson to accomplish more than the average man who starts life with only a pair of willing hands and a heart courageous for any fate. Mr. Gibson is now one of the large land owners in Platte Township of Andrew County, has a large family of boys and girls, and most of them are married and occupying homes of their own which he gave them. Forty years ago James Gibson came to Andrew County with a wife and an infant child six months old. He had very little money, but most men at the present time would consider it hardly enough for running expenses. What he has accomplished since then is a remarkable testimonial to his diligence and general business ability.

James Gibson was born in Ayrshire, Scotland, June 4, 1849, a son of Alex and Jane (Howitt) Gibson. Both parents were born in the same county, and spent their lives there, chiefly on a farm. Their nine children were: Jane Miller, deceased; David, who lives in Kansas; William, who died in Scotland; James; John, who lives in Scotland; Mary Jimeson of Scotland; Alex, of Scotland; Peter, who died in childhood; Agnes, who died in girlhood; and one that died in infancy.

James Gibson received an education in the old country, and earned his support while working as a farmhand until 1869. He gave his people half his wages, but by careful economy managed to save £9, and with this sum started for the United States. Large numbers of Ayrshire people had settled in the State of Wisconsin, and that was his destination. When he arrived at Milwaukee he had 25 cents in his pockets, and though an exceedingly homesick boy lost no time in securing work as a farmhand and going ahead until he had some degree of financial independence. In 1875 Mr. Gibson came to Andrew County, and for five years rented and operated a farm, and then bought the nucleus of his present homestead. At the present time Mr. Gibson owns 640 acres, divided into seven different farms, each with a set of improvements. In his home place he operates 120 acres, and also uses forty additional acres for pasturage. His success has come from general grain and stock farming, and after acquiring his land he has kept improving it and by his own work has added much of the value which his farms now represent. While his sons were at home assisting him, he usually fed about a carload of cattle every year.

Mr. Gibson is an independent republican, and is a member of the Lower Empire Presbyterian Church, and has fraternal affiliations with the Independent Order of Odd Fellows and the A. H. T. A. In 1874 he married Agnes Booth. Mrs. Gibson was born January 28, 1852, in Waukesha County, Wisconsin, where they were married. Her parents were James and Elizabeth (Welch) Booth, both natives of Scotland, but married in New York, and immediately afterward came West and settled in Waukesha County, Wisconsin, securing land from the Government. The five children in the Booth family were: Robert, James, Janet, now deceased, Agnes and Elizabeth.

Mr. and Mrs. Gibson have a family of eight children. William lives in Platte Township; Ella is the wife of Myron Johnson of Platte Township; Elizabeth is the wife of Le Roy Wilkerson of Platte Township; James; Myron; Robert; Charles, who died at the age of four years; and Jennie, at home. The six oldest children are all married and each occupies a farm of eighty acres on Empire Prairie, originally a part of their father's estate. The homestead farm of Mr. and Mrs. Gibson is known as Plain View.

DAVID GEBHART. During the forty-five years of his residence in Andrew County, David Gebhart has lived from early manhood to mature age and has acquired those things most appreciated by a man of industry and ambition. He has a fine farm in Platte Township. which represents his diligence and good business judgment, has provided liberally for home and family, and has gained the esteem of all citizens in that locality for his uprightness and solid work.

David Gebhart is a native of Indiana, born in Henry County, on Christmas Day of 1851. His parents were George and Mary (Baker) Gebhart, both natives of Pennsylvania, where they were married. They removed to Indiana during the '40s and spent the rest of their lives there. The mother died when David was two years old and the father lived to be nearly eighty-two years of age, passing away in 1903. George Gebhart, who was of German ancestry, was a shoemaker by trade while living in Pennsylvania and followed the old-time custom of making boots and shoes to order, and traveling first from one home to the next, doing all the cobbling required by one family before passing on to the next place in his itinerary. After removing to Indiana he took up a farm in the midst of the timber and cleared it up and followed farming for the most part. He and his wife were members of the United Brethern Church. There were five sons and one daughter: John B., who died at Hagerstown, Indiana, in 1906; Josiah, who died in Andrew County, Missouri, in 1912; Elizabeth Covalt, who died in Henry County, Indiana, in 1911; George W., now living in California, who served four years in the Thirty-sixth Regiment of the Indiana Infantry during the Civil war, having been chiefly under the command of General Rosecrans, and Isaiah, who a number of years ago took up a homestead near Wichita, Kansas, and still lives there.

David Gebhardt grew up in Indiana, received his education in the public schools of Henry County, and in the spring of 1870, when about nineteen years old, came to Andrew County, Missouri. Since then his best energies have been devoted to farming and stock raising. He is the owner of 160 acres in section 10 of Platte Township, located partly in the bottoms of the Platte River. This land he operates through a tenant.

His home place, comprising forty-two acres, adjoins the little Village of Whitesville on the south and is located in section 27. The house stands on an elevation which is the highest point of land in this vicinity. Many people in this part of the state associate this farm with the name Jersey Stock Farm. Until he sold out about two years ago Mr. Gebhart was a successful raiser of high grade Jersey cattle, and kept a herd of about twenty-five head.

Politically Mr. Gebhart acts with the republican party, is a member of the Baptist Church and has fraternal affiliations with the Masonic Order and the Independent Order of Odd Fellows. On January 2, 1876, he married Emily M. Crockett, who was born in Andrew County, Missouri, October 1, 1857. Her parents are Milton and Sarah E. (West) Crockett. Some of the chief facts in this family's history will be found on other pages of this work. Mr. and Mrs. Gebhart have two children: Oliver C., who was born January 14, 1879, was educated for the profession of medicine at St. Louis, and is now a well-known practicing physician in St. Joseph, being a specialist in tuberculosis cases. The son, Ezra, born February 25, 1887, is also a resident of St. Joseph, and by his marriage to Nell Howitt has one child, Helen, born February 10, 1912.

JOHN W. HOWITT. Though Mr. Howitt has recently retired from the Village of Whitesville to his farm in Platte Township he has made his chief record of success and achievement in Andrew County as a banker. For eleven years he held the position of cashier and was practically in executive management of the Farmers Bank of Whitesville. While capital and resources are always considered an important element in banking, an even more important factor is the personality of the men in active charge. Under the progressive administration of Mr. Howitt the Farmers Bank of Whitesville is now one of the most substantial institutions in Andrew County. When he took charge it had a capital stock of $10,000 and a surplus of $1,200. He left it with the capital stock the same but with a surplus of $10,000 and undivided profits of like amount. Mr. Howitt retired from active banking on account of ill health, but still has a block of stock in the bank and is one of its directors.

John W. Howitt was born in Waukesha County, Wisconsin, February 21, 1868, but has spent practically all his life in Andrew County, where his parents were early settlers. His parents were James and Elizabeth (Weaver) Howitt. His father was born in Ayrshire, Scotland, December 27, 1823, was brought to America by his parents at the age of twelve years in 1835, and from New York State moved out to Wisconsin about the time he reached his majority. He lived in Wisconsin until 1858 and then came to Missouri and located on the prairie five miles east of Whitesville. That was his home until his death in 1899. He was a practical farmer and owned and directed the management of about three hundred acres. He always took a keen interest in local affairs, was a republican voter, and though reared in the Presbyterian Church belonged for many years to the Methodist. His wife was born December 27, 1831, in Oneida County, New York, and went with her parents to Wisconsin in 1839, and was married there December 25, 1851. She died in Andrew County in 1908. Of the five children two died in infancy, and the other three are: A. J., of Platte Township; Agnes E., widow of James Colville of Platte Township; and John W.

John W. Howitt received his education in the common schools, and in 1891 was graduated from the Gem City Business College at Quincy,

Illinois. While he was reared on a farm and has always had some interests in the country, his active career has been spent mainly along commercial lines. He had a general merchandise store at King City until it was burned out, and he then returned to a farm in Andrew County. For a year and a half he gained some valuable experience as a clerk in St. Joseph and then returned to Whitesville and became cashier of the bank. He is now living on a well improved small farm of sixty acres 4½ miles north of Whitesville.

Mr. Howitt is a republican, a citizen of influence in his part of Andrew County, and has long been identified with the Baptist Church, having served as superintendent of Sunday school and teacher of a class. Fraternal matters have made a strong appeal to him and he is affiliated with the Masonic Order, the Independent Order of Odd Fellows, the Modern Woodmen of America, the Woodmen of the World and the Order of Yeomen.

On May 1, 1889, Mr. Howitt married Jennie McAllaster of Gentry County, Missouri. They have one daughter of their own, Stella, who is the wife of V. L. Townsend, living 2½ miles south of Whitesville. Mr. and Mrs. Townsend have two children, Francis Marion and Josephine Victoria, both of whom are the pride and delight of their grandparents. Mr. Howitt is also rearing an orphan boy, named Raymond Howitt, who was taken from an orphan home in St. Louis at the age of thirteen months and is now eight years of age and attending school.

RALPH STINSON. A life of quiet effectiveness, marked by a record of many duties well done and many responsibilities faithfully fulfilled, has been that of Ralph Stinson, one of the venerable citizens of Andrew County, and still living on his fine old farm on section 10 of Platte Township, in his eighty-third year. Mr. Stinson was one of the men who developed and made Andrew County what it is. As an early settler, a soldier, a farmer, and in the round of commonplace accomplishments which fill every life, he has given a faithful and intelligent performance of each task, and has a record which may well be admired by the generations that follow him.

Ralph Stinson was born in Sandusky County, Huron Township, Ohio, December 11, 1832, and much of his life was spent in new countries and close to the western frontier. His parents were Seth and Elizabeth (Stull) Stinson, his father a native of New York and his mother of Pennsylvania. His father died December 19, 1885, aged seventy-five years, ten months and twenty-eight days, and the mother passed away June 13, 1890, aged seventy-nine years, eleven months and fourteen days. Both died at Marion in Linn County, Iowa. They were married in Sandusky County, Ohio, moved to Williams County in the same state, and out to Iowa about 1843. Seth Stinson bought a claim in Iowa and entered a large amount of land in Linn County, and spent the rest of his career as a pioneer farmer. There were eight children in the family, briefly mentioned as follows: Ralph; Robert, who still lives at the old home place near Marion, Iowa, and saw three years of service in the Civil war as captain of an Iowa company; George, a resident of Oklahoma, was also three years a soldier and in his brother's company; Franklin, of California, spent three years with an Iowa regiment; Marion is now deceased; Mary Jane is the wife of Mr. Mills of Tama, Iowa; Mrs. Sarah Black, now deceased; and Laura, who died after her marriage to Wane Leuts.

Ralph Stinson lived with his parents, first in Williams County, Ohio, and later in Iowa, until 1854. In that year he came to Andrew County, Missouri, and identified himself actively with the work of improvement that was then converting the wilderness into a landscape of farms. He improved two farms on the prairie in Andrew County, and since 1864 has lived on his present estate in Platte Township, all of which he cleared and put under cultivation. A residence of half a century in one community is in itself a distinction, and in the case of Mr. Stinson it has been accompanied by much effective service both in his own interests and for the benefit of the community. His farm in section 10 in the north half comprises 327 acres; and is known as the Forest Home Farm. General farming has been the feature of his industrial efforts, and he has also long been identified with the milling interests. He operates a sawmill and a sorghum works. Mr. Stinson is an all round mechanic, and by trade is a millwright and patternmaker. For a number of years he kept on his farm a fine herd of Angus cattle. His sorghum mill is the best equipped in the state with a capacity of 500 gallons daily, and good years the output is about five thousand gallons. The average output of his sawmill is about five thousand feet daily.

Mr. Stinson can recall many of the interesting experiences of pioneer times. As a boy he lived in the heavy woods of Williams County, Ohio, where it was necessary to construct buildings to protect live stock from the bears and other wild animals. The nearest neighbors at one time were nine miles away. After his experience in Ohio he had some more pioneer life on the prairies of Iowa Territory. At one time he and his brother George were looking after a sugar camp in the woods of Iowa, and one night they were awakened when a panther rummaging about, got on them as they lay asleep on the ground, with their heads under cover. The Indians killed the panther, strung its nails and put them around their necks. Panthers and wolves and other animals were numerous in those days, and particularly dangerous to live stock. During the war Mr. Stinson was a member of a regiment of Missouri State Militia. He is independent in politics, but it may be recalled that in 1864, during the presidential campaign of that year, he made a speech at Richmond, in Rea County, before his regiment, favoring the election of Mr. Lincoln, and helped to win over most of his comrades to support the republican candidate. His prosperity as a farmer has not been kept all to himself, but it is known that any undertaking for the general good in Andrew County will have his support and liberal donation. He gave money for the building of the hall at Whitesville for the Interstate Corn and Poultry Show, and has donated to the cause of many churches and other purposes.

In 1854 at Marion, Iowa, Mr. Stinson married Ruann Tomlinson. She was born in Scioto County, Ohio, September 13, 1835, and died in Andrew County, October 25, 1912. They were the parents of a large family of children: Warren lives in St. Joseph; Worth died in childhood; Minerva is the wife of John Whetsel of King City, Missouri; Anna, now deceased, married John Whetsel; Bell is the wife of Evert Goforth of Flagg Springs, Andrew County; Franklin died January 18, 1871, in childhood; Minnie is the wife of John Potts of Guilford, Missouri; Katie is the wife of John Redkey, now deceased; and Scott lives in Platte Township, on his farm adjoining the home place.

NORTON BURKEHOLDER. The cashier of the Bank of Spickardsville at Spickard, Mr. Burkeholder is a prominent business man and land owner in Grundy County, and represents one of the old and prominent families of this section of Northwest Missouri, his father being the Hon. Abraham H. Burkeholder of Trenton.

Norton Burkeholder was born at Trenton, Missouri, March 2, 1870. His father, Abraham H. Burkeholder, was born June 27, 1835, in York

County, Pennsylvania, and is now in his eightieth year. The maiden name of the mother was Rebecca A. Waltner, who was born July 3, 1840, in Putnam County, Ohio. Abraham H. Burkeholder was a soldier of the Union army during the Civil war, being quartermaster lieutenant of the One Hundred and Eighty-eighth Ohio Infantry, and was in the army three years. During a considerable part of his service he was stationed at Nashville, Tennessee, and after the war was for a time in the Tod Barracks at Columbus, Ohio. He was a lawyer by profession, and in 1865 moved from Putnam County, Ohio, to Trenton, and engaged in the practice of law at which he continued many years until his retirement. Abraham H. Burkeholder was elected on the republican ticket as prosecuting attorney and also as judge of the Probate Court in Grundy County, served two terms as state senator, and in 1892 was a candidate for Congress from the Second Missouri District. He was also president of the Trenton Board of Trade, and took an active and influential part in getting the Rock Island to locate its shops and division point in Trenton, and later was one of the leaders in the movement which also secured the location of the shops of the O. K. Railway at the same place.

Norton Burkeholder acquired his early education in the Trenton schools, graduating from the high school in 1888, and in 1891 completed a commercial course at the Gem City Business College at Quincy, Illinois. His first work was with the Rock Island Railway as chief timekeeper of the Southwestern Division, extending between Kansas City and St. Joseph and Davenport, Iowa. He was in the railway service until August, 1903, at which time he was elected and took charge of the Bank of Spickardsville, as cashier. This bank has a capital stock and surplus of $30,000, and its other officers are Michael Wolz, president, and Henry Waltner, vice president.

Mr. Burkeholder is a stockholder in six different banks in this section of Missouri, and is also well known in Grundy County as a farmer and stockraiser, being the owner of 620 acres of fine fertile land. Politically he is a progressive republican, is president of the Spickard school board, secretary of the Chautauqua Association, and is a deacon in the Baptist Church. His fraternal associations are with the Independent Order of Odd Fellows and the Knights of Pythias, and he is a past grand of Grand River Lodge No. 52 of the Odd Fellows at Trenton.

On June 11, 1903, Mr. Burkeholder married Miss Sarah J. Wolz, daughter of John F. and Sarah (Evans) Wolz. Her father was one of the largest land owners in this section of Missouri, and the family is still prominently represented here. Mr. and Mrs. Burkeholder are the parents of three children: Elizabeth Nadeen, Martha Bliss and John Hudson.

EDGAR M. HARBER. During an active practice at Trenton for nearly forty years Mr. Harber has won a position through his ability and repeated successes which ranks him among the leading lawyers of Missouri. Much of his practice has been in corporation work, and he is regarded as pre-eminent in this sphere. While devoted to the jealous mistress of the law, he is hardly less prominent as a democratic leader. It has been his lot to reside in a republican county of a democratic state, and while official honors have been consequently restricted he has for a number of years been recognized as one of the strongest and most eligible men in the party for the larger honors. His friends have again and again urged him as a candidate for governor, and his name is spoken with favor in every district of Missouri and through the press has become well known in many quarters where he is personally unacquainted.

Edgar M. Harber was born on a farm three miles from Richmond,

Madison County, Kentucky, a region which sent more sturdy pioneers to early Missouri than came from any other part of the United States. His father, Thomas B. Harber, was born in the same county in 1829, and was a son of Thomas Harber. The latter was a planter and slaveholder and spent all his life in Kentucky. About 1856 Thomas B. Harber, who had been reared and educated in Kentucky, migrated to Northwest Missouri, and was one of the first men to engage in mercantile business at the little village of Osborn in DeKalb County. He sold general merchandise to his friends and neighbors in that country until the breaking out of the war, when he moved out to the Territory of Nebraska, locating in Nebraska City. The Seymour Hotel of which he was proprietor was in that day one of the largest and best-known houses of public entertainment in Nebraska. Returning to Missouri at the close of the war, he bought a farm on the north line of Clinton County, 2½ miles south of Osborn, and was engaged in its cultivation until 1872, when he moved to Trenton. He was first known to the people of that town as a landlord, but being a man well versed in politics and public affairs was appointed by Governor Phelps presiding judge of the County Court and later held the position of postmaster at Trenton until his death. Judge Harber married Mildred A. Phelps, who was also a native of Madison County, Kentucky, a daughter of George T. Phelps. She departed this life in Chicago, July 27, 1914. For years she spent her summers with her daughters, Mrs. Rella H. Wright and Bessie Hough in Chicago, and her winters were usually passed with her daughter, Mrs. Witten, in Okmulgee, Oklahoma, also spending a goodly portion of her time with her son, Edgar, in Trenton. Her nine children were named as follows: George T., now deceased; James B., of Butte, Montana; Edgar M.; Tevis S., of Leavenworth, Kansas; Nannie L., wife of Judge W. W. Witten, Okmulgee, Oklahoma; Kate, who married Frank H. Glover, and both are now deceased; Bessie, the wife of Millie Hough, of Kansas City and Chicago; Rella Wright, a widow living in Chicago; and Charles C., of Leavenworth.

Edgar M. Harber partly with the aid of his father and partly through his own efforts acquired a substantial education. He attended school in Nebraska City, also the Trenton high school, and then took up the study of law with H. J. Herrick. With his admission to the bar in 1875 he opened an office at Trenton, and in a very short time was making a living and winning recognition for an alert ability and thoroughness of knowledge and preparation of cases which made his success a certainty. Much of his practice has come as the attorney for the Rock Island Railroad Company, and until he resigned in 1911 he also represented the Chicago, Milwaukee & St. Paul Road.

Mr. Harber in 1881 married Miss Lizzie D. Austin, a native of Trenton and daughter of Col. James Austin. She died September 23, 1907. Mr. Harber has been prominent in the Knights of Pythias Order, having been grand chancellor of the state lodge and is now in his third term as supreme representative. His interest in public affairs began before he was qualified by age for the exercise of the franchise. His influence has always been directed to the support of democratic principles and candidates, and as a campaigner, a forceful and convincing speaker he has few equals in his part of the state, and has filled engagements in nearly every district of the state. Mr. Harber holds a high place of esteem in his home community, and his popularity led to his choice as city solicitor of Trenton and also as prosecuting attorney of Grundy County. For nearly twenty-five years he has been chairman of the Central District Democratic Committee, has been a delegate to numerous county and district conventions, and was honored as a delegate to every state con-

vention from 1878 until the primary law took effect. In the national
convention of 1888 he supported Cleveland, and went to Baltimore in
1912. In 1880 he was the youngest member of the electoral college, and
was an elector in 1892 when he cast his ballot for Cleveland for the
latter's second term. While possessing the strength requisite for gubernatorial candidate, Mr. Harber has never found it possible to enter
actively upon a campaign for the nomination. In 1907 he would probably have received the nomination had not sickness in his family caused
him to refuse to have his name considered. In his private life Mr.
Harber, like many successful professional men, finds diversion from his
vocation in outdoor life. His interest in agriculture has been keen
and practical since his youth, and he is the owner of extensive farming
property, which he operates chiefly through renters, but to his favorite
country estate of nearly three hundred acres, near Trenton, he gives
his personal attention, and farms both for pleasure and profit. His
herd of Jerseys is one of the best in Grundy County. On the 16th
of December, 1914, Mr. Harber was appointed collector of internal
revenue for the Sixth District of Missouri and shortly thereafter unanimously confirmed by the Senate and is now in charge of this important
office at Kansas City, Missouri.

LUTHER COLLIER has been a member of the Grundy County bar
more than forty years. Success and official distinctions have come
to him in the course of his long and honorable career. He fought
for the Union in the Civil war, and the duties of patriotism and
good citizenship have always been conspicuous features of his character.
His is a pioneer stock in that part of Northwest Missouri. His father
built the first courthouse at Trenton, and in many other ways the family
have earned a proper place in the history and regard of this quarter of
the great commonwealth.

Though he was born in Howard County, Missouri, June 19, 1842,
Luther Collier has lived in Grundy County practically all his life, and
his memories cover practically the entire course of local history and
development. His father, William Collier, was born on a farm in Madison County, Kentucky, in 1790. James Collier, the grandfather, was an
early settler in the Bluegrass State, owned and operated a plantation in
Madison County, where his life came to a close. His widow, who was a
Miss Easton, survived him, married a Mr. Mills, and came to Missouri to
end her days. The four children of her first marriage were William,
Lewis, Stephen and Millie.

In his native state William Collier grew up and married. In 1827,
accompanied by his wife and six children, he came to Missouri. This was
then the newest of all the states in the Union, and it was a long journey
from Kentucky to Howard County. Wagons and teams conveyed the
family and all their goods from one stage to another, and at night they
often camped by the wayside. The Mississippi River was crossed at St.
Louis, and from there they followed up the valley of the Missouri to
Howard County, which received a great bulk of its early population from
Madison County, Kentucky. William Collier was a building contractor
and brickmaker, a business in which he found much employment in the
new country. His contracts took him far beyond the borders of Howard
County. Grundy County was organized in 1841, and soon afterward
the local officials awarded William Collier the contract for constructing
the courthouse. In 1842 he came to Trenton and set up a plant for the
manufacture of the brick. In the following year his family followed.
The courthouse was finished in 1844, and stood, a venerable reminder
of early days, until it was replaced a few years ago by the present mod-

ern building. After that Mr. Collier continued his business headquarters at Trenton, and altogether was in active business as contractor and builder for nearly half a century. His death occurred at Trenton October 10, 1870. When a young man he had seen service in the War of 1812, and the Government gave his widow a pension during her last years.

Her maiden name was Susan Higbee. She was born in Jessamine County, Kentucky. Joseph Higbee, her father, was a soldier of the Revolution, and from Kentucky moved to Missouri and found an early home in Randolph County. A church was built on his land, and when the railroad was constructed Higbee Church became also a location for a station, and the village has since been Higbee. Mrs. William Collier, who died at the advanced age of ninety-one, was the mother of thirteen children: Sally Ann, Rebecca, Joseph F., James M., Elizabeth, Susan, William, Kitty Ann, Charles L., Martha J., David A., Robert A. and Luther. David died when about five years old, but all the others married and had families of their own, who have carried the name and family relationship into many parts of the country.

A child of about twelve months when the family located at Trenton, Luther Collier grew up in the early surroundings of the county seat, and attended the early schools. He was a pupil of a well remembered educator, Prof. Joseph Ficklin, and later of Prof. W. D. Stewart, and as a young man for a time assisted the latter in school instruction. The outbreak of the war called him away to more serious duties. In 1861 he enlisted in Colonel King's regiment of State Troops, and was discharged at the end of six months. In August, 1862, he enlisted for the regular service in Company B of the Twenty-third Missouri Infantry. For a time he was in the Twentieth Army Corps under General Rousseau and later in the First Brigade, Third Division of the Fourteenth Army Corps. His regiment joined Sherman's army at the Chattahoochee River, and was in much of the fighting which led up to the fall of Atlanta, went on with the victorious army to Savannah and the sea, and thence made the great movement through the Carolinas which brought the right wing of the Federal forces into the rear of Virginia. When Lee surrendered and Johnston's army capitulated, he was with the hosts that went on to Washington and marched in the grand pageant down Pennsylvania Avenue. Mr. Collier was at that time acting adjutant and in his tattered uniform rode a strawberry roan in the parade. He was given his honorable discharge in June, and reached Trenton after an absence of nearly three years on June 20th.

The next two years were spent in farming. This was followed by his appointment as road commissioner, in which office he surveyed all the roads of Grundy County and laid out many new ones. Taking up the study of law in the office of Shanklin, Austin & Herrick, he continued until admitted to the bar on February 15, 1870. His practice as a lawyer has been continuous since that time except so far as official duties have prevented.

On March 27, 1862, before he went away to the war, he married Miss Martha B. Carter. She was born in Twiggs County, Kentucky, a daughter of Dr. Benjamin and Elizabeth Carter. Her father was an old-time physician, and spent his last years in practice at Lafayette, Indiana, where he died. His widow then married again and brought her family to Missouri. Mrs. Collier died June 16, 1878. On October 29, 1879, Mr. Collier married Fannie C. Brawner, who was born in Clinton County, Missouri, a daughter of Jacob and Susan Brawner, the former a native of Kentucky and the latter of Missouri. The second Mrs. Collier died March 30, 1893, and on February 28, 1895, he was united in marriage with Alexa W. Marshall. Clay County, Missouri, was the place of her birth, a daughter of Alexander and Fannie E. Marshall. Mr. Collier was the father of five children by his first wife, namely: Annie D., Oscar L., Kittie, Jewett N. and Luther C. The four by the second wife were: Leland H., Cora B., Joseph N. and Susie D. There are two children of the present union, Woodson E. and John W. All are living except Joseph N., who died in 1909 aged twenty-six. The children's marriages and the names of the grandchildren are given brief record as follows: Annie D. married Clifton M. Brawner, and has Leon, Luther N., Audley and Hilda, Audley being married and the father of one child. Oscar L. married Bessie Lowen, and their three children are Raymond, Ruth and Clifton. Kittie is the wife of Charles N. Mason. Jewett N. married Effie Black, and has two children, Audrey and Fred. Luther C. married Dollie Warner, and has a child, Florence. Leland H. married Adelle Gennett, and has a son, Luther T. Cora B. is the wife of Bryant C. Biggerstaff, and her three children are Curtis Lee, Luther C. and Katharine Ann.

Mr. Collier has been a stanch upholder of republican doctrines ever since casting his first ballot for Abraham Lincoln. His official record is perhaps the least of his public service to the community where he has spent his life. He has been a justice of the peace, upwards of thirty years was a member of the school board, was city attorney fourteen years, and mayor two years. He affiliates with Grand River Lodge, I. O. O. F., and the Woodmen of the World. Mr. Collier has been an elder in the Christian Church for forty years.

WILLIAM A. ODELL. A veteran of the Civil war, William A. Odell is probably the oldest living native son of Caldwell County, and with the exception of the period spent in the war has lived about eighty years in that county, and as a soldier, citizen, a farmer and industrious worker has long been held in high esteem by all his community.

A log cabin in the vicinity of Kingston was the place in which he first saw the light of day, and his birth occurred on February 10, 1831. To anyone familiar with the history of settlement in Northwest Missouri, that date is sufficient to fix the pioneer establishment of the Odell family in this section. Only ten years had passed since Missouri's admission to the Union, and Northwest Missouri was just beginning to be settled. His father, Isaac Odell, was a native of Pulaski County, Tennessee, and came to Northwest Missouri with his father, Calip Odell, who was one of the prominent pioneers in Daviess County. Isaac Odell lived for some years near Gallatin, and then established a home in Caldwell County, built a log cabin, and hewed a farm out of the wilderness. He was married at Independence, Missouri, to Elizabeth Adams, who was born in Kentucky, a daughter of Richard Adams. Isaac Odell and wife had twelve children, and five sons and two daughters are still living. The family made a notable record during the war, and William A., Solomon, Frank L., Pleasant C. and Andrew M. were all soldiers. The father of the family died at the age of forty-six, and his widow married Andrew Welker, and became the mother of two children. Isaac Odell was a democrat in politics, and a member of the Baptist Church.

William A. Odell grew up in a pioneer country, and in his early youth and manhood hunted all kinds of wild game, including bear, wolf, turkeys, and did his own part in developing this section of Missouri from its original wilderness condition. When the war came on, his sympathies were with the Union, and he went to Quincy, Illinois, and there enlisted in an Illinois regiment. His brother, Andrew, was in the same regiment. He saw some of the most strenuous campaigns of the war, was with Sherman's army in its campaign from Chickamauga to Atlanta, then marched on to the sea and up through the Carolinas, and finally participated in the grand review of the victorious troops at Washington. He received his honorable discharge at Quincy and lived in that vicinity for several years. In 1869 Mr. Odell returned to his native County of Caldwell, and that has ever since been his home.

Mr. Odell married Mary Jane Wright. To their marriage were born twelve children, three of whom are living: William, of Braymer, Missouri; Rufus; and John, who lives at Hinton, Oklahoma. Mrs. Odell, who died in 1886, was an active member of the Methodist Episcopal Church. For his second wife Mr. Odell married Mrs. Mary Holms. They have two children: Mrs. Myrtle Bryant, of Breckenridge, Missouri; and Frank L. Mr. Odell now lives quietly, enjoying the fruits of a long and well spent life, is one of the popular old soldiers, a man of frank and genial personality, and delights in the recollections and tales of pioneer days in Caldwell County.

JOHN W. BAKER. Both in Caldwell and Ray counties the name Baker Brothers signifies exceptional success and prosperity in the agricultural and stock-raising industry. The firm is made up of John W. and James Baker, both of whom are natives of this section of Missouri, and have employed their well-trained judgment and industry in developing a fine farming property and various other important interests both in Missouri and elsewhere. They have lived in Grant Township in section 25 since 1870.

John W. Baker was born on the old homestead in Ray County, December 10, 1841, while his brother James was born at the same place in 1839. Their father was John Baker, a pioneer settler in Ray County, and the owner of a large amount of property in that vicinity. John Baker was born in Bedford County, Tennessee, July, 1804, a son of William Baker, who died when his son John was three years of age. William Baker's wife was a Miss Bullard, a sister of Kit Bullard, a prominent man in his time in Tennessee. John Baker was married in Tennessee to Mary F. Hanna, a native of Tennessee. While living in that state two children were born to them, one of whom, William H., died in Ray County in 1858, and the other was Martha L. Hunt, also now deceased. After the birth of these two children, in 1831, John Baker and wife left Tennessee, loaded their family and possessions in a wagon drawn by a yoke of oxen, and spent ten weeks driving across the country, camping at night by the roadside, cooking their meals over a camp fire, and shooting game for provisions. They finally arrived and settled near Knoxville, in Ray County, where John Baker began a career which ultimately gave him both prosperity and influential position. He owned 463 acres of valuable land in Ray County. After the family came to Ray County the following children were born: Lucinda Petty, deceased; Mary F., widow of W. H. Stone, and living in Polo; Mrs. Nancy Houston, of Polo, whose husband died in 1868; James C. and John W., of Cowgill, Missouri; Robert M., who died in 1861 at the age of seventeen; Thomas J., who lives in Washita County, Oklahoma; and Mrs. S. M. Good, of Cooper, Texas. The mother died in 1891 at the age of eighty-four, while the father was ninety-two years of age when death called him from his labors. Both were members of the Presbyterian Church, and lived lives in keeping with their religious profession. The father was a Henry Clay whig in early life and later a democrat.

John W. Baker grew up in Ray County, and has many interesting recollections of his boyhood, which was spent in almost a pioneer community. He attended one of the old log schoolhouses so frequent in that time, and sat on a slab bench and rested his feet on a puncheon floor. His brother James had similar experiences as a boy, and both early became acquainted with industry and the hard work of making a living in a new country, and have witnessed many remarkable developments in the country since their boyhood. The Baker Brothers now have two farms in Caldwell County, aggregating 400 acres, and have such improvements in the way of buildings and other facilities as constitute a valuable property and specially adapted for its purposes of general farming and stock raising. The brothers are also heavily interested as investors in Texas lands, and own 770 acres in Delta County and 900 acres in another section of that state.

James Baker was married in 1870 to Mary C. Thompson, now deceased. In 1875 John W. Baker married Caroline Hemery, a daughter of Reason and Elizabeth Hemery, both now deceased. Mrs. John W. Baker died in 1885 at the age of thirty-four. She was a member of the United Brethren Church. She was survived by three children: James V., who died at the age of seven; and John W. and Reason H. John W. Baker, Jr., is a prominent farmer and dairyman with a large farm near Polo. He married Nellie M. Seiss, and their five children are John S., L. Carson, Robert B., Raymond and James V. The son Reason H. married Nellie Stone, a daughter of Mr. W. C. Stone, president of the Farmers Bank of Polo, and their two children are Floyd and Carrie. The Baker Brothers and their families are members of the Methodist Episcopal Church South.

J. B. BATHGATE. The First National Bank of Polo is one of the well organized and substantial financial institutions of Northwest Missouri, and in its business record and in the personnel of its stockholders and officers offers the strongest possible guarantee for the safe and conservative management of its funds. The First National Bank of Polo was incorporated September 4, 1905. It has a capital stock of $30,000, its surplus is $13,000 and its officials are all men of prominence in the community. The officers are: J. B. McVeigh, president; W. M. Estes, first vice president; Elbert Zimmerman, second vice president; J. B. Bathgate, cashier; and H. C. Zimmerman, assistant cashier. All these are well-known business men, farmers and stockmen in both Caldwell and Ray counties.

J. B. Bathgate, the efficient and popular cashier of the institution, was born on a farm ten miles south of Polo, a son of the late Thomas Bathgate, one of the most successful men in Northwest Missouri, who gained prominence as a farmer and stockman, and at his death in 1911 left an estate estimated to be worth two hundred and fifty thousand dollars. He was a man who had made his fortune through his own efforts and good management. He was a native of Scotland, came in youth to the United States, and was married at the age of thirty-five to Rachel Shepneck, who was of a Virginia family. They were the parents of six children. Dr. H. T. Bathgate, now deceased, was formerly physician and surgeon at Chicago; W. S. is in the hardware business at Kingston; J. B., the subject of this sketch; Charles A., a merchant of Polo; L. B., a farmer and stockman; and Mary, wife of James T. Moffett, farmer and stockman living near Polo. The father was a strong republican, and besides successfully managing his own private interests, did much to promote the welfare of Ray County.

J. B. Bathgate was reared on a farm, was taught to work from early youth, and acquired his education in the public schools and Central Business College at Sedalia, Missouri. For about twelve years he was associated with his brother in the hardware business at Polo, and then became one of the organizers of the First National Bank of Polo, in the management of which his keen business judgment and financial ability have been important factors.

Mr. Bathgate has lived in one of the modern homes of Polo since 1910. His wife, Eva Slack, is a daughter of Judge Job Slack, a prominent citizen of this section. Mr. and Mrs. Bathgate were the parents of three children, a son and two daughters who died in infancy. Both Mr. and Mrs. Bathgate are active members of the Methodist Church, in which he is serving as superintendent of the Sunday School and treasurer of the church, while Mrs. Bathgate is also active in church and Sunday School, and has done much to maintain the activities and influence of her church home. Mr. Bathgate is affiliated with the Masonic Lodge at Polo, the chapter at Hamilton, and belongs to Orient Commandery No. 35 of the Knights Templar at Kansas City.

DAVID A. KELMEL. When mention is made of the leading stockmen of Northwest Missouri the name of David A. Kelmel is sure to receive some attention, since there are few men in that industry whose activities are more extensive and whose judgment is held in higher esteem. Mr. Kelmel has his large farm in Knoxville Township of Ray County, while his business headquarters are at Polo, in Caldwell County. His farm is about three miles south of Polo. Mr. Kelmel is proprietor of two highly improved farms, aggregating 800 acres of some of the best soil to be found in Ray County. His operations in stock raising comprise on the average the feeding of a hundred head of cattle and two hundred or more hogs.

His farm equipment and home are an evidence of the well-ordered prosperity which prevails on his estate. When his father William built the residence some years ago it was considered the finest country home in Ray County. It is a large substantial modern house, containing nine rooms, built in modern style and with such conveniences as hot and cold water, furnace heat, and other facilities that up to a few years ago were found only in the better city houses. The house is surrounded by blue grass lawn, and ample porches both in the front and rear are inviting attractions. On the home farm is an immense barn, 80x100 feet, besides a cattle shed 25x100 feet, and large and well-kept feed lots, with stock scales, and all the water for the barns, lots and the house is pumped by windmill power. Mr. Kelmel usually plants and cultivates about two hundred and fifty acres of corn, and all his grain is fed to his own stock. There is also a large expanse of blue grass pastures and fine meadows, and there is no farmer in that vicinity who keeps up his fences better and looks more carefully after the many details of his business. Besides what he does in the raising and feeding of cattle on his farm, Mr. Kelmel is an extensive stock buyer and shipper, and his headquarters for that business are in Polo.

David A. Kelmel comes of the substantial and thrifty German stock, and was born near Polo, in Caldwell County, December 15, 1861. His father, William Kelmel, who died at the age of seventy-eight, was born in Baden, Germany, and was brought when a boy to America, his family locating in Central Illinois, near Galesburg, where he grew up, and from there moved to Caldwell County, Missouri. He married Miss Martha Holman, a daughter of David Holman. She was a capable helpmate and mother to her family, and died at the age of thirty-one years. David A. is the only one now living of the two children. The mother was a member of the Baptist Church. The father came to Caldwell County prior to the Civil war, settled on land that had scarcely any improvement, and in time became an extensive farmer and stockraiser. William's brother Thomas, now deceased, was associated with him for some years in helping to clear up the wild lands. Thomas died at Liberty, in Clay County.

David A. Kelmel, though a well educated and informed man, having received the advantages of the public schools and a course in a business college at St. Joseph, has had all his experience and has concentrated his attention on the industry which has been the foundation of his generous success. As a boy he helped in the plowing, planting and harvesting seasons on the farm, and manifested a strong inclination for the stock department of farm enterprise. His characteristics remind one of a typical westerner, and in fact Mr. Kelmel spent some years of his earlier career in the far West. At the age of twenty-two he went out to Colorado, locating at Gunnison City, in the western part of that state, and spent the years 1881-82 in that part of the country, engaging in the livery and stock business. On returning to Missouri he remained only a short time, until the call of the West again proved too strong to resist, and this time he went to the western frontier of Kansas, and there had many interesting experiences on the ranch and range. After several years in Kansas, Mr. Kelmel returned to Ray County, and has since been steadily engaged in the stock business and farming.

On December 13, 1884, Mr. Kelmel married Allie Taylor, a daughter of M. G. Taylor. Mr. and Mrs. Kelmel are the parents of three children: Wilma, the wife of M. G. Roberts, who is a former county attorney of Ray County and now practicing law in St. Joseph; Logan, a young man of twenty-three and already a practical and successful farmer, being the right-hand man to his father; Edna is a student in a seminary at St. Joseph, Missouri.

Besides his extensive business activities, Mr. Kelmel has for a number of years been regarded as one of the wheel horses of the democratic party in this part of Missouri. He has attended as a delegate many of the county, congressional and state conventions, and has done much not only to keep up the party organization and promote its success, but has always shown himself public spirited and ready to assist in any movement for the local welfare of his home district. He is also active in the Masonic fraternity, has membership in the lodge, chapter and commandery, and also the Temple of the Mystic Shrine at Kansas City. Mr. Kelmel is a man of generous physical proportions, stands five feet ten and weighs about two hundred pounds, and has the frank and open countenance and the general air of the western cattle man.

JACOB O. MILLER. Among the public officials of Andrew County who have won the commendation and favorable criticism of their fellow citizens by the manner in which they have discharged the duties of office, Jacob O. Miller is entitled to more than passing consideration. In the capacity of superintendent of the county farm, now one of the best equipped and most commodious in the state, he has not only demonstrated his entire capacity to successfully handle the business end of his office, but has also shown an interest in the personal welfare of his charges, which has done much to lighten their burdens and make life more comfortable for them.

Mr. Miller has been a resident of Andrew County all of his life, having been born here on his father's homestead, November 6, 1875, a son of William K. and Louisa (Flesher) Miller. His grandfather, a well-known character, and universally spoken of as "Uncle Daniel" Miller, was born in Ohio, and from that state made the journey to Missouri at an early day, entering land near Cosby, Andrew County, to

1840 HISTORY OF NORTHWEST MISSOURI

which he added from time to time as the years passed, until at one time he owned and operated 900 acres and was known as one of the sub-stantial men of his community. When he came to Missouri he was the owner of fifteen or twenty slaves, and with the German thrift that he had inherited from his ancestors he placed these to work operating a mill at Rochester, of which he was the owner for several years. He was the father of five sons and three daughters.

This was one of the families which divided upon the issues of the Civil war, all of the sons joining the ranks of the Confederacy as soldiers except William K., who served in the Union army. One of the boys, Samuel, met a soldier's death, being mortally wounded in action. The maternal grandfather of Jacob O. Miller was a native of either Germany or Ohio and emigrated to Missouri at an early day, there passing the rest of his life as a farmer and machinist. He had a large family, and one of his sons, Capt. Adam Flesher, raised a com-pany which was first put into the Missouri State Militia and later joined the regular service at Lexington. There were nine sons and two daugh-ters in the family of William K. and Louisa Miller, and of these all are living except one boy, and all, with the exception of one in California, live in Missouri.

Jacob O. Miller was given the advantages of a public school educa-tion, and was brought up to the pursuits of the farm, being engaged on the homestead until his marriage. At that time he bought a farm in Rochester Township, on which he carried on operations until ap-pointed to his present position, January 1, 1914. The buildings on the county farm were formerly of frame and rather small, but the county has just completed a new $30,000 home, into which the county charges moved in December, 1914. This is a large, modern, fire-proof building, with every convenience and comfort for the inmates. Under Mr. Mil-ler's management the affairs of the farm are progressing in a very sat-isfactory manner. While he is a strict disciplinarian, he also takes a kindly and genuine interest in the welfare of his people, who, in turn, have come to respect and esteem him. Politically a republican, Mr. Miller was at one time a candidate for sheriff of Andrew County, but the opposing party was heavily in the majority, and he met defeat at the polls, although he received a very gratifying vote. He is a member of the Christian Church at Long Branch, and has been very active in Sunday school work. Fraternally he is connected with the local lodges of the Independent Order of Odd Fellows and the Knights of Pythias.

On May 3, 1899, Mr. Miller was united in marriage with Miss Eva Dickson, who was born in Andrew County, Missouri, January 7, 1883, daughter of John B. and Mary C. (Hurst) Dickson, the former born in Tennessee in 1859. He came to Missouri with his parents at the age of ten years, and was engaged in farming in Clay Township, Andrew County, until his death, which occurred March 23, 1900. Mrs. Dickson, who is a daughter of Elijah Hurst, formerly of Savannah, and one of the earliest pioneers of the county, lived in this county, where she was born in 1862, until 1914, when she moved to her present residence in the vicinity of Los Angeles, California. Mr. and Mrs. Miller are the parents of two children: Raymond and Neva.

JAMES R. WILSON. The largest mercantile establishment and the most prosperous merchant at Lawson at once suggests the name of James R. Wilson. About twenty years ago he located in Lawson, after some experience in merchandising which began in the humble capacity of clerk and had already taken him into independent operations, and since that time his progress has been steadily upward, until now his success is a matter of common reputation throughout Ray County. Mr. Wilson did not start life in affluence, and the resources contained within himself and his remarkable industry have been the factors which have brought him to his present position. Mr. Wilson is one of the popular men in politics in Ray County, and at the present time is a candidate before the primaries for the office of county clerk. His previous political service and experience are of themselves the best assurance to the people of his value and usefulness in one of the most important county offices.

James L. Wilson was born near Millville, in Ray County, March 31, 1865. His father, Phillip Wilson, who was born in Clay County, Kentucky, died in Ray County, March 4, 1877, at the age of sixty-four. The mother, whose maiden name was Charlotte Link, also a native of Clay County, Kentucky, died February 10, 1901, at the age of seventy-four. Of their eight children, five are living, namely: Fred, in Texas; Pleasant, of Sacramento, California; Jerry T., of Richmond, Missouri; James R.; and Mary, wife of David Kinter, of Denver, Colorado. The Wilson family moved from Kentucky to Missouri in 1858, settling near Millville, where the father purchased some new land, developed a farm and remained upon it until his death.

James R. Wilson grew up in the country surroundings of Ray County, attended the country schools for several years, but at the age of thirteen became self-supporting, and has made his own way ever since. His first work on the beginning of his business experience was in Craven Brothers' store at Millville. Four years later he entered the employ of John P. Grimes of Millville, under whose superintendence his business training was perfected. This was followed by an independent mercantile venture at Millville, and he began selling goods on his own account there before he reached the age of twenty-one. In 1889 his stock was moved to Hardin, in Ray County, and at the end of three years he sold out, returned to Millville and was once more numbered among the merchants of that village. In 1894, having sold out his Millville interests, Mr. Wilson came to Lawson and established his present business. His large stock of general merchandise, now comprising practically everything for the use of farm and home, occupies a double room, 40x80 feet, and on two floors.

Mr. Wilson for a number of years has taken an active part in local politics, served two terms as mayor of Lawson, and for several years was a member of the board of aldermen. He was also for some time secretary of the Democratic County committee, and has been an ardent democrat since casting his first vote. He affiliates with the Independent Order of Odd Fellows, and is a charter member of the Modern Woodmen of America at Lawson.

On September 20, 1887, was celebrated the marriage of Mr. Wilson to Miss Dora Campbell, who was born near Russellville, Missouri, in June, 1867. Her parents, James T. and Mary Campbell, are retired farming people now living in Lawson. Mr. Wilson and wife have three children: Gordon C., Bayard C. and Iras M., all at home.

CHRIS BACHMAN. For more than thirty years Chris Bachman has been a prosperous and progressive farmer of Andrew County and has one of the best improved places in Monroe Township, located on section 6, with mail facilities from the rural route of Cosby. Mr. Bachman represents the hardy Swiss stock in Northwest Missouri, and though he began his career in this part of the state as a renter, he has long since been numbered among the independent farmers, with a record of unusual prosperity to his credit.

Chris Bachman was born in Switzerland, September 16, 1848, a son of Chris and Elizabeth (Dummarmut) Bachman. His parents were substantial Swiss people, and his father was employed as a carpenter in that country. In 1868 all the family except one daughter left Switzerland and emigrated to America and came direct to Andrew County, locating on a farm north of Amazonia. The father died there in April, 1898, at the age of eighty years and seven months, and the mother passed away in December, 1888, at the age of sixty-one. After coming to this country the father followed farming. He was a republican in politics, and a member of the German Reform Church at Amazonia. Their ten children were: Chris; John, a grocery merchant in St. Joseph; Jacob, who lives in Andrew County on a farm; Fred, a resident of the State of Ohio; Charles, who died unmarried; Gottlieb, a resident of Idaho; Elizabeth Zahnd, of Andrew County; Maggie Martha; Anna, who is a widow living in Amazonia; and Rosa, deceased.

Chris Bachman lived with his parents until after his marriage, and on starting out for himself became a renter, and operated another man's farm two years. His first purchase of land in Andrew County was fifty acres south of Savannah, and thirty years ago he sold that property and bought his present place. He has in his homestead 165 acres, besides 100 acres three miles north in Rochester Township. On his home farm Mr. Bachman has done much work of improvement, and has two sets of buildings, and devotes his land to grain and stock farming.

Politically he acts with the republican party, and is a member of the German Reform Church at Cosby. Mr. Bachman was married March 19, 1878, to Rosa Elise Strasser. She was born in Switzerland, October 16, 1853, and came to this country with her widowed mother in 1873. Barbara (Ott) Strasser, the mother, died on the 22d of January, 1882, and her husband, Joseph Strasser, died in 1861, in Switzerland. To Mr. and Mrs. Bachman have been born two children: Otto and Alfred, the latter at home. Otto lives on a part of the homestead farm, occupying the second group of buildings, and by his marriage to Elsie Snowden has one child, Imogene.

JAMES A. WATERMAN, M. D.   Northwest Missouri has no more loyal and useful citizen than Dr. James A. Waterman, of Breckenridge, where for more than twenty-five years he has practiced medicine. Along with success and prestige as a doctor he has also been distinctive in his community and in the state for service both in and out of his profession. Doctor Waterman has served in an official capacity in connection with several of the state institutions. He is a scholarly and cultured physician, a man of broad and thorough experience in affairs, and has enjoyed high standing in the citizenship of Breckenridge and Caldwell County.

Dr. James A. Waterman was born at Frankfort, Kentucky, August 12, 1862, a son of Rev. J. H. Waterman, who is now pastor and canon of the Episcopal Church at Fresno, California, having reached the venerable age of eighty-three years, most of which time has been spent in the service of the church. He was educated at Dartmouth College, graduating with honors in 1859, was ordained to the ministry, came to Northwest Missouri and held pastorates both in Hamilton and Chillicothe, and in 1890 moved to Fresno, California, where he is still active. There were nine children in the family, six sons and three daughters. Doctor Waterman is the only one still living in Missouri, one being a resident of Georgia, another of Texas, and the others in California.

Doctor Waterman was well educated, at first in the public schools, later as a student in St. Paul's College at Palmyra, Missouri, took up the study of medicine under Doctor Brown, an old and noted physician of

Hamilton, and finished his education by graduation from the St. Louis Medical College with the class of 1887. Doctor Waterman spent eighteen months in practice at Spring Hill, Missouri, and since 1889 his home has been in Breckenridge. His practice has been of a general character, both in town and country, and for many years he has been one of the familiar figures in that section, in his rounds of professional duties, in earlier years making his trips on horseback and in buggy, and latterly having taken up the fashion of the modern physician and traveling much by automobile.

Doctor Waterman is a stanch republican. Governor Hadley appointed him superintendent of the Insane Asylum at Farmington, Missouri, and during his administration he won favorable comment from both parties. He also served for two years and five months as physician and surgeon in the penitentiary at Jefferson City.

Doctor Waterman was married in 1889 to Albina F. Murphy, daughter of Henry Murphy. They are the parents of two sons: Lloyd S., who is in the second year at William Jewell College at Liberty, and during his college career has made a record as an athlete, particularly in baseball; and Henry, who is now eleven years of age. Doctor Waterman affiliates with the Masonic Lodge, and the Knights of Pythias. At the present time he is representative of his county at Jefferson City, Missouri.

JACOB WEDDLE. More than thirty years a resident of Andrew County, Jacob Weddle, long a substantial and prosperous farmer in Platte Township, is now best known in that community as president of the Farmers' Bank of Whitesville. Mr. Weddle became head of this institution at the beginning of the second year of its existence, and has since given most of his time and attention to its management. He is one of Andrew County's prominent citizens and came to Northwest Missouri in the early days when a boy.

Jacob Weddle was born in Hendricks County, Indiana, June 24, 1848, a son of Aaron and Mary (Dodd) Weddle. His parents were both natives of Virginia, the father born in 1821, and the mother in 1822. Aaron Weddle went with his family to Indiana when young, and was married in that state. In 1859 the family set out to find a new home in Western Missouri. Jacob Weddle and his father walked almost the entire distance, driving a bunch of cattle to Buchanan County. They located on a farm eight miles east of St. Joseph. The father was a Douglas democrat and early in the war served in the six months service in Major Joseph's Battalion, and in March, 1862, enlisted with the regular volunteers in the Twenty-fifth Missouri Infantry. A few months later, at the battle of Corinth, Mississippi, he died in August, 1862. His widow lived with her only son Jacob for the last five years of her life, dying at the age of eighty-two.

Jacob Weddle was about eleven years of age when he came to Missouri, had a somewhat limited education, and had to begin work for his self-support at an early age. From Buchanan County he moved to Andrew County in 1882 and was actively identified with farming here until 1909. Mr. Weddle is the owner of a fine place of 180 acres in Platte Township five miles northeast of Whitesville. After leaving the farm and removing to Whitesville, he was engaged in the hardware business about a year, in addition to his service as president of the Farmers Bank. Politically he acts with the republican party, is a trustee of the Methodist Episcopal Church at Walnut Grove, is affiliated with the Independent Order of Odd Fellows.

In 1871 Mr. Weddle married Helen Brierly, who was born in Iowa, and died in 1880. Her daughter, Luella, is the wife of Dr. A. M. Peter, of Whitesville. Two children died young, Howlit at the age of four and a half years, and Myrtie when one year of age. In 1881 Mr. Weddle married a sister of his first wife, Mary Brierly. There are no children by the second marriage. The Brierly sisters were both born in Keokuk, Iowa, the daughters of James and Sarah (Cabble) Brierly. The father was a native of Ohio, and the mother of Kentucky, and in the early days James Brierly moved to Iowa and was married near Quincy, Illinois, to Miss Cabble. Both spent their last years with Mr. and Mrs. Weddle, and died on the farm in Platte Township. James Brierly was a pilot on the Mississippi River during the early days and a man of no little prominence in any community which he called his home. He was in Iowa before it became a state and served in the territorial Legislature, and later was a member of the Missouri State Legislature, and was captain of state troops during the Civil war from Buchanan County. Politically he was a Douglas democrat before the war, but was elected to the Missouri Legislature on the republican ticket. In 1853 the Brierly family, including both wives of Mr. Weddle, started out for California, making the trip overland with an ox-team. On account of the hostility of the Indians, they spent the winter in Salt Lake City, and resumed the journey and arrived in California in the spring of 1854. After three years in that western state they returned East in 1857, and soon afterwards moved to Kirksville, Missouri, and in 1859 to Buchanan County, where both the daughters lived until their marriage.

HAMILTON: ITS HISTORY.* Herein is presented a record of the early colonization of Hamilton, including the distinctive features of the early settlement and appropriate honor to the father, founders and builders of the city. The name Davis is so woven into the history of Hamilton and Caldwell County that no apology is needed for introducing it at the beginning. Since all the land at Hamilton and Nettleton was entered under that name, it appears oftener in court records than any other. When A. G. Davis arrived here he found a land of marvelous beauty, an extended prairie with luxuriant verdure, and rarely traversed save by Indians and hunters. He found no friends to greet him, nothing but the genial heavens and the generous earth to give him consolation and hope.

In his determination to build a town he was well fortified for the undertaking by his skill as a surveyor. Late in the fall of 1854, while yet a resident of Mirabile, he heard that the projected line of the Hannibal & St. Joseph Railroad had been surveyed. He shared his plan of locating a town on the line with Edward M. Samuel, of Liberty. A town company was organized, with Mr. Samuel as president, and other members as follows: Greenup Bird, John Berry, Michael Arthur, Simpson McGaughey and Stephen Ritchey, of Liberty; John Ardinger and Ephraim B. Ewing, of Richmond; Albert G. Davis and John Burrows, of Mirabile; Charles J. Hughes, of Kingston; Thomas J. Frame, of Gallatin; Jeff Thompson, of St. Joseph.

Mr. Davis believed a certain tract of land along the route of the proposed railroad was still owned by the Government, though generally supposed to have been acquired by the railroad. After two days spent in surveying, he found, true to his surmise, that section 13 had never been entered. He sent his nephew, Tilton Davis, to the land office at Plattsburg, where the section was entered in the name of Edward Samuel, president of the land company. Mr. Samuel then deeded to Mr. Davis, as

---

*This sketch as published is the substance of a History of Hamilton, written by Mrs. Anna B. Korn, of Trenton, a granddaughter of A. G. Davis.—Editor.

trustee of the company, forty acres, which was laid off into blocks and lots. Subsequently eighty acres were added to the original plat.

The honor of naming the town devolved upon Mr. Davis, who called it Hamilton, partly, he says, in honor of Alexander Hamilton and partly for Joseph Hamilton, a brilliant lawyer and a soldier under General Harrison, killed at the battle of the Thames October 5, 1813. The first sale of town lots was advertised far and near for October, 1855, and the promise of free dinner and plenty of whisky brought a tremendous crowd. The auctioneer was Judge Parrott of DeKalb County. John Berry of Liberty bought the first lot. On the average the lots brought $33 apiece. There was a second sale of lots in June, 1856.

Mr. Davis then built a two-story frame house, into which his family moved in April, 1856. The lumber was brought from St. Louis by river to Camden in Ray County, thence by wagon, and cost, delivered $70 per thousand feet. While the town was beginning to grow this house was used and conducted as a hotel, the Lone Star House. At that time Porter Ward ran a stage between Gallatin and Hamilton, and Judge Green ran one south from Hamilton to Lexington. It took a day to go and one to come. Transient travelers stopped overnight with Mr. and Mrs. Davis.

The original streets of the town were named for members of the town company; thus, Davis (commonly called Main), McGaughey, Berry, Bird, Arthur, Samuel, Burrows, Ewing, Ritchie, etc. The second house in town, built by Mr. Davis in 1857, was a log building, rented to Henry Holmes, a German brickmaker, who had the first brickyard and his was the second family. In the summer of 1857 Mr. Davis put up the first storehouse, a two-story frame, and opening a stock of general merchandise was soon doing a large and profitable business.

How the more substantial families secured educational advantages for their children is illustrated in the case of Mr. Davis. He introduced to his home a governess from Carrollton, Missouri, and she lived in the Davis home and taught the children for a number of years. In order to encourage education and the building of good schoolhouses he donated two lots to the city in 1857. When the first postoffice was established in 1858, he was appointed postmaster and kept the office in his store.

February 14, 1859, the railroad was completed through Hamilton and the first locomotive came through the next day. Mr. Davis was the first railroad and express agent. As no depot was built until the fall of that year, he built a pen for the storage of freight and express, paying a guard to watch it until the owners came and carried it away. Mr. Davis was commissioned notary public July 26, 1859, and for four years performed the duties of the office with a diligence and exactitude that left his record free from error or complaint.

Among other early settlers were: William P. Steele, deputy under Mr. Davis and second postmaster; Samuel Baldwin, who owned the first lumber yard in 1858; David Buster, who in the fall of 1858 put up a small box saloon, conducting it in connection with a stock of groceries; Robert Owens, another merchant of 1858; Samuel Hill, who in 1859 laid off forty acres as Hill's addition or Hillsboro; Otis B. Richardson, who came in 1860 and was the third postmaster; William Napier, who brought his family to town in 1860 and whose sister Sallie was a popular teacher in the county; Presley Thomas, who came in 1860 and opened the first blacksmith shop; other families that followed closely upon these were Claypool, Elliott, Logan, Crist, Johnson and Graer.

In 1860 the first piano was bought by Mr. Davis for his only daughter. It was a Chickering of fine tone and quality. He then sent for a music teacher, Miss Mary Payne, who lived in the Davis home and taught the daughter several years during the summer vacation.

These pioneer fathers and mothers were a busy, active people, but they had their times for rest, and during these restful times they found much solace in song. The violin was their main instrument. They listened to its melody, danced to it, sang to it. In the days of the pioneer, every community had its singing school with a professional singing master in charge. For music they were restricted to old melodies found in "Carmina Sacra," "The New Lute of Zion," "The Triumph," "The Revivalist," long since out of date. Some of the best books were written in the old square note system so the people could learn it more easily.. Familiar airs were "The Land of Canaan," "Mary to the Saviour's Tomb," "Jesus Lover of my Soul," "Happy Days." Through the art of song patriotism became a part of the life of the community in the days of the Civil war. The singing school led to the popular camp meeting. When a man fails to solve a difficult problem with his head, he instinctively undertakes to solve it with his heart. At a time the camp meeting could not conflict with sowing and reaping, people met, mingled, and their hearts were mellowed by the divine message they heard preached from the Bible. Accordingly' this was a season of heart culture and social and religious meeting place of early pioneers whose wisdom and eloquence were voiced and penned by the pioneer pulpiteers among whom were Rev. Eli Penney and Jimmy Reed. Their influences have quickened the pulpit and given fresh inspiration to every form of literary effort. So we revere and recognize in these untitled messengers our first religious influence. Another notable place of meeting was the old-fashioned barbecue, which usually was given on the Fourth of July or after the harvest season. It was a time of amusement, when people reveled in speaking, baseball, racing and feasting.

In 1861, at the breaking out of the Civil war and the ensuing depression, the town ceased to grow but held its own well. In the fall of that year the first Federal troops were stationed here, and remained throughout the war. They were a company of the Fiftieth Illinois and James Battalion of the Home Guards. The few rebel sympathizers were made to take the oath of allegiance. Sometime during the summer of 1863 two of Gallatin's prominent citizens were shot down on the streets of Hamilton by Federal sympathizers. Both men had been drinking freely and openly announcing their views as Confederates. This deed plunged both Hamilton and Gallatin into the most intense excitement.

Henry Thornton took up his residence in 1862 and was thereafter proprietor of a livery stable. A dentist, Doctor Kelley, and a physician, Doctor Cavanaugh, hung out their signs in that year. Religious services were held in the depot before and during the early period of the war, and Rev. Eli Penney, Baptist, and Reverend Mr. Fine, of the Christian Church, were the first ministers. About 1863 James Kemper erected a fine home, still standing. Mrs. Post also set up the first dress-making shop. The first newspaper was started in 1863. John Burrows and A. G. Davis were the financial backers, but the editor soon left town in debt to his benefactors. Marcus A. Low took charge of the paper in 1865 and conducted it successfully. In the same year the war closed, and Hamilton began to spread her domain owing to the steady influx of settlers.

James Penney and John R. Penney, all locating on farms; William Atherton and Marion C. Martin, builders and contractors, and a little before them came S. F. Martin, Henry Partin, Elijah Altman, who furnished service also as builders. April 1, 1866, Jacob Brosius and William Ervin opened the Hamilton House, a hotel widely known during its existence for its good management, furnishings, excellent cooking and cleanliness. The popular dances, feasts and social functions are often recalled in pleasant retrospection by the people of those times. W. J. Ervin, who opened the second drug store in 1867, continued in the same business upwards of forty years.

From 1867 to 1871 names of individuals and heads of families locating in Hamilton were as follows: Rev. William Wilmot, Robert Ogden, Marion Reed, L. B. Moore, Henry Reed, G. G. Perkins, W. W. Orr, J. S. Orr, J. L. Filson, H. C. Farabee, Billy Dodge, George Pickel, William Pickel, Ben Pickel, Andy Harrah, Rev. James Penney, John R. Penney, A. G. Howard, druggist; O. O. Brown, merchant; James Stone, hardware; A. C. Menefee and C. C. Green, meats; H. C. Hughes, restaurant; Phil Rogers and James Lunn, shoe shops; Henry Thorton, plasterer; Sam McBrayer and Paxton Bros., livery; Anthony Rohrbaugh, head of Rohrbaugh, Moore & Company; John Minger, who in 1867 established the first bakery; Lee M. Cosgrove, painter and paper hanger; Joseph Allen, contractor; C. M. Morrow, William Wagonseller, J. J. Hooker, Henry Leeper.

In 1868 Hamilton was incorporated as a town. The trustees were Anthony Rohrbaugh, F. P. Low, George Lamson, John Morton, and William Partin, with Mr. Low as chairman, or mayor, and his son M. A. Low as secretary and city attorney. Charles Stephenson was first marshal. In 1868 Alston and Vincent Bowman as a committee circulated a petition for the purchase of ground for a cemetery. Mr. Davis surveyed the ground into lots. This is called the old cemetery. Other events of this same year were: The erection of the first M. E. Church building at a cost, including bell, of $4,000; chartering of Eden Lodge No. 190, I. O. O. F., and Chapter No. 45, R. A. M.

Other names and business concerns that deserve mention in 1868-69 were: R. D. Dwight, Israel Gee, B. F. Holmes and T. E. Tuthill, farmers and stock raisers; Col. J. W. Harper, who had the first furniture store; John C. Griffing, wagon maker; A. C. Cochran, who in 1868 established the first bank, his successors in that business being Houston, Spratt and Menefee; Major Higgins, who started the second lumber yard; Hiram Markham, real-estate and insurance; Dr. S. V. Stoller; William McCoy and George Hastings, grocers; Mrs. Lutitia Dodge, first milliner; J. J. C. Guy and J. F. Naugle, who in 1869 erected the first elevator and were the first to engage in the grain trade; William Goodman, who started a hotel; S. H. Swartz, a produce merchant, who remained a resident for many years; Asa Thompson, a cabinet maker; J. E. Colby, who had the third lumber yard, which by his son was developed later into a flourishing hardware and implement business; the Broadway Hotel, built in 1869; T. H. Hare, who came in 1869 and the next year opened the first photograph gallery; Dr. R. D. King and Dr. J. W. Tuttle, who had been

dent in the town was a boiler explosion in the Hamilton Mills, which had recently been bought by Henry Clark. The explosion occurred in October, 1870, killing two men and injuring several. This mill was destroyed by fire in 1878, but was rebuilt, the roller process installed in 1882, and some years later the electric light plant was added to the mill equipment. In 1871 Hamilton began the erection of its high school building on a block a portion of which had been donated for that purpose the previous year by A. G. Davis. The members of the school board that year were S. F. Martin, George Brosius, L. B. Moore and James McAdoo. In 1870 the first Episcopal Church edifice was erected, and consecrated April, 1871. The first fire of consequence occurred May 27, 1871, resulting in the destruction of several stores; other bad fires were on July 5, 1884, and September 30, 1886. In 1877 the Hamiltonian was founded by William Morton, a paper that never missed a weekly issue from the start. Ten years later it was sold to W. J. Clark. In 1877 the Baptists put up a frame church, and the following year the first Christian Church was built.

Up to this time Hamilton had been governed by a board of trustees, but on October 5, 1880, was organized as a city of the fourth class. That act may be said to have brought the pioneer period of history to a close. As grand as were their deeds and memorable their lives, the days of the pioneers are past. Homes have been built and farms improved; Indians have been civilized. Having passed through the home-seeking period and entered into the home, social and commercial development era, the town began to extend her boundaries. Having recovered from the unrest and troublesome times of the war, the people once more returned to the peaceable and industrial pursuits of life.

Hamilton has never boomed, but has steadily marched onward, carving out a place for itself in the ranks of the cities of the state, building solidly and permanently as it advanced. Private enterprise has kept pace with the public purse, and erected many imposing business buildings, hotels, and churches, city hall, schools and residences, that for uniform beauty and evidence of affluence combined with culture have made Hamilton a home owning community. Particular attention is given to education, and the benefits of the best instruction in. public schools. Her park and Chautauqua grounds are the pride and admiration of her citizens. Her streets are 100 feet wide, and alleys eighty feet, and are well kept and in sanitary condition. Her press—and best friend and agent for diffusing knowledge and advertising her resources and advantages to the world—is an indispensable power in the community. Her railroad facilities for marketing her products are the best. Excellent roads in first class condition, in every direction, can be traversed for twenty miles and connect with four of the great railways of the state. Hamilton is surrounded with the best agricultural country and the best soil the sun ever shone on. Her modern country homes are the marvel of all. She has an electric light plant and telephone system; miles of granitoid walks, a flouring mill and elevator. She has two beautiful cemeteries, where repose her honored dead. Hamilton invites homeseekers to settle within her boundaries, believing—

> "This is indeed the land of forest tree
>   And sweet clinging vine;
> Where flowers ever blossom
>   And beams ever shine;
> Where light wings of zephyr
>   Oppressed with perfume
> Wax faint o'er the gardens
>   Of city in its bloom.

Where apple and peach are fairest of fruit,
And tones of the wild bird never are mute;
Where tints of the earth and hues of the sky
In color though varied in beauty may vie.''

A. G. DAVIS. As the founder of Hamilton, the name of A. G. Davis has been frequently mentioned in the historical sketch of that Northwest Missouri City. Of his own career, it is in keeping with the purposes of this work, that some memorial should be given. He was a man, aside from his practical achievements, whose excellent character and sterling worth made him a central figure in Caldwell County for over half a century. He was a member of an old and aristocratic family. Great executive ability has distinguished members of his kindred, who have served this country from time to time in various official positions which rendered them prominent in the business and social life of their times. Earlier family connections were with the nobility of both France and Great Britain.

Albert Gallatin Davis was born near Old Franklin, Howard County, Missouri, March 12, 1819. His father was Augustus Cave Davis, a Virginian by birth, and one of the number who followed Daniel Boone's trail to Missouri. He was a son of Louis Cave Davis, who in turn was one of seven sons that emigrated from England. A. G. Davis'·mother was Mrs. Elizabeth Colson Holliday of Kentucky; her mother was a Hampton, niece of General Wade Hampton of Revolutionary fame, a cousin to General Wade Hampton, who was a Confederate officer, twice governor of South Carolina and a Federal senator from that state. Mr. Davis' mother was an own cousin to one of Missouri's early governors, Lilburn W. Boggs. Mr. Davis' cousin Ben Holliday was famous in early western annals, was proprietor of Holliday's stage line from Omaha to San Francisco, ran a line of steamships from the latter city to Portland, and also built the Oregon connections of the Southern Pacific Railway and while operating them established the Wells, Fargo & Company's Express. Two of his daughters married French counts. Ben Holliday and Nan Patton started the first printing office in Missouri outside of St. Louis at Franklin, Howard County, issuing a paper called The Missouri Intelligencer and Boon's Lick Advertiser. The only copy of this first newspaper published west of St. Louis now in existence has been purchased by the Missouri Historical Society and is now in Columbia. On April 23, 1819, the first copy of The Missouri Intelligencer and Boon's Lick Advertiser was issued at Franklin, Howard County, Missouri Territory, by Nathaniel Patton and Ben Holliday. It was published weekly, and the subscription was $3 per annum, payable in advance. The paper was four pages—printed in large type with copious use of capitals.

The paper continued to be published at Franklin until 1823, when it was moved to Fayette, the new county seat of Howard County. In 1835 the type and presses were taken to Columbia by M. Patton, who started the Patriot, which in 1843 was succeeded by The Missouri Statesman, edited by Col. William F. Switzer and John B. Williams.

Another cousin was J. A. Holliday, of Hamilton, a lawyer and well known in political life. Mr. Davis' nephew, Tilton Davis, was prominent as a lawyer, and his brother Jeff Davis is well remembered as an attorney and public official at Kingston. Mr. Davis himself had eight brothers and one sister, and was the last survivor but one. His brother, Dr. Owen Davis, laid out the town of Sulphur Springs, Texas, and had previously distinguished himself in the Mexican and Civil wars.

Mr. Davis was the son of a farmer, and took to that vocation himself. On the outbreak of the Mormon war he enlisted in 1838 under Gen. John

B. Clark of Howard County, and was commissioned captain. At the end of the war he returned home. November 27, 1844, Gov. John E. Edmonds commissioned him captain of the First Company, Fourteenth Regiment, Second Battalion, First Brigade, First Division of Missouri Militia, and he served two years in that capacity. In 1846 Mr. Davis became traveling salesman for a drug house in Saline County, and it was while in Mirabile visiting his nephew, Matison T. Hines, that he met Miss Julia Ann Penney, who afterwards became his wife.

Mr. Davis had much skill as a surveyor, which proved of great value to him when it came to the founding of Hamilton. He was the chief promoter of that settlement, and its mainstay for many years. He built and conducted the first hotel; became the first merchant and built the first store building, and with the expansion of the business established branch stores in Breckinridge and Kingston. He was also the first postmaster and the first railroad agent and express agent. He was also a notary public and carried on a business in real estate. For years he held a record of which he was justly proud, as in no instance was there an error made in transferring property or a case contested. In time he became the largest landowner of the county, his holdings aggregating 2,000 acres, which taken in connection with his other interests made him the wealthiest man in the county. His name appears oftener in the records than that of any other early citizen of Caldwell County.

He was an advocate of education, and recognized the fact that intelligence in communities is essential to progress and reform and the soundest bulwark of institutions and civilization. As a means of manifesting this interest in a practical manner, he donated much of the ground on which the public schools in Hamilton were built. He was likewise a man of charity, ready to respond to the needs of the less fortunate, a strong man "of light and leading" in his community. He has been described as a man of urbane manners, chivalrous nature, agreeable spirit, and careful disposition, characteristics that were the results of solid culture and experience in the social arts. His brilliant intellect and retentive memory acquired from study and travel made him both an interesting conversationalist and a useful friend. His life was a call to manly living, obedience to law, faith in right, fair dealing with men, and peace in God. He was not a communicant of a church until towards the end of his life, when he united with the Methodist faith. He had long reverenced the principles and practice of Masonry, and was credited with being the oldest Mason in the state. He was a charter member of Hamilton Lodge No. 224, A. F. & A. M., of Royal Arch Chapter No. 45, R. A. M., and an honorary member of the Eastern Star.

In the fullness of years and maturity and fruitfulness of his works he passed away February 26, 1906. Schools and business houses closed on the afternoon of his funeral, which was conducted by the pastor of the Methodist Church and other ministers assisting and with the impressive auspices of the Masonic fraternity. In the words of a local paper: "In passing judgment upon the merits of the Father of Hamilton we take into account the quality as well as the quantity of what he has done, and we take just pride in his achievements, in his indomitable will, his skilful adaptation and application of the forces that brought him success. As the spire on some lofty cathedral seen at close view, where neither its true height nor its majestic proportions can be accurately measured, so is Albert Gallatin Davis, whose splendid life will be the more appreciated as time exposes its intrinsic worth, and symmetry, strength and beauty of his character."

JULIA ANNA DAVIS, the wife of the late A. G. Davis of Hamilton, was born April 18, 1828, and died September 27, 1891. She was the daughter of the Baptist clergyman, Rev. Eli Penney, and was born in Anderson County, Kentucky, twelve miles from Frankfort, where she was educated. Born of such stock we might expect a conscientious woman, and her life vindicated the expectation. She was cultured also, a woman of remarkable judgment and ability.

She fitted herself for teaching, so that when she left her Kentucky home and emigrated with her parents to Mirabile, Missouri, she was well equipped for the frontier life they were to follow. She opened a school over which she presided several years. She was industrious and an adept in the art of tailoring, and made many of the fashionable coats and vests for the gentlemen of those days. Besides this, like many women of the older generation, she was taught carding, spinning and weaving of cloth, which furnished pleasant employment for summer vacation hours and amply compensated her labors. Thus she laid the foundation for the useful career she was destined to lead.

It was in 1846 that Albert Gallatin Davis visited his nephew, Matison T. Hines, for the first time. He was traveling salesman for John Sappington & Brother, druggists of Arrow Rock, Saline County, Missouri. It was while here he met, wooed and married the belle of the village, Miss Julia Anna Penney, and then settled on a farm adjoining Mirabile, the wedding gift of Reverend Mr. Penney to his daughter. After conducting this farm until 1855, Mr. Davis turned his attention to other pursuits which brought them more renown. Mrs. Davis assumed the management of the farm during her husband's absence in superintending the first sale of town lots in Hamilton and until he had completed the first house in the town, when she severed her connection with farm life and opened a hotel to provide shelter and entertainment to those seeking homes in a new and undeveloped country. As manager of this new business, she proved successful, and at the end of two years invested her earnings in a lumber yard; forming a partnership with James A. Brown, they acquired the business of Samuel Baldwin, and conducted it with profit for two years. Mr. Joseph Davis—youngest son—has the distinction of being the first white child born in the first house in Hamilton—June 13, 1857.

Mrs. Davis was a woman of executive ability, enabling her to preside at meetings, speak before audiences, and carry forward any plans her conscience approved. She joined the Baptist Church in 1843, but later accepted the truth of the Seventh Day Adventists in 1870 and faithfully lived up to the principles of the church. She was exceedingly lovely and amiable. All active, philanthropic and Christian enterprises met with her sympathy, encouragement and cooperation. Mrs. Davis was one of the first and earnest workers in the Order of the Eastern Star when it was instituted here. As an entertainer she was gifted; for charity she was noted; and for hospitality had no superiors.

She was the mother of eight children, five dying in infancy. Three survived her: Mary Frances Brosius, Albert G., Jr., and Joseph H.; and two grandchildren: Anna Brosius Korn and Ben. H. Brosius.

MARY FRANCES BROSIUS, the oldest child of Albert G. Davis and wife, and herself the oldest citizen of Hamilton in point of residence, died at the home of her daughter, Mrs. Frank N. Korn, in Trenton, March 10, 1914. She was born in Mirabile, and was still a child when she went to the first house built in Hamilton. On the beautiful prairie surrounding that home and the village in company of her colored nurse-girl she gathered the flowers of summer and romped and played as only children can.

Later, in the absence of educational facilities in the pioneer village, her parents engaged a governess to instruct her, Miss Mollie Carroll of Carrollton. Several years later Miss Julia Payne came to the home and taught the child piano and music. After the stage line was in operation between Gallatin and Richmond, Mary Frances was sent to school in Gallatin. Several years later she entered a young woman's seminary at Liberty, and later a finishing school at St. Joseph. On her return to Hamilton she became a progressive social spirit in the town, working with church and school in their entertainments.

February 16, 1865, she married James Henry Brosius. To this union three children were born: Lillian, who died at the age of eighteen months; Anna Lee, now Mrs. Frank N. Korn of Trenton; and Ben Holliday Brosius of Council Bluffs, Iowa. Mrs. Brosius was converted and joined the Methodist Church in 1875, and for nearly forty years journeyed in the faith of the Lord. She showed both the spirit and practice of an older generation of Christians, exemplifying her doctrine in a kindliness and charity that had no proxy and went directly to all in need, irrespective of class or color. At the same time she was an exemplar in the virtues of the home, and through her household and through her relations with the life outside did much to enrich and ennoble her community. She was active in the orders of the Eastern Star and the Pythian Sisters. Her life was the expression of a beautiful character, and since the influence of a single deed is beyond the computation of the finite mind, who can attempt to measure the influences that went out from that steady-burning flame which was unquenched through her long life?

ALBERT GALLATIN DAVIS, JR., one of the two sons who survive Mr. and Mrs. A. G. Davis, was born at Mirabile, October 9, 1854. He grew to manhood in Hamilton, entered his father's mercantile store, learning the business when not in school. Like that of his brother and sister, his education was under private instructors engaged in the home. Later he went to school in Gallatin, finishing his education in the Missouri State University. On returning home he engaged in farming and stock raising, and also mastered surveying, a business he still pursues. In politics he is a democrat, and was elected city and township assessor in 1909, and was the first democrat elected to that office since his father held it, forty years before.

JOSEPH HAMILTON DAVIS, the youngest child of Mr. and Mrs. A. G. Davis, was born June 13, 1857, and has the distinction of being the first child born in Hamilton in the first house built in the town—"The Lone Star"—in recognition of which fact he was named after the town. He was graduated from the high school under Prof. David Ferguson. He was taught the mercantile business, and assisted his father in the store. Later he attended Moore's Business College at Chillicothe, and subsequently taught school several years in the county. October 2, 1901, he was united in marriage with Miss Laura Hardman of Polo. Missouri, by Rev. J. E. Ellenberger. He engaged in farming near Polo until 1907, when he sold his place and bought the Moffat farm a

Anderson County, Kentucky, April 6, 1799, and died in Hamilton, Missouri, June 13, 1872. When he and his wife, Polly Burruss Penney, left Kentucky to emigrate to Missouri, they sold a fine estate, well improved, with brick two-story house, brick outbuildings and walks, everything to make life comfortable and happy. The parting with these possessions and old friends filled the members of the household with sorrow as they embarked upon their journey in covered wagons, drawn by mule and horse teams, driven by negro servants.

In 1841 they purchased and settled upon a farm near Mirabile, now Colonel Frost's farm, where they prospered and continued to live until 1868, when they sold their farm and came to Hamilton to live near their several children located in that town. As their children married they gave to each of them $2,000 and a negro servant, which was an excellent start in life, and at their deaths the children shared equally in the final division of the estate.

They were people of strong characters, indomitable energy, and strictest integrity. Kinder and more obliging neighbors never lived; while the poor were always certain of their warmest sympathy, together with something more substantial. Elder Penney was among the first pulpit orators of pioneer days. He was an old-school Baptist, very earnest in his convictions, living his belief with the utmost fidelity. Of the ten children born to Eli Penney and wife, only one survives, Edward of Kansas City. The others were: Dr. Eli Penney; Frances, wife of Captain David Thompson of Kingston; Julia Anna, wife of A. G. Davis of Hamilton; John R., of St. Joseph; Mary Jane, wife of Doctor Adams of St. Joseph; Mildred, wife of Dr. J. H. McClintock, of Houston, Texas; Elizabeth, wife of William Partin of Hamilton; William, who died at the age of twenty-one; and Rev. James C., a Baptist minister of Hamilton.

ANNA BROSIUS KORN. One of Missouri's distinguished women is Mrs. Anna Brosius Korn, of Trenton. Mrs. Korn is a very talented woman, a leader in club, social, patriotic and civic activities, and her name is perhaps familiar to most Missouri people as a charming and graceful writer of both prose and poetry.

She is renowned as a versatile song writer.. A song written by her entitled, "The Missouri Carol," was unanimously endorsed by the Forty-seventh General Assembly of the Missouri Legislature for use on state occasions, national holidays, and in schools and .colleges. A patriotic song entitled, "Guard the Flag of Our Republic," written by her, was received with every demonstration of enthusiasm when rendered by a quartette at the state encampment of the Grand Army of the Republic at the Lyceum Theater, St. Joseph, and at the dedication of Patriots Hall, Valley Forge, Pennsylvania, February 22, 1914, by the choir of Washington Memorial Chapel.

Mrs. Korn is the originator of a movement for the inauguration of a Missouri Day in state life. Resolutions drafted by her designating first Monday in October Missouri Day have been adopted by the State Teachers' Association; Missouri Daughters American Revolution; Missouri Federated Commercial Clubs; Missouri Society United States Daughters of 1812; Women's Federated Clubs; Group Two, Bankers Association; Missouri Society of Colorado; Missouri Society of Washington, District of Columbia. She is the author of the bill that has been introduced in the Forty-eighth General Assembly to create the first Monday in October Missouri Day, by official act. The bill known as Waterman House Bill 112, passed both houses March 19, 1915. While a resident of Oklahoma for three years, she was elected vice president of the Missouri Society of Oklahoma, organized at Oklahoma City, April 22, 1909.

On October 1, 1909, her work received high recognition at the Oklahoma State Fair. The Daily Oklahoman mentions her as first prize winner among the state's artists to capture champion prize in pastel in fine arts exhibit.

Mrs. Korn is a student of the William Heacock School of Journalism. As a descriptive writer she has achieved success on articles of travel, published in serial form; penal institutions, pottery, etc., articles appearing in western publications.

Mrs. Korn's ancestors assisted in establishing independence. Mrs. Korn is the daughter of James Henry Brosius, born September 20, 1839. His father, Jacob Brosius, born August 19, 1808, died September 13, 1878, was married to Lorenza Hoblitzell at Hancock, Maryland, on September 14, 1830. She was born May 20, 1812; died July 13, 1886.

Jacob Brosius was the son of Jacob Brosius, Sr., and Marie Eva Meyer. Jacob Brosius, Sr., born August 7, 1774, died July 13, 1862. Marie Eva Meyer, born January 28, 1785, died November 24, 1846. They were married May 25, 1804. The said Jacob, Sr., was a son of Abraham and Margaret Brosius. The former, born in 1722, and died in 1802, was private in Captain Peter Decker's Company, Fifth Pennsylvania Battalion, in 1776. Marie Eva Meyer, wife of Jacob, Sr., was a daughter of Henry Meyer, born in 1750, and Katharina Diehl. They were married in 1783. Katharina Diehl was the daughter of Nicholas Diehl, born in Chester County, Pennsylvania, June 8, 1725, and died in Maryland February 1, 1805. Nicholas Diehl was a member of the Chester County, Pennsylvania, Committee of Observation and Soldiers and was commissioned captain of a company of the Third Battalion, Chester County Associates, 1776.

James Henry Brosius acquired his early education in the country schools of Cooper County and for many years was a well-known hotel man and was also engaged in mercantile pursuits. Politically he was a democrat and affiliated with the Episcopal Church. He served in the Confederate army under General Price. He was married February 16, 1865, to Miss Mary Frances Davis, daughter of Albert Gallatin Davis and Julia Anna (Penney) Davis, the pioneer family of Hamilton, Missouri, and founders and builders of the town. James H. Brosius and ·wife were the parents of three children: Lillian, who died in infancy; Ben Holliday Brosius; and Anna Lee.

Anna Lee Brosius was married at Hamilton, Missouri, October 28, 1891, to Frank Nicholas Korn, by Rev. R. T. Mathews. To this union two children were born: Frank Marvin, who died at six weeks, September 12, 1892; Mildred Lillian, who was born May 31, 1894, died November 11, 1904.

Mrs. Korn traces her ancestry back to Gen. Wade Hampton of Revolutionary fame, through her mother's ancestors. Mrs. Korn is best known by her literary name as Anna Brosius Korn. She is a graduate, widely traveled, and thoroughly cultured woman and from early years has manifested great talent in literary and artistic movements. Has written many short stories in addition to her poems and songs. As a student and traveler, has assimilated much knowledge and is thoroughly informed on the prominent social and political questions of the day. She is a member of the Missouri Daughters of the American Revolution, the United Daughters of the Confederacy, of which she is president of Trenton Chapter, and Missouri Society United States Daughters of 1812. Mrs. Korn organized the Dorcas Richardson Chapter, Daughters of the American Revolution, of Trenton, Missouri, May 29, 1912, at her home, and is now commissioned to organize a chapter of the United Daughters of the Confederacy.

FRANK NICHOLAS KORN, a thorough railroad man, was born and reared in Breckenridge. At the early age of fourteen years he started his railroad career as messenger boy on the Hannibal & St. Joe Railroad. Learning telegraphy at the same time, he was promoted as a telegraph operator, with his first position at St. Joe, August, 1886, remaining with that company in capacity of operator and station agent until 1890, when he entered the service of the Santa Fe Railroad as operator at Las Vegas, New Mexico, where he remained until April, 1891, when he entered the service of the Rock Island Railway at Trenton, Missouri, as operator. In May he was promoted to the position of train dispatcher.

On October 28, 1891, he was united in marriage to Miss Anna Lee Brosius, of Hamilton, Missouri. A residence was established in Trenton and maintained until October, 1895, when he entered the service of the St. Louis & Southwestern Railway, and served that company in capacity as operator, station agent and train dispatcher for five years. In June, 1900, he entered the service of the Kansas City Southern Railway at Pittsburg, Kansas, which position he held until August 6, 1902, when he was promoted to the position of chief dispatcher, which position he relinquished to accept a position with the Denver & Rio Grande Railway, under General Superintendent William Coughlin, who resigned his position recently with the Kansas City Southern. The following article may be here quoted:

"It appears that the Kansas City Southern is the training school for the railroads of the country. Whenever a road wants a good man they take one from the Kansas City Southern offices. The latest man selected is the genial, hard-working chief dispatcher, F. N. Korn. He has accepted a position with the Denver & Rio Grande. Next Monday he leaves for his new home in Salida, Colorado. The whole office force hate to see him go. They feel as bad about it as they did when Superintendent Coughlin left, and that is saying a great deal for the popularity of Mr. Korn. He has been employed here a number of years and was promoted to his present position on the 6th of last August. From that day on he has borne the responsibilities of the office and never failed. The hours are long, the work hard and delicate, but he didn't falter nor lose temper. His subordinates are his greatest admirers, for he was always kind, generous, a good fellow, and an excellent chief. His successor has not been named."

Mr. Korn commenced duties at Salida, Colorado, for the Denver & Rio Grande Railway as dispatcher and chief dispatcher in April, 1903, and continued in service until November 16, 1905, when he resigned his position as chief dispatcher with that company to accept a position with the Rock Island Railway at Little Rock, Arkansas, in capacity of train master of construction, and built that part of the road from Haskel into Crosset, Arkansas. When the work was completed he was transferred to Chickasha, Oklahoma, where he was employed as dispatcher for ten months, when he was transferred to El Reno, Oklahoma, where he was made chief dispatcher, and later promoted to trainmaster of transportation, which position he held until January 1, 1911, when he was transferred to the Missouri division of the Rock Island lines as chief dispatcher at Trenton, where he and wife at present reside.

Frank N. Korn received his education in the schools of Breckenridge, Missouri. His father, J. N. Korn, a cabinet maker, is a native of Saxe Coburg, Germany, born March 17, 1829. His mother, Alida (Van Allen)

Korn, was a native of Canajoharie, New York. Frank N. is one of six children born to this union.

GEORGE S. TUGGLE. Tuggle is a pioneer name in Northwest Missouri and has been identified particularly with Daviess County for more than half a century. George S. Tuggle is proprietor of the South View Stock and Chicken Farm in Davis Township of Caldwell County, adjoining the little City of Braymer. This farm is becoming famous in this part of Missouri for its fine stock, and particularly for its poultry. It comprises 129 acres of land, and with the continued growth of Braymer will no doubt at some time be largely included within the city limits. Mr. Tuggle has spent both time and money and experience and care in selecting and looking after his fine stock. He has a herd of fine Poland China hogs, but his prize stock is his white Orpington chickens, some of the finest to be found in Northwest Missouri of the Kellerstrass strain. The conveniences of his home and the general arrangement and equipment of the farm are all in keeping with his stock. He has a fine eight-room modern residence, situated only a block from the public school, and the situation is such that he has all the facilities and conveniences of country life combined with what amounts to a residence in a growing town.

George S. Tuggle was born in Daviess County, Missouri, on a farm in Monroe Township, April 24, 1875. His father is William S. Tuggle, who was born in Kentucky, June 22, 1848, a son of Spencer H. Tuggle, who became one of the pioneer settlers of Northwest Missouri. William S. Tuggle married Annie C. Railsback, April 3, 1872, who was born in Estill County, Kentucky, January 24, 1854, and died May 28, 1906. Their children were: George S., Dora B., deceased; Beulah, Dennis A., Jesse W.; Mary A., deceased, Josie M. and James S. William S. Tuggle, the father, is still living. He has been a farmer, is a member of the Christian Church, is affiliated with the Masons and Independent Order of Odd Fellows, and in politics is a democrat.

George S. Tuggle was reared on a farm, acquired his education in the local schools and Grand River College, Gallatin, Missouri, and on June 4, 1902, married E. Belle Steenrod. To their marriage have been born two children, Nina Belle, born February 23, 1904; and Anna Evelyn, born January 29, 1911. Mrs. Tuggle was born in Des Moines County, Iowa, March 11, 1875, and moved with her father's family, when six years of age, to the farm in Caldwell County, Missouri, where a few years later the town of Braymer was surveyed. She acquired her education in the local schools. Her father, Robert Steenrod, now deceased, at one time owned the land on which the greater part of the town of Braymer is built, and the present South View Farm is a portion of the 350 acres originally owned by this pioneer. Robert Steenrod was a native of Virginia, and located at Braymer in 1881. He died June 23, 1910, at the age of seventy-five. He was a son of Ephraim Steenrod, who came from Virginia. Robert Steenrod married Elizabeth J. Deam, who was born in Clark County, Ohio, October 20, 1827, and died March 19, 1907. Robert Steenrod lived here before the coming of the railroad on land for which he paid eighteen dollars an acre and had about three hundred and fifty acres in Caldwell County, and much of it was sold at a later day for fifty dollars an acre. The children in the Steenrod family were: Elizabeth Jane Moorman; Nelson of Oklahoma; Ephraim D. of El Reno, Oklahoma; John F., of Missouri; Amelia I. Shiner; and E. Belle Tuggle. Mrs. Tuggle's father was a democrat, a member of the Independent Order of Odd Fellows for more than forty years, and one of the foremost citizens in this section of Northwest Missouri.

Mr. Tuggle has part of his land laid out in lots, and it offers an exceedingly attractive situation for homes, being well drained, and every lot a perfect site for buildings, within easy distance of schools, churches and the business center of town. Mr. and Mrs. Tuggle are members of the Baptist Church, and they have always maintained the South View Farm as a home of hospitality and good cheer, and both are actuated by that public spirit which gives support to churches, schools and all movements to promote the moral and material benefit of the community.

N. W. CROCKETT. The Spring Hill Farm in section 13 of Platte Township, Andrew County, has as its owner one of the foremost agriculturists and stockmen of this section, a man who has spent all his life in this one community, is a farmer by training and inclination, and has made himself a progressive factor in those affairs and activities which lie outside the immediate limits of an individual farm. Mr. Crockett has been known in this section of Andrew County as a banker, and as a stock exhibitor his name is familiar among stockmen over several states.

Nathan W. Crockett was born on the old homestead farm in Platte Township, November 19, 1860, a son of that splendid old pioneer, Milton Crockett. On other pages of this publication will be found the essential facts in the career of the late Milton Crockett and his family.

Nathan W. Crockett has always lived in Platte Township, grew up on the home place, and remained at home until two years after his marriage. He then came to his present farm, and is the owner of forty acres included in his father's estate. His Spring Hill farm, which takes its name from the presence of several springs of living water on the land, comprises 285 acres, and owing to the general lay of the land is unusually well adapted for stock raising. Mr. Crockett for a number of years has featured the thoroughbred Hereford cattle, the registered Percheron horses, keeps a stable with some imported jacks and jennets, raises mules and Chester White hogs. This has been his business for the past thirty years, and his reputation as a stock breeder and farmer is not confined to the limits of his home county. His jacks, jennets and horses have been frequently exhibited at the Des Moines State Fair and in the stock shows at St. Joseph and Sedalia, and his horses always won premiums. Mr. Crockett has been one of the directors of the Whitesville Interstate Corn and Poultry Association since the organization of that now famous institution. For a number of years he was also a director and president of the Rea Banking Company. To his farm management he has brought the same degree of enterprise and good judgment which would have enabled him to make a success in commercial lines, and has a property that in value and improvements favorably compares with any country place in Andrew County. Mr. Crockett began his career on 120 acres, which he bought at twenty-five dollars an acre, and it is now worth at an average $150 an acre. In politics Mr. Crockett is a republican.

In 1882 he married Emma Ewing, who was born at Whitesville, in Andrew County, May 30, 1861. When she was three years old her parents moved to Kentucky, but returned to Missouri when she was nine years of age, and she grew up in this county. Her parents were Daniel and Lou Ann (Riley) Ewing. Her father was born in Kentucky, May 12, 1825, and her mother in Clinton County, Missouri, August 1, 1837, representing one of the pioneer families in that section of Northwest Missouri. Her mother is now living at a venerable age in Saline County, Missouri. Her father, who died in 1864 while temporarily in Illinois, was a miller all his active career, and had a financial interest in and was the manager of the old mill at Whitesville at the time of his death. Mrs. Crockett was one of three children, the other two being John, now deceased, and Lizzie, also deceased. Mr. and Mrs. Crockett have no children.

J. F. TAYLOR. Under the modern conditions of American society there is no more important factor than the teacher, the head or the instructor in the great public school system. The public school has been an institution of American society almost from the beginning of government, but never until the present era has its scope of importance and usefulness reached out so far and broad as in the present generation. One of the able educators of Northwest Missouri is the present superintendent of the Braymer schools, Professor J. F. Taylor. Mr. Taylor has been connected with the schools at Braymer for the past four years. He has done much to improve and systematize the school work in that time, and has a well-equipped educational plant under his direction. The Braymer school building is a large ten-room brick structure, occupying a beautiful site, with ample ground. Mr. Taylor has a corps of nine teachers, and his assistants during the year 1914 were: Helen Nixon, P. G. Davis, G. W. Pool, Edna Glick, Ethel Williams, Grace Messenbaugh and Ethelyn Stubblefield.

Professor Taylor was born in Green City, Sullivan County, Missouri, and comes from a family of teachers and educators. His father, T. C. Taylor, was for many years identified with school work in this state. He was born, reared and educated in Ohio, and now lives in West Plains, Missouri. He married Jane Edson, and both of them finished their courses in the Kirkville Normal School, and have taught in different sections of Northwest Missouri. The Edson ancestors came from Michigan and the Taylors from Virginia. T. C. Taylor and wife were the parents of five sons and five daughters. A. E. Taylor is instructor in the high school at Cameron; Mrs. P. H. Proops lives at Weiser, Idaho, and is a graduate of the Missouri Wesleyan College; Leah Taylor lives at West Plains, Missouri; Adaline is in the Missouri Wesleyan College at Cameron; Thomas C., Jr., is a student in the Illinois State University; Ruth has her home in West Plains; Maynard is at home.

J. F. Taylor grew up in Northwest Missouri, and was carefully educated for his profession. He attended high school and college, is a graduate in the class of 1911 from the Missouri Wesleyan College at Cameron, and was also a student in the Maryville State Normal School. Mr. Taylor for one year was assistant instructor of science in the Missouri Wesleyan College, and in the fall of 1911 accepted the call to take charge of the high school at Braymer, and in the following year was promoted to superintendent of the entire public school system of the town.

In July, 1912, at Granger, Missouri, Professor Taylor married Helen Farwell. She was a graduate from the Missouri Wesleyan College with the class of 1912. Her father, Frank Farwell, is a resident of Granger, Missouri, and came from Iowa. Professor Taylor and wife have one child, John F., Jr., now one year old. Mr. Taylor is a republican in politics and he and his wife are members of the Methodist Episcopal Church. He is a man of athletic build, and during his college career made a record in football and on the track.

PETER GLENN FULKERSON. More than seventy-two years have passed since Judge Peter Glenn Fulkerson came with his parents from the Old Dominion State to the wilderness of Grundy County, Missouri. During this nearly three-quarters of a century he has witnessed a marvelous growth and development, a transformation in which he has shared and borne a full part. Few, indeed, are those now surviving who were here when he came, and among the younger generations who have grown up about him he still survives in hale and hearty old age, taking a keen interest in the affairs which affect his community, although the time has long since passed when it was necessary for him to engage in active labors, and his declining years are being passed at Trenton in the ease and quietude which his long period of labor won him.

Judge Fulkerson was born in Lee County, Virginia, May 16, 1833, and is a son of Benjamin Franklin and Mary J. (Ewing) Fulkerson, the former born in Lee County, Virginia, and the latter in Bath County, Kentucky. Both Judge Fulkerson's paternal and maternal grandfathers served as soldiers during the War of 1812, and he also has a military record, having been subject to call throughout the Civil war as a member of the Missouri State Militia, in which he enlisted in 1861. In 1842 his parents started on the long and dangerous overland journey to the newly-opened country in Missouri, the father entering 640 acres of prairie and timber land from the Government. Here both he and his courageous and faithful wife continued to reside during the remainder of their lives, making a home for their children and winning the respect and affection of those in the new country among whom their lives were cast.

Peter Glenn Fulkerson was but nine years of age when he accompanied his parents to Grundy County, and such education as he was able to secure was obtained in the primitive schools. He experienced every hardship and witnessed every incident of pioneer life, and is frequently prevailed upon today to speak of the times when he lived in the little log cabin in the midst of a country filled with wild game and in which the Indians still roamed in great numbers. The little home of the Fulkersons, like those of other pioneers, boasted of neither floor nor door. The hard earth served for the former, while a quilt in the winter months was used to keep out the cold. A wooden mallet was used to crush the corn, although hominy was the chief cereal used, as most easily secured; the leather for the family shoes was tanned by some member of the family and then kept until the shoemaker made his rounds and fashioned it into footwear. About the year 1852 the community began to become more thickly settled, many families coming here by way of ox-teams, and about that year the father freed his slaves, who were sent to Liberia and there given a generous portion of land. But while neighbors became more numerous, it was many years before primitive conditions ceased to exist. Sugar was a luxury not to be thought of, and honey was accordingly used to sweeten the food, this being gathered in the timber. Money was scarce, and but one store was located on the present site of the City of Trenton, while such mail as was received was paid for at the rate of twenty-five cents per letter. Tea and coffee being too expensive, the inventive settlers made a good brew from bark, boiled over a fire started by striking flints. The home-made candle furnished the light by which the mother made the summer clothes from flax, carded the wool, wove the cloth therefrom, or knitted the socks for the family, the latter commodity often being exchanged for the family bacon, at a ratio of one cent per pound, money being too scarce to pay for this article.

It was amid such surroundings that Judge Fulkerson grew to manhood. He worked on the home farm until he was twenty-eight years of age, at which time his father gave him 100 acres of land, located ten miles north of Trenton, on which he built a log house of one large

room, and there all of his children were born. As the years passed he
added from time to time to his property, paying from thirty cents to
five dollars per acre for his land, until he owned 640 acres of prairie
land and was known as one of the substantial men of his community.
He is now living in quiet retirement at Trenton, is still in the best of
health and spirits, and has the appearance of a man many years his
junior. A long life of integrity and honorable dealing have made him
known and respected all over this part of the county, and at various
times he has been called upon to serve in important offices. For many
years he has been a member of the school board, and in 1875 was
elected county judge from the Second Judicial District, serving efficiently in that capacity for four years. He is a member of the Independent Order of Odd Fellows, and his religious connection is with the
Methodist Episcopal Church.

In 1861 Mr. Fulkerson was married to Miss Eliza Carns, daughter
of Thomas and Anna (Peery) Carns, and to this union there have been
born six children, one daughter, who is deceased, and five sons, all living and married. The boys are as follows: Dr. William Daw, who
married Miss Ina Johnson, who died shortly afterwards, and he married Miss Sallie Weldon, daughter of William Weldon, and has one
son, George; Walter P., who married Miss Sarah Harper, of Carthage,
Missouri; Thomas F., who married Miss Mamie Milbank, of Chillicothe,
Missouri, daughter of George Milbank; Emmet, who married Miss
Louise Peery, daughter of Joseph Peery, of Ogden, Utah; and Henry
Cartz, who married Miss Ida Shoemaker, daughter of John Shoemaker,
of Perrin, Missouri.

GEORGE W. DAVIS. From the earliest pioneer times down to the
present Caldwell County has been continuously honored and benefitted
by the presence within her borders of the Davis family. In the character of its individual members and in their public services no family
in the county probably has been more distinguished, and it is impossible to estimate the strength and diversity of the influences which
emanate from such a family and affect the social and business affairs
of the county even to its most remote bounds.

George W. Davis is a representative in the third generation of this
family, and has himself lived here a period of three score years and
ten. His home is in Davis Township, named in honor of his grandfather, and in his career he has gained his success by farming and
stock raising. He has a fine farm of 350 acres, with Cowgill as his postoffice and market town. Mr. Davis is regarded in this county as the
best informed man on current topics and particularly on English
history.

He was born in a log cabin near the present place of his residence
on March 15, 1844. His father was John T. Davis, a native of Kentucky,
who grew up in Greene and Macoupin counties, Illinois. Grandfather
Dennis Davis brought his family to Caldwell County, Missouri, in 1837.
The township, which was named Davis in his honor, at one time comprised a quarter of the entire area of the county. The county was
practically an unbroken wilderness, and most of it heavy forest lands.
The first settlers had extreme difficulty in clearing off the virgin timber in order to have space for their crops, but abundant materials for
living were at hand in the woods and in the streams in the shape of
wild game and fish. Almost any day a deer could be shot within a few
rods of a pioneer cabin, and Mr. George W. Davis himself has hunted
such game as deer and wild turkey in the woods about his home in this
section of Missouri. Grandfather Dennis Davis was a volunteer soldier

during the Black Hawk war. John T. Davis married Margaret Moore, who was born in Macoupin County, Illinois. Their children were: Mary Ann Hauks of Kansas City; Elizabeth J. Ross, now deceased; George W.; D. J., deceased; John T., a prominent farmer of Davis Township; Margaret Brown, who lives in Kansas; and Mrs. Hannah P. Etherton of Davis Township. John T. Davis died at the age of seventy-one, was a democrat in politics, and a member of the Methodist Church, with which his wife also had communion. She died at the age of seventy-three.

George W. Davis grew up on the old homestead, and some of his earlier recollections center about the log cabin schoolhouse, which he attended for a number of terms, chiefly in the winter seasons. He was only eighteen when the war broke out between the states, and was one of the young men in this section of Northwest Missouri who volunteered for service in the Union army. He enlisted in 1861 in Captain Phillips company, and in 1864 joined the Forty-fourth Missouri Infantry. He was in the fight at Rolla, Missouri, and afterwards took part in some of the heavy campaigning in Tennessee. He was at Franklin and Nashville, two of the bloodiest battles of the Mississippi Valley, and also was at Mobile and participated in the capture of Forts Blakely and Spanish. Later he was in Montgomery, Alabama, and various other points in the South. He made a record of efficiency and fidelity as a soldier, and remained in the army until honorably discharged in August, 1865, after he had been out nearly four years.

After returning home, a veteran soldier, he took up farming and stock raising, and that has been the vocation which has brought him a substantial success and enabled him to provide liberally for his growing family. Mr. Davis was married October 5, 1865, to Pauline Noffzinger, of Ray County. Her parents were David and Mary Noffzinger, who came as early settlers from Virginia to Ray County, Missouri. Mr. Davis is justly proud of his children, brief mention of whom is made as follows: Rosetta Taylor, who lives in Oklahoma; Mary E., wife of L. McBee of Oklahoma; Rev. A. D., a preacher in the Methodist Church; Ola, of Braymer, Missouri; I. G., of Davis Township; Lute, of Oklahoma; Joshua, of Enid, Oklahoma; Clyde, of Davis Township; Charles B., in Caldwell County; M. J., who lives in Oklahoma City; H. A., of Cowgill; Ellen, wife of R. Sabin of Enid, Oklahoma; Emon, who died at the age of thirty-three; and Laura, who died when one year of age. The mother of these children died April 9, 1884. She was a devout member of the Methodist faith. On November 19, 1896, Mr. Davis married Mrs. Mary Alice West, a daughter of J. J. Lane, who was a soldier in the Civil war and is now deceased, dying at the age of sixty-eight years, and he was an active member of the Grand Army and of the Methodist Church. Mrs. Davis' mother was Mary F. Smith, now living at the age of sixty-nine. Mrs. Davis was reared in Caldwell County, Missouri, and by her first marriage had four children, Effie May, Stella L., Minnie F. and Eva B. Mr. Davis and wife have the following children: Gertrude, George W., Jr., Opal G. and Roscoe L.

The Davis home is one of the attractive estates of Davis Township, and the residence is a comfortable seven-room house, surrounded with barns, and with all the conveniences and facilities of a model country home. Mr. Davis has made a specialty of the raising of high-grade Norman horses, and keeps good grades of cattle and hogs. He annually feeds about a hundred head of cattle and three hundred hogs. Mr. Davis is a member of the Methodist Church, and in his community has always stood for good schools and churches, good roads, and everything that will make country life more attractive and lighten the economic burdens. Mr. Davis is a popular member of the Grand Army of the Republic.

CATHERINE (KENNISH) BISSETT, whose husband was the late William Henry Bissett, was born in the Isle of Man, December 7, 1851, being the third child of William Kennish, who was the fifth heir of the Corroney and of Catherine Callow, his wife. William Kennish, on the side of his paternal grandmother, was a descendant of the Lewellyn family, a family distinguished throughout all the British Isles. His great-aunt, Belle Lewellyn, was the lady chosen on one occasion to open the ball in her father's house with the Duke of Atholl, "King in Man." William Kennish identified himself with the early Methodists, and with the Temperance and Rechabite Order. He was a great student of religious history and read his Bible in three languages. He was earnestly solicited to represent the people in the House of Keys, but upon his refusal the people offered to meet his expenses, if that would be any inducement to him to accept the honor. He still refused, believing he could not afford to be away from his home duties during the long sessions of the Legislature. It is a matter of interest to note that this position in the "House of Keys" was for several years filled by the celebrated novelist, Hall Caine, and at the present time by a cousin of Mrs. Bissett, Robert Kerruish. Shortly after his declination of this honor, having met with some losses, William Kennish decided to sell his home and embark with his wife and twelve children to America. Thus, about forty-five years ago, the family was established in Missouri.

The children of William Kennish and wife were: William, the first born, was laid away in the family cemetery at Kirk Manghold, Isle of Man, at the age of eight years. The second, Annie, was married to J. W. Cairns near Greeley, Colorado. Margaret married Charles Allen in Denver, Colorado. Christian married David Kelly of Greeley, Colorado. Robert married Dora Skeels. John married Nellie Offutt. Ellen married William Tyson. Janie married Frederick Wrench. James marred Gertrude Saunders. Alice is single. Edward married Alice Collison. Thomas married Jessie Lawrence.

Catherine Kennish was educated in the parochial school of the Church of England and in a ladies' seminary in Douglas, Isle of Man. She was married to William Henry Bissett on September 9, 1883. On August 2, 1884, was born to them a daughter, who died shortly after birth. William Edward was born July 20, 1885. John Haken was born February 28, 1887.

William Henry Bissett, who died January 12, 1888, was born in Nova Scotia, April 9, 1846, and came from Kewanee, Illinois, to Holt County, Missouri, in February, 1883. His father was Edward Bissett, of French Huguenot descent, and by occupation a farmer and miller. The name originally was spelled Bizet in France, but after the family came to Canada the form was anglicized. In 1674 a record tells that Clara Bissot became the wife of one of America's greatest soldiers of fortune, Louis Joliet, who received a title to the Island of Anticosta. Some time later the English swooped down upon this island home in 1690, captured it, destroyed the fort and the houses erected by Joliet, seized his entire fortune and took his wife a prisoner. William H. Bissett's mother was Mary Cummins, who came with her parents to Nova Scotia when a child from Glasgow, Scotland. They were strict adherents of the Presbyterian Church.

The older of Mrs. Bissett's two living sons, William Edward Bissett, was educated at Ross Grove School, the Mound City High School and the State University at Columbia. His education was interrupted at different periods in order to carry on the work of the home farm. He passed the state ·bar examinations in Jefferson City in December, 1912. John Haken Bissett, the younger son, was married to Nellie Criswell, September 20, 1904. To their union were born Harold C. Bissett on June 20, 1905, and Catherine Bissett on October 19, 1910.

HON. FRANCIS M. WELLS. Among the venerable men of Northwest Missouri who have stepped aside from the paths of labor to let pass the members of the younger generation, with their hopes and ambitions, may be mentioned Judge Francis M. Wells, an honored veteran of the great Civil war, a pioneer settler of Andrew County, and a man who for a long period of years has been identified with the life of this locality both as a private citizen and a public official. Judge Wells was born in Morgan County, Illinois, September 14, 1835, and is a son of Jonathan and Letitia (Way) Wells, natives of Orange County, North Carolina.

Jonathan Wells was born in Orange County, North Carolina, January 4, 1800, and was fifteen years of age when he was taken by his parents to Orange County, Indiana. There he was married to Letitia Way, who was born September 1, 1806, in Orange 'County, North Carolina, and was a child when taken to Indiana. Some time after their marriage Mr. and Mrs. Wells moved to Morgan County, Illinois, where they resided until 1842, then moving to Monroe County, Iowa. In 1857 they came to Andrew County, Missouri, and settled at Lower Neely Grove, midway between Bolckow and Rosendale, and there the father died April 18, 1883, the mother following him to the grave May 2, 1884. Mr. Wells was a farmer all of his life, and a pioneer in four states, Indiana, Illinois, Iowa and Missouri. He and his brother-in-law, Enoch Way, were the first two settlers in Monroe County, Iowa, where Mr. Wells' land, in the southeastern corner of the county, a quarter section, was known as Wells Prairie. This he divided among his children. They were as follows: Peter H., who died in September, 1914, at Topeka, Kansas, having reached the advanced age of eighty-nine years; Margaret Ellsworth, who died September 24, 1896; Joseph, who was captain of the Missouri State Militia for a time, and later entered the Fifty-first Regiment, Missouri Volunteer Infantry, for service during the Civil war as a lieutenant, and is now living at an advanced age at Spearfish, South Dakota; Enoch, who died February 8, 1894; Francis M., of this review; George, who died June 24, 1904, served in Captain Johnson's Light Artillery and later in the Fifty-first Infantry during the Civil war;. Martha Jane, who is the widow of Charles Wheeler of Appleton City, Saint Clair County; Nancy Louisa, the widow of William Wilson, of Oakley, Kansas; Mary Lavina, who died in childhood, in 1847; and Zachary Taylor, of Springfield, Missouri.

Francis M. Wells received ordinary educational advantages in the public schools of Morgan County, Illinois, and Monroe County, Iowa, and remained under the parental roof until he was twenty-five years of age, at which time he established a home of his own by marrying, and at that time began farming for himself. He continued to be thus engaged until 1862, when he joined Captain Johnson's Light Artillery, and after seeing some active, arduous and dangerous service, was taken ill and was eventually honorably discharged because of disability. Returning to his farm, Mr. Wells continued to be engaged in agricultural pursuits until 1889, when he retired and moved to Bolckow, where he has since continued to make his home. A republican in politics, he served four years as postmaster of Bolckow, under Benjamin Harrison. For two terms of four years each, Judge Wells served as county judge of the First, or Eastern District. He is a deacon in the Baptist Church at Bolckow, is a Master Mason, and until its disbandment was a member of the local post of the Grand Army of the Republic. A man of the strictest integrity and probity of character, in his dealings with his fellow men he has been guided by high ideals, and his name is one that is honored in business, political and social circles.

In 1860 Mr. Wells was united in marriage with Miss Elizabeth Richard, who was born in Macoupin County, Illinois, May 13, 1838, and when three years of age was brought to Andrew County, Missouri, by her parents, Zachary and Mary (Field) Richard. The father was born in Western Tennessee and the mother in Alabama, and following their marriage they removed to Macoupin County, Illinois, coming to Andrew County, Missouri, May 10, 1841, where both passed away after spending years in agricultural pursuits. Mrs. Wells remembers when there were only Indian trails to follow instead of the excellent roads of today, and on one occasion about 500 of the red men stopped at the Richard farm. She can relate many interesting experiences of the early days, and remembers distinctly the laying out of St. Joseph, Savannah and other places which have since grown to importance. To Mr. and Mrs. Wells there have been born the following children: Margaret Ellen, who is the wife of Israel Knuppenberger of Bolckow, and was born June 18, 1861; Lavina Jane, born February 18, 1868, who is the wife of John M. Townsend, residing two and one-half miles south of Bolckow; Samuel E., born in 1864, who died in infancy; Alzina A., born in 1865, in Putnam County, Missouri, married Charles G. Townsend, and died January 14, 1908; William H., born February 17, 1867, who died in infancy; and Emma Izella, born June 29, 1869, wife of John W. Montgomery, of Bolckow.

In 1874 Judge Wells purchased a quarter section of land in Benton Township at $30 an acre, and this land he still owns, it being valued today at $100 an acre more than he paid for it. He also has a number of good pieces of land in Bolckow, and, on the whole, has been eminently successful. His substantial position in life has been attained through the medium of his own efforts, and he is worthily entitled to be called one of the self-made men of his community.

OTTO GEHLBACH. Located four miles north of Trenton, in Lincoln Township, is found Good View Farm, which is known as one of the finest agricultural properties in Grundy County. Its owner, Otto Gehlbach, has been a resident of this community since a time when the present site of Trenton was but a cow pasture, with one building, a primitive school, standing on the property now occupied by the Farmers Store, and during the years that have passed since his arrival he has fostered this locality's interests, grown with their growth and prospered with their prosperity.

Mr. Gehlbach was born at Zweibrucken, Germany, June 18, 1848, and is a son of Jacob and Anna Mary (Mueller) Gehlbach, natives of the same place. He was granted good educational advantages in his youth, first attending the country school while assisting his father in the work of the homestead farm, and then going to an agricultural college for one and one-half years. Thus prepared, in 1867 he turned his face toward America and on his arrival here spent a short time in Pennsylvania. In the fall of 1867 he moved to Illinois, but after a short stay in that state decided to come still further west, and accordingly journeyed to Grundy County, in 1868, where he purchased 100 acres of land at a cost of $18 an acre. On this property was located a small log house, in which he made his home during the earlier years, while he was improving his

property, and in 1875 added to his original purchase 72½ acres, which
cost him $28 an acre. In 1883 he added 87½ acres and in 1891 bought
and added to the land 320 acres, a part of this property being located in
township 62, range 24, known as Lincoln Township. Subsequently Mr.
Gehlbach sold twenty acres of this land which was in timber, but still
retains 560 acres, this being considered one of the finest improved farms
in Grundy County, and comparing favorably with any in the state. In
addition to general farming, Mr. Gehlbach has been much interested in
stock raising, specializing in the very best breeds, including thoroughbred Shorthorn cattle and Percheron horses, and even in his poultry has
only the best and purest bred chickens. In his operations he has shown
himself as a man of the utmost capacity, both as an agriculturist and a
business man, and the honorable manner in which he has always carried
on his operations has given him a high standing in the esteem of his
fellow-men. He is a democrat in politics, and at various times has been
called upon to serve his community in official position. In 1892 he was
elected a trustee of Lincoln Township, which is nominally a republican
stronghold, and was re-elected to that office in 1894, also serving on the
school board for a number of years. With his family he is identified
with the Presbyterian Church, and has given that body his support in its
various movements.

Mr. Gehlbach was married in 1873 to Miss Elizabeth Wolz, a daughter
of George C. and Mary Ann (Fischer) Wolz, the father born in Wurttemburg, and the mother in Baden, Germany, while Mrs. Gehlbach is a
native of Missouri. The children born to Mr. and Mrs. Gehlbach are as
follows: Emma, who married Frank F. Butler, of Grundy County, and
has one daughter—Emma F.; Mary, who married Ray Jackson, a merchant at Garden City, Kansas; Nora; Lula, who married Charles Pennell,
of Trenton, Missouri; Albert R., who is assisting his father in the work
of the homestead, and has a diploma from the Trenton Business College;
Gustav S., a farmer and stockraiser of Howard County, Missouri, and
the owner of 220 acres of land, married Emma Lowery, and graduated
last year from the agricultural college at Columbia, Missouri; Florence,
who resides with her parents; and Charles H., who is attending the
agricultural school at the University at Columbia, Missouri, and will
graduate next year. Mr. Gehlbach is a popular member of the local
lodge of the Fraternal Order of Eagles.

J. W. ZIMMERMAN. A traveler through Andrew County, Missouri,
cannot fail being impressed with the signs of thrift and prosperity presented all through the agricultural sections, together with the genial and
hearty hospitality of the people. He may be fortunate enough to become acquainted with J. W. Zimmerman, one of the prominent and substantial citizens of Rochester Township, who owns a finely improved farm
of 166 acres, situated in section 16, which through his own efforts has
been developed from its original unproductive state. Mr. Zimmerman
is not only a successful farmer and stockraiser, but he is also a veteran
of the great Civil war, and has been a resident of Andrew County for
forty-six years.

J. W. Zimmerman was born in Highland County, Ohio, April 2, 1846,
and is a son of Samuel and Maria (Smith) Zimmerman, and a grandson
of Jacob Zimmerman, who was born in Germany and was brought to the
United States by his parents. They settled first in Maryland, moved
then to Virginia and later to Ohio, the grandfather dying in Fayette
County, that state, in his sixty-sixth year. Of his thirteen children,
eleven grew to maturity. One son, Joseph, left home to serve in the
Mexican war and was never afterward heard from. Samuel Zimmerman

was born in Virginia, November 2, 1819, and lived mainly in Ohio until he came to Andrew County, Missouri, in 1869. He lived upon his farm until 1901, after which he resided with his son, J. W., until his death, which occurred January 21, 1905. He was twice married, first to Maria Smith, and second to Mrs. Angeline (Binegar) Wilson, a widow. Mrs. Maria Zimmerman was born in Ohio, December 2, 1822, and died in that state in July, 1859. Her mother belonged to the Woodson family and married Rev. Adam Smith, a Methodist preacher, of the Kentucky Smiths, who later removed to Ohio. To the first marriage of Samuel Zimmerman, the following children were born: Alsina, who married Irving McVey, left ten children when she died; Sally, who married Elmer Welchmermer, and they now live at Washington Court House, Fayette County, Ohio; J. W.; Jacob, who is a farmer in Ohio; A. C., who is a resident of Rochester Township, Missouri; Lyda Jane, who died in 1871, was the wife of Joseph Ellis, of Fayette County, Ohio; Lizzie, who is the wife of John Aber, a blacksmith at Linden, Ohio; Charles Emery, who died in childhood; and Martha, who died in infancy. Three children were born to his second union: Effie, who is the wife of Lewis Castle, of Avenue City, Andrew County; Ettie, who is the wife of Joseph Castle, of Andrew County; and Emma, who died in infancy. Angeline Zimmerman, the second wife, died in July, 1908, at the residence of J. W. Zimmerman.

J. W. Zimmerman attended the district schools in boyhood and remained with his father on the Ohio farm until 1863, when he enlisted for service in the Civil war, entering Company G, Seventy-third Ohio Volunteer Infantry, and was in active service until the close of hostilities. He took part in all the battles and marches of his regiment, fought at Lookout Mountain and Missionary Ridge, was with Sherman's forces on the memorable march to the sea and can vividly recall the long tramp back through the Carolinas and the splendors of the great final review of the home-coming victorious troops at Washington, District of Columbia. Although he never consented to leave the regiment to be cared for, Mr. Zimmerman three times suffered bullet wounds, and no doubt a less courageous man would have considered them serious enough for hospital care. After the close of his military life he returned to Ohio.

On January 1, 1866, Mr. Zimmerman was married to Miss Mary M. Wilson, who was born in Indiana, August 14, 1850. In girlhood she had accompanied her parents to St. Clair County, Missouri, but after the death of her father, she and her mother returned East and located in Fayette County, Ohio, where she married. Following marriage, Mr. Zimmerman and wife, with the former's brother, Jacob Zimmerman, started for Missouri, driving over the prairies and finally locating near Oregon, in this state. As everything was not satisfactory, in the spring of 1868, Mr. Zimmerman and family went back to Ohio and remained there one year, in 1869 returning to Missouri and locating on the present farm in Andrew County. He recognized the value of this land and as he had no fear of not being able to develop it if given time, he borrowed the money with which to make his first payment, of $35 per acre, and it has proved a wise investment as he would not at present accept $150 an acre for any of it. He bought the farm from Samuel Ensworth, a well-known character, who subsequently died on this place, having been cared for in his old age by Mr. Zimmerman and family. General farming is carried on here, Mr. Zimmerman devoting himself to his industries very closely and making them profitable through his good judgment and practical methods. He has greatly improved his property and has every reasonable comfort and convenience.

Mr. and Mrs. Zimmerman have had seven children born to them:

Elisha, whose death, at the age of twenty-two years, was a crushing blow to the family, was a young man of bright promise and a successful school teacher; Emma Estella, who is the wife of Harry McElwain, of Helena, Andrew County; Elmer, who died at the age of four years; Arthur, who is a meat inspector for the United States Government, at St. Joseph, Missouri; Emelius and Gamelius, twins, who did not survive infancy; and a babe that also died.

Mr. Zimmerman is a well-balanced, thoughful man and keeps thoroughly posted on public questions. Until 1896 he cast his votes with the republican party, but in that year voted for Hon. William Jennings Bryan for President, and since then has used his own judgment in supporting candidates. He is a representative citizen of Andrew County.

FRANK A. JOHNSON. A resident of Andrew County since 1903, Frank A. Johnson has been engaged in agricultural pursuits in Benton Township with a full measure of success since that time, and as the owner of Maple Hill Farm has one of the nicest properties in this locality. That men of broad and varied experience are best fitted for the vocation of farming is doubted by no one familiar with the intellectual and general demands placed upon present day exponents of scientific agriculture, and especially is a knowledge of general business an important item in the equipment of those who conduct farming operations. The possession of this advantage has contributed largely to Mr. Johnson's success.

Frank A. Johnson was born in Henry County, Illinois, September 21, 1859, and is a son of Hans and Eliza (Nord) Johnson, natives of Sweden. The father, who came to the United States alone, located on a farm in Henry County, Illinois, where he was married, and there continued to be engaged in agricultural pursuits during the remainder of his life, passing away about the year 1865, when he was forty-two years of age. Mrs. Johnson, who survived her husband until June, 1910, and was seventy years of age at the time of her demise, came to the United States and to Illinois with her parents, when she was eleven years of age. She was a daughter of John Nord, who located in Henry County, and who was twice married, having three children by each wife. One of Mrs. Johnson's brothers, John M. Nord, served as a Union soldier during the Civil war and is now retired and a resident of Nebraska, while a stepbrother, Charles Johnson, was also a soldier in that struggle and is now a resident of California. Mrs. Johnson was married a second time, after the death of her first husband, to Charles Peterson, and by each union had six children, Frank A. being the third child by her first marriage. Charles Peterson served in the Civil war three years.

Frank A. Johnson was something more than five years of age when his father died, and he was largely reared by his stepfather who sent him to the public schools of Henry County, Illinois. There he assisted Mr. Peterson in the work of the homestead until 1889, in which year he went to Wayne County, Nebraska, where he spent some fifteen years. Mr. Johnson came to Andrew County, Missouri, in March, 1903, selling his 240-acre Nebraska farm, and here purchasing a property of 445 acres, on which he has put three separate sets of modern farm improvements, of the most highly approved character. He has devoted himself to the raising of grain and the growing of livestock, and each year feeds three cars of cattle and two cars of hogs. Maple Hill Farm is named from the maple grove about the home, which is situated on an elevation, giving an excellent view of the country for miles around. This is mostly valley or bottom land, a rich sandy loam which yields bumper crops. Mr. Johnson keeps fully abreast of the times in his calling, and is skilled in the use of the most modern methods and machinery. He has established a reputation not only as a good and practical agriculturist, but as a man of the highest integrity, whose fidelity to engagements and straightforward dealing have won the confidence of his associates. A democrat in his political views, he has not been an office seeker, but has always been anxious to do his part as a good citizen. He is a Master Mason and a member of the Modern Woodmen of America, and his religious connection is with the Christian Church at Bolckow.

On August 15, 1889, Mr. Johnson was united in marriage with Miss Mary C. Classman, who was born at McGregor, Clayton County, Iowa, May 9, 1871, a daughter of Henry and Caroline (Helming) Classman, natives of Germany, who were born near Hanover. Mrs. Classman came to the United States at the age of eighteen years, while her husband was twenty-five years old at the time of his arrival, and they were married at Clinton, Iowa. After a long career passed in agricultural pursuits, Mr. Classman died June 21, 1908, at Wayne, Nebraska, at the age of seventy years, and Mrs. Classman still makes her home there, being now seventy years old.

Three sons and six daughters have been born to Mr. and Mrs. Johnson, all of whom are living except one: Frank E., who is the proprietor of an automobile garage at Bolckow, Missouri; Blanche R., who is the wife of Lyle Chamberlain, of Dwyer, Wyoming; Grace E., who resides with her parents; Laverne; Mary; Sadie; Loren; Royal and Jennie. Mr. and Mrs. Johnson have one granddaughter: Mary Louise Johnson.

CAPT. ISAAC B. BAKER. During a long lifetime, most of it spent in Hardin Township of Clinton County, Capt. Isaac B. Baker has accomplished those things which are considered most worth while by ambitious men—years of honorable activity in business, with satisfying material reward, the esteem of his fellow men, and a public spirited share in the social and civic life of his community. Captain Baker gained his title by gallant service as an officer during the Civil war on the Confederate side, and the qualities which enabled him to fight a good fight in that struggle between the states have been exemplified in his career as a farmer and stock man, and as a good citizen.

Isaac B. Baker was born December 28, 1837, in Bracken County, Kentucky, a son of Isaac Baker. Isaac Baker was a native of Virginia, and the son of a Tennessee pioneer who served as a soldier in the War of 1812. Isaac Baker, Sr., with his brother, Abram Baker, took a very prominent part in the very early industrial activities of St. Joseph, where they built the first packing house west of St. Louis. In the early years when the Missouri River was the outskirts of civilization and the central point where the great supply trains of the West met the markets of the East, they operated their packery to supply Government transportation trains and the large parties of emigrants departing for the gold fields of California. It was for a number of years one of the leading institutions of St. Joseph. These brothers besides their packing plant owned about three thousand acres of land in Northwest Missouri and had large herds of cattle and were among the leading moneyed men of this section. Abram finally took his share of the business and returned to Kentucky, but Isaac remained in Northwest Missouri and lived on his large plantation in Clinton County, where he had extensive slave quarters and did business on a large scale. Isaac Baker married Elizabeth Hutchinson, who was born in Kentucky. Their thirteen children were: Captain John F., who died in St. Louis at the age of eighty-six; Dr. J. S., a well-known physician now deceased; Henry B., a retired business man; Martha, wife of Rev. Joseph Hopkins; Iliza J., who lives in the West, wife of G. W. Guyon; Abram Baker, who died in Clinton County; Mrs.

Elizabeth Lang, deceased, who was the wife of G. W. Lang; Minerva, who died at the age of eighty-eight in Logan County, Kentucky; Captain Isaac B.; James, a well-known citizen of Clinton County; Mrs. Helen Moore; George H., who lives with his brother, Captain Isaac; Jesse, of Kansas City. The father died at the age of eighty-seven years. He was a broad-minded and successful business man, liberal in all things, and was one of the finest examples of the old slave-holding aristocracy in Missouri. He was a member of the Methodist Episcopal Church South. For many years the Baker homestead was noted for its hospitality, and friends and strangers were entertained there on the lavish scale characteristic of older times.

Capt. Isaac B. Baker was reared on the old plantation, and a young man at the outbreak of the war enlisted in the Confederate service and became a member of Company M, in the Third Kentucky Infantry, under Col. J. T. Hughes. His regiment was with the command under Gen. Joseph Johnston, and also with Gen. John Morgan, and during the Ohio expedition Captain Baker was captured. For gallant service on the field of battle he was promoted from private in the ranks to captain of a company, and is now one of the few surviving Confederate officers still living in this section of Missouri.

After the war he returned home and engaged in the more peaceful pursuits of agriculture and stock raising, and his activities in that line are well known to the people of Clinton County. In 1866 he married Frances D. Stoutimore, a sister of D. L. Stoutimore of Plattsburg, and further details concerning this well-known old family will be found on other pages of this work. Mrs. Baker was a daughter of Josiah and Amelia (Lincoln) Stouteman. Captain Baker has two children: Jefferson Davis, who is prominent as a farmer and cattle raiser in Clinton County, with a place of 550 acres; and Margaret, wife of C. Gryson of Bates County, and they have a child, John C. Gryson.

Captain Baker now lives on his farm of 224 acres, which in its improvements and its long associations with the substantial agricultural activities of the county stands as one of the best known and most valuable places. Captain Baker has lived a long life of seventy-five years, and while always positive in his convictions and vigorous in his activities has lived a life of honor among men.

SAMUEL CROWLEY. More than three-quarters of a century have passed since Samuel Crowley first took up his residence in Andrew County, and here his life has been passed in the pursuits of the soil. He has been successful in the accumulation of a large body of land in Jefferson Township, and his personal influence and financial stability are the result of patient application to farming, prudent investment and the habit of always living within his income. Mr. Crowley was born May 21, 1830, five miles from Excelsior Springs, Clay County, Missouri, and is a son of Samuel and Sarah (Macinnich) Crowley.

John Crowley, the grandfather of Samuel Crowley, was born in England, from whence he emigrated to America during Colonial days, and took up his residence in Ray County, Georgia, where he passed his active years in the pursuits of agriculture. He was married twice and reared a large family, and in his declining years moved to the home of one of his children in Clay County, Missouri, where he died in 1847. Samuel Crowley, father of Samuel of this review, was born near Savannah, Georgia, in June, 1794, and migrated to Howard County, Missouri, with his brother, Jerry Crowley, at a time when the state was still the home of hostile tribes of Indians, the white settlers for the most part living at forts under the protection of the soldiers. Later he moved on to Clay

County, locating in the vicinity of Excelsior Springs, but in the spring of 1837 came to Andrew County and pre-empted the land on which his son Samuel now lives. That year he grew a crop, and in the same fall his family joined him, his wife dying here in 1848. Mr. Crowley resided in Andrew County until about the close of the Civil war, when he went to Oregon, and there died at the home of one of his children, in April, 1877. An excellent business man and an industrious worker, he accumulated about 600 acres of land, and was known as one of the substantial men of his community. He served during the War of 1812 and fought under Stonewall Jackson. In politics a democrat, he was influential in the ranks of his party in this part of the state, and was appointed by the governor as presiding judge of the Andrew County Court, which was held at that time under an old elm tree, there being no court-house. This office Mr. Crowley held for two or three terms, and during this time named the City of Savannah in honor of the place of his birth in Georgia. He and his wife were the parents of twelve children, as follows: James, who for many years was a farmer in Andrew County and died a bachelor when past fifty-seven years of age; Louise, who married Willis Gaines and crossed the plains to the Pacific coast in 1852 in an ox-team, her subsequent life being spent in Oregon, where she died; Jane, who died in Colorado as the wife of Dean B. Holman, also crossed the plains in 1852; Matilda, who was married the first time to Elvis Sloan and second to James Shields, and died in California; John W., who was a member of the party which crossed to the coast, contracted mountain fever on the journey, from the effects of which he died; Louisa, who died in Oregon as the wife of William Hudson; Mary Ann, who married Francis M. Holman, a brother of Dean B., and died in California; George Washington, who died in Jefferson Township, Andrew County, married Maggie Dysart, of Andrew County; Benjamin Franklin, who died at the age of two years; Samuel, of this review; Thomas McClain, who died in Jefferson Township, married Elizabeth Smith, of Suisun City, Solano County, California; and Susan, who married Judge John L. Stanton, and died at Oregon, Missouri.

Samuel Crowley, who is the only one of his parents' twelve children still living, has resided in Andrew County, Missouri, all of his life with the exception of the period when he was crossing the plains and in the West during the excitement over the discovery of gold in California and the resultant rush to that state. He received a good public school education, and when he reached manhood adopted farming as his life's vocation, and in this has continued to be engaged to the present time. At this time Mr. Crowley is the owner of about one thousand acres of land, much of which he has himself put under cultivation, although a large part has been gained through wise investment and the exercise of foresight and good judgment. At the age of eighty-four years he is still active in body and alert in mind and is able to manage his large affairs himself, although he has an able assistant in his nephew, Samuel W. Crowley, named for him, and who has a son, also named Samuel.

Mr. Crowley has never married. He has been a democrat in politics all of his life, but has not been an office seeker, preferring to devote his activities to the peaceful pursuits of farming and stockraising. For many years he has been connected with the Masonic fraternity, and has many friends in that order, as he has in business and agricultural circles of Andrew County.

HON. WILLIAM DALE. While his long and busy career has been devoted primarily to the vocation of farming, Hon. William Dale, of Rochester Township, has found the time, inclination and ability to serve his community faithfully in high public offices, and his record both in public and private life is such as to fully entitle him to the respect and esteem in which he is held. Mr. Dale is a native of Dane County, Wisconsin, and was born February 16, 1869, a son of Edward and Elizabeth (Rowe) Dale, natives of Cornwall, England, where the father was born March 28, 1822, and the mother July 30, 1822. Mrs. Dale was the oldest of her parents' children, and with them migrated to Canada, settling in the City of Toronto, where she married Mr. Dale. In 1847 they moved to Wisconsin, securing land from the United States Government near Blue Mound, Dane County, and in 1852 Mr. Dale left his pioneer farm and joined the adventurous throng which made its way tortuously across the great sandy plains to the land of promise in California. There he spent two years in gold mining, with some measure of success, and at the end of that time returned to his Wisconsin home by way of the Isthmus and New York. He was engaged in farming until in 1862, in which year he enlisted for service in the Union Army, serving under General Thomas with a captain's commission in the commissary department, and participated in the battles of Chattanooga and Chickamauga. He remained in the service until 1866, and had an excellent record as a soldier, being brevetted major at the time of his discharge and then returning again to his farm. In 1866 Mr. Dale came to Missouri and located on a farm in sections 5 and 8, Rochester Township, Andrew County, purchasing 400 acres of land, which had been partly fenced, and on which there was a log house. Here he passed the remainder of his life, engaged in the pursuits of the soil, and died in September, 1869, Mrs. Dale surviving until January, 1911. Mr. Dale was a hard and industrious worker, and during his life was successful in the accumulation of a handsome property. In addition to general farming, he was largely occupied in feeding stock, branding his cattle and turning them loose over the prairie. A republican in his political views, he stood high in the confidence of the people, and at the time of his death was serving as county judge of Andrew County. He was an active and valued member of the local post of the Grand Army of the Republic. To Mr. and Mrs. Dale there were born the following children: Jane E., the widow of Horace A. Woodbury, of Rochester Township, residing on a part of the old home place; Sarah, who is the wife of N. Zink, of Nebraska; Edward J.; Emma, a resident of Oklahoma; Kate, who died at the age of ten years; Mary A., who is the wife of A. J. Holt, of Stanberry, Missouri; and William.

William Dale has been a resident of his present property ever since he was brought to Missouri by his parents. He was given fair educational advantages, attending both the country schools and the high school at Savannah, and for four or five years was engaged in teaching school during the winter months. He is now the owner of 230 acres, the most of which is a part of the old homestead, and here he has erected fine buildings and made many substantial improvements. This may be said to be a stock farm, and Mr. Dale raises and feeds thoroughbred Shorthorn cattle and Duroc Jersey hogs. The farm, which is known as Inwood Dale, is possessed of a fine grove of locust trees, also thirty-five acres of oak and elm forest.

Mr. Dale is one of the republican leaders of his county, being at present chairman of the County Central Committee, and in public life is known as a conscientious and honorable official. He served very capably for two years in the capacity of county judge, and was subsequently elected to the lower house of the State Legislature, gaining much prestige through the able manner in which he looked after the interests of his community and his constituency. Fraternally, Judge Dale is affiliated with the Masons and the Modern Woodmen of America. His religious faith, and that of his family, is that of the Methodist Episcopal Church.

Judge Dale was married in September, 1884, to Margaretta Millen, who was born in Gentry County, Missouri, August 6, 1861, and came to Andrew County, Missouri, in 1865, with her parents, Andrew G. and Sarah Elizabeth (White) Millen, the former a native of Kentucky and the latter of Morgan County, Illinois. Both died in 1877, at Savannah, Missouri, the father being fifty-three years of age and the mother forty-eight. They were married in Illinois, where Mr. Millen was a railroad man, but after coming to Missouri, in 1857, engaged in farming. Four children have been born to Judge and Mrs. Dale, as follows: Harry Edward; Sarah Elizabeth, who died at the age of five months; Dorothy M., and Esther J.

W. H. LILE. The business possibilities and advantages of country life in Northwest Missouri are capable of no better illustration than in the enterprise of W. H. Lile, a farmer and stock man and stock dealer, whose home is in Lincoln Township of Caldwell County. The Lile farm comprises 450 acres of highly improved land, and is located midway between Cowgill and Polo. In that section of country are few farms that compare with it in value and excellence of management. Mr. Lile usually keeps about a hundred head of cattle and four hundred hogs, and is one of the largest buyers and shippers in Caldwell County. His home is an unusually attractive place, a residence of nine rooms, situated on a well selected building site, and surrounded by a blue grass lawn, shade trees, orchard, and with ample barns and cattle sheds. Mr. Lile cultivates a large acreage of corn and other grains, and though his training has been an intensely practical one, he follows the best methods of farm and animal husbandry.

W. H. Lile was born in Missouri February 6, 1855, was reared on a farm, and has been acquainted with the details of its management by practical experience since boyhood. His father was Henry W. Lile, who was born in Tennessee, June 11, 1811, and married Elizabeth King, who was born in Kentucky of an old family in that state in 1827. There were five children, two of whom are deceased, while the three living are: Wiley, who served as a soldier in the Union Army during the Civil war; W. H.; and Martha Elizabeth, whose home is in Camden, Missouri. The father died February 9, 1873, at the age of sixty-two. Throughout his active career he had prospered as a farmer and stock man.

W. H. Lile received his education from the public schools, and learned the lessons of industry and honesty and has always practiced them and that has been a contributing source of his success. In 1881 Mr. Lile was married in Ray County to Jessie A. Kinkaid, who was born, reared and educated in that county, daughter of Frank L. Kinkaid. Mrs. Lile's mother is still living in this county at the age of eighty-one. Mr. Lile is a democrat, and is affiliated with the Cowgill Lodge No. 557 of the Masonic fraternity. He is a man of strong and vigorous physique, of frank and genial temperament and his home is a recognized center of substantial hospitality in Caldwell County.

WILLIAM L. CHAFFIN, M. D. Representing the first class ability and skill of his profession and with a large general practice, Doctor Chaffin is one of the young physicians and surgeons of Breckenridge who have quickly taken front rank in their profession. He began practice with an excellent equipment, and the test of real practice found him qualified for this important service to society.

Dr. William L. Chaffin was born at Breckenridge, Missouri, April 28, 1881. His father, John H. Chaffin, is a carpenter and contractor, and was born at Roanoke, Virginia, of an old Virginia family. He married M. Trosler, whose parents came from Kentucky. Besides Doctor Chaffin the parents had these children: O. L., a farmer and stock man; R. E., in the merchandise business; James lives at Lock Spring; and Eugene L. is a teacher.

Dr. William L. Chaffin was reared in Breckenridge, attended the public schools, finished the high school course, and in 1908 entered the Bennett Medical College of Chicago, where he continued his medical studies until graduating as one of the leaders in his class in 1912. With this preparation Doctor Chaffin returned to Breckenridge, and has since been favored with a large general practice. His offices are in the Post-office Building, and he is one of the few physicians who have the X-ray apparatus, and his other equipment and library indicate his thorough preparation for his work and his ambition to keep in close touch with modern advances made in the same. He is a member of the Caldwell County Medical Society.

Louis W. Reed. A member of the Caldwell County bar since 1909, L. W. Reed possesses and has exercised qualities that are not far from brilliant, and in a community where he grew up from childhood, where he knows everybody and everybody knows him, has securely established a reputation for ability as a lawyer and has started on a public career which his friends believe will carry him far in local and state politics. Mr. Reed has been continuously in the office of mayor of Breckenridge since 1908, and in that time has done much to make the town a good place to live, and also a center of increasing commercial activity. Mr. Reed is also president of the Commercial Club of Breckenridge. In 1912, after an exciting campaign and against a normal republican majority in Caldwell County, he was elected to the office of county attorney of Caldwell County and the county has had no more vigorous and effective official in that position for a number of years.

Louis W. Reed comes of a family which has been identified with this section of Missouri since pioneer days. He was born in Daviess County, on a farm a few miles north of Breckenridge, on July 6, 1878. His father was the late Thomas W. Reed, a Kentuckian by birth, came to Northwest Missouri in the early days, and had to clear up a portion of the land and make a farm, and spent the years of a long life as an industrious farmer and a citizen of more than ordinary influence. He married Abigail Dewey, who was born and educated in Indiana, and is a relative of the Dewey family which gave to the American nation Admiral George Dewey, the hero of Manila Bay. Mrs. Reed is still living, a venerable and lovable old lady, and keeps her home with her son Louis, at Breckenridge. Thomas W. Reed died in 1901 at the age of eighty-two. He had for a number of years been prominent in democratic politics, and served in the office of county judge. Of the seven children, most of them are still living in Northwest Missouri, and are people of prominence. Thomas P. Reed, one of the oldest, is a farmer in Daviess County, and one of the most successful men as an agriculturist and stock raiser in the vicinity of Breckenridge. Another son is Phil Reed, a prominent business man of Cameron. Dr. Charles W. Reed, the brother next older than Louis, is a graduate of the medical department of Washington University at St. Louis, and for the past seven years has practiced with growing success and prestige in Grand Junction, Colorado.

Louis W. Reed grew up in Breckenridge, was educated in the local high school, and largely dependent upon his own resources has secured a thorough education and has a broad and accurate knowledge of the law. Mr. Reed was a student in the Missourian Wesleyan College at

Cameron, and in his early days excelled as an athlete, especially in baseball.

Mr. Reed has served four terms as mayor of Breckenridge. He is affiliated with the Independent Order of Odd Fellows and has filled a number of positions in fraternal orders, was elected president of the Commercial Club in 1912, and is a member of the Methodist Church. Louis W. Reed is still a young man, and with a thorough foundation as a lawyer has the ability to push himself into a larger life of the state. He possesses a ready wit, and the eloquence of the born orator, is acquainted with men and with practical politics, and has all the direct and wholesome qualities which make for success in modern politics.

Dr. W. A. Long. A veteran of the Civil war, Dr. W. A. Long has spent over forty years in Northwest Missouri, in the vicinity of Mound City in Holt County, and has had a long and active career as a soldier, dentist, farmer and as a good citizen. He is perhaps one of the best known men in both Holt County and Northwest Missouri, one of the landmarks of his community, and has always enjoyed the high esteem of every place in which a portion of his life has been spent.

Dr. W. A. Long was born in Franklin County, Pennsylvania, January 22, 1837, a son of David and Mary (Shoemaker) Long. His parents were married in Pennsylvania, and his father was descended from Scotch stock and his mother from Dutch people. The Doctor was one of their seven children, of whom four are still living. The father and mother spent their lives in Pennsylvania, the former a farmer.

Doctor Long acquired his education in Pennsylvania, and in early manhood, in 1862, went out to fight the battles of the Union with the One Hundred and Fiftieth Pennsylvania Infantry, but was discharged at Harrisburg, Pennsylvania, in October, 1863, on account of ill health. Previous to his military career he had taken up photography as a profession, at a time when the old daguerreotype and ambrotype were in the height of their popularity and represented the farthest advance of photography at that time. But after the war Doctor Long turned his attention to the study of dentistry, took a course at Baltimore, and began practice at Philadelphia, later practicing in several different places. In 1872 he came to Northwest Missouri, and has since been successfully identified with this section as a dentist and as a farmer. He owns 240 acres of land, which he rents, his son, William E., assisting in its operation. During the past fifteen years the doctor has been practically retired from his profession, and he resides on his estate near Mound City, which has been his home since 1872. He has made many of the improvements which classify his farm as one of the best in the county.

Doctor Long first married, in Franklin County, Pennyslvania, Elizabeth Swanger, a daughter of Henry Swanger. She died a few years after the birth of her children, who are also deceased. After coming to Northwest Missouri Doctor Long married Anna Meyer Griffith, who was born and reared in Holt County, a daughter of one of the distinguished old citizens, Judge Andrew Meyer, who lived to near the age of ninety years, and was active until two years before his death. By her first husband Mrs. Long had one child, Maud B., who is the wife of Leslie Thompson, of Oklahoma, both of whom were reared and married in Holt County. They have five children, two daughters and three sons. Mrs. Long's first husband was a farmer, and came to Northwest Missouri from Virginia. Mrs. Long's people were of German stock, and her father was a prosperous farmer, and was also judge of the County Court. As one of the early settlers in Northwest Missouri he went out with the troops from this section to the Mexican war, having been one of the first to enlist and one of the last to leave the ranks. He was a whig in politics, and in addition to serving a number of years as county judge was also a member of the school board. He was reared a Lutheran, but subsequently became a member of the Presbyterian Church, in which Dr. and Mrs. Long are also active members. Doctor Long and wife have two sons. The elder, Dr. Thomas Long, married Alice Patterson, and they have three children: Adessa, who married B. M. Terhune, and has a son, John; Fannie, who married A. J. Wells; and Gothe, who married R. E. Cottier and has a daughter, Elizabeth. The younger son of Doctor and Mrs. Long, William Ellis Long, is unmarried and living at home. Both sons were born in Holt County. Doctor Long is a democrat, and has had affiliation with the Independent Order of Odd Fellows for more than half a century.

JOHN C. BAGBY. To Mr. Bagby belongs the honor of being a native son of Holt County, and having spent all his life in one community he has many pleasant associations with the country and its people, and has won that esteem which is paid to prosperous and right living. He owns one of the large farms near Mound City, and the name Bagby has for many years been identified with large land holding and agricultural activities.

John C. Bagby was born in Holt County June 13, 1866, a son of Richard R. Bagby. His father was an early settler in Holt County. His original home was Kentucky, from which state he migrated with wagon and team, spent a time in Illinois, and then came to Buchanan County, Missouri. He took up land in Buchanan County, but left it and homesteaded about two miles east of where his son John C. now lives. Mr. Richard Bagby's brother James also homesteaded 160 acres in the same locality. The first home they put up for their family was a log cabin, and it was necessary to contend with many difficulties before the land was fenced and brought under cultivation. During the war Richard Bagby moved to Nebraska and spent a couple of years in that state, but then returned to Holt County and steadily followed his vocation as an agriculturist until the death of his wife. He had married Margaret J. Gibson, and their marriage was celebrated in Holt County. To their union were born eight children, and the three now living are: Sallie M., the widow of Chester C. Fuller; Ella M., widow of Frank Zachary; and John C. All the children were born in Holt County. Both parents were members of the Christian Church and were upright people and good neighbors. The father had come to Holt County with very limited capital, and for the first ten years had employed much of his time in work for others at $10 a month. Possessing good habits, thrift and industry, he steadily prospered, and now at the age of eighty-four looks back upon a career which has covered both the pioneer and modern activities of Northwest Missouri, and among the substantial rewards of his life was the accumulation of an aggregate of 1,400 acres of land, all of which represented his own industry and business ability, and a large part of which has since been sold or distributed among his children. Throughout his life he has been noted as a man who never uses profane language.

John C. Bagby grew up in Holt County, had his schooling in the brief months when work on the farm was slack, and has been successful without higher training than that given by the country schools. He lived at home and helped his father until his marriage to Flora Anselment, a daughter of Charles Anselment. They were among the early settlers, and her grandfather had the first grist mill in Holt County. Mr. and Mrs. Bagby have three children: Lucile, Blanche and Sallie, all of whom were born in this county. Blanche married Ray

Cardinell, and has two children, Thomas and Elizabeth. Lucile married Fred Burk. Mr. Bagby has lived on his present estate since 1893, at which time he bought the land in an improved condition and has since increased it to an aggregate of 400 acres, all of it under cultivation except forty-five or fifty acres. He has gone ahead with the improvements, has erected a good house and barns and several outbuildings, and has one of the most attractive farmsteads in the vicinity of Mound City. Mr. Bagby is a member of the Christian Church and in politics is a democrat, the same political allegiance as his father.

E. L. SCHNEIDER. One of the sterling citizens and prominent business men of Avenue City is Emil L. Schneider, proprietor of a general store here, owner of a fine farm in Jefferson Township, and a member of the board of directors of the Farmers and Traders Bank of St. Joseph, Missouri. He was born three miles southeast of Avenue City, in Monroe Township, Andrew County, Missouri, November 15, 1868, and is a son of Frederick and Elizabeth (Schindler) Schneider. The father was born in Switzerland, in September, 1839, a son of Christopher Schneider, and accompanied his parents to the United States when thirteen years of age.

Christian Schneider located in Monroe Township, Andrew County, Missouri, on the farm on which his grandson, Emil L., was born many years later, and there spent the rest of his life. Frederick Schneider followed farming on the large tract his father had bought and was one of the five sons to be given a farm. He died there August 29, 1911. He married Elizabeth Schindler, who was born in Ohio and had accompanied her parents to Andrew County, in childhood. After she became a widow she removed to St. Joseph and now lives there with a daughter. There were ten children in the family: Rosetta, who is the wife of Stephen Hug, of Holton, Kansas; Anna, who is the wife of Charles Ritter, of Rochester Township; Pauline, who is the widow of Frank Heggeman, of St. Joseph, Missouri; Harry H., who is a merchant of Crosby, Missouri; L. F., who is a farmer in Jefferson Township; W. G., who is a resident of Denver, Colorado; Oscar C., who remains on the home farm; Flora, who is the wife of Henry Bolliger, of Monroe Township; Frederick, who died at the age of four years; and Emil L., who was the second born.

Emil L. Schneider remained with his father until he was twenty-one years of age, in the meanwhile attending the country schools. Afterward he was a student for two years in the Chillicothe Normal School, where he was graduated in 1892. Finding his tastes ran in the direction of a mercantile life, Mr. Schneider then entered a general store at St. Joseph, where he continued until January 1, 1895, when he embarked in his present business at Avenue City. He carries a very complete assortment of general merchandise, including agricultural implements, everything a farmer needs being found in his stock. He has a large trade, partly on this account, but largely because of his accommodating manner and honorable business methods.

Mr. Schneider was married April 7, 1896, to Miss Emma Ritter, who was born in Monroe Township, Andrew County, and is a daughter of Joseph Ritter. They have three children: Leola, Russell and Louis. Mr. Schneider is giving his children many advantages. With his family he belongs to the German Reformed Church at Cosby, and all are active and interested in the Sunday school. He takes no very active part in

GEORGE P. HARTMAN. A mile and a half west and half a mile south of the Village of Cosby, in section 10 of Monroe Township, Andrew County, is located the fine dairy farm known as the Holstein Dairy Farm. Its proprietor is George P. Hartman, who has spent practically all his life in Andrew County, and of whose success as a dairyman and general farmer the best proof is in the fine establishment he has built up in the last twenty or twenty-five years. He is one of the best known citizens of Monroe Township, and likewise one of the most successful.

George P. Hartman was born half a mile west of his present farm on January 29, 1865. His family has been identified with Andrew County for more than half a century. His parents were Charles W. and Ellen Nora (Shanka) Hartman, his father a native of Indianapolis and his mother of Virginia. They were brought to Northwest Missouri when children, grew up and were married in Andrew County, and both passed away in this locality. The father died October 20, 1889, at the age of sixty-seven, and the mother was at the same age when she died on June 6, 1896. Charles W. Hartman started out with his only possession a horse, and yet long before the end of his life had acquired a property of about five hundred acres in Andrew County. He was a member of the Baptist Church and a democrat in politics. In the family were eight sons and two daughters, named as follows: Harvey, who died at the age of seventeen; John Wesley, who died in 1908; William, who died in 1899; Leander Jackson, who lives in Buchanan County; Catherine, widow of John Kelley of Monroe Township; Lucinda Jane, wife of Nathaniel Lewis of DeKalb County; James Daniel, of DeKalb County; Oscar, of Flag Springs, Andrew County; George P.; and Charles, who lives in St. Joseph.

George P. Hartman grew up in Monroe Township, received his education in the public schools, and after a training as a boy on the farm was ready for an independent career as soon as he reached his majority. Mr. Hartman owns 165 acres of land in his farm, and runs a fine dairy, his herd numbering about fifty head of high grade Holstein cattle. He has his barn equipped with all the modern facilities for dairying, and separates the cream and sells it through the Cosby Creamery to the St. Joseph market. Besides Holstein cattle he makes a specialty of Hampshire hogs, and keeps about sixty-five head. He has his farm equipped with four barns and two houses, and all these improvements have been placed there since Mr. Hartman took possession of the land.

Mr. Hartman is a democrat, and is affiliated with the Masonic Lodge at Cosby. In 1901 he married Miss Lillian Kelley. She was born in Monroe Township, Andrew County, in 1870, a daughter of Frank and Lydia Kelley of this county. Mr. and Mrs. Hartman are the parents of two children, Viola and Elsie.

JAMES A. SLADE. Prominent among the men who are ably representing the farming interests of Andrew County is found James A. Slade, proprietor of Fairview Farm, a handsome tract of land lying in Rochester Township. Mr. Slade is well known to the people of his locality, where he has spent his entire life, and bears the reputation of being a business man of sterling integrity and a citizen who is always found favoring advancement in any direction. He was born on his father's farm, one mile south of Helena, in Rochester Township, January 6, 1861, and is a son of William W. P. and Isabella (McDonald) Slade.

The Slade family is of Scotch-Irish descent, and has been in America from colonial times. John Slade, the grandfather of James A. Slade, was a son of John Slade, a Revolutionary soldier, participated himself in the War of 1812 and saw service in the battle of New Orleans, under

Jackson, and his only brother, Thomas Slade, was killed in the naval engagement in Chesapeake Bay, in 1813. James A. Slade's maternal great-grandfather was Maj. John Cartmell, a well-known officer of the Revolution. William W. P. Slade was born near Franklin, Bedford County, Tennessee, August 4, 1825, and was four years of age when his parents brought him to Lafayette County, Missouri. There he was reared and educated, and was living on his father's farm when the Mexican war commenced, and he at once enlisted for service under General Lanigan, continuing in the service for two years. He then returned to Andrew County, whence his father had preceded him, and here he entered two farms, comprising 164 acres, in the cultivation of which he was engaged during the remainder of his active life. In his declining years he retired from activity and moved to Helena, Missouri, where his death occurred March 24, 1912. Mrs. Slade, who was born in Indiana, March 10, 1826, died on the farm, March 9, 1899. Mr. Slade played an active part in local events during the Civil war, he serving all through that struggle as a member of the Twelfth Missouri Cavalry, his term expiring April 6, 1866. Later he went on expeditions against the Sioux Indians, and remained in the regular army, being appointed by Governor Fletcher as drillmaster and recruiting officer. He drilled the Ninety-seventh Missouri Cavalry, the drill grounds being near his home, and a large part of his life was devoted to military matters. A democrat in politics, he served at times as justice of the peace, township collector, school director and a member of various commissions. He was an elder in the Cumberland Presbyterian Church from the time of his eighteenth year until his death.

The children born to William W. P. and Isabella (McDonald) Slade were as follows: T. D., who met his death in a railroad accident, June 26, 1903, leaving a widow and five daughters; Sophia, who is the wife of J. F. Beeler, of Helena; Betty, who is the wife of Albert Wilkerson, of Union Township; Mary S., who is the wife of A. J. Mathersead, of Wallace, Nebraska; Susie, a resident of Helena; John, a wealthy and prominent farmer of Andrew County; James A., of this review; Abbie, who is the wife of L. D. Fisher, of Union Station; R. W., who is in the United States Secret Service, and is located at Denver, Colorado; and two children who died in infancy.

James A. Slade secured a public school education, and while he has always been engaged in farming, he was also for twenty-three years engaged in teaching school, becoming well and prominently known as an educator in Buchanan and Andrew counties. At this time he is the owner of a farm of 135½ acres, one-half mile south of Helena, which is, under a high state of cultivation, and which he devotes to general farming, the raising of hay and grain, and the breeding of a fine strain of livestock. Here he has erected modern, substantial buildings, including a comfortable eight-room house, and has his own water and light works. He is a good agriculturist, using practical and modern methods, and in business circles his name is honored on commercial paper. In politics Mr. Slade is a democrat, his religious faith is that of the Presbyterian Church, and fraternally he is connected with the Masons, the Odd Fellows and the Knights of Pythias.

On June 29, 1910, Mr. Slade was married to Miss Ella Bermond, who was born March 19, 1866, in Buchanan County, Missouri, a daughter of George and Martha (Castle) Bermond, he a native of France and she of Missouri. He was an early settler of Missouri, and both he and his wife died on their farm in Buchanan County. Mr. and Mrs. Slade have had no children.

BOURTER LEGG. Among the old and honored residents of Grundy County, Missouri, one who has long held a substantial place in the community is Bourter Legg, who is now living retired at Tindall, after many profitable years passed in agricultural pursuits. Mr. Legg was born in Pickaway County, Ohio, January 29, 1834, and is a son of Seldon and Rachael (Deckard) Legg, natives of Virginia.

Bourter Legg was a child when his parents removed from their Ohio home to Edgar County, Illinois, and there he received his education in the country schools while growing to manhood on his father's farm. In 1855 he came to Grundy County, Missouri, purchasing forty acres of prairie land at prices ranging from three to five dollars per acre, and so well were his labors prosecuted during the years that followed that he became the owner of 520 acres of land. At the time of his retirement he divided this property equally among his five children, who still retain and operate it. At the present time Mr. Legg is living in retirement at Tindall, although he still has extensive interests under his supervision, including 101 building lots. He was at all times known as a practical and progressive farmer, whose operations not only brought him a handsome competence but also served to advance the development of the community. While he was shrewd and businesslike, never neglecting an opportunity to add to his holdings, his transactions were carried on in a strictly honorable manner, and he never advanced himself by taking advantage of another's misfortune. Thus it is that he is held in high esteem by those who have had dealings with him.

Not long after arriving in Missouri, in 1855, Mr. Legg enlisted for service in the Union army during the Civil war, as a member of the Fourth Regiment, Provisional Missouri State Militia, from Tindall, Grundy County. He was subject to call throughout the war and was mustered out of the service in 1864, with the rank of third sergeant. He has never lost interest in the affairs of his old army comrades, and still retains his membership in the Grand Army of the Republic. Mr. Legg's three brothers, William, Mathias and Elijah, all served in the Union army, enlisting from Edgar County, Illinois, and the last-named endured the hardships and privations of Andersonville Prison, in which he was confined for fifteen months after his capture by the Confederates. Mr. Legg is a republican in his political views, and at various times has been called upon to serve his fellow-citizens in offices both at Tindall and in the country, and his official record is that of a conscientious and capable public servant. He is a devout member of the Baptist Church, in the faith of which all his children were reared.

In 1864 Mr. Legg was united in marriage with Miss Cemira Woods, daughter of Jarvis and Amanda (DeVaul) Woods, natives of Ray County, Missouri, of German and Welsh descent. Mrs. Legg has two brothers living at Edinburg, Missouri, and one in Trenton. Of the five children born to Mr. and Mrs. Legg four are living: Rachel, wife of J. W. Tracy, of Tindall, Missouri, and they have one daughter, Miss Venice Tracy, now a teacher in the Trenton public schools; Marion, who married Miss Mollie Tracy, daughter of Nathan and Addie Tracy, has two children: Miss Cleatis Legg, a student in the Trenton high school, and Agel, a son attending school at Tindall, Missouri; Annie, wife of Fred Thompson, of Des Moines, Iowa; Dr. Grace O'Doan, who is engaged in the practice of medicine in Des Moines is a daughter of Mrs. Thompson by a former marriage; Jennie, wife of W. R. Crockett, a successful business man of Trenton, Missouri, their daughter, Miss Willie Lee, being a student in the Trenton high school; Mrs. Minta Legg Jordan, youngest daughter of Mr. and Mrs. Bourter Legg, died in Kansas City in 1910, leaving a

husband and two children, Helen and Donald, who are attending school
in Vancouver, Washington.

THOMAS PETTIGREW. The career of Thomas Pettigrew, a venerable
resident of Helena, Andrew County, is one well worthy of consideration
by the younger generation. Born in Ireland, he emigrated to the United
States as a young man, but before he could start on a career of his own
he was forced to serve five years for another to clear off an indebtedness. Subsequently he saw service in the great war between the North
and the South, in which he sustained severe injuries, and finally, when
he came to Missouri, it was as a laborer. His experiences, however,
had given him self reliance and courage, and with determination he
set forth to make a place for himself among the men of substance of
his community. How well his ambitions were realized is evidenced by
the high esteem in which he is held in his county and the handsome
property which he has accumulated for his declining years.

Thomas Pettigrew was born in County Tyrone, Ireland, in 1831, and
is a son of William and Margaret (Aken) Pettigrew, the latter of
whom died when Thomas was a baby, while the former, a farmer all
his life, passed away in New Jersey. The following children were in the
family: William, Eliza, James, George, Charles, all deceased, Thomas,
Mary, deceased, and Margaret, of Orange New Jersey. Mr. Pettigrew
received only a public school education in his native land and was a
young man of twenty-four years when he emigrated to the United States.
He was bound to his brother William for five years, in the manufacture
of hats, and served the time at Milburn, New Jersey, following which
he secured a position as conductor on a street railway in Brooklyn and
was thus engaged for three years. The outbreak of the Civil war found
Mr. Pettigrew a resident of New Jersey, and in May, 1861, he enlisted
in Company K, Second Regiment, New Jersey Volunteer Infantry.
This regiment was attached to the Army of the Potomac, which participated in the great and sanguine battle of the Wilderness, five miles
from Richmond, when Mr. Pettigrew was severely wounded by a bullet
in the left leg below the knee. He fell into the hands of the Confederates,
and for six days lay on the field without having anything done for
his injury, but subsequently went to Chesapeake Hospital, and was
discharged therefrom and from the service after one year and eleven
months as a soldier.

Mr. Pettigrew, with an excellent war record, came to Missouri to
see his sister, Mrs. Eliza Atkinson. He was at once struck with the
opportunities offered in this rich and fertile region, locating in Nodaway County, where he decided to remain. For three years he worked
as a laborer, but in 1866 established a home of his own, when he was
married to Mary C. Pattison, who was born in Indiana, May 27, 1844,
and came to Nodaway County, Missouri, with her parents, in 1858.
After his marriage Mr. Pettigrew engaged in farming ventures on his
own account, and for twenty-four years resided on one farm, this
adjoining the town of Rosendale, on the east. He still owns this property, which consists of 120 acres, on which there are numerous substantial buildings and modern improvements. For ten years Mr.
Pettigrew resided at Woodston, Kansas, and for eleven years at El
Reno, Oklahoma, and he still owns properties at both of these places.
He is also interested in the Woodston State Bank, the Rooks County
(Kansas) State Bank and the First National Bank of Stockton, Kansas. Mr. Pettigrew also owns 960 acres of fine land in the Pan Handle
district of Texas, on which he has a well 340 feet deep. In all his business

ventures he has been honorable and upright, and as a result he stands high in the esteem of his community.

Mr. Pettigrew has no professed religious connection, although he has always supported movements which have made for morality and education. He has been a lifelong republican, but is, at the same time, an ardent admirer of President Wilson.

Hon. Abraham H. Burkeholder. On July 12, 1865, a new member was added to the bar of Trenton and Grundy county. He had many competitors then, all more or less acquainted with the community by virtue of some residence. Not one of those lawyers with whom he had his first associations is longer in practice, a fact which leaves Abraham Hudson Burkeholder as the dean of the legal profession at Trenton. Previous to his location in Trenton he had acquitted himself worthily as a soldier and in minor capacities, and since then many honors and important services have come within the scope of his years and attainments.

Abraham H. Burkeholder was born on a farm in York County, Pennsylvania, June 27, 1835. His father was Joseph Latshaw Burkeholder, born also in York County in 1797, while Grandfather Abraham was likewise a native of that portion of Pennsylvania. However, it is believed that the head of the next previous generation was from Lancaster County, and of early German stock. Abraham Burkeholder owned and cultivated a farm about five miles from Petersburg in York County, and lived there till death. His wife was named Brown and was of English and French stocks.

Joseph L. Burkeholder, the father, after a training on a farm, left York County in 1839, and in Perry County of the same state bought a farm on the Juniata River near Newport. Selling out there in 1860, in the following year he moved to Ohio and secured a new home in Putnam County. That was his home until his death at the age of seventy-one. He had married Barbara Harmon. Her birthplace was a farm near the Village of Gettysburg, Pennsylvania, and some of the actual fighting between the armies of Lee and Meade during the first three days of July, 1863, occurred on that farm. Her father, John Harmon, spent all his days in that state. Barbara Burkeholder died in 1859, leaving a family of ten children, all of whom grew to manhood and womanhood.

The veteran Trenton attorney had the training of an average Pennsylvania farm boy during the '40s and '50s. When the strength of his body was sufficiently mature, he was given plenty of work on the farm, but his studious nature and strong inclination for learned pursuits caused him to make the most of his educational opportunities. When nineteen he entered the Markville Normal Institute, paid his own tuition and the most of his living expenses, and on graduating in 1859 was well qualified for a position as teacher. While teaching in Perry County he also studied in the law office of McIntire & Son at New Bloomfield, and at the April term of the Court of Common Pleas in Perry County, in 1862, obtained admission to the bar. He then went to Ohio, following his father, and the winter of 1862-63 was spent in teaching in Putnam County. Then in June, 1863, the interests of the school and of his profession were put aside, and he became one of the many units who were fighting for the union of states. He enlisted in Company I of the Eighty-eighth Ohio Infantry, and soon afterward was sent south. After fifteen months of service he was promoted to the rank of lieutenant, and later became quartermaster of the One Hundred and Seventy-ninth Ohio Regiment. He remained with his command and in active service until peace came between the North and South, and was granted his honorable discharge at Nashville, Tennessee, on June 30, 1865.

Though he went back to Ohio, he almost at once took leave of his home folks and on the 12th of July arrived at Trenton. Opening his office as a lawyer, he has since been in continuous practice except so far as his official duties have interfered. Mr. Burkeholder brought his wife with him to Trenton. In 1862 he had married Rebecca A. Waltner, who was born in Wayne County, Ohio, July 3, 1840, a daughter of Jacob and Rebecca Waltner, and who died December 20, 1912. Of their marriage are two sons and one daughter still living, namely: Poe, Norton and Bliss. Poe married Laura L. Hubbell, and has two children, Wolcott Hudson and George Waltner. Norton married Sarah Wolz, and their three children are Elizabeth N., Martha B. and John Hudson. Bliss is unmarried.

While as a lawyer Mr. Burkeholder has long been one of the leaders of the Grundy County bar, he has given many years of his career to unselfish public service. He was ten years president of the board of trustees of the Grand River College and for a similar period a member of the Trenton Board of Education. In 1866, the year following his arrival in Trenton, he was elected judge of probate, an office which he filled admirably four years. In 1871 occurred his appointment to the office of prosecuting attorney, and in the following year his administration was endorsed by a popular election. In 1876 he was elected to represent the fourth district in the Missouri Senate. In that body he was a member of the committee on criminal jurisprudence and others, and in the thirtieth assembly was chairman of the committee to revise all tax and assessment laws relating to railroad property. He was author of the law permitting an increased levy for the support of schools and for the erection of school buildings, and a number of other acts that became laws of the state.

In 1892 he was nominated by his party for Congress from the second district, made a canvass of six weeks, but was defeated by his democratic opponent.

Mr. Burkeholder still lives in Trenton, and is in his eightieth year.

HENRY A. CRAWFORD. What Henry A. Crawford has accomplished in acquiring a home and building up substantial prosperity as a farmer may well prove a stimulus and incentive to others. He is an Indiana man who a little more than thirty years ago found himself possessed of a family but no capital and with restricted opportunities for getting ahead in the world. He accordingly determined to come out to Northwest Missouri. He had to borrow money to ship his household effects, and arrived in Andrew county with no special credentials except a willingness to work and an ambition which has steadily propelled him forward to better things. His first attempt at getting a home of his own was the buying of half an interest in four acres, with two years to pay for it at ten per cent interest, then a prevailing and not unusual rate for the use of money, but before the note was due he bought out his partner. By thrift, hard work and close economy he managed to pay for the four acres, and by repeating the same process bought two acres, later buying another four acres. He has never been afraid to assume liability, having the courage and the self-reliance necessary to meet obligations as they fall due. After getting ten acres he bought another tract of land of twenty-five acres nearby, and then followed that with the purchase of eight acres. He next bought 9½ acres, and then bought fifteen acres. His transactions included at that time 67½ acres and he later bought 100 acres, and after selling sixty acres two years ago he still has a farm of 107½ acres, all paid for with a surplus in the bank, and with a credit carefully maintained that entitles him to the trust and confidence of every business man in Andrew County. Mr. Crawford spent a number of years in the heavy task of clearing up brush land, since practically all his acreage when he secured it was raw land and had to be cleared before it could be cultivated. His first home was a small box house unplastered, and hardly worth $25. Mr. Crawford is a mechanic, having built all of his buildings, which are modern. He now owns a fine home with all the conveniences of good living, has provided liberally for his family, has at different times been a factor in community enterprise, and has also helped several of his relatives to get started in the same section of Missouri.

Henry A. Crawford was born in Jefferson County, Indiana, May 8, 1860, a son of John R. and Joeta (Cox) Crawford. His father was born in Thomastown, Maine, April 2, 1832, and his mother was born in Gallatin County, Kentucky, February 26, 1838. His father grew up in Maine and Massachusetts, and was married in Frankfort, Kentucky, April 20, 1854. From Kentucky they removed to Indiana, and spent the rest of their lives there on a farm. John R. Crawford served three years in the Civil war, having enlisted in the Sixth Indiana Infantry, and after his term of service was over he reentered the service as a veteran. He lived to a good age and died in January, 1901, while his wife passed away in February, 1889. They were the parents of six sons: Adalbert, of Platte Township; James S., of Parnell, Missouri; Henry A., of Platte Township; George A., who was born September 3, 1865, and died at the age of ten years; Samuel, of Columbus, Indiana; and Edward, who died at the age of five years.

Henry A. Crawford grew up on the Indiana farm, received the training of a country boy, and in country schools, and lived there until 1882. He was the first of his family to come to Andrew County, Missouri, and has been at his present location in Platte Township since 1883. His farm is one of exceptional improvements, and is well deserving the title of West Lawn Farm. It is noted as a breeding farm for Poland China hogs, though Mr. Crawford is also a general grain raiser and stock farmer.

In affairs outside his home place, he has taken an interest in several business enterprises. For the past nine years he has been on the board of directors of the Andrew County Mutual Fire, Lightning and Tornado Insurance Company, and for several years served as a director of the Andrew County Mutual Telephone Company. For nine years he was a member of the local school board. Politically he gives his support to the republican party.

February 7, 1877, Mr. Crawford married Amelia Jane Bivens, who was born in Jefferson County, Indiana, October 11, 1859, and grew up and was married there. Her parents were James and Lydia Bivens. Mr. and Mrs. Crawford have a fine family of children, there having been eight births, the three first in Indiana and the others in Andrew County. Edward M., the oldest, is a farmer in Platte Township, and by his marriage to Lulu Beatie has three children; John O., who was born October 3, 1880, was murdered in Lewistown, Montana, November 8, 1913, leaving a widow and two children by his first wife; Frank A., a resident of Minneapolis, married Minnie Bryant and has one child; Orpha is the wife of George Silvers of Platte Township, and has three children; Archie B. married Lillie Beattie, and has one child by a former marriage; Goldie M. is the wife of Earnest Deal of Platte Township, and has one child; Elsie died in infancy; and Freeman, the youngest, lives at home.

LEONARD A. SAUNDERS. The development of a sound optimism and intelligence throughout the country has brought the vocation of agriculture to something between a profession and a science, the great possibilities of which can be but partially mastered by any one individual during his years of endeavor. Thus it is that in the various departments of agricultural work, men have arisen who are experts in their special lines, and through their labors the farming interests of the country are receiving great encouragement. Among the men who have attained prominence in this way in Northwest Missouri, none perhaps is better known than Leonard A. Saunders, whose connection with agricultural organizations and expositions has made him so familiar to the people that he has acquired the title of the "Corn Show Man of Missouri." He has been a resident of Andrew County all of his life, is a farmer of experience and practical training, and at the present time is the owner of a valuable farm in Benton Township.

Mr. Saunders was born at Whitesville, Andrew County, Missouri, September 29, 1877, and is a son of Orris B. and Mary A. (Combest) Saunders. He was born in Norfolk, Virginia, and in his younger years was a seafaring man, traveling extensively for his day. He was still a young man when he removed from the East to Saint Joseph, Missouri, there taking up the trade of tinner as one of the first men to engage in that business in that city. He was married at Whitesville, Missouri, January 31, 1856, to Miss Mary A. Combest, who was born in Kentucky, and not long after their marriage they set out to make the journey across the plains to California. Soon, however, they returned to Mrs. Saunders' father's farm, three miles east of Whitesville, and there made their home for many years, Mr. Saunders accumulating 500 acres of good land and engaging in grain and stockraising. In his later years he retired from active pursuits and went to Savanah, where he continued to make his home until his death, in February, 1908. Mrs. Saunders, who survives him, resides at Pasadena, California. After his retirement, Mr. Saunders was much interested in the five-gaited, saddle horse, horse back riding being his chief enjoyment. He was prominent in local democratic politics, was a man held in high esteem as a citizen, was prominent in Masonic circles, and was a faithful member of the Christian Church. Mr. and Mrs. Saunders were the parents of the following children: Pauline C. Powell, who is deceased; William S., also deceased; Archie D., who is a resident of Maryville; Lula A., the wife of U. D. Jennings, of Bolckow; Virdie, who is the wife of J. R. White, of Whitesville; Edith A., the wife of William M. Holt, of Leeton, Missouri; Dollie V., the wife of Fred Camp, of Los Angeles, California; Mollie, who is the wife of Ed Fisher, of Warrensburg, Missouri; Mildred, the wife of William Bailey, of Suffolk, Virginia; Leonard A., of this review; and Crystal, who is the wife of J. W. Thompson, of Pasadena, California.

Leonard A. Saunders received his early education in the public schools, following which for three years he attended Drake University. He grew up on his father's farm and resided under the parental roof until the time of his marriage, when he rented and operated his father's farm of 500 acres, conducting it for about six years. When his father died the farm was sold, and Mr. Saunders purchased his present property, a tract of seventy-five acres, adjoining the corporate limits of the Town of Bolckow, on the south, in section 11, Benton Township. Here Mr. Saunders has erected modern buildings and a substantial residence, and in his farming operations has met with decided success. He uses the most up-to-date methods and modern improved machinery, and as a business man has won the confidence of those with whom he has had dealings. In 1909 Mr. Saunders leased a part of his farm to be used as Fair Grounds, but in 1914 sold out to J. O. Dougan, this being a tract of thirty acres.

In the encouragement of agriculturists and agricultural interests there are few men who have contributed in greater degree than has Mr. Saunders. An energetic, progressive man, and an enthusiastic "booster" for his community, he has been secretary of the Whitesville Interstate Corn and Poultry Association since its organization, superintendent of the Corn Show and manager of the Corn Show News, and the only salaried man connected with the association. This organization, formed to protect and foster the interests of the agriculturists of Whitesville and the surrounding locality, started in a modest manner, but has yearly grown in importance, so that today it interests farmers all over the state, and attracts many from other commonwealths. Its annual feature, the Corn Show, is ably handled by Mr. Saunders, and the Corn Show News, as edited by him, is a bright and newsy sheet, telling of the happenings of the exposition and those who attend and exhibit at it. The Futurity Corn Show is a new feature, entirely Mr. Saunders' idea, and is a distinct departure from the old cut and dried methods.

It may not be inappropriate to here quote from an article which appeared in the Kansas City Star, date November 18, 1914, which said, in part: "Eight years ago the farmers near Whitesville, Missouri, rebelled. For years they had had their recreation and entertainment wrapped up and delivered to them by the Whitesville merchants in much the same way they got their sugar and dry goods. Then someone asked why, and the rebellion was on. 'Yes, why?' asked the farm dwellers, discovering at the same time they possessed the power to make up their community mind for themselves and without the aid of any town. 'Why should anyone try to do anything for us?' they asked. 'Are we not plenty able to do things for ourselves? Farming is the most important part of the community life hereabouts, so why not put farming to the front?' And so it was done. The farmers organized a farmers' club and the merchants joined in and were glad to belong and content to see the farmers occupying all the club offices. Whitesville is not on a railroad. It was not distinguished for one single thing when the farmers' club took charge of its destinies eight years ago, so they proceeded to formulate a plan to make it famous. A corn show was decided on as the vehicle of greatness, and the club provided liberal cash prizes and said to the world: 'Come on with your corn. If you can win our money you are welcome to it.' That was taking in lots of territory— fact is, Whitesville took on too much territory at first, but it was the making of the show and the eighth annual Interstate Corn Show, at Whitesville, December 7 to 10 (1914) will perhaps be the greatest of the state. Corn is expected to be entered from several states, and Whitesville does not expect to pay out all the prize money to strangers by a good deal. Whitesville farmers are conspicuous winners each year at the state fair and they take prizes at all the great shows of the nation. Two years ago a member of their club had the honor of showing the best peck of wheat at Charleston, South Carolina. 'World competition is what has made our show,' declares Len A. Saunders, secretary of the club. 'Outside competition has developed our own corn breeders as nothing else would. I have been to many corn shows where the territory was limited and have thought it did the exhibitor in small classes more harm than good to get a first. It made him satisfied with medium quality. I can truthfully say competition is the life of corn shows.' The second year of the Corn Show it grew too big for the Odd Fellows Hall. The club organized a $10,000 stock company and built itself a permanent home. An example of the efficiency of the farmers' club is the fact that for eight years it has had no change of officers. J. F. Roberts has been the president continually and under him and Mr. Saunders it has prospered amazingly. Another thing, the secretary has always been paid for his work, the theory being that he was worth it—and he is." "The Corn Show Man of Missouri" has been frequently called upon to organize other associations of this kind, his ability in this direction being generally acknowledged throughout the state. He has found time to serve efficiently as a member of the school boards of Whitesville and Bolckow, having acted in this capacity almost from the time he attained his majority. His political support is given to the democratic party. Mr. Saunders is a member of the Christian Church at Bolckow, and for a number of years has served as superintendent of the Sunday school.

In December, 1902, Mr. Saunders was united in marriage to Miss Kate L. Bartholomew, who was born at Whitesville, in 1881, daughter of Henry and Martha Bartholomew. Mr. Bartholomew, who was an early settler of Whitesville, and one of the first harness makers at that place, died after many years of industrious labor there, Mrs. Bartholomew surviving. Four children have been born to Mr. and Mrs. Saunders, namely: Mary Olive, Vincent Henry, Leonard Clayton and Harry Irving, all residing at home.

JAMES E. ETHERTON. Born in one of the pioneer homes of Ray County, James E. Etherton has for many years been identified with the farming community of Davis Township in Caldwell County. By good judgment and industry he has provided his declining years with a comfortable home and a sufficient prosperity, and he and his good wife have reared a family who do them honor. Mr. Etherton has a farm of eighty acres, and lives in peace and comfort. His house contains seven rooms, surrounded by lawns, shade trees and fruit orchard, and under his management his fields have been regularly producing the staple crops of Caldwell County for an entire generation.

James E. Etherton was born six miles northeast of Knoxville in Ray County in 1848. His father, William Etherton, was born in Kentucky, October 2, 1818, and was brought to Ray County in 1832 by his father, William Etherton, Sr. The last named was one of the first settlers in this section of Missouri, and built and operated the first water power grist mills in northern Ray County. William Etherton, Jr., married in Ray County, Mary Ann Thogmartin, who was born in Tennessee, and came with her father, Joseph Thogmartin, from that state to Ray County in 1833. Thus on both sides of the house Mr. Etherton is connected with some of the earliest families who helped to make history in Ray County. William Etherton and wife were the parents of the following children: William, who enlisted in the Confederate army in the Civil war and was killed while fighting with Gen. Sterling Price in the battle of Franklin in 1864; Thomas, who is also deceased; Mary J., who lives in Topeka, Kansas; Henry, who died at the age of fourteen; James, of this review; and Warren, who died in October, 1914, leaving a widow and children. Mr. Etherton's mother died at the age of thirty-two, and his father later married Margaret Watson, and that union resulted in five children: Thomas, deceased; John, deceased; Mary Ann; Sally, deceased; and Dr. William C., who practices at Millville, Missouri. The father of these children died at the age of eighty-eight years. He was a democrat in politics and a member of the Methodist Episcopal Church, South.

James E. Etherton grew up on the old farm in Ray County, and had his experiences in the log cabin days of this section. He attended a school kept in a log cabin, but his career is only one of many illustrations that prove how such primitive schools did not fail to produce useful men and women and the citizens who bore the brunt of progress during the last century.

At the age of twenty-seven, on January 10, 1877, Mr. Etherton married Hannah P. Davis, of one of the oldest and most prominent families
in Caldwell County. She was born in Davis Township April 10, 1859, a
daughter of John T. Davis and a granddaughter of Dennis Davis, the
pioneer in whose honor the township was named. John T. Davis married
Margaret Moore, who was born in Illinois, and they became the parents
of the following children: Rose, deceased; Mary A., of Kansas City;
Elizabeth, deceased; George W., a prominent Davis Township citizen;
Dennis, deceased; Joanna, deceased; John T., Jr.; Margaret H., of Baldwin, Kansas; Walter S., deceased; and Mrs. Etherton. Mr. Davis died at
the age of eighty-four years. He was a democrat and a member of the
Methodist Church.

Mr. and Mrs. Etherton have lived on their present farm for thirty-
seven years, and in that time have won prosperity from the cultivation
of its acres, have had a happy and contented home life and are now in
a position to enjoy the comforts of declining years. Their first child,
Henry C., has followed a career as an educator and married a popular
teacher of St. Louis, and both have made a name in educational affairs.
William F. died at the age of three years. Margaret E. lives at home.
John Luther, an active farmer of Taney County, is married and is the
father of one child, Morris C., aged three years. James T. farms at home
with his father. Mr. Etherton is a democrat, and has served on the
home school board.

JOHN H. VIRDEN, one of the well known farmers and stockmen of
Harrison County, Missouri, is a native of the community in which he now
resides, his birth having occurred December 6, 1854, and the old birthplace now being owned by his sister, Mrs. Naomi Kinkade. The tradi-
tional history of the Virdens is that they came from England, the direct
progenitor being the great-grandfather of John H. Virden, who took
up his residence in the State of Delaware.

John W. Virden, the father of John H. Virden, came to Missouri from
Ohio, where he was temporarily located for two years. He was born
in the little Commonwealth of Delaware, and was a country boy with
the usual educational and business training, and was perhaps thirty-two
years of age when he came to Missouri, entering 160 acres of land in
Harrison County, which he improved into a good farm, and on which he
carried on agricultural operations during the remainder of his life.
He was rather past the age to take part in the Civil war, but was a
Union man and a strong republican. A Presbyterian in his religion,
he was an officer of his church and aided in the building of the Foster
Church, the first one erected in this locality, to which he was a large
contributor. He also gave more than any other man to the building of
the church of that faith at New Hampton. Mr. Virden was a quiet,
reserved man, taking but little interest in business matters beyond his
control, but was at all times known as a good and practical farmer and as
a public-spirited and dependable citizen. Mr. Virden married Miss Caroline Black, who was born in Surry County, North Carolina, a daughter of
a farmer, and she came to Missouri with her widowed mother and a
brother, Valentine Black. They settled just west of the Virden farm
and she married John W. Virden during the '40s and made him a faithful
and helpful wife until her death in 1902. Their children were as follows:
William M., who spent his life in Harrison County and died in 1900,
unmarried; Eliza, who died in childhood; John H., of this review; Naomi,
the wife of James Kinkade, of Harrison County; and Amy, who married
Frank Pruden, also of this county.

John H. Virden was reared in the vicinity of his birth and there received his education in the country school which bore the family name. He was reared as an agriculturist and began his career as such, remaining under the parental roof until he reached his majority and then settling on a farm adjoining his present home in section 21. Two years later he moved to his present place in section 16 and erected the first house ever built on this place, the two main rooms of his present home comprising the original dwelling. Here he has resided since the '70s, and as a farmer he has engaged in grain growing and stock feeding, and in the early days in dealing and shipping, while he still ships what he feeds. He owns land in sections 15, 16, 17, 20, 21 and 22, aggregating nearly twelve hundred acres, through which the Inter-State Trail passes, as well as two other laid-out trails.

Mr. Virden became identified with the banking business of New Hampton when it started as a stockholder of the Farmers Bank, and has continued as a director of this institution ever since, also spending several years as its president. As a builder of New Hampton he aided in the erection of one of the leading mercantile houses of this thriving community. Mr. Virden has not been identified with the politics of his locality, save as a voter, and, having been brought up under a republican roof supports the principles and candidates of that party. He is one of the directors of the New Hampton school and served his country school efficiently in a like capacity prior to becoming a resident of the town.

Mr. Virden was married to Miss Angie Chipp, a daughter of John W. Chipp, an ante-bellum settler of Harrison County from Indiana. The following children have been born to Mr. and Mrs. Virden: Lizzie, who is the wife of Curtis Larmer, of Albany, Missouri, who died in 1910, and has three children, Louise, John and Margaret; Stella, who married Charles A. Rowland, of New Hampton; Amy J., who married Lewis T. Gibbs, of Kosse, Texas; and Paul H. These daughters were educated beyond the public schools, Mrs. Larmer attending the Albany Institute and the female college at Liberty, Missouri, where her sister Stella attended later, while the other daughter acquired a liberal education in different schools at home and elsewhere.

BEN F. WOOD. In the thriving little community of Laredo in Grundy County no one family has had more intimate and active relations during the past thirty years than the Woods, who were among the early settlers. Ben F. Wood has been particularly prominent in this locality, has been a teacher, a farmer, a banker and business man, and many times has accepted the responsibilities and honors of public position.

Ben F. Wood was born in Grant County, Indiana, November 17, 1856. His father, William Wood, was born in Kentucky, August 15, 1827, and married Marinda Braffett, who was born in Ohio, October 30, 1834. The paternal grandparents were Joseph Wood and wife, and the maternal grandparents were Silas and Mary (Woods) Braffett. William Wood had an unusual military record. Early in his career he enlisted for service in the Mexican war in the army under General Scott, and some years later while living in Indiana entered the service of the Union army in 1861 as second lieutenant in Company I of the Twelfth Regiment, Indiana Volunteers. At the end of one year he was honorably discharged and afterward reenlisted in Company I of the One Hundred and First Indiana Regiment, and was promoted from second lieutenant to captain, and commanded a company until his final discharge from service in 1865. He was in the battle of Chickamauga, and in the historic fight at Missionary Ridge on September 6, 1863, was wounded. From Indiana he moved out to Grundy County, Missouri, in

1871, went back to the old state in 1872, but in 1874 located permanently in Grundy County and bought a farm of 179 acres two miles east of the present site of Laredo.

Ben F. Wood received most of his education in country schools in Indiana, and was about fifteen years of age when the family first came to Grundy County, and was eighteen when they located here permanently. In 1874 Mr. Wood began teaching school in Grundy County, and for seventeen years followed that vocation in this and surrounding counties and there are many people now in mature years who recall him as one of their instructors when children. In 1891 Mr. Wood was elected cashier of the Bank of Laredo, and for practically a quarter of a century has been one of the vital factors in the growth and development of this little town. He is at present a member of the board of directors of the Citizens Bank, of Laredo. In 1894 he established an insurance and loan business, and in 1896 bought the Laredo Tribune, and continued in active newspaper work for fourteen years and still owns a third interest in that paper.

Mr. Wood has always been a stanch republican, and for twelve years served as a member of the Republican County Central Committee, and during ten years of that time was secretary of the committee. He has held a commission as notary public for twenty-eight years, served as a justice of the peace sixteen years, and for the past ten years has been mayor of Laredo. He was also township clerk and assessor for six years, and has been a member and secretary of the local board of education for nineteen years. This is an unusual record of public service, and indicates how high in the esteem of the community Mr. Wood stands. Fraternally he is identified with the Masons and with the Modern Woodmen of America, having affiliation with Lodge No. 253, A. F. & A. M., and is now the secretary of this lodge. For thirty-nine years he has been an active member of the Baptist Church, and is now serving as trustee and deacon in the church at Laredo.

On May 8, 1878, Mr. Wood married Miss Mary McKay, a daughter of Moses and Roxana (Fenn) McKay. Her father was born in Switzerland County, Indiana, August 28, 1833, and her mother was born in Fairfield County, Ohio, September 7, 1836. Mr. and Mrs. Wood are the parents of six children: Althea, Orion, Claud, Icy, Susan and William McKay Wood. The son Claud died in infancy. Althea married George Snyder of Colorado, and now lives at Long Beach, California. Orion married Margaret Hill, daughter of Andrew J. and Katie Hill of Worth County, Missouri, and they have four children, Lemuel, Mary K., James L. and Buford N. The daughter Icy married Dr. Charles Nair of Pennsylvania, and now living in Linneus, Missouri. Susan is the wife of William B. Schweizer of California, and has one child, Mary M., and they too live at Long Beach, California.

CHARLES BENNETT. Long life and prosperity have been given to Charles Bennett, of Andrew County, who has already passed the seventy-fifth milestone of life's journey, and while on the way has accumulated more than an average share of this world's goods, represented in substantial lands and farm improvements in section 15 of Platte Township. His home has been in this one locality since the spring of 1867, and in all these years he has succeeded not only in living peaceably with his neighbors but in making himself a positive factor for good to others as well as his own family, from whom he enjoys all the honors of old age.

Charles Bennett is a native of Canada, born in the Province of

Quebec, October 17, 1838, the third of thirteen children whose parents were Andrew and Ann (Abbott) Bennett. All the children grew to maturity, and two of the sons and two of the daughters are now deceased. The parents were natives of County Cork, Ireland, his father born in 1797 and his mother in 1817. They were married in Canada in 1833, Andrew Bennett having emigrated to America at the age of thirty-four. His death occurred in 1865, having for many years followed farming both in the old country and in Canada. In 1867 the widowed mother with her children removed to Andrew County, Missouri, and some years later she removed to Gentry County, and died at Stanberry at the home of her youngest daughter June 4, 1911, at advanced years.

Charles Bennett grew up on a Canadian farm, and as his parents were poor and burdened with the responsibilities of a large household, his educational advantages were somewhat neglected, and during his active manhood he has acquired most of his learning by close and attentive reading and observation. For several years after coming to Andrew County he and his brother Andrew worked together and engaged in farming on a partnership basis. Mr. Bennett now owns a well improved farm of 250 acres in Platte Township, but at one time his possessions amounted to 500 acres, part of which he distributed among his children. On October 1, 1912, he suffered a heavy loss by fire which destroyed a fine barn 168 by 42 feet, with a hundred tons of hay and all the farming implements. He carried $1,500 insurance, but the total loss was more than six thousand dollars. Mr. Bennett is an interesting talker, a man of broad views gained by practical acquaintance with the world and with men, and possesses a philosophic turn of mind. As a result of an accident and advancing years he has almost lost his eyesight, and now has to see the printed page through the eyes of other members of the household.

In 1881 Mr. Bennett married Mrs. Susanna H. (Nugent) McComb. She brought him one son by a former marriage, Thomas Leroy McComb, who is now in the grocery business in Kansas City. Mr. and Mrs. Bennett have four children of their own: Andrew, a farmer in Gentry County, who married Flora Ingles and has three children; Anna, who is the wife of Frank Troupe of DeKalb County, and has four children; Joseph Emerson, who married Ada Van Natta and has two sons; and Winnie, living at home.

JAMES M. VAN METER. A successful career has been that of James M. Van Meter of Rochester Township, Andrew County. Many things constitute success, and it is not alone in his material possessions, ample though they are, that the success of Mr. Van Meter is measured. When just entering manhood he went away to the war, spent three years in fighting for the Union, and the close of the war came with an honorable record as a soldier but with the serious struggle of life before him. He came out to Northwest Missouri about this time, and in face of obstacles which few young men of the present century would willingly face began making a home. There followed many years of unremitting toil, often handicapped by discouragements, but with perseverance and persistence he has several years passed that point where independence is established, and in addition to serving his own ends has been a valuable citizen to the community, and served as one of the county judges of Andrew County.

James M. Van Meter was born in Pike County, Ohio, March 8, 1843, and two years ago passed the age of three score and ten. His parents were Noble and Helen (Cruze) Van Meter. The grandparents were

Jacob and Susan (Moore) Van Meter, the former a Virginian, and the latter from Pennsylvania, the daughter of a man of Irish birth. The grandparents spent their lives in Ohio farming. Noble Van Meter was born in Pike County, Ohio, September 17, 1818, while his wife was born in Cumberland County, Virginia, May 4, 1818, and at the age of fifteen was brought by her parents to Ohio, where she grew up and was married. She died in 1899, and Noble Van Meter passed away in 1901, after a long career as a farmer. In the early days he had his share of strenuous toil, lived and made a home in a district covered with hardwood timber, of size and quality that would now yield a considerable wealth, though at that time the forests were considered an incumbrance, and Mr. Van Meter as other early settlers spent many years in the heavy task of clearing off the trees from their land. Noble Van Meter had an exceedingly meager education, but was a man of industry, honest and straightforward, and did well by his home and his community. He served in the State Militia but save as a voter participated little in politics or public affairs. James M. Van Meter was the oldest of eight children, the others being mentioned as follows: Catherine Ann, the widow of Warren Miller, lives in Oklahoma; Martha Jane, deceased wife of Thomas Remmel; John, deceased; Eliza, deceased wife of Thomas Greenwalt; Susan, now deceased, who married Robert Irons; Charles, deceased; America, deceased wife of Thomas' Greenwalt.

Judge Van Meter grew up in Pike County, Ohio, lived with his parents and received the advantages of the local schools, and at the age of nineteen volunteered his services to help put down the rebellion. He enlisted August 6, 1862, at Bainbridge in Ross County, Ohio, in Company H of the Eighty-ninth Ohio Volunteer Infantry. Senator Foraker was a sergeant in the regiment, and Mr. Van Meter and this distinguished Ohio statesman have many times stood picket duty together. He continued in the war until its close and was mustered out at Columbus, April 14, 1865. He had many narrow escapes, and can relate many interesting incidents of the war, particularly in the campaigns involving the subjugation of Tennessee and Northern Georgia, during 1863-64. In the battle of Chickamauga he was wounded in the left leg, but only a flesh wound, and was not out of service on that account. At Eutaw Creek in Georgia a ball passed through his right thigh on August 6, 1864, and this sent him to the hospital for four months, and after he was able to be up and around but still convalescent he was placed in charge of a ward in the hospital, and the war was over before he was able to resume active duty. Mr. Van Meter participated in the Tullahoma campaign, was at Chickamauga, Lookout Mountain, Missionary Ridge, at Ringgold, Georgia, and until wounded and disabled was in the famous Atlanta campaign under Sherman, involving ninety days of almost continuous fighting from Dalton to the capital city of Georgia. At the close of the war his blanket had thirty-two bullet holes, and on one occasion while he was asleep a bullet pierced his knapsack under his head.

On November 24, 1865, a few months after his honorable discharge from military duties, Mr. Van Meter landed in St. Joseph, Missouri, and there took a stage to Albany, where he remained until the following March. He then came into Andrew County, and with the exception of a short time spent in Colorado working in the mines he has been a resident of this county ever since. For forty years he has lived in Rochester Township, and his home has been at his present farm thirty-one years. Until a few years ago Mr. Van Meter owned 420 acres in one body, but has since given his son 207 acres, and now has only 190 acres under his active control. This farm is located on the east side of Platte River, and under his management has had a splendid record of production through many years. He has raised mules, cattle, horses and hogs, has specialized in the Hereford cattle and the Duroc red hogs. A considerable part of his land is in the river bottoms, especially valuable for corn, and the uplands have been utilized for stock pasturage. When Mr. Van Meter came into Andrew County he started with exceedingly modest resources, on ten acres of ground and with a two-room house built from the native lumber. He had no place for his cattle, tied his cows up in the night, and had a rough log shelter for his mules. The experiences of his early boyhood in the timber districts of Ohio stood him in good stead when he came to Northwest Missouri, and all the extensive clearing and improvements on his home farm and those of his sons constitute a splendid testimonial to his efforts and enterprise. He cleared up 200 acres, and removed the stumps from the fields.

Naturally Mr. Van Meter has affiliated with the republican party since casting his first vote while with the army in the South. He served with efficiency in the office of county judge one term, and for thirty years has been clerk of the district school board. He is a member of the Masonic order and of the Independent Order of Odd Fellows, and has interested himself in Grand Army organizations. Mr. Van Meter is a director of the Peoples Bank at Union Star.

April 9, 1871, he married Charlotte Jane Courter, who was born in Delaware County, Ohio, June 2, 1855, and came to Andrew County with her parents September 6, 1864. Her parents were Edward S. and Mary Elizabeth (Rolson) Courter. Her father was born in New Jersey and her mother in Delaware County, Ohio, and both died in Andrew County. Her father was born May 16, 1833, and died January 20, 1891, and her mother was born April 29, 1833, and died April 20, 1884. Mrs. Van Meter's father was a carpenter and shoemaker by trade, which he followed in Ohio, but was a farmer after coming to Missouri. In 1861 he went out to California, accompanying a freighting outfit from St. Joseph. Mrs. Van Meter is one of three children, the other two being deceased, named Eliza and Wingenand Courter.

Mr. and Mrs. Van Meter have special reasons to be proud of their family of children, ten in number, mentioned briefly as follows: Gordon C., who is a progressive young farmer on a part of the old homestead; Alonzo F., also on the home farm; Mary Ethel, wife of Robert Humphrey of Alvin, Texas; Julius A., of Chaseley, North Dakota; Ellen, wife of Edward Huffaker, of Andrew County; Rosa, wife of Jackson Gates of Rochester Township; Catherine, living at home with her parents; Grace, wife of John Courley of Grand City; Lillian, wife of Lloyd White of Conception, Missouri; and Etta, wife of M. J. Cross of DeQuincey, Louisiana.

HON. KEERAN MCKENNY. When Judge Keeran McKenny came to Gentry County for his permanent settlement, in 1871, he was possessed of a serviceable team of horses and enough cash to purchase the land he needed for a home. In the forty-three years that have followed he has accumulated more than eleven hundred acres of land, and in addition to being extensively interested in farming and stock raising operations has large holdings in other enterprises, commercial and financial, and occupies an important place among the men who have developed this part of Northwest Missouri. Mr. McKenny's career has been an active, industrious and interesting one, and he has used the implements of destruction as well as those of construction, for during the Civil war he served his adopted land as a soldier, and following the close of that struggle remained in the employ of the Government for several years. He is a native of Ireland, born in Kings County, June 25, 1844, a son of John and Catherine (Guinan) McKenny.

The paternal grandfather of Judge McKenny was Andrew Mc-Kenny, who passed his life in Etin, his only child being John Mc-Kenny. The latter was born in Kings County, and was there married to Catherine Guinan, who died in Ireland, their children being: Bridget, who died in Gentry County as Mrs. James Rourke; Mary, who married Chris Cummings and died in Nodaway County, Missouri; Thomas A., a farmer and stockman of Gentry County; Judge Keeran, of this review; and Kate, who died at Laramie, Wyoming, as Mrs. John Guinan. The father immigrated to the United States in 1854, settling in Ohio, where he was first engaged as a contractor in public highways, but later adopted the vocation of a farmer, to which he devoted his energies to the time of his death, in 1902, when he was seventy-six years of age. He married a second wife after coming to this country, in Clark County, Ohio, in 1858. Mr. McKenny was too old to participate in the Civil war as a soldier, and never desired public office, being content to live his life merely as an industrious agriculturist and good citizen of the land of his adoption.

Judge Keeran McKenny left his native land as a boy of twelve years, two years after his father had come to America. He was granted only ordinary educational advantages in the public schools, but made the most of his opportunities and acquired a good mental training. Under the capable preceptorship of his father he learned the duties of farmer and stock raiser, vocations to which he has given the best years of his life. When the Civil war came on his sympathies were with the Union, and in August, 1862, when but eighteen years of age, he enlisted at South Charleston, Ohio, in Company C, Captain Smith, the 110th Regiment of the Ohio Volunteer Infantry, Col. J. Warren Keifer. His regiment first belonged to General Millroy's army, and after the battle of Winchester, in June, 1863, they joined the Army of the Potomac and belonged to the Third Army Corps. They got to the front at Winchester, Virginia, and participated in the engagement that made "Sheridan's Ride" famous. In 1864 Mr. McKenny was made a member of the Sixth Army Corps, and went up the Shenandoah Valley with that intrepid general, participating in the Strasburg fight and later in the battle of Cedar Creek, where Gen. Jubal Early's army was victorious in the forenoon and later met with defeat. Then the 110th did no more campaigning until the spring of 1865, when the campaign for the capture of Richmond began and Judge McKenny with his regiment participated in such noted battles as the Wilderness, Mine Run, Chancellorsville, Spottsylvania, Cold Harbor, Petersburg and Appomattox, at which last named the 110th was in the lead with the Sixth Army Corps when General Lee surrendered his broken army. Judge McKenny accompanied his regiment to the grand review at Washington, D. C., and was mustered out at Columbus, Ohio, in June, 1865. He was twice wounded during his service, first at Winchester, and a second time at Cedar Creek. One bullet, which he still keeps, was taken from his side, and the other one bored through his left thigh in its flight. Judge McKenny was discharged as corporal of his company, and has since taken an active interest in Grand Army matters, being at this time a popular comrade of Tyler Post, at Ford City.

Following the close of the Civil war Judge McKenny continued to pass some six years in the employ of the United States as a freighter and wagon-master. He joined the Forde company at Leavenworth, Kansas, in April, 1866, and made his first trip across the plains to Salt Lake City, his train taking out the Thirty-sixth Infantry to relieve what was known as the "galvanized Yankees," Southern prisoners who went out West instead of returning to the South. Judge McKenny remained in that western country until 1871, making two trips to Texas, and during his various trips across the plains the red man was in hostile evidence frequently, but no serious encounters occurred.

Judge McKenny wound up his service for the Government at Fort Hayes, Kansas, and returned to Missouri and engaged in farming on Grand River, Gentry County. After spending eight years in that locality he came to his present farm, three miles northeast of Ford City, here taking up 160 acres of land, which he improved and developed. As the years have passed he has continued to add to his land holdings, and now has a farm and a ranch, more than eleven hundred acres of land. His general farming operations are extensive, and stock raising has been a conspicuous factor in his activities, he showing marked success as a cattle feeder, while his pasture and ranch are well stocked with Mammoth steers.

In politics Judge McKenny is a republican, and has attended state conventions and helped to nominate a candidate for governor of his state at Springfield. He has also served on the republican county committee, and nearly thirty years ago was elected presiding judge of Gentry County, a position in which he served four years. He helped to promote the Citizens National Bank of King City, of which he is at this time president, and was one of the organizers of the Ford City Bank. Reared a Catholic, he has continued to hold membership in that denomination.

On February 10, 1874, Judge McKenny was married in Gentry County, Missouri, to Miss Mary Elizabeth Flood, a daughter of Michael Flood and a sister of John Flood of King City, whose history appears on another page of this work. Judge and Mrs. McKenny have been the parents of the following children: Frank, who is cashier of the Citizens Bank of King City; Catherine, who died here as Mrs. Frank Downey, and left a child, Michael; Thomas A., who died at the age of five years; James, a bookkeeper at Casper, Wyoming, who married Marie Vadonna; Thomas Leo, who died at the age of eight years; Mary, who married Mr. O'Malley, of Albany, and has two children, Kathline and Elizabeth; Charles, of this locality, who married Madge Handley; Annalaura, who died at the age of two years; and Veronica Grace, who died when seventeen years of age.

WILLIAM M. HUNT. One of the oldest business men of Polo is William M. Hunt, proprietor of the Pioneer Drug Store. Mr. Hunt has lived in this vicinity for fifty-three years, and whether as a business man or citizen his relations have always been straightforward and public-spirited, and in this section where he has spent so many years he has practically as many friends as acquaintances.

William M. Hunt was born October 30, 1849. His father was Rev. John W. Hunt, who is now living at the advanced age of eighty-five years at Polo, and who was born in Fleming County, Kentucky, in 1829. The grandfather was James M. Hunt, of Kentucky, who saw some active service as a soldier during the War of 1812 and the Indian wars. Reverend Mr. Hunt was one of a family of ten sons and three daughters. He married Susan Lebo, a native of Kentucky and a daughter of John D. Lebo. Reverend Mr. Hunt and wife were the parents of ten children, five sons and five daughters, namely: William M.; John F.; Daniel M.; James R.; Sarah L.; Mary L.; Martha J., who died young; George W., of Richmond, Missouri; and Frances, who died as a girl. The Reverend Mr. Hunt has for many years been a Baptist preacher, but is now retired from active service, while his wife is deceased.

William M. Hunt was reared in Western Missouri, received his education in the public schools, and ten years of his earlier career were spent in the active work of teaching, for which he was especially well qualified. Many of his pupils are now successful business men and are represented also in the professions. After leaving the schoolroom Mr. Hunt engaged in the drug business, and now for many years has kept the Pioneer Drug Store at Polo, and is a reliable pharmacist and as a merchant believes in the principles of fair dealing to all customers.

He was married November 11, 1882, at Polo, to Hattie A. Clarkson. She was born, reared and educated in Caldwell County, a daughter of T. B. Clarkson, who is a relative of James Clarkson, now holding a place in the Federal Government as assistant postmaster general. Mr. and Mrs. Hunt are the parents of three children. George C. is engaged in the jewelry business at Polo, has a well established store. is married and the father of three children, Nellie, Fern and Ralph. Mr. Hunt's second son is W. V., who lives in Sulphur Springs, Missouri, and has two children, William C. and a baby. The third son is W. H.

Mr. Hunt in politics is a democrat. He has served as a member of the school board, and his best public service was in leading the campaign and providing ways and means for the erection of the handsome schoolhouse which is now one of the chief features of the town. It was built at a cost of $14,000. What he has done in behalf of the school board is characteristic of all his civic relations with the community.

J. T. KENOWER. A newspaper which has had a fine and vitalizing influence in its community is the Bulletin of Breckenridge, the editor and publisher of which, J. T. Kenower, has had a long and active career both in educational work and as a newspaper publisher. The Bulletin was established in 1875, and for many years has held the field in competition with a number of other journals of more temporary existence. The Bulletin is the home paper of Breckenridge, and under the management of Mr. Kenower, who has been its editor since 1895, it has not only published the news and furnished an available medium of advertising, but has been an influence in politics and for local civic improvements.

J. T. Kenower was born in Xenia, Clay County, Illinois, September 12, 1860. He comes of Pennsylvania German stock, and his father, George Kenower, was born in Carlisle, Pennsylvania, and married Anna Shelly, also a native of Pennsylvania, in Carlyle, Illinois. They moved to Xenia, Clay County, Illinois, where the subject of this sketch was born; from there to Huey, Illinois, and from there, in 1884, to Bolivar, Polk County, Missouri. In 1892 they moved to Breckenridge, Missouri, where the father died at the age of eighty-eight years, and the mother at seventy-six. He was a republican in politics, and both were Methodists. There were four children, two sons and two daughters, and the other son is George F. Kenower, editor of the Chronicle, of Wisner, Nebraska.

J. T. Kenower grew up on a farm, had the wholesome environment and training of a farmer boy, had his early education in the public schools, and graduated from the University of Illinois in 1883. After his graduation he was for ten years identified with educational matters and for two years was a teacher and superintendent in the Cherokee

Indian schools in the Indian Territory. He also taught for two years in the Bolivar, Missouri, schools, and from 1891 to 1895 was superintendent of the public schools of Breckenridge. Many of the men and women now active in affairs in this section of Northwest Missouri and in other states were pupils under him at Breckenridge.

Since 1895 Mr. Kenower has had charge of the Bulletin, and has made it a journal that always stands for the best things in the community life, and the Breckenridge schools owe, to a large extent, their present high standing to the impetus given them by Mr. Kenower, both as teacher and as editor.

On August 25, 1891, Mr. Kenower married Ola Russell, a daughter of J. E. Russell, a prominent farmer near Bolivar, Missouri. Mr. Kenower and wife have four children: Pansy, attending Stephens College at Columbia; Pauline, also a student in Stephens College; Fred Russell and Ethel Estell, both at home. The family are members of the Methodist Church, and Mrs. Kenower is active in club and social affairs in Breckenridge.

Mr. Kenower is affiliated with the Masonic and other fraternal orders, standing as he does, for the educational, moral and religious uplift of the community.

In the fall of 1914 Mr. Kenower built a substantial brick building with three floors, including the basement, designed especially for the permanent home of the Bulletin on the corner of Sixth and Main streets, all of which is occupied by the different departments of his model, up-to-date printing office.

THOMAS JACKSON BUTTS. Prominent among the old and honored residents of Kingston is found Thomas Jackson Butts, justice of the peace, retired agriculturist, lawyer, and ex-soldier of the Civil war. In the course of a long and useful life, he has at all times proved his good citizenship, and although now past the age of three score and ten, still takes a lively and active interest in the affairs of the community, and discharges the duties of his office in an able and efficient manner. Judge Butts was born at Mirabile, Caldwell County, Missouri, January 26, 1845, and is a son of Col. Thomas N. O. Butts.

Colonel Butts, his father, was born in Culpepper County, Virginia, a member of an old and honored family of the Old Dominion State, and was married in 1832 to Harriet C. Ellis, who was born in Woodford County, Kentucky. In 1840 they moved to Mirabile, Missouri, where Colonel Butts engaged in farming until the outbreak of the Civil war. He was loyal to the South and enlisted in the Confederate army, subsequently serving in the commands of Generals Price and Marmaduke, and participating in battles in Missouri, Arkansas and other parts of the Southland. On his return from the war he settled down to farming and continued to be so engaged until his death at the age of sixty years. He took a prominent part in democratic politics for some years and was known as one of the influential men of his community. Both he and Mrs. Butts, who died when eighty years of age, were faithful members of the Baptist Church. They were the parents of three sons and six daughters: Samuel J. who died in 1880; William M.; Thomas

Company C, Forty-fourth Regiment, Missouri Volunteer Infantry, under Gen. A. J. Smith, and took part in a number of hard-fought engagements, including the battle of Franklin, Tennessee, in which he was shot through the right arm. He was removed to the hospital at Cairo, Illinois, and upon his recovery received his honorable discharge and returned to the home farm.

Mr. Butts studied law under such distinguished preceptors as General Doniphan and C. T. Garner, and was admitted to practice in October, 1867. For two years he was a lawyer in Calhoun, Texas, but since that time has been more or less actively identified with the bar at Kingston. For many years Mr. Butts was engaged in successful agricultural pursuits, but eventually retired from active business. In 1911 he was elected justice of the peace, and this office he has continued to hold to the present time, presiding over his court with an impartiality, ability and judgment which have won him the esteem and respect of his fellow citizens. He is a prominent member of Ben Loan Post No. 33, Grand Army of the Republic, and has served in a number of official capacities therein, and at the present time is adjutant of the post. His fraternal connection is with the Independent Order of Odd Fellows, and his religious belief that of the Christian Church. In all the duties of life Judge Butts has displayed a conscientious devotion to high principles, and the general confidence in which he is held by all who know him is well merited.

Judge Butts was married in Daviess County, Missouri, in 1873, to Miss Kate Stirman, who passed away August 12, 1876. They had one son, T. N. O. Butts, who died August 21, 1876. On January 15, 1885, he was married to Mary A. Reynolds of Kingston, who was born at Warrensburg, Missouri. Their children are briefly mentioned by name as follows: Effie May, who is employed in Pocatello, Idaho; Harriet Clark; William M., of Idaho; Thomas Jackson, Jr., deceased; George G.; Francis Marion Cockrell, at home; and Abbie Maurine, deceased.

TRENTON CHAPTER, P. E. O. While the P. E. O. is, as the following article shows, one of the strongest woman's organizations in the country, it has manifested a special strength in Missouri, and nearly all the larger towns and cities have chapters. For this reason it is deemed appropriate to include in this work a brief sketch of the order in general and in particular concerning the work and activities of the local chapter at Trenton. The following article has been prepared and contributed to this publication by one of the members of the Trenton Chapter.

The P. E. O. Sisterhood, the largest secret organization of women independent of men's organizations, was founded at the Iowa Wesleyan University of Mount Pleasant, January 21, 1869, by seven bright young girls, members of the graduating class of that year, whose one desire at that time was to perpetuate their love and friendship by the tie of fraternity. They chose the star, whose five points represent faith, love, purity, justice and truth, as a means of recognition, and a motto represented by the letters P. E. O., the meaning of which is spoken only when initiating new members.

The Sisterhood has grown until today it has over twenty-two thousand

desire to complete their higher education with the view to become self-supporting. We have 130 now in the colleges and universities of the different states preparing themselves for the duties of life.

The local chapter, A. D., P. E. O., was organized November 23, 1903, by Mrs. Sophia McLean of Hamilton, state organizer, at the home of Mrs. Addie Shreeve with ten charter members as follows: Miss Lena Conrads, Mrs. Retta Ginn, Mrs. Nettie Hoffman, Mrs. Cora Merrill, Mrs. Mabel Stepp, Mrs. Addie Shreeve, Mrs. Emma Melvin, Mrs. Della Allen, Mrs. Belle Easterday. Miss Conrads was chosen first president as it was largely through her efforts and zeal that the organization was effected.

Chapter A. D. has been visited by three state inspectors, Mrs. Addie Mauzer of Kansas City, Mrs. Charles Iddiols of St. Louis, and Mrs. Vina Bowden of Brookfield, charming sisters, thoroughly familiar with their work, and A. D. enjoyed their presence and received much inspiration from their visits.

The most important event in A. D.'s history was the entertaining of Missouri Grand Chapter convention. It was a big undertaking for the sixteen resident members, but by a united effort and a unanimous purpose, and with the generous assistance given by many loyal citizens, it was possible for Trenton and Chapter A. D. to boast of having the best convention ever held in the state. More than one hundred and ten officers and delegates from all over the state were in attendance, besides visitors from other states, including Mrs. Winona Reeves of Keokuk, Iowa, supreme president, and Mrs. Helen D. Townsend of Albia, Iowa, chairman of educational fund committee. From this array of talent, P. E. O.'s naturally would receive much enthusiasm and encouragement, and A. D. will always cherish the memory of those three days with guests as the brightest of the chapter's existence.

The local chapter has been honored by the State Grand Chapter in electing two of her members to state office. Miss Conrads served three terms as second vice president and chairman of the reciprocity bureau, and Mrs. Hoffman served two terms as state treasurer and one term as first vice president. While serving in this office she was elected treasurer of Supreme Chapter, which necessitated her resigning state work. She served four years as supreme treasurer and is now first vice president of Supreme Chapter.

A. D.'s program has been varied and interesting. The first year was devoted to the study of the constitution, P. E. O. history and initiation ceremony; one year with American history, another, the study of woman's work in the world, women in literature, women in business, women in politics, women as composers, etc. The chapter has studied Ireland and her people, Japan and her people, prominent women of the Bible, our cities' needs, our schools, Russia, parliamentary law. Other features have been debates, constitutional quiz, etc. Alternating with current events, all this interspersed with vocal and instrumental music, making each year's work pleasing and instructive.

The social events have been many and most enjoyable. The first effort was a reception, given at the home of Mrs. Merrill, when 150 guests responded to invitations. Refreshments were served in three

guests were surprised and somewhat embarrassed, but as it was all for fun, greatly enjoyed. An elaborate luncheon, music and glee followed, and each guest expressed himself as having had the "best time of his life."

Two nights of each year are set aside for pleasure, when programs and work are forgotten, the anniversary when the work is initiation and banquet, and a winter picnic for the B. I. L.'s, which is usually the occasion for the initiation of some new brother, making a delightful evening of feasting, fun and frolic.

On February 8, 1910, the members of A. D. were entertained by the B. I. L.'s at Cook's Hall, when they gave a burlesque on the P. E. O. initiation, a mock banquet, then a trip to the Gem Theater, where a special program had been arranged, very personal and of ridiculous nature. Souvenir spoons eighteen inches long were presented as favors. We were then taken to the home of E. M. Harbor, where an elaborate banquet with everything from turkey and cranberry sauce to brick ice cream and cake was served. The evening was full of surprises and a great success.

On Thursday, October 2, Chapter A. D. gave a beautiful and elaborate luncheon at the home of Mrs Austin in honor of Mrs. H. F. Hoffman, who was reelected supreme treasurer at the supreme convention held in St. Louis the week before. The house was adorned with potted ferns and cut flowers and the dining-room was a bower of marguerites, the P. E. O. flower. A six-course luncheon was served, Miss Conrads being toast mistress. Four toasts were given as follows: To Chapter A. D., Mrs. Range; to P. E. O., Mrs. Asher; Our Star, Miss Austin; and a toast to the guest of honor, Mrs. Hoffman, by Mrs. Fulkerson.

On November 21 the same year A. D. gave a chrysanthemum party at the spacious home of Mrs. Hoffman, in honor of the ladies of Trenton who so graciously opened their homes to the delegates during the convention in June. A chrysanthemum contest was greatly enjoyed. The home was profusely decorated with chrysanthemums, southern smilax and a profusion of marguerites. Handsome chrysanthemums in yellow and white were given as favors.

Last but not least was an evening with "Our Mothers" at the home of Mrs. Austin on November 23, 1914. An interesting program of music and papers appropriate to the occasion was given, followed by a social hour, and refreshments served in the dining-room, a bower of beauty in yellow and white.

As to charity work, A. D. has always contributed her part to every worthy cause, from giving $10 to a poor crippled boy to assist him in buying an artificial limb to filling Christmas baskets with food and groceries, sending toys and dolls and good warm clothing to the poor and needy. The sisters have given to the local Charity Union, the Soldiers' Monument, to the Red Cross and Belgian sufferers, and to many more worthy causes, but the main charity work is in giving to the order's own chosen work, the education fund, to which A. D. contributes lovingly and most generously.

Chapter A. D. has been fortunate, as death has but once entered the chapter. On August 19, 1912, the blessed spirit of Della Allen passed to the joys of the beyond. In the loss of Della Allen A. D. mourns, as she was the dearest and sweetest of our number. To know her was to love her.

Chapter A. D. regrets the loss by dimit of four—Mrs. Sally B. Patton, Mrs. Cordelia Green, Mrs. Belle Easterday and Mrs. Bertha Engle. The chapter has maintained a slow and careful growth and it is a pardonable boast that our relations have always been harmonious and our labor one of love. The following is the personnel of the chapter: Mrs. Mabel Stepp, president; Mrs. Ida Austin, vice president; Miss Ima Austin, secretary; Mrs. Olive Asher, corresponding secretary; Mrs. Rètta Ginn, treasurer; Mrs. Sarah Fulkerson, chaplain; Mrs. Cora Merrill, journalist; Miss Elizabeth Carnes, guard; Mrs. Emma Melvin, Mrs. Nettie Hoffman, Miss Lena Conrads, Mrs. Katie Wolz, Miss Blanche Bartlett, Mrs. Katherine Mallett, Mrs. Anna Range, Mrs. Estella Hemley, Mrs. May Temple West, Miss Anna Melvin, Miss Mildred Melvin; Mrs. Nellie Roberts, nonresident; Mrs. Addie Shreeve, nonresident; Miss Emma Webster, nonresident.

PROF. S. F. BONNEY. For the past two years superintendent of the Breckenridge public schools, Professor Bonney is a Missouri educator of thorough qualifications and successful experience, and has been actively identified with the work of teaching and school supervision for the past seven years. Professor Bonney was fortunate in entering the field of education at the beginning of the great modern uplift movement in this department of human affairs, and has already demonstrated the true spirit of service which is at the foundation of the highest usefulness in this calling. The public schools of Breckenridge are now housed in a modern eight-room building, constructed in 1911 at a cost of about twenty thousand dollars, and with the best of standard equipment and facilities for progressive work. In 1914 about three hundred and twenty-five pupils were enrolled, and a large enrollment found in the high school, while eight teachers comprised the staff of instruction. A thorough course of instruction is given in agriculture in addition to the usual curriculum.

Prof. S. F. Bonney was born at Osceola, Missouri, September 27, 1887, and comes of a family whose members have usually been identified with professional life. His grandfather was Dr. S. F. Bonney, a native of Maine. The father, Dr. E. J. Bonney, was formerly a resident of Quincy, Illinois, and after a long and successful career as a physician and surgeon is now living retired. He was a graduate of the Keokuk Medical College at Keokuk, Iowa. Dr. E. J. Bonney married in Osceola, Missouri, Ida Darden, who was reared and educated in Missouri, a daughter of Maj. Samuel Darden, who gained his rank by distinguished service in the Confederate army in Virginia. The mother died at the age of thirty-two.

Professor Bonney was well educated, and after finishing the high school entered college and graduated in 1906 A. B. He taught his first school at Emden, Missouri, for one year, and finished the normal course at Kirksville in the class of 1908. For four years Mr. Bonney was connected with the Jamesport schools, and came to Breckenridge to his present position with a record as a successful and well-seasoned teacher. His management of the local schools has been exceptionally efficient, and for a town of its size Breckenridge now has one of the best public schools in Northwest Missouri.

Mr. Bonney was married in July, 1911, to Agnes Delany. Mr. Bonney

J. E. BOATRIGHT. One of the oldest homesteads in Nodaway Township of Andrew County is the Boatright farm, in section 36, which has been under cultivation and improvement for more than half a century, and its present proprietor, J. E. Boatright, was born there more than half a century ago. He is a farmer and stock raiser, a thorough business man, and among other good things that come into his life is the head of a happy home and the father of a large family of children.

J. E. Boatright was born on his present farm September 10, 1863, a son of Joseph and Sarah (Davidson) Boatright. His father, who was a native of Gentry County, Missouri, enlisted in the Confederate army at the beginning of the war and was killed in service. This son is the only child. The mother was born in Tennessee, was brought to Andrew County by her parents when she was a child, and lived on the old farm until her death in December, 1900, at the age of sixty-three.

J. E. Boatright grew up on the homestead farm, gained his education in the country schools, and has been a practical farmer and manager of the resources of the soil since boyhood. His farm comprises 150 acres of good land in Nodaway Township, and in 1911 he improved it with a handsome modern home of ten rooms. He also rents another farm, and the chief feature of his business is the raising of cattle and hogs.

Politically Mr. Boatright is a democrat and is a member of the Mount Vernon Baptist Church. His fraternal affiliations are with the Modern Brotherhood of America and the Independent Order of Odd Fellows. On October 24, 1890, he married Eunice Jane Deming. Mrs. Boatright was born in Andrew County October 21, 1871, a daughter of William W. and Isyphenia (Files) Deming, her father a native of Vermont and her mother of Andrew County. Her parents were married in 1870, and the father died in March, 1894, while the mother is still living in this county. The children of Mr. and Mrs. Boatright are: Ernest, who died at the age of one year; Elmer, a farmer in Nodaway Township; Glenna; Floyd; Marie; Harold; Arthur; Mildred, who died at the age of three months; Margaret; and Marjorie, who died when one year of age.

FREDERICK DEBO FULKERSON. Here is a name that has been identified with Grundy County settlement and history for nearly three-quarters of a century. It has become honored and respected through long years of successive industry, business integrity and Christian and moral character. Few Grundy County families have been longer established and none have borne their part in community affairs with greater credit to themselves and with more practical usefulness to the community than the Fulkersons. Love of land and the industry based upon it have been the controlling factors in their lives, and mention of the name at once suggests an extraordinary degree of success in handling resources of the soil and in all departments of farm and animal husbandry.

Frederick Debo Fulkerson, who represents the third generation of residence in this section of Northwest Missouri, is the active manager of the splendid stock farm near Brimson, in Grundy County. He was born in this county, in Taylor Township, July 28, 1870, and is a son of Joshua Frederick and Margaret Frances (Fulkerson) Fulkerson.

It was in 1842 that the paternal grandparents, Franklin and Polly (Ewing) Fulkerson, came to Grundy County. Franklin Fulkerson was

in that structure. Northwest Missouri had hardly begun to be settled in the early '40s, and the people who lived there were put to the most primitive methods of industry and living conditions. In the home one of the conspicuous features were the spinning wheel and other implements used for carding the wool, spinning the woolen threads and the flax, and the looms used for weaving the homespun cloth. All the cooking was done at the fireplace, and the children had nothing but corn bread on week days, while on Sundays they were feasted with flour biscuits sweetened with honey taken from the bee trees in the surrounding forest. While the Indians were numerous they were peaceable, and the principal relations the settlers had with these original residents of the forest were trading, though the Indians were notorious as beggars and if not watched were inclined to petty thieving. All this country in the '40s had an abundance of wild game of all kinds—turkey, deer and other animals— and wolves were the chief obstacle to the raising of live stock, the cattle and hogs having to be carefully watched until well grown. The most convenient market for supplies was at that time at Brunswick. Money was a very scarce commodity and the method of doing business was largely by barter and exchange. It was with wagon and ox teams that the Fulkersons came from Virginia to Missouri, and for a number of years all the farm work was performed by the slow plodding oxen, and the plow was made of wood shod with iron. When the grandparents came to Northwest Missouri they brought with them one slave, whom they afterwards liberated and paid his passage to the Liberian Republic, where all American slaves were welcomed, and he was given 160 acres of land and reached a considerable degree of prosperity before his death. Franklin and Polly Fulkerson were the parents of twelve children: Eliza Jane, Amanda, Evelina, Rachel, Peter Glen, Putnam Samuel, Joshua Frederick, Theophilus, Preston, James Evans, Ewing Wirt and Dow. The four still living are Peter Glen, James, Wirt and Theophilus, all of them residents of Missouri.

On the maternal side the grandparents were Frederick Fulkerson and wife, who were also Virginians, and came to Missouri in 1842 and located on the south side of the Missouri River, in Lafayette County. Because of their pronounced sympathy with the general opinion in the North antagonistic to slavery, they suffered a great deal of persecution, and finally moved to Grundy County, where they were safer from such attacks. After the war they returned to Lafayette County, and died near Higginsville.

Joshua Frederick Fulkerson, father of Frederick D., was born in Kentucky October 8, 1838, and his wife, Margaret Frances Fulkerson, was born in Tazewell County, Virginia, in 1846. Joshua F. Fulkerson enlisted in the Missouri State Militia during the war, held the rank of captain, but most of his service was only subject to call and some skirmish duty. He was mustered out at Chillicothe in 1865. He had received from his father eighty acres of land, and began his career as a farmer with a team of oxen and one horse. He had his father's talent for farming, and added to his place until it comprised 339 acres, most of which was thoroughly improved. In 1866 he built on his land a log house of one large room, and there his family of children were reared. The shingles on this house were of walnut, and many of the older settlers recall how plentiful walnut timber was in those days and so little thought of that it was used for firewood. Some of those great walnut logs would now be worth a considerable sum of money. Many facts might be recalled as typical of early times in Northwest Missouri and all of which have been part of the experience of the Fulkerson family. Forty or fifty years ago wild eagles were very numerous and they were a pest to farmers, particularly to those who attempted to raise sheep, since these eagles frequently carried away and destroyed the young lambs. There were few neighbors in the community and families as a rule lived far apart. The Fulkersons had a queer old character as a neighbor, and one incident is recalled. When this old settler came to the Fulkerson home it was customary to give him some present, and on one occasion they sent him away with as many cherries as he could take. The old man put these cherries in his shirt bosom in absence of anything better in which to carry them. Somewhat later a member of the household was visiting at the Fulkersons and was asked how they liked the cherries. She replied that they were very good, but "a little greasy." The very finest land now operated in the farm of Frederick D. Fulkerson was at one time under water, comprising a veritable lake or swamp. There is now hardly any better land in Northwest Missouri. Frederick D. Fulkerson undertook a number of years ago to tile all the bottom land, and since it has been drained it is unexcelled for the growing of corn and other crops. Among the improvements on his estate is a system of private water works. Mr. Fulkerson keeps two men employed the year around and hires considerable extra help during the summer season.

In Grundy County Mr. Fulkerson is regarded as one of the most progressive farmers and stock raisers. His cattle are all thoroughbred shorthorns, he keeps a large number of Shropshire sheep, fine Poland China hogs, and has a yardfull of black Langshan chickens. For a number of years he has been an exhibitor at county fairs and other stock shows, and has won prizes in the State Fair, in the fair at Canton and the Interstate Fair at St. Joseph. His cattle won prizes in the interstate shows and a number of blue ribbons have been awarded his sheep. The ram for his herd was bought in England at a cost of $500 and has won first prizes in Iowa, Illinois, Missouri and Nebraska state fairs. Mr. Fulkerson takes especial pride in his hogs and has spent a great deal of time and care and money in improving and grading up his Poland Chinas until his herd is one of the best in Missouri. The first Poland China hog he ever owned he got by cutting and binding ten acres of corn. He is an expert in all departments of animal husbandry, and among stockmen his name is one of the most familiar in Missouri. He exhibited some of his finest animals in the World's Fair at St. Louis about ten years ago and 'has some premiums from that exposition. He is likewise a lover of good horses and keeps a number of high grade animals.

Frederick D. Fulkerson grew up in Grundy County, attended the country schools, later the Grand River College at Edinburg, and completed his education in the University of Missouri. Mr. Fulkerson studied law, but at the death of his parents came home and has since applied himself to farming and stock raising with a success which is probably greater than he could have reached in that profession, and he has a business and income such as few of the best lawyers in the state enjoy. After the death of his parents he managed the farm so as to educate the younger members of the family, and he and his brother and sister have since kept up the household. Frederick Fulkerson is proprietor of the old home place and has a large amount of town property. He is also engaged in the hardware business at Brimson, under the name of Dent & Fulkerson. Mr. Fulkerson is a republican in politics and has held the offices of justice of the peace, tax collector and town trustee. Fraternally his relations are with the Independent Order of Odd Fellows and the Benevolent and Protective Order of Elks.

DAVID HENRY CLARK. From the position of a country school teacher to proprietor of one of the largest grain and elevator enterprises in

Northwest Missouri indicates a progress and advancement worthy of any ambitious career. While that is the chief business accomplishment of David Henry Clark, it does not measure to the full the civic relations and influences which he has exercised as one of the sterling men of Sullivan and Grundy counties. Mr. Clark has for several years been a resident of the town of Galt, is known to everyone in that community, and his name is familiar to grain dealers all over the state.

David Henry Clark was born in Sullivan County, near the Town of Milan, October 10, 1865. His father was Benjamin Thomas Clark, a native of Kentucky. His mother's maiden name was Elizabeth Peters, who was born in Sullivan County, a daughter of Silas Peters, who was a Kentuckian and one of the first settlers in Sullivan County, having entered land three miles north of Humphreys at a cost of $1.25 per acre. At the time of his death Silas Peters owned a splendid estate of 320 acres, all of it well improved, having been cleared off from the dense wilderness which covered it when he first secured it. Silas Peters was also a prominent man in Sullivan County in the early days, and held a number of local offices. Benjamin Thomas Clark was a resident of Missouri before the war, and in 1861 enlisted as a soldier in the Twenty-second Missouri Volunteers and saw four years of service. He was once wounded, was mustered out and given an honorable discharge in 1865.

David Henry Clark grew up in Sullivan County, attended the country schools there, and in 1886 entered the college at Humphreys. In 1888 he began his career as a teacher, and for several terms had charge of schools in Sullivan County.

It was in 1899 that Mr. Clark became identified with the grain and seed business at Osgood. In the ten years that he was located there his own business became a factor in making that section one of the largest millet producing regions in the United States. Mr. Clark has specialized to a large degree in the handling of millet seed and is still recognized as one of the largest dealers in this commodity in the United States. This brief outline of what he has accomplished in a business way does not suggest the difficulties which he has overcome and the problems he has mastered, but it can be stated that he is a thoroughly self-made man and has achieved success as a result of enterprise and hard work. After some years his business at Osgood became so extensive that he found it necessary to remove to Galt in order to secure better railroad accommodations. At Galt he has the finest and best equipped elevator in that section of Missouri. Mr. Clark is also a farmer, though he operates his land by tenant.

As a republican and a good citizen he has made himself a valuable factor in his home community. Mr. Clark is president of the board of aldermen and president of the school board, also president of the Electric Light Company of Galt, and has served in an official capacity in connection with the town council and the board of education for a number of years. As a feature of his political opinion it is noteworthy that he favors woman's rights. Mr. Clark is a member of the Methodist Episcopal Church and one of its trustees. Fraternally he is affiliated with the Masonic Lodge and the Independent Order of Odd Fellows.

In March, 1889, Mr. Clark married Miss Louisa Jacobs, daughter of

and Nina Ethel. The daughter Lena is the wife of Howell Pollock, son of Judge George W. Pollock of Grundy County.

OTTO HAMILTON. One of the active business men of Spickard, engaged in the grain, coal and feed and general implement trade, Otto Hamilton has spent all his life in Northwest Missouri and has connections with some of the oldest families in this part of the state.

Otto Hamilton was born in Mercer County, Missouri, June 8, 1875, a son of James L. and Matilda (Chilcoat) Hamilton, both of whom were natives of Ohio, and moved to Grundy County, Missouri, in 1866. His father worked on a farm until 1878 and then bought 320 acres in Mercer County for $16 per acre. This land had been entered by a Southern slave holder, who occupied it and worked the land with his slaves. Under Mr. Hamilton's direction the farm was greatly improved, and in 1907 was sold as one of the highly developed farms of that community, bringing a price much higher than was paid for it thirty years before. James L. Hamilton is now living at Chillicothe, Missouri, at the age of seventy-seven. One of his sons, Robert, is a farmer in Howell County, Missouri, and a younger son, J. L., lives with his father in Chillicothe.

Otto Hamilton received his education in one of the country schools of Mercer County, and then became associated with his father in farming until 1901. At that date he bought 100 acres in Mercer County, sold it in 1905 to George Spickard, and then bought 150 acres four miles northwest of Spickard, half of which lies in Mercer County and the other half in Grundy County. In 1907 Mr. Hamilton sold his farm and moved into Spickard, and has since been engaged in business. He was clerk in the hardware and grocery store of T. W. Ballew for a time, and in 1908 was employed at the carpenter's trade in Spickard. In 1911, having given up the work of his trade, Mr. Hamilton engaged in the grain and feed business, to which he afterwards added a stock of implements and hardware. He now has a prosperous business and distributes these various products throughout the surrounding country, and does a good deal of buying and shipping.

Politically he has always been identified with the republican party, but in 1913 was elected on the progressive ticket as township trustee. He is a member of the Christian Church. September 27, 1897, Mr. Hamilton married Mirtie B. Barnes, daughter of Thomas W. and Purcella (Austin) Barnes, of Grundy County. Mrs. Hamilton's parents are among the oldest settlers of Grundy County.

NOBLE J. YOUNG. One of the active and enterprising young business men of Spickard, Noble J. Young is manager of the T. W. Ballew Lumber Company at that point, and began his work in the lumber business at Gallatin several years ago. Mr. Young also has a diploma as an embalmer and undertaker.

Noble J. Young was born at Cedar Falls, Iowa, March 3, 1888, a son of Dr. James W. and Anna (Scham) Young. His father was born in Virginia in 1846 and when only a boy in 1862 enlisted at Batavia, New York, in the Eighth New York Regiment of Heavy Artillery, being assigned to the division commanded by General Hancock. He was pre-

schools of Union County, Iowa, where his parents lived from 1897 until
1902. In the latter year the family moved to Daviess County, Missouri,
and lived on a farm, but he attended school in Gallatin. Doctor Young
moved into Gallatin in 1907, and the son soon afterwards took up business life as clerk in the Farmers store. In 1908 he entered Grand River
College at Gallatin, being graduated in 1910, and in the fall of the same
year entered a school of embalming at Kansas City and was graduated
and given a diploma. Since then his attention has been given chiefly to
the lumber business. In 1911 he became second man with the firm of
T. W. Ballew Lumber Company at Gallatin, and on January 1, 1913,
was sent to Spickard to take charge of the local yards as manager.

Mr. Young is a democrat and is affiliated with the Masonic fraternity
and the Knights of Pythias. He was married June 12, 1913, to Myra A.
Newman, daughter of Albert A. and Winifred (Kegrice) Newman,
formerly of Illinois, but locating at Breckenridge, Missouri, in 1896.
Mrs. Young's father is a large land owner in that section of Missouri.

JOHN D. HOBSON. For nearly three-quarters of a century Andrew
County has been continuously honored and benefited by the presence
within its borders of the Hobson family. In the character of its individual members and in their public services no family in the county has
enjoyed higher esteem, and as the first generation were of the fine pioneer
type which create homes out of the wilderness, so those that have followed
have taken up in turn their destinies in the world and have been home-
makers, industrious providers and capable citizens.

John D. Hobson, who represents the second generation, was born in
the City of Savannah November 19, 1852. His parents were John and
Elizabeth Jane (Phillips) Hobson, both of whom were natives of North
Carolina, were of English descent, and in the earliest generations all
Quakers. John Hobson was born in Raleigh County, North Carolina,
June 29, 1813, a son of Hadley Hobson, who spent all his life in North
Carolina. John Hobson early in his career started for the West, lived a
time in Indiana, later in Illinois, and while in that state helped lay off a
portion of the present City of Chicago, and then with horse and wagon
journeyed on to the western frontier and thus arrived in Andrew
County in 1841. In 1844 he was married in Ray County, Missouri, to
Elizabeth Phillips, who was born in North Carolina in 1824, and was
brought to Andrew County when a child, the Phillips having been among
the very first to locate in this section of Missouri. John and Elizabeth
Hobson lived for a time in Rochester Township, and later moved to Savannah, where he was associated with his brother Stephen in conducting
a brick yard and kiln, and they furnished the material and also the building service in the construction of many of the old homes in Savannah.
John Hobson had acquired land from the Government situated six miles
northeast of Savannah, in Empire Township, being the owner of a quarter
section of prairie land and also forty acres of timber land on the Platte
River. After leaving the brick business in Savannah he retired to his
farm and spent the rest of his life there, where he died in 1892 at the
age of about sixty-nine. His wife passed away March 13, 1877, aged
fifty-four. After he had lived several years in Northwest Missouri, John
Hobson. returned to North Carolina, making the trip with a one-horse
wagon and having another horse which he rode half the time and the
other half drove the wagon. The family were members of the Baptist
Church. Their five children were: C. L. of Whitesville; Sarah Ellen,
wife of Asbury Pendry of Benton Township, and she is now deceased;
Mary E., wife of John Bombarger of Rea; John D.; and Breckenridge B.
of Empire Township.

John D. Hobson has spent all his life in Andrew County, and lived at home and assisted his parents in operating the old farm until twenty-seven. He then married and began farming for himself, and now owns an excellent estate in section 14 of Platte Township of 160 acres, known as Woodside Farm. It is devoted to general grain and stock farming and Mr. Hobson is one of the successful representatives of agricultural activities in this part of the state. He is a republican in politics and is a member of the Methodist Episcopal Church at Walnut Grove.

In 1880 Mr. Hobson married Margaret Crockett, a member of a well known family of that name in Andrew County. She died in 1895. Her father was Nelson Crockett. In 1901 Mr. Hobson married Cynthia Adkins, who died in 1906. In 1908 he married Emma Jones, daughter of Isaac N. and Susan (Bowman) Jones. Mr. Hobson has no children by any of his wives.

Isaac N. Jones, father of Mrs. John D. Hobson, is one of the oldest native sons of Andrew County, where he was born December 18, 1849. Two years later his father was killed by lightning, and the mother then took her eight children up to the old home in Indiana, lived there several years, and at the close of the war returned with three of her children, the other one still living having remained in Indiana, and she continued to reside in Andrew County until her death in 1875. The three children now living are: Elizabeth Blanchard of Barnard, William F. of St. Joseph and Isaac N.

Isaac N. Jones received his education in the country schools and has been a continuous resident of Andrew County since 1865, a period of fifty years. His active career was spent as a farmer and a few years ago he retired and is now living on the farm with his son-in-law, Mr. Hobson. Mr. Jones was married in 1871 to Susan Bowman, who was born in Andrew County December 30, 1848, and has spent practically all her days within the limits of this county. Her parents were Casper and Mary Ann (Hutchinson) Bowman, both natives of Kentucky. Her father was born in 1802 and died at the age of eighty-seven, and her mother was born in 1811 and died at the age of eighty-nine. They moved from Kentucky to Northwest Missouri with five children during the latter '30s, and spent the rest of their days on a farm six miles northeast of Savannah, on land that had been entered by John Bowman, father of Casper. Isaac N. Jones and wife are the parents of four children: Emma L., wife of John D. Hobson; George Ernest, of Rochester Township; Mary Lou, wife of George Bailey, and now living with her father; Alonzo Newton, of St. Joseph.

C. L. Hobson, an older brother of John D., is also one of the older native sons of Andrew County. He was born in Rochester Township November 7, 1847, and all his years have been spent in this county except three, during which time he was a farmer in Brown County, Kansas. He was reared on a farm, followed that as a vocation until 1882, then spent sixteen years in conducting the mill at Whitesville, and has since been engaged in the carpenter trade. C. L. Hobson is affiliated with Whitesville Lodge No. 313 of the Independent Order of Odd Fellows.

On May 4, 1882, he married Adelia Harlan. She was born in Clinton County, Ohio, February 25, 1857, and came with her parents, R. M. and Mary (Downer) Harlan, to Andrew County in 1868. Both her parents are now deceased and were natives of Ohio. There were three sons and six daughters in the Harlan family. Mr. and Mrs. C. L. Hobson are the parents of three children: Anna Flossie is the wife of E. R. Smith of Whitesville; Nellie Grace is the wife of C. B. Allen of High Prairie, Platte Township, and their three children are named Duane

Hobson, Loren Plato and Robert R.; and C. L., Jr., who lives in Salt Lake City, Utah, married Gertrude Thompson of Denver.

L. F. NOELLSCH. One of the vigorous and enterprising younger farmers of Holt County, L. F. Noellsch, has spent practically all his life in this section, and his career illustrates what may be accomplished by young men of industry and ambition in the fertile farming district of Holt County.

L. F. Noellsch was born in this county December 16, 1879, a son of Joseph and Louisa (Hoffman) Noellsch. There were six children, and all of them are still living. Mr. Noellsch married Blanche Bucher, daughter of Jacob Bucher. By their marriage they have become the parents of three children: Kenneth, Louis and Ethel, all of whom were born in Holt County.

Mr. L. F. Noellsch graduated in the high school at Oregon and since that time has taken his place as a hard working member of the agricultural community. His first farm was one that he rented from his father, and his present place is a portion of the estate of Jacob Bucher. Mr. Noellsch has done much to improve the farm, which comprises 160 acres of land, and is prospering along general lines of agriculture and stock raising. In politics he is a republican and his father was of the same political faith.

BENJAMIN CLAY NICHOLS. For forty-five years Benjamin C. Nichols has been engaged in mercantile business at Trenton. He recently retired from a long service in the office of postmaster and has in many different ways been identified with this community. During the war he was a soldier in a Missouri regiment fighting for the Union cause. His family was one of the earliest to make settlement in this section of Northwest Missouri, and the name is one always spoken with respect and appreciation of its dignified position in the community.

Benjamin C. Nichols was born on a farm in Grundy County two miles north of the courthouse, November 22, 1844. His father was Benjamin Nichols, who was born at Bellefontaine, in Logan County, Ohio, in 1802. Grandfather Ninian Nichols was born probably in Virginia, lived for some years in Kentucky, finally settled in Ohio, and bought a tract of land near Bellefontaine, where he was a farmer. Late in life he went out to Iowa, and at the home of a daughter died, aged eighty-eight. His wife had died in Ohio, and they had a large family.

Benjamin Nichols, the father, was reared on an Ohio farm and followed farming in Ohio until 1839. In that year he came and made settlement in Grundy County. His wife and four children accompanied him, and, as there were no railroads across the Mississippi at that time, they made the entire journey from Ohio by wagons and teams, driving over the rough roads and taking several weeks for a journey which could now be accomplished in twenty-four hours. His location was a tract of timber land two miles north of where the courthouse now stands in Trenton. A previous settler had cleared off an acre or so, and the Nichols family located in a log house where the son Benjamin C. was born five years later. At that time all Northwest Missouri was sparsely settled and the greater part of the land was still owned by the Government. There were many Indians, and all the early settlers were on more or less familiar terms with the red men. About half a mile from the old Nichols homestead was a grist mill operated by horse-power. Settlers came from miles around with their grain and kept the little mill going night and day in order to turn out the grist. Oftentimes those who brought grain had to camp in the vicinity and wait their turn several

days before getting the meal and flour for their households. After a
few years Benjamin Nichols sold out that farm and bought a place five
miles north of Trenton, where he was employed in general farming and
stock raising until his death, at the age of seventy-one years. Benjamin
Nichols married Anna Huston. She was born near Bellefontaine, Ohio,
in which vicinity her parents were pioneer settlers. She survived her
husband a few years and reared eleven children, whose names are briefly
as follows: James T., who was a soldier in the Mexican war and who
died at the venerable age of eighty-three years; Mary Jane; Melinda;
Susan Matilda; Martha; William Harrison; John C.; Elizabeth C.; Benjamin Clay; Lucetta; Robert Huston.

Benjamin Clay Nichols grew up in a country which still had much of
the characteristics of the virgin wilderness, and as he was born in a log
cabin he also attended a school taught in a log house, heated from a fireplace, with home made furniture. There were no desks in front of the
rude slab benches on which the pupils sat, and a broad board set at an
incline against the wall served for purposes of writing. While his
scholastic training might have been deficient in some ways, he had no
lack of practical training. He worked on the farm, developed his physical
constitution, and before he reached manhood had seen active service as a
soldier, fighting the battles of the Union. Some time after the breaking
out of the war he enlisted in the state militia and served two years, and
then entered Company A of the Forty-fourth Regiment of Missouri
Infantry. After a brief time spent at Rolla, the regiment went south
and joined the Army of the Cumberland. Its principal battle was at
Franklin in the latter months of the war, and while this was a Federal
victory, Mr. Nichols was one of those captured by the Confederates, and
as a prisoner of war he assisted in burying the dead on that battlefield. He
saw six Confederate generals taken dead from the battlefield. As a
prisoner he was removed to Meridian, Mississippi, and thence to Selma,
Alabama, to Cahaba, and was finally sent with others to Vicksburg to be
exchanged. The Confederate prisoners refused exchange, and the Union
men were placed on neutral ground and kept until the close of the war.
Mr. Nichols then went to St. Louis and received his honorable discharge
in May, 1865. Returning home, he continued his schooling for two years
in the Trenton High School, taught for two years, and then began his
long and active service as a merchant. He was at first a clerk in a general store, and finally got into business on his own account. In 1880 he
formed a partnership with Henry F. Carnes, under the name of B. C.
Nichols and Company. In 1885 this was changed, when R. E. Boyce
and James Fulkerson joined Mr. Nichols, and they conducted a prosperous dry goods house until 1898. Selling out, Mr. Nichols then entered
a partnership with W. E. Patterson under the firm name of Patterson
& Nichols. They were engaged in the shoe business until 1906, when
they sold their stock and acquired the men's furnishing store from T. H.
Roder & Co. As Patterson & Nichols they have sold goods to a large
trade ever since.

Mr. Nichols was married in 1878 to Miss Mary E. Moberly. She was
born in Trenton, a daughter of George W. and Margaret B. Moberly.
Her death occurred in 1883, and in 1895 he married Laura A. Yakey.
She was born at Sidney, Shelby County, Ohio, daughter of Peter and
Jane Yakey. Mr. Nichols cast his first presidential vote for Abraham
Lincoln while a soldier in the army and has been a stanch republican
ever since. In many ways he has been one of the leading republicans of
Grundy County, and in June, 1913, retired from his administration of
postmaster at Trenton after a service of eight years and five months.
He affiliates with Grand River Lodge No. 52, I. O. O. F.; Trenton Lodge

No. 111, A. F. & A. M.; Godfrey De Bouillon Commandery No. 24, Knights Templars, and the Temple of the Mystic Shrine at St. Joseph; also with Trenton Lodge No. 15, Daughters of Rebekah, and with the Order of the Eastern Star.

OLIVER GREEN BAIN. This name, of a prominent lawyer of Trenton, where he has practiced with success and participated in public affairs for more than thirty years, is also suggestive of one of the most interesting pioneer families in this section of Northwest Missouri. The Bains were among the very first to establish homes in the virgin wilderness of Grundy County before a county of that name had been created.

The family in 1837 located in what is now Lincoln Township, Grundy County, and in a log cabin near the present site of Tindall Oliver Green Bain was born January 4, 1850. His father was Jesse Bain, who was born in a fort on the Muskingum River, in Muskingum County, Ohio, June 21, 1812. Riason Bain, father of Jesse, was born on the east side of the Ohio River, in the little valley shut in by hills where now stands the City of Wheeling, West Virginia, in 1791, and came of good old American colonial stock. About 1808 the Bain family crossed the Ohio River, moved west along the National road, and finally arrived in the wilds of Muskingum County. Though Ohio had been a state for half a dozen years, the greater part of the country was a wilderness enjoyed as a hunting ground by Indians. Near where the Bains settled stood a fort for the protection of the scattered inhabitants, and at the first note of Indian alarm all gathered behind its stockade for protection. Riason Bain grew up and was married in Ohio, and lived there until about 1830.

The westward movement was in the blood of this family, and practically every generation has furnished men of the pioneer type. Riason Bain with his family followed out the course of empire and moved first to Rush County, Indiana, and in the spring of 1837 again set out for a still more remote point on the frontier. With his sons Jesse and Jacob he made a journey overland to Missouri, using ox-teams for transportation and carrying all the moveable possessions in wagons. The Mississippi River was crossed at St. Louis on April 9, and they pushed on to Pulaski County, Missouri, where they hastily prepared ground and put in a crop. Then they resumed exploration over the surrounding country. While traveling as prospectors, they met a Government surveyor, Lisbon Applegate, who had finished some work for the Government in the Grand River country. When asked about that section he replied that in his report he should credit the land with being better than first rate. On hearing this the Bains at once returned to Pulaski County and, having harvested their grain, started with a team and wagon for Grand River. On arriving at the confluence of Shoal Creek, in Livingston County, they met Samuel Kelso, Henry Foster and William Dille. The water was high and the creek unfordable. Kelso had been delayed by the water some time and was discouraged and ready to quit. Riason Bain took the lead, constructed a raft and ferried the entire party across. They all proceeded westward until they reached what is now Grundy County. There Riason Bain selected the southwest quarter of section 25, township 62, range 24, now designated as Lincoln Township. At that time most of this country was owned by the Government and much of Grundy County still unsurveyed. Two years later he entered his pre-emption right in the land office at Lexington.

In a history of Grundy County the authors say: "Lincoln township was first settled in 1837. The first settlers pitched their tent November 12th of that year. The colony consisted of Riason Bain, Samuel Kelso, Jesse Bain, Henry Foster and William Dille. Their camping ground was on the northwest quarter of section 22, three hundred yards east of the site of the Bain schoolhouse. They traveled many hundred miles to reach their new home and were water bound and compelled to remain encamped many days.''

Riason Bain was a Methodist and was a leader of the first class meetings in the neighborhood. In 1838 it was in his house that Rev. Thomas Peery preached the first sermon heard in Lincoln Township. Riason Bain died in 1839. His wife, whose maiden name was Nellie Crow, a native of Virginia, died in 1830. Her parents were pioneers of Western Virginia, and later of Muskingum County, Ohio. While the Crow family and others were sheltered in the fort previously mentioned, two of Nellie's sisters and a brother ventured into the woods for hickory nuts. Indians fell upon them, scalped the girls and knocked the boy senseless. He recovered, got back to the fort, and lived several years, but the girls died soon after being brought within the shelter.

Jesse Bain was a vigorous young pioneer of twenty-five when he arrived in Grundy County. The little home which he established in Lincoln Township was for a long time an isolated outpost of civilization. All kinds of wild game were in abundance, deer and wild turkey furnished meat for the table, and one of the favorite sports among the settlers was "bee hunting," a bee-tree supplying the larder with sweets for several weeks. The women of the household did many tasks now unknown to womanly accomplishment, such as carding and spinning and weaving of the cloth which furnished raiment for all the family. As soon as the land was put on the market Jesse Bain walked all the way to Lexington and entered the southeast quarter of the northwest quarter of section 22, and then constructed the log cabin in which the present Trenton attorney first saw the light of day. He hewed a farm from the wilderness, and was one of the strong men in that day of rugged frontier virtues. Little money was in circulation in the first ten or fifteen years of Grunty County history, and though it was a heavy task to produce a crop lack of convenient market kept prices down. When a farmer of that community had some hogs or hides to sell, they were carried by wagon to Brunswick, seventy-five miles away, and there sold at from one dollar and fifty cents to one dollar and seventy-five cents per hundred weight. In spite of early disadvantages, Jesse Bain prospered, added to his land until he owned 320 acres, and left it well improved with buildings and under perfect cultivation.

The pioneering which brought him to Grundy County did not satisfy him, and in 1850 he joined in the great exodus to the California gold fields. He joined a party that went overland with wagons and teams, staid about a year on the coast, and returned by sea, around Cape Horn, and after many adventures, including the wreck of a vessel, he once more took his place in the little Missouri community. During the war between the states he was in Company E of the Seventh Missouri Militia. His later years were passed in quiet and comfort on his farm, where he died September 22, 1894.

In Pulaski County on August 10, 1837, Jesse Bain married Catherine Ogletree. She was born in Overton County, Tennessee, in November, 1818, and died in 1857, leaving two sons, Pleasant W. and Oliver Green. November 10, 1858, he married Mary Rock. By this marriage there were four: Walter G., Anna, Jesse D. and Helen A. From the formation of the party Jesse Bain was a strong republican.

Fifty years ago Grundy County was still a half wilderness, and the boyhood of Oliver G. Bain was encompassed by an environment which seems primitive compared with present conditions. He attended a school taught in a log cabin and has a vivid recollection of old-time books and methods. Later he studied in the Trenton high school, and began his self-supporting career as a teacher, a vocation he followed through seven terms. In the meantime he had applied himself to the study of law, and in 1878 was admitted to the bar. His has been one of the honorable careers in the law in Grundy County for an entire generation. After a brief practice in the country, and one year in the Town of Spickard, he moved to Trenton, where he has been in practice ever since.

In 1884 he was elected prosecuting attorney of Grundy County, and in 1890 was again elected and re-elected in 1892. He has long been a leader in republican ranks, and cast his first vote for Grant in 1872.

February 14, 1878, Mr. Bain married Miss Rosa Brunson, who represents an old family of Southern Iowa. She was born in Lee County, Iowa, September 17, 1859. Her father, Thomas, was born in Hamilton County, Ohio, in 1835. Thomas Rennick Brunson, her grandfather, was born in New York State in 1784, a son of Barefoot Brunson, who came from Holland and settled in the Province of New York before the Revolution. This Dutch settler married Margaret Bell, a native of Ireland. Thomas R. Brunson learned the trade of stonemason, and when a young man went to Tennessee and assisted in laying the foundation of the state capitol at Nashville. Later he settled in Clermont County, Ohio, and in 1841 moved out to the Territory of Iowa. As a pioneer in Lee County he bought a tract of land near the present site of West Point, and combined farming with his trade until his death in 1866. His wife, Susan Miller, was born in Pennsylvania in 1796 and died in 1874. David Miller, her father, was born in Germany, settled in Pennsylvania, where he was a miller, and died there in 1845. He married Susan Humlong, also a native of Germany, born in 1741 and died in 1844. Thomas Brunson, father of Mrs. Bain, was six years old when the family settled in Lee County, where he was reared and learned the trade of plasterer. That and farming were his means of support in Lee County until 1867, when he sold out and went to Clark County, Iowa. That section of the state was still new, and he was able to trade a horse for eighty acres of land, which he began to improve, and he lived there to see settlement and civilization become established all around him. After twenty-eight years he again sold, and moved into the new country of the Southwest. In Washita County, Oklahoma, he became one of the early white settlers, bought a quarter section of raw land, and built a frame house which he plastered with his own hands. It was the first house with plastered walls in the county, and attracted much attention for this modern innovation. He followed farming and stock-raising for some years, and finally moved to the Town of Foss, where he is now retired at the age of seventy-eight. Thomas Brunson married Arline Clark, a native of Ohio. Her father was Cullen Clark, born in Vermont, in 1810, and a son of Johnson Clark, of Scotch ancestry, who died in 1820, and whose wife Sally (Bent) Clark, died in 1817. Cullen Clark in young manhood went to Ohio, where he married Rozella Case. Her father, Chauncey Case, who was born in 1788 and died in 1868, and was a New York farmer, married Nancy Van Heining, who died in 1884. Thomas and Arline Brunson had five children, namely: Rosa, Cullen, Clark, Bent H. and Thurman. To the marriage of Mr. and Mrs. Bain has been born one child, Homer Judson.

HOMER JUDSON BAIN. The only son of Oliver G. and Rosa (Brunson) Bain, Homer J. Bain is one of the successful younger lawyers of Grundy County, and has practiced with his father at Trenton since his admission to the bar.

He was born at Trenton, September 9, 1879, attended the city schools, graduating from the high school with the class of 1896, and the following year entered the University of Missouri. He graduated LL. B. in 1901, and was admitted to the bar before the Supreme Court in the same year.

An active republican, casting his first vote for William McKinley, he has interested himself in local affairs and has been honored with positions of trust. In 1905 he was elected city attorney, and by re-election served three terms. In 1910 he was elected prosecuting attorney of Grundy County, and added to the honors previously gained by his father in the same office.

June 16, 1908, he married Fern Hibbird, who was born at Sigourney, Keokuk County, Iowa. Mr. Bain belongs to the university honorary fraternity, Beta Theta Pi, and to Lodge No. 801, B. P. O. E. He is much interested in agriculture, owns a stock farm in Lincoln Township, where the Bain family history centers, and supervises his estate as a pastime and recreation, though he also makes his land pay good profits.

HON. THOMAS B. COOK, M. D. It is scarcely possible, in these modern days, for a man to be a successful practitioner of medicine without being also a man of learning and of solid, scientific acquirements. Often the youth who feels the inspiration that ultimately leads him into the medical profession finds his progress one of difficulty from lack of encouragement, opportunity or capital, and when all these drawbacks are overcome, through personal effort, battles have been won that make firm the foundations of character. One of the leading physicians of Ray County, Dr. Thomas B. Cook, of Rayville, has not only gained a high place in his profession through individual effort and merit, but has also won distinction in public life, and as the representative of his people has been able to secure the enactment of some legislation of a decidedly beneficial character to his community.

Doctor Cook has been a lifelong resident of Ray County, being a member of a family which came here in pioneer days. He was born on a farm in the vicinity of Lawson, May 6, 1855, and is a son of Joseph and Melvina (Underwood) Cook, natives of Orange County, North Carolina, the former born January 12, 1809, and the latter December 15, 1812. In 1838 Joseph Cook and his wife started on their long journey to the far west, as then represented by Missouri, packing their possessions in one wagon and being accompanied by their children, one of whom died on the way, while in Tennessee. The hard, tedious and dangerous trip consumed six weeks, but finally the little party of immigrants reached their destination in Audrain County, and there the father established their primitive home. The family continued to reside in that community until 1844, in which year Mr. Cook purchased a tract of land in Ray County, on the present site of Lawson, and there became a fairly well-to-do farmer. The contentions and animosities growing out of the struggle between the North and the South, however, caused him to remove to Illinois in 1864, and there he remained until peace was declared between the warring factions in 1865. On his return to Missouri, he located on a property in Caldwell County, near Polo, and this continued to be his home until his death, March 2,

of Joseph McCowan, of Elmira, Missouri; Sallie, who is the wife of William P. Pryor, of Ray County, and Dr. Thomas B., of this review.

Doctor Cook was reared on the home farms and attended the common schools of the country and the high school at Lathrop, and while he was not employed with his studies gave his services to his father on the home place. It was his ambition to become a physician, but was not possessed of the finances necessary, and accordingly, to secure the needed means, took up school teaching as a vocation. From 1874 until 1880 he taught in the country schools of the community, and in the latter year, having carefully saved his means, began reading medicine in the office and under the preceptorship of Dr. W. C. James, at Lawson. Subsequently he entered the medical department of the University of Louisville, Kentucky, and in 1883 saw his ambitions realized when he was graduated with the degree of Doctor of Medicine. He at once came to Rayville, and in this city established himself in practice, his subsequent activities having been centered here. At this time Doctor Cook is in the enjoyment of an excellent professional business, built up by his ability, his thorough knowledge of his profession and his deep sympathy and kindliness. He has attained high standing in his profession as a strict adherent of medical ethics, and among his fellow-practitioners is accounted a valued assistant in consultation. He belongs to the various organizations of his profession and keeps himself thoroughly in touch with the discoveries and inventions constantly being made in the field of his calling. Doctor Cook has been successful in a business way, being the owner of a flourishing drug business at Rayville and a stockholder in the Commercial Bank at Lawson and the Savings Bank at Richmond. A lifelong democrat, he has been active in the ranks of his party, and in 1906 was honored by election to the Missouri Legislature. His district returned him as representative to the Forty-fourth General Assembly, in which he introduced and had passed a measure granting to circuit clerks the power to fix bail of persons charged with criminal acts during the vacation of courts. He was also made chairman of the committee on accounts and in that capacity acquired the suggestive sobriquet of "Watch-dog of the Treasury." He took at all times a leading part in placing on the Missouri statutes some of its most important laws during his terms of office, and conscientiously protected the interests of his constituents.

On January 31, 1888, Doctor Cook was married to Miss Maud Massberger, who was born in Carroll County, Missouri, May 15, 1868, a daughter of Frank M. and Anna (Taylor) Massberger, natives of Missouri, who are now living at Bogard, this state. One son has been born to Doctor and Mrs. Cook, Thomas B., Jr., who is a member of the senior class, 1914, at the University of Missouri.

MRS. MARY S. NAUMAN. The Nauman family took up its residence in Holt County more than thirty years ago, and during his lifetime the late Hiram Godfrey Nauman was one of the prosperous agriculturists of Liberty Township. Though he came to Missouri a poor man, he exhibited the thrift and enterprise which bring success in any vocation and in any locality and has left his widow and children well provided, and theirs is now one of the largest individual estates in Liberty Township.

The late Hiram Godfrey Nauman, who died January 17, 1913, and whose death took away one of the best and most successful citizens of Liberty Township, was born in Page County, Virginia, a son of Reuben and Elizabeth Nauman. He was married in his native county to Mary S. Dovell, a daughter of David M. and Elizabeth (Booton) Dovell. Mrs. Nauman had seven brothers and four sisters, while her husband was

one of a family of twelve sons and daughters. Mr. and Mrs. Nauman
became the parents of six children, mentioned as follows: Stella, unmarried; Lelia Clyde; Emma V., who married Albert L. Walkup; Bessie G.,
who married Lester Griffith, and has one child, Roseland Virginia; C.
Victor, unmarried; Hiram Elmer, who married Blanche Conner, and
has two children, Robert Sheldon and B. Louise. The children are all
still living, and all of them were born in Virginia, except the two
youngest, one of whom was born in Holt County and the other in Atchison
County.

Mr. and Mrs. Nauman brought their family to Holt County in 1881,
and he began here as a renter. Subsequently he bought a farm in Atchison County but sold that and secured the 200 acre farm in Liberty
Township from David Kelly. This was the nucleus of his enterprise,
which before his death had accumulated a large estate comprising 600
acres. During that time he also erected a substantial residence now
occupied by Mrs. Nauman and her unmarried children, and perfected
many other improvements about the farm.

The late Mr. Nauman was a member of the Presbyterian Church,
while Mrs. Nauman belongs to the old school Baptist. Politically he
was a democrat. Mrs. Nauman and her children now have the active
management of the farm, and are people who enjoy the highest regard
of the community.

Hon. John E. Carter. Now in the seventy-eighth year of his life,
Mr. Carter is one of the oldest and best known citizens of Trenton in
Grundy County, and with firm step and unclouded mind still walks the
streets and attends to his daily routine of affairs, and only recently
retired from his active duties as county treasurer. Mr. Carter was
in business in Trenton before the Civil war, served on the Union side in
the great struggle between the states, and during the past forty years
has given much of his time to official duties. He still manifests a keen
and intelligent interest in all that effects the welfare of his home county
and city, and is known as a man of progress and public spirit.

John E. Carter was born in the one-time Village of Cleveland in
Tippecanoe County, Indiana, December 21, 1836. His father was Dr.
Benjamin Carter, who was born in Whitefield, Lincoln County, Maine,
and the grandfather was Joseph Carter, of an old English family and
a farmer in Lincoln County, Maine. Dr. Carter acquired a good education as a young man, and studied medicine in Bowdoin College, where
he was graduated with his degree and went west to take up practice.
He lived in Indiana for a time, and taught school as well as looked
after his patients. From Indiana he moved to Kentucky, later went
to Arkansas, but without making a permanent home in either state he
returned to Indiana and settled in the Town of Monroe, Tippecanoe
County, where he died at the age of fifty years. Doctor Carter, Sr.,
married Elizabeth Eddy, who was born in Dearborn County, Indiana,
in 1818. Her father, John Eddy, a native of New York State, was one
of the early settlers of Dearborn County, a few years later moved to
Tippecanoe County and from there to Lawrence County in Arkansas,
where his last years were spent. Mrs. Carter, after the death of Doctor
Carter, married James LaCount, and spent her last years in the City of
Trenton. By her first marriage there were three children: John E.,
Martha and Frances. The second union resulted in two sons, Benjamin
and Fred.

John E. Carter was reared neither in affluence nor in poverty, but
in a time and among circumstances which forced him early into the
struggle of life, and what he has accomplished is almost entirely the

result of his well directed efforts. The Indiana schools which he attended as a boy were conducted on the subscription plan and the teacher boarded around among the families of his patrons. This school, such as it was, afforded him the rudiments of training, but at the age of twelve he became self-supporting and earned his living at various kinds of work for several years. When he was seventeen he apprenticed himself to the blacksmith's trade, and at the end of one year was given twenty-five dollars for the twelve months' work. Mr. Carter came to Trenton, Missouri, at the age of nineteen, nearly fifty-nine years ago. At that time the Hannibal and St. Joseph Railway was in process of construction, but not yet completed entirely across the state. His trip' west, from Indiana to Trenton, with all his belongings, was performed in the old "prairie schooner," and was not very eventful, except the loss of a horse which somewhat delayed the journey, until a horse could be bought, and the journey westward could be resumed. The country was new and untamed, and many were the times they enjoyed the luxury of camping out, and the game which came in the way of his rifle. They reached Trenton at last, a hamlet of 800 inhabitants, peculiarly characteristic of southern life, "niggers" and the "divine" institution. After two years of work as a journeyman, he opened a shop of his own and did a good business until the breaking out of the war.

In 1861 Mr. Carter enlisted in the Missouri State Militia, and spent six months with the Grundy County Battalion. He then served with a regiment of state troops, all of whose service was in Missouri. At the close of the war he resumed his business at Trenton and directed it personally until 1870. Since that time much of his energies have been absorbed by official duties.

On January 30, 1860, Mr. Carter married Mary E. Wethered. She was born near Pontiac, Michigan, a daughter of George Wethered. The happy married companionship of Mr. and Mrs. Carter has continued for fifty-three years, and they are one of the most venerable couples in Northwest Missouri. They have reared six children, named Minnie, Elizabeth, Frances, Luther, Mattie and Myrtle. Minnie married William Marden, and has one daughter, Carrie. Elizabeth married J. L. Marden, and their one daughter is Edna. Frances married John Rose, and has a son named John Conrad. Luther married Maude Hall, and has a son, Dale. Mattie married John R. Brazelton, and has a daughter, Frances. Myrtle is the wife of P. R. Durdy. Both Mr. and Mrs. Carter have been members of the Christian Church for more than half a century.

Mr. Carter cast his first presidential vote for Abraham Lincoln, and was one of sixteen republicans in all Grundy County in the year 1860. He has been one of the wheel-horses of the party in Grundy County for half a century. In 1881 he was elected a member of the State Legislature, and was three times re-elected. During his four terms at the state capital he did much for his home district, was a student and a worker for progressive legislature affecting the entire Commonwealth, and gave suitable service on various committees. In 1904 came his election to the office of county treasurer, and by re-election his ministration was continued until January, 1913. Mr. Carter belongs to the Jacob Smith Camp No. 72, G. A. R., and he also affiliates with the Grand River Lodge No. 52, I. O. O. F.

JACOB F. PHILLIPS. With the passing years the descendants of the old soldiers of the Civil war will prize more and more the gallant records made by their forefathers who fought in the campaigns of the South which brought about a united country. There are many families now which take special pride in referring to their Revolutionary ancestors, and in course of time even greater respect will be paid to those who fought for the integrity of the Union during the dark days of the '60s. One of the fine old soldiers who still survive from that dark and stormy time of civil strife is Jacob F. Phillips, a prominent citizen and farmer of Davis Township in Caldwell County.

Jacob F. Phillips was born in Washington County, Indiana, February 27, 1840. His birthplace was a log cabin, located on an early farm in that section of Indiana. His father was Andrew Phillips, who came from North Carolina and was one of the first settlers in Indiana. Grandfather Phillips died in Caldwell County, Missouri, in about 1870. Andrew Phillips was reared in Indiana, and was married there to Jemima Ratts, who died in Illinois in about 1901. She was born in North Carolina, a daughter of Rinehart Ratts, who died in Indiana. Andrew Phillips in 1854 moved to Logan County, Illinois, settling on a farm near Atlanta, and he died there in 1856, at the age of thirty-seven, leaving his widow with seven sons, whose names are: Jacob F.; Rinehart, who was a soldier of the Twenty-eighth Illinois Infantry, died in 1863, in Mississippi, and was buried at Oxford, that state; Ransom, who was also a soldier, now lives at Atlanta, Illinois; Abraham, who died at Kingfisher, Oklahoma; John M., who died at Atlanta, Illinois; Thomas F., whose home is in Kingfisher, Oklahoma, and who was also a soldier; and George A., who died in Illinois when but five months old.

Jacob F. Phillips was reared in Illinois and was educated in the schools of Logan County. He was twenty-one years of age when the war came on, and in August of 1861 he enlisted for service in Company F, Thirty-eighth Illinois Infantry. He went with the regiment to Missouri, took part in some operations around Pilot Knob, and at different times was under the command of General Scofield, General Grant, General Rosecrans and others of the great leaders of the Union Army. He fought at Murfreesboro, Tennessee, at Rome, Georgia, in the various battles and skirmishes about Chickamauga, and during that campaign was taken prisoner. He endured all the hardships and sufferings of life in the Southern prisons, was confined in the notorious Libby Prison at Richmond, Virginia, and then the no less famous Andersonville, and was confined at five different places before his exchange. When he went into prison he weighed 190 pounds and about one hundred and twenty-five when he came out. He was exchanged in December, 1864. In one of his battles, that of Chickamauga, he was wounded in the left leg. He served in the Missouri Militia in 1866, as a non-commissioned officer, with the rank of orderly sergeant.

As a Missouri farmer Mr. Phillips has been unusually successful and owns a fine place of 320 acres, a part of which is bottom land well situated for alfalfa. His industry has been largely stock raising, and he keeps about one hundred and fifty hogs and horses, mules and cattle.

Mr. Phillips married, February 21, 1867, Martha Rathbun, a sister of Samuel Rathbun, a prominent Caldwell County farmer whose history will be found on other pages of this work. Her father was Allen Rathbun, one of the early pioneers of Caldwell County. Mrs. Phillips died March 11, 1909, at the age of sixty-three. She was a member of the Church of Christ. They became the parents of nine children, three of whom died in infancy, and five are now living. Mary M., who is living in Kansas, is married and has two children; James A., who is on the old homestead farm, married and has three children; Edgar L., Effie and Eva May, all at home. Dora A. died at the age of twenty-eight years. Since the death of his wife Mr. Phillips has lived with his children and grandchildren. Politically he is a republican, and has supported that party since war times. He is also active in the Grand Army of the Republic, and is a member of and an elder in the Church of Christ. He is devoted to his home and family, but is also a man of popular character in the community, and has hosts of friends in this section of Northwest Missouri.

CYRUS JASPER PATTISSON. One of the most beautiful properties in Andrew County is that of Cyrus J. Pattisson, a tract of 125 acres and 20 acres of timber land, lying in section 19, Platte Township. "The Evergreens," as this farm is known, has been developed under the supervision of Mr. Pattisson, who has resided here since 1870, and is known as one of the township's substantial men. While the property is equipped with every modern appliance for practical farming and stock raising, it has been so beautified by the planting of shade and ornamental trees, shrubs, roses, etc., and occupies such a notable position on a ridge that it is one of the show-places of this part of Northwest Missouri.

Cyrus J. Pattisson was born in Jefferson County, Indiana, April 4, 1843, and is a son of John and Leah (Walker) Pattisson, the former a native of Indiana and the latter of Maryland. His grandfather, John C. Pattisson, was born in London, England, within 200 feet of the north end of the historic London bridge over the Thames. He was twice married, and by both unions reared families. The grandmother of Cyrus J. Pattisson was the second wife, formerly Mary Bloor, a native of England, but of a family said to have been of Holland origin. John C. Pattisson was a physician and early settler of Indiana, in which state he located after his emigration to the United States. His pill bag, which he carried on his saddle, is one of his grandson's highly prized possessions. He died in Jefferson County, Indiana, in 1837, the grandmother surviving him many years, and passing away in September, 1876, at the home of one of her daughters (Josephine Snider) in Nodaway County, Missouri, near Barnard and is buried in the Lower Neely Grove Cemetery near Rosendale in Andrew County.

John Pattisson grew up in Jefferson County, Indiana, and was there married June 16, 1842, to Leah Walker, who had been brought from her native Maryland by her parents as a child. In May, 1858, the family came to Nodaway County, Missouri, where John Pattisson engaged in farming until 1859, then going to St. Joseph, where he was engaged in merchandising during that and the following year. In the spring of 1861 he returned to his farm in Nodaway County, and afterwards came to Andrew County, and died on his farm there June 27, 1875, aged fifty-eight years eight months and seventeen days, having been born October 10, 1816. His widow survived until March 17, 1896, being eighty-five years of age at the time of her demise. John Pattisson was a strong and unswerving Union man and one of the 410 Lincoln voters in St. Joseph in 1860. Because of his outspoken views in behalf of a free state, he made numerous enemies, and June 19, 1861, was the night set as the date upon which he was to have been hanged by Southern sympathizers. However, some information as to the plot leaked out, and on the night set for the tragic work the plotters were met by a much superior force of armed men and completely foiled and defeated. Having escaped this fate John Pattisson subsequently for a time served in the Home Guard during the war. While not a member of any church John Pattisson's religious views and sentiments inclined him to Universalism, and his wife did not take up with any particular creed of religion. John Pattisson and wife were the parents of seven children, of whom three died in infancy, the others being: Cyrus J.; Mary C., who became the wife of Thomas Pettigrew, a sketch of whose career will be found in this work; Hannah Thirsa, who is the widow of George Boharm of Rosendale, Missouri; William Bonaparte, deceased, who was a soldier in the Fifty-first Regiment, Missouri Volunteer Infantry, during the Civil war, died May 13, 1871. The three children who died in infancy were: John, who died December 6, 1849, aged eleven days; Solomon, who died January 10, 1852, aged one year, one month and fifteen days; and Worcester Daniel, who died May 28, 1858, aged two years, ten months and fifteen days.

Cyrus J. Pattisson received his education in the public schools of Jefferson County, Indiana, and was a lad of fifteen when, in May, 1858, he came to Missouri with his parents. He then lived in Nodaway County a year, in the City of St. Joseph two years, and again for about nine years in Nodaway County, and with these exceptions has spent the rest of his life in Andrew County, and since March, 1870, has lived on the farm which he now owns. He was successful in his agricultural ventures from the start and succeeded in the accumulation of 240 acres, but has since sold or deeded some land to his son, and his farm now consists of 125 acres, on which he resides. This he has appropriately named "The Evergreens" from the large number of evergreen trees growing about the property. In 1871 he brought from Indiana and set out a number of red cedar trees and later secured more, which were placed in rows, resembling an orchard. Here also are found numbers of American Arbor Vitae trees, used as a shelter belt, with Austrian pine and blue spruce, giving the estate a most pleasing appearance. Mr. Pattisson takes great pleasure in anything that grows and has a small greenhouse, in which he cultivates tropical plants. That he is a practical man, however, is shown by his well cultivated fields and large herds of well-fed, contented stock. He is a natural mechanic, and when a young man, from 1860 to 1864, manufactured four violins, two of which are of especially fine tone. In his little workshop on the farm he is able to make all the repairs necessary on his farming equipment, and has studied invention quite a little and has perfected several devices with some success. Mr. Pattisson leads a quiet, home life, taking his greatest interest in his farm, and not caring to mix in public matters, although he has always been ready to cooperate with his fellow citizens in movements for the general public welfare. While not a member of any church denomination, or any order, he has been a steadfast upholder of right and morality, is tolerant of the creeds and beliefs of others, and carries out his principles into practice in his everyday life and in his politics. He has the esteem of his community because of a life of straightforward dealing, and during his long residence in Platte Township has attracted to himself a wide circle of friends.

Mr. Pattisson was married December 26, 1867, to Miss Mary Elizabeth Atkinson, who was born in New Jersey, May 20, 1851, and who came to Andrew County in 1857 with her parents, Hugh M. and Eliza (Pettigrew) Atkinson, natives of Armagh, Ireland. Eight children have been born to Mr. and Mrs. Pattisson: Laura, born February 9, 1869, is the wife of Newton Hershberger, of Bolckow, Missouri; one daughter, Helen Honor, died in infancy; Amanda May, born August 9, 1873, died March 17, 1907, as Mrs. Claude Rea, leaving two children, Ruth and Clifford; John William, born April 3, 1876, lives at Savannah, and by his marriage to Eva Cooper has two sons, aged four and two years; Daniel Edwin, who now lives in Platte Township, was born November 2, 1878, and married Miss Emma Rea; Cyrus Chester, born June 15, 1880, lives in Nodaway County, and by his marriage to Miss Ada Stewart has one boy, Lawrence, aged eleven years. Estella Ethel, born April 19,

1886, is the wife of Charles Hauensteine of Grand River, Iowa; Mary Etta, born December 25, 1870, died at the age of one year, three months.

FREDERICK W. KORNEMANN. One of the valuable farms of Andrew County which represent German thrift and industry is the Kornemann homestead, near the Village of Clarksdale, on section 13 of Monroe Township. Its proprietor, Frederick W. Kornemann, has lived on this one place and has been a factor in community affairs more than thirty years and his name is familiar to many stockmen in various parts of Northwest Missouri.

Frederick W. Kornemann was born in Hesse Cassel, Germany, November 17, 1850. His parents were Franz and Mary Christina (Kaseburg) Kornemann. In 1868 all the family left Germany, went first to St. Louis, and soon afterwards located in Clinton County, Missouri, near Cameron. There Franz Kornemann followed the vocation of farming until his death in 1871, when about fifty-nine years of age. His widow lived with her son Frederick until her death May 17, 1901, at the age of seventy-four. Franz Kornemann spent all his life as a farmer, and before leaving Germany served three years in the army. The children were: Frederick W.; Mary, wife of Fred Krull of Monroe Township; Henry, who lives near Walla Walla, Washington; George, whose home is near Warrensburg, Missouri; and Minnie, deceased, who married Conrad Neth.

Frederick W. Kornemann was about seventeen years of age when the family came to America, and his education had been acquired in German schools. He learned the English language after coming to America, and for several years was a substantial farmer in Clinton County. In 1879 he and his mother bought the Andrew County farm from Thomas Aston, and took possession in 1880. Since then for a period of thirty-four years Mr. Kornemann lived in Andrew County, has prospered in the general lines of agricultural activity, and has stood well in his civic relations and as a helpful member of the community. At the present time he is owner of 240 acres, the homestead comprising 160 acres. Much of his revenue as a farmer comes from live stock. At the time of the Spanish-American war he and his brother George rode all over this section of Missouri buying mules for the Government, and this established an extensive acquaintance among stockmen over several counties and proved an experience subsequently valuable to him as an individual stock raiser. Mr. Kornemann is a director in the Platte Valley Bank at Cosby, having been identified with that institution since its organization. Politically he is a republican and is a member of the German Methodist Church. Mr. Kornemann is unmarried.

GEORGE L. HOBSON. A good citizen, a prosperous business man, and an honor to his family name and community was the late George L. Hobson, who died at his home in Empire Township, Andrew County, February 11, 1915. He left an estate which illustrated Northwest Missouri farm enterprise at its best. A part of his property in that township was entered by his grandfather many years ago direct from the Government. Mr. Hobson was no man to hide his talents in a napkin. The inheritance he received from his family has been multiplied and increased, and his energy, sound judgment and alert ability enabled him to build up a fine business and accumulate property which in extent and value would do credit to a most successful manufacturer or merchant.

George L. Hobson was born on a part of his present farm, 2½ miles southeast of Rea on August 17, 1854. He represented two old and substantial families of Northwest Missouri. His parents were John M. and

Martha (Colburn) Hobson. The paternal grandfather George Hobson was a native of North Carolina, left that state and became a pioneer in Indiana, and some years later came to Northwest Missouri and entered Government land, a part of which is now included in the estate of his grandson. The Hobsons were English Quakers, and the first Americans of the name came over to this country with William Penn. Grandfather George Hobson was born June 5, 1791, and died near Oregon, Holt County, Missouri, December 29, 1865. He married Deborah Marshall, who died September 15, 1862, at the age of sixty-nine years, one month, twenty-three days. John M. Hobson, the father, was born near Newcastle, Indiana, January 17, 1826, and was about twenty-two years of age when he came to Northwest Missouri. He was a farmer and acquired about one hundred and forty acres, now included in the farm of George L. Hobson. John M. Hobson was reared a Quaker but married outside that church. He was a republican in politics, and during the Civil war served in the Missouri State Militia for a time and was a soldier in the regular army during the last six months of the war. He died on the old homestead April 28, 1902. He was married on the Colburn farm to Martha Colburn, who was also born near Newcastle, Indiana, June 28, 1829. Miss Colburn came to Andrew County when thirteen years of age with her parents, John R. and Elizabeth (Petty) Colburn. Her father located four miles northeast of Savannah, entering land from the Government, and spent the rest of his life on that farm. John R. Colburn was a circuit rider of the Methodist Church, and combined preaching and farming. There were eight children in the Colburn family. Mrs. Martha Hobson died December 15, 1900. Their four children were: Esther, who died at the age of sixteen years; Margaret, wife of Isaac Silvers of Savannah; George L.; and John F., who lives near El Reno, Oklahoma.

George L. Hobson grew up on the old home farm, received his education in the local schools, and from early boyhood manifested those traits of industry and enterprise which carried him so far in a business way. During his early childhood his parents removed to Oregon in Holt County, where his father for 4½ years operated a mill. With that exception his home was in Andrew County practically all his life. As a farmer he was careful, methodical, and practiced the rule of keeping all his land in productive use and at the same time conserving and upbuilding his resources. The surplus from his business was reinvested in more land, and the old home place has gradually been extended until at his death he was owner of 745 acres of the fertile soil of Empire Township. His home place is situated in section 7. All of this land is in one body, and there are three sets of farm buildings. After acquiring the land Mr. Hobson put up two sets of buildings, and these are used by his tenant operators, who in this case are his own children. One of the best country homes in Andrew County is found on his old home site, and he built the residence in 1900. Mr. Hobson lived on one spot for thirty-eight years, and it is interesting to recall that his first building was a double log cabin. His well ordered enterprise is shown in the substantial character of his farm buildings, comprising large barns, silos and all other equipment needed for the sheltering of his crops and stock. His success came from combined grain and stock farming and he keeps a large number of high grade stock. Mrs. Hobson has also interested herself in the poultry department of farming, and takes much pride in her chickens, geese, ducks and canary birds. Mr. Hobson was a republican, and a member of the Methodist Episcopal Church at Wyatt.

On December 27, 1876, George L. Hobson married Eliza A. Johns.

She was born in Madison County, Iowa, July 13, 1854, and came to Andrew County with her parents in 1863. She is a daughter of Andrew B. and Mary A. (Smith) Johns, both natives of Ohio. Mrs. Johns died in Iowa when Mrs. Hobson was eight years of age. Andrew Johns was born July 7, 1829, and his wife October 3, 1830, and she died in 1862. Mr. Johns married for his second wife Mahala Bradford. He died in Andrew County, January 8, 1895. By the first marriage there were eight children and eleven by the second union, and Mrs. Hobson is the oldest among the nineteen children of her father's family.

Mr. and Mrs. Hobson had five children, but two of them, Marshall Andrew and George Byron, died in infancy. The three living are: Homer F., who is a city mail carrier at Quincy, Illinois; Walter M., who occupies and operates a part of the homestead of his father; and Ethel M., wife of W. M. Lanning, they occupying another of the two groups of farm buildings on Mr. Hobson's estate.

WILLIAM HUTCHEON. The career of William Hutcheon, one of the substantial farmers and livestock raisers of Nodaway County, is illustrative of the great rewards which are granted those who follow lives of industry and integrity. He was thrown upon his own resources when but fourteen years of age, and since then has worked his way to a substantial position among the men of the various communities in which he has been located, being principally known as the owner of Mapleton Stock Farm, where have been bred a number of national champions in White Faced cattle.

Mr. Hutcheon is a native of Scotland, born at Aberdeenshire, November 19, 1862, a son of Alexander and Isabella (Brodie) Hutcheon. His father, who was a modest farm laborer, died in 1874, but the lad continued at his studies in the public schools for two years more, at which time he entered upon a career of his own, from the outset of which he was connected in some way with the raising of thoroughbred cattle. When he was eighteen years of age, Mr. Hutcheon left his native land and emigrated to the Province of Quebec, Canada, where he arrived with something less than five dollars. He had energy, ability and ambition, and soon found employment with a stockman, in whose employ he continued for nearly ten years. Mr. Hutcheon then emigrated to the United States and for two years was employed on a stock farm in Indiana, then coming to Jackson County, Missouri, where, in partnership with an Englishman, John J. Stewart, under the firm style of Stewart & Hutcheon, he engaged in the breeding of cattle. This association continued uninterruptedly until the fall of 1894, when Mr. Stewart died, and since that time Mr. Hutcheon has continued alone. In 1902 he came to his present property, Mapleton Stock Farm, a tract of 320 acres, located in sections 31 and 32, Grant Township, and half of which lies in Andrew County, the other half being in Nodaway County. This is one of the best farms in this part of the state and is exceptionally well improved, the greater number of improvements having been put on by Mr. Hutcheon.

In the raising of White Faced cattle, Mr. Hutcheon has had a grand success. Here was reared the famous "Mapleton," named after the farm, champion bull of the World's Fair at St. Louis in 1904. In 1905 at the Portland (Oregon) Exposition, Mr. Hutcheon was awarded the grand championship prize for the best herd of White Faced cattle, having four females and one male, the male being the son of "Mapleton." One year at the International, Mr. Hutcheon showed two animals from one cow, and was awarded first prize in each class, both senior and junior championships, joined together for grand championship, this never having been done before or since. Mr. Hutcheon exhibits annually in nine state fairs and the American Fair, at Kansas City, and for twelve years has exhibited annually at the International Stock Show, Chicago. Mr. Hutcheon keeps a herd of from seventy to one hundred animals on his place all the time, all thoroughbred stock, and these animals bring the highest prices in the markets and at sales. He also carries on general farming to some extent, and has met with a full measure of success in this department. In his business transactions he has always displayed straightforward dealing that has won him the confidence and respect of his associates, and as a citizen he is foremost in promoting beneficial measures. Mr. Hutcheon is a member of the Presbyterian Church at Bolckow, and also holds membership in the Masonic Lodge there. Since becoming a citizen of the United States, he has been a republican, his first presidential vote being cast for William McKinley.

In January, 1908, Mr. Hutcheon was married to Miss Margaret Lee, who died without issue in 1911.

SAMUEL EDWARD LEE began newspaper work at the age of twelve by setting type in the newspaper office of his mother, Mrs. Martina Christina Lee, who was editor and publisher of the Hasting (Iowa) Record for two years. Mr. Lee was a printer for several years in Iowa and went to Holton, Kansas, following the same work and later going to Chicago where he attended school. He came from there to Savannah and took up the foremanship of The Reporter in November, 1906. This he continued until 1910 when he purchased a half interest in The Reporter printing plant, established by O. E. Paul in 1876. On January 4, 1912, he married Mrs. Lilah Townsend Paul, who purchased a third interest in the same plant in 1902 and in 1905 purchased a half interest. Mr. Lee's father was James Monroe Lee, who was the son of Henry Lee, who was a descendant of the Virginia Lees. He was born in Blount County, Tennessee, in September, 1821, and married Miss Mary Catherine McConnell, daughter of James and Peggy McConnell. Henry Lee moved to Indiana and then to Michigan for a short time, coming to Shelby County, Iowa, where he died September 8, 1890. His sons, Sam and Annon, yet live in that county but the father of the subject of this sketch, who was a carpenter and contractor, went to Texas, near Houston, during the land boom of 1897 and died in January, 1899. Mr. Lee's mother is yet living in College View, Nebraska. Her father was Lars Weien, born in Denmark, February 4, 1827. He was a tailor by trade and he and his wife, Mette Petrine Christensen, who was born in 1831, came to America in 1861 and lived three years in Wisconsin, coming to Shelby County, Iowa, in 1864, when their daughter, Martina Christina, was nine years old. Samuel Edward Lee was born in Calhoun County, Iowa, on February 7, 1886. He and his wife continue to publish The Savannah Reporter, county seat weekly. Their only child, a daughter, died September 21, 1914.

COL. ELIJAH GATES. A venerable and highly esteemed citizen of St. Joseph, Col. Elijah Gates served throughout the Civil war as one of the most brave and gallant soldiers of the Confederate army, and has since served the state in various capacities, in each position to which he has been elected performing the duties devolving upon him efficiently and satisfactorily. A son of John Gates, he was born, December 17, 1827, in Garrard County, Kentucky.

John Gates, a farmer, spent his last years in Garrard County, Kentucky, dying in 1829, while yet in manhood's prime. The maiden name of his wife was Mary Maupin. She was a native of Madison County,

Kentucky. She survived him, married a second time, and spent her last days in Lexington, Kentucky.

Brought up and educated in Kentucky, Elijah Gates remained in his native state until 1848, when he followed the tide of emigration westward to Missouri. Purchasing a tract of wild land in Livingston County, he occupied it until 1857, when he sold, and bought a tract in Fremont Township, Buchanan County. In 1861 Colonel Gates enlisted for three months in the Confederate service, becoming captain of Company A, State Militia, and took part in the engagements at Carthage, Dry Wood, Lexington, and Springfield. He subsequently organized a regiment of soldiers at Springfield, and was commissioned colonel of the regiment, which was assigned to General Price's army. At the head of his regiment, the Colonel was at the front in the engagement at Elkhorn, Arkansas, and was later with General Beauregard at Corinth. He afterwards took an active part in the Battle of Iuka, the second engagement at Corinth, and in those at Grand Gulf, Champion Hills, and Big Black River. At the latter battle he was captured, but two days later he made his escape, and joined his command. He assisted in the defense of Atlanta, and participated in the Battle of Jonesboro, after which he went with Hood's army to Franklin, Tennessee, where he was in the thickest of the fight. He was there severely wounded, captured, and had his arm amputated. After remaining a prisoner twenty-four days, the Colonel escaped, and at Mobile again joined his command. In April, 1865, Colonel Gates was again captured by the enemy, and was held in confinement until the close of the war. Serving throughout the conflict, Colonel Gates was five times wounded, three times captured, twice making his escape, and had many narrow escapes from death, having had three horses shot from under him.

Soon after his return from the seat of war Colonel Gates embarked in business at St. Joseph, and continued until 1872, when he was elected sheriff, a position which he filled for five years. In 1876 he was elected state treasurer, and served for four years, from 1877 until 1881. He then bought an interest in an omnibus and transfer line, with which he was connected a few years. In December, 1885, Colonel Gates was appointed United States marshal for the Western District of Missouri, and served in that capacity for five years. The past few years the Colonel has lived retired from active business cares, having accomplished much work in his long and busy life.

Colonel Gates married, in 1852, Maria Stumper, who was born in Monroe County, Missouri, of pioneer ancestry, and to them twelve children have been born.

ANDREW FRANCIS McCRAY. For many years A. F. McCray, by which initials he is best known, has been one of the prominent citizens of Caldwell County. A veteran of the war, in which he lost a leg, he has been for over forty years one of the busiest and most energetic men in the county, has an unusual reputation as a successful auctioneer, has been engaged in the grain, real estate and insurance business, and in public affairs has served as county assessor two terms and as county treasurer one term, and as postmaster of Cowgill for more than twenty years. Mr. McCray has known Caldwell County and this section of Northwest Missouri since pioneer times, and his own home has been in the county since 1848.

He was born in Millersburg in Callaway County, Missouri, July 1, 1843. His birthplace was a log house, and his father, William McCray, was a native of Bourbon County, Kentucky, and of an old Kentucky family that emigrated to Missouri in 1829 when he was only ten years old.

William McCray married Nancy Carroll, a daughter of John Carroll, a descendant of that famous Carroll who affixed his name to the Declaration of Independence in 1776. William McCray was a man of strong character, an influential pioneer of Caldwell County, a whig and republican in politics, and a great admirer of General Zachary Taylor. He died at the age of eighty-four, and his wife passed away in 1885, aged sixty-three. He was loved and respected by all who knew him, and for many years served as a justice of the peace, his decisions being invariably sustained by the higher courts. He possessed both the physical vigor and strength of character which well fitted him for life in a new country. In 1861 he took a strong stand for the preservation of the Union, and such a position in Caldwell County was attended with more difficulties and had to combat more opposition than a similar stand in the more northern state. He was also an ideal man for a new country in his work of organizing and maintaining public schools and in helping to build up the moral and educational interests. His own education had been limited to three months of school privileges, but among his associates he passed as one of the best informed men of his community. He was a great reader of books, kept himself informed on everyday affairs of the nation, and his reading and practical experience fortified him for the position of leadership which he long held. In earlier years he was a blacksmith, but gave that up for the farm and he was noted for the excellence of the fruits grown in his orchard. Like many Kentuckians his name was a synonym for openhanded hospitality. His home never closed its door to friend or stranger alike, and passing travelers always found a welcome entertainment with food and shelter. The living children of William McCray and wife are: A. F.; James C., of Leavenworth, Kansas, who was a soldier in the Forty-fourth Missouri Infantry; Millard F., of Cowgill, Missouri; Warren, of Gurneville, California; David O., who is a well known newspaper correspondent and former publisher of many republican papers in Missouri and Kansas, and is now a resident of Topeka, Kansas; Charles C., of Redding, California, now a member of the California Legislature; and Mrs. G. B. Cowley, of Cowgill, Missouri.

A. F. McCray was reared on a farm in Caldwell County, attended the old time district schools but acquired most of his education from practical experience. When a young man in March, 1862, he enlisted for service in the Sixth M. S. M. Cavalry, and served until the battle of Lone Jack August 16, 1862, where he lost his left leg. He was removed to Lexington, Missouri, remained in the hospital until September 10, 1862, and was then taken to the old home by his father, who had been with the son while in the hospital, and received an honorable discharge November 25, 1862. After his return home Mr. McCray busied himself with work in different lines. He taught school during the winter of 1865-1866, and in the summer of 1866 embarked in the cattle business, which he followed successfully for many years. In November, 1866, Gov. Thos. C. Fletcher issued an order for the enrollment of all of the Militia forces in Missouri to suppress the bushwhacking that prevailed in many parts of the state. A. F. McCray was appointed enrolling officer for Caldwell County, with the rank and pay of a first lieutenant in the army. He proceeded to enroll all of the men in the county and organized them into companies and a regiment for actual service, but the regiment was never called into service. In 1868 he was elected to his first public office, as county assessor. In 1872 came his election to the office of county treasurer, and in that office as in every other public relation he showed his efficiency, competence and honesty. He was postmaster at Cowgill during President Harrison's administration, and in 1897 President McKinley appointed him postmaster again, and he served through the McKinley, Roosevelt and Taft administrations, until February 14, 1914. Mr. McCray had charge of the office during the institution of the various new departments of the postal service, including rural free delivery, and always administered the office beyond reasonable criticism. For forty years Mr. McCray has been engaged in business as auctioneer, and is one of the best known men in that profession over Northwest Missouri. His son, C. F. McCray, is now associated with his father, and his engagements call him to all parts of the country, frequently to Kansas City and Chicago to sell stock at the stock yards. Both father and son are known to all the prominent stock men in Northwest Missouri.

Mr. McCray married Miss Hortensia J. Rhoades, a prominent teacher in the public schools before her marriage, and born in Erie County, New York, but reared in Pennsylvania, her family being prominent in the Oil City district. By their marriage Mr. and Mrs. McCray are the parents of the following children: Harry B., who is connected with the Badger Lumber Company of Kansas City; Miss Merle; Mrs. J. O. Denton of Sapulpa, Oklahoma; William S., of Sapulpa, Oklahoma; and C. Frank, his father's partner.

Mr. McCray has prospered in business affairs and the competent fulfillment of obligations during his long and active career constitute him one of the leading men of Northwest Missouri. He is a member of the Independent Order of Odd Fellows, and for many years has been one of the leading republicans in his section of the state. For twenty years he served as commander and adjutant of the Grand Army Post at Cowgill.

CLYDE SID JONES, editor of the Polo Missouri Weekly News, is one of Caldwell County's most popular citizens. Engaged in newspaper work since 1901, he has steadily advanced in the ranks of Missouri journalism as well as in the esteem and confidence of the people with whom he has come into contact, and as a public-spirited and helpful citizen has done much to advance the interests of his chosen town.

Mr. Jones was born in Caldwell County, Missouri, in 1876, and is a son of J. M. Jones. His father, born in Coshocton County, Ohio, migrated to Missouri as a young man, and here enlisted for service during the Civil war, through which he served. When his military career was completed he returned to his vocation of farmer, in Missouri, but at this time is a resident of Oklahoma and is retired from active pursuits. He is a republican in his political views, and a member of the Grand Army of the Republic. There were seven children in the family: Eliza Jane Douglass, of Tulsa, Oklahoma; William, a farmer of Caldwell County; M. G., a merchant of this county; Charles M., engaged in the hardware business at Polo; J. E., a farmer of Caldwell County; Clyde Sid, of this review; and Fred, a farmer.

Clyde Sid Jones was educated in the public schools, and was reared to manhood on the home farm. From his early youth he displayed a predilection for newspaper work, and in 1901 embarked upon his real career in this field, being at that time connected with the Polo Post, with which he remained for two years. In 1903, when the Polo Missouri Weekly News was founded, Mr. Jones became its editor, and in this capacity has remained to the present time. This publication is issued every Thursday, and at the present time has a paid-up circulation of eight hundred readers. Since 1908 it has been consolidated with the Vindicator, and reaches a class of people that gives it its sub-title: "Read by Home Folks." The office equipment is of the best, including a complete job printing department, where work of the finest nature is done, this feature of the business having developed rapidly during the past several years. In his capacity of editor of this flourishing publication, Mr. Jones has done and is doing much for Polo, influencing the people along the lines of progress and good citizenship and supporting every measure for the advancement of education and morality. A man of pleasant personality, as fluent and ready a talker as he is a writer, he has made numerous friends since coming to Polo. Physically he is a strong, virile man, six feet tall, and weighing two hundred pounds. In political matters Mr. Jones is a republican, and while he has not sought public office on his own account, has done much for his party in Caldwell County.

Miss Nettie Maytum, the publisher of the News, is a lady of exceptional business ability, with broad experience in newspaper work. She knows her public and her field, and during her residence at Polo has become widely and favorably known to the people of this thriving community.

C. P. DORSEY. The name Dorsey has for many years been identified with the press of Northwest Missouri, and C. P. Dorsey is editor of the Braymer Bee, an influential newspaper of Caldwell County, which was for a number of years owned and edited by his father, the late Dr. Dennis Dorsey, who was distinguished in Northwest Missouri as a successful physician, minister, orator, editor, and a keen and incisive writer, who was thoroughly informed not only in his individual profession, but on civic and social affairs generally.

Dr. Dennis B. Dorsey was a graduate of the Medical College at Keokuk, and for many years practiced his profession. During the Civil war he served as surgeon in the Union Army. He was born in Baltimore, Maryland, and represented a family which had been founded in America by three brothers of French Huguenot stock who located on this side of the Atlantic during the Colonial times. Doctor Dorsey was married in Center County, Pennsylvania, to Margaret Gray, daughter of Jacob Gray, who was a native of Pennsylvania. In 1868, Doctor Dorsey located at Chillicothe, Missouri, where he later became editor of the Tribune. For many years he was one of the most active members and ministers of the Missouri Conference of the Methodist Episcopal Church. He stood strongly for the principles advocated by the republican party, and was a leader both for the economic policies advocated by that party, and also for the temperance movement. His death occurred September 2, 1901, at the age of seventy-one years. Personally he was a man of professional bearing, stood five feet ten inches, weighed 170 pounds, and was a man of accomplishments and a genial personality. His widow died in 1900, being then sixty-seven years of age. Their children were: Dr. F. B. Dorsey, who is a surgeon at Keokuk, Iowa; Dr. J. G. Dorsey, a physician at Wichita, Kansas; Luella Dorsey; Eva Dorsey, and C. P. Dorsey of Braymer, Missouri.

The Braymer Bee is a paper that has been read and quoted in Northwest Missouri for a number of years, and has an individuality and influence impressed upon it by the different members of the Dorsey family who have controlled its destiny. It is republican in politics, but has worked without partisanship for the upbuilding and welfare of Braymer and Caldwell County. It has a large circulation, the plant occupies a building of its own, and it is one of the rural newspapers of Northwest Missouri that represents a profitable business.

C. P. Dorsey was born in Chillicothe, Missouri, July 11, 1874, and has been in the newspaper business most of his active career after leaving school. From 1909 to 1911 he was editor of the Keokuk, Iowa, Constitution-Democrat, and then became identified with journalism in St.

Louis. He resigned his work there in order to take charge of the Bray-mer Bee, the health of his sister, Miss Eva, who had edited the paper for two years, making it inadvisable for her to continue the full man-agement of the journal.

Mr. C. P. Dorsey was married June 7, 1911, at Kansas City, to Miss Mary Lankford, daughter of the late Thomas H. Lankford, for many years a prominent Chillicothe newspaper man. Mr. and Mrs. Dorsey have two children: Dennis B. and Florence Margaret. Mr. Dorsey is a member of the Methodist Episcopal Church and active in its Sunday school, and he and his family stand high in local society.

JUDGE CHESLEY A. MOSMAN. An able and influential member of the Missouri bar and for nearly half a century a resident of St. Joseph, the late Judge Chesley A. Mosman won unmistakable prestige in his chosen profession, his scholarly attainments and comprehensive knowl-edge of the law gaining him success in the legal world. He was born July 29, 1842, in Chester, Illinois, but was brought up and educated in St. Louis, Missouri, where his parents settled when he was an infant.

At the outbreak of the Civil war Mr. Mosman, fired with patriotic zeal and enthusiasm, enlisted in a St. Louis company which was assigned to an Illinois regiment, and with his command went South to join the Union forces. Although he started with General Sherman's army on its march to the sea, his company did not go beyond Atlanta with the gallant hero, but he, with his command took an active part in the engage-ments at Murfreesboro and Chickamauga, and later, having joined Gen-eral Thomas, was at the front in the Battle of Nashville. After the surrender of Lee, on April 9, 1865, Mr. Mosman was ordered with his command to Texas to look after the Mexican situation, and after the execution of Maximilian, the French having been driven out, his regi-ment was discharged, he having in the meantime been promoted to the rank of first lieutenant. While in the army he was wounded twice, on one occasion his shoulder blade having been broken by a bullet.

On his return to Illinois, Mr. Mosman accepted a position as a clerk in a mercantile establishment, and while thus employed took up the study of law, and shortly after coming to St. Joseph, in 1868, was admitted to the bar. Subsequently, under Judge Albin, he served as clerk of the Circuit Court, and in 1870 was elected prosecuting attor-ney of Buchanan County. He later became junior attorney for the Kansas City, St. Joseph & Council Bluffs Railroad, now a part of the Burlington system, and held the position until 1875, when the senior attorneys, Hall & Oliver, retired. Mr. Mosman then formed a partner-ship with the late J. D. Strong, with whom he was associated sixteen years as senior attorneys for the Burlington Railroad. On the retire-ment of Mr. Strong, on account of ill health, in 1891, Judge Mosman became junior member of the firm of Spencer, Burnes & Mosman, which was continued until the election of Mr. Burnes to Congress. Messrs. Spencer & Mosman, however, continued as general solicitors for the Burlington until 1900, when Judge Mosman retired from the firm, and resumed private practice. In 1904 the Judge was elected judge of Division No. 1 of the Circuit Court, on the republican ticket, and served most acceptably for one term of six years.

For several months prior to his death, which occurred at his home, 619 South Thirteenth Street, St. Joseph, Judge Mosman was forced to give up business, but though he remained at home he still retained his interest in local affairs, and took great pleasure in seeing his friends. A man of high principles and sterling character, the cordial upright nature of the Judge won him a host of sincere friends, and made him highly honored and beloved in the city where he was best known.

Politically Judge Mosman was identified with the republican party, and he served wisely and well in the offices to which he was called. He had the distinction of being the last president of the St. Joseph School Board under the old law, which provided for ward representation, serving from June, 1894, until 1896, when the membership of the board was reduced from eighteen to six. He was prominent in social, fraternal and religious circles, serving each organization to which he belonged in an official capacity. He was a member, and past commander, of Custer Post No. 7, Grand Army of the Republic; and belonged to St. Joseph Chapter, Sons of the American Revolution; and to the Military Order of the Loyal Legion of the United States. Standing high in Masonic circles, Judge Mosman was a member of St. Joseph Lodge No. 78, Ancient Free and Accepted Order of Masons; of Mitchell Chapter No. 14, Royal Arch Masons; and of Hugh de Payen Commandery, Knights Templar; and of Radiant Chapter No. 88, Order of the Eastern Star. He was deputy grand master of the Ancient Free and Accepted Order of Masons, and had he lived a few months longer would have been made grand master. On December 30, 1874, the Judge united with the First Congregational Church, of which he was a trustee at the time of his death.

Judge Mosman married in 1869, Miss Rocelia Norton, at Kewanee, Illinois, and she survives him. Four children blessed the union of Judge and Mrs. Mosman, namely: Oliver C. Mosman, an attorney at Kansas City; Burroughs N. Mosman, also successfully engaged in the practice of law at Kansas City; Mrs. Fred Sweeney, of Washington, D. C., and Mrs. Frank Worth, of St. Joseph.

JACOB NEWTON WILSON. The mercantile interests of Grundy County, Missouri, are well represented at Tindall by Jacob Newton Wilson, an energetic and progressive business man of the younger generation, who, while still comparatively a newcomer to this community, has already thoroughly established himself in the confidence and good will of the people here. He has had long and practical experience in various lines of endeavor, and in adding his name to its citizenship this ambitious little city has gained an individual who has both the ability and the desire to assist his locality's interests while bettering his own.

Mr. Wilson is a native of the State of West Virginia, and was born in Roane County, in 1882, his parents being Jacob and Virginia (Cox) Wilson, natives of Virginia (now West Virginia), the latter of Lewis County. Mrs. Wilson is of Revolutionary stock, while Jacob Wilson enlisted in 1861 in the state militia of West Virginia and was subject to call at any time throughout the war between the North and the South. Jacob Newton Wilson was reared amid rural surroundings, his father being a West Virginia farmer, and while growing to manhood divided his time between attending the country schools and assisting in the work of the homestead. He resided with his mother in Roane County, West Virginia, where all of his eleven brothers and sisters still live, until he reached his majority, and in 1903 bought a farm of his own there, but only operated it for one year, when he decided to seek other fields of endeavor, and accordingly went to Pennsylvania. Still with his face toward the West, after a short experience in farming in Pennsylvania, he moved on to Akron, Ohio, where he became identified with the Diamond Rubber Company, remaining with that concern until 1909, in which year he made his advent in Missouri. First locating in Sullivan County, he again resumed agricultural operations, first as a hand and in 1911 as the owner of 150 acres of Sullivan County land. This he continued to operate with some measure of success until 1914, when accepting a promising opportunity, he came to Tindall and established himself in business as the proprietor of a general mercantile business. Mr. Wilson carries a complete stock of first-class, reliable goods, suitable to the wants of the community, whose people's needs he has studied. He is at all times courteous and obliging, endeavoring in every way to satisfy his customers' wishes, and these traits, combined with the excellence of his goods, have attracted to him a generous trade from all over the surrounding territory. Mr. Wilson is possessed of more than the ordinary business ability and has a wealth of ideas and his transactions are carried on in a manner that demonstrates his integrity and fair-mindedness. A republican in his political views, he has not yet found time to engage actively in public affairs, but has expressed his willingness to aid in movements which have the betterment of the community as their ultimate aim. He has shown some interest in fraternal matters, and at the present time is a member of the local lodges of the Modern Woodmen of America and the Yeomen.

On September 17, 1902, Mr. Wilson was united in marriage with Miss Bessie Hoff, daughter of William A. and Rena (Ward) Hoff, of West Virginia, and to this union there was born one child: Ruby. who died at the age of one year.

FRED G. HARRISON. A member of the younger generation of business men, who through energy, industry and well-applied effort is making a place for himself in trade circles of Richmond, is Fred G. Harrison, proprietor of a thriving hardware business. Like a number of the younger men engaged in commercial pursuits, he was brought up to agricultural pursuits, but has shown himself capable of competing with those whose entire training has been along business lines. Mr. Harrison was born on a farm located four miles north of Richmond, in Ray County, January 20, 1888, and is a son of Samuel A. and Emma (Seek) Harrison.

Samuel A. Harrison was born in Kentucky in 1832, and was there reared to manhood, securing his education in the public schools. When he was twenty years of age he left the Blue Grass State and came to Ray County, Missouri, locating on a farm situated two miles west of Richmond, but subsequently removing to the property on which our subject was born. The father was a man of industry and enterprise, and carried on his operations in such a manner that he not alone won material rewards, but also the esteem and confidence of his neighbors and associates in business. When he retired from active pursuits he took up his residence at Hardin, and there his death occurred in 1904, when he was seventy-two years of age. He was a democrat in his political views, but did not care for public life, being content to devote his activities to the tilling of his fields. Mr. Harrison was married in Ray County to Miss Emma Seek, who was born in Missouri, and she survives him and now makes her home at Richmond with her son. Three children were born to Samuel A. and Emma Harrison, namely: J. B., who is a resident of Hardin, Missouri; Maud, who is the wife of J. T. Haynes, an agriculturist of Ray County; and Fred G.

Fred G. Harrison was still a child when his parents removed to Hardin, and there he was given good educational advantages in the public and high schools. He embarked upon his own career in 1905. the year after his father's death, when he started operations on the homestead on which he had been born. After five years of successful operation of this property he came to Richmond. and here became identified with mercantile lines by purchasing the hardware stock of Jesse Child. At this time Mr. Harrison has a complete and attractive stock of hardware, harness, farming implements, buggies and wagons, and caters to the best and most representative trade of the city. He is a young man of excellent business ability, sagacious and far-sighted, and by his earnest desire to please his customers and by his courteous treatment and fair dealing, he has secured a liberal patronage, of which he is deserving. Although he has not sought public preferment, the best interests of the community receive his support, and he withholds his cooperation from no worthy undertaking calculated to promote the general welfare. Like his father he is a democrat, and can be depended upon to support his party's policies and candidates. During his residence in Richmond, Mr. Harrison has gained a wide acquaintance, in which he numbers many sincere friends.

On December 11, 1910, Mr. Harrison was united in marriage with Miss Beulah Meadows, who was also born in Ray County, and to this union has been born one son: Grover.

H. C. WALKER, JR. Occupying a position of note among the public officials of Clinton County is H. C. Walker, Jr., county recorder. Careful conscientious, and competent, he can always be depended upon to fulfill his exacting duties in an intelligent and satisfactory manner. Coming from honored pioneer ancestry, he was born July 12, 1870, in Clinton County, on a farm situated two miles west of Plattsburg.

His father, H. C. Walker, Sr., was born in Clinton County, Missouri, of Holland ancestry. His parents came from Kentucky to Missouri about 1838, in early pioneer days, and having bought land in what was then known as the Platt Purchase, cleared and improved a homestead. H. C. Walker, Sr., became a farmer from choice and was actively engaged in agricultural pursuits until his death, in 1913, at the age of seventy-three years. He was held in high respect as a man and a citizen, his death being a loss to the community. In his political affiliations he was a stanch democrat, and religiously he was a member of the Christian Church. To him and his good wife, whose maiden name was Emily Carter, three children were born, namely: Jacob A., of Osborn, Missouri; H. C., Jr.; and Alberta, living at home. The mother, who came to Missouri from Virginia with her parents when a girl, is still living.

Brought up on the home farm, H. C. Walker, Jr., became familiar with its many duties while yet a boy. He obtained the rudiments of his future education in the rural schools, after which he attended the old Plattsburg College and the State Normal School. Having prepared himself for a teacher, he secured a position in a district school when but nineteen years old, and for several years taught with good success. Being then urged to take charge of the Clinton County schools, Mr. Walker accepted the position of county supervisor of schools, for which he was amply fitted, and filled it most acceptably until January 1, 1911, when he entered upon the duties of his present office.

On February 29, 1904, Mr. Walker was united in marriage with Mary West, a daughter of the late Jackson West, of Plattsburg. Her mother still lives in Plattsburg. Mr. and Mrs. Walker have one child, a daughter named Emily. They are identified by membership with the Methodist Episcopal Church, South, and are active in its Sunday school work.

JOHN A. ASHER, M. D. More than thirty years in the active membership of the medical fraternity of Northwest Missouri has brought Doctor Asher all the better distinctions that come to the physician and surgeon, and his success has been in proportion to the length of his practice. For many years he has practiced at Trenton, is one of the best known physicians of Grundy County, and his family have been known in that vicinity nearly half a century.

John A. Asher was born on a farm near Zanesville, Muskingum County, Ohio. His father, Solomon Asher, was born in Muskingum County, November 24, 1827. The grandfather was John S. Asher, also a native of Muskingum County, and the son of Luke Asher, who was born either in the north of Ireland or in this country of Scotch-Irish parents. Luke Asher was an Ohio pioneer, and identified himself with that new country probably about the time Ohio was detached from the original Northwest Territory and made into a state. Luke Asher married Rachael Scott.

John S. Asher bought a farm in Muskingum County, five miles a little southeast from Zanesville, and there spent the rest of his life. He married Jane Shumaker, a daughter of Adam and Rachael Shumaker, who were probably born in Germany, or were at least of German parentage. John S. Asher and wife reared two sons and four daughters, namely: Solomon, Caroline, Sarah, Catharine, Rachael and William, while of two other children, a daughter Mary died in early childhood, and another daughter died in infancy. Of this list of children, William was a soldier and was killed in the Battle of the Wilderness during the Civil war.

Solomon Asher, father of Doctor Asher, was reared on the Ohio farm, and when ready to start out for himself his father gave him two horses and two cows and a little furniture. With that equipment he bought on time sixty acres from his father, and he and his wife began housekeeping in a log cabin, and from that humble beginning they eventually achieved success. After farming for a few years, he bought a portable sawmill, and moved from place to place sawing up tracts of timber. That work was carried on in the intervals of his farm labor. After the death of his father he returned to the old homestead, but in the fall of 1868 sold out his Ohio interests and moved to Northwest Missouri, settling in Grundy County. He bought a farm in Lincoln and Trenton townships, and remained there until his death in 1905. On December 27, 1848, he married Elizabeth Ellen Birch. She was born on a farm in the northeast part of Muskingum County, Ohio, February 26, 1827. William Birch, her father, was an early settler of Muskingum County, a farmer, and married Emily Wickham. The latter was born in Ohio, a daughter of Ebenezer and Sarah Wickham. Ebenezer Wickham came from England. After the death of William Birch, Emily, his widow, married Elijah Eaton, and by that union had one son, Elijah Eaton, Jr. After the death of Mr. Eaton she married for her third husband John Emmons, and died a few years later, leaving a son John W. Emmons. Her last years were spent on a farm about six miles east of Zanesville. Elizabeth Ellen Birch was the only child of her first marriage.

Solomon Asher and wife lived together fifty-seven years, and celebrated among their children, grandchildren and friends their golden wedding anniversary. Both joined the Baptist Church when they were young, and for many years he continued a deacon and active worker in that denomination. Their eight children were named as follows: Milton Clarence, Howard Benton, John Alvin, Alice Jane, Edwin F., Benjamin Franklin, Arthur E. and Solomon Scott.

Dr. John A. Asher received his early training in the rural schools of Ohio and of Grundy County. Later he was a student in the Grand River College. One term of school teaching was a feature of his early experience and he took up the study of medicine with Dr. Thomas Kimlin. Later he was a student in the medical department of the University of Iowa at Iowa City, and then entered the medical school of the University of Michigan at Ann Arbor, and also attended the University Medical College of New York City, where he was graduated M. D. in 1881. Returning to Trenton he took charge of Doctor Kimlin's drug store, and was a druggist and physician in combination until 1894. Since that time he has devoted his attention strictly to his large private practice in Trenton and vicinity.

On January 18, 1888, Doctor Asher married Sallie M. Graham. She was born at Gentryville, Gentry County, Missouri. Her father, Dr. George D. Graham, was born in White County, Illinois, in 1836, a son of John M. Graham, who was a White County farmer and on coming to Missouri settled in Grundy County, buying land near Edinburg, where he operated his farm with slave labor and lived until his death. John M. Graham married Rebecca Phillips, who died two months after her husband. They reared six sons and one daughter: James, William, Emily W., John M., Alfred, George D. and Oliver. Dr. George D. Graham attended Grand River College and graduated from the Missouri Medical College at St. Louis in 1857, beginning practice at Gentryville, where he lived until his death in 1883. Doctor Graham married Martha Dobbins. She was born in Sullivan County, Missouri, in 1838, and her father, Thomas E. Dobbins, came from the vicinity of Springfield, Illinois, and settled in Sullivan County in early days. He bought large tracts of land on the line between Sullivan and Grundy counties, and was a prominent farmer and stock raiser there before his death. Thomas E. Dobbins married Sarah Kirkpatrick, who was the mother of fifteen children, thirteen of whom grew to maturity. Mrs. Doctor Graham died in May, 1913. She reared five children, namely: David T., Emma J., Sallie M., Leota and James. Doctor and Mrs. Asher have two children, Vera and Arthur Graham.

Doctor Asher has membership in the Grundy County and the Missouri State Medical societies, and fraternally he is affiliated with Grand River Lodge No. 52, I. O. O. F. He is a director in the Citizens State Bank at Trenton. Reared on a farm, he has never lost his fundamental interest in agriculture, and is the owner of a fine place three miles east of Trenton, and takes much pleasure in its cultivation and management. Doctor Asher was elected coroner of Grundy County in 1906, and again elected in 1912, in the meantime having served two years as deputy coroner. In 1888 he was appointed a member of the pension examining board, and with the exception of four years served to the present time. Mrs. Asher is a member of the Daughters of Rebekah, and is also connected with such representative social organizations as the Ninety-Nine Club, the Shakespeare and the Sans Souci clubs.

JOHN STEPHENS. A home of comfort, thrift and enterprise is that of John Stephens in Lincoln Township of Caldwell County. Mr. Stephens has spent practically all his life in this section of Northwest Missouri, learned the details of farming when a boy, and has applied his experience and industry to the making of a good home. His farm comprises 160 acres, and is devoted to general agriculture and stock raising. Their residence is a substantial seven-room house, all well furnished, and with surroundings that indicate the taste and thrift of the owners. Mr. Stephens has as the business department of his farm a large barn, 30 by 40 feet, for horses, cattle and hay, and has all his fields well fenced and improved, and the general management of the place indicates a high order of farm management. One department of his farming is the raising of fine chickens, and he keeps a flock of some of the best white Leghorns and white Wyandotte fowls in Caldwell County.

John Stephens was born on the old homestead forty years ago, a son of Edward and Eliza Stephens. Both his parents were natives of Wales, grew up and were married there, and in 1870 came across the ocean on a sailing vessel to find homes in the New World. Edward's brother, Thomas, had been the first of the family to come to Missouri and acquire a homestead. Edward and Eliza Stephens were the parents of nine children, as follows: Mary Jane, deceased; John; Edward; Sarah; William; Thomas R., who is a lawyer; George; Ann Eliza, and Matilda Ann. Edward Stephens, the father, was a man of marked intelligence and industry, was a republican in politics, and he and his wife were members of the Baptist Church.

John Stephens grew up on the home farm, learned the lessons of industry while attending the local schools, and as the years gave his body strength was able to assist in cultivating and keeping up the old farm. Mr. Stephens has always kept in touch with the movements of the world and of politics and affairs, and has read especially along the lines of history and is a well informed and pleasant man to meet.

On March 10, 1897, he was married in Cowgill, Missouri, to Lydia A. McClellan. She was born in Saline County, Missouri, a daughter of T. W. and Matilda (Lynn) McClellan, her father a native of Johnston County, Missouri, and her mother of Kentucky. Her father was born November 14, 1839, a son of a Tennesseean who located early in Missouri. T. W. McClellan married his wife in Saline County, and she died at the age of fifty-seven. In the McClellan family were two sons and seven daughters, named as follows: Ruth F.; Kate Murphy; Lydia Stephens; John L.; Lucy Kelly; Florence Norton; Taylor; Sarah Couch, besides one that died in infancy.

Mr. and Mrs. Stephens had one child, J. W., who was born April 19, 1903, and died August 17, 1910. He was a bright boy, the life of the home and the joy of his parents. Mr. Stephens is affiliated with Cowgill Lodge No. 561, I. O. O. F. He and his wife are active members of the Baptist Church and are people of the highest standing and esteem in their community.

H. K. MILLER. The substantial character of a family can in no better way be indicated than through long residence and a constant progressiveness in its work and influence. For half a century the Miller family has lived in Liberty Township of Holt County, and the homestead now occupied by H. K. Miller is the same which his father bought when he first came to the county, and which has been under the management of three successive generations.

H. K. Miller was born in Liberty Township, of Holt County, September 19, 1882, and is a son of Frank and Jennie (Kay) Miller. He was the only child, and after the death of his father on the old home farm he continued to live with his grandfather, Henry C. Miller, and wife, and was under their care from the age of two years. After the death of his grandfather Mr. Miller continued on the farm and his grandmother lived part of the time with him and part of the time in Kansas. She is now eighty-three years of age. Mr. Miller received his education by attending the public schools of Liberty Township.

Grandfather Henry C. Miller located this farm in Liberty Township in 1864. It was land that at that time had practically no improvements, and the plowed fields, the fences, the substantial buildings, and all other evidences of material progress represent the enterprise of this one

time regarded as an expert in the handling of tools and the operation of machinery. Politically he was a republican.

Mr. H. K. Miller married Mary Lambert, daughter of David and Fannie (Price) Lambert. To their marriage have been born two children, Irene and Bonita, both of whom were born on the homestead in Liberty Township. Mr. Miller is affiliated with the Independent Order of Odd Fellows, and politically his relations have been with the republican party since casting his first vote.

JOHN W. HYDER. An experienced and practical journalist, editor, litterateur and churchman, John W. Hyder has long occupied a high position in the estimation of the public, particularly at Excelsior Springs and vicinity. His energy, enterprise and desire to please the public have been liberally rewarded, both as to his reputation among Missouri newspaper men and also from a financial standpoint.

John W. Hyder was born in Clay County, Missouri, September 6, 1862. His father, John B. Hyder, a native of Tennessee, came to Missouri when only ten years of age. He became a farmer, and though with little or no capital to start with, through his own efforts and with the aid of his industrious and economical wife acquired a competency. John B. Hyder married Miss Caroline Spearro, who was born in 1844, a short time after her parents arrived in this country from Germany. John W. Hyder was the eldest of their twelve children, five of whom died in infancy, the others being mentioned as follows: Lula F., now the wife of G. W. Lord of Excelsior Springs; Mollie, the wife of R. L. Beckett of Excelsior Springs; Ida M., wife of Frank Campbell of St. Joseph; Tena; Henry H.; and Sadie Zula, the wife of Jesse L. Myers of Kansas City.

Unfortunately the early life of John W. Hyder was almost wholly without opportunities for obtaining an education, and eight months comprised the sum total of his school days. This is largely due to the fact that his services were so badly needed on the home farm, on which he spent many a day in hard manual labor. During this time, while his mind lay fallow, his constitution was strengthened by outdoor life, and his powers of eager observation supplied him with a useful fund of general information. It was his steadfast ambition that enabled him to break down the barriers of circumstance and to elevate himself beyond his opportunities. Many hours usually wasted by other boys were spent by him in reading every book, paper and periodical that came in his way. At the age of eighteen young Hyder procured an amateur outfit of printers' type, and that was the beginning of his career as a printer and journalist. Using his father's residence as an office, with characteristic energy he began soliciting job work, and did all the work alone. In a short time he commenced the publication of his first paper, a monthly journal called Glad Tidings, which was a four-page 7 by 10 inch sheet. The liberal patronage received encouraged him to persevere in the enterprise, and it was soon necessary to move the "plant" to more convenient and commodious quarters.

At Excelsior Springs, in 1883, Mr. Hyder began the publication of a six-column weekly paper called the Sentinel of Truth, which was con-

enterprise. He has been connected with every newspaper in the city, and in connection with Doctor Flack is the founder of the Christian Union Herald, a non-sectarian weekly, and since 1906 has been sole editor and publisher of this religious journal.

Having sold the Daily Phunn in 1893, Mr. Hyder in 1894 established the Daily Call and conducted it until selling out his interest in 1903. Later a partnership was formed with the purchaser, and they also acquired the Journal, a weekly publication. Mr. Hyder's partner played a one-handed game and the partnership was dissolved. Mr. Hyder retained the Journal plant, to which, in the meantime, he had added a standard linotype, one of the first one-machine plants in the West.

Mr. Hyder now devotes his entire time to the publication of his own papers, to his literary work, and to a large book and job trade. In 1889 he began writing short stories and sketches for eastern papers, and his productions were soon accepted and published by such leading journals as the Boston Globe, New Orleans Times-Democrat, Epoch, Comfort, San Francisco Wasp, West Shore and others. He has written a few serial stories, one of which, "The Fair Enchantress," was published in book form in 1893.

In politics Mr. Hyder is a stanch prohibitionist, with strong progressive republican tendencies. For a number of years he has been an active member and supporter of the Christian Union Church, and has been identified with church work since 1878. In 1890 he was appointed a delegate to the general council of the church held at Crawfordsville, Indiana, and proved one of the most useful and influential members of the council. In 1898 he was again a delegate to the general council at Holt, Missouri, in 1906 was sent as a delegate to Homer, Indiana, again in 1910 at the council in Excelsior Springs, and in 1914 at West Union, Ohio, was elected assistant secretary of the general council. During the past twelve years Mr. Hyder has been regularly elected secretary of the Missouri Council, and in eight years has visited nine different state councils each year, serving as secretary of several of these.

Personally Mr. Hyder possesses a suave and polite manner, is modest, unselfish and careful of the feelings and opinions of others, is a pleasant conversationalist, always approachable and of prepossessing appearance. He has long been one of the most useful and best known citizens of Clay County.

GEORGE EDWIN GIRDNER. Among the families whose activities and lives have been distinctive contributions to the communities of Harrison and Mercer counties, probably none deserve more credit than that of Girdner. It has been established in this section of Northwest Missouri for fully sixty-five years, and from that time to the present the name has been associated with the best virtues of manhood and social character. They came into the country in time to do their share of the hard work involved in the clearing of the forests and the laying of substantial foundations of civilization. To an unusual degree material success has been their lot, and they have also stood in important relations with the civic affairs of the locality.

George Edwin Girdner, who represents the third generation of the family residence in this section of Missouri, has lived in the Mount Moriah community since childhood, and he grew up on the farm he now owns, situated on Rural Free Delivery Route No. 3 out of Ridgeway. His birth occurred in Mercer County, near Princeton, June 23, 1874. His grandfather was James Girdner, who came from Kentucky to Missouri, and spent his life as a farmer. He was one of the men of extensive interests in Mercer County and widely known as a good citizen. His death occurred at the age of seventy-six. He married a Miss Prichard, who died about six years before him. Their children were: James Brittan; Polly Ann, the wife of Morris Perry; Andrew Jackson; Frank, who was killed during the war; Joseph, who died in Oklahoma; John R.; Sarah, who is the wife of John Boyd and lives on the old Girdner home near Princeton.

John R. Girdner, the father of George E., was born November 28, 1848, and it was about that time that the grandfather settled near Princeton. John R. Girdner is now a resident of Princeton, but was brought up on a farm near there and has spent all his active life as a farmer. He was successful, did a large business as a stock man and was able to provide liberally for his children. He was too young to serve in the army during the war, has been little identified with politics except as a democratic voter, and was brought up in the Christian Church, though his tendencies are now toward the Methodists. John R. Girdner married Miss Maria Isabel Granlee. Her father, Joseph B. Granlee, came to Missouri about the close of the war from near Spraggs, Pennsylvania, and was distantly related to the numerous Spragg family of that locality, many representatives of which are found in Northwest Missouri. The children of John R. Girdner and wife are: George Edwin; Jennie A., the wife of Stoton Boxley, of Princeton; Charles, of Cainesville, Missouri; Bessie M., wife of Fred Clemands, of Princeton; and Cleo L., of Princeton.

George Edwin Girdner while growing up on his present farm acquired an education in the country schools, also attended school at Cainesville and Edinburg, Missouri, and finally at the old Stanberry Normal. From school he graduated at once into the work of the farm, and continued at home with his parents until past his majority. He was married February 26, 1899, to Miss Elizabeth Leazenby.. Her father is William V. Leazenby, of Ridgeway, Missouri, a nephew of Wesley Leazenby, one of the pioneers of Harrison County. William V. Leazenby was reared in Pickaway County, Ohio, and came to Missouri in the '80s. He married Sarah Keys, and their children were: Mrs. Girdner, who was born January 29, 1880; Etta, who died at the age of fifteen; Ethel, wife of William Norwood, near Ridgeway; Minnie, wife of Max Burgin, of Maryville, Missouri; Ola, who died at the age of four years; Wilda, wife of Herman Waswo, of Ridgeway; and Miss Laura. William V. Leazenby by his second wife, whose maiden name was Mary Harrison, has two children: Truman and Ray. Mr. George E. Girdner and wife have four children: Forrest W., Charles Dorrell, Lois May and Elizabeth Lee.

Recently Mr. Girdner has engaged in the lumber business at Cainesville, Missouri, having joined his brother Charles in purchasing the principal lumber yard at that place, that of C. F. Fransham & Son. Both as a farmer and a citizen Mr. Girdner has had an important part in local affairs. He is now serving as township trustee and has held that office to the benefit of the community for five years. A democrat, he cast his first vote for William J. Bryan in 1896, and has voted for all the democratic candidates in the past eighteen years. As a delegate he was present at the judicial convention in St. Joseph in 1904. Fraternally he is affiliated with the Independent Order of Odd Fellows, is a past Noble Grand in his local lodge, and his household centers its religious interests in the Methodist Church.

As a man of affairs Mr. Girdner owns a farm of 368 acres, and like most successful farmers in Missouri he obtained his profits from stock. His progressive enterprise is shown in the various improvements of his farm. He is also known in local banking, and was one of the original stockholders of the First National Bank of Cainesville, but has since withdrawn his connection with the institution.

JONATHAN TOWNSEND. Andrew County has its full quota of men who have stepped aside from participation in active affairs to let pass the younger generation with its hopes and ambitions, and in this class is found Jonathan Townsend, who is now living in retirement after many years passed in agricultural pursuits. Mr. Townsend was born in Morgan County, Indiana, June 17, 1827, and is a son of William and Mary (Voyles) Townsend, born within fourteen days of each other, in February, 1797, in Cabarrus County, North Carolina. William Townsend, the grandfather of Jonathan, was also born in that county, and was about seventeen years of age at the outbreak of the Revolutionary war. Although he belonged to an old English family, his heart was with the colonists, and during the entire period of the war he served as a private under General Greene. He died in Indiana about the year 1837.

William Townsend was ten years of age when he accompanied his parents to Morgan County, Indiana, and there he was living at the time of the outbreak of the War of 1812, in which he fought valiantly as a soldier. Both he and his wife attained advanced years, and passed away in Indiana, after a long period passed in farming. They were the parents of fourteen children, namely: Elison; Alfred; William C.; Lucy, who died young; Jesse; Joseph, who died young; Jonathan; Rachel Simmons; Elizabeth Elliott; Andrew Jackson; Catherine; Thomas Jefferson; Lafayette; and Benjamin Franklin.

Jonathan Townsend received his education in the public schools of Indiana, and remained on the homestead farm there until he reached the age of nineteen years, at that time, in 1847, coming to Andrew County, Missouri. Locating on a property two miles north of Savannah, he continued to reside thereon and to add thereto until his retirement, February 24, 1894, at which time he was the owner of 190 acres of land, of which he disposed, and since then has made his home at Savannah. During the period of the Civil war Mr. Townsend served as a private in the Missouri State Militia, under Col. William Herrin, and the last year under Capt. John Majors of Savannah. He sustained the family reputation for courage and military prowess, discharging his duties in a manner that has always been characteristic, whether in war or peace. At the age of eighty-seven years he is still in the enjoyment of perfect health and has all his faculties, it even being unnecessary for him to wear glasses. He attributes his long and healthy life to the fact that he has always lived sensibly, has never been intoxicated and has never used tobacco. He has been a great lover of home and simple things, and has never played cards or danced. He has been a consistent democrat since the time he cast his first vote for General Cass, but has never sought public preferment. Fraternally, he is connected with the Masons, which he joined before the Civil war. He has been a member of the Baptist Church for sixty-seven years, and at this time is serving as deacon thereof.

On January 24, 1849, Mr. Townsend was married to Miss Katie Ann Landers, who was born in Platt County, Missouri, and died in Andrew County in 1861. Their children were as follows: William Burnett, a resident of Andrew County; Francis Marion, living at Whitesville, Missouri; James S., who is the owner of a large farm in the vicinity of Cawood, Missouri; Hamilton Smith, an undertaker and monument dealer at Warrensburg; and Louisa Jane, who died as Mrs. Ephraim Todd, leaving four children. Mr. Townsend was again married April 5, 1863, to Miss Amanda J. Parker, who was born February 28, 1839, in Bartholomew County, Indiana, and came West with her parents in 1855, the family settling first in Nodaway County, Missouri, and three years later removing to a farm west of Savannah. She was a daughter of William and Miriam

(Critchfield) Parker, the former a native of Kentucky and the latter of Tennessee, and the parents of nine children. Three of Mrs. Townsend's brothers, Reuben, Nathaniel and John, served as soldiers during the Civil war, the first two in the Missouri State Militia, and the last-named in the United States service. Reuben met a soldier's death in battle at Springfield, Missouri. Four children have been born to Mr. and Mrs. Townsend: Nathaniel, who died as a child; one infant which died unnamed; Elison Eugene, who is a resident of Savannah; and Laura Nettie, who is the wife of John Rowe, living one and one-half miles north of Savannah. Mr and Mrs. Townsend celebrated their golden wedding anniversary April 5, 1913.

THE XCIX CLUB, TRENTON. A women's club with a record of notable accomplishment and influence since its establishment is that known as the XCIX Club in Trenton. While the club was originally in purpose a study club, its aim and scope were soon broadened to bring it into more vital relations with the life of the community. It is now not only the medium through which its members work for their individual advancement and culture, but also turn their united efforts to the improvement and betterment of their home city.

The club was organized in February, 1899, and its name is derived from the year of its establishment. The first president was Mrs. George Hall. At first the membership was limited to fifteen, but later to twenty-five, and in 1906 the study club feature was broadened to a department club, comprising three departments: Home and education, art and literature, history and music. At that time the membership was made unlimited.

At the present time the chief object of achievement before the club is to aid in the establishment of a Y. M. C. A. The first hundred dollars subscribed to the fund was given by this club some years ago, and the club's contributions have since been increased until they now aggregate four hundred dollars. Besides this, much philanthropic and civic work has been accomplished by the home and education department. This includes the establishment of a children's reading room at the Jewett Norris Library at a cost of $300; a contribution of fifty dollars to the White Way; the annual gift to the Missouri' Loan Scholarship Fund which assists poor girls to secure a college education; an annual gift to the Charity Union; the contribution to the Monument to the Civil War Veterans; the inspection of dairies, bakeries, meat markets and groceries, and the censoring of picture shows and pool halls.

The club has also done some effectual work in connection with the public schools, and has conducted parents' and teachers' meetings which have served to bring into closer relations the schools and the homes. The Trenton Clean City Club, an outgrowth of the XCIX Club, provided a public playground and installed drinking fountains in the public schools. The club-members on one Arbor Day visited the schools and made talks on the planting of trees and the conservation of nature's resources, and at another time they observed the Safety First day.

The other departments of the club have studied the history, music, art and literature of the United States and of most of the European countries. Many of the musical programs have been worthy of mention, including the "Evening with American Composers," and "Selections from Grand Opera." The art and literature department secured the Turner Art Exhibit and has given dramas by authors whose countries were being studied. Guest day is the first of May and has been celebrated by many unique social affairs; notably the May Day breakfast at the

Riverside Country Club and the Commercial Club Banquet at which Governor Hadley was the guest of honor.

The motto of the club is: "Slumber not in the tents of your fathers; the world is advancing, advance with it." The club flower is the carnation and the club colors red and white. A list of the past presidents of the club is as follows: Mrs. Rachel Hall, Mrs. Nettie Hoffman, Mrs. Ida Austin, Mrs. Sarah Steckman, Mrs. Lida M. Cook, Mrs. Sallie M. Asher, Mrs. Sallie B. Patton, Mrs. Rachel Hall, Mrs. Bessie S. Witten, Mrs. Carrie Rogers Clark, Mrs. Eva M. Wright, Mrs. Rose H. McGrath, Dr. Lulu Herbert, Dr. Erie Herbert, Mrs. Sallie M. Asher, Mrs. Carrie Rogers Clark, Mrs. Bessie S. Witten, Mrs. Rose Preston, Mrs. Sarah Steckman, Mrs. Pansy Prewitt McCollom and Mrs. Mae Brandt.

The club now has 100 members and is affiliated with the Missouri State Federation and the General Federation of Women's Clubs.

HOMER CROCKETT. A representative of that class who have been most efficient in bringing prosperity and in creating the modern twentieth century conditions in Northwest Missouri, Homer Crockett has spent his active career as a farmer, merchant and horseman, his chief reputation outside the county being due to the successful enterprise which he conducts in partnership with his brother Nathan W. in the breeding and raising of thoroughbred imported horses, jacks, jennets and mules. In Platte Township of Andrew County is a community where the name Crockett has been synonymous with enterprise and successful ability since the early days. In section 14, in the same neighborhood as are located other Crockett farms, is the home place of Homer Crockett.

Homer Crockett is the second of five children born to Milton and Sarah (West) Crockett, who came out to Northwest Missouri in 1857 and were among the early settlers of Andrew County. Milton Crockett was a fine character among the older settlers, and the chief facts in his life and his lineage will be found in the sketch of Le Roy Crockett. Homer Crockett was born in Seneca County, Ohio, August 2, 1855, and has spent most of his life in Andrew County. During the war his parents returned to Ohio, where his father enlisted and served in the Union army. Homer Crockett lived on the old home farm until his marriage, and has since been actively identified with farming with the exception of four years during the '80s when he and his brother Wallace A. were in partnership in merchandising at Whitesville. Homer Crockett occupies a farm of 120 acres, and owns another eighty acres nearby, also 320 acres in Hartley County, Texas. The home farm is the old Rodkey Place, formerly owned by Mrs. Crockett's father. Since 1890 Mr. Crockett and his brother Nathan have been engaged jointly in the business of breeding Percheron horses, jacks and jennets, also high grade Tennessee and Kentucky stock. Their enterprise has brought them a considerable reputation, and their animals have been exhibited as prize winners in a number of shows and fairs. Homer Crockett has been a stockholder in the Farmers Bank of Whitesville since its organization. He is known all over this community as a capable man of affairs and an alert and public spirited citizen, and a hard worker in any cause which he enlists. He is a member of the Methodist Episcopal Church at Walnut Grove, in which he is a trustee, and in politics is a republican.

On September 1, 1878, Homer Crockett married Jennie Rodkey, who was born in Carroll County, Indiana, July 17, 1855, and came with her parents to Andrew County in the spring of 1866. Her life since that time has been spent on the home farm where she now lives with the exception of four years in Whitesville while her husband was engaged in merchandising there. Mrs. Crockett is a daughter of David and Elizabeth (Eller)

Rodkey, her father a native of Pennsylvania and her mother near Dayton, Ohio. They were married in Ohio, from there moving to Carroll County, Indiana, and her father came to Andrew County in 1865 and brought his family in the following spring. Mrs. Crockett's mother died in 1879, at the age of fifty-eight, and her father in 1883, at the age of sixty-two. Mr. Rodkey was a carpenter by trade, an occupation he followed for a number of years, but later engaged successfully in farming. He also conducted a nursery, and supplied the young trees for a large number of the early orchards in Andrew County. The five children in the Rodkey family were: Lodiska, widow of J. A. Williams, of Kokomo, Indiana, and she now resides in Bolckow, Missouri; Newton, deceased; Wirt, deceased; Mrs. Crockett; and Esther, wife of Lyman Stingley, of King City. Mr. and Mrs. Stingley formerly owned a 160 acre farm in this neighborhood, just east of the Homer Crockett place, and he was a successful farmer and stock raiser, handling a good many fine mules. In January, 1913, however, he sold his farm and moved to King City, where he is now living retired.

Mr. and Mrs. Crockett have three children: Maggie, the wife of C. O. Townsend, of Colorado Springs, Colorado, and they have one child, Gladys; the second child, a son, died in infancy; Lena is the wife of Ewing D. Clark. of Omaha, Nebraska, and has one son, Edwin D. Mrs. Clark graduated from the Savannah high school and was one of Andrew County's successful school teachers. She attended the Maclean School of Expression and Dramatic Art in Chicago, Illinois, in 1912, and she has won high honors for her ability. She was awarded the silver medal at the W. C. T. U. contest, and she afterward won the gold medal at the contest held at Albany, Missouri. Mrs. Crockett takes much interest and is an active worker in the Walnut Grove Methodist Episcopal Church, and has been president of the Ladies Aid Society since its organization.

JOHN W. GRESHAM. Many years of steady industry, growing prosperity and influential citizenship have marked the career of John W. Gresham in Holt County. Mr. Gresham owns fine farming property in Bigelow Township, and for a man who began life with little education and who gave the benefit of his early struggling years to paying off debts and supporting a family, he has well earned all the comforts and the esteem which the world can bestow.

John W. Gresham was born in Johnson County, Missouri, July 13, 1857, but has lived in Holt County since infancy. His parents, John J. and Elizabeth (Catron) Gresham, were the parents of seven children, one of whom is now deceased. John J. Gresham, a farmer, came to Holt County about 1858 and settled on land about two miles southwest of Bigelow. It was an unimproved place, and for a number of years his labors were directed to the clearing up of the land and to the establishment of a home. About 1876 John J. Gresham made a trip to Wyoming, leaving his wife and children on the farm. It was a disastrous expedition, and the party with which he traveled turned back before reaching its destination, but they were overtaken by Indians and in the fight which ensued John J. Gresham was killed, and his body never recovered. This calamity befell when John W. Gresham was about nineteen years of age. At once there devolved upon his shoulders the responsibilities of managing the farm and assisting his mother and brothers and sisters in making a living and paying off the debt which incumbered the homestead. Mr. Gresham thus remained at home until his marriage, and afterwards his mother lived with her younger sons.

After his marriage in 1879 Mr. Gresham began as a renter, worked in that way for three years, and then bought seventy-seven acres comprising his present farm and also the forty acres on which his son Earl now lives. It was improved land, but all the building has been done since he took possession thirty-five years ago.

Mr. John W. Gresham is a member of the Methodist Episcopal Church, is affiliated with the Woodmen of the World and the Fraternal Union of America, and his course in both public and private affairs has always identified him with the betterment and advancement of his community. He has served on the home school board, and is a democrat in politics, with which party his father was also affiliated. As a farmer Mr. Gresham is successful in the raising of stock and the staples of Holt County. Mr. Gresham credits the success that he has won largely to the possession of good health, industrious habits and honorable dealings with his fellow men. His father was a man of exemplary habits, and never used tobacco in all his life.

John W. Gresham married Belle Bridgeman, daughter of John W. Bridgeman. They have one son, Allen Earl Gresham, who was born in the village of Bigelow, Holt County, October 6, 1884. He was reared and educated in his native county, obtained his schooling at Mound City and Bigelow, and continued at home with his parents until his marriage. He married Virginia Flowers, daughter of W. L. and Martha Ellen (Dawson) Flowers. After his marriage he was located on the Frank Sauer farm until 1914, and then moved to his present place of forty acres, comprising a part of his father's estate in Bigelow Township. He does a general farming business. Mr. and Mrs. Allen Earl Gresham are the parents of three children, Farell F., Rex F. and Forest B., all of whom were born in Holt County.

CHARLES W. SCOTT. Among the venerable citizens of Grundy County whose lives have long since passed the mark of three score and ten, Charles W. Scott, of Brimson, is worthy of mention. His life has been a long and full one, including experiences in California during the "days of old, the days of gold, the days of '49," as a soldier during the Civil war, in which he won promotion for valiant service, and, in later years, as a farmer and stock raiser whose energetic and well-directed efforts won him material fortune, while his good citizenship won him personal esteem. Today, at the age of more than eighty-one years, he goes about his daily round of affairs, a striking and helpful example of a long life well lived.

Charles W. Scott was born August 2, 1833, in Daviess County, Missouri, and is a son of John and Charlotte (Meeks) Scott, natives of Virginia. His father's family included members who participated in the War of 1812, while on his mother's side he is related to Joseph and Butler Meeks, who many years ago went to the Hudson's Bay country, where they engaged in hunting and trapping, and where many bearing the name are still to be found. Mr. Scott obtained his education in the public schools of Grundy County, but at the age of seventeen years the spirit of adventure and the oft-repeated stories of the great fortunes to be secured in the gold country called him to California, and he safely made the long and hazardous journey across the plains. A short experience, however, convinced him that money was not to be secured as quickly as he had been led to believe, and he gave up the vocation of miner for that of tender of a ranch. In 1853 Mr. Scott returned to Grundy County, and, realizing the need of further education, attended Grand River College. In that same year he entered upon his agricultural career by purchasing eighty acres of land, locating in Grundy County and erecting a small log cabin. This land, which cost him $2.50 per acre, he improved, and was able, in 1856, to dispose of it at a good price. He next moved to Harrison Township, in the same county, where he purchased sixty acres, at $1.25 per acre, and this formed the nucleus for his present magnificent farm.

The distress of his country and its need for men called Mr. Scott to the ranks of the Union army in 1861, when he enlisted in the Missouri State Militia, which organization was held to subject to call at any time during the war. Under Colonel Shanklin, Mr. Scott participated in a number of battles in Missouri, was promoted to orderly sergeant of his company, and was honorably discharged at the close of hostilities with an excellent record as a soldier. Returning at that time to his home he resumed the duties of peace, taking up his agricultural labors where he had left off, and as the years have passed he has continued to devote himself to general farming and stock raising, with a full measure of success. At this time he is the owner of 420 acres of land, on which are located substantial and architecturally handsome buildings, a modern frame residence, valuable improvements of every kind, and large herds of well-fed cattle. The very air of the place denotes its prosperity and the property is a substantial monument to the labors, good management and ability of its owner. Mr. Scott is a republican and has labored efficiently and conscientiously in his community's behalf as justice of the peace and in other offices. With his family he attends the Methodist Episcopal Church and takes a helpful part in its work.

Mr. Scott was married December 3, 1854, to Miss Sarah Thornburg, who was born in Alabama, a daughter of William and C. (Rickey) Thornburg. Nine children have been born to this union, as follows: Laura, who married George Drummond, and has five children—Floyd, Ray, Musie, Irene and Francis; Flora, who married Charles M. Bowman, of Grundy County, a native of Ohio, and has three children—Velta, Dale and Scott; Hannah, who married J. P. Lynch, of Grundy County, and has one son—Frank; Lottie, who married Louis Shaw, of Grundy County, and has four children—Lyman, Gard, Paul and Bart; Charles S., who married a young lady of Iowa; Thomas T., who married a California lady and has one daughter—Yuba; Hugh, who married Luella Frazier, of Gallatin, Daviess County, Missouri, daughter of Dr. and Mrs. Lillian Frazier, of that place, and has six children—Wilson, Hulda, Anna L., Elsie B., James and Francis L.; Bart, who married Elizabeth Coppel, of Ludlow, Missouri, daughter of Mose Coppel; and Porter, who married Callie Cires, of Grundy County, daughter of Columbus and Mary Jane Cires, and has three children—Gertrude, Helen and Columbus.

PHILIP ERNEST WENZ. Many of the most thrifty and prosperous business men of Buchanan County have come from the land beyond the sea, noteworthy among the number being Philip Ernest Wenz, who has been actively identified with the manufacturing and mercantile interests of St. Joseph for more than half a century, and is eminently deserving of mention in this biographical work. He was born, October 23, 1831, at Beisinger, three miles from Bodelshausen, Hohenzollern, Germany, in the same house in which his father, Conrad Wenz, was born and reared. His paternal grandfather served in the German army, under Karl Herzog, and was afterwards appointed chief forester, with two assistants under him. He subsequently bought a house in Beisinger, and there spent his remaining years.

Conrad Wenz learned the trade of a baker when young, and spent his entire life in the town in which his birth occurred. He married, and of the six children he reared, five came to America, as follows: Philip Ernest, George, Fred, Catherine, and Rosa.

Having attended school steadily from the age of six years until fourteen years old, Philip Ernest Wenz then served an apprenticeship of four years at the trade of a boot and shoe maker in the City of Zurich, after which he followed his trade in various European cities. In 1854, desirous of trying life in a new country, he went from Stuttgart, Germany, to Havre, France, where he sailed for America, arriving at the end of sixty-seven days after leaving the fatherland. Mr. Wenz immediately came to St. Joseph, which was then a small frontier city, Missouri having at that time no railways, while Kansas had just been opened to settlers. His only capital when he came to this country was good health, willing hands, and a set of tools. Finding employment at his trade, he worked as a journeyman for twenty-one months, and then embarked in business on his own account, establishing on Edmund Street the business now owned by his brother, it being one of the first of the kind established in the city, or in Northwestern Missouri. Selling out in 1860, Mr. Wenz purchased property at No. 1003 Frederick Avenue, and there conducted a general store a few years, but has since, at the same location, been actively engaged in his present business.

Mr. Wenz married, in 1859, Christiana Frederica Bauman, who was born in the village of Backnang, in Wurtemberg, Germany, in the same house in which the birth of her father, John Bauman, occurred. Reared and educated in his native village, John Bauman married Frederica Schwaterer, a native of Marbach, Wurtemberg. She died in 1844, in early womanhood, leaving seven children, Christina F., George, Caroline, Gottlieb, Jacob, Dorothy, and Ludwig, all of whom, with the exception of Dorothy, came to America. In 1858 Mr. Bauman emigrated with his family to this country, settling in Andrew County, Missouri, where he purchased 150 acres of land, one half of which had been cleared. Immediately assuming possession of the log buildings standing on the place, he began adding to the improvements already inaugurated, and was there a resident until his death, at the age of seventy-two years. Mrs. Wenz died September 28, 1902, leaving four children, namely: Emma, Rosa, Annie, and Nellie. Mr. Wenz has four grandsons, William Wenz, Herbert Wenz, Edwin Wenz, and Ernest Beihl. Mr. and Mrs. Wenz were both brought up in the Lutheran Church, and have reared their family in the same religious faith.

CAPT. JOHN HARNOIS. A veteran of the Civil war, and a highly respected citizen of St. Joseph, Capt. John Harnois has had a varied career in life, having been associated with different industries, and having served in army and navy, and also having filled with ability and fidelity numerous public offices. A son of Peter Harnois, he was born, November 12, 1844, in what is now the State of Nebraska, coming from pure French ancestry, the founder of the family in this country having settled in Nova Scotia on leaving France, becoming one of the Acadian colonists.

His paternal grandfather, John Baptiste Harnois, was born in the Province of Quebec, Canada, where his father, Charles Harnois, an Acadian by birth, spent his last years. He embarked in farming when young, owning and managing a farm near Lavaltrie, in the Province of Quebec, about thirty miles below Montreal, and there spent his life. He married Mary Maible, a lifelong resident of the Province of Quebec.

Peter Harnois was born on the parental farm near Lavaltrie, in 1814, and as a young man served an apprenticeship at the trade of a blacksmith. He subsequently came to the United States, and found employment in the lumber camps along the lakes, a part of the time being engaged in selecting ship timber. He later located in Cleveland, where he was driver on the canal. Going from there to Detroit, he followed his trade for awhile in that city, and then went South, first to Louisville, Kentucky, thence to New Orleans, where he spent one winter selling produce on the wharves. In 1836 he entered the employ of the American Fur Company, and for two years was located at the head waters of the Missouri River. The ensuing ten years he was in the employ of the United States as a blacksmith among the Indians, spending five years with the Otoes and Omahas, and five years among the Pawnees, after which he was in business for himself one year at Sarpy's trading post, a few miles below Omaha. Locating in St. Joseph in 1849, he kept a hotel at No. 815 North Second Street for a time, and continued his residence in that place until his death, in 1894. The maiden name of the wife of Peter Harnois was Sarah Holcomb. She was born in Gallia County, Ohio, and died in St. Joseph, Missouri, in 1889. She was of Welsh ancestry, her immigrant ancestor having come from Wales in the ship "Mary John" soon after the "Mayflower" at Plymouth.

A boy of five years when he came with his parents to St. Joseph, John Harnois attended school quite regularly until sixteen years old, when he began life as a wage-earner, clerking in a store. On November 12, 1862, he enlisted in the enrolled militia, and served as orderly under Gen. Oden Guitar. He was later made corporal of Company M, from that organization enlisting, in August, 1863, in Company G, Fifteenth Kansas Cavalry. He was subsequently with his command in Missouri, Arkansas, Kansas, and the Indian Territory, being promoted to the rank of first sergeant, and continuing in service until honorably discharged, October 19, 1865, when he returned home ill in health. On November 11, 1867, Mr. Harnois enlisted in the United States Navy, in which he served until receiving his honorable discharge, July 14, 1868.

Mr. Harnois married in 1869, and after that important event kept a store for awhile. He then assumed charge of his father's farm for a few months, after which he served as a letter carrier for three years. In 1877 he went to the Black Hills, but seeing no prospect of acquiring a fortune in that region soon returned, and during the ensuing seven years was bookkeeper in a bottling house. In 1885 Mr. Harnois was appointed United States gauger, and held the position until a change of administration. The following two and one-half years he was in the employ of an express company, afterwards being bookkeeper for a hay and grain firm. In 1889 he was again appointed United States gauger, and served in that capacity thirteen months. He was then deputy collector of internal revenue for seventeen counties in Northwestern Missouri, continuing in that office until another change in the presidential administration. Mr. Harnois was subsequently variously employed until 1900, when he went to Oklahoma, where he spent seven years. Returning to St. Joseph in 1907, he has since been busily employed at the courthouse.

Mr. Harnois has been twice married. He married first Alice A. White, in 1869. She was born in Zanesville, Ohio, a daughter of Frederick W. and Alice (Stewart) (Pharis) White, and died November 10, 1884. Mr. Harnois married second, December 6, 1885, Laura Holcomb, who was born in Ottumwa, Iowa, a daughter of Zephaniah Holcomb. Mrs. Holcomb is a noted preacher in the United Brethren Church, and a widely known temperance lecturer. By his first marriage Mr. Harnois reared two children, Sarah Alice and George P. Sarah Alice Harnois was one of the youngest graduates of the St. Joseph High School. She married, and at her death left one child, Etta Freeman, who now lives with her grandparents. George P. Harnois was educated in the St. Joseph High School, the Christian Brothers' School, and at Glencoe, after which he taught for awhile in the Christian Brothers' School. He is a veteran of the Spanish war, and was in service in the Philippines for two years. He has served five years as a member of the National Guard of Missouri, two years of the time being captain of the Grant Guards.

Mr. Harnois is a member of the Custer Post, Grand Army of the Republic, and has served as chief mustering officer of the Department of Missouri, and has been on the national and department staff several times, now, in 1914, being adjutant of the post.

G. B. COWLEY, M. D. During his many years of residence in Caldwell County, Doctor Cowley has performed varied and useful service, as physician and surgeon, as editor and publisher, as a member of the State Legislature, and one of the leaders in every movement that concerns the development and progress of his home town and county. Doctor Cowley is editor and proprietor of the Cowgill Chief, one of the most influential papers in Caldwell County. He has been identified with the medical profession for about thirty years, and has been proprietor of the newspaper at Cowgill since 1889. He has made this newspaper not only a medium for the current news and the business announcements of the town and vicinity, but also a force for good in the community, upholding clean and honest civic movements, purity in politics, and moral and religious progress. He has also for several years been identified with the rural letter carrier service out of Cowgill.

Dr. George B. Cowley represented his district in the Thirty-ninth Missouri Assembly, as a republican, and was one of the very active members of that body, a member of the ways and means committee, the Committee on Banks and Banking, and in many ways showed himself a hard working and intelligent member of the law making body. Doctor Cowley was born near Rio, Wisconsin, May 16, 1861. His father, Alfred Cowley, who was born in England in 1827, was brought to this country in 1838. In 1856 Alfred Cowley married Hannah A. Carter, who was born in New Jersey in 1833. Coming from Wisconsin, they became in 1869 early settlers of Caldwell County, and lived as farmers near Polo. They had a large family and seven grew to maturity: Charles A., a resident of Cottonwood Falls, Kansas; A. A., of Polo; Joseph H., died in 1893; John H., in the lumber business at Hamilton; B. F., of Leesville, Louisiana; S. R., of Cedar Point, Kansas; Dr. George B. The mother died in 1890, and the father in 1899, at the age of seventy-two. In politics he was a republican.

Dr. George B. Cowley was reared on a farm, attended the public schools, and in 1882 graduated in medicine from the Missouri Medical College at St. Louis. He was first located at Polo, but soon after came to Cowgill where he has long enjoyed a high position in his profession as well as in business and civic affairs.

Doctor Cowley was married August 29, 1886, to Mary Alice E. McCray, a member of one of the prominent families in Caldwell County, and a daughter of William and Nancy (Carroll) McCray. They were natives of Kentucky, who settled in Caldwell County in 1846 and died there in 1903 and 1885 respectively. Doctor Cowley and wife became the parents of six children: Luella J., who is secretary and registrar of Phillips University, in Enid, Oklahoma; Harry, who was married in 1913 to Maurine Todd of this county, and they have one son, Kenneth Carl; Lucile, wife of M. K. Simpson, a merchant in Thomas, Oklahoma, and they have two children, Margaret R. and William; Joy Louise, who is connected with the First National Bank of Cowgill; George B., Jr., and Eva May, at home. All the children but one are graduates of the Cowgill High School, and all have shown themselves useful workers in the world. In addition to their Cowgill property and some holdings in Texas and Oklahoma, Doctor Cowley and wife own a fine fruit and stock farm of 160 acres in the "Shepherd of the Hills Country" of Southern Missouri. He and family are active in the Christian Church, and he is at this time president of its official board, and interdenominational superintendent of adult Sunday School work for Caldwell County. He affiliates with Masonic Lodge No. 561, the M. W. A., R. N. A. and W. O. W., and Lodge No. 483 of the Independent Order of Odd Fellows at Cowgill. He is also a member of the Missouri Press Association, the county and state medical societies and is a registered pharmacist. For the past seventeen years Doctor Cowley has served as a member of the Board of Education, and was from 1897 to 1914 secretary of the County Board of U. S. Pension Examining Surgeons. These are only a few of the major facts in his active career, and there has hardly been a movement for the advancement of Cowgill and Caldwell County in the past twenty-five years with which his name has not been influentially identified.

The name of Cowley is an ancient and honorable one in English history, Abraham Cowley, the famous poet of the restoration, having been the personal friend and confidant of King Charles I, and on his (Cowley's) death in 1667 was honored by burial in Westminster Abbey, London, near the present tombs of Wellington and Nelson. Mrs. Cowley also has a notable ancestry, her mother, Nancy Carroll, being the daughter of John Carroll of Virginia and Kentucky, a soldier of the War of 1812, he being a son of John Carroll, born in Virginia in 1754, who afterward saw distinguished service in the Revolutionary war. (See Collins' History of Kentucky, (Vol. 2) Census of 1840, Rev. Pensioners). Mrs. Cowley is a member of the National Chapter, Daughters of the American Revolution.

Doctor Cowley, among his many accomplishments, has the faculty of wielding a graceful pen in literary composition, and both as an illustration of his style and for the intrinsic beauty of the lines the following poem, dedicated to the old Union soldiers' of Caldwell County, under the title "On Decoration Day," which appeared in the St. Louis Globe-Democrat, is herewith quoted:

"It was an aged veteran, with locks all thin and gray,
Who sat within the village church on Decoration Day;
He came upon his crutches, with tottering step and slow,
And many winters on his brow had cast their fleeting snow;
His eyes were sunk and feeble, his cheek was pale and wan,
Not like the boy who went out when the cruel war began.

The organ pealed out grandly: "My Country, 'Tis of Thee,"
And youthful voices sang aloud the anthem of the free.
With listless air he watched them, from the old, familiar pew,
A sad example of the old supplanted by the new.
No wife or child sat by him—all dead or far away;
Amid the throng he was alone, on Decoration Day.

Too weak and lame for walking for many years of late,
A friendly auto bore him to the cemetery gate;
Here, sitting in the welcome shade, he watched his comrades come—
A piteous few, but keeping step behind the fife and drum;
Then, leaning on a marble shaft, his dead wife's grave a-nigh,
He gave salute, and waved his hat, as the starry flag went by.

The graves were strewn with blossoms, the little flags all placed;
His comrades to the busy town their halting steps retraced;
And the dead slept on in silence, beneath the flowers of May,
Heedless alike of fife and drum, and Decoration Day;
But, lingering there among them, till red the sunset gleamed,
His head sank down upon his breast; he fell asleep and dreamed.

He dreamed of childhood's hour; he heard the robin sing
And culled again the violets that blossomed by the spring;
With sisters and with brothers, in his happy northern home,
He watched the war cloud gather, and heard its thunders come.
His mother's clasp, his sweetheart's kiss, still thrilled him as of yore,
When proudly, down the village street, he marched out to the war.

He dreamed of soldiers marching—he saw the deadly fray
'Round Vicksburg's walls, on Lookout's height, and Shiloh's bloody
    day:
"Tramp, tramp!" Is this the boy he was, who marches, blithe and
    free,
With Sherman and with Sherman's men through Georgia to the sea?
"Tramp, tramp!" It is the Grand Review, and Grant is looking on!
Then "Taps" were blown, the lights went out, and night and death
    came down!

They found him there next morning; his locks were wet with dew
And his dead face wore a peaceful smile, as if the angels knew
That this brave old Union soldier had struck his earthly tent
And marched on to that blissful shore, where old Elijah went.
Perhaps, from that great camping-ground where summer shines for
    aye,
He still looks down, and waves his hat, on Decoration Day.''

THOMAS JEFFERSON TOWNSEND.   Since its establishment in Northwest
Missouri in 1846 the Townsend family has been identified with its agricultural interests, and its numerous members have attained substantial
positions in this fertile farming community.   Its men have shown in
their own careers the worth of industry and integrity in the affairs of life,
and have contributed materially to the development of the locality's
resources.   A worthy representative of the name is found in the person
of Thomas Jefferson Townsend, who is now the owner of a well cultivated
farm in section 24, Benton Township.
    Mr. Townsend was born January 22, 1856, on the original homestead
of his parents, located four miles northwest of Savannah, in Andrew
County, Missouri, a son of William Calvin and Mary Ann (Judd) Townsend.   William C. Townsend was born on an Indiana farm, was there
reared and educated, and married in that state Mary Ann Judd, who was
born in Dearborn County, Indiana, in 1825, four years her husband's
junior.   They were married May 26, 1842, and about the year 1846
migrated to the State of Missouri, taking up their residence on a new,
undeveloped farm, four miles northwest of Savannah.   Here the father
made the usual pioneer improvements, and the little log house continued
to be the family home until 1861, when removal was made to Iowa, Thomas
J. being then a lad of five years.   Two years later, however, the family
returned to Andrew County, Missouri, and took up their residence on a
farm two and one-half miles south of the town of Bolckow.   William C.
Townsend continued to be identified with agricultural pursuits on this
property during the remainder of his life, and through industry and
earnest effort made a success of his grain and stock raising operations,
accumulating over three hundred acres of good land. He was a republican
in his political views, but took only a good citizen's interest in affairs of a
public character.   Both he and Mrs. Townsend were charter members of
the Baptist Church at Bolckow, in which Mr. Townsend was a deacon for a
number of years, and since their deaths their children have placed there
in their memory a beautiful memorial window, one of the largest in the

church. William C. Townsend passed away, honored and respected by the community, July 12, 1882, the mother surviving him until August 29, 1907. Ten children were born to William C. and Mary A. Townsend, as follows: Sarah, who is the widow of the late George H. Sexton and resides in Oklahoma; Emeline, deceased, who was the wife of David H. Headley; Nancy A., deceased, who was the wife of James C. Campbell; John M., whose sketch will be found elsewhere in this work; William Calvin, a resident of Benton Township; Thomas Jefferson, of this review; Harriet F., who is the wife of G. F. Wilson and resides at Warrensburg; Charles G., who lives in Benton Township; Elizabeth E., deceased; who was the wife of T. J. Officer; and Ida B., whose death occurred at the age of four years.

Thomas J. Townsend received his education in the public schools of Benton Township and has been a resident of Andrew County all of his life with the exception of four years. In early manhood he decided to devote his career to agricultural pursuits, and his training in his youth was along this line. At the present time he is the owner of ninety-five and one-half acres, this being a part of his father's homestead. He has brought his land under a high state of cultivation, and it is devoted to the raising of grain and live stock, and in both lines Mr. Townsend has met with excellent success. His buildings are of a substantial character, his stock is of a good grade, his improvements are new and modern, and his good management is reflected in every department. He has been content to devote his energies to farm work and has kept out of politics, save as a republican voter, but maintains an interest in matters that affect the welfare of his community and can be relied upon to support good and progressive movements. Mr. Townsend is a member of the Baptist Church at Bolckow, to which the members of his family belong.

In 1883 Mr. Townsend was united in marriage with Miss Dora E. Dorrel, who was born September 25, 1866, in Andrew County, a daughter of James and Eliza J. Dorrel, a history of the family being found in the sketch of Judge A. Dorrel, elsewhere in this work. Four children have been born to Mr. and Mrs. Townsend, namely: Anna Ethel, who is the wife of Blaine Townsend and resides in Wyoming; Eva Ruth, who is at home; and Warren Irl and Mary Dorrel, who reside with their parents.

JUDGE WILLIAM McAFEE. In Hamilton and Caldwell County for more than thirty years there has been perhaps no abler attorney than Judge William McAfee. His successes have all been worthily won, he has built up a large and prosperous practice through solid ability, and has served his community with disinterested devotion to the public welfare.

William McAfee was born September 19, 1850, at Blue Lick, Indiana, and comes of an old Scotch-Irish ancestry. In the earlier generations the family were planters and slave holders, but subsequently liberated their negroes, lived in the northern states, and were chiefly industrious and high-minded farmers. On the maternal side Judge McAfee's grandfather was a native of Vermont. The Judge was one of six children. His brother James was a railroad man and was killed in a railroad accident. Thomas is deceased. John lived in the State of New Mexico until his death. The father died at the age of seventy-three. He was a farmer and cooper, a member of the Christian Church, and affiliated with the Independent Order of Odd Fellows.

William McAfee received practically no schooling till the winter of his eighteenth year, when he began working for himself and secured his education by home study and attending college at Macon City, Missouri, two years. After coming to Northwest Missouri he taught in the high school at Kingston for four years while studying law.

In 1875 Judge McAfee married Marian Johnson, daughter of Capt. E. D. Johnson, of prominent family in Northwest Missouri, but coming here from Coshocton County, Ohio. Judge McAfee and wife have three children: Agnes, wife of W. O. Keeney; Emmet, who is employed in the laboratory of the Dr. Price Baking Powder Company; and Floyd L. Two children died in childhood, Effie and Ernest. The children were all liberally educated, most of them in college, and one of them was a student in the Missouri Wesleyan College at Cameron.

Judge McAfee was admitted to the bar in 1876, and has been engaged in active practice ever since that time. He was prosecuting attorney of Caldwell County three terms, of two years each, from 1876-1880; 1887-1889. He has held a commission as notary public from all the governors of Missouri since that time. Judge McAfee served four years as judge of the Probate Court of Caldwell County, and at one time declined a nomination for Congress. He is affiliated with the Royal Arch Chapter of Masonry, with the Independent Order of Odd Fellows and the Knights of Pythias, and his church is the Methodist. In politics he is a republican.

ISAAC M. NEFF, of Fox Creek Township, R. F. D. No. 2, Gilman City, is the oldest living member of this pioneer and numerous family of Harrison County. He has resided in the county since April 6, 1858, when he came to it as a young man with a small family, settling where he' is now located and where he patented a small piece of school land, and here he has spent his life with his farm and with the manifestation of a genius for invention and for doing new things which has marked him among the interesting and useful men of his community. Mr. Neff came hither from Franklin County, Indiana, where he was born November 15, 1834. His environment as a youth was such as inspired him with mechanical inclinations, for his father was a mechanic, made plows with wooden moldboards, made cradles for harvesting grain, manufactured wagons and worked in iron as well, and had a shop on his farm about two miles from Andersonville, Indiana, having worked at wagon-making in Andersonville, and had a wagon shop in Andersonville itself.

The father of Isaac M. Neff was Elihu S. Neff, who moved into Rush County, Indiana, in 1822, his parents coming from Clinton County, New York, where he was born March 6, 1811. He picked up his trade by himself, being naturally skilled in and having an eye for mechanics, and worked at his several vocations until late in life. Mr. Neff manufactured seventy-two coffins after coming to Missouri, from time to time in his community as they were needed to bury its dead. Mr. Neff had been granted only such education as was afforded by the public schools, but early developed an inventive turn of mind such as is evidenced by his sons and daughters, and his judgment was of a superior order, enabling him to succeed notwithstanding the fact that a portion of his career covered a period of national monetary and commercial depression that severely tried the metal of business men. An example of his industry is shown in the fact that in Indiana he paid for the clearing of his farm by making all kinds of agricultural implements, and this work he did with his own hands. Elihu Neff was an earnest whig in his political views, but was never possessed of ability as a speaker, and did not seek the honors of public office. He voted for Henry Clay for president in 1832, and in 1836 and 1840 for William Henry Harrison. In coming from New York to Indiana, the Neffs made the trip by boat much of the way, coming down the Ohio River to the mouth of the Miami, where Gen. William H. Harrison lived in his log cabin, and with the general the family stopped while the father, Daniel Neff, went on to Indiana and selected his location for settlement. General Harrison, or "'Old Tippecanoe," as he was after that called, lived in a typical pioneer cabin, with coon-skins stretched about over it, and the hospitality of the general's home so impressed young Elihu S. that he held the Harrison family in grateful remembrance ever after. During the campaigns which the general made later, Mr. Neff cast his ballot for the gallant soldier, and when the grandson of "Old Tippecanoe" became a candidate for president, in 1888, Elihu S. Neff, then an old man, built a replica of the old Harrison cabin, loaded it on a wagon, provided a live coon for one of his decorations, and drove the wagon and cabin about over Harrison County as a campaign feature in aid of Benjamin Harrison for the presidency. When the latter was elected the live coon was sent to him at the White House. Elihu S. Neff's only military experience was as a teamster in the Missouri militia during the Civil war.

Daniel Neff, the grandfather of Isaac M. Neff, was a Quaker and although according to his faith not a believer in warfare, was old enough to haul supplies for the Revolutionary army of the colonies. He lived at that date in New York and was only ten years old when the war ended. He was a native of the Empire State and his life's activities were devoted to the cultivation of a farm. In all that he did Daniel Neff was noted for his accuracy, a trait noticeable in his descendants. He lived the Quaker faith, always spoke the truth and let it make its own defense, and was courageous in reproving those who he believed needed reproof, although he did it in a mild and inoffensive way. His death occurred in Rush County, Indiana, some time after the Civil war. Mr. Neff's first wife was Charity Sherman, who was of Quaker stock, and it is doubtless from her that subsequent generations have inherited their inventive genius, for she fashioned her own spinning wheels and looms and was a conspicuous figure in her community. She died before her husband, who subsequently married Mrs. Deborah Howell. The children born to Daniel Neff were: Orange H., Elihu S., Ebenezer, Daniel, Jane, Sophira, Jeanette, Sophrona and Ann. Of these, Jane married Henry Cook, Sophira became the wife of John Allen, and Jeanette married James Yates.

Elihu S. Neff was married July 5, 1832, to Amanda Howell, a daughter of Isaac and Deborah (Barnett) Howell, the father being a native of Wales, a farmer by vocation and an early pioneer of the State of Kentucky, where he died. After his death his widow moved to Indiana, and there passed away, being buried in Franklin County, at the age of ninety-six years and five months. Mrs. Neff died in August, 1887, aged seventy-three years, while Mr. Neff survived until April 6, 1896. Their children were as follows: Oliver H., who met his death by a stroke of lightning in 1868 and left a wife and three sons; Isaac M.; Lydia J., who married Richard Utter and died in Nebraska; Francis M., of Ridgeway, Missouri; Charles H., who died in childhood; Daniel B., a resident of San Diego, California; Deborah, who died at the age of seven years; Orange T., who reared a family and died in Caldwell, Kansas; Elihu O., a farmer near Ridgeway, Missouri; Mary, who married Daniel Pilcher; Emily C., who first married Thomas Wiley, and second John Adkinson and died near Caldwell, Kansas; Sarah, who married Frank Reaksecker and died in Harrison County; and Laura, who married Jo Stephens, of Caldwell, Kansas.

Isaac M. Neff received his education mainly at home, aided somewhat by his father who was too constantly at his work to give much aid, and his mother learned to read and write after he did from the same source. He possessed an inherited mathematical turn, as well as a fondness for books, and became a teacher himself despite the fact that he had seldom been a pupil of school. As a teacher he taught in the Walnut School, where Gardner Station is now situated, December 6, 1862. Of the eighty pupils who enrolled in and out of the district, only one is now a resident of the district and none of the parents of those students survive. The number of pupils now in that district is less than half the number who attended his school, and the farm houses now occupied are fewer than one-fourth of what they were then as a result of the development and growth of the "larger farm." Mr. Neff taught in five different districts in Missouri, but his earliest work was done in Indiana as a youth of eighteen years. The total of the young folks who have attended his public and private schools is 1,470, the Sabbath school teaching spanning almost the period of his active life. He educated mainly for the farm, and a wonderfully successful lot of men went out of his schools as farmers, but in spite of this his teaching was with him rather a side line, for he was engaged in careful farming ventures at the same time. He has continued his studies through life, and learned the laws governing the solar system by securing a complete treatise on astronomy, and at the age of eighty can commit to memory better than at an earlier age.

The early boyhood of Mr. Neff had been passed in the days of financial depression that marked President Jackson's administration and the years that immediately followed. Labor was then worth but twenty cents a day, wheat after being cut with the hand sickle and threshed by hand brought only forty cents a bushel, half in goods and half in money, at Cincinnati, sixty miles away; a suit of clothes could be had for four dollars, and rich and poor were obliged to work hard to make both ends meet. This early experience without doubt bred in him a spirit of thrift and industry that enabled him to make a success of his later labors. He was always able to give at least one-third of his earnings to help the needy. In the matter of agriculture Mr. Neff is able as a result of numerous experiments to teach many of the teachers of the colleges of agriculture. He has been able to produce on one sweet potato vine three bushels of potatoes by irrigation, and four good ears on one stalk of his "Yellow Dent" corn. His experiments have covered the conservation of moisture, subirrigation and the handling of different plants at any season of the year, transplanting trees and plants to determine how readily they would recover and produce fruit. One pear tree which he moved at four years old, produced within eighteen months 100 pears that weighed forty-seven pounds. He then lifted this pear tree which, with the roots and leaves intact, weighed thirty-six pounds, and reset it with the leaves not wilting, and in less than two years gathered 102 pears from its branches and picked up twenty-three windfalls. According to Mr. Neff this demonstrates that any plant or tree in foliage can be transplanted successfully if the roots are not injured. In another field of agriculture Mr. Neff is also a pioneer, for he brought the first Poland-China hogs to Harrison County in 1858, when hogs were worth only $1.25 per hundred pounds.

As a mechanical engineer and practical mechanic Mr. Neff was active for more than forty years, moving eighty-one houses between July 10 and November 17, 1876. His work as a mover included three large grist mills. One conspicuous case was the moving of the Cainesville mill from its props on the edge of Grand River to the high bank, where it was lifted twelve feet to form a basement. The mill contained eighty tons of grain at the time of moving. He built the first bridge over Grand River, making the water itself cut or excavate the ground for the abutments, a new and cheap method of doing that sort of work. At the same time he straightened the channel of Grand River. He has had experience in all kinds of excavation, straightening up and repairing, putting additional stories on houses and erecting new homes for the people of his county, and has used as many as forty-four horses on some of his loads, and employed as many as twenty-five men on a job, and never had a man nor an animal to lose its temper and fail to do good work.

In his politics, Mr. Neff first voted for John C. Fremont, and cast two ballots for President Lincoln, and has voted for all the republican candidates since. In 1864, while in the military camp at Chillicothe, as a member of Captain Frisby's company, Col. James Neville's regiment, in which he largely did hospital work, he had some difficulty in returning home to cast his vote. While he was ready to fight as a soldier, he has always favored universal peace, but his sentiments in regard to slavery and the defense of the home caused him to take up arms. His mission in politics of recent years is to aid in the correction of the evil which has come to dominate portions of our government and to restore the truth to power everywhere. He confesses allegiance to no man or party and reserves for himself the right to expose error in public affairs and to lend a hand in its overthrow. He makes addresses, speeches and talks on occasions, and writes freely and extensively upon the great opportunities men have to combat evil and to correct error in private as well as in public life. In this connection it may be said that he is also well known on the lecture platform before bodies of farmers and agricultural investigators as well as students, upon subjects pertaining to farming. Mr. Neff is a strong temperance man, and favors the county unit law as proposed, as well as votes for women. Throughout his life he has continued to engage in Sabbath school work, and on numerous occasions has been a delegate to conventions and conferences of Sabbath school workers.

In addition to bringing up his own family, Mr. Neff has reared seven orphan children, educated them in a business way, taught them all kinds of domestic work, and never an unkind word has ever escaped any one of them toward him. One of them, Nona, enumerated the citizens of the township in 1909 and was the first enumerator to report her work as completed. These children were: Zula Neff, who is the wife of Alexander Bond; Vernie Neff, who is the wife of Jesse Little; Nona Neff, who still resides with Mr. Neff; Bert I., who is a successful farmer of Fox Creek Township; and Juna Neff, who married Rev. Floyd Morgan of Mercer, Missouri; Ollie Ballew, who is the wife of Thomas Arney, of Harrison County, Missouri; and Wilma Barnes Chuning, of Clayton, New Mexico.

Mr. Neff was married February 6, 1856, in Franklin County, Indiana, to Miss Barbara A. Maple, daughter of Elijah and Sarah (Coon) Maple. She was born August 28, 1834, and died August 8, 1897, was a devout Christian woman, a member of the United Brethren Church, and a woman of clear thought and careful speech, who took a great interest in doing her work well and was a most domestic and home-loving woman. She possessed great attraction for her children and grandchildren, and when she died left many sorrowing friends in the community. The children born to Mr. and Mrs. Neff were as follows: William H., residing on the old homestead, who married Nellie Good, and has three children; Alvah, who married Grace Hubbard; Lillie, who married James Childers, and Joseph, who married Edna Bryant; Sarah Amanda, who married J. I. Straight, of Bonesteel, South Dakota, and has seven children—Elma, Merlin, Walter, Van, Lucile, Forest and Ronda; Thomas V., a farmer of Harrison County, married Allie McGowin and has three children,

Ethel, Mon and Van. Their mother died eleven years ago and four years ago their father married Jennie Dewit, a widow with three children. He has one son from this marriage. John P., of Gilman, Missouri, who married Delila Gibson and has a daughter, Merle; Rhoda, who married Henry Leazenby of Bethany, Missouri; and Franklin E., who married Minnie McGowin and has four children, Hazel, Edith, Delbert and Elgin.

In the very month that Mr. Neff celebrated his eightieth birthday anniversary, he entered upon a personal campaign which lasted for many days in his efforts to secure the establishment of certain principles and certain reforms which his study and observation have led him to believe essential to the proper working of government and the administration of justice. Mr. Neff has also been greatly stirred by the events of the European war, and having little patience with the superficial aspects and causes which have been so prominently emphasized by statesmen and political philosophers, he is one of those who recognize that the war primarily and fundamentally is the result of a perversion of truth and those divine principles upon which the welfare and health of society must always rest. In his home district Mr. Neff has exerted his influence to secure the abrogation of rules and methods by which the administration of justice in the courts is too often turned aside and perverted in the interests of attorneys, who, he claims, have too often ruled the court and have made of judicial procedure little more than a game of chance.

Mr. Neff at the patriarchal age of eighty is still one of the most valuable citizens of Harrison County, and a man whose conversation is always interesting and enlightening. Much more might be written of his activities and the influence which he has exerted in his community, but the limits assigned to this sketch have already been passed and it will be necessary to close.

J. A. ROBERTS. For nearly a half century the Roberts family have been conspicuous members of the rural community half a dozen miles west of Savannah in Lincoln Township, where J. A. Roberts has his home in section 3. The name bespeaks a large relationship with both the older and later generations of Andrew County people and while the lives of most of them have been spent in the normal and inconspicuous walks of life, they have been none the less useful, have walked upright in the sight of men and God, and those that have gone have left the world a little better for their presence.

J. A. Roberts, though a resident of Andrew County most of his life, was born in Richardson County, Nebraska, July 27, 1857. His family were among the pioneers of Nebraska Territory, and his birth occurred shortly after the historic debate on and settlement of the Kansas-Nebraska question. Mr. Roberts is a son of the late J. W. and Sarah Ann (Walker) Roberts. The paternal grandparents were Arnett and Ann (Thompson) Roberts, both of whom were born in Kentucky and both died at Salem, Nebraska. Some facts that will contribute to the family history are found in an obituary of Ann (Thompson) Roberts, who died in Salem, Nebraska, at the home of her daughter, Mrs. J. C. Lincoln, October 15, 1892, aged eighty-four years nine months and fourteen days. She was the daughter of Gideon and Jane Thompson, and was born in Todd County, Kentucky, and was married to Arnett Roberts when sixteen years of age. They removed from Kentucky to Cooper County, Missouri, in the spring of 1826, lived there a year or

first settlers in the vicinity of Salem. Arnett Roberts died at Salem in February, 1862, his widow surviving him thirty years. They were the parents of eight children, four sons and four daughters, and only three of them survived their mother. Those who grew up were three sons and two daughters: James W.; Obediah, Samuel, Eliza Lincoln and Carrie Holt.

The late J. W. Roberts, father of J. A. Roberts, was born in Cooper County, Missouri, May 22, 1826, and was about sixteen years of age when his parents came to Andrew County in February, 1842. He was married February 25, 1849, to Sarah A. Walker, who was born in Estill County, Kentucky, July 22, 1829, moved with her parents to Clay County, Missouri, in 1830, and thence to Andrew County in 1837, the Walkers having been among the very first settlers in that section of Northwest Missouri. In October, 1854, J. W. Roberts and wife removed to Richardson County, Nebraska, and helped to establish the frontier line of civilization in that state. They lived there about a dozen years, and in November, 1866, returned to Andrew County. Here J. W. Roberts bought a farm on Hackberry, six miles west of Savannah, and lived there working as a farmer and increasing his revenues by employment as a carpenter among the neighbors throughout the rest of his active career. J. W. Roberts and wife traveled through life together nearly fifty-eight years, and died within thirty-six hours of each other. Mr. Roberts died at his old home February 3, 1907, aged seventy-nine years eight months and seven days, and less than two days later his wife passed away February 5, 1907. She had united with the Christian Church in 1858 and remained steadfast in its membership until her death. She is remembered as a faithful wife, a devoted mother and a kind neighbor. J. W. Roberts, who was long affectionately known in his community as "Uncle Billy," was a man who had gone through some of the hard experiences of pioneering, but always retained an optimistic attitude towards life, and his death marked the passing of one of Andrew County's oldest and best citizens. He had become identified with the Masonic order in 1848, and for many years was in good standing in his lodge. J. W. Roberts and wife were the parents of ten children: Mary Martin, deceased; Susan Martin, deceased; Alexander D., of the State of Washington; J. A.; Frank, a resident of Washington; David, of Andrew County; Samuel, who died in 1878; William, of Andrew County; Jennie Patterson, of Warrensburg, Missouri; and Carrie Evans of Savannah. The late J. W. Roberts was the first man to carry the mail between Sparta in Andrew County and Rockport in Atchison County, and performed this service during 1844 to 1848.

Mr. J. A. Roberts has lived in Andrew County since the return of his parents to this section from Nebraska in October, 1866. He was about ten years of age at that time and finished his education in the public schools of this county. His home has been on the farm where his father died west of Savannah with the exception of the first four years after his marriage, when he lived in another locality west of Savannah. Mr. Roberts owns 104 acres, utilized for general farming purposes. He has been a progressive and successful citizen. He is affiliated with the Modern Woodmen of America and belongs to the Christian Church in Savannah.

On March 9, 1882, he married Nannie Caroline Waterson, who was born in Brown County, Kansas, June 20, 1861, a daughter of James

Mrs. Roberts have eight children: Minnie Bell, who died January 25, 1814, was the wife of J. J. Hall; James W. was graduated from the law department of the University of Missouri in 1910, was nominated for the office of prosecuting attorney in Andrew County before receiving his diploma, was elected as a democrat, succeeding in overcoming a normal republican majority of about three hundred, and was nominated for a second term in that office, but withdrew from the campaign in order to remove to Muskogee, Oklahoma, where he is now one of the successful members of the bar; Jesse L. is a farmer in Andrew County; Joseph Ernest died January 20, 1883, at the age of four years; Claude V. is a farmer in Andrew County; Ruth Lucile is the wife of Clarence Christianson, an Andrew County farmer; Lloyd W. and Loren L. are both at home.

WILLIAM THORNE. The owner of a fine farm on section 5 of Lincoln Township in Andrew County, William Thorne represents the sturdy stock of old Devon, England. It was in that section of Southern England, noted for its stock and dairy industries, that William Thorne spent his boyhood and early manhood, and has exemplified the qualities of his race in his career in Andrew County, which has been his home for over forty years.

William Thorne was born in Devonshire in May, 1842, the son of Henry and Mary (Thorne) Thorne. His parents spent all their lives in Devonshire, where his father was a carpenter and later a farmer. There were seven children: John, deceased; Mary Lord of England; Anna Carey, deceased; William; Edwin, who lives in England; and Jacob of England, and one that died in infancy.

William Thorne is the only member of his family to come to America. He came direct to Savannah in the spring of 1870 and has spent most of his life in this locality since that year. Two or three years he was engaged in mining near Georgetown, Colorado, but otherwise his work has been along the line of farming. His success is due to his individual enterprise and industry. For several years he was known in Andrew County as a hard-working, sober and intelligent farm hand, then rented a farm for several years, and finally bought his present place in Lincoln Township. Mr. Thorne is the owner at the present time of 330 acres, which in its cultivation and improvements measures up to the high standards of Andrew County agriculture. It is devoted to general farming and stock raising.

Mr. Thorne since becoming an American citizen has affiliated with the democratic party. He is a member of the Independent Order of Odd Fellows. In 1875 he married Martha J. Hunter, who was born in Kentucky, a daughter of Samuel Hunter, and came to Andrew County during childhood. She died at the old home in Lincoln Township in 1914 at the age of sixty-two. She was the mother of ten children: Henry, who lives at Long Branch; Ina, of Fillmore; Clara, wife of Donald Turner, of Lincoln Township; Charles, who is living on the farm; Kate, at home; Thomas, of Fillmore; Arlene, wife of Chester G. Turner, of Jackson Township; Clyde, at home; Myrtle, at home; and Benjamin, who is still in the home circle.

L. A. AEBERSOLD. Representing an Andrew County family that has been identified with that section for a half century, L. A. Aebersold has exhibited the sturdy qualities of his Swiss ancestors and has established himself securely both in material circumstances and in the esteem of his community. Mr. Aebersold has accomplished those things that are most worth while, has provided a home, has reared a family, has lived amicably with his friends and neighbors and enjoys esteem both at home and abroad.

L. A. Aebersold was born in Tuscarawas County, Ohio, October 30, 1859, a son of John and Barbara (Yenni) Aebersold. Both parents were born in Switzerland, and his father is still one of the honored old residents of Andrew County, and a sketch of his life and family will be found on other pages in this publication. L. A. Aebersold was the oldest of five children, three of whom are still living. He was five years old when his parents in 1864 left Ohio and after spending the following winter in Indiana came into Andrew County in the spring of 1865 and located in Lincoln Township. Here Mr. Aebersold grew up, attended the local schools, and learned the lessons of industry on his father's farm. He remained at home with his parents until 1881, and then spent a year in Colorado employed by a railroad contractor in getting out ties. On his return to his father's place he farmed a year, then married, and took his bride to a rented place in Nodaway Township, where he spent one year. In 1883 Mr. Aebersold came to his present homestead in section 36 of Jackson Township. His first purchase was 160 acres, and he subsequently added another eighty acres, making a fine farm of 240 acres, nearly half of section 36. This has been his home ever since with the exception of one year which he spent in Texas. Mr. Aebersold has invested his surplus in the lands of Western Texas, and owns two sections in Gray and Parson counties, and has brought that land into an improved condition and employs it both for grazing and for the staple crops of that part of the Lone Star State. When Mr. Aebersold located on his home farm in Jackson Township a little more than thirty years ago, the house was a small one of four rooms, and there was also a small pole barn. His own progress and prosperity is exemplified in the changed conditions in these two classes of improvements. There now stands a fine modern nine-room dwelling, with attractive surroundings, and with well equipped and substantial barns and other outbuildings. Mr. Aebersold has found success in general farming and stock feeding and shipping.

Politically he is a republican, and has served his community as a school and road officer. He was brought up in the faith of the German Reform Church and is a member of that denomination in Amazonia. Fraternally he is identified with the Modern Woodmen of America. On December 31, 1882, Mr. Aebersold married Lizzie Maag, who was born at Savannah, Missouri, October 5, 1860, a daughter of Casper and Margaret (Smith) Maag. Her father was a native of Switzerland and her mother was born in Canada, and both died in Lincoln Township of Andrew County. Mr. and Mrs. Aebersold have a fine family of children, most of whom are established for themselves and by their lives are honoring father and mother. Their names and stations in life are: Albert Aaron, who lives on one of his father's farms in Texas and by his marriage to Georgia Goodloe has one child, Herman L.; John Alexander married Frances Cottrell, lives near Fillmore in Andrew County, and has one child, John C.; Roy Tillman, lives in Texas, and by his marriage to Emma Yenni has two children, Devere and Lawrence Sheldon; Robert Carl, who lives on the homestead with his father, married Emily Faires, and has one child, Warren G.; Louis Emmett is cashier of the Farmers Bank of Nodaway; Walter Ray lives at home; Emma Elizabeth died in 1900 at the age of two years; Barbara Elizabeth died at the age of eight months.

JAMES PLEASANT GILLISPIE. A resident of one locality for more than half a century is not an unimportant distinction, especially when the years are filled with useful efforts, with satisfying accomplishment in material things and the esteem of fellow citizens; and such is the position of James Pleasant Gillispie in Andrew County, Missouri, where he was born, where he spent his school days and early youth, where he has accumulated a sufficient property for advancing age, and where he has been honored as one of the judges of the county.

Judge Gillispie was born at Lincoln Creek in Jackson Township, Andrew County, March 16, 1858, a son of J. H. and Marion (Cornelison) Gillispie. His father was born in Madison County, Kentucky, and as a child was brought to Andrew County by his widowed mother during the '40s. He died July 13, 1895, at the age of sixty-nine, and his wife passed away January 13, 1884. J. H. Gillispie was first married to a sister of his second wife, and the one child of the first union, Andrew, is now deceased. By his second marriage there were five sons and three daughters: W. T., of Jackson Township; Susan Frances, wife of William Hoffman, of Jackson Township; Judge James P.; John M., of Jackson Township; Mary Elizabeth, deceased, who married David Roberts; Edward Lafayette, of Jackson Township; Margaret Rebecca, wife of Jesse Robinson, of Fillmore; and Benjamin B., who died in 1906. J. H. Gillispie spent most of his life on a farm in Jackson Township, where his son John now resides. During the California gold excitement he made a journey overland to California with ox team in 1849. He was a democrat, served as justice of the peace many years, was affiliated with the Masonic fraternity and belongs to the Christian Church.

Judge Gillispie has spent all his life in Andrew County, had a country school education, and the first year after his marriage worked as a renter, and then conducted a farm owned jointly with his brother, John M., for seven years. They owned 140 acres in partnership. Since that time he has been an independent farmer. Judge Gillispie now has a fine stock farm well known in Lincoln Township, situated on sections 1 and 2, comprising 186¾ acres. All its improvements except the residence represents his own enterprise. For about ten years Judge Gillispie did a profitable business as a breeder of Shropshire sheep, and now specializes in Poland China hogs.

He has been an active democrat since casting his first ballot back in the '70s, was a candidate for sheriff in 1900, and served as county judge from his district for one term of two years, 1902-04. He is affiliated with the Masonic order.

On September 10, 1882, Judge Gillispie married Susannah Elizabeth Bohart. Mrs. Gillispie comes of one of the wealthy and prominent old families of Andrew County and was born in this county October 29, 1862. Her parents were William and Mary (Burns) Bohart, both natives of Indiana. Her father was born in 1842 and her mother in the same year, and her father came to Missouri in 1860 and her mother in 1858. They were married in Andrew County and were prosperous farmers there. Her father died February 25, 1874, and her mother April 17, 1903. The four Bohart children were: Mrs. Gillispie; Sally, wife of N. S. Dickson, of Andrew County; Philip Emery, deceased; and Jennie, wife of J. L. Martin, of Andrew County. Judge Gillispie and wife had only one child, Carl Emery, who died in April, 1887, at the age of four years.

E. M. WATERSON. For more than forty-five years E. M. Waterson has been a resident of Andrew County, and has lived at his present home place in section 2 of Lincoln Township since 1883, has prospered like the majority of Andrew County farmers, has been a liberal provider for his family, has been interested in business affairs, and is honored in his community for his private success and for his value as a citizen.

E. M. Waterson was born at Marysville, Kansas, August 2, 1858. That date of itself indicates an early residence in the Sunflower State, and Mr. Waterson has the distinction of having been the first white child born in Marshall County. A few hours after his birth the first white girl was born in that community, named Hattie McGill. Mr. Waterson's parents were James and Artemisia (Cameron) Waterson, his father a native of Ohio and his mother of Kentucky. Both the Waterson and Cameron families were Kansas pioneers, having gone to that territory in 1844. The grandfather, Thomas W. Waterson, who died at Marysville, Kansas, September 5, 1889, was born in Pennsylvania in 1811, went from there to Cincinnati and in 1854 settled in Doniphan County, Kansas, and in 1860 took up his residence at Marysville. It is said that he was the first justice of the peace appointed in the Territory of Kansas, his appointment coming in 1854. He was a member of the Territorial Legislature in 1855 and in 1857 and was four times mayor of the City of Marysville besides other offices of trust. From 1860 until the year of his death he was a Marysville merchant, finally selling out and spending his last days in retirement. His success as a business man was measured by the accumulation of a property estimated at upwards of a hundred thousand dollars. .Combined with this was a thorough public spirit and liberality which caused him to contribute in many ways both to the public good and to individual needs.

James and Artemisia were reared in Kansas, were married in 1857 in Brown County, and soon afterwards took up pioneer claims in Marshall County. James Waterson was killed at Marysville, Kansas, in 1868, while driving a team. He was then thirty-four years of age. His widow survived him many years, and died near Savannah in Andrew County, Missouri, August 6, 1884, at the age of forty-four. There were three children: E. M.; Nannie, wife of J. A. Roberts, of Andrew County; and John, a resident of St. Joseph.

In 1863, when E. M. Waterson was five years of age, the family moved to Andrew County, Missouri, owing to the troubles incident to the war. After the war the family returned to Kansas, lived there until the death of the father, when the mother once more brought her children to Andrew County. During his residence in these two states E. M. Waterson spent his boyhood and acquired his education in the common schools. He has lived in Andrew County since 1868, and has been a farmer since reaching his majority. He now owns 160 acres, and has had his home on this farm since March 15, 1883. Its improvements are to be credited to his own management and labor, and he has prospered through the work of general farming and stock raising. For one year he was a director of the Andrew County Mutual Telephone Company, and for the past eighteen years has been a director and agent for the Andrew County Mutual Fire, Lighting & Wind Storm Insurance Company. In politics a democrat, Mr. Waterson twice led his party ticket as candidate for the offices of county judge and county collector. His only fraternal affiliations are with the Modern Woodmen of America.

In March, 1883, Mr. Waterson married Sarilda Mackey. She was born on the farm where she now lives, November 30, 1856, and has never lived in any other locality longer than eleven months. Her parents were John O. and Sarah (Cameron) Mackey. Her father was born in Kentucky, March 10, 1811, and her mother in Clay County, Missouri, in 1824. John O. Mackey came to Clay County when a youth, was married there in December, 1842, and in 1844 came to Andrew County as a pioneer. He died on the old farm in Lincoln Township in 1857, while his widow survived him fifty years, passing away in 1907. John O. Mackey was not only a pioneer farmer but a blacksmith by trade, and

had one of the shops which supplied a service to a large country community. He worked in the fields during the day time, and would usually
spend several hours doing his work as a blacksmith in the night. There
were six Mackey children, as follows: Eliza Mary, widow of C. M.
Rumburg, of California; Anderson, of Andrew County; Elizabeth,
deceased wife of W. W. Bussell; Mrs. Waterson; James, who died at
the age of sixteen years; and Frances, who died at the age of four
years. Mr. and Mrs. Waterson are the parents of five children: Lola
May, wife of C. F. Clark, of Loveland, Colorado, and who died March 1,
1915; Alice, wife of Henry Ordnung, of Andrew County; John Ray,
who died at the age of four years; Ralph and Ada, both at home.

WILLIAM ENT. In point of years of continuous residence William
Ent is the oldest citizen of Lincoln Township, Andrew County. More
than fifty-five productive and useful years have been spent in this community. It is difficult to measure the work and influences that can
properly be ascribed to such a man as William Ent. If he has prospered beyond the average of men, his success is only a just desert, since
through all these years he has gone about among his fellow men with the
uprightness of conduct and the incorruptible integrity which more than
justify any material reward that has followed his labors.

William Ent is a native of Ohio, born in Knox County, December 25,
Christmas Day, 1836, a son of John and Susanna (Baxter) Ent. His
father was born in Pennsylvania, and his mother in Knox County, Ohio.
John Ent was taken by his parents when a child to Knox County, Ohio,
grew up there, became a farmer, and died in March, 1847, when his son
William was only ten years of age. The Ent family was established in
Andrew County by the grandparents, Peter and Elizabeth (Davis) Ent.
Grandfather Ent was a native of New Jersey, lived in Pennsylvania and
in Knox County, Ohio, but in 1847 settled among the pioneers of Andrew
County. He bought a farm, a portion of which is now owned by his
grandson, William Ent. Peter Ent died in Andrew County in 1862, and
his wife passed away within the same week of his death, both being
advanced in years, past eighty. All their ten children came out to
Andrew County except John Ent, who had died in Ohio the same year
the rest of the family went to the West. William Ent's mother died in
Savannah, Missouri.

William Ent grew up in Knox County, received a limited education
from the local schools, and in 1854 started out to satisfy the usual long-
ings of a boy for travel and adventure. His chosen destination was the
Pike's Peak gold district, but he never reached Colorado. His mother
had gone to Iowa to live with her people and the son met her in that state
in 1856, and in November, 1858, he arrived in Andrew County, with
an ox team and wagon. On the way he had encountered the typical
Missouri mud, and it was all he could do to make progress with an
empty wagon and three yoke of cattle. Arriving in Andrew County he
never proceeded further west, since his grandfather managed to hold
him in this part of Missouri. William Ent was one of a family of five
children, the others being: Delilah Graham, of Iowa City, Iowa; John,
deceased; Samantha, deceased; and Mary Webber of Albia, Iowa. The
mother of this family came to Andrew County about 1870.

William Ent has lived in Andrew County continuously since 1858.
His career has been one of effective endeavor, not only as a farmer, but
also as a business man. At the present time he owns and occupies eighty
acres in section 12 of Lincoln Township, land formerly owned by his
grandfather. He bought this land in 1865, and developed it as a splendid
fruit orchard. Much of the old orchard has since been cleared away

and is now used for other purposes. For fifteen years Mr. Ent was engaged in the fruit packing business at Savannah and packed as high as twenty thousand barrels of apples in a single season besides manufacturing about a thousand barrels of cider. During 1864-65 he conducted a sawmill in Andrew County. From these facts it can be seen that Mr. Ent has lived and worked in such a way as to profit himself and to furnish a service to the community.

As a citizen voter Mr. Ent's record goes back nearly sixty years. His first presidential vote was cast for James Buchanan in 1856, but on the whole he has been identified with the republican party, having voted the democratic ticket only three times in the course of fifty years. He is a member of the Methodist Episcopal Church, and has been particularly prominent in the Independent Order of Odd Fellows, a fraternity with which his membership has been identified more than half a century. He is the oldest member in good standing of Savannah Lodge No. 14, and has represented his home lodge both in the Grand Encampment and in the Grand Lodge in the State of Missouri. During the Civil war he served nine months in the Missouri State militia on the Union side.

In 1859 Mr. Ent married Miss Annie Spencer, who was born in Portage County, Ohio, and died in 1870. She was the mother of three children: Perry, who died in 1905; Kitty, who died at the age of twenty years; and Flavia, wife of James Harless, of Wichita, Kansas. In 1872 Mr. Ent married Mrs. Artemisia Cameron Waterson, a widow who brought him three children of her own, and who died in 1883, the mother of four children by Mr. Ent, two of whom died in infancy, and the other two are: Bertie, of St. Joseph; and Frank, of St. Joseph. On December 7, 1886, Mr. Ent married Mrs. Louisa S. Piper. She was also the mother of two daughters by her former marriage, one of them now deceased. By his third wife Mr. Ent has a son, Lawrence S., who is now engaged in the active management of the home farm in Lincoln Township. Mr. Ent's son Perry left four children, and three of these have been reared by their grandfather and are now living with him, named Ruby, Beulah and William. Mr. Ent sometimes speaks of his homestead in Lincoln Township as the orphans' home. Besides his own children it has been a home for half a dozen children by the previous marriages of his two wives and also the home of his three grandchildren.

WALTER KURZ. The Kurz family has a record of more than thirty years' residence in Andrew County. In the cultivation and improvement of land and in the raising of the fruits thereof it is only a matter of justice to say that they have not only kept pace with but have been leaders in raising the general agricultural standards of this section of the state. Mr. Walter Kurz, whose home is in section 11 of Lincoln Township, is one of the younger representatives of this family, and what he has accomplished in the last quarter of a century will serve to indicate the substantial things associated with this name.

Walter Kurz was born in Canton Bern, Switzerland, July 18, 1871, one of the younger children of Benedict and Elizabeth (Biegler) Kurz. His father was born in the same canton in 1831, and his mother in 1832. Benedict Kurz was a man of education and of no little prominence in his native country. He taught school for a number of years and then on account of his health took up farming. He was active in local politics, served as mayor three terms, each term four years in duration, of his home Village of Wattenwyl and was representative of his home district, Seftigen, in the Federal Government six years, having resigned his post when he left Switzerland for America. He had many friends, stood high in the community, and it was on account of financial troubles brought about by his generosity in attaching his name to bonds for his friends that led him in 1883 to leave Switzerland and come to America. He came direct to Andrew County, where many of his fellow countrymen had located, and bought 158 acres of land in Lincoln Township, and lived there as a farmer until his death in 1899. His wife passed away in 1896. The old home place is now occupied by their son, Fred E. After coming to America Benedict Kurz took out citizenship papers, and voted with the democratic party. He was a member of the German Reform Church. Brief mention of the nine children in the family is as follows: Fred E., the present proprietor of the old homestead; John, who lives in Lincoln Township; Elizabeth, who died in 1888 at the age of twenty-eight; Ernest, a resident of Texas; Alexander, who lives with his brother, John; Joseph, a resident of Kansas; Gottfried, of Texas; Walter; Millie, who lives with her brother, Ernest, in Texas.

Walter Kurz was twelve years old when the family came to America, and most of his education was acquired in the national schools of Switzerland. He lived at home with his parents until the age of twenty-three, and then for three years was a farmer in partnership with his brother, Joseph. After his marriage he bought a farm of eighty acres, and applied himself industriously and with characteristic vigor to the task of paying for the land and improving it. When that was accomplished he bought an adjoining eighty acres, and on the second eighty he has his present homestead. The second purchase was a well improved farm. His success has come from general farming and stockraising, and no man stands higher in that community than Walter Kurz.

Politically he is identified with the democratic party, and has served his community as a school and road officer. He is a member of the German Reform Church at Amazonia.

In 1899 Mr. Kurz married Rosa Lee Durtchi, who was born in Canton Bern, Switzerland, in 1872, and in 1883 came to this country with her parents, Adolph and Rosa Durtchi. Her father is still living, a resident of Fillmore, Andrew County. Mr. and Mrs. Kurz are the parents of seven children: Benjamin, Edna, Selma, Aline, Ernest, Clarence and Irma Lee.

The oldest brother of Walter Kurz, Fred Emil Kurz, was born in Switzerland, July 10, 1856, and has lived on the old farm in Lincoln Township since 1883. He is likewise one of the successful general farmers and stock raisers of this county. He was well educated in his native land, but for more than thirty years has been a loyal and patriotic American citizen. He is a democrat and a member of the German Reform Church in Amazonia. In 1891 he married Minnie Segessemann, who was born in Lincoln Township, Andrew County, in 1870, a daughter of Gottlieb and Catherine Schneider Segessemann. Both her parents were natives of Switzerland and are now deceased. Fred E. Kurz and wife have the following children: Elizabeth, Fred H., Paul (who died at the age of thirteen years), Eric, Ada, Gertrude (died at the age of nine), Wilma, Alma, and Heinz.

JOHN AEBERSOLD. The possibilities of a human life and the wide opportunities of America are well illustrated in the career of John Aebersold, one of the most substantial citizens of Andrew County. Like many other residents around Amazonia he is of Swiss birth and parentage, came to the United States a young man with knowledge and skill in a trade, but entirely unfamiliar with the English language or the customs of the New World. He had courage and determination, but no financial resources, and for a number of years battled manfully with circumstances, and not only mastered a new tongue but acquired by slow and painful effort the capital which he brought with him into Andrew County.

John Aebersold was born in Canton Bern, Switzerland, December 25, 1835, a son of John and Catherine (Buhler) Aebersold, likewise natives of Canton Bern. His father was born in 1810, and died in the old country when the son, John, was seven years of age. The mother, who was born November 17, 1811, followed her son to America in the summer of 1867, and spent the last thirty years of her life in the Aebersold home in Andrew County. She died in March, 1900. Her children were John; Jacob, who died at the age of twenty; Elizabeth Steiner, of Switzerland; and Caroline, deceased.

John Aebersold spent the first twenty-four years of his life in Switzerland, where he was educated in the national schools, and learned two trades, first the baker's occupation, and later the miller's trade. In 1859 he came to America, spent five years in Tuscarawas County, Ohio, and in 1864 reached Andrew County. Here he invested the capital which represented his savings since coming to America in a tract of raw land, forty acres, north of Amazonia. Later he sold that and bought his present place in section 14 of Lincoln Township. At the present time Mr. Aebersold owns 125 acres, and at one time his farm comprised 285 acres, but it was too much for his individual management, and he sold more than half of it. He did much pioneer work in Andrew County, having cleared about one-third of his land, and developed it into a farm that has long yielded regular returns in grain, fruit, and livestock.

Mr. Aebersold has been a republican voter ever since his naturalization as an American citizen, and has been one of the leaders and most generous contributors to the German Reform Church at Amazonia. He helped build the church of that denomination in Amazonia, and gave more for its construction than any other member. With success as a farmer he has naturally been called upon to take his part in other public affairs, and at one time was vice president of the Exchange Bank at Savannah, and also a director in the Commercial Bank at Savannah. At the present time he retains no active business interests, his son-in-law operating the farm, and in the eightieth year of his life is enjoying those comforts and the leisure which are the merited reward of his earlier efforts.

In 1859 in Ohio Mr. Aebersold married Anna Barbara Yenni, who was born in Canton Bern, Switzerland, September 13, 1840. She died at the Aebersold homestead in Andrew County, February 17, 1914. Her parents were John and Barbara Yenni, a family long well known in Andrew County. Mr. and Mrs. Aebersold were the parents of five children: Louis A., who lives in Jackson Township, Andrew County; Emma Catherine, wife of Mike Ordnung, of Nodaway Township; Mary, wife of Frank Ruhl, who manages the Aebersold farm; Fred A., who died at the age of eleven years; and John A., who died in childhood.

When John Aebersold landed in Ohio he possessed only fifty cents in American money. For five years he worked at day wages on farms in Eastern Ohio, and spent the winter months as a coal miner. He learned the English language by the rough and ready method of actual conversation and by hearing others speak it, and learned to read and write by the help of newspapers. He has mastered the language, and for many years has been a devoted reader of the county and the daily metropolitan papers, and also has taken several agricultural journals. He takes no German papers, and has completely transformed himself into an American citizen, and is one of the most loyal Americans to be found in Northwest Missouri. When Mr. Aebersold reached Andrew County he had about three hundred dollars, representing his hard earned savings during his residence in Ohio. Aside from what his hard labor has accomplished, Mr. Aebersold gives the credit for his success in life to his good wife. She was an industrious homemaker, always ready with valuable counsel to her husband in his affairs, and is remembered by all the people of her community in Andrew County for her kindness of heart and practical charity. When people were in trouble she was always sympathetic, and turned her sympathy into deeds of practical helpfulness and was a welcome visitor at every home in times of affliction.

JUDGE CHRISTIAN YENNI. A representative of that sterling Swiss people, a large colony of whom have been identified with the development of a section of Northwest Missouri lying north of St. Joseph, Judge Christian Yenni has lived in Andrew County a half century, and he himself and other members of the family are men of prominence and distinctive leadership in affairs. Judge Yenni has been singularly prosperous as a farmer, and owns one of the fine estates in Lincoln Township near Amazonia. His home place is in section 23 of that township. While engaged in the productive activities of farming he has not neglected public affairs, and among other responsibilities was for eight years one of the county judges of Andrew County.

Christian Yenni was born in Canton Bern, Switzerland, June 30, 1850, a son of John and Barbara (Lichti) Yenni, natives of the same canton. His father was born in 1809 and his mother in 1826. In 1859 the family emigrated to America, and after five years spent in Tuscarawas County, Ohio, they moved to Northwest Missouri, arriving in Andrew County in the fall of 1864. Here the parents spent the rest of their lives on a farm in Lincoln Township. The father died in 1869 and the mother in 1886. John Yenni, while most of his time was devoted to agricultural efforts, was a useful citizen, and held several offices in the democratic republic which was his native land. He was a lifelong member of the German Reformed Church. Judge Yenni was the seventh in a family of twelve children, three of the sons and four of the daughters being still alive. Barbara, the oldest, is the deceased wife of John Aebersold of Lincoln Township; Elizabeth married John Vetter of the same township; Rosa is the deceased wife of E. Oppliger; Verena is the wife of Peter Bauman of Lincoln Township; Mary married John Graff of Bedford, Iowa; John lives in Chicago; Judge Yenni is the next in order of birth; Magdaline died at the age of twenty-two years; Fred is deceased; Gottlieb lives in Jackson Township; Caroline is the wife of William Bawman of Dade County; and Emma is the wife of Fred Beverly of Los Angeles, California.

Judge Yenni has had his home in Andrew County since 1864. He was a boy of nine years when the family came to this country, and the education which had been begun in Switzerland was continued in the public schools of Tuscarawas County, Ohio. After the death of his father he managed the home farm for his mother until his marriage, and then spent three years as a renter. Thrift, industry, and the thoroughness and adaptability for agriculture which he probably inherited from his long line of Swiss ancestors have brought Judge Yenni to a place among the most successful men of Andrew County. After his work as a renter he bought a place of ninety-eight acres, but sold that in 1890 and came to his present farm in section 23. This comprises two hundred and forty acres, all highly improved and valuable land. Besides this he owns a hundred and two acres of bottom land in the county and has a half section of land in Hartley County in the Texas Panhandle. From the superficial appearance of the Yenni homestead anyone may quickly judge the excellence of its improvements and may understand how thoroughly its owner has conducted his business affairs. One of the conspicuous features on the farm is a large bank barn, on a basement foundation 40 by 80 feet, with a stock shed 80 by 10 feet. It is a grain and stock farm, and has been so conducted for many years. At one time Judge Yenni had a large area devoted to fruit. Having worked hard and being able to see the fruits of his efforts, Judge Yenni gives only nominal supervision to his farming interests, and two of his sons rent and manage the home place.

Judge Yenni assisted in the organization of the Amazonia State Bank, and has been its president, with the exception of two years, since its organization. He is president of the Amazonia Fruit Growers' Association. In early life he was a republican, but for the past twenty-five years has been affiliated with the democratic party. As a democrat he was three times elected county judge, at a time when Andrew County regularly returned a normal majority between three and six hundred to its republican candidate. He served two two-year terms and one term of four years, thus making eight years of service in the most important administrative office within the gift of his fellow citizens. It was during his term as judge that the present courthouse and jail were built at Savannah, and it has been frequently said that no county ever received better value for the money expended than Andrew County in its present chief public buildings.

Judge Yenni is an active member and is an elder of the German Reformed Church at Amazonia. In 1877 he married Bertha Zimmerman, who was born in Ohio, September 20, 1856, and in 1858 came to Andrew County with her parents, John and Magdalena (Ziset) Zimmerman. Her father was a native of Switzerland, while her mother was born in Ohio. Both are now deceased. Mr. and Mrs. Yenni may take pride in their fine family of children, and have had ten in number: John Henry of Andrew County; Marie M., wife of Walter Ryan of Andrew County; Emma L., wife of Roy Abersold of White Deer, Texas; Leonard L., of Andrew County; Anna, who died at the age of seventeen; Edward F. and Albert Christian, who are now the active managers of the Yenni home farm in Lincoln Township; Ida Lalah, who lives at home; Minnie Helen, attending the State Normal School at Maryville; and Clarence. at home. The children were all born in Andrew County, and received their preparatory education in the Liggett school district, which Judge Yenni has served in an official capacity for many years.

D. C. ALLEN. For the greater part of a lifetime of near eighty years D. C. Allen has lived in Clay County, Missouri. His active retrospect over affairs in his part of the state covers more than half a century, and in his work as a lawyer he has come into close touch with the more important events which have shaped political history and local progress.

DeWitt Clinton Allen was born at Upper Liberty Landing in Clay County, Missouri, November 11, 1835. His family on both sides is one of more than ordinary distinction. His grandfather was Thomas Allen, whose wife was Bathsheba Stodhart. These people were from Massachusetts near Groton, and belonged to an old Massachusetts lineage. Col. Shubael Allen, father of D. C. Allen, was born near Goshen, Orange County, New York, on February 28, 1793. He came to Missouri in 1817, several years before the territory was admitted to the union and settled in Clay County, far out on the western frontier of civilization, May 10, 1820. By profession he was a civil engineer, and built the first bridge over the Susquehanna River at Columbia, Pennsylvania, about 1814, and also constructed the first bridge over the Kentucky River, at Frankfort. in 1816. In Clay County, in 1825, he established a steamboat

landing on the Missouri River. He was colonel of the Clay County
regiment of militia and commanded that body of troops in the Heatherly
war and in the expedition to observe Black Hawk in 1836. Mr. Allen's
mother was Dinah Ayres Trigg, and she was born in Estill County,
Kentucky, February 19, 1803, and came to Howard County, Missouri,
with her father, Gen. Stephen Trigg, in 1818. She was married to
Colonel Allen, in Howard County, September 19, 1822. She died June
25, 1886. She was a communicant of the Baptist Church, a woman of
high intelligence, very fond of books and literature and was well read.
The Trigg family came originally from Cornwall, England, settling in
Virginia about 1710. In the old dominion members of the Trigg family
intermarried with the Clark, Johns, Henderson, Anthony, Moorman,
Preston, Leftwich and Ayres families. Mr. Allen's great-grandfather
on the maternal side was Maj. John Trigg, of Bedford County, Virginia.
He was in the Continental Army, commanding a battery under Washington at Yorktown. He subsequently had a distinguished position in
public life. He was a member of the Virginia convention of 1788 which
ratified the Federal Constitution, and was subsequently a member from
Virginia in the fifth, sixth, seventh and eighth congresses. While in
Congress he voted against the alien and sedition law.

D. C. Allen was educated in the common schools as they existed in
Clay County during the '40s and '50s. All of these schools were maintained by subscription, and for only a few months each year. At the
age of fourteen he entered William Jewell College at Liberty and was
graduated from that old institution at the age of nineteen in June,
1855, receiving the degree A. B. In 1898 the Missouri State University
awarded him the degree LL. D. Like many successful professional men,
Mr. Allen has had his share of experience as a teacher. During 1855-56
he taught in the Masonic College at Lexington, Missouri. In 1856 he
took up the study of law and was licensed to practice in Missouri in
1857. From August 1, 1858, to April, 1860, he practiced in Leavenworth,
Kansas, in partnership with Richard R. Rees. In April, 1860, he returned to Liberty and has lived in that city and practiced law ever since.
His professional career has been successful, though not marked with
unusual incidents. He bears the reputation of a studious, hard-working
lawyer, and for many years has owned a very fine law library. He
served as attorney for the Kansas branch of the Chicago, Burlington &
Quincy Railroad Company from 1865 to 1870, and since September,
1871, has been an attorney for the Wabash Railway Company and its
predecessors in Missouri. From November, 1860, to December 17, 1861,
he served as circuit attorney for the Fifth Judicial Circuit of Missouri.

Probably his most noteworthy public service was as a member of the
Missouri Constitutional Convention of 1875, which framed the present
organic law of the state. Concerning his political opinions and the
direction of his influence in public life it may be said that Mr. Allen
stanchly represents those time-tried principles of the old Jeffersonian
democracy. He confesses an active opposition to the initiative and
referendum, the recall and all similar developments of socialism, and
believes in upholding the Constitution, first, last and all the time. He
is also opposed to woman suffrage.

Mr. Allen is a member of several Masonic bodies, including the Blue
Lodge, the Royal Arch Chapter, and the Knights Templar Commandery,
and in earlier years served, officially, as secretary, but has held no office
for the past thirty-six years. He is a member of the Liberty Commercial
Club, of the Missouri Historical Society at St. Louis, of the Missouri
Valley Historical Society at Kansas City, the Missouri Bar Association
and the American Bar Association. He is not connected with any

church, though reared in a Baptist family, and with sympathies and belief inclining to that denomination.

In Ray County, Missouri, May 18, 1864, Mr. Allen married Emily Elizabeth Settle, who was born at Culpeper Court House, Virginia, January 18, 1843, a daughter of Hiram Perry and Juliet Adelaide (Duval) Settle. The Settle family is one of early settlement and many influential associations with the old state of Virginia. The Duvals were of French descent, and their first ancestry in Virginia was one of Lafayette's soldiers during the Revolutionary war. Mr. and Mrs. Allen became the parents of three children: Lee, who was born August 26, 1865, and died November 4, 1897; Juliet Rushbrooke, born September 30, 1867, is the wife of Lyman H. Howard of Unionville, Missouri; Perry Settle, born June 24, 1869.

JUDGE HENRY C. KORNEMAN. An eminently useful and esteemed citizen of Clinton County, Judge Henry C. Korneman, ex-county judge, is an important member of the agricultural community in which he resides, owning and managing one of the best and most extensive farms in Shoal Township. He not only carries on general farming with most satisfactory results, but is known as one of the largest and most successful stock feeders and dealers in the vicinity of Cameron, his home city. Coming to this township somewhat more than thirty years ago with but $20 to his name, he put into actual practice those lessons of industry, economy and integrity in which he had been so well trained by his parents, and in due course of time had saved a sufficient sum to buy a piece of land. As his means increased he bought other near-by tracts, and now holds high rank among the more prosperous and enterprising farmers of this part of the state.

He was born in Hesse, Germany, and was there bred and educated, attending school regularly until fourteen years old. He came to the United States in 1873, accompanying his parents, John and Minnie Korneman, the former of whom died aged thirty-nine while the latter is still living, her home being in Muscatine, Iowa.

In 1881 Henry C. Korneman located in Clinton County, and later, having accumulated some money, he bought 160 acres of land in Shoal Township, where he at once began the improvement of a farm. Although the location was a fortunate one, the clearing and cultivation of a good farm was a work of no small moment; but as the years sped on field after field was added by purchase; a well furnished and convenient house of nine rooms was erected; a general utility barn, 40 by 90 feet, was built; a horse barn, 20 by 40 feet, was also put up; and subsequently Mr. Korneman, with his usual foresight and business acumen, began the buying and feeding of cattle on an extensive scale. Meeting with well merited success, he has continued his operations until the present day, and is now one of the large landholders of his township, having a well improved farm of 640 acres, and an extensive stock feeder, keeping on an average two hundred head of fine cattle in his herd.

Judge Korneman married, in 1882, Christine Stein, who was born in Shoal Township, a daughter of William Stein, who came to this country from Germany when young, and settled as a farmer in Clinton County, near Cameron. Mr. and Mrs. Korneman have eight children, namely: Minnie, Lizzie, Emma, Susan, Charles, Herman, Mary and John. One of the leading democrats of the county, Judge Korneman has been active in the interests of his party, serving as a delegate to several county conventions. He was also county judge for two years, serving in that position with credit to himself, and to the honor of his constituents.

FATHER F. X. HOCHGESANG. Into the commonplace, everyday life of each man comes problems and perplexities, frequently difficult of solution, although these are usually entirely personal, pertaining to the small circle to which his interests are bound. In the adjustment of these his interests and energies are often taxed to their utmost. Heavy as their sum is ordinarily, their total weighs little when compared with the aggregation of responsibilities that are placed upon the members of the priesthood of the Roman Catholic Church. The great, distinctive doctrines of the mother church for ages have been cherished and perpetuated by those who have been especially prepared for this important task, and, the world over, no more scholarly, zealous, pious, broad-minded men can be found than the priests of this great religious body. Their burdens are heavy, the responsibilities great, their influence wide-spreading, their value to civilization incalculable.

The Holy Trinity Parish of the Catholic Church, embracing the large church at Weston and the mission churches at Platte City and Parkville, are under the able care of the Rev. Father F. X. Hochgesang. He was the fourth son of J. B. Hochgesang, his parents being of German extraction, although born in the United States, and he himself first saw the light of day here, being born at St. Anthony, Du Bois County, Indiana, August 22, 1876. He was reared at St. Anthony and received a collegiate education at St. Meinrad's, Indiana, and later resumed his studies at St. Mary's Seminary, East Cincinnati, Ohio, where he received his training for the priesthood, on the completion of which he was ordained a priest. The solemn ceremony of ordination took place at St. Peter's Cathedral, in Cincinnati, under the auspices of the Most Rev. Henry Miller, D. D., archbishop of the Diocese of Cincinnati, Wednesday, June 16, 1909, and shortly thereafter Father Hochgesang entered fully upon his life work.

Coming West, Father Hochgesang was appointed by the Rt. Rev. M. F. Burke, D. D., bishop of the Diocese of St. Joseph, to mission labors, which he continued for about two years, and during this time he was connected with and taught Latin in the Christian Brothers' College, St. Joseph, and was also chaplain in the Sisters' Hospital in that city. He finally received his appointment to Weston, his first parish, in 1911, coming to that town in March of that year.

It soon became apparent to Father Hochgesang that a new building was needed here. The old structure, erected in the years from 1844 to 1847, had served Holy Trinity congregation faithfully for over sixty years, but was showing unmistakable signs of going the way of all things material, and was becoming unsafe for public usage. So Father Hochgesang and his people pitched in and went to work, and in a few short months the present beautiful and stately building arose on the site of the old one. That Father Hochgesang is a man of ability and resource no one will doubt after a visit to the splendid sacred edifice that has been erected under his supervision. A plain man of the people he is, also, and one not afraid to labor with his hands, as the lovely landscape gardening about the church amply testifies, for it is all the result of his

Rev. F. R. Hochgesang.

It is exceedingly appropriate to give in this connection a history of
Holy Trinity Parish of the Roman Catholic Church, and the following
article was taken from the Weston Chronicle, issue of May 31, 1912:
"Through the grace of Almighty God and the excellent will of our
parishioners, as well as our esteemed non-Catholics of Weston and
friends at large, we have the great honor on Thursday, May 30, 1912,
Decoration day, to hold the solemn services of laying the cornerstone
for our new church. More than an honor, for such an edifice that is
built solely to the glory and honor of God with the greatest sacrifices
of the worshipers of the Creator of heaven and earth. With the blessing of God it is but once that such a calling is in request to the present
generation, and owing to such a rare calling, it is but proper to execute
such a voice with the utmost zeal for a collective home where to gather
and pay due respects and worship of their Maker.

"It is due to the age of the timbers and brick, with which our old
church had been constructed, that served to countless worshipers, from
the year 1847, to abandon it November 5, 1911. By request of the
Rev. F. X. Hochgesang, the present pastor, to the Rt. Rev. M. F. Burke,
bishop of the diocese, we held the solemn closing service on the evening
of November 8, 1911. Father Hochgesang was assisted on the occasion
by Rev. J. J. McLaughlin and Rev. P. Arensberg, both of whom had
been pastors of this church in past years. The services in the evening
consisted of solemn benediction with the most blessed sacrament and a
most eloquent sermon by Rev. J. J. McLaughlin, who spoke on the subject: 'What a Church designates—its true members and the good
results coming from those faithful to God in this world and their reward
in the next world,' and concluding his eloquence with God's blessing and
the good will of the parishioners in erecting the new building.

"The following morning a high mass was sung by Rev. P. Arensberg, assisted by the Rev. J. J. McLaughlin as deacon and Rev. F. X.
Hochgesang as subdeacon of the mass. This closed all services in the
building, which had stood through the long years from 1844, at which
time the erection was begun, until Thursday, November 9, 1911. Immediately after the solemnity began the work of moving into the school-
hall nearby for the future services until the new and modern edifice will
be completed.

"While parishioners and visitors are interested in watching the
progress of the new church building, the minds and hearts of all—but
especially those of the older members—will revert to the early days,
when Holy Trinity parish was first established. As early as 1842 a
Jesuit missionary, Rev. Father Eisvogel, who attended to the spiritual wants of the Kickapoo Indians on the opposite side of the Missouri river, came at intervals to administer the rites of the church to
members of the faith who resided here. At that time there was no
church building, so mass was said at the home of Edward Diffley, a
pioneer loghouse on Rock street. At this time Weston was in the
Archdiocese of St. Louis, presided over by Bishop Kenrick, who was
on a pastoral visit and a guest at the house of Mr. and Mrs. Peter Blanc-
jour when he received word from Rome that he had been made Archbishop of St. Louis. Among the first of the new archbishop's duties
was the establishing of a new parish at Weston and giving it the name
Holy Trinity. He appointed Rev. Father Ruttkowski to take charge.
He was a native of Poland, who with his parents had fled to France
from his native land after the Polish insurrection against Russia in order
to keep from being exiled to Siberia. Father Ruttkowski was the
descendant of a noble family and held the rank of captain of cavalry
in the French army before studying for the priesthood. He left parents

and friends at Havre de Grace, France, and sailed to America, arriving at New Orleans. From there he proceeded by boat, the only means of travel in those days, up the Mississippi to St. Louis, and was soon sent on up the Missouri to the gateway of the West, at Weston, where he began his labors in the Master's vineyard. How well he laid the foundation is shown not only by the building which was torn down last fall, but also by the zeal and faithfulness shown in the building of the new. As in most pioneer towns, the people were poor, but willing, happy in working for the betterment of conditions for themselves and their descendants. As early as 1844 the site was purchased by the archbishop, excavating was begun, trees cut and hewed into timbers, bricks made during the summer time, the pastor living in a barn that was first put up for himself and team, the members dividing themselves into shifts in attending the kilns of burning brick. At last the little brick church of happy memory was completed in 1847, and the first baptism in it recorded October 3rd of that year. This Polish father so full of zeal for his people continued here until 1852, when he was succeeded by Rev. Mathew Dillon, an Irish priest, who continued the good work and was kindly remembered for his cheerfulness and his native music on the hornpipe.

"In 1854 Rev. William Fish took up the labor, and during his administration built the little brick parochial residence, in 1856. In 1857 Rev. Conrad Tintrup, whose death occurred in April, 1912, at Arcadia, Missouri, at the advanced age of eighty-one, took up the work and did faithful service for the next two years. At this time the Catholic school was in charge of several sisters of the Order of St. Joseph of Carondelet, near St. Louis, among whom Mother Justine and Mother Francis died the past year at the mother house. They always cherished fond memories for the years spent at Holy Trinity parish. In 1859 Rev. Francis Schreiber was given charge, and is yet kindly remembered by the older members. He was of a literary turn and was the author of several volumes. He was present at the celebration of the Golden Jubilee, in 1897, and celebrated the Requiem High Mass for the deceased members of the parish. In 1860 a Benedictine Rev. Father Severin came and remained one year, when another priest of the same order, Father Philip, was sent and stayed until the close of the Civil War, 1865. During that time Rev. Charles Linnenkamp, at present Vicar General of this diocese, came to inspire and edify, and by his untiring efforts gave an impetus not only to the parish at Weston, but also to the missions at Plattsburg and Easton, where he built churches, and also started the church at Platte City. In 1866 he built the brick schoolhouse which is now serving as chapel during the erection of the new church. No other priest of the diocese is so familiar with the history of Holy Trinity parish as Monsignor Linnenkamp, for he is well acquainted with the humble beginning, the efforts of the first pastors, the trials and tribulations both priest and people endured, as well as the progress and successes the pastor and people now enjoy. In 1869 Father Linnenkamp was called to Immaculate Conception parish in St. Joseph, where he was made irremovable rector and where he erected one of the most handsome church edifices in the West several years ago. This is a grand monument to the life work of this noble priest. He holds various offices of honor in the diocese, being raised in 1900 by the Pope to the dignity of Monsignor; beside this he is vicar general, diocesan consultor, a judge of the ecclesiastical and canon law in matters pertaining to discipline, and also matrimony. He is now advanced in age, but his people pray that he may be spared many years, as his broad experience, combined with good mentality, continues to be a guiding lamp of usefulness.

"For part of the year 1869 Father Philip was returned, and built the mission church now standing and still used at Platte City. Next came Rev. Joseph Seybolt, who baptised, taught and married many of the present congregation. In 1872 Father Fintan Mundweiler, O. S. B., sent from the mother house at St. Meinard, Indiana, took charge and continued two years, during which time he was prior of the order, afterwards being made abbot, the highest office of the order. A happy coincidence occurs right here, for when the present pastor of Trinity parish, Rev. F. X. Hochgesang, was a boy and living near St. Meinard's Abbey, Indiana, it was his delight to drive with the different abbots from place to place, and often went with this Abbot Mundweiler, little thinking that he himself would one day be pastor of the same church at Weston over which the good pastor had presided in previous years. He died in 1898.

"For the next few years the parish was presided over by another member of the Benedictine order, Rev. Francis Nigsch. In 1879 Rev. Beatus Ziswyler, Order of the Precious Blood, gave his earnest endeavors for the promotion of the faith through both school and church. From 1881 until 1883 Rev. L. M. Porta, the only Italian priest ever in charge of this parish, did much to promote the growth of Catholicity by his kindness and his warm-heartedness. His next place was assistant to Right Reverend J. J. Hogan, but was given a parish at Springfield, Missouri, where he built a beautiful church, which became his sepulchre, as his remains now rest beneath the main altar.

"In 1883 Rev. P. J. Cullen, now of Marceline, was given Weston for his field of labor, and he is kindly remembered for his fine sentiment of feeling, his courteous treatment to all. Father Cullen is now author of many beautiful lyrics which show much delicacy in poetic power. Following Father Cullen came the big-hearted Father F. C. Becker, who had done so much missionary work in the far west and whose delight was to be among his non-Catholic friends. His last years were spent at the Soldiers' Home, at Leavenworth, where he was chaplain at the time of his death. For the next thirteen years the parish was directed by Rev. C. Schaaf, whose instructions in church music and in the more solemn ceremonies of the Catholic church, not often performed in small parishes on account of lack of essentials, were of much benefit to the congregation. Near the close of his administration, in 1897, the church observed its Fiftieth Anniversary, or Golden Jubilee, in a three-day observance, at which time a sermon in German was delivered by Monsignor Linnenkamp, of St. Joseph, a sermon in English by Rev. Father Dalton, of Kansas City, and a sermon on the Congregation's Departed Ones by Father Schreiber, of Streator, Illinois.

"For a short time in 1893, during the pastor's absence in Mexico for his health, Father Boniface, O. S. B., of Atchison, was chosen spiritual adviser of this parish. His appealing sermons on the Love of God were among the best ever delivered within the walls of the old church building. From 1898 to 1910 Rev. J. J. McLaughlin gave the first dozen years of his pastoral duties to the congregation at Weston. The simplicity of his manner, the earnest sincerity of the man so impressed all with whom he came in contact, resulted in untold good for the uplift of the parish, which showed that his efforts were not in vain. His going away was regretted by both Catholics and non-Catholics. At present he is pastor of Holy Rosary Church at St. Joseph. In 1900 he replaced the little brick parish house by the present modern two-story building. His successor was Rev. P. Arensberg, who, for the following ten months, presented the truths of religion in his own pleasing, affable way, which holds the attention and convinces reason and intellect. At present he is pastor of the Cathedral at St. Joseph. Ash Wednesday, 1911, the present pastor, Rev. F. X. Hochgesang, began his service in Holy Trinity parish. He is full of zeal for the spiritual welfare of the parish, and his energy for the cause of the church knows no bounds, as is shown in the efficient manner in which he directs the erection of the new building and the active hand he takes personally in any part of the work. He is a living example of unselfishness which proves quite an inspiration to his followers. The handsome edifice now going up will long be a monument to his labors for the honor and glory of God.''

The cornerstone of the edifice above referred to was laid May 30, 1912, and the structure was completed and dedicated October 27, 1912. The property includes a good-sized plot of ground on the north side of East Market Street, three blocks east of Main, high up on the slope of the Pinnacles. The land has been leveled and terraced and beautified by landscape gardening, and is one of the loveliest spots around Weston. From the churchyard one can see out over Weston and far up the river valley, and the view is grand in the extreme. The church building is a huge and beautiful structure of stone, with two tall spires, each of which is surmounted with a large gold cross. The interior is richly and exquisitely decorated and finished, and is lighted by large memorial windows of stained glass. The great altar was formerly used in the old church and was a memorial gift of Eberhard and Dora Bons, and cost $1,000. It is of Gothic design, with a central statue of the Holy Trinity in carved wood. On either side are statues of SS. Boniface and Eberhard. Two angelic figures also adorn this altar. The two beautiful side altars were given by Mr. and Mrs. Winabald Rumpel, one in their own memory and the other as a memorial of their daughter, Pauline Rumpel Robbins. This couple also gave the statue of St. Anthony. The church has a nice set of stations, candelabra and other equipment necessary in the various ceremonies, many of which are personal gifts. Outside of the church building the parish owns a nice, modern frame parsonage and a brick school building. It also has a set of sweet-toned angelus bells. They were the gifts of Peter and Mary Blancjour, and hang in the church towers. The church has a large Ladies' Altar Society.

FREDERICK GOTTLIEB GRAF. The owner and editor of the Ravenswood Gazette, Frederick Gottlieb Graf, like many of his contemporaries of Northwest Missouri, began his connection with matters journalistic with an apprenticeship at the printer's trade. Gradually he has worked his way upward through the laborious stages that mark the career of the men upon whom the public depends for the distribution of the world's news, and today, when still in the prime of vigorous manhood and the ripeness of his powers, he is the managing head of a paper which is recognized as a distinct influence in the forming of pubic opinion in one of Missouri's most flourishing communities.

Mr. Graf was born at Frankfort-on-Main, Germany, December 7, 1872, and is a son of Gottlieb and Elizabeth (Hambrecht) Graf, the former of whom died at the age of forty-two years, in 1891, at Ottumwa, Iowa, where the latter still makes her home. Gottlieb Graf left the Fatherland alone in 1882 and upon his arrival in the United States took up his residence at Ottumwa, Iowa, where he established himself as an architect, a profession which he had learned in his native land, and designed several of the important buildings of Ottumwa. The mother

paper man in the shop of the Journal and Free Press of that place, and was with this paper for three years, a period which will aways remain in the memory of Mr. Graf, who for his first year received $1 per week wages, $2 a week the second year and $3 a week in the third year. In 1889 he began work as a compositor for the Omaha Bee, and subsequently was connected with the Chicago Tribune, following which he traveled as a journeyman printer, visiting all the important cities west of the Mississippi and eventually landing, in 1900, at Buffalo, Wyoming. Mr. Graf conducted a cafe for two years with such a measure of success that he was able to purchase a ranch of 380 acres, which he leased, and afterwards sold, and this was followed by the purchase of a dairy farm of 33 1-3 acres, which he operated successfully for two years. Mr. Graf entered the office of the Ravenwood Gazette as a compositor, and July 1, 1913, purchased the newspaper and entire plant from its former owner, Oliver F. Smith. This is now an independent newspaper, with a paid-up subscription of 520 readers, at $1.00 per annum, and the plant includes a power press of Diamond manufacture and the most up-to-date equipment to be secured. In addition it has a well-equipped job office, which branch of the business is bringing excellent returns. Mr. Graf is giving the people of Ravenwood a well-printed, carefully-edited news-paper, which aims to print all the news all the time, unbiased and reliable. His cogent, well-written editorials have always supported the town's best interests, and in this way he has done much to advance the community's interests. In 1913 Mr. Graf was appointed city clerk of Ravenwood, a capacity in which he still acts. He is a splendid type of the energetic, wide-awake, pushing westerner, and has already gained a high place in the confidence of the people. He belongs to the North-west Missouri Press Association, Cost Congress and the Missouri State Press Association.

On December 16, 1893, Mr. Graf was married to Miss Minnie V. Peckham, daughter of Charles Peckham, who is now a successful farmer of Montana. Charles Peckham was born in Meigs County, Ohio, in 1843, a son of Joseph Peckham, a farmer of near Plymouth, Massachusetts, where his father had landed from England at an early day. Joseph Peckham was born in Massachusetts in 1811, and died in Lee County, Iowa, in 1900. Charles Peckham was nine years of age when he accompanied his parents to Lee County, Iowa, and there he grew to manhood and secured his education. The family subsequently came to Clark County, Missouri, locating near the Town of Revere, where Mr. Peckham homesteaded 120 acres of land and cultivated an excellent farm, which he is now renting to tenants. In 1909 he went to Fort Shaw, where he is serving in the capacity of postmaster. In 1865 Mr. Peckham enlisted in the Missouri State Militia, and was stationed at Hannibal, as a guard, being honorably discharged after three months of service. There have been five children in his family: Mrs. Graf, Mrs. Lenora M. Cutting, Mrs. Matilda Cutting, David and Bartlett. Mrs. Graf's mother bore the maiden name of Amelia Mauck, and was a daughter of David and Matilda (Philips) Mauck, her father being a soldier throughout the Civil war and a captain in command at the battle of Athens, Missouri.

Mrs. Graf is an active member of the Christian Church, and is well known in social circles of Ravenwood. She is a lady of superior attain-

Elizabeth Minnie; and Frederick LeRoy, born March 11, 1897, and a graduate of the Ravenwood High School.

MICHAEL NESTER. A short time before the war the Nester family became identified with Andrew County. The parents were thrifty and capable Irish people, were both from County Limerick, and the course of their destiny finally directed them to this section of Northwest Missouri. For many years the Nester home in Lincoln Township has possessed the distinctions associated with upright and thrifty people, members of church, moral, law abiding members of the community, and people who have added something to the community in which they live.

The family was founded here by the late Patrick Nester, who was born in County Limerick, Ireland, a son of Patrick Nester. Patrick senior died in this country, while his wife subsequently returned and died in Ireland. Patrick junior was an only child. He learned the trade of shoemaker, though he never followed that to any extent. For several years he worked as a laborer in Washington, D. C., and while there in 1853 married Margaret Lysaught, who was born in County Limerick, August 15, 1835, and came to Washington, D. C., at the age of twelve years, with a younger sister Jane. Their mother had died and she and her sister came to this country to join an older brother, John Lysaught, who was at that time married and living in Washington. Patrick Nester during his residence in Washington was employed for the most part by a florist, and was a competent man in that business. He finally removed to Kansas City, Missouri, and there continued along the same line, then went up the river to St. Joseph, and a short time before the war located on Nodaway Island in Lincoln Township of Andrew County. That was the locality in which his business as a farmer was carried on until 1881, when the high waters in the Missouri Valley of that year almost completely destroyed his farm. He then bought a place away from the river, comprising 126 acres, and his wife bought forty acres more. By that time he and his wife had a family of vigorous young sons and daughters, and the management of the land was largely in the hands of the sons. In that home Patrick Nester died September 6, 1901. He was an active democrat, and a member of the Catholic Church. There was no church in his locality, but a priest came from St. Joseph once a month to hold services, and that custom has prevailed for thirty years or more. The Nester home is the center of worship for all the Catholic communicants residing in that vicinity. Patrick Nester and wife were the parents of nine children, only two of whom married. James, who was born in Washington, D. C., in 1856, and died at the age of seventeen in Andrew County; Patrick, who was born in 1858 in Kansas City and died on the home farm in Andrew County, June 4, 1911; Maggie, who is the wife of Frederick Wigham of St. Joseph; Michael; William, who lives at home; John; Thomas; David; and Mary. Four of the children died in early childhood. Mrs. Patrick Nester is a daughter of Patrick and Johanna (Knurth) Lysaught, both of whom spent all their lives in County Limerick. There were three sons and eight daughters in the family, and they all came to the United States, their names being as follows: John, Michael, Patrick, Bridget, Johanna, Ellen, Ann, Kate, Honora, Jane and Margaret.

Michael Nester, whose fine farm home is located in section 17 of Lincoln Township, was born on the Nodaway Island farm of his father in 1867, and has lived in Andrew County all his life. After his marriage he began his independent efforts as a farm renter, continued in that way three years, and then bought sixty-eight acres where he now resides. The purchase price of this was $1,200, and he was able to pay only $400 down, and at once began the task of making a living and paying off the indebtedness. It was a place that had long been occupied, and the house and other improvements were old and in a poor condition. He bettered the improvements as rapidly as possible, paid off the debt, and with the surplus of his increasing prosperity invested in more land, until he now has 219 acres, all well improved. At one time Mr. Nester had sixty acres of apple orchard but has reduced this to about eighteen acres. The rest of his farm is devoted to grain and stock, and he is considered one of the most successful farmers in Lincoln Township. Politically he has always been identified with the democratic party. His mother is now living at Nodaway Station, and is about eighty years of age.

Michael Nester was married in 1891 to Ida Elizabeth Steeby, who was born in Lincoln Township, March 24, 1873, a daughter of Gottlieb and Mary (Moser) Steeby. Mr. Steeby was one of the fine old pioneer citizens of Andrew County, and a sketch of his career will be found on other pages of this publication. He died November 8, 1913, and his wife July 26, 1893. Mr. and Mrs. Nester lost six children in infancy and three still living are John Harold, Lola Margaret and Alexander W.

GOTTLIEB STEEBY. One of the rugged pioneer citizens of Andrew County passed away in death at his home on November 8, 1913. Gottlieb Steeby had a place of no small influence during his residence of sixty years in this county of Northwest Missouri. His life was marked by simplicity, by honest and industrious effort, capable dealings in a business way, and the utmost integrity in all his relations with society and his fellow men.

In Tuscarawas County, Ohio, February 17, 1834, he was born as the oldest of four children in the family of George and Mary (Schwendeman) Steeby. His father was of English stock and his mother of German descent, and both were born in Pennsylvania, the former on July 20, 1813, and the latter on July 25, 1807. They were married in their native state and at once removed to Ohio where they entered forty acres of raw land in Tuscarawas County. George Steeby in early life worked at the millwright's trade, but later was a furniture dealer in Ragersville, where he died in 1867. Throughout his life he voted consistently with the democratic party, and was a member of the Presbyterian Church. His wife survived him and was past eighty years of age at the time of her death.

Gottlieb Steeby grew up in a home of modest comfort and yet his surroundings were such as to encourage his self reliance and his determination to effect something in life. His education was that supplied by the country schools of his time and place, and at the age of sixteen he began learning the carpenter's trade and was employed in that line for three years in Ohio. It was in 1853 that he sought a home on the frontier, and on arriving in Savannah, Missouri, had only fifty cents and an extra suit of clothes. In a short time by his trade he was earning nine dollars a week, and continued industriously in that work in Savannah for three years. He then went to Nebraska Territory, but was satisfied to remain there only one year, after which he returned to Amazonia in Andrew County, and worked as a carpenter four years, part of the time in St. Joseph. In 1862 he bought forty acres of land near Amazonia, and attempted to divert his energies to farming as a permanent occupation. He soon found that his farm was too small, and accordingly sold out in the fall of 1864 and in February of the next year removed to Lincoln Township, which was subsequently the scene of his exceptionally successful efforts as a farmer and land holder. His first purchase was 120 acres, and for several years he combined his trade with the tilling of his fields and harvesting of his crops. In the meantime he prospered and his surplus capital was reinvested in additional lands, until within less than twenty-five years after his service as a farmer he was the owner of nearly eight hundred acres in Andrew County.

Gottlieb Steeby was not a man to restrict his influence and efforts to his own interests, but was a man of power in the community. In November, 1880, he was elected a member of the County Court for one term, and in April, 1866, had been chosen a school director in his district, and held that position for many years.

On February 12, 1857, Mr. Steeby married Miss Mary Moser of Ohio, who was reared in Andrew County. Gottlieb Steeby was an active republican and he and his wife belonged to the Presbyterian Church. He had survived more than twenty years, her death having occurred on July 26, 1893. Gottlieb Steeby and wife were the parents of fourteen children, mentioned briefly as follows: William Columbus, who died in June, 1873; Eli Franklin, of Lincoln Township, Andrew County; Alice, wife of R. T. Turner of Andrew County; Sarah, now deceased, who was the wife of Joseph Mann; John Sherman, of Arkansas; Peter Gottlieb, deceased; Alexander Lee; Henry Grant, of Jefferson Township; Ella May, wife of Ed Mann of Nodaway Township; Ida, wife of Michael Nester of Lincoln Township; Susan, deceased wife of John Martie; Lulu, wife of Oliver Martie of Lincoln Township; Ombra Davis of Oklahoma; Lena, wife of Ernest Zahnd of Lincoln Township.

ALEXANDER LEE STEEBY. One of the children of the fine old pioneer, the late Judge G. Steeby, Alexander Lee Steeby has spent his life in Andrew County and is one of the most capable farmers and public spirited citizens of Lincoln Township, his valuable homestead being located in section 8.

Alexander Lee Steeby was born January 19, 1869, near his present home in Lincoln Township. After his marriage he bought a farm in Jackson Township of one hundred acres, and increased its extent until he had over two hundred acres. He lived there twelve years and then sold and bought his present farm, comprising 221 acres. This is only part of his land holdings, however, since he owns a good farm of 140 acres in Jackson Township, which is worked on the shares under his direct supervision. He also has a quarter section of land in Palmer County, Texas. Mr. Steeby's farm shows the well ordered enterprise which has characterized his career as a Northwest Missouri farmer. He and his family reside in a large eight-room house, surrounded with barns and other equipment, and his efforts have taken the direction of grain and stock farming. He is also a stockholder in the Farmers Bank of Nodaway.

Mr. Steeby is a republican in politics and he and his family worship in the Methodist Church. Their church home is known as Union Chapel, and was erected on land donated by Mr. Steeby, and he also gave an additional $400 as part of the building fund. Mr. Steeby shared in the division of the splendid estate of 900 acres formerly owned by his father, but much of his success has come from his own efforts and capable management.

Mr. Steeby was married November 30, 1890, to Mary Elizabeth Moser, who was born in Ohio, but came to Northwest Missouri when a child with her parents, Jacob and Mary Moser, both of whom died in this

locality. To this union have been born three children, George W., Mary and Herbert.

ELI FRANKLIN STEEBY. On other pages is recited the career and long continued activities of Judge Gottlieb Steeby, who lived in Andrew County sixty years and built up a splendid estate, aggregating about nine hundred acres of land. The oldest of his living children is Eli Franklin Steeby, who in his own career has exemplified the same rugged qualities and successful judgment that characterized his father, and now has a large stock and grain farm in section 17 of Lincoln Township.

Eli Franklin Steeby was born in Lincoln Township, Andrew County, December 27, 1859, the second of the fourteen children born to Gottlieb and Mary (Moser) Steeby. Lincoln Township has been his only home through all the years since his birth, and he continued with his parents through boyhood and early manhood, gaining his education in the local schools and disciplining his body and mind by active contact with the duties of a farm. After his marriage Mr. Steeby bought his first place of 172 acres. A number of years ago he made a specialty of apple raising, and at one time had sixty acres in orchard. As the trees have become burdened with age and have largely ceased bearing, he has cut away most of the orchard and now devotes the ground to grain and stock farming, in which he has been peculiarly successful.

Mr. Steeby is a republican in politics and with his family worships in the Christian Church at Nodaway. On January 19, 1881, he married Mary Wilson, who was born in Lincoln Township October 4, 1863, and like her husband has always lived in this one locality. Her parents were Milus and Lucinda Anna (Baldwin) Wilson. Both her parents were also natives of Northwest Missouri. Her mother died in 1865, after having two children, and her father married again and had eight children by his second wife. Mr. and Mrs. Steeby are the parents of six children: Effie May, wife of Milus Wilson of Lincoln Township; William Lewis, of Lincoln Township; Alexander Ray; Aaron Ira; Milus Gottlieb; and Opal Marie.

THEODORE L. ROBINSON. The years of his life which were most fruitful in accomplishment and in broad and effective service to himself and his fellow men, the late Theodore L. Robinson passed at Maryville, in Nodaway County. There his memory is likely to endure long, and the inspiration of his career and its example are effective lessons that may be read with profit by all. After many years spent in battle against adversity, he lived to accomplish those things which are considered most worth while by ambitious men—honorable activity in business with satisfying material rewards, the esteem of his fellow men and a public-spirited share in the social and civic life of his community.

Theodore L. Robinson was a native Missourian, born in Callaway County February 8, 1833. Three years later his mother died, and he was left in the care of his paternal grandparents by his father, who went to Texas and whom he never afterwards saw. When eleven years of age his grandparents moved to the vicinity of St. Joseph, and at the age of twelve he began work in a hotel in that city. He made himself useful, and soon attracted the attention of a St. Joseph merchant, in whose employ he remained for five years. The agreement as to salary was $60 per year, with the privilege of three months' schooling during each of three years. However, his school attendance all told aggregated only six months, and so far as books and instruction in the "literary arts" was concerned he had an exceedingly limited education. When the discovery of gold in California was heralded throughout the world he was sixteen years of age, and at once caught the "gold fever," and went West. His employer furnished him with goods, mostly cheap clothing, to sell in the West, and in company with another young man he crossed the plains with a wagon drawn by oxen. His mercantile venture was ill-starred, since everyone seemed to have supplied himself with clothing and other needed supplies, and all the stock he carried across the plains was disposed of at a sacrifice. However, by hard work in mining and otherwise he earned enough to pay his old employer for all the goods and for the team furnished for transportation. Six years were spent on the Pacific Coast in varied experience and hardships, and in 1855 he returned to Missouri, without money, and with his constitution impaired by exposure and the rough existence of the West. On his return to Missouri he received news that his father had recently died in Texas, leaving his second wife a widow with three little children. His elder brother had also died in the same state, while a younger brother had died in 1844. Mr. Robinson at once reentered the employ of his merchant friend at St. Joseph, and remained until he could equip himself with a wagon and team for the long journey to Houston, Texas. He went to that state and brought back his father's widow and her three small children, in order the better to provide for them. This was only an incident of his long career, but it illustrates remarkably well the general character of his mind and heart. Soon after returning from Texas Mr. Robinson was furnished a stock of goods by his old and always friendly employer, and in August, 1857, established a store in Maryville, Missouri. That little city remained his home the rest of his days, where he was honored not only as one of the early merchants, but as one of the finest citizens. He prospered in mercantile trade and also as a lumberman. In 1873 Mr. Robinson became actively connected with the Nodaway Valley Bank of Maryville, as a partner with James B. Prather, Mr. Robinson having active charge of the business. On the death of Mr. Prather in 1892, Mr. Robinson made his son, James B. Robinson, cashier of the bank, the latter having previously been book-keeper and assistant cashier. The bank was incorporated April 7, 1894, and Mr. Robinson remained its president until his death a few weeks later, on May 28, 1894.

This brief outline of facts only suggests the remarkable struggle of a poor boy against adverse circumstances and emphasizes his later success. He acquired a considerable fortune and died both wealthy and respected. Personally he was a plain and unassuming gentleman, wide awake in his attitude of affairs, and even tempered and well poised. His progressiveness and public spirit were as marked as his business ability. While he himself had succeeded in life without an education, he was none the less a stanch friend of schools and learning, and for twenty years was a member and treasurer of the Maryville School Board. Politically he was a democrat, had fraternal affiliations with the Independent Order of Odd Fellows, and died a member of the Christian Church.

On October 9, 1859, Mr. Robinson married Rebecca J. Ray. She was born in Bardstown, in Nelson County, Kentucky, and when a child was brought to Nodaway County by her father, James Ray, a pioneer

welfare and in the pleasures of home and in his many friendships was a strong characteristic.

JAMES B. ROBINSON. A son of the late Theodore L. Robinson, whose varied and interesting career as a merchant and banker has been described on other pages, James B. Robinson succeeded his father as president of the Nodaway Valley Bank of Maryville, and for twenty years has been active head of that substantial institution. He has exhibited the same quality of business enterprise and high civic ideals which characterized his father, and is one of Maryville's most prominent men.

James B. Robinson was born in Maryville, Missouri, November 24, 1864, was reared and educated in his native city, attending the public schools. His business training was begun under the direction of his father, and at the age of eighteen he entered the Nodaway Valley Bank as bookkeeper and assistant cashier. In 1892 he was promoted to the post of cashier, and on the death of his father in 1894 was elected president, which has since been his chief distinction in the business community of Nodaway County. Mr. Robinson also owns large holdings in farm lands, and is extensively engaged in agriculture and stock raising.

Though a stanch democrat politically, he has never sought any political honors. His most imporant service in official position has been as a member for fifteen years of the Maryville School Board. Mr. Robinson is affiliated with the Knights of Pythias and is a member of the Christian Church.

In 1894 Mr. Robinson married Maggie Garrison of Albany, Missouri. Their three children are named Theodore Garrison, James B., Jr., and Chilton K. The Robinson home is one of the largest and most attractive residences in Maryville.

SAMUEL G. GILLAM. A little over twenty-five years ago Samuel G. Gillam left the home farm in Nodaway County and as a boy of fifteen began his business experience as clerk in a title and abstract office at Maryville. Few of the successful men in financial affairs in Northwest Missouri have had a more notable rise and steady progress than Mr. Gillam, who is now president of the Gillam-Jackson Loan & Trust Company and with other important financial and property interests in that section of the state.

Samuel G. Gillam was born in McDonough County, Illinois, April 21, 1871, a son of Hachaliah and Amelia L. (Herzog) Gillam. His father was a native of Indiana and his mother of New York City. In 1882 the parents moved out to Iowa, and in 1884 came to Missouri and settled on a farm in Nodaway County.

It was in the rural communities of the different states mentioned that Samuel G. Gillam spent his childhood and early youth, and his educational equipment was largely supplied by district schools. At the age of fifteen he came to Maryville, took up the work as clerk already mentioned, and perhaps one of the reasons for his success, outside of his native talent and energy, has been the fact that he has applied himself almost to one line through all the years, and title and abstract work

the First National Bank, and both have offices in the same building. The company transacts an extensive business as a loan, trust, savings, abstract and title concern, and its growth and success are largely to be credited to the long experience and able management of Mr. Gillam. He is also the owner of farm lands, and a part of his income is derived from agriculture.

In politics Mr. Gillam is a democrat, has held several minor offices, and at one time was presidential elector for his congressional district. Governor Folk during his administration appointed Mr. Gillam a member of the board of managers for State Asylum No. 2 at St. Joseph, and during the latter part of his term he was president of the board. Governor Major appointed him the Missouri delegate to the commission to investigate foreign rural credits.

Mr. Gillam was married in 1894 to Miss Emma Trueblood, daughter of William E. and Tuiza Trueblood. Mrs. Gillam was born and reared in Maryville, and is the mother of one son, Forest T. Trueblood Gillam. Mr. and Mrs. Gillam are members of the Presbyterian Church, in which he serves as a ruling elder.

JOHN FRED HULL. Few members of the journalistic fraternity in Northwest Missouri had an earlier introduction to the practical work of printing than John F. Hull, now editor and publisher of the Maryville Tribune, with a weekly issue, and the Maryville Daily Tribune. Mr. Hull has been connected with printing and newspaper work since thirteen years of age, practically acquired his education in that unexcelled school, and for about twenty years has been in the newspaper business at various points in Northwest Missouri.

John Fred Hull was born in Boone County, Iowa, October 10, 1874, a son of Henry W. and Kate (Swift) Hull. His father has the distinction of having been the first white child born in Boone County, while the mother was a native of New York State. When Mr. Hull was about a year old his parents moved to Grant City, Missouri, where his father was successfully engaged in the practice of law until 1891. His wife having died the previous year, he went to Des Moines, Iowa, and later spent the closing years of his life in Boone County, Iowa. During the Civil war he was a soldier of the Union, enlisting in Company F of the Thirteenth Iowa Volunteer Infantry, and for about two years followed the fortunes of his regiment in various campaigns through the South.

John Fred Hull spent most of his boyhood in Grant City, where he was educated in the public schools, and at the age of thirteen began training himself for his future career in a printing office at that town. Later he was employed for a time in Des Moines, and in 1895 returned to Grant City and was employed on the Grant City Star for three years, at the end of which time he bought an interest in the paper. In 1899 Mr. Hull moved to Maysville and bought the Maysville Pilot and conducted it for two years. His next location was at Gallatin, Missouri, and on June 1, 1909, he came to Maryville and became city editor of the Maryville Daily Tribune. A year later he acquired the entire plant, and has since given active direction to this well known and influential daily and weekly paper.

Mr. Hull is a republican in politics, and has fraternal affiliations with the Knights of Pythias, the Benevolent and Protective Order of Elks and the Masonic lodge. On March 6, 1900, he married Miss Urith Matteson of Grant City. Their little family of four children are Clifford M., Robert Ray, Elizabeth Katherine and Kenneth Frederick.

JOHN WILLIAM KENNEDY. A splendid type of progressive citizen, conservative, yet broad-minded, and a leading factor in the business, financial and agricultural life of the Maryville community of Nodaway County, John William Kennedy, president of the Farmers State Bank of Parnell, is eminently worthy of extended mention in a work dealing with the representative men of Northwest Missouri. The labor of compiling the biographies of the living successful men of any locality is frequently made difficult by the prevailing modesty of the man of business, who almost invariably manifests a certain unwillingness to force his personality to the front, and thus in a manner discourages even friendly attempts to secure a record of the events which have led to his success. The lesson told in the lives of these men, however, is one of the greatest assistance, and there is, therefore, a due measure of satisfaction in presenting even a brief review of the life of such a man, which will not alone prove interesting because of his personal achievements, but because he is a native son of his community, and a member of a family which has been honored and respected here for many years.

John William Kennedy was born April 20, 1853, on his father's farm, five miles west of Maryville, Nodaway County, Missouri, and is a son of Samuel Thomas and Lucretia Webster (Smith) Kennedy, the former of whom died in September, 1909, while the latter still survives and is a resident of Maryville. Samuel Thomas Kennedy was born in 1829, in Union County, Indiana, and when he was fourteen years of age he went with his parents to Rush County, Indiana, the family later migrating to Platte County, Missouri, and locating near Weston, this trip being made by oxen. His father, John Kennedy, rented land in Platte County for four years, and in 1849 removed to Nodaway County, where the grandfather entered 320 acres on the southwest corner of section 16, township 64, range 36, and there continued to reside until his death in August, 1864. He had been a devout member of the Baptist Church. John Kennedy was married in North Carolina to Miss Charity McMichael, a native of that state, and they became the parents of the following children: Archibald, William, James, Mrs. Margaret Bell, Mrs. Sarah Jane Kane, Mrs. Ross, and Samuel Thomas. Mrs. Ross's only son, Benjamin Ross, was adopted by his grandparents and inherited considerable of his grandfather's property.

When the family came to Nodaway County, in 1849, Samuel Thomas Kennedy entered some Government land located in section 9, township 64, range 36, four miles west of Maryville, where he built a home of logs and broke 120 acres of the 320 acres of prairie of which the tract consisted. There he continued to make his home until the spring of 1897, and at that time retired from active agricultural pursuits. Mr. Kennedy was a democrat in his political proclivities, and as such served his county as judge of the County Court for three terms, as presiding judge two terms and as township commissioner of Pope Township. He was a man who took a keen and active interest in anything which promised to be of benefit to the community, and among other services acted as a working director of the Nodaway County Fair. His religious connection was with the Methodist Episcopal Church. A Mason of Maryville Lodge No. 165, he was district deputy and grand master, and organized Kennedy Lodge (named in his honor), at Elmo, Missouri, then called "Possum Walk." He organized a number of other lodges, was prominent in some Grand Lodge meetings, and was also affiliated with the Independent Order of Odd Fellows, being past noble grand of Maryville Lodge. In 1850, prior to the establishment of Skidmore as a town, Mr. Kennedy was married there to Lucretia Webster Smith, who was born on a farm located on the townsite of Plattsburg,

Missouri. To this union there were born the following children: Mrs.
Mary J. Wilhoyte, residing on the old home place west of Maryville;
John William; Henry Newton, a resident of Keywood, Missouri; Mrs.
Margaret Alice Miller, of St. Petersburg, Florida; Mrs. Dora Taylor, of
Des Moines, Iowa; Mrs. Henrietta Lingenfelter, of Seattle, Washing-
ton; and Mrs. Belle Booth, of Maryville, Missouri. The mother of these
children resides with the last named.

John William Kennedy attended the "Shellgrove" school, located
near Maryville, intermittently until 1872, during which time he worked
on the home farm, and he later attended school at Rushville, Indiana.
In the spring of 1874 he bought sixty acres of partly improved land in
section 24, township 64, range 37, which he sold in the fall of 1880 to
John Smith, and then purchased 120 acres on section 13, township 65,
range 34. This farm he brought to a high state of development, residing on it for seventeen years, and still owns the property, which he has
added to until it now consists of 240 acres, and is being farmed on
shares by his son, Wallace. In the spring of 1891 Mr. Kennedy bought
eighty acres of land near Orrsburg, in partnership with J. D. Ford,
and set out seventy acres to apples. While this orchard venture was a
success, Mr. Kennedy's activities were demanded elsewhere, and he has
since sold his interest.

While Mr. Kennedy has been successful as an agriculturist he has
not confined his activities to that field of endeavor, for he is also well
known in business and financial circles. He is president of the Farmers
Bank of Parnell, which was organized in 1910, and which is capitalized
at $20,000, with a surplus of $10,000, with W. W. Morgan as vice president and Otis Gray as cashier. The bank is known as one of the substantial and prosperous institutions of Nodaway County, and much of
its success may be accredited to Mr. Kennedy's excellent abilities. He
is also doing a very satisfactory business in the line of real estate and
insurance, and in every way bears a high reputation among those with
whom he has had dealings of any nature.

A stalwart democrat, Mr. Kennedy was elected judge of the north
district of Nodaway County in 1896, and has also served capably and
conscientiously as a member of the school board, having at all times
displayed a keen interest in educational matters. A devout member of
the Methodist Episcopal Church, he has supported its movements liberally, and at this time is a member of the board of trustees. Mrs. Kennedy is also a member of this church and has been a helpful factor in
its work, being presiding officer of the Ladies' Aid Society at Parnell.

On October 19, 1873, Mr. Kennedy was married to Miss Susan Mary
Ford, daughter of Marshall and Lucy (Hutchinson) Ford, the former
of whom is deceased, while the latter now lives with her son, Albert,
and is eighty-seven years of age. Marshall Ford was one of the pioneers
of Nodaway County, coming to this locality after his marriage in
Pulaski County, Kentucky. Their children were as follows: Mrs.
Catherine Shell, Mrs. Susan Mary Kennedy, Mrs. Nettie Kennedy, Mrs.
Fanny Hanna, Mrs. Belle Hogan, Jefferson Davis, Albert Sidney
Johnston, and Marshall, Jr. Two children have been born to Mr. and

Nodaway County, he is inveterately young in his enthusiasm and professional outlook, and is today regarded as one of the most capable physicians in that section of the state. He began practice in the county in 1870, having his residence at Pickering until about ten years ago, since which time he has been located at Maryville, and now has two capable associates in his sons.

Dr. Wallis was born in Genesee County, New York, January 12, 1848, one of six children whose parents were Miles and Lavinia (Tuller) Wallis, both natives of New York State. The father was a farmer and stock raiser and dealer, had a large farm in Genesee County, and there his children grew up. After the death of his first wife he married a second time, and finally moved out to Nodaway County, Missouri, for several years was proprietor of a hotel at Pickering, and then retired from business activities. His death occurred at Pickering at the age of ninety-three. There were no children by his second marriage.

Dr. Wallis while a boy in New York received an academic education in the Genesee and Wyoming Seminary in his native county, and prepared for professional work in the medical department of the University of Buffalo, where he was graduated at the end of the session of 1869-70. In the fall of the latter year, when a young man of twenty-two years, Dr. Wallis came out to Missouri and located at Pickering, which was his home for thirty-four years. Throughout that time he was actively engaged in general practice, and his patients lived in all directions from the town so that he was compelled to cover a large territory in his daily rounds. When Dr. Wallis began practice in Nodaway County there were few of the improvements and facilities which make the life of the modern physician comparatively pleasant. In the early days he even mixed his own drugs, and usually carried a general supply of medicines about the country with him. He rode horseback and drove a buggy over the country roads both summer and winter, and was already one of the older physicians of that section before the introduction of the telephone and many years more passed before the era of improved highways and automobiles. Dr. Wallis is a physician who has never failed to keep up with the rapid advance in professional attainments, and has gained an enviable reputation as an able and skillful physician. Several times he was honored with office as president of the Nodaway County Medical Society, and is an active member of the Missouri State Medical Society and the American Medical Association. In 1904 Dr. Wallis, after a course of post-graduate study in the Post-Graduate School of Medicine at Chicago, returned home and moved his office and residence to Maryville, where he now practices with his two sons.

Though a stanch democrat, Dr. Wallis has never shown extreme partisanship, and has never sought political honors. He worships in the Christian Church, and is a Master Mason. In 1875 in Nodaway County Dr. Wallis married Augusta H. Leach. She is a native of New York State. Their three children are Frank C., William M. and Helen Augusta.

Dr. Frank C. Wallis, the older of the sons of the senior Dr. Wallis, was born at Pickering in Nodaway County February 2, 1876. After

Scottish Rite Masonry, is also affiliated with the Benevolent and Protective Order of Elks, and is a member of the Christian Church.

Dr. William M. Wallis, Jr., was born in Pickering September 4, 1880, was educated in the public schools of his native town and the high school of Des Moines, and at Drake University. In 1903, after the regular course of study, he was graduated M. D. from the Central Medical College of St. Joseph, Missouri, and the following two years were spent as an interne in the Sisters Hospital in that city. He continued in regular practice of medicine at St. Joseph for four years, and then joined his father and brother at Maryville. His special reputation is based upon skillful work as a surgeon. Dr. Wallis is a member of the county and state medical societies, the Missouri Valley Medical Society and the American Medical Association. He is affiliated with the Benevolent and Protective Order of Elks and is a member of the Christian Church. In 1907 he married Miss Nettie Douglas of Kansas City, Missouri.

GEORGE S. BAKER. The pioneer banker of Nodaway County, now retired from an active control of affairs which he directed forty years, George S. Baker has been one of the group of business men chiefly responsible for the direction and management of the larger commercial and financial interests in and about Maryville. His success and position have been honorably won, and his beginnings were made in an environment where the labor of his hands was the chief source of his livelihood. Mr. Baker represents one of the older families of Nodaway County, and himself has lived there since boyhood.

George S. Baker was born in Madison County, Kentucky, June 19, 1836, a son of Charles and Fannie (Saunders) Baker. His parents, who were also natives of Kentucky, came to Missouri in 1846, and after five years in Buchanan County located in Nodaway County, where the father died soon afterward at the age of fifty-three. The mother passed away in 1879 aged eighty years. There were three daughters and one son in the family.

Reared on a farm, educated in country schools, and with little opportunity to gain an education, George S. Baker had to create his own destiny. In 1854, at the age of eighteen, he left the farm and found a position as a poorly paid and hard working clerk in a store at Maryville. That was the start of a business career which the subsequent years have marked with unusual success. His business was interrupted during 1861-62, in the course of the war, when he served as a quartermaster of the Missouri State Troops under General Price. Returning to Maryville, he continued employment in different stores, and in 1867 engaged in the livestock business. It was his operations in that line that developed the need of a bank at Maryville, and he became one of the most active among several associates who organized the private banking firm of Geo. S. Baker & Company. His associates in that company were Joseph E. Alexander, E. S. Stephenson, W. C. O'Rear and J. B. Prather. Mr. Baker remained at the head of the bank until 1873, and after he sold his interests the Nodaway Valley Bank was organized to succeed the private company. In 1873 Mr. Baker and others organized the banking firm of Baker, Saunders & Company. This was succeeded by the Maryville National Bank, which was organized February 1, 1890, and that institution in turn gave way in 1913 to the present Farmers Trust Company of Maryville. Mr. Baker was president of the Maryville National Bank until 1893, when he was succeeded by Mr. George L. Wilfley. Then for three years Mr. Baker was out of active banking and spent his time in looking after his farming interests. In September, 1896, Mr. Baker and others organized the Real Estate Bank of Maryville, accepted the position of president, and continued to give active direction to its affairs until 1906, since which time his place has been among the retired business men of Maryville, though he still looks after his private investments and various holdings. His has been an enviable reputation, not only as a pioneer banker, but as a man who for many years has assisted to uphold and maintain the integrity of business in his home city.

Mr. Baker was reared under the influences of the whig party in politics, but for many years has been identified with the democratic interests and always active in political affairs. In later years he has reserved a choice in casting his ballot, which classifies him almost as an independent. He has never sought office, but at one time was honored by appointment to the office of postmaster at Maryville, and gave that position a creditable administration, though he resigned after a short time. He is a member of Maryville Lodge No. 165, A. F. & A. M. His church is the Episcopal.

April 14, 1863, Mr. Baker married Margaret Ellen Prather, who passed away September 4, 1878. Few families in Northwest Missouri are better known and more prominent than the Prathers, and Mrs. Baker was a daughter of Isaac Newton Prather, one of Nodaway County's pioneers, and long prominent in business, farming and stock raising. Mr. Prather is given credit as having been the first to introduce blue grass pasture and thoroughbred horses into Northwest Missouri. Mr. and Mrs. Baker became the parents of five children: Maud, wife of M. G. Tate of Maryville; George B. Baker, now president of the Real Estate Bank of Maryville; and the three, Fannie, Hubert, and Charles, who died in infancy.

GEORGE BASIL BAKER. A son of the retired banker of Maryville, George S. Baker, and the active successor of his father in financial affairs, being now president of the Real Estate Bank, George B. Baker practically grew up in banking and for twenty-seven years has given almost undivided attention to the banking business in Maryville.

George Basil Baker was born at Maryville February 19, 1871, a son of George S. and Margaret Ellen (Prather) Baker. He was educated in the public schools of Maryville, and for six years was identified with the old banking house of Baker, Saunders & Company, which in 1890 was succeeded by the Maryville National Bank. With the reorganized institution he continued until 1896, and then became one of the group of men who established the Real Estate Bank, in which he accepted the post of cashier. Mr. Baker was cashier of the Real Estate Bank until June 26, 1911, at which time he was elected president to succeed the late Mr. E. J. Williams, who had been president after the retirement of George S. Baker. Mr. Edward E. Williams succeeded Mr. Baker as cashier. Besides his banking interests Mr. Baker owns a large area of farm lands, and until a few years ago found a great deal of pleasure and profit in maintaining a herd of fine thoroughbred horses and Hereford cattle.

Mr. Baker is a democrat, a Knight Templar Mason, a member of the Nobles of the Mystic Shrine and of the Benevolent and Protective Order of Elks. His church home is the Methodist. Of public service he has given his time to the Maryville Library Board for some time, and at the present time is serving by appointment from Governor Major as a member of the board for the State Insane Asylum No. 2 at St. Joseph.

On October 12, 1892, Mr. Baker married Miss Sarah Scott Campbell, daughter of the late Dr. Smith V. and Carrie S. Campbell of Maryville. Mr. and Mrs. Baker have a daughter, Carrie Margaret, who is now a student in the Northwestern University at Evanston, Illinois.

THOMAS FOSTER STONE. Of citizenship and individual character that must be described of more than representative degree, the position of the Stone family in Platte County is second to none among those solid and excellent people who have been most closely identified with this community during the past seventy years. The late Thomas F. Stone was a fine old pioneer, measuring well up in personal qualities with those ideal pictures of western early settlers so often depicted in history. His widow is still living, and Northwest Missouri has no finer example of venerated motherhood and womanly character.

Thomas Foster Stone was born in Bourbon County, Kentucky, January 1, 1821, and died on his farm in Platte County, Missouri, May 21, 1896. His father, Elijah, who was the oldest son of Kinsey Stone of Virginia, was an early settler of Bourbon County, locating within a mile of Paris. Elijah married Eliza Foster, whose father, Thomas Foster, was from Maryland and located near Frankfort, Kentucky, where he died.

The only child of his parents, Thomas F. Stone was seven months old when his father died, and after that lived with his grandfather Stone until his mother married a Mr. Mitchell. His stepfather gave him a common school education and taught him the value of honest toil as a means of advancement in the world. It was in 1844, at the age of twenty-three, that he first came to Missouri, visiting his stepfather in Lincoln County and later an uncle in Platte County. While here his grandfather, who was getting old and wished to retire, sent for his grandson to come and live with him the rest of his days. Mr. Stone accordingly remained in Kentucky with his grandfather until his death, and then in 1846 set out for Platte County, which was to be his future home for the half century remaining to him of life. Platte County then had a heavy forest covering that can hardly be imagined by the present generation. His purchase of 320 acres is included in the present homestead. It had a growth of fine black walnut timber, which, if still standing, would be worth a fortune in itself. The two-room frame house on the land was the second house of frame in Platte County. The larger timbers were hewed out of walnut logs, the siding was of walnut boards, the shingles were hand-riveted and also walnut, and a whipsaw had been used to make the interior finishing, also of walnut. This remarkable structure, of a timber that is now used only in more expensive furniture and interior finishing, is still standing, and part of the fine old residence on the Stone farm.

Into this home came Mrs. Stone as a young bride. They had been married in Kentucky on May 31, 1846, and at once left by stage for Maysville, and from there embarked on a river boat and came by water to the landing at Weston, where they arrived on June 15th. Mrs. Stone recalls that when the boat stopped at Westport, now Kansas City, the hills were covered with Indians, and in the early days she saw as many as six hundred of the red men in Weston at one time.

Mr. Stone set to work with an industry that was characteristic of him to make a home in this wilderness. He cleared off many acres for cultivation, and from time to time bought more land until at his death his estate comprised 425 acres. This is now owned by Mrs. Stone and her son, Thomas F., Jr. In 1872 Mr. Stone began breeding thoroughbred Shorthorn cattle, and in time had one of the finest herds in Northwest Missouri, and that branch of the business is still carried on by his son. How early Mr. Stone was a factor in affairs in this part of Missouri is well indicated by the fact that he was present at the first sale of lots at what was then called Roubidaux's Mills, the present City of St. Joseph. When he first began voting he was a whig, and a stanch

Mary A. Stone

admirer of the great Kentuckian, Henry Clay, but afterwards allied his fortunes with the democratic party.

Mrs. Stone, who before her marriage was Miss Mary Anne Flanagan, was born in London, England, November 25, 1831. Her father, Francis John Flanagan, was a man of remarkable attributes and experiences. He had the brilliant qualities of the Irish race, refined and cultured by association with great people and by extensive travel. He studied law under the noted Daniel O'Connell at Dublin, and for a number of years practiced in England. In early youth he was present in Belgium when the battle of Waterloo was fought. He had accompanied a sister whose husband was an officer in the Scotch Greys, and who held herself in readiness to aid her husband should he be wounded or to carry away his body should he be among the slain. Many years afterward he was a friend of Louis Napoleon during his exile and poverty in London, and gave him many a goldpiece to buy clothes and food, and when the tide of politics and fortune turned in his favor was present at Paris at the crowning of the second Napoleon as emperor of France. The emperor gave Mr. Flanagan a prominent seat as a spectator of the ceremony and also presented him with a set of valuable books, which Mr. Flanagan donated to the College of Notre Dame. In the course of his career he visited every civilized country except South America, and could speak fourteen languages and dialects. After coming to the United States he became interested in some of the pork packing concerns at Louisville and St. Louis. He was the author of several books, and while a resident of Louisville became a friend of Henry Clay and entertained that statesman at his home in Louisville. The Flanagans were an aristocratic house, and the family crest was a bent armored arm with a dagger in the hand, and a motto, meaning "Fortune favors the Brave."

Mr. Flanagan was first married September 3, 1819, to Catherine Malloy, who died October 23, 1823. Of their children a son, John, entered the priesthood and spent his life in a monastery at Birmingham, England. February 18, 1831, Mr. Flanagan married Catherine Knight Greening, a native of England. They were married in the Warwick Street Catholic Church in London, and on the same day had the service repeated before a Protestant minister, as the English laws then required. Of this marriage there were six children, and the two still living are Mrs. Stone and Mrs. Catherine Healy, the latter of Philadelphia. When Mrs. Stone was an infant she was brought to America, the voyage from Liverpool to Sandy Hook lasting six weeks. Her father first went to Zanesville, Ohio, and later to Louisville, where her mother died October 6, 1844, at the age of thirty-six. Mr. Flanagan married for his third wife Agnes Carter of Bourbon County, Kentucky. He finally moved to St. Louis, where he died February 21, 1861.

Three of Mr. Flanagan's sons were educated in the College of Notre Dame. Mrs. Stone was educated in a Catholic convent in Louisville. Now in her eighty-fourth year, she has lived not only many years, but a life remarkable for her interests both at home and in the world. She has always been a reader, and is informed on the history of the day as well as the past, and knows the fashions, too. She thoroughly enjoys every minute of her life, and it is a delight to hear her recount her early experiences in Platte County. Her home and children have been the shrine of her life, and it has been a matter of careful study and pride that her house should be the most attractive place in the world for her boys, and she kept it open for the young people of the community while those men now in the prime of their powers were growing to manhood.

Mr. and Mrs. Stone became the parents of nine children, and there are five sons still living. All of them were educated in the Christian Brothers' College in St. Louis, and the five of them sat on the platform at one time and received their degrees. The Stone family are devout members of the Catholic faith. The sons are: Elijah Francis, an attorney in St. Louis; Walter, librarian of the law school at the University of Missouri; Terence, president of the United States Banking and Trust Company at Grand Junction, Colorado; Thomas F., who conducts the old homestead and has made a success as farmer and stockman; and Robert Lee, who lives in Reno, Nevada.

HON. CHARLES HYSLOP. Now serving as representative from Nodaway County, in the State Legislature, Charles Hyslop has lived in this section of Northwest Missouri and has taken an active part in business, public and church and social affairs for more than forty years. He is a veteran of the great Civil war, and the same qualities which made him an efficient soldier have been exhibited in his work as a business man, his fidelity to the responsibilities of public office, and he is easily one of the best known and most highly esteemed citizens of Nodaway County.

Charles Hyslop was born in New York at Penn Yan, July 21, 1843, and represents a fine Scotch ancestry. His father, William Hyslop, was born in New Galloway, Scotland, and his mother, whose maiden name was Mary McAdam, was born at Castle Douglas in Scotland. After their marriage the parents emigrated to America, arriving in the spring of 1843, and after a brief residence in New York moved on to Illinois and in June, 1844, settled at Carthage in Hancock County. In the year of their arrival, in August, the father died, and a few years later the mother married James Baird, who was also a Scotchman and a successful Hancock County farmer.

It was on the Baird farm in Hancock County that Charles Hyslop grew up, and while there attended the common schools. On July 21, 1861, the day he was eighteen years of age, Mr. Hyslop was sworn in as a private in Company G of the Black Hawk Cavalry, which was later consolidated with the Seventh Volunteer Cavalry of Missouri. He saw some hard campaigning in the states of Missouri, Arkansas and Louisiana and also in Indian Territory and along the western frontier. He was out a little more than two years, and on account of physical disability was honorably discharged. For many years Mr. Hyslop has taken a prominent part in Grand Army circles, and has filled all the positions in his post, Sedgwick Post, No. 21, G. A. R. In 1882 he was commissioned captain of Company G, M. N. G., by Governor Crittenden, and served three years.

In February, 1873, Mr. Hyslop moved to Northwest Missouri, and has since had his home in Maryville. For several years he was a merchant, but in 1880 opened an office to handle real estate, loans and general insurance, and that has been his principal line of business activity down to the present time. Always a republican in politics, Mr. Hyslop has been frequently honored with positions of trust, and in 1884 was elected public administrator for Nodaway County, and gave a capable administration of its affairs for eight years. He also served as justice of the peace. In 1914 he was elected a member of the Legislature to represent Nodaway County, and the interests of this section of Missouri will be well taken care of as long as he remains in the legislative body.

Fraternally Mr. Hyslop is a Knight Templar Mason, has taken thirty-two degrees in the Scottish Rite, is past high priest of the Royal

Arch Chapter and at the present time commander of the Knights Templar. For many years he has been identified with the Knights of Pythias, and has filled all the chairs in the local lodge. Mr. Hyslop is well known for his prominence in the Baptist Church in this section of Missouri, has served as clerk of the local church, and has been a member of several state boards, being now on the Board of Curators for William Jewell College at Liberty. In December, 1867, Mr. Hyslop married Delia M. Mann. Her father was Miles B. Mann, a prominent citizen of Hancock County, Illinois, who was postmaster at Carthage at the time Joe Smith, the Mormon leader, was killed.

LIONEL CLARENCE GOODEN. A veteran journalist of Northwest Missouri, Lionel Clarence Gooden, editor and proprietor of the Sentinel, of Parnell, has been connected with the newspaper business throughout practically his entire career, and is not alone a shaper of public opinion in connection with his journalistic activities, but also occupies a prominent place in public life, having served almost continuously in offices of responsibility and trust since his arrival in Parnell in 1900.

Mr. Gooden was born at Willow Grove near Dover, Delaware, December 14, 1864, and is a son of John Cooper and Elizabeth Ann (Broadaway) Gooden, and a member of an old family which originated in Wales and which originally spelled the name "Godyn." John Cooper Gooden was born March 3, 1839, and for many years was engaged in educational capacities. He is still a resident of Dover, Delaware, and is a man of scholarly mind and marked literary attainments, being a frequent contributor to newspapers and magazines. A democrat in politics, he has held various public positions, being recorder of deeds of Kent County, Delaware, and in 1877 was appointed state librarian by Gov. Benjamin Biggs. He is a Lodge and Chapter Mason. Mrs. Gooden died at Dover, in 1890, the mother of two children: Lionel Clarence, of this review; and Mrs. Anna Evelyn Culver, of Dover.

After attending the public schools of his native place, Lionel C. Gooden took a course at Wilmington Conference Academy, and, inheriting a predilection for literary and newspaper work, was in 1880 apprenticed to the printing trade in the book and job printing office of James Kirk & Son. Four years later, in partnership with his father, he engaged in the general merchandise business at Willow Grove, but in 1887 decided to seek his fortune in the West, and accordingly went to Stevens County, Kansas, locating at Dermot, and there establishing a newspaper known as the Enterprise. This he conducted successfully for two years and then moved to Nodaway County, Missouri, but soon went to Fairfax, Atchison County, where he established the Fairfax Star. In 1891 he disposed of this paper and went to Maryville, where he purchased a one-half interest with W. M. Carr, of Mound City, in the Evening News. A short time later he sold his interest and moved to Burlington Junction, there becoming half-owner of the Post, from that place going to Stanberry where he was foreman of the Sentinel for six months. In 1892 he established the Westboro Wave. After six months he disposed of his interest therein and accepted the position of foreman with the Tarkio Independent, but after six months returned to Stanberry and became connected with the Sentinel. Mr. Gooden in March, 1894, went to Sheridan, Missouri, where he purchased the Advance, from J. L. West, and remained there six years, in the meantime serving in the capacity of mayor and as a member of the town board. Still he had not yet found the locality which he wished to make his permanent field of activity but this was discovered in 1900, in July of which year he came to Parnell and purchased from Charles J. Colden the Sentinel, which he has continued to publish to the present time with much success. He has built up an excellent circulation, attracted by a neatly-printed, thoroughly reliable newspaper, independent in its policies as to politics and aiming to give its readers an unbiased view of the leading questions of the day, together with a comprehensive and interesting account of local happenings, the latest national and international news, and well-written editorials. Mr. Gooden's efforts have been appreciated by the people of Parnell and Nodaway County, who have supported him generously, both in the matter of subscriptions and advertising, and the Sentinel is today recognized as one of the influential newspapers of this part of the state. Mr. Gooden is a charter member of the Northwest Missouri Press Association, and the high regard in which he is held by members of the craft was eloquently evidenced in 1906 when he was chosen president of this organization. He has been interested in various other enterprises here, being at this time owner and manager of the Parnell Opera House, owner of the building in which his newspaper plant is located, and of a handsome residence property. Formerly for six years he was manager of the Parnell Telephone Exchange and for four years was secretary of the Worth Mutual Telephone Company.

While he has conducted his newspaper as an independent sheet, Mr. Gooden has democratic tendencies and generally gives his support to that party. During the past twelve years he has served as a member of the town board, and during 1907, 1909, 1910, 1911 and 1912, acted in the capacity of mayor of the city. In March, 1913, he was elected justice of the peace and was appointed notary public in 1900 and holds both of these positions at the present time. He has also served as clerk . of school district No. 57, as secretary and director of the board of education, and in 1896 was a delegate to the senatorial convention. In each of his public capacities he has displayed a commendable desire to be doing something in behalf of his community and its people, and few men have accomplished more for the development and advancement of Parnell. He is well known in fraternal circles, having been secretary and senior warden of Gaynor City Blue Lodge, No. 465, A. F. & A. M., . and at the present time is worshipful master; a member of Parnell Lodge, No. 484, Independent Order of Odd Fellows, of which he is past noble grand, and attended the assembly from 1904 to 1908 for district No. 74, at Kirksville, St. Louis, Excelsior Springs and Springfield, and during these four years being district deputy, as well as lodge deputy at Parnell for three years; secretary of Rebekah Lodge of Parnell; and consul of the Modern Woodmen of America Lodge No. 2859, of which he has also been banker and trustee. He is likewise worthy patron of the Eastern Star Chapter at Parnell.

On January 1, 1889, Mr. Gooden was married to Miss Elma DuBois, daughter of Jonathan and Mary Angeline (Jones) DuBois, formerly of Ross County, Ohio, and now of Dos Palos, California. Jonathan DuBois came to Nodaway County, Missouri, from Ohio, in 1886, and farmed near Hopkins for eight years, following which he returned to his Ohio home. He and Mrs. DuBois were the parents of four children: Mrs. Gooden, Peter E., Samuel and Mrs. Mary True. Mrs. Gooden belongs to the Christian Science Church, and is also well known in fraternal circles, being worthy matron of the Eastern Star Chapter at Parnell and past noble grand of the Rebekah Lodge, and in 1906 was a delegate to Kirksville Assembly Convention. Mr. and Mrs. Gooden have one son: Harold Elting, born at Maryville, Missouri, in December, 1890, and now conducting a business of decorating and paper-hanging at Dos Palos, California.

THOMAS ALEXANDER BRASHEAR. A resident of Parnell for more than a quarter of a century, having come here prior to the laying out of the town, Thomas Alexander Brashear is known as one of his community's most progressive and enterprising citizens and one who has led an active and successful career. Born March 30, 1840, in Hancock County, Illinois, Mr. Brashear is a son of William G. and Rosa (Wood) Brashear. His father was born January 13, 1807, in the Spartanburg District of South Carolina, and died May 10, 1862, in Adair County, Missouri, while the mother was born September 22, 1809, and died August 29, 1900. They were married in their native community, where they were reared.

The Wood and Brashear families came to Ralls County, Missouri, in the spring of 1827, and in 1841 the parents of Mr. Brashear moved to Adair County, locating near the present site of the Town of Brashear, which place was named in honor of R. M. Brashear, now of Kirksville, Missouri. The father was a man who took the utmost pride in the development of his locality, and was never too busy to show a stranger Government land. He was hospitable, with a keen faith in human nature, and often, when he took the word of a stranger for security, he was sadly imposed upon. He was a man of temperate habits, a stanch supporter of the church and very aggressive, hesitating at no obstacles in advocating better educational facilities, even giving up a portion of his own home to be used as a schoolhouse. He was a devout member of the Baptist Church. His children were as follows: Coleman, a resident of California; Mrs. Mary J. Patterson, of Illinois; Richard M., who lives at Kirksville, Missouri; Mrs. Cynthia Hoasly, who is living in Oklahoma; John W., of Hutchinson, Kansas; Mrs. Martha Conkle, of Brashear, Missouri; George B., of Oklahoma; Thomas Alexander, of this review; and Millicent, James W., Susan A. and Nancy, who are all deceased.

Thomas Alexander Brashear spent his boyhood on the home place in Adair County, Missouri, and when the Civil war came on his sympathies were with the Union. He was twenty-one years of age when he enlisted, July 12, 1861, from Adair County, Missouri, in Company A, Fourteenth Regiment Illinois Volunteer Infantry, under Captain Thompson and Col. John M. Palmer, with which organization he served three years and three months. Mr. Brashear participated in much of the most important warfare of the great struggle between the North and the South, and his record was that of a hard-fighting, reliable and faithful soldier. After seeing service in the vicinity of Springfield, Missouri, and at Wilson Creek, in the fall of 1861, in the spring of 1862 his command fought General Price's troops, and was at Forts Henry and Donelson, February 6 and February 15-16; Shiloh, April 6; Corinth, October 3-4, 1862; Vicksburg, May 18 to July 4, 1863; Champion Hills, February 4, 1864, and Sherman's raid to Meridian. The Fourteenth and Fifteenth regiments were consolidated in July, 1864, and became known as a veteran battalion, which marched between Tallahachie, Holly Springs, Memphis, Bolivar, Corinth, Vicksburg, Meridian, Chattanooga and Marietta, Georgia, and was honorably discharged August 24, 1864, at Chattanooga, Tennessee. At that time Mr. Brashear returned to his home at Paulville, located twelve miles east of Kirksville, Missouri. He had earned the respect and gratitude of his country by his faithful service, and now, still the good soldier, was ready to resume the responsibilities of private citizenship and to engage in the battles of peace.

Mr. Brashear was married October 27, 1866, to Miss Laura L. Grayson, daughter of Oren and Eveline (Wooley) Grayson, of Adair County,

Missouri, who had come to that county in 1862. Mrs. Brashear was born near Three Rivers, Michigan, August 29, 1849. After their marriage Mr. and Mrs. Brashear resided in Buchanan County, where he rented some land and engaged in railroading, and also, while at Hill Station, engaged in the manufacture of ties, railway timber, etc. In 1888 Mr. Brashear purchased the first lot sold at Parnell, and after moving to this place built a dwelling and place of business, in which he successfully conducted a butcher shop for six years. He then turned his attention to farming, purchasing 240 acres of land, partly improved, southwest of Parnell, from Mr. Jones of Maryville. He engaged extensively in buying and shipping stock, and in this line became one of the best known men in this part of Nodaway County, but in 1902 disposed of his land to W. S. Wright, of Parnell. In the meantime, January 19, 1898, Mr. Brashear had been appointed postmaster at Parnell, by President McKinley, and held this office continuously until July 22, 1914. At the present time Mr. Brashear is the owner of twenty-seven acres of land adjoining Parnell, and here he has his comfortable modern residence.

Mr. Brashear is a member of Parnell Lodge No. 484, Independent Order of Odd Fellows, having first joined in DeKalb, Buchanan County, in 1867, and now being past noble grand. He and Mrs. Brashear belong to the Rebekahs, Mrs. Brashear being delegate to the State Assembly of Rebekahs, May 21, 22, 23, 1901, and being past noble grand therein. Mr. Brashear is connected with Parnell Post No. 517, Grand Army of the Republic, having been a charter member at the time of its organization twenty-five years ago, and acting in various official capacities. Nine children have been born to Mr. and Mrs. Brashear, namely: Anna, the wife of George W. Korell, of Savannah, Andrew County, Missouri, has had five children,—Georgia Vera, Vollie Alexander, Johnny Brashear, Harold and Lucille, but Harold is deceased; Rose Adelia, the wife of Charles C. Evans, an auctioneer and stockman of Parnell, has one daughter—Matie Fraulein; Benjamin H., who married Josephine Bowles, of Savannah, has one son—James Thomas; and Charles C., Lewis, Markie, Bruce, Willie and Wilbur, who are deceased.

Mrs. Brashear's father was born in Canada and her mother at Three Rivers, Michigan, and they were married in Canada, and subsequently moved in 1849 to Dane County, Wisconsin, Mr. Grayson buying a tract of prairie land. There he resided and carried on operations until 1856, when the family moved to Labelle, Lewis County, Missouri, the trip being made with teams and wagons, and there Mr. Grayson bought 100 acres of improved prairie land and continued to reside thereon until about 1859. In that year he removed to Adair County, about nine miles southeast of Kirksville, where in addition to farming he carried on a blacksmith and wagon making shop. Mr. and Mrs. Grayson were the parents of eight children: Mrs. Anna Emmons, Mrs. Carrie Rhoads, Andrew, Mrs. Brashear, Frank, Grant L., Mrs. Louisa McKinney and George W., but Mrs. Carrie Rhoads, Mrs. Louisa McKinney, Frank and George W. are deceased.

BENTON SMITH. Prominent among the old and respected families of Nodaway County, Missouri, whose members have contributed materially to the upbuilding and development of this section, and particularly from a practical wilderness to a flourishing business and agricultural community, and a center of education and religion. Whether handling the tools of destruction or the implements of construction he has always proved himself a sincere, reliable and public-spirited citizen, with a keen interest in the advancement of his locality, and exercising his influence for good citizenship and morality in all things.

Benton Smith was born February 27, 1841, in Bartholomew County, Indiana, and is a son of Elon and Minerva (McCall) Smith. His father, a native of South Carolina, early left the Old South state for Indiana, locating in Bartholomew County, where he was married. After spending several years on a rented farm, he decided that the country still farther west offered better opportunities, and in the fall of 1845 brought his family to Andrew County, Missouri. There he rented a farm near Whitesville and had started to develop a home for his children, when, in 1846, he was suddenly stricken by death. The children were: Hamilton, Eliza Ann, Benton, Andrew J. and Elon. After the death of her husband, the mother, in brave determination to keep her children about her, moved to Guilford, Nodaway County, in 1846, and there Benton Smith was given his educational training in a primitive subscription school of the log cabin type. The boys rented small patches of land, and in 1851 the mother purchased a tract of 160 acres near Ravenwood, to which the family moved. Continuing to attend school during the short winter terms, and passing the summer months in the work of the farm, Benton Smith arrived at his twenty-first year with a good mental training, and strong in body, thoroughly conversant with every detail of farm work. With this equipment he entered upon his own career on a farm of sixty acres of prairie land, partly covered with timber, and this he cleared and broke with oxen. This land, located near Ravenwood, on section 24, township 64, range 34, he subsequently sold to S. P. Joy, and in 1873 purchased 100 acres of slightly improved land on section 23, in the same township. There he resided from 1873 until 1889 at which time he retired from active agricultural operations, being the owner of 300 acres, which property has since been divided among his children, while Mr. Smith is living a quiet life.

In 1861 Mr. Smith enlisted in Company G, Missouri State Militia, under Captain Swinford, for service during the Civil war. He was honorably discharged in April, 1862, after some time passed in guard duty near St. Joseph, and returned home, where he worked by the month for a short period. The war fever had gripped him, however, and he again enlisted, this time at Independence, Missouri, in the Fourth Missouri Cavalry, under Col. George H. Hall. He subsequently saw service, at all times active. from the Osage River to Kansas City, coming into frequent contact with the troops of the Confederate General Price, and later going south to Fort Scott, and participating in the battle which culminated in the surrender of General Marmaduke. He received his honorable discharge at St. Louis, July 8, 1865, and returned to his farm at Ravenwood, with an excellent record as a good and faithful soldier.

In political matters Mr. Smith is a democrat, and has frequently been a candidate to county conventions. Duties at home prevented him attending the state convention in 1906 to which he had been elected as a delegate. He is a charter member of Ravenwood Post, an outpost

daughter of Kilburn and Agnes (Neenan) Basford, of Edgar County, Illinois. Mr. Basford was a pioneer farmer of Illinois, and in his latter years went to California, where both he and his wife passed away. Their children were: Mrs. Smith, Delilah, Mary Ann and Harriet. To Mr. and Mrs. Smith there have been born the following children: Oliver E.; Harriet A., who married Thomas M. Curry, a merchant at Hillsdale, Wyoming, has two children, Oliver B. and Harold A.; Charlotte A., who died in 1904; Willis, deceased; Lourinda M. and Joseph J.

Oliver E. Smith, eldest son of Benton Smith, was born December 28, 1868, and has worked out his career at Ravenwood. After attending the country schools, in 1888 he entered the Maryville school, and after one term returned to the home place. On June 16, 1899, Mr. Smith purchased the Ravenwood Gazette, which he conducted successfully as an independent paper until July, 1913, when he sold the plant to F. G. Graf, of Kansas City, who had been his assistant for three years. Mr. Smith served as postmaster of Ravenwood for four years, in President Cleveland's second term, and for five years was representative to the assemblies of the Independent Order of Odd Fellows, at Columbia, Jefferson City and Excelsior Springs, having been recording secretary of Ravenwood Lodge No. 464, and at this time past noble grand thereof. Mr. Smith is now engaged in the real estate and insurance business at Ravenwood, in which he is meeting with well-deserved success. He is known as one of his town's progressive and public-spirited citizens. Mr. Smith holds membership in the Woodmen of the World and in the Northwest Missouri Press Association, of which latter he was president during 1912. He was married June 20, 1900, to Miss Ida Strider, of Montgomery County, Illinois, daughter of Isaac and Eglantine (Matkin) Strider, both of whom are now deceased.

Joseph J. Smith, the youngest son of Benton Smith, is the owner of 140 acres of land at Ravenwood, a part of the old homestead, which he now has rented, as well as 160 acres of homestead land near Hillsdale, Wyoming, the northeast one-quarter of section 8, township 14, range 63. He is now acting in a clerical capacity at the Platte Valley Bank, and is the owner of a garage at Ravenwood, which he erected. Fraternally, Mr. Smith is connected with Ravenwood Blue Lodge No. 201, of the Masonic fraternity.

GEORGE PATTERSON WRIGHT. Among the active members of the Nodaway County bar, George P. Wright has gained a notable reputation for success as a trial lawyer, and his services have been enlisted in behalf of the county, which he served as prosecuting attorney until 1915, and his two terms of experience in that office did much to develop and improve his power before court and jury and fixed his place among the successful lawyers of Maryville. Prior to taking up the law as a profession, Mr. Wright was for a number of years one of the most popular and successful educators in Nodaway County.

George Patterson Wright was born in Louisa County, Iowa, March 30, 1873, a son of Cyprian L. and Sarah A. (Patterson) Wright. His father was a native of Indiana and his mother of Ohio, they were married in Iowa, and for a number of years lived on a farm near Morning Sun, but in 1879 came to Nodaway County, Missouri, and located near Ravenwood. They moved from their farm into Maryville in 1898, and the father died in that city in 1913 at the age of seventy-one, while the mother is still living. The father was a soldier during the Civil war, having enlisted in 1861 in the Nineteenth Ohio Regiment of Infantry, and his service continued for a few days longer than three years. He was a man of well balanced character and judgment, was

Mrs Alice Layton Gabbert

Benton Gabbert

highly esteemed in the different communities where he made his home, and both he and his wife were active members of the Methodist Church, South.

George P. Wright grew up on a farm, had his preliminary training in country schools and subsequently finished both the literary and commercial courses in the Maryville Seminary, and for one year was a student in the Stanberry Normal. Before the completion of this educational course he had begun his work as a country school teacher, and alternately attended and taught school for a period of about ten years. His last work as a teacher was as principal for three years of the schools at Graham, and the previous two years had been spent at Quitman. While in active work in the schoolroom at Graham Mr. Wright was elected county commissioner of schools for Nodaway County, and during his term in that office he did much to improve the personnel and morale of the teaching staff of the county, and in every way made a creditable record. In the meantime Mr. Wright had begun the private study of law, and in June, 1903, was admitted to the bar, and at once began general practice at Maryville. He was soon in possession of a good business as a lawyer, and in 1910 when his name was placed on the democratic ticket as candidate for prosecuting attorney his personal popularity and high professional standing were the recommendations which caused his election. He was reelected in 1912 and his second term expired January 1, 1915. Since retiring from office Mr. Wright and Mr. M. E. Ford formed the law firm of Wright & Ford.

Mr. Wright is a Master Mason, also affiliated with the Independent Order of Odd Fellows, and is a member of the Christian Church. What he has accomplished in two professions has been the result of his determined ambition to make himself useful in the world, and he has won the honor and respect of his community. On November 26, 1902, Mr. Wright married Miss Mamie Wilson, daughter of W. G. Wilson, of Graham, Missouri.

BENTON GABBERT. It is a distinction which history will always associate with Benton Gabbert that his enterprise was primarily responsible for making Dearborn one of the thriving business centers of Platte County. While his reputation among many people is rather based on his prominence as a Hereford cattle breeder, he must be given credit for having given Dearborn its first bank and having used his means and influence to upbuild that town as no other individual has been concerned.

Long and useful lives have been a characteristic of the Gabbert family for generations. No name is better known for its substantial achievements in this section of Northwest Missouri. Benton Gabbert was born in Bartholomew County, Indiana, December 3, 1842. His parents were William and Frances (Hamner) Gabbert, both natives of Kentucky, and living almost the extreme limit of years. William was born October 8, 1817, and died January 19, 1908, when past ninety-one, while she was born September 3, 1819, and died January 14, 1914, when past ninety-four. The four of their eight children still living are: Benton; M. H., of Platte County; Ira T., of Caldwell, Kansas; and Elnora, wife of William Calvert, of Weston.

Both the Gabbert and Hamner families removed from Kentucky to Indiana in 1819, and in that state Mr. Gabbert's parents grew up and were married, December 27, 1838. Not long afterward, James Gabbert, the grandfather, set out for Western Missouri, in the early '40s, to seek cheaper land for his children. The Platte Purchase had only been open to settlement a few years, and it was within the limits of Platte

County that he found what he wanted and bought a tract near what is now Pleasant Ridge. In October, 1844, William and Frances Gabbert packed their possessions in a wagon and started on the long journey from Indiana to Platte County. Arriving there in October, 1844, they began accommodating themselves to the circumstances of a frontier community on a piece of eighty acres, with a small house, and five acres of land cleared for the first crops. The rest of the farm was a dense timber of oak and walnut. In 1848 William Gabbert removed to an adjoining place of fifty acres, which he had bought, including what was then a very substantial two-story house. William Gabbert had the character and industry which would succeed anywhere. He acquired new tracts of land, and frequently loaned out his surplus capital to advantage. He took a peculiar delight in helping his children, and before his death most of his property had been wisely distributed among them. He was influential in local politics, before the war as a democrat, but after that a republican. He and his wife were originally Baptists, but died in the faith of the Christian Church. He was known in his community as a great reader, and especially as a Bible student.

Benton Gabbert was an infant when the family came to Platte County. His youth was spent on the farm, and he attended school with fair regularity until the outbreak of the war. In 1864 he went to Kansas, living there two years, and in the meantime taking unto himself a wife. In 1866 he moved to a farm near Woodruff, and two years later to a farm a mile and a half east of that town. The year 1881 was the date of his coming to his present homestead. This comprises 437 acres, fine land and with fine improvements.

It was in 1883 that Mr. Gabbert introduced to this section several fine specimens of thoroughbred Herefords, and began breeding and building up a herd, which now numbers about two hundred, the largest of the kind in Platte County. He is now regarded as the oldest man in the business in Missouri in point of continuous activity for more than thirty years. His Herefords are famous wherever that strain of cattle is known. It will be recalled that a few years ago at a public auction in Kansas City Frank Rockefeller, a brother of John D., paid $5,500 for a yearling bull from the Gabbert herd. Another branch of his farming enterprise that should be specially mentioned is tobacco culture. Since beginning to grow the plant in 1909, he has increased his fields to about twenty-five acres, and now has two large sheds for the curing and keeping of the tobacco.

In 1888 Mr. Gabbert and W. C. Wells, the well known banker of Platte City, organized the Bank of Dearborn. Dearborn then had a depot and one store. Mr. Gabbert recalls how he drove to the village with a stalk cutter, using it to clear off the stalks from the old corn field which was the site of the proposed bank building. The bank was soon in operation, and in 1889 Mr. Gabbert bought the interests of his associate, and conducted a private bank until 1908, when it was reorganized under a state charter and Mr. Gabbert resigned the presidency. For twenty-five years he has stood ready on every occasion to forward anything of advantage to this locality. He owns much of the real estate of the village, and the principal owner of stock in the canning factory. Politically he is a stanch democrat, was affiliated with the lodge of Odd Fellows.

On March 21, 1865, Mr. Gabbert married Miss Alice Layton. Mrs. Gabbert was born in Platte County, November 27, 1843, a daughter of J. H. and Sarah (Smither) Layton, both natives of Mason County, Kentucky. Her father was born in 1813 and died in February, 1867, and her mother was born January 8, 1818, and died April 24, 1903.

Mrs. Gabbert was one of eight children; of these Mrs. Mary Kirkpatrick lives in Weston; D. B. in Platte County; Mrs. Gabbert; P. S., of Weston; Amney, wife of M. L. Newby, of Lees Summit, Missouri; Elvira, wife of Edgar Hull, of Platte County; Judge J. W., of Platte County. The Layton family came to Platte County in the fall of 1843, by boat as far as Weston. J. H. Layton pre-empted land, became a successful farmer, was one of the prominent early democrats, and held the office of county judge when there was only one such official for the entire county.

Mr. and Mrs. Gabbert are the parents of four children: Eva, wife of E. E. Pumphrey, of Dearborn; William H., of Dearborn; S. J., at home; and L. C., an attorney engaged in practice of law at St. Joseph.

The golden wedding anniversary of Mr. and Mrs. Benton Gabbert was appropriately celebrated in Dearborn last Sunday. The condition of the roads made it impossible for their many friends to reach their country homestead, so, for their convenience Mr. and Mrs. Gabbert received their friends here.

The festivities began with a family dinner at the home of their eldest son, W. H. Gabbert, and this beautiful home was artistically decorated in honor of the event. The colors in the dining room were yellow, the centerpiece being a huge wedding cake, and suspended from the chandelier were golden wedding bells, with a profusion of jonquils in the room. At this table the honor guests, with their brothers and sisters were seated.

In the parlor a table was spread for the children. The decorations were white and yellow, a cluster of yellow roses being the centerpiece on this table, over which was suspended white wedding bells.

In the reception room around a large square table fifteen grandchildren and one great grandchild were seated, the centerpiece being a beautiful shepherdess basket of jonquils. On each table were yellow candles in crystal candelabras and the favors were yellow daisies.

A four course dinner was served, the ices being in the form of wedding bells.

At 2 o'clock the Gabbert family assembled at the Gabbert Hall where during the remainder of the afternoon they were greeted and congratulated by several hundred friends. A string band from St. Joseph furnished music. "Silver Threads Among the Gold" was beautifully sung by Mr. Fred S. Hamm, leader of the orchestra. Mrs. L. C. Gabbert, of St. Joseph, served each guest with the bride's cake, and Misses Mildred and Nadine Gabbert served punch from a beautiful hand painted punch bowl, done in white and yellow, the work of our talented artist. Mrs. C. M. Ward.

Wednesday, March 21, 1865, at 7 o'clock P. M., with Mr. Benjamin Vineyard and Miss Fannie Barbee as attendants, the Rev. Oliver Steele united in marriage Miss Alice Layton and Mr. Benton Gabbert, and we dare say they were no happier on that day than they were in celebrating their fiftieth anniversary.

Mr. and Mrs. Gabbert began their married life by creating a happy home. There have been no thistles in this home vase, but always flowers of love and sympathy and cheerfulness have been there in great profusion. Their genial and lovable nature, their cheering smile and unchanging amiability has attracted friends to them always. Nothing could have proclaimed more surely and emphatically the high regard and affection of our people for Mr. and Mrs. Gabbert than the response to the invitation to the celebration of their fiftieth anniversary. At the request of Mr. and Mrs. Gabbert there were no presents. The only gift was a handsome gold brooch with pearl settings from Mr. Gabbert to his beloved wife.

Among the visitors were Dr. Ira Gabbert, of Caldwell, Kansas, and M. H. Gabbert, of Weston, brothers of Mr. Benton Gabbert; Mrs. M. H. Gabbert, W. B. Calvert and wife, George H. Calvert, Mrs. Mary Farra, Weston; L. C. Gabbert and family, W. P. Hoehen, V. D. Hawkins, J. D. Heffley, Albert S. McGee, Mrs. Margaret Smythe and children, St. Joseph; Mrs. Olive J. Carlton, Kendrick, Idaho; George R. Lewis and wife, of Kansas City.

The following poem was received from Miss Lindsey Barbee, of Denver, Colorado, a niece of Mrs. L. C. Gabbert:

As those who journey 'long a winding way,
Who gain at best the mountain's lofty crest—
And weary, pausing for a moment's rest,
View there the beauty of departing day—
To you, dear aged ones, 'neath sunlight's ray,
'Neath shade, have traveled far. Each joy, each test
Has urged you onward—taught you what is best,
Till now in Life's last season you delay
And silently behold the rainbow clouds
Of yesterday. With eyes uplift, you see
Beyond the winter's cold and snowy shrouds,
Into the endless promise of eternity;
And as the ev'ning shadows fade away,
"The sky is filled with stars, invisible by day."

WILLIAM H. GABBERT. Mention of the name Gabbert in Platte County at once suggests business enterprise as farmers, stock men, bankers and large property owners. As has been related in a sketch of Benton Gabbert on other pages, the thriving little Town of Dearborn owes its chief impetus and upbuilding to that prominent farmer and stock man and banker. While Benton Gabbert is still one of the efficient factors in local affairs about Dearborn, the banking interests of the family are now largely in the hands of his son, William H. Gabbert, who is cashier of the Bank of Dearborn, in the founding of which his father had so important a part.

William H. Gabbert was born near Woodruff in Platte County, Missouri, July 1, 1867. As the history of his family has been recounted on other pages it will be unnecessary to refer to it in this connection. Mr. Gabbert grew up on the farm of his father, was educated in the common schools, and spent three years in the University of Missouri at Columbia, finishing his preparation for a business career by a course in the Gem City Business College at Quincy, Illinois.

In 1890 he entered the Bank of Dearborn as assistant cashier. His father and Mr. Wells had established this as a private bank about two years before, and in 1889 it became the property of Benton Gabbert. William H. Gabbert continued his active connection with the institution as assistant cashier until 1906, when he was chosen cashier, and has remained with the institution since it was incorporated under a state charter a few years ago. Mr. Gabbert for a number of years has been closely associated with his father in the latter's various enterprises as a farmer, a noted Hereford cattle grower and also a tobacco raiser. He and his father also own the controlling interest in the Dearborn Canning Factory, which was organized in 1895 for the chief purpose of packing tomatoes, apples and pumpkins.

Mr. Gabbert has affiliations with the Masonic Order, the Knights of

Pythias and the Independent Order of Odd Fellows, and like his father is a democrat. On February 24, 1898, he married Miss Anna Bone, who was born in Platte County, Missouri, August 22, 1879, a daughter of Rev. D. F. and Ellen (Devlin) Bone. Rev. Mr. Bone was born in Carroll County, Missouri, January 5, 1843, and is still active in the ministry of the Methodist Episcopal Church, his present residence being at St. Joseph. For what he has accomplished and the service he has rendered in this profession his has been a truly remarkable career. He was self educated, having attended school regularly not more than three months in his life. That was at Mt. Vernon, Missouri. Most of his education came from close study and diligent reading in the night hours by the light of a pine knot. He has been an active member of the Missouri Conference of the Methodist Church for forty-four years. During the war between the states he served four years in the Confederate army as chaplain of a regiment under the command of General Price. On one occasion he was taken prisoner and kept under guard by northern soldiers for some time. Ellen Devlin, his wife, was born November 11, 1851, and died in June, 1884. Her father, Rev. J. M. Devlin, was also a minister of the Methodist Episcopal Church South and one of the pioneer circuit riders in Missouri. Rev. Mr. Devlin died at Lawson, Missouri, in 1879 at the age of seventy-eight, and his wife, whose maiden name was Sarah Cable, was born at Wilmington, Delaware, and died at Richmond, Missouri, in March, 1908, at the age of ninety-four. She had a recollection covering almost a century of our national history, and recalled among other incidents of early times the visit of Lafayette to the United States, and was among the school children who greeted him on his triumphal tour, and was one of those upon whose heads he placed his hand in benediction.

Mr. and Mrs. Gabbert are the parents of four children: Nadine, born February 6, 1901; Rosemary, born on Friday the 13th of March, 1903, and by a peculiar coincidence the thirteenth grandchild of Benton Gabbert; George, who was born June 6, 1907; and Lewis, born December 15, 1911.

JOSEPH JACKSON. For more than seventy years the Jackson family have been identified with the growth and development of Nodaway County. One of the first officials of the county was the father of Joseph Jackson, who has himself lived in this county since infancy, gave nearly four years of valiant service to the Union during the Civil war, was afterwards honored with various official positions, and for more than forty-one years has been prominent as a banker, being now president of the First National Bank of Maryville.

Joseph Jackson was born at Smithfield in Jefferson County, Ohio, September 20, 1842. His parents were John and Harriett (Dunn) Jackson. His father was born in Jefferson County, Ohio, October 10, 1810, and was a son of John and Rachael (Orr) Jackson. Harriet Dunn was born in Jefferson County December 19, 1819. From the old home in Eastern Ohio John Jackson brought his family out to Northwest Missouri, and first located at Newmarket in Platte County, while in October, 1843, they moved to Nodaway County, locating near Maryville, where John Jackson was one of the real pioneers and soon showed himself a leader in community affairs. The chief scope of his business activity was as a farmer, and he lived a life of usefulness and honor until his death on January 27, 1875, on his farm a mile and a half north of Maryville, the place he had settled in 1843. The history of Nodaway County will always preserve his name from the fact that he was the first county treasurer, and was elected three times to that office and served altogether six years. He was a member of the Presbyterian Church and in politics a democrat. John and Harriett Jackson were married in 1840, and she was a daughter of Joseph and Sarah (Colvin) Dunn, both natives of Pennsylvania. Mrs. Jackson died July 9, 1892, at the age of seventy-three. When the family came to Northwest Missouri they brought two children, Sarah and Joseph, and in Nodaway County ten others were born. Four of the children died in infancy, and the eight reared to maturity were: Sarah Holt, Joseph Jackson, Louise Trueblood, Rachel Bentley, Benton Jackson, Sophrona Hawkins, Ada Manuel and Oliver Jackson. Sophrona and Oliver died in 1904.

Joseph Jackson grew up in Nodaway County from the time he was a year old, has many interesting recollections of this country when it was almost a wilderness, and until the age of eighteen lived just north of Maryville, and attended school in town during the winter and worked on the farm in the summer. In October, 1861, during the first year of the war, he enlisted for service in the state in Kimbles Regiment of the Union army for six months, and afterwards enlisted in the Thirty-sixth Missouri Militia, with which he served a year and a half, and finally in the Twelfth Missouri Cavalry. He was orderly sergeant in Company F. His chief service outside of the state was with the Twelfth Missouri Cavalry, in which he enlisted on October 3, 1863. The regiment was a part of General Wilson's Cavalry, and went South and joined the army of General Thomas at Gravel Springs, Alabama. This was soon after the fall of Atlanta, when General Thomas was in pursuit of Hood's army back through Tennessee. From that time Mr. Jackson was in active service and saw a great deal of hard campaigning. The two great battles in which his regiment participated were those at Franklin, on November 30, 1864, and at Nashville, on December 15, 16 and 17, 1864. During the third day's fighting at Nashville, as the Confederate army was falling back, he was shot through the right arm and the right leg, and his leg was amputated just above the ankle. He was in a hospital at Franklin until January 20, 1865, and at Nashville until April 4, 1865. He was mustered out on July 1, 1865, and returned home.

On September 1, 1865, Mr. Jackson was appointed county clerk of Nodaway County, Dr. G. B. Ford having resigned in his favor, and for this help in a time of need Mr. Jackson has always cherished a high regard for that estimable citizen. He was elected to the office in the fall of 1865 at a special election, and thereafter was retained at his post year after year until he had completed 13½ years of efficient service as county clerk, finally going out of office on January 1, 1879.

Mr. Jackson has been more or less actively identified with banking at Maryville for forty years. In July, 1873, he and John C. Terhune bought out H. C. French, of the banking firm of Fisher & French, and reorganized as Fisher, Jackson & Company. The bank at that time stood on Third Street where the Democrat Forum office is now located. In 1874 the site now occupied by the First National Bank of Maryville was secured and the firm erected the building there. In 1877 H. C. Fisher sold his interest to Messrs. Terhune and Jackson, and the bank was then reorganized as the Farmers Bank. In 1884 another reorganization occurred, and the bank became the First National Bank of Maryville, with a capital of $100,000. The first directors and officers were: Joseph Jackson, president; John C. Terhune, cashier; and William Per-

poration. As a banker and business man Mr. Jackson has won and merits the thorough confidence and respect of his fellow citizens, and by his counsel and practical assistance has done much to help men struggling to get a firm foothold on the path to success.

Mr. Jackson was married April 29, 1866, at the home of Washington Downing, three miles east of Hopkins, to Amanda Broyles. She was born in Andrew County, Missouri, December 9, 1847, the daughter of William W. and Sarah Broyles. Both her parents were natives of Tennessee and came to Northwest Missouri in 1845. After 1867 Mr. and Mrs. Jackson lived for twenty-four years on the site now occupied by the Methodist Episcopal Church in Maryville, and in the meantime had bought five acres in Southwest Maryville and in 1891 moved to the home which has since been the center of family associations and hospitality. Mrs. Jackson died in January, 1912. She was the mother of six children, one of whom died in infancy, the others being: Lola C., wife of J. F. Colby; Laura, now Mrs. Miles Saunders; Mary, wife of Paul Ream; Nellie, Mrs. George E. Alexander; and Joseph, Jr., who is cashier of the First National Bank of Maryville. In politics Mr. Jackson is a republican, and since August, 1880, has been a member of the Presbyterian Church of Maryville.

ALBERT P. FRY. This family name is one of the most familiar in Clinton County, it is associated with many pioneer memories and activities, and has been closely associated with farming, stock raising and community affairs in that section of Northwest Missouri for more than three-quarters of a century.

The family was established here by Solomon Fry, one of the most remarkable of the pioneers of Clinton County. He came to the county in 1838, and made his first entries of Government land soon after the Platte Purchase was acquired. He has especial distinction in the history of both Clay and Clinton counties, since he built the first jail at Liberty and also the first at Plattsburg. He acquired by entry and purchase about three thousand acres of land in Clinton County, and for a number of years was one of the largest land holders and planters in that section. Solomon Fry was born November 24, 1794, in Virginia, and came of an old Virginia family. His father was Isaac Fry, born June 14, 1765, a son of Benjamin Fry, also a native of Virginia, and the first settlers were of German stock. Solomon Fry was reared in Virginia and in Kentucky, his family having located in the latter state in Shelby County when Solomon was three years of age. At the age of twenty he followed the line of frontier advance as far as Clay County, Missouri. Solomon Fry married Susie Snapp, who was born at Old Vincennes, Indiana, and came of one of the French families that comprised the original colony about Vincennes. Her father was Abram Snapp. The children of Solomon Fry and wife were: Helen; Abram S., who died at the age of eighty-five; Harriet Hockaday; Lewis S., who died at the age of seventy-five; Anna, who married Speed Thurman; India, who married Rev. Thomas Todd; Emanuel Shelby. Solomon Fry died when eighty-two years of age. He was a member of the Baptist Church. A man of rugged physique though not large in build, he was as noted as a hunter as farmer and land owner, and in the early days of Northwest Missouri killed many deer and other wild game. Solomon Fry acquired his land

many of the old time practices and genial characteristics still survive
into this later generation.

The present proprietor of the old homestead and one of the most
active and successful farmers and stock men of Clinton County is Albert
P. Fry, a grandson of the pioneer Solomon. Albert P. Fry owns 600
acres in two farms located in Clinton Township, and is one of the best
managed and equipped estates in the county. His home is located seven
miles south of Plattsburg. Much of his enterprise is directed to the
raising of stock, and he keeps about one hundred and fifty head of cattle
and two hundred hogs, besides a number of horses and mules.

Albert P. Fry was born on the old homestead May 30, 1867. His
father was Abram S. Fry, who was born in Clay County, Missouri, in
1828 and died in 1913 at the advanced age of eighty-five. Abram Fry
married for his first wife Anna Bland, sister of Dr. Bland, another
Clinton County pioneer. The child of that marriage was William, who
died in infancy. For his second wife he married Alice Lindsy, and they
had one child, Perry H., who was a druggist in Plattsburg for a number of years and died in 1898. Abram Fry later married Emma Simpson, who was born in Kentucky. The children of this marriage were:
Cora, wife of J. Bland; Emma, wife of W. R. Wright; Albert P.; Mary
H., wife of O. A. Adams, of Smithville, Missouri. Albert P. Fry's
mother died at the age of forty-six. She was a member of the Presbyterian Church. Abram Fry was four times married, and his last wife
was Margaret Trimble and is still living at Plattsburg. He was one of
the well known citizens of Clinton County, a successful business man,
and left an honored name. Politically he was a democrat.

Albert P. Fry was reared on the old farm, was educated in the public
schools, and after reaching manhood began life as a farmer on 105
acres of land, representing a portion of the old homestead. Since then
he has acquired land to the total of 600 acres, and now owns the old
homestead. On January 16, 1890, Mr. Fry married Bertha Ann Froman, a daughter of Abram and Eleanor Froman. Mrs. Fry was one of
a family of children named as follows: Ida Brown; Lillian, who lives
in Kansas City; Mrs. Fry; Rose, of Kansas City; and Perry, who lives
in DeKalb County, near Cameron. Mrs. Fry's father is a republican.

Mr. and Mrs. Fry have two children: Alice, wife of P. C. Breckenridge of Turney, Missouri; and Eleanor, now a student in Randolph
College, Virginia. Mr. Fry has a delightful home, a residence of ten
rooms, well furnished and in modern style, surrounded by large shade
trees and a fine orchard. The farm equipment also comprises well built
barns and there is no more attractive place in Clinton Township. Mr.
Fry is affiliated with the Masonic order, a member of the Knight
Templar Commandery No. 162 at Plattsburg, and of the Moila Temple
of the Mystic Shrine, of St. Joseph.

FRANK DUNCAN. The conclusion of the negotiations resulting in the
Platte Purchase and the advent of the Duncan family to this section of
Western Missouri occurred in the same year. While a number of
"squatters" had come into this district in preceding years, the Duncans
may properly claim credit as among the very first prominent pioneers.
A residence of more than three quarters of a century has been accompanied by the hard working diligence and the capable citizenship which
make the presence of any family a useful factor in the community. The
present presiding judge of the County Court of Platte County is Frank
Duncan, whose grandfather in the early days also sat as a member of
the County Court, and was otherwise distinguished as a justice of the
peace and for two terms a member of one of the early state legislatures.

Frank Duncan is one of the prominent farmers in the western part of Platte County, and was born a mile south of his present residence near Dearborn on September 23, 1860. His grandfather, Edward P. Duncan, a native of Virginia, came out to Platte County with his family in 1838, making the long journey overland with wagon and team. He located on land near the present town of Dearborn, and lived there until his death. Richard Frederick Duncan, father of Judge Duncan, was born in Culpeper County, Virginia, November 14, 1830, and was a boy of about eight years when brought to Western Missouri. He grew up in the then existing, wilderness conditions of Platte County, and after his marriage began farming on 160 acres lying a mile south of Judge Duncan's home. He was a man of considerable business ability, thrifty and energetic, accumulated much property, and at the time of his death in 1907 was owner of 600 acres. He possessed a characteristic fondness with many southern gentlemen of the time for fine horses, and the older residents many of them can identify his personality most distinctly in association with the fine team which he always drove about the country. While not a member of any church he assisted in the building of several local places of worship, and was kindly neighbor and in every way a model citizen. Politically he was a democrat. Richard Frederick Duncan married Sarah Ann St. John, who was born in Tennessee November 14, 1838, and is now living at a good old age in St. Joseph, Missouri. She was a small child when the St. John family emigrated to Clay County, Missouri. She became the mother of nine children, named as follows: Frank; A. B., of St. Joseph; William, deceased; Mrs. Etta Carson, of St. Joseph; R. E., of Platte County; B. W., of Sedalia, this state; C. B., of Edgerton Junction, Missouri; J. R., also of Edgerton Junction; and Mrs. W. B. Smith, of Colorado Springs.

Judge Frank Duncan was reared on a farm, attended the common schools, and finished his education by two years in William Jewell College at Liberty. His early life was on a farm, and he had a thorough training in agricultural methods. In 1888 he removed to St. Joseph and for five years was in the livery business in that city. On October 15, 1893, he took possession of his present fine homestead near Dearborn. His farm contains 153 acres, and all its building improvements have been the result of Judge Duncan's management since he took possession. A capable farmer, he has always stood high in the esteem of his fellow citizens, and this brought about his election in 1911 as a county judge from the western district of Platte County. In November, 1914, he was reelected, this time as presiding judge of the County Court. Politically he is a democrat.

Judge Duncan was married February 9, 1889, to Margaret H. Meloan, who was born at Paynesville, in Pike County, Missouri, December 14, 1860. Her father, Joseph Meloan, was born at Mount Sterling, Kentucky, in 1819 and died in 1873. The maiden name of her mother was Margaret Patton, who was born at Cynthiana in Harrison County, Kentucky, in November, 1833, and died in 1911, having been brought by her parents to Pike County, Missouri, when five years of age. Mr. and Mrs. Duncan are the parents of three children: Richard M., of St. Joseph; Margaret Helen and Etta Wells, both at home.

ADOLPH P. DOPPLER. There is no town in Northwest Missouri that has more intimate and interesting relations with early commercial history along the Missouri River than Weston. A firm that has been identified with commercial undertakings there since Weston was a metropolis and Kansas City was an insignificant village is that of Doppler. Adolph

P. Doppler is the second generation in Weston, and has himself been prominent in mercantile circles for thirty years or more.

Adolph P. Doppler was born at Weston, Missouri, January 6, 1857. His father was the late George M. Doppler, who was born in Wacheheim, Germany, October 11, 1830, and died July 20, 1900. In early manhood he came to the United States, and in 1854 was married at St. Louis to Salome Brandenburg, who was born in the same part of Germany and came to the United States on the same ship with her future husband. From St. Louis they came out to the Western Missouri frontier, locating at Weston, where George Doppler, being a tailor by trade, opened a shop. He continued working at his trade until his savings amounted to $500, and they were then invested in a small stock of dry goods. He used half of a small room for his stock, and displayed this merchandise to the public in the spring of 1865. From that humble beginning as a merchant his enterprise steadily grew until his was the largest dry goods and grocery house in Weston, drawing trade from a country miles around. In 1900 he retired, turning over his business to his two sons, Phillip and Frank, and died during the same year. His wife passed away in February, 1901, at the age of seventy. There were seven children: Adolph P.; Frank, deceased; Mrs. Emma Bacote of California; George of St. Joseph; Phillip of Weston; Laura, wife of C. W. Bowen, of Brunswick, Missouri; and Nellie, wife of John Brill of Weston. The father of these children had affiliations with the Masonic Order, the I. O. O. F. and the German Benevolent Association, and was one of the founders and charter members of the German Methodist Episcopal Church at Weston.

In his native town of Weston Adolph P. Doppler grew to manhood, attended the local schools about four months in each year until twelve years of age, and then entered upon his practical business career in his father's store, where he remained ten years. From the spring of 1879 until October, 1883, Mr. Doppler was cashier in the office of the United States Internal Revenue Collector at Kansas City. He then returned to Weston, and bought out the Chicago Lumber Company. In 1894 he bought the grocery business formerly conducted by T. A. Gilbert, and continued both enterprises until 1896. The lumber business was then sold, and his time has since been devoted to the grocery trade, with a success proportionate to the increasing years. In 1910 Mr. Doppler bought the site of his present business house, and erected a modern store 25x80 feet, a two-story building of brick. This store is built on the solid rock. Its thoroughness of construction is such that the building may probably stand for generations as a landmark in Weston. On a concrete base 36 inches wide was laid the foundation of rock, giving a basement 7 feet in clear, with a 10-inch solid concrete floor. On top of that was erected the two-story brick building, the second floor being a seven room modern home. The basement he uses as an adjunct to his store for the keeping of vegetables and general storage. The building is fitted with a private water works, with hot and cold pressure tanks in the basement. While this is now one of the substantial business structures of the Weston commercial district, the site is of considerable interest as one of the landmarks of Weston. The old building torn down by Mr. Doppler preparatory to the erection of the present structure was one owned by an uncle of Buffalo Bill, and in that store the noted Buffalo Bill worked for a time as a clerk. Even Mr. Doppler can recall a time in the early days of Weston when the old counter in this building had a pile of gold dust on it that would fill a peck measure. In those days Weston was one of the first points of civilization between

the Missouri River and the extreme western gold fields, and much of the currency of financial circulation was the unminted gold dust.

As a merchant Mr. Doppler is an unqualified success and carries a splendid stock of groceries and queensware. He has also served the community as treasurer of the school board thirteen years. Fraternally he is affiliated with the Masonic order and the Independent Order of Odd Fellows, and he and his wife are Methodists. In April, 1879, Mr. Doppler married Anna Ilkenhaus, who was born at Weston, a daughter of Emanuel Ilkenhaus, who was born in Germany and was an old time jeweler in Weston. Mr. and Mrs. Doppler have two children: Adella, wife of R. D. How, of Weston; and Adolph, living at home.

.MORRIS ADELBERT REED. With a conspicuous place in the legal profession of Northwest Missouri, and prominent both by his professional attainments and his services in public affairs, Morris A. Reed has been practicing as a member of the St. Joseph bar for the past forty-five years, and is one of the oldest attorneys in this quarter of the state. As a lieutenant he made a brilliant record on the Union side during the Civil war, and was admitted to the bar in New York State, a few years after the war closed.

Morris Adelbert Reed was born at Watertown, New York, in 1838, a son of Lewis and Angeline (Spinning) Reed. Through his father's mother Mr. Reed is a descendant from the Ball family, who saw conspicuous service in the Revolutionary war. Mr. Reed was educated at the Jefferson County Institute in Watertown, New York, and in the Belleville Academy at Belleville, New York, graduating from the latter in 1861. After a year at home, he enlisted in September, 1862, in Company A of the Tenth New York Heavy Artillery, receiving his commission as second lieutenant and was afterward promoted to first lieutenant. Soon afterwards came his appointment on the staff of General Piper, who at that time was division commander in the defences of Washington, as acting assistant inspector general of said division. During the last year of the war he served in the Shenandoah Valley, under General Sheridan and under General Grant at the siege of Petersburg. With a record as a faithful and efficient soldier, Lieutenant Reed returned to his old home town of Watertown, studied law in the office of Brown & Beach, and on his admission to the bar in 1867 located at St. Joseph, Missouri, where forty-five years of his active professional work and his residence have been.

Mr. Reed up to 1888 was associated in partnership with Colonel John Doniphan, under the firm name of Doniphan & Reed. That was one of the foremost law firms in St. Joseph, during its existence. After 1888 Mr. Reed became associated with Mr. W. K. James, under the firm name of Reed & James. That firm, which lasted until 1898, was also one of special ability and with a large clientage among the most important interests. Mr. James in 1898 was elected circuit judge, and since that time Mr. Reed has devoted himself alone to the practice of law. At the present time all his work is office counsel practice, and his time is taken up by several large private interests, among which may be mentioned the Burnes National Bank of St. Joseph.

In 1873 Mr. Reed was appointed register in bankruptcy, which position he held until the repeal of the Bankruptcy Act. In 1882 he entered politics on the republican ticket as candidate for Congress against Colonel James Burnes, and gave the latter the closest race he had through his congressional career. Mayor Englehart in 1888 appointed Mr. Reed city counselor of St. Joseph, and his service in that capacity lasted two years. In January, 1892, Mr. Reed was appointed general attorney for the St. Joseph and Grand Island Railway Company, and represented that corporation until 1904.

During the recent general election in 1912, Mr. Reed was republican candidate for Congress in his district. His social relations are with the Sons of the American Revolution, to which his membership was granted by his connection with Revolutionary sires already mentioned. His church is the Christ Episcopal church of St. Joseph.

On October 15, 1872, Mr. Reed married Miss Margie R. Kimball, a daughter of Lotus Kimball, a banker of Bath, Maine, and representing one of the old families of shipbuilders in Bath during the period when sailing ships were much in vogue. Mrs. Reed died July 1, 1904, leaving two children. Clara A., wife of Owen B. Knight of St. Joseph, and Morris H. Reed, who with his brother-in-law, comprised the firm of Knight-Reed Millinery Company at St. Joseph. Mr. Reed and family reside at 547 North Sixth street, and' his offices are at 414½ Francis Street.

JAMES W. COX. One of Platte County's oldest institutions, and which stands second to none as to reputation for solidity and straightforward dealing, is the Railey & Brother Banking Company, at Weston. Much of the prestige held by this institution may be credited to the able and energetic activities of its vice president, James W. Cox, a resident of Weston since 1891, from which time to the present he has been connected with various prominent enterprises, all connected with the growing financial and industrial interests of the town.

Mr. Cox was born in Platte County, Missouri, February 5, 1860, and is a son of W. G. and Sallie A. (Stone) Cox. His father was born at Georgetown, Kentucky, in November, 1820, and was there married, the mother having been born at Paris, Bourbon County, Kentucky, in June, 1837. In 1855 they left their southern home and came to Platte County, Missouri, settling seven miles north of Weston, bringing with them four negro slaves and a small outfit of house furnishings. While W. G. Cox began his life in this state in a modest way, through inherent ability, enterprise and perseverance he became one of his community's substantial men, and through his natural capacity as a trader succeeded in the accumulation of 1,500 acres of land. Both he and Mrs. Cox were faithful members of the Baptist Church, in the belief of which the father died in 1877. The mother, who still survives him, makes her home at Kansas City, Missouri. They were the parents of eight children, of whom six are living, namely: D. K., a resident of Platte County, Missouri; James W., of this review; Lizzie J., who is the wife of Charles Markle, of Galveston, Texas; Mattie, who is the wife of D. G. Main, of Kansas City, Missouri; Edwin G., of Craig, Missouri; and Minnie, the wife of S. B. Hall, of Colorado.

James W. Cox was reared on his father's farm, and after attending the country schools entered William Jewell College, at Liberty, Missouri, which he attended during 1878 and 1879. During the years 1880, 1881 and 1882 he was a student at the State University, Columbia, then returning home to take charge of the farm, in order that his mother might move to Plattsburg that the younger children might be given better educational advantages. Mr. Cox continued to operate the homestead until 1887, when he moved to a property of his own, east of Weston, and remained there until 1891. In that year he became identified with the business interests of Weston, buying the two lumber yards here and consolidating them, and remained at the head of that industry until February, 1911, when he sold out to the Lambert Lumber Company.

In the meantime, in 1906, Mr. Cox had become vice president of Railey & Brother Banking Company, a business to which he has given his best energies since 1907. This bank was founded in 1867 by J. M. and E. W. Railey, the latter being president. In 1897 the bank was incorporated and the name was changed to Railey & Brother Banking Company, a style which it has since retained. In the capacity of vice president of this institution Mr. Cox has shown himself a man of marked financial capacity, shrewd, far-seeing and of excellent judgment. His own well-known integrity has done much to inspire confidence in the depositors, without which no monetary enterprise may survive. Mr. Cox is a democrat, but has confined his activities in politics to casting his vote for good men and measures. He is a Knight Templar Mason and has been treasurer of his lodge for twelve years, and he and Mrs. Cox are members of the Baptist Church and interested actively in its work.

Mr. Cox was married September 3, 1885, to Miss Lizzie Noble, who was born at Weston, Missouri, a daughter of W. G. Noble, a native of Boone County, Missouri, and one of the early merchants of Weston, where he died in 1904. Two children have been born to Mr. and Mrs. Cox: Forrestine, who is the wife of J. S. Sitlington, of Kansas City, Missouri; and Neva, the wife of Ed Thorn, of Weston, Missouri.

M. H. GABBERT. One of the oldest native sons of Platte County is M. H. Gabbert, whose life of nearly seventy years has been spent in this county, and whose boyhood recollections associate themselves with the heavy forests and the wilderness surroundings of pioneer times. As a farmer, like other members of the family, his career has been one of substantial and prosperous industry, and in a quiet way he has been an effective influence for the advancement of the community.

M. H. Gabbert was born in Weston Township of Platte County, April 30, 1846. His father, William Gabbert, was born in Kentucky, October 8, 1817, and died January 19, 1908, while his wife, whose maiden name was Frances Hamner, was born in the same state, September 3, 1819, and died January 14, 1914. Long lives have been characteristic of the Gabbert family, and it will be seen that both parents were more than ninety years of age when summoned by death. Of eight children four are still living: Benton, of Platte County; M. H.; Ira T., of Caldwell, Kansas; and Elnora, wife of William Calvert, of Weston. The Gabbert and Hamner families removed from Kentucky to Bartholomew County, Indiana, in 1819, and there William Gabbert and Frances Hamner grew up in the same neighborhood and were married December 27, 1838. That section of Indiana was then well settled and lands were increasing in value on account of the numerous population they had to support. In consequence the Gabbert family during the early '40s began planning for a removal to the western frontier. Early in the '40s the grandfather of M. H. Gabbert set out on a prospecting tour to examine the lands in the new Platte Purchase of Missouri. He was accompanied by his oldest son, and in Platte County, near what is now known as Pleasant Ridge, bought a good sized tract of land, sufficient to give each of his sons eighty acres. Then in 1844 was accomplished the general removal of the family from Indiana to Missouri. The household goods and the children and women rode in wagons, and after many days of journeying they reached Platte County in October, 1844. William Gabbert's eighty acres had a small house and five acres were all cleared for cultivation, but the rest was in the midst of the heavy walnut and oak timber. In 1848 he removed to an adjoining place of fifty acres, improved with a substantial two-story frame house. He was one of the men of exceptional ability during the pioneer times of Platte County, and accumulated both land and money, loaning the latter to advantage among his neighbors. One of the chief incentives to him in his work was to provide liberally for his children, in whom he always took a great interest, and much of his estate was distributed among them before his death. He and his wife in early life were Baptists, but later both joined the Christian Church. William Gabbert was well versed in Bible literature. Politically he was identified with the republican party.

M. H. Gabbert grew up on the old homestead in Weston Township, attended country schools until they were suspended on account of the war, and then applied himself to the practical duties of the home farm. He lived at home until his marriage on March 25, 1868, to Henrietta Cox. Mrs. Gabbert was born in Platte County April 21, 1849, a daughter of Jacob and Susan (Pettigrew) Cox. To the marriage of Mr. and Mrs. Gabbert have been born five children: Nannie, wife of James Risk, of Platte County; Jessie, wife of A. E. McGlashan, of Trinidad, Colorado; Bessie L., wife of B. A. Gow, of Trinidad, Colorado; Jakie, wife of G. M. Hamm, of Waterloo, Iowa; and Elnora, wife of G. B. Park, of Platte City, Missouri.

Mr. Gabbert has worked out his destiny on prosperous proportions as a farmer, and has occupied his present fine farm near Weston since 1884. His place of 240 acres is well known in the community for its capable management, and its crops of grain, tobacco and stock. The Gabbert home is one of the attractive places in that community. Mr. Gabbert is affiliated with the Independent Order of Odd Fellows at Weston, and he and his family are Baptists. Politically his support is given to the republican party.

EDWIN E. PUMPHREY. Any mention of pioneer families in Platte County must include reference to the Pumphreys, who have lived here usefully and actively practically since the Platte Purchase was opened for settlement. Edwin E. Pumphrey is a prosperous citizen of Dearborn, where he is cashier of the Bank of Wallace, was identified with the Bank of Dearborn from its organization until a few years ago, and in his earlier life was a teacher.

Edwin E. Pumphrey was born in Green Township of Platte County, Missouri, February 5, 1854, and his home has been within three miles of his birthplace all his life. His grandparents, Elijah and Olive (Wilson) Pumphrey, came from Kentucky to Platte County in the very early days, making the journey by wagon and locating near the Town of Dearborn. There Elijah Pumphrey pre-empted a tract of land and subsequently bought more. His death occurred in Platte County in 1875. William J. Pumphrey, father of the banker, was born in Kentucky and died near Camden Point, Missouri, in May, 1865, at the age of forty-five. He grew up on the old Platte County homestead, having been brought to Missouri when a boy, and after his marriage located on the farm where Edwin E. was born, and subsequently removed to another place six miles south, where his death occurred. He was a raiser of stock and also a hemp grower. In the early days the family were all democrats and Southern sympathizers, and members of the Baptist Church. William J. Pumphrey married Sarah A. (Malotte) Smith.

Mr. Pumphrey was engaged in teaching, and had schools both in Platte and Buchanan counties. Many of his former pupils are now men and women in this section of Missouri with families of their own. In 1888, at the organization of the Bank of Dearborn by Benton Gabbert and W. C. Wells, Mr. Pumphrey became identified with the institution as cashier. He continued to hold that office and to a large degree handled the business until 1906. Failing health then compelled him to resign, and he spent several years in outdoor life and in recuperating. In 1910 Mr. Pumphrey took the position of cashier in the Bank of Wallace and has since handled its affairs.

Mr. Pumphrey has been a leader in public affairs, and is one of the stanch democrats of Platte County. He represented this county in the Forty-third and Forty-fourth general assemblies, and during the second term was chairman of the Committee on Banks and Banking and a member of the House Appropriation Committee and other committees. He became a member of the town board of Dearborn when it was first organized, and served twelve years on the school board. Fraternally he is affiliated with the Masonic order, including the Mystic Shrine at St. Joseph. His wife is a member of the Christian Church.

On December 28, 1887, Mr. Pumphrey married Eva Gabbert, daughter of Benton Gabbert, farmer, stockman and banker of Dearborn, whose prominent career is sketched on other pages. Mr. and Mrs. Pumphrey have had seven children: Max M., of Dearborn; Alice, deceased; Edwin G., Margaret, Benton, Smith and Eva Lucile, all at home.

JAMES WATSON. In the death of James Watson at Dearborn, Missouri, October 7, 1906, Platte County was bereaved of a citizen it could ill afford to lose. Mr. Watson was a valuable worker wherever his sphere of duty lay, and for a number of years was the able director and publisher of one of the influential newspapers of Northwest Missouri.

Born at Paris, Bourbon County, Kentucky, October 26, 1863, he was not quite forty-three years old when death summoned him. His parents were Dr. J. M. and Elizabeth (Taylor) Watson, both of Bourbon County, whence they moved to Missouri, spending 1867-68 in Halleck, then lived some years in Kansas City, and located at Dearborn in 1881. James Watson died just twenty-five years to the day from the arrival of the family in Dearborn. Doctor Watson was a well educated gentleman and capable physician, and practiced until his death in November, 1909, at the age of seventy-eight. He was a man of literary tastes, and was a student all his life.

James Watson received most of his education in the public schools of Kansas City, and also spent a year in the University of Missouri. His first regular position was as station agent for the Great Western at Faucett, Missouri, to which he was appointed in 1886, but was soon transferred to Dearborn. On November 1, 1896, he bought the Dearborn Democrat, and continued it as editor and publisher until his death, with the exception of four years spent as chief clerk in the insurance department in the state capitol during the administration of Governor Dockery. On returning to Dearborn he bought back the Democrat from the party he had previously sold to. The late Mr. Watson was a vigorous democrat in politics, belonged to the Christian Church, and was a member of the Independent Order of Odd Fellows.

January 26, 1892, he married Miss Gene Stagner, of an old and prominent Platte County and Kentucky family. She was born at Dearborn, Missouri, February 1, 1865. Her father, Andrew J. Stagner, was born in Madison County, Kentucky, December 11, 1830, and died January 29, 1874. He was a son of Thomas J. and Nancy (Maupin) Stagner. Thomas J., who was a son of James Stagner, was born in Kentucky June 13, 1792, while his wife, who was a daughter of Thomas Maupin, a soldier of the Revolution, was born December 2, 1803. Thomas J. Stagner was a pioneer in Kentucky. He followed the business of cattle drover, buying stock and driving it to the southern markets. He died in 1860 possessed of an estate of $100,000, consisting of lands, stocks and slaves. While Madison County, Kentucky, was his birthplace, his parents came out of North Carolina and settled near old Boonesboro.

Andrew J. Stagner was a boy when his parents located in Missouri, and in 1851, when about grown, was led in a spirit of adventure to make a visit to California, where he had many experiences, but returned in 1858 to Platte County and bought the land on which the Town of Dearborn now stands. After his death his wife platted and sold much of it in town lots. A. J. Stagner married Cynthia A. Davidson, who was born in Lewis County, Kentucky, May 15, 1832, and died April 4, 1910. She was the mother of five children: Thomas J., of Artesia, New Mexico; Mrs. James Watson; Mary E., wife of E. L. Wells, of St. Joseph; Andrew N., of Dearborn; and Miss Julia A., of Dearborn. She was the daughter of Joseph and Nancy Davidson of Lewis County, Kentucky, who emigrated to Platte County in 1840, by river as far as Liberty, from which point a wagon conveyed him and his possessions to Platte County. Here he pre-empted 320 acres in timber.

The late James Watson had a brother and sister, Dr. Bruce Watson being a physician at Perry, Oklahoma, and Lena, the wife of A. C. Baker, of Des Moines, Iowa.

Mr. and Mrs. Watson were the parents of just one child, John M., who was born December 13, 1893. He was married June 7, 1911, to Mabel June Irene Spratt, who was born in Platte County August 28, 1895, a daughter of W. C. and Lewellyn (Bryan) Spratt, her father a druggist at Dearborn. John M. Watson and wife have one child, Maurine, born December 22, 1912.

Since the death of Mr. Watson, Mrs. Watson, with the help of her son, has continued the publication of the Dearborn Democrat, and has kept it up to the standard set by its former proprietor, as one of the best and cleanest country papers in this quarter of the state. Mrs. Watson is a good business woman, and also supervises her farm near Dearborn.

ISAIAH TWADELL. To enter somewhat into the details of the life of Isaiah Twadell is to describe a career which illustrates the successful farming enterprise of Northwest Missouri and a typical character among the successful men of this region. . Years of residence, from before the war, experience of soldiering and hardship and roughing it on the west plains, the breaking up and conquest of wild lands, the growing scope of prosperity, and useful and helpful relations with a community—such are some of the more important incidents in the career of this well known citizen of the country adjoining Mount Moriah in Harrison County, with home on Rural Free Delivery Route No. 2 out of Ridgeway.

The Twadell family has lived in this section of Missouri since 1851. when Amos Twadell, the father of Isaiah, settled west of Goshen and entered 120 acres, developed it as a farm, and died when almost eighty-seven years of age. Amos Twadell was a brick and stone mason by trade, having learned it in Jennings County, Indiana, but most of his years were spent in the quiet and effective duties of farm and agriculture.

Amos Twadell was born just below Madison, Indiana, on the Ohio River, October 4. 1818. His father was James Twadell, who at the age of one year was brought from Ireland in 1775 by his father Daniel, who settled in Genesee County, New York. James moved from New York to the West and became one of the pioneers in Switzerland County, Indiana, and was a farmer there and in Jennings County, where he and his wife died. James Twadell married Annie Risley, of New Hampshire. Their children were: Hiram; Eber; Chauncey; Amos; Julia, who married Gideon Underwood and died in Jennings County; Frances, who married Rufus Carpenter and died in Dickinson County, Kansas; and Martha, who married David Johnson and died at Red Bluffs, California. James Twadell was a soldier in the War of 1812 in the army of General Dearborn, and it is believed that Daniel, his father, was a Revolutionary patriot.

Amos Twadell grew up in Southern Indiana and had an education that was almost altogether practical, with a minimum of reading, writing and arithmetic. In 1832 his parents moved to Jennings County, and their home was on Sand Creek, eleven miles from Vernon, the county seat. Amos Twadell, though without special training, had a fine memory, and the events of his life and times were woven into his ready recollection. It was by team and wagon that he came to Missouri in 1851, arriving at Cainsville May 9, 1851, and entered land in Mercer County the same year. He was a republican, but held no office except school director, and was a director of his home school for twenty-four years. During the war he was in the militia two years, in Major King's regiment and Captain Alley's company. He was out one summer with his company, but otherwise went to duty only when called. A Methodist, he assisted in building the Goshen Church, and in later times took considerable part in Sunday school activities.

Isaiah Twadell was about four years of age when brought to Missouri. He was born in Jennings County, Indiana, February 15, 1847. His education came from the schools of Mercer County. Youth kept him out of the ranks of soldiers in the first part of the war, but during the winter of 1864-65 he was accepted in Company D of the Fifty-first Missouri Infantry, under Capt. George W. Herrick and Colonel Moore. An older brother was serving in Company F of the Thirty-fifth Regiment. He was kept in St. Joseph until May, and then ordered with his company to Pilot Knob, and did guard duty at the fort and along the Iron Mountain Railway and other property. He returned to St. Louis for muster out on August 31, 1865, and the only enemy he saw were the rebels and bushwhackers captured by his command and turned into the stockade at Pilot Knob.

Then followed several years of comparative quiet and monotony, passed on the farm in Mercer County. When past his majority Mr. Twadell and his brother joined a party for the West. They started on foot without means, and at Omaha joined an outfit engaged in construction work along the Union Pacific Railroad. The brothers worked three months on this road west of Cheyenne and Laramie, spent the fall chopping wood on Elk Mountain, and in the winter returned to Cheyenne, and a few weeks later reached Pine Bluff, Colorado. There they worked on a ranch, cutting and hauling wood to the railroad, and the following summer and fall were spent employed in Government contract work about Julesburg. The Government was engaged in building, during the summer of 1869, Fort Sedgewick, and when that was finished the brothers drove a six-mule and a four-mule team back to Fort Leavenworth, reaching home in the spring of 1870.

Having returned to civilization, Mr. Twadell was again content with the plain life of farmer in Mercer County until the spring of 1873, when he once more went out on the plains, to Nevada, and remained in the West for another year. For much of the time he was located at White Pines, engaged in chopping and hauling cordwood and other duties about a mining camp. Returning to Missouri, he resumed his station on the farm in 1874, and remained near Goshen until he came to Harrison County in 1900. He bought the old Sam Ross farm, near Mount Moriah, one of the early settled places of the prairie, and also is owner of a farm of 160 acres on Grand River. His prosperity is the result of solid accomplishment, and his career, while outwardly quiet and unassuming, has been one of real achievement. He has never cared for the honors of politics, though usually found aligned with the republican cause, and has never filled an office, nor been delegate to a convention. He is a member of no church, nor social organization, though his wife is a Baptist.

Mr. Twadell was first married in Mercer County, March 11, 1890, to Sarah J. Kilbourn, a daughter of Calvin Lloyd. She died September 27, 1894, leaving a daughter, Miss May, who is a graduate of the Kirksville Normal School and a teacher in the Harrison County public schools. On March 26, 1902, Mr. Twadell married Miss Mollie Fletcher, a daughter of Hiram and Mary Ann (Bruce) Fletcher. Her father, who was born in Harrison County, Kentucky, in 1816, early went to Indiana, and about 1840 came to Missouri, where he was married in 1845 in Mercer County. He was a cooper by trade, but farming was his occupation for many years, and he died in Mercer County March 19, 1886, on land he had entered. He was a democrat and a member of the Christian Church. His first wife died February 23, 1853, leaving two children: Sarah A., who married Bert Sullivan, of Cass County, Iowa; and Mrs. Twadell. In 1854 Mr. Fletcher married Mary A. Clark, who was the mother of the following: Nancy, wife of Tillman Stanley, of Mercer County; Phoebe, deceased, wife of Ben Baker; Miss Jennie, of Mercer County; Andrew, deceased, who first married a Miss Hammock and later Miss Sarah Moore; Kate, who married her sister Phoebe's husband, Ben Baker; Alta, who married George Owens, of Mercer County; Estella, wife of John Black, of Mercer County; and Dona, who married Thomas Cain, of Mercer County. Mr. and Mrs. Twadell have had no children.

JUDGE SHELBY FRY THURMAN. A former county judge of Clinton County, Judge Thurman is a member of the prominent firm of Thurman Brothers, farmers and stock raisers in Hardin Township. Judge Thurman represents a family that has been identified usefully and prominently with Clinton County for more than half a century.

His father, Jefferson S. Thurman, came to Clinton County in 1856. He was born in Lincoln County, Kentucky, March 19, 1834, and represented old Kentucky and Colonial stock. His father was Willis G. Thurman, who was born in the same county of Kentucky, and was the son of a Georgian, who had seen active service as a soldier in the Revolutionary war and was of English stock. Willis G. Thurman married Louisa Peyton, who was born in Kentucky. Both were members of the Christian Church. They became parents of seven children, four sons and three daughters. Jefferson S. Thurman was reared in Kentucky on the old plantation, was taught the value of industry and honesty, and came to Missouri in 1856 and took up farming. He was married in Clinton County to Miss Anna Fry, whose name suggests one of the oldest pioneer families in Northwest Missouri. She was a daughter of Solomon Fry, who was born in Kentucky about 1794, came to Clay County, Missouri, in early manhood, and among his varied activities in this pioneer section he built the first jail at Liberty and also the first jail at Plattsburg. He made the first cash entry of land in Clinton County, and at one time owned about three thousand acres in that section. Jefferson S. Thurman and wife were the parents of seven sons, as follows: Eugene, Lee, Hill, Paul, Emmett, James, and Judge Shelby F. Mrs. Anna (Fry) Thurman died in 1871, on the 14th of July, at the age of thirty-four. Mr. Thurman married for his second wife Sarah Arnold, and by that union there is one son, James, a partner in the firm of Thurman Brothers. Jefferson S. Thurman and wife are still among the respected and honored citizens of Clinton County, active workers in the Christian Church, and he has served as a church officer and has always been ready to identify himself with those movements which give strength and wholesomeness to community life.

Judge Shelby F. Thurman was born on the old homestead of his father June 12, 1869. He grew up as a farm boy, was educated in the public schools and by study at home, and being of a scholarly disposition, qualified himself for teaching higher mathematics. He taught in public schools and colleges for seven years in Ohio and Illinois, but eventually left that vocation in favor of farming and stock raising. He and his brother, James Thurman, now have a splendid industry as farmers and stockmen, and own and operate 500 acres of the rich land of Hardin Township. They keep about a hundred head of cattle and three hundred hogs. It is an admirably equipped farm for stock purposes, has a large extent of blue grass meadows, plenty of shade and water, and for a number of years the fields have been made to produce a high average of crops yield.

Judge Thurman was married October 4, 1894, to Miss Alice B. Cook, a woman of education and refinement who has done much to give character to their home life. Her father was the late George Cook, who married Elizabeth Fry, who is still living and occupied the old Cook homestead in Clinton County. Mrs. Thurman finished her education in the Fulton Female College. They are the parents of three children: E. Burke, aged nineteen; Helen F., aged thirteen; and Hill C., Jr., aged four.

It was through an appointment from Governor Dockery that Mr. Thurman was appointed to fill out the unexpired term of Judge George Hall in the office of county judge of Clinton county, and he performed his duties with a capacity and fairness which commended him as a useful and able citizen. Judge Thurman is an active democrat, has long been identified with the Christian Church, and fraternally is affiliated with the Masonic lodge, the Knights Templar Commandery No. 162 at Plattsburg. He and his family reside in a fine home of ten rooms, surrounded with lawn and shade trees, large barns, and all the improvements of an up-to-date twentieth century Missouri home.

JAMES THURMAN. Associated with his brother, Judge Thurman, under the firm name of Thurman Brothers, James Thurman is one of the proprietors of the splendid farm and stock ranch operated under the partnership in Hardin Township. As a farmer of judgment and ability he has shown himself one of the most capable in the county and has a successful record both in business and as a home maker and citizen.

James Thurman was born on the old homestead December 21, 1872, a son of Jefferson S. Thurman, whose sketch with other particulars of family history are found in preceding paragraphs. James Thurman was reared on the farm, attended the local schools, and has concentrated practically all his time and energies on farming since reaching manhood.

In 1891 Mr. Thurman married Georgia Cook, a daughter of the late George W. Cook. Mr. and Mrs. Thurman are the parents of four children: Hazel, aged twelve; Keyron, aged eleven; Howard S., and Geraldine.

George W. Cook, father of Mrs. James Thurman, was for many years one of the leading citizens and farmers and stockmen of Clinton County. He was born in 1806 in Virginia, and died in Clinton County after a residence of many years at the age of sixty-four. He left a large and valuable farm, and it represented the many years of his industrious life. He was a child when he came to Missouri with his father, David Cook, who was one of the pioneers. George W. Cook married Elizabeth Fry, who was a daughter of Thomas Fry, a prominent early settler of Clay County, Missouri. Thomas Fry was a brother of Solomon Fry, and that family is sketched on other pages of this publication. Thomas Fry married Elizabeth McCulloch, who was born in North Carolina. Thomas Fry died at the age of eighty-three, and his wife at the advanced age of ninety-two. George W. Cook and wife had five children, one of whom died in infancy, while the others are: Nettie Pearson, of Hardin Township; Alice B., wife of Judge Shelby F. Thurman; Georgia, wife of James Thurman; and W. M., a prominent farmer and stockman of Clinton County, who occupies the old homestead, and gives a home to his widowed mother.

JULIUS RUMPEL. Among the business men of Weston few are better known or more highly esteemed than is Julius Rumpel, owner of the Weston Telephone System, half owner of the R. & B. Grain Elevator, and for the past twenty-nine years proprietor of a retail liquor business that is one of Weston's oldest established enterprises. Mr. Rumpel has done much to aid and encourage the growth and development of the community in both a commercial and civic way, and has done his full share in building up its varied interest.

Julius Rumpel was born at Leavenworth, Kansas, September 7, 1862, and is a son of William and Josephine (Emhart) Rumpel, natives of Wurttemburg, Germany. The father had served an apprenticeship to the blacksmith's trade in his native land, but never followed that vocation after coming to this country. In 1857 he came to the United States, landing at New York City after forty-five days on the ocean in a sailing vessel, and at once went to Milwaukee, Wisconsin, where he was married. In the following year he went to Leavenworth, Kansas, and there followed the trade of cooper, also experiencing some exciting adventures during the rough days of border warfare. He came to Weston in 1864, where he took charge of the cooper shop for Charles Perry, but later became the proprietor of an establishment of his own, which he conducted for a number of years. His declining years were passed in the hardware store of his son, at Weston. In politics Mr. Rumpel was a democrat, and both he and Mrs. Rumpel were devout members of the Catholic Church, in the faith of which they passed away.

Julius Rumpel was two years of age when brought by his parents to Weston, and here his education was secured in the public schools. He began business life as a lad in his father's cooper shop, and for a short time owned and conducted a shop of his own at Tracy, Missouri, but subsequently returned to Weston and established himself as proprietor of a tobacco store. In 1886 he disposed of this business to become owner of his present retail liquor business, which had been established in 1858 by the original owner. Mr. Rumpel owns his building, which is of brick, with a frontage of forty-five feet on the south side of West Thomas Street, the western part containing the main salesroom, two stories high, while the eastern part is three stories in height, the first floor being used for storage and office purposes. Across the alley west on Thomas Street, Mr. Rumpel owns another two-story brick building, the upper part of which is used by the German Benevolent Society as a hall for meeting purposes, this making a total frontage of seventy-five feet on Thomas Street. Mr. Rumpel believes in keeping strictly up-to-date, and in addition to his local retail trade, he makes a special feature of pure liquors for family and medicinal use, and has a large mail order trade that extends throughout the Middle West.

In 1900 Mr. Rumpel established the Weston Telephone System and built it from the ground up. From a comparatively small beginning it has developed until now it has 380 phones in operation in Weston, equipped with all metallic lines, besides long distance connection everywhere, and many rural lines. The telephone central office is located in the third story of Mr. Rumpel's building on the south side of Thomas Street, two doors west of Main Street, where it is fully equipped with the latest improved apparatus. The business is ably looked after by a chief operator, four assistant operators, a repair man, a superintendent of construction and a general assistant, and in the hands of this force the system is kept in good shape, and first class, courteous service is given the patrons. The exchange is kept open all night, and to Platte City and other neighboring places free service is given at all times. On the whole, Weston has every reason to be proud of its telephone system, for it is one that is a credit to the community. A recent review, in commenting upon this system, said in part: "The telephone business in the United States has had a most astounding growth, and from being merely an interesting toy in the early '70s, it has developed until now it is absolutely essential in almost all the affairs of life. The telephone systems of the nation and its cities and towns can be likened to the nervous system of a living being, in that they are the means of instantaneous communication from one part to another. A marvelous invention it was, but it is now such an everyday affair with everybody that little thought is given to it, and it is hard to imagine what the conditions would be without it, yet middle-aged and older people can remember the days before it came, when the methods of local communication were solely by messenger or in person, and when more distant places could be reached only by mail or telegraph. A stranger in Weston would naturally expect a town of this size and importance to have first-class telephone service, and he would not be disappointed in this expectation if he should investigate the matter, for it can truthfully be said that it is in the top rank when it comes to telephones."

Mr. Rumpel is a half owner of the R. & B. Grain Elevator, at Weston, having, in partnership with B. J. Bless, erected a new and modern elevator of 24,000 bushels capacity, and opened it for business July 12, 1914. This business has taken a leading place among the enterprises of Weston, and includes the buying and shipping of wheat, corn, oats and hay, and the handling of hard and soft coal in a retail way. Mr. Rumpel is also the owner of several business properties, has always stood for public improvements, and has been ready at all times to contribute of his means, influence, time or ability in securing the success of movements which promise to benefit Weston and its people. For ten years Mr. Rumpel served in the capacity of chief of the Weston Fire Department, and its present efficiency is largely due to his efforts and executive ability. Mr. Rumpel has invented and patented recently the Rumpel cold lunch bag, a sanitary, waterproof and almost airtight lunch bag; a bag that will keep food and liquid cold for ten hours, which make all outings more enjoyable.

On December 10, 1907, Mr. Rumpel was married to Miss Blanche

Sebus, who was born at Stewartville, Missouri, and to this union there has come one son: Julius E.

CHARLES H. HILLIX. There can be no better recommendation advanced of a community's solidity and real worth than the substantiality of its monetary institutions. The banking house always has been, and will continue to be, the directing center of business interests; through its coffers must flow the moneys which keep alive the transactions of the marts of commerce and trade. It is the medium through which diversified activities are brought into contact, and, in large extent, with it these interests must stand or fall. To ably and conservatively play its destined part in the representation of the finances of county, state, corporation and individual has been the realized ambition of the men who have had under their direction the affairs of the Bank of Weston, and in this realization none has been more gratified than the able and popular cashier of the institution, Charles H. Hillix, by profession an attorney, who gave up his work in that calling to devote his entire time to finance.

Charles H. Hillix was born in Leavenworth County, Kansas, July 15, 1863, and is a son of William Walker and Ellen R. (Whittington) Hillix. His father was born in Bourbon County, Kentucky, October 9, 1830, and in 1854 first came to Missouri, where he sought the opportunity of supporting his widowed mother and his three sisters. He soon established himself well, and in 1856 was married to Ellen R. Whittington, who was born in Eastern Tennessee, November 10, 1840, and they began life together in Buchanan County, but soon moved to Leavenworth County, Kansas, where they remained until the fall of 1863, then returning to Missouri and settling 2½ miles northeast of Weston, on a tract of timber land. This place the father cleared and improved, and for forty years was engaged in general farming and the raising of cattle and hogs, from time to time adding to his land until he was the owner of 260 acres. In 1905 he retired from active participation in agricultural labors and located at Weston, where he passed away June 6, 1907, Mrs. Hillix having died November 13, 1893. Mr. Hillix was a democrat, and in religious belief a Christian, serving as elder in that church for some years. He and his wife were the parents of eight children, of whom two died in infancy, the others being: William, of St. Joseph, Missouri; Allen A., a resident of Platte County; Charles H., of this review; Frank, of Weston, Missouri; Minnie, who is the wife of W. C. Polk, of Weston; and Albert Sidney Johnston, of Weston.

Charles H. Hillix was reared amid agricultural surroundings, and after completing the course of study in the district schools entered William Jewell College at Liberty, remained one year and then entered La Grange College, from which he was graduated in 1885, then entering the law department of Washington University, St. Louis, where he received his degree in 1888. After one year of practice at St. Joseph, he came to Weston and opened an office, and in 1897 was made cashier of the Bank of Weston, and still holds that position. In 1899 he discontinued his law practice to give his entire and undivided attention to the affairs of the bank. Aside from his interests of a financial nature, Mr. Hillix has served Weston long and well. When he resigned, in 1914, he had been city attorney and clerk for twenty-one years, and as a member of the school board gave the city his best services for eighteen years. For thirty-one years a member of the Christian Church, he has for twenty years of that time held an official position, and at present is an elder. He is well known in Masonry, having passed through the chapter and council degrees. Mr. Hillix has a number of business connections, and is the owner of farming land in Buchanan County, Missouri, and in Kansas.

On May 29, 1894, Mr. Hillix was united in marriage with Miss Clara M. Nelson, who was born May 20, 1866, in Platte County, Missouri, a daughter of Nels P. and Entra T. (Hoverson) Nelson, natives of Norway, who came to Platte County, Missouri, in 1860 and later removed to Buchanan County. Mr. Nelson died in 1888, at the age of sixty years, while Mrs. Nelson still survives at the age of seventy-six years, and makes her home at St. Joseph. Four children have come to Mr. and Mrs. Hillix, born as follows: Charles Nelson, October 27, 1895; Minnie Christine, July 25, 1898; Catherine Rebecca, January 27, 1900, and Enger A., October 11, 1903.

It is within the province of this sketch to include a review of the life of the Bank of Weston, this being quoted verbatim from an article published in Weston's leading newspaper: ''Weston's location as the commercial center for a large surrounding territory that is rich in natural resources and thickly populated, has necessitated the establishing of reliable banking concerns to meet the demands of its trade, and because of its prominence and close connection with the business affairs of West Platte County, the sketch of the Bank of Weston will be given a leading position in this edition. The history of this institution is contemporary with, and a part of, the history of Platte County for the past twenty-one years. It opened its doors for business April 1, 1893, and was at that time a private institution with a capital of $5,000. Success attended its efforts from the first, and, in order to adjust itself to the demands of its steadily growing business, its capital has since increased several times. In December, 1896, it was changed to $7,000, and on March 26, 1898, the bank was incorporated under the state laws with a capital stock of $10,000, and this continued until 1905 when it was still further increased. to $25,000, its present amount. The officers and directors of this bank are: Allen A. Hillix, president; John U. Dale, vice president; Charles H. Hillix, cashier; William C. Polk, assistant cashier, and Canby Hawkins.

''This bank owns its building, which is located at the southwest corner of Main and Thomas streets. It is a handsome, modern, two-story brick structure, with a frontage of 25 feet on Main street, and extending back along Thomas street 60 feet. The banking apartments have a full glass front, which gives excellent light, and the interior is divided into main lobby, counting room and private office, all beautifully finished in pleasing designs. The walls and ceiling are of steel paneling, the floor of the main lobby is of mosaic tiling in colors, and the counter extensions are finished in the natural wood with bases of polished marble, and are surmounted with rich panels of frosted glass. To the rear of the business apartments is a large, comfortable rest room, containing writing table and easy chairs, and open to the public at all times during business hours. The building is heated by natural gas and coal fires, is lighted by both gas and electricity, and is supplied with electric fans for use during hot weather. A full-sized basement beneath is used for storage purposes, for fuel, etc. The equipment still further embraces a massively-constructed vault 12x14 feet in size, with double walls of heavy masonry having an air space in the center and a ventilating system, thus rendering it entirely fire and damp proof. The vault is closed with Mosler double-steel doors, secured with combination locks, and is used for the protection of valuable papers and as a safe deposit for patrons. In addition to the vaults, the bank equipment includes a Mosler screw-door, triple-time lock of the latest design, which furnishes absolute protection for treasure. The routine work of the bank is facilitated by the necessary devices, including typewriters and a Burroughs adding machine. It is also supplied with a telephone.

"The Bank of Weston does a general banking business in all its branches. It handles exchange, makes collections, receives deposits, and places loans, the latter being made principally on personal security and real estate, although it handles tobacco and live stock paper to some extent. Its deposits, in round numbers, range from $85,000 to $150,000, its loans at present about $100,000, and it now has a surplus of $6,500, and undivided profits $1,000. Its correspondents are the First National Bank, Kansas City; Burnes National Bank, St. Joseph; Mechanics American National Bank, St. Louis, and the National City Bank of New York. It is a member of the Missouri Bankers' Association, and is insured against burglary and daylight holdups in the Ocean Accident and Guarantee Corporation, of London, England. Ample fire insurance is also kept up.

"This bank is, without doubt, one of the foremost business institutions of Platte County. It has, from the first, exerted a large influence upon the commercial interests of this section of Missouri, and this influence has always been for the betterment and building up of this part of the state. Conservatism and careful transactions have always been promi- ·nent features of its management, consequently it has ever had the full confidence of the public, and its career has been a most honorable and successful one since it opened its doors for business."

EDWIN CLIFTON HILL, M. D. The senior member of the medical fra- ternity at Smithville, Doctor Hill claims Northwest Missouri as his native home, and has been in practice more than twenty years, his home having been in Smithville since 1898. One of his brothers is a physician, and by marriage the doctor is connected with a family which has given pro- fessional service in medicine to this part of Missouri for more than sev- enty years.

Edwin Clifton Hill was born near Plattsburg, Clinton County, Mis- souri, August 31, 1868. His father is Thomas R. Hill, now a venerable resident of Plattsburg, who was born in Henry County, Kentucky, August 29, 1837. He was married to Julia F. Sparks, who was born in Owen County, Kentucky, September 16, 1838, and died August 25, 1908. In 1857 they moved to Missouri, locating near St. Joseph, and in 1861 going to Clinton County, where he bought a farm 4½ miles from Plattsburg. On that homestead the children were reared and the mother died. In 1913 the father left the farm and has since had his home in retirement at Plattsburg. He was very successful as a farmer. An ardent democrat, he has interested himself in politics and public affairs, and at one time served as presiding judge of the Clinton County Court. His wife and most of the family were of the Baptist faith. There was a large family of children, comprising eight sons and three daughters, named as follows: A. Henry, of El Reno, Oklahoma; Dr. W. H., of St. Joseph; Lou P., wife of J. D. Smith, of Knox County, Missouri; Georgia L., wife of Robert Smithers, of Kansas City; Dr. E. C., of Smithville; Molly F., wife of R. L. Eberts, of Plattsburg; H. W., of Liberty, Missouri; A. W., of Woodlake, Kentucky; Ben P., of Pomona, California; T. Russ and A. Lester, both of whom are dentists in practice at St. Joseph and Kansas City, Missouri.

Edwin C. Hill reverts to the Clinton County farm as the scene of his early recollections and experiences, and while there he had the discipline and instruction of the common schools. Having made up his mind to prepare for medicine as a profession, he contrived the means and opportunity for attending college, and took his course in the Eclectic

Medical College of Cincinnati, where he was graduated M. D. in 1891. His first location was at Gower, in Clinton County, and after seven years he moved to Smithville, in Clay County. He has enjoyed a large practice both in town and country, and with each year of experience his skill is more in demand and his position more securely established in the confidence of the people.

Doctor Hill has professional associations with the Clay County and Missouri State Medical societies, with the American Medical Association and the National Eclectic Association. Fraternally he is affiliated with the Masonic order and the Mystic Shrine, with the Independent Order of Odd Fellows, Knights of Pythias and Benevolent and Protective Order of Elks. In politics he is a democrat.

September 2, 1891, Doctor Hill married Miss Annie E. May, and they are the parents of six children, two of whom, Edwin R. and George D., are deceased. The others are Julia May, Ben Lester, David W. and Howard W.

Mrs. Hill was born at Barry, in Clay County, March 4, 1870, a daughter of Dr. Ben L. and a granddaughter of Dr. Ware May, both prominent in their profession. Her grandfather came from Kentucky, being a graduate of the Lexington Medical College, and was for many years in practice at Liberty and in Platte County. He served as a surgeon with Missouri troops in the Mexican war. He married Elizabeth Burnett, a sister of former Gov. Peter Burnett of California. Dr. Ben L. May, father of Mrs. Hill, was born in Platte County, Missouri, June 17, 1841, and died April 25, 1882. In 1865 he graduated from the Bellevue Hospital Medical College of New York City, and had previously been a Confederate soldier under Gen. Sterling Price. He began his practice at Barry, in Clay County, and that was his home until his death. A man of large physical frame and broad mental capacity, equaled by a jovial temperament, he was beloved by everyone in that entire community. He was married September 28, 1865, to Mary A. Nicol. She was born near Platte City, Missouri, April 4, 1846, and is now living with her only daughter, Mrs. Hill. Her parents, David and Ellen (Peyton) Nicol, were born in Rappahannock County, Virginia, and settled in Platte County, Missouri, in the fall of 1846, and lived on a farm there the rest of their lives. Besides Mrs. Hill the other children of Dr. and Mrs. May were: George E., of Charles City, Iowa; David W., in Government service in Porto Rico; and B. Wood, of Charles City, Iowa.

W. B. HARRIS. The best small town paper in Clay County is the distinction given by its readers and the general public to the Democrat-Herald at Smithville. Its editor and proprietor, W. B. Harris, is a newspaper man from the ground up, and has had little experience in any other field since boyhood.

W. B. Harris was born in Corning, Kansas, January 6, 1877, a son of Robert A. and Lucy (Rucker) Harris. His father, who was born in Indiana, moved out to Kansas in 1867, and homesteaded land in that state, where he lived the life of a practical farmer until his death in 1890 at the age of thirty-nine. He was the father of four children: W. B.; Roscoe, of Corning, Kansas; Inez, wife of Earl R. Short, of Colorado; and Robert, of Corning. The mother is now living at Corning as the wife of D. B. Garver.

While on the Kansas farm Mr. Harris attended school in town, and in 1893 finished the course in the high school at Corning. Two years before, in 1891, he began his newspaper apprenticeship in all-round work in the office of the Corning Gazette. On May 11, 1896, he attained to the dignity of proprietor by the purchase of a half interest in the plant, but a year later sold out and bought the Times at Vermillion, Kansas. After publishing it 3½ years, he moved the plant to Kelly, Kansas, and issued the Reporter, with which he was actively identified 3½ years. Following this Mr. Harris came to Missouri, and from March, 1905, to December, 1912, was foreman on the Jeffersonian at Higginsville. Since December, 1912, his home has been in Smithville, where he bought the Democrat-Herald.

Mr. Harris was reared a republican, but is now of the democratic party. He is affiliated with the Independent Order of Odd Fellows, the Knights of Pythias and the Mystic Workers of the World. His church is the Presbyterian, while Mrs. Harris is a Baptist. He was married March 8, 1898, to Miss Gertrude Warner, of Kansas. She died June 19, 1905, leaving a daughter, Bernice. December 12, 1908, Mr. Harris married Anna Mount, of Higginsville. Her parents are Charles and Samantha (Carel) Mount, the former a native of Alabama and the latter of Indiana, and both now residents of Kansas City, Missouri. Mr. and Mrs. Harris are the parents of one son, Howard.

H. M. MARSH. The Clear Creek Valley Stock Farm of 196 acres is one of the noteworthy country places of Clinton Township, in Clinton County. It has been the home of high class stock and has illustrated practical farm management for many years. Its proprietor, H. M. Marsh, is a man who through his interest has done much to elevate the standards of general farming and stock husbandry in Clinton County. There are many attractive features about the place. One of the first to be noted is the fine modern residence of nine rooms standing well back from the road, with ample and enticing porches, surrounded by a fine and well shaded lawn. The farm also has another residence of six rooms, and there is every facility for convenience and comfort as well as for profitable business. The pastures are of blue grass, there are extensive fields of corn and other grain, and alfalfa is one of the crops upon which Mr. Marsh places his dependence. There is a fine barn 33x36 feet, granaries, and a number of large sheds for the drying and curing of tobacco. This is one of the few farms in Clinton County where tobacco is grown on a commercial scale. Mr. Marsh raises on the average about twelve thousand pounds of tobacco every year, and is an expert in its cultivation. As a stockman he gives special attention to Percheron horses and jacks. These are only a few of the things which make the Clear Creek Valley Stock Farm one of the best in Clinton County. Mr. Marsh is regarded as one of the most capable judges of stock in his section. One hundred and twenty acres of his farm lies in the fertile Valley of Clear Creek, and this is the land that yields the large crops of alfalfa. Mr. Marsh was one of the early alfalfa growers in Clinton County, and by his example has done much to popularize that crop.

H. M. Marsh was born on the old homestead in Clinton County May 23, 1868. He was reared in a home of substantial comfort, was educated in the public schools, and trained himself for his successful

ton County's estimable citizens and useful workers. There were two children in the McFarland family, and the son, Frank McFarland, is now an official in the postal service, being superintendent of the Seventh Division of United States Railway Mail Service.

Mr. and Mrs. Marsh are the parents of three children: Clinton is eighteen years of age and a student in the high school; Albert, who is thirteen; and Wilma, aged seven. Mr. Marsh is an active member of the Baptist Church, and has served for a number of years as superintendent and teacher in the Sunday school. He is one of the frank and genial citizens of Clinton County, a man who commands respect wherever he goes, and has shown himself a friend of schools, community morality, and all improvements and institutions which make life better.

V. P. MARSH. The enterprise of the Marsh family is exhibited in two of the best known stock farms in Clinton County, and V. P. Marsh is proprietor of the Jersey Hill Dairy Farm. This comprises 183 acres, divided between hill and valley lands, with improvements that make it second to no similar estate in that vicinity. Mr. Marsh gets most of his profit from a fine herd of Jerseys, seventeen in number, with a thoroughbred pedigreed bull at the head. Seventy acres of his land lie in the bottoms, and is excellently adapted for alfalfa, of which he grows several crops a year, and that is a large part of his stock feed. He has the other advantages of a good stock farm, plenty of shade and water, and has a fine sanitary barn 28x34 feet. Mr. Marsh shipped his cream to the Blue River Creamery Company in Kansas City. His shipping station is Holt in Clay County, which is 2½ miles from his farm. Mr. Marsh and family have an attractive and comfortable home, a seven-room house, well furnished, and with the delightful surroundings of a blue grass lawn and large shade trees.

V. P. Marsh was born in Clinton County July 15, 1878. His father is Hon. W. S. Marsh, a former member of the Legislature, who during his term at Jefferson City introduced the best banking bill ever brought forward for the regulation of Missouri banks, and one that provided for the rigid inspection of loans and for the guarantee of deposits. W. S. Marsh has long been one of the able democrats in this section, and as a farmer and stock man developed a large property. He retired from active affairs in 1903 and has since lived in Holt, being now seventy-eight years of age. He married Dulcina Alnutt. To their marriage were born thirteen children, and eight are still living: D. B., of Plattsburg; W..A., of Kansas, where he is a farmer and stock man; W. L., also of Kansas, and a farmer and stock man; Mrs. Fanny McComas, of Holt; H. M., proprietor of the Clear Creek Valley Stock Farm in Clinton County; Grace Kennedy, of Lexington, Kentucky; Lizzie Brown, of Jackson Township; and Virgil P. The father is a prominent Mason, being affiliated with the Royal Arch Chapter of Lathrop.

Virgil P. Marsh was reared on the old farm, and received his education in the local public schools. He has been a practical business man and farmer since early manhood, and has been peculiarly successful as a dairyman. On September 21, 1902, he married Roxana Harris, who was one of six children, four sons and two daughters, born to Moses G.

mans moved to Buchanan County in 1841, and J. F. Bridgman himself
was born in Buchanan County May 7, 1841. His career since early manhood has been that of a farmer and stock raiser, he owns and controls
extensive interests in Bigelow Township of Holt County, and is one of
the solid, enterprising and prosperous men of that section.

He was the second in a family of eight children born to John W.
and Lucinda (Gibson) Bridgman. His father, a native of Tennessee,
moved to Buchanan County, Missouri, in 1841, with an ox and horse
team. He preempted land there aggregating 160 acres, and became
extensively identified not only with agricultural operations but with the
buying, raising and trading in live stock. In the early days he made
a practice of driving his cattle from Buchanan County to the better
pasturage found along the river bottoms in Holt County, around Bigelow. Some years after settling in Missouri he joined in the exodus to
California, during the exciting days of 1849, and after investigating
conditions in the far West returned to Missouri. Cattle were very cheap
in the middle West at that time, but commanded high prices in California and his next venture was to drive a herd of cattle across the plains.
It took from May until the following September to complete the trip,
and after disposing of his cattle to an advantage in the mining districts
of the Pacific coast he returned East by the water route. In 1852 John
W. Bridgman located permanently in Holt County, establishing a farm
on the river bottoms. Later he lived for a couple of years in Kansas,
but Holt County was his home most of the years until death, and he
gained a reputation as a successful farmer and cattle raiser.

J. F. Bridgman was schooled largely in the university of experience,
since public schools hardly existed in his locality while a boy and his
instruction so far as books were concerned was comparatively meager.
He has been a practical, hard working and judicious manager of such
resources as came to his hand, and has made a success in spite of the
handicap of little book learning. His father's homestead was hardly
sufficient to accommodate the energies of all the sons, and at the age
of eighteen he and his brother engaged in partnership in working a
farm. After a few years he had some capital of his own, and has since
continued farming, investing his surplus in more land, and now owns
a good estate.

Mr. Bridgman married for his first wife Sarah Catron, daughter of
Christopher Catron. The one child of this union was Belle, wife of
W. J. Schatz. There was also a son named William, who died at the
age of three years. After the death of his first wife Mr. Bridgman
married Mary Catron, the widow of Joseph E. Hoffman. By her first
marriage there were four children: Martha, wife of Richard Utt; Anna,
who married Bert Basinger; Carrie, who married W. S. Thompson; and
Fannie, who died in infancy. Mr. and Mrs. Bridgman have the follow-
ing children by their marriage: Richard B., who is an attorney at
Oregon and married Mattie Groves; Thomas J., who married Stella
Fike; John Britton, who married Blanche Caldwell; Edna, who married
C. S. McKee. All these children are living, and all were born in Bigelow
Township.

with many of the distinguished men of the state and country, and to a large extent his time has been taken up with public duties. For twelve years Mr. Schmitz served as postmaster at Chillicothe and has filled a number of other offices in his home community and county.

John L. Schmitz was born in Tuscarawas County, Ohio, a son of George and Sarah Van Lehn Schmitz, both natives of Ohio. His father spent all his active life as a Tuscarawas County farmer. On the old farm in Northeastern Ohio Mr. Schmitz grew up to manhood, and developed a sound physical constitution at the same time he was training his intellect in the country schools. Following a period spent as a teacher in the common schools he entered the National Normal University at Lebanon, Ohio, graduating in 1878. He then was employed as a teacher in the Western Normal College at Ladoga, Indiana, one year, and for the following three years returned to his alma mater at Lebanon as a teacher. During his residence at Ladoga Mr. Schmitz became acquainted with Gen. Lew Wallace, the celebrated Indiana soldier, statesman and author, and also with Maurice Thompson, also distinguished as an author.

Mr. Schmitz removed to Chillicothe in 1884, having come here to become superintendent of the public schools, a position he filled two years. He then took up the study of law in the office of L. A. Chapman and in 1888 by examination before the court of Caldwell County was admitted to practice. He at once opened an office in Chillicothe, and has been as closely identified with the practice of law as his varied public responsibilities would permit. He has practiced not only in the state but in the federal courts.

In politics he has been a stanch republican all his life, and in 1888-89 served as mayor of Chillicothe, was police judge from 1889 to 1891, and city attorney during 1891-93. In 1894 he was elected prosecuting attorney of Livingston County. His early work as superintendent of the schools made his services and counsel useful to the school board, and he served on that board from 1887 to 1893. In 1902 Mr. Schmitz was candidate of his party for Congress, but unable to overcome the large democratic majority. On March 1, 1903, President Roosevelt appointed him postmaster at Chillicothe, and by reappointment he filled that office continuously until the expiration of his term under a democratic administration on March 1, 1915. The relief from the duties of the postmastership gives Mr. Schmitz an opportunity to devote himself unreservedly to his profession. His appointment as Chillicothe postmaster was a matter of surprise to him personally, since he had in no wise been a candidate for the position, and it came as a compliment to his popularity and high standing. Mr. Schmitz probably has as extensive an acquaintance with men of state and national prominence as almost any man in this section of Missouri. He has long been recognized as one of the republican leaders of the state.

Mr. Schmitz married Miss Lillian Felton, whose death occurred in 1896. She was the mother of three children, two of whom are living. Helen is her father's housekeeper and Laura is a teacher in the Chillicothe public schools. Mr. Schmitz is fraternally identified with the Benevolent and Protective Order of Elks.

HON. FRED S. HUDSON. One of the lawyers of highest rank and standing in Northwest Missouri is Fred S. Hudson, of Chillicothe. Mr.

attorney for a number of railways, banks and other corporations in his section of the state.

Fred S. Hudson represents an old family of Northwest Missouri, and was born near Hale, Carroll County, Missouri, January 27, 1868. His parents were Milton Jefferson and Mary (Hanna) Hudson. His grandfather, William Hudson, came from Ohio to Missouri in 1852, locating near Hale. He had left his native state because of differences of opinion in the family regarding the slavery question. While he himself was favorable to slavery, and for that reason had come to Missouri, when the Civil war began he enlisted in the Union army. Curiously enough his relatives back in Ohio identified themselves with the cause of the Confederacy. While living in Ohio William Hudson married Nancy Hurd, and their four children were: William, who enlisted in the Union army and died after the battle of Pea Ridge; Milton Jefferson; Bentley, who lives in Carroll County; and Susanna, wife of J. W. Jamison of Hale, Missouri. Grandfather William Hudson died during the early '70s.

Milton Jefferson Hudson, the father, was born in Southeastern Ohio March 3, 1845, and came with his family to Missouri at the age of seven years. He attended country schools, lived on a farm and developed his strength there, and in April, 1861, though only sixteen years of age, enlisted as a private in the Union army in the Eighteenth Missouri Volunteer Infantry, going out from Livingston County. He was mustered out as a sergeant. Few Missouri volunteers sacrificed more and endured more hardships in behalf of the Union cause. He was taken prisoner at the battle of Shiloh, and for fourteen months was confined in various Southern prisons, at Libby, Andersonville and at Macon, Georgia. He had his full share in the hardships and sufferings endured by Union prisoners in these notorious places of confinement. At the time of his exchange he weighed only ninety-eight pounds. In spite of this self-sacrificing service, for many years he refused to accept a pension, saying his services were willingly offered and given, and it was only on the insistence of his family that during his late years he consented to apply for and received a pension of $12.00 per month. One morning after breakfast he walked out on his front porch, and died suddenly of heart failure. His wife was a native of New York State, was reared at Oberlin, Ohio, and is now living at Hale, Missouri. Fred S. Hudson was one of four children, the others being: Charles B., an attorney at Wichita, Kansas; Clyde M., an attorney at Wichita, Kansas; and Mrs. Edna Fisk, of Colorado Springs, Colorado.

Fred S. Hudson grew up in Carroll County, attended the common schools, and in 1885 was graduated from the Northwestern Normal School at Stanberry. Several years of business experience preceded his entrance into the law, and it was while bookkeeper in a bank at Hale that he took up his law studies at such intervals of leisure as occurred, and subsequently was a student in the office of S. J. Jones at Carrollton. Mr. Hudson was admitted to the bar in 1897, and began his practice at Hale. In 1902 he came to Chillicothe, and though for a time engaged in general practice soon began specializing along the line of corporation law, and on the basis of his present connection and his general standing is without doubt one of the ablest corporation attorneys in Northwest Missouri. He was first employed by the Milwaukee Railroad Company, and his services were so valuable to that corporation that he was promoted in 1911 to be general solicitor for the State of Missouri. He is

road, the legal department of the company in Missouri has been reorganized, and Mr. Hudson is now its head. He has ten men under him in the state, and Chillicothe, being the most centrally located city on the road, has been selected for headquarters. Mr. Hudson's office is on the second floor of the Citizens National Bank Building, where he has one of the best equipped offices and one of the most complete law libraries in the state.

In 1892 Mr. Hudson married Miss Ida Fink of Hale, Missouri, daughter of Capt. C. Fink, who was one of the early settlers at Utica, Livingston County, but subsequently moved to Hale. Two children were born to Mr. and Mrs. Hudson: Arthur Carroll and Henry Walter, both of whom died in infancy.

Mr. Hudson is a member of the Christian Church and fraternally is a Mason, being past master of his lodge, past high priest of the chapter, past eminent commander of the Knights Templar, and a member of the Mystic Shrine. He has taken an active part in republican politics, and in 1904 was candidate of his party for Congress. In 1906 he was nominated and elected state senator from the Fourth Senatorial District, and his term of four years was characterized by much valuable work in the interests of the state and of his constituency. For several years he has served as a member of the State Central Committee, and his name has been frequently associated with the honors of a gubernatorial nomination, and he is regarded as one of the strongest eligibles in North Missouri for that office. As he is only in the prime of his powers his future possesses much potential value and service to his state.

LEWIS A. CHAPMAN. This name is one that will be recognized over Northern Missouri as that of a highly successful lawyer for more than a generation engaged in practice at Chillicothe, and a man who has used his profession not only as a means of performing his individual work in the world, but in many ways for community betterment. Mr. Chapman has lived in Livingston County since childhood, and has witnessed all the important developments in that section since the beginning of the railroad era.

Lewis A. Chapman was born in Rappahannock County, Virginia, October 1, 1852, and though a Virginian has for years been one of the leading republicans of his county. His parents were John and Jemima (Nolen) Chapman, the former a native of Newmarket, Virginia, and the latter of Rappahannock County. John Chapman was a cabinet maker and wheelwright by trade, and in 1856 brought his family out from Virginia to Utica, Livingston County, Missouri. The greater part of the distance was covered by passage on river boats. The father worked at his trade in Utica for a time and then moved to a farm owned by his wife's father, Gustavus A. Nolen, who was a man of considerable means, a farmer and slave owner, who had come to Livingston County, Missouri, in 1855. Thus the family was established in that section of Missouri a short time before the first railroad was constructed. Lewis A. was the second of four children: Gustavus A., formerly a lawyer at Bentonville, Arkansas, but not now engaged in practice; Lewis A.; Oliver J., a lawyer of Kansas City; and a daughter who died at the age of two years.

In 1858 Mr. Chapman's mother died, and the family was then broken up. The father removed from the county, and died of the cholera at

ston County, receiving very little schooling during that time. At the age of fifteen he went to Chillicothe and entered the academy conducted by Hezekiah Ellis, attending for about a year, and when not in school working on a farm and at other employment. After this year's schooling he earned his way as a farm hand, and then returned to Chillicothe and took up the study of law with the firm of Dixon & Sloane, and subsequently with Broaddus & Pollard. In October, 1870, when only eighteen years of age, Mr. Chapman was examined by a committee appointed by the local court and was admitted to practice, although three years under his majority. He was soon taken into a partnership with Thomas J. Dent, and for six months was at Breckenridge attending to the business of the firm.

In the meantime Mr. Chapman had decided that his education was not yet sufficient to enable him to cope successfully with his profession, and he accordingly returned to Livingston County and for six years taught school, using part of his earnings for the purchase of law books and carrying on his studies on holidays and vacation times. In 1876, when Judge Broaddus was elected to the circuit bench, Mr. Chapman became clerk and assistant in the law office of Judge Pollard. At the end of one year Judge Pollard was elected from this district to a seat in Congress, and a partnership was then formed under the name Pollard & Chapman, the business of which Mr. Chapman managed while his partner was attending to his legislative duties in Washington. This firm enjoyed the largest practice of any law firm in that section of Missouri. Following his term in Congress Judge Pollard moved to St. Louis, and since that time Mr. Chapman has had no associations. He has practiced in all the higher courts, both state and federal, and his long and prominent record can be read in the dockets of the local and district courts and in the reports of the higher court.

His political career has been one of large service and activity. Mr. Chapman was a member of the Republican State Central Committee, and has been chairman of his congressional, county, city and township committees. For eighteen years he served as United States commissioner, has been a member of the city council of Chillicothe, was city attorney three times, and a member of the school board fifteen years, three years its secretary and eleven years its president. On three different occasions he was the nominee of his party for prosecuting attorney, and while receiving a very complimentary vote was unable to overcome the large democratic majority. In 1910 he was tendered the nomination for justice of the Supreme Court, without opposition, but declined that honor, which was paramount to election, since the candidate of his party was chosen to the bench in that campaign.

Mr. Chapman has been identified with the Baptist Church since he was fifteen years of age. He has served as a deacon and trustee, and has devoted the first day of every week for years to the work of the Sunday school, having served as superintendent, for forty years as a teacher, and at the present time is Sunday school treasurer. Mr. Chapman was one of the organizers and the first vice president of the Citizens National Bank of Chillicothe, in which he is now a stockholder and its attorney.

On March 13, 1877, soon after beginning his professional career, Mr. Chapman married Miss Luella Florence Benson, daughter of Ira Benson,

M. is a graduate in law from the University of Missouri and now in practice at Chillicothe; Donaldson, a graduate from the collegiate department of the University of Missouri, is now taking his law course in the same institution; Van is in the Chillicothe High School; Thomas H. is a student in William Jewell College at Liberty; Marion is attending the Central College for Women at Lexington, Missouri; Arthur G. died at the age of two years; Grace when nine years old, and William at birth.

SCOTT J. MILLER. Though for more than a quarter of a century recognized as one of the foremost trial lawyers of North Missouri, Scott J. Miller has been content to confine his abilities entirely to one line of work, has given much public service to his home county and state, and some years ago, having ventured as a diversion into a special field of live stock husbandry, is now pronounced the leading breeder of Missouri jacks and mules and has one of the largest industries of the kind in the Middle West if not in the entire country.

Col. Scott J. Miller was born in Columbus, Ohio, December 29, 1867, a son of J. W. and Mary Elizabeth (Bland) Miller. The Millers were originally from Germany, first locating in Pennsylvania, and from there moving to Ohio. Colonel Miller's father was a farmer, and in 1869 brought his family to Caldwell County, Missouri, and in 1872 to Livingston County, locating in Jackson Township, where he was engaged as a farmer and stock raiser until shortly before his death, when he retired and lived in Chillicothe, until his passing in 1909. His widow still survives. There were four sons and three daughters in the family.

Scott J. Miller spent his early life in the country and its associations established in him a thorough love of rural life and its activities. He attended country schools, taught for a time, and in 1883 entered the University of Missouri, taking an elective course and devoting his time principally to the study of languages for two years. The following year was spent as teacher in the tenth grade of the Chillicothe public schools. He began the study of law in the office of Judge Elbridge J. Broaddus, who afterwards became a justice of the Court of Appeals at Kansas City. He also studied law with Hon. Charles H. Mansur, who was subsequently elected to Congress.

Admitted to practice in 1888 by examination before a committee appointed by the local courts, Colonel Miller at once opened an office in Chillicothe and the succeeding years have brought him an enviable fame and position as a lawyer. He has always preferred independent practice, and his only associate in all this time was his brother Frank for two years. He has been admitted to practice in all the state and federal courts and has tried cases in fifteen different states. A large share of his practice has been damage cases, and his ability has shown itself most conspicuously as what may be called a jury lawyer. In criminal cases he has attended nearly all the murder trials in Livingston County for twenty years or more. His practice is not confined to one county, but extends all over the northern part of Missouri, and as a trial lawyer it is doubtful if any other member of the North Missouri bar has so extended a clientele. He is one of the scholarly members of the bar, and has a very complete law library.

In politics he has affiliated with the democrats, but has never sought nor desired any of the honors of public office. However, in 1912 he

regents of the State Normal School at Kirksville, and was reappointed at the same position by Governors Stephens and Dockery. This was his longest and most important public service, continuing for ten years, eight years of which he was president of the board. In this time he sacrificed his professional interests in many ways to give his time and attention to the upbuilding and improvement of the Normal. Much of his own time and money were spent in planning a model country schoolhouse during the last two years of his administration, and this building is now on exhibition at the State Normal in Kirksville. During his absence the other members of the board gave it the name by which it is known, the Scott J. Miller Model School.

Colonel Miller in the course of his career has acquired large tracts of land in Livingston County. A number of years ago he began the breeding of thoroughbred stock, taking his avocation as a means for recuperation and diversion from the exacting duties of his profession. He was peculiarly successful, and what had been begun as a pastime developed into a large and profitable industry, so that he is now the largest breeder of Missouri jacks in the state. He also breeds thoroughbred Poland-China hogs and Percheron horses. While thus a general stock man, Colonel Miller has a national reputation for having developed a particular strain and marking of mules. In 1905 he undertook to breed mules with the object of producing black mules with white faces. It took four generations to produce such an animal, which was the first of its kind, and the oldest animal with these markings was two years old November 1, 1912. Since that time he has continued his efforts and now has the black white-faced mule practically a fixture. It is his intention to continue the breeding of this animal until it shall become known the world over. He is now planning to extend the market for his jacks to Argentine, South America, which promises an exceptionally good market for such animals.

On January 6, 1897, Colonel Miller married Miss Oakland Leeper of Chillicothe. They have one son, Roger Stone. Fraternally Mr. Miller is a Knight Templar and thirty-second degree Mason, and is chairman of the board of stewards in the Methodist Episcopal Church South. Professionally he is a member of the State and National Bar Association. For a man who has accomplished so much in his profession and in other ways, it is only natural that he should be a big man both physically and mentally.

REUBEN BARNEY, SR., M. D. A man of the highest professional attainments was the late Dr. Reuben Barney, Sr., who for thirty-five years was engaged in the active practice of medicine and surgery at Chillicothe. That city never had a citizen more loved and respected than Doctor Barney. This esteem was shown him in many ways during his lifetime in honors and responsibilities heaped upon him by his fellow men, and at his death a final tribute was paid him when every business house in the city closed its doors, a thing, it is said, never before done for any other departed citizen.

Reuben Barney, Sr., was born in the State of Vermont and received his medical education at the Albany Medical College in Albany, New York. He enlisted in the Union army during the Civil war, and served as a surgeon in the Massachusetts General Hospital during the last year of the conflict. Following that he engaged in active practice at Hoffman's Ferry, New York, three years and in October, 1868, arrived in Chillicothe, Missouri. From that time until his death, on July 15, 1903, he was continuously associated with his profession in Livingston County.

The late Doctor Barney was a member of the Chillicothe Episcopal

Church and served as its senior warden more than thirty years. Politically a republican, with the exception of the Cleveland administration, he served almost continuously as president of the United States Board of Pension Examiners in his district. He was also for eight years president of the Chillicothe Board of Education.

The late Doctor Barney was one of the organizers of the Chillicothe Building Association, and from its origin to the time of his death its president. He was surgeon for the Chicago, Milwaukee & St. Paul, the Chicago, Burlington & Quincy and the Wabash railroads. His professional relations were with the Livingston County, the Grand River Valley and the Missouri State Medical societies and the American Medical Association. He was one of the organizers of the Grand River Valley Society, and was honored as president both of that society and of his county society. Fraternally he had a high standing in Masonic circles, was grand commander of the state, grand high priest of the Royal Arch Chapter, a grand patron of the Order of the Eastern Star, and had taken thirty-two degrees in the Scottish rite.

The memory of the late Doctor Barney is cherished by many men and women in Northwest Missouri, and his character and ideals are continued to the active benefit of mankind through his sons, all of whom are professional men. Doctor Barney married Miss Mattie Prindle, who is still living. She has served as state grand matron of the Eastern Star, and is now one of the board of control of the Masonic Home at St. Louis. Of their four sons, three are physicians and one a civil engineer. Dr. Reuben Barney, Jr., lives in Chillicothe, and a sketch of him follows. P. C. Barney, the second son, attended the Missouri State University, later graduated in civil engineering at the Rensselaer Politechnic Institute in Troy, New York, for a time served in the engineering department of the United States navy, but for several years past has been a civil engineer connected with the water supply department of New York City. Dr. M. D. Barney, the third son, is a graduate of the Bellevue Hospital Medical College at New York City, but is now retired from practice and is operating a farm and creamery at Powell, Wyoming. The youngest son, Dr. H. N. Barney, graduated from the Bellevue Hospital Medical College and is engaged in practice at Richmond, California.

REUBEN BARNEY, JR., M. D. For more than forty-five years the City of Chillicothe has enjoyed the professional services in the field of medicine and surgery of a Doctor Barney, and Dr. Reuben Barney, Jr., has made a name and reputation in the sphere so highly dignified by the late Doctor Barney, Sr.

Reuben Barney, Jr., was born in Chillicothe, a son of Dr. Reuben and Mattie (Prindle) Barney. His early education was received in the local schools, and after leaving high school he entered the St. James Military Academy at Macon, Missouri, and pursued his medical studies in the University Medical College at Kansas City. As soon as he graduated he took up practice at Chillicothe, and was associated professionally with his father until the latter's death twelve years ago. Since that time he has practiced alone. Doctor Barney is especially proficient in the field of surgery, and a large part of his practice is of that nature. Since his first graduation he has taken post-graduate work in the Bellevue Hospital Medical College of New York City, from which noted institution he has a degree, and has done other post-graduate work in New York City and Chicago.

Doctor Barney married Miss Anna Reynolds of Chillicothe, daughter of R. W. Reynolds. They are the parents of two children: Reuben

Reynolds and Olive. Doctor Barney is a member of the Episcopal Church and politically is a republican. His public service includes work as a United States pension examiner, as county coroner, and for several terms as president of the city board of health. He has also been interested in military affairs, and was one of the organizers of the Leach Rifles, which became Company H of the Fourth Missouri National Guard. At the organization of the company he was its first sergeant, and was later transferred to the regimental staff, being commissioned assistant surgeon of the regiment. Fraternally he is affiliated with the Benevolent and Protective Order of Elks and the Masonic Order.

Doctor Barney has been particularly active in the Livingston County and the Grand River Valley Medical societies, and like his father has been honored as president of both these organizations. He also is a member of the Missouri State Medical Society and the American Medical Association. He is surgeon of the Chicago, Burlington & Quincy, Chicago, Milwaukee & St. Paul and the Wabash railroads.

GEORGE EMMETT WALTER. One of Northwest Missouri's successful men is George Emmett Walter, who laid the foundation for his prosperity as a farmer out in Holt County, and who for the past ten years has been identified with the management of the Farmers Bank of Rockport, and in general financial judgment and business ability he is accounted one of the strongest men in that section of the state. While energy and judgment are important factors in the business of banking, the foundation of confidence is in integrity of character, and it is his unsullied reputation for absolute honesty and fair dealing that has made Mr. Walter so influential a factor in local business circles.

George Emmett Walter was born in Holt County, January 12, 1866, the third in a family of four children born to Frederick and Mary Walter. There are two brothers, Len and Andrew, and one sister, Alice, all of whom were born in Holt County. His father was one of the early settlers of what is known as the Corning Settlement in Holt County, and is still living, the owner of a fine home and farm near Corning, where he has for a number of years conducted a general store, and is the owner of extensive lands both in Holt and Atchison counties. Mr. Walter's mother died August 12, 1901.

George E. Walter spent his life to his twenty-fifth year on his father's farm, and takes a pardonable pride in the fact that his youth was compassed by the wholesome environment of rural surroundings. While developing his muscle in the fields at home he also attended school at Corning, and later graduated from the National Business College at Kansas City, Missouri. At the age of twenty-five he began farming for himself, and has since acquired a fine property of 320 acres, located in sections 1 and 2, township 63, range 41, with forty acres in section 5 of the same township and range. On his farm he has a seven-room house, a substantial barn, 40 by 80 feet, with a full equipment of sheds, cribs, scales, and all the improvements found on the best farms in Northwest Missouri. His arrangements for feeding stock are specially excellent, and he is one of the large stock feeders and shippers in Atchison County, usually sending about one carload of fat cattle to market every year, and from one hundred to two hundred head of fat hogs. Among other improvements on that model homestead is an orchard and vineyard affording an ample supply of fruit for family use.

30, 1868, a daughter of Benjamin and Wilhelmina Bowers. Benjamin
Bowers came from Hanover, Germany, and located in Atchison County
in 1845, as one of the early settlers and prominent German farmers of
Benton Township. He died in 1892 and his widow now lives in Corning.
Mr. and Mrs. Walter are members of the German Lutheran Church, and
in politics he is a democrat, has taken much interest in political affairs,
though chiefly for the benefit of good government, has served as delegate
to various conventions, and in 1900 was elected county collector of
Atchison County and reelected in 1902. For ten years, while living
on the farm, he was a director and clerk of the school district. He was
also at one time a director of the Creamery Company of Corning, and
vice president and assistant cashier of the Farmers Bank of Corning.

In the Farmers Bank of Rockport Mr. Walter is one of the chief
stockholders, a director, and his genial and accommodating services as
cashier have proved invaluable to the institution since its organization.
The Farmers Bank of Rockport was organized in 1905, by Doctor Strick-
land, John H. Traub, J. S. Bennett, J. J. McCartney, C. O. Robinson,
G. E. Walter. Originally its capital stock was $20,000, which has since
been increased to $30,000. The president is John H. Traub, J. S. Bennett
is vice president, H. G. Cooper is second vice president, G. E. Walter
is cashier and S. M. Clark is assistant cashier.

JOSEPH DURFEE. One of the most prominent names in banking
circles in Atchison County is that of Durfee. The present Joseph Durfee, cashier of the Citizens State Bank of Rockport, is a son of the late
Col. A. B. Durfee, who was one of the founders and for many years
president of that institution. In the broader fields of citizenship, as
well as in business, the late Colonel Durfee performed much useful
service, which has properly identified him for all time with the history
of this locality. Colonel Durfee was a type and example of one who
succeeds in life, though his youth was passed in comparative poverty,
and with only such advantages as he could procure by his own labors
and ambitions.

The late Col. Aaron B. Durfee was born at Marion, Ohio. When he
was quite young his father died, and he and other children were assisted
in gaining an education by an uncle. Aaron's brothers, Joseph and
Charles, were soldiers during the Civil war, Joseph being a lieutenant-
colonel. Aaron B. Durfee in early years was a civil engineer and also
a lawyer, and was a man of thorough scholarship, though acquired
through self study, possessed splendid financial judgment, and was
noted for the thoroughness with which he carried through every undertaking. He was one of the early members of the Rockport bar, and
identified himself actively with all the important developments of the
town. Though coming to Missouri a poor young man, by admirable
foresight and business methods he acquired a fortune. He was one
of the pioneer bankers of the county, and the old private banking house
of Durfee, McKillop & Wyatt was the first firm that furnished a general
banking service in Atchison County. Colonel Durfee died June 11,
1891. His wife, whose maiden name was Sallie Todd, died in February, 1881.

Joseph Durfee, who since his father's death has succeeded in large

2032 HISTORY OF NORTHWEST MISSOURI

At the death of his father Joseph Durfee was about twenty-one years of age, and then became the largest stockholder and a director. For several years he served, as assistant cashier, and was then elected cashier, a post he now fills, and looks after a large share of the executive details.

Mr. Durfee is a member of the Presbyterian Church and a deacon in that organization. His fraternal associations are with the Independent Order of Odd Fellows and the Knights of Pythias at Rockport, and in politics he is a republican. He is a member of the executive board of the Rockport Lecture Association, and his interest in local affairs brought him the honor of election in 1905 as mayor of the city without an opposing candidate.

Mr. Durfee married Miss Leona Oliver on June 9, 1892. She was born December 2, 1872, and has spent practically all her life in Rockport. She is a graduate of the high school, and was also a student in the Hardin College at Mexico, Missouri. Mr. and Mrs. Durfee have had two children: Otis, born April 9, 1893, and died April 29, 1900; and Joseph Eugene, born September 11, 1894. Mr. and Mrs. Durfee reside in one of the most elegant homes of Rockport.

CLAUDE M. DONOVAN. The cashier of the Citizens Exchange Bank at Orrick in Ray County is one of the ablest bankers in that section of the state and is familiar with every practical detail of banking from the work of janitor and office boy up to the responsibilities of executive management. Mr. Donovan is also a popular citizen and has some interesting family connections with the earlier times in Northwest Missouri.

Claude M. Donovan was born at Missouri City, in Clay County, July 30, 1875. His parents were A. K. and Elizabeth (Marsh) Donovan. His father was born at Maysville, in Mason County, Kentucky, and died in 1906 at the age of sixty-three. The mother was born in Lafayette County, Missouri, and is still living at Kansas City. There were eight children in the family, and the four still living are: Elmer A., married and living at Kansas City; Claude M.; Luke E., of Missouri City; and Francis, of Kansas City. The parents of these children were married in Clay County, Missouri, and the father owned a small farm near Missouri City. He was known as a breeder and a dealer in live stock, and that was his chief vocation through his active career, though for years he was in the boot and shoe business at Missouri City. He was a man of quiet and retiring disposition, and though a loyal democrat never sought office.

Claude M. Donovan was reared in Missouri City, attended the public schools there, and began his career as clerk in a grocery store. November 13, 1893, he began his banking career, when he found work in a humble position for the Norton Brothers Bank at Missouri City. From the fall of 1893 until the following April he worked without any pay, getting experience only. He then began drawing a salary of $15 a month, and that was gradually increased and his responsibilities likewise, until his promotion to the post of cashier. He held that office eight years, and was cashier both for the bank at Missouri City and the Citizens Exchange Bank at Orrick, both of which banks were then controlled by the Norton brothers. Mr. Donovan had to divide his time between two banks, spending a part of each day at the two places, and when the press of business required it often worked far into the night. This was a thorough apprenticeship, and few Northwest Missouri bankers have had a more practical and valuable experience. In 1906 Mr. Donovan was made cashier of the Citizens Exchange Bank at Orrick, after the change of management and ownership, and has held that office ever since.

On June 30, 1902, Mr. Donovan married Edna S. Ralph. Mrs. Donovan was born at Missouri City, June 23, 1874. They have two children: Ellen E., born November 5, 1904; and Margaret R., born March 14, 1909. Mr. Donovan votes with the democratic party and he and his wife are members of the Methodist Church.

Mrs. Donovan's father was the late Dr. Arthur B. Ralph, one of the prominent old-time physicians of this section of the state. He was born near Orrick, in Ray County, February 29, 1836, and died at the home of Mr. and Mrs. Donovan February 17, 1911. Doctor Ralph married Ellen Hardwick who was born near the present site of Excelsior Springs, in Clay County, April 9, 1844, and is now deceased. Her parents were Lewis and Elizabeth (Smith) Hardwick, her father born in Virginia, June 20, 1807, and died November 7, 1863. Elizabeth (Smith) Hardwick was born in St. Charles County, Missouri, October 15, 1805, and died June 29, 1888. Of the ten children in the Hardwick family the two still living are Mrs. Margaret Moffett, a widow, at Kansas City, and Mrs. Caroline Sublett, also a widow, of Kansas City. Lewis Hardwick and wife were married in St. Charles County, Missouri, and were among the earliest pioneers who settled in Clay County, locating here in 1829. He was a farmer, and in 1860 removed to Missouri City, were he died. The late Dr. A. B. Ralph was a son of Dr. A. B. and Mary E. (Brasher) Ralph, both natives of North Carolina, where they married, and in 1829 came to Northwest Missouri and located in Ray County. The senior Doctor Ralph was born December 25, 1800, and died June 9, 1888, while his wife was born in 1809 and died June 8, 1870. They had three sons and four daughters, and the two still living are: Lucy, widow of Dr. William Campbell of Kansas City, and Belle, wife of J. B. Gant of Kansas City. The late Doctor Ralph, father of Mrs. Donovan, was reared in Northwest Missouri, was well educated for the time, and in 1865 graduated M. D. from the St. Louis Medical College. His first location for practice was at Camden. He was married October 7, 1868, and a year later removed to Missouri City, where he was long engaged in the practice of his profession, and gave his services to the people of that entire vicinity. After his wife's death he spent his remaining years with his daughter at Orrick. Doctor Ralph was a member of the Masonic fraternity and for years belonged to the Christian Church. He was a strong democrat in politics, was honored several times with the office of mayor of Missouri City, and was otherwise prominent in that locality. The two children of Doctor Ralph and wife were: Lois, wife of E. L. Hunt, of Orrick, and Mrs. Donovan.

WILLIAM L. PIGG. Few Ray County families have longer and more interesting connections with this section of Missouri than the one represented by the above named farmer and banker of Orrick. It was fully three quarters of a century ago that the pioneer arrived on the banks of the Missouri River, and the flowing waters of that stream have since witnessed many transformations in the fortunes of the family and in the country.

William L. Pigg, who was born August 6, 1860, on the farm he still occupies, is a grandson of Lewis Pigg and his wife, Sallie (McWhorter) Pigg, both natives of Kentucky, whence they came on to Northwest Missouri in 1839, to Ray County. He located a quarter section of school land on the banks of the river, and being a blacksmith by trade established a little shop and, while clearing off the brush and timber supported his family by doing custom blacksmithing for the neighboring settlers. Five years after the arrival, came the historic flood of 1844, inundating the entire Missouri Valley. When it passed all the improvements and possessions were gone, too, and the family was left destitute. The grandfather in the face of this misfortune permitted the land to revert to the county, and moved to Southpoint, where he found work at his trade to provide a living for his family. In the spring of 1845 he returned to his former location, but in April of the same year died. His wife, who was a daughter of John McWhorter, a member of the North Carolina Volunteers during the Revolution, after the death of her husband petitioned the county to allow the farm to be put up at auction. Her request was granted, and she bid in the 160 acres at $2.00 an acre, and had it deeded to her oldest son, Reuben. It was heavily timbered land, and it was a tremendous task to clear it up and prepare it for cultivation. A house built of logs was the family residence until 1871, when it was replaced by the present modern home. Mrs. Lewis Pigg died November 5, 1857, and all her five sons and five daughters are also deceased.

Reuben Pigg, the oldest of the second generation and the father of William L., was born in Casey County, Kentucky, November 3, 1821, and died on the homestead December 24, 1900, being then in his eightieth year. He was old enough to take an active part in the task of pioneering when the family came to Ray County, and took charge of affairs and became head of the family after his father's death, which occurred when he was about twenty-three years old. He had learned the blacksmith trade under the eye of his father, and for many years kept a shop on the farm. Owing to his heavy responsibilities he did not marry until the age of thirty-five, when Miss Susan Writesman became his wife. Her family was one of the first in Clay County, where she was born February 23, 1834, a daughter of Peter and Polly (Officer) Writesman, who were natives of Virginia and came out to Clay County in 1823 or 1824.

Reuben Pigg was noted for his vigorous activity, which he maintained almost to the end of his life. In the early days he was known for his skill and eagerness as a hunter and fisherman. This pursuit did not prevent him from clearing up and improving the 220 acres in his farm, and he gained much of his profits from the raising of stock. He was an active member of the Christian Church, and though a strong democrat was loyal to the Union during the war. He once said: "I have seen my fences lined with McClellan's men, who helped themselves to what they could find, and my family was obliged to take what was left." Of his eight children, three sons are living: William L., George H. and Charles, all in or near Orrick.

William L. Pigg grew up on the farm which his father had improved, and as a boy became acquainted with all branches of farm management, and did not a little clearing on his own account. His education came from the country schools and one year in the State University at Columbia. When schools days were over he elected to remain on the farm, and has found farming the most satisfying and independent as well as a very profitable vocation.

November 26, 1884, Mr. Pigg married Miss Maggie Kirkpatrick. She was born in Virginia, March 15, 1864. Her father, Charles Boyd Kirkpatrick, was born in the same state October 13, 1819, and died there March 12, 1875, while his wife, whose maiden name was Isabelle McDowell Kerr, was born in Virginia April 25, 1822, and died April 25, 1873. The Kirkpatricks came out to Ray County in 1869, but afterwards returned to Virginia. There were four sons and three daughters in their family. Mr. and Mrs. Pigg have one son, Elmer L. He is cashier of the Missouri City Bank, Missouri City, and has a son, Elmer L., Jr., born September 30, 1911.

Mr. Pigg's homestead, comprising 280 acres, has a beautiful location along the banks of the Missouri, with a fine view over that valley. In 1890 Mr. Pigg assisted in the organization of the Citizens Exchange Bank of Orrick, and was one of its directors until the death of A. D. Brasher, the first president, since which time he has held the post of president. Mr. Pigg is one of the most popular and progressive citizens in Ray County. He is a Democrat, and with his wife a member of the Christian Church. His mother is still living and makes her home with him.

JOHN M. PIGG. The career of John M. Pigg, a farmer and banker at Orrick, began with excitement and adventure during the Civil war, when he was only a boy, but the later years have been marked with a steady and quiet industry, with steadily rising prosperity, and a secure place in the esteem of his community.

He was born on a farm located three miles north of his present place, November 8, 1846, a son of Jefferson and Julia (Roy) Pigg. His father was born in Casey County, Kentucky, a son of Lewis and Sally (Mc-Whorter) Pigg, who, when he was a boy, moved to Ray County and settled a tract of school land on the banks of the Missouri. They came in 1839, and five years later Lewis Pigg died, leaving the development of the homestead to his sons. Jefferson, who was one of five sons and five daughters, all now deceased, grew to manhood in Ray County, was a farmer for many years, and later started a general store and was also in the hotel business at Orrick, where he died.

Julia Roy, the wife of Jefferson Pigg, was born at Independence, Missouri, a daughter of Joseph and Mary Louise (Shackleford) Roy. Both were of French ancestry, and their families lived near St. Louis in St. Charles County. When they married there in 1813, there were thirty-six witnesses at the wedding, and not one could read or write, signing the marriage record with "their marks." The wedding was a thirteen-day celebration, and it required a barrel of whisky and a fat hog every day. Joseph Roy was one of the early French traders in Western Missouri, locating at Independence, where he owned more than six hundred acres of land. Jefferson and Julia Pigg were the parents of four children: Mary, widow of Charles Freeman, of Ray County; John M.; N. B., of Orrick; and George W., of Oklahoma.

John M. Pigg had his education in the country schools with two terms in high school, and was less than fifteen years old when the entire country became involved in civil war. On account of the war he left home in the spring of 1862 and went to the far West with a freighting outfit to Utah. Of the twenty-six in the party, only two are now alive. After two years of roughing it in the West, he returned to Missouri, and for six months was driver of a stage out of Independence. Such were the strained relations growing out of the war that he was warned to leave the country, and did so in a hurry. On his last trip a woman had given him $3.00 to buy her some fruit cans. There was no time to perform the errand, and he kept the money and after his return lost track of its owner. The interesting part of the incident is that about two years ago Mr. Pigg learned of a man bearing the same name as the woman who had given him the money, and by correspondence found that he was a son of the woman, and that the latter was still living. Thus after a lapse of forty-eight years he was able to restore the $3.00 with which he had been entrusted. On leaving the second time he again went to Utah, and stayed in the West until all hostilities had ceased.

February 22, 1872, Mr. Pigg married Nellie Tucker, who was born

September 16, 1853, in the same house that was her husband's birthplace. Her father, Daniel H. Tucker, was born in Marion County, Kentucky, October 21, 1816, and came with his parents to Ray County in 1835. On November 10, 1836, he married Milly Elliott, who was born in North Carolina November 21, 1820, a daughter of John and Susana Elliott. There were fourteen Tucker children, and those now living are: James L., of Ray County; Mrs. Martha Grider, of Ray County; Mrs. Lena Bryan, of Oklahoma; Ben F., of Ray County; Mrs. Pigg; Andrew, of Ray County; Daniel, of the same County; Mrs. Eliza Wolf, of Ray County; Mrs. Sallie Hall and William, of Ray County.

To the marriage of Mr. and Mrs. Pigg were born twelve children, and the eight living are: Julia, wife of T. E. Dudgeon of Ray County; Sallie, at home; Joseph, a physician practicing in Alaska; W. B., of Ray County; Eliza, wife of H. E. Potter of Orrick; John M., Jr., Louis F. and Maggie, all at home.

The greater part of his career since the war Mr. Pigg has spent as a farmer, though for six years he was in the hardware business at Orrick. He has occupied his home farm for thirty years, and nearly all its improvements represent his individual energy and management. In 1890 he was one of the financiers who organized the Citizens Exchange Bank of Orrick, and for twenty-five years has served as its vice president. He was also one of the organizers and has since been treasurer of the Patrons Telephone Company of Orrick. His farm comprises 160 acres. Fifty acres are in alfalfa, and he has been one of the most successful in introducing this crop in Ray County. Another large crop with him is potatoes, and he has long been a raiser and feeder of cattle and hogs. In politics a democrat, he is serving as a justice of the peace, and has been a member of the Christian Union Church since he was twenty-two years of age.

WILLIAM N. KIRKHAM. The quiet life and substantial accomplishment of the farmer have been the lot of William N. Kirkham, whose home is in the Orrick neighborhood of Ray County. Besides his farm holdings he is a banker, and has accumulated sufficient against the days that are to come, and the respect in which he is held is not less than his material accomplishment.

A Missourian by birth, he was born in Montgomery County November 1, 1847, a son of David and Ann M. (Freeland) Kirkham. His grandfather Kirkham was a native of England, and on coming to Virginia settled on the James River and followed the vocation of fisherman. David Kirkham was born at Petersburg, Virginia, in February, 1820, and died May 8, 1873. His first wife, above named, was a native of Rockingham County, Virginia, and died in 1850 at the age of twenty-four, leaving the two sons, William N. and Charles R., both of Ray County. Later the father married at St. Louis Adelaide Cowen, a native of England, and of the four children of this union two are living, one in New York City and the other in Galveston, Texas. David Kirkham after moving to Missouri was a merchant at Portland in Callaway County, in 1864 became a tobacco dealer in St. Louis, and in the same year came to Ray County, where he bought and sold and manufactured tobacco, and remained here until his death.

William N. Kirkham received most of his schooling in St. Louis, and also in Montgomery County. He was reared for the most part by his mother's parents, the Freelands, who lived in Montgomery County. Since his boyhood he has been largely dependent on his own exertions. On December 22, 1869, he married Miss Susan A. Gooch, and they have now lived together as man and wife for forty-five years. She was born

October 2, 1852, on adjoining farm now occupied by Mr. and Mrs. Kirkham. Her father, Alexander Gooch, was from Kentucky, and an early settler in Ray County. The three children comprising the family of Mr. Kirkham are: Emma A., wife of Will R. Vanhoozer, of Orrick; Archibald, a physician practicing in Jasper County, Missouri; and Maggie, at home.

In the prosperous agricultural district around Orrick Mr. Kirkham has spent his active career as a farmer, and since 1880 has occupied his present farm of 200 acres, situated in the rich alluvial bottoms of the Missouri. He has inaugurated many improvements, and has found both the comforts and the profits of life in country communities. His farm is now rented, and he enjoys the leisure of semi-retirement. At the organization of the Bank of Orrick he contributed some of the funds, was one of its directors from the beginning, and for the last twelve years has served as vice president and now president. Politically he is a democrat.

CHARLES R. KIRKHAM. While for more than forty years Mr. Kirkham has followed the routine of the efficient farmer and good citizen in the vicinity of Orrick, Ray County, he was for several years of his youth a Texas cowboy on the open ranges of that great state, and in order to lay the foundation of his present prosperity he had to work hard from the time he was fourteen years old.

Charles R. Kirkham was born in Montgomery County, Missouri, July 22, 1849. His brother, William, also of Orrick, and himself were the only children of David and Ann M. (Freeland) Kirkham. His mother died in 1850 at the age of twenty-four, and his father was again married. David Kirkham, who was born in Virginia, where his father settled on coming from England, died May 8, 1873, at the age of fifty-three. During his residence in Missouri he was chiefly engaged in the mercantile and tobacco business, having moved to Ray County in 1869, and from that time until his death bought and sold and manufactured tobacco.

Charles R. Kirkham and his brother were reared chiefly by the maternal grandparents, the Freelands, who lived in Montgomery County. His education was finished at the age of fourteen, and at sixteen he and his brother as partners began working the farm of Joe Dorton. Two years later he went to Texas, in 1869. Hardly a fourth of that state was then settled up, the rest of it being occupied by the cattlemen and the Indians and buffaloes. He worked as a cowboy on the ranches until 1873, and had some interesting experiences. Returning to Ray County in 1873, he began his career as independent farmer by purchasing forty acres north of his present place. In 1877, after his marriage, he moved to the location which has been his home for the past forty years. He now has over three hundred and fifty acres under his management, eighty of which lie in the rich and fertile bottoms. He is a farmer who knows his business thoroughly, and while improving his property to the highest point of productiveness has also put up many buildings that increase the comforts and convenience of country life. Mr. Kirkham is a democrat, is affiliated with the Independent Order of Odd Fellows, and his wife is a member of the Christian Church.

November 9, 1875, Mr. Kirkham married Elizabeth A. Blyth, who was born just a mile west of where they now live, on October 10, 1854. They have a fine family of seven children: William H., of Richmond, Missouri; Albert, of Ray County; Alene, wife of William Wholf, of Ray County; V. B., of Nebraska: Dallas, wife of Claud Heath, of Jackson County, Missouri; Ross and Lillian, both at home.

Mrs. Kirkham's father, William R. Blyth, was one of the prominent pioneers and large landholders in Ray County. He was born in Tennessee January 18, 1803, and died March 27, 1886. He was in the very advance guard of pioneers in Ray County, having arrived in 1823. He did little more than look over the country then, and went back to his native state. In 1826 he came on for permanent settlement, bringing his mother with him. He entered a tract of Government land and bought more, paying only twenty-five cents an acre for some of it. A 160 acres included in the present homestead of Mr. Kirkham was entered in 1822 by John Keeney, and was later bought by Mr. Blyth for $250, a sum that would now represent the value of only three or four acres. William R. Blyth was in every way a successful man. All his education came from his own studies, during the night hours, when he applied his mind to books by the light of a fireplace. Besides a landed proprietorship at one time comprising 1,400 acres in Ray County, he was prominent as a citizen. He served as first lieutenant in Captain Clark's company during the Black Hawk war of 1832. He represented Ray County in the Missouri Legislature during 1840-42 and in the State Senate from 1842 to 1846. His first wife, whom he married in 1830, was Didama Fletcher, a daughter of David and Rebecca Fletcher of Maryland. She was born June 9, 1811, and died November 3, 1845. Of her five children the two living are Mrs. Becky J. Stokes of Ray County and Thomas of Kansas City. January 5, 1848, Mr. Blyth married Leannah Riffe, who was born in Casey County, Kentucky, January 24, 1826, and died July 23, 1910, a daughter of John and Polly Riffe. Five of her nine children are living: John L., of Floyd, Missouri; Mrs. Kirkham; Mattie, wife of L. A. Vandiver, of Orrick; Laura, wife of Charles H. Branham, of Orrick; and Robert, of Ray County. The late Mr. Blyth among other activities had at one time taught school in Ray County. He was a member of the Christian Church at the time of his death.

EVERT ENDSLEY. One of the fine farms of Ray County, near Orrick, has been under cultivation by one family more than half a century, and its present owner and proprietor, Evert Endsley, has done much to improve his ancestral acres and increase in value and productiveness a farm with which he has been familiar from his earliest recollection.

On this farm he was born November 22, 1869. His is one of the oldest families of Ray County, with a continuous residence of ninety-five years. His grandparents were John and Hannah (Wells) Endsley, who came to Ray County in 1819, the same year that Congress passed the law enabling Missouri to come into the Union of states. Ethbert Endsley, father of Evert, was born in Ray County, June 18, 1834, and died October 30, 1908. He was reared on a farm and had a career of quiet uneventfulness until 1852, when he joined in the exodus to California. The party with which he traveled to the gold coast went across the plains, and six months elapsed between the starting and the arrival. After five years as a miner he set out again for the states, coming by way of the Isthmus of Panama, and up the river to St. Louis and thence to Ray County. In 1864 he against went West to Salt Lake City, and from there to Montana, where he was in the early mining activities of that state, but followed business as a freighter. After a year he returned home, and thereafter the responsibilities of a Missouri farm afforded him a satisfactory outlet for his energies. He did well as a general farmer and stock raiser, acquired about four hundred and eighty acres of land, and made the breeding of Short-horn cattle a feature of his industry. He had begun farming on eighty acres situated in the midst of the timber, with only a log house to live in. He was a member of the Masonic fraternity, and politically an active democrat.

On December 27, 1857, the father married Eliza M. Vance, who was born in North Carolina April 1, 1836, and died June 8, 1873. She was the mother of nine children, and the three still living are: Alice, wife of J. M. Heilfer of Belleville, Kansas; Evert; and Fannie, wife of Jack Dudgeon, of Sibley, Missouri. September 15, 1875, Ethbert Endsley married Mary L. Owens. Five children were born of that union, and the two living are Arthur, of Ray County, and Callie, wife of Henry Coons, of Ray County.

Evert Endsley spent his boyhood on the farm, and all his education came from the local schools. The practical training of his youth served him well when he took up the independent life of a farmer, and since acquiring the homestead he has done much to improve its acres and has erected some substantial buildings. The place contains 145 acres, and is devoted to general farming.

On December 9, 1891, Mr. Endsley married Jennie Estelle Black. She is of Scotch lineage, and was born at Sharon, Mercer County, Pennsylvania, June 9, 1873, a daughter of Frank and Jeanette (Russell) Black. Her father, who was born in Scotland June 25, 1850, was brought by his parents to America in 1854. After a year and a half spent in Maryland the family returned to Scotland, but in a short time came again to this country, locating in Knox County, Illinois. Frank Black afterwards went East from Illinois and was married in Pennsylvania, where his wife was born October 8, 1852. Later the Black family moved to Jefferson County, Kansas. Mrs. Endsley's parents are still living, and are residing in Ray County, north of Evert Endsley's farm, on a part of the Jackie Frazier farm. Mr. and Mrs. Endsley have two children: Beatrice, who was born July 10, 1896, and is at home; and Birdie Franklin, born February 5, 1903.

EDGAR D. BROWN. When the roll is called of the men who have done most to add to the value, the productiveness and beauty of the Northwest Missouri country, a place of peculiar honor must be awarded to Edgar D. Brown. He had the genius and persistence for doing things that others thought impossible or impracticable. For generations thousands of acres in the Missouri bottoms have been left uncultivated, worthless to mankind, a miasmatic swamp, breeding malaria and mosquitoes. Hundreds have wished that the fertility of that land might be made available, and protected against the superabundance of moisture. But Edgar D. Brown combined vision with practical means, lost little time in dreaming, and by his individual work and leadership has reclaimed many thousand acres in Ray and Carroll counties, and has actually created a wealth that will continue to yield revenue for all the generations to come.

The fact that he was born near Danville, Illinois, may have some significance, since in that district reclamation of submerged river lands was begun a number of years ago with remarkable results. He was born April 25, 1868, a son of William H. and Lydia (Lusk) Brown, was reared on a farm, attended common schools and then entered Knox College at Galesburg, but on account of ill health did not graduate. As the six sons became of age their father divided among them his property, so that each had a fair capital to begin with.

For a time Mr. Brown lived in Kansas, and then came to Missouri and began operations in the Missouri bottoms around Hardin in Ray County and Norborne in Carroll. He showed his faith in the future by purchasing some five thousand acres of swamp land. After surmounting some huge obstacles he succeeded in draining it, and then sold it off in small tracts. Some of the best farms in that section are on the tract that he developed. After finishing his plans there he came to Orrick and secured a tract of 1,100 acres, in swamp and lake. He formed a drainage district, and almost the entire area is now in cultivation, raising remarkable crops of wheat and corn. He began his enterprise at Orrick in 1906, and it was in the face of bitter opposition that he carried out his project. The same thing was true in other states when the reclamation movement began, and it was necessary partly to convince and partly to ignore the many who said the thing was impossible. He was a man of few words and these he uttered after due deliberation and careful analysis. Therefore he made but few mistakes. He was slow in reaching conclusions, but once he had decided upon a course of action he put his shoulder to the wheel and used every art and energy to achieve success. He was a man of great foresight and planned far into the future, and reaped a golden harvest as the fruits of his perspicacity. He sought to build up, never to destroy. His life was helpful to those around him. He was a man of remarkable memory and was known as "the walking abstract," since he knew every piece of land from the beginning and had no need to consult the records. It is said that no other one man has done so much to benefit Ray and Carroll counties.

The tragic aspect of his career is that after all his successful work he passed away in prime of life on March 20, 1915, after an illness of ten months. Few men deserve a higher tribute of respect and esteem from their fellow citizens. He was a member of the Masonic order.

Mr. Brown was married in Kansas City, Missouri, to Lillie A. Bastman. She was born in Kansas City, a daughter of K. T. and Hannah (Lidman) Bastman, both of whom were born in Sweden but lived in Kansas City thirty-five years. Mr. and Mrs. Brown are the parents of two children, William H. and Lolita.

HON. JAMES H. HULL. Platte County is the home district of James H. Hull, who will be remembered over the state at large for his services as a legislator. Mr. Hull represented his home county in the forty-fifth, forty-sixth and forty-seventh general assemblies, and during his last term was elected speaker of the house. In the forty-seventh assembly he was also chairman of the judiciary committee and a member of the committee on rules and the committee on clerical force. He was an able parliamentarian, and was one of the strong and influential men in the house.

By profession Mr. Hull is a lawyer, and has long been active in the Platte City bar. He was born at Weston, Platte County, October 20, 1861, was educated in the public schools of his native town and at LaGrange College at LaGrange, Missouri, and was graduated from the law department of Washington University, at St. Louis. Mr. Hull was prosecuting attorney of Platte County for two terms, from 1903 to 1907. Mr. Hull was married May 22, 1899, to Miss Frankie E. Wells of Platte City. She was the daughter of Hon. William C. Wells, a pioneer of Platte County. She died May 20, 1901. On September 3, 1907, Mr. Hull married Miss Jessie Wilson of St. Joseph, Missouri.

Mr. Hull has been a Mason since early manhood, a Knight Templar, a member of Mystic Shrine of Moila Temple of St. Joseph, Missouri; also

means, broad experience and ability, and a capacity for effective action, as well as the faculty of deliberation. The Chesnut family has been prominent in Plate County for more than half a century, and the honors of public office have been held by two generations.

David A. Chesnut is of fine old Kentucky stock, and was born at London, Laurel County, in that state, July 23, 1857, a son of William and Lucinda (Garrard) Chesnut, and grandson of Abraham and Elizabeth (Blakely) Chesnut. The Garrards will be recognized as a historic Kentucky name. Lucinda Garrard was a granddaughter of Governor Garrard, while her maternal grandfather, Harry Tolman, served as secretary of state under Governor Garrard. Lucinda was a daughter of Daniel Garrard, who was a soldier in the War of 1812. William Chesnut was born at London, Kentucky, June 5, 1826, and died in Platte City, Missouri, March 5, 1895. He was married November 2, 1847, to Lucinda Garrard, who was born at a place called Union Salt Works, Clay County, Kentucky, December 28, 1827, and died at St. Joseph, Missouri, September 5, 1894. Their five children were: Garrard, of Kansas City; Kate, wife of Frank G. Clemings, of Platte City; Bettie, wife of Thomas G. Cockrill, of Platte County; Delia, widow of C. O. French, of Kansas City; and David A.

Judge William Chesnut was a man who in character and activities measured up to the best conceptions of the fine old Kentucky gentleman. Well educated, he followed merchandising in Kentucky until 1859, when he brought his family to Platte County, coming by wagon and river boats, and settling on land six miles east of Platte City. He had exceptional judgment and success in managing land and stock, and accumulated large tracts of farm property and other tangible wealth. At the beginning of the war he raised part of a company for Weston's Confederate Regiment, but after a short service returned home. In November, 1878, he was elected judge of the County Court, was re-elected in 1880 and 1882, and resigned the office March 1, 1884. During 1880-81 he was president of the Platte County Agricultural Association. In June, 1884, Judge Chesnut left the farm and moved into Platte City. He served several terms as alderman, and spent much time and his own means in improving the streets, and it is said that no one did more as an individual to that purpose than Judge Chesnut.

David A. Chesnut was reared in a fortunate environment, and has well utilized his advantages. He attended the district schools while on the farm, and later completed a commercial course in the Christian Brothers College at St. Joseph. Returning home, he became a farmer by profession. Having inherited part of his father's place, he bought the rest, and now owns more than six hundred and twenty acres, a splendid farmstead to the management of which he gives his supervision. During his active career as a farmer he made a specialty of mules and shorthorn cattle. Since 1897 his home has been in Platte City, where he owns a fine residence. Mr. Chesnut has varied business interests, and since 1896 has been vice president in the Wells Banking Company of Platte City.

He has given valuable public service in the same office earlier held by his father. In 1906 he was elected presiding judge of the County Court, and by reelection in 1910 completed eight years of office, and

son. This son, W. Pryor, born July 19, 1880, now lives at Fargo, North Dakota. The present Mrs. Chesnut, whom he married September 2, 1886, was Miss Maggie Dye. She was born near Weston, in Platte County, a daughter of James and Lucy J. (Guthrie) Dye. Her father, who is living at a venerable age in Weston, was born in Mason County, Kentucky, February 13, 1834, and came with his parents to Platte County in 1844. He was married October 9, 1856, to Miss Guthrie, who was born January 1, 1840, and died September 2, 1882, leaving four children. Mr. and Mrs. Chesnut have two daughters: Edna, born in 1887, is the wife of J. B. Dillingham, of Platte City; Elizabeth, born October 2, 1889, is the wife of H. R. Farnsworth of Neligh, Nebraska.

SPENCE REDMAN, M. D. Since 1850, with the exception of an interval of a few years, Platte County has always had the services of a Redman in the medical profession. One of the pioneer doctors was the late Elias C. Redman, who was a familiar figure, making his rounds in the sparsely settled district in the years before and after the war, and few of his contemporaries performed so valuable a service. Dr. Spence Redman, his son, has continued the profession and has spent more than thirty years in active practice in Platte County. In point of years, only one other physician in the county now ranks as his senior in continuous service.

Dr. Spence Redman was born two miles west of Platte City, on January 25, 1862. His father, Dr. Elias C., was born at Bardstown, Kentucky, May 2, 1822, and died in 1892. On November 28, 1849, he married Margaret E. Spence, who was born in Boone County, Missouri, March 16, 1821, and died in 1901. Their five children were: Annie, widow of J. M. Cockrell, of Texas; Ben R., who died March 12, 1861; Minnie, wife of Dr. J. A. Baldwin, of Fayetteville, Arkansas; Spence; and Maggie, wife of Joseph W. Clark, of Liberty.

When Elias C. Redman was seven years old his parents moved to Ralls County, Missouri, where he grew to manhood. He was well educated in the fundamentals, and in June, 1849, was graduated from the St. Louis Medical College with his degree doctor of medicine. After his marriage in the fall of the same year he sought a field for his work in the comparatively new and unsettled section of Western Missouri, locating at Platte City. His office was in town until 1860, when he removed to a farm west of town, and continued making his professional rounds until 1875. He then retired from active practice, and devoted himself steadily to his farm until 1885, when he moved into Platte City and lived there until his death. A democrat, he was much interested in politics, in behalf of good government and his friends, but never for an office himself. He was active in the Christian Church.

Dr. Spence Redman spent his early life on his father's farm near Platte City, and after attending the public schools and the Gaylord Institute of Platte City took up the study of medicine under his father's direction. His regular courses were taken in that old and high-class institution, the Jefferson Medical College of Philadelphia, where he was graduated M. D. April 2, 1883. He had barely turned his majority, and with the prestige of a thorough training and a good family name returned to Platte City to make this the scene of a professional career which has had no important interruption down to the present time. For a number of years he practiced over a wide radius of country, and rode and drove over country roads in all kinds of weather, long before the telephones, good roads, and automobiles came to lighten the burdens of the doctor. His services are now given to many people whose parents were among his early patients. Doctor Redman is a man of broad and accurate knowledge, and has an excellent professional and general library and a good office equipment. His professional associations are with the County and State Medical societies and the American Medical Association.

Doctor Redman's first wife was Camilla S. Burnes, who died leaving two children, Margaret E. and Spence, Jr., both at home. On April 15, 1908, Doctor Redman married Myrtle Higgins, a member of one of the oldest and leading families of this section of Missouri. She was born near Parkville, in Platte County, November 14, 1880. Her grandfather, A. J. Higgins, was born in Howard County, Missouri, in 1816, five years before the admission of Missouri to the Union, and at the age of twenty-one, in 1837, became a pioneer in the Platte Purchase, recently opened for settlement. In Platte County he preempted three farms. On his father's advice, and on the understanding that he would be recompensed, he turned over two of the farms to his brothers, but owing to his father's sudden death he was left without recourse for much of his pioneer enterprise. In 1850 he began the clearing of his third farm, and lived there until his death in 1894. A. J. Higgins married Susan Gregg, who was born in Clay County, Missouri, September 28, 1823, and died August 8, 1899. The date of her birth indicates the pioneer advent of the Gregg family to Northwest Missouri. Her father was David Gregg, who in 1837 moved from Clay County to Platte County and settled on a place adjoining the Higgins farm. She was married to Mr. Higgins January 5, 1842, and became the mother of five children, three of whom are still living.

David B. Higgins, the father of Mrs. Redman, was born in Platte County, December 4, 1850, was reared on a farm, attended country school and the St. Joseph High School, and at the age of nineteen began teaching, a vocation for which he was well qualified and which he followed in various localities for ten years. After that he conducted the home farm, and in 1891 took the lead in organizing the Platte County Farmers Mutual Fire Insurance Company, in which he was elected secretary. With the exception of one year he has held that post ever since. In 1902 he moved from the farm to Platte City, and now gives all his time to the affairs of the company. It now has insurance in force in Platte County aggregating $2,540,000. Mr. Higgins is a member of the Masonic fraternity, and in politics a democrat. On February 7, 1878, he married Sarah M. Noland, who was born in Platte County in January, 1860, and died in 1902. Their two children are A. J., of Platte City, and Mrs. Doctor Redman.

CAMPBELL WELLS. The cashier of the Wells Banking Company of Platte City has had a purposeful career. While thirty years have been spent in active banking, Mr. Wells has had many relations outside of his private business.

Born at New Market, Platte County, Missouri, May 23, 1864, Campbell Wells is a son of William C. and Eliza Jane (Strother) Wells, and a grandson of William and Elizabeth (Thorp) Wells. His grandfather, who was a physician, came from Kentucky to Platte County in 1843. Back in Kentucky he had formerly been well to do, but met with business reverses, and unwilling to remain in his home county a poor man he came west to Platte County during its early development and started life anew. During the cholera epidemic in this section of Missouri he was incessant in his efforts to attend the stricken people and contracted the disease himself. While convalescent, owing to the insistent calls of his patients, he took up his round of duties too soon.

While riding on duty near Parkville his horse stumbled and threw him, breaking his neck.

The late William C. Wells, who was born in Madison County, Kentucky, September 12, 1834, and died at Platte City, Missouri, March 21, 1898, was nine years old when his parents moved to this state. Although his regular schooling was all compressed within portions of two years, he always passed among his associates as a man of education, due to his wide reading and keen knowledge of men and affairs. His career began as a merchant in the inland village of New Market. His store was burned during the war. At the close of hostilities he was appointed deputy sheriff, and while engaged in those duties took up the study of law and was qualified and admitted to practice in the Platte County courts. His best service as a lawyer was in keeping his clients and neighbors out of court. As arbiter and adviser he practiced the rule of getting the litigants together and settling their difficulties without resort to legal procedure. In 1879 he started the Exchange Bank of Wells & Company, and six months later bought the other bank then existing in Platte City. From January 1 to December 1 of 1887 he was out of business, and at the latter date organized the Wells Banking Company, of which he was president until his death, and which has been successfully carried on by his sons for the last fifteen years. Besides his service in business and the law, he occupied a prominent place in public affairs, and represented Platte County in the twenty-ninth and thirtieth assemblies and was state senator at the time of his death. By his marriage to Eliza Jane Strother, who was born at Richmond, Kentucky, December 25, 1837, and died December 28, 1890, there were six children. The three now living are William S., Campbell and Samuel Rollyn, the last being a resident of Leavenworth, Kansas.

Campbell Wells was liberally educated, first in the public schools of Platte City, then in the Gaylord Institute and finally in the old school established by Alexander Campbell, the Bethany College of West Virginia, where he was graduated in June, 1884. From a college boy he soon turned himself to practical affairs, becoming assistant cashier of the Exchange Bank of Wells & Company, and has been cashier of the Wells Banking Company since its organization in 1887.

While never a seeker for official honors, he has worked on the board of education in Platte City and gives much time to the local schools. His most important service began with his appointment in 1897 as one of the curators of the state university. Governor Stephens first selected him for this position, and he continued on the board during the administrations of Governors Dockery and Folk. It was partly through the efforts of Mr. Wells that the school of journalism was organized, the first among American universities requiring a four years course. He is also the head of a happy household. November 11, 1891, he married Mattie Callahan, who was born in Platte County, a daughter of H. T. Callahan. Their two children are: Catherine Jane, who was born in May, 1893, and graduated from the University of Missouri in June, 1913; and William C., born December 14, 1896, and now a student in the state university.

WILLIAM STROTHER WELLS. It has been frequently remarked that no stronger booster for Platte County interests lives than this prominent Platte City banker, William S. Wells, now president of the Wells Banking Company. While his active career of more than thirty years has been devoted to banking, through all the grades from clerk to president, he has in countless ways given practical direction and effect to his public spirit, and his name has been associated with the principal undertakings of the last two decades for the advancement of his home county.

William S. Wells was born at New Market, Platte County, August 6, 1862, but was reared in Platte City, where his father was a lawyer and banker. After leaving the public schools he became a student in what was then known as Gaylord Institute, spent two years in Woodland College at Independence, Missouri, and finished his education in Bethany College, West Virginia, where he was graduated in June, 1882.

Beginning October 1, 1882, he was clerk in the Exchange Bank of Wells & Company at Platte City for one year, and on October 1, 1883, became cashier of the Bank of Edgerton, Missouri, and filled that office exactly two years. In March, 1886, Mr. Wells became bookkeeper in the Citizens National Bank of Kansas City, where his knowledge and training in his chosen vocation were broadened under metropolitan conditions. On January 1, 1887, he was elected cashier of the Bank of Independence, and remained in that city until March 4, 1891, when he returned to his home town to accept the vice presidency of the Wells Banking Company. With the death of his father in 1898 he succeeded to the presidency of a bank which, for soundness and service, is one of the strongest institutions in Platte County.

Mr. Wells was married October 18, 1893, to Miss Maud Gates, who was born at Port Byron, Illinois, but from the age of two years was reared in Independence, Missouri. They are the parents of four children: Louise Elizabeth, William Gates, Oscar and Strother.

Mr. Wells comes of good old southern and Kentucky stock. His grandparents were William and Elizabeth (Thorp) Wells. His grandfather, a physician, was a prosperous man in Kentucky, but as a result of business reverses was unwilling to remain in his home county a poor man, and in 1843 sought a new country and located in Platte County, Missouri. During the cholera epidemic in this section of Missouri his incessant efforts to attend the stricken people caused him to contract the disease, and had not regained his strength when he was again in the saddle endeavoring to relieve the suffering all around him. While riding near Parkville his horse stumbled and threw him, breaking his neck.

William C. Wells, father of William S., was born in Madison County, Kentucky, September 12, 1834, and died at Platte City, March 21, 1898, after a long and successful career. He was nine years old when he came to Missouri, and his regular schooling was confined to portions of two years. By self study he became a well educated man, and stood among the foremost men of Platte County. His career began as a merchant in the inland village of New Market. His store was burned during the war. A little later he was appointed deputy sheriff and while engaged in those duties took up the study of law and was admitted and began practice in the Platte County courts. His best service as a lawyer was in keeping his clients and neighbors out of court. As arbiter and adviser he used his influence to get the litigants together and settle their difficulties without resort to legal procedure. In 1879 he started the Exchange Bank of Wells & Company, and six months later bought the other bank in the town. From January 1 to December 1 of 1887 he was out of business, and at the latter date organized the Wells Banking Company, of which he was president until his death.

Besides his service in business and law he occupied a prominent place in public affairs, and represented Platte County in the Twenty-ninth and Thirtieth General Assemblies and was state senator at the time of his death. William C. Wells married Eliza Jane Strother. She was born at Richmond, Kentucky, December 25, 1837, and died December

28, 1890. Of the six children three are still living: William S.; Campbell, cashier of the Wells Banking Company; and Samuel Rollyn, of Leavenworth, Kansas.

HENRY L. DILLINGHAM. No name is spoken with more respect in Platte County than that of Dillingham. The family have lived in this locality about half a century, and as farmers, business men and public officials have been factors in making the county what it is. Henry L. Dillingham is a prosperous young business leader in Platte City, and is a son of the late John H. Dillingham, whose tragic end while engaged in the performance of his official duties is an event in local history that will not soon be forgotten.

The grandparents came from Kentucky to Clay County some years before the war, settling near Mosby, but four years later moved to Platte County and located on a farm five miles east of Platte City. The grandfather was both a farmer and, like many Kentuckians, a fancier of fine stock.

The late John H. Dillingham was born at Richmond, Madison County, Kentucky, September 29, 1853, and was brought to Missouri when a baby. He grew up to manhood in this state and from an early age was noted for physical and moral courage and a readiness to engage in any undertaking promising adventure. Soon after reaching his majority he went out to Nevada in charge of some fine stock for his father, and remained in the West for some time. While at Butte, Montana, he was appointed an officer and for several months assisted in keeping law and order in that new and wild country. Following his return to Missouri he married and turned his attention to the quiet vocation of farmer, which he continued until the failing health of his wife caused to leave Missouri. Starting in a wagon, they made a health trip to Colorado, but soon after their return to Platte City Mrs. Dillingham died. He then engaged in the livery business at the county seat, and was soon appointed city marshal, a post he held until April, 1896. He resigned to begin an active campaign for the sheriff's office, and was elected in the following fall, taking office January 1, 1897. In 1898 he was unanimously reelected. In his capacity of sheriff, while engaged in making an arrest, he was shot and killed on August 20, 1900. His death was quickly avenged by his own son, Henry, who after a hand to hand struggle killed his father's slayer. John H. Dillingham was a man without fear and without reproach, and his courage was tempered by the kindliness and tenderness which have so often marked heroic natures. No death was more widely and sincerely mourned in Platte County. At the time of his sudden passing, he was also serving as manager of the Platte County Agriculture and Live Stock Association, and was the owner of some of the finest saddle horses and mules in Missouri. Prior to his terms as sheriff he had served as deputy under Sheriffs Synamon and Berry. One incident is related as showing his persistence in the performance of duty. A valuable horse was stolen in Platte City. Deputy Dillingham started in pursuit, and stopping only to eat, snatch a few hours' sleep and change horses, he followed the trail across the country to Indian Territory, where he caught his man and brought him and the stolen horse home without extradition papers. The prisoner made his escape from the local jail, and again Mr. Dillingham took up the chase, and finally caught the fugitive at Vicksburg, Mississippi, and this time had the satisfaction of seeing him convicted and sent to the penitentiary.

John H. Dillingham married Anna L. Oldham, who was of a pioneer family, originally from Kentucky. Their six children were: Henry

L.; W. W., of Platte City; John C., deceased; Joseph B., E. S., and Bessie A., all of Platte City.

While growing up in Platte City Henry L. Dillingham attended both the public schools and the Gaylor Institute. In 1898 he built and installed the first telephone exchange at Platte City, starting with fifty subscribers, and at the end of two years sold the plant. After his father's death he was appointed to fill out the unexpired term of sheriff, although at the time only twenty-three years old. His next venture was the purchase of a drug store, and he studied pharmacy and passed the examination for a registered pharmacist. After selling his business in 1909, he was engaged in handling real estate and farming until May 1, 1913, when he again acquired his former business as a druggist and now has one of the best stores in that line in the county.

No citizen takes a more public spirited interest in his home community. He is a member of the city council, has served as a justice of the peace, and in 1914 was president of the Platte County Fair Association and has been elected to the same post for 1915. The Platte County Fair is the oldest institution of its kind in the state, having been established fifty-one years. For twelve years Mr. Dillingham served as chairman of the Platte County Democratic Committee, and represented for a time the Fourth Congressional District in the state committee. He is a member and treasurer of the Presbyterian Church, while his wife belongs to the Christian Church. In July, 1901, he married June C. Cockrill, a native of Platte County and daughter of Thomas G. Cockrill, one of the county's leading farmers. Their two children are named Bessie Lucile and Mary Wanda.

ALVA NAYLOR, M. D. In addition to building up and looking after an excellent practice at Platte City, Doctor Naylor has been fully responsive to the duties and privileges of citizenship, and is one of that active group of men who stand for material and civic betterment in one of the best communities of Northwest Missouri. Doctor Naylor is of a family that has been identified with Platte County for sixty-five years.

His grandparents, Ignatius and Elizabeth (Arsmith) Naylor, left Kentucky and by means of wagon and team crossed the intervening country and located in Platte County in 1850. Their settlement was near Waldron in the timber, which had to be cleared off before cultivation was possible. The grandfather lived there and made a home and reared his family.

Abner Naylor, father of Doctor Naylor, was born in Bath County, Kentucky, August 12, 1843, and was a boy of seven when brought to Platte County, where he was educated in the old-fashioned subscription schools. After his marriage he bought a tract of land near his father, and remained there, a prospering farmer and good neighbor, until his death in April, 1902. For several years he served as a justice of the peace, was a democrat in politics, and with his wife worshiped in the Methodist Church South. He married Elizabeth Brink, who was born in Missouri March 17, 1857, and is now living with her son, Doctor Naylor. Her family comprised six sons and one daughter, and the five now living are: A. J., of Kansas City; Mary, wife of C. W. Babcock, of Hickman Mills, Missouri; Alva; W. W. and Chester, both of Waldron.

Dr. Alva Naylor had a youth surrounded with the usual conditions of a farm, and when its duties did not demand his presence he attended the neighboring country school. His ambition was for other things than farming, and after a course in the Stanberry Normal College he began clerking in a drug store at Waldron and at the same time studied pharmacy both in books and practical experience, and passed the examination before the state board. After some years as a druggist, in 1901 he entered the University Medical College at Kansas City, and was graduated M. D. in 1905. Since then he has found his field of practice in Platte City, and has also served as county physician. His professional associations are with the Platte County and the Missouri State Medical societies and the American Medical Association.

Doctor Naylor is affiliated with the Masonic fraternity, the Independent Order of Odd Fellows and the Modern Woodmen of America. In his home city he was member of the school board. During his service on the school board he took the lead in the campaign for the erection of the present modern schoolhouse, and its establishment is credited largely to his vigorous efforts.

November 11, 1894, Doctor Naylor married Flora Grey. She was born in Platte County, and her parents, Henry H. and Eliza (Gargus) Grey, are both natives of Missouri and Mrs. Grey lives in Kansas City; Mr. Grey died in August, 1905. Doctor Naylor and wife have two children, Leota and O. A., both at home.

COL. W. T. JENKINS.   For nearly a quarter of a century Col. William Talliaferro Jenkins has been editor and publisher of that influential Platte City journal, the Landmark, a paper read in the majority of Platte County homes and frequently quoted by the Missouri press for the keen paragraphs and incisive editorials that brighten its pages. Colonel Jenkins represents a ''first family'' in this section of Missouri, and his own career has been notable for varied activities and honors outside of his useful sphere as a newspaper man.

Born near Platte City, August 12, 1853, he is the son of Howell and Charlotte (Evans) Jenkins, and the only one of their four sons and two daughters still living. His father was born in Merthyr Tydvil, Wales, July 17, 1812, and was married in London, England, June 30, 1838, to Charlotte Evans. In 1841 they embarked on a sailing vessel in the Thames, and were two months in crossing the Atlantic, one of their children dying in the meantime and being buried at sea. From New York City they came West, following the slow routes of river and canal to St. Louis, and thence by steamboat up the Missouri to Platte County, where they landed in the fall of 1842. Howell Jenkins was a marble cutter by trade, having served his apprenticeship in his native land. Today are standing monuments in the Platte City Cemetery which were cut by his hands from the native stone. Later he became a California '49er, crossing the plains with a party of gold seekers. His skill at his trade got him a position as gang boss in blasting operations in the mines. One day a charge exploded prematurely, and in consequence of his injury he returned to the states in 1851, coming by sea and across the Isthmus of Panama. He then engaged in the mercantile business at Platte City until the late '60s. He also owned a drug store, and for twelve years was postmaster. During the war he turned his business over to his sons. He voted with the democratic party, and was a charter member of Nebraska Lodge No. 12, I. O. O. F.

Colonel Jenkins grew up in Platte City, and his acquaintance with the people, with politics and general business affairs is based on close personal experience covering nearly half a century. For his education he attended the public schools, the Gaylord Institute and for a time the Washington and Lee University in Virginia. Leaving school in 1872, he returned home and spent eleven years with his brother Thomas in the mercantile business. Then followed his election to the office of county collector of Platte County, and his two terms covered eight years.

In October, 1890, the ownership of the Platte City Landmark passed into the hands of Colonel Jenkins, and he has been at his desk and directing the policies and writing the leading articles ever since. A number of times the people of the community have sought his services for public duty, and he has been one of the democratic leaders and interested in both county and state party affairs. He has been a county and state committeeman, and has gone to several national conventions as a delegate and his name has appeared on the tickets as presidential elector.

Colonel Jenkins is well known in the Masonic fraternity, having affiliation with the York bodies of Royal Arch and Knights Templar and for twenty-seven consecutive years has been prelate in the commandery. He is also a member of the Independent Order of Odd Fellows. He is a former president of the Northwest Missouri Press Association and has been its historian for many years; he is also a member of Missouri State Press Association and a member of several clubs.

On May 1, 1888, he married Sallie Guthrie, who was born in Callaway County, Missouri, at New Bloomfield, a daughter of Ewing and Mary Jane (Chalfant) Guthrie, early settlers in that section of Missouri. Colonel Jenkins has one daughter, Ruth Mary, living at home.

GUY B. PARK. One of the able and learned members of the legal profession of Northwest Missouri during the past fifteen years, Guy B. Park has taken a forceful and stirring participation in the affairs of Platte City, both as professional man and private citizen. He is a legist by inheritance, inclination, training and experience, for his father was a lawyer, and he was brought up amid surroundings that tended to train his thoughts along professional lines, having been born at Gaylord Institute, Platte City, July 10, 1872.

Mr. Park's father, Thomas Woodson Park, was born in Madison County, Kentucky, October 12, 1842, and died December 8, 1908, at Platte City, Missouri. He was a son of Elihu and Mary (Ballou) Park, natives of Kentucky, the former of whom died when Thomas W. Park was a child. Mrs. Park subsequently married Prof. F. G. Gaylord, who was from the Empire State and a school teacher by profession, being the principal of a private school at Irvine, Estill County, Kentucky. In 1857 the family migrated to Platte City, Missouri, where Professor Gaylord established the Platte City Academy for Boys, and afterwards, for years, he conducted what was known as Daughters' College at Platte City. Professor Gaylord and his wife passed away at Platte City, universally respected and esteemed.

Thomas Woodson Park was fifteen years of age when he accompanied his mother and stepfather to Platte City, and here he completed his excellent training under the tutelage of his father. When the Civil war broke out, his sympathies were with the cause of the South, and this caused him to enlist as a private under the flag of the Confederacy. He was in the army of Gen. Sterling Price, and his brave and faithful services gained him promotion to the rank of lieutenant, but illness forced his retirement from service before the close of the war. On his return home he took up the study of law, and after being graduated from the law department of the University of Louisville, Kentucky, was admitted to practice, November 16, 1867. However, Mr. Park never gave his active attention to practicing his profession, although his knowledge thereof was a great help to him in succeeding years when he held numerous positions of high trust.

The rank of major, to which Mr. Park was entitled, was acquired by service on the staff of Governor Woodson. In 1868 he entered the newspaper field, at Platte City, Missouri, when he founded the Reveille, one of the first democratic newspapers to be published in Northwest Missouri. On June 2, 1871, this paper was consolidated with the Landmark, and Mr. Park continued its editor and owner until February, 1881. He was a fine and forceful writer, supporting the measures which he believed just with fire and energy, and attacking what he believed to be bad movements with courage and a trenchant pen. As a finished orator he was also well and widely known, and as president of the State Editorial Association of Missouri, in the session at Fredericktown, where Eugene Field was the guest of honor, he was presented, by Mr. Field, with the humorous poem entitled, "Tom Park at Fredericktown."

In 1870 Thomas W. Park was elected county clerk of Platte County, and in 1874 received the reelection, but resigned March 27, 1877. From 1881 to 1890 he was chief clerk of the labor commission at Jefferson City under Governor Marmaduke; in the latter year was appointed chief clerk to Secretary of State Alex Leasuer, and in 1903 became assistant to Secretary Stevens of the St. Louis World's Fair, continuing in this position until about one year after the close of that exposition. At that time he retired from the active affairs of life, and so lived until his death.

On November 15, 1866, Major Park was united with Miss Maggie E. Baxter, who was born at Liberty Landing, Clay County, Missouri, in 1849, and is still living at Platte City. Two children were born to this union: Fred G., born March 21, 1868, a resident of Las Vegas, Nevada, who held the same position as his father, that of chief clerk, under Secretary of State Roach, and after five years of service resigned; and Guy B.

Mrs. Thomas W. Park is a daughter of John and Sarah (Wallis) Baxter, pioneers of Clay County, Missouri, the latter of whom was born in 1812 and died January 12, 1879. The father was for some years well known among the business men at Liberty Landing, where he was the proprietor of a hotel and owner of a hemp warehouse. Mrs. Park was finely educated in art, music and literature, at Professor Love's girls' seminary at Liberty. Subsequently she went to teach in Professor Gaylord's Academy at Platte City, and there became acquainted with Mr. Park, whom she subsequently married. In 1892 Mrs. Park opened Gaylord Institute, at Platte City, primarily known as Daughters College, and this she continued to conduct until 1909, when, because of advancing years, she abandoned her educational labors. She is widely known not only in her own city, but throughout this part of the state in educational circles, and her friends are many in social life.

Guy B. Park received his early education in Gaylord Institute, from whence he went to enter the law department of the University of Missouri. He was graduated therefrom in June, 1896, and for 2½ years held a position in a law office at Denver, Colorado, but in 1899 returned to Platte City, where he has since continued successfully in the practice of his profession. His practice is broad and general in character and includes the best kind of business that a lawyer can enjoy, and he holds a high place in the esteem of his fellow practitioners here. He has been successful in a number of cases of importance, and is generally accounted a capable, painstaking and conscientious legist. In official life he has served two terms as prosecuting attorney of Platte County, and at the present time is attorney for Platte City. In addition to the organizations of his profession, Mr. Park is an Odd Fellow and has attained high rank in the Masonic fraternity, belonging to the various orders up to and including the Mystic Shrine at St. Joseph.

Mr. Park was married November 16, 1909, to Miss Eleanora Gabbert, who was born July 27, 1889, in the vicinity of Weston, Platte County, Missouri, a daughter of M. H. and Henrietta (Cox) Gabbert, natives of Missouri who are still living near Weston. To this union there has come one daughter, Henrietta, who was born December 26, 1910. Mr. Park and his mother are members of the Christian Church. Mrs. Guy B. Park is affiliated with the Baptist denomination.

HON. ALONZO D. BURNES. A member of the bar of Northwest Missouri during a period of thirty years, and for more than half that time judge of the Circuit Court of the Fifth Judicial District, including the counties of Platte, Clinton, DeKalb, Andrew and Holt, Hon. Alonzo D. Burnes occupies a conspicuous and distinguished position in his community. Possessed of a mind of the judicial order, it would seem that Nature had intended him for service upon the bench, to which he would have probably been sent in any locality in which he prosecuted his legal labors. In his reelections to office Judge Burnes had no opponent, either republican or democratic, and received the endorsement of every attorney in all the counties comprising his district. This high esteem in which he is held as a jurist among the entire profession is the result of a rare combination of fine legal ability and culture, and incorruptible integrity, with the dignified presence, absolute courage, and graceful urbanity which have characterized all his official acts.

Judge Burnes was born near Platte City, Missouri, October 27, 1864, and is a son of Fielding and Elizabeth (Summers) Burnes. His father was a native of Indiana and his mother of Kentucky, and they were married in Platte County, Missouri, the father having come here with his parents in 1836, when he was seventeen years of age. When he entered upon a career of his own he adopted the vocation of his father, that of agriculturist, and continued to be so engaged during a long, active and useful life, which was characterized by honesty, integrity and fidelity to high principles, and which terminated in 1897, when he was seventy-five years of age. Mrs. Burnes passed away in 1892, at the age of sixty-five years. Mr. Burnes was well known in fraternal circles, being a Knight Templar Mason, and in his political views was a democrat He and Mrs. Burnes were devout members of the Methodist Episcopal Church, to the teachings of which they were always faithful. Of their children, two are living: Judge Alonzo D., of this review, and Alice, who is the wife of H. A. Koster, of Kansas City, Missouri.

Alonzo D. Burnes was reared amid the surroundings of the farm and received his primary education in the district schools, but as a lad he had decided upon a professional career, and when he had completed the course of the country schools his father sent him to Gaylord Institute, at Platte City. Later he became a student at Vanderbilt University, Nashville, Tennessee, being graduated from the academic department in 1881. Returning to Missouri, he entered the law department of the state university, from which he received his degree in 1885, was admitted to practice that same year, and returned to Platte City to enter upon the duties of his calling. Here he was soon recognized as an able lawyer and took a prominent position at the bar. He served as city attorney of Platte City for a period of eight years, and as prosecuting attorney four years, and in the fall of 1898 came his call to the bench, reelections following in 1904 and 1910. Judge Burnes is said to be one of the most capable and popular jurists in Northwest Missouri. To occupy a position on the bench worthily, it is not enough that one be learned in the principles of jurisprudence, familiar with precedents and thoroughly honest, and possess legal acumen. The majority of individuals are unable to entirely divest themselves of prejudice, even when acting with conscientious fidelity, their own mental characteristics unconsciously warping their judgments. This unconscious influence is a variable factor, a disturbing power, and it is because this factor is not discernible and practically does not exist in the nature of Judge Burnes that he has attained such high standing in the esteem of the bench and bar throughout this part of the state. In political matters he is a democrat, but because he holds that a judge should not be partisan in anything and not lower the dignity of his office, or render himself subject to a charge of favoritism or prejudice, he has refrained from taking any active part in politics. In fraternal circles he is well and favorably known, being a Shriner Mason at St. Joseph, a Pythian Knight and a member of the Odd Fellows. Since 1881 he has been a member of the Christian Church and has endeavored to live up to its teachings.

Judge Burnes was married to Miss Rowena Boone, a native of Howard County, Missouri.

W. Z. JONES. Of the industries allied with agriculture, the developing of fine livestock is one of the most interesting and profitable, and particularly, in these days, is the breeding of superior horses carried on, to meet the demand for standard animals. Partly by environment and partly by science, has the present magnificent saddle horse been developed from the primitive type, and with its fine, glossy skin and clean limbs it is beautiful to look at and it does not require a horseman to recognize its superiority to the common type, its graceful movements and its look of intelligence proving to anyone that it is thoroughbred. For a number of years W. Z. Jones, a representative citizen of Platte County, has devoted much attention to livestock, and since 1908 has been in the business of breeding saddle horses and jacks at Platte City.

W. Z. Jones was born in Montgomery County, Kentucky, November 14, 1861, and is a son of James H. and Fannie (Ragan) Jones. James H. Jones was born January 27, 1835, and died April 4, 1894. He was reared on a farm and attended the country schools. At the outbreak of the war between the states, he entered the Confederate service and served under General Morgan. In the Ohio raid he was captured and was taken first to Camp Chase, Ohio, and from there to Lexington, Kentucky, and was held there until the close of the war. In 1869 he came to Platte County and located six miles southeast of Platte City, where he bought 160 acres of improved land and made that place his permanent home, occupying himself in agricultural pursuits. He was a strong democrat all his life, but desired no political rewards. From the age of eighteen years he was a member of the Christian Church. He was a man of sterling character and of strong convictions and, believing them right, had the courage to uphold them. In Kentucky he married Fannie Ragan, who was born November 17, 1840, and died June 26, 1911, in the faith of the Christian Church. They had but one child.

W. Z. Jones spent boyhood and youth assisting his father on the farm and attending the country schools. Afterward he had collegiate advantages for three years at Platte City, later spent one year at the University of Kentucky, at Lexington, and in 1881 returned home to give his father assistance again and soon decided to seek no further for a congenial occupation. After his father's death, his mother bought more land and Mr. Jones now owns 560 acres of some of the most productive land in Platte County. He bred and dealt heavily in livestock while on the farm, owning a fine herd of shorthorn cattle and successfully breeding French coach horses. In 1908 Mr. Jones left the farm and came to Platte City, where he has accommodations for continuing in the horse business, as mentioned.

On April 17, 1884, Mr. Jones was married to Miss Junie E. Oldham, who was born at Mount Sterling, Montgomery County, Kentucky, and is a daughter of F. M. and Sarah E. (Reynold) Oldham. The parents of Mrs. Jones were both born in Montgomery County, the father on September 22, 1830, and the mother on July 24, 1835. The latter resides with Mr. and Mrs. Jones, but the former died December 18, 1907. They came from Kentucky to Platte County in 1873, settling on a farm southeast of Platte City. They belonged to the Methodist Episcopal Church and in that faith Mrs. Jones was reared. In politics Mr. Jones has always been identified with the democratic party, supporting it from principle and not for political favor. Like his parents before him, he is a member of the Christian Church. Mr. Jones is not only one of the substantial men of Platte County, but one of the most dependable and reliable, his fellow citizens always knowing his attitude on public questions will be in favor of peace, justice, morality and temperance.

J. F. SEXTON. As county superintendent of schools of Platte County, Missouri, J. F. Sexton occupies a position of importance and responsibility, secured through his scholarly attainments and further justified by his executive ability. He is a native of the great State of Missouri, born in Platte County, four miles north of Platte City. His parents were Joseph E. and Jennie (Brown) Sexton, and they had two sons: James H. and J. F.

Joseph E. Sexton was born in Mason County, Kentucky, July 8, 1836, and died on his farm in Platte County, Missouri, November 28, 1904. In 1860 he came to Platte County and on the outbreak of war between the states in the following year, enlisted for service in the Confederate army as a private in the command of General Marmaduke. He was a gallant soldier, was twice wounded and was promoted for his valor, and at the close of the war held rank as captain. Shortly afterward he married Miss Jennie Brown, who was born in Platte County, October 25, 1846, and still resides on the home farm. Her father, James L. Brown, came early to Platte County from Tennessee and preempted land and made the tract his permanent home. After marriage, Joseph E. Sexton followed farming successfully for many years. He was zealous in his support of the democratic party and was a man honest and upright in thought and action. During the greater part of his life he was a member of the Methodist Episcopal Church and his influence was beneficial in his community.

J. F. Sexton has practically resided on the home farm all his life. After his preliminary training in the country schools he attended Gaylord Institute, Platte City, and later the Missouri State Normal School, at Warrensburg. He started to teach in the country schools in 1892 and finding this a congenial profession, has continued in educational work until the present. For two years he taught at Platte City and also taught at Tracy. In 1909 he was elected and qualified as county school commissioner, and in 1911 was elected county superintendent of schools for a term of four years and reelected in 1915 for another term of four years. Mr. Sexton is an earnest, conscientious official who cherishes the ambition to see the public schools of Platte County the best in the state. He maintains a high standard and expects his teachers to live up to it, being ever ready to advise with them and give encouragement, his appreciation of their efforts being one reason for the high esteem they all feel for him, both personally and officially.

Mr. Sexton belongs to various educational bodies and is fraternally identified with the Masons and the Knights of Pythias. He is unmarried and resides on the farm with his mother.

A. C. HAMILTON. Among the old and substantial banking institutions of Platte County is the Park Bank of Parkville, founded more than a quarter of a century ago, and whose continuous existence and practically uninterrupted prosperity are due to the business integrity and financial judgment of the Hamilton family. A. C. Hamilton, who has been cashier of this bank almost since it was founded, is a most capable bank official, and his father before him was founder and long the president of the Park Bank.

A. C. Hamilton was born in Cleveland, Ohio, in April, 1869, a son of the late A. J. Hamilton. His father was also a native of Cleveland, born in January, 1834, and died at Parkville, Missouri, March 31, 1896. He was reared in Cleveland, educated in the common schools, and in his young manhood, in 1861, enlisted in the One Hundred and Seventy-seventh Ohio Volunteer Infantry and served two years as a defender of the Union cause. He was in the real estate business until 1888, and then came to Parkville, Missouri, and established the Park Bank. He was its first president, with J. P. Tucker vice president, and A. C. Hamilton soon became cashier. A. J. Hamilton was a splendid citizen, gave his entire attention to banking, and outside of his own place of business was noted for his quiet and retiring disposition, but was keen and efficient in business matters. A. J. Hamilton was married in Cleveland to Miss Emma C. Brooks, a native of the same city. Mrs. Hamilton succeeded her husband in the office of president of the Park Bank, and is still living at Parkville. Their three sons are: A. C. Hamilton; H. A. Hamilton of Springfield, Missouri; and H. B. Hamilton, assistant cashier of the Park Bank.

A. C. Hamilton grew up in Cleveland, attended the common and high schools of that city, and was about twenty years of age when his parents came to Parkville. In April, 1889, he entered his father's bank as cashier, and with growing experience has gradually accepted the chief responsibilities of its management. Like his father, he has no disposition to indulge in politics and other conspicuous events of the community, and does his best public service as a banker. He is a republican, as was his father.

Mr. Hamilton was married in February, 1894, to Miss Kate Clark, a native of Chariton County, Missouri. They are the parents of two daughters, Helen and Irene, both at home.

JOHN T. McCORMICK. A prominent distiller and business man of Platte County and Kansas City, John T. McCormick is one of the youngest veterans of the Confederate army, has lived in Northwest Missouri since the war, and has been a farmer, merchant, banker and manufacturer during the course of his progressive career.

John T. McCormick was born in Culpeper County, Virginia, August 4, 1847. His grandfather's brother was Cyrus McCormick, whose name will always be associated with the invention and perfection of the harvesting machinery. His father was Randall McCormick, also a native of Virginia.

The period of the Civil war thrust itself into the early youth of John T. McCormick, interrupted his work in the common schools and at the age of fifteen turned him into a soldier. He was with the armies of the South during the last three years of the war. After his service he came out West in 1866 and began farming in Platte County near Camden

Point. That was his regular vocation until 1879, when he sold his place and came into Waldron. There he established and operated a general mercantile enterprise until 1884. With Cleveland's election to the presidency he was appointed collector of internal revenue for the Sixth District, and held that office four years until a change of administration. In 1888 Mr. McCormick established the McCormick Mercantile and Distilling Company at Waldron, and his active management and business energy have built that up to an important industry, with an output of 2,000 barrels of distilled products per year.

In August, 1909, he established the Waldron State Bank, and has owned the controlling interest and is president of that institution. Since 1909 Mr. McCormick has had his home in Kansas City, from which city he manages his various interests, with occasional visits to Waldron, where the business is under the direction of his sons, E. R. and W. T.

Mr. McCormick first married Miss Mary Stallard, who was born in Platte County, Missouri, of Virginia parents. She died in 1882 leaving four children: Miss Lou J., assistant cashier of the Waldron State Bank; E. R., who manages the Kansas City office of the distilling company; J. R., deceased; and W. T., at Waldron. The second wife was Jennie Miller. The present Mrs. McCormick was Elizabeth Burdette. Of three children born to this union, two are living, Louis B. and Helen, both at home. Mr. McCormick has always been identified with democratic politics.

C. H. ATCHISON, M. D. A physician at Waldron and formerly engaged in practice for a number of years at St. Joseph, Doctor Atchison bears an honored name in Northwest Missouri, and is related to those Atchisons who stood as foremost leaders in thought and action in the early days.

Dr. C. H. Atchison was born in Clinton County, Missouri, February 2, 1873. His father, the late David R. Atchison, was namesake of his noted uncle, General Atchison, Missouri lawyer, soldier and statesman, who was, as will be recalled, a bachelor and introduced his namesake into the comforts and luxuries of his home and made him part heir to his estate. Gen. David R. Atchison spent twelve years as speaker of Congress and for one day was acting President of the United States. He was educated for the Presbyterian ministry, and afterwards said he had the education but not the religion, though he died in the Presbyterian faith.

The grandfather of Doctor Atchison, and hence a brother to General Atchison, was William Atchison, who also came to Missouri and settled in Clay County near Kearney. David R. Atchison, Jr., who was born near Lexington, Kentucky, August 9, 1840, and died on his farm December 4, 1904, came to his uncle's home in Clinton County in 1849, and afterwards while living on his father's place in Clay County went to school with the subsequently notorious Jesse James of that neighborhood. He was also given the advantages of an academy, but did not take kindly to learning, and never took up a profession, perhaps to the disappointment of his uncle. During the war he enlisted for the Confederate service at Liberty, and was with the troops under General Price until wounded at Carthage, Missouri. He was a man of no little influence and power in his community, and for three terms, twelve years in all, was a judge of the County Court of Clinton County. After his marriage he devoted himself to farming, and thereafter lived plain and unadorned, making his fields and his home his primary interest. He and his wife were members of the Christian Church. Her maiden name was Laura Screace, who was born in Clinton County near Plattsburg, October 21, 1842, and died September 17, 1902.

Doctor Atchison, the only one now living of the four children of his parents, grew up on the Clinton County farm, attended local schools and in 1893 graduated from the Military School at Mexico, Missouri. The following four years were spent at home, in the routine of farm duties. In that time he had taken definite stock of his inclinations, and in 1897 entered the Ensworth Medical College at St. Joseph, where he was graduated M. D. in 1901. He was attracted to the opening of the Kiowa and Comanche reservations in Southwestern Oklahoma that year, and was the second physician to hang out his shingle at Lawton, the metropolis of the new country, his rival having anticipated that action by about two hours. After eight months of experience as a practitioner and in the varied life of the new Southwest, Doctor Atchison returned to civilization, and for ten years was located at St. Joseph with growing rank in his profession. In February, 1913, Doctor Atchison removed to Rushville, Missouri, and October 21, 1914, bought a drug store and located at Waldron.

December 10, 1910, he married Beatrice York, who was born in Harrison County, Missouri, January 31, 1879. Dr. and Mrs. Atchison are members of the Christian Church, and in politics he adheres to the democratic faith of his fathers.

D. A. COLVIN. One of Atchison County's oldest and most honored citizens is D. A. Colvin, who in the course of a long and useful life has been a soldier, clerk, several years was a public official and freighter in the northwestern mining countries of the early days, has filled a number of county offices in Atchison with ability and efficiency, and for more than thirty years has been identified with the Citizens Bank of Atchison County at Rockport.

D. A. Colvin is a native of New York State, born in Chautauqua County, February 24, 1840. His parents, Welcome and Elmira (Munn) Colvin, were also born in New York, and in 1847 the family removed west to Milwaukee, Wisconsin, lived there six years, then located in Brookfield in the same state, and in 1859 came to Missouri and located at Hemme's Landing in Holt County. D. A. Colvin acquired his education chiefly in Wisconsin, and after his arrival in Holt County worked as a clerk until the beginning of the war, being employed by F. N. Thompson and another merchant. In the spring of 1861 he enlisted in the Missouri State Militia for six months, after which he helped recruit Company C for the Fifth Missouri Regiment, became first lieutenant in his company, and continued in active service with that command about eighteen months. At the expiration of that time he assisted in the recruiting of another company for the Twelfth Missouri United States Cavalry, but on account of his father's death was compelled to resign his commission and remain at home and give his work for the support of his mother and family at Rockport.

In 1864 Mr. Colvin went to the newly opened mining region of the Northwest, in Montana and Idaho, and participated in the stirring activities of that time and place. He was a freighter, a miner, a trader, and came into close contact with the people and interests and activities of the country. In the summer of 1865, owing to his qualities as a leader he was elected the first county recorder at Helena, Montana. In 1867 he located at Fort C. F. Smith on the Big Horn River, and was engaged in contracting to furnish hay and wood for that post.

After nearly four years of life in the mountainous country of the Northwest, Mr. Colvin returned to Atchison County, Missouri, in 1868, and in the fall of the same year was elected sheriff and collector of the county, an office he held until 1872. He then engaged in the livery business, and in that connection ran a transfer line between Rockport and Phelps. He was in that business until the spring of 1882, and in the meantime, in 1880, had been elected to the office of county collector.

Since 1883 Mr. Colvin has been continuously identified with the banking business at Rockport. He was one of the officers and organizers of the private bank of Durfee, Smith & Colvin, which in 1883 was incorporated under a state charter, with a capital stock of $15,000. The Citizens Bank of Atchison County has a continuous record of sound financial management and business service in this community of more than thirty years, and has always been located in the same place. At the present time its capital stock is $20,000, with a large sum representing surplus and undivided profits.

On February 22, 1872, Mr. Colvin married Ella Bennett, who was born in New York State in March, 1848, and was educated in the states of Mississippi and Illinois. Her father and mother were natives of New York, the maiden name of her mother being Diana Howard. Mr. Colvin had two children. His oldest son, Welcome R. Colvin, died when about thirty-three or thirty-four years of age, and was at that time at the outset of a promising career and serving as assistant cashier of the Citizens Bank. He married Miss Gertrude Kurtz of Marion, Iowa, and left one son, Roy Welcome. The other son, still living, is Don M. Colvin, who married Miss Hazel Bunting, daughter of William Bunting, and they have two children, Margie and Don M., Jr.

The presence of such a citizen as D. A. Colvin in one community for more than forty years has an actuating and vitalizing influence in many ways. Few movements for the public welfare have been undertaken in this time without his cordial cooperation and support. Among other things he was instrumental in the building of the privately owned railroad through Rockport, and is still financially interested in that enterprise. As a banker his well known conservatism, his thorough integrity and popular relations as a citizen with the community have helped to give poise and stability to local business affairs. Mr. Colvin is a member of the Grand Army of the Republic, is a past chancellor in the Knights of Pythias, and in politics a republican.

PARK COLLEGE. There are probably few residents of Northwest Missouri who are not familiar with at least the name of Park College, an institution which for forty years has been doing the service of enlightenment and of Christian education in its picturesque location on the rugged hills bordering the Missouri River in western Platte County. For the purpose of making the readers of this work better acquainted with the material facts, the ideals and the influence of this institution, the following sketch finds an appropriate place in these pages.

Park College was founded in 1875 by Col. George Park and Rev. John A. McAfee. The latter was its president for a number of years, and was succeeded by his son, Lowell M. McAfee, and since the latter's retirement the acting president has been Dr. Arthur L. Wolfe. The fundamental idea of the founders was to provide a school for the training of young men and young women of limited means so as to make them efficient factors in Christian leadership. John A. McAfee had been conducting a private institution with similar aims, but without financial support, and Col. George Park was a business man who had long been interested in educational work and agreed to furnish the resources for such an undertaking. Professor McAfee brought seventeen students to Parkville, and the college was opened May 12, 1875. Colonel Park had donated land for the campus and an old stone hotel building. Since that date there has been a steady unfolding and growth, both in financial means of the institution and in its facilities and purposes of educational service.

Park College lies just east of the Town of Parkville, and nine miles from Kansas City. The campus contains eighty acres on the rugged bluffs of the Missouri River, a site of many attractive features, greatly improved by simple methods of landscape gardening. The buildings are nearly all of brick and stone, and most of them were built by student labor, only the more difficult technical parts having been performed by skilled artisans. The original building is Woodward Hall, which was formerly located on the river front. It was remodeled in 1894 and used as a men's dormitory until 1908, when the land was bought by the Burlington Railroad Company and the new hall constructed on the campus, much of the old material having been used. One of the older buildings is McCormick Chapel, of brick and stone, the gift of Mrs. Cyrus McCormick of Chicago, and erected in 1886. This chapel has seating capacity for 900, and is used for many of the college services and also for the services of the Presbyterian Church of the Sabbath School. Mackay Hall, three stories, was occupied in March, 1893, and contains lecture halls, laboratories and executive offices. In 1898 was erected the Charles Smith Scott Astronomical Observatory, located on the summit of a hill overlooking the campus and containing a complete equipment of superior instruments. The Carnegie Library, gift of Andrew Carnegie, built in 1909, provides room for a library of over twenty-five thousand volumes. As a result of gifts from the Alumni Association one of the newer and handsome structures on the campus is the Alumni Building, containing an auditorium, offices, banqueting hall and other facilities for social purposes. A pumping station was built in 1897, and in 1906 a heating, lighting and power plant was completed, furnishing power and light both to the college and to the Town of Parkville. Another building, the headquarters of the industrial features of the college life, is Labor Hall, built in 1906. From funds supplied by the late Anthony Dey of New York, Waverly Hospital was completed in 1912. There are also nine dormitory buildings, and shop buildings preserve the aims of industrial and vocational education, including printing office, planing mill, storage building, etc.

The first class was graduated from the college in 1879, and in that year the state granted a charter and its government has since been under control of a self-perpetuating board of trustees, with affiliations with the Presbyterian Church. While not a sectarian school, the religious feature has always been emphasized, and the college maintains several strong organizations, the Young Men's Christian Association and the Young Women's Christian Association, and also a student volunteer band for foreign missions. Over one hundred of the alumni are scattered in foreign mission service in all the countries of the globe. Another organization that deserves mention is the Park College Chapter of the Association of Cosmopolitan Clubs, whose object is the cultivation of fraternal spirit among students of different nationalities and the promotion of universal peace. While under the same general control, Park College has two distinct departments, one for the regular collegiate work, and the other of academic scope. There are six college literary societies, and four societies in the academy. Ample facilities are given for athletic work, but athletic competition is confined to the college bodies, without participation in intercollegiate sports. Park College has graduated nearly nine hundred young men and young women, who are now found in twenty-three different countries of the world, and at least five thousand others have been students for longer or shorter periods, and have gained there some of the inspiration and efficiency for the work of their lives.

Aside from the work of Park College in its regular academic and collegiate departments, and its persistent influence in the training of men and women for Christian citizenship, there are two distinctive features which deserve some notice.

The first is what is called the "College Family Idea," continuing the early purpose of the founders to make it a school for the education of people of moderate means. As a result of the evolution of this idea a larger part of the students of Park College are found enrolled in its students' service, reducing the expenses of a college education by contributing three hours daily labor in some branch or other of the work of maintenance. Thus the students are to a large degree a family circle, to some extent self-supporting, and standing in the relation of giving as well as receiving the benefits of college life.

Out of this first idea, with the continued growth of the school, have necessarily been developed a great variety of utilities for the practical services of the student body which are not only an integral working part of the institution, but furnish a means of practical education to those engaged. This industrial work is esteemed of the highest value as giving wholesome physical exercise, developing practical efficiency, and producing a symmetrical training for life. Many students become expert workmen at their special crafts, but few choose them as permanent vocations. The largest department is the farm, where much of the food consumed by the college family is produced and prepared for use. The farm consists of 1,200 acres of fertile Platte County land adjacent to the campus. Five hundred acres are under cultivation, and the students themselves perform much of the labor of the fields. An immense amount of grain, hay, garden vegetables and other farm products are raised, and a striking feature is the apple orchard of 160 acres. The farm has a dairy herd of sixty-seven Holstein cattle, and the young farmers thus gain a practical experience in a modern sanitary dairy. This farm in its equipment of machinery, livestock and general management is a model institution of itself, and it is performing a great service in the training of young men who go from Park College to places on farms of their own. An auxilliary to the farm is a canning factory, where the raw products of the land are preserved. The surplus products are sold at the regular market rate. In the printing shop opportunities are given to those who are inclined to this particular line of industry, and all the publications of the college are printed there. Other college shops are carpenter shop, planing mill, broom factory, and also the light and power plant.

From this sketch it will be seen that Park College has succeeded in fitting its service closely into relationship with the demands of modern life, and in the forty years since its founding the influences emanating therefrom have helped to mold and direct the activities of many thousands of the world's workers.

ARTHUR L. WOLFE, Ph. D. The present acting president of Park College is Arthur L. Wolfe, who was born at Montclair, New Jersey, September 16, 1866, and has been identified with this institution continuously for twenty-six years.

Doctor Wolfe was reared at Montclair, attended the common and high schools, graduated in 1885 and then entered the New York University, where he took his degree A. B. in 1889. In the fall of the same year he came to Park College as professor of Latin. While an undergraduate at New York University he had won a fellowship, and by post-graduate

study he obtained from his alma mater in 1892 the degree Ph. D.   He
is the author of a handbook of Latin Syntax and of the Elements of
the Science of Language.   Aside from his professorship he has always
been interested in college activities.   In 1913 he was elected dean of the
faculty, and on July 1, 1913, was made acting president.

During 1901-02 Doctor Wolfe was given leave of absence from his
work, and spent some months in the University of Leipsic, Germany,
and in the American Classical School of Rome.

In 1890 at Montclair, New Jersey, he married Gertrude R. Snow, who
was born at Albany, New York, January 28, 1867.   They are the parents
of five children: Arthur Whiting, now a student in Chicago; Austin
Robert, a student in Park College; Herbert Snow, also in Park College;
Edward Winslow and Hugh Campbell.

Dr. and Mrs. Wolfe are both active members of the Presbyterian
Church, and Doctor Wolfe is a member of the Parkville Board of
Education.

WILLIAM HENRY CONN.   Probably few men in Northwest Missouri
have better exemplified the principle of self-help or have made better
use of the opportunities of life in spite of the limitations of physical
powers than the present probate judge of Nodaway County and judge
of the Juvenile Court, William Henry Conn.   His has been a career of
loyal usefulness and service, and his general popularity is based not
only upon his personal character and his gallant fight against difficulties,
but upon his practical value as a working member of his community.

Judge Conn has been a resident of Nodaway County since 1890, in
which year he located at Ravenwood and spent four years in the milling
business, followed by activity as a real estate man.   In 1906 he received
the republican party's nomination for the office of probate judge, was
elected, four years later was renominated and again elected, and in
1914 was again his party's nominee for a third term.   Throughout the
eight years of his official service the citizens of Nodaway County have
felt that the interests of widows and orphans were safely intrusted, and
he has also made the Juvenile Court an agency of reform and improvement and has corrected the wayward course of many boys not naturally
vicious.

Judge Conn was born in Hancock County, Illinois, November 4, 1846,
being the youngest of four children of Henry and Permelia (Miles)
Conn.   The parents were born, reared and married in the State of
New York, and moved to Illinois in 1840.   When Judge Conn was about
five years of age his parents located in Lee County, Illinois, and it was
in that section of the prairie state that he was reared and educated.
Following the discovery of gold in California his father left Illinois,
and after a varied career there of about four years, died in that state.
Judge Conn received his education in the public schools of Lee County,
was graduated from the Teachers' Institute and Classical Seminary at
Paw Paw, Illinois.   In 1866 his widowed mother and her other children
moved out to Worth County, Missouri, and Judge Conn followed them
in 1870.   He was a teacher in Worth County, and also served four years
as county superintendent of public schools.   Fraternally he is affiliated
with the Independent Order of Odd Fellows and is a Baptist in religious
faith.

When a child of two years Judge Conn sustained an injury from a
fall that weakened his spine, and since then he has never had the use
of his lower limbs.   It was with this severe handicap he had to face the
world, and few careers better illustrate the efficiency of a well-trained

mind and well-poised character than the life of Judge Conn, as briefly outlined in this sketch.

CHILLICOTHE BUSINESS COLLEGE. To many thousand people in Missouri and elsewhere Chillicothe is best known for its associations with the old Chillicothe Normal School, which in recent years has become the Chillicothe Business College. This institution is a monument to the late Allen Moore, a sketch of whose life has been briefly outlined in following paragraphs.

The late Allen Moore came to Chillicothe early in 1890 from Stanberry, Missouri, where he had been successfully identified with the Stanberry Normal as instructor and half owner. He was attracted to Chillicothe because of the progressive spirit of its citizens, the wealth of the surrounding agricultural territory, and the superior railroad facilities. Another influence, already noted, was the fact that his wife's people lived in the adjoining County of Linn. Mr. Moore made a proposition for the establishment and maintenance of the normal school, provided a stock company among the local citizens would purchase desirable ground and construct a building suitable for school purposes. Furthermore Mr. Moore guaranteed to erect on the chosen site a dormitory of three stories and to pay rental to the stock company for the use of the college building. The citizens accepted his proposition, and following a campaign of determined effort and enthusiasm the sum of $25,000 was raised. The first building was hurriedly but substantially erected, and in 1890 the institution was incorporated as the Chillicothe Normal School and Business Institute, with thirteen of Livingston County's well known citizens on the board of directors. The building was completed in the fall of 1890, and the school opened about the same time.

In the scope of the work the institution at first offered courses in common school branches, pedagogy, science, classics, bookkeeping, stenography, penmanship, elocution, music and photography. The first year's enrollment was 600. With the growing reputation of the school and its head, the attendance increased, the faculty was enlarged, and additional courses added. The school grew more rapidly than its material facilities and the financial resources of the local stock company. As a result Mr. Moore, in 1899, purchased the outstanding stock, and became sole owner. In 1900 the third building was erected on the campus, supplying facilities which had been urgently needed for fully eight years. All that time the work of instruction in the normal school had been maintained at the highest standards, such that the State University and other normal colleges accepted the grades and allowed full credit for work done at Chillicothe. But with the beginning of the present century conditions changed. The State University, with its large income from the state, introduced and expanded its academic and normal work, several new state normal schools were established with liberal appropriations, and the high schools were graded up and made more efficient and offering more courses. Thus the private normal school had to compete with a growing number of institutions supported by local and state government. While the services of a private normal became correspondingly less important, the complexity of modern civilization offered other fields for a private school. There was a demand for telegraph operators, and the Chillicothe Normal was the first institution of its kind to introduce telegraphy and courses in practical railroad work as regular departments of its curriculum.

The death of the founder of the Chillicothe Normal, Allen Moore, Sr., occurred January 9, 1907. His life had centered in the institution, and it represented his highest ambitions and efforts. He had planned for its continuation, and had reared his sons with the idea that they should continue the work when he should retire. After his death Allen Moore, Jr., became president and Ralph LeRoy Moore became vice president. The institution under their management was continued along the original lines for almost three years, but as the demand for business education increased with more and more competition in the normal department from state institutions, the young men wisely placed additional emphasis upon the business departments. In the fall of 1910 the normal department was abandoned, and the new title of the school became the Chillicothe Business College and College of Telegraphy. At first, however, only the advanced work in the normal department was dropped, otherwise classes being maintained in all branches required for the different grades of certificates in Missouri. With the opening of the school year in September, 1911, this feature was also abandoned, and since that time the Chillicothe Business College has conformed strictly to its name. There has been a marvelous growth of the business college, and its attendance has increased to such proportions that additional buildings became necessary, leading to the erection of Dryden Hall, a modern dormitory of twenty-four rooms for young men. The Chillicothe Business College occupies the largest plant in America devoted exclusively to business education. Its patronage is national in scope, and each year some students are enrolled from foreign countries. Approximately thirty thousand men and women have attended the Chillicothe institution since it was founded, and a large number of them have reached positions of business prominence and success. While the present institution is a monument to the efforts of its founder, the spirit of his work has been ably continued by his sons, who are equally well qualified as educators and administrators.

ALLEN MOORE. One of the foremost educators of Missouri was the late Allen Moore, who was distinguished not only as a teacher, but as an educational executive and administrator, and during his active life in North Missouri founded, built up and gave remarkable prestige to the Chillicothe Normal School and was also owner and president of the Stanberry Normal School at Stanberry, and part owner of the Springfield Normal School at Springfield, Missouri (a private normal). The late Allen Moore exerted a larger influence on the life of the state than many men whose names more frequently appeared in the current press. Under his regime the Chillicothe Normal maintained the highest standards of instruction and life in general. A long procession of students passed through its halls, and there are hundreds of successful men and women in the world who have grateful memories of the kindly and helpful influence exercised by Mr. Moore as an executive and teacher.

Allen Moore was born July 4, 1853, at Huntington, Huntington County, Indiana, and died January 9, 1907. His parents were Samuel and Elizabeth (Wiley) Moore, the former a native of North Carolina and the latter of Ohio. His father was a farmer, and spent his active career in Huntington County, Indiana. It was in that state and county that the late Allen Moore spent his early boyhood, and had training in the district schools. At a early age one of those adversities befell him which often serve to bring up and refine the highest qualities of manhood. At the age of fourteen he contracted white swelling, and for seven years walked on crutches, and never entirely recovered the use of one leg. This affliction unfitted him for the so-called active work of the world, but limited in one direction, there was proportionate enlargement and expansion of his intellectual horizon and he always showed a splendid faculty for organization and for effective carrying out of plans formu-

lated in his own mind. At an early age he was given a certificate as a
teacher, and taught twenty-six terms in the public schools of Indiana.
In the meantime he had continued his education in higher institutions,
at the National Normal University at Lebanon, Ohio, and later the
Northern Indiana Normal School at Valparaiso, Indiana, from which
institution he was a graduate. His expenses in these colleges were
defrayed by his work as a teacher.

Mr. Moore came to Missouri in 1881, locating at Stanberry, where
he became principal of the commercial department and teacher of
English in a school conducted there by Professor Morris. After the
death of Professor Morris, who was the founder of the school, Mr. Moore
and J. E. Fesler became joint owners of the institution, and after the
retirement of Mr. Moore, Mr. Fesler was sole proprietor for a number
of years. Mr. Moore came to Chillicothe in 1890, and organized the
stock company which built the Chillicothe Normal. In 1899 Mr. Moore
became sole owner of the institution which he conducted until his death.
He is remembered for his especial gifts as a teacher of English, and was
also a polished speaker and one of the most popular lecturers before
teachers' institutes and assemblies in the state. In the autumn before his
death he had addressed twenty-nine county teachers' meetings in addition to the heavy burdens involved in the management of his own schools.

At the time of his death Mr. Moore was also owner of the Stanberry
Normal at Stanberry, and half owner of the Springfield Normal at
Springfield. The old Stanberry School has since burned, while the lease
of the Springfield Normal was sold to the state when the State Normal
was located there. After buying the Springfield Normal, Mr. Moore
divided his time between that institution and the Chillicothe Normal for
one year, at the end of which time J. A. Taylor purchased a one-half
interest and took active charge of the Springfield school. Mr. Moore
also owned a farm in Livingston County, and at his death left a splendid
property to Mrs. Moore and the children.

Though a democrat, he was never active in politics. He had been
reared in the faith of the Quaker Church, and always regarded that
faith as his own.

In 1883 Allen Moore married Miss Emma J. Dryden of Linneus,
Missouri. Mrs. Moore had grown up in that section of Missouri, and
her presence in the state was one of the factors that influenced him to
locate here permanently. Mrs. Moore died January 19, 1908, a little
more than a year after her husband. To their marriage were born seven
children, two of whom died in infancy, and the others are mentioned as
follows: Allen, Jr., Ralph LeRoy, Irene, Elizabeth, and George Dryden,
who died at the age of fourteen, not long after his father.

After the death of their father the sons, Allen, Jr., and Ralph LeRoy,
came into the possession and management of the Chillicothe Normal
School, which they continued as a normal until 1910. It was then converted into a business college, and has since been known as the Chillicothe
Business College and College of Telegraphy. The attendance has increased largely since the change, and the daily enrollment is now 600
pupils with a yearly attendance of 1,200. As an exclusive business
college it has the largest plant in the state. When the Springfield
Normal School was leased to the state, Allen Moore (senior) and J. A.
Taylor built the Springfield Business College, a one-half interest of
which was left to the five children and which interest is still held by the
estate. The institution has a yearly attendance of about one thousand
pupils. In 1915 the two brothers and J. A. Taylor established at Joplin,
Missouri, the Joplin Business College, which, profiting by the experience
and prestige of the names associated with its ownership, now has a yearly

attendance of 700 pupils. Mr. Taylor has charge of the Springfield and Joplin schools. The young men, Allen and Ralph LeRoy Moore, are numbered among the leading educators of the state, and like their father, have been identified with this profession since early manhood.

JAMES B. McVEIGH. The prominent position of James B. McVeigh in the business community of Ray County is indicated by his presidency of the First National Bank of Polo and his successful activities as a farmer and stock raiser on a fine estate of 380 acres in Knoxville Township.

Mr. McVeigh's father was Alexander McVeigh, who died in Ray County more than forty years ago. His mother was the late Mrs. Harriet (Brody) McVeigh, one of Ray County's most venerable women and whose life came to a close on March 29, 1913, when she was past eighty-four years of age. Alexander McVeigh was born in Belfast, Ireland, and became an early resident of Ray County in 1852. He was of Scotch-Irish ancestry, and of Episcopalian family. Many of his family had served as soldiers and officers in the English army, and both his maternal and paternal grandfathers were colonels in the English army and received medals for conspicuous bravery on the field of battle. Alexander's brother, James, for whom the Polo banker was named, was an officer in the English army and was in the famous charge of the Six Hundred at Balaklava, and went through the Crimean war and was honored by promotion and by a medal betokening gallantry in active service. Alexander McVeigh was born in 1836, was reared and educated in Belfast, and after coming to America was engaged in the mercantile business for a time in New York. He then came to Ray County, and lived here as a farmer until his death in 1873.

Alexander McVeigh was married April 3, 1860, to Mrs. Harriet (Brody) Creason. She was born in Ohio, January 21, 1829, the second daughter of Jesse and Eleanor Brody. Her death occurred at the family home, 5½ miles southeast of Polo, March 29, 1913, at the age of eighty-four years, two months and eight days. The Brodys were among the pioneer families of Ray County, having moved to the vicinity of Morton in 1838 and afterwards settling in the neighborhood of Knoxville. Mrs. McVeigh's mother died at the advanced age of ninety-two years on May 29, 1898. Mrs. McVeigh left surviving her four sisters and one brother. She was first married on February 12, 1852, to Oliver Perry Creason, who by a previous marriage had three children. To the marriage of Mr. and Mrs. Creason was born one daughter, Miss Emma. Oliver P. Creason died August 5, 1853. Mrs. McVeigh had the companionship of her second husband, Alexander McVeigh, thirteen years, and she was then left with one daughter, Mary Eleanor, and two sons, Perry Alexander and James B. After the death of her second husband Mrs. McVeigh courageously assumed the task of widowhood again and set about to support, train and educate her children. For forty years she led an active and purposeful life. She took the active management of the farm, and did much to direct and assist her two boys when they were still too young to be independently trusted with the farm work. In her community she will be long remembered as a good mother, a kind and loving wife, and a very thoughtful and helpful neighbor. In early life she had been converted at a camp meeting near Knoxville, conducted by a Presbyterian minister, but she joined the Knoxville Methodist Church, and afterwards, in 1874, transferred her membership to the Polo church, and for the last thirty-nine years of her life had been a member of that society. Her Christian example and influence meant much in her own home, and she trained her children and grandchildren in her piety and faith, and carried her Christian virtues into practice in relation to all her friends and neighbors. Her daughter, Mary Eleanor, now deceased, was a young woman of education and refinement and for a number of years a popular teacher in Ray County. The daughter, Emma Creason, by her first marriage, now lives with James B. McVeigh on the old homestead.

James B. McVeigh was reared in Ray County, had an education in the local schools, and for several years was a teacher and made an excellent record in that department of work. Since reaching his majority he and his half-sister, Miss Creason, have looked after the old homestead and maintained its character for hospitality and the best Christian virtues as exemplified by their mother. His material success has come from general farming and stock raising, and he feeds cattle, hogs and horses, and for several years has concentrated his business interests in the First National Bank of Polo and has helped to make that a sound and successful institution.

C. J. WINGER. An honored resident of Caldwell County, C. J. Winger has now retired from his activities as a farmer and stock raiser, and has his home in section 21 of Grant Township near Polo. When in the prime of his business activities Mr. Winger did an important service to this community as a breeder and raiser of fine shorthorn cattle. He kept a herd of about thirty-four head, containing some of the finest shorthorns to be found anywhere in Northwest Missouri. He also dealt extensively in cattle and made a very successful record in the line of business for which he showed special proficiency.

C. J. Winger is a native of Virginia and was born on a farm near Roanoke in 1846. His father was David Winger, a native of Virginia and of German extraction, and the maiden name of his mother was Laura Peterman, also a native of Virginia. In 1852 the family left Virginia and found a home in the new country of Missouri, locating in Ray County, where ·the father built a log cabin as his first habitation, and in time developed a good farm and provided well for his children. David Winger died in 1866, and his wife passed away at the age of seventy-eight. They were the parents of six children: C. J., Elizabeth, Griffin, Jacob W., Letitia, and one that died in early childhood. The father was a whig in politics and afterwards a republican, and both parents were members of the Baptist faith.

C. J. Winger grew up in the Ray County homestead, and as a boy his school associations were with one of the early schoolhouses conducted in that vicinity. He learned the value of industry, and has always been a hard worker as well as a capable business executive. Mr. Winger was married September 12, 1871, in Clinton County, to Matilda Cooper. Mrs. Winger was well educated and was a successful teacher before her marriage. She comes of a family of educators, and both her parents and other members of her family were engaged in that vocation. Her father was John A. Cooper, a native of North Carolina, who was married in Tennessee to Miss Susan E. Law. Both parents taught some of the early schools of Clinton County, Missouri. Mrs. Winger was one of a family of ten children, the names of the others being: Lafayette, John A., Jane, W., Alice Hill, James, David, Ellen and Frances. The son, John A., was a soldier in the Union army. The father of these children died at the age of seventy-six and spent twenty years as a teacher. His wife died at the age of sixty-seven. Mr. and Mrs. Winger are the parents of two sons. The older, Morris Homer, is now a well known attorney in Kansas City. He married Nora Ridelin, and their three children are Morris, George and Robert. The second son is Mayor Herbert, now manager of the Polo Telephone Exchange, and an active young business man of that town. He married Ada Reed, and their two children are Euleva and Charles. Mr. and Mrs. Winger also lost three children by death.

Mr. Winger has paid much attention to stock of all kinds, and has the fondness of a Yankee for trading. He has owned some fine horses, and during his active career had business relations with practically all the leading stock men in this section of Missouri. Mr. Winger is a democrat in politics, is a deacon in the Baptist Church, and has accumulated in the course of his lifetime those things which constitute real success, ample material prosperity, the esteem of a community, and a character of honorable rectitude.

E. L. HUNT. One of the prosperous merchants of Orrick in Ray County is E. L. Hunt, who never had a failure yet, and between farming, merchandising and other activities he has come a long distance on the road to success and is not yet ready to close his journey. One special reputation enjoyed by Mr. Hunt is due to his extensive operations as a potato grower, and he is almost entitled to the position of Potato King in the Orrick district.

E. L. Hunt was born in Warren County, Missouri, in February, 1863, the second of five children, the others being: Miss Lou, of Missouri City; C. A. Hunt, of Clay County; Minnie, wife of J. A. Courtney, of Missouri City; and Laura, wife of G. E. Bell, of Liberty. Their parents were W. H. and Susan (Hayes) Hunt, the former a native of Kentucky and the latter of Missouri. The father died in Clay County in 1907 aged seventy, and the mother in 1898 aged sixty-eight. When six years old W. H. Hunt was brought by his parents from Kentucky to Warren County, Missouri, where he grew up and married. In 1869 he moved to Clay County and bought 160 acres of slightly improved land located east of Excelsior Springs Junction. A man who employed a great deal of energy in his endeavors, he succeeded as a farmer, and at one time owned 300 acres of Clay County soil. He was of southern family, a sympathizer with the struggles of the South during the war, and a democrat.

Mr. E. L. Hunt was just about old enough to remember the removal of the family to Clay County, where he grew to manhood, had the practical experiences of a farmer boy, and acquired his education in the common schools with one year in the State Normal at Warrensburg. He was for a time clerk for a clothing firm and then went back to the farm. After five years of active farm management Mr. Hunt traded, in 1898, for a hardware store in Missouri City, becoming a principal in the firm of Owens-Hunt Hardware Company. Four years later they bought a stock of hardware at Orrick, and Mr. Hunt took charge of the branch establishment, followed a year later by his purchasing it and dissolving the partnership. Since then he has been a leading merchant of this town, and handles a large stock of general hardware, machinery, implements and buggies.

Mr. Hunt owns the old homestead, comprising 159 acres, at Excelsior Springs Junction, and has specialized in the growing of potatoes. In five seasons he sold from ninety-five acres potatoes to the value of $39,000, and in 1914 had 120 acres in that crop. In political affairs Mr. Hunt is a democrat, and a citizen who does his proper part toward supporting movements of public benefit. For twelve years he has been a member of the school board. Fraternally he belongs to the Masonic and Odd Fellows fraternities, and with his wife is a member of the Christian Church.

March 14, 1893, Mr. Hunt married Miss Lois Ralph, of a well known and prominent old family in this section of Missouri. She was born in Missouri City, November 23, 1869. Their five children are: William Ralph, born December 15, 1896; Edward Paul, born July 18, 1898, both these sons being students in the Kemper Military Academy at Boonville; Arthur B., born February 5, 1902; Eleanor Lee, born February 23, 1907; and Evelyn Lois, born August 11, 1909.

Mrs. Hunt is a daughter of the late Dr. Arthur B. Ralph, who was born near Orrick, February 29, 1836, and died there February 17, 1911. He was a son of Dr. A. B. and Mary E. (Brasher) Ralph, both natives of North Carolina, the former born December 25, 1800, and died June 9, 1888, and the latter born in 1809 and died June 8; 1870. Doctor Ralph, the younger, was one of three sons and four daughters, and of this family the only two now living are Lucy, widow of Dr. William Campbell of Kansas City, and Belle, wife of J. B. Gant of Kansas City. The late Doctor Ralph was liberally educated, and after graduating from the St. Louis Medical College in 1865 located at Camden, Missouri, and in 1870 transferred his practice to Missouri City, where he devoted himself actively to his profession until five years before his death. His last years were spent with his daughter at Orrick. He was a Mason, for many years connected with the Christian Church, and a strong and loyal democrat. Several times he was honored with the office of mayor in Missouri City.

Doctor Ralph was married October 7, 1867, to Ellen Hardwick, whose family, like her husband's, was among the first in Clay County. She was born near what is now Excelsior Springs, April 9, 1844, a daughter of Lewis and Elizabeth (Smith) Hardwick. Her father was born in Virginia, June 20, 1807, and died November 7, 1863. He was married in St. Charles County, Missouri, where his wife was born October 15, 1805, and she died June 29, 1888. Mrs. Ralph was one of ten children, and the two still living are Mrs. Margaret Moffett and Mrs. Caroline Sublette, both widows, living at Kansas City. The Hardwicks moved to Clay County in 1829, were among the pioneers, and Lewis Hardwick was a substantial farmer, an occupation he followed until 1860, after which his home was in Missouri City. Dr. and Mrs. Ralph had two daughters: Mrs. E. L. Hunt and Edna S., the wife of Claude M. Donovan of Orrick.

B. J. BLESS. No enterprising community worthy the name has gained any position of recognized importance without the stimulative aid and encouraging assistance of the press. It is within the province and power of the fourth estate to so mold public opinion and direct public effort that the community is led to accomplish great achievements, and thus it is that the newspaper is one of a city's chief institutions. Such power, however, placed in unscrupulous or incapable hands becomes at once dangerous—a menace, and for this reason the people of Weston and Platte County are to be congratulated that so strong and influential a paper as the Weston Chronicle is under the management and direction of such an able journalist, public-spirited citizen and honorable man as B. J. Bless has shown himself to be during the twenty-nine years that he has had charge of this journal's destinies.

Mr. Bless is a native son of Platte County, Missouri, and was born February 21, 1863, his parents being Bartholomew and Gertrude (Giebels) Bless, natives of Germany, the former born in 1825, and the latter March 5, 1824, at Dusseldorf. The parents left Germany in 1857, and after a stormy trip of seven weeks in a sailing vessel made port at New Orleans, from whence they made their way up the Mississippi and Mis-

souri rivers to the little Town of Weston. There they settled on a piece
of bottom land, which was soon swallowed up by the river, and the father
moved his little home farther back. He soon saw that the river would
again destroy his property and he tore his home down, intending to move
elsewhere. His plans were put to naught, however, by a scratch which he
received from a dog, and which developed into blood poisoning, from
which Mr. Bless died in September, 1862, five months before the birth
of his son, B. J. He had one other child, Mary, who is now the wife of
Peter Seeger, of Weston. Mrs. Bless subsequently married again, her
husband being Matt Derks, but they had no children.

B. J. Bless spent his boyhood and youth in the Town of Weston,
where his stepfather operated a truck garden. He was given a good
educational training, attending Kemper Military Academy, at Boonville,
Missouri, and the Catholic schools of Jefferson City, and in 1876 received
his introduction to the vocation which he has made his life work, when
he was employed on a German paper at Jefferson City, the Volksfreund.
Succeeding this he passed three years as a clerk in a Weston grocery
store, but, while this training undoubtedly was of much value as a business experience, he could not resist the call of the craft and once more
became associated with newspaper work. He was connected with various
dailies and weeklies from New Orleans to the Dakotas, and held positions
on such well-known papers as the Kansas City Times and the Omaha
Bee. Eventually he returned to Weston, and here became identified
with the Weston Chronicle, which had been established in July, 1872, by
H. Howard, as the Missouri Commercial. In August, 1883, this was
superseded by the Chronicle, Mr. J. B. Mundy buying Mr. Howard's
interest, and Mr. Mundy continued to publish the paper until April 17.
1886, when he sold out to Mr. Bless, who has continued uninterruptedly
as its editor and publisher to the present time.

The Weston Chronicle is an eight-column folio in size, strongly democratic in politics, and the plant occupies its own building on the southwest corner of Main and Market streets, a large two-story brick structure.
The mechanical equipment of the office includes a Taylor cylinder book
press, two Peerless jobbers, a Sanborn paper cutter, a fine lot of type for
all classes of high-grade news and job work, and everything else necessary in a first-class printing establishment. In addition to its editor
the paper has a full corps of assistants, who enthusiastically labor in an
effort to produce the best newspaper in Platte County. The plant has
its own waterworks system, is heated by its own steam plant and lighted
by gas, and power is furnished by a 2½-horsepower gas engine. It is
without a doubt the best-equipped enterprise at Weston. It has always
been the editor's effort and ambition to give his readers all the news,
and while the policy of the paper is democratic, he endeavors to present to
the reading public an impartial and unbiased opinion upon the important
political topics of the day. That his efforts have been appreciated is
made evident by a circulation which, by reason of its size and class,
makes the Chronicle one of the best advertising mediums in Platte
County.

First and foremost, Mr. Bless has been for Weston. He has encour-

bushels, while the business includes the buying and shipping of wheat, corn, oats and hay, and the retailing of hard and soft coal. Mr. Bless is also the owner of a valuable farm in Southern Missouri, one-half section of land in Michigan's famous fruit belt and various real estate properties in the Town of Weston, and is the heaviest taxpayer in Weston.

On October 4, 1886, Mr. Bless was united in marriage with Miss Lizzie How, who was born in Platte County, Missouri, and to this union there was born one son, B. J. Bless, Jr., who is associated with his father in business as junior editor of the Chronicle, a capacity in which he has also charge of the job printing department. Mr. Bless is a capable and energetic young business man and very popular among the people of Weston. He married Miss Bertha Iseman, and they have one child, C. A., a bright and interesting lad now in his third year.

B. W. SPRY. One of the well known attorneys of Caldwell County, B. W. Spry, has practiced at Braymer since 1908. He is a widely experienced lawyer, and for a number of years was identified with the law and with educational work before coming to Braymer. It was through the avenue of school teaching that he finally acquired the means to prepare himself for his profession and to enter upon his active practice, and since his admission to the bar he has enjoyed many of the successes of the able lawyer.

B. W. Spry was born September 4, 1871. His father, Samuel Spry, a farmer and stockman, was born near Zanesville, in Muskingum County, Ohio. Two of Samuel's brothers saw service as soldiers during the Civil war. The paternal grandfather was William Spry. Samuel Spry was educated in Ohio, and married Miss C. Lamb, who was born and reared in Ohio.

B. W. Spry was reared on a farm, acquired a country school education, also enjoyed the advantages of the Methodist College at Mount Pleasant, Iowa, and of the State University at Columbia, Missouri. He studied law under Judge William E. Ellison, and since locating at Braymer has built up a good practice and a reputation as a successful lawyer. Mr. Spry was married in 1901 and has a fine family of children. He is a progressive in politics, and in every community where he has lived has identified himself with the more progressive element, and has been a factor in the community upbuilding and progress. He is a thorough student and devotes all his time and attention to his profession.

JAMES F. GORE. Now one of the ablest and most successful members of the Rockport bar, Mr. Gore may be said to have begun his practical career in Atchison County as a hard-working student and teacher. He was not sent to college as the son of a prosperous farmer, but his education, like everything else he has attained, was the result of his determined purpose and industrious labor. Mr. Gore has gained distinction both at the bar and in public affairs, and it is only natural that such a man should interest himself in the political questions, and he is one of the recognized leaders in the democratic party of Atchison County.

James F. Gore was born in Fremont County, Iowa, November 15, 1873, and is the oldest in a family of six children born to William T. and Mary E. Gore. The other children in the family were: Ada, who left that state and finally located on a farm in Atchison County, Missouri.

James F. Gore remained at home with his father on the farm until 1891, and in the meantime had received an education in the country schools. In 1891 he began a course in Tarkio College, as an academic student, and paid part of his tuition by teaching in country schools for one year. He remained in Tarkio College until 1897, and during the last two years of his course there was an instructor. After graduating in Tarkio he accepted the principalship of the Westboro public schools, and held that position one year. In 1898 Mr. Gore was elected circuit clerk of Atchison County for a term of four years, and was re-elected to that office in 1902. He was first elected on the fusion ticket, as the representative of both the people's party and the democrats, and the second time was elected as a straight democrat. During his second term as circuit clerk, in January, 1905, at the regular term of Circuit Court, Mr. Gore was admitted to the bar, the Hon. W. C. Ellison being on the bench at the time. Mr. Gore began the active practice of law at Rockport in 1907, after the expiration of his second term as circuit clerk, and has since enjoyed a large share of the legal business in this county.

Mr. Gore is the type of man who believes that his talents and abilities should be exerted to the full capacity, not only for the interests of himself, but also in whatever way he can best serve the community in which he lives. Outside of his profession and public affairs he has been particularly occupied with religious work. He is active in the Baptist Church at Rockport, has served as superintendent of the Sunday school since 1900, as secretary and treasurer of the Sunday School Association of Atchison County since 1905, and since 1903 has been secretary of the Rockport Lecture and Chautauqua Association. In politics he is a sterling democrat, but during the '90s, while the people's party was at the climax of its strength, he worked with that organization. In 1900 he was treasurer of the fusion committee representing both the people's party and democratic party. Regardless of party affiliations he has the complete confidence and respect of all the people of Atchison County.

Mr. Gore was married May 1, 1900, to Miss Flora B. Hughes, a daughter of George L. and Mary A. Hughes. She was born in Atchison County, October 8, 1874, was a student in the Rockport High School and also in Tarkio College, and was a teacher for several years in the Atchison County schools and for several years was connected with the Westboro public schools, where her husband was principal. Mr. and Mrs. Gore have four children, all of whom were born at Rockport: Genevieve, the oldest, who was born February 27, 1904; James F., Jr.; Clark; and George William.

CHARLES P. BREEN. One of Parkville's best citizens is Charles P. Breen, who has spent his life in Platte County in a progressive rise from stonemason's apprentice when a boy to independent contractor and builder, and finally to executive control of one of the county's leading banks. No small amount of his business service has gone in practical helpfulness to the community. Such men as Charles P. Breen typify the best in any locality.

Born at Weston, Missouri, June 29, 1858, he was the second child of James and Mary (Collins) Breen, who were early settlers of Platte County. His father was born at Wexford, Ireland, and died at Weston in 1891, aged sixty-two, while his mother was born in County Limerick, Ireland, and died at the age of sixty-five in 1907. All their nine children are still living. James Breen was twenty-two when he came to the United States, and was married at Maysville, Kentucky, his wife having come over at the age of eighteen. In Ireland he had served apprenticeship as a stonemason, and that was the trade he followed in Maysville until 1858. He then brought his family to Weston, Missouri, traveling by boat, and here continued his chosen work the rest of his active years.

Charles P. Breen took up the responsibilities of life at an early age. His schooling ended at fourteen, and he helped pay his way at home and also learned a useful trade by assisting his father. With skill and experience as a stonemason, he was not long in starting independently as contractor. His removal to Parkville in 1886 was in order to take charge of all construction work for Park College, and he has erected all the substantial buildings on the campus of that institution, structures of brick and stone that for many years to come will be monuments to the man who fabricated them.

In the course of years his business interests have expanded, while others have been laid by. In 1905 he was elected president of Park Bank, which had his services in that capacity four years. In 1909 Mr. Breen retired from mason contracting as a regular business, and his only resumption of activities was during 1912, when he took the contract and built the Weston Catholic Church. He donated his own services, only taking pay for the actual wages of his workmen. In 1911 he organized the Farmers Exchange Bank at Parkville, of which he is the owner and president, and now gives all his time to the management of that institution. His interest in home affairs has prompted him to give twenty years' service as member of the city council and school board. All his life he has affiliated with the democratic party, and he and his wife are Catholics.

In 1887 Mr. Breen married Miss Mary Nall, who was born at Weston, Missouri, October 5, 1861. Her parents were Mathias and Grace Nall, both natives of Germany, her father having come to Weston in 1848 and for many years following his trade as wagonmaker. Mr. and Mrs. Breen have a family of five children: Edward N. is vice president of the bank at Parkville and an employe of the new National Reserve Bank at Kansas City; Everett J. is cashier of the Farmers Exchange Bank at Parkville; Howard M. has also begun a banking career and is now connected with one of the banks of Kansas City; Charles and Grace, the younger children, are both in school.

Hon. CHARLES M. DAILY. Honored in public life, eminently successful in business and deeply beloved not only by his kindred but by everyone who knew him, the late Charles M. Daily was a citizen of Andrew County, whose loss will long be deplored. The natural capacities and the sterling traits which made him an admirable judge, were combined with personal qualities which endeared him, in every phase of life, to those with whom he was brought into contact. Just and impartial in public office, in private life he was warm-hearted, genial, charitable and hospitable, and exemplified in his everyday life the best that is in manhood those things which are worthy, useful, helpful and lasting.

Charles M. Daily was born near Greensburg, Decatur County, Indiana, September 1, 1837, and died on his home farm in Andrew County,

who is a resident of St. Joseph; Mrs. Cora Holt, who is deceased; William, who is a resident of Greensburg, Indiana; Samuel and Abraham, both of whom are deceased; and Wilson, who is a resident of Benton, Kansas.

Charles M. Daily had attended school in Indiana and when he accompanied his parents to Andrew County was ready to go into business. He owned 1,500 acres of land and the raising of stock was his object in holding so much. He became connected with the stock yards at St. Joseph, operating there a long time before the present commission system was established, and drove stock in the early days, before railroads were built, all over the country. He bought and sold and raised the finest horses, mules and hogs in the country, carrying on all his agricultural operations on a vast scale. Judge Daily continued in the commission business with the St. Joseph yards for many years, one of his sons, Benjamin Daily, now of St. Joseph, succeeding him in that relation.

Judge Daily came to what continued his home place in sections 1 and 5, Rochester Township, in 1860. The original owner of the place, now known as Cherry Grove Farm, was the father of his second wife, Benjamin Holt, who entered the land from the Government and built the commodious, old-fashioned brick house still standing. The bricks used in its construction were made by Joseph Selecman. Here Judge Daily spent his most enjoyable years. While his business interests were large he became very prominent in public affairs in Andrew County and served three terms as county judge. It was during his administration that the county courthouse was built, a fine structure creditable to its builders and the county alike, and the name of Judge Daily, with two other county judges, is inscribed on the building, they composing the construction committee. Within the building also is hung a portrait of Judge Daily.

The first marriage of Judge Daily took place September 23, 1858, to Miss Nancy R. Murphey, who came to Andrew County a short time previously with her parents. Three children were born to this union: Gates, who is a resident of St. Joseph, Missouri; John Frank, who lives at Moncraft, Wyoming; and Julia, who died at the age of three years. Judge Daily's second marriage took place November 28, 1864, to Miss Mary Ann Holt, and the six children of this marriage were: Benjamin, who is a resident of St. Joseph and prominent in the meat packing business; Julia, who is the wife of Jacob Carson, of Kodiak, Missouri; Charles M., who is a farmer in Andrew County; Robert, who is also a farmer in this county; and Abraham and Florence, both of whom are deceased, the former dying at the age of five years and the latter at three years. On September 27, 1881, Judge Daily was married to Miss Mary E. Selecman, who was born two miles north of the present homestead, October 23, 1856, and has resided in Andrew County all her life. There were four children born to the above marriage: George William, who divides his time, living partly with his mother and partly at St. Joseph, where he is in the cattle commission business; Henry Redman, who resides at home; Sally, who is the wife of John Easley, residing near Savannah; and Mollie, who died when aged fourteen months. The large estate left by Judge Daily, including the home place of 700 acres, has not yet been completely settled, the heirs being the widow and nine children. Judge Daily owned the above farm for over forty years.

In politics Judge Daily was a democrat but during the Civil war he was in sympathy with the Union cause. He never was swayed by politics in public life and was always so busily concerned in other directions that he did little seeking for public office, serving faithfully, however, when elected. He was known all over the state and at his hospitable table many distinguished men were frequently entertained. It was his custom to make a feast for all who cared to come, on the day his birthday was celebrated, when, with other special dainties, a young pig was roasted in true southern style. He was affectionately called "uncle Charley" by those who had known him long and appreciated his generosity and open-hearted kindness. There are many in Andrew County and elsewhere who can recall his words of encouragement and also his practical help when lack of money seemed to mean also lack of friends. He was identified with the Masonic fraternity and for many years was a member of the Methodist Episcopal Church, South.

JOHN L. ZEIDLER. A man of prominence and recognized ability, John L. Zeidler, of St. Joseph, has ever taken an active and intelligent interest in local affairs, and his influence for good has been felt in nearly all of the progressive movements for the betterment of city and county. A son of John Zeidler, he was born in Scranton, Pennsylvania, of German ancestry.

John Zeidler was born in the Town of Selb, Bavaria, Germany, where his parents were life-long residents. Three of his brothers immigrated to America, Christian settling first in Poughkeepsie, New York, but later settling in Scranton, Pennsylvania, as did the other two brothers, Oswald and Loreny. John Zeidler was reared and educated in the Fatherland, and there served an apprenticeship at the baker's trade. Embarking on a sailing vessel he landed in New York after a long and tedious voyage of 103 days. He first found work on the Erie Canal, and later was engaged in lumbering in the forests of New York. In 1853 he went to Scranton, Pennsylvania, then a small city, and was there for a time employed in a sawmill. Establishing himself then in the bakery business he was very successful, and after a few years opened a hotel in a brick building in Scranton. He subsequently conducted both a hotel and the bakery, continuing in active business until his death.

The maiden name of the wife of John Zeidler was Maria Bechtold. She was born in Zweibrucken, Hesse Darmstadt, Germany. Her father, John Bechtold, was born in the same locality. In 1800 he came to America as a young man, and for a time was employed on the Erie Canal. Going then to Pittston, Pennsylvania, he found work in the Butler mine, which was the first mine to ship anthracite coal, and was foreman in the mine for upwards of forty years. He lived to the remarkable age of 105 years, retaining his mental faculties and good health until the last, passing away after an illness of three days. He was three times married, and reared three families. John Zeidler and his wife reared five children, as follows: Maria, Wilhelmina, John L., Margaret, and Emma.

Receiving his preliminary education in private schools, John L. Zeidler was fitted for college at Hoboken Academy, and later entered Mihlenberg College, in Allentown, Pennsylvania, but as he had decided not to engage in any profession he did not complete the course of study at that institution. Instead of being graduated, Mr. Zeidler left college and a good home and in 1878 started westward in search of fame and fortune. At Kansas City he hired out to go South with a herd of cattle, and in that capacity made several drives over the trail to Dodge City, Kansas, where the cattle were shipped West. A year later he came to St. Joseph, where he was variously employed for awhile, first at the Atlantic House, then one of the leading hotels, and later at the Colorado House. In 1885 Mr. Zeidler embarked in the real estate business, and having added a line of insurance in 1887 soon built up an extensive business in that line, and now represents several of the strongest insurance companies in the country.

Since taking up his residence in St. Joseph, Mr. Zeidler has been actively interested in the welfare of his adopted city. In 1888 he visited his old home in Scranton, and there first saw street cars operated by electricity. On his return he called the attention of the president of the St. Joseph Street Railway Company to it, with the result that the system of this city was changed from horses to electricity. At that time the trolley wheel ran on top of the rail, each car carrying a detached pole with which to shift the wheel whenever necessary to do so. It was in the car barns at St. Joseph that the wheel under the wire was devised.

Mr. Zeidler was one of the first to talk of interurbans, and to interest parties willing to build if a franchise could be obtained. He labored hard to secure the franchise, and the promoters then went to Indianapolis, where they established one of the greatest interurban systems of the world. For years Mr. Zeidler has talked and worked for good roads in Missouri, and was a member of the driving club that built the boulevard. He is a member of the Interstate Trail Association, of the Hannibal and St. Joseph Cross State Highway Association, and represents Buchanan County as a member of the executive committee of the Hannibal and St. Joseph Highway Association.

Mr. Zeidler married, in 1885, Josephine Wagner, who was born in Wilkes-Barre, Pennsylvania. On coming to America her parents settled in Pennsylvania, where the death of Mr. Wagner occurred, Mrs. Wagner, who survived him, passing away in Missouri. Fraternally Mr. Zeidler is a member of the Scranton Lodge, No. 345, Ancient Free and Accepted Order of Masons; of St. Joseph Lodge, No. 40, Benevolent and Protective Order of Elks; and of St. Joseph Aerie, No. 49, Fraternal Order of Eagles.

JOHN KURTH. For nearly forty years John Kurth has been an estimable citizen of Andrew County, has spent most of his active career in farming, and is now living retired at Cosby. As a young man he served during the closing months of the Civil war with a Union regiment, and his record as a citizen has been in keeping with the loyal qualities he displayed while fighting for his adopted country.

John Kurth is a native of Switzerland, born in Canton Berne, November 12, 1840, a son of John and Elizabeth (Lontz) Kurth. His father was born in 1810 and his mother in 1812. In 1850, when the son John was ten years of age, the family left Switzerland, embarked on a sailing vessel at Havre, France, and after a long and tedious voyage of forty-three days arrived at New Orleans. From there they came up the Mississippi River to St. Louis, and then found a home with a colony of Swiss people at the old Town of Highland thirty miles east of St. Louis, in Madison County, Illinois. Highland was established by Swiss people, and has always retained its characteristic as a Swiss and German town. At Highland the father worked at his trade as a gunsmith for about twenty years, and then spent the rest of his career as a farmer. He died at the age of eighty-three, and his wife passed away at seventy-five. They were the parents of a large family of children, twelve in number, named as follows: Elizabeth, deceased, who married Rev. Jacob Tanner; John; Jacob, of Portland, Oregon; Barbara, who died at Effingham, Illinois, was first the wife of Jacob Kooch and later married Mr. Barthold; Andrew, who died at the age of eighteen; Caroline, deceased, who married a Mr. Joice; Godfried, who died in infancy; Eddie; Godfried, who lives as a farmer in Chase County, Kansas; Emilia, widow of Jonas Tontz of Portland, Oregon; William, of Highland, Illinois; and Mary, wife of Jacob Hollinger, of Grand Fork, Illinois.

Mr. John Kurth was ten years of age when the family located at Highland, and had only one year of schooling after that, since it was necessary for him to go to work and help his father support the large family of children. He was employed on a farm, and was an industrious worker at home until 1864, when he enlisted in Company B of the Fifteenth Missouri Infantry at St. Louis. He served in the Army of the Cumberland, went South to Texas in the latter months of his service, and was mustered out in that state, and discharged at St. Louis in February, 1866, with the rank of sergeant.

After the war Mr. Kurth continued farming in Illinois until 1876, and in October of that year arrived in Bates County, Missouri. He rented a farm there one year, then ran a mail route, and on September 1, 1878, arrived in St. Joseph and worked as a teamster until the following spring. Mr. Kurth then bought a small place of forty-five acres north of Cosby, and some time later bought an improved farm of ninety acres in Rochester Township. For many years he continued the cultivation and operation of this farm, but after retiring from active life went to Cosby to live.

Mr. Kurth is a member of the Methodist Episcopal Church, in which his wife is also a member, and is well known in Grand Army circles. On October 20, 1870, John Kurth married Mary Elizabeth Kline, who was born in Vinton County, Ohio, August 19, 1848, a daughter of Godlove and Nancy (Byerly) Kline. The Kline family has some interesting connections with this section of Northwest Missouri, and a more complete sketch of the family will be found on other pages. Mr. and Mrs. Kurth are the parents of a family of nine children whose names and brief mention of whom are as follows: John G., who was drowned in the Platte River at the age of thirty years; Anna Oretta, wife of George McKee of Fort Scott, Kansas; Sally, who married William McKee, a rural mail carrier and brother of George, and they live at Cosby; Nancy is the wife of Frank Krull of Bates County; Mollie is the wife of John McKee of Hemple, Missouri; Emma died at the age of twelve years; William E., a farmer near Cosby; Charles lives at Lathrop, Missouri; and Nellie is the wife of Bud J. Thomas of Andrew County.

DAVID WILLIAM HARVEY. In the field of agriculture it has often happened that the fathers and grandfathers have secured the broad and fertile tracts of land which the sons and grandsons have brought to their full capacity of productiveness. The rough, preliminary labors of the pioneers were necessary, but it has been the work of those who have come later which has made the various agricultural sections have such an important place in the life of any state. David William Harvey is one of the agriculturists of Andrew County who is living on land which was cultivated by his father and from which he is bringing excellent results. He was born on this property, which lies in section 15, Nodaway Township, about one mile south of the courthouse at Savannah, February 27, 1865, and is a son of Richard Jacob and Margaret Agnes (Abbott) Harvey.

The maternal grandparents of David W. Harvey were David P. and Celestine (Phelps) Abbott, the former a native of Indiana and the latter of Delaware. They came to Missouri as early as April 2, 1842, traveling overland with ox-teams from the Hoosier State, and bringing beside their six children all their household effects and $3,000 in gold and silver with which to purchase their land in the new country. Settling down in Andrew County they engaged in agricultural pursuits and established a home and here two other children were born to them. In 1849 when there came the thrilling news of the discovery of gold in California, Mr. Abbott joined a caravan of fifty wagons and made the long and dangerous journey across the plains, only to die shortly after his arrival at Sacramento City. Of his children, none survive.

Richard Jacob Harvey was born at Norfolk, Virginia, in 1822, and about the year 1858 came West to the Platte Purchase in Missouri and engaged in farming, in connection with which he was for many years one of the best known educators of this part of the state. He died in 1885 at the age of sixty-three years, and in the faith of the Methodist Church. In political matters he was a democrat, and an influential man in his community. By his first marriage he had one daughter: Elizabeth, who is the widow of Sam Porter, of Whitesville, Andrew County. After coming to Missouri, Mr. Harvey was married to Margaret Agnes Brown, who had been twice married before and who was born in Leesville, Indiana, in 1829. By her first marriage she was the mother of two children, Henry Green Caples and Mary A. Caples, both of whom are now deceased. By her second marriage she had one daughter, Fannie Brown, who died at the age of one year. Two children were born to Mr. and Mrs. Harvey: David William, of this review; and Richard A., a banker of Lincoln, Nebraska. Mrs. Harvey was thirteen years of age when she came to Missouri with her parents who at that time bought the farm of A. Walters, that had been entered in 1840. Mrs. Harvey died in 1892, in the faith of the Christian Church.

David William Harvey received his education in the public schools of Savannah, and as a young man was interested in mercantile pursuits for about three years, when he acted as clerk in a grocery store at Barnard, Missouri. At the end of that period, however, he returned to farming, and secured ninety acres of the homestead, of which he at present retains seventy acres. He is engaged successfully in general farming and stockraising, and has good improvements on his land, the greater number of buildings having been erected by himself. He has various other interests, and is a stockholder in his brother's bank at Hebron, Nebraska, the Hebron State Bank. Mr. Harvey is a member of the Christian Church and of its official board, and has shown his interest in the cause of education by serving efficiently as a member of the board of school directors of his township. Progressive measures and movements have his support, and in every respect he is entitled to be named as one of his community's substantial men.

In 1894 Mr. Harvey was married to Miss Jennie Miller, who died in 1899, at the age of thirty-five years, having been the mother of two children, Margaret, who died at fourteen months; and Abbot, who died when three months old. Mr. Harvey was again married in 1901, when he was united with Mrs. Sadie Clark Horton, and to this union there have been born three children: Richard Clark, who is twelve years of age and a student in the Savannah schools; John W., aged ten years, and also attending the public schools; and Caroline, who died at the age of eight months.

CHARLES B. NEWBURN. A resident of Andrew County more than forty years, Charles B. Newburn has been known as a successful farmer, for several years was identified with merchandising in Cosby, and is now living retired in that village.

Charles B. Newburn was born in Marshall County, Illinois, April 19, 1861, only a few days after the beginning of the Civil war. His parents were David and Lucinda (Van Winkle) Newburn, both of whom were natives of Preble County, Ohio. David Newburn, the great-grandfather of Charles B. Newburn, was born January 18, 1756, and died June 2, 1820, his ancestors being from Wales in England. Tamer Newburn, his wife, was born March 30, 1761, and died August 15, 1837. To them were born eleven children as follows: John, Rachel, Sarah Newburn Yarnell, Dorothy, Nemiah, Jacob, David, George, William, Mary Newburn Vore, Ann Newburn Vore. David Newburn, the grandfather, was born July 27, 1792, and died March 28, 1855. Beulah (Brown) Newburn, his wife (and daughter of John Brown and Virgin (Gaskell) Brown), was born February 17, 1787, and died February 22, 1829. David Newburn was married twice, and to the first marriage was born four children as follows: Rachel, John, Virgin B. Newburn Hofford and David Newburn. He was again married and to himself and Gule Elma Newburn were born six children: William H., Mary Ann, Warner Leads, Amy Newburn Carney, George and Lydia Newburn Grable, the last mentioned at this writing is still living with her family near Abilene, Kansas.

David Newburn, the father of Charles B. Newburn, was born near the old Quaker Church, about ten miles south of Eaton, in Preble County, Ohio, on the 22d day of January, 1829. He moved out to Illinois when a boy, and first married Jane Reddick, who was the mother of one daughter, Louisa J., now deceased. David Newburn returned to Ohio and married Miss Van Winkle on February 2, 1860, and then returned to Marshall County, Illinois. In March, 1872, he brought his family to Andrew County, Missouri, locating a mile and a half from Cosby, and one year later bought a farm near the Platte River in Rochester Township. He lived as a farmer for a number of years, finally retiring to the Village of Cosby, where he died June 2, 1914. His wife, who was born November 27, 1827, passed away in July, 1911. From the age of sixteen David Newburn had been a blacksmith by trade, combining his trade with farming until he came to Missouri, after which he devoted all his time to his agricultural interests. At one time he owned 700 acres in Andrew County. Politically he acted with the whig party in early life, later with the republican, and held several minor township offices. He and his wife were the parents of three children: Charles B., Warner L., who lives in Mankato, Jewell County, Kansas; and Sarah B., the deceased wife of J. N. Addington.

Charles B. Newburn has been a resident of Andrew County since eleven years of age, acquired some education in the public schools of Illinois, and after coming to Missouri combined practical experience on the farm with some attendance in the local schools. On reaching his majority he took up farming as a practical vocation, and followed it with substantial success until 1900. Since that year his home has been in Cosby, and for five years he was engaged in the hardware and implement business with J. P. Anderson under the firm name of Anderson & Newburn. Mr. Newburn has some valuable property which measures his life accomplishments as a farmer and business man, owning 240 acres in Rochester Township and a quarter section of land in Western Kansas in Jewell County. Mr. Newburn is a republican in politics, and has been a member of the Cosby town council since its organization. His church home is the Christian, and he is affiliated with the Masonic fraternity and the Independent Order of Odd Fellows.

On September 6, 1882, Mr. Newburn married Florence M. Newton. She was born in Preble County, Ohio, October 10, 1861, and was brought to Andrew County when seven years of age. Her parents were Thomas and Lucinda (Leach) Newton. Thomas Newton, Sr., the great-grandfather of Mrs. Florence M. Newton Newburn, was born in Ireland. He came to America, and on the 28th of March, 1818, bought a carding mill of his son Thomas Newton, Jr., the consideration being $1,000, which is shown by the original contract still in the possession of the family. The mill was on Beaver Creek, in Preble County, Ohio, and was used for carding wool for many years. Thomas Newton, Jr., was married in 1823 to Mrs. Rebecca Anderson (her former husband being dead). To them was born two children: Elizabeth Newton (Early) and Thomas Newton. The father, Thomas Newton, Jr., died in 1840. The mother, Rebecca Newton, lived with her children until her death in 1862 at the age of seventy-five years. Thomas Newton, Jr., had two sons by a former marriage, Isaac and Asa Newton; and Rebecca Newton, wife of Thomas Newton, Jr., also had five children by the name of Anderson, from a former marriage. Thomas Newton, the father of Mrs. Florence M. Newton Newburn, was born in Preble County, Ohio, on October 31, 1829, and died in Andrew County, Missouri, July 2, 1905. Lucinda Leach Newton, his wife, was born in Tennessee August 18, 1830, and died in Andrew County, Missouri, December 11, 1900. Thomas Newton and Lucinda Leach were married in Eaton, Preble County, Ohio. In 1867 Thomas Newton and wife and three children and William Leach (his wife's brother) drove through in a wagon from Eaton, Ohio, to Rochester, Andrew County, Missouri, the trip taking six weeks. Jacob Leach, the grandfather of Mrs. Newburn on the mother's side, was married in Tennessee in 1826, to Matilda Jennings (who with her brother, Pleasant Jennings, had come from England). About the year 1831 Jacob Leach and wife with two small children left Tennessee and came through on horseback to near Eaton, Preble County, Ohio, where they spent the rest of their lives. They were parents of eleven children, as follows: Luelsa Leach Jellison, Lucinda Leach Newton, Sarah Jane Leach Charles, Julia A. Leach Potterf, Mary Ellen Leach Krug, Susanna Leach White, Peter Leach, who died in infancy, William Leach, John P. Leach, Matilda Leach Wilson and Thomas N. Leach. Jacob Leach died near Eaton, Ohio, in the year 1880, and his wife Matilda Leach died in 1882. Thomas Newton followed farming most of his life, but when a young man had learned the trade of cooper, and also worked at various times at carpentry. He possessed a natural genius for mechanical work, and that was a factor in his success as a farmer. The children in the Newton family were: Sarah, deceased wife of Richard Skinner; Thomas W., who lives at St. Joseph; Mrs. Newburn; Eva, wife of Edward Kelsey, of Rochester Township; James E. Newton, born April 8, 1852, died March 6, 1853, and William A. Newton, born October 11, 1853, and died August 28, 1855.

Mr. and Mrs. Newburn have one son, Percy E., who was born on a farm in Rochester Township, July 22, 1883. He received his education in the country schools and after finishing a course in a commercial college at Savannah became an employe of the Cosby State Bank, and is now a director and assistant cashier of that institution. Percy Newburn married Clara E. Hartman, a daughter of J. W. Hartman, now deceased.

RUDOLPH C. MANDLER. An industry that has grown and flourished in Northwest Missouri during the past several decades is the operation of farm lands for the production of dairy goods. Ever since the necessity for pure milk has been recognized many of the most progressive agriculturists of this section have devoted their activities to dairying, and that industry is the chief feature of the farm enterprise of Rudolph C. Mandler, a prosperous and well known citizen of section 12, Monroe Township, Andrew County. Mr. Mandler has spent practically all his life in Andrew County, and has won his present standing as a business man and farmer by close attention to business, and a well seasoned judgment in the management of his affairs.

Rudolph C. Mandler was born near Berlin, Germany, February 1, 1870, a son of John and Louisa (Reschke) Mandler, natives of the same country. Three months after his birth his parents emigrated to America, locating at St. Joseph. The father died in this country in September, 1871, at the age of thirty-eight. His widow subsequently married Christian Harr, and she lived until 1910, passing away at the age of sixty-six. By her first marriage there were three children: Mrs. Christina Ochse, deceased; Rudolph; and Louisa, wife of Louis Bepper of Fall City, Nebraska. By her marriage to Mr. Harr there were four children: Christian Harr of Easton, Missouri; Eva, wife of William Bunse, Godfried, and Herman, all of Cosby.

Rudolph C. Mandler was brought to Andrew County before the beginning of his conscious recollections, and after his education found employment on farms, and has steadily advanced to a substantial prosperity. He is now proprietor of a farm of 120 acres, and most of its improvements have been placed there by Mr. Mandler. He keeps a dairy of eighteen graded Jersey cows, and ships cream to the St. Joseph market. The other bi-products and farm produce are fed to Poland China hogs, and he also has been successful as a poultry raiser, the barred rock fowls being his specialty. Mr. Mandler is also a director in the Cosby State Bank.

In politics he voted with the republican party, and is a member of the Evangelical Association. On March 3, 1893, Mr. Mandler married Mary Bunse. She was born on the farm where she now lives July 31, 1871, and has never had any other home than this place. Her parents were Christian and Minnie (Zimmerman) Bunse, both of whom were born in Waldec, Germany, were married there, and in 1866 emigrated to America and settled in Andrew County. There her mother died in 1875 and her father passed away in 1910. Mr. and Mrs. Mandler are parents of four children now living: Elsie, Wesley, Freda and Ada, besides one named Selma and an infant who are deceased.

FATHER HENRY B. TIERNEY. As a poet-priest and lecturer, Father Tierney's reputation and recognition have been growing steadily for the past ten years, and while he is claimed as a product of Northwest Missouri, the influence of his oratory and his song has spread afar. He has been in Trenton nine years, where in addition to the upbuilding of St. Joseph's parish there, he has made himself an important factor in the civic and social affairs of that community. He has spread throughout the country this motto: "Get acquainted with your neighbor, you might like him." He was particularly active in the Trenton Commercial Club, and prepared much of the literature for the publicity committee of that club, as a result of which "The Trenton Idea" has made Trenton perhaps the most talked of town in the State of Missouri. In fact, "The Trenton Idea," of which Father Tierney is the originator, is now nationally known and is being adopted throughout the country as a practical plan of real union between town and country.

Father Tierney was born in St. Joseph, Missouri, July 13, 1878, of Irish-American parentage. His father was Mark Tierney and his mother Margaret Gleason, both of them natives of Indiana, but of Irish parents. Father Tierney attended the public schools of St. Joseph, going through the grammar and high schools of that city. His inclinations were early turned toward literary work. His first poem appeared in the old St. Joseph Gazette in 1888, when he was only ten years of age. A few years later he became reporter and special writer for several of the

St. Joseph daily papers, and also contributed to papers in other American cities and also to a London paper in England. He now entered the Benedictine College, St. Benedict's, at Atchison, Kansas, and finished with honors the six-year classical course. During all this time his writings were appearing regularly in leading periodicals. He then returned to practical journalism on the St. Joseph Press and the Gazette Herald for one year, at the expiration of which he resumed his theological studies and a course in sacred oratory at Kenrick Seminary in St. Louis. While in the seminary he revealed his unusual powers as a speaker and also an extraordinary ability as a writer of prose and verse. By this time his poems were being published in periodicals not only in the United States, but by magazines abroad. In 1903 he received a gold medal from King Christian of Denmark as the grand prize for the best royal poem in the international literary contest celebrating the remarkable visit of the Dowager Czarina of Russia to her royal father, King Christian, in Denmark.

Father Tierney was ordained by Rt. Rev. M. F. Burke in January, 1906, at St. Joseph Cathedral, the church in which he had been a member all his life and in which his parents were married July 4, 1877, by Bishop John J. Hogan. The young priest's mother was at the point of death at the time of her son's ordination, and as a special privilege from Bishop Burke he was permitted to say his first mass at the bedside of his dying mother. February 1, 1906, Father Tierney was sent to Brook field, Missouri, and January 1, 1907, was assigned to the pastorate of St. Joseph's Church in Trenton, Missouri, and the St. John's Mission Church in Gillman City. His parish now extends over territory comprising five counties, i. e., Grundy, Harrison, Mercer, Daviess and part of Livingston. He holds services at nine points in these five Northwest Missouri counties, in four of which he has churches.

As an American poet Father Tierney has been frequently called the successor of Father Abram Ryan, the late poet-priest of the South. His published poems if collected would fill several volumes. Neale & Co., Union Square, New York, have just published (May, 1915) the first volume of his poems. Five thousand copies of the first edition have been sold. He is noted as an orator, and has appeared on the lecture platform in all parts of the country. Some of the subjects of his lectures are: "Shams and Hypocrites, a Constructive Lecture;" "Back to God, the Moral Revolt;" "Is God Dead? a Plea for the Common Man;" "Thou Shalt Not—a Lecture on Marriage;" "Literature and Life;" "True Education;" "Unity of Christendom;" "The Scarlet Woman, a Lecture on the Catholic Church;" "Money, Women and Whisky." He is an active member of the International Lyceum Association of America, the Catholic Writers' Guild, and Council No. 571 of the Knights of Columbus at St. Joseph. Father Tierney's poetry is characterized by a rare charm of expression as well as a wonderful delicacy of sentiment. He furnished the words and the music to an ancient Irish lullaby from a Gaelic fragment, entitled "S-Hoh-Heen Shoh," a ballad which was sung by one of the principals of the Irish National Theater Company at St. Louis World's Fair, and has since been published and had a large sale. His best known poems are: "Mother o' Mine," "The American Flag," and "The Heart of God."

THE AMERICAN FLAG

Unfurl the flag of freedom, lo, behold!
The ensign of a people young and bold;
    Repeat our banner's story,
    Salute the flag of glory
Which reveals the stars of freedom in each fold.

REFRAIN

The Stars and Stripes shall never kiss the dust,
The sword of Justice never sleep in rust,
   O, our hearts are loyal, true
   To our old red, white and blue
Love for God and home and country is our trust.

Every true heart of the nation deep must feel
The thrilling, patriotic vim and zeal
   Which has shaped our glorious fate,
   Making each new grateful state
In Old Glory's azure field a living seal!

God has made our land a nation rich and great,
He inspired our fathers with a nation's fate,
   Their principles were few,
   Immortal, simple, true—
Eternal, are His laws for man and state.

Americans we are, and brave at heart,
And every man of us will do his part,
   Let our declaration stand,
   Soul aflame and flag in hand,
We will serve in peace and war with willing heart.
      —Father H. B. Tierney, in Leslie's Weekly.

SAMUEL TENNESSEE FUNK. A worthy and capable representative of the agricultural interests of Harrison County is found in the person of Samuel Tennessee Funk, who is the owner of 300 acres of well-developed land in sections 16 and 17, township 63, range 29, and in section 11, of the same township and range. Mr. Funk was born March 10, 1874, on the old Funk homestead at New Hampton, upon which Riley N. Funk now resides and which the latter owns.

The paternal grandfather of Samuel T. Funk was Martin Funk, who was born December 25, 1800, in Rockingham County, Virginia, of German descent, his remote ancestor being one of four brothers who came to America from Germany and probably settled in Virginia. It is not known that they owned slaves, and for the most part they were agriculturists, although Henry Funk, one of the early members of the family became a scholarly man and was the publisher of an almanac. The Funks were originally Mennonites. Martin Funk had a fair education, was a democrat in politics, although he never held political office, had no military record, and was not a professed member of any church. He followed farming throughout his life and died in June, 1881, when he was eighty years of age.

Nathaniel Funk, the father of Samuel T. Funk, was born in Rockingham County, Virginia, August 25, 1826, and was a child when he accompanied his parents to Henry County, Indiana. There he was reared, educated and married, and was living there when the Civil war came on, but the township in which he resided furnished the money necessary to provide the troops called for by the Government, and he was not drafted for military service. He came to Harrison County, Missouri, in 1865, and purchased the homestead at New Hampton, in section 17, township 63, range 29, and there passed his remaining years and died December 23, 1909. He was a democrat in politics, but not a politician, and only held the offices of member of the district school board and postmaster, the latter when the office was situated in his home, before the location of the Town of "Hamptonville," now New Hampton. He was one of the substantial men of his community and aided in the building of the Foster church. He was a Universalist in religious belief, but as there was no church of that denomination in his neighborhood, he divided his labors, and never failed to donate to religious movements. He belonged to no secret or fraternal order. Mr. Funk was married the first time to Eliza J. Courtney, a daughter of John Courtney, of Indiana, and three children were born to them: Joseph, a leading farmer of Harrison County; Mart, of El Paso County, Colorado; and Margaret, who became the wife of J. W. Sevier, of Portland, Oregon. Mr. Funk's second marriage was to Miss Catherine Huffman, who was born August 15, 1832, and who died in June, 1890, daughter of Jonathan Huffman, a Virginian, who died in Rockingham County, his native state. Three children were born to Mr. and Mrs. Funk: Riley Napoleon, who lives on the old homestead; Gillie A., the wife of Sam Claytor, of Harrison County; and Samuel T., of this notice.

Samuel T. Funk grew to manhood on the homestead farm at New Hampton, and received his education in the district school, in the meantime learning the elements of farm work and assisting his father and brothers. He left the parental roof at the age of twenty-one years, at which time he was married and located upon a portion of the homestead. He has continued to be successfully identified with the raising of grain and the breeding of stock, and through industry and intelligent effort has made himself one of the substantial men of his township. His improvements are of the most substantial character, and his commodious and conspicuously large two-story house is one of the best farm residences in the locality. In his political affiliations Mr. Funk is a democrat, but he is without experience in public office. His religious connection is with the Christian Church, and at the present time he is acting as deacon of the New Hampton church.

In February, 1895, Mr. Funk was married to Miss Nannie Clabaugh, a daughter of Isaiah J. Clabaugh, and to this union there have been born seven children: Bernice, Ed Ray, Edith May, Doris, Lucille, Robert S. and Lois. Mr. Funk's interests outside of his farm are as a stockholder in the Farmers Lumber Association of New Hampton, the Farmers Scales and the Worth Mutual Telephone Company here.

Isaiah J. Clabaugh, who passed away at New Hampton in September, 1907, at the age of sixty-four years, came here in the fall of 1876 and was a farmer south of the village for several years, when he moved to the town and was engaged in the hardware business for two decades. He was a man of prominence in church matters, being a preacher of the Primitive Baptist faith, and was a reader and great student of the Bible. He had no military record during the Civil war, and his only public service was as postmaster during the early days of New Hampton, his political belief being that of the democratic party.

The Clabaughs originated in Pennsylvania, and Mrs. Funk's grandfather was Henry Clabaugh, who spent his life in Ohio. He married Rebecca Hofert, and their children were: Joseph S. A., who died at Albany, Missouri; Isaiah J.; Lavina, who married William Laferty and died in Oklahoma; and John D., of Wieser, Idaho. Isaiah J. Clabaugh was born in Ohio, and as a young man left the state and went to Iowa, where he was married, subsequently going to Nebraska, where he homesteaded land near Beatrice, and finally coming to Missouri. His wife was Miss Nancy Beebe, a daughter of Arch Beebe, and she died in 1881, the mother of these children: Arch L., a lawyer and real estate man of New Hampton; Charles C., of Canon City, Colorado; and Nancy, who is Mrs. Funk. Mr. Clabaugh was married a second time, his wife being Anice Highnote, and they had four children: Worthy, John, William, and Ruth.

Arch L. Clabaugh, son of Isaiah J. Clabaugh, and brother of Mrs. Funk, was born near Beatrice, Nebraska, April 4, 1870. He received his early education in the public schools, following which he attended the Stanberry Normal School, and entered upon his career as a teacher. He followed the profession in the public schools of Harrison County for four years, his last school being at Bell, just east of New Hampton, and next engaged in farming for three years in Worth County, Missouri. This was followed by a period in the hardware business with his father at New Hampton, and finally he engaged in real estate transactions which have occupied his attention to the present time. Mr. Clabaugh read law alone in his own office and was admitted to the bar before Judge Wanamaker, examined by a committee composed of Alex Cummins, Ezra Frisby and Carl Winslow, and was examined in a class with Polk Oxford of Cainsville. His admission occurred May 18, 1905, but he has practiced little, using his legal knowledge in his own private business and in advising people to keep out of lawsuits.

CHARLES A. EVANS. It requires some exceptional ability and talent to run successfully a country journal anywhere, and the problem is no less difficult in Northwest Missouri. One of the men who have ventured with success in this special field is Charles A. Evans, now editor and proprietor of the Edgerton Journal in Platte County. Mr. Evans began working in a printing office when a boy, contributing his wages to the support of the family, which had been deprived of its head through the affliction of blindness. Mr. Evans has been connected with a number of newspapers in Northwest Missouri, and though a product of the older school of journalism, has adapted himself to the modern usages and requirements and is conducting a live and prosperous paper at Edgerton.

Charles A. Evans was born at Liberty in Clay County, Missouri, February 20, 1861, a son of Lafayette and Sarah (Huff) Evans. There were three other children: Mary, deceased; Margaret, wife of Fred Gordon, of Nevada, Missouri; and Annie, deceased. The parents were married in Tennessee, moved from there to Springfield, Illinois, and thence to Liberty in Clay County, Missouri. The father was a tailor by trade, and followed that vocation a number of years. He and his wife are Baptists, he a democrat, and served in the Home Guard during the war.

Charles A. Evans grew up in Liberty, and had little schooling. In 1878 his father went blind, and as the only son the burden of family support largely fell on his youthful shoulders. He spent his years of apprenticeship and also earned journeyman's wages with the old Liberty Advance, spending ten years there, and then became foreman for the Liberty Tribune, filling that post ten years. Removing to Nevada, Missouri, he bought a half interest in the Nevada Noticer, but five years later sold out and returned to Liberty with the Herald. In 1900 Mr. Evans went to Triplet, Missouri, bought the Tribune there, and there showed his special ability as a newspaper man, since he was the first editor who had succeeded in running that paper for more than a year. The party from whom he acquired it had lasted only eleven weeks. He made the enterprise self-supporting and profitable, and continued its management for six years. Selling out, he went to Richmond, Missouri, to become manager of the Democrat, and somewhat later this paper was sold and the plant removed to Independence, Mr. Evans going along with it. A year later he became connected with the Dearborn Democrat, and in

February, 1908, bought the Edgerton Journal, which he now owns and publishes.

Mr. Evans is a democrat in politics. He was married December 23, 1891, to Gertrude I. Mosby, a graduate of Liberty Ladies' College, who was born northeast of Liberty in Clay County. They have two sons: Estes of Kansas City, and Jack M. of Kansas City.

JOHN DONOVAN. On November 18, 1913, sudden death brought to a termination the career of this honored and influential citizen of St. Joseph. It was said of John Donovan that probably no man had done more to further the interests of his home city, at least during its modern epoch of upbuilding, since it was through his efforts and influence in a conspicuous degree that St. Joseph became an important cattle center and the location of several of the extensive packing house industries. All his life he was a hard worker, beginning with the time when as a small boy he drove cattle to earn a meagre support, and the results he accomplished in less than sixty years of life are a tribute to a marvelous energy and fine personality. His character was the positive expression of a strong nature, and he fully merited the confidence and esteem reposed in him in the city to whose advancement he contributed in such practical and generous measure. For a number of years John Donovan was one of the substantial capitalists and men of affairs in Northwest Missouri. He was president of the St. Joseph Railway, Light, Heat & Power Company, vice president of the St. Joseph Stock Yards Company, was a banker, built or helped to build a number of St. Joseph's most conspicuous architectural monuments, and was interested in enterprises of a varied character that did much to uphold the civic and material welfare of St. Joseph. Essentially a practical and rugged business man, blunt in his speech, vigorous and effective in all his manners and actions, he was nevertheless a man among men, and has many pleasing associations with the friends who had been attracted to him by his sincerity, genialty and sterling worth of character.

John Donovan was born at Easton, Talbot County, Maryland, July 28, 1854, a son of John and Evelina M. (Robinson) Donovan. Both parents were born in Maryland, the father at Cambridge, Dorchester County, in February, 1828, and the mother was a daughter of a substantial planter and honored citizen of Talbot County in the same state, where she was reared, and where her marriage to the senior John Donovan was celebrated on September 1, 1850. John Donovan, Sr., represented the fourth generation of the family in Maryland, and the original American progenitors of the name emigrated from Ireland during colonial history, settling in Virginia, from which colony representatives of the name served as patriot soldiers in the War of the Revolution. At an early day one branch of the family moved to Maryland, and from that branch is descended the St. Joseph family. John Donovan, Sr., was given a liberal education, and fitted himself for the bar. Though admitted to practice in Maryland, he gave little attention to his profession, since his energies were better directed in other channels. In Maryland he built up a prosperous industry in the canning of oysters, fruits, vegetables, etc., and was one of the pioneers in what is now a great and valuable commercial enterprise. In the spring of 1861 he came to Missouri with St. Joseph as his destination, and his family joined him in that city in the following June. His attention here was especially paid to real estate, and he found a great field for his business acumen and energy in the rapidly developing city and county, and while he achieved for himself a large success, at the same time he aided greatly in the civic and industrial progress of his generation. John

Donovan, Sr., was one of the best known and most honored citizens of St. Joseph until his death, which occurred in 1897. His wife passed away March 31, 1895. Both were communicants of Christ Episcopal Church, and he was a member of its vestry for many years.

John Donovan, Jr., acquired his first educational training in the public schools of his native town, and later in the City of Baltimore. His business career began in the winter of 1868, when he was fourteen years of age. He found employment as errand boy in the shoe store of William T. Stone, of St. Joseph, and was later employed as a clerk in the offices of the Hannibal & St. Joseph Railroad Company. On leaving that work, and taking a position with the firm of Hastings & Saxton, contractors, he was employed in buying ties and other equipment for the construction of the St. Joseph & Denver City Railroad, now known as the St. Joseph & Grand Island. His next position was with the Kansas Land and Town Company, and his duties were such as were involved in the company's work in establishing and laying out towns along the route of the present St. Joseph & Grand Island Railroad. These different positions were a fine training school for the future capitalist and business builder, and his administrative and executive powers were rapidly matured.

It was in the spring of 1871 that his independent business career may be said to have begun. Buying cattle throughout Northwestern Missouri, he drove most of his stock to the vicinity of Maryville, and sold it to the farmers. On the 17th of May in the same year, after having had a varied experience for one of his years, and having profited by the practical test through which he had passed, he laid the foundation for the more substantial and lasting part of his business career by entering the State National Bank of St. Joseph in the capacity of a messenger. He remained with this institution exactly ten years, and resigned in May, 1881, to accept the management of the Hemphill County Cattle Company, in Hemphill County, Texas, an enterprise projected by St. Joseph capital. When the company disposed of its holdings and business in Texas in the fall of the same year, Mr. Donovan bought the land on which the South St. Joseph stock yards and packing houses now stand.

This land was level and in many parts swampy, and except for an industrial site, had little potential value. The new owner, with complete confidence in the outcome and with the courage of his convictions, first directed his attention to the ditching, draining and reclaiming of the land, which had previously been unavailable for practical uses. Through his sound arguments and earnest efforts, the representative men in packing house industry were induced to erect immense plants at St. Joseph, and Mr. Donovan's reclaimed land thus acquired a magnificent value as an industrial location. On the original Donovan tract now stand the most modern of packing houses, as well as the fine Live Stock Exchange Building, which was considered at the time of its erection as the handsomest structure of its kind in the world. The grounds reclaimed by Mr. Donovan contain also many acres of sheds for the shelter of the thousands of cattle, hogs, sheep, etc., shipped annually to the great packing houses at St. Joseph from the grazing pastures and farms of the western states. To Mr. Donovan is thus due in large measure the development of the great industrial center, which more than any other one factor has brought about the great increase in population and economic wealth of his home city. Mr. Donovan was connected with the old St. Joseph Stock Yards as a director, from the date of its organization in 1884. On July 1, 1893, he took active charge of the affairs of the Stock Yards Company as vice president and general manager, and though several years ago he gave up the management because of numerous other responsibilities, he held the office of vice president until his death.

Mr. Donovan was one of the founders of the German-American Bank of St. Joseph, and served as vice president from its organization early in 1887 until July 1, 1893. Mr. Donovan, since January 1, 1903, had held the office of president of the St. Joseph Railway, Light & Power Company, which owns and operates the street railway system of St. Joseph, besides supplying electricity and power for the general public. He held the executive position in the company since the St. Joseph Traction System was sold by E. H. Harriman to the Clarks of Philadelphia, who subsequently sold it to the present owners. He is said to have negotiated the sale to the Clarks, and at one time brought suit against the late Mr. Harriman for a large commission, that case having been dropped at Harriman's death. Mr. Donovan was a promoter of the Union Terminal Railway, which is closely allied with the live stock enterprises. He was a director of the St. Joseph and Savannah Interurban Railroad Company, was president of the South St. Joseph Town Company, and a stockholder in many other industrial and commercial corporations. He owns much valuable real estate in the vicinity and city. He was associated with William E. Spratt in the purchase of the Ballinger Building at Seventh and Edmond Street. He built the block on South Fourth Street occupied by the Horigan Supply Company, and owned a number of buildings in South St. Joseph. To the end of his life he never lost his keen interest in live stock, and owned the King Hill Stock Farm several miles northeast of the city, where he had many head of fine horses and cattle, and a handsome summer residence. His name merits enduring credit for his work in making St. Joseph an important center of the live stock and packing industry, and is not to be soon forgotten in the community for which he did so much. As a business man he had broad views and great initiative, and his success was the more gratifying because it represented the results of his own ability and efforts. As a citizen he was always liberal and progressive, ready to give his influence and cooperation to everything for the advancement of the social and material welfare of the community.

Mr. Donovan was active for a number of years in the state militia. He was one of the organizers of the Saxton Rifles, a fine military body, which he served as first lieutenant. Later a battalion was formed under the same title, and he was captain of Company A in that organization. From that position he was promoted to the rank of major, in command of the battalion, but resigned his commission when he went to Texas in connection with the business interests already mentioned. The military organization with which he was identified is still one of the most important in the Missouri National Guards. When the metropolitan police system was inaugurated in St. Joseph Mr. Donovan was appointed a member of the first board of police commissioners, an honor accorded him by Governor Marmaduke on April 28, 1887. He organized the police force of the city, for two years gave personal supervision to the drilling of its members, in military tactics, and other service work, and served altogether on the police commission for six years. He was always an earnest supporter of the democratic party, both in the county and state.

As a man the late John Donovan was direct, emphatic and positive in nature, placing true estimates on men and affairs, and never seeking public plaudits, being well content with that splendid reserve of resources and ability which made him master of every situation. There might be enumerated many other incidents of his career, showing how closely he was identified with his home city. In the fall of 1907 and 1908 it was his personal effort that made St. Joseph the scene of the big military tournaments, when about five thousand soldiers from ports all over the Middle West assembled and engaged in their maneuvers. So much had Mr. Donovan done for St. Joseph that the citizens decided that some special tribute should be paid him, and on December 28, 1908, he was presented with a handsome silver loving cup, the presentation being made in the auditorium before thousands of his home people.

On October 5, 1875, John Donovan married Miss Emma C. Patee, granddaughter of the late John Patee, whose part as a St. Joseph pioneer has familiar memorial in one of the city's streets. Mrs. Donovan died December 7, 1909, and left one daughter, Emma. On December 30, 1910, Mr. Donovan married Mrs. Elizabeth A. Tracy, of Weymouth, Massachusetts. Mrs. Donovan presides over the beautiful home at 508 North Fifth Street. The daughter of Mr. Donovan is the wife of Douglas McCaskey, a captain in the United States army.

BIOGRAPHY OF JOHN W. S. DILLON

BIRTHPLACE

John William Sherman Dillon was born May 4, 1868, in Allen Township, Worth County, Missouri, twelve miles southeast of Grant City. The place of his birth was a farm on which his father and mother settled in 1867. Here he grew to manhood and gained a country school education, proving himself an average student in most studies, excepting arithmetic, in which he excelled his fellow students. The first day he went to a country school was at what is called the Stormer Schoolhouse, 2½ miles from his home. This was only a few days after he had passed his fifth birthday. His first teacher was F. A. Roche, who was a college student in the New England states before coming to Missouri. He continued to walk to and from this school until he was ten years of age, when the district was divided, and from thence on he went to what was called the Williams School, which was 1½ miles from his home.

ENTERS HIGH SCHOOL

On account of being overheated in the harvest field when he was fifteen years of age, he suffered from a heart injury for a few years and did not go to school again until he was nineteen years of age, when he entered the high school at Albany, Missouri, under G. M. Castor as superintendent, and there, by hard study, brought up the various common school studies in which he found himself considerably lacking. In practical and higher arithmetic he excelled all his fellow students here, as he had done in the country school. Following this he spent six months in the Stanberry Normal School, which was a private school managed by Allen Moore and John E. Fesler. Here he succeeded in bringing up his knowledge of English to a point that enabled him to pass an entrance examination to the Missouri State University covering two years of English in that institution.

The following fall and winter he spent largely in debating societies at the Williams Schoolhouse, the Dry Schoolhouse and the Pine Schoolhouse.

ENTERS STATE UNIVERSITY

In September, 1889, he entered the Missouri State University and pursued what was called the bachelor of letters course of study, and included the courses in military science and in pedagogy. In 1892 he graduated in the military course, which at that time was considered equal to one-half the military course at West Point. He also graduated in the junior course in pedagogy, which entitled him to a state certificate as teacher. During the last semester of his work at the university he was carrying thirty-seven hours of recitations per week, which was nearly double the regular course prescribed for students. Among the eminent teachers under whom he studied in the state university were Doctor Fisher and Doctor Jones in Latin; Doctor Allen in English; Dr. William Benjamin Smith and Professor Tyndall in mathematics; Professor Broadhead in geology; Doctor Blackwell and Professor Hoffman in modern languages; Dr. J. P. Blanton in psychology and pedagogy. He attained first rank and distinction grades in most of his studies and led some of his classes with a one hundred grade on every examination. He was enabled to carry the large number of studies and attain the high grades only through the most constant and diligent application, utilizing all his spare hours during the summer, as well as every spare moment during the student year.

University Building Burns

It was during his last year at the university that the large main building of the university burned, and as a result an extra session of the State Legislature was called by Governor Francis and a movement was set on foot to remove the state university to Sedalia, Missouri. Finally this matter was settled by the people of Columbia contributing $50,000 and a large appropriation being made by the Legislature, which, added to the insurance of $247,000 on the building, enabled the university curators to rebuild on a much more elaborate scale.

Teaches Prairie Home School *

In September, 1892, he began teaching at the Prairie Home School, four miles north of Blackburn, in Saline County, Missouri, and continued teaching here through a second year, or until the spring of 1894. He attained a very high degree of success at this place in teaching and brought away with him recommendations from members of the school board and others to the effect that he was the best disciplinarian and instructor the school had had. His salary the first year was $60 per month and the second year was $70 per month, and he was offered $80 per month to teach the school the third year, which at that time was an unprecedented wage for a country school anywhere in Missouri.

Elected Superintendent of Grant City Schools

However, owing to the death of his father the previous fall, he returned to his home in Worth County, where his mother and two sisters still resided on the home farm. He was then hired by the Grant City School Board as superintendent of the Grant City School, of which he took charge in the fall of 1894, having passed an examination for state teacher's certificate under State Superintendent Wolfe and Professor Muir at a state institute at Moberly, Missouri, where he was highly complimented by his instructors as having written the best papers on the examinations they had had in the same studies.

Prepares School for Articulation with University

Within the first two months of his teaching in Grant City he succeeded in changing all the text books in the high school, and with the cooperation of the school board started the new course of study, fulfilling the requirements for articulation with the state university. It was at this time that Latin was first studied in the Grant City schools, and Mr. Dillon found much opposition to this study, even from the better classes of the city; some of the professional men argued that it was a dead language and that there was no practical use for it, but before he closed his work as a teacher in Grant City he saw Latin become very popular.

ELECTED TO UNIVERSITY CHAIRS

In the fall of 1896 he was elected to the chair of Latin and the chair of political economy in the Campbell University at Holton, Kansas, an institution which was said to stand next to the Kansas University in course of study, requirements and capabilities at that time. Mr. Dillon was not to take active charge of his duties in this university until the Grant City School closed, in May, 1897. During the winter intervening Mr. Dillon had due time to consider the ten year contract he had for the chairs in the Campbell University and decided that if he fulfilled that engagement it would make him a teacher for lifetime, as he would then be too old to adapt himself readily to a new profession, and for that reason he resigned the chairs of Latin and political economy in February, 1897, with the determination to give up teaching entirely, although he was very much in love with the work and closed his last year in the school at Grant City with a unanimous recommendation from the school board as one of the best instructors and disciplinarians that had ever occupied the position.

CONDUCTED FATHER'S FARM

During the three years that he was superintendent of the Grant City School he conducted and operated his father's farm, where his mother and two sisters lived, and put into cultivation considerable acreage of new land.

WAS COLUMBIAN GUARD AT WORLD'S FAIR

Reverting to the first years of teaching, in April, 1893, he went to Chicago and became a member of the Columbian Guards at the World's Fair held in commemoration of the four hundredth anniversary of the discovery of America by Columbus. He remained nearly four months at the World's Fair, serving about three months as a member of Company No. 24 of the Columbian Guards. His duties engaged him at the Woman's Building, the entrance to the Midway Plaisance, the Children's Building, the Puck Building, and the White Star Line Steamship's Building. He proved himself capable and efficient in this position and still possesses recommendations from both the captain and the first sergeant of his company, testifying as to his ability and honesty and good character during his service at the World's Fair.

ELECTED COMMANDER MISSOURI DIVISION SONS OF VETERANS

In the latter part of 1896 he was elected captain of Shiloh Camp No. 48, Sons of Veterans, which was at that time organized in Grant City. In 1897 he attended the state encampment of the Sons of Veterans at Warrensburg, Missouri, where he was elected junior vice commander of the state division. This was the third official position of the order in the state. The next year, in 1898, at the annual encampment held at Carthage, Missouri, he was elected commander of the Missouri Division, Sons of Veterans, which included the states of Missouri, Arkansas and Texas. In this position he was quite active and devoted a large part of his time to the interest of his division. The annual encampment the next year, under his command, was held at Kirksville, Missouri. He still holds the rank of past commander in the order.

TOURS CANADA AND EASTERN UNITED STATES

Having given up the profession of teaching in 1897, he decided to take a vacation and also to give his two sisters some recreation and change after their long vigil at the bedside of their mother, who died the 27th day of March, 1897, and consequently, in July, the three started on a tour of the East, landing first at Buffalo, New York, where they spent a week with the Grand Army Encampment, and at Niagara Falls; thence to Hamilton, Toronto, Montreal and Quebec, Canada; thence to Mount Washington; Portland, Maine; Boston, Massachusetts; Albany, Newburg, New York City, Philadelphia, Washington, District of Columbia, and numerous other points. On this trip Mr. Dillon made a special effort to become acquainted with the professions of law and journalism, and the opportunity for the study of each in the East. At the University of Cincinnati he heard two lectures on law by W. H. Taft. The next time he saw Mr. Taft was at the White House at Washington, District of Columbia, when Mr. Taft was President of the United States, and Mr. and Mrs. Dillon were on their wedding tour of the East.

MAKES GENEALOGICAL INVESTIGATIONS

It was on the return part of the trip in 1897, when Mr. Dillon and his sisters reached Lawrence County, Ohio, where their parents were both reared and where many of their relatives still lived, that Mr. Dillon spent considerable time in gathering all the genealogical data known to the living relatives. Acknowledgment of much valuable information is due to his great-uncle, John Dillon, and to his uncles, Peter H. Dillon and William Dillon, and to H. J. Dennison for the genealogical record of his grandparents, Vincent and Mrs. Hannah Dillon. Also acknowledgment is due to the step-grandmother, Mrs. Elizabeth Rapp; to his uncles, August and Abner Rapp, and to John Snyder, as well as to numerous others for much valuable information concerning his grandparents, John Rapp and Catharine Rapp.

DILLON ANCESTRY—PATERNAL

His grandfather, Vincent Dillon, was born in Green County, Pennsylvania, on January 1, 1809. Vincent Dillon's father was John Dillon, who was born in the same county and on the same homestead, shortly after the close of the Revolutionary war of America. John Dillon's father was Thomas Dillon, who was born in the County of Mayo on the Shannon River in Ireland, and arrived in America in time to take part in the latter struggles in the Revolutionary war. He was a weaver by trade and followed this trade to the time of his death. His son, John Dillon, took part in the War of 1812.

NORTHMEN FROM DENMARK

The Dillon genealogy extends back almost indefinitely, but later writers confine themselves mainly to that part beginning with the year

885 A. D., when Siegfried, a noted sea king of the Danish Vikings, ascended the Seine River with 40,000 Vikings, composed of Danish Northmen, in 700 vessels, and besieged Paris for ten months. Many of these Vikings or Northmen remained in Southern France, and among them was one who was so strong and agile that the natives of France called him DeLion. Through the wear of years this was gradually shortened to Dillon. Two hundred years later, or in the year 1185, Chevalier Henry Dillon of Aquitiane, a descendant of the Northman who came over with Seigfried came to Ireland in the train of Henry II and acquired large possessions on the River Shannon, which were granted and confirmed to him by the king, and which became known as "Dillon's Country." This was the beginning of the race of Dillons in Ireland, and it was from this Dillon's Country that Thomas Dillon came to Green County, Pennsylvania.

Dillons in Medieval Wars

Among the Dillons who attained distinction in the medieval wars was Viscount Theobald Dillon and his son, Count Arthur Dillon, Chevalier James de Dillon and Count Henry de Dillon. The last four named had the famous Dillon Regiment in France. Their living in France was due to the fact that their ancestors had been expatriated from Ireland at the time of Cromwell's usurpation, about 1649. A fifth brother became Archbishop of Toulouse and also Archbishop of Norborne, but at the time of the French revolution was beheaded. At the guillotine a court lady under sentence to be beheaded terrifiedly turned to Archbishop Dillon and asked him to go first, to which he replied, "Certainly; anything to favor the lady." Another one of the Dillons, a little later in the line, who attained distinction in the military service, was Col. Arthur Dillon, whose regiment was connected with that of Count D'Estaing in assisting the American revolutionists to defeat the British.

Grand Maternal Ancestry English

The wife of Vincent Dillon was Hannah Jackson. Her grandfather was Henry Jackson, who was of pure English descent. He was a man weighing over two hundred pounds and lived to be eighty or ninety years of age. Before the revolution he lived where Washington, District of Columbia, now stands, and often herded his horses on the "Old Poison Fields," which has since become the location of the capitol of the United States. During the Revolutionary war he and his family were at a fort near his farm. Afterward they removed to Green County, Pennsylvania, and then to Guernsy County, Ohio, where he died.

The above references to the Dillon genealogy show that J. W. S. Dillon was of Irish, French and English descent on his father's side.

Maternal Lineage

In his genealogical search at the time referred to when in Southern Ohio, Mr. Dillon found that both his mother's parents were born at Felbach, near Stuttgart, in the Kingdom of Wurtemburg, Germany. He found that his grandmother's maiden name was Catharine Elsasser, and that some time in earlier centuries that their ancestors had been given that name because of the fact that they had come from the Province of Alsace-Lorraine.

RAPPS IN NAPOLEONIC TIMES

Mr. Dillon found that his mother's father, John Rapp, was born at Schlaght, seventy-two miles from Stuttgart. Tradition has it that many centuries before this the ancestors of Rapp had lived in the southern part of Gaul, later known as Aquitania, and probably were among the original Franks of the first and second centuries. And it was said that about the time of the Sicilian Vespers, in 1282, that the Rapps moved across the Rhine to the Kingdom of Wurtemburg. John Rapp's father's name was John Rapp, who had what at that time was quite a large landed estate of 1,100 acres, and his standing with the Austrian Royalty conferred on him the task of furnishing herds of cattle to the Austrian armies while fighting Napoleon's armies. The contract with the Austrian emperor was that Rapp should be paid for all the cattle which he attempted to take to the Austrian armies, whether they were delivered or captured by the French armies, but in later years the claims for cattle not delivered were repudiated, because of the very serious financial straits of the Austrian Government. Hence the claims amounting to 200,000 guilders worth of cattle, which had been captured from Rapp by the French army at different times, were repudiated. The last and one of the largest losses suffered by Rapp in this way was when he was driving 80,000 guilders worth of cattle to General Mack, whose army had suddenly been besieged at Ulm by Napoleon. This herd of cattle was captured by Napoleon's troops. In 1807, John Rapp was murdered by the French soldiers.

RETURNED FROM MOSCOW

John Rapp, Jr., was impressed into the French service when Napoleon began his march to Moscow in Russia, and Rapp was one of the few of Napoleon's troops who returned from that terrible retreat of the grand army. Later John Rapp enlisted in Blucher's army, and at the Battle of Waterloo was fighting against the soldiers who had killed his own father, and there helped defeat Napoleon. Immediately after this battle John Rapp came to America and settled at Barboursville, Kentucky, and later in Lawrence County, Ohio, where Jane Rapp, the mother of the subject of this sketch, was born and raised.

MOTHER OF J. W. S. DILLON

Miss Jane Rapp was married to Isaac Dillon, August 4, 1867, and joined with her husband in building a home and raising a family on their farm in Worth County. Mrs. Dillon was a woman of wonderful perseverance and had the strict German training from her parents that caused her to train her children not only to be scrupulously honest and honorable in every respect, but to be considerate of both persons and property. The financial success of her husband was doubtless due almost as much to her efforts as to his. She was an unusually good manager and sacrificed her life largely in her ambition to raise her children in the way she thought they ought to go. Her death on March 27, 1897, at the age of sixty-one years, was due very largely to the fact that she had never found time to rest during her whole lifetime. She had the independent spirit and the efficiency that comes from being raised by the higher class of Germans.

FATHER OF J. W. S. DILLON

The fourth child and the third son of Vincent Dillon was Isaac Dillon, born in Monroe County, Ohio, June 11, 1835, and raised and reared to manhood on his father's farm, which is located one mile east of Scott Town, in Lawrence County, Ohio. He taught school near his home and prepared to go to college, but this arrangement was broken into by a desire to go West with his brother, P. H. Dillon, and his brother-in-law, J. Q. Hagerman, all of whom came to Missouri, starting April 12, 1859. At Kansas City, Missouri, P. H. Dillon and Isaac Dillon came near purchasing ten acres of land for $1,000; the only thing that prevented them from making this purchase was the fact that P. H. Dillon was attacked with a case of malaria and was afraid that he could not live there in case they purchased the land. Had they completed this purchase of the ten acres, situated in what is now the heart of Kansas City, Missouri, it would have made them millions of dollars. Isaac Dillon came on to Worth County, Missouri, and taught school in that county and in Ringgold County, Iowa, until the spring of 1862, having, in the meantime, purchased eighty acres of land twelve miles southwest of what is now Grant City. He was teaching school at the Dry Schoolhouse in the spring of 1862, when the war excitement became so great and the soldiers passing by the schoolhouse and through the vicinity so greatly occupied the attention of, not only the scholars, but the patrons as well, that it was decided to discontinue the school. He immediately went to St. Joseph and enlisted in the Fifth Missouri Cavalry under General Penick, with whom he served until the regiment was mustered out fourteen months later.

During this service he was in many of the skirmishes with Quantrell's guerrillas, and Isaac Dillon was one of the special guard to go to the home of Mrs. Samuels, who at that time was Mrs. James, the mother of Frank and Jesse James, and investigate an attack which was the result of a bomb being thrown into the house and tearing off the arm of Mrs. James. The guard, of which Isaac Dillon was a member, arrested certain parties who were presumed to have been connected with this deed, and these parties were given a trial by the Military Court, a result of which the writer does not know.

FATHER IN CIVIL WAR

Upon being mustered out of General Penick's Regiment, Isaac Dillon immediately reenlisted at Fort Leavenworth, Kansas, in the Second Kansas Cavalry, with which he served until the spring of 1864, when he was taken prisoner at Poison Springs, Arkansas, while in a guard of 1,500 men accompanying 300 foraging wagons filled with corn. A part of the guard was surrounded by General Price's army of eight or ten thousand men, and just before being taken prisoner Isaac Dillon was shot through the right arm, just above the elbow; from this wound he suffered several months in the prisons, and on account of it his arm was disabled for life. At the close of the war he was at Camp Ford, Texas, where, on account of their isolation, it was not learned that the war was over for several months, and he continued as a prisoner of the Confederates. Finally he was discharged and went to New Orleans and embarked on a boat to St. Louis, Missouri, and thence to Fort Leavenworth, Kansas, on the Missouri River, where he was mustered out on the 8th of September, 1865, and compelled to prove that he was alive, as his captain had marked him dead in the report of the battle at Poison Springs, Arkansas.

MARRIAGE OF PARENTS

From Leavenworth, Kansas, he returned to Worth County, Missouri, where he taught school until 1867. He was married on August 4, 1867, to Miss Jane Rapp, and they settled on the farm which he had purchased before the war, and there underwent the struggle of the pioneers and raised a family of one son, J. W. S. Dillon, and two daughters, Avonia and Greta Dillon. Although he failed in his ambition to be a college man, Isaac Dillon was a student and all his life kept in intelligent touch with all current events. He and his wife were ambitious in that their children have a good education and that their son become a graduate of the Missouri State University. Isaac Dillon was a man five feet ten inches in height with very dark hair; slender, weighing about one hundred and twenty-four pounds; was always active and energetic and directed his business in an intelligent and systematic manner. At his death, which occurred October 30, 1893, it was said by all who knew him that he did not have an enemy among all with whom he had become acquainted while he lived in Worth County. He was fifty-eight years old at the time of his death and his death was brought on by sciatica, which was the result of an attack of grippe about a year previous. He and his wife both had very high ideals of honesty and integrity and were very diligent in instilling these qualities into their children.

Besides the above outline of genealogical facts in the Dillon, Jackson, Rapp and Elsasser families, John W. S. Dillon secured about one hundred pages of typewritten data concerning these families that is of interest to relatives, and many stirring events would be of interest to the public were there time and space for relating them.

HAS WATERLOO SABER

Among the mementoes of the Napoleonic period in Europe found on this trip by J. W. S. Dillon was the saber carried by John Rapp in the Battle of Waterloo and probably carried by him on his march to Moscow in earlier years. In 1908 J. W. S. Dillon was again in Lawrence County, Ohio, and was presented with this sword by his uncle, Abner Rapp, to whom it had been presented at an earlier date by Mrs. Naomi Whitley of Huntington, West Virginia. Mr. Dillon now has it at his home in Grant City. At one time on his return march from Moscow John Rapp secured a loaf of bread, which doubtless stood between him and starvation on that march with both winter and the cossacks on their heels and killing the French troops by the hundreds of thousands. Another soldier saw Rapp with the loaf of bread and entered into a saber battle with him for the possession of the bread. The soldier caught Rapp on the chin with his saber, which threw him off his guard; Rapp took advantage of this opportunity to dispatch the soldier and thereby retained the loaf of bread, which may have been the slender thread of nourishment that enabled him to keep up his march until safe within his own country.

At the close of his genealogical search, J. W. S. Dillon and his two sisters returned to their home farm in Worth County, Missouri, in the latter part of 1897, where Mr. Dillon lived for about a year and conducted the farm.

PURCHASES GRANT CITY STAR

One afternoon about the 1st of August, 1898, he drove to Grant City on business. He found, accidentally, that the Grant City Star was for sale and in twenty-four hours he and J. F. Hull had purchased it. They edited and managed the paper five years, the circulation had doubled from the time of his purchase. Since 1903, the Star has had a larger circulation in proportion to county population than any local weekly newspaper in Missouri. Such an accomplishment is not so difficult as it might seem, as Worth County is the smallest in the state and hence the population is more compactly situated near the county seat.

NEWSPAPER POLICIES

Mr. Dillon's newspaper policy has always been to give the best service to its subscribers. He has always been on the square with all of them and their friendship is largely due to his honest dealing and hard work. It has not been his policy to attack unjustly or indulge in personalities, but he has fearlessly stood for justice and right regardless of personal interests, but wraps the mantle of charity about the mistakes of the earnest but misguided. The politics of the paper has been republican from its founding in 1867 and so ably has Mr. Dillon fought the political battles of his party that it has won many victories.

IN POLITICS

In politics Mr. Dillon has been a republican from the time of his first vote, but not so strict that he would vote for any kind of man just because he was on his own ticket. In 1898 he made a short campaign of 2½ weeks in the Third Congressional District for the republican nomination for Congress. At the convention at Excelsior Springs, August 22d, he was defeated by J. E. Goodrich, a former classmate at the state university. Mr. Goodrich won by one-half of a vote, but was defeated by the large democratic majority in the November election.

CHAIRMAN OF REPUBLICAN COMMITTEE

Mr. Dillon was elected chairman of the Republican Committee of Worth County three successive terms and finally gave up the position because of pressing official duties. At the three elections held while he was chairman of the committee, more republicans were elected than at any other three elections in the history of the county.

POSTMASTER AT GRANT CITY

On December 17, 1903, Mr. Dillon was commissioned postmaster at Grant City to succeed J. F. Okey, resigned. This commission was signed by President Roosevelt. On January 13, 1908, he was re-commissioned by President Roosevelt. On March 18, 1912, he was commissioned for a third term by President Taft. The office is a middle third class office and its receipts have increased by about two thousand dollars a year since Mr. Dillon took possession of the office. He also moved the office into his building on the west side of the square, where he fitted up modern equipment. This was in 1904. Again in the beginning of 1915 he re-furnished the office with new equipment in the main, making it one of the best equipped offices of its size in the state. It has been referred to as a model postoffice by inspectors. Mr. Dillon's first two appointments were made without opposition. His third appointment was made after a long political fight, which was carried up to the President, personally, and to the United States Senate. His excellent record as postmaster saved the position for him. His work was specially investigated by inspectors and by Frank Hitchcock, postmaster general; Charles Nagel, secretary of the Department of Commerce and Labor, and by Senator Bradley, of Kentucky, and Senator Bourne, of Oregon. All these gentlemen passed the record as good. His last term will soon expire and he will be succeeded by a democrat.

MARRIED TO MISS FRANCES MULLINS

On June 16, 1909, J. W. S. Dillon was married to Miss Frances Mullins, daughter of Major and Mrs. A. W. Mullins, of Linneus, Missouri. Major Mullins and wife were formerly Kentuckians and Major Mullins served with distinction in the Civil war. He has been one of the leading lawyers of the state and is also a banker. Mrs. Dillon is a graduate of Christian College at Columbia, Missouri, and of the Central College at Lexington, Missouri. She specialized in English literature, music and art. Mrs. Dillon is interested in literary work and is active in working for local civic improvements.

ALL PEOPLE TRACE BACK TO FIRST OF HUMAN RACE

An epitome of the nationalities from which J. W. S. Dillon sprang show that his origin is about equally from the English, Irish, French and German races. The analysis of the above branches shows that they are in turn derived from the various earlier nations and tribes of Europe, such as the Franks, the Iberians, the Scandinavians, especially the Danish Northmen, and some of these were descended from the Goths; also the Romans, the Teutons, Saxons are among the races from which the subject of this sketch descended. All of these in turn would be traced to still earlier nationalities, if history existed, and would go finally to the beginning of the human race. This is merely the history of every human being of the present time and none in America believe in the classes as they used to exist in Europe, but in the merit of the individual.

AMERICAN SPIRIT

As a result of this American spirit most people forget their ancestors. Mr. Dillon claims no merit from his ancestors, excepting that in all of his tracings he was unable to find a single instance of a crime of any sort committed by an ancestor, and all were honorable and honest. Mr. Dillon feels that he is even more American in spirit after having made a study of his European ancestors than he was before he knew anything of them. He has asked that some mention be made in this biography in order that the descent of the average human being may be illustrated.

AMERICA'S BULWARK

Mr. Dillon believes that if Americans will continue to be honest individually and collectively that America will never meet the fate of the republics whose downfall have inevitably resulted from dishonesty and corruption that has gradually crept among the people as they saw how opportunities opened easily where everyone was free to do as he wished. If America will avoid this one pitfall he believes that nothing can destroy the Government.

CPSIA information can be obtained
at www.ICGtesting.com
Printed in the USA
BVHW041709110620
581231BV00003B/18

9 780342 512782